Goldmine's Price Guide To Collectible Jazz Albums 1949-1969

By Neal Umphred

The painting by David Stone Martin, which appears on the back cover of this book, was used on a Billie Holiday album.

Published by

krause publications

700 E. State Street • Iola, WI 54990-0001
Telephone: 715/445-2214

Library of Congress Catalog Number: 92-71452
ISBN: 0-87341-288-5
Printed in the United States of America

Table of Contents

Acknowledgements

While I am rather loathe to list the contributors quantitatively, I do believe th some sectioning is necessary to adequately do justice to those who were able take the time from their hectic schedules and contribute "above and beyond t call of duty." The two gentlemen that carried me through the first edition we also the backbone of this book:

Bill Shonk
Issaquah, WA

Armand "Mr. Blue Note" Lewis
N. Hollywood, CA

Two other aficionados contacted me through the mail and then proceeded to i undate my post office box with page after page of hand-written notes:

Brian Izin
Los Angeles, CA

Frederic Klinger
New York, NY

Certain individuals offered specific input: Bill Bickham of McLean, VA, conce trated on jazz vocals; Robert Campbell of Clemson, SC, provided the primary da for Sun Ra; David Jessup of Elmira, NY, completely redid the Benny Goodman ar Glenn Miller sections; and Uwe Weiler of Nordestedt, Germany, address problems with Debut Records listings. The following provided addition corrections, additions and suggestions the reader will find in these pages:

Frederick Cohen
Jazz Record Center
New York, NY

John David
Elmsford, NY

Marv Edwards
Mt Ephraim, NJ

Charles Gutierrez
Jonesborough, TN

John Knapp
Rockville Center, NY

Bruce Krohmer
Silver Spring, MD

Joseph Leung
Vancouver, BC, Canada

Jim Murphy
Ridgecrest, CA

Roderick O'Neil
Waltham, MA

Mark Oyloe
Fergus Falls, MN

Jack Shadolan
Amherst, MA

Alan Shebroe
Walnut, CA

Dan Shellenbarger
Marshall, MI

Ed Tataryn
Hatchville, MA

Tony Verdi
Washington, DC

Lars Walter
Stockholm, Sweden

General advice, suggestions and background were provided by Manek Daver Tokyo, Japan; Stephen Hartig of the Jazz Record Exchange, Jamaica, NY; Mart Levy of Smogtown Records, Los Angeles, CA; and Brendan Meade of New York, NY

The illustrations in this book were taken from the collections of Bill Shon (photography by John Christensen), Armand Lewis, and Mark Pomerantz of Va Nuys, CA. Finally, special thanks to Anthony & Margo Martin, Brooklyn, NY, fo their cooperation in providing me with artwork from David Stone Martin's files.

Foreword Into The Past

A lot has happened in the world of collectible jazz since the first edition of this book appeared in 1992. Initial response was more or less what I expected and best illustrated by an anecdote: In May of 1993 I sojourned to the mysterious East and did a couple of shows in the New York/New Jersey area. After setting up my table with assorted price guides for sale I was accosted by an irate jazz fan who let me know in less than subtle terms what a disservice I had done the hobby with the preposterously low prices I had assigned the records, more or less across the board. As I attempted to deal with this man's [genuine and heartfelt] criticisms, a second jazz buff approached and asked for a word or two with me.

Excusing myself from the first person, I then sat back and listened as I was criticized again for the pricing of the jazz book. "And what, exactly, is your complaint, sir?," says I. "Well, they're too damned high! You're pricing the average collector out of the market," says he. At which point I introduced the two collectors to one another. . . Accompanying me that day was the inimitable Ms. Jan Bittenbender, who was appalled by the directness of the gentlemen's attacks and inquired if this was normal behavior for record collectors. I wasn't sure how to answer. . .

At another show, a collector approached me and politely inquired as to how I had arrived at a value of $100 for a certain female vocalist's album. "Why, is it too low?" I asked. "Oh, no. I would think it's way too high," he replied. To which I asked my favorite retort: "And do you have a near mint copy in your collection?" And he assured me that he had scored a virtually unplayed mint copy a couple of years ago. "I'll give you $100 for it right now," I said, offering him five twenties. "I'd *never* sell it for that!" at which point he paused, then added "Uh, I see your point."

Now, neither of these accountings are meant to insult the intelligence nor the integrity of the individuals involved. Rather, it is an attempt to provide the reader with a glimpse into some of the pitfalls that accompany the issuance of a price guide in [probably any field of] collectibles. In fact, each of the three men above, after venting their honest criticisms, spent some time talking with me, and, I believe, left with a greater appreciation for the problems inherent in any my undertaking.

The single most repeated remark concerning the book went something like "I don't care about the prices; just get the listings right." And, I can assure you, the listings in this edition are far more complete and accurate than those of the previous. In fact, they are so different in so many ways that they render the first edition all but useless! Aside from the expanded discographies (I have added over 1,000 new mono/stereo listings along with more than 4,000 second pressings, dramatically altering the listings for many labels, especially Blue Note), many factual and judgmental errors have been corrected (the most glaring, perhaps, being the listing of the Pepper/Knepper Quintet under Pepper Adams instead of Art Pepper).

One collector wrote "One subject that was not addressed explicitly in the previous volume was that of imports. For many out-of-print titles, imports were often the only available source of the music. Fortunately, their sound quality often exceeded that of their [original] American counterpart, particularly the

Japanese pressings, long in favor with may audiophile oriented listeners. On many labels the import cover and label designs often replicate the originals with only the catalog numbers differing." This is an excellent point, but, unfortunately, the lack of foreign pressings remains true for this edition, although I do hope to address this situation in future editions. Also, I have not included such items as V-Discs (absolutely essential to the big band/swing collectors), radio air-shots, and bootlegs (excepting the legendary Jolly Roger label).

As for future editions, aside from additions, corrections or suggestions regarding the data already published here, I am especially in need of listings and information on reissues from the past twenty years (1970-1992) on the albums in this edition, including notes telling me what album is being reissued; extending the discographies of the artists; Latin jazz albums of the '50s through the '90s; and the many small labels of the '70s and '80s—most of whom were rapidly absorbed by the majors—involved in everything from traditional and bop through funk and fusion. I am also planning the definitive book on Blue Note, tentatively titled *The Blue Note Blue Book*, that will address every aspect of this most collectible label, including general music data (albums recorded, song titles, personnel,etc.) and the minutia of collector related lore (all known label variations, reissues, test pressings, foreign pressings, et al). If you would like to contribute your knowledge to either project, please address letters to: Neal Umphred, *Jazz Price Guide*, P.O. Box 40116, Bellevue, WA 98015.

"Jazz records are, alas, ephemeral products. They go in and out of print with breathtaking speed, in an apparently random and haphazard manner. The only inviolable rule seems to be that the more you desire a given record, the more likely it is that record will soon go out of print. There is one consolation: if you wait long enough, the record you want will probably be reissued by somebody, somewhere, some time—usually just after you've bought a scratched copy of the original release at an outrageous price on the second-hand market." Author Robert Gordon penned those undying words for the discography in the back of his excellent little tome *Jazz West Coast* , and I find them rather apropppriate for closing this foreword. . ..

Neal Umphred
January 1994

Things Ain't What They Used To Be

An Introduction by Neal Umphred

Brian Priestly writes in *Jazz On Record* that a record "preserves a likeness of the music in live performance which record collectors, if they have sufficient experience of hearing music live, can re-create in their mind's ear. Unlike photographs of musicians and press reports of their activities, [records] at least tell us what the music sounds like. Despite the deliberate unreality of their sound picture. . . and despite the more subtle distortions of the recording situation and its philosophy, records are an invaluable source of pleasure. They are also an inexhaustible subject for study and, unlike music heard live, they can be repeated. Records are the audible documentation for a history of jazz."

In *The 101 Best Jazz Albums*, Len Lyons states, "Jazz has no better friend than records. As the music is characterized by spontaneous, emotional improvising, a jazz performance can never be repeated with exactly the same feeling. . . The music's foremost heroes have peak periods of creativity, freshness of imagination, and technical skill which they themselves cannot recapture once the delicate web of circumstances is altered. Nor can the best jazz, which always involves an element personal to the musicians involved, be written down in all its nuances for 'duplication' by others. Thus sound recording is the only means of documenting jazz's development and its artistic triumphs."

Each book has boundaries (size, page count, etc.) in which the author or editor must work. The more these boundaries can be defined, the more likely it is that the individual goals will be met. As most collectible records are the older ones, I have centered the listings of this book on those albums released between 1949, the beginning of the LP era, and 1969. While the development of the LP was complete by 1948, the first jazz LPs did not reach the market until the following year. 1969 was chosen for several reasons: It marks the demise of mono (that is, the practice of *recording* and issuing new titles in mono *and* stereo was over), it can be seen as the beginning of the post-modern era in which free, funk and fusion predominate, *and* it ends the decade, giving the book a twenty year span.

The book you hold in your hands, the second edition of *Goldmine's Price Guide To Collectible Jazz Albums*, is the closest thing to a complete discography regarding this time period ever published. While intended primarily to serve the needs of the collectors market (those people who collect the actual artifact of the era versus those who simply desire to have the music available for their listening) this book also exists as a discographical source book, providing both hobbyists and historians with more than 20,000 listings of first and later pressings of 33 1/3 RPM long playing albums issued between 1948 and 1969. A book intending to cover the entire field of recorded jazz (all of the 78 rpm singles and albums, 45 rpm singles and EPs, 33 1/3 rpm LPs issued during the past eighty or so years) would be a monumental task requiring several huge volumes *and* more years of labor than the reader may care to wait. . .

This book can be read by an observer articulate in the recorded history of jazz in many ways: As the separate discographies are laid out individually by artist in more or less chronological order by label, these listings detail the move from the 10" album to the 12"; the shift from independent jazz-based labels to the larger corporations and their broader market; the slow march from exclusively mono to exclusively stereo; etc. . . *And* the addition of second pressings indicates what was considered "good" enough to kept on the retailers' shelves, at least by the record company accountants.

The market for collectible jazz albums has been kept relatively secret over the years. While the demand for the old line sounds (traditional/Dixieland and big band "swing") has toned down considerably, the interest in hard bop and post bop, particularly by black artists, has grown across the board (and across the Atlantic and Pacific). *And,* aside from individual styles and artists, certain labels, now have their collectors. Of course, completists who want to "run a label" (i.e., collect an original of each number released by the label from beginning to end) must then collect every artist and every period (traditional, bop, funk, fusion, etc.) that particular label released.

This is difficult with major labels (Capitol, Columbia, Decca, Mercury, RCA Victor, etc.) where the jazz titles are interspersed with other fields as diverse as rock, country, comedy and soundtracks. Such a goal is attainable—and still affordable!—with the smaller, independent jazz labels such as Blue Note, Pacific Jazz or Impulse. But even such indies as Fantasy and Prestige often veered well outside of the jazz medium, lessening the desire to run the label.

But this is digression; I'd rather tell you what this book is not. This book is *not* the bible for jazz collectors; it is *not* the blue book of vinyl junkies. And it is certainly not the "Official" price guide for anything. Nor does this book reflect my opinions of what your records are worth. The prices quoted here are an attempt to reflect the broad differences in markets from region to region, state to state and city to city. The prices here are an attempt *to document what collectible records are worth on the open collectors' market.*

Please note that the prices quoted reflect the market during the period in which this book was assembled; *I cannot guarantee that they will remain the same for any length of time following the publication of this book.* In fact, a good price guide tends to have a direct, and often immediate, effect on the very market that it attempts to chronicle. That is, the release of the new information from such a book into the general market can influence what collectors collect and, consequently, what prices are paid. Prices listed here may be made obsolete *by their very listing,* especially when the listing offers new information or information that contradicts previously published (erroneous) information.

As for the fluctuations in the market, well, for those readers who expect values to rise automatically, the collectibles market is not all that different from the commodities market or the stock market, and *everyone* knows the insanities that occur there. So, while most prices do remain stable, or rise gradually, some rise dramatically while others actually go down. Value is established solely by supply and demand: Prices go up when the current demand is greater than the available supply; prices go down when the available supply is greater than the current demand. (Period!)

There *are* going to be instances where the information here is incomplete or wrong; it is almost unimaginable for any book listing 20,000 records not to make errors. These may range in nature from common typographical errors—from pressing the wrong character on the keyboard to transferring data from an error filled source—to incomplete research (missing catalog numbers or incorrect values assigned to records).

What's Here and What's Not!

There is no attempt to define jazz by the records listed in this book; I am neither so brave nor so foolhardy. Rather, this book attempts to list those records enjoyed and collected by people who dig jazz. Non-jazz artists are listed when a particular release has significance to the jazz enthusiast. While the most notable may be the three albums by Henry Mancini from the "Peter Gunn" series, the usual is for a popular vocalist attempting to broaden his or her range (read: market) by covering jazz-oriented tunes with appropriate arrangements and musicians. Thus albums by Dinah Shore (with Red Norvo), Tony Bennett (with Count Basie), and that most controversial of non-jazz singers, Frank Sinatra (with both the Count and the Duke), are listed. As these albums are definitely the singer's, they are listed under the singer's name, although the session musicians are listed when known. References are made under the separate musicians calling the reader's attention to these listings.

I have included in the "Jazzy Soundtracks" section those soundtracks of a jazz nature, not necessarily by a jazz artist. That is, *soundtracks with jazz-based music that would be of interest to a jazz collector,* such as the aforementioned Mancini "Gunn" albums. Not listed are non-jazz soundtracks by jazz artists.

Also included are select spoken word recordings. While those that are narratives or documentations/histories are common for such a book, less common are listings of poetry readings. Notable are those from the poets of the "beat generation," who found inspiration in jazz solos and attempted to emulate the "jazz feeling" into both the words they wrote and the way they read. It is not surprising that some (Kenneth Rexroth, Lawrence Ferlinghetti) found their way onto Fantasy Records, one of the West Coast's premier jazz labels of the '50s. Certainly one of the most unique of all spoken word artists, and one inextricably linked to jazz, as everything about his work would be inconceivable without the music, is the now legendary "word jazz" recordings from Ken Nordine. Also included are jazz linked comedians, such as Lenny Bruce and Lord Buckley.

In jazz, identifying a "group" with a specific name can be rather awkward. For instance, in 1959 Joe Castro, Billy Higgins, Leroy Vinnegar and Teddy Edwards formed a quartet, a co-operative unit. They landed a gig on ABC TV's "Stars of Jazz" as the Leroy Vinnegar Quartet, scored a recording contract with Atlantic Records as the Joe Carter Quartet and, in mid 1960, recorded for Contemporary Records as the Teddy Edwards Quartet.

For this book, I have kept instances such as this lumped together when it seemed the logical thing to do. For instance, Eddie Davis and Johnny Griffin recorded both as the Eddie Davis Quintet and as the Johnny Griffin Quintet; in this book both groups are listed together under "Eddie Davis & Johnny Griffin." The reader will find a note under Griffin referring him or her to the Davis & Griffin listings. Other instances such as this are treated similarly.

This helped me meet one of the book's basic criteria: Each album is listed once! While it is entirely reasonable to list many albums under two (or more) artists' names, I have opted to avoid redundancy and make a solitary entry per title. Where, exactly, the title is listed has less to due with the prominence of the artists' names on the cover (or the prominence of the artist in the field) and more to due with which label it is on. That is, an album with two or more featured artists *is listed under the artist's name who regularly records with that label,* since it is assumed that the sessions that led to the album were initiated due to the artist under the label's contract.

When both of the artists record for the label, I listed them where they made the most sense to me. For instance, Gerry Mulligan, Ben Webster and Johnny Hodges all recorded for Verve. *Gerry Mulligan Meets Ben Webster* and *Gerry Mulligan Meets Johnny Hodges* are listed under Mulligan's name not because his name is first but because they are part of a series of "Gerry Mulligan Meets. . ." Other artists in this series include an album with Stan Getz which was originally issued as *Getz Meets Mulligan In Hi Fi* and should probably be listed under Getz but, for the sake of clarity— and sanity— is listed under Mulligan!

There are cases where this criteria has not been followed religiously: For some of Norman Granz' sessions, Oscar Peterson's group would function as a house band, backing another artist. The resulting album, while recorded for Peterson's label using his group and often featuring him prominently on the cover and/or title, would be listed under the featured soloist, as the album is quite obviously meant *as* the soloist's.

First Pressings, Second Pressings & Reissues

This second edition adds more than 4,000 second pressings. For this book I define a second pressing as occurring when the record company originally releasing the album makes a physical change in the pressing of the album: Label color or design, the cover art or even the album's title, *provided the catalog number remains the same.* There *are* instances where an album has an identical label and front cover but the back cover varies from pressing to pressing. Often, as new titles came into print, ads were placed on the back cover alerting the consumer to other titles that might interest him or her.

For instance, original pressings of Columbia CL-1085, *Ellington Indigos* (1958), came with a set of liner notes taking up three columns with a note on Columbia LPs taking up the fourth. Later pressings replace the note with a list of other Ellington albums available up to CL-1323, *Ellington Jazz Party* (1959). This list also notes the availability of stereo versions of several titles, including 1085, which was not available in stereo on release. Thus we can ascertain this: First pressings of 1085 were issued only in mono with a back cover that does not list other Ellington albums. Second pressings, apparently released in 1959 or 1960, were in mono *and* stereo; the back cover of the monos, otherwise identical to the first pressings, *do* advertise other Ellington albums.

I assume that this occurred for many more albums than this lone Ellington release. So, a rule of thumb (that is a part of the fabric of the assumptions upon which the pricings in this book are based) is: Whenever an album cover advertises other, later album releases, it is assumed to be a second pressing *and the price listed in this book does not apply to that pressing!* Please highlight this section now that you've read it; as a buyer or a seller, this is imperative in determining the value of a given release in a particular transaction.

"Reissues" occur when 1) the record company deletes the original album and then places it back in circulation with a new catalogue number, often changing the title and the packaging but leaving the contents [essentially] unchanged, or 2) the music is repackaged and sold by another record company, either a subsidiary of the original label or an entirely different company which leases or otherwise acquires temporary or permanent legal use of the masters.

By 1954 it was obvious that the 12" LP had beat the 10" for the public's fancy (and spending money) and many labels reissued 10" titles as 12" albums. (12" reissues were usually track for track duplications of the 10" although many companies did add new tracks to fill out the extra space and to make the packaging more alluring.) I have dispensed with the notes as these should be fairly obvious. For example, aside from adding two inches to the disc's diameter, the only thing Capitol did was to change the prefix, usually from "H" to "T." With Fantasy, the 10" titles were given new 12" catalog numbers, but that really shouldn't baffle anyone.

One Channel vs. Two: The Mono & Stereo Debate

As a rule, jazz collectors of '50s and early '60s albums prefer the mono pressings to the stereo. Therefore, in this book, monos are priced higher than their stereo counterparts. There is one major exception: Those vocalists who recorded pop-oriented material for the major labels; their value is greatly affected by non-jazz collectors. In these cases (and there are many, with Peggy Lee, Julie London, June Christy and Jo Stafford coming immediately to mind), the stereo version is generally in far more demand than the mono and the price is subsequently affected. For those vocalists who record jazz more or less exclusively, usually for exclusively jazz labels, the mono remains the more desirable. Also, in cases where an artist in this book had a chart hit, the stereo version also attracts collectors and the price may or may not be affected. . .

While the major labels kept their mono stampers going through 1968, the press runs for these were miniscule, with distribution and sales correspondingly low. But this may not be true for smaller, independent labels, who, more wary of the bottom line, began deleting monos from their catalog as early as 1967. There may be considerably more mono titles from 1968 than this book lists; one would assume that they are rarer than their stereo counterparts. And, the fact that most jazz listeners prefer mono to stereo, they should be in more demand.

While jazz collectors cringe at early "true" stereo, virtually every record collector enters a paroxysm of rage at the mention of electronically rechanneled stereo (i.e., where the engineers took a mono signal and created a stereo effect with the use ofboosted treble and bass, echo, phase, etc. Those albums that underwent these tortures are listed with an "(E)." Should the reader find that an album listed as "(S)" but, in, fact, plays phony stereo, reduce the listed stereo price 20-40% *at least.*

There are often non-annotated differences between the mono and stereo versions of an album. While many, if not most, of the studios recording jazz in the '50s began using two tracks as far back as 1956-57, most of them did so only for the increased latitude it allowed in mixing down to mono. When stereo became a viable commercial medium toward the end of the decade, many companies returned to the original multi-track tapes and mixed them for stereo release. Thus hundreds of titles, recorded with only mono in mind, were issued to the new stereo enthusiasts. Many of these contain the most rudimentary form of stereo, with little or none of the stereophonic imaging that makes the enjoyment of stereo essential to most listeners. For that matter alone, aside from having the *original* mix, most jazz collectors prefer the mono over the stereo, even when the stereo is the rarer of the two.

More importantly, completely different takes may be used on mono and stereo versions (Atlantic and Verve appear to be the main culprits in this area), *or* the artist may actually go back into the studio and re-record the entire album for stereo! For instance, the aforementioned *Ellington Indigos* features two different sets of takes for each cut on the mono and the stereo albums. Thus, while this might seem trivial to a non-fan, to an Ellingtonian, this is the same as having two different albums. To further complicate matters, when CBS reissued the album as part of its digitally remastered "Jazz Masterpieces," they used the stereo mixes and included previously unreleased outtakes. So for the Duke completist, one would need a mono pressing, a stereo pressing *and* the digital stereo pressings!

Similarly, when Capitol decided to issue June Christy's *Something Cool* in stereo in 1960, they whisked the singer and a band back into the studios and recorded the entire album from scratch. And, while almost all collectors prefer to performance of the original, it nonetheless functions as an entirely "new" album for Christy collectors. Collectors who have information concerning other such re-recorded albums are invited to submit the data for future editions.

While the major labels kept their mono stampers going through 1968, the press runs for these were miniscule, with distribution and sales correspondingly low. But this may not be true for smaller, independent labels, who, more wary of the bottom line, began deleting monos from their catalog as early as 1967. There may be considerably more mono titles from 1968 than this book lists; one would assume that they are rarer than their stereo counterparts. And, the fact that most jazz listeners prefer mono mixes to stereos, they should be in more demand.

Page Breakdown

Artists are listed using fairly standard alphabetization; albums are listed more or less chronologically by label with the intention of presenting a *sem-blance* of the artist's recording career. As an example, I'll use Phil Woods. (The reader should note that the discography below is incomplete and merely for the purpose of illustration.)

WOODS, PHIL
Philip Woods is a modern jazz alto and soprano saxophone and clarinet player. For additional listings refer to The Manhattan Jazz All Stars; Zoot Sims; and the Various Artists section under Prestige.

New Jazz NJLP-1104	*(10")*	**Phil Woods New Jazz Quintet**	*1954*	**125.00**	**250.00**
Prestige PRLP-204	*(10")*	**Phil Woods New Jazz Quintet**	*1955*	**100.00**	**200.00**
		(Prestige 204 is a reissue of New Jazz 1104.)			
New Jazz NJLP-8304	*(M)*	**Sugan**	*1963*	*Unreleased*	
Impulse A-9143	*(M)*	**Greek Cooking**	*1967*	**12.00**	**30.00**
Impulse AS-9143	*(S)*	**Greek Cooking**	*1967*	**10.00**	**25.00**
		—Impulse albums above have orange & black labels.—			
Impulse AS-9143	*(S)*	**Greek Cooking**	*1968*	**4.00**	**10.00**
		—Impulse albums above have red & black labels with the "abc" logo on top.—			

WOODS, PHIL, & GENE QUILL

Epic LN-3521	*(M)*	**Phil Talks With Quill**	*1959*	**20.00**	**50.00**
Epic BN-554	*(S)*	**Phil Talks With Quill**	*1959*	**16.00**	**40.00**

WOODS, PHIL, & GENE QUILL / JACKIE McLEAN & JOHN JENKINS / HAL McKUSICK

New Jazz NJLP-8204	*(M)*	**Bird Feathers**	*1958*	**40.00**	**100.00**

After the artist's name, a brief note tells the reader more or less what instrument(s) he, she or they are noted for, followed by any references to other listings that may apply. References throughout the book are kept to a bare minimum; the line "For additional listings. . ." refer the reader to another listing when the artist in question is named in the title of an album or is inseparably linked with the recording. A parenthetical note reading "also features" indicates that the artist noted was listed on the cover or label in such a way as to call attention to his or her presence, more or less as a special guest whose appearance could boost sales. Listing references for artists who appeared on other artist's recording is a book in itself. . .

An example (not pictured here) is Prestige 7181, *Soul Junction*, whose cover credits "the red garland quintet featuring john coltrane and donald byrd." As this was Garland's session with an expanded trio, the listing in this book notes parenthetically "(Prestige 7181 also features John Coltrane and Donald Byrd.)" This does not mean to take away from the contributions of the two regular members of the trio, Paul Chambers and Art Taylor, both of whom have recorded albums as leaders. It merely is an expedient way for me to deal with guest appearances in a sane, orderly manner.

As for the actual listings, the first column indicates the label and catalog number. The second features a notation for the record's sound: "(M)" denotes monaural, while "(S)" means the entire record is in "true" stereo (essentially, a live recording with two mikes and no over-dubs) or multi-track stereo (the stereo signal emanating from your speakers was manipulated by the engineer after the fact). An "(E)" indicates that the stereo effect of the album has been electronically created from the original monaural source using a variety of engineering tricks. "(10")" indicates a 10" album, originally issued 1949-56, and is always mono.

The record's title is the middle column followed by the year of release. I make no claims for the exact order of the listings; these are approximations. Some artists' discographies are so complex that I couldn't even begin to place the records in anything resembling a sane chronology! Specific notes short enough to place on the same line follow the title, usually identifying a colored vinyl pressing or a cover variation. Notes too long are indented, in parentheses and italicized on the line below. For instance, the note in the example tells the reader that Prestige 204 is a reissue of New Jazz 1104.

Notes in italics that are centered and open (i.e., lacking parentheses but framed on each side by a "— ") refer to the album or albums above and deal exclusively with label specifications. These notes include the qualifier "above" when referring to more than one title! Glancing at the Verve releases, the reader should note that the stereo 6000 series are actually reissues released in 1960, often two or three years after the original monos. The centered note "Original Impulse albums above. . ." informs the reader of the particularities of identifying first pressings. The note applies to *all of the albums above it.* Similarly, second pressings are listed immediately afterword with a centered notation detailing the label's characteristics.

When an album is credited to two (or more) artists, usually as co-leads of a quarter/quintet/etc., the albums are listed under the first artist's last name followed by an ampersand ("&") and the other artist's name. When a compilation album features the work of two— usually with one side devoted to each— or more artists, the names are listed with a slash ("/") between them, as per the New Jazz 8204 listing above, where the album collects individual tracks from three groups: Woods & Quill, McLean & Jenkins, and McKusick.

The values, one for "Very Good Plus" (VG+) and one for "Near Mint" (NM) follow. Occasionally the reader will encounter either "Unreleased" or "See below" in the pricing columns. The first is self-explanatory and the title is listed with the note to inform the reader that, while the title and catalog number had been listed in the past— generally in a company catalog, on an inner sleeve or back cover, in one of the trade publications, or in *Schwann*, the record was, to the best of my ability to decipher data, not released to the public for sale. The "See below" note refers the reader to a parenthetical note beneath the listing that calls attention to something extraordinary pertaining to the selection.

Pricing the Records

The records listed here are taken from a variety of printed sources plus the input of the contributors. This input and a constant scrutiny of the set-sale and auctions placed in the pages of *Goldmine* also played a part in the make-up of this book. I strived for a sense of internal consistency with the pricing so that the book as a whole works as a guideline for each region of the country to use as on outline for their own market. *Every item in this book has been scrutinized by several contributors.* The values that were decided upon represent a ball park value that takes into account each of the prices submitted by those contributors.

The price that anyone will buy (or sell) an item for is often linked closely with the geographic/economic environment he or she is living in. A collector in New York City *should expect to pay more* for a given item than a collector from Wilkes-Barre, PA. After all, the Manhattan collector pays more for rent, for a restaurant dinner, for tickets to the Mets or Yankees, etc., because a New York City resident will be paid commensurately more for his job. Similarly, just as a dealer takes for granted that he or she will pay less for records when stocking his or her shop in Wilkes-Barre, they should also expect to sell them for less *in the same market.*

My own opinion varies greatly with some of the values listed here, so I have a bit of advice for any *serious* collector: *"When you are offered a record for which you have been actively searching for over five years, do not argue with the price, pay it."* The corollary to this little bit of wisdom would be: *"If you don't, you may not see it again for another five years, and it will cost even more."*

There are some cases where records are so rare in collectible condition realistic values could not be assigned. In those cases no figure was assigned to the price column but an estimated range was noted parenthetically beneath the title. This is not to imply that the record is worth either the highest or the lowest of the estimated range but rather that this range is a reasonable assessment of the discrepancies in the submitted values.

If a price on a record *with which you are familiar* seems ludicrously wrong, don't feel obliged to accept it. If other dealers and collectors are puzzled by the same discrepancy, it may be just that, an error of mine. But, at the same time, the *average* dealer or collector is often years (at least months) behind the reality of the market when it comes to the specialized knowledge of truly rare records, mainly because they are so rare that few, if anyone, ever see them for sale at any price. For example, the prices that are quoted for West Coast jazz 10" LPs may appear preposterous to a hard-bop specialist; but cool collectors know that certain titles are difficult to find at any price! *The more knowledgeable that you are, the more useful and informative this book will be,* if only that the informed reader will be be better able to assimilate the information and make use of it on a day to day basis.

Many collectors have expressed concern over the effects the overseas buyer has had on American records. To ignore these events would be both futile and counter-productive. Thus, a reasonably common item that goes for a bigger dollar overseas is not unduly affected because the foreign collectors only purchase a fraction of the copies put up for sale each year!

But. . . a record that turns up infrequently (only a few times a year), and invariably leaves the country to an overseas collector who bids two or three times what American collectors believe the record is "really" worth, then those prices *do* determine the value of those records. I would, in effect, be doing you, the user of this book, a disservice were I to choose any other option. *The average American collector needs to know what he or she should expect to have to bid to win a truly rare and desirable record in an open auction on the open market.* Please bear in mind that many of the records listed here, especially those with three figure values, will sell for considerably more overseas than here.

There are two prices listed for each record: the last and most important is the "Near Mint" price. I use a scale that evaluates the Very Good Plus, or Excellent, condition record as a sliding percentage of the NM value. For lesser condition records, VG prices are, for easy reference, approximately one-half (50%) of the listed VG+ value. The normal rule of thumb for pricing is that the cover makes up 40-50% of the value and the record 50-60%, although there are many, many exceptions to this rule.

Please note that the prices quoted are for opened copies in either VG+ or NM condition. Many collectors are willing to pay a premium for still-sealed copies. Two major points on purchasing still-sealed albums: first, shrink-wrapping of albums at the factory was not a common practice until the early to mid-'60s. A label as large as Capitol was using the fact that their albums were "poly-wrapped in the factory" as late as January 1964 as a selling point to the consumer. Thus, should you be offered an album from the '50s or early '60s still sealed in shrink-wrap, think twice. *A dealer cannot be held responsible for what is inside a sealed jacket.*

There is also the practice of re-sealing albums. This was done over the years by the record companies and by firms specializing in cut-outs. Prior to the sales boom of the mid-'70s, the industry had a very loose policy regarding returns; many of us over "thirty something" grew up able to test a purchase out on the store's turntable before taking it home (and were often able to return records that we just plain didn't like). Of course, those were pre-corporate days when retail operations were independently owned and the proprietor knew most of his customers and catered to their needs.

When purchasing a valuable sealed collectible at a shop or show, pay for the record *with the mutual understanding* that you will open it *immediately after purchase, in front of the dealer,* and if the record inside is not what it should be, *you may return it on the spot.* Do not purchase a sealed record, leave the store or dealer's table, and return later claiming that you got the wrong record or a damaged copy. Very few dealers will offer a refund in such a case. On a less savory note, there are a few dealers and shops that do their own shrink-wrapping. . .

Grading the Records

Records are graded by visual standards, not aural. The biggest complaints against the visual method are 1) the subjectivity of the grader's eyes or viewpoint, and 2) the fact that records do not always play as good, or bad, as they look. Both of these are justifiable arguments and, of course, it is the first point that causes the need for articles such as this: *records always look better when selling than when buying.* Arguments against play-grading are similar: The subjectivity of the listener is also a factor that is multiplied by the type of equipment being used. So, for the sake of convenience and necessity, your eyes are the method by which your records are graded.

When grading a disc, *grade the overall wear of the vinyl.* A record advertised as "NM" or "VG" should tell the prospective buyer the shape of the playable vinyl (although common sense should be used: un-played records that are warped cannot be Mint). Such defects as name stickers on the label, tape on the jacket, etc., should be addressed separately with abbreviated notations. A reliable set of these notations have been developed over the years covering virtually every type of defect that can occur to a record or its cover; a list of most of the more common abbreviations and their meanings follow the grading definitions below. When defining the grades, it is difficult to describe several without discussing certain defects and/or the way the disc plays; these are included to help define the grade, not to cause confusion.

Visual grading is most important in mail-order transactions where a buyer doesn't see his purchase until his check has cleared the bank. Grading needs to be as strict, as accurate as possible. Put simply, the aim of grading is to make the buyer visualize the record he or she is purchasing through an advertisement and not be disappointed when that record arrives! A record that is accurately graded will play the same (or better) than the grading! In-person deals do not require a grade of any sort; if you are holding a record that has obviously been played a hundred times, you don't need a grade to determine whether or not you are going to purchase that disc.

Always grade records under a good, steady light. A 100 watt light bulb in a common desk lamp will do an adequate job; most major defects will jump out at you and allow you to make an accurate assessment of the vinyl. Grading a record using light from the ceiling or from deflected sunlight entering the window will often "hide" paper scuffs, discoloration, groove wear and even some fingerprints. Everyone makes mistakes in grading. This is a problem all dealers and collectors are prone to make and must be aware of. Do not condemn a dealer for one mistake; but, when the mistake is the norm, find someone else to buy your records from. . .

A ***Mint*** record (abbreviated as "M") should appear to have just left the manufacturer without any handling; that is, it should appear perfect! No scuffs or scratches, blotches or stains, labels or writing, tears or splits; nothing. *Perfect.* And age has nothing to do with it; *the same standards for Mint apply to a Prestige 10" from 1954 as they do to a 12" reissue on that company's Original Jazz Classics series from the '80s!* There are no sliding values for Mint.

A Mint album cover should appear to have never have had a record in it; no ring-wear, dog-eared corners, writing, seam-splits. I define ring-wear as any imprint on the cover from the record that it formerly held. *Any* imprint. To many dealers and collectors the ink has to be worn off for them to recognize ring-wear and grade a cover down. Uh-uh. Mint means perfect and nothing else.

A ***Near Mint*** record (NM) appears Mint but has one or two tiny, inconsequential flaws that do not affect the play is Near Mint and should command 85-95% of the Mint price. For many, Near Mint and Mint-Minus mean the same thing; for the sake of this article, they are interchangeable. When dealing with a seller that discriminates between the two grades, inquire as to what the dealer means when he calls one record M- and another NM. Many dealers and collectors take the position that any used (opened) record cannot be verified as Mint so they use M- to describe what appears to be a perfect record that has been opened. Covers should still be close to perfect with minor signs of wear or age just becoming evident: slight ring-wear, minor denting to a corner, or writing on the cover should all be noted properly.

Many records *are available* in Near Mint/Mint condition, although these are generally more recent and the prices are nominal. That is, most dealers set a minimum price on the records they sell in their store, usually dollars ($3.99-4.99), just for normal, everyday, all-too-readily-available records. Whether they are unplayed or "merely" near mint the price will be the same: it wouldn't be worth the dealer's time to stock the single unless that minimum price was met.

A ***Very Good Plus*** record (VG+) has been handled and played either infrequently or very carefully (this grade is sometimes referred to as "Excellent"). On a disc, this could mean that there are light paper scuffs from sliding in and out of a sleeve; the vinyl may have lost some— *not all*— of its original luster. A slight scratch that did not affect the play in an otherwise nearly Mint disc would be acceptably VG+ for most collectors; a scratch of any sort that audibly clicked throughout at a level greater than or equal to the music would not be acceptable. Always list the flaws in a VG+ record or cover.

As a rule of thumb, a VG+ item is worth 50%, or one-half, of the Near Mint value, although this ratio varies with the rarity of the item. That is, a record that is fairly common in NM/M condition has little real value in VG+ to most collectors; consequently 25-35% may be more appropriate. On the other hand, truly rare records will fetch 75% in VG+. (By rare, I am referring to items in which the supply is merely a fraction of the demand and the record sells for hundreds of dollars. . .) On covers, some wear from storage is acceptable, especially light wear that does not affect the beauty of the artwork. Again, listing the flaws when selling is safest.

Very Good (VG) records will display visible signs of handling and playing, such as loss of vinyl luster, light surface scratches, groove wear, and spindle trails from countless spins on the turntable. A VG record looks like it will have some audible surface noise when it is played, although any such noise should not overwhelm the music or ruin the listening experience. A VG record should appear to have been well-played by a responsible owner. Gouges, cracks, and maple syrup in the grooves are unacceptable.

As more and more collectors spend more and more money on their acquisitions, the lower limits of acceptability for an item to be admitted into their collection rises. That is, to many collectors, a record in VG condition is not acceptable unless the item is truly rare and virtually unavailable in any other condition! And then, it is accpetable only if the price is scaled appropriately to match the condition. "Used but not abused" might sum up this grade. A VG record should command approximately 20-30% of the Near Mint price.

This is a difficult grade when discussing paper goods. Like a disc, usually a cover is VG when a variety of problems are evident: ring wear, seam splits, bent corners, loss of gloss on the photo, stains, etc. An aggravated combination of two of these problems— never all of them— would cause a sleeve to be graded VG.

Good (G) in record collecting parlance all too often means a beat, trashed, take-it-to-the-flea-market frisbee. Good should mean that the record is well-played with any number of defects that collectors normally shy away from, such as an almost complete loss of surface sheen, aggravating surface noise, etc. Still, the purchaser, knowing full well that he or she is buying a Good record, should be able to take it home, slap it onto the turntable and have a good time listening to it. Records that do not provide this most fundamental requirement are just no good. A Good record should command 10-15% of the Near Mint price.

A Good cover has seen considerable handling over a course of years and displays the obvious physical signs: ring-wear on the front and back; some seam-splitting, particularly along the bottom, which would receive the brunt of the record's sliding in and out; corners may be dog-eared to a light degree; an infatuated owner may have written his or her name somewhere; etc. If a record or cover is beneath your contempt, it is not in "G" condition; look below for the appropriate grade.

Any record or cover that does not qualify for a "Good" grading should be seen as ***Poor***. A "P" record should command 0-5% of the Mint price. Make a friend: Give any "P" record away as a freebee to anyone who expresses interest in it. . .

Finally, bear in mind that visual evidence can be deceiving: the quality of the vinyl and the plating make all the difference in the world. A record properly manufactured with a high quality plating may look VG+ and play Near Mint; this is particularly true of records from the '50s through the mid-'60s, when print runs were dramatically smaller, vinyl was fresher and more care was paid to the entire procedure. Records from this period are a better investment in VG+ condition than the more recent American product. In fact, many 45s from the '50s can be purchased in VG condition at reasonable prices and will play far better than the price paid would indicate. A record manufactured from recycled vinyl with poor plating may look Mint and play VG. Still, most dealers do not have the time to listen to each item in their inventory, so visual standards remain.

Record Collecting Abbreviations

Listed here are common abbreviations used when advertising to describe flaws and their locations on a record or cover. Different dealers have different ways of using these abbreviations; some capitalize them ("DJ"), some use periods after each letter ("n.a.p.") and some use a slash ("c/o"). Those defects marked with an asterisk (*) should *always be listed* when advertising an item for sale or auction.

"cc" .... cut corner*
"co" .... cut out*
"coh" .... cut-out hole*
"c-33" .... compact-33 1/3 rpm single or EP
"cvr" .... cover
"dj" .... promotional disc jockey copy
"imp" .... import
"ips" .... inches per second
"lbl" .... label
"lp" .... 12" 33 1/3 rpm long playing album
"mo" .... mono, or monaural
"nap" .... (does) not affect play
"ol" .... on label
"org" .... original
"pln cvr" .... plain paper jacket (no picture or titles)
"promo" .... promotional copy
"quad" .... quadraphonic
"re" .... reissue
"reel" .... reel to reel tape
"repro" .... reproduction, or counterfeit
"sdtk" .... soundtrack
"se" or "e" .... stereo effect electronically produced
"2nd pr" .... second pressing
"slt wrp" .... slight warp*

"sm splt" .... seam split*
"sol" .... sticker on the label*
"sr" .... slight ring-wear on the front cover*
"ss" .... still sealed
"st" .... stereo
"stkr" .... sticker
"t&ts" .... (disc jockey) title & timing strip
"toc" .... tape on the cover*
"tol" .... tape on the label*
"ts" .... taped seams*
"wlp" .... white label promo
"wol" .... writing on the label*

Jazz At 16 2/3 RPM

In 1957 Prestige began issuing titles in 16 2/3 rpm, "the modern speed in phonograph records." Each album was capable of containing the music of two regular, 33 1/3 rpm LPs, with an average playing time of 45 minutes per side. These 12" albums featured black on white versions of the familiar black on yellow Prestige label and were issued in jackets with artwork and liner notes. A legend on the back notes that these records were compatible with any turntable "equipped with a playing speed of 16 2/3 rpm. You are not required to buy a new needle. . ." and credits Rudy Van Gelder as the engineering consultant for this system.

The program did not take off with the public, although the reviews of the time were rather favorable, noting no discernible loss of sound quality. The first four titles were reviewed by *downbeat* writer Dom Cerulli, who noted "With these four Prestige LPs. . . the era of jazz on superlongplay records has begun. . . Whether the majors intend to go into 16 rpm remains to be seen. I can't see how they can avoid it, if this system will hold up as well with, say, symphony orchestras as well as small groups." [His article noted the release of other musical types on 16 2/3 rpm by Vox.}

These records have not been previously listed in a price guide and the general awareness of their existence among collectors is negligible. The values assigned below are based on the few sales reported to me; they seem rather conservative given their relative rarity.

16-1 The Modern Jazz Quartet / Milt Jackson, **Concorde** *1957* **50.00** **125.00**
(16-1 is a reissue of Prestige 7005, MJQ's "Concorde," and 7003, "Milt Jackson.")

16-2 Billy Taylor, **Let's Get Away From It All** *1957* **50.00** **125.00**
(16-2 is a reissue of Prestige 7015 and 7016, "Billy Taylor Trio, Volume 1 and 2.")

16-3 ***Miles Davis And The Modern Jazz Giants*** *1957* **50.00** **125.00**
(16-3 is a reissue of Prestige 7109, "Bags Groove," and a first pressing of "Miles Davis And The Modern Jazz Giants," later to be issued as 7150.)

16-4 J.J. Johnson & Kai Winding / Bennie Green, **Trombone By Three** *1957* **50.00** **125.00**
(16-4 is a reissue of Prestige 7023, "Trombone By Three," and 7030, "J.J. Johnson, Kai Winding, Bennie Green.")

16-5 **Modern Jazz Survey 1—New York Jazz** *1958* **60.00** **150.00**
(16-5 is a reissue of New Jazz 8207, George Wallington's "New York Scene," and a first pressing of Phil Woods' "Sugan," later issued as New Jazz/Status 8304.)

16-6 **Modern Jazz Survey 2—Baritones And French Horns** *1958* **60.00** **150.00**
(16-6 consists of material that would eventually be issued as Prestige 7280, John Coltrane's "Dakar," and New Jazz/Status 8305, "Curtis Fuller And Hampton Hawes With French Horns.")

Record Company Label Directory

This section will define the evolution of record company label designs, hopefully assisting the reader in identifying originals from later pressings. Many labels have various ways of identification; I have kept the explanations as brief and to the point as possible. The companies are listed alphabetically. Years and issue numbers are approximate; you may find that you have pressings of an album on an earlier label than I have either here or in the listings.

Promotional versions of albums were manufactured exclusively for distribution among radio stations. The most common method of printing promotional records has been to press them on white labels with plain black print, hence the term "white label promo." Some labels used their regular label, or a modified version, and had such mottos as "Audition Copy" or "Promotional Copy" incorporated into the label's typesetting; *labels with such notices stamped on after the fact are not the same!*

Promotional records are usually pressed in small runs on quality vinyl, generally commanding a premium above the normal value of the record. Not so in the jazz market. . . The reader should assume that a promo has little or no value differential with the price listed for a stock copy (in fact, to many collectors, the promo is *less* desirable).

<u>A&M</u>: From 1963 through mid-'73, A&M used a brown label. From then until 1985 the label was a silver gray with a large brown "AM" fading into the background.

<u>ABC-Paramount</u>: From 1956 through 1961 (101-400), a black label was issued with ABC-Paramount on top and "A Product of Am-Par Record Corp" on the bottom. From 1962 through 1966 (400-560s), the black label reads "A Product of ABC-Paramount Records Inc." During 1966 and 1967, the logo was changed to "abc records" in a box at the top. Throughout these years, mono albums bore an "ABC" prefix; stereo, "ABCS." White label promos were issued.

From 1968-74, the label was black with "abc" on top and "New York, NY" on the bottom. Other labels: black one with the logo in children's blocks (1973) and purple on gold (1974-78). In 1979, ABC was acquired by MCA.

<u>American Recording Society</u>: A mail-order firm that leased masters from other companies. Each album was issued without a cover in plastic sleeves and included an insert (folded into four pages) with liner notes and ordering information. A.R.S. appeared to serve as a branch of Norman Granz' operations, with many recordings appearing simultaneously—if not earlier—on this imprint than on the regular series, although it is the Verve pressing that is the more desirable to collectors.

<u>Argo</u>: From inception through 1964, Argo used a black label with silver print. The final year, 1965, is confusing, as along with the original label, the company issued a silver label with black print and a brown label with pink print. Throughout these years, mono albums bore an "LP" prefix; stereo, "LPS." By 1966 Argo became Cadet, which lasted into the early '70s.

Atco: A subsidiary of Atlantic, initial pressings from 1958 through the latter part of 1961 were on a solid yellow label with a harp in the upper left (101-138). Stereo pressings on this label are very rare! From 1961 through 1968, mono albums had a gold and gray label with a white stripe through the center with "ATCO" in large print. Stereo albums were purple and brown with the white stripe.

In 1969, after the demise of mono, all (stereo) albums returned to a solid yellow with an 1841 Broadway, NYC address printed on the bottom. When Atlantic was sold to the Warner conglomerate, the address was changed to 75 Rockefeller Plaza, NYC. From 1978 through 1984 the company used a solid gray label; since then, a gray label made up of countless tiny "Atco" logos was used. By the '80s, Atlantic/Atco had become a part of Warner Communications, now known as the corporate giant WEA (Warner/Elektra/Atlantic.)

Atlantic: From 1950 through mid 1960, mono albums were issued on a black label with silver print (8000-8040 and 1200-1332). In 1958 select titles were mixed into stereo and issued on a green label, all of which are rather rare! A transition label, referred to as the "bullseye label," was in use briefly: Mono albums had an orange, purple and black fan around the spindle hole with "Atlantic" in an orange and purple band on top. For stereo albums there is a green and blue border around the label; the fan around the hole is also green and blue. These "bullseye" labels were used on at least 8026 through 8036 and are all very rare.

From 1960 through 1962 (8040-8059 and 1330-1378), Atlantic switched to a banded, multi-color label: mono albums were orange and purple; stereo albums were green and blue. Each label had a white band through the center with a white pinwheel logo (known as the "fan") in a black box on the right side. Stereo albums on this label are generally more difficult to find than the monos.

From 1962 through 1966 (8060-8125 and 1379-1463) the fan switched to black on white with "Atlantic" running vertically alongside it. In 1966 through 1968 (8126-8178 and 1464-1499) "Atlantic" ran horizontally beneath the fan. After 1968, the label, now stereo only, switched to green and orange with the company's 1841 Broadway, NYC address on the bottom.

From 1973 through 1975 a Rockefeller Plaza address appeared at the bottom and, from 1975 through the end of the '80s "A Warner Communications Company" appeared on the bottom. White label promos were issued from the mid-'60s on. By the '80s, Atlantic/Atco was a part of Warner Communications, now the corporate giant Warner/Elektra/Atlantic, known acronymically as WEA.

Bethlehem: Throughout the 1950s, Bethlehem mono albums carried a "BCP" prefix and featured a maroon label with silver print with the "Bethlehem" logo in an arc across the top. In the latter years of that decade, the "Bethlehem" logo changed to black letters in a silver border across the top. The stereo albums wre identified as "SBCP" with a blue label. Stereo albums on Bethlehem are very rare! In the 1960s, after they were acquired by King Records, the new covers and LPs carried King's Cincinnati, Ohio address. Finally, Bethlehem appears to have issued only one album that would be of apparently and absolutely no interest to a jazz collector: 6057, *A Treasury Of Spicy Sea Songs,* by The Shantymen.

Blue Note: Blue Note is the most collectible of jazz labels, if not the single most collectible LP label on all music fields. While the previous edition of this book made a passable effort at delineating the most obvious variance, that of the varying company address that appeared on the label, there are many as yet undocumented aspects of the Blue Note label that are sought out by the highly specialized collector. These include the weight of the actual disc and the depth of the grooves; the cut of the platter's edge ("squared" or "rounded"); the appearance of the registry mark ("®") on the label (which I made a stab at in the first edition but have dropped this time around until more is made manifest); whether or not the front cover is laminated; the company address on the back cover; and more. I am attempting to wade through this morass of arcana step by step.

So. . . through 1957 (the 7000 and 5000 series of 10" albums and 12" albums on the 1200 and 1500 through 1543), blue on white labels with the company's Lexington Ave., NYC address in an arc in the upper right between 1 and 3 o'clock were used. Only mono albums were issued during these years, carrying a "BLP" prefix.

From mid 1957 through 1961 the company's address was on West 63rd Street, NYC. First pressings of the remaining 1500 series (1544-1599) and the first few 4000s (through approximately 4014) carry the new address. These first pressings apparently do not bear a registry mark on the bottom of the label nor does "Blue Note, Inc" appear on the back of the covers.

All original Blue Note pressings through early 1960 (1200s, 1500s, 4000-4049) were originally pressed with what is referred to as a "deep groove label." That is, the pressers used would push the vinyl through the manufacturing process and leave a deep circle in the vinyl beneath the label on both sides. This circle was approximately the size of a 50¢ piece.

Original copies of Blue Note 4015 through 4074 have the W. 63rd Street address while 4074 through approximately 4100 have a W. 61st Street address, with some overlapping: 4074 and 4077 apparently exist with both addresses, and others, such as 4078, are rumored to exist with the 63rd Street label.

In early 1959 Blue Note incorporated, adding the now familiar registry mark ("®") below the "E" in "BLUE NOTE" on the bottom of the label, and the back covers read "Blue Note, Inc." All of the earlier W. 63rd Street pressings were reissued with this new label variation.

It was also during 1959 that the company's first stereo titles appeared. These initial releases used a "BST" prefix and the four digit mono catalog number. For example, *Art Blakey & The Jazz Messengers*, commonly referred to as the *Moanin'* album, was issued in mono as BLP-4003 and in stereo as BST-4003. Later that year, new stereo titles bore a "BST-8" prefix. Using Blakey again, *Buhaina's Delight* was issued in mono as BLP-4104 and in stereo as BST-84104. Note that the earlier stereo titles were reissued with the new numbering system: *Art Blakey & The Jazz Messengers*, appeared as BST-84003. These, too, are often confused for first pressings.

Tiring of the need to continually change their address on the label, the company witched over to a more broader location by printing "New York, USA" in lieu of a specific address. This label was used through the duration of Blue Note's stature as an independent. The company did add thier new address to the back of the album covers; New York, USA labels can be found in 61st Street covers.

Note: Copies with a different label on each side exist; these sports have no real value at this time to aficionados. Similarly, the "deep groove" pressings can be found with the groove on just one side. These are later pressings with no premium attached to them. . .

In 1966 Blue Note was sold to Liberty, who kept the blue on white label and essentially reissued the entire line (in stereo, real or electronic) with the address replaced by "A Division Of Liberty Records." When Liberty was absorbed by United Artists in 1970, a dark blue, almost black, label with the Blue Note logo in a box on the left side was also in effect. This transition label carried the "Liberty/UA, Inc" motto on the bottom.

U.A. then returned to the classic blue on white label and from 1970 through 1972, "A Division Of United Artists Records" appeared where the address used to be. From 1973 through 1978, a solid blue label with the company logo on upper right was issued. Throughout the 1970s a blue label with "Re-Issue Series" on top was issued. In 1985, U.A. was purchased by Capitol and the label returned to the original blue on white with the motto "The Finest In Jazz Since 1939."

<u>Blue Thumb</u>: The first four LPs had a black label. From the fifth release through approximately the mid-60s the off-white label had a thumb print on top. This was finally replaced with a purple label with the "abc" logo on top in 1974.

<u>Bluesville</u>: Originals on this subsidiary of Prestige had bright blue labels with the logo in block print on top. Second pressings had flat blue labels with the Prestige trident logo on the right side.

<u>BluesWay</u>: During the first year, 1967 and 1968, the label was blue. This was replaced by a black label with a blue perimeter.

<u>Brunswick</u>: From 1950 through the early '60s, Brunswick used a black label with silver print. Yellow label promos were issued. In late 1962 through 1972, the company switched to a black label with a rainbow through the center and "A Division of Decca Records" along the perimeter. Throughout these years, mono albums bore a "BL" prefix while stereo carried a "BL-7". Since 1972, a black label with the rainbow and "Manufactured by Brunswick Record Corp" along the perimeter was used.

<u>Cadence</u>: From inception through 1962 a maroon label was used with a silver top. During the company's final year the label was red with a black border.

<u>Cadet</u>: From 1965, when Argo became Cadet, through 1968, a blue label was used. In 1969 a blue label fading into white was issued. A pink and yellow label was in effect in the early '70s, replaced briefly by a pink and orange label.

<u>Camden</u>: A subsidiary of RCA Victor, Camden's original label was a pink/purple. From 1958 through 1964, a blue label with a purple perimeter. From 1964-68, a blue label with a dark blue fading into light blue perimeter was in print. Throughout this time, mono albums bore a "CAL" prefix; stereo titles had a "CAS" prefix. Stereo numbers ending with an "e" denote reprocessed stereo. From 1969-75 a dark blue label was in effect. In 1976 the entire line was turned over to Pickwick.

<u>Cameo</u>: From 1959-61 the label was orange with a cameo logo on top. From 1961 through the rest of the decade it was a red and black label with the cameo on the right. In the late '60s a purple label was used with the cameo on top.

<u>Capitol</u>: From 1949 through 1953 (100-344), they basically issued a green label with "Long Playing Microgroove" on the bottom. From 1953 through 1958 (345-1010) a turquoise label with "Long Playing" on the bottom was in effect, with gray/black label also used during this time. Yellow label promos were issued.

From 1958-1959 (1021-1225), Capitol switched to a black label with a "rainbow" perimeter and the Capitol dome logo on the left side. From 1959-1962 (1225-1700), the black/rainbow label had the logo and a silver line on the left. Black label promos with "Not For Sale" on the bottom were issued.

From 1962 through 1969 (1700-2999 and 100-261), Capitol issued a black label with the dome logo on top. From 1969 through 1972, Capitol's albums were issued on a lime green label. Capitol has since used red, yellow, and purple labels before returning to the black rainbow label of the '60s.

The early 10"s albums bore an "H" prefix. Throughout the above years, 12" mono albums bore a "T" or "W" prefix with "ST" or "SW" for stereo. A "DT" or "DW" prefix indicates reprocessed stereo, the "D" referring to Capitol's "Duophonic" method of altering the mono signal beyond recognition. Special packaging, such as gatefold cover, were often designated as "TAO/STAO" or "KAO/SKAO."

The Capitol group now owns or controls the catalogs of Blue Note, Transition, Imperial, Liberty, Aladdin, Pacific Jazz and United Artists.

<u>Chancellor</u>: Initial releases in 1958-59 had pink labels; after that, black.

<u>Charles Mingus</u>: In an attempt to overcome the inequities of recording for the established labels, Mingus started this eponymous label to sell his work through the mail via ads placed in the trades. Four albums were issued: JWS 001/002, 005, 009, and 013/014. After the mail-order business failed, the remaining copies were distributed to the stores through Fantasy Records in 1967, with each copy containing a photo-copy of a letter from Mingus pleading for financial contributions. (The letter is worth an additional $50.) When these few copies were gone, the first three titles were then reissued on Fantasy, keeping the same "JWS" numbers.

<u>Circle</u>: Throughout the 1950s, Circle issued a white label with "Circle" in script on top. In the latter part of the decade the logo appeared in block print.

<u>Clarion</u>: This budget subsidiary of Atlantic/Atco repackaged material from the parent label's catalog.

<u>Clef</u>: Originals on Norman Granz' first label had black labels with a line drawing of a trumpet player in the upper left with "Clef Records, Inc" on the bottom. These were distributed by Mercury Records with Mercury's familiar "MG" as part of its prefix, and are often referred to as Mercury/Clefs. After being consolidated into Verve in 1956, the new label inaugurated the "Clef Series," many of which were reissues of earlier titles. During the first years, "Verve Records" was at the top of the label with the trumpeter and "Clef Series" beneath.

<u>Colpix</u>: From inception through the early '60s the company used a gold label with "Colpix" in large red letters on top. In 1963 a strip of movie film was added. Later pressings were on a blue label. Stereo numbers are decidedly rarer than their mono counterparts.

<u>Columbia</u>: From 1949 through 1955, Columbia used a red label with gold print and "Long Playing" on the bottom (through 650). A variety of prefixes, "CL," "GL" and "ML," were used before the company settled on "CL." From 1955 through 1962 (650-1779), these mono albums had red labels with six white-on-black, highly stylized camera "eye"-on-a-tripod logos on each side of the label.

From 1962 through 1965 (1780-2379), the eye logos were replaced with two white eye logos, one on each side of the spindle hole, and read "Guaranteed High Fidelity" on the bottom. From 1965 through 1968 (2380-2811), the red mono label read "360 Sound Mono" in white on the bottom. [Note that some later pressings—late 1967-1968—read only "Mono."]

Columbia apparently began manufacturing stereo albums (8000 series) in early 1959; the initial 8000 numbers were assigned randomly as mono albums were mixed into stereo and released. By 1960, designating stereo was simple: CS-6800 was added to the mono catalog number to denote stereo. Thus, a Columbia CL-2127 (Brubeck's *Time Changes)* would be CS-8927!

8000-8579 featured the red label with the six white on black camera-on-a-tripod logos, known as the "eye" logo. From 1962 through 1965 (8630-9128), stereo labels featured the two white eye logos with "360 Sound Stereo" in black on the bottom. From 1965 through 1970 (9130-9999, 1-30, and 30000-30050), stereo labels read "360 Sound Stereo" in white at the bottom.

From 1970 on, the red label reads "Columbia" in orange/gold letters a half-dozen times around the perimeter. Columbia subsidiaries include Epic, listed separately below, and their budget reissue series, Harmony, also below.

<u>Concert Hall Jazz</u>: *Refer to* Jazztone

<u>Contemporary</u>: From 1950 through the mid-'60s, mono albums on the 3000 series had yellow labels with black print and bore a "C" prefix. In 1958, ads appeared in trade journals announcing that Stereo Records would be releasing a number of Contemporary titles in stereo. Stereo Records was a Contemporary imprint created to showcase the company's new equipment—designed in house—and conceived as a high-end line for the "audiophile" market. Bearing a 7000 number with an "S" prefix and assigning the numbers as titles were mixed into stereo, the labels were black with gold print and similar to Contemporary's in layout.

By 1959 Contemporary was issuing stereo albums with an "S" prefix and the same last three digits as the 3000 monos; this included reissuing the Stereo Records titles with their original 7000 numbers. The mono 3000 series received an "M" prefix. The label was defunct through the late '60s, picking up again in the early '70s. New titles and reissues from the '70s have green labels; from the '80s, a light orange-gold label. Contemporary is currently a part of Fantasy Records.

<u>Coral</u>: From inception through 1963, albums from Coral, a subsidiary of Decca Records, were issued on a maroon label. Blue label promos were issued. From 1963 through 1968 a black label with a rainbow center and "A Subsidiary of Decca Records" was in used. From 1968 through 1970 "A Subsidiary of MCA" replaced the original Decca motto. Throughout these years, mono albums bore a "CRL" prefix; stereo albums, a "CRL-7." Coral is now a part of MCA.

<u>Cotillion</u>: From 1969 till late 1972 this Atlantic subsidiary used a grey label with an "1841 Broadway" address on the bottom. The address was changed to "75 Rockefeller Plaza" in the mid-'70s. Finally, Cotillion switched to a purple label.

<u>Crown</u>: Arising from the ashes of Modern Records, Crown used a black label with silver print through 1960, often reissuing the earlier label's titles. By 1960, Crown specialized in low budget reissues, pressed on the cheapest vinyl available and often with completely misleading credits.

<u>Decca</u>: From 1949 through 1954, Decca used a black label with gold print. From 1954 through 1960 (the 8000 series), a black label with silver print. Pink label promos were issued. From 1960 through 1966 (4000-4830s), the label was black with a rainbow stripe and reads "Mfrd. by Decca Records."

From 1967 through 1971, "A Division of MCA" was printed beneath the rainbow. White label promos were issued. For approximately one year, 1971-1972, "Mfd. by MCA" was added. After that, reissues appeared on the MCA label. Mono albums bore a "DL" prefix; stereo albums were designated with a "DL-7." By 1973 MCA had entirely subsumed the Decca imprint.

<u>Del-Fi</u>: Original label (1201) were blue with a black border containing blue circles. The next label (1202-1246) was basically black with blue/gold diamonds around the border. Reissues from the '80s have a gold label.

<u>Deram</u>: From inception through the early '70s the label was basically white with "London" beneath the Deram logo on top. During the '70s the white label had a brown top. The '80s versions read "Manufactured by Phonogram, Inc" on top.

<u>Dot</u>: During 1955-56 (the 3000 series), Dot issued a maroon label with "Gallatin, Tennessee" on the bottom. During late 1956 through 1957 the address was "Hollywood, California." From 1957 through 1967 (3030-3050), a black label was used with "Long Play" and "Dot" in script on the top. In 1968 "A Division of Paramount" appeared on the bottom. Throughout these years, mono albums bore a "DLP" prefix with a 3000 number; stereo albums bore the same "DLP" but were a 25000 series (the last three digits of the mono and stereo releases were identical).

From 1968 through 1970 the Paramount mountain logo appeared in a box with the Dot logo at the top of the label. From 1970 through 1974, the Dot logo appeared in a box on top with "A Division of Famous Music Corp" on the bottom. During 1974-78, a purple and yellow label was in effect. From 1978 on, select Dot titles were reissued on ABC.

<u>Elektra</u>: During the '50s a white label was used with an electron logo on top. This was replaced with a grey label a small guitar player on top. From 1961 until 1966 a gold label was used with a large guitar player on top. The gold label was replaced from 1966 until 1969 (#4007-4040s) with a flat brownish label. During 1969 and 1970 the label was red (#4040s-5007). Throughout the rest of the decade the label was multi-colored with a butterfly in the upper right. This was replaced by a red label with a Warner Bros. logo on the bottom. After 1983 the label was black.

<u>EmArcy</u>: From 1954 through 1958, EmArcy used a blue label with silver print with a David Stone Martin "drummer" at the top. Like other Mercury subsidiaries, an "MG" prefix was used on the mono 36000 series. When titles were released in stereo, an "SR" prefix and an 80000 number was used. [Note that some titles were reissued on special blue Mercury/EmArcy Jazz labels, often appearing here in stereo for the first time.] In the 1960s, a gray label was issued. Reissues in the 1980s featured a brown and gold label with the drummer.

<u>End</u>: The label was originally gray with a dog on top that read "Product of End Music, Inc" at the bottom. This was replaced with a gray "dog" label that read "A Division of Roulette Records, Inc" on the bottom. This was replaced in the early '60s with a label that had "End" on end on either side.

<u>Epic</u>: As Columbia's primary subsidiary, from inception through 1962, Epic carried a yellow label with black lines radiating out along the perimeter; stereo issues read "Stereorama" across the top. During 1962-63, a yellow label with "Epic" appearing eight times around the perimeter was used for mono albums; stereos read "Stereo" and "Epic" three times each around the perimeter. From 1963-65 a yellow label with "A Product of CBS" on the bottom was used. From 1965 through 1972 the yellow label without the CBS motto was in print.

Initially, mono albums bore an "LG" or "LN" prefix. When titles from the 3000 series were issued in stereo, they carried a "BN" prefix and were part of the 500 series. By the '60s, the bulk of the releases were either in the LN-24000 series (mono) or the BN-26000 series (stereo). From 1973-78 Epic issued an orange label and replaced that with a black label in 1978.

<u>Fantasy</u>: From inception through the 1960s, mono albums had a red/maroon label. 10" albums bore a number "3" prefix. 12" albums began with 200 and also bore the "3" prefix. When the label added stereo in the early 1960s, they used an 8000 series number; these originals had a blue label with silver print and were pressed on stiff, non-flexible vinyl. White label promos were issued.

Fantasy began pressing its albums on colored vinyl with their 10" series; copies of these albums have been seen on red, blue, green and purple vinyl; some were on rainbow-like pressings of different colors; these are rather rare. With the inception of their 12" line in 1955, all new albums were pressed on red vinyl. This book assumes that *all* of the original mono releases from 1955 through 1957 were pressed on thick, dark red vinyl, often with a mottling effect of the red dye in the vinyl. For a brief period, approximately twelve months during 1957-58, new releases were pressed on black vinyl. By '58 red wax was back. . . Pressings from this point on were still on the thick vinyl but were a lovely, translucent red. In-print titles were pressed on this wax before reverting the black in the early '60s.

When Fantasy began issuing stereo in 1962, these were pressed on the same thick vinyl as the mono only using a translucent blue. These would then revert to modern black vinyl for the duration of the decade.

A popular title such as Dave Brubeck's *Jazz At The College Of Pacific* could have been pressed first on thick, dark red vinyl in 1956. Second pressings in 1957 would have been on the thick black vinyl of the '50s with little or no "grooveguard" around the disc's perimeter to keep the stylus from sliding off. Third pressings in 1958/59 would be on the thick translucent red vinyl while final mono pressings from the early '60s would have been on thinner, more modern black vinyl with the now familiar grooveguard. Then a blue stereo pressing in 1962 followed by a black vinyl stereo reissue through the rest of the decade.

From 1972 through 1978, Fantasy used a brown label on both their new original releases and their various reissues, including the jazz label, Milestone. Eventually, Fantasy absorbed a number of labels and *their* subsidiaries, including Prestige, New Jazz, Bluesville, Moodsville, Swingville, Riverside, Debut, Milestone, Pablo and Galaxy. Much of this music was reissued as new titles on Milestone in the '70s (often as annotated two-fers) or as part of their Original Jazz Classic series ("OJC" prefix) of reissues in the '80s.

<u>Harmony</u>: Columbia's budget subsidiary used a maroon label from 1957 through 1959 (7000-7150). For the next twelve years they issued a black label.

Hifijazz: Actually Los Angeles' High Fidelity Records, virtually everyone refers to it as "hifijazz" because of the prominence of that motto on the label; it is listed in this book as such.

Imperial: From 1950 through 1958 (9000-9040s), Imperial featured a maroon label with silver print. From 1958 through 1964 (9045-9260), they used a black label with stars and colored rays on top. White label promos were issued. From 1964 through 1966 (9260-9320s), a black and pink label was in effect. From 1966 through 1969, a black and green label with "Product Of Liberty Records" on the bottom was issued. After Liberty was purchased by United Artists in 1970, "Liberty/UA, Inc" was added.

Mono albums bore an "LP" prefix and were part of the 9000 series. When stereo was added in the late 1950s, these albums carried the same "LP" prefix but were part of the 12000 series. Original stereo albums featured a black label with silver print; later pressings had the black label with the stars and bars. Imperial merged with Liberty, then became a part of United Artists and is now under the Capitol umbrella.

Impulse: Originally a subsidiary of ABC, Impulse albums (1-100 and the first few titles on the 9000 series) through 1968 had an orange and brown label. Mono albums bore an "A" prefix while stereos carried an "AS." From 1969 through 1972, the label was red and black; from 1973-74, black; and, from 1974-78, purple and green. Impulse is now a part of the MCA Corporation.

Jazztone: The Concert Hall Society, a classical music appreciation group, formed the Jazztone Society. While they specialized in reissuing classic jazz material leased from other labels, they did commission some original works. Albums on the Concert Hall label were sold through retail outlets; the same material was sold through the mail to subscribers on the Jazztone label.

Jolly Rogers: An early bootleg company lifting its catalog from previously released 78s. They are listed in this book 'cause they are listed everywhere else. . .

Josie: From inception through the early '60s the label was a cream color with blue print. Through the latter '60s and into the '70s the label was light brown.

Jubilee: From inception through 1958, Jubilee used a blue label. From 1958 through 1960, a black label with "jubilee" in a silver "sun burst" oval on top was in effect. Throughout the '60s, a black label with "jubilee" in a multi-colored "sun burst" was in print. Mono albums carried a "JGL" prefix; stereos, "JGS."

Kapp: From 1956 through 1959, Kapp used a maroon (or blue) label. From 1959 through 1962, a black and blue label with a "K" logo was in effect. From 1962 through 1964, a black and blue label with a red major's hat was used. From 1964 through 1971 a black label was in print with the major's hat on top.

Throughout these years, mono albums bore a "KL" prefix and were part of the 1000 series (white label promos were issued); stereo albums were part of the "KS-5000" series. From 1971-73 an orange and purple label was used.

King: From inception through 1966, original King albums had a black label with silver print. From 1966 through the mid 1970s, a blue or black label was used with a crown on top. Throughout the rest of the label's run, a gold/brown or black label with a "K" logo on top was in service.

King 10" albums bore a "295" prefix (the suggested retail price of $2.95). The first 12" albums carried a "395" prefix ($3.95) through 1960, after which the monos were simply designated "LP." Stereo albums on this label were virtually non-existent until 1966; those in true stereo from this period (1960-66) are rare and highly sought after by non-jazz collectors running the label.

Laurie: The original label (1002) was gold with black lettering, "Laurie" in a semi-circle on top and "Mastersound" around the bottom. After that it gets confusing: The labels of originals and reissues are essentially the same except on the original pressings the dots in the five points of the star are large with plenty of white space. On later pressings the dots are noticeably smaller with considerably less white space.

Liberty: From inception through 1960 (3000-3140s), Liberty boasted an aqua blue label with silver print. When stereo albums, many reprocessed, were issued on the 7000 series in the late '50s, a black label with silver print was in effect. Throughout these years, mono albums bore an "LRS" prefix (white label promos were issued); some titles were issued as part of the 6000 series with an "LRS" prefix. Stereo albums were designated with "LST."

From 1960 through 1966 (3150-3440 and 13/14000s), a black label with a rainbow and a gold logo was in use. From 1966 through 1969 (3440-7620s and 13/14000s), a "Liberty Records, Inc" was added beneath a blue logo. Off-white, or creme, label promos were issued. By 1970, the Liberty group included Blue Note, Transition, Aladdin and Imperial. After Liberty was purchased by United Artists in 1970, "Liberty/UA, Inc" was added beneath the blue logo. In the 1980s, a gray label was in use.

London: From inception through 1964, mono albums had a red/maroon label with silver print and featured an "ffrr"/ear logo on top. White label promos were issued. When stereo was issued, a blue label was issued with "ffss" in a circle on top (all are true stereo). From 1963 through 1965, mono albums had a red/maroon label, and stereo LPs had a blue label with a plain "London" in silver print on top. From 1965-69, "London" appeared in a box on top. After that, "London" appeared in blue print in a silver box at the top.

Throughout these years, mono albums bore an "LL" prefix and carried a four digit number. Stereo releases had a "PS" prefix and a three digit number, usually dropping the first number from the mono designation.

Mainstream: Original albums (1965-66) bore a light, silvery-blue label. White label promos were issued. Later pressings bore a "Red Lion Production."

MCA: The MCA Corporation currently owns the catalogs of many former labels, including Decca and Coral. From 1973 through 1978 (#2000-2300s) a black label was used with a rainbow. A light brown label with a darker perimeter was in used from 1977 until 1979 (the 3000 series and the early 5000s). After 1980 the label showed a blue sky and clouds motif. Note: A blue label with rainbow was used on the MCA reissues.

Mercury: Original albums on the 1000 series had a black label with gold print. From the mid-'50s through 1963 (20000-20700), mono albums had a black label with silver print and a plain logo on top. Mono albums carried an "MG" prefix; yellow label promos were issued. The first stereo albums appeared in 1957 with a 60000 number and bore an "SR" prefix. They had a black label with silver print.

From 1961 through 1964 (20600-20900), a black label with an oval logo on top was in effect. From 1964 through 1968 (20900-61190), a red label with Mercury's head on top was used. White label promos were issued. From 1969 through 1973 (61200-61300s and 600-670s), a red label with 12 oval logos around perimeter was in service. During 1973-74 (680-on), Mercury issued a red label with seven oval logos around perimeter. From 1974 through 1982 (1000s), a colored label with a skyscraper was in print. From 1982 on, a black label with "Marketed by Polygram" on the bottom was in effect.

Mercury's budget label was Wing. Labels distributed by them were primarily the Norman Granz labels, Clef, Down Home, Norgran and Verve (through 1960) along with Savoy and Regent. Along the way they also picked up Keynote and Limelight before becoming a part of the Polygram group.

Metrojazz: MGM's jazz label, originals have a red label; mono albums bore an "E" prefix with stereos an "SE."

MGM: Original MGMs (3000-3770) have a yellow and black label. Yellow label promos were issued. From 1960 through 1968 (3770-4515), MGM used a black label with a multi-color logo. White label promos were issued. Throughout these years, mono albums bore an "E" prefix; stereo albums carried an "SE."

From 1968 through 1976, a blue and gold swirl label with "A Division of Metro-Goldwyn-Mayer" on the bottom was in print. From 1976 through the end, a blue and gold swirl label with a street address on the bottom was in service. Yellow label promos were issued.

MGM's subsidiaries include Metrojazz and, later, the budget label, Metro. In 1961 they purchased Verve from Norman Granz, altering that label's cataloging system. (For more information refer to Verve below.) MGM is currently part of Polygram Records.

Monument: 1961 and 1962 releases had a copper and white swirl label. This was replaced in 1962 and 1963 with a white and rainbow swirl label. From 1963 until 1976 a light green label was used with a gold perimeter and a Henderson, Tenn, address on the bottom. From 1966 until 1971 the Tenn. location was dropped. A brownish orange label was used from 1971 until 1976. This was replaced in 1976 with a black label. Finally, a silver label was used in the early '80s.

Moodsville: Originals on this subsidiary of Prestige had green labels with the logo in block print on top. Second pressings had flat blue labels with the Prestige trident logo on the right side.

Music Minus One: This innovative label hired musicians from sundry fields to provide background music by which the "listener" could learn by playing along. That is, the recorded music was minus one part, which the listener would supply. This label was operative from the late '50s into the '70s or '80s. While there was not a lot of information at the time of publication, several jazz artists (notably Mal Waldron) were involved. There is little demand for these records at this time.

New Jazz: Original albums on this Prestige subsidiary were 10" LPs. This label was halted and the 10" albums were reissued on the Prestige label. When the label was reintroduced in 1958 (the 8200 series), the first four releases—8201, 8202, 8203 and 8204—were originally issued with the yellow Prestige label. These were then reissued with the standard purple New Jazz label. Later pressings from the mid '60s had flat blue labels with the Prestige trident logo on the right side.

Stereo versions of New Jazz titles apparently do not exist! From 8303 on, the numbering was carried on the Status label, also a subsidiary of Prestige, although many discographies the later numbers as both New Jazz *and* Status. New Jazz titles were reissued in stereo in the '80s on Fantasy's Original Jazz Classics line with new catalog numbers.

Pacific Jazz/World Pacific: Original 10" albums started with number "1" and carried a "PJ LP" prefix. Throughout the 1950s, Pacific Jazz mono albums (the PJM-400 and PJ-1200 series) had a plain black label with silver print. In late 1957, the company changed its name to World Pacific. Early reissues and the first few new titles issued bear the older "PJ" prefix. By 1958, the albums carried the now familiar "WP" prefix, and each of those first few PJ releases were changed. Along with new titles, the majority of the catalog was reissued on World Pacific label in 1958 with their original catalog numbers, using a "WP" prefix for the "1200s and "WPM" for the 400s.

In this book, the two pressings are listed consecutively, the PJ with a 1957 release date while the WP is 1958. This should tell the reader what's up. It is also possible that some of the first reissues on World Pacific of the Pacific Jazz titles may have also been issued with a PJ. When stereo titles were introduced in late 1958, they issued a 1000 number with an "ST" prefix.

Pacific Jazz pressed early 12" albums on colored vinyl; red was the most prevalent. These colored gems appear to have been pressed [perhaps] no later than 1956; collectors should assume that these are rare. . .

From 1960-65, the Pacific Jazz label was back, starting all over with number "1." Mono albums ("LP" prefix) had a black label with silver print; stereo albums ("ST") were blue. Pacific Jazz/World Pacific became a part of Liberty Records, eventually being absorbed by United Artists who were then swallowed by Capitol. From 1965-70, a black, orange and yellow label was in effect. During the late '70s and early '80s, a blue and green "waves" label was used.

In *Jazz West Coast*, Robert Gordon notes "[Owner Richard] Bock produced a great many fine albums over the years, but one wishes he could have resisted the urge to splice and otherwise tamper with his tapes, a temptation to which he all too often succumbed." An example is Jim Hall's *Jazz Guitar:* The original sessions (on Pacific Jazz/World Pacific 1227) featured a trio with Red Mitchell, bass, and Carl Perkins, piano. When Bock reissued the album in 1963 (Pacific Jazz 79), he overdubbed a drum track, making the recording a quartet. Tampering with the integrity of the original recording arouses the ire of most listeners. Of course, collector-wise, it does create a new version to be sought. . .

Paramount: In 1969 the label was gray with "A Division of Paramount Pictures" on the bottom. In the early '70s the gray label read "A Division of Famous Music." A few titles in 1971 and 1972 featured a blue label. Note: This company is not affiliated with ABC-Paramount.

Philips: From inception through 1963 (2/600001-120s), Philips used a black label with "Chicago 1, Illinois" on the bottom. From 1964-66, the black label had "Vendor: Mercury" on the bottom. From 1966-70, the black label with no print extra disclaimers on the bottom was used. Throughout this time, mono albums bore a "PHM" prefix and were part of the 200-000 series; stereo titles had a "PHS" prefix and were part of the 600-000 series. Gold or white label promos were issued. From 1970-74, a black label was used with "Manufactured and Distributed by Mercury" on the bottom. Philips is now a part of Polygram.

Polydor: From 1969 until 1978 the label was red with no street address. From 1978 until 1982 the red label carried a Seventh Ave. address on the bottom.

Prestige: From inception through 1956 (7000-7140), Prestige albums had a black on yellow label with the company's "W. 50th Street, NYC" address on top. From 1957-1964 (7141-7320s), the same black on yellow label featured a "Bergenfield, NJ" address. In 1960 stereo titles were released on a black on silver Bergenfield label carrying a "PRST" prefix.

From approximately 1964 through 1967, titles were issued with a blue label with the company's new trident logo on the right; a few titles were reissued on this label and are rather hard to find. From 1967 through '69, the blue label carried the trident in a circle on top.

From 1969 through 1972, the label was purple with the encircled trident on top. After the label was purchased by Fantasy, a green label was used (white label promos were issued). In the '80s, select titles were reissued, often in stereo, with a facsimile of the original yellow label and with an OJC ("Original Jazz Classic") prefix.

Prestige subsidiaries include New Jazz, Moodsville, Swingville and Status, the latter reissuing earlier titles. These labels are listed in this book. Another label, one that stepped outside the jazz field, was Bluesville, which released over eighty titles before inexplicably turning to Ravi Shankar. . . The Bluesville series is not included in this volume.

RCA Victor: From 1950 through 1954, RCA Victor albums had a green label. For one year, 1954-55, the company switched to a glossy black label with Nipper (the dog) on top in outline only. The 10" albums bore an "LPT" or "LPM" prefix and were issued with a 3000 number. Titles on the "LJM" jazz series have silver labels.

From 1955 through 1963 (LPM 2000-2700s), the classic shiny black label with the full-bodied Nipper on top appeared with "Long Play" on the bottom. During 1963-64, (LPM 2700-2999), "Mono" was printed on the bottom and from 1964-1968 (LPM 3000-3900s), "Monaural." [Note that some albums issued in 1966-67 read "Mono Dynagroove."]

Stereo albums: From 1958 through 1964 (LSP 2000-2999), the classic shiny black label with the full-bodied Nipper on top appeared with "Living Stereo" on the bottom. From 1964 through 1968 (LSP 3000-4000s), only "Stereo" appeared on the bottom. [Note that some albums issued in 1966-67 read "Stereo Dynagroove."]

From late '68 through '71 (LSP 4000-4460s), an orange label was issued on stiff, non-flexible vinyl. Many, if not most, of these were reissued with identical labels on RCA's ridiculously flimsy "dynaflex" vinyl. From 1971 through 1976 (LSP 4460s-1039), the same orange label was in effect but with "dynaflex" printed on the bottom. During 1975-76, a light brown label was used. In 1976, they returned to a black label with Nipper located in the upper right at approximately 1-2 o'clock.

The label issued a "vintage series" (LPV 500 series) of mono albums with purple labels within 1965-66. Remastered from old 78s for modern cartridges, most, if not all, of this material was previously uncollected on LP. RCA Victor's subsidiaries include both the Vik and the "X" label and the budget Camden.

Regent: A subsidiary of Savoy, Regent was distributed by Mercury and carried an "MG" prefix. Original Regent releases used a green label; red labels are reissues.

Reprise: Initially Frank Sinatra's pet, Reprise was incorporated into Warner Bros. within a few years. From inception through 1968, Reprise used a pink, gold and green label with a large steamboat in the upper left. [Note that Reprise had a jazz series that was yellow, red and green with an angel in the upper left in print during the early '60s.] From 1968 through 1970, a brown and orange label with a smaller steamboat and the "W7" logo on top was in effect. White label promos were issued.

Throughout this time, mono albums on the 1000 series had an "F" prefix; stereos, an "FS." Mono titles on the 6000 series had an "R" prefix; stereo titles were originally issued with an "R6" and then an "RS." From 1970 through 1976, a brown label without the "W7" logo was in effect. White label promos were issued.

Riverside: From inception through early 1957 (100-240s), Riverside used a blue on white label. From 1956 through 1963 (240s-476), a blue label with a logo that displayed a mike and two reels of tape on top was issued. Stereo titles (beginning in approximately late '58) had a black label with the mike and reels logo. For a brief period in 1963-64, mono and stereo labels were blue without the mike and reels logo; this was definitely used on 477 and may have turned up on a few others and some reissues; more information is needed. These labels read "Bill Grauer Productions" on the bottom.

Initially, the mono albums began with 100 and carried an "RLP-12" prefix. Initial stereo releases were on a 1100 series, numbers assigned as the stereo remixes for previous titles were made available. When new titles were automatically released in both mono and stereo, the monos retained the three digit figure (approximately in the late 200s or early 300s) and the "RLP" prefix. Stereo titles had the same three digit number but bore an "RS-9" prefix. In 1962-63 the mono prefix was changed to "RM."

From 1964 through '67 (478-499), the label was turquoise with "Orpheum Prod." on the bottom. After ABC took over distribution of the label in 1967, the earlier material was reissued with black on brown labels. In the mid-'80s, select titles were reissued, often in stereo, by Fantasy with a facsimile of the original blue on white label but with an OJC ("Original Jazz Classic") prefix.

Roost: While the cover credits Roost Records and the label reads "Manufactured by Roost Records" on the bottom, the label prominently displays "Royal Roost" at the top. For the sake of convenience, the records are listed as Roost. Roost eventually sold out to Roulette.

Roulette: Original issues in 1957-58 (25000-25050) had black labels. White label promos were issued. From 1959 through 1962 (25050-25180 and 52000-52050), a white label with criss-crossed color bars (*ala* the roulette wheel) was in effect. For a brief period in 1962-63, an orange and pink label was issued. From 1963 on, Roulette used an orange and yellow label with a roulette wheel design. Throughout this time, mono albums bore a "R" prefix (white label promos were issued); stereo titles had a "SR" prefix. Since 1977, the orange and yellow label with a roulette wheel label has added "Made in USA by Roulette Inc" to the bottom.

Royal Roost: *Refer to Roost.*

Saturn: Owned and operated by the legendary Sun Ra, formerly Herman "Sonny" Blount. Saturn reflected the personalities of its founder: The original serial numbers are unfathomable to those not versed in numerology. In 1967, however, after LP issues had begun to proliferate, a three-digit series of catalog numbers was instituted to simplify ordering. These three-digit numbers are given for releases from 1967 onward but the old numbers were retained on the label or the jacket. Pressing runs could be extremely small— as few as 75 at a time! Certain Saturns, however, received wider distribution through Royal Disc between 1971 and 1973, and were produced in larger quantities.

The original Saturn label (from 1956 through 1964) was yellow or gold with red or black print. The Saturn logo was displayed in block letters across the top or in script letters down the left side. Matrix numbers were stamped in the trail-off vinyl instead of being incised or etched. From 1965 to 1967, Saturn used a red label with silver lettering with the Saturn logo in block letters across the top. In 1968 a green label with black print appeared (sometimes with a Minneapolis address). From 1969 though the early '70s, many Saturn labels bore the motto "Thoth Intergalactic." These Thoth labels were black with silver print, or blue and white with black print. Labels that read "El Saturn" down the left side and include an ankh over an animated sun were used from 1969 until the shutdown of the Chicago label in 1985.

All Saturns prior to 1974 were issued by the Chicago Saturn operation, run by Alton Abraham. Most of these carried the address PO Box 7124, Chicago 7, Illinois (later Chicago, Illinois 60607) on the label. Saturn albums were issued in a confusing variety of covers; many early LPs were sent out in blank covers, often hand-decorated.

Savoy: All original issues from 1950 through ??? had bright, "blood" red label. By the '60s the label was an opaque maroon. Distributed by Mercury, this label also used an "MG" prefix. Their subsidiary was Regent. When titles were reissued in the '70s, a red or brown label with "Distributed by Arista" on the bottom was issued. Savoy's catalogue is currently controlled by Arista.

Scepter: The original label (501) was red with "Scepter" in black script outlined in silver. From 1962 until 1971 the label was orange with an oval-like center. Although a few titles had solid white or red labels. In 1972 and 1973 a multi-color label was in use on general releases with the special "Citation Series" carrying a yellow label. From 1974 until 1976 the label was blue.

Smash: From 1961 through 1968 a flat red label was used with black print. From 1968 until 1971 the red label carried a Mercury logo in an oval on top.

Specialty: From 1957 through the early '70s the label was gold with a black top. The '80s reissues had a white label with a black top.

Status: This subsidiary of Prestige was inaugurated in 1965, carrying on the numbering system of the New Jazz label with 8303 on. Status primarily reissued previous New Jazz titles, including several that had been scheduled years earlier for release on New Jazz but were pulled prior to release. Stereo versions of New Jazz titles apparently do not exist!

Stereo Records: *Refer to Contemporary*

Sue: From 1961 through the mid-'60s the label was orange; later titles and reissues are black.

Sunset: This budget subsidiary of Liberty repackaged material from the parent label's catalog. Original releases through 1969 had a black and blue label that read "A Division of Liberty Records" on the bottom. After 1970 the same label read "Liberty/U.A." on the bottom.

Swingville: Original monos on this subsidiary of Prestige had purple/red labels with the logo in block print on top; stereos had maroon/red labels. Second pressings had flat blue labels with the Prestige trident logo on the right side.

Tampa: Original labels through 1957 were black with colored vinyl pressings. As I have not been able to identify all of these, the reader will find one listing for these titles. Later black vinyl pressings have pink labels. Stereo pressings apparently also exist, although, again, information at this time is sketchy.

Tower: This subsidiary of Capitol used a dull orange label from 1965 until 1968. Several titles were reissued in 1968 on a striped label. Mono albums carried a "T" prefix while stereo LPs were "ST" and rechanneled stereo, "DT."

20th Century Fox: From inception through the early '60s, a light blue label with "20th Fox" on top was in effect. From the early '60s through the early '70s, a black label was issued. During the '70s, an aquamarine label was in print. From 1977 though the '80s, a light brown/tan label with spotlights on top was used.

United Artists: In 1958-59, U.A. used a red & black label for monos (40000s) and a gold & black label for stereo (30000s). In mid-'59, mono albums switched to red labels, while stereos were blue. In 1960, a black label with a large "UA" logo on top was issued briefly. From 1960 through 1968 (3120-6640), the label was black with "United Artists" in a box on top. From 1968 through 1970 (6640-6710s), a purple and orange label was in effect. White label promos were issued. Throughout this period, mono albums (3000 and 4000 series) bore a "UAL" prefix and stereos (6000s for the 3000 series and 5000s for the 4000) a "UAS."

In 1962 the company inaugurated the United Artists Jazz label with a UAJ-14000 mono series and a UAJS-15000 stereo series. The distinctive label was gray with a silhouette of a sax player bent backwards blowing over the spindle hole. These are all difficult to find today.

During 1970-71 (6710-6700s and early 5500s and 5200s), a black and orange label was in effect. From 1971 through 1975 (6780 on and 100-540), a brown label. From 1975 through 1977 (540-760), "Music & Record Group" was added to the bottom of the brown label. From 1977 on, a "sun burst" design was used on the label. After acquiring the Liberty group of labels, U.A. was subsequently purchased by Capitol.

Vanguard: From inception through 1963 (the 9000 series), Vanguard used a maroon label with silver print and a horseman logo on top. Stereo albums (2000s and 9000s) had a black label with silver print. From 1963 through 1970, the company issued a gold-brown or silvery-gray label with a white horseman logo on the bottom. White label promos were issued. Throughout these years, monos bore a "VRS" prefix while stereos had a "VSD7." During the 1970s, a marble "swirl" effect label was issued.

Vee Jay: From inception through 1959 the first few albums (#1000-1013?) had a maroon label with silver print; the few stereo releases were gray with black print. From 1960 through 1963 a glossy black label was used with a rainbow perimeter and the Vee Jay logo in an oval at the top of the label (#1010s-1070s and the 3000 series). From 1963 through 1965 (#1060-1070s) the glossy black rainbow label featured the logo in brackets. During 1965 and 1966, a flat black label was used with silver print. Throughout these years Vee Jay's basic prefix was the common "LP" while the almost always rare stereo issues carried either an "LPS" of "SR" prefix. White label promos were issued.

When Vee Jay went belly up in 1966, the demand for a lot of their product remained and was met. . . illegally. Many Vee Jay titles remained in print *(sic)* throughout the '70s with black/maroon labels in pressings that are dramatically inferior to the originals. In fact, they resemble barely professional counterfeits: The covers are photo-reproductions of the originals and the pressings are abominable, with poor sound and noticeable noise from recycled vinyl. Several jazz titles proliferated, including 2504, *Eric Dolphy Memorial Album*, 3015, Lee Morgan's *Ex-phoobi-dent*, and the ubiquitous 3013, *The Young Lions*. During the 1970s "VJ International" and a "Vintage Series" appeared. During the 1970s and the '80s, a red label with the brackets logo was also in effect.

<u>Verve/Verve Clef</u>: Verve was Norman Granz' flagship label, which he began by consolidating his previous labels, Clef, Down Home and Norgran, and reissuing the bulk of the earlier titles. On the 2000 series, Verve used an orange or a blue label prior to switching to black with "Verve Records, Inc" on the bottom. For the 8000 series, the label was black with silver print and "Verve Records, Inc" on the bottom from 1956 through 1960, when the label was sold to MGM.

Most of the early printings through approximately 8390 featured the outline of a trumpet player (courtesy of David Stone Martin and a carry-over from the Clef and Norgran labels) in the upper left. Later mono albums had a large "T" design (that looks somewhat like a thumb tack) splitting the label in three.

Note: The trumpet player on a later number does not automatically mean that it is a first pressing. Granz apparently used whatever label was available to him at the time of pressing. Nonetheless, the "trumpet player labels" are highly sought after and usually commands a premium when there is a choice between the "T" label and the "trumpet player."

The 1000 series was for traditional jazz while the 2000 series was used primarily for "pop" oriented selections, although some jazz, especially vocals, found their way here. Early pressings of the 2000s have an orange label, replaced by a light blue label and then, finally, the familiar silver on black "T" label. The 4000 series was created for Ella Fitzgerald's protean output.

What each of the above label variations had in common (with the 8000s) was an "MGV" prefix and "Verve Records, Inc." along the bottom perimeter of the label. When select titles were remixed in stereo and issued on the 6000 series in late '59 and '60, an "MGVS" prefix was used.

When the label was purchased by MGM in 1960, most of the catalog was reissued with the monos designated with a "V" and the stereos a "V6," the original 8000 series number being kept for both. The new parent company retained the original label (black with silver print) but "MGM Records-A Division Of Metro-Goldwyn-Mayer, Inc." was included on the bottom. A reissue series using a "VSP/VSPS" prefix was issued in the mid-'60s with most, if not all, of the stereo being rechanneled. From 1966 through 1971, MGM's Sunset address is also on the bottom. From 1972-75, a white label with blue MGM and Verve logos was used. White label promos were issued.

Vik: This RCA subsidiary had black labels with a multi-color logo on top.

Warner Brothers: From 1958 through 1962 (1200-1470), W.B. used gray label with a black and yellow logo on top. From 1962-65 (1470-1620), a gray label with a black and white logo on top was in print. From 1966 through 1968 (1920-1730), a gold label was in effect. From 1968 through 1970, a green label with the Warner Bros./7 Arts "W7" logo on top was in print. Throughout these years, mono albums carried a "W" prefix; stereos, a "WS." White label promos were issued.

From 1970 through 1977, a green label with the "WB" logo on top was in effect. From 1973-75, the label featured a Burbank street scene. From 1978 through the '80s, a tan label was issued. Warner/Reprise eventually became Warner Communications before merging with Elektra and Atlantic into WEA.

Wing: As a subsidiary of Mercury, from inception through the 1950s, Wing had a blue label with silver print and the "Wing" logo in an oval on top, often with "Jazz" above it, was used. (Several titles were issued simultaneously on Mercury or EmArcy and on Wing.) Throughout the '60s, when Wing was exclusively a budget label, a blue or black label with "Mercury" above the "Wing" logo was in print. Mono albums were on the 12000 series with an "MGW" prefix while stereos carried an "SRW" prefix on the 16000 series. From 1970 through 1971, a blue label featured both the Wing and the oval Mercury logo alongside it on top.

World Pacific: *Refer to Pacific Jazz.*

"X": The RCA subsidiary had white labels with a huge red "X" on top.

A.

ABDUL-MALIK, AHMED

Ahmed Abdul-Malik, formerly Samuel Gill, is a modern jazz bassist who also plays a variety of Eastern instruments. For additional listings refer to Odetta.

Riverside RLP-12-287	*(M)*	**Jazz Sahara**	*1958*	**20.00**	**50.00**
Riverside RLP-1121	*(S)*	**Jazz Sahara**	*1958*	**16.00**	**40.00**
		(Riverside 287 also features Johnny Griffin.)			
		—Riverside albums above have blue mono or black stereo labels with a reel & mike logo on top.—			
RCA Victor LPM-2015	*(M)*	**East Meets West**	*1959*	**20.00**	**50.00**
RCA Victor LSP-2015	*(S)*	**East Meets West**	*1959*	**16.00**	**40.00**
		—RCA albums above have black labels with "Long Play" or "Living Stereo" on the bottom.—			
New Jazz NJLP-8266	*(M)*	**The Music Of Ahmed Abdul-Malik**	*1961*	**20.00**	**50.00**
New Jazz NJLP-8282	*(M)*	**Sounds Of Africa**	*1962*	**20.00**	**50.00**
New Jazz NJLP-8298	*(M)*	**Eastern Moods**	*1963*	*Unreleased*	
New Jazz NJLP-8303	*(M)*	**Spellbound**	*1963*	*Unreleased*	
		—New Jazz albums above have purple labels.—			
New Jazz NJLP-8266	*(M)*	**The Music Of Ahmed Abdul-Malik**	*1965*	**10.00**	**25.00**
New Jazz NJLP-8282	*(M)*	**Sounds Of Africa**	*1965*	**10.00**	**25.00**
		—New Jazz albums above have blue labels with a trident logo on the right side.—			
Prestige PRLP-16003	*(M)*	**Eastern Moods**	*1963*	**16.00**	**40.00**
Status ST-8303	*(M)*	**Spellbound**	*1965*	**16.00**	**40.00**
		(Status 8303 also features Ray Nance and Seldon Powell.)			

ABRAMS, RICHARD (MUHAL RICHARD ABRAMS)

Delmark DS-413	*(S)*	**Levels And Degrees Of Light**	*1968*	**10.00**	**25.00**
Delmark DS-423	*(S)*	**Young At Heart, Wise In Time**	*1969*	**10.00**	**25.00**

ADAMS, JERRI

Ms. Jerri Adams is a modern jazz vocalist.

Columbia CL-916	*(M)*	**It's Cool Inside**	*1956*	**16.00**	**40.00**
Columbia CL-1258	*(M)*	**Play For Keeps**	*1958*	**16.00**	**40.00**
		—Columbia albums above have six white on black "eye" logos on each label.—			

ADAMS, PEPPER

Park "Pepper" Adams is a modern jazz baritone, tenor and alto saxophone and clarinet player. For additional listings refer to Thad Jones & Pepper Adams; The Prestige Blues Swingers; and the Various Artists section under Bethlehem and Savoy.

Transition TRLP-8	*(M)*	**Pepper Adams Quintet Introducing Curtis Fuller**	*1956*	*Unreleased*	
Mode LP-112	*(M)*	**Pepper Adams 5**	*1957*	**40.00**	**100.00**
		(Mode 112 also features Mel Lewis.)			
World Pacific PJM-407	*(M)*	**Critic's Choice**	*1957*	**40.00**	**100.00**
World Pacific WPM-407	*(M)*	**Critic's Choice**	*1958*	**20.00**	**50.00**
		(World Pacific 407 also features Mel Lewis.)			
Regent MG-6066	*(M)*	**The Cool Sound Of Pepper Adams**	*1958*	**30.00**	**75.00**
Riverside RLP-12-265	*(M)*	**10 To 4 At The 5 Spot**	*1958*	**20.00**	**50.00**
Riverside RLP-1104	*(S)*	**10 To 4 At The 5 Spot**	*1958*	**20.00**	**40.00**
		—Riverside albums above have blue mono or black stereo labels with a reel & mike logo on top.—			
Interlude MO-502	*(M)*	**Pepper Adams 5**	*1959*	**20.00**	**50.00**
Interlude ST-1002	*(S)*	**Pepper Adams 5**	*1959*	**16.00**	**40.00**
		(Interlude 502 is a reissue of Mode 112.)			
Warwick W-2041	*(M)*	**Out Of This World**	*1961*	**20.00**	**50.00**
Warwick W-2041ST	*(S)*	**Out Of This World**	*1961*	**16.00**	**40.00**
		(Warwick 2041 also features Donald Byrd.)			
Warwick W-5003	*(M)*	**The Soul Of Jazz Percussion**	*1963*	**20.00**	**50.00**
Warwick WST-5003	*(S)*	**The Soul Of Jazz Percussion**	*1963*	**16.00**	**40.00**
Workshop Jazz JWS-219	*(M)*	**Pepper Adams Plays The Compositions Of Charles Mingus**	*1963*	**20.00**	**50.00**
Savoy MG-12211	*(M)*	**The Cool Sound Of Pepper Adams**	*196?*	**8.00**	**20.00**
		(Savoy 12211 is a reissue of Regent 6065.)			

Label & Catalog #		Title	Year	VG+	NM
ADAMS, PEPPER, & JIMMY KNEPPER					
Metrojazz E-1004	(M)	**The Pepper-Knepper Quintet**	1958	30.00	75.00
Metrojazz SE-1004	(S)	**The Pepper-Knepper Quintet**	1958	20.00	50.00
ADAMS, PEPPER, & ZOOT SIMS					
Prestige PRST-7677	(S)	**Encounter!**	1969	10.00	25.00
		— Prestige albums above have blue labels with a trident logo on top.—			
ADDERLEY, CANNONBALL					
Julian "Cannonball" Adderly is a modern alto and tenor sax, trumpet, clarinet and flute player who achieved fame with Miles Davis' Quintet on Columbia. Brother Nat has been a featured member of Cannonball's groups whether or not he is credited on the cover. For additional listings refer to Ray Brown; Eric Dolphy / Cannonball Adderley; Kenny Dorham; Gil Evans; The Nutty Squirrels; Nancy Wilson.					
Savoy MG-12018	(M)	**Presenting Cannonball**	1955	30.00	75.00
EmArcy MG-36043	(M)	**Julian "Cannonball" Adderley**	1955	24.00	60.00
EmArcy MG-36063	(M)	**Julian "Cannonball" Adderley And Strings**	1956	24.00	60.00
EmArcy MG-36077	(M)	**In The Land Of Hi-Fi**	1956	24.00	60.00
EmArcy MG-36110	(M)	**Sophisticated Swing**	1957	24.00	60.00
EmArcy MG-36135	(M)	**Cannonball's Sharpshooters**	1958	24.00	60.00
EmArcy MG-36146	(M)	**Jump For Joy**	1958	24.00	60.00
		— EmArcy albums above have blue labels with silver print.—			
Mercury MG-20449	(M)	**Cannonball Adderley Quintet In Chicago**	1959	20.00	50.00
Mercury SR-60134	(S)	**Cannonball Adderley Quintet In Chicago**	1960	16.00	40.00
		(Mercury 20449 also features John Coltrane and Wynton Kelly.)			
Mercury MG-20530	(M)	**Jump For Joy**	1960	16.00	40.00
Mercury SR-60207	(S)	**Jump For Joy**	1960	12.00	30.00
		(Mercury 20530 is a reissue of EmArcy 36146.)			
Mercury MG-20531	(M)	**Cannonball's Sharpshooters**	1960	16.00	40.00
Mercury SR-60208	(S)	**Cannonball's Sharpshooters**	1960	12.00	30.00
		(Mercury 20531 is a reissue of EmArcy 36135.)			
Mercury MG-20616	(M)	**Cannonball Enroute**	1961	16.00	40.00
Mercury SR-60616	(S)	**Cannonball Enroute**	1961	12.00	30.00
Mercury MG-20652	(M)	**The Lush Side Of Cannonball Adderley**	1961	16.00	40.00
Mercury SR-60652	(S)	**The Lush Side Of Cannonball Adderley**	1961	12.00	30.00
		(Mercury 20652 is a reissue of EmArcy 36063.)			
		— Mercury albums above have black labels with "Long Playing Microgroove" on the bottom.—			
Blue Note BLP-1595	(M)	**Somethin' Else** *(Deep groove)*	1958	60.00	150.00
Blue Note BLP-1595	(M)	**Somethin' Else**	1958	40.00	100.00
Blue Note BST-1595	(S)	**Somethin' Else** *(Deep groove)*	1959	40.00	100.00
Blue Note BST-1595	(S)	**Somethin' Else**	1959	30.00	75.00
		— Blue Note albums above have blue on white labels with a W. 63rd Street, NYC address.—			
Blue Note BLP-1595	(M)	**Somethin' Else**	1963	10.00	25.00
Blue Note BST-81595	(S)	**Somethin' Else**	1963	8.00	20.00
		— Blue Note albums above have blue on white labels with a New York, USA label.—			
Blue Note BST-81595	(S)	**Somethin' Else**	196?	5.00	12.00
		— Blue Note albums above have blue on white labels with "A Division of Liberty Records."—			
Riverside RLP-12-269	(M)	**Portrait Of Cannonball**	1958	20.00	50.00
Riverside RLP-12-286	(M)	**Things Are Getting Better**	1958	20.00	50.00
Riverside RLP-1128	(S)	**Things Are Getting Better**	1958	16.00	40.00
		(Riverside 286 also features Milt Jackson.)			
Riverside RLP-12-303	(M)	**Cannonball Takes Charge**	1959	20.00	50.00
Riverside RLP-1148	(S)	**Cannonball Takes Charge**	1959	16.00	40.00
Riverside RLP-12-311	(M)	**Cannonball Adderley Quintet In San Francisco**	1959	20.00	50.00
Riverside RLP-1157	(S)	**Cannonball Adderley Quintet In San Francisco**	1959	16.00	40.00
Riverside RLP-12-322	(M)	**Them Dirty Blues**	1960	20.00	50.00
Riverside RLP-1170	(S)	**Them Dirty Blues**	1960	16.00	40.00
Riverside RLP-344	(M)	**Cannonball Adderley Quintet At The Lighthouse**	1960	16.00	40.00
Riverside RS-9344	(S)	**Cannonball Adderley Quintet At The Lighthouse**	1960	12.00	30.00
Riverside RLP-355	(M)	**Cannonball Adderley And The Poll-Winners**	1960	16.00	40.00
Riverside RS-9355	(S)	**Cannonball Adderley And The Poll-Winners**	1960	12.00	30.00
Riverside RLP-377	(M)	**African Waltz**	1961	16.00	40.00
Riverside RS-9377	(S)	**African Waltz**	1961	12.00	30.00
Riverside RLP-388	(M)	**Cannonball Adderley Quintet Plus**	1961	16.00	40.00
Riverside RS-9388	(S)	**Cannonball Adderley Quintet Plus**	1961	12.00	30.00
Riverside RLP-404	(M)	**Cannonball Adderley Sextet In New York**	1962	16.00	40.00
Riverside RS-9404	(S)	**Cannonball Adderley Sextet In New York**	1962	12.00	30.00
		(Riverside 404 also features Yusef Lateef.)			

Label & Catalog #		Title	Year	VG+	NM
Riverside RLP-416	(M)	**Cannonball's Greatest Hits**	1962	16.00	40.00
Riverside RS-9416	(S)	**Cannonball's Greatest Hits**	1962	12.00	30.00
Riverside RLP-433	(M)	**Know What I Mean?**	1962	16.00	40.00
Riverside RS-9433	(S)	**Know What I Mean?**	1962	12.00	30.00
		(Riverside 433 also features Bill Evans.)			
Riverside RLP-444	(M)	**San Francisco Revisited**	1963	16.00	40.00
Riverside RS-9444	(S)	**San Francisco Revisited**	1963	12.00	30.00
		(Riverside 444 also features Yusef Lateef.)			
Riverside RLP-455	(M)	**Cannonball's Bossa Nova**	1963	16.00	40.00
Riverside RS-9455	(S)	**Cannonball's Bossa Nova**	1963	12.00	30.00
— Riverside albums above have blue mono or black stereo labels with a reel & mike logo on top.—					
Riverside RM-477	(M)	**Nippon Soul—Recorded In Concert In Tokyo**	1963	12.00	30.00
Riverside RS-9477	(S)	**Nippon Soul—Recorded In Concert In Tokyo**	1963	10.00	25.00
— Riverside albums above blue labels with "Bill Grauer Productions" on the bottom.—					
Riverside RM-499	(M)	**Cannonball In Europe**	1967	10.00	25.00
Riverside RS-9499	(S)	**Cannonball In Europe**	1967	8.00	20.00
Riverside RS-3038	(S)	**The Best Of Cannonball Adderley**	1968	6.00	15.00
Riverside RS-3041	(S)	**Planet Earth**	1969	6.00	15.00
		(Riverside 3041 also features Yusef Lateef.)			
— Riverside albums above blue labels with "Orpheum Productions" on the bottom.—					
Capitol T-2203	(M)	**Domination**	1965	8.00	20.00
Capitol ST-2203	(S)	**Domination**	1965	6.00	15.00
Capitol T-2216	(M)	**Fiddler On The Roof**	1965	8.00	20.00
Capitol ST-2216	(S)	**Fiddler On The Roof**	1965	6.00	15.00
Capitol T-2284	(M)	**Live Session**	1965	8.00	20.00
Capitol ST-2284	(S)	**Live Session**	1965	6.00	15.00
		(Capitol 2884 also features Ernie Andrews.)			
Capitol T-2399	(M)	**Cannonball Adderley—Live!**	1965	8.00	20.00
Capitol ST-2399	(S)	**Cannonball Adderley—Live!**	1965	6.00	15.00
Capitol S-2531	(M)	**Great Love Themes**	1966	8.00	20.00
Capitol ST-2531	(S)	**Great Love Themes**	1966	6.00	15.00
Capitol T-2617	(M)	**Why Am I Treated So Bad?**	1966	8.00	20.00
Capitol ST-2617	(S)	**Why Am I Treated So Bad?**	1966	6.00	15.00
Capitol T-2663	(M)	**Mercy, Mercy, Mercy! Live At "The Club"**	1967	10.00	25.00
Capitol ST-2663	(S)	**Mercy, Mercy, Mercy! Live At "The Club"**	1967	6.00	15.00
Capitol T-2822	(M)	**74 Miles Away / Walk Tall**	1967	10.00	25.00
Capitol ST-2822	(S)	**74 Miles Away / Walk Tall**	1967	6.00	15.00
Capitol ST-2987	(S)	**Accent On Africa**	1968	6.00	15.00
Capitol ST-162	(S)	**Cannonball In Person**	1969	6.00	15.00
— Capitol albums above have black rainbow labels with the logo on top.—					

ADDERLEY, CANNONBALL, & JOHN COLTRANE

Limelight LM-82009	(M)	**Cannonball And Coltrane**	1964	10.00	25.00
Limelight LS-86009	(S)	**Cannonball And Coltrane**	1964	8.00	20.00
		(Limelight 82009 is a reissue of Mercury 20449.)			

ADDERLEY, CANNONBALL & NAT

Limelight LM-82032	(M)	**Them Adderleys**	1966	10.00	25.00
Limelight LS-86032	(S)	**Them Adderleys**	1966	8.00	20.00
		(Limelight 82032 reissues Mercury material.)			

ADDERLEY, NAT

Nathaniel Adderley is a modern jazz cornet, flugel horn, mellophone and trumpet player who played with brother Cannonball's group from 1959-1975. For additional listings refer to Buddy Johnson; King Curtis; and the Jazzy Soundtracks section under Reprise.

Savoy MG-12021	(M)	**That's Nat**	1955	30.00	75.00
EmArcy MG-36091	(M)	**Introducing Nat Adderley**	1955	30.00	75.00
EmArcy MG-36100	(M)	**To The Ivy League From Nat**	1956	30.00	75.00
— EmArcy albums above have blue labels with silver print.—					
Wing MGW-60000	(M)	**Introducing Nat Adderley**	1956	20.00	50.00
		(Wing 60000 is a reissue of EmArcy 36091.)			
Riverside RLP-12-285	(M)	**Branching Out**	1958	20.00	50.00
		(Riverside 285 also features Johnny Griffin and The Three Sounds)			
Riverside RLP-12-301	(M)	**Much Brass**	1959	20.00	50.00
Riverside RLP-1143	(S)	**Much Brass**	1959	16.00	40.00
Riverside RLP-12-318	(M)	**Work Song**	1960	20.00	50.00
Riverside RLP-1167	(S)	**Work Song**	1960	16.00	40.00

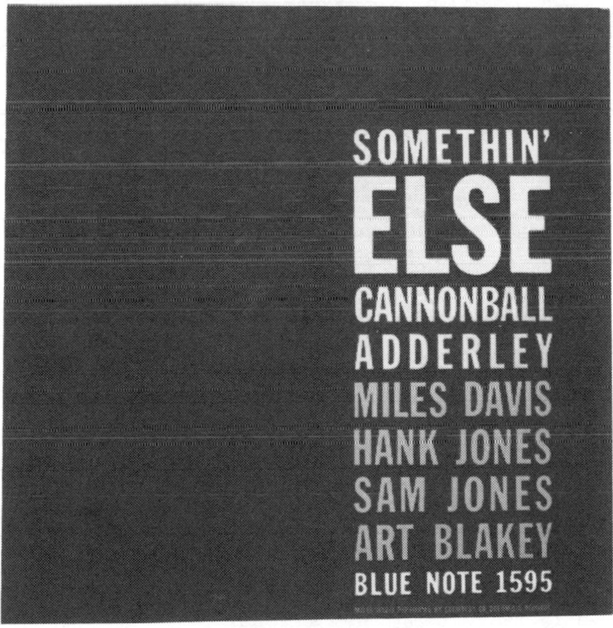

Cannonball Adderley began his jazz career by sitting in with Oscar Peterson in 1955, after which he was signed by EmArcy and toured with a group that featured brother Nat. He spent 1957-59 as part of Miles Davis' first Columbia combo, also recording with Blue Note and Mercury before starting a lengthy stay with Riverside (1958-63) and Capitol, with whom he had a top ten chart hit, "Mercy, Mercy, Mercy," in 1967. Aside from his work with Davis, he has recorded as a featured guest with Ray Brown, Kenny Dorham, and Gil Evans. He can also be heard backing Sarah Vaughan and Dinah Washington, both on Mercury, Nancy Wilson on Capitol, and The Nutty Squirrels on Columbia, and as a sideman with Paul Chambers on Vee Jay and Philly Joe Jones on Riverside.

Label & Catalog #		Title	Year	VG+	NM
Riverside RLP-330	(M)	**That's Right!**	1960	16.00	40.00
Riverside RS-9330	(S)	**That's Right!**	1960	12.00	30.00
		—Riverside albums above have blue mono or black stereo labels with a reel & mike logo on top.—			
Jazzland JLP-47	(M)	**Naturally!**	1961	16.00	40.00
Jazzland JLP-947	(S)	**Naturally!**	1961	12.00	30.00
Jazzland JLP-75	(M)	**In The Bag**	1962	16.00	40.00
Jazzland JLP-975	(S)	**In The Bag**	1962	12.00	30.00
Riverside RM-474	(M)	**Little Big Horn!**	1964	16.00	40.00
Riverside RS-9474	(S)	**Little Big Horn!**	1964	12.00	30.00
		—Riverside albums above have blue mono or black stereo labels with a reel & mike logo on top.—			
Atlantic 1439	(M)	**Autobiography**	1965	8.00	20.00
Atlantic SD-1439	(S)	**Autobiography**	1965	6.00	15.00
Atlantic 1460	(M)	**Sayin' Something**	1966	8.00	20.00
Atlantic SD-1460	(S)	**Sayin' Something**	1966	6.00	15.00
Atlantic 1475	(M)	**Live At Memory Lane**	1967	8.00	20.00
Atlantic SD-1475	(S)	**Live At Memory Lane**	1967	6.00	15.00
		—Atlantic albums above have multi-color labels with a black fan logo.—			
Milestone MSP-9009	(S)	**Natural Soul**	1968	6.00	15.00
Milestone MSP-9016	(S)	**The Scavenger**	1969	6.00	15.00
A&M SP-3005	(S)	**You, Baby**	1968	4.00	10.00
A&M SP-3017	(S)	**Calling Out Loud**	1969	4.00	10.00

AKIYOSHI, TOSHIKO: ***Refer to*** **TOSHIKO**

ALBAM, MANNY

Emanuel Albam is a modern jazz baritone and tenor saxophone player, arranger and composer whose work can be found on TV and movie soundtracks. For additional listings refer to Steve Allen & Manny Albam.

Label & Catalog #		Title	Year	VG+	NM
RCA Victor LPM-1211	(M)	**The RCA Victor Jazz Workshop**	1956	20.00	50.00
RCA Victor LPM-1279	(M)	**The Drum Suite**	1956	20.00	50.00
		—RCA albums above have black labels with "Long Play" on the bottom.—			
Coral CRL-57142	(M)	**Jazz Greats Of Our Time, Volume 2**	1958	16.00	40.00
Coral CRL-57173	(M)	**Jazz Greats Of Our Time, Volume 1**	1958	16.00	40.00
Coral CRL-57207	(M)	**West Side Story**	1958	16.00	40.00
Coral CRL-57231	(M)	**Sophisticated Lady— The Songs Of Duke Ellington**	1958	16.00	40.00
Coral CRL-59101	(M)	**The Blues Is Everybody's Business**	1958	16.00	40.00
		—Coral albums above have maroon labels.—			
Mercury MG-20325	(M)	**With All My Love**	1958	16.00	40.00
Dot DLP-9004	(M)	**Jazz New York**	1958	16.00	40.00
Dot DLP-29004	(S)	**Jazz New York**	1958	12.00	30.00
Dot DLP-9008	(M)	**Steve's Song**	1958	16.00	40.00
Dot DLP-29008	(S)	**Steve's Song**	1958	12.00	30.00
Top Rank RM-313	(M)	**Double Exposure**	1959	16.00	40.00
Top Rank RS-613	(S)	**Double Exposure**	1959	12.00	30.00
United Arts. UAL-3079	(M)	**Drum Feast**	1959	16.00	40.00
United Arts. UAS-6079	(S)	**Drum Feast**	1959	12.00	30.00
Vocalion VL-3678	(M)	**West Side Story**	1960	6.00	15.00
		(Vocalion 3678 is a reisssue of Coral 57207.)			
RCA Victor LPM-2432	(M)	**More Double Exposure**	1961	10.00	25.00
RCA Victor LSA-2432	(S)	**More Double Exposure**	1961	8.00	20.00
RCA Victor LPM-2508	(M)	**I Had The Craziest Dream**	1962	10.00	25.00
RCA Victor LSA-2508	(S)	**I Had The Craziest Dream**	1962	8.00	20.00
		—RCA albums above have black labels with "Long Play" or "Living Stereo" on the bottom.—			
Impulse A-19	(M)	**Jazz Goes To The Movies**	1962	12.00	30.00
Impulse AS-19	(S)	**Jazz Goes To The Movies**	1962	10.00	25.00
		—Impulse albums above have orange & black labels.—			
Impulse AS-19	(S)	**Jazz Goes To The Movies**	1969	4.00	10.00
		—Impulse albums above have red & black labels with the "abc" logo on top.—			
Decca DL-4517	(M)	**West Side Story**	1964	6.00	15.00
Decca DL-74517	(S)	**West Side Story**	1964	5.00	12.00
		(Decca 4517 is a reissue of Coral 57207.)			
Solid State SM-17000	(M)	**Brass On Fire**	1966	6.00	15.00
Solid State SS-18000	(S)	**Brass On Fire**	1966	5.00	12.00
Solid State SM-17009	(M)	**The Soul Of The City**	1966	6.00	15.00
Solid State SS-18009	(S)	**The Soul Of The City**	1966	5.00	12.00

Label & Catalog #		Title	Year	VG+	NM
ALBANY, JOE					
Joseph Albany is a modern West Coast jazz pianist.					
Riverside RLP-12-270	(M)	**The Right Combination**	1958	**30.00**	**75.00**
		(Riverside 270 also features Warne Marsh.)			
– Riverside albums above have blue mono or black stereo labels with a reel & mike logo on top.–					
Riverside RS-3023	(E)	**The Legendary Jazz Pianist**	1968	**5.00**	**12.00**
ALBRIGHT, LOLA					
Lola Albright is a vocalist backed on her Columbia debut by Henry Mancini's jazz combo.					
Columbia CL-1327	(M)	**Dreamsville**	1959	**16.00**	**40.00**
Columbia CS-8133	(S)	**Dreamsville**	1959	**20.00**	**50.00**
– Columbia albums above have six white on black "eye" logos on each label.–					
ALBRIGHT, MAX					
Max Albright is a modern jazz vibraphone player and drummer best known for his session work on television scores. For additional listings refer to the Various Artists section under Tampa.					
Motif 502	(M)	**Mood For Max**	1956	**24.00**	**60.00**
ALESS, TONY					
Anthony Alessandrin, aka Tony Aless, is a tradional jazz based pianist.					
Roost LP-2202	(M)	**Long Island Suite**	1955	**30.00**	**75.00**
ALEXANDER, BOB: ***Refer to*** **AL KLINK / BOB ALEXANDER**					
ALEXANDER, JOE, & BOBBY TIMMONS					
Joseph Alexander is a modern jazz tenor saxophone player.					
Jazzland JLP-23	(M)	**Blue Jubilee**	1960	**16.00**	**40.00**
Jazzland JLP-923	(S)	**Blue Jubilee**	1960	**12.00**	**30.00**
ALEXANDER, MONTY					
Montgomery Alexander is a modern jazz pianist.					
Pacific Jazz LP-86	(M)	**Monty Alexander**	1965	**10.00**	**25.00**
Pacific Jazz ST-86	(S)	**Monty Alexander**	1965	**8.00**	**20.00**
Pacific Jazz PJ-10094	(M)	**Spunky**	1965	**10.00**	**25.00**
Pacific Jazz ST-20094	(S)	**Spunky**	1965	**8.00**	**20.00**
ALEXANDER, ROLAND					
Roland Alexander is a modern jazz soprano and tenor saxophone player.					
New Jazz NJLP-8267	(M)	**Pleasure Bent**	1962	**20.00**	**50.00**
– New Jazz albums above have purple labels.–					
New Jazz NJLP-8267	(M)	**Pleasure Bent**	1965	**10.00**	**25.00**
– New Jazz albums above have blue labels with a trident logo on the right side.–					
ALEXANDRIA, LOREZ					
Lorez Alexandria is a modern jazz vocalist.					
King 542	(M)	**This Is Lorez**	1958	**40.00**	**100.00**
King 565	(M)	**Lorez Sings Prez**	1958	**40.00**	**100.00**
King 656	(M)	**The Band Swings, Lorez Sings**	1959	**40.00**	**100.00**
King 676	(M)	**Lorez Sings Songs Everybody Knows**	1959	**40.00**	**100.00**
– King albums above have black labels without a crown on top.–					
Argo LP-663	(M)	**Early In The Morning**	1960	**20.00**	**50.00**
Argo LPS-663	(S)	**Early In The Morning**	1960	**16.00**	**40.00**
		(Argo 663 also features The Ramsey Lewis Trio.)			
Argo LP-682	(M)	**Sing No Sad Songs For Me**	1961	**20.00**	**50.00**
Argo LPS-682	(S)	**Sing No Sad Songs For Me**	1961	**16.00**	**40.00**
Argo LP-694	(M)	**Deep Roots**	1962	**20.00**	**50.00**
Argo LPS-694	(S)	**Deep Roots**	1962	**16.00**	**40.00**
Argo LP-720	(M)	**For Swingers Only**	1963	**20.00**	**50.00**
Argo LPS-720	(S)	**For Swingers Only**	1963	**16.00**	**40.00**
Impulse A-62	(M)	**Alexandria The Great**	1964	**12.00**	**30.00**
Impulse AS-62	(S)	**Alexandria The Great**	1964	**10.00**	**25.00**
Impulse A-76	(M)	**More Of The Great Lorez Alexandria**	1965	**12.00**	**30.00**
Impulse AS-76	(S)	**More Of The Great Lorez Alexandria**	1965	**10.00**	**25.00**
– Impulse albums above have orange & black labels.–					
Impulse AS-62	(S)	**Alexandria The Great**	1968	**4.00**	**10.00**
Impulse AS-76	(S)	**More Of The Great Lorez Alexandria**	1968	**4.00**	**10.00**
– Impulse albums above have red & black labels with the "abc" logo on top.–					

Label & Catalog #		Title	Year	VG+	NM

ALFRED, CHUZ, & OLA HANSON & CHUCK LEE

Savoy MG-12030	(M)	**Jazz Young Blood**	1955	**24.00**	**60.00**

—Savoy albums above have red labels with silver print.—

ALLEN, BRYON

Paul Bryon Allen is a modern jazz alto saxophone player.

ESP-Disk' 1005	(M)	**The Bryon Allen Trio**	1965	**10.00**	**25.00**
ESP-Disk' 1005	(S)	**The Bryon Allen Trio**	1965	**8.00**	**20.00**

ALLEN, DAVID

David Allen is a jazz-based vocalist who originally recorded as David Allyn with Boyd Raeburn's orchestra.

Pacific Jazz PJM-408	(M)	**A Sure Thing**	1957	**30.00**	**75.00**
Pacific Jazz ST-1006	(S)	**A Sure Thing**	1958	**20.00**	**50.00**
World Pacific WP-1250	(M)	**Let's Face The Music And Dance**	1958	**16.00**	**40.00**
World Pacific WP-1295	(M)	**David Allen Sings The Jerome Kern Songbook**	1960	**12.00**	**30.00**
World Pacific ST-1295	(S)	**David Allen Sings The Jerome Kern Songbook**	1960	**10.00**	**25.00**

(World Pacific 1295 is a reissue of Pacific Jazz 408.)

ALLEN, RED / RED NORVO

Brunswick BL-58044	(10")	**Battle Of Jazz, Vol. 6**	1953	**20.00**	**50.00**

ALLEN, RED

Henry "Red" Allen Jr. is a traditional jazz trumpet player, singer and composer. For additional listings refer to George Lewis; Pee Wee Russell.

"X" LVA-3033	(M)	**Ridin' With Red**	1955	**20.00**	**50.00**
RCA Victor LPM-1509	(M)	**Ride, Red, Ride In Hi-Fi**	1957	**20.00**	**50.00**
		—RCA mono albums above have black labels with "Long Play" on the bottom.—			
Verve MGV-1025	(M)	**Red Allen Plays King Oliver**	1957	**20.00**	**50.00**
		—Verve albums above have "Verve Records, Inc." on the bottom of the label.—			
Verve V-1025	(M)	**Red Allen Plays King Oliver**	1961	**8.00**	**20.00**
Verve V6-1025	(S)	**Red Allen Plays King Oliver**	1961	**6.00**	**15.00**
		—Verve albums above have black labels with "MGM Records" on the bottom.—			
Swingville SWLP-2034	(M)	**Mr. Allen**	1962	**20.00**	**50.00**
Swingville SWST-2034	(S)	**Mr. Allen**	1962	**16.00**	**40.00**
		—Swingville albums above have purple mono or red stereo labels.—			
Swingville SWLP-2034	(M)	**Mr. Allen**	1965	**10.00**	**25.00**
Swingville SWST-2034	(S)	**Mr. Allen**	1965	**8.00**	**20.00**
		—Swingville albums above have blue labels with a trident logo on the right side.—			
RCA Victor LPV-556	(M)	**Henry "Red" Allen**	1965	**8.00**	**20.00**
Columbia CL-2447	(M)	**Feeling Good**	1966	**8.00**	**20.00**
Columbia CS-9247	(S)	**Feeling Good**	1966	**6.00**	**15.00**

—Columbia albums above have "360 Sound" in white on the bottom of the label.—

ALLEN, RED, & KID ORY

Verve MGV-1018	(M)	**Henry "Red" Allen Meets Kid Ory**	1957	**20.00**	**50.00**
Verve MGVS-6076	(S)	**Henry "Red" Allen Meets Kid Ory**	1960	**16.00**	**40.00**
Verve MGV-1020	(M)	**We've Got Rhythm**	1957	**20.00**	**50.00**
Verve MGVS-6121	(S)	**We've Got Rhythm**	1960	**16.00**	**40.00**
		—Verve albums above have "Verve Records, Inc." on the bottom of the label.—			
Verve V-1018	(M)	**Henry "Red" Allen Meets Kid Ory**	1961	**8.00**	**20.00**
Verve V6-1018	(S)	**Henry "Red" Allen Meets Kid Ory**	1961	**6.00**	**15.00**
Verve V-1020	(M)	**We've Got Rhythm**	1961	**8.00**	**20.00**
Verve V6-1020	(S)	**We've Got Rhythm**	1961	**6.00**	**15.00**

—Verve albums above have black labels with "MGM Records" on the bottom.—

ALLEN, RED, & JACK TEAGARDEN & KID ORY

Verve MGV-8233	(M)	**Red Allen, Jack Teagarden & Kid Ory At Newport**	1958	**20.00**	**50.00**
		—Verve albums above have black labels with "Verve Records, Inc." on the bottom.—			
Verve V-8233	(M)	**Red Allen, Jack Teagarden & Kid Ory At Newport**	1961	**8.00**	**20.00**

—Verve albums above have black labels with "MGM Records" on the bottom.—

ALLEN, STEVE

Steve Allen is a pianist and composer of jazz and pop tunes (not included here). For additional listings refer to Terry Gibbs; Mary Anne Jackson; Jack Kerouac; and the Various Artists section under Coral.

Decca DL-8151	(M)	**Steve Allen's All Star Jazz Concert, Vol. 1**	1955	**12.00**	**30.00**
Decca DL-8152	(M)	**Steve Allen's All Star Jazz Concert, Vol. 2**	1955	**12.00**	**30.00**
Coral CRL-57018	(M)	**Jazz For Tonight**	1956	**12.00**	**30.00**

Label & Catalog #		Title	Year	VG+	NM
Coral CRL-57028	(M)	**Let's Dance**	1956	12.00	30.00
		("Let's Dance" features songs from the film version of Benny Goodman's life with Allen backed by Goodman alumni.)			
Roulette R-25033	(M)	**At The Roundtable**	1958	10.00	25.00
Roulette SR-25033	(S)	**At The Roundtable**	1958	8.00	20.00
Forum F-9014	(M)	**Steve Allen At The Round Table**	196?	8.00	20.00
Forum FS-9014	(S)	**Steve Allen At The Round Table**	196?	6.00	15.00
Dot DLP-3515	(M)	**Gravy Waltz**	1963	6.00	15.00
Dot DLP-25515	(S)	**Gravy Waltz**	1963	5.00	12.00

ALLEN, STEVE, & MANNY ALBAM

Dot DLP-3194	(M)	**....And All That Jazz**	1959	10.00	25.00
Dot DLP-25194	(S)	**....And All That Jazz**	1959	8.00	20.00

ALLISON, MOSE

Mose Allison modern jazz vocalist and pianist. For additional listings refer to The Manhattan All Stars.

Prestige PRLP-7091	(M)	**Back Country Suite**	1957	24.00	60.00
Prestige PRLP-7121	(M)	**Local Color**	1958	24.00	60.00
Prestige PRLP-7137	(M)	**Young Man Mose**	1958	24.00	60.00
		—Prestige albums above have W. 50th St. NYC address on the label.—			
Prestige PRLP-7152	(M)	**Creek Bank**	1959	16.00	40.00
Prestige PRLP-7189	(M)	**Autumn Song**	1960	16.00	40.00
Prestige PRLP-7215	(M)	**Ramblin' With Mose**	1961	16.00	40.00
Prestige PRLP-7279	(M)	**The Seventh Son—Mose Allison Sings**	1963	16.00	40.00
Prestige PRST-7279	(S)	**The Seventh Son—Mose Allison Sings**	1963	14.00	35.00
		—Prestige albums above have yellow mono or silver stereo labels with a Bergenfield, NJ address.—			
Prestige PRLP-7423	(M)	**Down Home Piano**	1966	10.00	25.00
Prestige PRST-7423	(S)	**Down Home Piano**	1966	8.00	20.00
Prestige PRLP-7446	(M)	**Mose Allison Plays For Lovers**	1967	10.00	25.00
Prestige PRST-7446	(S)	**Mose Allison Plays For Lovers**	1967	8.00	20.00
		—Prestige albums above have blue labels with a trident logo on the right side.—			
Columbia CL-1444	(M)	**The Transfiguration Of Hiram Brown**	1960	10.00	25.00
Columbia CS-8240	(S)	**The Transfiguration Of Hiram Brown**	1960	8.00	20.00
Columbia CL-1565	(M)	**I Love The Life I Live**	1960	10.00	25.00
Columbia CS-8365	(S)	**I Love The Life I Live**	1960	8.00	20.00
		—Columbia albums above have six white on black "eye" logos on each label.—			
Epic LA-16031	(M)	**Take To The Hills**	1962	8.00	20.00
Epic BA-17031	(S)	**Take To The Hills**	1962	6.00	15.00
Atlantic 1389	(M)	**I Don't Worry About A Thing**	1962	8.00	20.00
Atlantic SD-1389	(S)	**I Don't Worry About A Thing**	1962	6.00	15.00
Atlantic 1398	(M)	**Swingin' Machine**	1962	8.00	20.00
Atlantic SD-1398	(S)	**Swingin' Machine**	1962	6.00	15.00
Atlantic 1424	(M)	**The Word From Mose**	1964	6.00	15.00
Atlantic SD-1424	(S)	**The Word From Mose**	1964	5.00	12.00
Atlantic 1450	(M)	**Mose Alive!**	1966	6.00	15.00
Atlantic SD-1450	(S)	**Mose Alive!**	1966	5.00	12.00
Atlantic 1456	(M)	**Wild Man On The Loose**	1966	6.00	15.00
Atlantic SD-1456	(S)	**Wild Man On The Loose**	1966	5.00	12.00
Atlantic SD-1511	(S)	**I've Been Doin' Some Thinkin'**	1969	5.00	12.00
		—Atlantic albums above have multi-color labels with a black fan logo.—			

ALMEIDA, LAURINDO

Brazilian born Laurindo Almeida is a guitarist and composer in the samba style. For additional listings refer to Herb Ellis; Stan Getz; The Modern Jazz Quartet; Bud Shank.

Capitol H-193	(10")	**Guitar Concert**	1950	30.00	75.00
Coral CRL-56049	(10")	**A Guitar Recital Of Famous Serenades**	1952	30.00	75.00
Coral CRL-56086	(10")	**Latin Melodies**	1952	30.00	75.00
Pacific Jazz PJLP-7	(10")	**Laurindo Almeida Quartet**	1953	50.00	125.00
Pacific Jazz PJLP-13	(10")	**Laurindo Almeida Quartet, Vol. 2**	1954	50.00	125.00
Pacific Jazz PJ-1204	(M)	**Laurindo Almeida Quartet Featuring Bud Shank**	1955	40.00	100.00
		(Pacific Jazz 1204 is a reissue of 7 and 13.)			
Coral CRL-57056	(M)	**A Guitar Recital Of Famous Serenades**	1956	20.00	50.00
World Pacific WP-1204	(M)	**Laurindo Almeida Quartet Featuring Bud Shank**	1958	24.00	60.00
World Pacific WP-1412	(M)	**Brazilliance, Volume 1**	1962	12.00	30.00
		(World Pacific 1412 is a reissue of 1204.)			
World Pacific WP-1419	(M)	**Brazilliance, Volume 2**	1962	12.00	30.00
World Pacific ST-1419	(S)	**Brazilliance, Volume 2**	1962	10.00	25.00
		(World Pacific 1419 also features Bud Shank.)			

Label & Catalog #		Title	Year	VG+	NM
World Pacific WP-1425	(M)	**Brazilliance, Volume 3**	1962	12.00	30.00
World Pacific ST-1425	(S)	**Brazilliance, Volume 3**	1962	10.00	25.00
		(World Pacific 1425 also features Bud Shank.)			
Capitol T-1759	(M)	**Viva Bossa Nova**	1962	6.00	15.00
Capitol ST-1759	(S)	**Viva Bossa Nova**	1962	5.00	12.00
Capitol T-1872	(M)	**Ole! Bossa Nova**	1963	6.00	15.00
Capitol ST-1872	(S)	**Ole! Bossa Nova**	1963	5.00	12.00
Capitol T-1946	(M)	**It's A Bossa Nova World**	1963	6.00	15.00
Capitol ST-1946	(S)	**It's A Bossa Nova World**	1963	5.00	12.00
Capitol T-2197	(M)	**Guitar From Ipanema**	1964	6.00	15.00
Capitol ST-2197	(S)	**Guitar From Ipanema**	1964	5.00	12.00

— Capitol albums above have black labels with the logo on top.—

ALMEIDA, LAURINDA, & RAY BROWN

Century City CCR-80102	(S)	**Back Ground Blues And Green**	1968	8.00	20.00

ALMEIDA, LAURINDO / CHICO HAMILTON

Jazztone J-1264	(M)	**Delightfully Modern**	1957	16.00	40.00
		(Jazztone 1264 reissues material from Pacific Jazz 1204 and 1209, "Chico Hamilton Quintet.")			

ALMOND, JOHNNY

Deram DES-18030	(S)	**Music Machine**	1969	6.00	15.00

ALPERT, TRIGGER

Herman "Trigger" Alpert is a modern jazz bass player primarily associated with TV scores. The all-star session below, "Trigger Happy!," was reissued as Jazzland 11, credited to Zoot Sims & Tony Scott & Al Cohn as "East Coast Sounds."

Riverside RLP-12-225	(M)	**Trigger Happy!**	1956	30.00	75.00
		— Riverside albums above have blue on white labels.—			
Riverside RLP-12-225	(M)	**Trigger Happy!**	195?	16.00	40.00

— Riverside albums above have blue mono or black stereo labels with a reel & mike logo on top.—

ALVIN, DANNY

Daniel Viniello, aka Danny Alvin, is a traditional jazz drummer.

Stephany MF-4002	(M)	**Club Basin Street**	1957	20.00	50.00

AMERICAN JAZZ ENSEMBLE, THE

Epic LA-16040	(M)	**New Dimensions**	1962	10.00	25.00
Epic BA-17040	(S)	**New Dimensions**	1962	8.00	20.00
RCA Victor LPM-2557	(M)	**The American Jazz Ensemble In Rome**	1962	10.00	25.00
RCA Victor LSP-2557	(S)	**The American Jazz Ensemble In Rome**	1962	8.00	20.00

— RCA albums above have black labels with "Long Play" or "Living Stereo" on the bottom.—

AMMONS, ALBERT

Albert Ammons is a traditional jazz and boogie-woogie piano player.

Mercury MG-25012	(10")	**Boogie Piano Stylings**	1950	60.00	150.00
Blue Note BLP-7017	(10")	**Boogie Woogie Classics**	1951	125.00	250.00

AMMONS, ALBERT / PETE JOHNSON

RCA Victor LPT-9	(10")	**8 To The Bar**	195?	40.00	100.00

AMMONS, GENE

Eugene "Jug" Ammons is a modern jazz tenor saxophone player. For additional listings refer to Richard Holmes; Jack McDuff; Sonny Stitt & Gene Ammons.

Prestige PRLP-112	(10")	**Tenor Sax Favorites, Volume 1**	1951	100.00	200.00
Prestige PRLP-127	(10")	**Gene Ammons Favorites, Volume 2**	1952	100.00	200.00
Prestige PRLP-149	(10")	**Gene Ammons Favorites, Volume 3**	1953	100.00	200.00
Prestige PRLP-211	(10")	**Gene Ammons Jazz Session**	1955	100.00	200.00
Prestige PRLP-7039	(M)	**Hi Fidelity Jam Session**	1956	40.00	100.00
Prestige PRLP-7050	(M)	**Gene Ammons All Star Session**	1956	40.00	100.00
		(Prestige 7050, a reissue of 107 and 127.)			
Prestige PRLP-7060	(M)	**Jammin' With Gene**	1956	40.00	100.00
Prestige PRLP-7083	(M)	**Funky**	1957	40.00	100.00
Prestige PRLP-7110	(M)	**Jammin' In Hi Fi With Gene Ammons**	1957	40.00	100.00
Prestige PRLP-7132	(M)	**The Big Sound**	1958	40.00	100.00

— Prestige albums above have yellow labels with a W. 50th St, NYC address.—

Eugene "Jug" Ammons, son of famed boogie-woogie piano player Albert Ammons, came into prominence as a member of Billy Eckstine's band (1944-47) and then replaced the departing Stan Getz in Woody Herman's group in 1949. He then formed a group with co-leader Sonny Stitt (1950-52) before moving onto his own combo. The bulk of his recording has been with Prestige, including the two samples above, both parts of his "high fidelity jam sessions." Aside from the Herman Capitol sides, he has also recorded as a sideman with the Basie band on RCA and with Bennie Green on Vee Jay and Blue Note.

Label & Catalog #		Title	Year	VG+	NM
Prestige PRLP-7039	(M)	**The Happy Blues**	196?	20.00	50.00
		(Prestige 7039 was originally issued as "Hi Fidelity Jam Session.")			
Prestige PRLP-7050	(M)	**Woofin' And Tweetin'**	196?	20.00	50.00
		(Prestige 7050 was originally issued as "All Star Session.")			
Prestige PRLP-7060	(M)	**Not Really The Blues**	196?	20.00	50.00
		(Prestige 7060 was originally issued as "Jammin' With Gene.")			
Prestige PRLP-7146	(M)	**Blue Gene**	1958	20.00	50.00
Prestige PRLP-7176	(M)	**The Twister**	1960	20.00	50.00
		(Prestige 7176 is a reissue of 7110.)			
Prestige PRLP-7180	(M)	**Boss Tenor**	1960	20.00	50.00
Prestige PRST-7180	(S)	**Boss Tenor**	1960	16.00	40.00
Prestige PRLP-7192	(M)	**Jug**	1960	20.00	50.00
Prestige PRST-7192	(S)	**Jug**	1960	16.00	40.00
Prestige PRLP-7201	(M)	**Groove Blues**	1961	20.00	50.00
Prestige PRLP-7208	(M)	**Up Tight!**	1961	20.00	50.00
Prestige PRST-7208	(S)	**Up Tight!**	1961	16.00	40.00
Prestige PRLP-7238	(M)	**Twistin' The Jug**	1962	20.00	50.00
Prestige PRST-7238	(S)	**Twistin' The Jug**	1962	16.00	40.00
Prestige PRLP-7257	(M)	**Bad! Bossa Nova**	1963	16.00	40.00
Prestige PRST-7257	(S)	**Bad! Bossa Nova**	1963	12.00	30.00
Prestige PRLP-7270	(M)	**Preachin'**	1963	16.00	40.00
Prestige PRST-7270	(S)	**Preachin'**	1963	12.00	30.00
Prestige PRLP-7275	(M)	**Soul Summit, Volume 2**	1963	16.00	40.00
Prestige PRST-7275	(S)	**Soul Summit, Volume 2**	1963	12.00	30.00
		(Prestige 7275 also features Etta Jones and Jack McDuff)			
Prestige PRLP-7287	(M)	**Late Hour Special**	1964	16.00	40.00
Prestige PRST-7287	(S)	**Late Hour Special**	1964	12.00	30.00
Prestige PRLP-7320	(M)	**Velvet Soul**	1964	16.00	40.00
Prestige PRST-7320	(S)	**Velvet Soul**	1964	12.00	30.00
—Prestige albums above have yellow mono or silver stereo labels with a Bergenfield, NJ address.—					
Prestige PRLP-7369	(M)	**Angel Eyes**	1965	12.00	30.00
Prestige PRST-7369	(S)	**Angel Eyes**	1965	10.00	25.00
Prestige PRLP-7400	(M)	**Sock!**	1965	10.00	25.00
Prestige PRST-7400	(S)	**Sock!**	1965	8.00	20.00
Prestige PRLP-7445	(M)	**Boss Soul!**	1967	10.00	25.00
Prestige PRST-7445	(S)	**Boss Soul!**	1967	8.00	20.00
Prestige PRLP-7495	(M)	**Gene Ammons Live In Chicago**	1967	10.00	25.00
Prestige PRST-7495	(S)	**Gene Ammons Live In Chicago**	1967	8.00	20.00
Prestige PRLP-7534	(M)	**Boss Tenor**	1967	5.00	25.00
Prestige PRST-7534	(S)	**Boss Tenor**	1967	8.00	20.00
		(Prestige 7534 is a reissue of 7180.)			
—Prestige albums above have blue labels with a trident logo on the right side.—					
Prestige PRST-7552	(S)	**Jungle Soul**	1968	6.00	15.00
		(Prestige 7552 is a reissue of 7257.)			
Prestige PRST-7654	(E)	**The Happy Blues—Jam Session, Vo. 1**	1969	6.00	15.00
		(Prestige 7654 is a reissue of 7039.)			
Prestige PRST-7708	(S)	**Best Of Gene Ammons For Beautiful People**	1969	5.00	12.00
—Prestige albums above have blue labels with a trident logo on top.—					
EmArcy MG-26031	(10")	**With Or Without**	1954	50.00	125.00
Vee Jay LP-3024	(M)	**Juggin' Around**	1961	16.00	40.00
Vee Jay LPS-3024	(S)	**Juggin' Around**	1961	12.00	30.00
		(Vee Jay 3024 is a reissue of 1005, Bennie Green's "The Swingin'est.")			
Savoy MG-14033	(M)	**Golden Saxophone**	1961	12.00	30.00
Moodsville MVLP-18	(M)	**Nice And Cool**	1961	20.00	50.00
Moodsville MVLP-28	(M)	**The Soulful Moods Of Gene Ammons**	1963	20.00	50.00
Moodsville MVST-28	(S)	**The Soulful Moods Of Gene Ammons**	1963	16.00	40.00
—Moodsville mono albums above have green labels with silver print.—					
Moodsville MVLP-18	(M)	**Nice And Cool**	1965	10.00	25.00
Moodsville MVLP-28	(M)	**The Soulful Moods Of Gene Ammons**	1965	10.00	25.00
Moodsville MVST-28	(S)	**The Soulful Moods Of Gene Ammons**	1965	8.00	20.00
—Moodsville albums above have blue labels with a trident logo on the right side.—					
Argo LP-697	(M)	**Dig Him**	1962	12.00	30.00
Argo LPS-697	(S)	**Dig Him**	1962	10.00	25.00
Argo LP-698	(M)	**Just Jug**	1962	12.00	30.00
Argo LPS-698	(S)	**Just Jug**	1962	10.00	25.00
Wing MGW-12156	(M)	**Light, Bluesy And Moody**	1963	6.00	15.00
Wing SRW-16156	(E)	**Light, Bluesy And Moody**	1963	4.00	10.00
		(Wing 12156 is a reissue of EmArcy 26031.)			

Label & Catalog #		Title	Year	VG+	NM
Cadet LP-783	*(M)*	**Make It Happen**	*1967*	**10.00**	**25.00**
Cadet LPS-783	*(S)*	**Make It Happen**	*1967*	**6.00**	**15.00**

AMRAM-BARROW QUARTET, THE

David Amram is a modern jazz composer and French horn player noted for his work for screen and stage..

Decca DL-8558	*(M)*	**Jazz Studio No. 6**	*1957*	**20.00**	**50.00**

AMY, CURTIS

West Coast jazz star Curtis Amy plays the alto, soprano and tenor sax as well as the flute.

Pacific Jazz PJ-62	*(M)*	**Tippin' On Through— Recorded "Live" At The Lighthouse**	*1962*	**12.00**	**30.00**
Pacific Jazz ST-62	*(S)*	**Tippin' On Through— Recorded "Live" At The Lighthouse**	*1962*	**10.00**	**25.00**
Palomar 24003	*(M)*	**Sounds Of Hollywood**	*1965*	**8.00**	**20.00**
Palomar 34003	*(S)*	**Sounds Of Hollywood**	*1965*	**6.00**	**15.00**
Verve V-8684	*(M)*	**Mustang**	*1966*	**6.00**	**15.00**
Verve V6-8684	*(S)*	**Mustang**	*1966*	**5.00**	**12.00**

— Verve albums above have black labels with "MGM Records" on the bottom.—

AMY, CURTIS, & DUPREE BOLTON

Pacific Jazz PJ-70	*(M)*	**Katanga!**	*1963*	**12.00**	**30.00**
Pacific Jazz ST-70	*(S)*	**Katanga!** *(Red vinyl)*	*1963*	**20.00**	**50.00**
Pacific Jazz ST-70	*(S)*	**Katanga!**	*1963*	**10.00**	**25.00**

AMY, CURTIS, & PAUL BRYANT

Pacific Jazz PJ-9	*(M)*	**The Blues Message**	*1960*	**16.00**	**40.00**
Pacific Jazz ST-9	*(S)*	**The Blues Message**	*1960*	**12.00**	**30.00**
Pacific Jazz PJ-26	*(M)*	**Meetin' Here**	*1961*	**16.00**	**40.00**
Pacific Jazz ST-26	*(S)*	**Meetin' Here**	*1961*	**12.00**	**30.00**
Kimberly 2020	*(M)*	**This Is The Blues**	*1963*	**10.00**	**25.00**
Kimberly 11020	*(S)*	**This Is The Blues**	*1963*	**8.00**	**20.00**

(Kimberly 2020 is a reisue of Pacific Jazz 9.)

AMY, CURTIS, & FRANK BUTLER

Pacific Jazz PJ-19	*(M)*	**Groovin' Blue**	*1961*	**16.00**	**40.00**
Pacific Jazz ST-19	*(S)*	**Groovin' Blue**	*1961*	**12.00**	**30.00**

AMY, CURTIS, & VICTOR FELDMAN

Pacific Jazz PJ-46	*(M)*	**Way Down**	*1962*	**12.00**	**30.00**
Pacific Jazz ST-46	*(S)*	**Way Down**	*1962*	**10.00**	**25.00**

ANDERSON, CAT

William "Cat" Anderson is a traditional jazz trumpet player.

EmArcy MG-36142	*(M)*	**Cat On A Hot Tin Roof**	*1958*	**20.00**	**50.00**

—EmArcy albums above have blue labels with silver print.—

Mercury MG-20522	*(M)*	**Cat On A Hot Tin Roof**	*1959*	**16.00**	**40.00**
Mercury SR-60199	*(S)*	**Cat On A Hot Tin Roof**	*1959*	**12.00**	**30.00**

(Mercury 20522 is a reissue of EmArcy 36142.)

ANDERSON, CHRIS

Jazzland JLP-57	*(M)*	**Inverted Images**	*1961*	**16.00**	**40.00**
Jazzland JLP-957	*(S)*	**Inverted Images**	*1961*	**12.00**	**30.00**

ANDERSON, ERNESTINE

Ernestine Anderson is a modern jazz vocalist.

Metronome ????	*(M)*	**It's Time For Ernestine**	*1956*	**20.00**	**50.00**
Mercury MG-20354	*(M)*	**Hot Cargo**	*1958*	**16.00**	**40.00**
Mercury MG-20400	*(M)*	**Ernestine Anderson**	*1959*	**16.00**	**40.00**
Mercury SR-60074	*(S)*	**Ernestine Anderson**	*1959*	**20.00**	**50.00**
Mercury MG-20492	*(M)*	**Fascinating Ernestine**	*1959*	**16.00**	**40.00**
Mercury SR-60171	*(S)*	**Fascinating Ernestine**	*1959*	**20.00**	**50.00**
Mercury MG-20496	*(M)*	**My Kinda Swing**	*1959*	**16.00**	**40.00**
Mercury SR-60175	*(S)*	**My Kinda Swing**	*1959*	**20.00**	**50.00**
Mercury MG-20582	*(M)*	**Moanin'**	*1960*	**16.00**	**40.00**
Mercury SR-60242	*(S)*	**Moanin'**	*1960*	**20.00**	**50.00**

—Mercury albums above have black labels with "Long Playing Microgroove" on the bottom.—

Wing MGW-12281	*(M)*	**Ernestine Anderson**	*1964*	**4.00**	**10.00**
Wing SRW-16281	*(S)*	**Ernestine Anderson**	*1964*	**5.00**	**12.00**

Label & Catalog #		Title	Year	VG+	NM
ANDERSON, IVIE, & LENA HORNE					
Ivie Anderson is a jazz-based vocalist.					
Jazztone J-1262	(M)	**Lena And Ivie**	1956	16.00	40.00
ANDERZA, EARL					
Earl Anderza is a modern jazz alto saxophone player.					
Pacific Jazz PJ-65	(M)	**Outa Sight**	1963	12.00	30.00
Pacific Jazz ST-65	(S)	**Outa Sight**	1963	10.00	25.00
ANDRE'S CUBAN ALL STAR					
For additional listings refer to Jack Costanzo / Andre's Cuban All Stars.					
Clef MGC-515	(10")	**Cubano**	1954	40.00	100.00
ANDREWS, ERNIE					
Ernest Andrews is a modern jazz vocalist. For additional listings refer to Cannonball Adderley.					
Gene Norman GNP-28	(M)	**In The Dark**	1957	16.00	40.00
Gene Norman GNP-42	(M)	**Ernie Andrews**	1959	16.00	40.00
Gene Norman GNP-43	(M)	**Travelin' Light**	1959	16.00	40.00
Gene Norman GNPS-1008	(S)	**Travelin' Light**	1959	16.00	40.00
ANDREWS, GAYLE					
Hi-Life HL-54	(M)	**Love's A Snap**	195?	12.00	30.00
ANDY & THE BEY SISTERS					
Andy Bey and his sisters are a modern jazz vocal ensemble.					
Prestige PRLP-7346	(M)	**Now! Hear!**	1964	20.00	50.00
Prestige PRST-7346	(S)	**Now! Hear!**	1964	16.00	40.00
Prestige PRLP-7411	(M)	**'Round About Midnight**	1965	20.00	50.00
Prestige PRST-7411	(S)	**'Round About Midnight**	1965	16.00	40.00
—Prestige albums above have blue labels with a trident logo on the right side.—					
ANNA MARIE					
Vesta LP-101	(10")	**Anna Marie**	1955	20.00	50.00
ANTHONY, RAY					
Raymond Antonini, aka Ray Anthony, is a traditional jazz-based trumpet player and big band leader whose primary output is pop.					
Capitol T-749	(M)	**Jam Session At The Tower**	1956	16.00	40.00
—Capitol albums above have turquoise labels.—					
APPLEYARD, PETER					
English born Peter Appleyard is a modern jazz vibraphone player and drummer.					
Audio Fidelity AFLP-1901	(M)	**The Vibe Sound Of Peter Appleyard**	1959	16.00	40.00
Audio Fidelity AFSD-5901	(S)	**The Vibe Sound Of Peter Appleyard**	1959	12.00	30.00
ARGO, TONY					
Savoy MG-12157	(M)	**Jazz Argosy**	1960	16.00	40.00
ARMSTRONG, LIL					
Lillian Hardin Armstrong is a traditional jazz pianist, vocalist, arranger and composer.					
Riverside RLP-12-120	(M)	**Satchmo And Me** *(Documentary)*	1956	24.00	60.00
—Riverside albums above have blue on white labels—					
Riverside RLP-12-120	(M)	**Satchmo And Me** *(Documentary)*	195?	16.00	40.00
Riverside RLP-401	(M)	**Lil Armstrong And Her Orchestra**	1962	12.00	30.00
Riverside RS-9401	(E)	**Lil Armstrong And Her Orchestra**	1962	6.00	15.00
—Riverside albums above have blue mono or black stereo labels with a reel & mike logo on top.—					
ARMSTRONG, LOUIS					
Louis Armstrong. aka "Satchmo" or "Pops," is a traditional jazz cornet and trumpet player and singer. For additional listings refer to Bing Crosby & Louis Armstrong; Duke Ellington & Louis Armstrong; Ella Fitzgerald & Louis Armstrong; King Oliver; Oscar Peterson; and the Jazzy Soundtracks section under Decca, Dot, Reprise, and United Artists.					
Brunswick BL-58004	(10")	**Armstrong Classics**	1950	30.00	75.00
Decca DL-5225	(10")	**New Orleans To New York**	1950	30.00	75.00
Decca DL-5279	(10")	**New Orleans Days**	1950	30.00	75.00
Decca DL-5280	(10")	**Jazz Concert**	1950	30.00	75.00
Decca DL-5401	(10")	**Satchmo Serenades**	1952	30.00	75.00
Decca DL-5509	(10")	**Louis Armstrong And The Mills Brothers**	1954	30.00	75.00

Label & Catalog #		*Title*	*Year*	*VG+*	*NM*
Decca DL-5532	*(10")*	**Latter Day Louis**	*1954*	**30.00**	**75.00**
Decca DL-5538	*(10")*	**Louis Armstrong-Gordon Jenkins**	*1954*	**30.00**	**75.00**
Decca DX-108	*(M)*	**Satchmo At Symphony Hall** *(2 LP box)*	*1954*	**30.00**	**75.00**
Decca DL-8037	*(M)*	**Satchmo At Symphony Hall, Volume 1**	*1954*	**16.00**	**40.00**
Decca DL-8038	*(M)*	**Satchmo At Symphony Hall, Volume 2**	*1954*	**16.00**	**40.00**
Decca DL-8041	*(M)*	**Satchmo At Pasadena**	*1954*	**16.00**	**40.00**
Decca DL-8126	*(M)*	**Satchmo Sings**	*1955*	**16.00**	**40.00**
Decca DL-8168	*(M)*	**Louis Armstrong At The Crescendo, Volume 1**	*1955*	**16.00**	**40.00**
Decca DL-8169	*(M)*	**Louis Armstrong At The Crescendo, Volume 2**	*1955*	**16.00**	**40.00**
Decca DL-8211	*(M)*	**Satchmo Serenades**	*1956*	**16.00**	**40.00**
Decca DX-155	*(M)*	**A Musical Autobiography** *(4 LP box)*	*1956*	**40.00**	**100.00**
Decca DL-8284	*(M)*	**Jazz Classics**	*1956*	**16.00**	**40.00**
Decca DL-8329	*(M)*	**New Orleans Nights**	*1957*	**16.00**	**40.00**
Decca DL-8330	*(M)*	**Satchmo On Stage**	*1957*	**16.00**	**40.00**
Decca DL-8488	*(M)*	**Louis And The Angels**	*1957*	**16.00**	**40.00**
Decca DL-8781	*(M)*	**Louis And The Good Book**	*1958*	**16.00**	**40.00**
Decca DL-8840	*(M)*	**Satchmo In Style**	*1958*	**16.00**	**40.00**
		—Decca albums above have silver on black labels.—			
Decca DL-4137	*(M)*	**Satchmo's Golden Favorites**	*1961*	**8.00**	**20.00**
Decca DL-4227	*(M)*	**I Love Jazz**	*1962*	**8.00**	**20.00**
Decca DL-4331	*(M)*	**Satchmo 1930-34**	*1962*	**8.00**	**20.00**
RCA Victor WPT-9	*(10")*	**Town Hall Concert '48**	*1951*	**30.00**	**75.00**
RCA Victor LJM-1005	*(M)*	**Louis Armstrong Sings The Blues**	*1954*	**20.00**	**50.00**
RCA Victor LPM-1443	*(M)*	**Town Hall Concert**	*1957*	**20.00**	**50.00**
RCA Victor LPM-2322	*(M)*	**A Rare Batch Of Satch**	*1961*	**10.00**	**25.00**
RCA Victor LPM-2971	*(M)*	**Louis Armstrong In The '30s/'40s**	*1964*	**8.00**	**20.00**
		—RCA albums above have black labels with "Long Play" on the bottom.—			
Columbia ML-4383	*(M)*	**The Louis Armstrong Story, Volume 1**	*1951*	**20.00**	**50.00**
Columbia ML-4384	*(M)*	**The Louis Armstrong Story, Volume 2**	*1951*	**20.00**	**50.00**
Columbia ML-4385	*(M)*	**The Louis Armstrong Story, Volume 3**	*1951*	**20.00**	**50.00**
Columbia ML-4386	*(M)*	**The Louis Armstrong Story, Volume 4**	*1951*	**20.00**	**50.00**
Columbia CL-591	*(M)*	**Louis Armstrong Plays W.C. Handy**	*1954*	**16.00**	**40.00**
Columbia CL-6335	*(10")*	**Louis Armstrong Plays W.C. Handy, Volume 2**	*1955*	**16.00**	**40.00**
		—Columbia albums above have "Long Playing" on the bottom of the label.—			
Columbia CL-708	*(M)*	**Satch Plays Fats**	*1955*	**16.00**	**40.00**
Columbia CL-840	*(M)*	**Ambassador Satch**	*1956*	**16.00**	**40.00**
Columbia CL-851	*(M)*	**The Louis Armstrong Story, Volume 1**	*1956*	**12.00**	**30.00**
Columbia CL-852	*(M)*	**The Louis Armstrong Story, Volume 2**	*1956*	**12.00**	**30.00**
Columbia CL-853	*(M)*	**The Louis Armstrong Story, Volume 3**	*1956*	**12.00**	**30.00**
Columbia CL-854	*(M)*	**The Louis Armstrong Story, Volume 4**	*1956*	**12.00**	**30.00**
Columbia CL-1077	*(M)*	**Satchmo The Great**	*1957*	**12.00**	**30.00**
		—Columbia albums above have six white on black "eye" logos on each label.—			
Riverside RLP-1001	*(10")*	**Louis Armstrong Plays The Blues**	*1953*	**4.00**	**100.00**
Riverside RLP-1029	*(10")*	**Louis Armstrong With King Oliver's Creole Jazz Band 1923**	*1953*	**40.00**	**100.00**
Riverside RLP-12-101	*(M)*	**The Young Louis Armstrong** *(Riverside 101 is a reissue of 1001.)*	*1956*	**30.00**	**75.00**
Riverside RLP-12-122	*(M)*	**Louis Armstrong 1923** *(Riverside 122 is a reissue of 1029.)*	*1956*	**30.00**	**75.00**
		—Riverside albums above have blue on white labels—			
Riverside RLP-12-101	*(M)*	**The Young Louis Armstrong**	*195?*	**16.00**	**40.00**
Riverside RLP-12-122	*(M)*	**Louis Armstrong 1923**	*195?*	**16.00**	**40.00**
		—Riverside albums above have blue mono or black stereo labels with a reel & mike logo on top.—			
Jolly Roger 50??	*(10")*	**Louis Armstrong, Vol. 1**	*195?*	**20.00**	**50.00**
Jolly Roger 50??	*(10")*	**Louis Armstrong, Vol. 2**	*195?*	**20.00**	**50.00**
Jolly Roger 5008	*(10")*	**Louis Armstrong, Vol. 3**	*195?*	**20.00**	**50.00**
Jolly Roger 50??	*(10")*	**Louis Armstrong, Vol. 4**	*195?*	**20.00**	**50.00**
Jolly Roger 5014	*(10")*	**Louis Armstrong, Vol. 5**	*195?*	**20.00**	**50.00**
Jolly Roger 7001	*(M)*	**Louis Armstrong, Vol. 6**	*195?*	**16.00**	**40.00**
Jolly Roger 7003	*(M)*	**Louis Armstrong, Vol. 7**	*195?*	**16.00**	**40.00**
Verve MGV-4012	*(M)*	**Louis Under The Stars**	*1957*	**20.00**	**50.00**
Verve MGVS-6044	*(S)*	**Louis Under The Stars**	*1960*	**16.00**	**40.00**
		(Verve 4012 also features Russell Garcia's orchestra.)			
Verve MGV-4035	*(M)*	**I've Got The World On A String**	*1959*	**20.00**	**50.00**
Verve MGVS-6101	*(S)*	**I've Got The World On A String**	*1960*	**16.00**	**40.00**
Verve MGV-8322	*(M)*	**Louis Armstrong Meets Oscar Peterson**	*1959*	**20.00**	**50.00**
Verve MGVS-6062	*(S)*	**Louis Armstrong Meets Oscar Peterson**	*1960*	**16.00**	**40.00**
		—Verve albums above have "Verve Records, Inc." on the bottom of the label.—			

Label & Catalog #		Title	Year	VG+	NM
Verve V-4012	(M)	**Louis Under The Stars**	1961	8.00	20.00
Verve V6-4012	(S)	**Louis Under The Stars**	1961	6.00	15.00
Verve V-4035	(M)	**I've Got The World On A String**	1961	8.00	20.00
Verve V6-4035	(S)	**I've Got The World On A String**	1961	6.00	15.00
Verve V-8569	(M)	**The Essential Armstrong**	1963	5.00	12.00
Verve V6-8569	(S)	**The Essential Armstrong**	1963	6.00	15.00
Verve V-8595	(M)	**The Best Of Louis Armstrong**	1964	5.00	12.00
Verve V6-8595	(S)	**The Best Of Louis Armstrong**	1964	6.00	15.00
— Verve albums above have black labels with "MGM Records" on the bottom.—					
Audio Fidelity AFLP-1930	(M)	**Louis Armstrong Plays King Oliver**	1960	12.00	30.00
Audio Fidelity AFSD-5930	(S)	**Louis Armstrong Plays King Oliver**	1960	10.00	25.00
Audio Fidelity AFLP-2132	(M)	**The Best Of Louis Armstrong**	1964	8.00	20.00
Audio Fidelity AFSD-6132	(S)	**The Best Of Louis Armstrong**	1964	6.00	15.00
Kapp KL-1364	(M)	**Hello, Dolly**	1964	6.00	15.00
Kapp KS-3364	(S)	**Hello, Dolly**	1964	8.00	20.00
Metro M-510	(M)	**Hello, Louis**	1965	5.00	12.00
Metro MS-510	(S)	**Hello, Louis**	1965	6.00	15.00
Mercury MG-21081	(M)	**Louis Armstrong Sings Louis Armstrong**	1965	6.00	15.00
Mercury SR-61081	(S)	**Louis Armstrong Sings Louis Armstrong**	1965	8.00	20.00
Vocalion VL-73851	(E)	**Here's Louis Armstrong**	1968	5.00	12.00
Vocalion VL-73871	(E)	**The One And Only Louis Armstrong**	1968	5.00	12.00
ABC ABCS-650	(S)	**What A Wonderful World**	1968	6.00	15.00

ARMSTRONG, LOUIS / EDDIE CONDON

Columbia CL-931	(M)	**American Jazz Festival At Newport '56**	1956	16.00	40.00
— Columbia albums above have six white on black "eye" logos on each label.—					

ARMSTRONG, LOUIS, & DUKE ELLINGTON

Roulette R-52074	(M)	**Louis Armstrong And Duke Ellington**	1961	10.00	25.00
Roulette SR-52074	(S)	**Louis Armstrong And Duke Ellington**	1961	8.00	20.00
Roulette R-52103	(M)	**The Great Reunion**	1963	10.00	25.00
Roulette SR-52103	(S)	**The Great Reunion**	1963	8.00	20.00

ARNOLD, BUDDY

Arnold Grishaver, aka Buddy Arnold, is a modern jazz tenor saxophone, clarinet and oboe player.

ABC-Paramount ABC-114	(M)	**Wailing**	1956	20.00	50.00

ARNOLD, HARRY

Swedish born Harry Arnold Persson is a modern jazz composer and band leader.

EmArcy MG-36139	(M)	**Harry Arnold And His Orchestra**	1958	20.00	50.00
EmArcy SR-80006	(S)	**Harry Arnold And His Orchestra**	1958	16.00	40.00
— EmArcy albums above have blue labels with silver print.—					
Jazztone J-1270	(M)	**The Jazztone Mystery Band**	1958	16.00	40.00
Atco 33-120	(M)	**I Love Harry Arnold (And All That Jazz)**	1960	12.00	30.00
Jazzland JLP-65	(M)	**Great Big Band And Friends**	1962	12.00	30.00
Jazzland JLP-965	(S)	**Great Big Band And Friends**	1962	10.00	25.00
Riverside RM-7526	(M)	**Let's Dance On Broadway**	196?	10.00	25.00
Riverside RS-97526	(S)	**Let's Dance On Broadway**	196?	8.00	20.00
Riverside RM-7536	(M)	**Dancing On Broadway To The Music Of Cole Porter**	196?	10.00	25.00
Riverside RS-97536	(S)	**Dancing On Broadway To The Music Of Cole Porter**	196?	8.00	20.00

ARTHUR, BROOKS

Verve V-8650	(M)	**Solo Forms**	1966	6.00	15.00
Verve V6-8650	(S)	**Solo Forms**	1966	5.00	12.00
— Verve albums above have black labels with "MGM Record" on the bottom.—					

ASH, MARVIN

Marvin Ashbaugh, aka Marvin Ash, is a traditional jazz pianist.

Capitol H-188	(10")	**Honky Tonk Piano**	1950	20.00	50.00
Jazz Man LPJM-335	(10")	**Marvin Ash**	1954	20.00	50.00
Jump JL-4	(10")	**Marvin Ash**	1954	20.00	50.00
Decca DL-8346	(M)	**New Orleans At Midnight**	1957	16.00	40.00

ASHBY, DOROTHY

Dorothy Ashby is a modern jazz harpist and pianist.

Regent MG-6039	(M)	**Dorothy Ashby—Jazz Harpist**	1957	24.00	60.00

Label & Catalog #		Title	Year	VG+	NM
Prestige PRLP-7140	(M)	**Hip Harp**	1958	24.00	60.00
		(Prestige 7140 also features Frank Wess.)			
—Prestige albums above have yellow mono or silver stereo labels with a Bergenfield, NJ address.—					
Jazzland JLP-61	(M)	**Soft Winds**	1961	12.00	30.00
Jazzland JLP-961	(S)	**Soft Winds**	1961	10.00	25.00
Argo LP-690	(M)	**Dorothy Ashby**	1962	12.00	30.00
Argo LPS-690	(S)	**Dorothy Ashby**	1962	10.00	25.00
Atlantic 1447	(M)	**The Fantastic Jazz Harp Of Dorothy Ashby**	1966	8.00	20.00
Atlantic SD-1447	(S)	**The Fantastic Jazz Harp Of Dorothy Ashby**	1966	6.00	15.00
—Atlantic albums above have multi-color labels with a black fan logo.—					
Savoy MG-12212	(M)	**Dorothy Ashby Jazz Harpist**	196?	6.00	15.00
		(Savoy 12212 is a reissue of Regent 6039.)			
Cadet LPS-809	(S)	**Afro Harping**	1969	6.00	15.00
Prestige PRST-7638	(E)	**The Best Of Dorothy Ashby**	1969	5.00	12.00
		(Prestige 7638 is a reissue of 7140.)			
Prestige PRST-7639	(E)	**Dorothy Plays For Beautiful People**	1969	5.00	12.00
		(Prestige 7639 is a reissue of New Jazz 8209.)			
— Prestige albums above have blue labels with a trident logo on top.—					

ASHBY, DOROTHY, & FRANK WESS

New Jazz NJLP-8209	(M)	**In A Minor Groove**	1958	24.00	60.00
—New Jazz albums above have purple labels.—					
New Jazz NJLP-8209	(M)	**In A Minor Groove**	1965	10.00	25.00
—New Jazz albums above have blue labels with a trident logo on the right side.—					

ASMUSSEN, SVEND

Danish born Sven Asmussen is a modern jazz violin player.

Brunswick BL-58051	(10")	**Hot Fiddle**	1953	30.00	75.00
Angel ANG-60000	(10")	**Svend Asmussen And His Unmelancholy Danes**	1955	20.00	50.00
Angel ANG-60010	(10")	**Rhythm Is Our Business**	1955	20.00	50.00
Epic LN-3210	(M)	**Skol!**	1955	16.00	40.00

ASTAIRE, FRED

Mercury/Clef MGC-1001-4	(M)	**The Fred Astaire Story**	1953		See below
		("The Fred Astaire Story" features the singer backed by the JATP All Stars featuring Ray Brown, Barney Kessel, Oscar Peterson, Flip Phillips and Charlie Shavers.Limited edition, spiral-bound album of four blue vinyl LPs limited to an edition of 1,384 numbered copies signed by Mr. Astaire. Each album contains 11 pages of photos by Gjon Mili and a folio of drawings by David Stone Martin. Rare with a suggested Near Mint value of $1,000-2,000.)			
Mercury MGC-1001	(M)	**The Fred Astaire Story, Volume 1**	1954	40.00	100.00
Mercury MGC-1002	(M)	**The Fred Astaire Story, Volume 2**	1954	40.00	100.00
Mercury MGC-1003	(M)	**The Fred Astaire Story, Volume 3**	1954	40.00	100.00
Mercury MGC-1004	(M)	**The Fred Astaire Story, Volume 4**	1954	40.00	100.00
Clef MGC-662	(M)	**The Fred Astaire Story, Volume 1**	1955	20.00	50.00
Clef MGC-663	(M)	**The Fred Astaire Story, Volume 2**	1955	20.00	50.00
Clef MGC-664	(M)	**The Fred Astaire Story, Volume 3**	1955	20.00	50.00
Clef MGC-665	(M)	**The Fred Astaire Story, Volume 4**	1955	20.00	50.00
Verve MGV-2010	(M)	**Mr. Top Hat**	1956	20.00	50.00
		(Verve 2010 contains selections from "The Fred Astaire Story.")			
— Verve albums above have "Verve Records, Inc." on the bottom of the label.—					

AULD, GEORGIE

Canadian born John Altwerger, aka Georgie Auld, is a tradionally based jazz tenor, alto and soprano saxophone and clarinet player. For additional listings refer to Coleman Hawkins / George Auld.

Discovery DL-3007	(10")	**That's Auld**	1950	30.00	75.00
Apollo 102	(10")	**Concert In Jazz**	1951	30.00	75.00
Roost LP-403	(10")	**George Auld Quintet**	1951	30.00	75.00
Coral CRL-56060	(10")	**Tenderly**	1952	30.00	75.00
Coral CRL-56085	(10")	**Manhattan**	1953	30.00	75.00
Coral CRL-57032	(M)	**Misty**	1956	16.00	40.00
Allegro ALL-3102	(M)	**Jazz Concert**	1953	16.00	40.00
EmArcy MG-36060	(M)	**In The Land Of Hi Fi**	1955	16.00	40.00
EmArcy MG-36090	(M)	**Dancing In The Land Of Hi Fi**	1956	16.00	40.00
—EmArcy albums above have blue labels with silver print.—					
ABC-Paramount ABC-287	(M)	**Georgie Auld Plays For Melancholy Babies**	1958	16.00	40.00
ABC-Paramount ABCS-287	(S)	**Georgie Auld Plays For Melancholy Babies**	1958	12.00	30.00

Label & Catalog #		Title	Year	VG+	NM
Top Rank RM-306	(M)	**George Auld With The Mellowlarks**	1959	16.00	40.00
Top Rank RS-606	(S)	**George Auld With The Mellowlarks**	1959	12.00	30.00
Top Rank RM-333	(M)	**Good Enough To Keep**	1959	16.00	40.00
Top Rank RS-633	(S)	**Good Enough To Keep**	1959	12.00	30.00
Philips PHM-300-096	(M)	**George Auld Plays To The Winners**	1963	8.00	20.00
Philips PHS-600-096	(S)	**George Auld Plays To The Winners**	1963	3.00	15.00
Philips PHM-300-116	(M)	**Here's To The Losers**	1963	8.00	20.00
Philips PHS-600-116	(S)	**Here's To The Losers**	1963	3.00	15.00

AUSTIN, CLAIRE

Augusta Austin, aka Claire Austin, is a traditional jazz based vocalist.

Good Time Jazz L-24	(10")	**Claire Austin Sings The Blues**	1954	50.00	125.00
Contemporary C-5002	(M)	**When Your Lover Has Gone**	1956	20.00	50.00

AUSTRALIAN JAZZ QUARTET, THE

The AJQ s a traditional jazz ensemble featuring Jack Brokensha. For additional listings refer to Joe DeRise.

Bethlehem BCP-1031	(10")	**The Australian Jazz Quartet**	1955	24.00	60.00
Bethlehem BCP-39	(M)	**The Australian Jazz Quartet**	1956	16.00	40.00
Bethlehem BCP-6002	(M)	**The Australian Jazz Quartet**	1956	16.00	40.00
Bethlehem BCP-6003	(M)	**The Australian Jazz Quartet**	1956	16.00	40.00
Bethlehem BCP-6012	(M)	**The Australian Jazz Quartet At The Varsity Drag**	1956	16.00	40.00
Bethlehem BCP-6015	(M)	**The Australian Jazz Quartet + One**	1957	16.00	40.00
Bethlehem BCP-6022	(M)	**The Australian Jazz Quartet Plays Rogers & Hammerstein**	1958	16.00	40.00
Bethlehem BCP-6029	(M)	**Free Style**	1959	16.00	40.00
Bethlehem BCP-6030	(M)	**Three Penny Opera**	1959	16.00	40.00
Bethlehem BCP-6070	(M)	**Jazz For Beach-Niks**	1961	12.00	30.00
Bethlehem BCP-6073	(M)	**Jazz For Surf-Niks**	1961	12.00	30.00

AYERS, ROY

Roy Ayers is a modern jazz vibraphone player.

United Arts. UAL-3325	(M)	**West Coast Vibes**	1964	10.00	25.00
United Arts. UAS-6325	(S)	**West Coast Vibes**	1964	8.00	20.00
Atlantic 1488	(M)	**Virgo Vibes**	1967	8.00	20.00
Atlantic SD-1488	(S)	**Virgo Vibes**	1967	6.00	15.00
Atlantic SD-1514	(S)	**Stoned Soul Picnic**	1968	8.00	20.00
Atlantic SD-1538	(S)	**Daddy's Back**	1969	8.00	20.00

—Atlantic albums above have multi-color labels with a black fan logo on the right side.—

AYLER, ALBERT

Albert Ayler is a modern jazz tenor and alto saxophone player and composer.

Fantasy 6016	(M)	**My Name Is Albert Ayler**	1965	10.00	25.00
Fantasy 86016	(S)	**My Name Is Albert Ayler**	1965	8.00	20.00
ESP-Disk' 1002	(M)	**Spiritual Unity**	1965	10.00	25.00
ESP-Disk' 1010	(M)	**Bells** *(Colored vinyl)*	1965	20.00	50.00
ESP-Disk' 1010	(M)	**Bells**	1965	10.00	25.00
ESP-Disk' 1010	(S)	**Bells**	1965	8.00	20.00
ESP-Disk' 1C20	(M)	**Spirits Rejoice**	1966	10.00	25.00
ESP-Disk' 1020	(S)	**Spirits Rejoice**	1966	8.00	20.00
Impulse A-9155	(M)	**Live At The Village Vanguard**	1967	12.00	30.00
Impulse AS-9155	(S)	**Live At The Village Vanguard**	1967	10.00	25.00

—Impulse albums above have orange & black labels.—

Impulse AS-9155	(S)	**Live At The Village Vanguard**	1968	4.00	10.00
Impulse AS-9165	(S)	**Love Cry**	1968	8.00	20.00
Impulse AS-9175	(S)	**New Grass**	1969	8.00	20.00
Impulse AS-9191	(S)	**Music Is The Healing Force Of The Universe**	1969	8.00	20.00

—Impulse albums above have red & black labels with the "abc" logo on top.—

AYLER—CHERRY—RUDD—TCHICAI—PEACOCK—MURRAY

This avante-garde alliance is led by Albert Ayler and Don Cherry.

ESP-Disk' 1016	(M)	**New York Eye And Ear Control**	1966	10.00	25.00
ESP-Disk' 1016	(S)	**New York Eye And Ear Control**	1966	8.00	20.00

AZAMA, ETHEL

Pop singer Ethel Azama is backed by Marty Paich's Orchestra featuring Art Pepper.

Liberty LRP-3142	(M)	**Cool Heat**	1959	16.00	40.00
Liberty LST-7142	(S)	**Cool Heat**	1959	20.00	50.00

B.

BABASIN, HARRY

Harry Babasin is a West Coast jazz bass and cello player. For additional listings refer to The Jazz Pickers and the Various Artists section under Savoy.

Nocturne NLP-3	*(10")*	**Harry Babasin Quintet**	*1954*	**50.00**	**125.00**
Mode LP-119	*(M)*	**Jazz Pickers**	*1957*	**40.00**	**100.00**

BABASIN, HARRY / TERRY GIBBS

Premier PM-2010	*(M)*	**Pick 'N' Pat**	*1963*	**6.00**	**15.00**
Premier PS-2010	*(E)*	**Pick 'N' Pat**	*1963*	**2.50**	**7.50**

BAGLEY, DON

Donald Bagley is a modern West Coast jazz bass player.

Regent MG-6061	*(M)*	**Jazz On The Rocks**	*1957*	**24.00**	**60.00**
Dot DLP-3070	*(M)*	**Basically Bagley**	*1957*	**20.00**	**50.00**
Dot DLP-25070	*(S)*	**Basically Bagley**	*1958*	**16.00**	**40.00**
Dot DLP-9007	*(M)*	**The Soft Sell**	*1959*	**20.00**	**50.00**
Dot DLP-29007	*(S)*	**The Soft Sell**	*1959*	**16.00**	**40.00**
Savoy MG-12210	*(M)*	**Jazz On The Rocks**	*196?*	**8.00**	**20.00**
		(Savoy 12210 is a reissue of Regent 6061.)			

BAILEY, BENNIE

Ernest "Bennie" Bailey is a modern jazz trumpet player.

Candid CD-8011	*(M)*	**Big Brass**	*1960*	**16.00**	**40.00**
Candid CS-9011	*(S)*	**Big Brass**	*1960*	**12.00**	**30.00**
Argo LP-668	*(M)*	**Bennie Bailey Plays The Music Of Quincy Jones**	*1961*	**12.00**	**30.00**
Argo LPS-668	*(S)*	**Bennie Bailey Plays The Music Of Quincy Jones**	*1961*	**10.00**	**25.00**

BAILEY, BUSTER

William "Buster" Bailey is a traditional jazz ckarinet player.

Felsted 7003	*(M)*	**All About Memphis**	*1958*	**20.00**	**50.00**
Felsted 2003	*(S)*	**All About Memphis**	*1959*	**16.00**	**40.00**

BAILEY, DAVE

Samuel David Bailey is a modern jazz drummer.

Epic LA-16008	*(M)*	**One Foot In The Gutter**	*1960*	**16.00**	**40.00**
Epic BA-17008	*(S)*	**One Foot In The Gutter**	*1960*	**12.00**	**30.00**
Epic LA-16011	*(M)*	**Gettin' Into Something**	*1960*	**16.00**	**40.00**
Epic BA-17011	*(S)*	**Gettin' Into Something**	*1960*	**12.00**	**30.00**
Epic LA-16021	*(M)*	**Two Feet In The Gutter**	*1961*	**16.00**	**40.00**
Epic BA-17021	*(S)*	**Two Feet In The Gutter**	*1961*	**12.00**	**30.00**
Jazztime JT-003	*(M)*	**Reaching Out**	*1961*	**16.00**	**40.00**
Jazztime JS-003	*(S)*	**Reaching Out**	*1961*	**12.00**	**30.00**
Jazzline 33-01	*(M)*	**Bash!**	*1961*	**16.00**	**40.00**
Jazzline 33-01	*(S)*	**Bash!**	*1961*	**12.00**	**30.00**

BAILEY, MILDRED

Mildred Bailey introduced the era of the big band singer with Paul Whiteman's Orchestra in 1929.

Columbia CL-6094	*(10")*	**Mildred Bailey Serenade**	*1950*	**30.00**	**75.00**
Decca DL-5133	*(10")*	**Mildred Bailey Memorial Album**	*1952*	**30.00**	**75.00**
Decca DL-5387	*(10")*	**The Rockin' Chair Lady**	*1953*	**30.00**	**75.00**
Allegro 4007	*(10")*	**Mildred Bailey Songs**	*1952*	**30.00**	**75.00**
Allegro 4040	*(10")*	**Mildred Bailey Songs**	*1954*	**30.00**	**75.00**
Allegro 3119	*(M)*	**Mildred Bailey Sings**	*1955*	**24.00**	**60.00**
Regent MG-6032	*(M)*	**Me And The Blues**	*1957*	**20.00**	**50.00**
Columbia C3L-22	*(M)*	**Mildred Bailey's Greatest Performances** *(3 LPs with booklet)*	*1962*	**20.00**	**50.00**
		– Columbia albums above have six white on black "eye" logos on each label. –			
Savoy MG-12219	*(M)*	**Me And The Blues**	*1964*	**8.00**	**20.00**
		(Savoy 12219 is a reissue of Regent 6032.)			

Label & Catalog #		Title	Year	VG+	NM

BAILEY, PEARL

Singer Pearl Bailey's repertoire spans a broad gamut of R&B and pop music with only those of interest to a jazz collector listed below For additional listings refer to the Jazzy Soundtracks section under Capitol.

Columbia CL-6099	(10")	**Pearl Bailey Entertains**	1950	20.00	50.00
Coral CRL-56068	(10")	**Say Si Si**	1953	20.00	50.00
Coral CRL-56078	(10")	**I'm With You**	1953	20.00	50.00
Coral CRL-57037	(M)	**Birth Of The Blues**	1956	16.00	40.00
Coral CRL-57162	(M)	**Cultured Pearl**	1958	16.00	40.00
Mercury MG-20187	(M)	**The One And Only Pearl Bailey Sings**	1957	16.00	40.00
Mercury MG-20277	(M)	**The Intoxicating Pearl Bailey**	1958	16.00	40.00
Vocalion VL-3621	(M)	**Gems By Pearl Bailey**	1958	10.00	25.00
Roulette R-25195	(M)	**All About Good Little Girls And Bad Little Boys**	1962	8.00	20.00
Roulette SR-25195	(S)	**All About Good Little Girls And Bad Little Boys**	1962	6.00	15.00
		(Roulette 25195 also features Louis Bellson.)			

BAKER, BUDDY

Verve MGV-2006	(M)	**Two In Love**	1956	20.00	50.00
		— Verve albums above have "Verve Records, Inc." on the bottom of the label.—			
Verve V-2006	(M)	**Two In Love**	1961	8.00	20.00
		— Verve albums above have "MGM Records, Inc." on the bottom of the label.—			

BAKER, CHET

Chesney "Chet" Baker is a West Coast jazz trumpet and fluegel horn player— and occasional vocalist— who made his name with the Gerry Mulligan Quartet. For additional listings refer to Russ Freeman; Stan Getz; The Mariachi Brass; Gerry Mulligan; Johnny Pace; Art Pepper; Bud Shank; and the Jazzy Soundtracks section under World Pacific.

Pacific Jazz PJLP-3	(10")	**Chet Baker Quartet**	1953	100.00	200.00
Pacific Jazz PJLP-6	(10")	**Chet Baker Quartet Featuring Russ Freeman**	1953	100.00	200.00
Pacific Jazz PJLP-9	(10")	**Chet Baker Ensemble**	1954	100.00	200.00
Pacific Jazz PJLP-11	(10")	**Chet Baker Sings**	1954	70.00	175.00
Pacific Jazz PJLP-15	(10")	**Chet Baker Sextet**	1954	100.00	200.00
Pacific Jazz PJ-1202	(M)	**Chet Baker Sings And Plays With Bud Shank, Russ Freeman And Strings**	1955	50.00	125.00
Pacific Jazz PJ-1203	(M)	**Jazz At Ann Arbor**	1955	50.00	125.00
Pacific Jazz PJ-1206	(M)	**The Trumpet Artistry Of Chet Baker**	1955	50.00	125.00
		(Pacific Jazz 1206 is a reissue of 3 and 6.)			
Pacific Jazz PJ-1218	(M)	**Chet Baker In Europe**	1956	50.00	125.00
Pacific Jazz PJ-1222	(M)	**Chet Baker Sings**	1956	40.00	100.00
		(Pacific Jazz 1222 is a reissue of 11.)			
Pacific Jazz PJ-1224	(M)	**Chet Baker & Crew**	1956	50.00	125.00
Pacific Jazz PJ-1229	(M)	**Chet Baker Big Band**	1957	50.00	125.00
World Pacific WP-1202	(M)	**Chet Baker Sings And Plays With Bud Shank, Russ Freeman And Strings**	1958	30.00	75.00
World Pacific WP-1203	(M)	**Jazz At Ann Arbor**	1958	30.00	75.00
World Pacific WP-1206	(M)	**The Trumpet Artistry Of Chet Baker**	1958	30.00	75.00
World Pacific WP-1218	(M)	**Chet Baker In Europe**	1958	30.00	75.00
World Pacific WP-1222	(M)	**Chet Baker Sings**	1958	30.00	75.00
World Pacific WP-1224	(M)	**Chet Baker & Crew**	1958	30.00	75.00
World Pacific ST-1004	(S)	**Chet Baker & Crew**	1958	24.00	60.00
World Pacific WP-1229	(M)	**Chet Baker Big Band**	1958	30.00	75.00
World Pacific WP-1249	(M)	**Pretty/Groovy**	1958	40.00	100.00
World Pacific WP-1826	(M)	**Chet Baker Sings**	1964	12.00	30.00
World Pacific ST-1826	(E)	**Chet Baker Sings**	1964	8.00	20.00
		(World Pacific 1826 is a reissue of 1222.)			
World Pacific WP-1847	(M)	**Quietly, There**	1966	10.00	25.00
World Pacific ST-1847	(S)	**Quietly, There**	1966	8.00	20.00
World Pacific WP-1858	(M)	**Into My Life**	1967	12.00	30.00
World Pacific ST-1858	(S)	**Into My Life**	1967	8.00	20.00
Columbia CL-549	(M)	**Chet Baker & Strings**	1954	30.00	75.00
		— Columbia albums above have "Long Playing" on the bottom of the label.—			
Columbia CL-549	(M)	**Chet Baker & Strings**	195?	20.00	50.00
		— Columbia albums above have six white on black "eye" logos on each label.—			
Harmony HL-7320	(M)	**Chet Baker & Strings**	1962	6.00	15.00
		(Harmony 7320 is a reissue of Columbia 549.)			
Riverside RLP-12-278	(M)	**It Could Happen To You—Chet Baker Sings**	1958	20.00	50.00
Riverside RLP-1120	(S)	**It Could Happen To You—Chet Baker Sings**	1958	16.00	40.00
Riverside RLP-12-281	(M)	**Chet Baker In New York**	1958	20.00	50.00
Riverside RLP-1119	(S)	**Chet Baker In New York**	1958	16.00	40.00

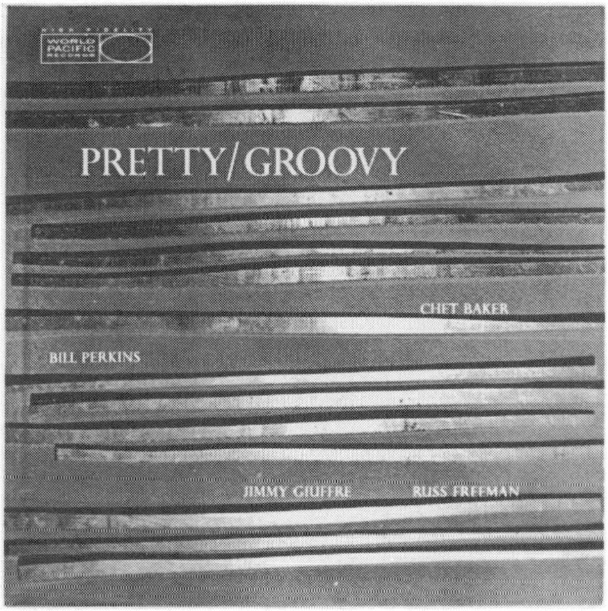

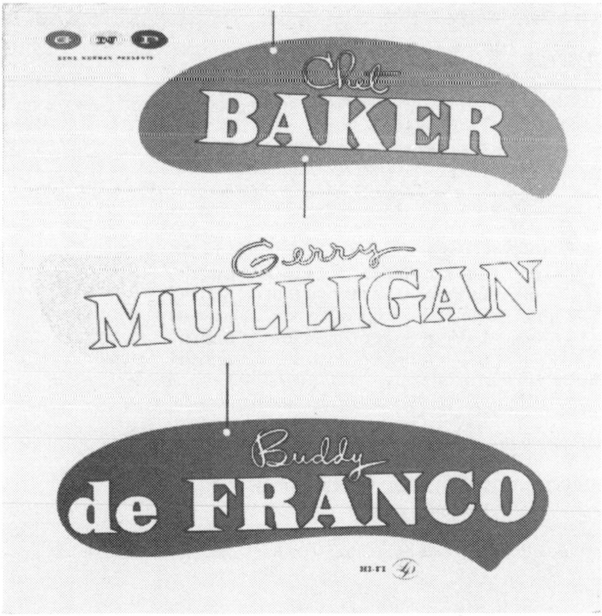

After playing some California dates with Charlie Parker's ill-fated tour of 1952, Chet Baker came into his own as a member of Gerry Mulligan's quartet. By 1953 he was on his own, where his good looks and easy style made him the virtual definition of the cool West Coast sound of the '50s. The albums above illustrate some of the problems of identifying jazz album artists by their covers: On the GNP cover he is given top billing, even though the album includes tracks from his stay with the Mulligan quartet, while the only thing that identifies the World Pacific title as Baker's is that his name is listed first. He has been a featured performer on albums by Russ Freeman, Stan Getz, The Mariachi Brass, Mulligan, Art Pepper, and Bud Shank.

Label & Catalog #		Title	Year	VG+	NM
Riverside RLP-12-299	(M)	**Chet**	1959	20.00	50.00
Riverside RLP-1135	(S)	**Chet**	1959	16.00	40.00
Riverside RLP-12-307	(M)	**Chet Baker Plays The Best Of Lerner & Loewe**	1959	20.00	50.00
Riverside RLP-1152	(S)	**Chet Baker Plays The Best Of Lerner & Loewe**	1959	16.00	40.00
—Riverside albums above have blue mono or black stereo labels with a reel & mike logo on top.—					
Jazzland JLP-11	(M)	**Chet Baker And Orchestra**	1960	20.00	50.00
Jazzland JLP-911	(S)	**Chet Baker And Orchestra**	1960	16.00	40.00
Jazzland JLP-18	(M)	**Chet Baker In Milan**	1960	20.00	50.00
Jazzland JLP-918	(S)	**Chet Baker In Milan**	1960	16.00	40.00
Jazzland JLP-21	(M)	**Chet Baker With Fifty Italian Strings**	1960	20.00	50.00
Jazzland JLP-921	(S)	**Chet Baker With Fifty Italian Strings**	1960	16.00	40.00
Crown CLP-5317	(M)	**Chet Baker Quintette**	196?	8.00	20.00
Crown CST-317	(E)	**Chet Baker Quintette**	196?	4.00	10.00
Colpix CP-476	(M)	**Chet Baker Sings & Plays**	1964	16.00	40.00
Colpix SCP-476	(S)	**Chet Baker Sings & Plays**	1964	20.00	50.00
		—Colpix albums above have gold labels.—			
Limelight LM-82003	(M)	**Baby Breeze**	1964	12.00	30.00
Limelight LS-86003	(S)	**Baby Breeze**	1964	10.00	25.00
Limelight LM-82019	(M)	**Baker's Holiday**	1965	16.00	40.00
Limelight LS-86019	(S)	**Baker's Holiday**	1965	12.00	30.00
Prestige PRLP-7449	(M)	**Smokin' With The Chet Baker Quintet**	1967	12.00	30.00
Prestige PRST-7449	(S)	**Smokin' With The Chet Baker Quintet**	1967	8.00	20.00
Prestige PRLP-7460	(M)	**Groovin' With The Chet Baker Quintet**	1967	12.00	30.00
Prestige PRST-7460	(S)	**Groovin' With The Chet Baker Quintet**	1967	8.00	20.00
Prestige PRLP-7478	(M)	**Comin' On With The Chet Baker Quintet**	1967	12.00	30.00
Prestige PRST-7478	(S)	**Comin' On With The Chet Baker Quintet**	1967	8.00	20.00
Prestige PRLP-7496	(M)	**Cool Burnin' With The Chet Baker Quintet**	1967	12.00	30.00
Prestige PRST-7496	(S)	**Cool Burnin' With The Chet Baker Quintet**	1967	8.00	20.00
Prestige PRLP-7512	(M)	**Boppin' With The Chet Baker Quintet**	1967	12.00	30.00
Prestige PRST-7512	(S)	**Boppin' With The Chet Baker Quintet**	1967	8.00	20.00
—Prestige albums above have blue labels with a trident logo on the right side.—					

BAKER, CHET, & ART PEPPER

Pacific Jazz PJ-1234	(M)	**Playboys**	1957	60.00	150.00
		(Pacific Jazz 1234 was issued in a World Pacific cover.)			
World Pacific PJ-1234	(M)	**Playboys**	1958	40.00	100.00
World Pacific WP-1234	(M)	**Playboys**	1958	30.00	75.00
Pacific Jazz PJ-18	(M)	**Picture Of Health**	1961	20.00	50.00
		(Pacific Jazz 18 is a reissue of World Pacific 1234.)			

BAKER, LaVERN

LaVern Baker is a rhythm 'n' blues singer who traces her roots to Bessie Smith.

Atlantic 1281	(M)	**LaVern Baker Sings Bessie Smith**	1958	75.00	125.00
Atlantic SD-1281	(S)	**LaVern Baker Sings Bessie Smith**	1958	90.00	150.00
—Atlantic albums above have black mono or green stereo labels.—					
Atlantic 1281	(M)	**LaVern Baker Sings Bessie Smith**	1961	12.00	30.00
Atlantic SD-1281	(S)	**LaVern Baker Sings Bessie Smith**	1961	16.00	40.00
—Atlantic albums above have multi-colored labels with a white fan logo.—					
Atlantic 1281	(M)	**LaVern Baker Sings Bessie Smith**	1962	6.00	15.00
Atlantic SD-1281	(S)	**LaVern Baker Sings Bessie Smith**	1962	8.00	20.00
—Atlantic albums above have multi-colored labels with a black fan logo.—					

BAKER, LaVERN / CHRIS CONNOR / HERBIE MANN / BOBBY SHORT

Atlantic 1383	(M)	**No Strings**	1962	8.00	20.00
Atlantic SD-1383	(S)	**No Strings**	1962	10.00	25.00
—Atlantic albums above have multi-colored labels with a black fan logo.—					

BAKER, SHORTY

Harold "Shorty" Baker is a traditional jazz trumpet player.

King 608	(M)	**Broadway Beat**	1959	24.00	60.00

BAKER, SHORTY, & DOC CHEATHAM

Swingville SVLP-2021	(M)	**Shorty & Doc**	1961	20.00	50.00
—Swingville albums above have purple mono or red stereo labels.—					
Swingville SVLP-2021	(M)	**Shorty & Doc**	1965	10.00	25.00
—Swingville albums above have blue labels with a trident logo on the right side.—					

Label & Catalog #		Title	Year	VG+	NM
BALES, BURT					
Burton Bales is a traditional jazz pianist and mellophone and baritone saxophone player..					
Cavalier 5007	*(10")*	**On The Waterfront**	*195?*	**20.00**	**50.00**
Good Time Jazz L-19	*(10")*	**New Orleans Joys**	*1954*	**20.00**	**50.00**
ABC-Paramount ABC-181	*(M)*	**Jazz From The San Francisco Waterfront**	*1957*	**16.00**	**40.00**
BALES & LINGLE					
Burt Bales and Paul Lingle.					
Good Time Jazz L-12025	*(M)*	**They Tore My Playhouse Down**	*1955*	**12.00**	**30.00**
BALL, KENNY					
Kapp KL-1276	*(M)*	**Midnight In Moscow**	*1962*	**8.00**	**20.00**
Kapp KS-3276	*(S)*	**Midnight In Moscow**	*1962*	**6.00**	**15.00**
BALL, RONNIE					
English born Ronald Ball is a modern jazz pianist.					
Savoy MG-12075	*(M)*	**All About Ronnie**	*1956*	**16.00**	**40.00**
BANJO KINGS, THE					
The Banjo Kings are a traditional jazz ensemble.					
Good Time Jazz L-15	*(10")*	**The Banjo Kings**	*1953*	**20.00**	**50.00**
Good Time Jazz L-12015	*(M)*	**The Banjo Kings**	*1955*	**16.00**	**40.00**
Good Time Jazz L-12029	*(M)*	**Nostalgia Revisited**	*1956*	**16.00**	**40.00**
Good Time Jazz M-12036	*(M)*	**The Banjo Kings Go West**	*1957*	**16.00**	**40.00**
Good Time Jazz L-12047	*(M)*	**The Banjo Kings Enjoy The Good Old Days**	*1958*	**16.00**	**40.00**
Good Time Jazz S-10047	*(S)*	**The Banjo Kings Enjoy The Good Old Days**	*1959*	**12.00**	**30.00**
BANKS, BILLY: *Refer to* PEE WEE RUSSELL / BILLY BANKS					
BARBARIN, PAUL					
Adolphe Paul Barbarin is a traditional jazz drummer, band leader and composer.					
Circle 408	*(10")*	**New Orleans Band**	*1951*	**30.00**	**75.00**
Concert Hall Jazz 1006	*(10")*	**New Orleans Jamboree**	*1954*	**20.00**	**50.00**
Jazztone J-1205	*(M)*	**New Orleans Jamboree**	*1955*	**16.00**	**40.00**
Atlantic 1215	*(M)*	**New Orleans Jazz**	*1955*	**20.00**	**50.00**
Atlantic SD-1215	*(S)*	**New Orleans Jazz**	*1958*	**16.00**	**40.00**
		—Atlantic albums above have black mono or green stereo labels.—			
Atlantic 1215	*(M)*	**New Orleans Jazz**	*1961*	**6.00**	**15.00**
Atlantic SD-1215	*(S)*	**New Orleans Jazz**	*1961*	**5.00**	**12.00**
		—Atlantic albums above have multi-color labels with a white fan logo.—			
Atlantic 1215	*(M)*	**New Orleans Jazz**	*196?*	**5.00**	**12.00**
Atlantic SD-1215	*(S)*	**New Orleans Jazz**	*196?*	**4.00**	**10.00**
		—Atlantic albums above have multi-color labels with a black fan logo.—			
BARBARIN, PAUL, & PUNCH MILLER					
Atlantic 1410	*(M)*	**Paul Barbarin And Punch Miller**	*1963*	**10.00**	**25.00**
Atlantic SD-1410	*(S)*	**Paul Barbarin And Punch Miller**	*1963*	**8.00**	**20.00**
		—Atlantic albums above have multi-color labels with a black fan logo.—			
BARBARIN, PAUL / SHARKEY BONANO					
Riverside RLP-12-217	*(M)*	**New Orleans Contrasts**	*1955*	**24.00**	**60.00**
		— Riverside albums above have blue on white labels.—			
Riverside RLP-12-217	*(M)*	**New Orleans Contrasts**	*1956*	**16.00**	**40.00**
		— Riverside albums above have blue mono or black stereo labels with a reel & mike logo on top.—			
BARBARIN, PAUL / JOHNNY ST. CYR					
John St. Cyr is a traditional jazz banjo and guitar player.					
Southland SLP-212	*(M)*	**Paul Barbarin And His Jazz Band / Johnny St. Cyr And His Hot Five**	*1955*	**16.00**	**40.00**
BARBER, CHRIS					
English born Donald Christopher Barber is a modern jazz trombone player and band leader.					
Atlantic 1292	*(M)*	**Here Is Chris Barber**	*1958*	**16.00**	**40.00**
		—Atlantic albums above have black mono or green stereo labels.—			
BARBIERI, GATO					
Gato Barbieri is a modern jazz tenor sax player. For additional listings refer to Jazz Composers Orchestra.					
ESP-Disk' 1049	*(S)*	**In Search Of The Mystery**	*1968*	**8.00**	**20.00**

Label & Catalog #		Title	Year	VG+	NM
BARKER, WARREN					
Warren Barker is a Hollywood composer and conductor known for his jazzy TV themes. For additional listings refer to the Jazzy Soundtracks section under Warner Brothers.					
Warner Bros. W-1290	(M)	**TV Guide—Top TV Themes**	1959	12.00	30.00
Warner Bros. WS-1290	(S)	**TV Guide—Top TV Themes**	1959	16.00	40.00
BARNES, EMIL					
American Music LP-641	(10")	**New Orleans Trad Jazz**	1952	20.00	50.00
BARNES, MAE					
Mae Barnes is a rhythm 'n' blues based vocalist.					
Atlantic ALS-404	(10")	**Fun With Mae Barnes**	1953	150.00	300.00
Vanguard VRS-9036	(M)	**Meet Mae Barnes**	1958	20.00	50.00
BARNET, CHARLIE					
Charles "Mad Mab" Bernett is a traditional jazz alto, soprano and tenor saxophone player and singer.					
Mercury MGC-114	(10")	**Charlie Barnet Plays Charlie Barnet**	1952	50.00	125.00
Clef MGC-114	(10")	**Charlie Barnet Plays Charlie Barnet**	1953	40.00	100.00
Clef MGC-139	(10")	**Dance With Charlie Barnet**	1953	40.00	100.00
Clef MGC-164	(10")	**Charlie Barnet Dance Session, Vol. 2**	1954	40.00	100.00
Clef MGC-165	(10")	**Charlie Barnet Dance Session, Vol. 1**	1954	40.00	100.00
Clef MGC-638	(M)	**One Night Stand**	1955	30.00	75.00
		(Clef 638 features cover art by David Stone Martin.)			
Verve MGV-2007	(M)	**Dance Bash**	1956	20.00	50.00
Verve MGV-2027	(M)	**Dancing Party**	1956	20.00	50.00
		(Verve 2027 is a reissue of Clef 638.)			
Verve MGV-2031	(M)	**For Dancing Lovers**	1956	20.00	50.00
Verve MGV-2040	(M)	**Lonely Street**	1957	20.00	50.00
—Verve albums above have "Verve Records, Inc." on the bottom of the label.—					
Verve V-2007	(M)	**Dance Bash**	1961	8.00	20.00
Verve V-2027	(M)	**Dancing Party**	1961	8.00	20.00
Verve V-2031	(M)	**For Dancing Lovers**	1961	8.00	20.00
Verve V-2040	(M)	**Lonely Street**	1961	8.00	20.00
—Verve albums above have black labels with "MGM Records" on the bottom.—					
RCA Victor LPT-3062	(10")	**Rockin' In Rhythm**	1954	30.00	75.00
RCA Victor LPM-1091	(M)	**Redskin Romp**	1955	20.00	50.00
—RCA albums above have black labels with "Long Play" on the bottom.—					
Decca DL-8098	(M)	**Hop On The Skyliner**	1954	20.00	50.00
Columbia CL-639	(M)	**Town Hall Jazz Concert**	1955	20.00	50.00
—Columbia albums above have "Long Playing" on the bottom of the label.—					
Columbia CL-639	(M)	**Town Hall Jazz Concert**	195?	16.00	40.00
—Columbia albums above have six white on black "eye" logos on each label.—					
Swing 103	(M)	**Charlie Barnet And His Orchestra**	195?	16.00	40.00
Capitol T-624	(M)	**Classics In Jazz**	1955	20.00	50.00
Everest LPBR-5008	(M)	**Cherokee**	1958	10.00	25.00
Everest SDBR-1008	(S)	**Cherokee**	1958	8.00	20.00
Crown CLP-5134	(M)	**On Stage With Charlie Barnet**	1959	6.00	15.00
Capitol T-1403	(M)	**Jazz Oasis**	1960	10.00	25.00
Capitol ST-1403	(S)	**Jazz Oasis**	1960	8.00	20.00
Vault LP-9004	(M)	**Charlie Barnet Big Band**	1967	8.00	20.00
Vault LPS-9004	(S)	**Charlie Barnet Big Band**	1967	6.00	15.00
BARRETT, EMMA					
Sweet Emma Barrett is a traditional jazz/rhythm 'n' blues pianist and vocalist.					
Riverside RLP-364	(M)	**Sweet Emma**	1960	16.00	40.00
Riverside RS-9364	(E)	**Sweet Emma**	1960	8.00	20.00
—Riverside albums above have blue mono or black stereo labels with a reel & mike logo on top.—					
BARRON, BILL					
Willaim Barron is a modern jazz tenor and soprano saxophone and flute player and composer.					
Savoy MG-12160	(M)	**The Tenor Stylings Of Bill Barron**	1961	20.00	50.00
Savoy MG-12163	(M)	**Modern Windows**	1962	16.00	40.00
Dauntless DM-4312	(M)	**West Side Story Bossa Nova**	1963	12.00	30.00
Dauntless DS-6312	(S)	**West Side Story Bossa Nova**	1963	10.00	25.00
Audio Fidelity AFLP-2123	(M)	**Now Hear This**	1964	10.00	25.00
Audio Fidelity AFSD-6123	(S)	**Now Hear This**	1964	8.00	20.00
Savoy MG-12183	(M)	**Hot Line**	1964	10.00	25.00

Label & Catalog #		Title	Year	VG+	NM

BARTLEY, CHARLENE

Vocalist Charlene Bartley is backed by Hal McKusick and Milt Hinton with Tito Puente's orchestra.

RCA Victor LPM-1478	(M)	**Weekend Of A Private Secretary**	1957	16.00	40.00
		—RCA albums above have black labels with "Long Play" on the bottom.—			

BARTZ, GARY

Milestone MSP-9006	(S)	**Libra**	1968	6.00	15.00
Milestone MSP-9018	(S)	**Another Earth**	1969	6.00	15.00

BASIE, COUNT

William "Count" Basie is a traditional jazz-based piano and organ player and band leader. For additional listings refer to Tony Bennett & Count Basie; Eddie Davis; Duke Ellington; Ella Fitzgerald; Dizzie Gillespie / Count Basie; Lambert, Hendricks & Ross; Arthur Prysock; Frank Sinatra; Kay Starr; Lester Young; Lester Young / Count Basie; and the Various Artists section under Savoy.

Columbia CL-6079	(10")	**Dance Parade**	1949	40.00	100.00
Decca DL-5111	(10")	**Count Basie At The Piano**	1950	40.00	100.00
Jazz Panorama 1803	(10")	**Count Basie And Lester Young**	1951	50.00	125.00
EmArcy MG-26023	(10")	**Jazz Royalty**	1954	30.00	75.00
		(EmArcy 26023 also features Earl Hines.)			
Decca DL-8049	(M)	**Count Basie & His Orchestra**	1954	20.00	50.00
Epic LG-1021	(10")	**The Old Count And The New Count—Basie**	1954	30.00	75.00
Epic LN-1117	(10")	**Rock The Blues**	1955	30.00	75.00
RCA Victor LPM-1112	(M)	**Count Basie**	1955	20.00	50.00
		—RCA albums above have black labels with "Long Play" on the bottom.—			
Epic LN-3107	(M)	**Lester Leaps In**	1955	20.00	50.00
Epic LN-3168	(M)	**Let's Go To Prez**	1955	20.00	50.00
		(Epic 3107 and 3168 also feature Lester Young.)			
Epic LN-3169	(M)	**Basie's Back In Town**	1955	20.00	50.00
Columbia CL-754	(M)	**Classics**	1955	16.00	40.00
Columbia CL-2560	(10")	**Basie Bash**	1956	20.00	50.00
Columbia CL-901	(M)	**Blues By Basie**	1956	16.00	40.00
Columbia CL-997	(M)	**One O' Clock Jump**	1956	16.00	40.00
		—Columbia albums above have six white on black "eye" logos on each label.—			
Brunswick BL-54012	(M)	**Count Basie**	1956	16.00	40.00
Mercury MG-25105	(10")	**Count Basie And His Kansas City Seven**	1952	40.00	100.00
Mercury MGC-120	(10")	**Count Basie And His Orchestra Collates**	1952	50.00	125.00
		(Mercury 120 features cover art by David Stone Martin.)			
Clef MGC-120	(10")	**Count Basie And His Orchestra Collates**	1953	40.00	100.00
Clef MGC-146	(10")	**Count Basie Sextet**	1954	40.00	100.00
Clef MGC-148	(10")	**Count Basie Big Band**	1954	40.00	100.00
		(Clef 148 features cover art by David Stone Martin.)			
Clef MGC-626	(M)	**Count Basie Dance Session #1**	1954	24.00	60.00
		(Clef 626 features cover art by David Stone Martin.)			
Clef MGC-633	(M)	**Basie Jazz**	1954	24.00	60.00
Clef MGC-647	(M)	**Count Basie Dance Session #2**	1955	24.00	60.00
		(Clef 647 features cover art by David Stone Martin.)			
Clef MGC-666	(M)	**Basie**	1955	24.00	60.00
		(Clef 666 features cover art by David Stone Martin.)			
Clef MGC-685	(M)	**The Count**	1956	24.00	60.00
Clef MGC-706	(M)	**The Swinging Count**	1956	24.00	60.00
Clef MGC-722	(M)	**The Band Of Distinction**	1956	24.00	60.00
		(Clef 722 is a reissue of 666.)			
Clef MGC-723	(M)	**Basie Roars Again**	1956	24.00	60.00
Clef MGC-724	(M)	**The King Of Swing**	1956	24.00	60.00
Clef MGC-729	(M)	**Basie Rides Again!**	1956	24.00	60.00
Clef MGC-734	(M)	**The Band Of Distinction**	1956	*Unreleased*	
Clef MGC-749	(M)	**Basie In Europe** *(2 LPs)*	1956	*Unreleased*	
		(Clef 749 was issued as Verve 8199.)			
American Rec. Soc. G-401	(M)	**Count Basie**	1956	16.00	40.00
American Rec. Soc. G-422	(M)	**Basie's Best**	1957	16.00	40.00
Verve MGV-8012	(M)	**April In Paris**	1957	20.00	50.00
Verve MGV-8018	(M)	**Basie Roars Again**	1957	20.00	50.00
		(Verve 8018 is a reissue of Clef 723.)			
Verve MGV-8070	(M)	**The Count!**	1957	20.00	50.00
		(Verve 8070 is a reissue of Clef 120 with the DSM cover.)			
Verve MGV-8090	(M)	**The Swinging Count!**	1957	20.00	50.00
		(Verve 8090 is a reissue of Clef 706.)			
Verve MGV-8103	(M)	**The Band Of Distinction**	1957	20.00	50.00
		(Verve 8103 is a reissue of Clef 722.with the DSM cover.)			

Label & Catalog #		Title	Year	VG+	NM
Verve MGV-8104	(M)	**King Of Swing**	1957	20.00	50.00
		(Verve 8104 is a reissue of Clef 724.)			
Verve MGV-8108	(M)	**Basie Rides Again!**	1957	20.00	50.00
		(Verve 8108 is a reissue of Clef 729.)			
Verve MGV-8199	(M)	**Basie In London**	1957	20.00	50.00
Verve MGV-8243	(M)	**Count Basie At Newport**	1958	20.00	50.00
Verve MGVS-6024	(S)	**Count Basie At Newport**	1960	16.00	40.00
Verve MGV-8291	(M)	**Hall Of Fame**	1958	20.00	50.00
		— Verve albums above have black labels with "Verve Records, Inc." on the bottom.—			
Verve V-8012	(M)	**April In Paris**	1961	8.00	20.00
Verve V-8018	(M)	**Basie Roars Again**	1961	8.00	20.00
Verve V-8070	(M)	**The Count!**	1961	8.00	20.00
Verve V-8090	(M)	**The Swinging Count!**	1961	8.00	20.00
Verve V-8103	(M)	**The Band Of Distinction**	1961	8.00	20.00
Verve V-8104	(M)	**King Of Swing**	1961	8.00	20.00
Verve V-8108	(M)	**Basie Rides Again!**	1961	8.00	20.00
Verve V-8199	(M)	**Basie In London**	1961	8.00	20.00
Verve V-8243	(M)	**Count Basie At Newport**	1961	8.00	20.00
Verve V6-8243	(S)	**Count Basie At Newport**	1961	6.00	15.00
Verve V-8291	(M)	**Hall Of Fame**	1961	8.00	20.00
Verve V-8407	(M)	**The Essential Count Basie**	1961	6.00	15.00
Verve V6-8407	(S)	**The Essential Count Basie**	1961	5.00	12.00
Verve V-8511	(M)	**On My Way & Shoutin' Again!**	1963	8.00	20.00
Verve V6-8511	(S)	**On My Way & Shoutin' Again!**	1963	6.00	15.00
Verve V-8549	(M)	**Li'l Ol' Groovemaker... Basie!**	1963	8.00	20.00
Verve V6-8549	(S)	**Li'l Ol' Groovemaker... Basie!**	1963	6.00	15.00
Verve V-8563	(M)	**More Hits Of The 50's And 60's**	1963	8.00	20.00
Verve V6-8563	(S)	**More Hits Of The 50's And 60's**	1963	6.00	15.00
Verve V-8596	(M)	**Verve's Choice—Best Of Count Basie**	1964	5.00	12.00
Verve V6-8596	(S)	**Verve's Choice—Best Of Count Basie**	1964	4.00	10.00
Verve V-8597	(M)	**Basie Land**	1964	8.00	20.00
Verve V6-8597	(S)	**Basie Land**	1964	6.00	15.00
Verve V-8605	(M)	**Our Shining Hour**	1964	4.00	20.00
Verve V6-8605	(S)	**Our Shining Hour**	1964	6.00	15.00
		(Verve 8605 also features Sammy Davis Jr.)			
Verve V-8616	(M)	**Basie Picks The Winners**	1965	4.00	20.00
Verve V6-8616	(S)	**Basie Picks The Winners**	1965	6.00	15.00
Verve V-8646	(M)	**Prysock/Basie**	1965	4.00	20.00
Verve V-8646	(S)	**Prysock/Basie**	1965	6.00	15.00
		(Verve 8646 also features Arthur Prysock.)			
Verve V-8659	(M)	**Basie's Beatle Bag**	1966	16.00	40.00
Verve V6-8659	(S)	**Basie's Beatle Bag**	1966	12.00	30.00
Verve V-8687	(M)	**Basie's Beat**	1967	4.00	20.00
Verve V6-8687	(S)	**Basie's Beat**	1967	6.00	15.00
Verve V6-8783	(S)	**Basie**	1968	6.00	15.00
		— Verve albums above have black labels with "MGM Records" on the bottom.—			
Verve VSP-12	(M)	**Inside Outside**	1966	4.00	20.00
Verve VSPS-12	(S)	**Inside Outside**	1966	6.00	15.00
Roulette R-52003	(M)	**Basie**	1958	14.00	35.00
Roulette SR-52003	(S)	**Basie**	1958	12.00	30.00
Roulette SR-52003	(S)	**Basie** *(Red vinyl)*	1958	40.00	100.00
Roulette R-52011	(M)	**Basie Plays Hefti**	1958	14.00	35.00
Roulette SR-52011	(S)	**Basie Plays Hefti**	1958	12.00	30.00
Roulette R-52024	(M)	**One More Time**	1959	14.00	35.00
Roulette SR-52024	(S)	**One More Time**	1959	12.00	30.00
Roulette R-52028	(M)	**Breakfast Dance And Barbecue**	1959	14.00	35.00
Roulette SR-52028	(S)	**Breakfast Dance And Barbecue**	1959	12.00	30.00
Roulette R-52029	(M)	**Basie/Eckstine, Inc.**	1959	14.00	35.00
Roulette SR-52029	(S)	**Basie/Eckstine, Inc.**	1959	12.00	30.00
Roulette R-52032	(M)	**Chairman Of The Board**	1959	14.00	35.00
Roulette SR-52032	(S)	**Chairman Of The Board**	1959	12.00	30.00
Roulette R-52036	(M)	**Dance With Basie**	1959	14.00	35.00
Roulette SR-52036	(S)	**Dance With Basie**	1959	12.00	30.00
Roulette R-52044	(M)	**Not Now—I'll Tell You When**	1960	12.00	30.00
Roulette SR-52044	(S)	**Not Now—I'll Tell You When**	1960	10.00	25.00
Roulette R-52051	(M)	**String Along With Basie**	1960	12.00	30.00
Roulette SR-52051	(S)	**String Along With Basie**	1960	10.00	25.00
Roulette RB-1	(M)	**The Count Basie Story** *(2 LP box with booklet)*	1960	20.00	50.00
Roulette SRB-1	(S)	**The Count Basie Story** *(2 LP box with booklet)*	1960	16.00	40.00

Label & Catalog #		Title	Year	VG+	NM
Roulette R-52056	(M)	**Benny Carter's Kansas City Suite**	1960	16.00	40.00
Roulette SR-52056	(S)	**Benny Carter's Kansas City Suite**	1960	12.00	30.00
Roulette R-52061	(M)	**Count Basie/Sarah Vaughan**	1960	12.00	30.00
Roulette SR-52061	(S)	**Count Basie/Sarah Vaughan**	1960	10.00	25.00
Roulette R-52065	(M)	**Basie At Birdland**	1961	12.00	30.00
Roulette SR-52065	(S)	**Basie At Birdland**	1961	10.00	25.00
Roulette R-52081	(M)	**The Best Of Basie**	1962	8.00	20.00
Roulette SR-52081	(S)	**The Best Of Basie**	1962	6.00	15.00
Roulette R-52086	(M)	**The Legend**	1962	10.00	25.00
Roulette SR-52086	(S)	**The Legend**	1962	8.00	20.00
Roulette R-52089	(M)	**The Best Of Basie, Volume 2**	1962	6.00	15.00
Roulette SR-52089	(S)	**The Best Of Basie, Volume 2**	1962	8.00	20.00
Roulette R-52099	(M)	**Count Basie In Sweden**	1962	10.00	25.00
Roulette SR-52099	(S)	**Count Basie In Sweden**	1962	8.00	20.00
Roulette R-52106	(M)	**Easin' It**	1963	10.00	25.00
Roulette SR-52106	(S)	**Easin' It**	1963	8.00	20.00
Roulette R-52111-3	(M)	**The World Of Count Basie** *(3 LPs)*	1964	12.00	30.00
Roulette SR-52111-3	(S)	**The World Of Count Basie** *(3 LPs)*	1964	10.00	25.00
		—Roulette albums above have white labels with crisscrossed color bars.—			
Camden CAL-395	(M)	**The Count**	1958	10.00	25.00
Camden CAL-497	(M)	**Basie's Basement**	1959	10.00	25.00
		(Camden 497 also features Jimmy Rushing.)			
Camden CAL-514	(M)	**Count Basie In Kansas City**	1959	10.00	25.00
Harmony HL-7229	(M)	**Count Basie Classics**	1960	6.00	15.00
Impulse A-15	(M)	**Kansas City Seven**	1962	16.00	40.00
Impulse AS-15	(S)	**Kansas City Seven**	1962	12.00	30.00
		—Impulse albums above have orange & black labels.—			
Impulse AS-15	(S)	**Kansas City Seven**	1968	4.00	10.00
		—Impulse albums above have red & black labels with the "abc" logo on top.—			
Reprise R-6070	(M)	**This Time By Basie!**	1963	10.00	25.00
Reprise RS-6070	(S)	**This Time By Basie!**	1963	8.00	20.00
Reprise R-6153	(M)	**Pop Goes The Basie**	1965	10.00	25.00
Reprise RS-6153	(S)	**Pop Goes The Basie**	1965	8.00	20.00
Metro M-516	(M)	**Count Basie**	1965	5.00	12.00
Metro MS-516	(S)	**Count Basie**	1965	4.00	10.00
ABC-Paramount ABC-570	(M)	**Basie's Swingin' Voices Singin'**	1966	10.00	25.00
ABC-Paramount ABCS-570	(S)	**Basie's Swingin' Voices Singin'**	1966	8.00	20.00
United Arts. UAL-3480	(M)	**Basie Meets Bond**	1966	12.00	30.00
United Arts. UAS-6480	(S)	**Basie Meets Bond**	1966	10.00	25.00
Dot DLP-25938	(S)	**Standing Ovation**	1968	6.00	15.00
BASIE, COUNT / DIZZY GILLESPIE					
Verve V-8560	(M)	**The Count Basie Band &The Dizzy Gillespie Band At Newport**	1963	10.00	25.00
Verve V6-8560	(S)	**The Count Basie Band & The Dizzy Gillespie Band At Newport**	1963	8.00	20.00
		—Verve albums above have black labels with "MGM Record" on the bottom.—			
BASIE, COUNT, & JOE WILLIAMS					
Vanguard VRS-8508	(M)	**A Night At Count Basie's**	1955	20.00	50.00
Clef MGC-678	(M)	**Count Basie Swings/Joe Williams Sings**	1955	20.00	50.00
		(Clef 678 features cover art by David Stone Martin.)			
Verve MGV-2016	(M)	**The Greatest! Count Basie Swings/ Joe Williams Sings Standards**	1956	20.00	50.00
Verve MGVS-6006	(S)	**The Greatest! Count Basie Swings/ Joe Williams Sings Standards**	1960	16.00	40.00
Verve MGV-8063	(M)	**Count Basie Swings/Joe Williams Sings**	1957	20.00	50.00
		(Verve 8063 is a reissue of Clef 678 with the DSM cover.)			
		—Verve albums above have "Verve Records, Inc." on the bottom of the label.—			
Verve V-8488	(M)	**Count Basie Swings And Joe Williams Sings**	1962	10.00	25.00
Verve V6-8488	(S)	**Count Basie Swings And Joe Williams Sings**	1962	8.00	20.00
		(Verve 8488 is a reissue of 8063.)			
		—Verve albums above have black labels with "MGM Record" on the bottom.—			
Roulette R-52021	(M)	**Memories Ad Lib**	1959	16.00	40.00
Roulette SR-52021	(S)	**Memories Ad Lib**	1959	12.00	30.00
Roulette R-52033	(M)	**Everyday I Have The Blues**	1959	16.00	40.00
Roulette SR-52033	(S)	**Everyday I Have The Blues**	1959	12.00	30.00
Roulette R-52054	(M)	**Just The Blues**	1960	16.00	40.00
Roulette SR-52054	(S)	**Just The Blues**	1960	12.00	30.00

Label & Catalog #		Title	Year	VG+	NM

BASIN STREET SIX, THE

The Basin Street Six are a traditional jazz band.

Circle L-403	(10")	**Dixieland From New Orleans**	1951	20.00	50.00
Mercury MG-25111	(10")	**The Basin Street Six**	1951	20.00	50.00
EmArcy MG-26012	(10")	**The Basin Street Six**	1954	20.00	50.00
Mercury MG-20151	(M)	**Strictly Dixie**	1957	16.00	40.00

BASSO-VALDAMBRINI OCTET, THE

Verve MGV-20009	(M)	**Jazz Festival, Milan**	1960	16.00	40.00
Verve MGV-20011	(M)	**New Sound From Italy**	1960	16.00	40.00
Verve MGVS-6152	(S)	**New Sound From Italy**	1960	12.00	30.00

—Verve albums above have "Verve Records, Inc." on the bottom of the label.—

Verve V-20009	(M)	**Jazz Festival, Milan**	1961	6.00	15.00
Verve V-20011	(M)	**New Sound From Italy**	1961	6.00	15.00
Verve V6-20011	(S)	**New Sound From Italy**	1961	5.00	12.00

—Verve albums above have black labels with "MGM Records, Inc." on the bottom.—

BAUDUC, RAY, & NAPPY LaMARE

Raymond Bauduc is a traditional jazz drummer and vocalist.

Capitol T-877	(M)	**Riverboat Dandies**	1957	12.00	30.00
Mercury MG-205??	(M)	**On A Swinging Date**	1960	10.00	25.00
Mercury SR-60186	(S)	**On A Swinging Date**	1960	8.00	20.00

BAUER, BILLY

William Bauer is a traditional jazz and big band guitar player.

Ad Lib AAL-5501	(10")	**Let's Have A Session**	1955	60.00	150.00
Norgran MGN-1082	(M)	**Billy Bauer Plectrist**	1956	30.00	75.00
Verve MGV-8172	(M)	**Billy Bauer Plectrist**	1957	20.00	50.00

—Verve albums above have black labels with "Verve Records, Inc." on the bottom.—

Verve MGV-8172	(M)	**Billy Bauer Plectrist**	1961	6.00	15.00

—Verve albums above have black labels with "MGM Record" on the bottom.—

BAY CITY JAZZ BAND, THE

The Bay City Jazz Band are a traditional jazz group.

Good Time Jazz L-12017	(M)	**The Bay City Jazz Band**	1955	12.00	30.00
Good Time Jazz L-12053	(M)	**Golden Days**	1957	12.00	30.00
Good Time Jazz S-10053	(S)	**Golden Days**	1960	10.00	25.00

BEAN, BILLY

Riverside RLP-380	(M)	**The Trio**	1961	20.00	50.00
Riverside RS-9380	(S)	**The Trio**	1961	16.00	40.00

—Riverside albums above have blue mono or black stereo labels with a reel & mike logo on top.—

BECHET, SIDNEY

Sidney Bechet is a traditional, New Orleans-based jazz soprano saxophone and clarinet player. For additional listings refer to Albert Nicholas / Sidney Bechet.

Blue Note BLP-7001	(10")	**Sidney Bechet's Blue Note Jazz Men**	1950	150.00	300.00
Blue Note BLP-7002	(10")	**Jazz Classics, Volume 1**	1950	125.00	250.00
Blue Note BLP-7003	(10")	**Jazz Classics, Volume 2**	1950	125.00	250.00
Blue Note BLP-7008	(10")	**Days Beyond Recall**	1951	125.00	250.00
		(Blue Note 7008 also features Bunk Johnson.)			
Blue Note BLP-7009	(10")	**Sidney Bechet With The Blue Note Jazz Men**	1951	125.00	250.00
Blue Note BLP-7014	(10")	**Sidney Bechet's Blue Note Jazz Men, Volume 2**	1951	125.00	250.00
Blue Note BLP-7020	(10")	**The Fabulous Sidney Bechet & His Hot Six**	1952	125.00	250.00
Blue Note BLP-7022	(10")	**The Port Of Harlem Six**	1952	125.00	250.00
Blue Note BLP-7024	(10")	**Jazz Festival Concert, Paris 1952—Volume 1**	1953	125.00	250.00
Blue Note BLP-7025	(10")	**Jazz Festival Concert, Paris 1952—Volume 2**	1953	125.00	250.00
Blue Note BLP-7026	(10")	**Dixie By The Fabulous Sidney Bechet**	1953	125.00	250.00
Blue Note BLP-7029	(10")	**Olympia Concert, Paris 1954—Volume 1**	1954	125.00	250.00
Blue Note BLP-7030	(10")	**Olympia Concert, Paris 1954—Volume 2**	1954	125.00	250.00
Blue Note BLP-1201	(M)	**Jazz Classics, Volume 1** *(Deep groove)*	1955	60.00	150.00
Blue Note BLP-1201	(M)	**Jazz Classics, Volume 1**	1955	40.00	100.00
		(Blue Note 1201 is a reissue of 7002 and 7008.)			
Blue Note BLP-1202	(M)	**Jazz Classics, Volume 2** *(Deep groove)*	1955	60.00	150.00
Blue Note BLP-1202	(M)	**Jazz Classics, Volume 2**	1955	40.00	100.00
		(Blue Note 1202 is a reissue of 7003 and 7022.)			
Blue Note BLP-1203	(M)	**Giant Of Jazz, Volume 1** *(Deep groove)*	1955	60.00	150.00
Blue Note BLP-1203	(M)	**Giant Of Jazz, Volume 1**	1955	40.00	100.00
		(Blue Note 1203 is a reissue of 7001 and 7005, "Art Hodes' Hot Five.")			

Label & Catalog #		Title	Year	VG+	NM
Blue Note BLP-1204	(M)	**Giant Of Jazz, Volume 2** *(Deep groove)*	1955	60.00	150.00
Blue Note BLP-1204	(M)	**Giant Of Jazz, Volume 2**	1955	40.00	100.00
		(Blue Note 1204 is a reissue of 7009 and 7014.)			
		—Blue Note albums above have blue on white labels with a Lexington Ave, NYC address.—			
Blue Note BLP-1207	(M)	**The Fabulous Sidney Bechet** *(Deep groove)*	1956	40.00	100.00
Blue Note BLP-1207	(M)	**The Fabulous Sidney Bechet**	1956	30.00	75.00
		(Blue Note 1207 is a reissue of 7020 and 7026.)			
		—Blue Note albums above have blue on white labels with a W. 63rd Ave, NYC address.—			
Jazz Panorama 1801	(10")	**Sidney Bechet, Vol. 1**	1951	40.00	100.00
Jazz Panorama 1809	(10")	**Sidney Bechet, Vol. 2**	1951	40.00	100.00
RCA Victor WPT-22	(10")	**Sidney Bechet**	1951	50.00	125.00
RCA Victor WPT-31	(10")	**Immortal Performances**	1952	50.00	125.00
Dial LP-301	(10")	**Black Stick**	1952	125.00	250.00
Dial LP-302	(10")	**Sidney Bechet With Wally Bishop's Orchestra**	1952	125.00	250.00
Savoy MG-15013	(10")	**Sidney Bechet**	1952	100.00	200.00
Atlantic ALS-118	(10")	**Sidney Bechet Solos**	1952	40.00	100.00
Atlantic 1206	(M)	**Sidney Bechet Duets**	1956	30.00	75.00
		(Atlantic 1206 also features Muggsy Spanier.)			
		—Atlantic albums above have black mono or green stereo labels.—			
Commodore FL-20020	(10")	**New Orleans Style, Old And New**	1952	50.00	125.00
Storyville STLP-301	(10")	**Sidney Bechet At Storyville, Vol. 1**	1954	70.00	175.00
Storyville STLP-306	(10")	**Sidney Bechet At Storyville, Vol. 2**	1954	70.00	175.00
Jolly Rogers 5028	(10")	**Sidney Bechet**	1954	20.00	50.00
		(Jolly Rogers 5028 also features Jelly Roll Morton.)			
"X" LVA-3024	(10")	**Sidney Bechet And New Orleans Feetwarmers**	1954	40.00	100.00
		("X" 3024 also features Sidney DeParis and Sid Catlett.)			
Riverside RLP-2516	(10")	**Sidney Bechet And His Soprano Sax**	1955	100.00	200.00
Good Time Jazz L-12013	(M)	**King Of The Soprano Saxophone**	1955	20.00	50.00
Storyville STLP-902	(M)	**Sidney Bechet At Storyville**	1955	20.00	50.00
London WV-91050	(10")	**La Nuit Est Une Sorciere**	1955	20.00	50.00
Columbia CL-836	(M)	**Grand Master Of The Soprano Sax & Clarinet**	1956	20.00	50.00
Columbia CL-1410	(M)	**Sidney Bechet In Concert At The Brussels Fair**	1960	12.00	30.00
		—Columbia albums above have six white on black "eye" logos on each label.—			
Riverside RLP-12-138/9	(M)	**In Memoriam** *(2 LPs)*	1961	12.00	30.00
Riverside RLP-12-149	(M)	**Bechet**	1961	10.00	25.00
		—Riverside albums above have blue mono or black stereo labels with a reel & mike logo on top.—			
Reprise R-7076	(M)	**The Immortal Sidney Bechet**	1963	10.00	25.00
Reprise RS-7076	(E)	**The Immortal Sidney Bechet**	1963	8.00	20.00
RCA Victor LPV-510	(M)	**Bechet Of New Orleans**	1965	8.00	20.00
RCA Victor LPV-535	(M)	**The Blue Bechet**	1965	8.00	20.00

BECHET, SIDNEY, & EDDIE CONDON

Savoy MG-12208	(M)	**We Dig Dixieland**	196?	8.00	20.00

BECHET, SIDNEY / OMER SIMEON

Jazztone J-1213	(M)	**Jazz A'la Creole**	1955	16.00	40.00

BECHET, SIDNEY, & MARTIAL SOLAL

World Pacific PJ-1236	(M)	**Young Ideas**	1957	30.00	75.00
World Pacific WP-1236	(M)	**Young Ideas**	1958	20.00	50.00

BECK, PIA

Vocalist Pia Beck is backed by a small combo including Barry Galbraith, Milt Hinton and Osie Johnson

Epic LN-3269	(M)	**Dutch Treat**	1956	16.00	40.00

BEE, DAVID

Bally BAL-12005	(M)	**Belgian Jazz**	1956	12.00	30.00

BEIDERBECKE, BIX

Leon "Bix" Beiderbecke is a traditional jazz cornet— and occasionally piano— player and composer. For additional listings refer to Jean Goldkette; Paul Whiteman.

Columbia ML-4811	(M)	**The Bix Beiderbecke Story, Volume 1**	1950	24.00	60.00
Columbia ML-4812	(M)	**The Bix Beiderbecke Story, Volume 2**	1950	24.00	60.00
Columbia ML-4813	(M)	**The Bix Beiderbecke Story, Volume 3**	1950	24.00	60.00
Columbia GL-507	(M)	**The Bix Beiderbecke Story, Volume 1**	1952	16.00	40.00
Columbia GL-508	(M)	**The Bix Beiderbecke Story, Volume 2**	1952	16.00	40.00
Columbia GL-509	(M)	**The Bix Beiderbecke Story, Volume 3**	1952	16.00	40.00
		—Columbia albums above have "Long Playing" on the bottom of the label.—			

Label & Catalog #		Title	Year	VG+	NM
Columbia CL-844	(M)	**The Bix Beiderbecke Story, Volume 1**	1956	12.00	30.00
Columbia CL-845	(M)	**The Bix Beiderbecke Story, Volume 2**	1956	12.00	30.00
Columbia CL-846	(M)	**The Bix Beiderbecke Story, Volume 3**	1956	12.00	30.00
		— Columbia albums above have six white on black "eye" logos on each label.—			
Jolly Roger 5010	(10")	**Bix Beiderbecke**	1954	20.00	50.00
Riverside RLP-1023	(10")	**Early Bix**	1954	30.00	75.00
Riverside RLP-1050	(10")	**Bix Beiderbecke And The Wolverines**	1954	30.00	75.00
Riverside RLP-12-123	(M)	**Bix Beiderbecke And The Wolverines**	1956	20.00	50.00
		(Riverside 123 is a reissue of 1023 and 1050.)			
		— Riverside albums above have blue on white labels.—			
Riverside RLP-12-123	(M)	**Bix Beiderbecke And The Wolverines**	195?	12.00	30.00
		— Riverside albums above have blue mono or black stereo labels with a reel & mike logo on top.—			
RCA Victor LPM-2323	(M)	**The Bix Beiderbecke Legend**	1961	10.00	25.00
		— RCA albums above have black labels with "Long Play" on the bottom.—			

BELL, AARON

Aaron Bell is a modern jazz bass, piano, trumpet and tuba player and composer. For additional listings refer to The Manhattan Jazz All-Stars.

Herald HLP-0100	(M)	**Three Swinging Bells**	1955	20.00	50.00
RCA Victor LPM-1876	(M)	**After The Party's Over**	1958	20.00	50.00
		— RCA albums above have black labels with "Long Play" on the bottom.—			
Lion L-70111	(M)	**Music From "77 Sunset Strip"**	1959	10.00	25.00
Lion L-70112	(M)	**Music From "Peter Gunn"**	1959	10.00	25.00
Lion L-70113	(M)	**Music From "Victory At Sea"**	1959	10.00	25.00

BELL, CHARLES

Charles Bell is a modern jazz pianist.

Columbia CL-1582	(M)	**The Charles Bell Contemporary Jazz Quartet**	1961	10.00	25.00
Columbia CS-8382	(S)	**The Charles Bell Contemporary Jazz Quartet**	1961	8.00	20.00
		— Columbia albums above have six white on black "eye" logos on each label.—			
Atlantic 1400	(M)	**Another Dimension**	1963	8.00	20.00
Atlantic SD-1400	(S)	**Another Dimension**	1963	6.00	15.00
		— Atlantic albums above have multi-color labels with a black fan logo .—			
Gateway 7105	(M)	**Charles Bell In Concert**	1964	6.00	15.00
Gateway 7105	(S)	**Charles Bell In Concert**	1964	5.00	12.00

BELL, GRAEME

Australian born Graeme Bell is a traditional jazz based pianist and band leader.

Angel ANG-60002	(10")	**Inside Jazz Down Under**	1954	20.00	50.00

BELL, MARTY

Martin Bell is a modern jazz based vocalist backed by Don Elliott..

Riverside RLP-12-206	(M)	**The Voice Of Marty Bell**	1956	24.00	60.00
		— Riverside albums above have blue on white labels.—			
Riverside RLP-12-206	(M)	**The Voice Of Marty Bell**	1957	16.00	40.00
		— Riverside albums above have blue mono or black stereo labels with a reel & mike logo on top.—			

BELLETTO, AL

Alphonse Belletto is a modern jazz alto and baritone saxophone and clarinet player.

Capitol T-6506	(M)	**The Al Belletto Sextette**	1955	20.00	50.00
Capitol T-6514	(M)	**Sounds And Songs**	1955	20.00	50.00
Capitol T-751	(M)	**Half & Half**	1956	20.00	50.00
Capitol T-901	(M)	**Whisper Not**	1957	20.00	50.00
		— Capitol albums above have turquoise labels.—			
King 716	(M)	**The Big Sound Of Al Belletto**	1961	20.00	50.00
		— King albums above have crownless black labels.—			

BELLSON, LOUIS

Louis Balassoni, aka Louis Bellson, is a modern jazz drummer, arranger and composer. For additional listings refer to Pearl Bailey; Benny Carter & Louis Bellson.; Meade Lux Lewis & Louis Bellson; Art Tatum; and the Various Artists section under Verve.

Capitol H-348	(10")	**Just Jazz All Stars**	1952	50.00	125.00
Norgran MGN-7	(10")	**The Exciting Mr. Bellson And His Big Band**	1954	70.00	175.00
Norgran MGN-14	(10")	**Louis Bellson With Wardell Gray**	1954	100.00	200.00
Norgran MGN-1007	(M)	**Journey Into Love**	1954	60.00	150.00
		(Norgran 1007 features cover art by David Stone Martin.)			
Norgran MGN-1011	(M)	**Louis Bellson And His Drums**	1954	70.00	175.00
Norgran MGN-1020	(M)	**The Driving Louis Bellson**	1955	30.00	75.00
Norgran MGN-1046	(M)	**Skin Deep**	1955	30.00	75.00

Label & Catalog #		Title	Year	VG+	NM
Norgran MGN-1095	(M)	**Concerto For Drums**	1956	Unreleased	
Norgran MGN-1099	(M)	**The Hawk Talks**	1956	30.00	75.00
		(Norgran 1099 is a reissue of 1020.)			
Verve MGV-8016	(M)	**Concerto For Drums**	1957	20.00	50.00
		(Verve 8016 is a reissue of Norgran 1011.)			
Verve MGV-8137	(M)	**Skin Deep**	1957	20.00	50.00
		(Verve 8137 is a reissue of Norgran 1011.)			
Verve MGV-8186	(M)	**The Hawk Talks**	1957	20.00	50.00
		(Verve 8186 is a reissue of Norgran 1099.)			
Verve MGV-8193	(M)	**Drumorama!**	1957	20.00	50.00
Verve MGV-8256	(M)	**Louis Bellson At The Flamingo**	1958	20.00	50.00
Verve MGV-8258	(M)	**Let's Call It Swing**	1958	20.00	50.00
Verve MGV-8280	(M)	**Music, Romance And Especially Love**	1958	20.00	50.00
Verve MGV-8354	(M)	**Drummer's Holiday**	1959	20.00	50.00
Verve MGV-2123	(M)	**The Brilliant Bellson Sound**	1960	20.00	50.00
Verve MGVS-6093	(S)	**The Brilliant Bellson Sound**	1960	16.00	40.00
Verve MGV-2131	(M)	**Louis Bellson Swings Jules Styne**	1960	20.00	50.00
Verve MGVS-6138	(S)	**Louis Bellson Swings Jules Styne**	1960	16.00	40.00
		— Verve albums above have black labels with "Verve Records, Inc." on the bottom.—			
Verve V-8016	(M)	**Concerto For Drums**	1961	8.00	20.00
Verve V-8137	(M)	**Skin Deep**	1961	8.00	20.00
Verve V-8186	(M)	**The Hawk Talks**	1961	8.00	20.00
Verve V-8193	(M)	**Drumorama!**	1961	8.00	20.00
Verve V-8256	(M)	**Louis Bellson At The Flamingo**	1961	8.00	20.00
Verve V-8258	(M)	**Let's Call It Swing**	1961	8.00	20.00
Verve V-8280	(M)	**Music, Romance And Especially Love**	1961	8.00	20.00
Verve V-8354	(M)	**Drummer's Holiday**	1961	8.00	20.00
Verve V-2123	(M)	**The Brilliant Bellson Sound**	1961	8.00	20.00
Verve V6-2123	(S)	**The Brilliant Bellson Sound**	1961	6.00	15.00
Verve V-2131	(M)	**Louis Bellson Swings Jules Styne**	1961	8.00	20.00
Verve V6-2131	(S)	**Louis Bellson Swings Jules Styne**	1961	6.00	15.00
		— Verve albums above have black labels with "MGM Record" on the bottom.—			
Roulette R-52087	(M)	**Big Band Jazz At The Summit**	1962	10.00	25.00
Roulette SR-52087	(S)	**Big Band Jazz At The Summit**	1962	8.00	20.00
Roulette R-52098	(M)	**The Mighty Two**	1962	10.00	25.00
Roulette SR-52098	(S)	**The Mighty Two**	1962	8.00	20.00
		(Roulette 52098 also features Gene Krupa.)			
Roulette R-65002	(M)	**Around The World In Percussion**	1962	10.00	25.00
Roulette SR-65002	(S)	**Around The World In Percussion**	1962	8.00	20.00
Impulse A-9107	(M)	**Thunderbird**	1966	12.00	30.00
Impulse AS-9107	(S)	**Thunderbird**	1966	10.00	25.00
		—Impulse albums above have orange & black labels.—			
Impulse AS-9107	(S)	**Thunderbird**	1968	4.00	10.00
		— Impulse albums above have red & black labels with the "abc" logo on top.—			

BELLSON, LOUIS, & LALO SCHIFRIN

Roulette R-52120	(M)	**Explorations**	1964	8.00	20.00
Roulette SR-52120	(S)	**Explorations**	1964	6.00	15.00

BELVIN, JESSE

Pop singer Jesse Belvin's sole jazz-tinged outing features Marty Paich's Orchestra with Art Pepper.

RCA Victor LPM-2105	(M)	**Mr. Easy**	1960	12.00	30.00
RCA Victor LSP-2105	(S)	**Mr. Easy**	1960	16.00	40.00
		— RCA albums above have black labels with "Long Play" or "Living Stereo" on the bottom.—			

BENNETT, BETTY

Betty Bennett is a traditional big band vocalist.

Trend TL-1006	(10")	**Betty Bennett Sings Previn Arrangements**	1954	40.00	100.00
Atlantic 1226	(M)	**Nobody Else But Me**	1956	40.00	100.00
		— Atlantic albums above have black mono or green stereo labels.—			
Atlantic 1226	(M)	**Nobody Else But Me**	1961	16.00	40.00
		— Atlantic albums above have multi-color labels with a white fan logo.—			
Kapp LP-1052	(M)	**Blue Sunday**	1957	16.00	40.00
United Arts. UAL-3070	(M)	**I Love To Sing**	1959	16.00	40.00
United Arts. UAS-6070	(S)	**I Love To Sing**	1959	20.00	50.00

BENNETT, MAX

Max Bennett is a modern jazz bassist.

Bethlehem BCP-1028	(10")	**Max Bennett**	1955	50.00	125.00

Label & Catalog #		Title	Year	VG+	NM
Bethlehem BCP-48	(M)	**Max Bennett Septet, Quartet & Trio**	1956	30.00	75.00
Bethlehem BCP-50	(M)	**Max Bennett Plays**	1956	30.00	75.00

BENNETT, TONY, & COUNT BASIE

Tony Bennett's considerable discography is primarily pop.

Roulette R-25072	(M)	**Count Basie Swings/Tony Sings**	1960	10.00	25.00
Roulette SR-25072	(S)	**Count Basie Swings/Tony Sings**	1960	12.00	30.00
Roulette R-25231	(M)	**Bennett And Basie Strike Up The Band**	1963	8.00	20.00
Roulette SR-25231	(S)	**Bennett And Basie Strike Up The Band**	1963	10.00	25.00

BENSON, GEORGE

George Benson is a modern jazz guitar player and singer.

Prestige PRLP-7310	(M)	**The New Boss Guitar Of George Benson**	1964	12.00	30.00
Prestige PRST-7310	(S)	**The New Boss Guitar Of George Benson**	1964	10.00	25.00
		(Prestige 7310 also features Jack McDuff)			

—Prestige albums above have yellow mono or silver stereo labels with a Bergenfield, NJ address.—

Columbia CL-2525	(M)	**Most Exciting**	1966	8.00	20.00
Columbia CS-9325	(S)	**Most Exciting**	1966	6.00	15.00
Columbia CL-2613	(M)	**The George Benson Cook Book**	1967	10.00	25.00
Columbia CS-9413	(S)	**The George Benson Cook Book**	1967	6.00	15.00

—Columbia albums above have "360 Sound" in white on the bottom of the label.—

Verve V6-8749	(S)	**Giblet Gravy**	1968	6.00	15.00
Verve V6-8771	(S)	**Goodies**	1969	6.00	15.00

—Verve albums above have black labels with "MGM Record" on the bottom.—

A&M SP-3014	(S)	**Shape Of Things To Come**	1969	4.00	10.00
A&M SP-3020	(S)	**Tell It Like It Is**	1969	4.00	10.00

BENTON, WALTER

Walter Benton is a modern jazz tenor saxophone player. For additional listings refer to the Various Artists section under EmArcy.

Jazzland JLP-28	(M)	**Out Of This World**	1960	20.00	50.00
Jazzland JLP-928	(S)	**Out Of This World**	1960	16.00	40.00

BERGER, KARL

Karl Berger is a modern jazz vibraphone player.

ESP-Disk' 1041	(M)	**Karl Berger**	1967	10.00	25.00
ESP-Disk' 1041	(S)	**Karl Berger**	1967	8.00	20.00
Milestone MSP-9026	(S)	**Tune In**	1969	6.00	15.00

BERIGAN, BUNNY

Rowland "Bunny" Berigan is a traditional jazz trumpet player and vocalist.

RCA Victor WPT-10	(10")	**Bunny Berigan 1937-38**	1951	30.00	75.00
RCA Victor LPT-1003	(M)	**Bunny Berigan Plays Again**	1952	20.00	50.00
Epic LN-3109	(M)	**Take It, Bunny!**	1955	20.00	50.00
RCA Victor LPM-2078	(M)	**Bunny Berigan & His Orchestra**	1959	16.00	40.00
RCA Victor LSP-2078	(S)	**Bunny Berigan & His Orchestra**	1959	12.00	30.00
RCA Victor LPV-550	(M)	**Bunny**	1966	8.00	20.00

BERIGAN, BUNNY, & WINGY MANONE

"X" LVA-3034	(10")	**Swing Sessions 1935**	1954	30.00	75.00

BERKLEE STUDENTS

Berklee Vol. IX	(M)	**Jazz In The Classroom— A Tribute To Oliver Nelson**	1965	20.00	50.00

BERMAN, SONNY

Sonny Berman is a West Coast jazz trumpet player.

Esoteric ES-532	(M)	**Sonny Berman 1946**	1954	50.00	125.00

BERNHART, MILT

Milt Bernhart is a West Coast trombone player. For additional listings refer to Boots Brown; and the Jazzy Soundtracks section under Chancellor.

RCA Victor LPM-1123	(M)	**Modern Brass**	1955	20.00	50.00

—RCA albums above have black labels with "Long Play" on the bottom.—

Decca DL-9214	(M)	**The Sounds Of Bernhart**	1959	16.00	40.00
Decca DL-79214	(S)	**The Sounds Of Bernhart**	1959	12.00	30.00

Label & Catalog #		Title	Year	VG+	NM
BERNSTEIN, LEONARD					
"What Is Jazz" is a documentary featuring Miles Davis' first recording for Columbia. For additional listings for the Maestro refer to Dave Brubeck.					
Columbia CL-919	(M)	**What Is Jazz?**	1956	16.00	40.00
		— Columbia albums above have six white on black "eye" logos on each label.—			
BERRY, BILL					
William Berry is a modern jazz trumpet and flugel horn player.					
Directional Sound 5002	(M)	**Jazz & Swinging Percussion**	1963	10.00	25.00
Directional Sound 5002	(S)	**Jazz & Swinging Percussion**	1963	8.00	20.00
BERRY, CHU					
Leon "Chu" Berry is a traditional jazz based tenor saxophonist. For additional listings refer to Lester Young / Chu Berry.					
Commodore FL-20024	(10")	**Chu Berry Memorial**	1952	100.00	200.00
Epic LG-3124	(M)	**Chu**	1955	30.00	75.00
Commodore DL-30017	(M)	**Chu Berry**	1959	30.00	75.00
		(Commodore 30017 is a reissue of 20024.)			
Mainstream 50038	(M)	**Sittin' In**	1965	12.00	30.00
Mainstream S-6038	(E)	**Sittin' In**	1965	6.00	15.00
		(Mainstream 50038 reissues Commodore material.)			
BERT, EDDIE					
Edward Bert is a modern trombone player.					
Discovery DL-3020	(M)	**Eddie Bert Quintet**	1953	40.00	100.00
Trans-World TWLP-208	(M)	**Let's Dig Bert**	1955	40.00	100.00
Savoy MG-12015	(M)	**Musician Of The Year**	1955	20.00	50.00
Savoy MG-12019	(M)	**Encore**	1955	20.00	50.00
Jazztone J-1223	(M)	**Modern Moods**	1956	16.00	40.00
Somerset SF-5200	(M)	**Like Cool**	1958	16.00	40.00
		(Somerset 5200 is a reissue of Trans-World 208.)			
BERT, EDDIE / BILLY BYERS & JOE NEWMAN					
Jazztone J-1276	(M)	**East Coast Sounds**	1959	16.00	40.00
BETTERS, HAROLD					
Harold Betters is a modern jazz based trombone player.					
Gateway 7001	(M)	**Harold Betters At The Encore**	1964	8.00	20.00
Gateway 7001	(S)	**Harold Betters At The Encore**	1964	6.00	15.00
Gateway 7009	(M)	**Harold Betters Meets Slide Hampton**	1964	8.00	20.00
Gateway 7009	(S)	**Harold Betters Meets Slide Hampton**	1964	6.00	15.00
Gateway 7014	(M)	**Do Anything You Want To**	1965	8.00	20.00
Gateway 7014	(S)	**Do Anything You Want To**	1965	6.00	15.00
Reprise R-6195	(M)	**Ram-Bunk-Shush**	1965	8.00	20.00
Reprise RS-6195	(S)	**Ram-Bunk-Shush**	1965	6.00	15.00
Reprise R-6208	(M)	**Out Of Sight And Sound**	1966	8.00	20.00
Reprise RS-6208	(S)	**Out Of Sight And Sound**	1966	6.00	15.00
Reprise R-6241	(M)	**Funk City Express**	1966	8.00	20.00
Reprise RS-6241	(S)	**Funk City Express**	1966	6.00	15.00
BIGARD, BARNEY					
Leon "Barney" Bigard is a traditional jazz clarinet and tenor saxophone player. For additional listings refer to Benny Carter & Ben Webster & Barney Bigard.					
Liberty LRP-3071	(M)	**Barney Bigard**	1957	16.00	40.00
BIRDLANDERS, THE: ***Refer to*** **HENRI RENAUD**					
BISHOP, JOHN					
Tangerine TRCS-1508	(S)	**Bishop's Whirl**	1969	5.00	12.00
BISHOP, WALTER, JR.					
Walter Bishop is a modern jazz pianist. For additional listings refer to Sidney Bechet.					
Jazztime JT-002	(M)	**Speak Low**	1961	12.00	30.00
Jazztime JS-002	(S)	**Speak Low**	1961	10.00	25.00
Cotillion SD-236	(S)	**Walter Bishop**	1969	8.00	20.00
Prestige PRST-7730	(S)	**The Walter Bishop Trio 1965**	1969	8.00	20.00
		— Prestige albums above have blue labels with a trident logo on top.—			

Label & Catalog #		Title	Year	VG+	NM

BLAIR, SALLIE

Sallie Blair is a modern jazz based vocalist.

Bethlehem BCP-6009	(M)	**Squeeze Me**	1957	30.00	75.00
MGM E-3723	(M)	**Hello, Tiger!**	1959	16.00	40.00
MGM SE-3723	(S)	**Hello, Tiger!**	1959	20.00	50.00

BLAKE, BETTY

Betty Blake is a modern jazz based vocalist.

Bethlehem BCP-6058	(M)	**In A Tender Mood**	1961	16.00	40.00
Bethlehem SBCP-6058	(S)	**In A Tender Mood**	1961	20.00	50.00

BLAKE, EUBIE

Eubie Blake is a traditional ragtiome piano player.

Columbia C2S-847	(S)	**The Eighty-Six Years Of Eubie Blake** *(2 LPs)*	1969	6.00	15.00

— Columbia albums above have "360 Sound" on the bottom of the label.—

BLAKE, RAN

Ran Blake is a modern jazz pianist and composer. For additional listings refer to Jeanne Lee & Ran Blake.

ESP-Disk' 1011	(M)	**Ran Blake Plays Solo Piano**	1965	8.00	20.00
ESP-Disk' 1011	(S)	**Ran Blake Plays Solo Piano**	1965	6.00	15.00
Milestone MSP-9021	(S)	**The Blue Potato**	1969	6.00	15.00

BLAKEY, ART

Art Blakey— also known by his Muslim name, Abdullah Ibn Buhaina— is a modern jazz drummer and the leader of The Jazz Messengers, whose recordings are listed separately following Blakey's. For additional listings refer to Paul Bley; Max Roach / Art Blakey.

EmArcy MG-26030	(10")	**Blakey**	1954	125.00	250.00
Blue Note BLP-5037	(10")	**A Night At Birdland, Volume 1**	1954	150.00	300.00
Blue Note BLP-5038	(10")	**A Night At Birdland, Volume 2**	1954	150.00	300.00
Blue Note BLP-5039	(10")	**A Night At Birdland, Volume 3**	1954	150.00	300.00
Blue Note BLP-1521	(M)	**A Night At Birdland, Volume 1** *(Deep groove)*	1956	100.00	200.00
Blue Note BLP-1521	(M)	**A Night At Birdland, Volume 1**	1956	60.00	150.00
Blue Note BLP-1522	(M)	**A Night At Birdland, Volume 2** *(Deep groove)*	1956	100.00	200.00
Blue Note BLP-1522	(M)	**A Night At Birdland, Volume 2**	1956	60.00	150.00

(Blue Note 1521 and 1522 reissue 5037, 5038 and 5039. The original covers for 1521 and 1522 feature drawings of two "birds," one enclosing the title of the album, the other, a photo of Blakey. Later pressings have the title on top top in blue for Volume 1 or red for Volume 2 while the bottom features seven photos of the musicians.)

— Blue Note albums above have blue on white labels with a Lexington Ave, NYC address.—

Blue Note BLP-1521	(M)	**A Night At Birdland, Volume 1**	1957	20.00	50.00
Blue Note BLP-1522	(M)	**A Night At Birdland, Volume 2**	1957	20.00	50.00
Blue Note BLP-1554	(M)	**Orgy In Rhythm, Volume 1** *(Deep groove)*	1957	60.00	150.00
Blue Note BLP-1554	(M)	**Orgy In Rhythm, Volume 1**	1957	40.00	100.00
Blue Note BLP-1555	(M)	**Orgy In Rhythm, Volume 2** *(Deep groove)*	1957	60.00	150.00
Blue Note BLP-1555	(M)	**Orgy In Rhythm, Volume 2**	1957	40.00	100.00
Blue Note BLP-4004	(M)	**Holiday For Skins, Volume 1** *(Deep groove)*	1958	70.00	175.00
Blue Note BLP-4004	(M)	**Holiday For Skins, Volume 1**	1958	50.00	125.00
Blue Note BST-4004	(S)	**Holiday For Skins, Volume 1** *(Deep groove)*	1959	50.00	125.00
Blue Note BST-4004	(S)	**Holiday For Skins, Volume 1**	1959	50.00	100.00
Blue Note BLP-4005	(M)	**Holiday For Skins, Volume 2** *(Deep groove)*	1958	70.00	175.00
Blue Note BLP-4005	(M)	**Holiday For Skins, Volume 2**	1958	50.00	125.00
Blue Note BST-4005	(S)	**Holiday For Skins, Volume 2** *(Deep groove)*	1959	50.00	125.00
Blue Note BST-4005	(S)	**Holiday For Skins, Volume 2**	1959	40.00	100.00

— Blue Note albums above have blue on white labels with a W. 63rd St, NYC address.—

Blue Note BLP-4097	(M)	**The African Beat**	1961	30.00	75.00
Blue Note BST-84097	(S)	**The African Beat**	1961	20.00	50.00

— Blue Note albums above have blue on white labels with a 61st St, NYC address.—

Blue Note BLP-1521	(M)	**A Night At Birdland, Volume 1**	1963	10.00	25.00
Blue Note BLP-1522	(M)	**A Night At Birdland, Volume 2**	1963	10.00	25.00
Blue Note BLP-1554	(M)	**Orgy In Rhythm, Volume 1**	1963	10.00	25.00
Blue Note BLP-1555	(M)	**Orgy In Rhythm, Volume 2**	1963	10.00	25.00
Blue Note BLP-4004	(M)	**Holiday For Skins, Volume 1**	1963	10.00	25.00
Blue Note BST-4004	(S)	**Holiday For Skins, Volume 1**	1963	8.00	20.00
Blue Note BLP-4005	(M)	**Holiday For Skins, Volume 2**	1963	10.00	25.00
Blue Note BST-4005	(S)	**Holiday For Skins, Volume 2**	1963	8.00	20.00
Blue Note BLP-4097	(M)	**The African Beat**	1963	12.00	30.00
Blue Note BST-84097	(S)	**The African Beat**	1963	10.00	25.00

— Blue Note albums above have blue on white labels with a New York, USA address.—

Label & Catalog #		Title	Year	VG+	NM
Blue Note BST-81521	(E)	**A Night At Birdland, Volume 1**	196?	4.00	10.00
Blue Note BST-81522	(E)	**A Night At Birdland, Volume 2**	196?	4.00	10.00
Blue Note BST-81554	(E)	**Orgy In Rhythm, Volume 1**	196?	4.00	10.00
Blue Note BST-81555	(E)	**Orgy In Rhythm, Volume 2**	196?	4.00	10.00
Blue Note BST-84004	(S)	**Holiday For Skins, Volume 1**	196?	5.00	12.00
Blue Note BST-84005	(S)	**Holiday For Skins, Volume 2**	196?	5.00	12.00
Blue Note BST-84097	(S)	**The African Beat**	196?	5.00	12.00
—Blue Note albums above have blue on white labels with "A Division of Liberty Records."—					
Mercury SR-6????	(S)	**Art Blakey Live!**	1968	8.00	20.00

BLAKEY, ART, & THE JAZZ MESSENGERS

The Jazz Messengers were a loose aggregate of musicians often serving as Blue Note's house band. The basic groups were Kenny Dorham, Hank Mobley, Horace Silver and Doug Watkins (1954-56); Spanky DeBrest, Sam Dockerly, Bill Hardaman and Jackie McLean (1956-57); Jymie Merritt, Lee Morgan, Wayne Shorter and Bobby Timmons (1958-60); and Curtis Fuller, Freddie Hubbard, Jymie Merritt, Wayne Shorter, Cedar Walton, and Reggie Workman (1961-64). Albums below may credit Art Blakey & The Jazz Messengers, Blakey's Jazz Messengers or The Jazz Messengers. For additional listings refer to Rita Reys; Horace Silver; and the Jazzy Soundtracks section under Colpix and Epic.

Label & Catalog #		Title	Year	VG+	NM
Blue Note BLP-1507	(M)	**At The Cafe Bohemia, Volume 1** *(Deep groove)*	1956	60.00	150.00
Blue Note BLP-1507	(M)	**At The Cafe Bohemia, Volume 1**	1956	40.00	100.00
Blue Note BLP-1508	(M)	**At The Cafe Bohemia, Volume 2** *(Deep groove)*	1956	60.00	150.00
Blue Note BLP-1508	(M)	**At The Cafe Bohemia, Volume 2**	1956	40.00	100.00
—Blue Note albums above have blue on white labels with a Lexington Ave, NYC address.—					
Blue Note BLP-1507	(M)	**At The Cafe Bohemia, Volume 1**	1957	20.00	50.00
Blue Note BLP-1508	(M)	**At The Cafe Bohemia, Volume 2**	1957	20.00	50.00
Blue Note BLP-4003	(M)	**Art Blakey & The Jazz Messengers** *(Deep groove)*	1958	60.00	150.00
Blue Note BLP-4003	(M)	**Art Blakey & The Jazz Messengers**	1958	40.00	100.00
Blue Note BST-4003	(S)	**Art Blakey & The Jazz Messengers** *(Deep groove)*	1959	40.00	100.00
Blue Note BST-4003	(S)	**Art Blakey & The Jazz Messengers**	1959	30.00	75.00
Blue Note BLP-4015	(M)	**At The Jazz Corner Of The World, Volume 1** *(Deep groove)*	1958	50.00	125.00
Blue Note BLP-4015	(M)	**At The Jazz Corner Of The World, Volume 1**	1958	30.00	75.00
Blue Note BST-84015	(S)	**At The Jazz Corner Of The World, Volume 1** *(Deep groove)*	1959	30.00	75.00
Blue Note BST-84015	(S)	**At The Jazz Corner Of The World, Volume 1**	1959	20.00	50.00
Blue Note BLP-4016	(M)	**At The Jazz Corner Of The World, Volume 2** *(Deep groove)*	1958	50.00	125.00
Blue Note BLP-4016	(M)	**At The Jazz Corner Of The World, Volume 2**	1958	30.00	75.00
Blue Note BST-84016	(S)	**At The Jazz Corner Of The World, Volume 2** *(Deep groove)*	1959	30.00	75.00
Blue Note BST-84016	(S)	**At The Jazz Corner Of The World, Volume 2**	1959	20.00	50.00
Blue Note BLP-4029	(M)	**The Big Beat** *(Deep groove)*	1960	40.00	100.00
Blue Note BLP-4029	(M)	**The Big Beat**	1960	30.00	75.00
Blue Note BST-84029	(S)	**The Big Beat**	1960	20.00	50.00
Blue Note BLP-4049	(M)	**A Night In Tunisia** *(Deep groove)*	1960	40.00	100.00
Blue Note BLP-4049	(M)	**A Night In Tunisia**	1960	30.00	75.00
Blue Note BST-84049	(S)	**A Night In Tunisia**	1960	20.00	50.00
Blue Note BLP-4054	(M)	**Meet You At The Jazz Corner Of The World, Volume 1**	1960	30.00	75.00
Blue Note BST-84054	(S)	**Meet You At The Jazz Corner Of The World, Volume 1**	1960	20.00	50.00
Blue Note BLP-4055	(M)	**Meet You At The Jazz Corner Of The World, Volume 2**	1960	30.00	75.00
Blue Note BST-84055	(S)	**Meet You At The Jazz Corner Of The World, Volume 2**	1960	20.00	50.00
—Blue Note albums above have blue on white labels with a W. 63rd St, NYC address.—					
Blue Note BLP-4090	(M)	**Mosaic**	1961	30.00	75.00
Blue Note BST-84090	(S)	**Mosaic**	1961	20.00	50.00
—Blue Note albums above have blue on white labels with a 61st St, NYC address.—					
Blue Note BLP-1507	(M)	**At The Cafe Bohemia, Volume 1**	1966	10.00	25.00
Blue Note BLP-1508	(M)	**At The Cafe Bohemia, Volume 2**	1966	10.00	25.00
Blue Note BLP-4003	(M)	**Art Blakey & The Jazz Messengers**	1966	10.00	25.00
Blue Note BST-4003	(S)	**Art Blakey & The Jazz Messengers**	1966	8.00	20.00
Blue Note BLP-4015	(M)	**At The Jazz Corner Of The World, Volume 1**	1966	10.00	25.00
Blue Note BST-84015	(S)	**At The Jazz Corner Of The World, Volume 1**	1966	8.00	20.00
Blue Note BLP-4016	(M)	**At The Jazz Corner Of The World, Volume 2**	1966	10.00	25.00
Blue Note BST-84016	(S)	**At The Jazz Corner Of The World, Volume 2**	1966	8.00	20.00

For a 1954 session for Blue Note pianist Horace Silver requested Art Blakey, Kenny Dorham, Hank Mobley and Doug Watkins as his sidemen. The five men found both the session and the experience so rewarding that they formed a loose aggregation for the express purpose of communicating modern jazz by combining the idiom of bop with the soul of the blues. Calling themselves, appropriately, the Jazz Messengers, their sound came to be associated with Blue Note. The albums above contain work for two other labels, both featuring different personnel backing leader Blakey.

Label & Catalog #		*Title*	*Year*	*VG+*	*NM*
Blue Note BLP-4029	*(M)*	**The Big Beat**	*1966*	**10.00**	**25.00**
Blue Note BST-84029	*(S)*	**The Big Beat**	*1966*	**8.00**	**20.00**
Blue Note BLP-4049	*(M)*	**A Night In Tunisia**	*1966*	**10.00**	**25.00**
Blue Note BST-84049	*(S)*	**A Night In Tunisia**	*1966*	**8.00**	**20.00**
Blue Note BLP-4054	*(M)*	**Meet You At The Jazz Corner Of The World, Volume 1**	*1966*	**10.00**	**25.00**
Blue Note BST-84054	*(S)*	**Meet You At The Jazz Corner Of The World, olume 1**	*1966*	**8.00**	**20.00**
Blue Note BLP-4055	*(M)*	**Meet You At The Jazz Corner Of The World, Volume 2**	*1966*	**10.00**	**25.00**
Blue Note BST-84055	*(S)*	**Meet You At The Jazz Corner Of The World, Volume 2**	*1966*	**8.00**	**20.00**
Blue Note BLP-4090	*(M)*	**Mosaic**	*1966*	**8.00**	**20.00**
Blue Note BST-84090	*(S)*	**Mosaic**	*1966*	**10.00**	**25.00**
Blue Note BLP-4104	*(M)*	**Buhaina's Delight**	*1962*	**16.00**	**40.00**
Blue Note BST-84104	*(S)*	**Buhaina's Delight**	*1962*	**12.00**	**30.00**
Blue Note BLP-4156	*(M)*	**The Freedom Rider**	*1963*	**16.00**	**40.00**
Blue Note BST-84156	*(S)*	**The Freedom Rider**	*1963*	**12.00**	**30.00**
Blue Note BLP-4170	*(M)*	**Free For All**	*1964*	**16.00**	**40.00**
Blue Note BST-84170	*(S)*	**Free For All**	*1964*	**12.00**	**30.00**
Blue Note BLP-4193	*(M)*	**Indestructible**	*1965*	**16.00**	**40.00**
Blue Note BST-84193	*(S)*	**Indestructible**	*1965*	**12.00**	**30.00**
Blue Note BLP-4245	*(M)*	**Like Someone In Love**	*1966*	**16.00**	**40.00**
Blue Note BST-84245	*(S)*	**Like Someone In Love**	*1966*	**12.00**	**30.00**
—Blue Note albums above have blue on white labels with a New York, USA address.—					
Blue Note BST-81507	*(E)*	**At The Cafe Bohemia, Volume 1**	*1963*	**4.00**	**10.00**
Blue Note BST-81508	*(E)*	**At The Cafe Bohemia, Volume 2**	*1963*	**4.00**	**10.00**
Blue Note BST-84003	*(S)*	**Art Blakey & The Jazz Messengers**	*1963*	**5.00**	**12.00**
Blue Note BST-84015	*(S)*	**At The Jazz Corner Of The World, Volume 1**	*1963*	**5.00**	**12.00**
Blue Note BST-84016	*(S)*	**At The Jazz Corner Of The World, Volume 2**	*1963*	**5.00**	**12.00**
Blue Note BST-84029	*(S)*	**The Big Beat**	*1963*	**5.00**	**12.00**
Blue Note BST-84049	*(S)*	**A Night In Tunisia**	*1963*	**5.00**	**12.00**
Blue Note BST-84054	*(S)*	**Meet You At The Jazz Corner Of The World, Volume 1**	*1963*	**5.00**	**12.00**
Blue Note BST-84055	*(S)*	**Meet You At The Jazz Corner Of The World, Volume 2**	*1963*	**5.00**	**12.00**
Blue Note BST-84090	*(S)*	**Mosaic**	*1963*	**5.00**	**12.00**
Blue Note BST-84104	*(S)*	**Buhaina's Delight**	*1963*	**5.00**	**12.00**
Blue Note BST-84156	*(S)*	**The Freedom Rider**	*1963*	**5.00**	**12.00**
Blue Note BST-84170	*(S)*	**Free For All**	*1963*	**5.00**	**12.00**
Blue Note BST-84193	*(S)*	**Indestructible**	*1963*	**5.00**	**12.00**
Blue Note BST-84245	*(S)*	**Like Someone In Love**	*1963*	**5.00**	**12.00**
Blue Note BLP-4258	*(M)*	**The Witch Doctor**	*1967*	**10.00**	**25.00**
Blue Note BST-84258	*(S)*	**The Witch Doctor**	*1967*	**8.00**	**20.00**
Blue Note BST-84347	*(S)*	**Roots & Herbs**	*1969*	**8.00**	**20.00**
—Blue Note albums above have blue on white labels with "A Division of Liberty Records."—					
Columbia CL-897	*(M)*	**The Jazz Messengers**	*1956*	**30.00**	**75.00**
Columbia CL-1002	*(M)*	**Drum Suite**	*1957*	**20.00**	**50.00**
Columbia CL-1040	*(M)*	**Hard Bop**	*1957*	**24.00**	**60.00**
—Columbia albums above have six white on black "eye" logos on each label.—					
Pacific Jazz PJM-402	*(M)*	**Ritual**	*1957*	**30.00**	**75.00**
Jubilee JLP-1049	*(M)*	**Cu-Bop** *(Jubilee 1049 also features Sabu.)*	*1957*	**30.00**	**75.00**
Elektra EKL-120	*(M)*	**A Midnight Session With The Jazz Messengers**	*1957*	**30.00**	**75.00**
Elektra EKS-120	*(S)*	**A Midnight Session With The Jazz Messengers**	*1958*	**20.00**	**50.00**
Vik LX-1103	*(M)*	**Art Blakey And The Jazz Messengers Play Selections From Lerner And Loewe**	*1957*	**40.00**	**100.00**
Vik LAX-1115	*(M)*	**A Night In Tunisia**	*1958*	**40.00**	**100.00**
Bethlehem BCP-6027	*(M)*	**Art Blakey's Big Band**	*1958*	**30.00**	**75.00**
Bethlehem BCP-6023	*(M)*	**Hard Drive**	*1958*	**30.00**	**75.00**
Savoy MG-12171	*(M)*	**Art Blakey And The Jazz Messengers** *(Savoy 12171 is a reissue of Elektra 120.)*	*1960*	**12.00**	**30.00**
Epic LA-16009	*(M)*	**Paris Concert**	*1960*	**16.00**	**40.00**
Epic BA-17009	*(S)*	**Paris Concert**	*1960*	**12.00**	**30.00**
Epic LA-16017	*(M)*	**Art Blakey In Paris**	*1961*	**16.00**	**40.00**
Epic BA-17017	*(S)*	**Art Blakey In Paris**	*1961*	**12.00**	**30.00**
Pacific Jazz PJ-15	*(M)*	**Ritual** *(Pacific Jazz 15 is a reissue of 402.)*	*1961*	**16.00**	**40.00**

Label & Catalog #		Title	Year	VG+	NM
Impulse A-7	(M)	**Art Blakey!!!!! Jazz Messengers!!!!!**	1961	16.00	40.00
Impulse AS-7	(S)	**Art Blakey!!!!! Jazz Messengers!!!!!**	1961	12.00	30.00
		—Impulse albums above have orange & black labels.—			
Impulse AS-7	(S)	**Art Blakey!!!!! Jazz Messengers!!!!!**	1968	4.00	10.00
		—Impulse albums above have red & black labels with the "abc" logo on top.—			
United Arts. UAJ-14002	(M)	**Three Blind Mice**	1962	20.00	50.00
United Arts. UAJS-15002	(S)	**Three Blind Mice**	1962	16.00	40.00
Josie JLPM-3501	(M)	**Cu-Bop**	1962	12.00	30.00
Josie JLPS-3501	(S)	**Cu-Bop**	1962	10.00	25.00
		(Josie 3501 is a reissue of Jubilee 1049.)			
Riverside RLP-438	(M)	**Caravan**	1962	12.00	30.00
Riverside RS-9438	(S)	**Caravan**	1962	10.00	25.00
Riverside RLP-464	(M)	**Ugetsu**	1963	12.00	30.00
Riverside RS-9464	(S)	**Ugetsu**	1963	10.00	25.00
		—Riverside albums above have blue mono or black stereo labels with a reel & mike logo on top.—			
RCA Victor LPM-2654	(M)	**A Night In Tunisia**	1963	14.00	35.00
RCA Victor LSP-2654	(E)	**A Night In Tunisia**	1963	8.00	20.00
		(RCA Victor 2654 is a reissue of Vik 1115.)			
		—RCA albums above have black labels with "Long Play" or "Reprocessed Stereo" on the bottom.—			
Impulse A-45	(M)	**A Jazz Message**	1963	16.00	40.00
Impulse AS-45	(S)	**A Jazz Message**	1963	12.00	30.00
		—Impulse albums above have orange & black labels.—			
Impulse AS-45	(S)	**A Jazz Message**	1968	4.00	10.00
		—Impulse albums above have red & black labels with the "abc" logo on top.—			
Cadet LP-4049	(M)	**Tough!**	1965	12.00	30.00
Cadet LPS-4049	(S)	**Tough!**	1965	10.00	25.00
Limelight LM-82001	(M)	**'S Make It**	1965	10.00	25.00
Limelight LS-86001	(S)	**'S Make It**	1965	8.00	20.00
Limelight LM-82019	(M)	**Soul Finger**	1965	10.00	25.00
Limelight LS-86019	(S)	**Soul Finger**	1965	8.00	20.00
Limelight LM-82034	(M)	**Buttercorn Lady**	1966	10.00	25.00
Limelight LS-86034	(S)	**Buttercorn Lady**	1966	8.00	20.00
Limelight LM-82038	(M)	**Hold On, I'm Coming**	1966	10.00	25.00
Limelight LS-86038	(S)	**Hold On, I'm Coming**	1966	8.00	20.00
Riverside RLP-493	(M)	**Kyoto**	1966	10.00	25.00
Riverside RS-9493	(S)	**Kyoto**	1966	8.00	20.00
		—Riverside albums above blue labels with "Orpheum Productions" on the bottom.—			
Riverside RS-3022	(S)	**Ugetsu**	1968	4.00	10.00

BLAKEY, ART, & THE JAZZ MESSENGERS / ELMO HOPE

Pacific Jazz PJ-33	(M)	**The Jazz Messengers & Elmo Hope**	1962	16.00	40.00
		(The Elmo Hope side also features Harold Land.)			

BLAKEY, ART, & THE JAZZ MESSENGERS, & THELONIOUS MONK

Atlantic 1278	(M)	**Art Blakey's Jazz Messengers With Thelonious Monk**	1958	20.00	50.00
Atlantic SD-1278	(S)	**Art Blakey's Jazz Messengers With Thelonious Monk**	1958	16.00	40.00
		—Atlantic albums above have black mono or green stereo labels.—			
Atlantic 1278	(M)	**Art Blakey's Jazz Messengers With Thelonious Monk**	196?	8.00	20.00
Atlantic SD-1278	(S)	**Art Blakey's Jazz Messengers With Thelonious Monk**	196?	6.00	15.00
		—Atlantic albums above have multi-color labels with a white fan logo.—			
Atlantic 1278	(M)	**Art Blakey's Jazz Messengers With Thelonious Monk**	196?	5.00	12.00
Atlantic SD-1278	(S)	**Art Blakey's Jazz Messengers With Thelonious Monk**	196?	4.00	10.00
		—Atlantic albums above have multi-color labels with a black fan logo.—			

BLEY, PAUL

Canadian born Paul Bley is a mdoern jazz piano and synthesizer player.

Debut DLP-7	(10")	**Introducing Paul Bley**	1954	125.00	250.00
		(Debit 7 also features Charles Mingus and Art Blakey.)			
EmArcy MG-36092	(M)	**Paul Bley**	1955	40.00	100.00
Wing WGW-60001	(M)	**Paul Bley**	1956	20.00	50.00
		(Wing 60001 is a reissue of EmArcy 36092.)			
Gene Norman GNP-31	(M)	**Solemn Meditation**	1957	10.00	25.00
Savoy MG-12182	(M)	**Footloose!**	1964	10.00	25.00

Label & Catalog #		Title	Year	VG+	NM
ESP-Disk' 1008	(M)	**Barrage**	1965	8.00	20.00
ESP-Disk' 1008	(S)	**Barrage**	1965	6.00	15.00
ESP-Disk' 1021	(M)	**Closer**	1966	8.00	20.00
ESP-Disk' 1021	(S)	**Closer**	1966	6.00	15.00
Limelight LM-82060	(M)	**Mr. Joy**	1967	8.00	20.00
Limelight LS-86060	(S)	**Mr. Joy**	1967	6.00	15.00

BLUE STARS OF FRANCE, THE

The Blue Stars of France are Christian Chevallier, Jeanine DeWaleyne, Roger Guerin, Christine Legrand, Jean Mercadier, Fats Sadi and Nadine Yound with Blossom Dearie.

EmArcy MG-36067	(M)	**Lullaby Of Birdland**	1956	16.00	40.00

—EmArcy albums above have blue labels with silver print.—

BLYHE, JIMMY

James Blythe is a traditional jazz pianist and composer.

Riverside RLP-1031	(10")	**Chicago Stomps And The Dixie Four**	1954	30.00	75.00
Riverside RLP-1036	(10")	**Chicago Jazz 1928**	1954	30.00	75.00

BOBO, WILLIE

William Bobo is a modern jazz based percussionist (bongos, congas and drums).

Roulette R-52097	(M)	**Bobo's Beat**	1962	12.00	30.00
Roulette SR-52097	(S)	**Bobo's Beat**	1962	10.00	25.00
Tico T-1108	(M)	**Do That Thing**	1963	12.00	30.00
Tico TS-1108	(S)	**Do That Thing**	1963	10.00	25.00
Verve V-8631	(M)	**Spanish Grease**	1965	12.00	30.00
Verve V6-8631	(S)	**Spanish Grease**	1965	10.00	25.00
Verve V-8648	(M)	**Uno, Dos, Tres**	1966	10.00	25.00
Verve V6-8648	(S)	**Uno, Dos, Tres**	1966	8.00	20.00
Verve V-8669	(M)	**Feelin' So Good**	1966	10.00	25.00
Verve V6-8669	(S)	**Feelin' So Good**	1966	8.00	20.00
Verve V-8685	(M)	**Juicy**	1966	10.00	25.00
Verve V6-8685	(S)	**Juicy**	1966	8.00	20.00
Verve V-8699	(M)	**Bobo Motion**	1966	12.00	30.00
Verve V6-8699	(S)	**Bobo Motion**	1966	10.00	25.00
Verve V-8736	(M)	**Spanish Blues Band**	1967	10.00	25.00
Verve V6-8736	(S)	**Spanish Blues Band**	1967	8.00	20.00
Verve V6-8772	(S)	**A New Dimension**	1968	8.00	20.00
Verve V6-8781	(S)	**Evil Ways**	1968	8.00	20.00

—Verve albums above have black labels with "MGM Record" on the bottom.—

BOCAGE, PETER

Peter Bocage is a traditional jazz banjo, trumpet, valve trombone, violin and xylophone player.

Riverside RLP-379	(M)	**Peter Bocage With His Creole Serenaders**	1961	12.00	30.00
Riverside RS-9379	(S)	**Peter Bocage With His Creole Serenaders**	1961	10.00	25.00

—Riverside albums above have blue mono or black stereo labels with a reel & mike logo on top.—

BOHANNON, GEORGE

George Bohannon is a modern jazz trombone, tenor saxophone, piano, bass and flute player.

Jazz Workshop JWS-214	(M)	**Bold Bohannon**	1963	20.00	50.00

BOLAND, FRANCY: ***Refer to*** **KENNY CLARKE & FRANCY BOLAND**

BOLLING, CLAUDE

French born Claude Bolling is a modern jazz based pianist.

Bally BAL-12003	(M)	**French Jazz**	1956	16.00	40.00
Omega OKL-6	(M)	**Rolling With Bolling**	1960	12.00	30.00
Omega OSL-6	(S)	**Rolling With Bolling**	1960	10.00	25.00

BOLTON, DUPREE: ***Refer to*** **CURTIS AMY**

BONANO, SHARKEY

Joseph "Sharkey" Bonano is a traditional jazz trumpet player and vocalist. For additional listings refer to Paul Barbarin / Sharkey Bonano.

Circle LP-422	(10")	**Sharkey Bonano**	1951	20.00	50.00
Capitol H-266	(10")	**Sharkey's Southern Comfort**	1951	20.00	50.00
Capitol T-266	(M)	**Kings Of Dixieland**	1954	16.00	40.00
Capitol T-792	(M)	**A Night In Old New Orleans**	1956	16.00	40.00

—Capitol albums above have turquoise labels.—

Southland SLP-205	(10")	**New Orleans Dixieland Session**	1954	20.00	50.00

BONANO, SHARKEY, & LIZZIE MILES

Label & Catalog #		Title	Year	VG+	NM
Capitol H-367	(10")	**Midnight On Bourbon Street**	1952	20.00	50.00
Capitol T-367	(M)	**Midnight On Bourbon Street**	1954	16.00	40.00

BOND SEXTETTE, JAMES

Label & Catalog #		Title	Year	VG+	NM
Mirwood M-7001	(M)	**James Bond Songbook**	1966	10.00	25.00
Mirwood S-7001	(S)	**James Bond Songbook**	1966	8.00	20.00

BONFA, LUIZ

Brazilian born Luiz Bonfa is a jazz-influenced guitar player and composer. For additional listings refer to Stan Getz; Paul Winter; and the Jazzy Soundtracks section under Epic and Mercury.

Label & Catalog #		Title	Year	VG+	NM
Atlantic 8028	(M)	**The Fabulous Guitar Of Luiz Bonfa/Amor!**	1959	16.00	40.00
Atlantic SD-8028	(S)	**The Fabulous Guitar Of Luiz Bonfa/Amor!**	1959	12.00	30.00
		—Atlantic albums above have black mono or green stereo labels.—			
Atlantic 8028	(M)	**The Fabulous Guitar Of Luiz Bonfa/Amor!**	1960	12.00	30.00
Atlantic SD-8028	(S)	**The Fabulous Guitar Of Luiz Bonfa/Amor!**	1960	10.00	25.00
		—Atlantic albums above have white "bullseye" labels.—			
Atlantic 8028	(M)	**The Fabulous Guitar Of Luiz Bonfa/Amor!**	1961	6.00	15.00
Atlantic SD-8028	(S)	**The Fabulous Guitar Of Luiz Bonfa/Amor!**	1961	5.00	12.00
		—Atlantic mono albums above have multi-color labels with a white fan logo.—			
Atlantic 8028	(M)	**The Fabulous Guitar Of Luiz Bonfa/Amor!**	196?	5.00	12.00
Atlantic SD-8028	(S)	**The Fabulous Guitar Of Luiz Bonfa/Amor!**	196?	4.00	10.00
		—Atlantic mono albums above have multi-color labels with a black fan logo.—			
Verve V-8522	(M)	**Luiz Bonfa Plays & Sings Bossa Nova**	1963	6.00	15.00
Verve V6-8522	(S)	**Luiz Bonfa Plays & Sings Bossa Nova**	1963	5.00	12.00
		— Verve albums above have black labels with "MGM Record" on the bottom.—			
Dot DLP-3804	(M)	**Luiz Bonfa**	1967	6.00	15.00
Dot DLP-25804	(S)	**Luiz Bonfa**	1967	4.00	10.00
Dot DLP-3825	(M)	**Luiz Bonfa Plays Great Songs**	1968	6.00	15.00
Dot DLP-25825	(S)	**Luiz Bonfa Plays Great Songs**	1968	4.00	10.00
Dot DLP-3881	(M)	**Bonfa**	1968	6.00	15.00
Dot DLP-25881	(S)	**Bonfa**	1968	4.00	10.00

BONNEMERE, EDDIE

Edward Bonnemre is a modern jazz based pianist.

Label & Catalog #		Title	Year	VG+	NM
Roost R-149	(10")	**Piano Mambo With Bonnemere**	1954	20.00	50.00
Roost LP-2236	(M)	**Piano Bon Bons**	1959	16.00	40.00
Roost SLP-2236	(S)	**Piano Bon Bons**	1959	12.00	30.00
Roost LP-2241	(M)	**The Sound Of Memory**	1960	16.00	40.00
Roost SLP-2241	(S)	**The Sound Of Memory**	1960	12.00	30.00
Prestige PRLP-7354	(M)	**Jazz Orient-ed**	1965	10.00	25.00
Prestige PRST-7354	(S)	**Jazz Orient-ed**	1965	8.00	20.00
		—Prestige albums above have blue labels with a trident logo on the right side.—			

BOOKER, BERYL

Ms. Beryl Booker is a modern jazz pianist. For additional listings refer to Don Byas.

Label & Catalog #		Title	Year	VG+	NM
Discovery DL-3021	(10")	**Beryl Booker Trio**	1953	125.00	250.00
EmArcy MG-26007	(10")	**A Girl Met A Piano**	1954	40.00	100.00
Cadence CLP-1000	(10")	**Beryl Booker**	1955	50.00	125.00

BOSTIC, EARL

Earl Bostic is a traditional jazz and rhythm 'n blues based alto saxophone player and band leader.

Label & Catalog #		Title	Year	VG+	NM
King 295-64	(10")	**Earl Bostic & His Alto Sax, Volume 1** *(Red vinyl)*	195?	40.00	100.00
King 295-64	(10")	**Earl Bostic & His Alto Sax, Volume 1**	195?	24.00	60.00
King 295-65	(10")	**Earl Bostic & His Alto Sax, Volume 2** *(Red vinyl)*	195?	40.00	100.00
King 295-65	(10")	**Earl Bostic & His Alto Sax, Volume 2**	195?	24.00	60.00
King 295-66	(10")	**Earl Bostic & His Alto Sax, Volume 3** *(Red vinyl)*	195?	40.00	100.00
King 295-66	(10")	**Earl Bostic & His Alto Sax, Volume 3**	195?	24.00	60.00
King 295-72	(10")	**Earl Bostic & His Alto Sax**	195?	24.00	60.00
King 295-76	(10")	**Earl Bostic & His Alto Sax**	195?	24.00	60.00
King 295-77	(10")	**Earl Bostic & His Alto Sax**	195?	24.00	60.00
King 295-78	(10")	**Earl Bostic & His Alto Sax**	195?	24.00	60.00
King 295-79	(10")	**Earl Bostic & His Alto Sax**	195?	24.00	60.00
King 295-95	(10")	**Earl Bostic Plays Old Standards**	195?	24.00	60.00
King 295-103	(10")	**Earl Bostic & His Alto Sax**	195?	24.00	60.00
King 395-500	(M)	**The Best Of Earl Bostic**	1956	14.00	35.00
King 395-503	(M)	**Bostic For You**	1956	14.00	35.00
King 395-515	(M)	**Alto-Tude**	1956	14.00	35.00
King 395-525	(M)	**Dance Time**	1956	14.00	35.00

Label & Catalog #		Title	Year	VG+	NM
King 395-529	(M)	**Let's Dance With Earl Bostic**	1958	12.00	30.00
King 395-547	(M)	**Invitation To Dance**	1958	12.00	30.00
King 395-558	(M)	**C'mon And Dance With Earl Bostic**	1958	12.00	30.00
King 395-571	(M)	**Bostic Rocks**	1958	12.00	30.00
King 395-583	(M)	**Showcase Of Swinging Dance Hits**	1958	12.00	30.00
King 395-597	(M)	**Alto Magic In Hi-Fi**	1958	12.00	30.00
King 395-602	(M)	**Sweet Tunes Of The Fantastic Fifties**	1959	12.00	30.00
King 395-613	(M)	**Workshop**	1959	12.00	30.00
King 395-620	(M)	**Sweet Tunes Of The Roaring Twenties**	1959	10.00	25.00
King 632	(M)	**Sweet Tunes Of TheSwinging Thirties**	1959	10.00	25.00
King 640	(M)	**Sweet Tunes Of The Sentimental Forties**	1959	10.00	25.00
King 662	(M)	**Musical Pearls**	1959	10.00	25.00
King 705	(M)	**Hit Tunes Of Big Broadway Shows**	1960	10.00	25.00
King 725	(M)	**25 Years Of Rhythm And Blues Hits**	1960	10.00	25.00
King 786	(M)	**By Popular Demand**	1962	10.00	25.00
King 827	(M)	**Earl Bostic Plays Bossa Nova**	1963	10.00	25.00
King 838	(M)	**Fantastic Fifties**	1963	10.00	25.00
King 846	(M)	**Jazz As I Feel It**	1963	10.00	25.00
King 881	(M)	**The Best Of Earl Bostic**	1964	10.00	25.00
King 900	(M)	**New Sound**	1964	10.00	25.00
King 921	(M)	**The Great Hits Of 1964**	1964	10.00	25.00

—King albums above have crownless black labels. Most, if not all, were reissued in stereo on the blue crown label in the late '60s.—

Philips PHM-200-262	(M)	**The Song Is Not Ended**	1967	10.00	25.00
Philips PHS-600-262	(S)	**The Song Is Not Ended**	1967	10.00	25.00
King KS-1048	(S)	**Harlem Nocturne**	1969	10.00	25.00

BOSWELL, CONNEE

Classically trained Conee Boswell of The Boswell Sisters is a traditional jazz-based pop vocalist and instrumentalist, including the cello, piano, alto sax and violin.

Decca DL-6013	(10")	**The Star Maker**	1951	30.00	75.00
Decca DL-5390	(10")	**Connee Boswell**	1951	30.00	75.00
Decca DL-5445	(10")	**Singing The Blues**	1951	30.00	75.00
Decca DL-8356	(M)	**Connee**	1956	20.00	50.00
Decca DL-4254	(M)	**The Star Maker**	1962	12.00	30.00
Decca DL-74254	(E)	**The Star Maker**	1962	6.00	15.00
RCA Victor LPM-1426	(M)	**Connee Boswell & The Original Memphis 5**	1957	16.00	40.00
Design DLP-68	(M)	**Connee Boswell Sings Irving Berlin**	196?	4.00	10.00
Design DLPS-68	(E)	**Connee Boswell Sings Irving Berlin**	196?	1.00	5.00
Design DLP-101	(M)	**The New Sound Of Connee Boswell**	196?	4.00	10.00
Design DLPS-101	(E)	**The New Sound Of Connee Boswell**	196?	1.00	5.00

BOTHWELL, JOHNNY

Johnny Bothwell is a traditional jazz alto saxophone player.

Brunswick BL-58033	(10")	**Presenting Johnny Bothwell**	1953	30.00	75.00

BOU LOU

4-Corners FCL-4211	(M)	**The 13 Year Old Sensation From France**	1966	8.00	20.00
4-Corners FCS-4211	(S)	**The 13 Year Old Sensation From France**	1966	6.00	15.00
4-Corners FCL-4234	(M)	**Jazz/Left Bank**	1967	8.00	20.00
4-Corners FCS-4234	(S)	**Jazz/Left Bank**	1967	6.00	15.00

BOWIE, LESTER

Nessa N-1	(S)	**Numbers 1 + 2**	1968	8.00	20.00

BOWIE, PAT

Ms. Pat Bowie is a modern jazz based vocalist.

Prestige PRLP-7385	(M)	**Out Of Sight**	1965	14.00	35.00
Prestige PRST-7385	(S)	**Out Of Sight**	1965	12.00	30.00
Prestige PRLP-7437	(M)	**Feelin' Good**	1967	12.00	30.00
Prestige PRST-7437	(S)	**Feelin' Good**	1967	10.00	25.00

—Prestige albums above have blue labels with a trident logo on the right side.—

BOWN, PATTI

Columbia CL-1379	(M)	**Patti Bown Plays Big Piano**	1959	12.00	30.00

—Columbia albums above have six white on black "eye" logos on each label.—

Label & Catalog #		Title	Year	VG+	NM
BOYD, ROCKY					
Rocky Boyd is a modern jazz tenor saxophone player.					
Jazztime JT-001	(M)	**Ease It**	1961	12.00	30.00
Jazztime JS-001	(S)	**Ease It**	1961	10.00	25.00
BRACE, JANET					
ABC-Paramount ABC-116	(M)	**Special Delivery**	1956	20.00	50.00
BRADFORD, CLEA					
Clea Bradford is a modern jazz vocalist.					
Tru-Sound TRU-15005	(M)	**These Dues**	1962	20.00	50.00
		(Tru-Sound 15005 also features Clark Terry.)			
New Jazz NJLP-8320	(M)	**Clea Bradford With Clark Terry**	1963	*Unreleased*	
Status ST-8320	(M)	**Clea Bradford With Clark Terry**	1965	16.00	40.00
		(Status 8320 is a reissue of Tru-Sound 15005.)			
Mainstream 56042	(M)	**Clea Bradford Now**	1965	10.00	25.00
Mainstream S-6042	(S)	**Clea Bradford Now**	1965	12.00	30.00
Cadet LPS-810	(S)	**Her Point Of View**	1969	5.00	12.00
BRADFORD, PERRY					
Perry "Mule" Bradford is a traditional jazz pianist, vocalist and composer.					
Crispus-Attackus 101	(M)	**The Perry Bradford Story**	1957	20.00	50.00
BRADLEY, WILL					
Wilbur Schwictenberg, aka William Bradley, is a traditional jazz trombone player and composer. For additional listings refer to Bobby Byrne / Will Bradley.					
Epic LG-1005	(10")	**Boogie Woogie**	1954	40.00	100.00
Epic LN-1127	(10")	**The House Of Bradley**	1954	40.00	100.00
Epic LG-3115	(M)	**Boogie Woogie**	1955	20.00	50.00
Epic LN-3199	(M)	**The House Of Bradley**	1955	20.00	50.00
RCA Victor LPM-2098	(M)	**Big Band Boogie**	1960	16.00	40.00
RCA Victor LSP-2098	(S)	**Big Band Boogie**	1960	12.00	30.00
—RCA albums above have black labels with "Long Play" or "Living Stereo" on the bottom.—					
BRADSHAW, EVANS					
Evans Bradshaw is a modern jazz pianist.					
Riverside RLP-12-263	(M)	**Look Out For Evans Bradshaw!**	1958	16.00	40.00
Riverside RLP-12-296	(M)	**Pieces Of Eighty-Eight**	1959	16.00	40.00
Riverside RLP-1136	(S)	**Pieces Of Eighty-Eight**	1959	12.00	30.00
—Riverside albums above have blue mono or black stereo labels with a reel & mike logo on top.—					
BRAFF, RUBY					
Reuben Braff is a traditional jazz trumpet player. For additional listings refer to Buck Clayton & Ruby Braff & Mel Powell; Joe Newman; Pee Wee Russell & Ruby Braff.					
Bethlehem BCP-1005	(10")	**Ruby Braff Swings**	1954	40.00	100.00
Bethlehem BCP-1032	(10")	**Holiday In Braff**	1955	40.00	100.00
Bethlehem BCP-1034	(10")	**Ball At Bethlehem With Braff**	1955	40.00	100.00
Storyville STLP-320	(10")	**Hustlin' And Bustlin'**	1955	30.00	75.00
Concert Hall Jazz 1210	(M)	**Little Big Horn**	1955	16.00	40.00
Jazztone J-1210	(M)	**Little Big Horn**	1955	16.00	40.00
Vanguard VRS-8504	(M)	**The Ruby Braff Special**	1955	16.00	40.00
Storyville STLP-908	(M)	**Hustlin' And Bustlin'**	1956	20.00	50.00
Bethlehem BCP-5	(M)	**A Ruby Braff Omnibus**	1957	20.00	50.00
		(Bethlehem 5 is a reissue of 1005.)			
RCA Victor LPM-1008	(M)	**To Fred Astaire With Love**	1955	16.00	40.00
RCA Victor LPM-1332	(M)	**The Magic Horn Of Ruby Braff**	1956	16.00	40.00
RCA Victor LPM-1510	(M)	**Salute To Bunny In Hi Fi**	1957	16.00	40.00
RCA Victor LPM-1966	(M)	**Easy Now**	1959	16.00	40.00
RCA Victor LSP-1966	(S)	**Easy Now**	1959	12.00	30.00
—RCA albums above have black labels with "Long Play" or "Living Stereo" on the bottom.—					
ABC-Paramount ABC-141	(M)	**Ruby Braff Featuring Dave McKenna**	1956	16.00	40.00
Epic LN-3377	(M)	**Braff!**	1957	16.00	40.00
Stereo-Craft RTN-507	(M)	**You're Getting To Be A Habit With Me**	1959	16.00	40.00
Stereo-Craft RTS-507	(S)	**You're Getting To Be A Habit With Me**	1959	12.00	30.00
Warner Bros. W-1273	(M)	**Ruby Braff Goes Girl Crazy**	1959	16.00	40.00
Warner Bros. WS-1273	(S)	**Ruby Braff Goes Girl Crazy**	1959	12.00	30.00
United Arts. UAL-3045	(M)	**Blowing Around The Around**	1959	16.00	40.00
United Arts. UAS-6045	(S)	**Blowing Around The Around**	1959	12.00	30.00

Label & Catalog #		Title	Year	VG+	NM
United Arts. UAL-4093	(M)	**Ruby Braff-Marshall Brown Sextet**	1960	16.00	40.00
United Arts. UAS-5093	(S)	**Ruby Braff-Marshall Brown Sextet**	1960	12.00	30.00
Bethlehem BCP-6043	(M)	**The Best Of Ruby Braff**	1960	12.00	30.00

BRAFF, RUBY, & ELLIS LARKINS

Label & Catalog #		Title	Year	VG+	NM
Vanguard VRS-8019	(10")	**Inventions In Jazz—Volume 1**	1955	30.00	75.00
Vanguard VRS-8020	(10")	**Inventions In Jazz—Volume 2**	1955	30.00	75.00
Vanguard VRS-8507	(M)	**Two By Two**	1956	16.00	40.00
Vanguard VRS-8516	(M)	**Pocketful Of Dreams**	1957	16.00	40.00

(Vanguard 8516 is a reissue of 8019 and 8020.)

BRAFF, RUBY, & PEE WEE RUSSELL / BOBBY HENDERSON

Label & Catalog #		Title	Year	VG+	NM
Verve MGV-8241	(M)	**The Ruby Braff Octet With Pee Wee Russell And Bobby Henderson At Newport**	1958	20.00	50.00

— Verve albums above have black labels with "Verve Records, Inc." on the bottom.—

Label & Catalog #		Title	Year	VG+	NM
Verve V-8241	(M)	**The Ruby Braff Octet With Pee Wee Russell And Bobby Henderson At Newport**	1961	8.00	20.00

— Verve albums above have black labels with "MGM Record" on the bottom.—

BRAITH, GEORGE

George Braith is a modern jazz tenor and soprano saxophone player.

Label & Catalog #		Title	Year	VG+	NM
Blue Note BLP-4148	(M)	**Two Souls In One**	1963	20.00	50.00
Blue Note BST-84148	(S)	**Two Souls In One**	1963	16.00	40.00
Blue Note BLP-4161	(M)	**Soul Dream**	1964	20.00	50.00
Blue Note BST-84161	(S)	**Soul Dream**	1964	16.00	40.00
Blue Note BLP-4171	(M)	**Extension**	1964	20.00	50.00
Blue Note BST-84171	(S)	**Extension**	1964	16.00	40.00

—Blue Note albums above have blue on white labels with a 61st St, NYC address.—

Label & Catalog #		Title	Year	VG+	NM
Blue Note BLP-4148	(M)	**Two Souls In One**	1966	10.00	25.00
Blue Note BST-84148	(S)	**Two Souls In One**	1966	8.00	20.00
Blue Note BLP-4161	(M)	**Soul Dream**	1966	10.00	25.00
Blue Note BST-84161	(S)	**Soul Dream**	1966	8.00	20.00
Blue Note BLP-4171	(M)	**Extension**	1966	10.00	25.00
Blue Note BST-84171	(S)	**Extension**	1966	8.00	20.00

—Blue Note albums above have blue on white labels with a New York, USA address.—

Label & Catalog #		Title	Year	VG+	NM
Blue Note BST-84148	(S)	**Two Souls In One**	196?	6.00	15.00
Blue Note BST-84161	(S)	**Soul Dream**	196?	6.00	15.00
Blue Note BST-84171	(S)	**Extension**	196?	6.00	15.00

—Blue Note albums above have blue on white labels with "A Division Of Liberty."—

Label & Catalog #		Title	Year	VG+	NM
Prestige PRLP-7474	(M)	**Laughing Soul**	1967	10.00	25.00
Prestige PRST-7474	(S)	**Laughing Soul**	1967	8.00	20.00
Prestige PRLP-7515	(M)	**Musart**	1967	10.00	25.00
Prestige PRST-7515	(S)	**Musart**	1967	8.00	20.00

—Prestige albums above have blue labels with a trident logo on the right side.—

BRASS ENSEMBLE OF THE JAZZ AND CLASSICAL MUSIC SOCIETY, THE

The Brass Ensemble includes Miles Davis, Urbie Green, J.J. Johnson and Osie Johnson.

Label & Catalog #		Title	Year	VG+	NM
Columbia CL-941	(M)	**Music For Brass**	1956	20.00	50.00

— Columbia albums above have six white on black "eye" logos on each label.—

BREGMAN, BUDDY

Buddy Bregman is a traditional jazz based pianist, composer and conductor whose more closely associated with television scores. For additional listings refer to Bing Crosby; Annie Ross.

Label & Catalog #		Title	Year	VG+	NM
Verve MGV-2042	(M)	**Swingin' Kicks**	1957	20.00	50.00
Verve MGVS-6013	(S)	**Swingin' Kicks**	1960	16.00	40.00
Verve MGV-2064	(M)	**Funny Face**	1958	20.00	50.00
Verve MGV-2093	(M)	**Gershwin Anniversary Album**	1959	20.00	50.00
Verve MGV-2094	(M)	**Dig Buddy Bregman In Hi Fi**	1959	20.00	50.00

— Verve albums above have "Verve Records, Inc." on the bottom of the label.—

Label & Catalog #		Title	Year	VG+	NM
Verve V-2042	(M)	**Swingin' Kicks**	1961	8.00	20.00
Verve V6-2042	(S)	**Swingin' Kicks**	1961	6.00	15.00
Verve V-2064	(M)	**Funny Face**	1961	8.00	20.00
Verve V-2093	(M)	**Gershwin Anniversary Album**	1961	8.00	20.00
Verve V-2094	(M)	**Dig Buddy Bregman In Hi Fi**	1961	8.00	20.00

— Verve albums above have black labels with "MGM Records" on the bottom.—

Label & Catalog #		Title	Year	VG+	NM
World Pacific WP-1263	(M)	**Swingin' Standards**	1959	16.00	40.00
World Pacific ST-1024	(S)	**Swingin' Standards**	1959	12.00	30.00

Label & Catalog #		Title	Year	VG+	NM

BRIGHT, RONNELL

Ronnell Bright is a modern jazz pianist.

Vanguard VRS-8512	(M)	**Bright Flight**	1957	16.00	40.00
Regent MG-6041	(M)	**Bright's Spot**	1957	16.00	40.00
Savoy MG-12206	(M)	**Bright's Spot**	196?	8.00	20.00
		(Savoy 12206 is a reissue of Regent 6041.)			

BRITT, PAT

Crestview CR-3075	(M)	**Jazz From San Francisco**	1967	8.00	20.00
Crestview CRS-3075	(S)	**Jazz From San Francisco**	1967	6.00	15.00

BROCK, HERBIE

Herbert Bock is a traditional jazz pianist.

Savoy MG-12066	(M)	**Herbie Brock Solo**	1956	16.00	40.00
Savoy MG-12069	(M)	**Brock's Tops**	1956	16.00	40.00

— Savoy albums above have red labels with silver print.—

BROKENSHA, JACK

Australian born John "Jack" Brokensha is a traditional jazz vibraphone player and drummer. For additional listings refer to The Australian Jazz Quartet.

Savoy MG-12180	(M)	**And Then I Said**	1962	12.00	30.00

BROOKMEYER, BOB

Robert Brookmeyer is a West Coast jazz valve trombone and piano player, arranger and composer. For additional listings refer to The Manhattan All Stars; Gerry Mulligan & Bob Brookmeyer; Jimmy Raney; Bud Shank; Phil Sunkel; Clark Terry; Phil Urso and the Various Artists section under United Artists.

Storyville STLP-305	(10")	**Bob Brookmeyer Featuring Al Cohn**	1954	125.00	250.00
Pacific Jazz PJLP-16	(10")	**Bob Brookmeyer Quartet**	1954	50.00	125.00
World Pacific PJ-1233	(M)	**Traditionalism Revisited**	1958	30.00	75.00
Prestige PRLP-214	(10")	**Bob Brookmeyer With Jimmy Raney**	1955	50.00	125.00
Prestige PRLP-7066	(M)	**The Dual Role Of Bob Brookmeyer**	1956	30.00	75.00
		(Prestige 7066 is a reissue of 214 and 178, Teddy Charles' "New Directions, Vol. 5.")			
		— Prestige labels above have a W. 50th St., NYC address on the label.—			
Clef MGC-644	(M)	**Bob Brookmeyer Plays Bob Brookmeyer & Some Others**	1955	40.00	100.00
		(Cleff 644 features cover art by David Stone Martin.)			
Clef MGC-732	(M)	**The Modernity Of Bob Brookmeyer**	1956	30.00	75.00
		(Clef 732 is a reissue of 644.)			
Verve MGV-8111	(M)	**The Modernity Of Bob Brookmeyer**	1957	20.00	50.00
Verve MGV-8385	(M)	**The Blues, Hot And Cold**	1960	20.00	50.00
		— Verve albums above have black labels with "Verve Records, Inc." on the bottom.—			
Verve V-8111	(M)	**The Modernity Of Bob Brookmeyer**	1961	12.00	30.00
Verve V-8385	(M)	**The Blues, Hot And Cold**	1961	12.00	30.00
Verve V6-8385	(S)	**The Blues, Hot And Cold**	1961	10.00	25.00
Verve V-8413	(M)	**7 X Wilder**	1961	12.00	30.00
Verve V6-8413	(S)	**7 X Wilder**	1961	10.00	25.00
Verve V-8455	(M)	**Gloomy Sunday And Other Bright Moments**	1962	12.00	30.00
Verve V6-8455	(S)	**Gloomy Sunday And Other Bright Moments**	1962	10.00	25.00
Verve V-8498	(M)	**Trombone Jazz Samba**	1962	12.00	30.00
Verve V6-8498	(S)	**Trombone Jazz Samba**	1962	10.00	25.00
		— Verve albums above have black labels with "MGM Record" on the bottom.—			
Vik LX-1071	(M)	**Brookmeyer**	1957	20.00	50.00
United Arts. UAL-4008	(M)	**Kansas City Revisited**	1959	20.00	50.00
United Arts. UAS-5008	(S)	**Kansas City Revisited**	1959	16.00	40.00
Atlantic 1320	(M)	**Portrait Of The Artist**	1960	20.00	50.00
Atlantic SD-1320	(S)	**Portrait Of The Artist**	1960	20.00	50.00
		— Atlantic albums above have black mono or green stereo labels.—			
Atlantic 1320	(M)	**Portrait Of The Artist**	196?	10.00	25.00
Atlantic SD-1320	(S)	**Portrait Of The Artist**	196?	8.00	20.00
		— Atlantic albums above have multi-color labels with a white fan logo.—			
Mercury MG-20600	(M)	**Jazz Is A Kick**	1960	12.00	30.00
Mercury SR-60600	(S)	**Jazz Is A Kick**	1960	10.00	25.00
		— Mercury albums above have silver on black labels.—			
New Jazz NJLP-8294	(M)	**Revelation**	1963	20.00	50.00
		(New Jazz 8294 is a reissue of Prestige 7066.)			
		— New Jazz albums above have purple labels.—			
New Jazz NJLP-8294	(M)	**Revelation**	1965	10.00	25.00

— New Jazz albums above have blue labels with a trident logo on the right side.—

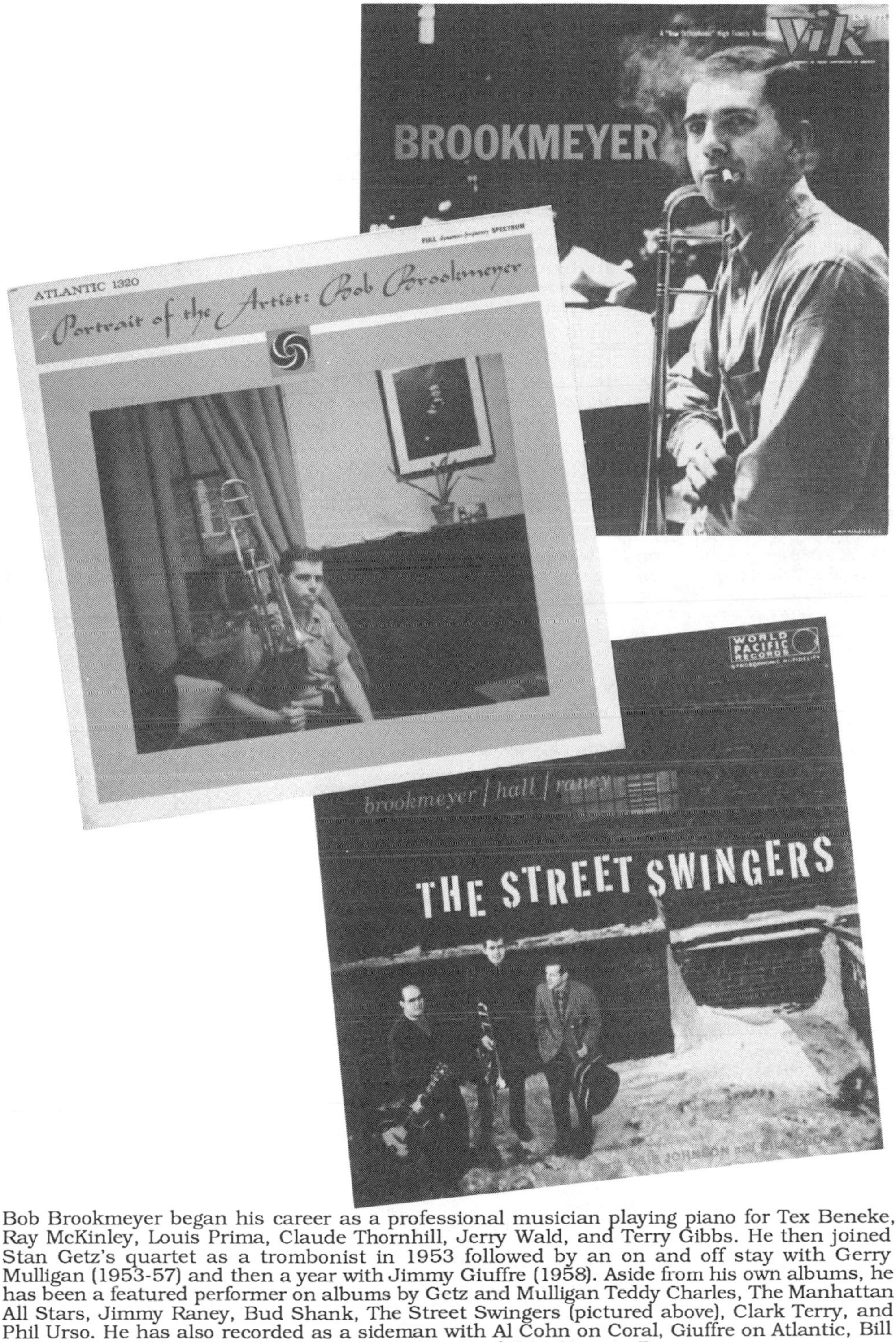

Bob Brookmeyer began his career as a professional musician playing piano for Tex Beneke, Ray McKinley, Louis Prima, Claude Thornhill, Jerry Wald, and Terry Gibbs. He then joined Stan Getz's quartet as a trombonist in 1953 followed by an on and off stay with Gerry Mulligan (1953-57) and then a year with Jimmy Giuffre (1958). Aside from his own albums, he has been a featured performer on albums by Getz and Mulligan Teddy Charles, The Manhattan All Stars, Jimmy Raney, Bud Shank, The Street Swingers (pictured above), Clark Terry, and Phil Urso. He has also recorded as a sideman with Al Cohn on Coral, Giuffre on Atlantic, Bill Potts on United Artists, George Russell on Decca, and Zoot Sims on Dawn.

Label & Catalog #		Title	Year	VG+	NM
Columbia CL-2237	(M)	**Bob Brookmeyer And Friends**	1965	8.00	20.00
Columbia CS-9037	(S)	**Bob Brookmeyer And Friends**	1965	6.00	15.00

—Columbia albums above have "360 Sound" in white on the bottom of the label.—

BROOKMEYER, BOB, & BILL EVANS

United Arts. UAL-3044	(M)	**The Ivory Hunters—Double Barrelled Piano**	1959	20.00	50.00
United Arts. UAS-6044	(S)	**The Ivory Hunters—Double Barrelled Piano**	1959	16.00	40.00

BROOKMEYER, BOB, & JIM HALL & JIMMY RANEY

World Pacific PJ-1239	(M)	**The Street Swingers**	1957	40.00	100.00
World Pacific WP-1239	(M)	**The Street Swingers**	1958	20.00	50.00
Kimberly 2021	(M)	**Brookmeyer And Guitars**	1963	12.00	30.00
Kimberly 11021	(S)	**Brookmeyer And Guitars**	1963	10.00	25.00

(Kimberly 2201 is a reissue of Pacific Jazz 1239.)

BROOKMEYER, BOB, & ZOOT SIMS

Storyville STLP-907	(M)	**Tonight's Jazz Today**	1956	30.00	75.00
Storyville STLP-914	(M)	**Whoo-eeee!**	1956	30.00	75.00
Jazztone J-1239	(M)	**Bob Brookmeyer and Zoot Sims**	1956	16.00	40.00

BROOKS, DONNA

Donna Brooks is a modern jazz based vocalist.

Dawn DLP-1105	(M)	**I'll Take Romance**	1956	50.00	125.00

BROOKS, JOHN BENSON

John Brooks is a modern jazz pianist and composer.

Vik LX-1083	(M)	**Folk Jazz U.S.A.**	1957	20.00	50.00
Riverside RLP-12-276	(M)	**The Alabama Concerto**	1958	20.00	50.00
Riverside RLP-1123	(S)	**The Alabama Concerto**	1958	16.00	40.00

—Riverside albums above have blue mono or black stereo labels with a reel & mike logo on top.—

Decca DL-75018	(S)	**Avant Slant**	1968	6.00	15.00

BROOKS, ROY

Workshop Jazz JWS-220	(M)	**Roy Brooks Beat**	1963	20.00	50.00

BROOKS, TINA

Tina Brooks is a modern jazz tenor saxophone player.

Blue Note BLP-4041	(M)	**True Blue**	1960	360.00	600.00
Blue Note BST-84041	(S)	**True Blue**	1960	*Unreleased*	
Blue Note BLP-4052	(M)	**Back To The Tracks**	1960	*Unreleased*	
Blue Note BST-84052	(S)	**Back To The Tracks**	1960	*Unreleased*	

—Blue Note albums above have blue on white labels with a W. 63rd St., NYC address.—

BROTHER MATTHEW

Before taking Orders, the good brother was known as Boyce Brown, a traditional jazz alto sax player..

ABC-Paramount ABC-121	(M)	**Brother Matthew**	1956	20.00	50.00

BROTHERS, THE: *Refer to* **STAN GETZ / ZOOT SIMS**

BROWN, BOOTS, & HIS BLOCKBUSTERS / DAN DREW & HIS DAREDEVILS

Boots and his band are Milt Bernhart, Bob Cooper, Roy Harte, Shelly Manne, Gerry Mulligan, Dave Pell, Frank Patchen, Shorty Rogers, Howard Rumsey and Bud Shank. Dan Drew & Co. feature Eddie Bert, Al Cohn, Osie Johnson, Buddy Jones, Elliott Lawrence, Charlie O'Kane and Nick Travis.

Groove LG-1000	(M)	**Rock That Beat**	1955	150.00	300.00

BROWN, CLIFFORD, & ART FARMER

Prestige PRLP-167	(10")	**Clifford Brown & Art Farmer With The Swedish All Stars**	1953	100.00	200.00

BROWN, CLIFFORD

Clifford Brown is a modern jazz trumpet player. For additional listings refer to Tadd Dameron; Lou Donaldson; Bob Gordon / Clifford Brown; Gigi Gryce & Clifford Brown; Max Roach; Sonny Rollins; and the Various Artists section under EmArcy.

Blue Note BLP-5032	(10")	**New Star On The Horizon**	1953	240.00	400.00
Blue Note BLP-5047	(10")	**Clifford Brown Quartet**	1954	240.00	400.00
Pacific Jazz PJLP-19	(10")	**The Clifford Brown Ensemble**	1955	100.00	200.00

(Pacific Jazz 19 also features Zoot Sims.)

EmArcy MG-36005	(M)	**Clifford Brown With Strings**	1955	40.00	100.00
EmArcy MG-36102	(M)	**Clifford Brown All Stars**	1956	40.00	100.00

Label & Catalog #		Title	Year	VG+	NM
Blue Note BLP-1526	(M)	**Clifford Brown Memorial Album** *(Deep groove)*	1956	100.00	200.00
Blue Note BLP-1526	(M)	**Clifford Brown Memorial Album**	1956	60.00	150.00
		(Blue Note 1526 reissues 5032 and 5030, "Lou Donaldson-Clifford Brown.")			
—Blue Note albums above have blue on white labels with a Lexington Ave., NYC address.—					
Blue Note BLP-1526	(M)	**Clifford Brown Memorial Album**	196?	20.00	50.00
—Blue Note albums above have blue on white labels with a W. 63rd Street address.—					
Blue Note BLP-1526	(M)	**Clifford Brown Memorial Album**	196?	10.00	25.00
—Blue Note albums above have blue on white labels with a "New York, USA" address—					
Blue Note BST-81526	(E)	**Clifford Brown Memorial Album**	196?	5.00	12.00
—Blue Note albums above have blue on white labels with "A Division Of Liberty Records."—					
Prestige PRLP-7055	(M)	**Clifford Brown Memorial**	1956	30.00	75.00
—Prestige albums above have yellow labels with a W. 50th St, NYC address.—					
Mercury MG-20827	(M)	**Remember Clifford**	1963	16.00	40.00
Mercury SR-60827	(E)	**Remember Clifford**	1963	10.00	25.00
		(Mercury 20827 reissues EmArcy 36005 and 36102.)			
—Mercury albums above have silver on black labels.—					
New Jazz NJLP-8301	(M)	**Clifford Brown**	1963	*Unreleased*	
Prestige PRLP-16008	(M)	**Clifford Brown**	1964	16.00	40.00
Limelight 2-8201	(M)	**The Immortal Clifford Brown** *(2 LPs)*	1965	16.00	40.00
Limelight 2-8601	(E)	**The Immortal Clifford Brown** *(2 LPs)*	1965	10.00	25.00
		(Limelight 8201 is a reissue of EmArcy 36005 and 36102.)			
Prestige PRST-7662	(E)	**Clifford Brown Memorial Album, Volume 1**	1969	4.00	10.00
		(Prestige 7662 is a reissue of 7055.)			
—Prestige albums above have blue labels with a trident logo on top.—					

BROWN, CLIFFORD, & MAX ROACH

EmArcy MG-26043	(10")	**Clifford Brown & Max Roach**	1954	150.00	300.00
EmArcy MG-36008	(M)	**Brown And Roach Incorporated**	1955	40.00	100.00
EmArcy MG-36036	(M)	**Clifford Brown & Max Roach**	1955	40.00	100.00
EmArcy MG-36037	(M)	**A Study In Brown**	1955	40.00	100.00
EmArcy MG-36070	(M)	**Clifford Brown & Max Roach At Basin Street**	1956	40.00	100.00
—EmArcy albums above have blue labels with silver print.—					
Gene Norman GNP-5	(10")	**Clifford Brown & Max Roach, Vol. 1**	1954	50.00	125.00
Gene Norman GNP-7	(10")	**Clifford Brown & Max Roach, Vol. 2**	1954	50.00	125.00
Gene Norman GNP-18	(M)	**The Best Of Max Roach & Clifford Brown In Concert**	1955	40.00	100.00
Mainstream MRL-386	(S)	**Daahoud**	196?	8.00	20.00

BROWN, LAWRENCE

Lawrence Brown is a traditional jazz trombone player.

Clef MGC-682	(M)	**Slide Trombone**	1955	40.00	100.00
		(Clef 682 features cover art by David Stone Martin.)			
Verve MGV-8067	(M)	**Slide Trombone** *(Cover art by DSM)*	1957	20.00	50.00
—Verve albums above have black labels with "Verve Records, Inc." on the bottom.—					
Verve V-8067	(M)	**Slide Trombone**	196?	8.00	20.00
—Verve albums above have black labels with "MGM Record" on the bottom.—					
Impulse A-89	(M)	**Inspired Abandon**	1965	12.00	30.00
Impulse AS-89	(S)	**Inspired Abandon**	1965	10.00	25.00
—Impulse albums above have orange & black labels.—					
Impulse AS-89	(S)	**Inspired Abandon**	1968	4.00	10.00
—Impulse albums above have red & black labels with the "abc" logo on top.—					

BROWN, LES

Lester Brown is a traditional jazz based band leader whose basic recordings are in the pop field.

Coral CRL-56026	(10")	**Over The Rainbow**	1951	20.00	50.00
Coral CRL-56030	(10")	**That Sound Of Renown**	1951	20.00	50.00
Coral CRL-56046	(10")	**You're My Everything**	1952	20.00	50.00
Coral CRL-56077	(10")	**Musical Weather Vane**	195?	20.00	50.00
Coral CRL-56094	(10")	**Le's Dance**	195?	20.00	50.00
Coral CRL-56108	(10")	**Invitation**	195?	20.00	50.00
Coral CRL-56109	(10")	**Time To Dance**	195?	20.00	50.00
Coral CRL-56116	(10")	**Le's Dream**	195?	20.00	50.00
Coral CX-1	(M)	**Les Brown Concert At The Palladium** *(2 LP box)*	1953	24.00	60.00
Coral CRL-57000	(M)	**Les Brown Concert At The Palladium—Part 1**	1954	12.00	30.00
Coral CRL-57001	(M)	**Les Brown Concert At The Palladium—Part 2**	1954	12.00	30.00
Columbia CL-2512	(10")	**I've Got My Love To Keep Me Warm**	1955	20.00	50.00
Columbia CL-2561	(10")	**The Cool Classics**	1955	20.00	50.00
Capitol T-657	(M)	**College Classics**	1955	12.00	30.00

Label & Catalog #		Title	Year	VG+	NM
Capitol T-659	(M)	**The Les Brown All Stars**	1955	12.00	30.00
		(Capitol 659 consists of three tracks each by Don Fagerquist, Ronny Lang, Dave Pell and Ray Sims, all members of Brown's band.)			
Capitol T-746	(M)	**Les Brown's In Town**	1956	12.00	30.00
Capitol T-886	(M)	**Composer's Holiday**	1957	12.00	30.00
		—Capitol albums above have turquoise labels.—			
Capitol T-1174	(M)	**The Les Brown Story**	1959	10.00	25.00
		—Capitol albums above have black "rainbow" labels with the logo on the left side.—			
Coral CRL-57311	(M)	**Jazz Song Book**	1959	10.00	25.00
Coral CRL-757311	(E)	**Jazz Song Book**	1959	5.00	12.00

BROWN, MARION

ESP-Disk' 1022	(M)	**Marion Brown Quartet**	1966	8.00	20.00
ESP-Disk' 1022	(S)	**Marion Brown Quartet**	1966	6.00	15.00
ESP-Disk' 1040	(M)	**Why Not?**	1967	8.00	20.00
ESP-Disk' 1040	(S)	**Why Not?**	1967	6.00	15.00

BROWN, MARSHALL: *Refer to* **RUBY BRAFF**

BROWN, ODELL

Cadet LP-775	(M)	**Raising The Roof**	1966	6.00	15.00
Cadet LPS-775	(S)	**Raising The Roof**	1966	5.00	12.00
Cadet LP-788	(M)	**Mellow Yellow**	1967	6.00	15.00
Cadet LPS-788	(M)	**Mellow Yellow**	1967	5.00	12.00
Cadet LP-800	(M)	**Ducky**	1967	6.00	15.00
Cadet LPS-800	(M)	**Ducky**	1967	5.00	12.00
Impulse A-9139	(M)	**3 For Shepp**	1967	10.00	25.00
Impulse AS-9139	(S)	**3 For Shepp**	1967	8.00	20.00
		—Impulse albums above have orange & black labels.—			
Impulse AS-9139	(S)	**3 For Shepp**	1968	4.00	10.00
		—Impulse albums above have red & black labels with the "abc" logo on top.—			

BROWN, PETE

James "Pete" Brown is a traditional jazz alto and tenor saxophone, trumpet and violin player. For additional listings refer to Coleman Hawkins & Roy Eldridge Pete Brown & Jonah Jones.

Bethlehem BCP-1011	(10")	**Peter The Great**	1954	50.00	125.00
Verve MGV-8365	(M)	**From The Heart**	1958	20.00	50.00
Verve MGVS-6133	(S)	**From The Heart**	1960	16.00	40.00
		—Verve albums above have black labels with "Verve Records, Inc." on the bottom.—			
Verve V-8365	(M)	**From The Heart**	196?	8.00	20.00
Verve V6-8365	(S)	**From The Heart**	196?	6.00	15.00
		—Verve albums above have black labels with "MGM Record" on the bottom.—			

BROWN, PETE / JONAH JONES

Bethlehem BCP-4	(M)	**Jazz Kaleidoscope**	1957	30.00	75.00
		(Bethlehem 4 is a reissue of 1011 and 1014, "Johanh Jones Sextet.")			

BROWN, RAY

Raymond Brown is a modern jazz bass player. For additional listings refer to Laurinda Almeida & Ray Brown; Fred Astaire; Blossom Dearie; The Poll Winners; Andre Previn & Herb Ellis.

Norgran MGN-1105	(M)	**Bass Hit!**	1956	*Unreleased*	
Verve MGV-8022	(M)	**Bass Hit!**	1957	20.00	50.00
Verve MGV-8290	(M)	**This Is Ray Brown**	1958	20.00	50.00
Verve MGV-8390	(M)	**Jazz Cello**	1960	20.00	50.00
		—Verve albums above have black labels with "Verve Records, Inc." on the bottom.—			
Verve V-8022	(M)	**Bass Hit!**	196?	8.00	20.00
Verve V-8290	(M)	**This Is Ray Brown**	196?	8.00	20.00
Verve V-8390	(M)	**Jazz Cello**	196?	8.00	20.00
Verve V-8444	(M)	**Ray Brown With The All Star Big Band Featuring Cannonball Adderley**	1962	12.00	30.00
Verve V6-8444	(S)	**Ray Brown With The All Star Big Band Featuring Cannonball Adderley**	1962	10.00	25.00
Verve V-8580	(M)	**Much In Common**	1964	12.00	30.00
Verve V6-8580	(S)	**Much In Common**	1964	10.00	25.00
		(Verve 8580 also features Milt Jackson.)			
Verve V-8615	(S)	**Ray Brown-Milt Jackson**	1965	12.00	30.00
Verve V6-8615	(S)	**Ray Brown-Milt Jackson**	1965	10.00	25.00
		—Verve albums above have black labels with "MGM Records" on the bottom.—			

Label & Catalog #		Title	Year	VG+	NM
Verve VSP-10	(M)	**Two For The Blues**	1966	5.00	12.00
Verve VSPS-10	(S)	**Two For The Blues**	1966	4.00	10.00
		(Verve 10 is a reissue of 8444.)			

BROWN, RONNIE

Philips PHM-200-130	(M)	**Jazz For Everyone**	1964	8.00	20.00
Philips PHS-600-130	(S)	**Jazz For Everyone**	1964	6.00	15.00

BROWN, RUTH

Ruth Brown is a rhythm 'n' blues based pop singer.

Atlantic 1308	(M)	**Late Date With Ruth Brown**	1959	60.00	150.00
Atlantic SD-1308	(S)	**Late Date With Ruth Brown**	1959	100.00	200.00
		—Atlantic albums above have black mono or green stereo labels.—			
Atlantic 1308	(M)	**Late Date With Ruth Brown**	1961	8.00	20.00
Atlantic SD-1308	(S)	**Late Date With Ruth Brown**	1961	10.00	25.00
		—Atlantic albums above have multi-color labels with a white fan logo.—			
Atlantic 1308	(M)	**Late Date With Ruth Brown**	196?	5.00	12.00
Atlantic SD-1308	(S)	**Late Date With Ruth Brown**	196?	6.00	15.00
		—Atlantic albums above have multi-color labels with a black fan logo.—			
Mainstream 16034	(M)	**Ruth Brown '65**	1965	6.00	15.00
Mainstream S-6034	(S)	**Ruth Brown '65**	1965	8.00	20.00

BROWN, TED

Theodore Brown is a modern jazz tenor saxophone player.

Vanguard VRS-8515	(M)	**Free Wheeling**	1956	200.00	400.00

BROWN, WINI: ***Refer to*** **COOTIE WILLIAMS**

BRUBECK, DAVE

David Brubeck is a pianist and leader of one of the West Coast's most influential groups of the '50s. Paul Desmond was a featured member of Brubeck's bands since 1948; his name was often as prominent on the covers as Brubeck's. For additional listings refer to Desmond; and the Jazzy Soundtracks section under Columbia and Epic.

Fantasy 3-1	(10")	**Dave Brubeck Trio** *(Colored vinyl)*	1951	60.00	150.00
Fantasy 3-1	(10")	**Dave Brubeck Trio**	1951	40.00	100.00
Fantasy 3-2	(10")	**Dave Brubeck Trio** *(Colored vinyl)*	1951	60.00	150.00
Fantasy 3-2	(10")	**Dave Brubeck Trio**	1951	40.00	100.00
Fantasy 3-3	(10")	**Dave Brubeck Octet** *(Colored vinyl)*	1951	60.00	150.00
Fantasy 3-3	(10")	**Dave Brubeck Octet**	1951	40.00	100.00
Fantasy 3-4	(10")	**Dave Brubeck Trio** *(Colored vinyl)*	1952	60.00	150.00
Fantasy 3-4	(10")	**Dave Brubeck Trio**	1952	40.00	100.00
Fantasy 3-5	(10")	**Dave Brubeck Quartet** *(Colored vinyl)*	1952	60.00	150.00
Fantasy 3-5	(10")	**Dave Brubeck Quartet**	1952	40.00	100.00
Fantasy 3-7	(10")	**Dave Brubeck Quartet** *(Colored vinyl)*	1952	60.00	150.00
Fantasy 3-7	(10")	**Dave Brubeck Quartet**	1952	40.00	100.00
Fantasy 3-8	(10")	**Jazz At Storyville** *(Colored vinyl)*	1953	60.00	150.00
Fantasy 3-8	(10")	**Jazz At Storyville**	1953	40.00	100.00
Fantasy 3-10	(10")	**Jazz At The Blackhawk** *(Colored vinyl)*	1953	60.00	150.00
Fantasy 3-10	(10")	**Jazz At The Blackhawk**	1953	40.00	100.00
Fantasy 3-11	(10")	**Jazz At Oberlin** *(Colored vinyl)*	1953	60.00	150.00
Fantasy 3-11	(10")	**Jazz At Oberlin**	1953	40.00	100.00
Fantasy 3-13	(10")	**Jazz At College Of Pacific** *(Colored vinyl)*	1954	60.00	150.00
Fantasy 3-13	(10")	**Jazz At College Of Pacific**	1954	40.00	100.00
Fantasy 3-16	(10")	**Old Sounds From San Francisco** *(Colored vinyl)*	1954	60.00	150.00
Fantasy 3-16	(10")	**Old Sounds From San Francisco**	1954	40.00	100.00
Fantasy 3-20	(10")	**Paul And Dave's Jazz Interwoven** *(Colored vinyl)*	1955	60.00	150.00
Fantasy 3-20	(10")	**Paul And Dave's Jazz Interwoven**	1955	40.00	100.00
Fantasy 3204	(M)	**Dave Brubeck Trio** *(Dark red vinyl)*	1956	30.00	75.00
		(Fantasy 3204 is a reissue of 1.)			
Fantasy 3205	(M)	**Distinctive Rhythm Instrumentals**	1956	30.00	75.00
		(Dark red vinyl. Fantasy 3205 is a reissue of 2.)			
Fantasy 3210	(M)	**Jazz At The Blackhawk** *(Dark red vinyl)*	1956	30.00	75.00
		(Fantasy 3210 is a reissue of 10.)			
Fantasy 3223	(M)	**Jazz At The College Of The Pacific**	1956	30.00	75.00
		(Dark red vinyl)			
Fantasy 3229	(M)	**Brubeck Desmond** *(Dark red vinyl)*	1956	30.00	75.00
		(Fantasy 3229 is a reissue of 5.)			
Fantasy 3230	(M)	**Dave Brubeck Quartet** *(Dark red vinyl)*	1956	30.00	75.00
		(Fantasy 3230 is a reissue of 7.)			

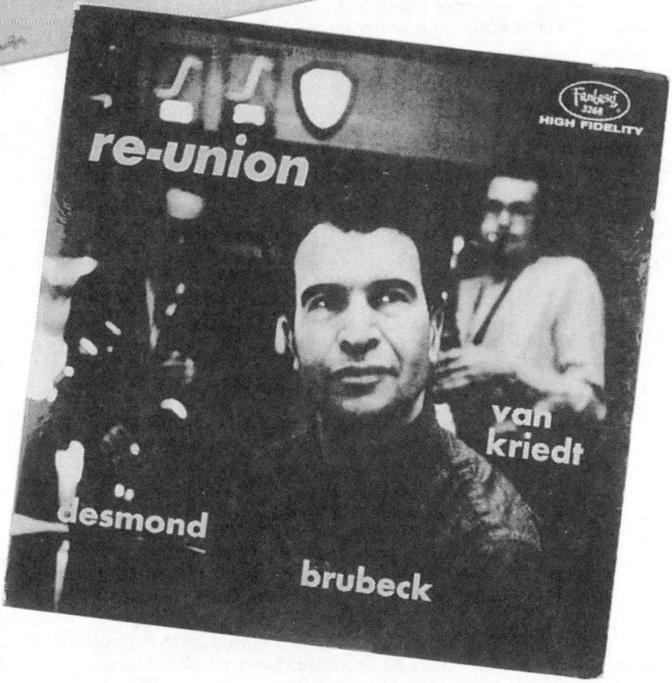

Dave Brubeck formed his first octet in 1946, although he did not record until 1949 (for Coronet but available on Fantasy). His style of playing has long been a source of controversy among critics and other musicians, although the record buying public took to him immediately. His groups have included many of jazz's finest musicians and often featured Paul Desmond.

Label & Catalog #		Title	Year	VG+	NM
Fantasy 3239	(M)	**Dave Brubeck Octet** *(Dark red vinyl)* *(Fantasy 3239 is a reissue of 3.)*	1956	30.00	75.00
Fantasy 3240	(M)	**Brubeck Desmond: Jazz At Storyville** *(Dark red vinyl. Fantasy 3240 is a reissue of 8.)*	1957	30.00	75.00
Fantasy 3245	(M)	**Jazz At Oberlin** *(Dark red vinyl)* *(Fantasy 3245 is a reissue of 11.)*	1957	30.00	75.00
Fantasy 3249	(M)	**Brubeck & Desmond At Wilshire-Ebell** *(Dark red vinyl)*	1957	30.00	75.00
—Fantasy mono albums above have red labels on dark red, non-flexible vinyl.—					
Fantasy 3204	(M)	**Dave Brubeck Trio**	195?	16.00	40.00
Fantasy 3205	(M)	**Distinctive Rhythm Instrumentals**	195?	16.00	40.00
Fantasy 3210	(M)	**Jazz At The Blackhawk**	195?	16.00	40.00
Fantasy 3223	(M)	**Jazz At The College Of The Pacific**	195?	16.00	40.00
Fantasy 8078	(E)	**Jazz At The College Of The Pacific** *(Blue vinyl)*	1962	16.00	40.00
Fantasy 8078	(E)	**Jazz At The College Of The Pacific**	196?	8.00	20.00
Fantasy 3229	(M)	**Brubeck Desmond**	195?	16.00	40.00
Fantasy 8092	(E)	**Brubeck Desmond** *(Blue vinyl)*	1962	16.00	40.00
Fantasy 8092	(E)	**Brubeck Desmond**	196?	8.00	20.00
Fantasy 3230	(M)	**Dave Brubeck Quartet**	195?	16.00	40.00
Fantasy 8093	(E)	**Dave Brubeck Quartet** *(Blue vinyl)*	1962	16.00	40.00
Fantasy 8093	(E)	**Dave Brubeck Quartet**	196?	8.00	20.00
Fantasy 3239	(M)	**Dave Brubeck Octet**	195?	16.00	40.00
Fantasy 8094	(E)	**Dave Brubeck Octet** *(Blue vinyl)*	1962	16.00	40.00
Fantasy 8094	(E)	**Dave Brubeck Octet**	196?	8.00	20.00
Fantasy 3240	(M)	**Jazz At Storyville**	195?	16.00	40.00
Fantasy 8080	(E)	**Jazz At Storyville** *(Blue vinyl)*	1962	16.00	40.00
Fantasy 8080	(E)	**Jazz At Storyville**	196?	8.00	20.00
Fantasy 3245	(M)	**Jazz At Oberlin**	195?	16.00	40.00
Fantasy 8069	(E)	**Jazz At Oberlin** *(Blue vinyl)*	1962	16.00	40.00
Fantasy 8069	(E)	**Jazz At Oberlin**	196?	8.00	20.00
Fantasy 3249	(M)	**Brubeck & Desmond At Wilshire-Ebell**	195?	16.00	40.00
Fantasy 8095	(S)	**Brubeck & Desmond At Wilshire-Ebell** *(Blue vinyl)*	1962	16.00	40.00
Fantasy 8095	(S)	**Brubeck & Desmond At Wilshire-Ebell**	196?	10.00	25.00
Fantasy 3259	(M)	**Dave Brubeck Plays And Plays And Plays...** *(Red vinyl)*	1958	20.00	50.00
Fantasy 3259	(M)	**Dave Brubeck Plays And Plays And Plays...**	195?	12.00	30.00
Fantasy 3268	(M)	**Re-union** *(Red vinyl)*	1958	20.00	50.00
Fantasy 3268	(M)	**Re-union**	195?	12.00	30.00
Fantasy 8007	(S)	**Re-union** *(Blue vinyl)*	1962	16.00	40.00
Fantasy 8007	(S)	**Re-union**	196?	10.00	25.00
Fantasy 3298	(M)	**Two Knights At The Black Hawk** *(Red vinyl)*	1959	20.00	50.00
Fantasy 3298	(M)	**Two Knights At The Black Hawk** *(Fantasy 3298 is a reissue of 210.)*	195?	12.00	30.00
Fantasy 8081	(E)	**Two Knights At The Black Hawk** *(Blue vinyl)*	1962	16.00	40.00
Fantasy 8081	(E)	**Two Knights At The Black Hawk**	196?	8.00	20.00
Fantasy 3301	(M)	**Brubeck A La Mode** *(Red vinyl)*	1960	20.00	50.00
Fantasy 3301	(M)	**Brubeck A La Mode**	196?	12.00	30.00
Fantasy 8047	(S)	**Brubeck A La Mode** *(Blue vinyl)*	1962	16.00	40.00
Fantasy 8047	(S)	**Brubeck A La Mode**	196?	10.00	25.00
Fantasy 3319	(M)	**Near-Myth** *(Red vinyl)*	1961	20.00	50.00
Fantasy 3319	(M)	**Near-Myth**	196?	12.00	30.00
Fantasy 8063	(S)	**Near-Myth** *(Blue vinyl)*	1962	16.00	40.00
Fantasy 8063	(S)	**Near-Myth**	196?	10.00	25.00
Fantasy 3331	(M)	**Dave Brubeck Trio Featuring Cal Tjader** *(Red vinyl)*	1962	20.00	50.00
Fantasy 3331	(M)	**Dave Brubeck Trio Featuring Cal Tjader** *(Fantasy 3331 is a reissue of 1.)*	196?	12.00	30.00
Fantasy 8073	(E)	**Dave Brubeck Trio Featuring Cal Tjader** *(Blue vinyl)*	1962	16.00	40.00
Fantasy 8073	(E)	**Dave Brubeck Trio Featuring Cal Tjader**	196?	8.00	20.00
Fantasy 3332	(M)	**Brubeck Tjader** *(Red vinyl)*	1962	20.00	50.00
Fantasy 3332	(M)	**Brubeck Tjader** *(Fantasy 3332 is a reissue of 2.)*	196?	12.00	30.00
Fantasy 8074	(E)	**Brubeck Tjader** *(Blue vinyl)*	1962	16.00	40.00
Fantasy 8074	(E)	**Brubeck Tjader**	196?	8.00	20.00
—Fantasy albums above have red mono or blue stereo labels on non-flexible vinyl.—					
Fantasy 3204	(M)	**Dave Brubeck Trio**	196?	6.00	15.00
Fantasy 3205	(M)	**Distinctive Rhythm Instrumentals**	196?	6.00	15.00

Label & Catalog #		Title	Year	VG+	NM
Fantasy 3210	(M)	**Jazz At The Blackhawk**	196?	6.00	15.00
Fantasy 3223	(M)	**Jazz At The College Of The Pacific**	196?	6.00	15.00
Fantasy 8078	(E)	**Jazz At The College Of The Pacific**	196?	4.00	10.00
Fantasy 3229	(M)	**Brubeck Desmond**	196?	6.00	15.00
Fantasy 8092	(E)	**Brubeck Desmond**	196?	4.00	10.00
Fantasy 3230	(M)	**Dave Brubeck Quartet**	196?	6.00	15.00
Fantasy 8093	(E)	**Dave Brubeck Quartet**	196?	4.00	10.00
Fantasy 3239	(M)	**Dave Brubeck Octet**	196?	6.00	15.00
Fantasy 8094	(E)	**Dave Brubeck Octet**	196?	4.00	10.00
Fantasy 3240	(M)	**Jazz At Storyville**	196?	6.00	15.00
Fantasy 8080	(E)	**Jazz At Storyville**	196?	4.00	10.00
Fantasy 3245	(M)	**Jazz At Oberlin**	196?	6.00	15.00
Fantasy 8069	(E)	**Jazz At Oberlin**	196?	4.00	10.00
Fantasy 3249	(M)	**Brubeck & Desmond At Wilshire-Ebell**	196?	6.00	15.00
Fantasy 8095	(S)	**Brubeck & Desmond At Wilshire-Ebell**	196?	5.00	12.00
Fantasy 3259	(M)	**Dave Brubeck Plays Solo**	196?	6.00	15.00
Fantasy 3298	(M)	**Two Knights At The Black Hawk**	196?	6.00	15.00
Fantasy 8081	(E)	**Two Knights At The Black Hawk**	196?	4.00	10.00
Fantasy 3301	(M)	**Brubeck A La Mode**	196?	6.00	15.00
Fantasy 8047	(S)	**Brubeck A La Mode**	196?	5.00	12.00
Fantasy 3319	(M)	**Near-Myth**	196?	6.00	15.00
Fantasy 8063	(S)	**Near-Myth**	196?	5.00	12.00
Fantasy 3331	(M)	**Dave Brubeck Trio Featuring Cal Tjader**	196?	6.00	15.00
Fantasy 8073	(E)	**Dave Brubeck Trio Featuring Cal Tjader**	196?	4.00	10.00
Fantasy 3332	(M)	**Brubeck Tjader**	196?	6.00	15.00
Fantasy 8074	(E)	**Brubeck Tjader**	196?	4.00	10.00
		—Fantasy albums above have red mono or blue stereo labels on flexible vinyl.—			
Crown CLP-5406	(M)	**Dave Brubeck— Paul Desmond—Cal Tjader Quartet**	196?	8.00	20.00
Crown CST-406	(E)	**Dave Brubeck— Paul Desmond—Cal Tjader Quartet**	196?	4.00	10.00
		(Crown 5406 reissues Fantasy material.)			
Columbia CL-566	(M)	**Jazz Goes To College**	1954	16.00	40.00
Columbia CL-6322	(10")	**Jazz Goes To College, Volume 2**	1954	16.00	40.00
Columbia CL-590	(M)	**Dave Brubeck At Storyville: 1954**	1954	16.00	40.00
Columbia CL-622	(M)	**Brubeck Time**	1955	16.00	40.00
		—Columbia albums above have "Long Playing" on the bottom of the label.—			
Columbia CL-566	(M)	**Jazz Goes To College**	195?	10.00	25.00
Columbia CL-590	(M)	**Dave Brubeck At Storyville: 1954**	195?	10.00	25.00
Columbia CL-622	(M)	**Brubeck Time**	195?	10.00	25.00
Columbia CL-699	(M)	**Jazz: Red, Hot And Cool**	1955	16.00	40.00
Columbia CL-878	(M)	**Brubeck Plays Brubeck**	1956	12.00	30.00
Columbia CL-984	(M)	**Jazz Impressions Of The U.S.A.**	1957	12.00	30.00
Columbia CL-1034	(M)	**Jazz Goes To Junior College**	1957	12.00	30.00
Columbia CL-1059	(M)	**Dave Digs Disney**	1957	12.00	30.00
Columbia CS-8090	(S)	**Dave Digs Disney**	1959	16.00	40.00
Columbia CL-1168	(M)	**Dave Brubeck Quartet In Europe**	1958	12.00	30.00
Columbia CS-8128	(S)	**Dave Brubeck Quartet In Europe**	1959	10.00	25.00
Columbia CL-1249	(M)	**Newport 1958**	1958	12.00	30.00
Columbia CS-8082	(S)	**Newport 1958**	1959	10.00	25.00
Columbia CL-1251	(M)	**Jazz Impressions Of Eurasia**	1958	12.00	30.00
Columbia CS-8058	(S)	**Jazz Impressions Of Eurasia**	1959	10.00	25.00
Columbia CL-1347	(M)	**Gone With The Wind**	1959	12.00	30.00
Columbia CS-8156	(S)	**Gone With The Wind**	1959	10.00	25.00
Columbia CL-1397	(M)	**Time Out Featuring "Take Five"**	1959	12.00	30.00
Columbia CS-8192	(S)	**Time Out Featuring "Take Five"**	1959	10.00	25.00
Columbia CL-1439	(M)	**Southern Scene**	1960	12.00	30.00
Columbia CS-8235	(S)	**Southern Scene**	1960	10.00	25.00
Columbia CL-1454	(M)	**The Riddle**	1960	12.00	30.00
Columbia CS-8248	(S)	**The Riddle**	1960	10.00	25.00
Columbia CL-1466	(M)	**Bernstein Plays Brubeck Plays Bernstein**	1960	12.00	30.00
Columbia CS-8257	(S)	**Bernstein Plays Brubeck Plays Bernstein**	1960	10.00	25.00
Columbia CL-1553	(M)	**Brubeck And Rushing**	1960	12.00	30.00
Columbia CS-8353	(S)	**Brubeck And Rushing**	1960	10.00	25.00
Columbia CL-1609	(M)	**Tonight Only!**	1961	12.00	30.00
Columbia CS-8409	(S)	**Tonight Only!**	1961	12.00	30.00
		(Columbia 1609 also features Carmen McRae.)			
Columbia CL-1690	(M)	**Time Further Out**	1961	12.00	30.00
Columbia CS-8490	(S)	**Time Further Out**	1961	10.00	25.00

Label & Catalog #		Title	Year	VG+	NM
Columbia CL-1775	(M)	**Countdown—Time In Outer Space**	1962	12.00	30.00
Columbia CS-8575	(S)	**Countdown—Time In Outer Space**	1962	10.00	25.00
		—Columbia albums above have six white on black "eye" logos on each label.—			
Columbia CL-566	(M)	**Jazz Goes To College**	196?	6.00	15.00
Columbia CL-590	(M)	**Dave Brubeck At Storyville: 1954**	196?	6.00	15.00
Columbia CL-622	(M)	**Brubeck Time**	196?	6.00	15.00
Columbia CL-878	(M)	**Brubeck Plays Brubeck**	196?	6.00	15.00
Columbia CL-984	(M)	**Jazz Impressions Of The U.S.A.**	196?	6.00	15.00
Columbia CL-1034	(M)	**Jazz Goes To Junior College**	196?	6.00	15.00
Columbia CL-1059	(M)	**Dave Digs Disney**	196?	6.00	15.00
Columbia CS-8090	(S)	**Dave Digs Disney**	196?	5.00	12.00
Columbia CL-1168	(M)	**Dave Brubeck Quartet In Europe**	196?	6.00	15.00
Columbia CS-8128	(S)	**Dave Brubeck Quartet In Europe**	196?	5.00	12.00
Columbia CL-1249	(M)	**Newport 1958**	196?	6.00	15.00
Columbia CS-8082	(S)	**Newport 1958**	196?	5.00	12.00
Columbia CL-1251	(M)	**Jazz Impressions Of Eurasia**	196?	6.00	15.00
Columbia CS-8058	(S)	**Jazz Impressions Of Eurasia**	196?	5.00	12.00
Columbia CL-1347	(M)	**Gone With The Wind**	196?	6.00	15.00
Columbia CS-8156	(S)	**Gone With The Wind**	196?	5.00	12.00
Columbia CL-1397	(M)	**Time Out Featuring "Take Five"**	196?	6.00	15.00
Columbia CS-8192	(S)	**Time Out Featuring "Take Five"**	196?	5.00	12.00
Columbia CL-1439	(M)	**Southern Scene**	196?	6.00	15.00
Columbia CS-8235	(S)	**Southern Scene**	196?	5.00	12.00
Columbia CL-1454	(M)	**The Riddle**	196?	6.00	15.00
Columbia CS-8248	(S)	**The Riddle**	196?	5.00	12.00
Columbia CL-1466	(M)	**Bernstein Plays Brubeck Plays Bernstein**	196?	6.00	15.00
Columbia CS-8257	(S)	**Bernstein Plays Brubeck Plays Bernstein**	196?	5.00	12.00
Columbia CL-1553	(M)	**Brubeck And Rushing**	196?	6.00	15.00
Columbia CS-8353	(S)	**Brubeck And Rushing**	196?	5.00	12.00
Columbia CL-1609	(M)	**Tonight Only!**	196?	6.00	15.00
Columbia CS-8409	(S)	**Tonight Only!**	196?	5.00	12.00
Columbia CL-1690	(M)	**Time Further Out**	196?	6.00	15.00
Columbia CS-8490	(S)	**Time Further Out**	196?	5.00	12.00
Columbia CL-1775	(M)	**Countdown—Time In Outer Space**	196?	6.00	15.00
Columbia CS-8575	(S)	**Countdown—Time In Outer Space**	196?	5.00	12.00
Columbia CL-1845	(M)	**Jazz: Red, Hot And Cool**	1963	8.00	20.00
Columbia CS-8645	(E)	**Jazz: Red, Hot And Cool**	1963	5.00	12.00
		(Columbia 1845 is a reissue of 699.)			
Columbia CL-1963	(M)	**Brandenberg Gate Revisited**	1963	8.00	20.00
Columbia CS-8763	(S)	**Brandenberg Gate Revisited**	1963	6.00	15.00
Columbia CL-1998	(M)	**Bossa Nova U.S.A.**	1963	8.00	20.00
Columbia CS-8798	(S)	**Bossa Nova U.S.A.**	1963	6.00	15.00
Columbia CL-2127	(M)	**Time Changes**	1964	8.00	20.00
Columbia CS-8927	(S)	**Time Changes**	1964	6.00	15.00
Columbia CL-2212	(M)	**Jazz Impressions Of Japan**	1964	8.00	20.00
Columbia CS-9012	(S)	**Jazz Impressions Of Japan**	1964	6.00	15.00
Columbia C2L-26	(M)	**Dave Brubeck Quartet At Carnegie Hall** *(2 LPs)*	1963	10.00	25.00
Columbia C2S-826	(S)	**Dave Brubeck Quartet At Carnegie Hall** *(2 LPs)*	1963	8.00	20.00
Columbia CL-2275	(M)	**Jazz Impressions Of New York**	1965	8.00	20.00
Columbia CS-9075	(S)	**Jazz Impressions Of New York**	1965	6.00	15.00
Columbia CL-2316	(M)	**Take Five**	1965	8.00	20.00
Columbia CS-9116	(S)	**Take Five**	1965	8.00	20.00
		(Columbia 2316 also featues Carmen McRae.)			
Columbia CL-2348	(M)	**Angel Eyes**	1965	8.00	20.00
Columbia CS-9148	(S)	**Angel Eyes**	1965	6.00	15.00
		—Columbia albums above have "Guaranteed High Fidelity" or "360 Sound Stereo" in black on the label.—			
Columbia CL-566	(M)	**Jazz Goes To College**	196?	5.00	12.00
Columbia CL-590	(M)	**Dave Brubeck At Storyville: 1954**	196?	5.00	12.00
Columbia CL-622	(M)	**Brubeck Time**	196?	5.00	12.00
Columbia CL-878	(M)	**Brubeck Plays Brubeck**	196?	5.00	12.00
Columbia CL-984	(M)	**Jazz Impressions Of The U.S.A.**	196?	5.00	12.00
Columbia CL-1034	(M)	**Jazz Goes To Junior College**	196?	5.00	12.00
Columbia CL-1059	(M)	**Dave Digs Disney**	196?	5.00	12.00
Columbia CS-8090	(S)	**Dave Digs Disney**	196?	4.00	10.00
Columbia CL-1168	(M)	**Dave Brubeck Quartet In Europe**	196?	5.00	12.00
Columbia CS-8128	(S)	**Dave Brubeck Quartet In Europe**	196?	4.00	10.00
Columbia CL-1249	(M)	**Newport 1958**	196?	5.00	12.00
Columbia CS-8082	(S)	**Newport 1958**	196?	4.00	10.00

Label & Catalog #		Title	Year	VG+	NM
Columbia CL-1251	(M)	**Jazz Impressions Of Eurasia**	196?	5.00	12.00
Columbia CS-8058	(S)	**Jazz Impressions Of Eurasia**	196?	4.00	10.00
Columbia CL-1347	(M)	**Gone With The Wind**	196?	5.00	12.00
Columbia CS-8156	(S)	**Gone With The Wind**	196?	4.00	10.00
Columbia CL-1397	(M)	**Time Out Featuring "Take Five"**	196?	5.00	12.00
Columbia CS-8192	(S)	**Time Out Featuring "Take Five"**	196?	4.00	10.00
Columbia CL-1439	(M)	**Southern Scene**	196?	5.00	12.00
Columbia CS-8235	(S)	**Southern Scene**	196?	4.00	10.00
Columbia CL-1454	(M)	**The Riddle**	196?	5.00	12.00
Columbia CS-8248	(S)	**The Riddle**	196?	4.00	10.00
Columbia CL-1466	(M)	**Bernstein Plays Brubeck Plays Bernstein**	196?	5.00	12.00
Columbia CS-8257	(S)	**Bernstein Plays Brubeck Plays Bernstein**	196?	4.00	10.00
Columbia CL-1553	(M)	**Brubeck And Rushing**	196?	5.00	12.00
Columbia CS-8353	(S)	**Brubeck And Rushing**	196?	4.00	10.00
Columbia CL-1609	(M)	**Tonight Only!**	196?	5.00	12.00
Columbia CS-8409	(S)	**Tonight Only!**	196?	4.00	10.00
Columbia CL-1690	(M)	**Time Further Out**	196?	5.00	12.00
Columbia CS-8490	(S)	**Time Further Out**	196?	4.00	10.00
Columbia CL-1775	(M)	**Countdown—Time In Outer Space**	196?	5.00	12.00
Columbia CS-8575	(S)	**Countdown—Time In Outer Space**	196?	4.00	10.00
Columbia CL-1845	(M)	**Jazz: Red, Hot And Cool**	196?	5.00	12.00
Columbia CS-6845	(E)	**Jazz: Red, Hot And Cool**	196?	4.00	10.00
Columbia CL-196?	(M)	**Brandenberg Gate Revisited**	196?	5.00	12.00
Columbia CS-8763	(S)	**Brandenberg Gate Revisited**	196?	4.00	10.00
Columbia CL-1998	(M)	**Bossa Nova U.S.A.**	196?	5.00	12.00
Columbia CS-8798	(S)	**Bossa Nova U.S.A.**	196?	4.00	10.00
Columbia CL-2127	(M)	**Time Changes**	196?	5.00	12.00
Columbia CS-8927	(S)	**Time Changes**	196?	4.00	10.00
Columbia CL-2212	(M)	**Jazz Impressions Of Japan**	196?	5.00	12.00
Columbia CS-9012	(S)	**Jazz Impressions Of Japan**	196?	4.00	10.00
Columbia C2L-26	(M)	**Dave Brubeck Quartet At Carnegie Hall** *(2 LPs)*	196?	6.00	15.00
Columbia C2S-826	(S)	**Dave Brubeck Quartet At Carnegie Hall** *(2 LPs)*	196?	5.00	12.00
Columbia CL-2275	(M)	**Jazz Impressions Of New York**	196?	5.00	12.00
Columbia CS-9075	(S)	**Jazz Impressions Of New York**	196?	4.00	10.00
Columbia CL-2316	(M)	**Take Five**	196?	5.00	12.00
Columbia CS-9116	(S)	**Take Five**	196?	4.00	10.00
Columbia CL-2348	(M)	**Angel Eyes**	196?	5.00	12.00
Columbia CS-9148	(S)	**Angel Eyes**	196?	4.00	10.00
Columbia CL-2437	(M)	**My Favorite Things**	1966	6.00	15.00
Columbia CS-9237	(S)	**My Favorite Things**	1966	5.00	12.00
Columbia CL-2484	(M)	**Dave Brubeck's Greatest Hits**	1966	5.00	12.00
Columbia CS-9284	(S)	**Dave Brubeck's Greatest Hits**	1966	4.00	10.00
Columbia CL-2512	(M)	**Time In**	1966	6.00	15.00
Columbia CS-9312	(S)	**Time In**	1966	5.00	12.00
Columbia CL-2602	(M)	**Anything Goes! Dave Brubeck Quartet Plays Cole Porter**	1966	6.00	15.00
Columbia CS-9402	(S)	**Anything Goes! Dave Brubeck Quartet Plays Cole Porter**	1966	5.00	12.00
Columbia CL-2695	(M)	**Bravo! Brubeck!**	1967	8.00	20.00
Columbia CS-9495	(S)	**Bravo! Brubeck!**	1967	5.00	12.00
Columbia CL-2712	(M)	**Jackpot**	1967	8.00	20.00
Columbia CS-9512	(S)	**Jackpot**	1967	5.00	12.00
Columbia CL-2872	(M)	**The Last Time We Saw Paris**	1968	12.00	30.00
Columbia CS-9672	(S)	**The Last Time We Saw Paris**	1968	5.00	12.00
Columbia CS-9704	(S)	**Compadres**	1969	5.00	12.00
Columbia CS-9897	(S)	**Brubeck In Amsterdam**	1969	5.00	12.00

—Columbia albums above have "360 Sound" in white on the bottom of the label.—

BRUBECK, DAVE / J.J. JOHNSON & KAI WINDING

Columbia CL-932	(M)	**American Jazz Festival At Newport '56**	1956	20.00	50.00

—Columbia albums above have six white on black "eye" logos on each label.—

BRUCE, LENNY

Lenny Bruce is a monologuist who took much of his schtick from the rhythm and slang of the '50s jazz life.

Fantasy 7001	(M)	**Interviews Of Our Times** *(Dark red vinyl)*	1959	30.00	75.00
Fantasy 7003	(M)	**Sick Humor** *(Dark red vinyl)*	1959	30.00	75.00
Fantasy 7007	(M)	**I Am Not A Nut, Elect Me** *(Dark red vinyl)*	1960	30.00	75.00
Fantasy 7011	(M)	**Lenny Bruce, American** *(Dark red vinyl)*	1961	30.00	75.00

—Fantasy albums above have red labels on dark red, non-flexible vinyl.—

Label & Catalog #		*Title*	*Year*	*VG+*	*NM*
Fantasy 7001	*(M)*	**Interviews Of Our Times** *(Red vinyl)*	*196?*	16.00	40.00
Fantasy 7001	*(M)*	**Interviews Of Our Times**	*1959*	10.00	25.00
Fantasy 7003	*(M)*	**Sick Humor** *(Red vinyl)*	*196?*	16.00	40.00
Fantasy 7003	*(M)*	**Sick Humor Of Lenny Bruce**	*1959*	10.00	25.00
Fantasy 7007	*(M)*	**I Am Not A Nut, Elect Me** *(Red vinyl)*	*196?*	16.00	40.00
Fantasy 7007	*(M)*	**I Am Not A Nut, Elect Me**	*1960*	10.00	25.00
Fantasy 7011	*(M)*	**Lenny Bruce, American** *(Red vinyl)*	*196?*	16.00	40.00
Fantasy 7011	*(M)*	**Lenny Bruce, American**	*1962*	10.00	25.00
Fantasy 7012	*(M)*	**The Best Of Lenny Bruce** *(Red vinyl)*	*1962*	16.00	40.00
Fantasy 7012	*(M)*	**The Best Of Lenny Bruce**	*1962*	8.00	20.00

—Fantasy albums above have red labels on flexible vinyl.—

Philles PHLP-4010	*(M)*	**Lenny Bruce Is Out Again**	*1966*	30.00	75.00
Lenny Bruce LB-3001/2	*(M)*	**Lenny Bruce Is Out Again** *(LB 3001/2 has the same cover as Philles 4101 except Bruce's address is on the back cover and the LP has plain white labels.)*	*196?*	125.00	250.00
Lenny Bruce LB-9001/2	*(10")*	**Recordings Submitted As Evidence In The San Francisco Obscenity Trial In March, 1962**	*196?*	250.00	500.00
United Arts. UAL-3580	*(M)*	**Lenny Bruce/Midnight Concert**	*1967*	10.00	25.00
United Arts. UAS-6580	*(E)*	**Lenny Bruce/Midnight Concert**	*1967*	6.00	15.00
Douglas SD-788	*(M)*	**The Essential Lenny Bruce**	*1968*	6.00	15.00
Verve/Forecast FTS-3035	*(E)*	**Lenny Bruce**	*1968*	*Unreleased*	
Bizarre 2XS-6329	*(M)*	**The Berkeley Concert** *(2 LPs)*	*1969*	10.00	25.00
Douglas 2	*(M)*	**To Is A Preposition, Come Is A Verb**	*196?*	8.00	20.00

BRUEL, MAX

Swedish born Max Bruel is a modern jazz baritone saxophone player.

EmArcy MG-36062	*(M)*	**Cool Bruel**	*1955*	20.00	50.00

—EmArcy albums above have blue labels with silver print.—

BRUNIS, GEORG

George Brunies, aka Georg Brunis, is a traditional jazz trombone player and vocalist.

Commodore FL-20008	*(10")*	**King Of The Tailgate Trombone**	*1950*	30.00	75.00
Riverside RLP-1024	*(10")*	**Georg Brunis & The Original New Orleans Rhythm Kings**	*1954*	30.00	75.00
Jolly Roger 5024	*(10")*	**Georg Brunis & The New Orleans Rhythm Kings**	*1954*	20.00	50.00
Commodore DL-30015	*(M)*	**King Of The Tailgate Trombone**	*1959*	16.00	40.00
Jazzology	*(M)*	**Georg Brunis And His Rhythm Kings**	*196?*	6.00	15.00

BRYAN, JOY

Joy Bryan is a modern jazz based vocalist.

Mode LP-108	*(M)*	**Joy Bryan Sings**	*1957*	30.00	75.00
Contemporary M-3604	*(M)*	**Make The Man Love Me**	*1961*	16.00	40.00
Contemporary S-7604	*(S)*	**Make The Man Love Me**	*1961*	20.00	50.00

—Contemporary stereo albums above have gold on black labels.—

BRYANT, BOBBY

Vee Jay LP-3059	*(M)*	**Big Band Blues**	*1964*	8.00	20.00
Vee Jay LPS-3059	*(S)*	**Big Band Blues**	*1964*	8.00	20.00
World Pacific ST-20159	*(S)*	**The Jazz Excursion Into "Hair"**	*1969*	6.00	15.00

BRYANT, CLORA

Clora Bryant is a modern jazz trumpet player and vocalist.

Mode LP-106	*(M)*	**Gal With A Horn**	*1957*	30.00	75.00

BRYANT, PAUL

For additional listings refer to Curtis Amy & Paul Bryant; Johnny Griffin.

Pacific Jazz PJ-12	*(M)*	**Burnin'**	*1961*	16.00	40.00
Fantasy 3357	*(M)*	**Something's Happening**	*1963*	10.00	25.00
Fantasy 8357	*(S)*	**Something's Happening**	*1963*	8.00	20.00
Fantasy 3363	*(M)*	**Groove Time**	*1964*	10.00	25.00
Fantasy 8363	*(S)*	**Groove Time**	*1964*	8.00	20.00

BRYANT, RAY

Raphael "Ray" Bryant is a modern jazz pianist and composer. For additional listings refer to The Prestige Blues Swingers.

Epic LN-3202	*(M)*	**Meet Betty Carter And Ray Bryant**	*1955*	40.00	100.00
Epic LN-3279	*(M)*	**Ray Bryant Trio**	*1956*	30.00	75.00
Prestige PRLP-7098	*(M)*	**Ray Bryant Trio**	*1957*	30.00	75.00

—Prestige albums above have yellow labels with a W. 50th St, NYC address.—

Label & Catalog #		Title	Year	VG+	NM
New Jazz NJLP-8213	(M)	**Alone With The Blues**	1959	20.00	50.00
New Jazz NJLP-8227	(M)	**Ray Bryant Trio**	1959	20.00	50.00
		(New Jazz 8227 is a reissue of Prestige 7098.)			
		—New Jazz albums above have purple labels.—			
New Jazz NJLP-8213	(M)	**Alone With The Blues**	1965	10.00	25.00
New Jazz NJLP-8227	(M)	**Ray Bryant Trio**	1965	10.00	25.00
		—New Jazz albums above have blue labels with a trident logo on the right side.—			
Signature SM-6008	(M)	**Ray Bryant Plays**	1960	125.00	250.00
Signature SS-6008	(S)	**Ray Bryant Plays**	1960	100.00	200.00
Columbia CL-1449	(M)	**Little Susie**	1960	10.00	25.00
Columbia CS-8244	(S)	**Little Susie**	1960	8.00	20.00
Columbia CL-1476	(M)	**Madison Time**	1960	10.00	25.00
Columbia CS-8276	(S)	**Madison Time**	1960	12.00	30.00
Columbia CL-1633	(M)	**Con Alma**	1961	10.00	25.00
Columbia CS-8433	(S)	**Con Alma**	1961	8.00	20.00
Columbia CL-1746	(M)	**Dancing The Big Twist**	1962	10.00	25.00
Columbia CS-8546	(S)	**Dancing The Big Twist**	1962	8.00	20.00
		—Columbia albums above have six white on black "eye" logos on each label.—			
Columbia CL-1867	(M)	**Hollywood Jazz Beat**	1962	8.00	20.00
Columbia CS-8667	(S)	**Hollywood Jazz Beat**	1962	6.00	15.00
		—Columbia albums above have "Guaranteed High Fidelity" or "360 Sound Stereo" in black on the label.—			
Sue LP-1016	(M)	**Groove House**	1963	20.00	50.00
Sue SLP-1016	(S)	**Groove House**	1963	20.00	50.00
Sue LP-1019	(M)	**Live At Basin Street**	1964	20.00	50.00
Sue SLP-1019	(S)	**Live At Basin Street**	1964	20.00	50.00
Sue LP-1032	(M)	**Cold Turkey**	1964	20.00	50.00
Sue SLP-1032	(S)	**Cold Turkey**	1964	20.00	50.00
Sue LP-1036	(M)	**Ray Bryant Soul**	1964	20.00	50.00
Sue SLP-1036	(S)	**Ray Bryant Soul**	1964	20.00	50.00
Cadet LP-767	(M)	**Gotta Travel On**	1966	8.00	20.00
Cadet LPS-767	(S)	**Gotta Travel On**	1966	6.00	15.00
Cadet LP-778	(M)	**Lonesome Traveler**	1966	8.00	20.00
Cadet LPS-778	(S)	**Lonesome Traveler**	1966	6.00	15.00
Cadet LP-781	(M)	**Slow Freight**	1967	8.00	20.00
Cadet LPS-781	(S)	**Slow Freight**	1967	6.00	15.00
Cadet LP-793	(M)	**The Ray Bryant Touch**	1967	8.00	20.00
Cadet LPS-793	(S)	**The Ray Bryant Touch**	1967	6.00	15.00
Cadet LP-801	(M)	**Take A Bryant Step**	1967	8.00	20.00
Cadet LPS-801	(S)	**Take A Bryant Step**	1967	6.00	15.00
Cadet LPS-818	(S)	**Up Above The Rock**	1968	6.00	15.00
Cadet LPS-830	(S)	**Sound Ray**	1969	6.00	15.00

BRYANT, RUSTY

Rusty Bryant is a traditional jazz based tenor and alto saxophone player.

Dot DLP-3006	(M)	**All Night Long**	1956	16.00	40.00
Dot DLP-3079	(M)	**Rusty Bryant Plays Jazz**	1957	16.00	40.00
Dot DLP-3353	(M)	**America's Greatest Jazz**	1961	8.00	20.00
Dot DLP-25353	(S)	**America's Greatest Jazz**	1961	6.00	15.00

BUCKNER, MILT

Milton Buckner is a traditional jazz piano, organ and vibraphone player and arranger.

Savoy MG-15023	(10")	**Milt Buckner Piano**	1953	40.00	100.00
Capitol T-642	(M)	**Rockin' With Milt**	1955	16.00	40.00
Capitol T-722	(M)	**Rockin' Hammond**	1956	16.00	40.00
Capitol T-938	(M)	**Send Me Softly**	1958	16.00	40.00
		—Capitol albums above have turquoise labels.—			
Argo LP-660	(M)	**Mighty High**	1960	8.00	20.00
Argo LPS-660	(S)	**Mighty High**	1960	6.00	15.00
Argo LP-670	(M)	**Please, Mr. Organ Player**	1961	8.00	20.00
Argo LPS-670	(S)	**Please, Mr. Organ Player**	1961	6.00	15.00
Argo LP-702	(M)	**Midnight Mood**	1962	8.00	20.00
Argo LPS-702	(S)	**Midnight Mood**	1962	6.00	15.00
Bethlehem BCP-6072	(M)	**The New World Of Milt Buckner**	1961	12.00	30.00
Prestige PRST-7668	(S)	**Milt Buckner In Europe**	1969	6.00	15.00
		—Prestige albums above have blue labels with a trident logo on top.—			

BUCKNER, TEDDY

John "Teddy" Buckner is a traditional jazz trumpet and flugel horn player and vocalist.

Gene Norman GNP-11	(M)	**Teddy Buckner**	1955	16.00	40.00

Label & Catalog #		*Title*	*Year*	*VG+*	*NM*
Dixieland Jubilee DJ-503	*(M)*	**In Concert At The Dixieland Jubilee**	*1956*	**16.00**	**40.00**
Dixieland Jubilee DJ-504	*(M)*	**Teddy Buckner And His Dixieland Band**	*1956*	**16.00**	**40.00**
Dixieland Jubilee DJ-505	*(M)*	**A Salute To Louis Armstrong**	*1956*	**16.00**	**40.00**
BUDIMIR, DENNIS					
Mainstream 56659	*(M)*	**Creeper**	*1966*	**10.00**	**25.00**
Mainstream S-6659	*(S)*	**Creeper**	*1966*	**8.00**	**20.00**
Revelation REV-M1	*(M)*	**Alone Together**	*1968*	**10.00**	**25.00**
Revelation REV-1	*(S)*	**Alone Together**	*1968*	**8.00**	**20.00**
Revelation REV-4	*(S)*	**A Second Coming**	*1968*	**8.00**	**20.00**
Revelation REV-9	*(S)*	**Sprung Free**	*1969*	**8.00**	**20.00**
BUNKER, LARRY					
Vault LP-9005	*(M)*	**Live At Shelly's Manne-Hole**	*1966*	**8.00**	**20.00**
Vault LPS-9005	*(S)*	**Live At Shelly's Manne-Hole**	*1966*	**6.00**	**15.00**
		(Vault 9005 also features Gary Burton.)			
BURGER, JACK					
Jack Burger is a modern jazz drummer and bongo player.					
Hifijazz J-804	*(M)*	**The End On Bongos**	*1962*	**16.00**	**40.00**
Hifijazz JS-804	*(S)*	**The End On Bongos**	*1962*	**12.00**	**30.00**
BURKE, RAY					
Raymond Barrois, aka Ray Burke, is a traditional jazz clarinet and saxophone(s) player.					
Southland SLP-209	*(10")*	**Contemporary New Orleans Jazz**	*1955*	**20.00**	**50.00**
BURKE, VINNIE					
Vincent Bucci, aka Vinnie Burke, is a modern jazz bass player. For additional listings refer to Eddie Costa & Vinnie Burke; Oscar Pettiford / Vinnie Burke; Bucky Pizzareli & Vinnie Burke.					
Bethlehem BCP-1010	*(10")*	**East Coast Jazz 2**	*1954*	**50.00**	**100.00**
ABC-Paramount ABC-139	*(M)*	**The Vinnie Burke All Stars**	*1956*	**20.00**	**50.00**
ABC-Paramount ABC-170	*(M)*	**The Vinnie Burke String Jazz Quartet**	*1957*	**20.00**	**50.00**
BURNS, RALPH					
Ralph Burns is a modern jazz pianist, arranger and composer. For additional listings refer to Fran Jeffries; Beverley Kenney; Sonny Stitt; Mary Lou Williams / Ralph Burns.					
Mercury MGC-115	*(10")*	**Free Forms**	*1952*	**100.00**	**200.00**
		(Mercury 115 features cover art by David Stone Martin.)			
Clef MGC-115	*(10")*	**Free Forms**	*1953*	**60.00**	**150.00**
Norgran MGN-1028	*(M)*	**Ralph Burns Among The JATP's**	*1955*	**40.00**	**100.00**
		(Norgran 1028 features cover art by David Stone Martin.)			
Verve MGV-8121	*(M)*	**Ralph Burns Among The JATP's**	*1957*	**20.00**	**50.00**
— Verve albums above have black labels with "Verve Records, Inc." on the bottom.—					
Verve V-8121	*(M)*	**Ralph Burns Among The JATP's**	*196?*	**8.00**	**20.00**
— Verve albums above have black labels with "MGM Records" on the bottom.—					
Period SPL-1105	*(10")*	**Spring Sequence**	*1955*	**40.00**	**100.00**
Period SPL-1109	*(10")*	**Bijou**	*1955*	**40.00**	**100.00**
Jazztone J-1228	*(M)*	**Spring Sequence**	*1956*	**20.00**	**50.00**
		(Jazztone 1228 is a reissue of Period 1105.)			
Bethlehem BCP-68	*(M)*	**Bijou**	*1957*	**20.00**	**50.00**
		(Bethlehem 68 is a reissue of Period 1109.)			
Decca DL-8235	*(M)*	**Jazz Studio 5**	*1956*	**30.00**	**75.00**
Decca DL-8555	*(M)*	**The Masters Revisited**	*1957*	**20.00**	**50.00**
Decca DL-9068	*(M)*	**New York's A Song**	*1959*	**20.00**	**50.00**
Decca DL-79068	*(S)*	**New York's A Song**	*1959*	**16.00**	**40.00**
Decca DL-9207	*(M)*	**Very Warm For Jazz**	*1959*	**20.00**	**50.00**
Decca DL-79207	*(S)*	**Very Warm For Jazz**	*1959*	**16.00**	**40.00**
Decca DL-9215	*(M)*	**Porgy And Bess**	*1959*	**16.00**	**40.00**
Decca DL-79215	*(S)*	**Porgy And Bess**	*1959*	**12.00**	**30.00**
MGM E-3616	*(M)*	**The Swinging Seasons**	*1958*	**20.00**	**50.00**
MGM SE-3616	*(S)*	**The Swinging Seasons**	*1958*	**16.00**	**40.00**
Warwick W-5001	*(M)*	**Where There's Burns There's Fire**	*1961*	**20.00**	**50.00**
Warwick W-5001ST	*(S)*	**Where There's Burns There's Fire**	*1961*	**16.00**	**40.00**
BURNS, RALPH / BILLIE HOLIDAY					
Clef MGC-718	*(M)*	**The Free Forms Of Ralph Burns/ The Songs Of Billie Holiday**	*1956*	**40.00**	**100.00**
		(Clef 718 is a reissue of 115 and 169, "Jazz At The Philharmonic.")			

Label & Catalog #		Title	Year	VG+	NM
Verve MGV-8098	(M)	**Jazz Recital**	1957	20.00	50.00
		(Verve 8098 is a reissue of Clef 718.)			
— Verve albums above have black labels with "Verve Records, Inc." on the bottom.—					
Verve V-8098	(M)	**Jazz Recital**	196?	8.00	20.00
— Verve albums above have black labels with "MGM Records" on the bottom.—					
BURNS, ROY					
Roulette R-52095	(M)	**Skin Burns**	1963	10.00	25.00
Roulette SR-52095	(S)	**Skin Burns**	1963	8.00	20.00
BURRELL, DAVE					
Douglas SD-798	(S)	**High**	1969	6.00	15.00
BURRELL, KENNY					
Kenneth Burrell is a modern jazz guitar player. For additional listings refer to Donald Byrd, Hank Mobley & Kenny Burrell; Coleman Hawkins; John Jenkins; Billie Poole; Shirley Scott; Ed Thigpen; Frank Wess & Kenny Burrell; Kai Winding; and the Various Artists section under Bethlehem, New Jazz, Prestige, and Savoy.					
Blue Note BLP-1523	(M)	**Introducing Kenny Burrell** *(Deep groove)*	1956	100.00	200.00
Blue Note BLP-1523	(M)	**Introducing Kenny Burrell**	1956	60.00	150.00
Blue Note BLP-1543	(M)	**Kenny Burrell, Volume 2** *(Deep groove)*	1957	100.00	200.00
Blue Note BLP-1543	(M)	**Kenny Burrell, Volume 2**	1957	60.00	150.00
		(Blue Note 1543 features cover art by Andy Warhol.)			
— Blue Note albums above have blue on white labels with a Lexington Ave., NYC address.—					
Blue Note BLP-1523	(M)	**Introducing Kenny Burrell**	1957	20.00	50.00
Blue Note BLP-1543	(M)	**Kenny Burrell, Volume 2**	1957	20.00	50.00
Blue Note BLP-1596	(M)	**Blue Lights, Volume 1** *(Deep groove)*	1958	50.00	125.00
Blue Note BLP-1596	(M)	**Blue Lights, Volume 1**	1958	30.00	75.00
Blue Note BST-1596	(S)	**Blue Lights, Volume 1** *(Deep groove)*	1959	30.00	75.00
Blue Note BST-1596	(S)	**Blue Lights, Volume 1**	1959	20.00	50.00
Blue Note BLP-1597	(M)	**Blue Lights, Volume 2** *(Deep groove)*	1958	50.00	125.00
Blue Note BLP-1597	(M)	**Blue Lights, Volume 2**	1958	30.00	75.00
Blue Note BST-1597	(S)	**Blue Lights, Volume 2** *(Deep groove)*	1959	30.00	75.00
Blue Note BST-1597	(S)	**Blue Lights, Volume 2**	1959	20.00	50.00
		(Blue Note 1596 and 1597 feature cover art by Andy Warhol.)			
Blue Note BLP-4021	(M)	**On View At The Five Spot Cafe** *(Deep groove)*	1960	50.00	125.00
Blue Note BLP-4021	(M)	**On View At The Five Spot Cafe**	1960	30.00	75.00
Blue Note BST-84021	(S)	**On View At The Five Spot Cafe**	1960	20.00	50.00
— Blue Note albums above have blue & white labels with a W. 63rd St., NYC address.—					
Blue Note BLP-1523	(M)	**Introducing Kenny Burrell**	1963	10.00	25.00
Blue Note BLP-1543	(M)	**Kenny Burrell, Volume 2**	1963	10.00	25.00
Blue Note BLP-1596	(M)	**Blue Lights, Volume 1**	1963	10.00	25.00
Blue Note BST-1596	(S)	**Blue Lights, Volume 1**	1963	8.00	20.00
Blue Note BLP-1597	(M)	**Blue Lights, Volume 2**	1963	10.00	25.00
Blue Note BST-1597	(S)	**Blue Lights, Volume 2**	1963	8.00	20.00
Blue Note BLP-4021	(M)	**On View At The Five Spot Cafe**	1963	10.00	25.00
Blue Note BST-84021	(S)	**On View At The Five Spot Cafe**	1963	8.00	20.00
Blue Note BLP-4123	(M)	**Midnight Blue**	1963	16.00	40.00
Blue Note BST-84123	(S)	**Midnight Blue**	1963	12.00	30.00
— Blue Note albums above have blue on white labels with a New York, USA address.—					
Blue Note BST-81523	(E)	**Introducing Kenny Burrell**	196?	4.00	10.00
Blue Note BST-81543	(E)	**Kenny Burrell, Volume 2**	196?	4.00	10.00
Blue Note BST-81596	(S)	**Blue Lights, Volume 1**	196?	5.00	12.00
Blue Note BST-81597	(S)	**Blue Lights, Volume 2**	196?	5.00	12.00
Blue Note BST-84021	(S)	**On View At The Five Spot Cafe**	196?	5.00	12.00
Blue Note BST-84123	(S)	**Midnight Blue**	196?	5.00	12.00
— Blue Note albums above have blue on white labels with "A Division of Liberty Records."—					
Prestige PRLP-7088	(M)	**Kenny Burrell**	1957	30.00	75.00
— Prestige albums above have yellow labels with a W. 50th St, NYC address.—					
Argo LP-655	(M)	**Night At The Vanguard**	1959	16.00	40.00
Argo LPS-655	(S)	**Night At The Vanguard**	1959	12.00	30.00
Columbia CL-1703	(M)	**Weaver Of Dreams**	1961	10.00	25.00
Columbia CS-8503	(S)	**Weaver Of Dreams**	1961	8.00	20.00
— Columbia albums above have six white on black "eye" logos on each label.—					
Kapp KL-1326	(M)	**Lotsa Bossa Nova**	1962	10.00	25.00
Kapp KS-3326	(S)	**Lotsa Bossa Nova**	1962	8.00	20.00
New Jazz NJLP-8276	(M)	**Kenny Burrell With John Coltrane**	1962	24.00	60.00
— New Jazz albums above have purple labels.—					
New Jazz NJLP-8276	(M)	**Kenny Burrell With John Coltrane**	1965	10.00	25.00
— New Jazz albums above have blue labels with a trident logo on the right side.—					

Label & Catalog #		Title	Year	VG+	NM
Moodsville MVLP-29	(M)	**Bluesy Burrell**	1963	20.00	50.00
Moodsville MVST-29	(S)	**Bluesy Burrell**	1963	16.00	40.00
		(Moodsville 29 also features Coleman Hawkins.)			
		—Moodsville mono albums above have green labels with silver print.—			
Moodsville MVLP-29	(M)	**Bluesy Burrell**	1965	10.00	25.00
Moodsville MVST-29	(S)	**Bluesy Burrell**	1965	8.00	20.00
		—Moodsville albums above have blue labels with a trident logo on the right side.—			
Prestige PRLP-7277	(M)	**All Day Long**	1963	20.00	50.00
Prestige PRST-7277	(E)	**All Day Long**	1963	14.00	35.00
		(Prestige 7277 is a reissue of 7081, a various artists album.)			
Prestige PRLP-7289	(M)	**All Night Long**	1964	20.00	50.00
Prestige PRST-7289	(E)	**All Night Long**	1964	14.00	35.00
		(Prestige 7289 is a reissue of 7073, a various artists album.)			
		—Prestige albums above have yellow mono or silver stereo labels with a Bergenfield, NJ address.—			
Prestige PRLP-7308	(M)	**Blue Moods**	1964	12.00	30.00
Prestige PRST-7308	(S)	**Blue Moods**	1964	10.00	25.00
		(Prestige 7308 is a reissue of 7088.)			
Prestige PRLP-7315	(M)	**Soul Call**	1964	12.00	30.00
Prestige PRST-7315	(S)	**Soul Call**	1964	10.00	25.00
Prestige PRLP-7347	(M)	**Crash**	1964	12.00	30.00
Prestige PRST-7347	(S)	**Crash**	1964	10.00	25.00
		(Prestige 7347 also features Jack McDuff.)			
Prestige PRLP-7448	(M)	**The Best Of Kenny Burrell**	1967	12.00	30.00
Prestige PRST-7448	(S)	**The Best Of Kenny Burrell**	1967	10.00	20.00
Prestige PRLP-7532	(M)	**Kenny Burrell Quintet With John Coltrane**	1967	12.00	30.00
Prestige PRST-7532	(E)	**Kenny Burrell Quintet With John Coltrane**	1967	8.00	20.00
		(Prestige 7532 is a reissue of New Jazz 8276.)			
		—Prestige albums above have blue labels with a trident logo on the right side.—			
Prestige PRST-7578	(E)	**Out Of This World**	1968	6.00	15.00
		(Prestige 7578 is a reissue of Moodsville 29.)			
		—Prestige albums above have blue labels with a trident logo on top.—			
Verve V-8553	(M)	**Blue Bash**	1963	8.00	20.00
Verve V6-8553	(S)	**Blue Bash**	1963	6.00	15.00
		(Verve 8553 also features Jimmy Smith.)			
Verve V-8612	(M)	**Guitar Forms**	1965	8.00	20.00
Verve V6-8612	(S)	**Guitar Forms**	1965	6.00	15.00
Verve V-8656	(M)	**A Generation Ago Today**	1966	10.00	25.00
Verve V6-8656	(S)	**A Generation Ago Today**	1966	8.00	20.00
Verve V-8746	(M)	**Blues—The Common Ground**	1968	8.00	20.00
Verve V6-8746	(S)	**Blues—The Common Ground**	1968	6.00	15.00
Verve V-8751	(M)	**Night Song**	1968	8.00	20.00
Verve V6-8751	(S)	**Night Song**	1968	6.00	15.00
Verve V6-8773	(S)	**Asphalt Canyon Suite**	1969	4.00	10.00
		—Verve albums above have black labels with "MGM Records" on the bottom.—			
Cadet LP-769	(M)	**Man At Work**	1965	8.00	20.00
Cadet LPS-769	(S)	**Man At Work**	1965	6.00	15.00
		(Cadet 769 is a reissue of Argo 655.)			
Cadet LP-772	(M)	**The Tender Gender**	1966	8.00	20.00
Cadet LPS-772	(S)	**The Tender Gender**	1966	6.00	15.00
Cadet LP-779	(M)	**Have Yourself A Soulful Little Christmas**	1966	8.00	20.00
Cadet LPS-779	(S)	**Have Yourself A Soulful Little Christmas**	1966	6.00	15.00
Cadet LP-798	(M)	**Ode To 52nd Street**	1967	8.00	20.00
Cadet LPS-798	(S)	**Ode To 52nd Street**	1967	6.00	15.00

BURRELL, KENNY / TINY GRIMES / BILL JENNINGS

Status ST-8318	(M)	**Guitar Soul**	1965	16.00	40.00

BURRELL, KENNY, & JIMMY RANEY

Prestige PRLP-7119	(M)	**Two Guitars**	1957	30.00	75.00
		—Prestige albums above have yellow labels with a W. 50th St., NYC address.—			

BURTON, GARY

Gary Burton is a modern jazz vibraphonist. For additional listings refer to Larry Bunker; Hank Garland.

RCA Victor LPM-2420	(M)	**New Vibe Man In Town**	1961	10.00	25.00
RCA Victor LSP-2420	(S)	**New Vibe Man In Town**	1961	8.00	20.00
RCA Victor LPM-2665	(M)	**Who Is Gary Burton?**	1963	10.00	25.00
RCA Victor LSP-2665	(S)	**Who Is Gary Burton?**	1963	8.00	20.00
		—RCA albums above have black labels with "Long Play" or "Living Stereo" on the bottom.—			

Label & Catalog #		Title	Year	VG+	NM
RCA Victor LPM-2880	(M)	**Something's Coming**	1964	8.00	20.00
RCA Victor LSP-2880	(S)	**Something's Coming**	1964	6.00	15.00
—RCA albums above have black labels with "Mono" or "Living Stereo" on the bottom.—					
RCA Victor LPM-3360	(M)	**The Groovy Sound Of Music**	1965	6.00	15.00
RCA Victor LSP-3360	(S)	**The Groovy Sound Of Music**	1965	5.00	12.00
RCA Victor LPM-3642	(M)	**The Time Machine**	1966	6.00	15.00
RCA Victor LSP-3642	(S)	**The Time Machine**	1966	5.00	12.00
RCA Victor LPM-3719	(M)	**Tennessee Firebird**	1966	6.00	15.00
RCA Victor LSP-3719	(S)	**Tennessee Firebird**	1966	5.00	12.00
RCA Victor LPM-3835	(M)	**Duster**	1967	8.00	20.00
RCA Victor LSP-3835	(S)	**Duster**	1967	5.00	12.00
RCA Victor LPM-3901	(M)	**Lofty Fake Anagram**	1967	8.00	20.00
RCA Victor LSP-3901	(S)	**Lofty Fake Anagram**	1967	5.00	12.00
RCA Victor LPM-3985	(M)	**Gary Burton In Concert**	1968	12.00	30.00
RCA Victor LSP-3985	(S)	**Gary Burton In Concert**	1968	5.00	12.00
RCA Victor LPM-3988	(M)	**A Genuine Young Funeral**	1968	12.00	30.00
RCA Victor LSP-3988	(S)	**A Genuine Young Funeral**	1968	5.00	12.00
—RCA albums above have black labels with "Monaural" or "Stereo" on the bottom.—					
RCA Victor LPM-4098	(S)	**Country Roads And Other Places**	1969	4.00	10.00
—RCA albums above have orange labels on non-flexible vinyl.—					
Atlantic SD-1531	(S)	**Throb**	1969	4.00	10.00

BURTON, GARY / SONNY ROLLINS / CLARK TERRY

RCA Victor LPM-2725	(M)	**3 In Jazz** *(Sampler)*	1963	8.00	20.00
RCA Victor LSP-2725	(S)	**3 In Jazz** *(Sampler)*	1963	6.00	15.00

BURTON, JOE

Joseph Burton is a traditional jazz based pianist.

Regent MG-6036	(M)	**Jazz Pretty**	1957	20.00	50.00
Coral CRL-57098	(M)	**Joe Burton Session**	1957	16.00	40.00
Coral CRL-57175	(M)	**Here I Am In Love Again**	1958	16.00	40.00
Coral CRL-757175	(S)	**Here I Am In Love Again**	1959	12.00	30.00
Joday J-1000	(M)	**The Subtle Sound Of Joe Burton**	1963	8.00	20.00
Joday JS-1000	(S)	**The Subtle Sound Of Joe Burton**	1963	6.00	15.00

BUSHKIN, JOE

Joseph Bushkin is a traditional jazz based piano and trumpet player and composer. For additional listings refer to Lennie Tristano / Joe Bushkin / Bobby Scott / Marian McPartland; Lee Wiley.

Atlantic ALR-108	(10")	**I Love A Piano**	1950	20.00	50.00
Columbia CL-6152	(10")	**Piano Moods**	1950	20.00	50.00
Columbia CL-6201	(10")	**After Hours**	1950	20.00	50.00
Royale 18118	(10")	**Joe Bushkin**	195?	20.00	50.00
Epic LN-3345	(M)	**Piano After Midnight**	1956	12.00	30.00
Capitol T-759	(M)	**Skylight Rhapsody**	1956	16.00	40.00
Capitol T-832	(M)	**A Fellow Needs A Girl**	1957	16.00	40.00
Capitol T-911	(M)	**Bushkin Spotlights Berlin**	1958	16.00	40.00
— Capitol albums above have turquoise labels.—					
Decca DL-4731	(M)	**Night Sounds Of San Francisco**	1965	6.00	15.00
Decca DL-74731	(S)	**Night Sounds Of San Francisco**	1965	5.00	12.00

BUTLER, BILLY

William Bulter is a modern jazz guitar player.

Prestige PRST-7622	(S)	**This Is Billy Butler!**	1969	10.00	25.00
Prestige PRST-7734	(S)	**Guitar Soul**	1969	10.00	25.00
—Prestige albums above have blue labels with a trident logo on top.—					

BUTLER, FRANK: *Refer to* CURTIS AMY; RED MITCHELL

BUTTERFIELD, BILLY

Charles William "Billy" Butterfield is a traditional jazz trumpet player. For additional listings refer to Bobby Hackett & Billy Butterfield & Luiz Henrique; The Dixie Stompers.

Capitol H-201	(10")	**Stardusting**	1950	20.00	50.00
Capitol H-424	(10")	**Classics In Jazz**	1953	20.00	50.00
Essex ESLP-111	(10")	**Far Away Places**	1954	20.00	50.00
Westminster WL-3020	(10")	**Billy Butterfield**	1954	20.00	50.00
Westminster WL-6006	(M)	**Dancing For Two In Love**	195?	16.00	40.00
Essex 401	(M)	**Billy Butterfield At Princeton**	1955	16.00	40.00
Essex 402	(M)	**Billy Butterfield Goes To N.Y.U.**	1955	16.00	40.00
Essex 403	(M)	**Billy Butterfield At Amherst**	1955	16.00	40.00

Label & Catalog #		Title	Year	VG+	NM
Essex 404	(M)	**Billy Butterfield At Rutgers**	1955	16.00	40.00
RCA Victor LPM-1212	(M)	**New York Land Dixie**	1956	16.00	40.00
RCA Victor LPM-1441	(M)	**They're Playing Our Song**	1957	16.00	40.00

—RCA albums above have black labels with "Long Play" on the bottom.—

Epic LA-12026	(M)	**Billy Plays Bix**	1962	16.00	40.00
Epic BA-16026	(S)	**Billy Plays Bix**	1962	12.00	30.00

BUTTERFIELD, ERSKINE

Erskine Butterfield is a traditional jazz pianist and composer.

Davis JD-104	(M)	**Piano Cocktail**	1951	16.00	40.00

BYARD, JAKI

John "Jaki" Byard is a modern jazz pianist.

New Jazz NJLP-8256	(M)	**Here's Jaki**	1961	20.00	50.00
New Jazz NJLP-8273	(M)	**Hi-Fly**	1962	20.00	50.00

—New Jazz albums above have purple labels.—

New Jazz NJLP-8256	(M)	**Here's Jaki**	1965	10.00	25.00
New Jazz NJLP-8273	(M)	**Hi-Fly**	1965	10.00	25.00

—New Jazz albums above have blue labels with a trident logo on the right side.—

Prestige PRLP-7397	(M)	**Out Front**	1965	10.00	25.00
Prestige PRST-7397	(S)	**Out Front**	1965	8.00	20.00
Prestige PRLP-7419	(M)	**Live! At Lennie's—Volume 1**	1966	10.00	25.00
Prestige PRST-7419	(S)	**Live! At Lennie's—Volume 1**	1966	8.00	20.00
Prestige PRLP-7463	(M)	**Freedom Together**	1967	10.00	25.00
Prestige PRST-7463	(S)	**Freedom Together**	1967	8.00	20.00
Prestige PRLP-7477	(M)	**Live! At Lennie's—Volume 2**	1967	10.00	25.00
Prestige PRST-7477	(S)	**Live! At Lennie's—Volume 2**	1967	8.00	20.00
Prestige PRLP-7524	(M)	**On The Spot**	1967	10.00	25.00
Prestige PRST-7524	(S)	**On The Spot**	1967	8.00	20.00

—Prestige albums above have blue labels with a trident logo on the right side.—

Prestige PRST-7550	(S)	**The Sunshine Of My Soul**	1968	6.00	15.00

(Prestige 7550 also features Elvin Jones.)

Prestige PRST-7573	(S)	**Jaki Byard With Strings!**	1968	6.00	15.00
Prestige PRST-7615	(S)	**The Jaki Byard Experience**	1969	6.00	15.00
Prestige PRST-7686	(S)	**Solo Piano**	1969	6.00	15.00

—Prestige albums above have blue labels with a trident logo on the right side.—

BYAS, DON

"Don" Carlos Byas is a traditional jazz tenor saxophone player. For additional listings refer to Mary Lou Williams & Don Byas.

Dial LP-216	(10")	**Tenor Saxophone Concerto**	1951	150.00	300.00
Atlantic ALR-117	(10")	**Don Byas Solos**	1952	100.00	200.00
Savoy MG-9007	(10")	**Don Byas Sax**	1952	60.00	150.00
Savoy MG-15043	(10")	**Tenor Sax Solos**	1955	50.00	125.00
Norgran MGN-12	(10")	**In France 'Don Byas Et Ses Rhythmes'**	1954	50.00	125.00
EmArcy MG-26026	(10")	**Don Byas Sax**	1954	50.00	125.00
Discovery 3022	(10")	**Don Byas With Beryl Booker**	1954	60.00	150.00
Seeco SLP-35	(10")	**Don Byas Favorites**	1955	50.00	125.00
Regent MG-6044	(M)	**Jazz—Free And Easy**	1957	30.00	75.00
Battle B-6121	(M)	**April In Paris**	1963	16.00	40.00
Battle BS-6121	(S)	**April In Paris**	1963	12.00	30.00
Savoy MG-12203	(S)	**Jazz: Free And Easy**	1969	8.00	20.00

(Savoy 12203 is a reissue of Regent 6044.)

Prestige PRST-7692	(S)	**Don Byas Meets Ben Webster**	1969	6.00	15.00

—Prestige albums above have blue labels with a trident logo on top.—

BYAS, DON / BERNARD PEIFFER

Clef MGC-748	(M)	**Jazz From Saint-Germain Des Pres**	1956	*Unreleased*	
Verve MGV-8119	(M)	**Jazz From Saint-Germain Des Pres**	1957	20.00	50.00

(Verve 8119 features cover art by David Stone Martin.)

—Verve albums above have black labels with "Verve Records, Inc." on the bottom.—

Verve V-8119	(M)	**Jazz From Saint-Germain Des Pres**	196?	8.00	20.00

—Verve albums above have black labels with "MGM Records" on the bottom.—

BYERS, BILLY

William Byers is a modern jazz trombone player. For additional listings refer to Eddie Bert / Billy Byers.

RCA Victor LPM-1269	(M)	**The Jazz Workshop**	1956	30.00	75.00

—RCA albums above have black labels with "Long Play" on the bottom.—

Concert Hall Jazz 1217	(M)	**Byers' Guide**	1955	20.00	50.00

Label & Catalog #		Title	Year	VG+	NM
BYRD, CHARLIE					
Charles Byrd is a jazz-based guitarist and composer. For additional listings refer to Stan Getz.					
Savoy MG-12099	(M)	**Jazz Recital**	1957	16.00	40.00
Savoy MG-12116	(M)	**Blues For Night People**	1957	16.00	40.00
Offbeat OLB-3001	(M)	**Jazz At The Show Boat, Volume 1**	1959	12.00	30.00
Offbeat OS-93001	(S)	**Jazz At The Show Boat, Volume 1**	1959	10.00	25.00
Offbeat OLB-3005	(M)	**Jazz At The Show Boat, Volume 2**	1959	12.00	30.00
Offbeat OS-93005	(S)	**Jazz At The Show Boat, Volume 2**	1959	10.00	25.00
Offbeat OLB-3006	(M)	**Jazz At The Show Boat, Volume 3**	1959	12.00	30.00
Offbeat OS-93006	(S)	**Jazz At The Show Boat, Volume 3**	1959	10.00	25.00
Offbeat OLB-3007	(M)	**Charlie's Choice**	1960	12.00	30.00
Offbeat OS-93007	(S)	**Charlie's Choice**	1960	10.00	25.00
Riverside RM-427	(M)	**Latin Impressions**	1962	12.00	30.00
Riverside RS-9427	(S)	**Latin Impressions**	1962	10.00	25.00
Riverside RM-436	(M)	**Bossa Nova Pelos Passaros**	1962	12.00	30.00
Riverside RS-9436	(S)	**Bossa Nova Pelos Passaros**	1962	10.00	25.00
Riverside RM-448	(M)	**Byrd's Word**	1963	12.00	30.00
Riverside RS-9448	(S)	**Byrd's Word**	1963	10.00	25.00
Riverside RM-449	(M)	**Byrd In The Wind**	1963	12.00	30.00
Riverside RS-9449	(S)	**Byrd In The Wind**	1963	10.00	25.00
Riverside RM-450	(M)	**Mr. Guitar**	1963	12.00	30.00
Riverside RS-9450	(S)	**Mr. Guitar**	1963	10.00	25.00
Riverside RM-451	(M)	**The Guitar Artistry Of Charlie Byrd**	1963	12.00	30.00
Riverside RS-9451	(S)	**The Guitar Artistry Of Charlie Byrd**	1963	10.00	25.00
Riverside RM-452	(M)	**Charlie Byrd At The Village Vanguard**	1963	12.00	30.00
Riverside RS-9452	(S)	**Charlie Byrd At The Village Vanguard**	1963	10.00	25.00
Riverside RM-453	(M)	**Blues Sonata**	1963	12.00	30.00
Riverside RS-9453	(S)	**Blues Sonata**	1963	10.00	25.00
Riverside RM-454	(M)	**Once More! Bossa Nova**	1963	12.00	30.00
Riverside RS-9454	(S)	**Once More! Bossa Nova**	1963	10.00	25.00
Riverside RM-467	(M)	**Byrd At The Gate**	1963	12.00	30.00
Riverside RS-9467	(S)	**Byrd At The Gate**	1963	10.00	25.00
—Riverside albums above have blue mono or black stereo labels with a reel & mike logo on top.—					
Riverside RM-481	(M)	**Byrd Song**	1966	8.00	20.00
Riverside RS-9481	(S)	**Byrd Song**	1966	6.00	15.00
Riverside RM-498	(M)	**Solo Flight**	1967	8.00	20.00
Riverside RS-9498	(S)	**Solo Flight**	1967	6.00	15.00
—Riverside albums above blue labels with "Orpheum Productions" on the bottom.—					
Riverside RS-3005	(S)	**The Guitar Artistry Of Charlie Byrd**	1968	5.00	12.00
Riverside RS-3044	(S)	**Byrd Man With Strings**	1969	5.00	12.00
Columbia CL-2337	(M)	**Brazilian Byrd**	1965	8.00	20.00
Columbia CS-9137	(S)	**Brazilian Byrd**	1965	6.00	15.00
—Columbia albums above have "Guaranteed High Fidelity" or "360 Sound Stereo" in black on the label.—					
Columbia CL-2337	(M)	**Brazilian Byrd**	1965	5.00	12.00
Columbia CS-9137	(S)	**Brazilian Byrd**	1965	4.00	10.00
Columbia CL-2435	(M)	**Travelin' Man Recorded Live**	1966	6.00	15.00
Columbia CS-9235	(S)	**Travelin' Man Recorded Live**	1966	5.00	12.00
Columbia CL-2477	(M)	**Hit Trip**	1966	6.00	15.00
Columbia CS-9277	(S)	**Hit Trip**	1966	5.00	12.00
Columbia CL-2504	(M)	**A Touch Of Gold**	1966	6.00	15.00
Columbia CS-9304	(S)	**A Touch Of Gold**	1966	5.00	12.00
Columbia CL-2555	(M)	**Christmas Cards For Solo Guitar**	1966	8.00	20.00
Columbia CS-9355	(S)	**Christmas Cards For Solo Guitar**	1966	6.00	15.00
Columbia CL-2592	(M)	**Byrdland**	1967	6.00	15.00
Columbia CS-9392	(S)	**Byrdland**	1967	5.00	12.00
Columbia CL-2652	(M)	**Hollywood Byrd**	1967	6.00	15.00
Columbia CS-9452	(S)	**Hollywood Byrd**	1967	5.00	12.00
Columbia CL-2692	(M)	**More Brazilian Byrd**	1967	6.00	15.00
Columbia CS-9492	(S)	**More Brazilian Byrd**	1967	5.00	12.00
Columbia CL-2782	(M)	**Music For "Villa Lobos"**	1968	8.00	20.00
Columbia CS-9582	(S)	**Music For "Villa Lobos"**	1968	5.00	12.00
Columbia CS-9667	(S)	**Delicately**	1968	5.00	12.00
Columbia CS-9747	(S)	**The Great Byrd**	1969	5.00	12.00
Columbia CS-9709	(S)	**The Greatest Hits Of The '60s**	1969	5.00	12.00
—Columbia albums above have "360 Sound" in white on the bottom of the label.—					

Label & Catalog #		Title	Year	VG+	NM

BYRD, DONALD

Donald Byrd is a modern jazz trumpet and flugel horn player. For additional listings refer to Pepper Adams; Kenny Drew & Donald Byrd & Hank Mobley; Art Farmer; Red Garland; Gigi Gryce & Donald Byrd; John Jenkins; Jackie McLean; Hank Mobley; Ernie Wilkins; Phil Woods; and the Various Artists section under Bethlehem and Prestige.

Label & Catalog #		Title	Year	VG+	NM
Transition TRLP-4	(M)	**Byrd's Eye View**	1956	300.00	600.00
		(Transition 4 was issued with a booklet, worth an additional $50.)			
Transition TRLP-5	(M)	**Byrd Jazz**	1956	300.00	600.00
		(Transition 5 was issued with a booklet, worth an additional $50.)			
Transition TRLP-17	(M)	**Byrd Blows On Beacon Hill**	1956	300.00	600.00
		(Transition 17 was issued with a booklet, worth an additional $50.)			
Savoy MG-12032	(M)	**Byrd's Word**	1956	40.00	100.00
Savoy MG-12064	(M)	**The Jazz Message Of...**	1956	50.00	125.00
Blue Note BLP-4007	(M)	**Off To The Races** *(Deep groove)*	1959	50.00	125.00
Blue Note BLP-4007	(M)	**Off To The Races**	1959	30.00	75.00
Blue Note BST-4007	(S)	**Off To The Races** *(Deep groove)*	1959	30.00	75.00
Blue Note BST-4007	(S)	**Off To The Races**	1959	20.00	50.00
Blue Note BLP-4019	(M)	**Byrd In Hand** *(Deep groove)*	1959	50.00	125.00
Blue Note BLP-4019	(M)	**Byrd In Hand**	1959	30.00	75.00
Blue Note BST-84019	(S)	**Byrd In Hand**	1959	20.00	50.00
Blue Note BLP-4026	(M)	**Fuego** *(Deep groove)*	1960	50.00	125.00
Blue Note BLP-4026	(M)	**Fuego**	1960	30.00	75.00
Blue Note BST-84026	(S)	**Fuego**	1960	20.00	50.00
Blue Note BLP-4048	(M)	**Byrd In Flight** *(Deep groove)*	1960	50.00	125.00
Blue Note BLP-4048	(M)	**Byrd In Flight**	1960	30.00	75.00
Blue Note BST-84048	(S)	**Byrd In Flight**	1960	20.00	50.00
Blue Note BLP-4060	(M)	**Donald Byrd At The Half Note Cafe, Volume 1**	1961	30.00	75.00
Blue Note BST-84060	(S)	**Donald Byrd At The Half Note Cafe, Volume 1**	1961	20.00	50.00
Blue Note BLP-4061	(M)	**Donald Byrd At The Half Note Cafe, Volume 2**	1961	30.00	75.00
Blue Note BST-84061	(S)	**Donald Byrd At The Half Note Cafe, Volume 2**	1961	20.00	50.00
		—Blue Note albums above have blue on white labels with a W. 63rd St., NYC address.—			
Blue Note BLP-4075	(M)	**The Cat Walk**	1961	30.00	75.00
Blue Note BST-84075	(S)	**The Cat Walk**	1961	20.00	50.00
		—Blue Note albums above have blue on white labels with a 61st St, NYC address.—			
Blue Note BLP-4007	(M)	**Off To The Races**	1963	10.00	25.00
Blue Note BST-4007	(S)	**Off To The Races**	1963	8.00	20.00
Blue Note BLP-4019	(M)	**Byrd In Hand**	1963	10.00	25.00
Blue Note BST-84019	(S)	**Byrd In Hand**	1963	8.00	20.00
Blue Note BLP-4026	(M)	**Fuego**	1963	10.00	25.00
Blue Note BST-84026	(S)	**Fuego**	1963	8.00	20.00
Blue Note BLP-4048	(M)	**Byrd In Flight**	1963	10.00	25.00
Blue Note BST-84048	(S)	**Byrd In Flight**	1963	8.00	20.00
Blue Note BLP-4060	(M)	**Donald Byrd At The Half Note Cafe, Volume 1**	1963	10.00	25.00
Blue Note BST-84060	(S)	**Donald Byrd At The Half Note Cafe, Volume 1**	1963	8.00	20.00
Blue Note BLP-4061	(M)	**Donald Byrd At The Half Note Cafe, Volume 2**	1963	10.00	25.00
Blue Note BST-84061	(S)	**Donald Byrd At The Half Note Cafe, Volume 2**	1963	8.00	20.00
Blue Note BLP-4075	(M)	**The Cat Walk**	1963	10.00	25.00
Blue Note BST-84075	(S)	**The Cat Walk**	1963	8.00	20.00
Blue Note BLP-4101	(M)	**Royal Flush**	1962	12.00	30.00
Blue Note BST-84101	(S)	**Royal Flush**	1962	10.00	25.00
Blue Note BLP-4118	(M)	**Free Form**	1962	12.00	30.00
Blue Note BST-84118	(S)	**Free Form**	1962	10.00	25.00
Blue Note BLP-4124	(M)	**A New Perspective**	1963	16.00	40.00
Blue Note BST-84124	(S)	**A New Perspective**	1963	12.00	30.00
Blue Note BLP-4188	(M)	**I'm Tryin' To Get Home**	1965	12.00	30.00
Blue Note BST-84188	(S)	**I'm Tryin' To Get Home**	1965	10.00	25.00
Blue Note BLP-4238	(M)	**Mustang!**	1966	12.00	30.00
Blue Note BST-84238	(S)	**Mustang!**	1966	10.00	25.00
		—Blue Note albums above have blue on white labels with a New York, USA address.—			
Blue Note BST-84007	(S)	**Off To The Races**	196?	5.00	12.00
Blue Note BST-84019	(S)	**Byrd In Hand**	196?	5.00	12.00
Blue Note BST-84026	(S)	**Fuego**	196?	5.00	12.00
Blue Note BST-84048	(S)	**Byrd In Flight**	196?	5.00	12.00
Blue Note BST-84060	(S)	**Donald Byrd At The Half Note Cafe, Volume 1**	196?	5.00	12.00
Blue Note BST-84061	(S)	**Donald Byrd At The Half Note Cafe, Volume 2**	196?	5.00	12.00
Blue Note BST-84075	(S)	**The Cat Walk**	196?	5.00	12.00
Blue Note BST-84101	(S)	**Royal Flush**	196?	5.00	12.00
Blue Note BST-84118	(S)	**Free Form**	196?	5.00	12.00
Blue Note BST-84124	(S)	**A New Perspective**	196?	5.00	12.00

Label & Catalog #		Title	Year	VG+	NM
Blue Note BST-84188	(S)	**I'm Tryin' To Get Home**	196?	**5.00**	**12.00**
Blue Note BST-84238	(S)	**Mustang!**	196?	**5.00**	**12.00**
Blue Note BLP-4259	(M)	**Blackjack**	1967	**10.00**	**25.00**
Blue Note BST-84259	(S)	**Blackjack**	1967	**8.00**	**20.00**
Blue Note BST-84292	(S)	**Slow Drag**	1968	**8.00**	**20.00**
Blue Note BST-84319	(S)	**Fancy Free**	1969	**8.00**	**20.00**
—Blue Note albums above have blue on white labels with "A Division of Liberty Records."—					
Verve V-8609	(M)	**Up With Donald Byrd**	1965	**10.00**	**25.00**
Verve V6-8609	(S)	**Up With Donald Byrd**	1965	**8.00**	**20.00**
— Verve albums above have black labels with "MGM Records" on the bottom.—					
BYRD, DONALD, & GIGI GRYCE / CECIL TAYLOR					
Verve MGV-8238	(M)	**The Gigi Gryce-Donald Byrd Jazz Laboratory/ The Cecil Taylor Quartet At Newport**	1958	**20.00**	**50.00**
— Verve albums above have black labels with "Verve Records, Inc." on the bottom.—					
Verve V-8238	(M)	**The Gigi Gryce-Donald Byrd Jazz Laboratory/ The Cecil Taylor Quartet At Newport**	196?	**8.00**	**20.00**
— Verve albums above have black labels with "MGM Records" on the bottom.—					
BYRD, DONALD, & HANK MOBLEY & KENNY BURRELL					
New Jazz NJLP-8317	(M)	**Donald Byrd, Hank Mobley & Kenny Burrell**	1963	*Unreleased*	
Status ST-8317	(M)	**Donald Byrd, Hank Mobley & Kenny Burrell**	1965	**16.00**	**40.00**
BYRNE, BOBBY					
Robert Byrne is a traditional jazz based trombone player.					
Grand Award GA-33-392	(M)	**Bobby Byrne Plays Great Themes**	1958	**20.00**	**50.00**
Grand Award GA-33-416	(M)	**The Jazzbone's Connected To The Trombone**	1959	**20.00**	**50.00**
BYRNE, BOBBY / WILL BRADLEY					
Grand Award GA-33-31?	(M)	**Muskrat Ramble**	1955	**20.00**	**50.00**
BYRNE, BOBBY / WILL BRADLEY / BUD FREEMAN					
Grand Award GA-33-313	(M)	**Jazz, Dixieland-Chicago**	1955	**20.00**	**50.00**
BYRON, GEORGE					
George Byron is a jazz based vocalist.					
Atlantic 1293	(M)	**George Byron Sings New And Rediscovered Jerome Kern Songs**	1958	**16.00**	**40.00**
Atlantic SD-1293	(S)	**George Byron Sings New And Rediscovered Jerome Kern Songs**	1958	**16.00**	**40.00**
—Atlantic albums above have black mono or green stereo labels.—					

C

CAIN, JACKIE, & ROY KRAL

Jacqueline Cain is a modern jazz-based vocalist; Roy Kral a pianist and vocalist. For additional listings refer to Charlie Ventura.

Storyville STLP-322	(10")	**Jackie & Roy**	1955	40.00	100.00
Storyville STLP-904	(M)	**Storyville Presents Jackie And Roy**	1955	24.00	60.00
Storyville STLP-915	(M)	**Sing Baby, Sing!**	1956	24.00	60.00
ABC-Paramount ABC-120	(M)	**The Glory Of Love**	1956	20.00	50.00
ABC-Paramount ABC-163	(M)	**Bits And Pieces**	1957	20.00	50.00
ABC-Paramount ABC-207	(M)	**Free And Easy**	1958	20.00	50.00
ABC-Paramount ABC-267	(M)	**In The Spotlight**	1959	16.00	40.00
ABC-Paramount ABCS-267	(S)	**In The Spotlight**	1959	20.00	50.00
Brunswick BL-54026	(M)	**Jackie Cain And Roy Kral**	1957	20.00	50.00
Regent MG-6057	(M)	**Jackie And Roy**	1957	20.00	50.00
Columbia CL-1469	(M)	**Sweet And Low Down**	1960	10.00	25.00
Columbia CS-8260	(S)	**Sweet And Low Down**	1960	12.00	30.00
Columbia CL-1704	(M)	**Double Take**	1961	10.00	25.00
Columbia CS-8504	(S)	**Double Take**	1961	12.00	30.00

—Columbia albums above have six white on black "eye" logos on the label.—

Columbia CL-1934	(M)	**Like Sing**	1963	8.00	20.00
Columbia CS-8734	(S)	**Like Sing**	1963	10.00	25.00

—Columbia albums above have "Guaranteed High Fidelity" or "360 Sound Stereo" in black on the label.—

Roulette R-25278	(M)	**By Jupiter/Girl Crazy**	1964	8.00	20.00
Roulette SR-25278	(S)	**By Jupiter/Girl Crazy**	1964	10.00	25.00
Verve V-8668	(M)	**Changes**	1966	8.00	20.00
Verve V6-8668	(S)	**Changes**	1966	10.00	25.00
Verve V-8688	(M)	**Lovesick**	1967	8.00	20.00
Verve V6-8688	(S)	**Lovesick**	1967	10.00	25.00

—Verve albums above have black labels with "MGM Records" on the bottom.—

Savoy MG-12198	(M)	**Jackie And Roy**	196?	8.00	20.00

(Savoy 12198 is a reissue of Regent 6057.)

CAIOLA, AL

Al Caiola is a guitar player, the bulk of whose work falls into the pop vein.

Savoy MG-12033	(M)	**Deep In A Dream**	1955	16.00	40.00
Savoy MG-12057	(M)	**Serenade In Blue**	1956	16.00	40.00
Chancellor CHL-5008	(M)	**Al Caiola And Don Arnone**	1960	12.00	30.00
Chancellor CHLS-5008	(S)	**Al Caiola And Don Arnone**	1960	10.00	25.00
United Arts. UAL-3299	(M)	**Cleopatra And All That Jazz**	1962	12.00	30.00
United Arts. UAS-6299	(S)	**Cleopatra And All That Jazz**	1962	10.00	25.00

(United Artists 3299 also features Clark Terry.)

CALLENDER, RED

George "Red" Callender is a traditional jazz bass and tuba player. For additional listings refer to Gene Krupa & Lionel Hampton & Teddy Wilson; Lester Young.

Modern MLP-1201	(M)	**Swingin' Suite**	1956	30.00	75.00
Crown CLP-5012	(M)	**Callender Speaks Low**	1957	16.00	40.00
Crown CLP-5025	(M)	**Swingin' Suite**	1957	16.00	40.00

(Crown 5025 is a reissue of Modern 1201.)

Metrojazz E-1007	(M)	**The Lowest**	1958	20.00	50.00
Metrojazz SE-1007	(S)	**The Lowest**	1958	16.00	40.00

CALLOWAY, CAB

Cabell Calloway is a traditional jazz-based vocalist and big band leader.

Brunswick BL-58101	(10")	**Cab Calloway**	1954	40.00	100.00
Epic LN-3265	(M)	**Cab Calloway**	1956	20.00	50.00
RCA Victor LPM-2021	(M)	**Hi De Hi, Hi De Ho**	1958	16.00	40.00
RCA Victor LSP-2021	(S)	**Hi De Hi, Hi De Ho**	1958	20.00	50.00

—RCA albums above have black labels with "Long Play" on the bottom.—

Gone LP-101	(M)	**The Cotton Club Revue Of 1958**	1959	30.00	75.00
Coral CRL-57408	(M)	**Blues Make Me Happy**	1962	12.00	30.00
Coral CRL-757408	(S)	**Blues Make Me Happy**	1962	10.00	25.00

Label & Catalog #		Title	Year	VG+	NM
CAMERON, JOHN					
Deram DES-18033	*(S)*	**Off Centre**	*1969*	**8.00**	**20.00**
CAMP, RED					
Red Camp is a modern jazz pianist.					
Cook LP-1087	*(M)*	**Camp Inventions— Bold New Design For Jazz Piano**	*1955*	**20.00**	**50.00**
Cook LP-1089	*(10")*	**Red Camp**	*1955*	**20.00**	**50.00**
Cook LP-5005	*(M)*	**Camp Has A Ball**	*1957*	**16.00**	**40.00**
CANADIAN ALL STARS, THE					
Discovery DL-3025	*(10")*	**The Canadian All Stars**	*1954*	**30.00**	**75.00**
CANDIDO					
Cuban born Candido Camero is a modern jazz-based drummer and congas player. For additional listings refer to Billy Taylor.					
ABC-Paramount ABC-125	*(M)*	**Candido Featuring Al Cohn**	*1956*	**20.00**	**50.00**
ABC-Paramount ABC-180	*(M)*	**The Volcanic Candido**	*1957*	**20.00**	**50.00**
ABC-Paramount ABC-236	*(M)*	**In Indigo**	*1958*	**20.00**	**50.00**
ABC-Paramount ABCS-236	*(S)*	**In Indigo**	*1959*	**16.00**	**40.00**
ABC-Paramount ABC-286	*(M)*	**Latin Fire**	*1959*	**20.00**	**50.00**
ABC-Paramount ABCS-286	*(S)*	**Latin Fire**	*1959*	**16.00**	**40.00**
RCA Victor LPM-2027	*(M)*	**Beautiful**	*1959*	**12.00**	**30.00**
RCA Victor LSP-2027	*(S)*	**Beautiful**	*1959*	**10.00**	**25.00**
—RCA albums above have black labels with "Long Play" or "Living Stereo" on the bottom.—					
Roulette R-52078	*(M)*	**Conga Soul**	*1962*	**10.00**	**25.00**
Roulette SR-52078	*(S)*	**Conga Soul**	*1962*	**8.00**	**20.00**
CANDOLI, CONTE					
Secondo "Conte" Candoli is a West Coast jazz trumpet player. For additional listings refer to The Five; Vince Guaraldi / Conte Candoli; Lou Levy / Conte Candoli.					
Bethlehem BCP-1016	*(10")*	**Sincerely, Conte Candoli**	*1954*	**50.00**	**125.00**
Bethlehem BCP-30	*(M)*	**Conte Candoli, Vol. 2**	*1955*	**30.00**	**75.00**
Mode LP-109	*(M)*	**Conte Candoli Quartet**	*1957*	**30.00**	**75.00**
Andex A-3002	*(M)*	**Mucho Calor**	*1958*	**20.00**	**50.00**
Andex AS-3002	*(S)*	**Mucho Calor**	*1958*	**16.00**	**40.00**
Crown CLP-5162	*(M)*	**Little Band, Big Jazz**	*1960*	**8.00**	**20.00**
Crown CST-190	*(E)*	**Little Band, Big Jazz**	*1960*	**4.00**	**10.00**
Crown CST-190	*(E)*	**Little Band, Big Jazz** *(Red vinyl)*	*1960*	**12.00**	**30.00**
CANDOLI, CONTE / STAN LEVEY					
Bethlehem BCP-9	*(M)*	**West Coasting** *(Bethlehem 9 is a reissue of 1016 and 1017, "Stan Levey Plays.")*	*1957*	**30.00**	**75.00**
CANDOLI, PETE					
Walter "Pete" Candoli is a West Coast jazz trumpet player. For additional listings refer to Henry Mancini; The Soundstage All-Stars and the Jazzy Soundtracks section under RCA Victor.					
Kapp KL-1230	*(M)*	**For Pete's Sake**	*1960*	**10.00**	**25.00**
Kapp KS-3230	*(S)*	**For Pete's Sake**	*1960*	**8.00**	**20.00**
Somerset SF-17200	*(M)*	**Blues, When Your Lover Has Gone**	*1963*	**10.00**	**25.00**
Somerset SFS-17200	*(S)*	**Blues, When Your Lover Has Gone**	*1963*	**8.00**	**20.00**
CANDOLI BROTHERS, THE					
Conte and Pete Candoli.					
Dot DLP-3062	*(M)*	**The Brothers Candoli**	*1957*	**20.00**	**50.00**
Dot DLP-3168	*(M)*	**Bell, Book And Candoli**	*1959*	**12.00**	**30.00**
Dot DLP-25168	*(S)*	**Bell, Book And Candoli**	*1959*	**10.00**	**25.00**
Mercury MG-20515	*(M)*	**Two For The Money**	*1959*	**12.00**	**30.00**
Mercury SR-60191	*(S)*	**Two For The Money**	*1959*	**10.00**	**25.00**
—Mercury albums above have silver on black labels.—					
Warner Bros. W-1462	*(M)*	**The Brothers Candoli**	*1962*	**10.00**	**25.00**
Warner Bros. WS-1462	*(S)*	**The Brothers Candoli**	*1962*	**8.00**	**20.00**
CAREY, MUTT					
Thomas "Mutt" Carey is a traditional trumpet player. For additional listings refer to Punch Miller / Mutt Carey.					
Riverside RLP-1042	*(10")*	**Mutt Carey Plays The Blues**	*1954*	**30.00**	**75.00**

Label & Catalog #		Title	Year	VG+	NM
CARISI, JOHN					
John Carisi is a jazz-based guitar player.					
Columbia CL-1419	(M)	**New Jazz Sounds Of "Showboat"**	1960	**10.00**	**25.00**
Columbia CS-8219	(S)	**New Jazz Sounds Of "Showboat"**	1960	**8.00**	**20.00**
— Columbia albums above have six white on black "eye" logos on each label.—					
CARMICHAEL, HOAGY					
Hoagland Carmichael is a traditional jazz-based pianist, singer and composer. For additional listings refer to John Carradine & Hoagy Carmichael & Bob Dorough.					
Decca DL-5068	(10")	**Stardust Road**	1950	**40.00**	**100.00**
RCA Victor LPT-3072	(10")	**Old Rockin' Chair**	1953	**40.00**	**100.00**
Pacific Jazz PJ-1223	(M)	**Hoagy Sings Carmichael**	1956	**30.00**	**75.00**
Jazztone J-1266	(M)	**Hoagy Sings Carmichael**	1957	**16.00**	**40.00**
		(Jazztone 1266 is a reissue of Pacific Jazz 1223.)			
Kimberly 2023	(M)	**The Legend Of Hoagy Carmichael**	1961	**12.00**	**30.00**
Kimberly 11023	(E)	**The Legend Of Hoagy Carmichael**	1961	**8.00**	**20.00**
		(Kimberly 2023 is a reissue of Pacific Jazz 1223.)			
Capitol T-1819	(M)	**I Can Dream, Can't I?**	1963	**8.00**	**20.00**
Capitol ST-1819	(S)	**I Can Dream, Can't I?**	1963	**10.00**	**25.00**
CARN, DOUG					
Savoy MG-12195	(M)	**The Doug Carn Trio**	1969	**8.00**	**20.00**
CARNEY, HARRY					
Harry Carney is a traditional jazz baritone saxophone, clarinet and bass clarinet player.					
Clef MGC-640	(M)	**Harry Carney With Strings**	1955	**30.00**	**75.00**
		(Clef 640 features cover art by David Stone Martin.)			
Verve MGV-2028	(M)	**Moods For Girl And Boy**	1956	**20.00**	**50.00**
		(Verve 2028 is a reissue of Clef 640 with the DSM cover.)			
— Verve albums above have "Verve Records, Inc." on the bottom of the label.—					
Verve V-2028	(M)	**Moods For Girl And Boy**	1961	**8.00**	**20.00**
— Verve albums above have black labels with "MGM Records" on the bottom.—					
CARPENTER, IKE					
Discovery DL-3003	(10")	**Dancers In Love**	1949	**60.00**	**150.00**
CARR, GEORGIA					
Georgia Carr is a jazz-based vocalist.					
Tops L-1617	(M)	**Songs By A Moody Miss**	1958	**12.00**	**30.00**
Roulette R-25077	(M)	**Shy**	1960	**10.00**	**25.00**
Roulette SR-25077	(S)	**Shy**	1960	**12.00**	**30.00**
Vee Jay LP-1105	(M)	**Rocks In My Bed**	1964	**8.00**	**20.00**
Vee Jay VJS-1105	(S)	**Rocks In My Bed**	1964	**10.00**	**25.00**
CARR, HELEN					
Helen Carr is a modern jazz-based vocalist.					
Bethlehem BCP-1027	(10")	**Down In The Depths On The 90th Floor**	1955	**40.00**	**100.00**
Bethlehem BCP-45	(M)	**.........Why Do I Love You**	1956	**20.00**	**50.00**
CARRADINE, JOHN, & HOAGY CARMICHAEL & BOB DOROUGH					
World Pacific WP-1409	(M)	**Poetry And Jazz**	1961	**20.00**	**50.00**
CARROLL, BARBARA					
Barbara Carole Coppersmith, aka Barbara Carroll, is a modern jazz pianist. For additional listings refer to Adelaide Robbins / Marian McPartland / Barbara Carroll.					
Atlantic ALR-132	(10")	**Piano Panorama**	1952	**30.00**	**75.00**
Livingston 1081	(10")	**Barbara Carroll Trio**	1953	**30.00**	**75.00**
RCA Victor LJM-1001	(M)	**Barbara Carroll Trio**	1954	**20.00**	**50.00**
RCA Victor LJM-1023	(M)	**Lullabies In Rhythm**	1955	**20.00**	**50.00**
RCA Victor LPM-1137	(M)	**Have You Met Miss Carroll?**	1956	**20.00**	**50.00**
RCA Victor LPM-1296	(M)	**We Just Couldn't Say Goodbye**	1956	**20.00**	**50.00**
RCA Victor LPM-1396	(M)	**It's A Wonderful World**	1957	**20.00**	**50.00**
— RCA albums above have black labels with "Long Play" on the bottom.—					
Verve MGV-2063	(M)	**Funny Face**	1957	**24.00**	**60.00**
		— Verve albums above have orange labels.—			
Verve MGV-2063	(M)	**Funny Face**	1957	**20.00**	**50.00**
Verve MGV-2092	(M)	**The Best Of George And Ira Gershwin**	1958	**16.00**	**40.00**
		(Verve 2092 is a reissue of 2063.)			

Label & Catalog #		Title	Year	VG+	NM
Verve MGV-2095	(M)	**Barbara**	1958	16.00	40.00
		—Verve albums above have black labels with "Verve Records, Inc." on the bottom.—			
Verve V-2092	(M)	**The Best Of George And Ira Gershwin**	1961	8.00	20.00
Verve V-2095	(M)	**Barbara**	1961	8.00	20.00
		—Verve albums above have black labels with "MGM Records" on the bottom.—			
Kapp KL-1113	(M)	**Flower Drum Song**	1958	10.00	25.00
Kapp KS-5113	(S)	**Flower Drum Song**	1958	8.00	20.00
SeSac N-3201	(M)	**Why Not?**	1959	16.00	40.00
SeSac SN-3201	(S)	**Why Not?**	1959	12.00	30.00
Warner Bros. W-1543	(M)	**"Hello, Dolly" & "What Makes Sammy Run?"**	1964	6.00	15.00
Warner Bros. WS-1543	(S)	**"Hello, Dolly" & "What Makes Sammy Run?"**	1964	5.00	12.00

CARROLL, BARBARA / MARY LOU WILLIAMS

Atlantic 1271	(M)	**Ladies In Jazz**	1958	20.00	50.00
		(Atlantic 1271 is a reissue of 132 and 114, Williams' "Piano Panorama.")			
		—Atlantic albums above have black mono or green stereo labels.—			
Atlantic 1271	(M)	**Ladies In Jazz**	1961	8.00	20.00
		—Atlantic albums above have multi-color labels with a white fan logo.—			

CARROLL, JOE

Joseph Carroll is a modern jazz-based vocalist.

Epic LN-3272	(M)	**Joe Carroll**	1956	20.00	50.00
Charlie Parker PLP-802	(M)	**The Man With The Happy Sound**	1962	12.00	30.00
Charlie Parker PLP-802S	(S)	**The Man With The Happy Sound**	1962	12.00	30.00

CARTER, BENNY

Bennett Carter is a traditional jazz alto and tenor saxophone, clarinet, trombone and piano player, arranger, composer and big band leader. For additional listings refer to Roy Eldridge & Benny Carter; Art Tatum, Benny Carter & Louis Bellson; and the Jazzy Soundtracks section under Reprise.

Clef MGC-141	(10")	**Cosmopolite**	1953	100.00	200.00
		(Clef 141 features cover art by David Stone Martin.)			
Norgran MGN-10	(10")	**The Urbane Mr. Carter**	1954	60.00	150.00
Norgran MGN-21	(10")	**The Formidable Benny Carter**	1954	60.00	150.00
Norgran MGN-1015	(M)	**Benny Carter Plays Pretty**	1955	40.00	100.00
		(Norgran 1015 featues cover art by David Stone Martin.)			
Norgran MGN-1025	(M)	**Benny Carter**	1955	*Unreleased*	
Norgran MGN-1044	(M)	**New Jazz Sounds**	1955	30.00	75.00
		(Norgran 1044 also features Dizzy Gillespie and Bill Harris)			
Norgran MGN-1058	(M)	**Alone Together**	1956	30.00	75.00
		(Norgran 1058 also features Oscar Peterson.)			
Norgran MGN-1070	(M)	**Cosmopolite**	1956	30.00	75.00
		(Norgran 1070 is a reissue of Clef 141 with the DSM cover.)			
Verve MGV-2025	(M)	**Moonglow—Love Songs By Benny Carter**	1956	24.00	60.00
		(Verve 2025 is a reissue of Norgran 1015 with the DSM cover.)			
Verve MGV-8135	(M)	**New Jazz Sounds**	1957	24.00	60.00
		(Verve 9=8135 is a reissue of Norgran 1044.)			
Verve MGV-8148	(M)	**Alone Together**	1957	24.00	60.00
		(Verve 8148 is a reissue of Norgran 1058 with the DSM cover.)			
Verve MGV-8160	(M)	**Cosmopolite**	1957	24.00	60.00
		(Verve 8160 is a reissue of Norgran 1070 with the DSM cover.)			
		—Verve albums above have black labels with "Verve Records, Inc." on the bottom.—			
Verve V-2025	(M)	**Moonglow—Love Songs By Benny Carter**	1961	8.00	20.00
Verve V-8135	(M)	**New Jazz Sounds**	1961	8.00	20.00
Verve V-8148	(M)	**Alone Together**	1961	8.00	20.00
Verve V-8160	(M)	**Cosmopolite**	1961	8.00	20.00
		—Verve albums above have black labels with "MGM Records" on the bottom.—			
Contemporary C-3555	(M)	**Jazz Giant**	1958	20.00	50.00
Stereo Records S-7028	(S)	**Jazz Giant**	1958	18.00	45.00
Contemporary S-7028	(S)	**Jazz Giant**	1959	16.00	40.00
Contemporary M-3561	(M)	**Swingin' The Twenties**	1959	20.00	50.00
Contemporary S-7561	(S)	**Swingin' The Twenties**	1959	16.00	40.00
		(Contemporay 3561 also features Earl Hines)			
		—Contemporary stereo albums have gold & black labels.—			
Audio Lab AL-1505	(M)	**The Fabulous Benny Carter**	1959	60.00	150.00
United Arts. UAL-3055	(M)	**"Can Can" And "Anything Goes"**	1959	16.00	40.00
United Arts. UAS-6055	(S)	**"Can Can" And "Anything Goes"**	1959	12.00	30.00
United Arts. UAL-4017	(M)	**Aspects**	1959	16.00	40.00
United Arts. UAS-5017	(S)	**Aspects**	1959	12.00	30.00

Label & Catalog #		Title	Year	VG+	NM
United Arts. UAL-4073	(M)	**"Can Can" And "Anything Goes"**	1960	10.00	25.00
United Arts. UAS-5073	(S)	**"Can Can" And "Anything Goes"**	1960	8.00	20.00
		(United Artists 4073 is a reissue of 3055.)			
United Arts. UAL-4080	(M)	**Jazz Calendar**	1960	10.00	25.00
United Arts. UAS-5080	(S)	**Jazz Calendar**	1960	8.00	20.00
		(United Artists 4080 is a reissue of 4017.)			
United Arts. UAL-4094	(M)	**Sax A La Carter**	1960	10.00	25.00
United Arts. UAS-5094	(S)	**Sax A La Carter**	1960	8.00	20.00
Impulse A-12	(M)	**Further Definitions**	1962	12.00	30.00
Impulse AS-12	(S)	**Further Definitions**	1962	10.00	25.00
Impulse A-9116	(M)	**Additions To Further Definitions**	1966	16.00	40.00
Impulse AS-9116	(S)	**Additions To Further Definitions**	1966	12.00	30.00
		—Impulse albums above have orange & black labels.—			
Impulse AS-12	(S)	**Further Definitions**	1969	4.00	10.00
Impulse AS-9116	(S)	**Additions To Further Definitions**	1969	4.00	10.00
		—Impulse albums above have red & black labels with the "abc" logo on top.—			
20th Cent. Fox TFM-3134	(M)	**Benny Carter In Paris**	1963	10.00	25.00
20th Cent. Fox TFS-4134	(S)	**Benny Carter In Paris**	1963	8.00	20.00
Prestige PRST-7643	(E)	**Benny Carter 1933**	1969	5.00	12.00
		—Prestige albums above have blue labels with a trident logo on top.—			

CARTER, BENNY, & BEN WEBSTER & BARNEY BIGARD

Swingville SVLP-2032	(M)	**B. B. B. & Co.**	1962	20.00	50.00
Swingville SVST-2032	(S)	**B. B. B. & Co.**	1962	16.00	40.00
		—Swingville albums above have purple mono or red stereo labels.—			
Swingville SVLP-2032	(M)	**B. B. B. & Co.**	1965	10.00	25.00
Swingville SVST-2032	(S)	**B. B. B. & Co.**	1965	8.00	20.00
		—Swingville albums above have blue labels with a trident logo on the right side.—			

CARTER, BETTY

Lillie Mae Jones, aka Betty Carter, is a modern jazz vocalist. For additional listings refer to Ray Bryant; Ray Charles & Betty Carter.

Peacock PLP-90	(M)	**Out There With Betty Carter—Progressive Jazz**	1958	40.00	100.00
ABC-Paramount ABC-363	(M)	**The Modern Sound Of Betty Carter**	1960	20.00	50.00
ABC-Paramount ABCS-363	(S)	**The Modern Sound Of Betty Carter**	1960	30.00	75.00
Atco 33-152	(M)	**'Round Midnight**	1963	16.00	40.00
Atco SD-33-152	(S)	**'Round Midnight**	1963	20.00	50.00
		—Atco albums above have a white stripe through the center of the label.—			
United Arts. UAL-3379	(M)	**Inside Betty Carter**	1964	20.00	50.00
United Arts. UAS-6379	(S)	**Inside Betty Carter**	1964	24.00	60.00

CARTER, JOHN, & BOBBY BRADFORD

Flying Dutchman FDS-108	(S)	**Flight For Four**	1969	6.00	15.00

CARTER, RON

Ronald Carter is a modern jazz bassist.

New Jazz NJLP-8265	(M)	**Where?**	1961	30.00	75.00
		(New Jazz 8265 also features Eric Dolphy and Mal Waldron.)			
		—New Jazz albums above have purple labels.—			
New Jazz NJLP-8265	(M)	**Where?**	1965	10.00	25.00
		—New Jazz albums above have blue labels with a trident logo on the right side.—			

CARY, DICK

Richard Cary is a traditional jazz piano, trumpet and alto horn player and arranger.

Golden Crest GC-3024	(M)	**Dixieland Goes Progressive**	1958	16.00	40.00

CASEY, AL

Albert Casey is a traditional jazz guitar player.

Moodsville MVLP-12	(M)	**The Al Casey Quartet**	1960	20.00	50.00
		—Moodsville mono albums above have green labels with silver print.—			
Moodsville MVLP-12	(M)	**The Al Casey Quartet**	1965	10.00	25.00
		—Moodsville albums above have blue labels with a trident logo on the right side.—			
Swingville SVLP-2007	(M)	**Buck Jumpin'**	1960	20.00	50.00
		—Swingville albums above have purple mono or red stereo labels.—			
Swingville SVLP-2007	(M)	**Buck Jumpin'**	1965	10.00	25.00
		—Swingville albums above have blue labels with a trident logo on the right side.—			

Label & Catalog #		Title	Year	VG+	NM
CASTLE, LEE					
Lee Castaldo, aka Lee Castle, is a traditional jazz trumpet player.					
Davis JD-105	(M)	**Dixieland Heaven**	1951	24.00	60.00
Celebrity CEL-203	(M)	**World Famous Dixieland Favorites**	1952	16.00	40.00
		(Celebrity 203 is a reissue of Davis 105.)			
CASTLE, PAULA					
Paula Castle is a jazz-based vocalist.					
Bethlehem BCP-1036	(10")	**Paula Castle**	1955	30.00	75.00
CASTRO, JOE					
Joseph Castro is a West Coast jazz pianist.					
Atlantic 1264	(M)	**Mood Jazz**	1957	20.00	50.00
Atlantic SD-1264	(S)	**Mood Jazz**	1958	16.00	40.00
Atlantic 1324	(M)	**Groove Funk Soul**	1960	20.00	50.00
Atlantic SD-1324	(S)	**Groove Funk Soul**	1960	16.00	40.00
		—Atlantic albums above have black mono or green stereo labels.—			
Atlantic 1264	(M)	**Mood Jazz**	1961	8.00	20.00
Atlantic SD-1264	(S)	**Mood Jazz**	1961	6.00	15.00
		—Atlantic albums above have multi-color labels with a white fan logo.—			
CATHCART, DICK					
Richard Cathcart is a traditional jazz trumpet player.					
Warner Bros. W-1275	(M)	**Bix/MCMLIX**	1959	12.00	30.00
Warner Bros. WS-1275	(S)	**Bix/MCMLIX**	1959	10.00	25.00
CAVANAUGH, PAGE					
Walter Page Cavanaugh is a traditional jazz-based pianist and vocalist.					
"X" LXA-3027	(10")	**Page Cavanaugh Trio**	1954	20.00	50.00
Capitol T-879	(M)	**Fats Sent Me**	1957	16.00	40.00
Capitol T-1001	(M)	**Swingin' Down The Road From Paris To Rome**	1958	16.00	40.00
		— Capitol albums above have turquoise labels.—			
CELESTIN, PAPA					
Oscar "Papa" Celestin is a traditional jazz trumpet player and vocalist.					
Southland SLP-206	(10")	**Papa's Golden Wedding**	1955	20.00	50.00
Imperial LP-9199	(M)	**Oscar "Papa" Celestin**	1962	8.00	20.00
Imperial LP-12199	(S)	**Oscar "Papa" Celestin**	1962	6.00	15.00
CELL BLOCK SEVEN					
Dixieland Jubilee DJ-506	(M)	**A Dixieland Riot**	195?	20.00	50.00
CESANA, OTTO					
Otto Cesana is a traditional jazz composer.					
Columbia GL-103	(10")	**Symphony In Jazz**	1950	20.00	50.00
CHALOFF, SERGE / OSCAR PETTIFORD					
Mercer LP-1003	(10")	**New Stars-New Sounds, Volume 2**	1951	60.00	150.00
CHALOFF, SERGE					
Serge Chaloff is a modern jazz baritone saxophone player. For additional listings refer to The Four Brothers.					
Storyville STLP-310	(10")	**Serge Chaloff And Boots Mussulli**	1954	100.00	200.00
Storyville STLP-317	(10")	**The Fable Of Mable**	1955	100.00	200.00
Capitol T-6510	(M)	**Boston Blow-Up!**	1955	30.00	75.00
Capitol T-742	(M)	**Blue Serge**	1956	30.00	75.00
		— Capitol albums above have turquoise labels.—			
CHAMBERS, PAUL					
Paul Chambers is a modern jazz bassist. For additional listings refer to Kenny Drew & Paul Chambers & Philly Joe Jones; Roy Haynes, The Jazz Modes; Phineas Newborn & Paul Chambers; and the Various Artists section under Bethlehem and Savoy.					
Jazz: West JWLP-7	(M)	**A Jazz Delegation From The East—Chambers' Music**	1956	360.00	600.00
Blue Note BLP-1534	(M)	**Whims Of Chambers** *(Deep groove)*	1956	60.00	150.00
Blue Note BLP-1534	(M)	**Whims Of Chambers**	1956	40.00	100.00
		—Blue Note albums above have blue on white labels with a Lexington Ave., NYC address.—			
Blue Note BLP-1564	(M)	**Paul Chambers Quintet** *(Deep groove)*	1957	50.00	125.00
Blue Note BLP-1564	(M)	**Paul Chambers Quintet**	1957	30.00	75.00

Label & Catalog #		Title	Year	VG+	NM
Blue Note BST-1564	(S)	**Paul Chambers Quintet** *(Deep groove)*	1959	30.00	75.00
Blue Note BST-1564	(S)	**Paul Chambers Quintet**	1959	20.00	50.00
Blue Note BLP-1569	(M)	**Bass On Top** *(Deep groove)*	1957	50.00	125.00
Blue Note BLP-1569	(M)	**Bass On Top**	1957	30.00	75.00
Blue Note BST-1569	(S)	**Bass On Top** *(Deep groove)*	1959	30.00	75.00
Blue Note BST-1569	(S)	**Bass On Top**	1959	20.00	50.00
		—Blue Note albums above have blue on white labels with a W. 63rd St., NYC address.—			
Blue Note BLP-1534	(M)	**Whims Of Chambers**	1963	10.00	25.00
Blue Note BLP-1564	(M)	**Paul Chambers Quintet**	1963	10.00	25.00
Blue Note BST-1564	(S)	**Paul Chambers Quintet**	1963	8.00	20.00
Blue Note BLP-1569	(M)	**Bass On Top**	1963	10.00	25.00
Blue Note BST-1569	(S)	**Bass On Top**	1963	8.00	20.00
		—Blue Note albums above have blue on white labels with a New York, USA address.—			
Blue Note BST-81534	(E)	**Whims Of Chambers**	196?	4.00	10.00
Blue Note BST-81564	(S)	**Paul Chambers Quintet**	196?	5.00	12.00
Blue Note BST-81569	(S)	**Bass On Top**	196?	5.00	12.00
		—Blue Note albums above have blue on white labels with "A Division of Liberty Records."—			
Score SLP-4033	(M)	**A Jazz Delegation From The East— Chambers' Music** *(Score 4033 is a reissue of Jazz West 7.)*	1958	30.00	75.00
Vee Jay LP-1014	(M)	**Go...**	1960	16.00	50.00
Vee Jay LPS-1014	(S)	**Go...**	1960	12.00	40.00
		—Vee Jay albums above have maroon labels.—			
Vee Jay LP-3012	(M)	**First Bassman**	1960	16.00	40.00
Vee Jay SR-3012	(S)	**First Bassman**	1960	12.00	30.00
		—Vee Jay albums above have gloosy black "rainbow" labels.—			
Imperial LP-9182	(M)	**A Jazz Delegation From The East— Chambers' Music**	1961	16.00	40.00
Imperial LP-12182	(E)	**A Jazz Delegation From The East— Chambers' Music** *(Imperial 9182 is a reissue of Jazz West 7.)*	1961	8.00	20.00

CHAMBLEE, EDDIE

Edward Chamblee is a modern jazz tenor saxophone player.

EmArcy MG-36124	(M)	**Chamblee Music**	1958	20.00	50.00
EmArcy MG-36131	(M)	**Doodin'**	1958	20.00	50.00
EmArcy SR-80007	(S)	**Doodin'**	1959	16.00	40.00
		—Mercury albums above have silver on black labels.—			
Mercury MG-20???	(M)	**Chamblee Music**	1960	12.00	30.00
Mercury SR-60127	(S)	**Chamblee Music** *(Mercury 20??? is a reissue of EmArcy 36124.)*	1960	10.00	25.00
Prestige PRLP-7321	(M)	**The Rocking Tenor Sax Of Eddie Chamblee**	1964	12.00	30.00
Prestige PRST-7321	(S)	**The Rocking Tenor Sax Of Eddie Chamblee**	1964	10.00	25.00
		—Prestige albums above have yellow mono or silver stereo labels with a Bergenfield, NJ address.—			

CHAPIN, JIM

James Chapin is a traditional jazz-based drummer.

Prestige PRLP-213	(10")	**Jim Chapin Sextet**	1955	100.00	200.00

CHARLES, RAY

R&B giant Ray Charles recorded as a modern jazz pianist, vocalist and composer, primarily on Atlantic's 1200 jazz series. For additional listings refer to Milt Jackson & Ray Charles; David Newman.

Atlantic 1259	(M)	**The Great Ray Charles**	1957	20.00	50.00
Atlantic SD-1259	(S)	**The Great Ray Charles**	1958	30.00	75.00
Atlantic 1289	(M)	**Ray Charles At Newport**	1958	16.00	40.00
Atlantic SD-1289	(S)	**Ray Charles At Newport**	1958	20.00	50.00
Atlantic 1312	(M)	**The Genius Of Ray Charles**	1960	16.00	40.00
Atlantic SD-1312	(S)	**The Genius Of Ray Charles**	1960	20.00	50.00
		—Atlantic albums above have black mono or green stereo labels.—			
Atlantic 1259	(M)	**The Great Ray Charles**	1961	5.00	12.00
Atlantic SD-1259	(S)	**The Great Ray Charles**	1961	6.00	15.00
Atlantic 1289	(M)	**Ray Charles At Newport**	1961	5.00	12.00
Atlantic SD-1289	(S)	**Ray Charles At Newport**	1961	6.00	15.00
Atlantic 1312	(M)	**The Genius Of Ray Charles**	1961	5.00	12.00
Atlantic SD-1312	(S)	**The Genius Of Ray Charles**	1961	6.00	15.00
		—Atlantic albums above have multi-color labels with a white fan logo.—			
Atlantic 1259	(M)	**The Great Ray Charles**	196?	4.00	10.00
Atlantic SD-1259	(S)	**The Great Ray Charles**	196?	5.00	12.00

Label & Catalog #		Title	Year	VG+	NM
Atlantic 1289	(M)	**Ray Charles At Newport**	196?	4.00	10.00
Atlantic SD-1289	(S)	**Ray Charles At Newport**	196?	5.00	12.00
Atlantic 1312	(M)	**The Genius Of Ray Charles**	196?	4.00	10.00
Atlantic SD-1312	(S)	**The Genius Of Ray Charles**	196?	5.00	12.00
Atlantic 1369	(M)	**The Genius After Hours**	1961	6.00	15.00
Atlantic SD-1369	(S)	**The Genius After Hours**	1961	8.00	20.00
		—Atlantic albums above have multi-color labels with a black fan logo.—			
Hollywood 504	(M)	**Ray Charles**	1959	60.00	150.00
Hollywood 505	(M)	**The Fabulous Ray Charles**	1959	60.00	150.00
		(Hollywood 504 and 505 contain Ray's pre-Atlantic recordings.)			
Impulse A-2	(M)	**Genius + Soul = Jazz**	1961	12.00	30.00
Impulse AS-2	(S)	**Genius + Soul = Jazz**	1961	10.00	25.00
		—Impulse albums above have orange & black labels.—			
Impulse AS-2	(S)	**Genius + Soul = Jazz**	1969	4.00	10.00
		—Impulse albums above have red & black labels with the "abc" logo on top.—			
Premier PM-2004	(M)	**The Great Of Ray Charles**	1962	4.00	10.00
Premier PS-2004	(E)	**The Great Of Ray Charles**	1962	1.00	5.00
Baronet B-111	(M)	**The Artistry Of Ray Charles**	1962	4.00	10.00
Baronet BS-111	(E)	**The Artistry Of Ray Charles**	1962	1.00	5.00
Baronet B-117	(M)	**The Great Of Ray Charles**	1962	4.00	10.00
Baronet BS-117	(E)	**The Great Of Ray Charles**	1962	1.00	5.00
Coronet CX-173	(M)	**Ray Charles**	1962	4.00	10.00
Coronet CXS-173	(E)	**Ray Charles**	1962	1.00	5.00
		(Premier, Design and Coronet recycle the Hollywood material.)			

CHARLES, RAY, & BETTY CARTER

ABC-Paramount ABC-385	(M)	**Ray Charles And Betty Carter**	1961	20.00	50.00
ABC-Paramount ABCS-385	(S)	**Ray Charles And Betty Carter**	1961	30.00	75.00

CHARLES, TEDDY

Theodore Charles Cohen is a modern jazz vibraphone player. For additional listings refer to Lee Konitz / Miles Davis / Teddy Charles; The Manhattan All Stars; The Prestige Jazz Quartet; and the Various Artists section under New Jazz and Prestige.

Prestige PRLP-132	(10")	**Teddy Charles Vibe Solos**	1952	70.00	200.00
Prestige PRLP-143	(10")	**New Directions, Vol. 1**	1953	70.00	200.00
Prestige PRLP-150	(10")	**New Directions, Vol. 2**	1953	70.00	200.00
Prestige PRLP-164	(10")	**New Directions, Vol. 3**	1953	70.00	200.00
Prestige PRLP-169	(10")	**New Directions, Vol. 4**	1954	70.00	200.00
Prestige PRLP-178	(10")	**New Directions, Vol. 5**	1954	70.00	200.00
		(Prestige 178 was reissued as part of 7066, "The Dual Role Of Bob Brookmeyer.")			
New Jazz NJLP-1106	(10")	**New Directions Quartet**	1955	125.00	250.00
Prestige PRLP-206	(10")	**New Directions Quartet**	1955	70.00	200.00
		(Prestige 206 is a reissue of New Jazz 1106.)			
Prestige PRLP-7028	(M)	**Collaboration: West**	1956	40.00	100.00
		(Prestige 7028 is a reissue of 169.)			
Prestige PRLP-7078	(M)	**Evolution**	1957	40.00	100.00
		(Prestige 7078 is a reissue of 164 and 206.)			
		—Prestige albums above have yellow labels with a W. 50th St, NYC address.—			
Prestige PRLP-7028	(M)	**Collaboration: West**	196?	12.00	30.00
Prestige PRLP-7078	(M)	**Evolution**	196?	12.00	30.00
		—Prestige albums above have blue labels with a trident logo on the right side.—			
Atlantic 1229	(M)	**The Teddy Charles Tentet**	1956	30.00	75.00
Atlantic 1274	(M)	**Word From Bird**	1956	30.00	75.00
		—Atlantic albums above have black mono or green stereo labels.—			
Atlantic 1229	(M)	**The Teddy Charles Tentet**	1961	12.00	30.00
Atlantic 1274	(M)	**Word From Bird**	1961	12.00	30.00
		—Atlantic albums above have multi-color labels with a white fan logo.—			
Elektra EKL-136	(M)	**Vibe-Rant**	1957	20.00	50.00
Jubilee JLP-1047	(M)	**Three For Duke**	1957	20.00	50.00
Jubilee JGS-1047	(S)	**Three For Duke**	1958	16.00	40.00
Bethlehem BCP-6032	(M)	**A Salute To Hamp**	1959	20.00	50.00
Bethlehem BCP-6044	(M)	**Teddy Charles On Campus**	1960	20.00	50.00
Warwick W-2033	(M)	**Jazz In The Garden Of The Museum Of Modern Art**	1960	20.00	50.00
Warwick W-2033ST	(S)	**Jazz In The Garden Of The Museum Of Modern Art**	1960	16.00	40.00
Savoy MG-12174	(M)	**The Rant Quintet**	1961	12.00	30.00

Label & Catalog #		Title	Year	VG+	NM
Josie JJM-3505	*(M)*	**Teddy Charles Trio Plays Duke Ellington**	*1963*	12.00	30.00
Josie JJS-3505	*(S)*	**Teddy Charles Trio Plays Duke Ellington**	*1963*	10.00	25.00
		(Josie 3505 is a reissue of Jubilee 1047.)			
United Arts. UAL-3365	*(M)*	**Russia Goes Jazz**	*1964*	12.00	30.00
United Arts. UAS-6365	*(S)*	**Russia Goes Jazz**	*1964*	10.00	25.00

CHERRY, DON
Donald Cherry is a West Coast jazz trumpet player. For additional listings refer to Ayler— Cherry— Rudd— etc.; John Coltrane; Jazz Composers Orchestra; Steve Lacy.

Blue Note BLP-4226	*(M)*	**Complete Communion**	*1966*	12.00	30.00
Blue Note BST-84226	*(S)*	**Complete Communion**	*1966*	10.00	25.00
Blue Note BLP-4247	*(M)*	**Symphony For Improvisers**	*1966*	12.00	30.00
Blue Note BST-84247	*(S)*	**Symphony For Improvisers**	*1966*	10.00	25.00
		—Blue Note albums above have blue on white labels with a 61st St, NYC address.—			
Blue Note BST-84226	*(S)*	**Complete Communion**	*196?*	5.00	12.00
Blue Note BST-84247	*(S)*	**Symphony For Improvisers**	*196?*	5.00	12.00
Blue Note BST-84311	*(S)*	**Where Is Brooklyn?**	*1969*	10.00	25.00
		—Blue Note albums above have blue on white labels with "A Division of Liberty Records."—			

CHILDERS, BUDDY
Marion "Buddy" Childers is a West Coast jazz trumpet player associated with Stan Kenton's groups.

Liberty LJH-6009	*(M)*	**Sam Songs**	*1956*	16.00	40.00
Liberty LJH-6013	*(M)*	**Buddy Childers Quartet**	*1956*	16.00	40.00

CHILDS, SUE

Studio-4 200	*(M)*	**Sue Childs**	*195?*	20.00	50.00

CHITTISON, HERMAN
Herman Chittison is a traditional jazz pianist.

Columbia CL-6134	*(10")*	**Herman Chittison**	*1950*	20.00	50.00
Columbia CL-6182	*(10")*	**Herman Chittison Trio**	*1951*	20.00	50.00

CHRISTIAN, CHARLIE
Charles Christian is a traditional jazz and big band guitarist. For additional listings refer to Dizzie Gillespie; Benny Goodman.

Esoteric ESJ-1	*(10")*	**Jazz Immortal** *(Red vinyl)*	*1951*	60.00	150.00
Esoteric 548	*(M)*	**Jazz Immortal**	*1956*	30.00	75.00
Counterpoint 548	*(M)*	**The Harlem Jazz Scene 1941**	*1956*	30.00	75.00
		(Esoteric and Counterpoint 548 are reissues of Esoteric 1.)			

CHRISTY, JUNE
June Christy is a big band vocalist associated with Stan Kenton. She is backed on many LPs by Pete Rugolo.

Capitol H-516	*(10")*	**Something Cool**	*1954*	30.00	75.00
Capitol T-516	*(M)*	**Something Cool**	*1955*	16.00	40.00
		(Original pressings have a black and white cover with blue tones.)			
Capitol T-656	*(M)*	**Duets**	*1955*	16.00	40.00
		(Capitol 656 also features Stan Kenton.)			
Capitol T-725	*(M)*	**The Misty Miss Christy**	*1956*	16.00	40.00
Capitol T-833	*(M)*	**June Fair And Warmer**	*1957*	16.00	40.00
Capitol T-902	*(M)*	**Gone For The Day**	*1957*	16.00	40.00
Capitol T-1006	*(M)*	**This Is June Christy!**	*1958*	16.00	40.00
		—Capitol albums above have turquoise labels.—			
Capitol T-516	*(M)*	**Something Cool**	*1958*	8.00	20.00
Capitol T-656	*(M)*	**Duets**	*1958*	8.00	20.00
Capitol T-725	*(M)*	**The Misty Miss Christy**	*1958*	8.00	20.00
Capitol T-833	*(M)*	**June Fair And Warmer**	*1958*	8.00	20.00
Capitol T-902	*(M)*	**Gone For The Day**	*1958*	8.00	20.00
Capitol T-1006	*(M)*	**This Is June Christy!**	*1958*	8.00	20.00
Capitol T-1076	*(M)*	**June's Got Rhythm**	*1958*	12.00	30.00
Capitol ST-1076	*(S)*	**June's Got Rhythm**	*1959*	16.00	40.00
Capitol T-1114	*(M)*	**The Song Is June!**	*1959*	12.00	30.00
Capitol ST-1114	*(S)*	**The Song Is June!**	*1959*	16.00	40.00
Capitol T-1202	*(M)*	**June Christy Recalls Those Kenton Days**	*1959*	12.00	30.00
Capitol ST-1202	*(S)*	**June Christy Recalls Those Kenton Days**	*1959*	16.00	40.00
Capitol T-1308	*(M)*	**Ballads For Night People**	*1960*	12.00	30.00
Capitol ST-1308	*(S)*	**Ballads For Night People**	*1960*	16.00	40.00
Capitol T-1327	*(M)*	**Road Show**	*1960*	12.00	30.00
Capitol ST-1327	*(S)*	**Road Show**	*1960*	16.00	40.00

Label & Catalog #		Title	Year	VG+	NM
Capitol T-1398	(M)	**The Cool School**	1960	12.00	30.00
Capitol ST-1398	(S)	**The Cool School**	1960	16.00	40.00
Capitol T-1498	(M)	**Off Beat**	1961	16.00	40.00
Capitol ST-1498	(S)	**Off Beat**	1961	20.00	50.00
Capitol T-1586	(M)	**Do Re Mi**	1961	16.00	40.00
Capitol ST-1586	(S)	**Do Re Mi**	1961	20.00	50.00
Capitol T-1605	(M)	**That Time Of Year**	1961	16.00	40.00
Capitol ST-1605	(S)	**That Time Of Year**	1961	20.00	50.00

—Capitol albums above have black labels with the Capitol logo on the left.—

Capitol T-1693	(M)	**The Best Of June Christy**	1962	10.00	25.00
Capitol ST-1693	(S)	**The Best Of June Christy**	1962	12.00	30.00
Capitol T-1845	(M)	**Big Band Specials**	1963	12.00	30.00
Capitol ST-1845	(S)	**Big Band Specials**	1963	16.00	40.00
Capitol T-1953	(M)	**The Intimate June Christy**	1963	12.00	30.00
Capitol ST-1953	(S)	**The Intimate June Christy**	1963	16.00	40.00
Capitol T-2410	(M)	**Something Broadway, Something Latin**	1965	12.00	30.00
Capitol ST-2410	(S)	**Something Broadway, Something Latin**	1965	16.00	40.00

—Capitol albums above have black labels with the Capitol logo on the top.—

CIRILLO, WALLY / BOBBY SCOTT

Wallace Cirillo is a modern jazz pianist and composer.

Savoy MG-15055	(10")	**Cirillo And Scott**	1955	30.00	75.00

CLARK, DOTTIE

Dorothea Clark is a modern jazz-based vocalist.

Mainstream 56006	(M)	**I'm Lost**	1966	8.00	20.00
Mainstream S-6006	(S)	**I'm Lost**	1966	10.00	25.00

CLARK, SONNY

Conrad "Sonny" Clark is a modern jazz pianist. For additional listings refer to Max Roach & Sonny Clark.

Blue Note BLP-1570	(M)	**Dial "S" For Sonny** *(Deep groove)*	1957	50.00	125.00
Blue Note BLP-1570	(M)	**Dial "S" For Sonny**	1957	30.00	75.00
Blue Note BST-1570	(S)	**Dial "S" For Sonny** *(Deep groove)*	1959	30.00	75.00
Blue Note BST-1570	(S)	**Dial "S" For Sonny**	1959	20.00	50.00
Blue Note BLP-1576	(M)	**Sonny's Crib** *(Deep groove)*	1957	60.00	150.00
Blue Note BLP-1576	(M)	**Sonny's Crib**	1957	40.00	100.00
Blue Note BST-1576	(S)	**Sonny's Crib** *(Deep groove)*	1959	40.00	100.00
Blue Note BST-1576	(S)	**Sonny's Crib**	1959	30.00	75.00
Blue Note BLP-1579	(M)	**Sonny Clark Trio** *(Deep groove)*	1958	50.00	125.00
Blue Note BLP-1579	(M)	**Sonny Clark Trio**	1958	30.00	75.00
Blue Note BST-1579	(S)	**Sonny Clark Trio** *(Deep groove)*	1959	30.00	75.00
Blue Note BST-1579	(S)	**Sonny Clark Trio**	1959	20.00	50.00
Blue Note BLP-1588	(M)	**Cool Struttin'** *(Deep groove)*	1958	50.00	125.00
Blue Note BLP-1588	(M)	**Cool Struttin'**	1958	30.00	75.00
Blue Note BST-1588	(S)	**Cool Struttin'** *(Deep groove)*	1959	30.00	75.00
Blue Note BST-1588	(S)	**Cool Struttin'**	1959	20.00	50.00
Blue Note BLP-1592	(M)	**Cool Struttin'—Volume 2**	1959	*Unreleased*	
Blue Note BST-1592	(S)	**Cool Struttin'—Volume 2**	1959	*Unreleased*	

—Blue Note albums above have blue on white labels with a W. 63rd St, NYC address.—

Blue Note BLP-4091	(M)	**Leapin' And Lopin'**	1961	30.00	75.00
Blue Note BST-84091	(S)	**Leapin' And Lopin'**	1961	20.00	50.00

—Blue Note albums above have blue on white labels with a 61st St, NYC address.—

Blue Note BLP-1570	(M)	**Dial "S" For Sonny**	1963	10.00	25.00
Blue Note BST-1570	(S)	**Dial "S" For Sonny**	1963	8.00	20.00
Blue Note BLP-1576	(M)	**Sonny's Crib**	1963	10.00	25.00
Blue Note BST-1576	(S)	**Sonny's Crib**	1963	8.00	20.00
Blue Note BLP-1579	(M)	**Sonny Clark Trio**	1963	10.00	25.00
Blue Note BST-1579	(S)	**Sonny Clark Trio**	1963	8.00	20.00
Blue Note BLP-1588	(M)	**Cool Struttin'**	1963	10.00	25.00
Blue Note BST-1588	(S)	**Cool Struttin'**	1963	8.00	20.00
Blue Note BLP-4091	(M)	**Leapin' And Lopin'**	1963	10.00	25.00
Blue Note BST-84091	(S)	**Leapin' And Lopin'**	1963	8.00	20.00

—Blue Note albums above have blue on white labels with a New York, USA address.—

Blue Note BST-81570	(S)	**Dial "S" For Sonny**	196?	5.00	12.00
Blue Note BST-81576	(S)	**Sonny's Crib**	196?	5.00	12.00
Blue Note BST-81579	(S)	**Sonny Clark Trio**	196?	5.00	12.00
Blue Note BST-81588	(S)	**Cool Struttin'**	196?	5.00	12.00
Blue Note BST-84091	(S)	**Leapin' And Lopin'**	196?	5.00	12.00

—Blue Note albums above have blue on white labels with "A Division of Liberty Records."—

Label & Catalog #		Title	Year	VG+	NM
Time T-70010	(M)	**Sonny Clark Trio**	1960	20.00	50.00
Time ST-70010	(S)	**Sonny Clark Trio**	1960	16.00	40.00
Time 52101	(M)	**Sonny Clark Trio**	1962	12.00	30.00
Time S-2101	(S)	**Sonny Clark Trio**	1962	10.00	25.00
		(Time 52101 is a reissue of 70010.)			

CLARKE, BUCK

Buck Clarke is a jazz-based congo player.

Offbeat OLP-3003	(M)	**Cool Hands**	1959	16.00	40.00
Offbeat OS-93003	(S)	**Cool Hands**	1959	12.00	30.00
Argo LP-4007	(M)	**Drum Sum**	1960	12.00	30.00
Argo LPS-4007	(S)	**Drum Sum**	1960	10.00	25.00
Argo LP-4021	(M)	**Sounds**	1963	12.00	30.00
Argo LPS-4021	(S)	**Sounds**	1963	10.00	25.00

CLARKE, KEN

Kenneth Clarke is a jazz-based pianist.

MGM E-205	(10")	**Jazz Piano**	1953	20.00	50.00

CLARKE, KENNY

Kenneth "Klook" Clarke is a modern jazz drummer. For additional listings refer to The Modern Jazz Quartet; The Trio; and the Various Artists section under Savoy.

Savoy MG-15051	(10")	**Kenny Clarke, Vol. 1**	1955	60.00	150.00
Savoy MG-15053	(10")	**Kenny Clarke, Vol. 2**	1955	60.00	150.00
Savoy MG-12006	(M)	**Telefunken Blues**	1955	30.00	75.00
		(Savoy 12006 is a reissue of 15033 and 15051.)			
Savoy MG-12017	(M)	**Bohemia After Dark**	1955	30.00	75.00
Savoy MG-12065	(M)	**Klook's Clique**	1956	30.00	75.00
		(Savoy 12065 also features John LaPorta.)			
Epic LN-3376	(M)	**Kenny Clarke Plays Andre Hodeir**	1957	16.00	40.00
Prestige PRST-7605	(E)	**Paris Bebop Sessions 1948-50**	1969	6.00	15.00

— Prestige albums above have blue labels with a trident logo on top.—

CLARKE, KENNY, & ERNIE WILKINS

Savoy MG-12007	(M)	**Plenty For Kenny**	1955	30.00	75.00

CLARKE, KENNY, & FRANCY BOLAND (THE CLARKE-BOLAND BIG BAND)

Blue Note BLP-4092	(M)	**The Golden Eight**	1961	30.00	75.00
Blue Note BST-84092	(S)	**The Golden Eight**	1961	20.00	50.00
		— Blue Note albums above have blue on white labels with a 61st St, NYC address.—			
Blue Note BLP-4092	(M)	**The Golden Eight**	1963	10.00	25.00
Blue Note BST-84092	(S)	**The Golden Eight**	1963	8.00	20.00
		— Blue Note albums above have blue on white labels with a New York, USA address.—			
Blue Note BST-84092	(S)	**The Golden Eight**	196?	5.00	12.00
		— Blue Note albums above have blue on white labels with a "A Division of Liberty Records."—			
Atlantic 1401	(M)	**Jazz Is Universal**	1963	16.00	40.00
Atlantic SD-1401	(S)	**Jazz Is Universal**	1963	12.00	30.00
Atlantic 1404	(M)	**The Clarke-Boland Big Band**	1963	12.00	30.00
Atlantic SD-1404	(S)	**The Clarke-Boland Big Band**	1963	10.00	25.00
		— Atlantic albums above have multi-color labels with a black fan logo.—			
Columbia CL-2314	(M)	**Now Hear Our Meanin'**	1965	8.00	20.00
Columbia CS-9114	(S)	**Now Hear Our Meanin'**	1965	6.00	15.00
		— Columbia albums above have "360 Sound" in white on the bottom of the label.—			
Prestige PRST-7634	(S)	**Fire, Soul, Heat & Guts**	1969	6.00	15.00
Prestige PRST-7699	(S)	**Let's Face The Music**	1969	6.00	15.00

— Prestige albums above have blue labels with a trident logo on top.—

CLAY, JAMES, & DAVID "FATHEAD" NEWMAN

Riverside RLP-12-327	(M)	**The Sound Of The Wide Open Spaces!!!**	1960	16.00	40.00
Riverside RLP-1178	(S)	**The Sound Of The Wide Open Spaces!!!**	1960	12.00	30.00

— Riverside albums above have blue mono or black stereo labels with a reel & mike logo on top.—

CLAY, JAMES

James Clay is a West Coast jazz tenor saxophone and flute player.

Riverside RLP-349	(M)	**A Double Dose Of Soul**	1961	16.00	40.00
Riverside RS-9349	(S)	**A Double Dose Of Soul**	1961	12.00	30.00

— Riverside albums above have blue mono or black stereo labels with a reel & mike logo on top.—

Label & Catalog #		Title	Year	VG+	NM

CLAYTON, BUCK

Wilbur "Buck" Clayton is a traditional jazz trumpet player and arranger. For additional listings refer to Harry Edison; Duke Ellington / Buck Clayton; Tommy Gwaltney; Coleman Hawkins; Odetta; Nat Pierce; Paul Quinichette; Mary Lou Williams & Don Byas.

Columbia CL-548	(M)	**Hucklebuck & Robbin's Nest**	1954	20.00	50.00
Columbia CL-567	(M)	**How High The Fi**	1954	20.00	50.00
Columbia CL-6325	(10")	**Moten Swing—Sentimental Journey**	1955	20.00	50.00
Columbia CL-6326	(10")	**How Hi The Fi**	1955	20.00	50.00
Columbia CL-614	(M)	**Buck Clayton Jams Benny Goodman**	1955	20.00	50.00
		—Columbia albums above have "Long Playing" on the bottom of the label.—			
Columbia CL-548	(M)	**Hucklebuck & Robbin's Nest**	195?	12.00	30.00
Columbia CL-567	(M)	**How High The Fi**	195?	12.00	30.00
Columbia CL-614	(M)	**Buck Clayton Jams Benny Goodman**	195?	12.00	30.00
Columbia CL-701	(M)	**Jumpin' At The Woodside**	1955	12.00	30.00
Columbia CL-808	(M)	**Jazz Spectacular**	1956	12.00	30.00
Columbia CL-882	(M)	**All The Cats Join In**	1956	12.00	30.00
Columbia CL-1320	(M)	**Songs For Swingers**	1959	12.00	30.00
Columbia CS-8123	(S)	**Songs For Swingers**	1959	10.00	25.00
		—Columbia albums above have six white on black "eye" logos on each label.—			
Jazztone J-1225	(M)	**Meet Buck Clayton**	1956	16.00	40.00

CLAYTON, BUCK, & RUBY BRAFF & MEL POWELL

Vanguard VRS-8008	(10")	**Buck Meets Ruby**	1954	20.00	50.00
Vanguard VRS-8514	(M)	**Buckin' The Blues**	1957	16.00	40.00
Vanguard VRS-8517	(M)	**Buck Meets Ruby And Mel**	1957	16.00	40.00

CLAYTON, BUCK, & BUDDY TATE

Swingville SVLP-2017	(M)	**Buck & Buddy**	1961	20.00	50.00
Swingville SVLP-2030	(M)	**Buck & Buddy Blow The Blues**	1962	20.00	50.00
Swingville SVST-2030	(S)	**Buck & Buddy Blow The Blues**	1962	16.00	40.00
		—Swingville albums above have purple mono or red stereo labels.—			
Swingville SVLP-2017	(M)	**Buck & Buddy**	1965	10.00	25.00
Swingville SVLP-2030	(M)	**Buck & Buddy Blow The Blues**	1965	10.00	25.00
Swingville SVST-2030	(S)	**Buck & Buddy Blow The Blues**	1965	8.00	20.00
		—Swingville albums above have blue labels with a trident logo on the right side.—			

CLAYTON, BUCK / "WILD" BILL DAVISON

Jazztone J-1267	(M)	**Singing Trumpets**	1957	16.00	40.00

CLEVELAND, JIMMY

James Cleveland is a modern jazz trombone player. For additional listings refer to Sonny Rollins / Jimmy Cleveland; and the Various Artists section under Savoy.

EmArcy MG-36066	(M)	**Introducing Jimmy Cleveland & His All Stars**	1956	20.00	50.00
EmArcy MG-36126	(M)	**Cleveland Style**	1958	20.00	50.00
		—EmArcy albums above have blue labels with silver print.—			
Mercury MG-20442	(M)	**A Map Of Jimmy Cleveland**	1959	16.00	40.00
Mercury SR-60117	(S)	**A Map Of Jimmy Cleveland**	1959	12.00	30.00
Mercury MG-20553	(M)	**Cleveland Style**	1960	16.00	40.00
Mercury SR-60121	(S)	**Cleveland Style**	1960	12.00	30.00
		(Mercury 20553 is a reissue of EmArcy 36126.)			
		—Mercury albums above have silver on black labels.—			
EmArcy MGE-26003	(M)	**Rhythm Crazy**	1964	10.00	25.00
EmArcy SRE-66003	(E)	**Rhythm Crazy**	1964	6.00	15.00

CLIFTON, BILL

William Clifton is a jazz-based pianist.

Columbia CL-6166	(10")	**Piano Moods**	1951	20.00	50.00

CLINTON, LARRY

Lawrence Clinton is a traditional jazz-based trumpet player, composer, arranger and big band leader.

Camden CAL-434	(M)	**Dance Date**	1958	8.00	20.00

CLOONEY, ROSEMARY

Rosemary Clooney is a big band based vocalist.

Columbia CL-6224	(10")	**Hollywood's Best**	1952	24.00	60.00
		(Columbia 6224 also features Harry James.)			
Columbia CL-2525	(10")	**Tenderly**	1955	24.00	60.00
Columbia CL-2572	(10")	**A Date With The King**	1956	24.00	60.00
		(Columbia 2572 also features Benny Goodman.)			

Label & Catalog #		Title	Year	VG+	NM
Columbia CL-2581	*(10")*	**On Stage**	*1956*	**24.00**	**60.00**
Columbia CL-585	*(M)*	**Hollywood's Best**	*1955*	**20.00**	**50.00**
		(Columbia 585 also features Harry James.)			
		—Columbia albums above have "Long Playing" on the bottom of the label.—			
Columbia CL-872	*(M)*	**Blue Rose**	*1956*	**12.00**	**30.00**
		(Columbia 872 also features Duke Ellington.)			
Columbia CL-969	*(M)*	**Clooney Tunes**	*1957*	**30.00**	**75.00**
Columbia CL-1230	*(M)*	**Rosemary Clooney's Greatest Hits**	*1957*	**16.00**	**40.00**
		—Columbia albums above have six white on black "eye" logos on each label.—			
Harmony HL-7123	*(M)*	**Rosemary Clooney In High Fidelity**	*195?*	**10.00**	**25.00**
Harmony HL-7213	*(M)*	**Hollywood Hits**	*195?*	**10.00**	**25.00**
Coral CRL-57266	*(M)*	**Swing Around Rosie**	*1958*	**12.00**	**30.00**
Coral CRL-757266	*(S)*	**Swing Around Rosie**	*1958*	**16.00**	**40.00**
MGM E-3834	*(M)*	**Rosie Swings Softly**	*1960*	**12.00**	**30.00**
MGM SE-3834	*(S)*	**Rosie Swings Softly**	*1960*	**16.00**	**40.00**
RCA Victor LPM-2133	*(M)*	**A Touch Of Tabasco**	*1960*	**8.00**	**20.00**
RCA Victor LSP-2133	*(S)*	**A Touch Of Tabasco**	*1960*	**10.00**	**25.00**
RCA Victor LPM-2212	*(M)*	**Clap Hands, Here Comes Rosie**	*1960*	**8.00**	**20.00**
RCA Victor LSP-2212	*(S)*	**Clap Hands, Here Comes Rosie**	*1960*	**10.00**	**25.00**
RCA Victor LPM-2265	*(M)*	**Rosie Solves The Swingin' Riddle**	*1961*	**8.00**	**20.00**
RCA Victor LSP-2265	*(S)*	**Rosie Solves The Swingin' Riddle**	*1961*	**10.00**	**25.00**
		—RCA albums above have black labels with "Long Play" or "Living Stereo" on the bottom.—			
Reprise R-6088	*(M)*	**Love**	*1963*	**12.00**	**30.00**
Reprise R9-6088	*(S)*	**Love**	*1963*	**16.00**	**40.00**
Reprise R-6108	*(M)*	**Thanks For Nothing**	*1964*	**12.00**	**30.00**
Reprise R9-6108	*(S)*	**Thanks For Nothing**	*1964*	**16.00**	**40.00**

CLOONEY, ROSEMARY, & BING CROSBY

Label & Catalog #		Title	Year	VG+	NM
RCA Victor LPM-1854	*(M)*	**Fancy Meeting You Here**	*1958*	**20.00**	**50.00**
		—RCA albums above black labels with "Long Play" on the bottom.—			
Capitol T-2300	*(M)*	**That Travelin' Two Beat**	*1965*	**10.00**	**25.00**
Capitol ST-2300	*(M)*	**That Travelin' Two Beat**	*1965*	**12.00**	**30.00**

CLOONEY, ROSEMARY, & THE HI—LO'S

Label & Catalog #		Title	Year	VG+	NM
Columbia CL-1006	*(M)*	**Ring Around Rosie**	*1957*	**16.00**	**40.00**
		—Columbia albums above have six white on black "eye" logos on each label.—			
Harmony HL-7236	*(M)*	**Young At Heart**	*195?*	**6.00**	**15.00**

COATES, JOHNNY JR.

Label & Catalog #		Title	Year	VG+	NM
Savoy MG-12082	*(M)*	**Portrait**	*1956*	**16.00**	**40.00**

COBB, ARNETT

Arnett Cobb is a traditional jazz tenor saxophone player. For additional listings refer to the Various Artists section under Prestige.

Label & Catalog #		Title	Year	VG+	NM
Apollo LP-105	*(10")*	**Swingin' With Arnett Cobb**	*1952*	**100.00**	**200.00**
Prestige PRLP-7151	*(M)*	**Blow Arnett, Blow**	*1959*	**20.00**	**50.00**
		(Prestige 7151 also features Eddie Davis.)			
Prestige PRLP-7165	*(M)*	**Party Time**	*1959*	**20.00**	**50.00**
Prestige PRLP-7175	*(M)*	**More Party Time**	*1960*	**20.00**	**50.00**
Prestige PRLP-7184	*(M)*	**Smooth Sailing**	*1960*	**20.00**	**50.00**
Prestige PRLP-7216	*(M)*	**Movin' Right Along**	*1961*	**20.00**	**50.00**
Prestige PRLP-7227	*(M)*	**Sizzlin'**	*1962*	**20.00**	**50.00**
Prestige PRST-7227	*(S)*	**Sizzlin'**	*1962*	**16.00**	**40.00**
		—Prestige albums above have yellow mono or silver stereo labels with a Bergenfield, NJ address.—			
Prestige PRLP-7151	*(M)*	**Blow Arnett, Blow**	*196?*	**10.00**	**25.00**
Prestige PRLP-7165	*(M)*	**Party Time**	*196?*	**10.00**	**25.00**
Prestige PRLP-7175	*(M)*	**More Party Time**	*196?*	**10.00**	**25.00**
Prestige PRLP-7184	*(M)*	**Smooth Sailing**	*196?*	**10.00**	**25.00**
Prestige PRLP-7216	*(M)*	**Movin' Right Along**	*196?*	**10.00**	**25.00**
Prestige PRLP-7227	*(M)*	**Sizzlin'**	*196?*	**10.00**	**25.00**
Prestige PRST-7227	*(S)*	**Sizzlin'**	*196?*	**8.00**	**20.00**
		—Prestige albums above have blue labels with a trident logo on the right side.—			
Moodsville MVLP-14	*(M)*	**Ballads By Cobb**	*1961*	**20.00**	**50.00**
		—Moodsville mono albums above have green labels with silver print.—			
Moodsville MVLP-14	*(M)*	**Ballads By Cobb**	*1965*	**10.00**	**25.00**
		—Moodsville albums above have blue labels with a trident logo on the right side.—			
Prestige PRST-7711	*(S)*	**The Best Of Arnett Cobb**	*1969*	**5.00**	**12.00**
		—Prestige albums above have blue labels with a trident logo on top.—			

Al Cohn got his start with the big bands of Joe Marsala in 1943 before moving on to Georgie Auld (1944-46), Alvino Rey (1947), Buddy Rich (1947), Woody Herman (1947-48), and Artie Shaw (1949) before "retiring." He returned in 1952 with Elliot Lawrence and then wrote for such popular TV shows of the times as Steve Allen and Pat Boone! He signed with RCA (1955-56) before forming the famed Al Cohn-Zoot Sims Quintet in 1957 (examples from both periods are pictured above). He has been a featured performer on albums by Bob Brookmeyer, Boots Brown, Candido, Ted McNabb, and Sims. He has also recorded as a sideman with Manny Albam on Coral, Miles Davis on Prestige, Art Farmer, Irene Kral and Bill Potts on United Artists, Lawrence on Fantasy, Gerry Mulligan on World Pacific, Jim Raney on ABC-Paramount, and backing Jack Kerouac on Hanover.

Label & Catalog #		Title	Year	VG+	NM

COBB, JUNIE C.

Junius Cobb is a traditional jazz piano, banjo, clarinet and saxophone(s) player and composer.

Riverside RLP-415	(M)	**Junie C. Cobb And His New Hometown Band**	1962	12.00	30.00
Riverside RS-9415	(E)	**Junie C. Cobb And His New Hometown Band**	1962	6.00	15.00

—Riverside albums above have blue mono or black stereo labels with a reel & mike logo on top.—

COHN, AL

Alvin Cohn is a modern jazz tenor saxophone player and arranger. For additional listings refer to Bob Brookmeyer; Boots Brown; Candido; The Four Brothers; The Four Most; Kent Harian; Jack Kerouac; Ted McNabb; Zoot Sims; Zoot Sims & Tony Scott & Al Cohn.; and the Various Artists section under Prestige and United Artists.

Progressive PLP-3002	(10")	**Al Cohn Quartet**	1953	125.00	250.00
Progressive PLP-3004	(10")	**Al Cohn Quintet**	1953	125.00	250.00
Savoy MG-12048	(M)	**Cohn's Tones**	1956	40.00	100.00
		(Savoy 12048 is a reissue of Progressive 3002 and 3004.)			
RCA Victor LJM-1024	(M)	**Mr. Music**	1955	30.00	75.00
RCA Victor LPM-1116	(M)	**The Natural Seven**	1955	30.00	75.00
RCA Victor LPM-1161	(M)	**Four Brass One Tenor**	1956	30.00	75.00
RCA Victor LPM-1207	(M)	**That Old Feeling**	1956	30.00	75.00
RCA Victor LPM-2312	(M)	**Son Of Drum Suite**	1960	20.00	50.00
RCA Victor LSP-2312	(S)	**Son Of Drum Suite**	1960	16.00	40.00
		—RCA albums above have black labels with "Long Play" or "Living Stereo" on the bottom.—			
Dawn DLP-1110	(M)	**Cohn On The Saxophone**	1956	40.00	100.00
Coral CRL-57118	(M)	**Al Cohn Quintet**	1957	20.00	50.00

COHN, AL, & RICH KAMUCA & BILL PERKINS

RCA Victor LPM-1162	(M)	**The Brothers**	1955	30.00	75.00

—RCA albums above have black labels with "Long Play" on the bottom.—

COHN, AL / SHORTY ROGERS

RCA Victor LJM-1020	(M)	**East Coast—West Coast Scene**	1954	60.00	150.00

—RCA albums above have black labels with "Long Play" on the bottom.—

COHN, AL, & ZOOT SIMS

RCA Victor LPM-1282	(M)	**From A To Z**	1956	30.00	75.00
		—RCA albums above have black labels with "Long Play" on the bottom.—			
Coral CRL-57171	(M)	**Al And Zoot**	1958	20.00	50.00
Abundant Sounds 1	(M)	**Either Way**	1960	30.00	75.00
Mercury MG-20606	(M)	**You 'N Me**	1960	16.00	40.00
Mercury SR-60606	(S)	**You 'N Me**	1960	12.00	30.00

COKER, JERRY

Gerald Coker is a modern jazz tenor saxophone player and arranger. For additional listings refer to the Various Artists section under Savoy.

Fantasy 3214	(M)	**Modern Music From Indiana U** *(Dark red vinyl)*	1956	24.00	60.00
		—Fantasy albums above have red labels on dark red, non-flexible vinyl.—			
Fantasy 3214	(M)	**Modern Music From Indiana U**	195?	16.00	40.00

—Fantasy albums above have red labels on non-flexible vinyl.—

COLE, COZY

William "Cozy" Cole is a traditional jazz-based drummer. For additional listings refer to Hot Lips Page.

Audition 33-5943	(M)	**Cozy Cole**	1955	20.00	50.00
Bethlehem BCP-21	(M)	**Jazz At The Metropole Cafe**	1955	20.00	50.00
Paris 122	(M)	**Cozy Cole And His All-Stars**	1958	20.00	50.00
King 673	(M)	**Cozy Cole**	1959	30.00	75.00
		—King albums above have black labels without a crown on top.—			
Love 500M	(M)	**Topsy**	195?	40.00	100.00
Love 500S	(S)	**Topsy**	195?	100.00	200.00
Charlie Parker PLP-403	(M)	**A Cozy Conaption Of Carmen**	1962	10.00	25.00
Charlie Parker PLP-403S	(S)	**A Cozy Conaption Of Carmen**	1962	8.00	20.00
Coral CRL-57423	(M)	**Drum Beat Dancing Feet**	1962	8.00	20.00
Coral CRL-757423	(S)	**Drum Beat Dancing Feet**	1962	6.00	15.00
Coral CRL-57457	(M)	**It's A Cozy World**	1964	8.00	20.00
Coral CRL-757457	(S)	**It's A Cozy World**	1964	6.00	15.00
Columbia CL-2553	(M)	**It's A Rockin' Thing**	1965	8.00	20.00
Columbia CS-9353	(S)	**It's A Rockin' Thing**	1965	6.00	15.00
Savoy MG-12197	(M)	**Concerto For Cozy**	196?	8.00	20.00

Label & Catalog #		Title	Year	VG+	NM
COLE, COZY / EARL HINES					
Felsted 7002	(M)	**Cozy's Caravan / Earl's Backroom**	1958	20.00	50.00
Felsted 2002	(S)	**Cozy's Caravan / Earl's Backroom**	1959	16.00	40.00
COLE, COZY / JIMMY McPARTLAND					
Grand Award GA-33-334	(M)	**After Hours**	1956	16.00	40.00
COLE, IKE					
Dee Cee LPM-4001	(M)	**Ike Cole's Tribute To His Brother Nat**	195?	20.00	50.00
COLE, NAT "KING"					
Nathaniel Coles, aka Nat King Cole, is a traditional jazz-based pianist and vocalist who moved into the world of popular song and international stardom. For additional listings refer to Lester Young; and the Jazzy Soundtracks section under Capitol.					
Capitol H-8	(10")	**The King Cole Trio**	1950	20.00	50.00
Capitol H-29	(10")	**The King Cole Trio, Volume 2**	1950	20.00	50.00
Capitol H-59	(10")	**The King Cole Trio, Volume 3**	1950	20.00	50.00
Capitol H-156	(10")	**Nat King Cole At The Piano**	1950	20.00	50.00
Capitol H-177	(10")	**The King Cole Trio, Volume 4**	1950	20.00	50.00
Capitol H-213	(10")	**Harvest Of Hits**	1950	20.00	50.00
Capitol H-220	(10")	**The Nat King Cole Trio, Volume 1**	1950	20.00	50.00
Capitol H-332	(10")	**Penthouse Serenade**	1952	20.00	50.00
Capitol H-420	(10")	**Nat King Cole Sings For Two In Love**	1952	20.00	50.00
Capitol T-332	(M)	**Penthouse Serenade**	1955	16.00	40.00
Capitol T-420	(M)	**Nat King Cole Sings For Two In Love**	1955	16.00	40.00
Capitol W-514	(M)	**10th Anniversary**	1955	16.00	40.00
Capitol T-592	(M)	**Instrumental Classics**	1955	16.00	40.00
Capitol W-689	(M)	**The Piano Style Of Nat King Cole**	1956	16.00	40.00
Capitol W-782	(M)	**After Midnight**	1956	16.00	40.00
—Capitol albums above have turquoise labels.—					
Capitol T-332	(M)	**Penthouse Serenade**	195?	8.00	20.00
Capitol W-514	(M)	**10th Anniversary**	195?	8.00	20.00
Capitol T-592	(M)	**Instrumental Classics**	195?	8.00	20.00
Capitol W-689	(M)	**The Piano Style Of Nat King Cole**	195?	8.00	20.00
Capitol W-782	(M)	**After Midnight**	195?	8.00	20.00
Capitol W-1675	(M)	**Nat King Cole Sings/George Shearing Plays**	1962	6.00	15.00
Capitol ST-1675	(S)	**Nat King Cole Sings/George Shearing Plays**	1962	8.00	20.00
Capitol W-1713	(M)	**Nat King Cole Sings The Blues**	1962	6.00	15.00
Capitol SW-1713	(S)	**Nat King Cole Sings The Blues**	1962	8.00	20.00
—Capitol albums above have black "rainbow" labels with the logo on the left side.—					
Capitol T-332	(M)	**Penthouse Serenade**	196?	5.00	12.00
Capitol W-514	(M)	**10th Anniversary**	196?	5.00	12.00
Capitol T-592	(M)	**Instrumental Classics**	196?	5.00	12.00
Capitol W-689	(M)	**The Piano Style Of Nat King Cole**	196?	5.00	12.00
Capitol W-782	(M)	**After Midnight**	196?	5.00	12.00
Capitol W-1675	(M)	**Nat King Cole Sings/George Shearing Plays**	196?	5.00	10.00
Capitol ST-1675	(S)	**Nat King Cole Sings/George Shearing Plays**	196?	5.00	12.00
Capitol W-1713	(M)	**Nat King Cole Sings The Blues**	196?	4.00	10.00
Capitol SW-1713	(S)	**Nat King Cole Sings The Blues**	196?	5.00	12.00
Capitol W-1929	(M)	**Nat King Cole Sings The Blues, Volume 2**	1963	5.00	12.00
Capitol SW-1929	(S)	**Nat King Cole Sings The Blues, Volume 2**	1963	6.00	15.00
Capitol T-2311	(M)	**The Nat King Cole Trio**	1965	6.00	15.00
—Capitol albums above have black "rainbow" labels with the logo on top.—					
Decca DL-8260	(M)	**In The Beginning**	1956	16.00	40.00
Verve VSP-14	(M)	**Nat Cole At JATP**	1966	5.00	12.00
Verve VSPS-14	(E)	**Nat Cole At JATP**	1966	4.00	10.00
Verve VSP-25	(M)	**Nat Cole At JATP 2**	1966	5.00	12.00
Verve VSPS-25	(E)	**Nat Cole At JATP 2**	1966	4.00	10.00
COLEMAN, CY					
Seymour Kaufman, aka Cy Coleman, is a modern jazz-based pianist.					
Benida LP-1023A	(10")	**Cy Coleman**	1955	20.00	50.00
Westminster WLP-15001	(M)	**Cool Coleman**	195?	16.00	40.00
COLEMAN, EARL					
Earl Coleman is a modern jazz-based vocalist.					
Prestige PRLP-7045	(M)	**Earl Coleman Returns**	1956	20.00	50.00
—Prestige albums above have yellow labels with a W. 50th St, NYC address.—					

Label & Catalog #		Title	Year	VG+	NM
Prestige PRLP-7045	(M)	**Earl Coleman Returns**	196?	10.00	25.00
—Prestige albums above have a blue labels with a trident logo on the right side.—					
Atlantic SD-8172	(S)	**Love Songs**	1968	6.00	15.00
—Atlantic albums above have multi-color labels with a black fan logo.—					

COLEMAN, ERNIE

Warner Bros. W-1261	(M)	**Be Gentle, Please**	1959	10.00	25.00
Warner Bros. WS-1261	(S)	**Be Gentle, Please**	1959	10.00	25.00

COLEMAN, GLORIA, & POLA ROBERTS

Gloria Coleman is a modern jazz organist.

Impulse A-47	(M)	**Soul Sisters**	1963	12.00	30.00
Impulse AS-47	(S)	**Soul Sisters**	1963	10.00	25.00
—Impulse albums above have orange & black labels.—					
Impulse AS-47	(S)	**Soul Sisters**	1968	4.00	10.00
—Impulse albums above have red & black labels with the "abc" logo on top.—					

COLEMAN, ORNETTE

Ornette Coleman is a modern jazz atlo saxophone player and composer,.

Contemporary C-3551	(M)	**The Music Of Ornette Coleman—Something Else!**	1958	40.00	100.00
Contemporary S-7551	(S)	**The Music Of Ornette Coleman—Something Else!**	1959	30.00	75.00
Contemporary M-3569	(M)	**Tomorrow Is The Question**	1959	30.00	75.00
Contemporary S-7569	(S)	**Tomorrow Is The Question**	1959	20.00	50.00
—Contemporary stereo albums have gold & black labels.—					
Atlantic 1317	(M)	**The Shape Of Jazz To Come**	1959	20.00	50.00
Atlantic SD-1317	(S)	**The Shape Of Jazz To Come**	1959	16.00	40.00
—Atlantic albums above have white "bullseye" labels.					
Atlantic 1317	(M)	**The Shape Of Jazz To Come**	1960	8.00	20.00
Atlantic SD-1317	(S)	**The Shape Of Jazz To Come**	1960	6.00	15.00
Atlantic 1327	(M)	**Change Of The Century**	1960	10.00	25.00
Atlantic SD-1327	(S)	**Change Of The Century**	1960	8.00	20.00
Atlantic 1353	(M)	**This Is Our Music**	1960	10.00	25.00
Atlantic SD-1353	(S)	**This Is Our Music**	1960	8.00	20.00
Atlantic 1364	(M)	**Free Jazz**	1961	10.00	25.00
Atlantic SD-1364	(S)	**Free Jazz**	1961	8.00	20.00
Atlantic 1378	(M)	**Ornette**	1961	10.00	25.00
Atlantic SD-1378	(S)	**Ornette**	1961	8.00	20.00
—Atlantic albums above have multi-color labels with a white fan logo.—					
Atlantic 1317	(M)	**The Shape Of Jazz To Come**	196?	5.00	12.00
Atlantic SD-1317	(S)	**The Shape Of Jazz To Come**	196?	4.00	10.00
Atlantic 1327	(M)	**Change Of The Century**	196?	5.00	12.00
Atlantic SD-1327	(S)	**Change Of The Century**	196?	4.00	10.00
Atlantic 1353	(M)	**This Is Our Music**	196?	5.00	12.00
Atlantic SD-1353	(S)	**This Is Our Music**	196?	4.00	10.00
Atlantic 1364	(M)	**Free Jazz**	196?	5.00	12.00
Atlantic SD-1364	(S)	**Free Jazz**	196?	4.00	10.00
Atlantic 1378	(M)	**Ornette**	196?	5.00	12.00
Atlantic SD-1378	(S)	**Ornette**	196?	4.00	10.00
Atlantic 1394	(M)	**Ornette On Tenor**	1962	8.00	20.00
Atlantic SD-1394	(S)	**Ornette On Tenor**	1962	6.00	15.00
—Atlantic albums above have multi-color labels with a black fan logo.—					
RCA Victor LPM-2982	(M)	**The Music Of Ornette Coleman**	1964	12.00	30.00
RCA Victor LSP-2982	(S)	**The Music Of Ornette Coleman**	1964	10.00	25.00
—RCA albums above have black labels with "Mono" or "Living Stereo" on the bottom.—					
Blue Note BLP-4210	(M)	**Town Hall Concert, Volume 1**	1965	*Unreleased*	
Blue Note BST-84210	(S)	**Town Hall Concert, Volume 1**	1965	*Unreleased*	
Blue Note BLP-4211	(M)	**Town Hall Concert, Volume 2**	1965	*Unreleased*	
Blue Note BST-84211	(S)	**Town Hall Concert, Volume 2**	1965	*Unreleased*	
Blue Note BLP-4224	(M)	**Ornette Coleman At The Golden Circle, Stockholm, Vol. 1**	1965	16.00	40.00
Blue Note BST-84224	(S)	**Ornette Coleman At The Golden Circle, Stockholm, Vol. 1**	1965	12.00	30.00
Blue Note BLP-4225	(M)	**Ornette Coleman At The Golden Circle, Stockholm, Vol. 2**	1965	16.00	40.00
Blue Note BST-84225	(S)	**Ornette Coleman At The Golden Circle, Stockholm, Vol. 2**	1965	12.00	30.00
Blue Note BLP-4246	(M)	**The Empty Foxhole**	1966	16.00	40.00
Blue Note BST-84246	(S)	**The Empty Foxhole**	1966	12.00	30.00
—Blue Note albums above have blue on white labels with a New York, USA address.—					

Label & Catalog #		Title	Year	VG+	NM
Blue Note BST-84224	(S)	**Ornette Coleman At The Golden Circle, Stockholm, Vol. 1**	196?	5.00	12.00
Blue Note BST-84225	(S)	**Ornette Coleman At The Golden Circle, Stockholm, Vol. 2**	196?	5.00	12.00
Blue Note BST-84246	(S)	**The Empty Foxhole**	196?	5.00	12.00
Blue Note BST-84287	(S)	**New York Is Now!**	1968	10.00	25.00
—Blue Note albums above have blue on white labels with "A Division of Liberty Records."—					
ESP-Disk' 1006	(M)	**Town Hall Concert, December 1962**	1965	10.00	25.00
ESP-Disk' 1006	(S)	**Town Hall Concert, December 1962**	1965	8.00	20.00
		(ESP 1005 contain material intended for Blue Note 4210 and 4211.)			
Impulse AS-9178	(S)	**Ornette At 12**	1968	10.00	25.00
Impulse AS-9187	(S)	**Crisis**	1969	10.00	25.00

COLES, JOHNNY

John Coles is a modern jazz trumpet player.

Epic LA-16015	(M)	**The Warm Sound**	1961	50.00	125.00
Epic BA-17015	(S)	**The Warm Sound**	1961	40.00	100.00
Blue Note BLP-4144	(M)	**Little Johnny C**	1963	20.00	50.00
Blue Note BST-84144	(S)	**Little Johnny C**	1963	16.00	40.00
—Blue Note albums above have blue on white labels with a New York, USA address.—					
Blue Note BST-84144	(S)	**Little Johnny C**	196?	5.00	12.00
—Blue Note albums above have blue on white labels with "A Division of Liberty Records."—					

COLLEGE ALL STARS, THE: ***Refer to*** **STAN RUBIN**

COLLETTE, BUDDY

William "Buddy" Collette is a West Coast jazz alto and tenor saxophone, clarinet and flute player. For additional listings refer to Chico Hamilton; Herbie Mann & Buddy Collette; Dick Marx; and the Various Artists section under Tampa.

Dig LP-101	(M)	**Tanganyika**	1956	30.00	75.00
Contemporary C-3522	(M)	**Man Of Many Parts**	1956	20.00	50.00
Contemporary C-3531	(M)	**Nice Day With Buddy Collette**	1957	20.00	50.00
Tampa TP-34	(M)	**Star Studded Cast**	1959	30.00	75.00
ABC-Paramount ABC-179	(M)	**Calm, Cool And Collette**	1957	20.00	50.00
Dooto DTL-245	(M)	**Buddy's Best** *(Red vinyl)*	1957	30.00	75.00
Dooto DTL-245	(M)	**Buddy's Best**	1957	20.00	50.00
Challenge CHL-603	(M)	**Everybody's Buddy**	1957	20.00	50.00
Specialty SP-5002	(M)	**Jazz Loves Paris**	1958	20.00	50.00
EmArcy MG-36133	(M)	**Swingin' Shepherds**	1958	20.00	50.00
EmArcy SR-80005	(S)	**Swingin' Shepherds**	1958	16.00	40.00
Mercury MG-20447	(M)	**At The Cinema**	1959	16.00	40.00
Mercury SR-60132	(S)	**At The Cinema**	1959	12.00	30.00
—Mercury albums above have silver on black labels.—					
Interlude MO-505	(M)	**Modern Interpretations Of Porgy & Bess**	1959	16.00	40.00
Interlude ST-1005	(S)	**Modern Interpretations Of Porgy & Bess**	1959	12.00	30.00
Music & Sound 1001	(M)	**Polynesia**	1959	12.00	30.00
Music & Sound S-1001	(S)	**Polynesia**	1959	10.00	25.00
World Pacific WP-1823	(M)	**Warm Winds**	1964	8.00	20.00
World Pacific ST-1823	(S)	**Warm Winds**	1964	6.00	15.00
Surrey S-1009	(M)	**Buddy Collette On Broadway**	1966	10.00	25.00
Surrey SS-3009	(S)	**Buddy Collette On Broadway**	1966	8.00	20.00

COLLINS, AL "JAZZBO"

For additional listings refer to The Six.

Coral CRL-57035	(M)	**East Coast Jazz Scene**	1956	40.00	100.00
Everest LPBR-5097	(M)	**Swingin' At The Opera**	1960	12.00	30.00
Impulse A-9150	(M)	**A Lovely Bunch Of Al "Jazzbo" Collins**	1967	16.00	40.00
Impulse AS-9150	(S)	**A Lovely Bunch Of Al "Jazzbo" Collins**	1967	12.00	30.00
—Impulse albums above have orange & black labels.—					
Impulse AS-9150	(S)	**A Lovely Bunch Of Al "Jazzbo" Collins**	1968	4.00	10.00
—Impulse albums above have red & black labels with the "abc" logo on top.—					

COLLINS, DICK

Richard Collins is a traditional jazz trumpet player and composer. For additional listings refer to Charlie Mariano / Dick Collins; Nat Pierce.

RCA Victor LJM-1019	(M)	**Horn Of Plenty**	1955	20.00	50.00
RCA Victor LJM-1027	(M)	**King Richard The Swing Hearted**	1955	20.00	50.00
—RCA albums above have black labels with "Long Play" on the bottom.—					

Label & Catalog #		Title	Year	VG+	NM

COLLINS, JOYCE
Joyce Collins is a jazz-based pianist and vocalist.

Jazzland JLP-24	*(M)*	**The Girl Here Plays Mean Piano**	*1960*	**12.00**	**30.00**
Jazzland JLP-924	*(S)*	**The Girl Here Plays Mean Piano**	*1960*	**10.00**	**25.00**

COLLINS, LEE: *Refer to* JACK DELANEY

COLONNA, JERRY

Liberty SL-9004	*(M)*	**Jerry Colonna Plays Trombone**	*1957*	**16.00**	**40.00**

COLTRANE, JOHN
John "Trane" Coltrane is a modern jazz tenor and soprano saxophone player. For additional listings refer to Cannonball Adderley; Cannonball Adderley; Cannonball Adderley & John Coltrane; Kenny Burrell; Tadd Dameron; Miles Davis; Ray Draper; Red Garland; Wilbur Harden; Milt Jackson & John Coltrane; Thelonious Monk; Cecil Taylor; Mal Waldron; and the Various Artists section under Bethlehem, New Jazz and Prestige.

Prestige PRLP-7105	*(M)*	**Coltrane**	*1957*	**40.00**	**100.00**
Prestige PRLP-7123	*(M)*	**John Coltrane With The Red Garland Trio**	*1957*	**40.00**	**100.00**
		—Prestige albums above have yellow labels with a W. 50th St, NYC address.—			
Blue Note BLP-1577	*(M)*	**Blue Train** *(Deep groove)*	*1957*	**60.00**	**150.00**
Blue Note BLP-1577	*(M)*	**Blue Train**	*1957*	**40.00**	**100.00**
Blue Note BST-1577	*(S)*	**Blue Train** *(Deep groove)*	*1959*	**40.00**	**100.00**
Blue Note BST-1577	*(S)*	**Blue Train**	*1959*	**30.00**	**75.00**
		—Blue Note albums above have blue on white labels with a W. 63rd St, NYC address.—			
Blue Note BLP-1577	*(M)*	**Blue Train**	*196?*	**12.00**	**30.00**
Blue Note BST-1577	*(S)*	**Blue Train**	*196?*	**10.00**	**25.00**
		—Blue Note albums above have blue on white labels with a New York, USA address.—			
Blue Note BST-1577	*(S)*	**Blue Train**	*196?*	**6.00**	**15.00**
		—Blue Note albums above have blue on white labels with "A Division of Liberty Records."—			
Prestige PRLP-7142	*(M)*	**Soultrane**	*1958*	**30.00**	**75.00**
Prestige PRLP-7158	*(M)*	**Cattin' With Coltrane & Quinichette**	*1959*	**30.00**	**75.00**
Prestige PRLP-7188	*(M)*	**Lush Life**	*1960*	**30.00**	**75.00**
Prestige PRLP-7213	*(M)*	**Settin' The Pace**	*1961*	**30.00**	**75.00**
Prestige PRLP-7243	*(M)*	**Standard Coltrane**	*1962*	**20.00**	**50.00**
Prestige PRST-7243	*(S)*	**Standard Coltrane**	*1962*	**16.00**	**40.00**
Prestige PRLP-7247	*(M)*	**Mating Call**	*1962*	**20.00**	**50.00**
Prestige PRST-7247	*(E)*	**Mating Call**	*1962*	**10.00**	**25.00**
		(Prestige 7247 is a reissue of 7070, Tadd Dameron's "Mating Call.")			
Prestige PRLP-7249	*(M)*	**Tenor Conclave**	*1962*	**20.00**	**50.00**
Prestige PRST-7249	*(E)*	**Tenor Conclave**	*1962*	**10.00**	**25.00**
		(Prestige 7249 is a reissue of 7074, a various artists album.)			
Prestige PRLP-7268	*(M)*	**Stardust**	*1963*	**20.00**	**50.00**
Prestige PRST-7268	*(S)*	**Stardust**	*1963*	**16.00**	**40.00**
Prestige PRLP-7280	*(M)*	**Dakar**	*1963*	**20.00**	**50.00**
Prestige PRST-7280	*(S)*	**Dakar**	*1963*	**16.00**	**40.00**
		(Prestige 7280 is a reisue of one half of "Modern Jazz Survey 2," listed in the "Jazz At 16 2/3 RPM" article.)			
Prestige PRLP-7292	*(M)*	**The Believer**	*1964*	**20.00**	**50.00**
Prestige PRST-7292	*(S)*	**The Believer**	*1964*	**16.00**	**40.00**
Prestige PRLP-7316	*(M)*	**Black Pearls**	*1964*	**20.00**	**50.00**
Prestige PRST-7316	*(S)*	**Black Pearls**	*1964*	**16.00**	**40.00**
		—Prestige albums above have yellow mono or silver stereo labels with a Bergenfield, NJ address.—			
Prestige PRLP-7105	*(M)*	**Coltrane**	*1964*	**12.00**	**30.00**
Prestige PRLP-7123	*(M)*	**Traneing In**	*1964*	**12.00**	**30.00**
		("Traneing In" is a reissue of "John Coltrane With The Red Garland Trio.")			
Prestige PRLP-7142	*(M)*	**Soultrane**	*1964*	**10.00**	**25.00**
Prestige PRLP-7158	*(M)*	**Cattin' With Coltrane & Quinichette**	*1964*	**10.00**	**25.00**
Prestige PRLP-7188	*(M)*	**Lush Life**	*1964*	**10.00**	**25.00**
Prestige PRLP-7213	*(M)*	**Settin' The Pace**	*1964*	**10.00**	**25.00**
Prestige PRLP-7243	*(M)*	**Standard Coltrane**	*1964*	**10.00**	**25.00**
Prestige PRST-7243	*(S)*	**Standard Coltrane**	*1964*	**8.00**	**20.00**
Prestige PRLP-7247	*(M)*	**Mating Call**	*1964*	**10.00**	**25.00**
Prestige PRST-7247	*(E)*	**Mating Call**	*1964*	**6.00**	**15.00**
Prestige PRLP-7249	*(M)*	**Tenor Conclave**	*1964*	**10.00**	**25.00**
Prestige PRST-7249	*(E)*	**Tenor Conclave**	*1964*	**6.00**	**15.00**
Prestige PRLP-7268	*(M)*	**Stardust**	*1964*	**10.00**	**25.00**
Prestige PRST-7268	*(S)*	**Stardust**	*1964*	**8.00**	**20.00**
Prestige PRLP-7280	*(M)*	**Dakar**	*1964*	**10.00**	**25.00**
Prestige PRST-7280	*(S)*	**Dakar**	*1964*	**8.00**	**20.00**

John Coltrane broke in with Eddie "Cleanhead" Vinson's R&B band in 1947-48 before joining the big bands of Dizzy Gillespie (1949-51), Earl Bostic (1952-53), and Johnny Hodges (1953-54). Joining Miles Davis in 1955-57 he established himself as one of the premier jazz saxophonists in the world. He finished the '50s with Prestige (both of the examples here are from this period) before recording the pivotal *Giant Steps* for Atlantic in 1959. He finished his career with Impulse!, recording some of the most profound music of the '60s before his unfortunate death in 1967. He also recorded albums with Cannonball Adderley, Tadd Dameron, and Milt Jackson and as a featured guest with Adderley, Kenny Burrell, Davis, Ray Draper, Red Garland, Wilbur Harden, Thelonious Monk, Cecil Taylor, and Mal Waldron. He also recorded as a sideman with Paul Chambers on Blue Note and Jazz West, Sonny Clark and Johnny Griffin, both on Blue Note, Art Taylor and Gene Ammons, both on Prestige, Michel LeGrand on Columbia, and George Russell on Decca.

Label & Catalog #		*Title*	*Year*	*VG+*	*NM*
Prestige PRLP-7292	*(M)*	**The Believer**	*1964*	**10.00**	**25.00**
Prestige PRST-7292	*(S)*	**The Believer**	*1964*	**8.00**	**20.00**
Prestige PRLP-7316	*(M)*	**Black Pearls**	*1964*	**10.00**	**25.00**
Prestige PRST-7316	*(S)*	**Black Pearls**	*1964*	**8.00**	**20.00**
Prestige PRLP-7353	*(M)*	**Bahia**	*1965*	**12.00**	**30.00**
Prestige PRST-7353	*(S)*	**Bahia**	*1965*	**10.00**	**25.00**
Prestige PRLP-7378	*(M)*	**The Last Trane**	*1965*	**12.00**	**30.00**
Prestige PRST-7378	*(S)*	**The Last Trane**	*1965*	**10.00**	**25.00**
Prestige PRLP-7426	*(M)*	**John Coltrane Plays For Lovers**	*1966*	**12.00**	**30.00**
Prestige PRST-7426	*(S)*	**John Coltrane Plays For Lovers**	*1966*	**10.00**	**25.00**
—Prestige albums above have blue labels with a trident logo on the right side.—					
Prestige PRLP-7531	*(M)*	**Soultrane**	*1967*	**10.00**	**25.00**
Prestige PRST-7531	*(E)*	**Soultrane**	*1967*	**5.00**	**12.00**
		(Prestige 7531 is a reissue of 7142.)			
Prestige PRST-7581	*(E)*	**Lush Life**	*1968*	**5.00**	**12.00**
		(Prestige 7581 is a reissue of 7188.)			
Prestige PRST-7609	*(E)*	**The First Trane**	*1969*	**5.00**	**12.00**
		(Prestige 7609 is a reissue of 7105.)			
Prestige PRST-7651	*(E)*	**Traneing In**	*1969*	**5.00**	**12.00**
		(Prestige 7651 is a reissue of 7123.)			
Prestige PRST-7670	*(E)*	**Two Tenors**	*1969*	**5.00**	**12.00**
		(Prestige 7670 is a reissue of 7043, Elmo Hope's "Informal Jazz.")			
—Prestige albums above have blue labels with a trident logo on top.—					
Atlantic 1311	*(M)*	**Giant Steps**	*1959*	**20.00**	**50.00**
Atlantic SD-1311	*(S)*	**Giant Steps**	*1959*	**16.00**	**40.00**
—Atlantic albums above have black mono or green stereo labels.—					
Atlantic 1311	*(M)*	**Giant Steps**	*1960*	**10.00**	**25.00**
Atlantic SD-1311	*(S)*	**Giant Steps**	*1960*	**8.00**	**20.00**
Atlantic 1354	*(M)*	**Coltrane Jazz**	*1960*	**12.00**	**30.00**
Atlantic SD-1354	*(S)*	**Coltrane Jazz**	*1960*	**10.00**	**25.00**
Atlantic 1361	*(M)*	**My Favorite Things**	*1961*	**12.00**	**30.00**
Atlantic SD-1361	*(S)*	**My Favorite Things**	*1961*	**10.00**	**25.00**
Atlantic 1373	*(M)*	**Ole' Coltrane**	*1961*	**12.00**	**30.00**
Atlantic SD-1373	*(S)*	**Ole' Coltrane**	*1961*	**10.00**	**25.00**
—Atlantic albums above have multi-color labels with a white fan logo.—					
Atlantic 1311	*(M)*	**Giant Steps**	*196?*	**6.00**	**15.00**
Atlantic SD-1311	*(S)*	**Giant Steps**	*196?*	**5.00**	**12.00**
Atlantic 1354	*(M)*	**Coltrane Jazz**	*196?*	**6.00**	**15.00**
Atlantic SD-1354	*(S)*	**Coltrane Jazz**	*196?*	**5.00**	**12.00**
Atlantic 1361	*(M)*	**My Favorite Things**	*196?*	**6.00**	**15.00**
Atlantic SD-1361	*(S)*	**My Favorite Things**	*196?*	**5.00**	**12.00**
Atlantic 1373	*(M)*	**Ole' Coltrane**	*196?*	**6.00**	**15.00**
Atlantic SD-1373	*(S)*	**Ole' Coltrane**	*196?*	**5.00**	**12.00**
Atlantic 1382	*(M)*	**Coltrane Plays The Blues**	*1962*	**12.00**	**30.00**
Atlantic SD-1382	*(S)*	**Coltrane Plays The Blues**	*1962*	**10.00**	**25.00**
Atlantic 1419	*(M)*	**Coltrane's Sound**	*1964*	**10.00**	**25.00**
Atlantic SD-1419	*(S)*	**Coltrane's Sound**	*1964*	**8.00**	**20.00**
Atlantic 1451	*(M)*	**The Avant Garde**	*1966*	**10.00**	**25.00**
Atlantic SD-1451	*(S)*	**The Avant Garde**	*1966*	**8.00**	**20.00**
		(Atlantic 1451 also features Don Cherry.)			
Atlantic SD-1541	*(S)*	**The Best Of John Coltrane**	*1969*	**4.00**	**10.00**
Atlantic albums above have multi-color labels with a black fan logo.—					
United Arts. UAJ-14001	*(M)*	**Coltrane Time**	*1962*	**20.00**	**50.00**
United Arts. UAJS-15001	*(S)*	**Coltrane Time**	*1962*	**16.00**	**40.00**
		(United Artists 14001 is a reissue of 4014, Cecil Taylor's "Hard Driving Jazz.")			
Impulse A-6	*(M)*	**Africa/Brass**	*1961*	**16.00**	**40.00**
Impulse AS-6	*(S)*	**Africa/Brass**	*1961*	**12.00**	**30.00**
Impulse A-10	*(M)*	**"Live" At The Village Vanguard**	*1962*	**16.00**	**40.00**
Impulse AS-10	*(S)*	**"Live" At The Village Vanguard**	*1962*	**12.00**	**30.00**
Impulse A-21	*(M)*	**Coltrane**	*1962*	**16.00**	**40.00**
Impulse AS-21	*(S)*	**Coltrane**	*1962*	**12.00**	**30.00**
Impulse A-30	*(M)*	**Duke Ellington And John Coltrane**	*1963*	**16.00**	**40.00**
Impulse AS-30	*(S)*	**Duke Ellington And John Coltrane**	*1963*	**12.00**	**30.00**
Impulse A-32	*(M)*	**Ballads**	*1963*	**16.00**	**40.00**
Impulse AS-32	*(S)*	**Ballads**	*1963*	**12.00**	**30.00**
Impulse A-40	*(M)*	**John Coltrane + Johnny Hartman**	*1963*	**20.00**	**50.00**
Impulse AS-40	*(S)*	**John Coltrane + Johnny Hartman**	*1963*	**16.00**	**40.00**
Impulse A-42	*(M)*	**Impressions**	*1963*	**12.00**	**30.00**

Label & Catalog #		Title	Year	VG+	NM
Impulse AS-42	(S)	**Impressions**	1963	10.00	25.00
Impulse A-50	(M)	**Coltrane Live At Birdland**	1963	12.00	30.00
Impulse AS-50	(S)	**Coltrane Live At Birdland**	1963	10.00	25.00
Impulse A-66	(M)	**Crescent**	1964	12.00	30.00
Impulse AS-66	(S)	**Crescent**	1964	10.00	25.00
Impulse A-77	(M)	**A Love Supreme**	1965	12.00	30.00
Impulse AS-77	(S)	**A Love Supreme**	1965	10.00	25.00
Impulse A-85	(M)	**The John Coltrane Quartet Plays**	1965	12.00	30.00
Impulse AS-85	(S)	**The John Coltrane Quartet Plays**	1965	10.00	25.00
Impulse A-94	(M)	**New Thing At Newport**	1965	12.00	30.00
Impulse AS-94	(S)	**New Thing At Newport**	1965	10.00	25.00
		(Impulse 94 also features Archie Shepp.)			
Impulse A-95	(M)	**Ascension—Edition I**	1965	40.00	100.00
Impulse AS-95	(S)	**Ascension—Edition I**	1965	30.00	75.00
Impulse A-95	(M)	**Ascension—Edition II**	1966	12.00	30.00
Impulse AS-95	(S)	**Ascension—Edition II**	1966	10.00	25.00
		(Second pressings—with a completely different take of the title song—have "Edition II" etched in the trail-off vinyl.)			
Impulse A-9106	(M)	**Kulu Se Mama**	1966	12.00	30.00
Impulse AS-9106	(S)	**Kulu Se Mama**	1966	10.00	25.00
Impulse A-9110	(M)	**Meditations**	1966	12.00	30.00
Impulse AS-9110	(S)	**Meditations**	1966	10.00	25.00
Impulse A-9120	(M)	**Expression**	1967	12.00	30.00
Impulse AS-9120	(S)	**Expression**	1967	10.00	25.00
Impulse A-9124	(M)	**"Live" At The Village Vanguard Again!**	1967	12.00	30.00
Impulse AS-9124	(S)	**"Live" At The Village Vanguard Again!**	1967	10.00	25.00
Impulse A-9140	(M)	**Om**	1967	12.00	30.00
Impulse AS-9140	(S)	**Om**	1967	10.00	25.00
		—Impulse albums above have orange & black labels.—			
Impulse AS-6	(S)	**Africa/Brass**	1968	5.00	12.00
Impulse AS-10	(S)	**"Live" At The Village Vanguard**	1968	5.00	12.00
Impulse AS-21	(S)	**Coltrane**	1968	5.00	12.00
Impulse AS-30	(S)	**Duke Ellington And John Coltrane**	1968	5.00	12.00
Impulse AS-32	(S)	**Ballads**	1968	5.00	12.00
Impulse AS-40	(S)	**John Coltrane + Johnny Hartman**	1968	5.00	12.00
Impulse AS-42	(S)	**Impressions**	1968	5.00	12.00
Impulse AS-50	(S)	**Coltrane Live At Birdland**	1968	5.00	12.00
Impulse AS-66	(S)	**Crescent**	1968	5.00	12.00
Impulse AS-77	(S)	**A Love Supreme**	1968	5.00	12.00
Impulse AS-85	(S)	**The John Coltrane Quartet Plays**	1968	5.00	12.00
Impulse AS-94	(S)	**New Thing At Newport**	1968	5.00	12.00
Impulse AS-95	(S)	**Ascension—Edition II**	1968	5.00	12.00
Impulse AS-9106	(S)	**Kulu Se Mama**	1968	5.00	12.00
Impulse AS-9110	(S)	**Meditations**	1968	5.00	12.00
Impulse AS-9120	(S)	**Expression**	1968	5.00	12.00
Impulse AS-9124	(S)	**"Live" At The Village Vanguard Again!**	1968	5.00	12.00
Impulse AS-9140	(S)	**Om**	1968	5.00	12.00
Impulse AS-9148	(S)	**Cosmic Music**	1969	8.00	20.00
Impulse AS-9161	(S)	**Selflessness**	1969	8.00	20.00
Impulse AS-9195	(S)	**Transition**	1969	8.00	20.00
		—Impulse albums above have red & black labels with the "abc" logo on top.—			
Solid State SM-17025	(M)	**Coltrane Time**	1968	10.00	25.00
Solid State SS-18025	(S)	**Coltrane Time**	1968	6.00	15.00
		(Solid State 17025 is a reissue of United Artists 14001.)			
Coltrane Music AU-4950	(S)	**Cosmic Music**	1968	125.00	250.00
Coltrane Music AU-5000	(S)	**Cosmic Music**	1968	100.00	200.00
		(Coltrane 5000 is a remastered reissue of 4950.)			

COLTRANE, JOHN / LEE MORGAN

Roulette R-52094	(M)	**The Best Of Birdland, Volume 1**	1962	12.00	30.00
Roulette SR-52094	(S)	**The Best Of Birdland, Volume 1**	1962	10.00	25.00

COLTRANE, JOHN, & FRANK WESS

New Jazz NJLP-8327	(M)	**Wheelin' & Dealin'**	1963	*Unreleased*	
Status ST-8327	(M)	**Wheelin' & Dealin'**	1965	16.00	40.00
		(Status 8327 is a reissue of Prestige 7131, a various artists album.)			

COLUMBO, CHRIS

Strand SL-1044	(M)	**Chris Columbo Quintette**	195?	16.00	40.00

Label & Catalog #		Title	Year	VG+	NM
COLYER, KEN					
English born Kenneth Colyer is a traditional jazz-based trumpet player.					
London PB-904	(10")	**New Orleans To London**	1954	**20.00**	**50.00**
London LL-1340	(M)	**Back To The Delta**	1956	**16.00**	**40.00**
London LL-1618	(M)	**Club Session With Colyer**	1957	**16.00**	**40.00**
COMMANDERS, THE					
Decca DL-8117	(M)	**Dance Party**	1955	**16.00**	**40.00**
CONDON, EDDIE					
Albert Edwin Condon is a traditional jazz guitar and banjo player and vocalist. For additional listings refer to Louis Armstrong / Eddie Condon; Sideny Bechet & Eddie Condon; and the Various Artists section under Verve.					
Decca DL-5246	(10")	**We Call It Music**	1950	**20.00**	**50.00**
Decca DL-5137	(10")	**George Gershwin Jazz Concert**	1950	**20.00**	**50.00**
Decca DL-5203	(10")	**Jazz Concert At Eddie Condon's**	1950	**20.00**	**50.00**
Decca DL-5218	(10")	**Jazz Concert At Eddie Condon's**	1950	**20.00**	**50.00**
Jazz Panorama 1805	(10")	**Eddie Condon**	1951	**16.00**	**40.00**
Jolly Roger 5018	(10")	**Eddie Condon & His Orchestra Featuring Pee Wee Russell**	1955	**20.00**	**50.00**
Jolly Roger 5025	(10")	**Eddie Condon**	1954	**20.00**	**50.00**
"X" LX-3005	(M)	**Eddie Condon's Hot Shots**	1954	**20.00**	**50.00**
Columbia CL-616	(M)	**Jammin' At Condon's**	1955	**16.00**	**40.00**
— Columbia albums above have "Long Playing" on the bottom of the label.—					
Columbia CL-719	(M)	**Bixieland**	1955	**16.00**	**40.00**
Columbia CL-881	(M)	**Eddie Condon's Treasury Of Jazz**	1956	**16.00**	**40.00**
Columbia CL-1089	(M)	**The Roaring Twenties**	1958	**16.00**	**40.00**
— Columbia albums above have six white on black "eye" logos on each label.—					
Decca DL-8282	(M)	**Ivy League Jazz**	195?	**16.00**	**40.00**
Savoy MG-12055	(M)	**Ringside At Condon's**	1956	**16.00**	**40.00**
Dot DLP-3141	(M)	**Dixieland Dance Party**	1958	**16.00**	**40.00**
MGM E-3651	(M)	**Eddie Condon Is Uptown Now**	1960	**12.00**	**30.00**
MGM SE-3651	(S)	**Eddie Condon Is Uptown Now**	1960	**10.00**	**25.00**
Mainstream 56024	(M)	**Eddie Condon: A Legend**	1965	**10.00**	**25.00**
Mainstream S-6024	(E)	**Eddie Condon: A Legend**	1965	**5.00**	**12.00**
CONNELLY, PEGGY					
Peggy Connelly is a jazz-based vocalist.					
Bethlehem BCP-53	(M)	**Peggy Connelly**	1956	**50.00**	**125.00**
CONNOR, CHRIS					
Chris Connor is a big band-based vocalist. For additional listings refer to LaVern Baker / Chris Connor / Herbie Mann / Bobby Short; Maynard Ferguson.					
Bethlehem BCP-1001	(10")	**Chris Connor Sings Lullabys Of Birdland**	1954	**30.00**	**75.00**
Bethlehem BCP-1002	(10")	**Chris Connor Sings Lullabys For Lovers**	1954	**30.00**	**75.00**
Bethlehem BCP-20	(M)	**This Is Chris**	1955	**24.00**	**60.00**
Bethlehem BCP-56	(M)	**Chris**	1956	**24.00**	**60.00**
Bethlehem BCP-6004	(M)	**Chris Connor Sings Lullabys Of Birdland**	1956	**24.00**	**60.00**
		(Bethlehem 6004 is a reissue of 1001 and 1002.)			
Atlantic 1228	(M)	**Chris Connor**	1956	**20.00**	**50.00**
Atlantic SD-1228	(S)	**Chris Connor**	1958	**24.00**	**60.00**
Atlantic 1240	(M)	**He Loves Me, He Loves Me Not**	1956	**20.00**	**50.00**
Atlantic SD-1240	(S)	**He Loves Me, He Loves Me Not**	1958	**24.00**	**60.00**
Atlantic 8014	(M)	**I Miss You So**	1956	**20.00**	**50.00**
Atlantic 2-601	(M)	**Chris Connor Sings The George Gershwin Almanac Of Song** *(2 LPs)*	1957	**40.00**	**100.00**
Atlantic 1286	(M)	**A Jazz Date With Chris Connor**	1958	**20.00**	**50.00**
Atlantic 1290	(M)	**Chris Craft**	1958	**20.00**	**50.00**
Atlantic 1307	(M)	**Ballads Of The Sad Cafe**	1959	**24.00**	**60.00**
Atlantic SD-1307	(S)	**Ballads Of The Sad Cafe**	1959	**30.00**	**75.00**
Atlantic 1309	(M)	**Chris Connor Sings The George Gershwin Almanac Of Song , Vol. 1**	1959	**16.00**	**40.00**
Atlantic SD-1309	(S)	**Chris Connor Sings The George Gershwin Almanac Of Song , Vol. 1**	1959	**20.00**	**50.00**
Atlantic 1310	(M)	**Chris Connor Sings The George Gershwin Almanac Of Song , Vol. 2**	1959	**16.00**	**40.00**
Atlantic SD-1310	(S)	**Chris Connor Sings The George Gershwin Almanac Of Song, Vol. 2**	1959	**20.00**	**50.00**
		(Atlantic 1309 ans 1310 are reissues of 601.)			

Label & Catalog #		Title	Year	VG+	NM
Atlantic 8032	*(M)*	**Witchcraft**	*1959*	20.00	50.00
Atlantic SD-8032	*(S)*	**Witchcraft**	*1959*	24.00	60.00
Atlantic 8040	*(M)*	**Chris In Person**	*1959*	20.00	50.00
Atlantic SD-8040	*(S)*	**Chris In Person**	*1959*	24.00	60.00
		—Atlantic albums above have black mono or green stereo labels.—			
Atlantic 1240	*(M)*	**He Loves Me, He Loves Me Not**	*1960*	16.00	40.00
Atlantic SD-1240	*(S)*	**He Loves Me, He Loves Me Not**	*1960*	20.00	50.00
Atlantic 8014	*(M)*	**I Miss You So**	*1960*	16.00	40.00
		—Atlantic albums above have white "bullseye" labels.—			
Atlantic 1228	*(M)*	**Chris Connor**	*196?*	8.00	20.00
Atlantic SD-1228	*(S)*	**Chris Connor**	*196?*	10.00	25.00
Atlantic 1240	*(M)*	**He Loves Me, He Loves Me Not**	*196?*	8.00	20.00
Atlantic SD-1240	*(S)*	**He Loves Me, He Loves Me Not**	*196?*	10.00	25.00
Atlantic 8014	*(M)*	**I Miss You So**	*196?*	8.00	20.00
Atlantic 2-601	*(M)*	**Chris Connor Sings The George Gershwin Almanac Of Song** *(2 LPs)*	*196?*	16.00	40.00
Atlantic 1286	*(M)*	**A Jazz Date With Chris Connor**	*196?*	8.00	20.00
Atlantic 1290	*(M)*	**Chris Craft**	*196?*	8.00	20.00
Atlantic 1307	*(M)*	**Ballads Of The Sad Cafe**	*1959*	8.00	20.00
Atlantic SD-1307	*(S)*	**Ballads Of The Sad Cafe**	*1959*	10.00	25.00
Atlantic 1309	*(M)*	**Chris Connor Sings The George Gershwin Almanac Of Song, Vol. 1**	*1959*	8.00	20.00
Atlantic SD-1309	*(S)*	**Chris Connor Sings The George Gershwin Almanac Of Song, Vol. 1**	*1959*	10.00	25.00
Atlantic 1310	*(M)*	**Chris Connor Sings The George Gershwin Almanac Of Song , Vol. 2**	*1959*	8.00	20.00
Atlantic SD-1310	*(S)*	**Chris Connor Sings The George Gershwin Almanac Of Song , Vol. 2**	*1959*	10.00	25.00
Atlantic 8032	*(M)*	**Witchcraft**	*1959*	8.00	20.00
Atlantic SD-8032	*(S)*	**Witchcraft**	*1959*	10.00	25.00
Atlantic 8040	*(M)*	**Chris In Person**	*1959*	8.00	20.00
Atlantic SD-8040	*(S)*	**Chris In Person**	*1959*	10.00	25.00
Atlantic 8046	*(M)*	**A Portrait Of Chris**	*1960*	16.00	40.00
Atlantic SD-8046	*(S)*	**A Portrait Of Chris**	*1960*	20.00	50.00
Atlantic 8049	*(M)*	**Double Exposure**	*1961*	12.00	30.00
Atlantic SD-8049	*(S)*	**Double Exposure**	*1961*	16.00	40.00
		(Atlantic 8049 also features Maynard Ferguson.)			
		—Atlantic albums above have multi-color labels with a white fan logo.—			
Atlantic 1228	*(M)*	**Chris Connor**	*196?*	5.00	12.00
Atlantic SD-1228	*(S)*	**Chris Connor**	*196?*	6.00	15.00
Atlantic 1240	*(M)*	**He Loves Me, He Loves Me Not**	*196?*	5.00	12.00
Atlantic SD-1240	*(S)*	**He Loves Me, He Loves Me Not**	*196?*	6.00	15.00
Atlantic 8014	*(M)*	**I Miss You So**	*196?*	5.00	12.00
Atlantic 2-601	*(M)*	**Chris Connor Sings The George Gershwin Almanac Of Song***(2 LPs)*	*196?*	8.00	20.00
Atlantic 1286	*(M)*	**A Jazz Date With Chris Connor**	*196?*	5.00	12.00
Atlantic 1290	*(M)*	**Chris Craft**	*196?*	5.00	12.00
Atlantic 1307	*(M)*	**Ballads Of The Sad Cafe**	*196?*	5.00	12.00
Atlantic SD-1307	*(S)*	**Ballads Of The Sad Cafe**	*196?*	6.00	15.00
Atlantic 8032	*(M)*	**Witchcraft**	*196?*	5.00	12.00
Atlantic SD-8032	*(S)*	**Witchcraft**	*196?*	6.00	15.00
Atlantic 8040	*(M)*	**Chris In Person**	*196?*	5.00	12.00
Atlantic SD-8040	*(S)*	**Chris In Person**	*196?*	6.00	15.00
Atlantic 8046	*(M)*	**A Portrait Of Chris**	*196?*	5.00	12.00
Atlantic SD-8046	*(S)*	**A Portrait Of Chris**	*196?*	6.00	15.00
Atlantic 8049	*(M)*	**Double Exposure**	*196?*	5.00	12.00
Atlantic SD-8049	*(S)*	**Double Exposure**	*196?*	6.00	15.00
Atlantic 8061	*(M)*	**Free Spirits**	*1962*	16.00	40.00
Atlantic SD-8061	*(S)*	**Free Spirits**	*1962*	20.00	50.00
		—Atlantic albums above have multi-color labels with a black fan logo.—			
FM 300	*(M)*	**Chris Connor At The Village Gate**	*1963*	24.00	60.00
FM S-300	*(S)*	**Chris Connor At The Village Gate**	*1963*	30.00	75.00
FM 312	*(M)*	**A Weekend In Paris**	*1964*	24.00	60.00
FM S-312	*(S)*	**A Weekend In Paris**	*1964*	30.00	75.00
ABC-Paramount ABC-529	*(M)*	**Gentle Bossa Nova**	*1965*	8.00	20.00
ABC-Paramount ABCS-529	*(S)*	**Gentle Bossa Nova**	*1965*	10.00	25.00
ABC-Paramount ABC-585	*(M)*	**Chris Connor Now**	*1966*	8.00	20.00
ABC-Paramount ABCS-585	*(S)*	**Chris Connor Now**	*1966*	10.00	25.00

Label & Catalog #		Title	Year	VG+	NM
CONNOR, CHRIS / CARMEN McRAE / JULIE LONDON					
Bethlehem BCP-6006	(M)	**Bethlehem Girl Friends**	1956	30.00	75.00
CONTEMPORARY JAZZ ENSEMBLE, THE					
Prestige PRLP-163	(10")	**New Sounds From Rochester**	1953	40.00	100.00
COOK, JUNIOR					
Herman "Junior" Cook is a modern jazz tenor saxophone player.					
Jazzland JLP-58	(M)	**Junior's Cookin'**	1961	20.00	50.00
Jazzland JLP-958	(S)	**Junior's Cookin'**	1961	16.00	40.00
COOL BRITONS, THE					
For additional listings refer to The Swinging Swedes.					
Blue Note BLP-5052	(10")	**New Sounds From Olde England**	1954	125.00	250.00
COOPER, BOB					
Robert Cooper is a West Coast jazz tenor sax and oboe player and composer. For additional listings refer to Boots Brown; The Video All Stars; and the Jazzy Soundtracks section under Chancellor and World Pacific.					
Capitol H-6501	(10")	**Bob Cooper**	1954	30.00	75.00
Capitol H-6513	(10")	**Shifting Winds**	1955	20.00	50.00
Capitol T-6501	(M)	**Bob Cooper**	1955	20.00	50.00
Capitol T-6513	(M)	**Shifting Winds**	1955	20.00	50.00
World Pacific WPM-411	(M)	**Bob Cooper Swings TV**	1958	20.00	50.00
Contemporary C-3544	(M)	**Coop!**	1958	20.00	50.00
Stereo Records S-7012	(S)	**Coop!**	1958	18.00	45.00
Contemporary S-7012	(S)	**Coop!**	1959	16.00	40.00
		—Contemporary stereo albums have gold & black labels.—			
Capitol T-1586	(M)	**Do Re Mi**	1961	12.00	30.00
Capitol ST-1586	(S)	**Do Re Mi**	1961	10.00	25.00
CORBIN, HAROLD					
Roulette R-52079	(M)	**Soul Brother**	1963	12.00	30.00
Roulette SR-52079	(S)	**Soul Brother**	1963	10.00	25.00
CORCORAN, CORKY					
Gene "Corky" Corcaron is a modern jazz tenor saxophone player.					
Epic LN-3319	(M)	**The Sound Of Love**	1956	30.00	75.00
Celestial Vol. 1	(M)	**Sounds Of Jazz** *(Red vinyl)*	1958	100.00	200.00
Celestial Vol. 1	(M)	**Sounds Of Jazz**	1958	50.00	125.00
COREA, CHICK					
Solid State SS-18039	(S)	**Now He Sings, Now He Sobs**	1969	6.00	15.00
Solid State SS-18055	(S)	**"Is"**	1969	6.00	15.00
CORWIN, BOB					
Robert Corwin is a modern jazz pianist.					
Riverside RLP-12-220	(M)	**Bob Corwin Quartet With Don Elliott**	1956	30.00	75.00
		—Riverside albums above have blue on white labels.—			
Riverside RLP-12-220	(M)	**Bob Corwin Quartet With Don Elliott**	195?	16.00	40.00
—Riverside albums above have blue mono or black stereo labels with a reel & mike logo on top.—					
CORYELL, LARRY					
Lawrence Coryell is a modern jazz guitar player. For additional listings refer to Jazz Composers Orchestra.					
Vanguard VSD-6509	(S)	**Larry Coryell**	1969	6.00	15.00
Vanguard VSD-6547	(S)	**Coryell**	1969	6.00	15.00
COSTA, EDDIE, & VINNIE BURKE					
Jubilee JLP-1025	(M)	**The Eddie Costa-Vinnie Burke Trio**	1956	30.00	75.00
COSTA, EDDIE					
Edwin Costa is a modern jazz piano and vibraphone player. For additional listings refer to The Manhattan Jazz Sextette; John Mehegan & Eddie Costa.					
Mode LP-118	(M)	**Eddie Costa Quintet**	1957	40.00	100.00
Coral CRL-57230	(M)	**Guys And Dolls Like Vibes**	1958	20.00	50.00
Dot DLP-3206	(M)	**The House Of Blue Lights**	1959	20.00	50.00
Dot DLP-25206	(S)	**The House Of Blue Lights**	1959	16.00	40.00
Interlude MO-508	(M)	**Eddie Costa Quintet**	1959	16.00	40.00
Interlude ST-1008	(S)	**Eddie Costa Quintet**	1959	12.00	30.00
		(Interlude 508 is a reissue of Mode 118.)			

Label & Catalog #		Title	Year	VG+	NM
COSTA, EDDIE, & ART FARMER					
Premier PM-2002	(M)	**In Their Own Sweet Way**	1962	6.00	15.00
Premier PMS-2002	(E)	**In Their Own Sweet Way**	1962	3.00	7.50
COSTA, EDDIE / MAT MATHEWS & DON ELLIOTT					
Verve MGV-8237	(M)	**Eddie Costa With Rolf Kuhn & Dick Johnson/ Mat Matthews & Don Elliott At Newport**	1958	16.00	40.00
— Verve albums above have black labels with "Verve Records, Inc." on the bottom.—					
Verve V-8237	(M)	**Eddie Costa With Rolf Kuhn & Dick Johnson/ Mat Matthews & Don Elliott At Newport**	1961	6.00	15.00
— Verve albums above have black labels with "MGM Records" on the bottom.—					
COSTA, JOHNNY					
John Costa is a modern "third stream" jazz pianist and composer.					
Savoy MG-15056	(10")	**Johnny Costa**	1955	30.00	75.00
Savoy MG-12052	(M)	**The Amazing Johnny Costa**	1956	20.00	50.00
COSTANZO, JACK					
Jack Costanzo is a West Coast jazz bongo player.					
Norgran MGN-32	(10")	**Afro-Cubano** *(Norgran 32 features cover art by David Stone Martin.)*	1954	60.00	150.00
Gene Norman GNP-19	(M)	**Mr. Bongo**	1955	20.00	50.00
COSTANZO, JACK / ANDRE'S CUBAN ALL STARS					
Norgran MGN-1067	(M)	**Afro-Cubano** *(Norgran 1067 is a reissue of 32 with the DSM cover and Clef 515, Andre's "Cubano.")*	1956	40.00	100.00
Verve MGV-8157	(M)	**Afro-Cubano**	1957	20.00	50.00
— Verve albums above have black labels with "Verve Records, Inc." on the bottom.—					
Verve V-8157	(M)	**Afro-Cubano**	1961	8.00	20.00
— Verve albums above have black labels with "MGM Records" on the bottom.—					
COTTRELL, LOUIS					
Louis Cottrell is a traditional jazz clarinet and saxophone(s) player.					
Riverside RLP-385	(M)	**Bourbon Street Parade**	1961	12.00	30.00
Riverside RS-9385	(E)	**Bourbon Street Parade**	1961	6.00	15.00
— Riverside albums above have blue mono or black stereo labels with a reel & mike logo on top.—					
COUNCE, CURTIS					
Curtis Counce is a West Coast jazz bass player. For additional listings refer to the Various Artists section under EmArcy and Tampa.					
Contemporary C-3526	(M)	**The Curtis Counce Group**	1957	30.00	75.00
Contemporary S-7526	(S)	**The Curtis Counce Group**	1959	20.00	50.00
Contemporary S-7526	(S)	**Landslide** *("Landslide" is a reissue of "The Curtis Counce Group.")*	196?	16.00	40.00
Contemporary M-3539	(M)	**You Get More Bounce With Curtis Counce**	1957	30.00	75.00
Contemporary S-7539	(S)	**You Get More Bounce With Curtis Counce**	1959	20.00	50.00
Contemporary M-3574	(M)	**Carl's Blues**	1960	20.00	50.00
Contemporary S-7574	(S)	**Carl's Blues**	1960	16.00	40.00
— Contemporary stereo albums have gold & black labels.—					
Dooto DTL-247	(M)	**Exploring The Future**	1958	20.00	50.00
COX, IDA					
Ida Cox is a traditional jazz-based vocalist. For additional listings refer to Tommy Ladnier.					
Riverside RLP-374	(M)	**Blues For Rampart Street**	1961	16.00	40.00
Riverside RS-9374	(S)	**Blues For Rampart Street** *(Riverside 374 also features Coleman Hawkins.)*	1961	12.00	30.00
— Riverside albums above have blue mono or black stereo labels with a reel & mike logo on top.—					
COX, KENNY					
Kenneth Cox is a modern jazz pianist.					
Blue Note BST-84302	(S)	**Introducing Kenny Cox**	1968	6.00	15.00
Blue Note BST-84339	(S)	**Multidirection**	1969	6.00	15.00
— Blue Note albums above have blue on white labels with "A Division of Liberty Records."—					
COX, SONNY					
Cadet LP-765	(M)	**The Wailer**	1965	8.00	20.00
Cadet LPS-765	(S)	**The Wailer**	1965	6.00	15.00

Label & Catalog #		Title	Year	VG+	NM

CRAWFORD, HANK

Henry Crawford is a modern jazz tenor, alto and baritone saxophone player, pianist and composer.

Atlantic 1356	(M)	**More Soul**	1960	10.00	25.00
Atlantic SD-1356	(S)	**More Soul**	1960	8.00	20.00
Atlantic 1372	(M)	**The Soul Clinic**	1961	10.00	25.00
Atlantic SD-1372	(S)	**The Soul Clinic**	1961	8.00	20.00
		—Atlantic albums above have multi-color labels with a white fan logo.—			
Atlantic 1356	(M)	**More Soul**	196?	5.00	12.00
Atlantic SD-1356	(S)	**More Soul**	196?	4.00	10.00
Atlantic 1372	(M)	**The Soul Clinic**	196?	5.00	12.00
Atlantic SD-1372	(S)	**The Soul Clinic**	196?	4.00	10.00
Atlantic 1387	(M)	**From The Heart**	1962	8.00	20.00
Atlantic SD-1387	(S)	**From The Heart**	1962	6.00	15.00
Atlantic 1405	(M)	**Soul Of The Ballad**	1963	8.00	20.00
Atlantic SD-1405	(S)	**Soul Of The Ballad**	1963	6.00	15.00
Atlantic 1423	(M)	**True Blue**	1964	8.00	20.00
Atlantic SD-1423	(S)	**True Blue**	1964	6.00	15.00
Atlantic 1436	(M)	**Dig These Blues**	1965	8.00	20.00
Atlantic SD-1436	(S)	**Dig These Blues**	1965	6.00	15.00
Atlantic 1455	(M)	**After Hours**	1966	8.00	20.00
Atlantic SD-1455	(S)	**After Hours**	1966	6.00	15.00
Atlantic 1470	(M)	**Mr. Blues**	1967	8.00	20.00
Atlantic SD-1470	(S)	**Mr. Blues**	1967	6.00	15.00
Atlantic SD-1503	(S)	**Double Cross**	1969	6.00	15.00
Atlantic SD-1523	(S)	**Mr. Soul Plays Lady Soul**	1969	6.00	15.00
		—Atlantic albums above have multi-color labels with a black fan logo.—			

CREVELING, CAROLE

Euterpean ETP-101	(M)	**Carole Creveling**	1955	20.00	50.00

CRISS, SONNY

William "Sonny" Criss is a West Coast jazz alto saxophone player. For additional listings refer to the Various Artists section under Savoy

Mercury MGC-122	(10")	**Sonny Criss Collates**	1953	Unreleased	
		(Jackets of Mercury 122 apparently contain copies of Clef 122.)			
Clef MGC-122	(10")	**Sonny Criss Collates**	1953	100.00	200.00
		(Cleff 122 also features Tommy Turk.)			
Imperial LP-9006	(M)	**Jazz - U.S.A.**	1956	100.00	200.00
Imperial LP-9020	(M)	**Go, Man! It's Sonny Criss And Modern Jazz**	1956	100.00	200.00
Imperial LP-9024	(M)	**Sonny Criss Plays Cole Porter**	1956	100.00	200.00
Peacock PLP-91	(M)	**At The Crossroads**	1959	60.00	150.00
Imperial LP-9205	(M)	**Criss Cross**	1962	30.00	75.00
Imperial LP-12205	(S)	**Criss Cross**	1962	20.00	50.00
Prestige PRLP-7511	(M)	**This Is Sonny Criss!**	1967	14.00	35.00
Prestige PRST-7511	(S)	**This Is Sonny Criss!**	1967	10.00	25.00
Prestige PRLP-7526	(M)	**Portrait Of Sonny Criss**	1967	14.00	35.00
Prestige PRST-7526	(S)	**Portrait Of Sonny Criss**	1967	10.00	25.00
Prestige PRLP-7530	(M)	**Up, Up And Away**	1967	14.00	35.00
Prestige PRST-7530	(S)	**Up, Up And Away**	1967	10.00	25.00
		—Prestige albums above have blue labels with a trident logo on the right side.—			
Prestige PRST-7558	(S)	**The Beat Goes On**	1968	8.00	20.00
Prestige PRST-7576	(S)	**Sonny's Dream**	1968	8.00	20.00
Prestige PRST-7610	(S)	**Rockin' In Rhythm**	1969	8.00	20.00
Prestige PRST-7628	(S)	**I'll Catch The Sun**	1969	8.00	20.00
		—Prestige albums above have blue labels with a trident logo on top.—			

CROSBY, BING

Bing Crosby is one of the most important vocal stylists in American popular music, drawing on traditional blues and jazz forms, among others. For additional listings refer to Rosemary Clooney & Bing Crosby.

Decca DL-5323	(10")	**Bing And The Dixieland Bands**	1951	20.00	50.00
Decca DL-8493	(M)	**Bing And The Dixieland Bands**	1957	16.00	40.00
Verve MGV-2020	(M)	**Bing Sings Whilst Bregman Swings**	1956	16.00	40.00
		—Verve albums above have "Verve Records, Inc." on the bottom of the label.—			
Verve V-2020	(M)	**Bing Sings Whilst Bregman Swings**	1961	6.00	15.00
		—Verve albums above have black labels with "MGM Records" on the bottom.—			
RCA Victor LPM-1473	(M)	**Bing With A Beat**	1957	16.00	40.00
		—RCA albums above have black labels with "Long Play" on the bottom.—			

Label & Catalog #		Title	Year	VG+	NM
CROSBY, BING, & LOUIS ARMSTRONG					
MGM E-3382	(M)	**Bing And Satch**	1956	16.00	40.00
MGM SE-3382	(E)	**Bing And Satch**	1958	8.00	20.00
CROSBY, BOB					
George Robert Crosby, brother of Bing, is a traditional jazz-based vocalist and band leader. For additional listings refer to the Jazzy Soundtracks section under Dot.					
Coral CRL-56000	(10")	**Swinging At The Sugar Bowl**	1950	20.00	50.00
Coral CRL-56003	(10")	**Dixieland Jazz 1**	1950	20.00	50.00
Coral CRL-56018	(10")	**Marches In Dixieland Style**	1950	20.00	50.00
Coral CRL-56039	(10")	**St. Louis Blues**	1950	20.00	50.00
Capitol H-293	(10")	**Bob Crosby & His Bobcats**	1952	20.00	50.00
Decca DL-8042	(M)	**Five Feet Of Swing**	1954	16.00	40.00
Decca DL-8061	(M)	**Bob Crosby's Bobcats**	1954	16.00	40.00
Capitol T-293	(M)	**Bob Crosby & His Bobcats**	1954	16.00	40.00
Coral CRL-57005	(M)	**The Bobcats' Ball**	1955	16.00	40.00
Coral CRL-57060	(M)	**Bobcats' Blues**	1956	16.00	40.00
Coral CRL-57061	(M)	**Bobcats On Parade**	1956	16.00	40.00
Coral CRL-57062	(M)	**Bob Crosby In Hi Fi**	1956	16.00	40.00
Coral CRL-57089	(M)	**Bob Crosby 1936-1956**	1957	16.00	40.00
Coral CRL-57170	(M)	**The Bobcats In Hi-Fi**	1958	16.00	40.00
Dot DLP-3170	(M)	**Petite Fleur**	1959	10.00	25.00
Dot DLP-25170	(S)	**Petite Fleur**	1959	8.00	20.00
Capitol T-1556	(M)	**The Hits Of Bob Crosby's Bobcats**	1961	8.00	20.00
Decca DL-4856	(M)	**Bob Crosby's Bobcats—Their Greatest Hits**	1966	6.00	15.00
Decca DL-74856	(E)	**Bob Crosby's Bobcats—Their Greatest Hits**	1966	4.00	10.00
CUOZZO, MIKE					
Michael Cuozzo is a jazz-based tenor saxophone player.					
Savoy MG-12051	(M)	**Mighty Mike**	1956	16.00	40.00
Jubilee JLP-1027	(M)	**Mike Cuozzo**	1957	16.00	40.00
CURRAN, ED					
Savoy MG-12191	(M)	**Elysa**	1967	8.00	20.00
CURSON, TED					
Theodore Curson is a modern jazz trumpet player.					
Old Town LP-2003	(M)	**Plenty Of Horn**	1961	100.00	200.00
Prestige PRLP-7263	(M)	**Fire Down Below**	1963	16.00	40.00
Prestige PRST-7263	(S)	**Fire Down Below**	1963	14.00	35.00
—Prestige albums above have yellow mono or silver stereo labels with a Bergenfield, NJ address.—					
Prestige PRLP-7263	(M)	**Fire Down Below**	1964	10.00	25.00
Prestige PRST-7263	(S)	**Fire Down Below**	1964	8.00	20.00
—Presitige albums above have blue labels with a trident logo on the right side.—					
Audio Fidelity AFLP-2123	(M)	**Now Hear This**	1964	8.00	20.00
Audio Fidelity AFSD-6123	(S)	**Now Hear This**	1964	10.00	25.00
Atlantic 1441	(M)	**The New Thing And The Blue Thing**	1965	8.00	20.00
Atlantic SD-1441	(S)	**The New Thing And The Blue Thing**	1965	6.00	15.00
—Atlantic albums above have multi-color labels with a black fan logo.—					

D.

D'AMICO, HANK

Henry D'Amico is a traditional jazz clarinet and saxophone(s) player.

Bethlehem BCP-1006	(10")	**Hank's Holiday**	1954	40.00	100.00

D'AMICO, HANK / AARON SACHS

Bethlehem BCP-7	(M)	**We Brought Our Axes**	1957	30.00	75.00

(Bethlehem is a reissue of 1006 and 1008, "Aaron Sachs Quintet.")

DAHLANDER, BERT

Swedish born Nils-Bertil Dahlander is a traditional jazz-based drummer.

Verve MGV-8253	(M)	**Skol**	1958	20.00	50.00

— Verve albums above have black labels with "Verve Records, Inc" on the btoom.—

Verve V-8253	(M)	**Skol**	1961	6.00	15.00

— Verve albums above have black labels with "MGM Records" on the btoom.—

DAILY, PETE

Peter Daily is a traditional jazz cornet player.

Capitol H-183	(10")	**Dixieland Band**	1950	20.00	50.00
Capitol H-385	(10")	**Dixie By Daily**	1953	20.00	50.00
Capitol T-183	(M)	**Dixieland Band**	1954	16.00	40.00
Capitol T-385	(M)	**Dixie By Daily**	1954	16.00	40.00

— Capitol albums above have turquoise labels.—

DAILY, PETE / PHIL NAPOLEON

Decca DL-5261	(10")	**Pete Daily / Phil Napoleon**	1950	20.00	50.00

DALEY, JOE

Joseph Daley is a modern jazz tenor saxophone, clarinet and flute player and composer.

RCA Victor LPM-2763	(M)	**Joe Daley At Newport '63**	1963	10.00	25.00
RCA Victor LSP-2763	(S)	**Joe Daley At Newport '63**	1963	8.00	20.00

DAMERON, TADD

Tadley Dameron is a modern jazz pianist, arranger and composer.

Prestige PRLP-159	(10")	**A Study In Dameronia**	1953	100.00	200.00
		(Prestige 159 also features Clifford Brown.)			
Prestige PRLP-7037	(M)	**Fontainebleau**	1956	400.0	100.00
Prestige PRLP-7070	(M)	**Mating Call**	1956	40.00	100.00
		(Prestige 7070 was reissued as 7247, credited to John Coltrane With Tadd Dameron.)			

— Prestige albums above have yellow labels with a W. 50th Street, NYC address.—

Riverside RLP-419	(M)	**The Magic Touch Of Tadd Dameron**	1962	20.00	50.00
Riverside RS-9419	(S)	**The Magic Touch Of Tadd Dameron**	1962	16.00	40.00

— Riverside albums above have blue mono or black stereo labels with a reel & mike logo on top.—

Jazzland JLP-50	(M)	**Fats Navarro Featured With The Tadd Dameron Quintet**	1962	20.00	50.00
Jazzland JLP-950	(E)	**Fats Navarro Featured With The Tadd Dameron Quintet**	1962	10.00	25.00
Jazzland JLP-68	(M)	**The Tadd Dameron Band**	1962	20.00	50.00
Jazzland JLP-968	(E)	**The Tadd Dameron Band**	1962	10.00	25.00
		(Jazzland 50 and 68 contain 1948 recordings featuring Navarro.)			
New Jazz NJLP-8300	(M)	**Dameronia**	1963	*Unreleased*	
Prestige PRLP-16007	(M)	**Dameronia**	1964	16.00	40.00
		(Prestige 16007 is a reissue of 7037.)			
Riverside RS-3019	(E)	**Good Bait**	1968	5.00	12.00

DANE, BARBARA

Barbara Dane is a traditional jazz-based guitar player and vocalist.

San Francisco 33014	(M)	**Trouble In Mind**	1957	20.00	50.00
Barbary Coast 33014	(S)	**Trouble In Mind**	1959	16.00	40.00
		(Barbary Coast 33014 is a reissue of San Francisco 33014.)			
Dot DLP-3177	(M)	**Livin' With The Blues**	1959	16.00	40.00
Dot DLP-25177	(S)	**Livin' With The Blues**	1959	12.00	30.00

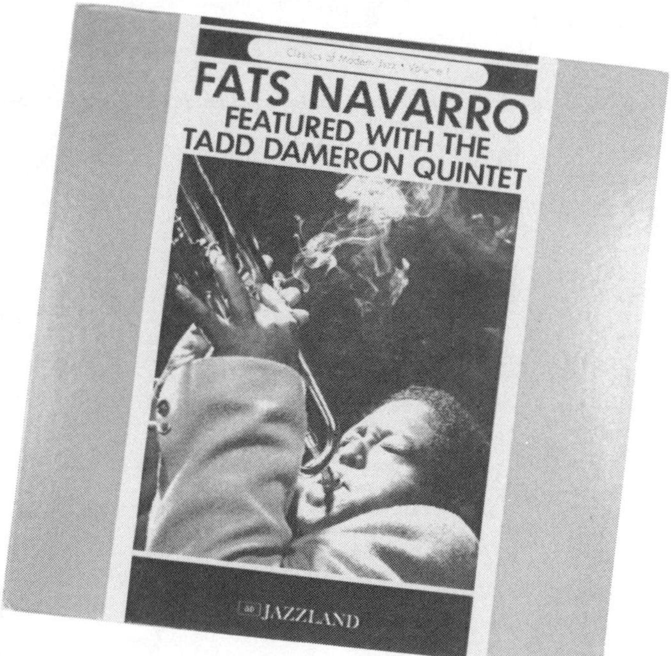

Tadd Dameron began with the bands of Freddie Webster, Zack White, Blanche Calloway, Vido Musso, and Harlan Leonard. In the late '40s he had his own quintet that featured Fats Navarro (the Jazzland album pictured here contains material from that period). He then worked with Miles Davis, Ted Heath, and Bull Moose Jackson before forming a group in 1953. He has recorded as a sideman with Navarro on Savoy and Blue Note, Clifford Brown on Prestige, and Dexter Gordon on Savoy.

Label & Catalog #		Title	Year	VG+	NM
Capitol T-1758	(M)	**On My Way**	1962	12.00	30.00
Capitol ST-1758	(S)	**On My Way**	1962	10.00	25.00
DANIELS, EDDIE					
Prestige PRLP-7506	(M)	**First Prize**	1967	14.00	35.00
Prestige PRST-7506	(S)	**First Prize**	1967	10.00	25.00
—Prestige albums above have blue labels with a trident logo on the right side.—					
DANIELS, HALL					
Jump JL-9	(10")	**Hall Daniels Septet**	1955	30.00	75.00
DANKWORTH, JOHN					
Roulette R-52096	(M)	**Jazz From Abroad**	1962	10.00	25.00
Roulette SR-52096	(S)	**Jazz From Abroad**	1962	8.00	20.00
Fontana MGF-27543	(M)	**Zodiac Variations**	1966	8.00	20.00
Fontana SRF-67543	(S)	**Zodiac Variations**	1966	6.00	15.00
DARCH, BOB					
Robert Darch is a traditional ragtime piano player.					
United Arts. UAL-3120	(M)	**Ragtime Piano**	1960	10.00	25.00
United Arts. UAS-6120	(S)	**Ragtime Piano**	1960	8.00	20.00
DARR, ALICE					
Alice Darr is a modern jazz-based vocalist.					
Charlie Parker PLP-811	(M)	**I Only Know How To Cry**	1962	12.00	30.00
Charlie Parker PLP-811S	(S)	**I Only Know How To Cry**	1962	12.00	30.00
DARTMOUTH INDIAN CHIEFS, THE					
Transition TRLP-23	(M)	**Chiefly Jazz**	1956	40.00	100.00
		(Transition 23 was issued with a booklet, worth an additional $15.)			
DAVIDSON, LOWELL					
Lowell Davidson is a modern jazz pianist.					
ESP-Disk' 1012	(M)	**Lowell Davidson Trio**	1965	8.00	20.00
ESP-Disk' 1012	(S)	**Lowell Davidson Trio**	1965	6.00	15.00
DAVIS, BOB					
Robert Davis is a modern jazz pianist.					
Stepheny 4000	(M)	**Jazz In Orbit**	1958	20.00	50.00
Zephyr 12001	(M)	**Jazz From The North Coast**	1959	20.00	50.00
DAVIS, "WILD" BILL					
William Davis is a traditional jazz-based organ and piano player, arranger and composer. For additional listings refer to Johnny Hodges & Bill Davis; Eddie Shu / Joe Roland / Bill Davis.					
Epic LN-1004	(10")	**Here's Wild Bill Davis**	1954	30.00	75.00
Epic LN-1121	(M)	**On The Loose**	1955	20.00	50.00
Epic LG-3118	(M)	**Wild Bill Davis At Birdland**	1955	20.00	50.00
Epic LN-3308	(M)	**Evening Concerto**	1956	20.00	50.00
Imperial LP-9010	(M)	**Wild Bill Davis On Broadway**	1956	20.00	50.00
Imperial LP-9015	(M)	**Wild Bill Davis In Hollywood**	1956	20.00	50.00
Everest LPBR-5052	(M)	**Flying High**	1959	12.00	30.00
Everest SDBR-1052	(S)	**Flying High**	1959	10.00	25.00
Everest LPBR-5094	(M)	**Dance The Madison**	1960	12.00	30.00
Everest SDBR-1094	(S)	**Dance The Madison**	1960	10.00	25.00
Everest LPBR-5125	(M)	**Dis Heah**	1961	12.00	30.00
Everest SDBR-1125	(S)	**Dis Heah**	1961	10.00	25.00
Everest LPBR-5133	(M)	**The Music From "Milk And Honey"**	1961	12.00	30.00
Everest SDBR-1133	(S)	**The Music From "Milk And Honey"**	1961	10.00	25.00
Coral CRL-57417	(M)	**One More Time**	1962	10.00	25.00
Coral CRL-757417	(S)	**One More Time**	1962	8.00	20.00
Coral CRL-57427	(M)	**Lover**	1962	10.00	25.00
Coral CRL-757427	(S)	**Lover**	1962	8.00	20.00
DAVIS, EDDIE "LOCKJAW"					
Edward Davis is a modern jazz tenor saxophone player. For additional listings refer to Mildred Anderson; Arnett Cobb; Coleman Hawkins; Sonny Stitt; and the Various Artists section under Prestige.					
Roost LP-422	(10")	**Goodies**	1954	60.00	150.00
Roost LP-2227	(M)	**Eddie Davis Trio**	1958	40.00	100.00
		(Roost 2227 is a reissue of 422.)			

Label & Catalog #		Title	Year	VG+	NM
King 506	(M)	**Modern Jazz Expression**	1958	40.00	100.00
King 526	(M)	**Jazz With A Horn**	1958	40.00	100.00
King 566	(M)	**Jazz With A Beat**	1958	40.00	100.00
King 599	(M)	**Big Beat Jazz**	1959	40.00	100.00
King 606	(M)	**Uptown**	1959	40.00	100.00
		—King albums above have black labels without a crown on top.—			
Roulette R-52007	(M)	**Count Basie Presents Eddie Davis**	1958	24.00	60.00
Roulette SR-52007	(S)	**Count Basie Presents Eddie Davis**	1958	20.00	50.00
Roulette R-52019	(M)	**Eddie Davis Trio**	1958	24.00	60.00
Roulette SR-52019	(S)	**Eddie Davis Trio**	1958	20.00	50.00
		—Roulette albums above have white labels with criss-crossed color bars.—			
Roulette R-52007	(M)	**Count Basie Presents Eddie Davis**	196?	10.00	25.00
Roulette SR-52007	(S)	**Count Basie Presents Eddie Davis**	196?	8.00	20.00
Roulette R-52019	(M)	**Eddie Davis Trio**	196?	10.00	25.00
Roulette SR-52019	(S)	**Eddie Davis Trio**	196?	8.00	20.00
		—Roulette albums above have orange labels with a checked roulette wheel.—			
Prestige PRLP-7141	(M)	**The Eddie "Lockjaw" Davis Cookbook**	1958	30.00	75.00
		(Original covers have a photo of a bareheaded Davis.)			
Prestige PRLP-7141	(M)	**The Eddie "Lockjaw" Davis Cookbook**	1959	20.00	50.00
		Later covers show Davis wearing a hat.)			
Prestige PRLP-7154	(M)	**Jaws**	1959	20.00	50.00
		(Prestige 7154 also features Shirley Scott.)			
Prestige PRLP-7161	(M)	**The Eddie "Lockjaw" Davis Cookbook, Vol. 2**	1959	20.00	50.00
Prestige PRLP-7171	(M)	**Jaws In Orbit**	1959	20.00	50.00
		(Prestige 7171 also features Shirley Scott.)			
Prestige PRLP-7178	(M)	**Bacalao**	1960	20.00	50.00
		(Prestige 7178 also features Shirley Scott.)			
Prestige PRLP-7206	(M)	**Trane Whistle**	1961	20.00	50.00
Prestige PRLP-7219	(M)	**The Eddie "Lockjaw" Davis Cookbook, Vol. 3**	1961	20.00	50.00
Prestige PRST-7219	(S)	**The Eddie "Lockjaw" Davis Cookbook, Vol. 3**	1961	16.00	40.00
		(Prestige 7219 also features Shirley Scott.)			
Prestige PRLP-7242	(M)	**Goin' To The Meeting**	1962	20.00	50.00
Prestige PRST-7242	(S)	**Goin' To The Meeting**	1962	16.00	40.00
Prestige PRLP-7261	(M)	**I Only Have Eyes For You**	1963	20.00	50.00
Prestige PRST-7261	(S)	**I Only Have Eyes For You**	1963	16.00	40.00
		(Prestige 7261 also features Paul Weston.)			
Prestige PRLP-7271	(M)	**Trackin'**	1963	20.00	50.00
Prestige PRST-7271	(S)	**Trackin'**	1963	16.00	40.00
		—Prestige albums above have yellow mono or silver stereo labels with a Bergenfield, NJ address.—			
Prestige PRLP-7301	(M)	**Smokin'**	1964	16.00	40.00
Prestige PRST-7301	(S)	**Smokin'**	1964	12.00	30.00
		(Prestige 7301 also features Shirley Scott.)			
Prestige PRLP-7407	(M)	**Live! The Breakfast Show**	1965	16.00	40.00
Prestige PRST-7407	(S)	**Live! The Breakfast Show**	1965	12.00	30.00
		(Prestige 7407 is a reissue of 7191)			
		—Prestige albums above have blue labels with a trident logo on the right side.—			
Moodsville MVLP-4	(M)	**Eddie "Lockjaw" Davis With Shirley Scott**	1960	20.00	50.00
		(Moodsville 4 also features Shirley Scott.)			
Moodsville MVLP-30	(M)	**Misty**	1963	20.00	50.00
Moodsville MVST-30	(S)	**Misty**	1963	16.00	40.00
		(Moodsville 30 also features Shirley Scott.)			
		—Moodsville mono albums above have green labels with silver print.—			
Moodsville MVLP-4	(M)	**Eddie "Lockjaw" Davis With Shirley Scott**	1965	10.00	25.00
Moodsville MVLP-30	(M)	**Misty**	1965	10.00	25.00
Moodsville MVST-30	(S)	**Misty**	1965	8.00	20.00
		—Moodsville albums above have blue labels with a trident logo on the right side.—			
Bethlehem BCP-6069	(M)	**Best Of Eddie "Lockjaw" Davis**	1961	16.00	40.00
Bethlehem SBCP-6069	(S)	**Best Of Eddie "Lockjaw" Davis**	1961	8.00	20.00
Riverside RLP-373	(M)	**Afro-Jaws**	1961	16.00	40.00
Riverside RS-9373	(S)	**Afro-Jaws**	1961	12.00	30.00
Riverside RLP-430	(M)	**Jawbreakers**	1962	16.00	40.00
Riverside RS-9430	(S)	**Jawbreakers**	1962	12.00	30.00
		(Riverside 430 also features Sweets Edison.)			
		—Riverside albums above have blue mono or black stereo labels with a reel & mike logo on top.—			
Jazzland JLP-97	(M)	**Alma Alegre**	1962	12.00	30.00
Jazzland JLP-997	(S)	**Alma Alegre**	1962	10.00	25.00
		(Jazzland 97 is a reissue of Riverside 373.)			
RCA Victor LPM-3652	(M)	**Lock The Fox**	1966	10.00	25.00
RCA Victor LSP-3652	(S)	**Lock The Fox**	1966	8.00	20.00

Label & Catalog #		Title	Year	VG+	NM
RCA Victor LPM-3741	(M)	**The Fox And The Hounds**	1967	10.00	25.00
RCA Victor LSP-3741	(S)	**The Fox And The Hounds**	1967	8.00	20.00
RCA Victor LPM-3882	(M)	**Love Calls**	1967	10.00	25.00
RCA Victor LSP-3882	(S)	**Love Calls**	1967	8.00	20.00
—RCA albums above have black labels with "Mono Dynagroove" or "Stereo Dynagroove" on the bottom.—					
Prestige PRST-7660	(S)	**In The Kitchen** *(Prestige 7660 is a reissue of 7141.)*	1969	6.00	15.00
Prestige PRST-7710	(S)	**The Best Of Eddie Davis And Shirley Scott**	1969	5.00	12.00
—Prestige albums above have blue labels with a trident logo on top.—					

DAVIS, EDDIE "LOCKJAW," & JOHNNY GRIFFIN (THE DAVIS-GRIFFIN QUARTET)

Prestige PRLP-7191	(M)	**The Tenor Scene**	1960	20.00	50.00
—Prestige albums above have a Bergenfield, NJ address on the label.—					
Jazzland JLP-31	(M)	**Tough Tenors**	1960	20.00	50.00
Jazzland JLP-931	(S)	**Tough Tenors**	1960	16.00	40.00
Jazzland JLP-39	(M)	**Lookin' At Monk**	1961	20.00	50.00
Jazzland JLP-939	(S)	**Lookin' At Monk**	1961	16.00	40.00
Jazzland JLP-42	(M)	**Griff & Lock**	1961	20.00	50.00
Jazzland JLP-942	(S)	**Griff & Lock**	1961	16.00	40.00
Jazzland JLP-60	(M)	**Blues Up & Down**	1961	20.00	50.00
Jazzland JLP-960	(S)	**Blues Up & Down**	1961	16.00	40.00
Jazzland JLP-76	(M)	**Tough Tenor Favorites**	1962	20.00	50.00
Jazzland JLP-976	(S)	**Tough Tenor Favorites**	1962	16.00	40.00
Prestige PRLP-7282	(M)	**Battle Stations**	1963	16.00	40.00
Prestige PRST-7282	(S)	**Battle Stations**	1963	12.00	30.00
Prestige PRLP-7309	(M)	**The First Set—Recorded Live At Minton's**	1964	16.00	40.00
Prestige PRST-7309	(S)	**The First Set—Recorded Live At Minton's**	1964	12.00	30.00
—Prestige albums above have yellow mono or silver stereo labels with a Bergenfield, NJ address.—					
Prestige PRLP-7330	(M)	**Live! The Midnight Show At Minton's Playhouse**	1964	12.00	30.00
Prestige PRST-7330	(S)	**Live! The Midnight Show At Minton's Playhouse**	1964	10.00	25.00
Prestige PRLP-7357	(M)	**The Late Show Recorded Live!**	1965	12.00	30.00
Prestige PRST-7357	(S)	**The Late Show Recorded Live!**	1965	10.00	25.00
—Prestige albums above have blue labels with a trident logo on the right side.—					

DAVIS, JACKIE

Capitol T-815	(M)	**Chasing Shadows**	1957	12.00	30.00
—Capitol albums above have black labels with the logo on the left side.—					

DAVIS, JOHNNY

John "Scat" Davis is a jazz-based vocalist.

King 626	(M)	**Johnny "Scat" Davis**	1959	30.00	75.00
—King albums above have black labels without a crown on top.—					

DAVIS, MEL

Melvin Davis is a traditional jazz-based trumpet player.

Epic LN-3268	(M)	**Trumpet With A Soul**	1956	16.00	40.00
Time 52087	(M)	**Shoot The Trumpet Player**	1962	10.00	25.00
Time S-2087	(S)	**Shoot The Trumpet Player**	1962	8.00	20.00
Time 52117	(M)	**Mel Davis**	1964	10.00	25.00
Time S-2117	(S)	**Mel Davis**	1964	8.00	20.00

DAVIS, MILES

Miles Dewey Davis III is a modern jazz trumpet player and band lader and the acknowledged giant of jazz since 1949. For additional listings refer to Leonard Bernstein; The Brass Ensemble; Michel LeGrand; Lee Konitz / Miles Davis / Teddy Charles; the Jazzy Soundtracks section under Fontana; and the "Jazz At 16 2/3 RPM" article..

Blue Note BLP-5013	(10")	**Young Man With A Horn**	1952	150.00	300.00
Blue Note BLP-5022	(10")	**Miles Davis, Volume 2**	1953	150.00	300.00
Blue Note BLP-5040	(10")	**Miles Davis, Volume 3**	1954	150.00	300.00
Blue Note BLP-1501	(M)	**Miles Davis, Volume 1** *(Deep groove)*	1955	100.00	200.00
Blue Note BLP-1501	(M)	**Miles Davis, Volume 1**	1955	60.00	150.00
Blue Note BLP-1502	(M)	**Miles Davis, Volume 2** *(Deep groove)*	1955	100.00	200.00
Blue Note BLP-1502	(M)	**Miles Davis, Volume 2** *(Blue Notes 1501 and 1502 collect 5013, 5022 and 5040.)*	1955	60.00	150.00
—Blue Note albums above blue on white labels with a Lexington Ave., NYC address.—					
Blue Note BLP-1501	(M)	**Miles Davis, Volume 1**	195?	20.00	50.00
Blue Note BLP-1502	(M)	**Miles Davis, Volume 2**	195?	20.00	50.00
—Blue Note albums above blue on white labels with a W. 63rd Street, NYC address.—					

While attending Juiliard in 1945, Miles Davis began dropping in on 52nd Street clubs and playing with Bird and Hawk. He toured with Benny Carter (1946-47) and Billy Eckstine (1947) before forming his own group with Parker in 1948. He then formed a group that included Gil Evans, Lee Konitz, John Lewis, Gerry Mulligan and Max Roach, among others, and recorded the ground breaking "birth of cool" sessions for Capitol. Recording for Prestige, Blue Note and Debut (examples above), his quintet and sextet (1952-56) are among the most influential small groups in jazz history. By 1957 he had signed with Columbia where, with albums such as *Miles Ahead*, *Kind Of Blue*, and *Sketches Of Spain* he not only retained his preeminence in the field but became the biggest selling modern jazz artist of the '60s. He has recorded as a member of The Brass Ensemble and The Metronome All Stars and, as a sideman with Charlie Parker on Savoy, Dial and Verve, Cannonball Adderley on Blue Note, and Sarah Vaughan on Columbia.

Label & Catalog #		Title	Year	VG+	NM
Blue Note BLP-1501	(M)	**Miles Davis, Volume 1**	196?	10.00	25.00
Blue Note BLP-1502	(M)	**Miles Davis, Volume 2**	196?	10.00	25.00
		—Blue Note albums above blue on white labels with a New York, USA address.—			
Blue Note BST-81501	(E)	**Miles Davis, Volume 1**	196?	4.00	10.00
Blue Note BST-81502	(E)	**Miles Davis, Volume 2**	196?	4.00	10.00
		—Blue Note albums above blue on white labels with "A Division of Liberty Records."—			
Capitol H-459	(10")	**Jeru**	1954	125.00	250.00
		(Capitol 459 contains the 1949 "Birth Of The Cool" sessions.)			
Capitol T-762	(M)	**Birth Of The Cool**	1956	60.00	150.00
		(Capitol 762 is a reissue of 459.)			
		—Capitol albums above have turquoise labels.—			
Capitol T-1974	(M)	**Birth Of The Cool**	1963	12.00	30.00
Capitol DT-1974	(E)	**Birth Of The Cool**	1963	6.00	15.00
		(Capitol 1974 is a reissue of 762.)			
Debut DEB-120	(M)	**Blue Moods**	1955	125.00	250.00
Fantasy 6001	(M)	**Blue Moods** *(Red vinyl)*	1962	20.00	50.00
Fantasy 6001	(M)	**Blue Moods**	196?	12.00	30.00
Fantasy 86001	(E)	**Blue Moods** *(Blue vinyl)*	1962	12.00	30.00
Fantasy 86001	(E)	**Blue Moods**	196?	6.00	15.00
		(Fantasy 6001 is a reissue of Debut 120.)			
		—Fantasy albums above have red mono or blue stereo labels.—			
Prestige PRLP-124	(10")	**The New Sounds Of Miles Davis**	1952	125.00	250.00
Prestige PRLP-140	(10")	**Blue Period**	1953	125.00	250.00
Prestige PRLP-154	(10")	**Miles Davis Plays Al Cohn Compositions**	1953	125.00	250.00
Prestige PRLP-161	(10")	**Miles Davis Featuring Sonny Rollins**	1953	125.00	250.00
Prestige PRLP-182	(10")	**Miles Davis Sextet**	1954	125.00	250.00
Prestige PRLP-185	(10")	**Miles Davis Quintet**	1954	125.00	250.00
Prestige PRLP-187	(10")	**Miles Davis Quintet Featuring Sonny Rollins**	1954	125.00	250.00
Prestige PRLP-196	(10")	**Miles Davis All Stars, Vol. 1**	1955	125.00	250.00
Prestige PRLP-200	(10")	**Miles Davis All Stars, Vol. 2**	1955	125.00	250.00
Prestige PRLP-7007	(M)	**Musings Of Miles**	1955	60.00	150.00
Prestige PRLP-7012	(M)	**Dig Miles Davis/Sonny Rollins** *(Grey cover)*	1956	60.00	150.00
Prestige PRLP-7012	(M)	**Dig Miles Davis/Sonny Rollins** *(Color cover)*	1957	50.00	125.00
Prestige PRLP-7014	(M)	**Miles—The New Miles Davis Quintet**	1956	60.00	150.00
Prestige PRLP-7025	(M)	**Miles Davis And Horns**	1956	60.00	150.00
Prestige PRLP-7034	(M)	**Miles Davis And Milt Jackson Quintet/Sextet**	1956	60.00	150.00
Prestige PRLP-7044	(M)	**Collectors' Item**	1956	50.00	125.00
Prestige PRLP-7054	(M)	**Blue Haze**	1956	50.00	125.00
Prestige PRLP-7076	(M)	**Walkin'**	1957	40.00	100.00
		(Prestige 7076 is a reissue of 182.)			
Prestige PRLP-7094	(M)	**Cookin' With The Miles Davis Quintet**	1957	40.00	100.00
Prestige PRLP-7109	(M)	**Bags Groove**	1957	40.00	100.00
Prestige PRLP-7129	(M)	**Relaxin' With The Miles Davis Quintet**	1957	40.00	100.00
		—Prestige albums above have a W. 50th St., NYC address on the label.—			
Prestige PRLP-7150	(M)	**Miles Davis And The Modern Jazz Giants**	1958	30.00	75.00
Prestige PRLP-7166	(M)	**Workin' With The Miles Davis Quintet**	1959	30.00	75.00
Prestige PRLP-7168	(M)	**Early Miles**	1959	30.00	75.00
		(Prestige 7168 is a reissue of 7025.)			
Prestige PRLP-7200	(M)	**Steamin' With The Miles Davis Quintet**	1961	30.00	75.00
Prestige PRLP-7221	(M)	**The Beginning**	1962	20.00	50.00
Prestige PRST-7221	(E)	**The Beginning**	1962	12.00	30.00
		(Prestige 7221 is a reissue of 7007.)			
Prestige PRLP-7254	(M)	**The Original Quintet**	1963	20.00	50.00
Prestige PRST-7254	(E)	**The Original Quintet**	1963	12.00	30.00
		(Prestige 7254 is a reissue of 7014.)			
Prestige PRLP-7281	(M)	**Diggin'**	1963	20.00	50.00
Prestige PRST-7281	(E)	**Diggin'**	1963	12.00	30.00
		(Prestige 7281 is a reissue of 7012.)			
		—Prestige albums above have yellow mono or silver stereo labels with a Bergenfield, NJ address.—			
Prestige PRLP-7034	(M)	**Miles Davis And Milt Jackson Quintet/Sextet**	1964	12.00	30.00
Prestige PRLP-7044	(M)	**Collectors' Item**	1964	12.00	30.00
Prestige PRLP-7054	(M)	**Blue Haze**	1964	12.00	30.00
Prestige PRLP-7076	(M)	**Walkin'**	1964	12.00	30.00
Prestige PRLP-7094	(M)	**Cookin' With The Miles Davis Quintet**	1964	12.00	30.00
Prestige PRLP-7109	(M)	**Bags Groove**	1964	12.00	30.00
Prestige PRLP-7129	(M)	**Relaxin' With The Miles Davis Quintet**	1964	12.00	30.00
Prestige PRLP-7150	(M)	**Miles Davis And The Modern Jazz Giants**	1964	12.00	30.00
Prestige PRLP-7166	(M)	**Workin' With The Miles Davis Quintet**	1964	12.00	30.00
Prestige PRLP-7168	(M)	**Early Miles**	1964	12.00	30.00

Label & Catalog #		Title	Year	VG+	NM
Prestige PRLP-7200	(M)	**Steamin' With The Miles Davis Quintet**	1964	12.00	30.00
Prestige PRLP-7221	(M)	**Beginning**	1964	12.00	30.00
Prestige PRST-7221	(E)	**Beginning**	1964	8.00	20.00
Prestige PRLP-7254	(M)	**The Original Quintet**	1964	12.00	30.00
Prestige PRST-7254	(E)	**The Original Quintet**	1964	8.00	20.00
Prestige PRLP-7281	(M)	**Diggin'**	1964	12.00	30.00
Prestige PRST-7281	(E)	**Diggin'**	1964	8.00	20.00
Prestige PRLP-7352	(M)	**Miles Davis Plays For Lovers**	1965	12.00	30.00
Prestige PRST-7352	(E)	**Miles Davis Plays For Lovers**	1965	8.00	20.00
Prestige PRLP-7373	(M)	**Jazz Classics**	1965	12.00	30.00
Prestige PRST-7373	(E)	**Jazz Classics**	1965	8.00	20.00
		—Prestige albums above have blue labels with a trident logo on the right side.—			
Prestige PRLP-7457	(M)	**Miles Davis' Greatest Hits**	1967	8.00	20.00
Prestige PRST-7457	(E)	**Miles Davis' Greatest Hits**	1967	5.00	12.00
Prestige PRST-7540	(E)	**Odyssey**	1968	5.00	12.00
		(Prestige 7540 is a reissue of 7034.)			
Prestige PRST-7580	(E)	**Steamin'**	1968	5.00	12.00
		(Prestige is a reissue of 7200.)			
Prestige PRST-7608	(E)	**Walkin'**	1969	5.00	12.00
		(Prestige 7608 is a reissue of 7076.)			
Prestige PRST-7650	(E)	**Miles Davis And The Modern Jazz Giants**	1969	5.00	12.00
Prestige PRST-7674	(E)	**Early Miles**	1969	5.00	12.00
		—Prestige albums above have blue labels with a trident logo on top.—			
Columbia CL-949	(M)	**'Round About Midnight**	1957	20.00	50.00
Columbia CL-1041	(M)	**Miles Ahead**	1957	30.00	75.00
		(Original covers feature a white woman with her child on a sailboat.)			
Columbia CL-1041	(M)	**Miles Ahead**	1957	20.00	50.00
		(Later covers show Miles aboard a sailboat sans instruments.)			
Columbia CL-1193	(M)	**Milestones...**	1958	20.00	50.00
Columbia CS-9428	(E)	**Milestones...**	1965	5.00	12.00
		(CS-9428 is a rechanneled stereo reissue with a "360 Sound" label.)			
Columbia CL-1268	(M)	**Jazz Track**	1958	30.00	75.00
		("Jazz Track" features performances for the French film "L'Ascenseur Pour l' Echafaud." Original covers feature an abstract drawing.)			
Columbia CL-1268	(M)	**Jazz Track**	1959	20.00	50.00
		(Later cover feature a photo of Miles with Jeanne Moreau.)			
Columbia CL-1274	(M)	**Porgy And Bess**	1958	20.00	50.00
Columbia CS-8085	(S)	**Porgy And Bess**	1959	16.00	40.00
Columbia CL-1355	(M)	**Kind Of Blue**	1959	20.00	50.00
Columbia CS-8163	(S)	**Kind Of Blue**	1959	40.00	100.00
Columbia CL-1480	(M)	**Sketches Of Spain**	1960	20.00	50.00
Columbia CS-8271	(S)	**Sketches Of Spain**	1960	30.00	75.00
Columbia CL-1656	(M)	**Someday My Prince Will Come**	1961	16.00	40.00
Columbia CS-8456	(S)	**Someday My Prince Will Come**	1961	12.00	30.00
Columbia C2L-20	(M)	**Friday And Saturday Nights In Person** *(2 LPs)*	1961	20.00	50.00
Columbia C2S-820	(S)	**Friday And Saturday Nights In Person** *(2 LPs)*	1961	16.00	40.00
Columbia CL-1669	(M)	**Friday Nights At The Blackhawk, San Francisco— Miles Davis In Person, Volume 1**	1961	12.00	30.00
Columbia CS-8469	(S)	**Friday Nights At The Blackhawk, San Francisco— Miles Davis In Person, Volume 1**	1961	10.00	25.00
Columbia CL-1670	(M)	**Saturday Nights At The Blackhawk, San Francisco— Miles Davis In Person, Volume 2**	1961	12.00	30.00
Columbia CS-8470	(S)	**Saturday Nights At The Blackhawk, San Francisco— Miles Davis In Person, Volume 2**	1961	10.00	25.00
Columbia CL-1812	(M)	**Miles Davis At Carnegie Hall**	1962	20.00	50.00
Columbia CS-8612	(S)	**Miles Davis At Carnegie Hall**	1962	16.00	40.00
		—Columbia albums above have six white on black "eye" logos on each label.—			
Columbia CL-949	(M)	**'Round About Midnight**	196?	8.00	20.00
Columbia CL-1041	(M)	**Miles Ahead**	196?	8.00	20.00
Columbia CL-1193	(M)	**Milestones...**	196?	8.00	20.00
Columbia CL-1274	(M)	**Porgy And Bess**	196?	8.00	20.00
Columbia CS-8085	(S)	**Porgy And Bess**	196?	6.00	15.00
Columbia CL-1355	(M)	**Kind Of Blue**	196?	8.00	20.00
Columbia CS-8163	(S)	**Kind Of Blue**	196?	6.00	15.00
Columbia CL-1480	(M)	**Sketches Of Spain**	196?	8.00	20.00
Columbia CS-8271	(S)	**Sketches Of Spain**	196?	6.00	15.00
Columbia CL-1656	(M)	**Someday My Prince Will Come**	196?	8.00	20.00
Columbia CS-8456	(S)	**Someday My Prince Will Come**	196?	6.00	15.00

Label & Catalog #		Title	Year	VG+	NM
Columbia CL-1669	(M)	**Friday Nights At The Blackhawk, San Francisco—Miles Davis In Person, Volume 1**	196?	8.00	20.00
Columbia CS-8469	(S)	**Friday Nights At The Blackhawk, San Francisco—Miles Davis In Person, Volume 1**	196?	6.00	15.00
Columbia CL-1670	(M)	**Saturday Nights At The Blackhawk, San Francisco—Miles Davis In Person, Volume 2**	196?	8.00	20.00
Columbia CS-8470	(S)	**Saturday Nights At The Blackhawk, San Francisco—Miles Davis In Person, Volume 2**	196?	6.00	15.00
Columbia CL-1812	(M)	**Miles Davis At Carnegie Hall**	1962	10.00	25.00
Columbia CS-8612	(S)	**Miles Davis At Carnegie Hall**	1962	8.00	20.00
Columbia CL-2051	(M)	**Seven Steps To Heaven**	1963	10.00	25.00
Columbia CS-8851	(S)	**Seven Steps To Heaven**	1963	8.00	20.00
Columbia CL-2106	(M)	**Quiet Nights**	1963	10.00	25.00
Columbia CS-8906	(S)	**Quiet Nights**	1963	8.00	20.00
Columbia CL-2183	(M)	**Miles Davis In Europe**	1964	10.00	25.00
Columbia CS-8983	(S)	**Miles Davis In Europe**	1964	8.00	20.00
Columbia CL-2306	(M)	**My Funny Valentine—Miles Davis In Concert**	1965	10.00	25.00
Columbia CS-9106	(S)	**My Funny Valentine—Miles Davis In Concert**	1965	8.00	20.00
Columbia CL-2350	(M)	**E. S. P.**	1965	10.00	25.00
Columbia CS-9150	(S)	**E. S. P.**	1965	8.00	20.00
—Columbia albums above have "Guaranteed High Fidelity" or "360 Sound Stereo" in black on the label.—					
Columbia CL-949	(M)	**'Round About Midnight**	196?	5.00	12.00
Columbia CL-1041	(M)	**Miles Ahead**	196?	5.00	12.00
Columbia CL-1193	(M)	**Milestones...**	196?	5.00	12.00
Columbia CL-1274	(M)	**Porgy And Bess**	196?	5.00	12.00
Columbia CS-8085	(S)	**Porgy And Bess**	196?	4.00	10.00
Columbia CL-1355	(M)	**Kind Of Blue**	196?	5.00	12.00
Columbia CS-8163	(S)	**Kind Of Blue**	196?	4.00	10.00
Columbia CL-1480	(M)	**Sketches Of Spain**	196?	5.00	12.00
Columbia CS-8271	(S)	**Sketches Of Spain**	196?	4.00	10.00
Columbia CL-1656	(M)	**Someday My Prince Will Come**	196?	5.00	12.00
Columbia CS-8456	(S)	**Someday My Prince Will Come**	196?	4.00	10.00
Columbia CL-1669	(M)	**Friday Nights At The Blackhawk, San Francisco—Miles Davis In Person, Volume 1**	196?	5.00	12.00
Columbia CS-8469	(S)	**Friday Nights At The Blackhawk, San Francisco—Miles Davis In Person, Volume 1**	196?	4.00	10.00
Columbia CL-1670	(M)	**Saturday Nights At The Blackhawk, San Francisco—Miles Davis In Person, Volume 2**	196?	5.00	12.00
Columbia CS-8470	(S)	**Saturday Nights At The Blackhawk, San Francisco—Miles Davis In Person, Volume 2**	196?	4.00	10.00
Columbia CL-1812	(M)	**Miles Davis At Carnegie Hall**	196?	5.00	12.00
Columbia CS-8612	(S)	**Miles Davis At Carnegie Hall**	196?	4.00	10.00
Columbia CL-2051	(M)	**Seven Steps To Heaven**	196?	5.00	12.00
Columbia CS-8851	(S)	**Seven Steps To Heaven**	196?	4.00	10.00
Columbia CL-2106	(M)	**Quiet Nights**	196?	5.00	12.00
Columbia CS-8906	(S)	**Quiet Nights**	196?	4.00	10.00
Columbia CL-2183	(M)	**Miles Davis In Europe**	196?	5.00	12.00
Columbia CS-8983	(S)	**Miles Davis In Europe**	196?	4.00	10.00
Columbia CL-2306	(M)	**My Funny Valentine—Miles Davis In Concert**	196?	5.00	12.00
Columbia CS-9106	(S)	**My Funny Valentine—Miles Davis In Concert**	196?	4.00	10.00
Columbia CL-2350	(M)	**E. S. P.**	196?	5.00	12.00
Columbia CS-9150	(S)	**E. S. P.**	196?	4.00	10.00
Columbia CL-2453	(M)	**'Four' & More—Recorded Live In Concert**	1966	8.00	20.00
Columbia CS-9253	(S)	**'Four' & More—Recorded Live In Concert**	1966	6.00	15.00
Columbia CL-2601	(M)	**Miles Smiles**	1966	8.00	20.00
Columbia CS-9401	(S)	**Miles Smiles**	1966	6.00	15.00
Columbia CL-2628	(M)	**Milestones**	1967	12.00	30.00
Columbia CS-9428	(S)	**Milestones**	1967	6.00	15.00
Columbia CL-2732	(M)	**Sorcerer**	1967	12.00	30.00
Columbia CS-9532	(S)	**Sorcerer**	1967	6.00	15.00
Columbia CL-2794	(M)	**Nefertiti**	1968	20.00	50.00
Columbia CS-9594	(S)	**Nefertiti**	1968	6.00	15.00
Columbia CL-2828	(M)	**Miles In The Sky**	1968	20.00	50.00
Columbia CS-9628	(S)	**Miles In The Sky**	1968	6.00	15.00
Columbia CS-9750	(S)	**Files De Kilimanjaro**	1969	6.00	15.00
Columbia CS-9808	(S)	**Miles Davis' Greatest Hits**	1969	6.00	15.00
Columbia CS-9875	(S)	**In A Silent Way**	1969	6.00	15.00
—Columbia albums above have "360 Sound" in white on the bottom of the label.—					
Columbia DS-417	(S)	**Miles Orbits** *(Columbia Record Club)*	1968	10.00	25.00

Label & Catalog #		Title	Year	VG+	NM

DAVIS, MILES , & JOHN COLTRANE

Label & Catalog #		Title	Year	VG+	NM
Moodsville MVLP-32	(M)	**Miles Davis & John Coltrane Play Richard Rodgers**	1963	20.00	50.00
		(Moodsville 32 reissues Prestige recordings.)			
—Moodsville mono albums above have green labels with silver print.—					
Moodsville MVLP-32	(M)	**Miles Davis & John Coltrane Play Richard Rodgers**	1965	10.00	25.00
—Moodsville albums above have blue labels with a trident logo on the right side.—					
Prestige PRLP-7322	(M)	**Miles Davis & John Coltrane Play Rodgers & Hart**	1964	16.00	40.00
Prestige PRST-7322	(E)	**Miles Davis & John Coltrane Play Rodgers & Hart**	1964	12.00	30.00
		(Prestige 7322 is a reissue of Moodsville 32.)			

DAVIS, MILES / DIZZY GILLESPIE / FATS NAVARRO

Label & Catalog #		Title	Year	VG+	NM
New Jazz NJLP-8296	(M)	**Trumpet Giants**	1962	20.00	50.00
—New Jazz albums above have purple labels.—					
New Jazz NJLP-8296	(M)	**Trumpet Giants**	1965	10.00	25.00
—New Jazz albums above have blue labels with a trident logo on the right side.—					

DAVIS, MILES / THELONIOUS MONK

Label & Catalog #		Title	Year	VG+	NM
Columbia CL-2178	(M)	**Miles And Monk At Newport**	1964	10.00	25.00
Columbia CS-8978	(S)	**Miles And Monk At Newport**	1964	8.00	20.00
		(Miles' Sextet features John Coltrane and Cannonball Adderley; Monk's Quartet features Pee Wee Russell.)			
—Columbia albums above have "Guaranteed High Fidelity" or "360 Sound Stereo" in black on the label.—					
Columbia CL-2178	(M)	**Miles And Monk At Newport**	1964	6.00	15.00
Columbia CS-8978	(S)	**Miles And Monk At Newport**	196?	5.00	12.00
—Columbia albums above have "360 Sound" in white on the bottom of the label.—					

DAVIS, SAMMY, JR.

Sammy Davis' is a pop vocalist. For additional listings refer to Count Basie.

Label & Catalog #		Title	Year	VG+	NM
Decca DL-8676	(M)	**Mood To Be Wooed**	1958	12.00	30.00
		(Decca 8676 features Mundell Lowe.)			
Decca DL-8981	(M)	**I Gotta Right To Swing**	1958	12.00	30.00
Decca DL-78981	(S)	**I Gotta Right To Swing**	1959	12.00	30.00
		(Decca 8981 features Eric Dolphy, Frank Foster, Thad Jones, Benny Powell and Snooky Young.)			

DAVIS, SHELBY: ***Refer to*** **ANNIE ROSS / DOROTHY DUNN / SHELBY SAVIS**

DAVIS, WALTER JR.

Walter Davis Jr. is a modern jazz pianist and composer. For additional listings refer to the Jazzy Soundtracks section.

Label & Catalog #		Title	Year	VG+	NM
Blue Note BLP-4018	(M)	**Davis Cup** *(Deep groove)*	1959	50.00	125.00
Blue Note BLP-4018	(M)	**Davis Cup**	1959	30.00	75.00
Blue Note BST-84018	(S)	**Davis Cup**	1959	20.00	50.00
—Blue Note albums above have blue on white labels with a W. 63rd St,, NYC address.—					
Blue Note BLP-4018	(M)	**Davis Cup**	196?	10.00	25.00
Blue Note BST-84018	(S)	**Davis Cup**	196?	8.00	20.00
—Blue Note albums above have blue on white labels with a New York, USA address.—					
Blue Note BST-84018	(S)	**Davis Cup**	196?	5.00	12.00
—Blue Note albums above have blue on white labels with "A Division of Liberty Records."—					

DAVISON, "WILD" BILL

William Davison is a traditional jazz cornet player. For additional listings refer to Buck Clayton / Wild Bill Davison; Helen Ward.

Label & Catalog #		Title	Year	VG+	NM
Commodore FL-20000	(10")	**Dixieland Jazz Jamboree**	1950	40.00	100.00
Commodore FL-30009	(M)	**Mild And Wild**	1959	24.00	60.00
Circle LP-405	(10")	**Showcase**	1951	30.00	75.00
Savoy MG-12035	(M)	**Jazz At Storyville**	1955	24.00	60.00
Savoy MG-12055	(M)	**Ringside At Condon's**	1955	24.00	60.00
Riverside RLP-12-211	(M)	**Sweet And Hot**	1956	24.00	60.00
—Riverside albums above have blue on white labels.—					
Riverside RLP-12-211	(M)	**Sweet And Hot**	195?	12.00	30.00
—Riverside albums above have blue mono or black stereo labels with a reel & mike logo on top.—					
Columbia CL-871	(M)	**Pretty Wild**	1956	16.00	40.00
Columbia CL-983	(M)	**Wild Bill Davison With Strings Attached**	1956	16.00	40.00
—Columbia albums above have six white on black "eye" logos on each label.—					

Label & Catalog #		Title	Year	VG+	NM
Savoy MG-12214	(S)	**Dixieland**	1969	6.00	15.00
		(Savoy 12214 also features Bill Stafford.)			
Jazzology 2	(M)	**Wild Bill Davison's Jazzologists**	196?	6.00	15.00
DAWSON, SID					
Delmar 109	(10")	**Sid Dawson's Riverboat Gamblers**	195?	20.00	50.00
DAY, CARA LEE					
Cara Lee Day is a jazz-based vocalist.					
Roulette R-52048	(M)	**My Crying Hour**	1960	12.00	30.00
Roulette SR-52048	(S)	**My Crying Hour**	1960	16.00	40.00
DeARANGO, BILL					
William DeArango is a jazz-based guitarist.					
EmArcy MG-26020	(10")	**Bill DeArango**	1954	20.00	50.00
DEARIE, BLOSSOM					
Blossom Dearie is a jazz-based pianist and vocalist.					
Verve MGV-2037	(M)	**Blossom Dearie**	1957	30.00	75.00
		(Verve 2037 also features Ray Brown, Herb Ellis and Jo Jones.)			
Verve MGV-2081	(M)	**Give Him The Ooh-La-La**	1958	30.00	75.00
Verve MGV-2109	(M)	**Blossom Dearie Sings Comden & Green**	1959	30.00	75.00
Verve MGVS-6050	(S)	**Blossom Dearie Sings Comden & Green**	1960	24.00	60.00
Verve MGV-2111	(M)	**Once Upon A Summertime**	1958	30.00	75.00
Verve MGVS-6020	(S)	**Once Upon A Summertime**	1960	24.00	60.00
		(Verve 2111 also features Ray Brown, Mundell Lowe and Ed Thigpen.)			
Verve MGV-2125	(M)	**My Gentleman Friend**	1959	30.00	75.00
Verve MGVS-6112	(S)	**My Gentleman Friend**	1960	24.00	60.00
Verve MGV-2133	(M)	**Broadway Song Hits**	1960	30.00	75.00
Verve MGVS-6139	(S)	**Broadway Song Hits**	1960	24.00	60.00
— Verve albums above have "Verve Records, Inc." on the bottom of the label.—					
Verve V-2037	(M)	**Blossom Dearie**	1961	12.00	30.00
Verve V-2081	(M)	**Give Him The Ooh-La-La**	1961	12.00	30.00
Verve V-2109	(M)	**Blossom Dearie Sings Comden & Green**	1961	12.00	30.00
Verve V6-2109	(S)	**Blossom Dearie Sings Comden & Green**	1961	10.00	25.00
Verve V-2111	(M)	**Once Upon A Summertime**	1961	12.00	30.00
Verve V6-2111	(S)	**Once Upon A Summertime**	1961	10.00	25.00
		(Verve 2111 also features Ray Brown, Mundell Lowe and Ed Thigpen.)			
Verve V-2125	(M)	**My Gentleman Friend**	1961	12.00	30.00
Verve V6-2125	(S)	**My Gentleman Friend**	1961	10.00	25.00
Verve V-2133	(M)	**Broadway Song Hits**	1961	12.00	30.00
Verve V6-2133	(S)	**Broadway Song Hits**	1961	10.00	25.00
— Verve albums above have black labels with "MGM Records" on the bottom.—					
DEDRICK, RUSTY					
Lyle "Rusty" Dedrick is a traditional jazz trumpet player and composer. For additional listings refer to Don Elliot & Rusty Dedrick.					
Esoteric ESJ-9	(10")	**Rhythm And Winds**	1955	40.00	100.00
Keynote 1103	(M)	**Rusty Dedrick**	1955	20.00	50.00
Counterpoint 552	(M)	**Salute To Bunny**	1957	20.00	50.00
Four Corners FC-4207	(M)	**The Big Band Sound**	1964	4.00	20.00
Four Corners FCS-4207	(S)	**The Big Band Sound**	1964	6.00	15.00
Monument MLP-6502	(M)	**A Jazz Journey**	1965	8.00	20.00
Monument SLP-16502	(S)	**A Jazz Journey**	1965	6.00	15.00
DeFRANCO, BUDDY					
Boniface "Buddy" DeFranco is a modern jazz clarinet player. For additional listings refer to Gerry Mulligan / Buddy DeFranco; Gerry Mulligan; Art Tatum & Buddy DeFranco.					
MGM E-177	(10")	**King Of The Clarinet**	1952	40.00	100.00
MGM E-253	(10")	**Buddy DeFranco With Strings**	1954	40.00	100.00
MGM E-3396	(M)	**Buddy DeFranco**	1956	30.00	75.00
		(MGM 3396 is a reissue of 177.)			
Clef MGC-149	(10")	**The Buddy DeFranco Quartet**	1954	Unreleased	
		("The Buddy DeFranco Quartet" was issued as Norgran 3.)			
Norgran MGN-3	(10")	**The Buddy DeFranco Quartet**	1954	60.00	150.00
		(Norgran 3 features cover art by David Stone Martin.)			
Norgran MGN-16	(10")	**Pretty Moods By Buddy DeFranco**	1954	60.00	150.00
		(Norgran 16 features cover art by David Stone Martin.)			
Norgran MGN-1006	(M)	**The Progressive Mr. DeFranco**	1954	40.00	100.00

Label & Catalog #		Title	Year	VG+	NM
Norgran MGN-1012	(M)	**Buddy DeFranco And His Clarinet**	1954	40.00	100.00
Norgran MGN-1016	(M)	**Buddy DeFranco And Oscar Peterson Play George Gershwin**	1955	40.00	100.00
		(Norgran 1016 features cover art by David Stone Martin.)			
Norgran MGN-1026	(M)	**Buddy DeFranco Quartet**	1955	40.00	100.00
		(Norgran 1026 features over art by David Stone Martin.)			
Norgran MGN-1068	(M)	**Jazz Tones**	1956	40.00	100.00
Norgran MGN-1069	(M)	**Mr. Clarinet**	1956	30.00	75.00
		(Norgran 1069 is a reissue of 1026.)			
Norgran MGN-1079	(M)	**In A Mellow Mood**	1956	30.00	75.00
Norgran MGN-1085	(M)	**The Buddy DeFranco Wailers**	1956	30.00	75.00
Norgran MGN-1094	(M)	**Odalisque**	1956	30.00	75.00
		(Norgran 1094 is a reissue of 1006.)			
Norgran MGN-1096	(M)	**Autumn Leaves**	1956	30.00	75.00
		(Norgran 1096 is a reissue of 1012.)			
Norgran MGN-1105	(M)	**Broadway Showcase**	1956	*Unreleased*	
Verve MGV-2022	(M)	**The George Gershwin Songbook**	1956	20.00	50.00
		(Verve 2022 is a reissue of Norgran 1016.)			
Verve MGV-2033	(M)	**Broadway Showcase**	1957	20.00	50.00
Verve MGV-2089	(M)	**Buddy DeFranco Plays Benny Goodman**	1958	20.00	50.00
Verve MGV-2090	(M)	**Buddy DeFranco Plays Artie Shaw**	1958	20.00	50.00
Verve MGV-2108	(M)	**I Hear Benny Goodman And Artie Shaw**	1958	20.00	50.00
Verve MGVS-6032	(S)	**I Hear Benny Goodman And Artie Shaw**	1960	16.00	40.00
		— Verve albums above have "Verve Records, Inc." on the bottom of the label.—			
Verve MGV-8158	(M)	**Jazz Tones**	1957	20.00	50.00
		(Verve 8158 is a reissue of Norgran 1068.)			
Verve MGV-8159	(M)	**Mr. Clarinet**	1957	20.00	50.00
		(Verve 8159 is a reissue of Norgran 1060.)			
Verve MGV-8169	(M)	**In A Mellow Mood**	1957	20.00	50.00
		(Verve 8169 is a reissue of Norgran 1079.)			
Verve MGV-8175	(M)	**The Buddy DeFranco Wailers**	1957	20.00	50.00
		(Verve 8175 is a reissue of Norgran 1085.)			
Verve MGV-8182	(M)	**Odalisque**	1957	20.00	50.00
		(Verve 8182 is a reissue of Norgran 1094.)			
Verve MGV-8183	(M)	**Autumn Leaves**	1957	20.00	50.00
		(Verve 8183 is a reissue of Norgran 1096.)			
Verve MGV-8210	(M)	**Buddy DeFranco And The Oscar Peterson Quartet**	1958	20.00	50.00
Verve MGV-8221	(M)	**Cooking The Blues**	1958	30.00	75.00
Verve MGV-8224	(M)	**Sweet And Lovely**	1958	20.00	50.00
Verve MGV-8279	(M)	**I Hear Benny Goodman And Artie Shaw**	1958	*Unreleased*	
Verve MGV-8315	(M)	**Bravura**	1959	20.00	50.00
Verve MGVS-6051	(S)	**Bravura**	1960	16.00	40.00
Verve MGV-8363	(M)	**Generalissimo**	1960	20.00	50.00
Verve MGVS-6132	(S)	**Generalissimo**	1960	16.00	40.00
Verve MGV-8375	(M)	**Wholly Cats**	1960	20.00	50.00
Verve MGVS-6150	(S)	**Wholly Cats**	1960	16.00	40.00
Verve MGVS-8382	(S)	**Closed Session**	1960	20.00	50.00
Verve MGVS-6165	(M)	**Closed Session**	1960	16.00	40.00
Verve MGV-8383	(M)	**Live Date!**	1960	20.00	50.00
Verve MGVS-6166	(S)	**Live Date!**	1960	16.00	40.00
Verve MGV-8384	(M)	**Buddy DeFranco**	1960	*Unreleased*	
Verve MGVS-6167	(S)	**Buddy DeFranco**	1960	*Unreleased*	
		— Verve albums above have black labels with "Verve Records, Inc." on the bottom.—			
Verve V-2033	(M)	**Broadway Showcase**	1961	8.00	20.00
Verve V-2089	(M)	**Buddy DeFranco Plays Benny Goodman**	1961	8.00	20.00
Verve V-2090	(M)	**Buddy DeFranco Plays Artie Shaw**	1961	8.00	20.00
Verve V-2108	(M)	**I Hear Benny Goodman And Artie Shaw**	1961	8.00	20.00
Verve V6-2108	(S)	**I Hear Benny Goodman And Artie Shaw**	1961	6.00	15.00
Verve V-8158	(M)	**Jazz Tones**	1961	8.00	20.00
Verve V-8159	(M)	**Mr. Clarinet**	1961	8.00	20.00
Verve V-8169	(M)	**In A Mellow Mood**	1961	8.00	20.00
Verve V-8175	(M)	**The Buddy DeFranco Wailers**	1961	8.00	20.00
Verve V-8182	(M)	**Odalisque**	1961	8.00	20.00
Verve V-8183	(M)	**Autumn Leaves**	1961	8.00	20.00
Verve V-8210	(M)	**Buddy DeFranco And The Oscar Peterson Quartet**	1961	8.00	20.00
Verve V-8221	(M)	**Cooking The Blues**	1961	8.00	20.00
Verve V-8224	(M)	**Sweet And Lovely**	1961	8.00	20.00

Label & Catalog #		Title	Year	VG+	NM
Verve V-8315	(M)	**Bravura**	1961	8.00	20.00
Verve V6-8315	(S)	**Bravura**	1961	6.00	15.00
Verve V-8363	(M)	**Generalissimo**	1961	8.00	20.00
Verve V6-8363	(S)	**Generalissimo**	1961	6.00	15.00
Verve V-8375	(M)	**Wholly Cats**	1961	8.00	20.00
Verve V6-8375	(S)	**Wholly Cats**	1961	6.00	15.00
Verve V-8382	(M)	**Closed Session**	1961	8.00	20.00
Verve V6-8282	(S)	**Closed Session**	1961	6.00	15.00
Verve V-8383	(M)	**Live Date!**	1961	8.00	20.00
Verve V6-8383	(S)	**Live Date!**	1961	6.00	15.00

—Verve albums above have black labels with "MGM Records" on the bottom.—

Gene Norman GNP-2	(10")	**Buddy DeFranco Takes You To The Stars**	1954	40.00	100.00
Dot DLP-9006	(M)	**Cross-Country Suite**	1958	16.00	40.00
Advance Guard 1001	(M)	**University Of New Mexico Stage Band**	1961	16.00	40.00
Decca DL-4031	(M)	**Pacific Standard Swingin' Time**	1961	10.00	25.00
Decca DL-74031	(S)	**Pacific Standard Swingin' Time**	1961	8.00	20.00
Hamilton HL-12133	(M)	**Cross-Country Suite**	1964	8.00	20.00
Hamilton HS-12133	(S)	**Cross-Country Suite**	1964	6.00	15.00

(Hamilton 12133 is a reissue of Dot 9006.)

DeFRANCO, BUDDY, & TOMMY GUMINA (THE DeFRANCO-GUMINA QUINTET)

Mercury MG-20685	(M)	**Presenting The Buddy DeFranco-Tommy Gumina Quintet**	1962	10.00	25.00
Mercury SR-60685	(S)	**Presenting The Buddy DeFranco-Tommy Gumina Quintet**	1962	8.00	20.00
Mercury MG-20743	(M)	**Kaleidoscope**	1962	10.00	25.00
Mercury SR-60743	(S)	**Kaleidoscope**	1962	8.00	20.00
Mercury MG-20833	(M)	**Polytones**	1963	10.00	25.00
Mercury SR-60833	(S)	**Polytones**	1963	8.00	20.00
Mercury MG-20900	(M)	**The Girl From Ipanema**	1963	10.00	25.00
Mercury SR-60900	(S)	**The Girl From Ipanema**	1963	8.00	20.00

—Mercury albums above have silver on black labels.—

DeJOHNETTE, JACK

Jack DeJohnette is a modern jazz bass player.

Milestone MSP-9022	(S)	**The DeJohnette Complex**	1969	6.00	15.00

DELANEY, JACK

Jack Delaney is a traditional jazz-based trombone player; Lee Collins a trumpet player.

Southland LP-214	(10")	**Jack Delaney With Lee Collins**	1954	20.00	50.00

DELANEY, JACK / GEORGE GIRARD

Southland LP-201	(10")	**Jack Delaney/George Girard In New Orleans**	1954	20.00	50.00

DELEGATES, THE

The Delegates—Mel Brown, Billy Larkin and Hank Swarn—are a modern jazz trio.

Aura 23002	(M)	**Pigmy**	1964	10.00	25.00
Aura 83002	(S)	**Pigmy**	1964	8.00	20.00
Aura 23003	(M)	**Blue Lights**	1965	10.00	25.00
Aura 83003	(S)	**Blue Lights**	1965	8.00	20.00

DeMANO, HANK

Freeway FLJP-1	(M)	**Hank DeMano Quartet With Don Friedman**	1955	20.00	50.00

DENNIS, JOHN

John Dennis is a modern jazz pianist.

Debut DEB-121	(M)	**New Piano Expressions**	1955	40.00	100.00

DENNY, DOTTY

"A440" AJ-505	(10")	**Tribute To Edgar Sampson**	1954	20.00	50.00
"A440" AJ-506	(10")	**Dotty Digs Duke**	1954	20.00	50.00

DePARIS, SIDNEY

Sidney DeParis is a traditional jazz trumpet and tuba player and vocalist. For additional listings refer to Sidney Bechet; Edmond Hall / Sidney DeParis.

Blue Note BLP-7016	(10")	**Sidney DeParis' Blue Note Stompers**	1951	125.00	250.00
Blue Note B-6501	(M)	**DeParis Dixie**	1969	6.00	15.00

(Blue Note 6501 is a reissue of 7016.)

Label & Catalog #		Title	Year	VG+	NM
DePARIS, SIDNEY / JAMES P. JOHNSON					
Blue Note B-6506	*(M)*	**Original Blue Note Jazz, Volume 2**	*1969*	**6.00**	**15.00**
DePARIS, WILBUR					
Wilbur DeParis, Sidney's sibling, is a traditional jazz trombonist and band leader.					
Atlantic ALS-141	*(10")*	**Wilbur DeParis & His Rampart Street Ramblers**	*1952*	**40.00**	**100.00**
Atlantic ALS-143	*(10")*	**Wilbur DeParis, Vol. 2**	*1953*	**40.00**	**100.00**
"A440" AJ-503	*(10")*	**New New Orleans Jazz**	*1954*	**20.00**	**50.00**
Heritage SS-1207	*(M)*	**Wilbur DeParis**	*1956*	**20.00**	**50.00**
Atlantic 1219	*(M)*	**Wilbur DeParis & His New Orleans Jazz**	*1956*	**20.00**	**50.00**
Atlantic SD-1219	*(S)*	**Wilbur DeParis & His New Orleans Jazz**	*1958*	**16.00**	**40.00**
Atlantic 1233	*(M)*	**Marchin' And Swingin'**	*1956*	**20.00**	**50.00**
Atlantic SD-1233	*(S)*	**Marchin' And Swingin'**	*1958*	**16.00**	**40.00**
Atlantic 1253	*(M)*	**Wilbur DeParis At Symphony Hall**	*1957*	**20.00**	**50.00**
Atlantic SD-1253	*(S)*	**Wilbur DeParis At Symphony Hall**	*1958*	**16.00**	**40.00**
Atlantic 1266	*(M)*	**New Orleans Blues**	*1957*	**20.00**	**50.00**
		(Atlantic 1266 also features Jimmy Witherspoon.)			
Atlantic 1288	*(M)*	**Wilbur DeParis Plays Cole Porter**	*1958*	**20.00**	**50.00**
Atlantic 1300	*(M)*	**Something Old, New, Gay, Blue**	*1958*	**20.00**	**50.00**
Atlantic SD-1300	*(S)*	**Something Old, New, Gay, Blue**	*1958*	**16.00**	**40.00**
Atlantic 1318	*(M)*	**That's A Plenty**	*1959*	**20.00**	**50.00**
Atlantic SD-1318	*(S)*	**That's A Plenty**	*1959*	**16.00**	**40.00**
		—Atlantic albums above have black mono or green stereo labels.—			
Atlantic 1233	*(M)*	**Marchin' And Swingin'**	*1961*	**8.00**	**20.00**
Atlantic SD-1233	*(S)*	**Marchin' And Swingin'**	*1961*	**6.00**	**15.00**
Atlantic 1253	*(M)*	**Wilbur DeParis At Symphony Hall**	*1961*	**8.00**	**20.00**
Atlantic SD-1253	*(S)*	**Wilbur DeParis At Symphony Hall**	*1961*	**6.00**	**15.00**
Atlantic 1266	*(M)*	**New Orleans Blues**	*1961*	**8.00**	**20.00**
Atlantic 1288	*(M)*	**Wilbur DeParis Plays Cole Porter**	*1961*	**8.00**	**20.00**
Atlantic 1300	*(M)*	**Something Old, New, Gay, Blue**	*1961*	**8.00**	**20.00**
Atlantic SD-1300	*(S)*	**Something Old, New, Gay, Blue**	*1961*	**6.00**	**15.00**
Atlantic 1318	*(M)*	**That's A Plenty**	*1961*	**8.00**	**20.00**
Atlantic SD-1318	*(S)*	**That's A Plenty**	*1961*	**6.00**	**15.00**
Atlantic 1336	*(M)*	**The Wild Jazz Age**	*1960*	**10.00**	**25.00**
Atlantic SD-1336	*(S)*	**The Wild Jazz Age**	*1960*	**8.00**	**20.00**
Atlantic 1363	*(M)*	**Wilbur DeParis On The Riviera**	*1961*	**10.00**	**25.00**
Atlantic SD-1363	*(S)*	**Wilbur DeParis On The Riviera**	*1961*	**8.00**	**20.00**
		—Atlantic albums above have multi-color labels with a white fan logo.—			
Atlantic 1233	*(M)*	**Marchin' And Swingin'**	*196?*	**5.00**	**12.00**
Atlantic SD-1233	*(S)*	**Marchin' And Swingin'**	*196?*	**5.00**	**10.00**
Atlantic 1253	*(M)*	**Wilbur DeParis At Symphony Hall**	*196?*	**5.00**	**12.00**
Atlantic SD-1253	*(S)*	**Wilbur DeParis At Symphony Hall**	*196?*	**5.00**	**10.00**
Atlantic 1266	*(M)*	**New Orleans Blues**	*196?*	**5.00**	**12.00**
Atlantic 1288	*(M)*	**Wilbur DeParis Plays Cole Porter**	*196?*	**5.00**	**15.00**
Atlantic 1300	*(M)*	**Something Old, New, Gay, Blue**	*196?*	**5.00**	**12.00**
Atlantic SD-1300	*(S)*	**Something Old, New, Gay, Blue**	*196?*	**5.00**	**10.00**
Atlantic 1318	*(M)*	**That's A Plenty**	*196?*	**5.00**	**12.00**
Atlantic SD-1318	*(S)*	**That's A Plenty**	*196?*	**5.00**	**10.00**
Atlantic 1336	*(M)*	**The Wild Jazz Age**	*196?*	**5.00**	**12.00**
Atlantic SD-1336	*(S)*	**The Wild Jazz Age**	*196?*	**5.00**	**10.00**
Atlantic 1363	*(M)*	**Wilbur DeParis On The Riviera**	*196?*	**5.00**	**12.00**
Atlantic SD-1363	*(S)*	**Wilbur DeParis On The Riviera**	*196?*	**5.00**	**10.00**
		—Atlantic albums above have multi-color labels with a black fan logo.—			
DeRISE, JOE					
Joseph DeRise is a jazz-based vocalist.					
Bethlehem BCP-1039	*(10")*	**Joe DeRise Sings**	*1955*	**40.00**	**100.00**
Bethlehem BCP-51	*(M)*	**Joe DeRise With The Australian Jazz Quintet**	*1956*	**20.00**	**50.00**
DESMOND, PAUL					
Paul Breitenfeld, aka Paul Desmond, is a West Coast jazz alto saxophone player long associated with Dave Brubeck. For additional listings refer to Dave Brubeck; Gerry Mulligan.					
Fantasy 3-21	*(10")*	**Paul Desmond**	*1955*	**40.00**	**100.00**
Fantasy 3235	*(M)*	**Paul Desmond Quartet Featuring Don Elliot**	*1956*	**30.00**	**75.00**
		—Fantasy mono albums above have red labels on dark red, non-flexible vinyl.—			
Fantasy 3235	*(M)*	**Paul Desmond Quartet Featuring Don Elliot**	*1957*	**16.00**	**40.00**
		—Fantasy mono albums above have red labels on non-flexible vinyl.—			
Fantasy 3235	*(M)*	**Paul Desmond Quartet Featuring Don Elliot**	*196?*	**6.00**	**15.00**
		—Fantasy mono albums above have red labels on flexible vinyl.—			

Label & Catalog #		Title	Year	VG+	NM
Warner Bros. W-1356	(M)	**First Place Again**	1960	16.00	40.00
Warner Bros. WS-1356	(S)	**First Place Again**	1960	12.00	30.00
RCA Victor LPM-2438	(M)	**Desmond Blue**	1961	16.00	40.00
RCA Victor LSP-2438	(S)	**Desmond Blue**	1961	12.00	30.00
RCA Victor LPM-2569	(M)	**Take Ten**	1962	16.00	40.00
RCA Victor LSP-2569	(S)	**Take Ten**	1962	12.00	30.00
RCA Victor LPM-2654	(M)	**Two Of A Mind**	1963	16.00	40.00
RCA Victor LSP-2654	(S)	**Two Of A Mind**	1963	12.00	30.00

(RCA Victor 2654 also features Gerry Mulligan.)

—RCA albums above have black labels with "Long Play" or "Living Stereo" on the bottom.—

RCA Victor LPM-3320	(M)	**Boss Antigua**	1965	12.00	30.00
RCA Victor LSP-3320	(S)	**Boss Antigua**	1965	10.00	25.00
RCA Victor LPM-3407	(M)	**Glad To Be Unhappy**	1965	12.00	30.00
RCA Victor LSP-3407	(S)	**Glad To Be Unhappy**	1965	10.00	25.00
RCA Victor LPM-3480	(M)	**Easy Living**	1965	12.00	30.00
RCA Victor LSP-3480	(S)	**Easy Living**	1965	10.00	25.00

—RCA albums above have black labels with "Monaural" or "Stereo" on the bottom.—

A&M SP-3015	(S)	**Summertime**	1969	4.00	10.00
A&M SP-3024	(S)	**From The Hot Afternoon**	1969	4.00	10.00
A&M SP-3032	(S)	**Bridge Over Troubled Water**	1969	4.00	10.00

DEUCHAR, JIMMY

Scottish born James Duechar is a traditional jazz-based trumpet and mellophone player and composer.

Discovery DL-2004	(10")	**New Sounds From England**	1953	30.00	75.00
Contemporary C-3529	(M)	**Pub Crawling**	1957	20.00	50.00

DICKENSON, VIC

Victor Dickenson is a traditional jazz trombone player and vocalist. For additional listings refer to Urbie Green / Vic Dickenson; Odetta.

Vanguard VRS-8001 (10")	(M)	**Vic Dickenson Septet, Vol. 1**	1953	20.00	50.00
Vanguard VRS-8002 (10")	(M)	**Vic Dickenson Septet, Vol. 2**	1953	20.00	50.00
Vanguard VRS-8012 (10")	(M)	**Vic Dickenson Septet, Vol. 3**	1954	20.00	50.00
Vanguard VRS-8013 (10")	(M)	**Vic Dickenson Septet, Vol. 4**	1954	20.00	50.00
Vanguard VRS-8520	(M)	**Vic Dickenson Showcase, Volume 1**	1958	16.00	40.00
		(Vanguard 8520 is a reissue of 8001 and 8002.)			
Vanguard VRS 8521	(M)	**Vic Dickenson Showcase, Volume 2**	1958	16.00	40.00
		(Vanguard 8521 is a reissue of 8012 and 8013.)			
Storyville STLP-920	(M)	**Vic's Boston Story**	1957	16.00	40.00

DICKENSON, VIC, & JOE THOMAS

Atlantic 1303	(M)	**Mainstream**	1958	20.00	50.00
Atlantic SD-1303	(S)	**Mainstream**	1958	16.00	40.00

—Atlantic albums above have black mono or green stereo labels.—

Atlantic 1303	(M)	**Mainstream**	196?	8.00	20.00
Atlantic SD-1303	(S)	**Mainstream**	196?	6.00	15.00

—Atlantic albums above have multi-color labels with a white fan logo .—

DICKERSON, WALTER

Walter Dickerson is a modern jazz vibraphone player and composer.

New Jazz NJLP-8254	(M)	**This Is Walter Dickerson**	1961	20.00	50.00
New Jazz NJLP-8268	(M)	**A Sense Of Direction**	1962	20.00	50.00
New Jazz NJLP-8275	(M)	**Relativity**	1962	20.00	50.00
New Jazz NJLP-8283	(M)	**To My Queen**	1962	20.00	50.00

—New Jazz albums above have purple labels.—

New Jazz NJLP-8254	(M)	**This Is Walter Dickerson**	1965	8.00	25.00
New Jazz NJLP-8268	(M)	**A Sense Of Direction**	1965	8.00	25.00
New Jazz NJLP-8275	(M)	**Relativity**	1965	8.00	25.00
New Jazz NJLP-8283	(M)	**To My Queen**	1965	8.00	25.00

—New Jazz albums above have blue labels with a trident logo on the right side.—

Audio Fidelity AFLP-2131	(M)	**Unity**	1963	10.00	25.00
Audio Fidelity AFSD-6131	(S)	**Unity**	1963	8.00	20.00
Dauntless DM-4313	(M)	**Jazz Impressions Of "Lawrence Of Arabia"**	1963	10.00	25.00
Dauntless DS-6313	(S)	**Jazz Impressions Of "Lawrence Of Arabia"**	1963	8.00	20.00
MGM E-4358	(M)	**Impressions Of "A Patch Of Blue"**	1965	10.00	25.00
MGM SE-4358	(S)	**Impressions Of "A Patch Of Blue"**	1965	8.00	20.00
Audio Fidelity AFLP-2217	(M)	**Vibes In Motion**	1968	10.00	25.00
Audio Fidelity AFSD-6217	(M)	**Vibes In Motion**	1968	6.00	15.00

Label & Catalog #		Title	Year	VG+	NM
DIXIE SMALL FRY, THE					
Liberty SL-3057	*(M)*	**Dixie Small Fry In Hi Fi**	*1957*	**16.00**	**40.00**
DIXIE STOMPERS, THE					
The Stompers are a group playing under individual pseudonyms and led by Billy Butterfield.					
Delmar DL-113 (10")	*(M)*	**Wake The Levee**	*195?*	**30.00**	**75.00**
Delmar DL-204	*(M)*	**Jazz At Westminster College**	*195?*	**20.00**	**50.00**
RCA Victor LPM-1212	*(M)*	**New York Land Dixie**	*1956*	**30.00**	**75.00**
—RCA albums above have black labels with "Long Play" on the bottom.—					
DIXIELAND RHYTHM KINGS, THE					
For additional listings refer to Tony Parenti / The Dixieland Rhythm Kings.					
Empirical LP-102 (10")	*(M)*	**The Dixieland Rhythm Kings**	*1954*	**30.00**	**75.00**
Riverside RLP-2505 (10")	*(M)*	**New Orleans Jazz Party**	*1954*	**30.00**	**75.00**
Riverside RLP-12-210	*(M)*	**Dixieland In Hi Fi**	*1956*	**24.00**	**60.00**
—Riverside albums above have blue on white labels.—					
Riverside RLP-12-210	*(M)*	**Dixieland In Hi Fi**	*195?*	**12.00**	**30.00**
Riverside RLP-12-259	*(M)*	**The Dixieland Rhythm Kings At The Hi-Fi Jazz Band Ball**	*1958*	**16.00**	**40.00**
Riverside RLP-12-289	*(M)*	**Jazz In Retrospect**	*1958*	**16.00**	**40.00**
—Riverside albums above have blue mono or black stereo labels with a reel & mike logo on top.—					
DIXON, BILL					
William Dixon is a modern jazz trumpet player. For additional listings refer to Archie Shepp & Bill Dixon.					
RCA Victor LPM-3844	*(M)*	**Intents And Purposes**	*1967*	**10.00**	**25.00**
RCA Victor LSP-3844	*(S)*	**Intents And Purposes**	*1967*	**8.00**	**20.00**
—RCA albums above have black labels with "Monaural" or "Stereo" on the bottom.—					
DODDS, BABY					
Warren "Baby" Dodds, Johnny's little brother, is a traditional jazz drummer.					
American Music 1	*(M)*	**Baby Dodds Drum Method—Band**	*1951*	**20.00**	**50.00**
American Music 2	*(M)*	**Baby Dodds Drum Method—Trio**	*1951*	**20.00**	**50.00**
American Music 3	*(M)*	**Baby Dodds Drum Method—Solo**	*1951*	**20.00**	**50.00**
Folkways FP-30 (10")	*(M)*	**Footnotes To Jazz, Volume 1—Baby Dodds' Drum Solos**	*1951*	**20.00**	**50.00**
DODDS, JOHNNY					
Johnny Dodds is a traditional jazz clarinet and also saxophone player.					
Brunswick BL-58016 (10")	*(M)*	**The King Of New Orleans Clarinets**	*1950*	**40.00**	**100.00**
Riverside RLP-1002 (10")	*(M)*	**Johnny Dodds, Vol. 1**	*1953*	**30.00**	**75.00**
Riverside RLP-1015 (10")	*(M)*	**Johnny Dodds, Vol. 2**	*1953*	**30.00**	**75.00**
Riverside RLP-12-104	*(M)*	**Johnny Dodds' New Orleans Clarinet**	*1956*	**24.00**	**60.00**
—Riverside albums above have blue on white labels.—					
Riverside RLP-12-104	*(M)*	**Johnny Dodds' New Orleans Clarinet**	*195?*	**12.00**	**30.00**
—Riverside albums above have blue mono or black stereo labels with a reel & mike logo on top.—					
"X" LX-3006 (10")	*(M)*	**Johnny Dodds' Washboard Band**	*1954*	**20.00**	**50.00**
Jolly Roger 5012 (10")	*(M)*	**Johnny Dodds**	*1954*	**20.00**	**50.00**
RCA Victor LPV-558	*(M)*	**Sixteen Rare Recordings**	*1965*	**8.00**	**20.00**
DODDS, JOHNNY / JIMMY NOONE					
Brunswick BL-58046 (10")	*(M)*	**Battle Of Jazz, Vol. 8**	*1953*	**20.00**	**50.00**
DODDS, JOHNNY, & KID ORY					
Epic LN-3207	*(M)*	**Johnny Dodds And Kid Ory**	*1956*	**20.00**	**50.00**
Epic LA-16004	*(M)*	**Johnny Dodds And Kid Ory**	*1960*	**10.00**	**25.00**
Epic BA-17004	*(E)*	**Johnny Dodds And Kid Ory**	*1960*	**6.00**	**15.00**
DODSON, MARGE					
Margorie Dodson is a jazz-based vocalist.					
Columbia CL-1309	*(M)*	**In The Still Of The Night**	*1959*	**16.00**	**40.00**
Columbia CL-1458	*(M)*	**New Voice In Town**	*1960*	**12.00**	**30.00**
Columbia CS-8258	*(S)*	**New Voice In Town**	*1960*	**16.00**	**40.00**
—Columbia albums above have six white on black "eye" logos on each label.—					
DOLDINGER, KLAUS					
German born Klaus Doldinger is a modern jazz tenor and soprano saxophone player.					
Philips PHM-200-125	*(M)*	**Dig Doldinger**	*1964*	**10.00**	**25.00**
Philips PHS-600-125	*(S)*	**Dig Doldinger**	*1964*	**8.00**	**20.00**
World Pacific WPS-20176	*(S)*	**Blues Happening**	*1969*	**6.00**	**15.00**

Eric Dolphy started his professional career with the bands of George Brown, Gerald Wilson, Buddy Collette, and Eddie Beal before achieving fame with Chico Hamilton in 1958-59. His short career as a leader began with the release of *Outward Bound* in 1960 and was over with his premature death in 1964. By then he had earned the nickname "the heaviest musician on earth" by Charles Mingus. He has recorded with The Jazz Artists Guild, The Latin Jazz Quintet and Orchestra U.S.A., and been a featured guest with Ron Carter, Ken McIntyre (above), Oliver Nelson and Mal Waldron.

DOLPHY, ERIC

Eric Dolphy is a modern jazz alto saxophone, bass clarinet and flute player. For additional listings refer to Ron Carter; Sammy Davis Jr; The Jazz Artists Guild; The Latin Jazz Quintet; Ken McIntyre; Oliver Nelson; Orchestra USA; George Russell; Mal Waldron.

Label & Catalog #		Title	Year	VG+	NM
New Jazz NJLP-8236	(M)	**Outward Bound**	1960	**40.00**	**100.00**
New Jazz NJLP-8252	(M)	**Out There**	1960	**40.00**	**100.00**
New Jazz NJLP-8260	(M)	**Eric Dolphy At The Five Spot**	1961	**30.00**	**75.00**
New Jazz NJLP-8270	(M)	**Far Cry**	1962	**30.00**	**75.00**
		(New Jazz 8270 also features Booker Little.)			
		—New Jazz albums above have purple labels.—			
New Jazz NJLP-8252	(M)	**Out There**	1965	**10.00**	**25.00**
New Jazz NJLP-8260	(M)	**Eric Dolphy At The Five Spot**	1965	**10.00**	**25.00**
New Jazz NJLP-8270	(M)	**Far Cry**	1965	**10.00**	**25.00**
		—New Jazz albums above have blue labels with a trident logo on the right side.—			
Prestige PRLP-7294	(M)	**Eric Dolphy At The Five Spot, Volume 2**	1964	**20.00**	**50.00**
Prestige PRST-7294	(S)	**Eric Dolphy At The Five Spot, Volume 2**	1964	**16.00**	**40.00**
Prestige PRLP-7304	(M)	**Eric Dolphy In Europe, Volume 1**	1964	**20.00**	**50.00**
Prestige PRST-7304	(S)	**Eric Dolphy In Europe, Volume 1**	1964	**16.00**	**40.00**
Prestige PRLP-7311	(M)	**Outward Bound**	1964	**16.00**	**40.00**
Prestige PRST-7311	(S)	**Outward Bound**	1964	**16.00**	**40.00**
		(Prestige 7311 is a reissue of New Jazz 8236.)			
		—Prestige albums above have yellow mono or silver stereo labels with a Bergenfield, NJ address.—			
Prestige PRLP-7294	(M)	**Eric Dolphy At The Five Spot, Volume 2**	1964	**10.00**	**25.00**
Prestige PRST-7294	(S)	**Eric Dolphy At The Five Spot, Volume 2**	1964	**8.00**	**20.00**
Prestige PRLP-7304	(M)	**Eric Dolphy In Europe, Volume 1**	1964	**10.00**	**25.00**
Prestige PRST-7304	(S)	**Eric Dolphy In Europe, Volume 1**	1964	**8.00**	**20.00**
Prestige PRLP-7311	(M)	**Outward Bound**	1964	**10.00**	**25.00**
Prestige PRST-7311	(S)	**Outward Bound**	1964	**8.00**	**20.00**
Prestige PRLP-7334	(M)	**Eric Dolphy Memorial Album**	1964	**10.00**	**25.00**
Prestige PRST-7334	(S)	**Eric Dolphy Memorial Album**	1964	**8.00**	**20.00**
Prestige PRLP-7350	(M)	**Eric Dolphy In Europe, Volume 2**	1965	**10.00**	**25.00**
Prestige PRST-7350	(S)	**Eric Dolphy In Europe, Volume 2**	1965	**8.00**	**20.00**
Prestige PRLP-7366	(M)	**Eric Dolphy In Europe, Volume 3**	1965	**10.00**	**25.00**
Prestige PRST-7366	(S)	**Eric Dolphy In Europe, Volume 3**	1965	**8.00**	**20.00**
Prestige PRLP-7382	(M)	**Here And There**	1965	**10.00**	**25.00**
Prestige PRST-7382	(S)	**Here And There**	1965	**8.00**	**20.00**
		—Prestige albums above have blue labels with a trident logo on the right side.—			
Prestige PRST-7611	(E)	**Live! At The Five Spot, Volume 1**	1969	**5.00**	**12.00**
		(Prestige 7611 is a reissue of New Jazz 8260.)			
Prestige PRST-7652	(E)	**Out There**	1969	**5.00**	**12.00**
		(Prestige 7652 is a reissue Of New Jazz 8252.)			
		—Prestige albums above have blue labels with a trident logo on top.—			
FM 308	(M)	**Conversations**	1963	**16.00**	**40.00**
FM S-308	(S)	**Conversations**	1963	**12.00**	**30.00**
Vee Jay LP-2503	(M)	**The Memorial Album**	1964	**16.00**	**40.00**
Vee Jay LPS-2503	(S)	**The Memorial Album**	1964	**12.00**	**30.00**
Limelight LM-82013	(M)	**Last Date**	1964	**16.00**	**40.00**
Limelight LS-86013	(S)	**Last Date**	1964	**12.00**	**30.00**
Blue Note BLP-4163	(M)	**Out To Lunch!**	1964	**20.00**	**50.00**
Blue Note BST-84163	(S)	**Out To Lunch!**	1964	**20.00**	**50.00**
		(BST-84163 may be worth $75-100 in the audiophile market.)			
		—Blue Note albums above have blue on white labels with a New York, USA address.—			
Blue Note BST-84163	(S)	**Out To Lunch!**	196?	**5.00**	**12.00**
		—Blue Note albums above have blue on white labels with "A Division of Liberty Records."—			
Douglas SD-785	(S)	**Iron Man**	1969	**10.00**	**25.00**

DOLPHY, ERIC / CANNONBALL ADDERLEY

Archive Of Folk & Jazz 227	(S)	**Eric Dolphy And Cannonball Adderley**	1968	**5.00**	**12.00**
		(Side 1 of AOF&J 227 reissues material from Vee Jay 2503.)			

DOMNERUS, ARNE / LARS GULLIN

Prestige PRLP-133 (10")	(M)	**New Sounds From Sweden, Volume 3**	1952	**125.00**	**250.00**

DOMNERUS, ARNE

Swedish born Arne Domnerus is a modern jazz alto saxophone and clarinet player. For additional listings refer to Bengt Hallberg / Arne Domnerus.

Prestige PRLP-134 (10")	(M)	**New Sounds From Sweden, Volume 4— Arne Domnerus Clarinet Solos**	1952	**125.00**	**250.00**

Label & Catalog #		Title	Year	VG+	NM
RCA Victor LPT-3032 (10")	*(M)*	**Around The World In Jazz—Sweden**	1953	100.00	200.00
Camden CAL-417	*(M)*	**Swedish Modern Jazz**	1958	12.00	30.00

DONAHUE, SAM

Samuel Donahue is a traditional jazz tenor saxophone and trumpet player and arranger.

Label & Catalog #		Title	Year	VG+	NM
Capitol H-613 (10")	*(M)*	**For Young Moderns In Love**	1955	20.00	50.00
Capitol H-626 (10")	*(M)*	**Classics In Jazz**	1955	20.00	50.00
Capitol T-613	*(M)*	**For Young Moderns In Love**	1956	16.00	40.00

DONALDSON, BOBBY

Robert Donaldson is a traditional jazz-based drummer.

Label & Catalog #		Title	Year	VG+	NM
Savoy MG-12128	*(M)*	**Dixieland Jazz Party**	1958	16.00	40.00

DONALDSON, LOU

Lou Donaldson is a modern jazz alto saxophone player. For additional listings refer to Clifford Brown; Jimmy Smith.

Label & Catalog #		Title	Year	VG+	NM
Blue Note BLP-5021 (10")	*(M)*	**Lou Donaldson Quintet-Quartet**	1953	150.00	300.00
Blue Note BLP-5030 (10")	*(M)*	**Lou Donaldson-Clifford Brown**	1954	150.00	300.00
Blue Note BLP-5055 (10")	*(M)*	**Lou Donaldson Sextet, Volume 2**	1955	150.00	300.00
Blue Note BLP-1537	*(M)*	**Lou Donaldson Quartet/Quintet/Sextet** *(Deep groove)*	1957	100.00	200.00
Blue Note BLP-1537	*(M)*	**Lou Donaldson Quartet/Quintet/Sextet**	1957	60.00	150.00
		—Blue Note albums above have blue on white labels with a Lexington Ave., NYC address.—			
Blue Note BLP-1537	*(M)*	**Lou Donaldson Quartet/Quintet/Sextet**	1957	20.00	50.00
Blue Note BLP-1545	*(M)*	**Wailing With Lou** *(Deep groove)*	1957	50.00	125.00
Blue Note BLP-1545	*(M)*	**Wailing With Lou**	1957	30.00	75.00
Blue Note BLP-1566	*(M)*	**Swing And Soul** *(Deep groove)*	1957	50.00	125.00
Blue Note BLP-1566	*(M)*	**Swing And Soul**	1957	30.00	75.00
Blue Note BST-1566	*(S)*	**Swing And Soul** *(Deep groove)*	1959	30.00	75.00
Blue Note BST-1566	*(S)*	**Swing And Soul**	1959	20.00	50.00
Blue Note BLP-1591	*(M)*	**Lou Takes Off** *(Deep groove)*	1958	50.00	125.00
Blue Note BLP-1591	*(M)*	**Lou Takes Off**	1958	30.00	75.00
Blue Note BST-1591	*(S)*	**Lou Takes Off** *(Deep groove)*	1959	30.00	75.00
Blue Note BST-1591	*(S)*	**Lou Takes Off**	1959	20.00	50.00
Blue Note BLP-1593	*(M)*	**Blues Walk** *(Deep groove)*	1958	50.00	125.00
Blue Note BLP-1593	*(M)*	**Blues Walk**	1958	30.00	75.00
Blue Note BST-1593	*(S)*	**Blues Walk** *(Deep groove)*	1959	30.00	75.00
Blue Note BST-1593	*(S)*	**Blues Walk**	1959	20.00	50.00
Blue Note BLP-4012	*(M)*	**LD + 3** *(Deep groove)*	1959	50.00	125.00
Blue Note BLP-4012	*(M)*	**LD + 3**	1959	30.00	75.00
Blue Note BST-4012	*(S)*	**LD + 3** *(Deep groove)*	1959	30.00	75.00
Blue Note BST-4012	*(S)*	**LD + 3**	1959	20.00	50.00
		(Blue Note 4012 also features The Three Sounds.)			
Blue Note BLP-4025	*(M)*	**The Time Is Right** *(Deep groove)*	1960	50.00	125.00
Blue Note BLP-4025	*(M)*	**The Time Is Right**	1960	30.00	75.00
Blue Note BST-84025	*(S)*	**The Time Is Right**	1960	24.00	50.00
Blue Note BLP-4036	*(M)*	**Sunny Side Up** *(Deep groove)*	1960	50.00	125.00
Blue Note BLP-4036	*(M)*	**Sunny Side Up**	1960	30.00	75.00
Blue Note BST-84036	*(S)*	**Sunny Side Up**	1960	20.00	50.00
Blue Note BLP-4053	*(M)*	**Light Foot**	1960	30.00	75.00
Blue Note BST-84053	*(S)*	**Light Foot**	1960	20.00	50.00
Blue Note BLP-4066	*(M)*	**Here 'Tis**	1961	30.00	75.00
Blue Note BST-84066	*(S)*	**Here 'Tis**	1961	20.00	50.00
		—Blue Note albums above have blue on white labels with a W. 63rd St., NYC address.—			
Blue Note BLP-4079	*(M)*	**Gravy Train**	1962	30.00	75.00
Blue Note BST-84079	*(S)*	**Gravy Train**	1962	20.00	50.00
		—Blue Note albums above have blue on white labels with a 61st St., NYC address.—			
Blue Note BLP-1537	*(M)*	**Lou Donaldson Quartet/Quintet/Sextet**	1963	10.00	25.00
Blue Note BLP-1545	*(M)*	**Wailing With Lou**	1963	10.00	25.00
Blue Note BLP-1566	*(M)*	**Swing And Soul**	1963	10.00	25.00
Blue Note BST-1566	*(S)*	**Swing And Soul**	1963	8.00	20.00
Blue Note BLP-1591	*(M)*	**Lou Takes Off**	1963	10.00	25.00
Blue Note BST-1591	*(S)*	**Lou Takes Off**	1963	8.00	20.00
Blue Note BLP-1593	*(M)*	**Blues Walk**	1963	10.00	25.00
Blue Note BST-1593	*(S)*	**Blues Walk**	1963	8.00	20.00
Blue Note BLP-4012	*(M)*	**LD + 3**	1963	10.00	25.00
Blue Note BST-4012	*(S)*	**LD + 3**	1963	8.00	20.00
Blue Note BLP-4025	*(M)*	**The Time Is Right**	1963	10.00	25.00
Blue Note BST-84025	*(S)*	**The Time Is Right**	1963	8.00	20.00

Label & Catalog #		Title	Year	VG+	NM
Blue Note BLP-4036	(M)	**Sunny Side Up**	1963	10.00	25.00
Blue Note BST-84036	(S)	**Sunny Side Up**	1963	8.00	20.00
Blue Note BLP-4053	(M)	**Light Foot**	1963	10.00	25.00
Blue Note BST-84053	(S)	**Light Foot**	1963	8.00	20.00
Blue Note BLP-4066	(M)	**Here 'Tis**	1963	10.00	25.00
Blue Note BST-84066	(S)	**Here 'Tis**	1963	8.00	20.00
Blue Note BLP-4079	(M)	**Gravy Train**	1963	10.00	25.00
Blue Note BST-84079	(S)	**Gravy Train**	1963	8.00	20.00
Blue Note BLP-4108	(M)	**The Natural Soul**	1962	16.00	40.00
Blue Note BST-84108	(S)	**The Natural Soul**	1962	12.00	30.00
Blue Note BLP-4125	(M)	**Good Gracious**	1963	16.00	40.00
Blue Note BST-84125	(S)	**Good Gracious**	1963	12.00	30.00
—Blue Note albums above have blue on white labels with a New York, USA address.—					
Blue Note BST-81537	(E)	**Lou Donaldson Quartet/Quintet/Sextet**	196?	4.00	10.00
Blue Note BST881545	(E)	**Wailing With Lou**	196?	4.00	10.00
Blue Note BST-81566	(S)	**Swing And Soul**	196?	5.00	12.00
Blue Note BST-81591	(S)	**Lou Takes Off**	196?	5.00	12.00
Blue Note BST-81593	(S)	**Blues Walk**	196?	5.00	12.00
Blue Note BST-84012	(S)	**LD + 3**	196?	5.00	12.00
Blue Note BST-84025	(S)	**The Time Is Right**	196?	5.00	12.00
Blue Note BST-84036	(S)	**Sunny Side Up**	196?	5.00	12.00
Blue Note BST-84053	(S)	**Light Foot**	196?	5.00	12.00
Blue Note BST-84066	(S)	**Here 'Tis**	196?	5.00	12.00
Blue Note BST-84079	(S)	**Gravy Train**	196?	5.00	12.00
Blue Note BST-84108	(S)	**The Natural Soul**	196?	5.00	12.00
Blue Note BST-84125	(S)	**Good Gracious**	196?	5.00	12.00
Blue Note BLP-4254	(M)	**Sweet Slumber**	1967	*Unreleased*	
Blue Note BST-84254	(S)	**Sweet Slumber**	1967	*Unreleased*	
Blue Note BLP-4263	(M)	**Alligator Boogaloo**	1967	12.00	30.00
Blue Note BST-84263	(S)	**Alligator Boogaloo**	1967	8.00	20.00
Blue Note BLP-84271	(M)	**Mr. Shing-A-Ling**	1967	12.00	30.00
Blue Note BST-84271	(S)	**Mr. Shing-A-Ling**	1967	8.00	20.00
Blue Note BST-84280	(S)	**Midnight Creeper**	1968	8.00	20.00
Blue Note BST-84299	(S)	**Say It Loud**	1968	8.00	20.00
Blue Note BST-84318	(S)	**Hot Dog**	1969	8.00	20.00
Blue Note BST-84337	(S)	**Everything I Play Is Funky**	1969	8.00	20.00
—Blue Note albums above have blue on white labels with "A Division of Liberty Records."—					
Argo LP-724	(M)	**Signifyin'**	1963	10.00	25.00
Argo LPS-724	(S)	**Signifyin'**	1963	8.00	20.00
Argo LP-734	(M)	**Possum Head**	1964	10.00	25.00
Argo LPS-734	(S)	**Possum Head**	1964	8.00	20.00
Argo LP-747	(M)	**Cole Slaw**	1964	10.00	25.00
Argo LPS-747	(S)	**Cole Slaw**	1964	8.00	20.00
Cadet LP-759	(M)	**Musty Rusty**	1965	10.00	25.00
Cadet LPS-759	(S)	**Musty Rusty**	1965	8.00	20.00
Cadet LP-768	(M)	**Rough House Blues**	1965	10.00	25.00
Cadet LPS-768	(S)	**Rough House Blues**	1965	8.00	20.00
Cadet LP-789	(M)	**Blowin' In The Wind**	1967	10.00	25.00
Cadet LPS-789	(S)	**Blowin' In The Wind**	1967	8.00	20.00
Cadet LP-842	(M)	**Fried Buzzard— Lou Donaldson Live**	1968	8.00	40.00
Cadet LPS-842	(S)	**Fried Buzzard— Lou Donaldson Live**	1968	8.00	20.00

DONEGAN, DOROTHY

Dorothy Donegan is a jazz-based pianist.

MGM E-278 (10")	(M)	**Dorothy Donegan Piano**	1954	30.00	75.00
Jubilee JLP-11 (10")	(M)	**Dorothy Donegan Trio**	1954	30.00	75.00
Jubilee JLP-1013	(M)	**September Song**	1956	20.00	50.00
Regina 285	(M)	**Swingin' Jazz In Hi Fi**	195?	16.00	40.00
Roulette R-25010	(M)	**Dorothy Donegan At The Embers**	1959	12.00	30.00
Roulette SR-25010	(S)	**Dorothy Donegan At The Embers**	1959	16.00	40.00
Capitol T-1155	(M)	**Dorothy Donegan Live!**	1959	12.00	30.00
Capitol ST-1155	(S)	**Dorothy Donegan Live!**	1959	16.00	40.00
Capitol T-1226	(M)	**Donneybrook With Dorothy**	1960	10.00	25.00
Capitol ST-1226	(S)	**Donneybrook With Dorothy**	1960	12.00	30.00

—Capitol albums above have black "rainbow" labels with the logo on the left side.—

Label & Catalog #		Title	Year	VG+	NM

DORHAM, KENNY

McKinley "Kenny" Dorham is a modern jazz trumpet player and composer. For additional listings refer to Art Blakey & The Jazz Messengers; The Jazz Artists Guild.

Label & Catalog #		Title	Year	VG+	NM
Debut DLP-9 (10")	(M)	**Kenny Dorham Quintet**	1954	150.00	300.00
Blue Note BLP-5065 (10")	(M)	**Afro-Cuban Holiday**	1955	150.00	300.00
Blue Note BLP-1524	(M)	**'Round About Midnight At The Cafe Bohemia** *(Deep groove)*	1956	100.00	200.00
Blue Note BLP-1524	(M)	**'Round About Midnight At The Cafe Bohemia**	1956	60.00	150.00
Blue Note BLP-1535	(M)	**Kenny Dorham Octet/Sextet** *(Deep groove)*	1956	100.00	200.00
Blue Note BLP-1535	(M)	**Kenny Dorham Octet/Sextet** *(Blue Note 1535 is a reissue of 5065.)*	1956	60.00	150.00
—Blue Note albums above have blue on white labels with a Lexington Ave., NYC address.—					
Blue Note BLP-4063	(M)	**Whistle Stop**	1961	30.00	75.00
Blue Note BST-84063	(S)	**Whistle Stop**	1961	20.00	50.00
—Blue Note albums above have blue on white labels with a W. 63rd St., NYC address .—					
Blue Note BLP-1524	(M)	**'Round About Midnight At The Cafe Bohemia**	1963	10.00	25.00
Blue Note BLP-1535	(M)	**Kenny Dorham Octet/Sextet**	1963	10.00	25.00
Blue Note BLP-4063	(M)	**Whistle Stop**	1963	10.00	25.00
Blue Note BST-84063	(S)	**Whistle Stop**	1963	8.00	20.00
Blue Note BLP-4127	(M)	**Una Mas—One More Time**	1963	16.00	40.00
Blue Note BST-84127	(S)	**Una Mas—One More Time**	1963	12.00	30.00
Blue Note BLP-4181	(M)	**Trompeta Toccata**	1964	16.00	40.00
Blue Note BST-84181	(S)	**Trompeta Toccata**	1964	12.00	30.00
—Blue Note albums above have blue on white labels with a New York, USA address.—					
Blue Note BST-81524	(E)	**'Round About Midnight At The Cafe Bohemia**	196?	4.00	10.00
Blue Note BST-81535	(E)	**Kenny Dorham Octet/Sextet**	196?	4.00	10.00
Blue Note BST-84063	(S)	**Whistle Stop**	196?	5.00	12.00
Blue Note BST-84127	(S)	**Una Mas—One More Time**	196?	5.00	12.00
Blue Note BST-84181	(S)	**Trompeta Toccata**	196?	5.00	12.00
—Blue Note albums above have blue on white labels with "A Division of Liberty Records."—					
ABC-Paramount ABC-122	(M)	**Kenny Dorham & The Jazz Prophets**	1956	30.00	75.00
Riverside RLP-12-239	(M)	**Jazz Contrasts**	1957	30.00	75.00
—Riverside albums above have blue on white labels.—					
Riverside RLP-12-239	(M)	**Jazz Contrasts**	1959	16.00	40.00
Riverside RLP-1105	(S)	**Jazz Contrasts**	1959	16.00	40.00
Riverside RLP-12-255	(M)	**2 Horns 2 Rhythm** *(Riverside 255 also features Ernie Henry.)*	1957	20.00	50.00
Riverside RLP-12-275	(M)	**This Is The Moment! Kenny Dorham Sings And Plays**	1958	20.00	50.00
Riverside RLP-12-297	(M)	**Blue Spring**	1959	20.00	50.00
Riverside RLP-1139	(S)	**Blue Spring** *(Riverside 297 also features Cannonball Adderley.)*	1959	16.00	40.00
—Riverside albums above have blue mono or black stereo labels with a reel & mike logo on top.—					
Jaro 5007	(M)	**The Arrival Of Kenny Dorham**	1959	250.00	500.00
Jaro 8007	(S)	**The Arrival Of Kenny Dorham**	1959	150.00	300.00
New Jazz NJLP-8225	(M)	**Quiet Kenny**	1959	30.00	75.00
—New Jazz albums above have purple labels.—					
New Jazz NJLP-8225	(M)	**Quiet Kenny**	1965	10.00	250.00
—New Jazz albums above have blue labels with a trident logo on the right side.—					
Time 52004	(M)	**Jazz Contemporary**	1960	20.00	50.00
Time S-2004	(S)	**Jazz Contemporary**	1960	16.00	40.00
Time 52024	(M)	**Showboat**	1960	20.00	50.00
Time S-2024	(S)	**Showboat**	1960	16.00	40.00
Jazzland JLP-3	(M)	**The Swingers**	1960	20.00	50.00
Jazzland JLP-93	(S)	**The Swingers** *(Jazzland 3 also features Frank Foster.)*	1960	16.00	40.00
Jazzland JLP-14	(M)	**Kenny Dorham And Friends**	1960	20.00	50.00
Jazzland JLP-914	(S)	**Kenny Dorham And Friends**	1960	16.00	40.00
Jazzland JLP-82	(M)	**Kenny Dorham And Friends**	1962	16.00	40.00
Jazzland JLP-982	(S)	**Kenny Dorham And Friends** *(Jazzland 82 is a reissue of 14.)*	1962	12.00	30.00
Pacific Jazz PJ-41	(M)	**Inta Somethin'— Recorded "Live" At The Jazz Workshop**	1962	16.00	40.00
Pacific Jazz ST-41	(S)	**Inta Somethin'— Recorded "Live" At The Jazz Workshop** *(Pacific Jazz 41 also features Jackie McLean.)*	1962	12.00	30.00
United Arts. UAJ-14007	(M)	**Matador**	1962	16.00	40.00
United Arts. UAJS-15007	(S)	**Matador**	1962	12.00	30.00

Label & Catalog #		Title	Year	VG+	NM
DORHAM, KENNY / CLARK TERRY					
Jazzland JLP-10	(M)	**Top Trumpets**	1960	20.00	50.00
Jazzland JLP-910	(S)	**Top Trumpets**	1960	16.00	40.00
DOROUGH, BOB					
Robert Dorough is a modern jazz pianist, vocalist and composer.					
Bethlehem BCP-11	(M)	**Devil May Care**	1957	40.00	100.00
Music Minus One 225	(M)	**Oliver**	1963	8.00	20.00
Focus FL-336	(M)	**Just About Everything**	1965	8.00	20.00
Focus FS-336	(S)	**Just About Everything**	1965	6.00	15.00
DORSEY, JIMMY					
James Dorsey of the Dorsey Brothers is a traditional jazz clarinet, alto saxophone and trumpet player.					
Decca DL 5091 (10")	(M)	**Latin American Favorites**	1950	20.00	50.00
Coral CRL-56004 (10")	(M)	**Contrasting Music, Volume 1**	1950	20.00	50.00
Coral CRL-56008 (10")	(M)	**Contrasting Music, Volume 2**	1950	20.00	50.00
Coral CRL-56033 (10")	(M)	**Gershwin Music**	1950	20.00	50.00
Columbia CL-6095 (10")	(M)	**Dixie By Dorsey**	1950	20.00	50.00
Columbia CL-6114 (10")	(M)	**Dorseyland Band**	1950	20.00	50.00
Columbia CL-608	(M)	**Dixie By Dorsey**	1955	16.00	40.00
—Columbia albums above have "Long Playing" on the bottom of the label.—					
Columbia CL-608	(M)	**Dixie By Dorsey**	195?	12.00	30.00
—Columbia albums above have six white on black "eye" logos on each label.—					
Decca DL-9153	(M)	**Latin American Favorites**	1959	16.00	40.00
DORSEY, JIMMY & TOMMY					
Riverside RLP-12-811	(M)	**A Backward Glance**	1956	24.00	60.00
—Riverside albums above have blue on white labels.—					
DORSEY, TOMMY					
Thomas Dorsey of the Dorsey Brothers is a traditional jazz trombone and trumpet player.					
RCA Victor LPT-3018 (10")	(M)	**This Is Tommy Dorsey**	195?	20.00	50.00
RCA Victor LPTM-22 (10")	(M)	**Tommy Dorsey Plays Cole Porter For Dancing**	195?	20.00	50.00
Decca DL-5317 (10")	(M)	**Tommy Dorsey Plays Howard Dietz**	1951	20.00	50.00
Decca DL-5448 (10")	(M)	**In A Sentimental Mood**	1952	20.00	50.00
Decca DL-5449 (10")	(M)	**Tenderly**	1952	20.00	50.00
Decca DL-5452 (10")	(M)	**Your Invitation To Dance**	1952	20.00	50.00
RCA Victor LPM-1425	(M)	**Tommy Dorsey Plays Cole Porter And Jerome Kern**	1956	16.00	40.00
Colpix CP-498	(M)	**A Man And His Trombone**	1966	8.00	20.00
Colpix SCP-498	(S)	**A Man And His Trombone**	1966	6.00	15.00
DORSEY, TOMMY, WITH FRANK SINATRA					
RCA Victor LPT-10 (10")	(M)	**Getting Sentimental**	1951	30.00	75.00
RCA Victor LPT-15 (10")	(M)	**All Time Hits**	1951	30.00	75.00
RCA Victor LPM-1229	(M)	**Yes Indeed**	1956	20.00	50.00
RCA Victor LPM-1432	(M)	**Tribute To Dorsey, Volume 1**	1956	16.00	40.00
RCA Victor LPM-1433	(M)	**Tribute To Dorsey, Volume 2**	1956	16.00	40.00
RCA Victor LPM-6003	(M)	**Sentimental Gentleman** *(2 LP box)*	1956	20.00	50.00
RCA Victor LPM-1569	(M)	**Frankie And Tommy**	1957	16.00	40.00
RCA Victor LPM-1632	(M)	**We Three**	1957	16.00	40.00
RCA Victor LPM-1643	(M)	**Having A Wonderful Time**	1957	16.00	40.00
—RCA Victor albums have "Long Play" on the bottom of the label.—					
Camden CAL-650	(M)	**The One And Only Tommy Dorsey**	196?	4.00	10.00
Camden CAL-800	(M)	**Dedicated To You**	196?	4.00	10.00
RCA Victor LPV-583	(M)	**This Love of Mine**	1965	8.00	20.00
DORSEY BROTHERS, THE					
The Dorsey Brothers are Jimmy and Tommy.					
Decca DL-6016 (10")	(M)	**Dixieland Jazz**	1951	30.00	75.00
Riverside RLP-1008 (10")	(M)	**Jazz Of The Roaring Twenties**	1953	30.00	75.00
Riverside RLP-1051 (10")	(M)	**The Dorsey Brothers With The California Ramblers**	1955	30.00	75.00
Columbia C2L-8	M)	**The Fabulous Dorseys In Hi-Fi** *(2 LPs)*	1958	12.00	30.00
—Columbia albums above have six white on black "eye" logos on each label.—					
Design DLP-20	(M)	**The Dorsey Brothers: Their Shining Hour**	196?	4.00	10.00
Design DLPS-20	(E)	**The Dorsey Brothers: Their Shining Hour**	196?	1.00	5.00

Label & Catalog #		Title	Year	VG+	NM

DOUBLE SIX OF PARIS, THE

The Double Six Of Paris also recorded with Dizzy Gillespie.

Capitol Int. T-10259	*(M)*	**The Double Six Of Paris**	*1961*	**10.00**	**25.00**
Capitol Int. ST-10259	*(S)*	**The Double Six Of Paris**	*1961*	**8.00**	**20.00**
Philips PHM-200-026	*(M)*	**Swingin' Singin'**	*1962*	**10.00**	**25.00**
Philips PHS-600-026	*(S)*	**Swingin' Singin'**	*1962*	**8.00**	**20.00**
Philips PHM-200-141	*(M)*	**The Double Six Of Paris Sings Ray Charles**	*1964*	**10.00**	**25.00**
Philips PHS-600-141	*(S)*	**The Double Six Of Paris Sings Ray Charles**	*1964*	**8.00**	**20.00**

DRAKE, DONNA

Donna Drake is a jazz-based vocalist.

Luxor LP-1	*(M)*	**The Wynton Kelly Trio Introduces Donna Drake— Donna Sings Dinah**	*1968*	**12.00**	**30.00**
Luxor LPS-1	*(S)*	**The Wynton Kelly Trio Introduces Donna Drake— Donna Sings Dinah**	*1968*	**10.00**	**25.00**

DRAPER, RAY

Raymond Draper is a modern jazz tuba player and composer.

Prestige PRLP-7096	*(M)*	**Tuba Sounds**	*1957*	**30.00**	**75.00**
		—Prestige albums above have yellow labels with a W. 50th Street, NYC address.—			
Jubilee JLP-1090	*(M)*	**A Tuba Jazz**	*1958*	**20.00**	**50.00**
New Jazz NJLP-8228	*(M)*	**Ray Draper Quintet Featuring John Coltrane**	*1959*	**24.00**	**60.00**
		—New Jazz albums above have purple labels.—			
New Jazz NJLP-8228	*(M)*	**Ray Draper Quintet Featuring John Coltrane**	*1965*	**10.00**	**25.00**
		—New Jazz albums above have blue labels with a trident logo on the right side.—			
Josie JLPM-3504	*(M)*	**A Tuba Jazz**	*1963*	**10.00**	**25.00**
Josie JLPS-3504	*(S)*	**A Tuba Jazz**	*1963*	**8.00**	**20.00**
		(Josie 3504 is a reissue of Jubilee 1090.)			

DREW, DAN: ***Refer to*** **BOOTS BROWN & HIS BLOCKBUSTERS / DAN DREW & HIS DAREDEVILS**

DREW, KENNY

Kenneth Drew is a modern jazz pianist. For additional listings refer to Leonard Feather; the Jazzy Soundtracks section under Charlie Parker; and the Various Artists section under EmArcy.

Blue Note BLP-5023 (10")	*(M)*	**Introducing The Kenny Drew Trio**	*1953*	**150.00**	**300.00**
Norgran MGN-29 (10")	*(M)*	**The Ideation Of Kenny Drew**	*1954*	**100.00**	**200.00**
		(Norgran 29 features cover art by David Stone Martin.)			
Norgran MGN-1002	*(M)*	**Progressive Piano**	*1954*	**100.00**	**200.00**
Norgran MGN-1066	*(M)*	**The Modernity Of Kenny Drew**	*1956*	**60.00**	**150.00**
		(Norgran 1066 is a reissue of 1002.)			
Verve MGV-8156	*(M)*	**The Modernity Of Kenny Drew**	*1957*	*See below*	
		(The existence of this record, both as an MGV-8156 original and an MGM V-8156 reissue, is in doubt. . .)			
		— Verve albums above have black labels with "Verve Records, Inc." on the bottom.—			
Jazz: West JWLP-4	*(M)*	**Walkin' And Talkin' With The Kenny Drew Quartet**	*1955*	**125.00**	**250.00**
Riverside RLP-12-811	*(M)*	**I Love Jerome Kern**	*1956*	**60.00**	**150.00**
Riverside RLP-12-224	*(M)*	**Kenny Drew Trio**	*1956*	**60.00**	**150.00**
Riverside RLP-12-236	*(M)*	**This Is New**	*1957*	**60.00**	**150.00**
		—Riverside albums above have blue on white labels.—			
Riverside RLP-12-224	*(M)*	**Kenny Drew Trio**	*195?*	**16.00**	**40.00**
Riverside RLP-12-236	*(M)*	**This Is New**	*195?*	**16.00**	**40.00**
Riverside RLP-12-249	*(M)*	**Jazz Impressions Of The Rodgers And Hart Stage And Screen Classic "Pal Joey"**	*1957*	**20.00**	**50.00**
Riverside RLP-1112	*(S)*	**Jazz Impressions Of The Rodgers And Hart Stage And Screen Classic "Pal Joey"**	*1959*	**16.00**	**40.00**
		—Riverside albums above have blue mono or black stereo labels with a reel & mike logo on top.—			
Judson L-3004	*(M)*	**A Harry Warren Showcase**	*1957*	**20.00**	**50.00**
Judson L-3005	*(M)*	**A Harold Arlen Showcase**	*1957*	**20.00**	**50.00**
Blue Note BLP-4059	*(M)*	**Undercurrent**	*1961*	**30.00**	**75.00**
Blue Note BST-84059	*(S)*	**Undercurrent**	*1961*	**20.00**	**50.00**
		—Blue Note albums above have blue on white labels with a W. 63rd St, NYC address.—			
Blue Note BLP-4059	*(M)*	**Undercurrent**	*196?*	**10.00**	**25.00**
Blue Note BST-84059	*(S)*	**Undercurrent**	*196?*	**8.00**	**20.00**
		—Blue Note albums above have blue on white labels with a New Yord, USA address.—			
Blue Note BST-84059	*(S)*	**Undercurrent**	*196?*	**5.00**	**12.00**
		—Blue Note albums above have blue on white labels with "A Division of Liberty Records."—			

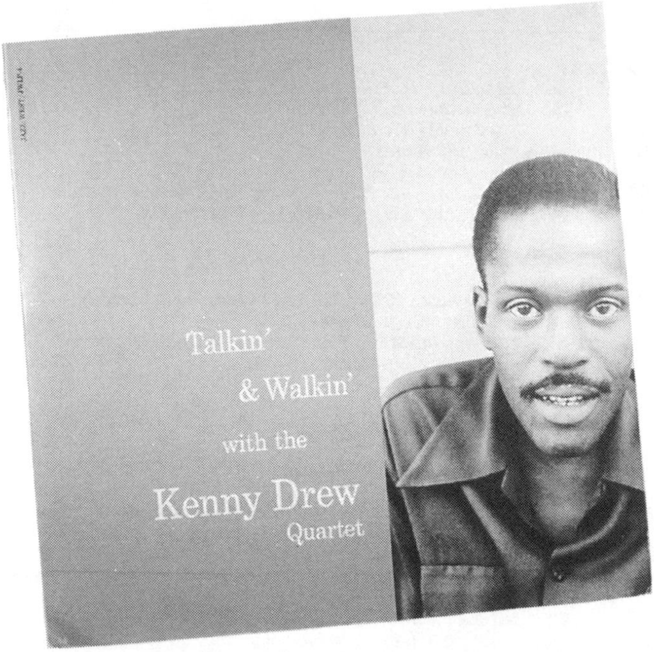

Classically trained Kenny Drew began his jazz career on record with a session for Howard McGhee on Blue Note in 1950. He then gigged with Coleman Hawkins, Lester Young, and Charlie Parker in 1950-51 and Buddy DeFranco in '52-53. After bouncing between coasts, he settled in with Buddy Rich for a year (1958-59). Aside from his own recordings as a leader he has recorded with Chet Baker, Johnny Griffin, Ernie Henry and Toots Thielemans, all on Riverside, Sonny Rollins and Sonny Stitt, both on Prestige, Art Farmer on New Jazz, Leonard Feather on ABC-Paramount, John Coltrane on Blue Note, Sonny Criss on Imperial, and Paul Chambers on Jazz West.

Label & Catalog #		Title	Year	VG+	NM
DREW, KENNY, & DONALD BYRD & HANK MOBLEY					
Jazzland JLP-6	(M)	**Hard Bop**	1960	20.00	50.00
Jazzland JLP-96	(S)	**Hard Bop**	1960	16.00	40.00
		(Jazzland 6 is a reissue of Riverside 236.)			
DREW, KENNY, & PAUL CHAMBERS & PHILLY JOE JONES					
Jazzland JLP-9	(M)	**The Tough Piano Trio**	1960	20.00	50.00
Jazzland JLP-99	(S)	**The Tough Piano Trio**	1960	16.00	40.00
		(Jazzland 9 is a reissue of Riverside 224.)			
DUKE, DOUGLAS					
Herald HLP-0102	(M)	**Sounds Impossible**	1956	16.00	40.00
DUKE'S MEN, THE					
Duke Ellington's band without the Duke.					
Epic LN-3108	(M)	**The Duke's Men**	1955	20.00	50.00
Epic LN-3237	(M)	**Ellington's Sidekicks**	1956	20.00	50.00
DUKES, JOE, & JACK McDUFF					
Joseph Dukes is a modern jazz drummer.					
Prestige PRLP-7324	(M)	**Soulful Drums**	1964	12.00	30.00
Prestige PRST-7324	(S)	**Soulful Drums**	1964	10.00	25.00
—Prestige albums above have blue labels with a trident logo on the right side.—					
DUKES OF DIXIELAND, THE					
The Dukes under the direction of Frank and Fred Assunto are a traditional jazz ensemble.					
Vik LX-1025	(M)	**The Dukes Of Dixieland At The Jazz Band Ball**	1957	12.00	30.00
Audio Fidelity AFLP-1823	(M)	**You've Got To Hear It To Believe It, Volume 1**	1957	6.00	15.00
Audio Fidelity AFSD-5823	(S)	**You've Got To Hear It To Believe It, Volume 1**	1957	8.00	20.00
Audio Fidelity AFLP-1840	(M)	**You've Got To Hear It To Believe It, Volume 2**	1957	6.00	15.00
Audio Fidelity AFSD-5840	(S)	**You've Got To Hear It To Believe It, Volume 2**	1957	8.00	20.00
Audio Fidelity AFLP-1851	(M)	**You've Got To Hear It To Believe It, Volume 3**	1958	6.00	15.00
Audio Fidelity AFSD-5851	(S)	**You've Got To Hear It To Believe It, Volume 3**	1958	8.00	20.00
Audio Fidelity AFLP-1861	(M)	**You've Got To Hear It To Believe It, Volume 4**	1958	6.00	15.00
Audio Fidelity AFSD-5861	(S)	**You've Got To Hear It To Believe It, Volume 4**	1958	8.00	20.00
Audio Fidelity AFLP-1862	(M)	**Mardi Gras Time**	1958	6.00	15.00
Audio Fidelity AFSD-5862	(S)	**Mardi Gras Time**	1958	8.00	20.00
Audio Fidelity AFLP-1891	(M)	**The Dukes Of Dixieland On Campus**	1959	6.00	15.00
Audio Fidelity AFSD-5891	(S)	**The Dukes Of Dixieland On Campus**	1959	8.00	20.00
Audio Fidelity AFLP-1892	(M)	**Up The Mississippi**	1959	6.00	15.00
Audio Fidelity AFSD-5892	(S)	**Up The Mississippi**	1959	8.00	20.00
Audio Fidelity AFLP-1956	(M)	**The Best Of The Dukes Of Dixieland**	1961	5.00	12.00
Audio Fidelity AFSD-5956	(S)	**The Best Of The Dukes Of Dixieland**	1961	6.00	15.00
Audio Fidelity AFLP-1964	(M)	**More Best Of The Dukes Of Dixieland**	1962	5.00	12.00
Audio Fidelity AFSD-5964	(S)	**More Best Of The Dukes Of Dixieland**	1962	6.00	15.00
RCA Victor LPM-2097	(M)	**The Dukes Of Dixieland**	1960	8.00	20.00
RCA Victor LSP-2097	(S)	**The Dukes Of Dixieland**	1960	6.00	15.00
—RCA albums above have black labels with "Long Play" or "Living Stereo" on the bottom.—					
Columbia CL-1728	(M)	**Breakin' It Up On Broadway**	1962	6.00	15.00
Columbia CS-8528	(S)	**Breakin' It Up On Broadway**	1962	5.00	12.00
—Columbia albums above have six eye logos on the label.—					
Columbia CL-2194	(M)	**Struttin' At The World's Fair**	1964	6.00	15.00
Columbia CS-8994	(S)	**Struttin' At The World's Fair**	1964	5.00	12.00
—Columbia albums above have "Guaranteed High Fidelity" or "360 Sound Stereo" in black on the label.—					
Decca DL-4653	(M)	**Live At Bourbon Street**	1965	6.00	15.00
Decca DL-74653	(S)	**Live At Bourbon Street**	1965	5.00	12.00
Decca DL-4807	(M)	**Sunrise, Sunset**	1966	6.00	15.00
Decca DL-74807	(S)	**Sunrise, Sunset**	1966	5.00	12.00
Decca DL-4863	(M)	**Come To The Cabaret**	1966	6.00	15.00
Decca DL-74863	(S)	**Come To The Cabaret**	1966	5.00	12.00
DUNCAN, DANNY					
"X" LVA-3040 (10")	(M)	**Ragtime Jamboree**	1955	20.00	50.00

DUNN, DOROTHY: ***Refer to*** **ANNIE ROSS / DOROTHY DUNN / SHELBY SAVIS**

Label & Catalog #		Title	Year	VG+	NM
DURAN, EDDIE					
Edward Duran is a modern jazz guitarist.					
Fantasy 3247	*(M)*	**Jazz Guitarist** *(Dark red vinyl)*	*1957*	**30.00**	**75.00**
		—Fantasy albums above have red labels on dark red, non-flexible vinyl.—			
Fantasy 3247	*(M)*	**Jazz Guitarist**	*195?*	**16.00**	**40.00**
		—Fantasy albums above have red labels on black, non-flexible vinyl.—			
DuSHON, JEAN					
Jean DuShon is a jazz-based vocalist.					
Argo LP-4039	*(M)*	**Make Way For Jean DuShon**	*1964*	**12.00**	**30.00**
Argo LPS-4039	*(S)*	**Make Way For Jean DuShon**	*1964*	**10.00**	**25.00**
Argo LP-750	*(M)*	**You Better Believe It**	*1965*	**12.00**	**30.00**
Argo LPS-750	*(S)*	**You Better Believe It**	*1965*	**10.00**	**25.00**
DUTCH SWING COLLEGE BAND, THE					
Epic LN-3211	*(M)*	**Dixieland Goes Dutch**	*1955*	**16.00**	**40.00**
Philips PHM-200-010	*(M)*	**Dixie Gone Dutch**	*1962*	**8.00**	**20.00**
Philips PHS-600-010	*(S)*	**Dixie Gone Dutch**	*1962*	**6.00**	**15.00**

Fred Astaire by David Stone Martin.

E.

EAGER, ALLAN

Allan Eager is a modern jazz tenor and alto saxophone player.

Savoy MG-9015	*(10")*	**New Trends In Modern Music, Volume 2**	*1952*	**100.00**	**200.00**
Savoy MG-15044	*(10")*	**Tenor Sax**	*1954*	**100.00**	**200.00**

EARDLEY, JON

Jon Eardley is a modern jazz trumpet player.

New Jazz NJLP-1105	*(10")*	**Jon Eardley In Hollywood**	*1954*	**100.00**	**200.00**
Prestige PRLP-205	*(10")*	**Jon Eardley In Hollywood**	*1955*	**60.00**	**150.00**

(Prestige 205 is a reissue of New Jazz 1105.)

Prestige PRLP-207	*(10")*	**Hey, There**	*1955*	**60.00**	**150.00**
Prestige PRLP-7033	*(M)*	**Jon Eardley Seven**	*1956*	**40.00**	**100.00**

—Presitge albums above have a W. 50th Street, NYC address on the label.—

EASY RIDERS JAZZ BAND, THE

Jazz Crusade 1002	*(M)*	**My Life Will Be Sweeter Someday**	*1963*	**8.00**	**20.00**

EATON, JOHNNY

John Eaton is a modern jazz pianist and composer.

Columbia CL-737	*(M)*	**College Jazz: Modern**	*1956*	**16.00**	**40.00**
Columbia CL-996	*(M)*	**Far Out, Far In**	*1957*	**16.00**	**40.00**

—Columbia albums above have six white on black "eye" logos on each label.—

ECHOES OF HARLEM

Royale LP-18128	*(10")*	**Echoes Of Harlem**	*195?*	**30.00**	**75.00**

(Royale 18128 does not identify the orchestra except for the LP title.)

ECKSTINE, BILLY

William "Mr. B" Eckstein, aka Billy Eckstine, is a traditional jazz-based vocalist—and occasional trumpet and valve trombone player—and band leader. For additional listings refer to Count Basie; Earl Hines.

National NLP-2001	*(10")*	**Billy Eckstine Sings**	*1949*	**60.00**	**200.00**
MGM E-523	*(10")*	**Songs By Billy Eckstine**	*1951*	**60.00**	**150.00**
MGM E-548	*(10")*	**Favorites**	*1951*	**60.00**	**150.00**
MGM E-153	*(10")*	**Billy Eckstine Sings Rodgers & Hammerstein**	*1952*	**60.00**	**150.00**
MGM E-219	*(10")*	**Tenderly**	*1953*	**60.00**	**150.00**
MGM E-257	*(10")*	**I Let A Song Go Out Of My Heart**	*1954*	**60.00**	**150.00**
MGM E-3176	*(M)*	**Mister B With A Beat**	*1955*	**20.00**	**50.00**
MGM E-3209	*(M)*	**Rendezvous**	*1955*	**20.00**	**50.00**
MGM E-3275	*(M)*	**That Old Feeling**	*1955*	**20.00**	**50.00**
King 295-12	*(10")*	**The Great Mr. B**	*1953*	**150.00**	**300.00**
DeLuxe 265-12	*(10")*	**The Great Mr. "B" & His All-Star Band**	*195?*	**60.00**	**150.00**
DeLuxe FA-2010	*(M)*	**Billy Eckstine And His Orchestra**	*195?*	**30.00**	**75.00**

(Deluxe 2010 also features Sarah Vaughan on several sides.)

EmArcy MG-26025	*(10")*	**Blues For Sale**	*1954*	**50.00**	**125.00**
EmArcy MG-26027	*(10")*	**The Love Songs Of "Mr. B"**	*1954*	**50.00**	**125.00**
EmArcy MG-36010	*(M)*	**I Surrender, Dear**	*1955*	**30.00**	**75.00**
EmArcy MG-36029	*(M)*	**Blues For Sale**	*1955*	**30.00**	**75.00**
EmArcy MG-36030	*(M)*	**The Love Songs Of "Mr. B"**	*1955*	**30.00**	**75.00**
EmArcy MG-36129	*(M)*	**Billy Eckstine's Imagination**	*1958*	**30.00**	**75.00**

—EmArcy albums above have blue labels with silver print.—

Regent MG-6052	*(M)*	**Prisoner Of Love**	*1957*	**20.00**	**50.00**
Regent MG-6053	*(M)*	**The Duke, The Blues And Me**	*1957*	**20.00**	**50.00**
Regent MG-6054	*(M)*	**My Deep Blue Dream**	*1957*	**20.00**	**50.00**
Regent MG-6058	*(M)*	**You Call It Madness**	*1957*	**20.00**	**50.00**
Lion L-70057	*(M)*	**The Best Of Billy Eckstine**	*1958*	**10.00**	**25.00**
Mercury MG-20333	*(M)*	**Billy's Best**	*1958*	**20.00**	**50.00**
Mercury MG-20637	*(M)*	**Broadway, Bongos And Mr. B**	*1961*	**12.00**	**30.00**
Mercury SR-60637	*(S)*	**Broadway, Bongos And Mr. B**	*1961*	**10.00**	**25.00**
Mercury MG-20674	*(M)*	**Billy Eckstine & Quincy Jones At Basin St. East**	*1962*	**12.00**	**30.00**
Mercury SR-60674	*(S)*	**Billy Eckstine & Quincy Jones At Basin St. East**	*1962*	**10.00**	**25.00**
Mercury MG-20736	*(M)*	**Don't Worry 'Bout Me**	*1962*	**12.00**	**30.00**
Mercury SR-60736	*(S)*	**Don't Worry 'Bout Me**	*1962*	**10.00**	**25.00**

Label & Catalog #		Title	Year	VG+	NM
Mercury MG-20796	(M)	**The Golden Hits Of Billy Eckstine**	1963	8.00	20.00
Mercury SR-60796	(S)	**The Golden Hits Of Billy Eckstine**	1963	6.00	15.00
		—Mercury albums above have black labels with silver print.—			
Audio Lab AL-1549	(M)	**Mr. B**	1960	60.00	150.00
Roulette R-52052	(M)	**No Cover, No Minimum**	1961	12.00	30.00
Roulette SR-52052	(S)	**No Cover, No Minimum**	1961	10.00	25.00
Roulette R-25104	(M)	**Once More With Feeling**	1962	12.00	30.00
Roulette SR-25104	(S)	**Once More With Feeling**	1962	10.00	25.00
Metro M-537	(M)	**Everything I Have Is Yours**	1965	6.00	15.00
Metro MS-537	(E)	**Everything I Have Is Yours**	1965	4.00	10.00
Motown MLP-632	(M)	**Prime Of My Life**	1965	12.00	30.00
Motown SLP-632	(S)	**Prime Of My Life**	1965	10.00	25.00
Motown MLP-646	(M)	**My Way**	1966	12.00	30.00
Motown SLP-646	(S)	**My Way**	1966	10.00	25.00
Motown MS-677	(S)	**For Love Of Ivy**	1969	10.00	25.00

ECKSTINE, BILLY, & SARAH VAUGHAN

Mercury MG-20316	(M)	**The Best Of Irving Berlin**	1958	16.00	40.00
Mercury SR-60002	(S)	**The Best Of Irving Berlin**	1959	12.00	30.00
Lion L-70088	(M)	**Billy And Sarah**	1959	10.00	25.00

EDISON, HARRY "SWEETS"

Harry "Sweets" Edison is a traditional jazz trumpet player. For additional listings refer to Eddie Davis; Roy Eldridge & Dizzy Gillespie & Harry Edison; Budd Johnson; Buddy Rich & Sweets Edison; Ben Webster & Harry Edison; Lester Young; Lester Young & Roy Eldridge and the Various Artists section under United Artists and Verve..

Pacific Jazz PJLP-4	(10")	**Harry Edison Quartet**	1953	60.00	150.00
Clef MGC-717	(M)	**Sweets**	1956	30.00	75.00
American Rec. Soc. G-430	(M)	**Sweets**	1957	16.00	40.00
Verve MGV-8097	(M)	**Sweets**	1957	20.00	50.00
		(A.R.S. 430 and Verve 8097 are reissues of Clef 717.)			
Verve MGV-8211	(M)	**Gee Baby, Ain't I Good To You?**	1958	20.00	50.00
Verve MGV-8293	(M)	**Harry Edison Swings Buck Clayton And Vice-Versa**	1958	20.00	50.00
Verve MGVS-6016	(S)	**Harry Edison Swings Buck Clayton And Vice-Versa**	1960	16.00	40.00
Verve MGV-8295	(M)	**The Swinger**	1959	20.00	50.00
Verve MGVS-6037	(S)	**The Swinger**	1960	16.00	40.00
Verve MGV-8353	(M)	**Mr. Swing**	1959	20.00	50.00
Verve MGVS-6118	(S)	**Mr. Swing**	1960	16.00	40.00
		(Verve 8353 features cover art by David Stone Martin.)			
		— Verve albums above have black labels with "Verve Records, Inc." on the bottom.—			
Verve V-8097	(M)	**Sweets**	1961	8.00	20.00
Verve V-8211	(M)	**Gee Baby, Ain't I Good To You?**	1961	8.00	20.00
Verve V-8293	(M)	**Harry Edison Swings Buck Clayton And Vice-Versa**	1961	8.00	20.00
Verve V6-8293	(S)	**Harry Edison Swings Buck Clayton And Vice-Versa**	1961	6.00	15.00
Verve V-8295	(M)	**The Swinger**	1961	8.00	20.00
Verve V6-8295	(S)	**The Swinger**	1961	6.00	15.00
Verve V-8353	(M)	**Mr. Swing**	1961	8.00	20.00
Verve V6-8353	(S)	**Mr. Swing**	1961	6.00	15.00
		— Verve albums above have black labels with "MGM Records" on the bottom.—			
Roulette R-52023	(M)	**Sweetenings**	1959	16.00	40.00
Roulette SR-52023	(S)	**Sweetenings**	1959	12.00	30.00
Roulette R-52041	(M)	**Patented By Edison**	1960	12.00	30.00
Roulette SR-52041	(S)	**Patented By Edison**	1960	10.00	25.00
Pacific Jazz PJ-11	(M)	**The Inventive Harry Edison**	1960	20.00	50.00
		(Pacific Jazz 11 is a reissue of 4.)			
Vee Jay LP-1104	(M)	**Sweets For The Sweet Taste Of Love**	1964	12.00	30.00
Vee Jay LPS-1104	(S)	**Sweets For The Sweet Taste Of Love**	1964	12.00	30.00
Sue LP-1030	(M)	**Sweets For The Sweet**	1965	16.00	40.00
Sue SLP-1030	(S)	**Sweets For The Sweet**	1965	16.00	40.00
Liberty LRP-3484	(M)	**When Lights Are Low**	1966	10.00	25.00
Liberty LST-7484	(S)	**When Lights Are Low**	1966	8.00	20.00

EDWARDS, EDDIE

Edwin Edwards is a traditional jazz trombone and violin player.

Commodore FL-20003	(10")	**Eddie Edwards' Original Dixieland Jazz Band**	1950	20.00	50.00

Label & Catalog #		Title	Year	VG+	NM
EDWARDS, TEDDY					
Theodore Edwards is a West Coast jazz tenor sax player. For additional listings refer to Heleyne Stewart.					
Pacific Jazz PJ-6	(M)	**It's About Time**	1960	16.00	40.00
Pacific Jazz ST-6	(S)	**It's About Time**	1960	12.00	30.00
		(Pacific Jazz 6 also features Les McCann.)			
Pacific Jazz PJ-14	(M)	**Sunset Eyes**	1961	16.00	40.00
Contemporary M-3583	(M)	**Teddy's Ready**	1960	12.00	30.00
Contemporary S-7583	(S)	**Teddy's Ready**	1960	10.00	25.00
Contemporary M-3588	(M)	**Together Again**	1961	16.00	40.00
Contemporary S-7588	(S)	**Together Again**	1961	12.00	30.00
		(Contemporary3592 also features Howard McGhee.)			
Contemporary M-3592	(M)	**Good Gravy**	1961	12.00	30.00
Contemporary S-7592	(S)	**Good Gravy**	1961	10.00	25.00
Contemporary M-3606	(M)	**Heart And Soul**	1962	12.00	30.00
Contemporary S-7606	(S)	**Heart And Soul**	1962	10.00	25.00
		— Contemporary stereo albums have gold & black labels.—			
Prestige PRLP-7518	(M)	**Nothin' But The Truth**	1967	12.00	30.00
Prestige PRST-7518	(S)	**Nothin' But The Truth**	1967	10.00	25.00
Prestige PRLP-7522	(M)	**It's Alright**	1967	12.00	30.00
Prestige PRST-7522	(S)	**It's Alright**	1967	10.00	25.00
		—Prestige albums above have blue labels with a trident logo on the right side.—			
ELDRIDGE, ROY					
David Roy "Little Jazz" Eldridge is a traditional jazz-based trumpet, flugel horn, and piano player, drummer, vocalist and composer. For additional listings refer to Benny Carter / Roy Eldridge; Russ Garcia; Coleman Hawkins & Roy Eldridge; Earl Hines & Roy Eldridge; The Jazz Artists Guild; Oscar Peterson; Art Tatum & Roy Eldridge; Lester Young & Roy Eldridge.					
Prestige PRLP-114	(10")	**Roy Eldridge In Sweden**	1951	100.00	200.00
Mercury MGC-113	(10")	**Roy Eldridge Collates**	1952	100.00	200.00
		(Mercury 113 features cover art by David Stone Martin.)			
Clef MGC-113	(10")	**Roy Eldridge Collates**	1953	60.00	150.00
		(Clef 113 is a riessue of Mercury 113.)			
Clef MGC-150	(10")	**The Roy Eldridge Quintet**	1954	60.00	150.00
Clef MGC-162	(10")	**The Strolling Mr. Eldridge**	1954	60.00	150.00
Dial LP-304	(10")	**Little Jazz Four: Trumpet Fantasy**	1953	150.00	300.00
Clef MGC-683	(M)	**Little Jazz**	1956	40.00	100.00
Clef MGC-704	(M)	**Rockin' Chair**	1956	40.00	100.00
Clef MGC-705	(M)	**Dale's Wail**	1956	40.00	100.00
Clef MGC-716	(M)	**Mr. Jazz—The Music Of Roy Eldridge**	1956	*Unreleased*	
American Rec. Soc. G-420	(M)	**Swing Goes Dixie**	1956	16.00	40.00
Verve MGV-1010	(M)	**Swing Goes Dixie**	1957	20.00	50.00
		(Verve 1010 is a reissue of A.R.S. 420 with cover art by David Stone Martin.)			
		— Verve albums above have "Verve Record, Inc." on the bottom of the label.—			
Verve MGV-8068	(M)	**Little Jazz**	1957	20.00	50.00
		(Verve 8068 is a reissue of Clef 683.)			
Verve MGV-8088	(M)	**Rockin' Chair**	1957	20.00	50.00
		(Verve 8088 is a reissue of Clef 704.)			
Verve MGV-8089	(M)	**Dale's Wail**	1957	20.00	50.00
		(Verve 8089 is a reissue of Clef 705.)			
Verve MGV-8389	(M)	**Swingin' On The Town**	1960	20.00	50.00
		— Verve albums above have black labels with "Verve Records, Inc." on the bottom.—			
Verve V-1010	(M)	**Swing Goes Dixie**	1961	8.00	20.00
Verve V-8068	(M)	**Little Jazz**	1961	8.00	20.00
Verve V-8088	(M)	**Rockin' Chair**	1961	8.00	20.00
Verve V-8089	(M)	**Dale's Wail**	1961	8.00	20.00
Verve V-8389	(M)	**Swingin' On The Town**	1961	8.00	20.00
		— Verve albums above have black labels with "MGM Records" on the bottom.—			
London PB-375	(10")	**Roy Eldridge Quartet**	1954	50.00	125.00
Discovery DL-2009	(10")	**Roy Eldridge With Zoot Sims**	1954	50.00	125.00
EmArcy MG-36084	(M)	**Roy's Got Rhythm**	1956	30.00	75.00
Metro M-513	(M)	**Roy Eldridge**	1965	6.00	15.00
Metro MS-513	(E)	**Roy Eldridge**	1965	3.00	7.50
ELDRIDGE, ROY, & BENNY CARTER					
American Rec. Soc. G-413	(M)	**The Urbane Jazz Of Roy Eldridge & Benny Carter**	1957	16.00	40.00

Label & Catalog #		Title	Year	VG+	NM
Verve MGV-8202	(M)	**The Urbane Jazz Of Roy Eldridge And Benny Carter**	1957	20.00	50.00
		— Verve albums above have black labels with "Verve Records, Inc." on the bottom.—			
Verve V-8202	(M)	**The Urbane Jazz Of Roy Eldridge And Benny Carter**	1961	8.00	20.00
		— Verve albums above have black labels with "MGM Records" on the bottom.—			

ELDRIDGE, ROY, & DIZZIE GILLESPIE

Clef MGC-641	(M)	**Roy And Diz**	1955	40.00	100.00
Clef MGC-671	(M)	**Roy And Diz, Volume 2**	1955	50.00	125.00
		(Clef 671 features cover art by David Stone Martin.)			
Clef MGC-730	(M)	**Trumpet Battle**	1956	40.00	100.00
Clef MGC-731	(M)	**The Trumpet Kings**	1956	40.00	100.00
Verve MGV-8109	(M)	**Trumpet Battle**	1957	20.00	50.00
		(Verve 8109 is a reissue of Clef 730.)			
Verve MGV-8110	(M)	**The Trumpet Kings**	1957	20.00	50.00
		(Verve 8110 is a reissue of Clef 731.)			
		— Verve albums above have black labels with "Verve Records, Inc." on the bottom.—			
Verve V-8109	(M)	**Trumpet Battle**	1961	8.00	20.00
Verve V-8110	(M)	**The Trumpet Kings**	1961	8.00	20.00
		— Verve albums above have black labels with "MGM Records" on the bottom.—			
Verve VSP-28	(M)	**Soul Mates**	1966	6.00	15.00
Verve VSPS-28	(E)	**Soul Mates**	1966	3.00	7.50

ELDRIDGE, ROY, & DIZZY GILLESPIE & HARRY EDISON

Verve MGV-8212	(M)	**Tour De Force**	1958	20.00	50.00
		— Verve albums above have black labels with "Verve Records, Inc." on the bottom.—			
Verve V-8212	(M)	**Tour De Force**	1961	8.00	20.00
		— Verve albums above have black labels with "MGM Records" on the bottom.—			

ELDRIDGE, ROY / SAMMY PRICE

Brunswick BL-58045	(10")	**Battle Of Jazz, Vol. 7**	1953	20.00	50.00

ELLINGTON, DUKE

Edward Kennedy "Duke" Ellington is a traditional jazz-based pianist, arranger, composer and band leader who bridged the gap into modern jazz. For additional listings refer to Louis Armstrong & Duke Ellington; Rosemary Clooney; John Coltrane; The Ellingtoniians; The Duke's Men; Ella Fitzgerald; Coleman Hawkins; Johnny Hodges; Frank Sinatra & Duke Ellington; and the Jazzy Soundtracks section under Columbia, Contact, Revue, and United Artists.

Columbia CL-6024	(10")	**Mood Ellington**	1949	40.00	100.00
Columbia CL-6073	(10")	**Liberian Suite**	1949	40.00	100.00
Columbia ML-4418	(M)	**Masterpieces By Ellington**	1951	40.00	100.00
Columbia ML-4639	(M)	**Ellington Uptown**	1951	40.00	100.00
Columbia CL-2522	(10")	**Duke's Mixture**	1955	30.00	75.00
Columbia CL-2562	(10")	**Here's The Duke**	1956	30.00	75.00
Columbia CL-2593	(10")	**Al Hibbler With The Duke**	1956	35.00	75.00
Columbia CL-558	(M)	**The Music Of Duke Ellington**	1954	20.00	50.00
		— Columbia albums above have "Long Playing" on the bottom of the label.—			
Columbia CL-558	(M)	**The Music Of Duke Ellington**	195?	16.00	40.00
Columbia CL-663	(M)	**Blue Light**	1955	16.00	40.00
Columbia CL-825	(M)	**Masterpieces By Ellington**	1956	16.00	40.00
Columbia CL-830	(M)	**Ellington Uptown**	1956	16.00	40.00
Columbia CL-848	(M)	**Liberian Suite**	1956	16.00	40.00
Columbia CL-934	(M)	**American Jazz Festival At Newport '56**	1956	16.00	40.00
Columbia CL-951	(M)	**A Drum Is A Woman**	1957	16.00	40.00
Columbia CL-1033	(M)	**Such Sweet Thunder**	1957	16.00	40.00
Columbia CL-1085	(M)	**Ellington Indigos**	1958	12.00	30.00
Columbia CS-8053	(S)	**Ellington Indigos**	1959	10.00	25.00
Columbia CL-1162	(M)	**Brown, Black And Beige**	1958	12.00	30.00
Columbia CS-8015	(S)	**Brown, Black And Beige**	1959	10.00	25.00
Columbia CL-1198	(M)	**The Cosmic Scene**	1958	30.00	75.00
Columbia CL-1245	(M)	**Newport 1958**	1958	12.00	30.00
Columbia CS-8072	(S)	**Newport 1958**	1959	10.00	25.00
Columbia CL-1282	(M)	**Duke Ellington At The Bal Masque**	1959	12.00	30.00
Columbia CS-8098	(S)	**Duke Ellington At The Bal Masque**	1959	10.00	25.00
Columbia CL-1323	(M)	**Duke Ellington Jazz Party**	1959	12.00	30.00
Columbia CS-8127	(S)	**Duke Ellington Jazz Party**	1959	10.00	25.00
Columbia CL-1400	(M)	**Festival Session**	1959	12.00	30.00

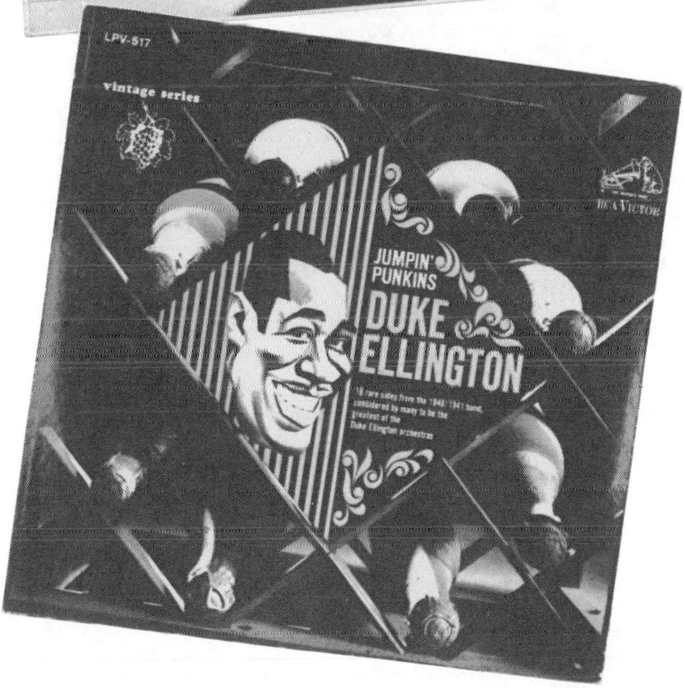

Even during his lifetime (1899-1974), Edward Kennedy Ellington, the single greatest composer the United States has ever produced, was considered a national resource and an international representative of what was great with this country. His first recordings were waxed in the mid 1920s as Ellington's Kentucky Club Orchestra. By 1930, Ellington's orchestra was nationally famous for its broadcasts emanating from Harlem's (in)famous Cotton Club. The Duke's primary recording affiliations have been with RCA in the '30s and '40s, Columbia and Capitol in the '50s, and Reprise in the '60s. The two albums here feature different artist's renditions of Ellington: The Capitol collection of '50s recordings depicts the debonair Duke while the RCA compilation of '30s sides is a caricature of the rascally band leader of the time.

Label & Catalog #		*Title*	*Year*	*VG+*	*NM*
Columbia CL-1445	*(M)*	**Blues In Orbit**	*1960*	**12.00**	**30.00**
Columbia CS-8241	*(S)*	**Blues In Orbit**	*1960*	**10.00**	**25.00**
Columbia CL-1541	*(M)*	**The Nutcracker Suite**	*1960*	**16.00**	**40.00**
Columbia CS-8341	*(S)*	**The Nutcracker Suite**	*1960*	**12.00**	**30.00**
Columbia CL-1546	*(M)*	**Piano In The Background**	*1960*	**16.00**	**40.00**
Columbia CS-8346	*(S)*	**Piano In The Background**	*1960*	**12.00**	**30.00**
Columbia CL-1597	*(M)*	**Peer Gynt Suite/Suite Thursday**	*1961*	**12.00**	**30.00**
Columbia CS-8397	*(S)*	**Peer Gynt Suite/Suite Thursday**	*1961*	**10.00**	**25.00**
Columbia CL-1715	*(M)*	**First Time**	*1962*	**12.00**	**30.00**
Columbia CS-8515	*(S)*	**First Time**	*1962*	**10.00**	**25.00**
		(Columbia 1715 also features Count Basie.)			
		— Columbia albums above have six white on black "eye" logos on each label.—			
Columbia CL-1790	*(M)*	**All American**	*1962*	**10.00**	**25.00**
Columbia CS-8590	*(S)*	**All American**	*1962*	**8.00**	**20.00**
Columbia CL-1907	*(M)*	**Midnight In Paris**	*1962*	**10.00**	**25.00**
Columbia CS-8707	*(S)*	**Midnight In Paris**	*1962*	**8.00**	**20.00**
Columbia CL-2029	*(M)*	**Piano In The Foreground**	*1963*	**12.00**	**30.00**
Columbia CS-8829	*(S)*	**Piano In The Foreground**	*1963*	**10.00**	**25.00**
Columbia C3L-27	*(M)*	**The Ellington Era, Vol. 1** *(3 LP box with book)*	*1963*	**16.00**	**40.00**
Columbia C3L-39	*(M)*	**The Ellington Era, Vol. 2** *(3 LP box with book)*	*1964*	**16.00**	**40.00**
		— Columbia albums above have "Guaranteed High Fidelity" or "360 Sound Stereo" in black on the label.—			
Columbia CL-558	*(M)*	**The Music Of Duke Ellington**	*195?*	**5.00**	**12.00**
Columbia CL-663	*(M)*	**Blue Light**	*196?*	**5.00**	**12.00**
Columbia CL-825	*(M)*	**Masterpieces**	*196?*	**5.00**	**12.00**
Columbia CL-830	*(M)*	**Ellington Uptown**	*196?*	**5.00**	**12.00**
Columbia CL-848	*(M)*	**Liberian Suite**	*196?*	**5.00**	**12.00**
Columbia CL-934	*(M)*	**American Jazz Festival At Newport '56**	*196?*	**5.00**	**12.00**
Columbia CL-951	*(M)*	**A Drum Is A Woman**	*196?*	**5.00**	**12.00**
Columbia CL-1033	*(M)*	**Such Sweet Thunder**	*196?*	**5.00**	**12.00**
Columbia CL-1085	*(M)*	**Ellington Indigos**	*196?*	**5.00**	**12.00**
Columbia CS-8053	*(S)*	**Ellington Indigos**	*196?*	**4.00**	**10.00**
Columbia CL-1162	*(M)*	**Brown, Black And Beige**	*196?*	**5.00**	**12.00**
Columbia CS-8015	*(S)*	**Brown, Black And Beige**	*196?*	**4.00**	**10.00**
Columbia CL-1245	*(M)*	**Newport 1958**	*196?*	**5.00**	**12.00**
Columbia CS-8072	*(S)*	**Newport 1958**	*196?*	**4.00**	**10.00**
Columbia CL-1282	*(M)*	**Duke Ellington At The Bal Masque**	*196?*	**5.00**	**12.00**
Columbia CS-8098	*(S)*	**Duke Ellington At The Bal Masque**	*196?*	**4.00**	**10.00**
Columbia CL-1323	*(M)*	**Duke Ellington Jazz Party**	*196?*	**5.00**	**12.00**
Columbia CS-8127	*(S)*	**Duke Ellington Jazz Party**	*196?*	**4.00**	**10.00**
Columbia CL-1400	*(M)*	**Festival Session**	*196?*	**5.00**	**12.00**
Columbia CL-1445	*(M)*	**Blues In Orbit**	*196?*	**5.00**	**12.00**
Columbia CS-8241	*(S)*	**Blues In Orbit**	*196?*	**4.00**	**10.00**
Columbia CL-1541	*(M)*	**The Nutcracker Suite**	*196?*	**5.00**	**12.00**
Columbia CS-8341	*(S)*	**The Nutcracker Suite**	*196?*	**4.00**	**10.00**
Columbia CL-1546	*(M)*	**Piano In The Background**	*196?*	**5.00**	**12.00**
Columbia CS-8346	*(S)*	**Piano In The Background**	*196?*	**4.00**	**10.00**
Columbia CL-1597	*(M)*	**Peer Gynt Suite/Suite Thursday**	*196?*	**5.00**	**12.00**
Columbia CS-8397	*(S)*	**Peer Gynt Suite/Suite Thursday**	*196?*	**4.00**	**10.00**
Columbia CL-1715	*(M)*	**First Time**	*196?*	**5.00**	**12.00**
Columbia CS-8515	*(S)*	**First Time**	*196?*	**4.00**	**10.00**
Columbia CL-1790	*(M)*	**All American**	*196?*	**5.00**	**12.00**
Columbia CS-8590	*(S)*	**All American**	*196?*	**4.00**	**10.00**
Columbia CL-1907	*(M)*	**Midnight In Paris**	*196?*	**5.00**	**12.00**
Columbia CS-8707	*(S)*	**Midnight In Paris**	*196?*	**4.00**	**10.00**
Columbia CL-2029	*(M)*	**Piano In The Foreground**	*196?*	**5.00**	**12.00**
Columbia CS-8829	*(S)*	**Piano In The Foreground**	*196?*	**4.00**	**10.00**
Columbia C3L-27	*(M)*	**The Ellington Era, Vol. 1** *(3 LP box with book)*	*196?*	**8.00**	**20.00**
Columbia C3L-39	*(M)*	**The Ellington Era, Vol. 2** *(3 LP box with book)*	*196?*	**6.00**	**15.00**
		— Columboa albums above have "360 Sound" in white on the bottom of the label.—			
Brunswick BL-58002	*(10")*	**Ellingtonia, Volume 1**	*1950*	**40.00**	**100.00**
Brunswick BL-58012	*(10")*	**Ellingtonia, Volume 2**	*1950*	**40.00**	**100.00**
Brunswick BL-54007	*(M)*	**Early Ellington**	*1954*	**20.00**	**50.00**
Jazz Panorama 1802	*(10")*	**Duke Ellington—Vol. 1**	*1951*	**40.00**	**100.00**
Jazz Panorama 1811	*(10")*	**Duke Ellington—Vol. 2**	*1951*	**40.00**	**100.00**
Jazz Panorama 1816	*(10")*	**Duke Ellington—Vol. 3**	*1951*	**40.00**	**100.00**
RCA Victor WPT-11	*(10")*	**Duke Ellington**	*1951*	**40.00**	**100.00**
RCA Victor LPT-3017	*(10")*	**This Is Duke Ellington And His Orchestra**	*1952*	**40.00**	**100.00**
RCA Victor LPT-3067	*(10")*	**Duke Ellington Plays The Blues**	*1953*	**40.00**	**100.00**
RCA Victor LJM-1002	*(M)*	**Seattle Concert**	*1954*	**20.00**	**50.00**

Label & Catalog #		Title	Year	VG+	NM
RCA Victor LPT-1004	(M)	**Ellington's Greatest**	1954	16.00	40.00
RCA Victor LPM-1092	(M)	**Duke And His Men**	1955	16.00	40.00
RCA Victor LPM-1364	(M)	**In A Mellotone**	1957	16.00	40.00
RCA Victor LPM-1715	(M)	**Duke Ellington At His Very Best**	1958	16.00	40.00
RCA Victor LPM-6009	(M)	**The Indispensable Duke Ellington**	1961	20.00	50.00
		—RCA albums above have black labels with "Long Play" on the bottom.—			
RCA Victor LPV-506	(M)	**Daybreak Express**	1964	8.00	20.00
RCA Victor LPV-517	(M)	**Jumpin' Punkins**	1965	8.00	20.00
RCA Victor LPV-541	(M)	**Johnny Come Lately**	1965	8.00	20.00
RCA Victor LPV-553	(M)	**Pretty Woman**	1965	8.00	20.00
RCA Victor LPV-568	(M)	**Flaming Youth**	1965	8.00	20.00
		—RCA albums above have purple labels.—			
RCA Victor LM-2857	(M)	**The Duke At Tanglewood**	1966	8.00	20.00
RCA Victor LSC-2857	(S)	**The Duke At Tanglewood**	1966	6.00	15.00
		(RCA 2857 also features Arthur Fiedler & The Boston Pops Orchestra.)			
RCA Victor LPM-3576	(M)	**The Popular Duke Ellington**	1966	8.00	20.00
RCA Victor LSP-3576	(S)	**The Popular Duke Ellington**	1966	6.00	15.00
RCA Victor LPM-3582	(M)	**Concert Of Sacred Music**	1966	8.00	20.00
RCA Victor LSP-3582	(S)	**Concert Of Sacred Music**	1966	6.00	15.00
RCA Victor LPM-3782	(M)	**Far East Suite**	1967	10.00	25.00
RCA Victor LSP-3782	(S)	**Far East Suite**	1967	6.00	15.00
RCA Victor LPM-3906	(M)	**And His Mother Called Him Bill**	1968	20.00	50.00
RCA Victor LSP-3906	(S)	**And His Mother Called Him Bill**	1968	6.00	15.00
		(RCA 3906 also features Billy Strayhorn.)			
		—RCA albums above have black labels with "Mono Dynagroove" or "Stereo Dynagroove" on the bottom.—			
Camden CAL-394	(M)	**Duke Ellington At Tanglewood**	1958	8.00	20.00
Camden CAL-459	(M)	**Duke Ellington At The Cotton Club**	1959	8.00	20.00
		—Camden albums above have blue labels with purple perimeters.—			
Royale 18143	(10")	**Duke Ellington & His Orchestra**	195?	20.00	50.00
Royale 18152	(10")	**Duke Ellington Plays Ellington**	195?	20.00	50.00
Allegro 3082	(M)	**Duke Ellington**	1953	20.00	50.00
Allegro 1591	(M)	**Duke Ellington**	1955	20.00	50.00
Allegro 4014	(10")	**Duke Ellington Plays**	1954	40.00	100.00
Allegro 4038	(10")	**Duke Ellington Plays**	1954	40.00	100.00
"X" LVA-3037	(10")	**Duke Ellington Plays**	1955	40.00	100.00
London AL-3551	(10")	**The Duke-1926**	195?	40.00	100.00
Capitol H-440	(10")	**Premiered By Ellington**	1953	40.00	100.00
Capitol H-477	(10")	**Ellington Plays Ellington**	1954	40.00	100.00
Capitol T-477	(M)	**The Duke Plays Ellington**	1954	16.00	40.00
Capitol T-521	(M)	**Ellington '55**	1954	16.00	40.00
Capitol T-637	(M)	**Dance To The Duke**	1955	16.00	40.00
Capitol T-679	(M)	**Ellington Showcase**	1956	16.00	40.00
		—Capitol albums above have turquoise labels.—			
Capitol T-477	(M)	**The Duke Plays Ellington**	195?	8.00	20.00
Capitol T-521	(M)	**Ellington '55**	195?	8.00	20.00
Capitol T-637	(M)	**Dance To The Duke**	195?	8.00	20.00
Capitol T-679	(M)	**Ellington Showcase**	195?	8.00	20.00
Capitol T-1602	(M)	**The Best Of Duke Ellington**	1961	8.00	20.00
Capitol DT-1602	(E)	**The Best Of Duke Ellington**	1961	5.00	12.00
		—Capitol albums above have black "rainbow" labels with the logo on the left side.—			
Bethlehem BCP-60	(M)	**Historically Speaking, The Duke**	1956	24.00	60.00
Bethlehem BCP-6005	(M)	**Duke Ellington Presents**	1956	24.00	60.00
Riverside RLP-12-129	(M)	**Birth Of Big Band Jazz**	1956	24.00	60.00
		—Riverside albums above have blue on white labels.—			
Riverside RLP-12-129	(M)	**Birth Of Big Band Jazz**	195?	12.00	30.00
Riverside RLP-475	(M)	**Great Times!**	1963	12.00	30.00
Riverside RS-9475	(S)	**Great Times!**	1963	10.00	25.00
		(Riverside 475 also features Billy Strayhorn.)			
		—Riverside albums above have blue mono or black stereo labels with a reel & mike logo on top.—			
Rondo-lette A-7	(M)	**Duke Ellington And Orchestra**	1958	12.00	30.00
Decca DL-9224	(M)	**Duke Ellington, Volume 1—In The Beginning**	1958	16.00	40.00
Decca DL-79224	(E)	**Duke Ellington, Volume 1—In The Beginning**	1958	10.00	25.00
Decca DL-9241	(M)	**Duke Ellington, Volume 2—Hot In Harlem**	1959	16.00	40.00
Decca DL-79241	(E)	**Duke Ellington, Volume 2—Hot In Harlem**	1959	10.00	25.00
Decca DL-9247	(M)	**Duke Ellington, Volume 3—Rockin' In Rhythm**	1959	16.00	40.00
Decca DL-79247	(E)	**Duke Ellington, Volume 3—Rockin' In Rhythm**	1959	10.00	25.00
		—Decca albums above have maroon labels.—			
SeSac N-2701	(M)	**Ellington Moods**	1959	20.00	50.00
SeSac SN-2701	(S)	**Ellington Moods**	1959	20.00	50.00

Label & Catalog #		Title	Year	VG+	NM
Reprise R-6069	(M)	**Afro Bossa**	1962	10.00	25.00
Reprise RS-6069	(S)	**Afro Bossa**	1962	6.00	15.00
Reprise R-6097	(M)	**The Symphonic Ellington**	1964	10.00	25.00
Reprise RS-6097	(S)	**The Symphonic Ellington**	1964	6.00	15.00
Reprise R-6122	(M)	**Hits Of The '60s**	1964	10.00	25.00
Reprise RS-6122	(S)	**Hits Of The '60s**	1964	6.00	15.00
Reprise R-6141	(M)	**Mary Poppins**	1965	10.00	25.00
Reprise RS-6141	(S)	**Mary Poppins**	1965	6.00	15.00
Reprise R-6154	(M)	**Ellington '66**	1965	10.00	25.00
Reprise RS-6154	(S)	**Ellington '66**	1965	6.00	15.00
Reprise R-6168	(M)	**Will Big Bands Ever Come Back?**	1965	10.00	25.00
Reprise RS-6168	(S)	**Will Big Bands Ever Come Back?**	1965	6.00	15.00
Reprise R-6185	(M)	**Concert In The Virgin Islands**	1965	10.00	25.00
Reprise RS-6185	(S)	**Concert In The Virgin Islands**	1965	6.00	15.00
Reprise R-6234	(M)	**Duke Ellington's Greatest Hits**	1966	8.00	20.00
Reprise RS-6234	(S)	**Duke Ellington's Greatest Hits**	1966	6.00	15.00
Verve V-8701	(M)	**Soul Call**	1967	6.00	15.00
Verve V6-8701	(S)	**Soul Call**	1967	5.00	12.00

— Verve albums above have black labels with "MGM Records" on the bottom.—

ELLINGTON, DUKE / BUCK CLAYTON

Columbia CL-933	(M)	**American Jazz Festival At Newport '56**	1956	16.00	40.00

— Columbia albums above have six white on black "eye" logos on each label.—

ELLINGTON, DUKE, & CHARLES MINGUS & MAX ROACH

United Arts. UAJ-14017	(M)	**Money Jungle**	1962	20.00	50.00
United Arts. UAJS-15017	(S)	**Money Jungle**	1962	16.00	40.00
Solid State SM-18022	(M)	**Money Jungle**	1968	6.00	15.00

(Solid State 18022 is a reissue of United Artists 15017.)

ELLINGTON, MERCER

Mercer Kennedy Ellington, Duke's son, is a traditional jazz-based trumpet player and composer.

Coral CRL-57225	(M)	**Stepping Into Swing Society**	1958	16.00	40.00
Coral CRL-757225	(S)	**Stepping Into Swing Society**	1958	12.00	30.00
Coral CRL-57293	(M)	**Colors In Rhythm**	1959	16.00	40.00
Coral CRL-757293	(S)	**Colors In Rhythm**	1959	12.00	30.00

ELLINGTONIANS, THE

The Ellingtonians are members of the Ellington orchestra. For additional listings refer to The Duke's Men.

Mercer LP-1004	(10")	**The Ellingtonians With Al Hibbler**	1951	40.00	100.00

ELLIOTT, DON

Donald Elliott Helfman is a modern jazz trumpet, vibraphone and mellophone player and composer. For additional listings refer to Marty Bell; Al Collins; Bob Corwin; Eddie Costa / Mat Mathews & Don Elliott; Paul Desmond; The Nutty Squirrels; Dinah Washington / Terry Gibbs & Max Roach & Don Elliott..

Savoy MG-9033	(10")	**The Versatile Don Elliott**	1953	60.00	150.00
Vanguard VRS-8016	(10")	**Doubles In Brass**	1954	40.00	100.00
RCA Victor LJM-1007	(M)	**Don Elliott Quintet**	1954	24.00	60.00

— RCA albums above have black labels with "Long Play" on the bottom.—

Bethlehem BCP-12	(M)	**Mellophone**	1955	20.00	50.00
Bethlehem BCP-15	(M)	**Don Elliott Sings**	1955	20.00	50.00
ABC-Paramount ABC-106	(M)	**Musical Offering**	1956	16.00	40.00
ABC-Paramount ABC-142	(M)	**Don Elliott At The Modern Jazz Room**	1956	16.00	40.00
ABC-Paramount ABC-190	(M)	**The Voice Of Don Elliott**	1957	16.00	40.00
ABC-Paramount ABC-228	(M)	**Jamaica Jazz**	1958	16.00	40.00
ABC-Paramount ABCS-228	(S)	**Jamaica Jazz**	1958	12.00	30.00
Hallmark 317	(M)	**Pal Joey**	1957	20.00	50.00
Decca DL-9208	(M)	**The Mello Sound**	1958	16.00	40.00
Decca DL-79208	(S)	**The Mello Sound**	1958	12.00	30.00
Design DLP-69	(M)	**Music For The Sensational 60s**	196?	5.00	12.00
Design DLPS-69	(S)	**Music For The Sensational 60s**	196?	4.00	10.00

ELLIOTT, DON, & RUSTY DEDRICK

Riverside RLP-2517	(10")	**Six Valves**	1955	40.00	100.00
Riverside RLP-12-218	(M)	**Counterpoint For Six Valves**	1956	40.00	100.00

(Riverside 218 is a reissue of 2517 plus four tracks.)

— Riverside albums above have blue on white labels.—

Riverside RLP-12-218	(M)	**Counterpoint For Six Valves**	195?	16.00	40.00

— — Riverside albums above have blue mono or black stereo labels with a reel & mike logo on top.—

Label & Catalog #		Title	Year	VG+	NM
Jazzland JLP-15	(M)	**Double Trumpet Doings**	1960	16.00	40.00
Jazzland JLP-915	(S)	**Double Trumpet Doings**	1960	12.00	30.00
		(Jazzland 15 is a reissue of Riverside 218.)			
ELLIOTT, DON / SAM MOST					
Vanguard VRS-8522	(M)	**Doubles In Jazz**	1957	24.00	60.00
		(Vanguard 8522 is an abridged reissue of 8106 and 8014.)			
Jazztone J-1256	(M)	**Doubles In Jazz**	1957	16.00	40.00
		(Jazztone 1256 is a reissue of Vanguard 8522.)			
ELLIOTT, DON / CAL TJADER					
Savoy MG-12054	(M)	**Vib-rations**	1956	24.00	60.00
		(Savoy 12054 is a reissue of 9033 and 9036.)			
ELLIS, ANITA					
Anita Ellis is a jazz-based vocalist.					
Epic LN-3280	(M)	**I Wonder What Became Of Me**	1956	20.00	50.00
Epic LN-3419	(M)	**Him**	1958	20.00	50.00
Elektra EKL-179	(M)	**The World In My Arms**	1960	16.00	40.00
Elektra EKS-7179	(S)	**The World In My Arms**	1960	20.00	50.00
ELLIS, DON					
Donald Ellis is a modern jazz trumpet player, composer and band leader.					
New Jazz NJLP-8257	(M)	**New Ideas**	1961	20.00	50.00
		—New Jazz albums above have purple labels.—			
New Jazz NJLP-8257	(M)	**New Ideas**	1965	10.00	25.00
		—New Jazz albums above have blue labels with a trident logo on the right side.—			
Pacific Jazz PJ-55	(M)	**Essence**	1962	16.00	40.00
Pacific Jazz ST-55	(S)	**Essence**	1962	12.00	30.00
Pacific Jazz PJ-10112	(M)	**Don Ellis 'Live' At Monterey**	1967	8.00	20.00
Pacific Jazz ST-20112	(S)	**Don Ellis 'Live' At Monterey**	1967	6.00	15.00
Pacific Jazz PJ-10123	(M)	**Live In 3 2/3 Time**	1967	8.00	20.00
Pacific Jazz ST-20123	(S)	**Live In 3 2/3 Time**	1967	6.00	15.00
Columbia CL-2785	(M)	**Electric Bath**	1968	12.00	30.00
Columbia CS-9585	(S)	**Electric Bath**	1968	6.00	15.00
Columbia CS-9668	(S)	**Shock Treatment**	1968	6.00	15.00
Columbia CS-9721	(S)	**Autumn**	1969	6.00	15.00
Columbia CS-9889	(S)	**The New Don Ellis Band Goes Underground**	1969	6.00	15.00
		—Columbia albums above have "360 Sound" in white on the bottom of the label.—			
Prestige PRST-7607	(S)	**New Ideas**	1969	6.00	15.00
		(Prestige 7607 is a reissue of New Jazz 8257.)			
		—Prestige albums above have blue labels with a trident logo on top.—			
ELLIS, HERB					
Mitchell Herbert Ellis is a modern jazz guitar player and composer. For additional listings refer to Blossom Dearie; Andre Previn & Herb Ellis.					
Norgran MGN-1081	(M)	**Ellis In Wonderland**	1956	40.00	100.00
Verve MGV-8171	(M)	**Ellis In Wonderland**	1957	20.00	50.00
		(Verve 8171 is a reissue of Norgran 1081.)			
Verve MGV-8252	(M)	**Nothing But The Blues**	1958	20.00	50.00
Verve MGV-8278	(M)	**Herb Ellis**	1958	*Unreleased*	
Verve MGV-8311	(M)	**Herb Ellis Meets Jimmy Giuffre**	1959	20.00	50.00
Verve MGVS-6045	(S)	**Herb Ellis Meets Jimmy Giuffre**	1960	16.00	40.00
Verve MGV-8381	(M)	**Thank You, Charlie Christian**	1960	20.00	50.00
Verve MGVS-6164	(S)	**Thank You, Charlie Christian**	1960	16.00	40.00
		—Verve albums above have black labels with "Verve Records, Inc." on the bottom.—			
Verve V-8171	(M)	**Ellis In Wonderland**	1961	8.00	20.00
Verve V-8252	(M)	**Nothing But The Blues**	1961	8.00	20.00
Verve V-8311	(M)	**Herb Ellis Meets Jimmy Giuffre**	1961	8.00	20.00
Verve V6-8311	(S)	**Herb Ellis Meets Jimmy Giuffre**	1961	6.00	15.00
Verve V-8381	(M)	**Thank You, Charlie Christian**	1961	8.00	20.00
Verve V6-8381	(S)	**Thank You, Charlie Christian**	1961	6.00	15.00
Verve V-8448	(M)	**Softly... But With That Feeling**	1962	12.00	30.00
Verve V6-8448	(S)	**Softly... But With That Feeling**	1962	10.00	25.00
		—Verve albums above have black labels with "MGM Records" on the bottom.—			
Epic LA-16034	(M)	**The Midnight Roll**	1962	12.00	30.00
Epic BA-17034	(S)	**The Midnight Roll**	1962	10.00	25.00

Label & Catalog #		Title	Year	VG+	NM
Epic LA-16036	(M)	**Three Guitars In Bossa Nova Time**	1963	10.00	25.00
Epic BA-17036	(S)	**Three Guitars In Bossa Nova Time**	1963	8.00	20.00

(Epic16036 also features Laurindo Almeida and Johnny Gray.)

Epic LA-16039	(M)	**Herb Ellis & "Stuff" Smith Together**	1963	12.00	30.00
Epic BA-17039	(S)	**Herb Ellis & "Stuff" Smith Together**	1963	10.00	25.00
Columbia CL-2330	(M)	**Herb Ellis Guitar**	1965	8.00	20.00
Columbia CS-9130	(S)	**Herb Ellis Guitar**	1965	6.00	15.00

—Columbia albums above have "360 Sound " in white on the bottom of the label.—

Dot DLP-3678	(M)	**The Man With The Guitar**	1965	8.00	20.00
Dot DLP-25678	(S)	**The Man With The Guitar**	1965	6.00	15.00

ELMAN, ZIGGY

Harry Finkelman, aka Ziggy Elman, is a traditional jazz multi-instrumentalist, specializing on the trumpet.

MGM E-163	(10")	**Dancing With Zig**	1952	20.00	50.00
MGM E-3389	(M)	**Sentimental Trumpet**	1956	16.00	40.00

ELSTAK, NEDLEY

ESP-Disk' 1076	(S)	**The Machine**	1969	6.00	15.00

EMMONS, BUDDY

Buddy Emmons is a country & western-based steel guitar player.

Mercury MG-20843	(M)	**Steel Guitar Jazz**	1963	30.00	75.00
Mercury SR-60843	(S)	**Steel Guitar Jazz**	1963	40.00	100.00

—Mercury albums above have silver on black labels.—

ENEVOLDSEN, BOBBY

Robert Enevoldsen is a West Coast jazz valve trombone player.

Nocturne NLP-6	(10")	**Bob Enevoldsen Quintet**	1954	60.00	150.00
Liberty LJH-6008	(M)	**Smorgasboard**	1956	20.00	50.00
Tampa TP-14	(M)	**Reflections In Jazz** *(Colored vinyl)*	1957	40.00	100.00
Tampa TP-14	(M)	**Reflections In Jazz**	1958	20.00	50.00

ENNIS, ETHEL

Ethel Ennis is a big band-based jazz vocalist.

Jubilee JLP-1021	(M)	**Lullabies For Losers**	1956	20.00	50.00
Jubilee JLP-5024	(M)	**Ethel Ennis Sings**	1963	8.00	20.00
Jubilee SDJLP-5024	(S)	**Ethel Ennis Sings**	1963	10.00	25.00
RCA Victor LPM-2984	(M)	**Eyes For You**	1964	8.00	20.00
RCA Victor LSP-2984	(S)	**Eyes For You**	1964	10.00	25.00

—RCA albums above have black labels with "Mono" or "Living Stereo" on the bottom.—

ERICSON, ROLF

Swedish born Rolf Ericson is a traditional jazz-based trumpet player.

EmArcy MG-36106	(M)	**Rolf Ericson And His All American Stars**	1957	20.00	50.00

—EmArcy albums above have blue labels with silver print.—

ERVIN, BOOKER

Booker Ervin Jr. is a modern jazz tenor saxophone player. For additional listings refer to Roy Haynes; Don Patterson; Mal Waldron.

Savoy MG-12154	(M)	**Cookin'**	1960	20.00	50.00
Candid CD-8104	(M)	**That's It**	1962	20.00	50.00
Candid CS-9104	(S)	**That's It**	1962	16.00	40.00
Blue Note BLP-4134	(M)	**Back From The Gig**	1963	*Unreleased*	
Blue Note BST-84134	(S)	**Back From The Gig**	1963	*Unreleased*	
Prestige PRLP-7293	(M)	**Exultation!**	1964	12.00	30.00
Prestige PRST-7293	(S)	**Exultation!**	1964	10.00	25.00
Prestige PRLP-7295	(M)	**The Freedom Book**	1964	12.00	30.00
Prestige PRST-7295	(S)	**The Freedom Book**	1964	10.00	25.00
Prestige PRLP-7318	(M)	**The Song Book**	1964	12.00	30.00
Prestige PRST-7318	(S)	**The Song Book**	1964	10.00	25.00
Prestige PRLP-7340	(M)	**The Blues Book**	1964	12.00	30.00
Prestige PRST-7340	(S)	**The Blues Book**	1964	10.00	25.00
Prestige PRLP-7386	(M)	**The Space Book**	1965	10.00	25.00
Prestige PRST-7386	(S)	**The Space Book**	1965	8.00	20.00
Prestige PRLP-7417	(M)	**Groovin' High**	1966	10.00	25.00
Prestige PRST-7417	(S)	**Groovin' High**	1966	8.00	20.00
Prestige PRLP-7455	(M)	**Settin' The Pace**	1967	10.00	25.00
Prestige PRST-7455	(S)	**Settin' The Pace**	1967	8.00	20.00

(Prestige 7455 also features Dexter Gordon.)

Label & Catalog #		Title	Year	VG+	NM
Prestige PRLP-7462	(M)	**The Trance**	1967	10.00	25.00
Prestige PRST-7462	(S)	**The Trance**	1967	8.00	20.00
Prestige PRLP-7499	(M)	**Heavy!**	1967	10.00	25.00
Prestige PRST-7499	(S)	**Heavy!**	1967	8.00	20.00
		—Prestige albums above have blue labels with a trident logo on the right side.—			
Pacific Jazz PJ-10199	(M)	**Structurally Sound**	1968	16.00	40.00
Pacific Jazz ST-20199	(S)	**Structurally Sound**	1968	8.00	20.00
Blue Note BST-84283	(S)	**The In Between**	1969	12.00	30.00
Blue Note BST-84314	(S)	**Booker Ervin**	1969	Unreleased	
		—Blue Note albums above have blue on white labels with "A Division of Liberty Records."—			
ERWIN, PEE WEE					
George "Pee Wee" Erwin is a traditional jazz trumpet player.					
Urania UJLP-1202	(M)	**Accent On Dixieland**	1955	16.00	40.00
Brunswick BL-54011	(M)	**The Land Of Dixie**	1956	16.00	40.00
Cadence CLP-1011	(M)	**Dixieland At Grandview Inn**	1956	16.00	40.00
EUREKA BRASS BAND, THE					
Pax LP-9001	(10")	**New Orleans Parade**	1954	20.00	50.00
Folkways FA-2642	(M)	**Music Of New Orleans**	195?	20.00	50.00
Atlantic 1408	(M)	**The Eureka Brass Band**	1963	8.00	20.00
Atlantic SD-1408	(S)	**The Eureka Brass Band**	1963	6.00	15.00
		—Atlantic albums above have multi-color labels with a black fan logo.—			
EUROPEAN JAZZ QUARTET, THE					
Pulse 3001	(M)	**New Jazz From The Old World**	1957	20.00	50.00
EVANS, BILL					
William Evans is a modern jazz pianist. For additional listings refer to Cannonball Adderley; Bob Brookmeyer & Bill Evans; Herbie Mann; Gary McFarland; and the Jazzy Soundtracks section under MGM.					
Riverside RLP-12-223	(M)	**New Jazz Conceptions** *(Photo cover)*	1958	250.00	500.00
		—Riverside albums above have blue on white labels.—			
Riverside RLP-12-223	(M)	**New Jazz Conceptions**	1958	12.00	30.00
Riverside RLP-12-291	(M)	**Everybody Digs Bill Evans**	1958	16.00	40.00
Riverside RLP-1129	(S)	**Everybody Digs Bill Evans**	1959	12.00	30.00
Riverside RLP-12-315	(M)	**Portrait In Jazz**	1959	16.00	40.00
Riverside RLP-1162	(S)	**Portrait In Jazz**	1959	12.00	30.00
Riverside RLP-351	(M)	**Explorations**	1961	12.00	30.00
Riverside RS-9351	(S)	**Explorations**	1961	10.00	25.00
Riverside RLP-376	(M)	**Sunday At The Village Vanguard**	1961	12.00	30.00
Riverside RS-9376	(S)	**Sunday At The Village Vanguard**	1961	10.00	25.00
Riverside RLP-399	(M)	**Waltz For Debby**	1961	12.00	30.00
Riverside RS-9399	(S)	**Waltz For Debby**	1961	10.00	25.00
Riverside RLP-428	(M)	**Moon Beams**	1962	12.00	30.00
Riverside RS-9428	(S)	**Moon Beams**	1962	10.00	25.00
Riverside RLP-445	(M)	**Interplay**	1963	12.00	30.00
Riverside RS-9445	(S)	**Interplay**	1963	10.00	25.00
Riverside RLP-473	(M)	**How My Heart Sings!**	1964	12.00	30.00
Riverside RS-9473	(S)	**How My Heart Sings!**	1964	10.00	25.00
		—Riverside albums above have blue mono or black stereo labels with a reel & mike logo on top.—			
Riverside RLP-487	(M)	**Bill Evans At Shelly's Manne-Hole, Hollywood, California**	1965	10.00	25.00
Riverside RS-9487	(S)	**Bill Evans At Shelly's Manne-Hole, Hollywood, California**	1965	8.00	20.00
		—Riverside albums above blue labels with "Orpheum Productions" on the bottom.—			
Riverside RM-3001	(M)	**Polka Dots And Moonbeams**	1967	6.00	15.00
Riverside RS-3001	(S)	**Polka Dots And Moonbeams** *(Riverside 3001 is a reissue of 9428.)*	1967	5.00	12.00
Riverside RM-3006	(M)	**Live At The Village Vanguard**	1967	6.00	15.00
Riverside RS-3006	(S)	**Live At The Village Vanguard** *(Riverside 3006 is a reissue of 9376.)*	1967	5.00	12.00
Riverside RS-3013	(S)	**Live At Shelly's Manne-Hole** *(Riverside 3013 is a reissue of 9487.)*	1968	5.00	12.00
Riverside RS-3042	(S)	**Peace Pieces**	1969	5.00	12.00
Verve V-8497	(M)	**Empathy**	1962	12.00	30.00
Verve V6-8497	(S)	**Empathy** *(Verve 8497 also features Shelly Manne.)*	1962	10.00	25.00
Verve V-8526	(M)	**Conversations With Myself**	1963	8.00	20.00
Verve V6-8526	(S)	**Conversations With Myself**	1963	6.00	15.00

Label & Catalog #		Title	Year	VG+	NM
Verve V-8578	*(M)*	**Bill Evans Trio '64**	*1964*	**8.00**	**20.00**
Verve V6-8578	*(S)*	**Bill Evans Trio '64**	*1964*	**6.00**	**15.00**
Verve V-8613	*(M)*	**Bill Evans Trio '65**	*1965*	**8.00**	**20.00**
Verve V6-8613	*(S)*	**Bill Evans Trio '65**	*1965*	**6.00**	**15.00**
Verve V-8640	*(M)*	**Bill Evans Trio With Symphony Orchestra**	*1965*	**6.00**	**15.00**
Verve V6-8640	*(S)*	**Bill Evans Trio With Symphony Orchestra**	*1965*	**5.00**	**12.00**
Verve V-8655	*(M)*	**Intermodulation**	*1966*	**6.00**	**15.00**
Verve V6-8655	*(S)*	**Intermodulation**	*1966*	**5.00**	**12.00**
		(Verve 8655 also features Jim Hall.)			
Verve V-8675	*(M)*	**A Simple Matter Of Conviction**	*1966*	**6.00**	**15.00**
Verve V6-8675	*(S)*	**A Simple Matter Of Conviction**	*1966*	**5.00**	**12.00**
		(Verve 8675 also features Eddie Gomez and Shelly Manne.)			
Verve V-8683	*(M)*	**Bill Evans At Town Hall**	*1966*	**6.00**	**15.00**
Verve V6-8683	*(S)*	**Bill Evans At Town Hall**	*1966*	**5.00**	**12.00**
Verve V-8727	*(M)*	**Further Conversations With Myself**	*1967*	**6.00**	**15.00**
Verve V6-8727	*(S)*	**Further Conversations With Myself**	*1967*	**5.00**	**12.00**
Verve V-8747	*(M)*	**The Best Of Bill Evans**	*1968*	**6.00**	**15.00**
Verve V6-8747	*(S)*	**The Best Of Bill Evans**	*1968*	**4.00**	**10.00**
Verve V6-8762	*(S)*	**Bill Evans At The Montreux Jazz Festival**	*1968*	**6.00**	**15.00**
Verve V6-8777	*(S)*	**What's New**	*1969*	**4.00**	**10.00**
		(Verve 8777 also features Jeremy Steig.)			
Verve V6-8792	*(S)*	**Bill Evans Alone**	*1969*	**4.00**	**10.00**

— Verve albums above have black labels with "MGM Records" on the bottom.—

EVANS, BILL, & JIM HALL

Label & Catalog #		Title	Year	VG+	NM
United Arts. UAJ-14003	*(M)*	**Undercurrent**	*1962*	**20.00**	**50.00**
United Arts. UAJS-15003	*(S)*	**Undercurrent**	*1962*	**16.00**	**40.00**
Solid State SS-18018	*(S)*	**Undercurrent**	*1968*	**6.00**	**15.00**
		(Solid State 18018 is a reissue of United Artists 15003.)			

EVANS, DOC

Paul "Doc" Evans is a traditional jazz cornet player.

Label & Catalog #		Title	Year	VG+	NM
Soma MG-100 (12")	*(M)*	**Dixieland Concert**	*1953*	**20.00**	**50.00**
Soma MG-101	*(10")*	**Dixieland Concert**	*1954*	**20.00**	**50.00**
Soma MG-1201	*(M)*	**Classic Jazz At Carleton**	*1954*	**16.00**	**40.00**
Audiophile AP-11	*(M)*	**Doc Evans & His Band, Vol. 1**	*1953*	**16.00**	**40.00**
Audiophile AP-12	*(M)*	**Doc Evans & His Band, Vol. 2**	*1953*	**16.00**	**40.00**
Audiophile AP-29	*(M)*	**Dixieland Session**	*1955*	**16.00**	**40.00**
Audiophile AP-31	*(M)*	**The Cornet Artistry Of Doc Evans**	*1955*	**16.00**	**40.00**
Audiophile AP-33	*(M)*	**Traditional Jazz**	*1955*	**16.00**	**40.00**
Audiophile AP-34	*(M)*	**Traditional Jazz**	*195?*	**16.00**	**40.00**
Audiophile AP-44	*(M)*	**Traditional Jazz**	*195?*	**16.00**	**40.00**
Audiophile AP-45	*(M)*	**Traditional Jazz**	*195?*	**16.00**	**40.00**
Audiophile AP-50	*(M)*	**Classics Of The '20s**	*195?*	**16.00**	**40.00**
Audiophile XL-328	*(M)*	**Traditional Jazz**	*195?*	**16.00**	**40.00**
Audiophile XL-329	*(M)*	**Traditional Jazz**	*195?*	**16.00**	**40.00**
Concert-Disc CS-48	*(S)*	**Muskrat Ramble**	*196?*	**8.00**	**20.00**
Audiophile APS-5968	*(S)*	**Reminiscing In Dixieland** *(Red vinyl)*	*196?*	**12.00**	**30.00**

EVANS, GIL

Ian Ernest Gilmore Green, aka Gil Evans, is a traditional jazz-based piano and keyboards player, arranger and composer.

Label & Catalog #		Title	Year	VG+	NM
RCA Victor LPM-1057	*(M)*	**There Comes A Time**	*1955*	**30.00**	**75.00**
		—RCA albums above have black labels with "Long Play" on the bottom.—			
Prestige PRLP-7120	*(M)*	**Gil Evans Plus Ten**	*1957*	**30.00**	**75.00**
		—Prestige albums above have yellow labels with a W. 50th St., NYC address.—			
World Pacific WP-1246	*(M)*	**New Bottle, Old Wine**	*1958*	**20.00**	**50.00**
World Pacific ST-1011	*(S)*	**New Bottle, Old Wine**	*1958*	**16.00**	**40.00**
World Pacific WP-1270	*(M)*	**Great Jazz Standards**	*1959*	**20.00**	**50.00**
World Pacific ST-1027	*(S)*	**Great Jazz Standards**	*1959*	**16.00**	**40.00**
New Jazz NJLP-8215	*(M)*	**Big Stuff**	*1959*	**20.00**	**50.00**
		(New Jazz 8215 is a reissue of Prestige 7120.)			
		—New Jazz albums above have purple labels.—			
New Jazz NJLP-8215	*(M)*	**Big Stuff**	*1965*	**10.00**	**25.00**
		—New Jazz albums above have blue labels with a trident logo on the right side.—			
Pacific Jazz PJ-28	*(M)*	**America's #1 Arranger**	*1961*	**12.00**	**30.00**
		(Pacific Jazz 28 is a reissue of World Pacific 1270.)			
Pacific Jazz PJ-40	*(M)*	**Cannonball Adderley/Gil Evans**	*1962*	**12.00**	**30.00**
Pacific Jazz ST-40	*(S)*	**Cannonball Adderley/Gil Evans**	*1962*	**10.00**	**25.00**

Label & Catalog #		Title	Year	VG+	NM
Impulse A-4	(M)	**Out Of The Cool**	1961	12.00	30.00
Impulse AS-4	(S)	**Out Of The Cool**	1961	10.00	25.00
Impulse A-9	(M)	**In The Hot**	1961	12.00	30.00
Impulse AS-9	(S)	**In The Hot**	1961	10.00	25.00
		—Impulse albums above have orange & black labels.—			
Impulse AS-4	(S)	**Out Of The Cool**	1968	4.00	10.00
Impulse AS-9	(S)	**In The Hot**	1968	4.00	10.00
		—Impulse albums above have red & black labels with the "abc" logo on top.—			
Verve V-8555	(M)	**The Individualism Of Gil Evans**	1963	10.00	25.00
Verve V6-8555	(S)	**The Individualism Of Gil Evans**	1963	8.00	20.00
		—Verve albums above have black labels with "MGM Records" on the bottom.—			

EVANS, LEE

Capitol T-1847	(M)	**The Lee Evans Trio**	1963	10.00	20.00
Capitol ST-1847	(S)	**The Lee Evans Trio**	1963	6.00	15.00

EVANS, RICHARD

Richard Evans is a modern jazz bass player.

Argo LP-658	(M)	**Richard's Almanac**	1960	16.00	40.00
Argo LPS-658	(S)	**Richard's Almanac**	1960	12.00	30.00

EWELL, DON

Donald Ewell is a traditional jazz pianist.

Windin' Ball LP-101	(10")	**Don Ewell**	1953	20.00	50.00
Windin' Ball LP-102	(10")	**Don Ewell & Mama Yancey**	1953	20.00	50.00
Windin' Ball LP-103	(10")	**Don Ewell Plays Tunes Played By The King Oliver Band**	1953	20.00	50.00
Good Time Jazz L-12021	(M)	**Music To Listen To Don Ewell By**	1955	16.00	40.00
Good Time Jazz L-12043	(M)	**The Man Here Plays Fine Piano**	1956	16.00	40.00
Good Time Jazz S-10043	(S)	**The Man Here Plays Fine Piano**	1960	10.00	25.00
Good Time Jazz L-12046	(M)	**Free 'N Easy**	1956	16.00	40.00
Good Time Jazz S-10046	(S)	**Free 'N Easy**	1960	10.00	25.00

EX-HERMANITES, THE: *Refer to* **TERRY GIBBS & BILL HARRIS**

EZELL, WILLIAM

Riverside RLP-1043	(10")	**Gin Mill Jazz**	1954	30.00	75.00

F.

FAGERQUIST, DON

Donald Fagerquist is a traditional jazz-based trumpet player. For additional listings refer to Les Brown.

Mode LP-124	*(M)*	**Music To Fill A Void**	*1957*	**40.00**	**100.00**

FAMOUS CASTLE JAZZ BAND, THE

Good Time Jazz L-12030	*(M)*	**The Famous Castle Jazz Band In Hi-Fi**	*1957*	**16.00**	**40.00**
Stereo Records S-7021	*(S)*	**The Famous Castle Jazz Band In Hi-Fi**	*1958*	**14.00**	**35.00**
Good Time Jazz S-7021	*(S)*	**The Famous Castle Jazz Band In Hi-Fi**	*1959*	**12.00**	**30.00**
Good Time Jazz L-12037	*(M)*	**The Five Pennies**	*1959*	**16.00**	**40.00**
Good Time Jazz S-10037	*(S)*	**The Five Pennies**	*1959*	**12.00**	**30.00**

FARLOW, TAL

Talmagde Farlow is a modern jazz guitarist. For additional listings refer to Red Norvo.

Blue Note BLP-5042	*(10")*	**Tal Farlow Quartet**	*1954*	**150.00**	**300.00**
Norgran MGN-19	*(10")*	**The Tal Farlow Album**	*1954*	**60.00**	**150.00**
		(Norgran 19 features cover art by David Stone Martin.)			
Norgran MGN-1014	*(M)*	**The Artistry Of Tal Farlow**	*1955*	**40.00**	**125.00**
Norgran MGN-1027	*(M)*	**The Interpretations Of Tal Farlow**	*1955*	**40.00**	**125.00**
		(Norgran 1027 features cover art by David Stone Martin.)			
Norgran MGN-1030	*(M)*	**A Recital By Tal Farlow**	*1955*	**40.00**	**125.00**
		(Norgran 1030 features cover art by David Stone Martin.)			
Norgran MGN-1047	*(M)*	**The Tal Farlow Album**	*1955*	**40.00**	**100.00**
		(Norgran 1047 is a reissue of 19 with the DSM cover.)			
Norgran MGN-1097	*(M)*	**Autumn In New York**	*1956*	**40.00**	**100.00**
		(Norgran 1097 is a reissue of 1014)			
Norgran MGN-1101	*(M)*	**Fascinating Rhythm**	*1956*	**40.00**	**100.00**
		(Norgran 1101 is a reissue of 1027.)			
Norgran MGN-1102	*(M)*	**Tal**	*1956*	**40.00**	**100.00**
Verve MGV-8011	*(M)*	**The Interpretations Of Tal Farlow**	*1957*	**20.00**	**50.00**
		(Verve 8011 is a reissue of Norgran 1027 with the DSM cover.)			
Verve MGV-8021	*(M)*	**Tal**	*1957*	**20.00**	**50.00**
		(Verve 8021 is a reissue of Norgran 1102.)			
Verve MGV-8123	*(M)*	**A Recital By Tal Farlow**	*1957*	**20.00**	**50.00**
		(Verve 8123 is a reissue of Norgran 1030 with the DSM cover.)			
Verve MGV-8138	*(M)*	**The Tal Farlow Album**	*1957*	**20.00**	**50.00**
		(Verve 8138 is a reissue of Norgran 1047 with the DSM cover.)			
Verve MGV-8184	*(M)*	**Autumn In New York**	*1957*	**20.00**	**50.00**
		(Verve 8184 is a reissue of Norgran 1097.)			
Verve MGV-8201	*(M)*	**The Swinging Guitar Of Tal Farlow**	*1957*	**20.00**	**50.00**
American Rec. Soc. G-418	*(M)*	**The Swinging Guitar Of Tal Farlow**	*1957*	**16.00**	**40.00**
Verve MGV-8289	*(M)*	**This Is Tal Farlow**	*1958*	**20.00**	**50.00**
Verve MGV-8370	*(M)*	**The Guitar Artistry Of Tal Farlow**	*1960*	**20.00**	**50.00**
Verve MGVS-6143	*(S)*	**The Guitar Artistry Of Tal Farlow**	*1960*	**16.00**	**40.00**
Verve MGV-8371	*(M)*	**Tal Farlow Plays The Music Of Harold Arlen**	*1960*	**20.00**	**50.00**
Verve MGVS-6144	*(S)*	**Tal Farlow Plays The Music Of Harold Arlen**	*1960*	*Unreleased*	
		— Verve albums above have black labels with "Verve Records, Inc." on the bottom.—			
Verve V-8011	*(M)*	**The Interpretations Of Tal Farlow**	*1961*	**6.00**	**15.00**
Verve V-8021	*(M)*	**Tal**	*1961*	**6.00**	**15.00**
Verve V-8123	*(M)*	**A Recital By Tal Farlow**	*1961*	**6.00**	**15.00**
Verve V-8138	*(M)*	**The Tal Farlow Album**	*1961*	**6.00**	**15.00**
Verve V-8184	*(M)*	**Autumn In New York**	*1961*	**6.00**	**15.00**
Verve V-8201	*(M)*	**The Swinging Guitar Of Tal Farlow**	*1961*	**6.00**	**15.00**
Verve V-8289	*(M)*	**This Is Tal Farlow**	*1961*	**6.00**	**15.00**
Verve V-8370	*(M)*	**The Guitar Artistry Of Tal Farlow**	*1961*	**6.00**	**15.00**
Verve V6-8370	*(S)*	**The Guitar Artistry Of Tal Farlow**	*1961*	**5.00**	**12.00**
Verve V-8371	*(M)*	**Tal Farlow Plays The Music Of Harold Arlen**	*1961*	**6.00**	**15.00**
		— Verve albums above have black labels with "MGM Records" on the bottom.—			
Prestige PRST-7732	*(S)*	**Tal Farlow Returns 1969**	*1969*	**6.00**	**15.00**
		—Prestige albums above have blue labels with a trident logo on top.—			

FARMER, ART

Arthur Farmer is a modern jazz trumpet and flugel horn player. For additional listings refer to Clifford Brown & Art Farmer; Eddie Costa & Art Farmer; Bennie Green; The Jazztet; The Prestige Blues Swingers; Andre Previn; the Jazzy Soundtracks section under MGM and United Artists; and the Various Artists section under Savoy.

Label & Catalog #		Title	Year	VG+	NM
Prestige PRLP-162	(10")	**Art Farmer Septet**	1953	100.00	200.00
Prestige PRLP-177	(10")	**Art Farmer Quintet Featuring Sonny Rollins**	1954	100.00	200.00
Prestige PRLP-181	(10")	**Art Farmer Quintet**	1954	100.00	200.00
Prestige PRLP-193	(10")	**Art Farmer Quartet**	1954	100.00	200.00
Prestige PRLP-209	(10")	**Art Farmer Quintet**	1955	100.00	200.00
Prestige PRLP-7017	(M)	**Art Farmer Quintet Featuring Gigi Gryce**	1956	40.00	100.00
Prestige PRLP-7031	(M)	**Art Farmer Septet**	1956	40.00	100.00
		(Prestige 7031 is a reissue of 162.)			
Prestige PRLP-7062	(M)	**Two Trumpets**	1956	40.00	100.00
		(Prestige 7062 also features Donald Byrd.)			
Prestige PRLP-7085	(M)	**When Farmer Met Gryce**	1957	40.00	100.00
		(Prestige 7085 is a reissue of 181 and 209.)			
Prestige PRLP-7092	(M)	**Three Trumpets**	1957	40.00	100.00
		(Prestige 7062 also features Donald Byrd and Idriss Suliman.)			
		—Prestige albums above have yellow labels with a W. 50th St, NYC address.—			
Prestige PRLP-7344	(M)	**Trumpets All Out** *(2 LPs)*	1964	20.00	50.00
Prestige PRST-7344	(E)	**Trumpets All Out** *(2 LPs)*	1964	14.00	35.00
		(Prestige 7344 is a reissue of 7062 and 7092.)			
		—Prestige albums above have blue labels with a trident logo on the right side.—			
New Jazz NJLP-8203	(M)	**Farmer's Market**	1958	40.00	100.00
		—New Jazz albums above have a yellow Prestige label.—			
New Jazz NJLP-8203	(M)	**Farmer's Market**	1958	20.00	50.00
New Jazz NJLP-8258	(M)	**Early Art**	1961	16.00	40.00
		(New Jazz 8258 is a reissue of Prestige 177 and 193.)			
New Jazz NJLP-8278	(M)	**Work Of Art**	1962	16.00	40.00
		(New Jazz 8278 is a reissue of Prestige 7031.)			
New Jazz NJLP-8289	(M)	**Evening In Casablanca**	1962	16.00	40.00
		(New Jazz 8289 is a reissue of Prestige 7017.)			
		—New Jazz albums above have purple labels.—			
New Jazz NJLP-8203	(M)	**Farmer's Market**	1965	10.00	25.00
New Jazz NJLP-8258	(M)	**Early Art**	1965	10.00	25.00
New Jazz NJLP-8278	(M)	**Work Of Art**	1965	10.00	25.00
New Jazz NJLP-8289	(M)	**Evening In Casablanca**	1965	10.00	25.00
		—New Jazz albums above have blue labels with a trident logo on the right side.—			
ABC-Paramount ABC-200	(M)	**Last Night When We Were Young**	1958	20.00	50.00
Contemporary C-3554	(M)	**Portrait Of Art Farmer**	1958	20.00	50.00
Stereo Records S-7027	(S)	**Portrait Of Art Farmer**	1958	18.00	45.00
Contemporary S-7027	(S)	**Portrait Of Art Farmer**	1959	16.00	40.00
		—Contemporary stereo albums have gold & black labels.—			
United Arts. UAL-4007	(M)	**Modern Art**	1958	20.00	50.00
United Arts. UAS-5007	(S)	**Modern Art**	1958	16.00	40.00
United Arts. UAL-4047	(M)	**Brass Shout**	1959	20.00	50.00
United Arts. UAS-5047	(S)	**Brass Shout**	1959	16.00	40.00
United Arts. UAL-4062	(M)	**Aztec Suite**	1959	20.00	50.00
United Arts. UAS-5062	(S)	**Aztec Suite**	1959	16.00	40.00
United Arts. UAL-4079	(M)	**Brass Shout**	1960	16.00	40.00
United Arts. UAS-5079	(S)	**Brass Shout**	1960	12.00	30.00
United Arts. UAL-4082	(M)	**Aztec Suite**	1960	16.00	40.00
United Arts. UAS-5082	(S)	**Aztec Suite**	1960	12.00	30.00
Argo LP-678	(M)	**Art**	1961	12.00	30.00
Argo LPS-678	(S)	**Art**	1961	10.00	25.00
Argo LP-738	(M)	**Perception**	1964	12.00	30.00
Argo LPS-738	(S)	**Perception**	1964	10.00	25.00
Mercury MG-20766	(M)	**Listen To Art Farmer & The Orchestra**	1963	10.00	25.00
Mercury SR-60766	(S)	**Listen To Art Farmer & The Orchestra**	1963	8.00	20.00
Atlantic 1412	(M)	**Interaction**	1963	12.00	30.00
Atlantic SD-1412	(S)	**Interaction**	1963	10.00	25.00
Atlantic 1421	(M)	**Live At The Half Note**	1964	12.00	30.00
Atlantic SD-1421	(S)	**Live At The Half Note**	1964	10.00	25.00
Atlantic 1430	(M)	**To Sweden With Love**	1964	10.00	25.00
Atlantic SD-1430	(S)	**To Sweden With Love**	1964	8.00	20.00
Atlantic 1442	(M)	**Sing Me Softly Of The Blues**	1965	10.00	25.00
Atlantic SD-1442	(S)	**Sing Me Softly Of The Blues**	1965	8.00	20.00
		—Atlantic albums above have multi-color labels with a black fan logo.—			

Label & Catalog #		Title	Year	VG+	NM
Scepter S-521	(M)	**The Many Faces Of Art Farmer**	1964	10.00	25.00
Scepter SS-521	(S)	**The Many Faces Of Art Farmer**	1964	8.00	20.00
Columbia CL-2588	(M)	**Baroque Sketches**	1966	10.00	25.00
Columbia CS-9388	(S)	**Baroque Sketches**	1966	8.00	20.00
Columbia CL-2649	(M)	**The Time And The Place**	1967	10.00	25.00
Columbia CS-9449	(S)	**The Time And The Place**	1967	6.00	15.00
Columbia CL-2746	(M)	**Art Farmer Plays The Great Jazz Hits**	1967	10.00	25.00
Columbia CS-9546	(S)	**Art Farmer Plays The Great Jazz Hits**	1967	6.00	15.00

—Columbia albums above have "360 Sound" in white on the bottom of the label.—

Prestige PRST-7665	(E)	**Early Art**	1969	5.00	12.00

(Prestige 7665 is a reissue of New Jazz 8258.)

—Prestige albums above have blue labels with a trident logo on top.—

FARMER, ART / ART TAYLOR

Prestige PRLP-7342	(M)	**Hard Cookin'** *(2 LPs)*	1964	16.00	40.00
Prestige PRST-7342	(E)	**Hard Cookin'** *(2 LPs)*	1964	10.00	25.00

(Prestige 7344 reissues 7017 and New Jazz 8219, "Taylor's Tenors.")

FAYE, FRANCES

Frances Faye is a jazz-based pianist and vocalist.

Capitol H-512	(10")	**No Reservations**	1954	30.00	75.00
Capitol T-512	(M)	**No Reservations**	1955	20.00	50.00

—Capitol albums above have turquoise labels.—

Capitol T-512	(M)	**No Reservations**	195?	12.00	30.00

—Capitol albums above have black "rainbow" labels with the logo on the left side.—

Bethlehem BCP-23	(M)	**I Am Wild Again**	1955	16.00	40.00
Bethlehem BCP-62	(M)	**Relaxin' With Frances Faye**	1956	16.00	40.00
Columbia CL-873	(M)	**The Beguiling Miss Francis Faye**	1956	16.00	40.00

(Columbia 873 also features Art Van Damme.)

—Columbia albums above have six white on black "eye" logos on each label.—

Bethlehem BCP-6017	(M)	**Frances Faye Sings Folk Songs**	1958	16.00	40.00
Gene Norman GNP-41	(M)	**Caught In The Act**	1958	16.00	40.00
Imperial LP-9059	(M)	**Frances Faye Swings Fats Domino**	1958	16.00	40.00
Imperial LP-12059	(S)	**Frances Faye Swings Fats Domino**	1959	16.00	40.00
Verve MGV-2147	(M)	**Frances Faye In Frenzy**	1961	16.00	40.00

—Verve albums above have "Verve Record, Inc." on the bottom of the label.—

Verve V-2147	(M)	**Frances Faye In Frenzy**	1961	8.00	20.00
Verve V-8434	(M)	**Swinging All The Way With Frances Faye**	1962	10.00	25.00
Verve V6-8434	(S)	**Swinging All The Way With Frances Faye**	1962	8.00	20.00

—Verve albums above have black labels with "MGM Records" on the bottom.—

Regina R-315	(M)	**You Gotta Go! Go! Go!**	1964	12.00	30.00
Regina RS-315	(S)	**You Gotta Go! Go! Go!**	1964	10.00	25.00

FAZOLA, IRVING

Irving Prestopnik, aka Irving Fazola, is a traditional jazz clarinet and saxophone(s) player.

Mercury MG-25016	(10")	**Irving Fazola & His Dixielanders**	1950	20.00	50.00

FAZOLA, IRVING / GEORGE HARTMANN

EmArcy MG-36022	(M)	**New Orleans Express**	1955	16.00	40.00

—EmArcy albums above have blue labels with silver print.—

FEATHER, LEONARD

Leonard Feather is a modern jazz pianist, arranger and composer.

MGM E-270	(10")	**Winter Sequence**	1954	50.00	100.00
ABC-Paramount ABC-110	(M)	**Swingin' On The Vibories**	1956	20.00	50.00

(ABC 110 features Sonny Clarke, Kenny Drew, Larry Marable and Leroy Vinnegar.)

Mode LP-127	(M)	**Leonard Feather Presents Bop**	1957	24.00	60.00
MGM E-3494	(M)	**Hi Fi Suite**	1957	20.00	50.00
MGM E-3650	(M)	**Oh, Captain!**	1958	20.00	50.00
Interlude 511	(M)	**Leonard Feather Presents 52nd Street**	1959	16.00	40.00
Interlude 1011	(S)	**Leonard Feather Presents 52nd Street**	1959	12.00	30.00

(Interlude 511 is a reissue of Mode 127.)

FELDMAN, VICTOR

English born Victor Feldman is a West Coast jazz piano and vibraphone player. For additional listings refer to Curtis Amy.

Mode LP-120	(M)	**Victor Feldman On Vibes**	1957	30.00	75.00
Contemporary C-3541	(M)	**Suite Sixteen**	1957	16.00	40.00

Label & Catalog #		Title	Year	VG+	NM
Contemporary C-3549	(M)	**The Arrival Of Victor Feldman**	1958	16.00	40.00
Contemporary S-7549	(S)	**The Arrival Of Victor Feldman**	1959	14.00	30.00
		— Contemporary stereo albums have gold & black labels.—			
Interlude MO-510	(M)	**With Mallets A Fore Thought**	1959	16.00	40.00
Interlude ST-1010	(S)	**With Mallets A Fore Thought**	1959	12.00	30.00
		(Interlude 510 is a reissue of Mode 120.)			
Vee Jay LP-1006	(M)	**Love Me With All Your Heart**	1960	12.00	30.00
Vee Jay LPS-1006	(S)	**Love Me With All Your Heart**	1960	12.00	30.00
Riverside RLP-366	(M)	**Merry Ole Soul**	1961	12.00	30.00
Riverside RS-9366	(S)	**Merry Ole Soul**	1961	10.00	25.00
		—Riverside albums above have blue mono or black stereo labels with a reel & mike logo on top.—			
World Pacific WP-1807	(M)	**Stop The World, I Want To Get Off**	1962	12.00	30.00
World Pacific ST-1807	(S)	**Stop The World, I Want To Get Off** *(Yellow vinyl)*	1962	20.00	50.00
World Pacific ST-1807	(S)	**Stop The World, I Want To Get Off**	196?	10.00	25.00
Contemporary M-5005	(M)	**Latinsville**	1963	16.00	40.00
Contemporary S-9005	(S)	**Latinsville**	1963	12.00	30.00
		— Contemporary stereo albums have gold & black labels.—			
Ava A-19	(M)	**Soviet Jazz Themes**	1963	10.00	25.00
Ava AS-19	(S)	**Soviet Jazz Themes**	1963	8.00	20.00
Vee Jay LP-2507	(M)	**It's A Wonderful World**	1965	8.00	20.00
Vee Jay LPS-2507	(S)	**It's A Wonderful World**	1965	8.00	20.00

FELICE, ERNICE

Ernice Felice is a jazz-based accordion player.

Capitol H-192	(10")	**Ernice Felice Quartet**	1950	20.00	50.00

FERGUSON, ALLYN

Ava A-32	(M)	**Pictures At An Exhibition Framed In Jazz**	1963	12.00	30.00
Ava AS-32	(S)	**Pictures At An Exhibition Framed In Jazz**	1963	10.00	25.00

FERGUSON, MAYNARD

Maynard Ferguson is a West Coast jazz trumpet player and big band leader. For additional listings refer to Chris Connor.

EmArcy MG-26017	(10")	**Maynard Ferguson's Hollywood Party**	1954	40.00	100.00
EmArcy MG-26024	(10")	**Dimensions**	1954	40.00	100.00
EmArcy MG-36009	(M)	**Jam Session Featuring Maynard Ferguson**	1955	20.00	50.00
EmArcy MG-36021	(M)	**Maynard Ferguson Octet**	1955	30.00	75.00
EmArcy MG-36044	(M)	**Dimensions**	1955	20.00	50.00
EmArcy MG-36046	(M)	**Maynard Ferguson's Hollywood Party**	1956	20.00	50.00
EmArcy MG-36076	(M)	**Around The Horn With Maynard Ferguson**	1956	20.00	50.00
EmArcy MG-36114	(M)	**Boy With Lots Of Brass**	1957	20.00	50.00
		(EmArcy 36114 also features Irene Kral.)			
		— EmArcy albums above have blue labels with silver print.—			
Mercury MG-20556	(M)	**Boy With Lots Of Brass**	1960	12.00	30.00
Mercury SR-60124	(S)	**Boy With Lots Of Brass**	1960	10.00	25.00
Roulette R-52012	(M)	**A Message From Newport**	1958	12.00	30.00
Roulette SR-52012	(S)	**A Message From Newport**	1958	10.00	25.00
Roulette R-52038	(M)	**Maynard Ferguson Plays Jazz For Dancing**	1959	12.00	30.00
Roulette SR-52038	(S)	**Maynard Ferguson Plays Jazz For Dancing**	1959	10.00	25.00
Roulette R-52047	(M)	**Newport Suite**	1960	12.00	30.00
Roulette SR-52047	(S)	**Newport Suite**	1960	10.00	25.00
Roulette R-52058	(M)	**Swingin' My Way Through College**	1960	12.00	30.00
Roulette SR-52058	(S)	**Swingin' My Way Through College**	1960	10.00	25.00
Roulette R-52068	(M)	**Two's Company**	1961	12.00	30.00
Roulette SR-52068	(S)	**Two's Company**	1961	16.00	40.00
		(Roulette 52068 also features Chris Connor.)			
Roulette R-52083	(M)	**Maynard '62**	1962	8.00	20.00
Roulette SR-52083	(S)	**Maynard '62**	1962	6.00	15.00
Roulette R-52084	(M)	**Si! Si! M.F.**	1962	8.00	20.00
Roulette SR-52084	(S)	**Si! Si! M.F.**	1962	6.00	15.00
Mainstream 56031	(M)	**Color Him Wild**	1965	8.00	20.00
Mainstream S-6031	(S)	**Color Him Wild**	1965	6.00	15.00
Mainstream 56045	(M)	**The Blues Roar**	1965	8.00	20.00
Mainstream S-6045	(S)	**The Blues Roar**	1965	6.00	15.00
Mainstream 56060	(M)	**Maynard Ferguson And Sextet**	1965	8.00	20.00
Mainstream S-6060	(S)	**Maynard Ferguson And Sextet**	1965	6.00	15.00
Prestige PRLP-7636	(S)	**Maynard Ferguson 1969**	1969	6.00	15.00
		—Prestige albums above have blue labels with a trident logo on top.—			

Label & Catalog #		Title	Year	VG+	NM

FERLINGHETTI, LAWRENCE

Lawrence Ferlinghetti. is a San Francisco "beat" poet. For additional listings refer to Kenneth Rexroth.

Fantasy 7004	(M)	**The Impeachment Of President Eisenhower**	1958	60.00	150.00
		—Fantasy albums above have red labels on dark red, non-flexible vinyl.—			
Fantasy 7004	(M)	**The Impeachment Of President Eisenhower**	195?	30.00	75.00
		—Fantasy albums above have red labels on non-flexible vinyl.—			

FIELDING, JANE

Jane Fielding is a jazz-based vocalist.

Jazz: West JWLP-3	(M)	**Jazz Trio For Voice, Piano And Bass**	1955	125.00	250.00
Jazz: West JWLP-5	(M)	**Embers Glow**	1956	125.00	250.00

FIELDING, JERRY

Joshua Felman, aka Jerry Fielding, is a jazz band leader, arranger and composer. For additional listings refer to The Hi-Lo's.

Trend TL-1000	(10")	**Great New Orchestra**	1953	40.00	100.00
Trend TL-1004	(10")	**The Jerry Fielding Orchestra**	1954	40.00	100.00
Kapp KL-1026	(M)	**A Dance Concert**	1956	20.00	50.00
Decca DL-8100	(M)	**Sweet With A Beat**	1955	12.00	30.00
Decca DL-8371	(M)	**Swingin' In Hi-Fi**	1956	12.00	30.00
Decca DL-8450	(M)	**Fielding's Formula**	1957	12.00	30.00
Decca DL-8669	(M)	**Hollywood Wind Jazztet**	1958	12.00	30.00
ABC-Paramount ABC-542	(M)	**Hollywood Brass**	1965	6.00	15.00
ABC-Paramount ABCS-542	(S)	**Hollywood Brass**	1965	5.00	12.00

FIELDS. HARRY

Caloric PB-2913/4	(M)	**Music For Cooking With Gas**	1964	6.00	15.00

FIELDS, HERBIE

Herbert Fields is a traditional jazz saxophone(s) and clarinet player.

Decca DL-8130	(M)	**Blow Hot—Blow Cool**	1955	16.00	40.00
RKO Unique 124	(M)	**A Night At Kitty's**	1957	16.00	40.00

FIREHOUSE FIVE (+ TWO), THE

The Firehouse gang is a loose confederation of employees from the Walt Disney Studios.

Good Time Jazz L-?	(10")	**The Firehouse Five Plus Two, Volume 1**	1953	30.00	75.00
Good Time Jazz L-?	(10")	**The Firehouse Five Plus Two, Volume 2**	1953	30.00	75.00
Good Time Jazz L-?	(10")	**The Firehouse Five Plus Two, Volume 3**	1953	30.00	75.00
Good Time Jazz L-16	(10")	**The Firehouse Five Plus Two, Volume 4**	1953	30.00	75.00
Good Time Jazz L-12010	(M)	**The Firehouse Five Story, Volume 1**	1955	16.00	40.00
Good Time Jazz L-12011	(M)	**The Firehouse Five Story, Volume 2**	1955	16.00	40.00
Good Time Jazz L-12012	(M)	**The Firehouse Five Story, Volume 3**	1955	16.00	40.00
Good Time Jazz L-12014	(M)	**The Firehouse Five + Two Plays For Lovers**	1955	16.00	40.00
Good Time Jazz L-12018	(M)	**The Firehouse Five + Two Goes South!**	1955	16.00	40.00
Good Time Jazz L-12028	(M)	**The Firehouse Five + Two Goes To Sea**	1956	16.00	40.00
Stereo S-7005	(S)	**The Firehouse Five + Two Goes To Sea**	1958	14.00	35.00
Good Time Jazz S-10028	(S)	**The Firehouse Five + Two Goes To Sea**	1960	12.00	30.00
Good Time Jazz L-12038	(M)	**The Firehouse Five + Two Crashes A Party**	1957	16.00	40.00
Good Time Jazz S-10038	(S)	**The Firehouse Five + Two Crashes A Party**	1960	12.00	30.00
Good Time Jazz L-12040	(M)	**Dixieland Favorites**	1957	16.00	40.00
Good Time Jazz S-10040	(S)	**Dixieland Favorites**	1960	12.00	30.00
Good Time Jazz L-12044	(M)	**Around The World**	1958	16.00	40.00
Good Time Jazz S-10044	(S)	**Around The World**	1960	12.00	30.00
Good Time Jazz L-12049	(M)	**The Firehouse Five + Two At Dixieland**	1958	16.00	40.00
Good Time Jazz S-10049	(S)	**The Firehouse Five + Two At Dixieland**	1960	12.00	30.00
Good Time Jazz L-12052	(M)	**The Firehouse Five + Two Goes To A Fire**	1959	16.00	40.00
Good Time Jazz S-10052	(S)	**The Firehouse Five + Two Goes To A Fire**	1960	12.00	30.00
Good Time Jazz L-12054	(M)	**Twenty Years Later**	1959	16.00	40.00
Good Time Jazz S-10054	(S)	**Twenty Years Later**	1960	12.00	30.00

FIRST JAZZ PIANO QUARTET, THE

The First Jazz Piano Quartet consists of Irving Joseph, Bernie Leighton, Morris Nanton and Moe Weschler.

Warner Bros. W-1274	(M)	**The First Jazz Piano Quartet**	1959	16.00	40.00
Warner Bros. WS-1274	(S)	**The First Jazz Piano Quartet**	1959	12.00	30.00

FISCHER, CLARE

Clare Fischer is a West Coast jazz piano and organ player. For additional listings refer to Bud Shank.

Pacific Jazz PJ-52	(M)	**First Time Out**	1962	12.00	30.00
Pacific Jazz ST-52	(S)	**First Time Out**	1962	10.00	25.00

Label & Catalog #		Title	Year	VG+	NM
Pacific Jazz PJ-67	(M)	**Surging Ahead**	1963	12.00	30.00
Pacific Jazz ST-67	(S)	**Surging Ahead**	1963	10.00	25.00
Pacific Jazz PJ-77	(M)	**Extension**	1963	12.00	30.00
Pacific Jazz ST-77	(S)	**Extension**	1963	10.00	25.00
World Pacific WP-1830	(M)	**So Danco Samba**	1964	10.00	25.00
World Pacific ST-1830	(S)	**So Danco Samba**	1964	8.00	20.00
Pacific Jazz PJ-10096	(M)	**Manteca**	1966	8.00	20.00
Pacific Jazz ST-20096	(S)	**Manteca**	1966	6.00	15.00
Columbia CL-2691	(M)	**Songs For Rainy Day Lovers**	1967	10.00	25.00
Columbia CS-9491	(S)	**Songs For Rainy Day Lovers**	1967	6.00	15.00

— Columbia albums above have red labels with "360 Sound" on the bottom.—

Revelation REV-2	(S)	**Easy Living**	1968	6.00	15.00
Revelation REV-6	(S)	**One To Get Ready, Four To Go**	1969	6.00	15.00
Atlantic SD-1520	(S)	**Thesaurus**	1969	5.00	12.00

FISELE, JERRY

Delmar DL-101	(10")	**Jerry Fisele And The Fabulous Windy City Six**	1954	20.00	50.00

FITCH, MAL

Mal Fitch is a jazz-based pianist, singer and composer.

EmArcy MG-36041	(M)	**Mal Fitch**	1956	20.00	50.00

—EmArcy albums above have blue labels with silver print.—

FITZGERALD, ELLA

Ella Fitzgerald is a jazz-based vocalist and composer. For additional listings refer to Peggy Lee and the Jazzy Soundtracks section under Decca and Verve.

Decca DL-5084	(10")	**Souvenir Album**	1950	50.00	100.00
Decca DL-5300	(10")	**Ella Fitzgerald Sings Gershwin Songs**	1951	50.00	100.00
Decca DL-8068	(M)	**Songs In A Mellow Mood**	1954	20.00	50.00
Decca DL-8149	(M)	**Lullabies Of Birdland**	1955	20.00	50.00
Decca DL-8155	(M)	**Sweet And Hot**	1955	20.00	50.00
Decca DL-8378	(M)	**Ella Sings Gershwin**	1957	16.00	40.00
Decca DL-8477	(M)	**Ella And Her Fellas**	1957	16.00	40.00
Decca DL-8695	(M)	**First Lady Of Song**	1958	16.00	40.00
Decca DL-8696	(M)	**Miss Ella Fitzgerald And Mr. Nelson Riddle Invite You To Listen And Relax**	1958	16.00	40.00
Decca DL-8832	(M)	**For Sentimental Reasons**	1958	16.00	40.00
Decca DXB-156	(M)	**The Best Of Ella** *(2 LPs)*	1958	16.00	40.00
Decca DXSB-156	(E)	**The Best Of Ella** *(2 LPs)*	1958	10.00	25.00

—Decca albums above have silver on black labels.—

Decca DL-4129	(M)	**Golden Favorites**	1961	8.00	20.00
Decca DL-74129	(E)	**Golden Favorites**	1961	6.00	15.00
Decca DL-4446	(M)	**Stairway To The Stars**	1964	6.00	15.00
Decca DL-74446	(E)	**Stairway To The Stars**	1964	5.00	12.00
Decca DL-4447	(M)	**Early Ella**	1964	6.00	15.00
Decca DL-74447	(E)	**Early Ella**	1964	5.00	12.00
Decca DL-4451	(M)	**Ella Sings Gershwin**	1964	6.00	15.00
Decca DL-74451	(E)	**Ella Sings Gershwin**	1964	5.00	12.00
Verve MGV-4001-2	(M)	**Ella Fitzgerald Sings The Cole Porter Songbook** *(2 LPs)*	1956	30.00	75.00
Verve MGV-4002-2	(M)	**Ella Fitzgerald Sings The Rodgers & Hart Songbook** *(2 LPs)*	1956	30.00	75.00
Verve MGV-4004	(M)	**Like Someone In Love**	1957	20.00	50.00
Verve MGVS-6000	(S)	**Like Someone In Love**	1960	16.00	40.00
Verve MGV-4008-2	(M)	**Ella Fitzgerald Sings The Duke Ellington Songbook, Vol. 1** *(2 LPs)*	1957	30.00	75.00
Verve MGV-4009-2	(M)	**Ella Fitzgerald Sings The Duke Ellington Songbook, Vol. 2** *(2 LPs)* *(Verve 4008 and 4009 feature the Ellington Orchestra.)*	1957	30.00	75.00
Verve MGV-4010-4	(M)	**Ella Fitzgerald Sings The Duke Ellington Songbook** *(Verve 4010 collects Verve 4008 and 4009 in a 4 album boxed set.)*	1957	50.00	125.00
Verve MGV-4013	(M)	**Ella Fitzgerald Sings The Gershwin Songbook**	1957	20.00	50.00
Verve MGV-8264	(M)	**Ella Fitzgerald At The Opera House**	1958	20.00	50.00
Verve MGVS-6026	(S)	**Ella Fitzgerald At The Opera House**	1960	16.00	40.00
Verve MGV-4019-2	(M)	**Ella Fitzgerald Sings The Irving Berlin Songbook** *(2 LPs)*	1958	30.00	75.00
Verve MGVS-6005-2	(S)	**Ella Fitzgerald Sings The Irving Berlin Songbook** *(2 LPs)*	1960	24.00	60.00

Label & Catalog #		Title	Year	VG+	NM
Verve MGV-4021	(M)	**Ella Swings Lightly**	1959	20.00	50.00
Verve MGVS-6019	(S)	**Ella Swings Lightly**	1960	16.00	40.00
Verve MGV-4022	(M)	**Ella Fitzgerald Sings The Rodgers & Hart Songbook, Vol. 1**	1959	20.00	50.00
Verve MGVS-6009	(S)	**Ella Fitzgerald Sings The Rodgers & Hart Songbook, Vol. 1**	1960	16.00	40.00
Verve MGV-4023	(M)	**Ella Fitzgerald Sings The Rodgers & Hart Songbook, Vol. 2**	1959	20.00	50.00
Verve MGVS-6010	(S)	**Ella Fitzgerald Sings The Rodgers & Hart Songbook, Vol. 2**	1960	16.00	40.00
		(Verve 4022 and 4023 are reissues of 4002.)			
Verve MGV-4024	(M)	**Ella Fitzgerald Sings The George & Ira Gershwin Songbook, Vol. 1**	1959	20.00	50.00
Verve MGVS-6077	(S)	**Ella Fitzgerald Sings The George & Ira Gershwin Songbook, Vol. 1**	1960	16.00	40.00
Verve MGV-4025	(M)	**Ella Fitzgerald Sings The George & Ira Gershwin Songbook, Vol. 2**	1959	20.00	50.00
Verve MGVS-6078	(S)	**Ella Fitzgerald Sings The George & Ira Gershwin Songbook, Vol. 2**	1960	16.00	40.00
Verve MGV-4026	(M)	**Ella Fitzgerald Sings The George & Ira Gershwin Songbook, Vol. 3**	1959	20.00	50.00
Verve MGVS-6079	(S)	**Ella Fitzgerald Sings The George & Ira Gershwin Songbook, Vol. 3**	1960	16.00	40.00
Verve MGV-4027	(M)	**Ella Fitzgerald Sings The George & Ira Gershwin Songbook, Vol. 4**	1959	20.00	50.00
Verve MGVS-6080	(S)	**Ella Fitzgerald Sings The George & Ira Gershwin Songbook, Vol. 4**	1960	16.00	40.00
Verve MGV-4028	(M)	**Ella Fitzgerald Sings The George & Ira Gershwin Songbook, Vol. 5**	1959	20.00	50.00
Verve MGVS-6081	(S)	**Ella Fitzgerald Sings The George & Ira Gershwin Songbook, Vol. 5**	1960	16.00	40.00
Verve MGV-4029-5	(M)	**Ella Fitzgerald Sings The George & Ira Gershwin Songbook**	1959	125.00	250.00
		(Five album set collects 6077-6081 with a bonus 10" album.)			
Verve MGVS-6082-5	(S)	**Ella Fitzgerald Sings The George & Ira Gershwin Songbook**	1960	100.00	200.00
		(Five album set collects 4024-4029 with a bonus 10" album.)			
Verve *(No number)*	(M)	**Ella Fitzgerald Sings The George & Ira Gershwin Songbook**	1959	300.00	500.00
		(Five albums in a leather pockets in a walnut box.)			
Verve MGV-4030	(M)	**Ella Fitzgerald Sings The Irving Berlin Songbook, Vol. 1**	1959	20.00	50.00
Verve MGVS-6052	(S)	**Ella Fitzgerald Sings The Irving Berlin Songbook, Vol. 1**	1960	16.00	40.00
Verve MGV-4031	(M)	**Ella Fitzgerald Sings The Irving Berlin Songbook, Vol. 2**	1959	20.00	50.00
Verve MGVS-6053	(S)	**Ella Fitzgerald Sings The Irving Berlin Songbook, Vol. 2**	1960	16.00	40.00
Verve MGV-4032	(M)	**Sweet Songs For Swingers**	1959	20.00	50.00
Verve MGVS-6072	(S)	**Sweet Songs For Swingers**	1960	16.00	40.00
Verve MGV-4034	(M)	**Hello, Love**	1959	20.00	50.00
Verve MGVS-6100	(S)	**Hello, Love**	1960	16.00	40.00
Verve MGV-4036	(M)	**Get Happy!**	1959	20.00	50.00
Verve MGVS-6102	(S)	**Get Happy!**	1960	*Unreleased*	
Verve MGV-4041	(M)	**Mack The Knife—Ella In Berlin**	1960	20.00	50.00
Verve MGVS-6163	(S)	**Mack The Knife—Ella In Berlin**	1960	16.00	40.00
Verve MGV-4042	(M)	**Ella Wishes You A Swinging Christmas**	1960	20.00	50.00
Verve MGV-4046-2	(M)	**Ella Fitzgerald Sings The Harold Arlen Songbook** *(2 LPs)*	1961	30.00	75.00
Verve MGV-4049	(M)	**Ella Fitzgerald Sings Cole Porter**	1961	20.00	50.00
Verve MGV-4050	(M)	**Ella Fitzgerald Sings More Cole Porter**	1961	20.00	50.00
Verve MGV-4052	(M)	**Ella In Hollywood**	1961	20.00	50.00
		— Verve albums above have "Verve Record, Inc." on the bottom of the label.—			
Verve V-4001-2	(M)	**Ella Fitzgerald Sings The Cole Porter Songbook** *(2 LPs)*	1961	8.00	20.00
Verve V-4004	(M)	**Like Someone In Love**	1961	10.00	25.00
Verve V6-4004	(S)	**Like Someone In Love**	1961	8.00	20.00
Verve V-4008-2	(M)	**Ella Fitzgerald Sings The Duke Ellington Songbook, Vol. 1** *(2 LPs)*	1961	8.00	20.00

Label & Catalog #		Title	Year	VG+	NM
Verve V-4009-2	(M)	**Ella Fitzgerald Sings The Duke Ellington Songbook, Vol. 2** *(2 LPs)*	1961	8.00	20.00
Verve V-8264	(M)	**Ella Fitzgerald At The Opera House**	1961	10.00	25.00
Verve V6-8264	(S)	**Ella Fitzgerald At The Opera House**	1961	8.00	20.00
Verve V-4019-2	(M)	**Ella Fitzgerald Sings The Irving Berlin Songbook** *(2 LPs)*	1961	8.00	20.00
Verve V6-4019-2	(S)	**Ella Fitzgerald Sings The Irving Berlin Songbook** *(2 LPs)*	1961	8.00	20.00
Verve V-4021	(M)	**Ella Swings Lightly**	1961	10.00	25.00
Verve V6-4021	(S)	**Ella Swings Lightly**	1961	8.00	20.00
Verve V-4022	(M)	**Ella Fitzgerald Sings The Rodgers & Hart Songbook, Vol. 1**	1961	10.00	25.00
Verve V6-4022	(S)	**Ella Fitzgerald Sings The Rodgers & Hart Songbook, Vol. 1**	1961	8.00	20.00
Verve V-4023	(M)	**Ella Fitzgerald Sings The Rodgers & Hart Songbook, Vol. 2**	1961	10.00	25.00
Verve V6-4023	(S)	**Ella Fitzgerald Sings The Rodgers & Hart Songbook, Vol. 2**	1961	8.00	20.00
Verve V-4024	(M)	**Ella Fitzgerald Sings The George & Ira Gershwin Songbook, Vol. 1**	1961	10.00	25.00
Verve V6-4024	(S)	**Ella Fitzgerald Sings The George & Ira Gershwin Songbook, Vol. 1**	1961	8.00	20.00
Verve V-4025	(M)	**Ella Fitzgerald Sings The George & Ira Gershwin Songbook, Vol. 2**	1961	10.00	25.00
Verve V6-4025	(S)	**Ella Fitzgerald Sings The George & Ira Gershwin Songbook, Vol. 2**	1961	8.00	20.00
Verve V-4026	(M)	**Ella Fitzgerald Sings The George & Ira Gershwin Songbook, Vol. 3**	1961	10.00	25.00
Verve V6-4026	(S)	**Ella Fitzgerald Sings The George & Ira Gershwin Songbook, Vol. 3**	1961	8.00	20.00
Verve V-4027	(M)	**Ella Fitzgerald Sings The George & Ira Gershwin Songbook, Vol. 4**	1961	10.00	25.00
Verve V6-4027	(S)	**Ella Fitzgerald Sings The George & Ira Gershwin Songbook, Vol. 4**	1961	8.00	20.00
Verve V-4028	(M)	**Ella Fitzgerald Sings The George & Ira Gershwin Songbook, Vol. 5**	1961	10.00	25.00
Verve V6-4028	(S)	**Ella Fitzgerald Sings The George & Ira Gershwin Songbook, Vol. 5**	1961	8.00	20.00
Verve V-4030	(M)	**Ella Fitzgerald Sings The Irving Berlin Songbook, Vol. 1**	1961	10.00	25.00
Verve V6-4030	(S)	**Ella Fitzgerald Sings The Irving Berlin Songbook, Vol. 1**	1961	8.00	20.00
Verve V-4031	(M)	**Ella Fitzgerald Sings The Irving Berlin Songbook, Vol. 2**	1961	10.00	25.00
Verve V6-4031	(S)	**Ella Fitzgerald Sings The Irving Berlin Songbook, Vol. 2**	1961	8.00	20.00
Verve V-4032	(M)	**Sweet Songs For Swingers**	1961	10.00	25.00
Verve V6-4032	(S)	**Sweet Songs For Swingers**	1961	8.00	20.00
Verve V-4034	(M)	**Hello, Love**	1961	8.00	20.00
Verve V6-4034	(S)	**Hello, Love**	1961	10.00	25.00
Verve V-4036	(M)	**Get Happy!**	1961	10.00	25.00
Verve V6-4036	(S)	**Get Happy!**	1961	8.00	20.00
Verve V-4041	(M)	**Mack The Knife—Ella In Berlin**	1961	10.00	25.00
Verve V6-4041	(S)	**Mack The Knife—Ella In Berlin**	1961	8.00	20.00
Verve V-4042	(M)	**Ella Wishes You A Swinging Christmas**	1961	10.00	25.00
Verve V-4049	(M)	**Ella Fitzgerald Sings Cole Porter**	1961	10.00	25.00
Verve V-4050	(M)	**Ella Fitzgerald Sings More Cole Porter**	1961	10.00	25.00
Verve V-4052	(M)	**Ella In Hollywood**	1961	10.00	25.00
Verve V-4053	(M)	**Clap Hands, Here Comes Charlie!**	1962	16.00	40.00
Verve V6-4053	(S)	**Clap Hands, Here Comes Charlie!**	1962	20.00	50.00
		(Verve V6-4053 may be worth $100-200 in the audiophile market.)			
Verve V-4054	(M)	**Ella Swings Brightly With Nelson**	1962	16.00	40.00
Verve V6-4054	(S)	**Ella Swings Brightly With Nelson**	1962	12.00	30.00
Verve V-4055	(M)	**Ella Swings Gently With Nelson**	1962	16.00	40.00
Verve V6-4055	(S)	**Ella Swings Gently With Nelson**	1962	12.00	30.00
Verve V-4056	(M)	**Rhythm Is My Business**	1962	16.00	40.00
Verve V6-4056	(S)	**Rhythm Is My Business**	1962	12.00	30.00
Verve V-4057	(M)	**Ella Fitzgerald Sings The Harold Arlen Songbook, Vol. 1**	1962	12.00	30.00

Label & Catalog #		*Title*	*Year*	*VG+*	*NM*
Verve V6-4057	*(S)*	**Ella Fitzgerald Sings The Harold Arlen Songbook, Vol. 1**	*1962*	**10.00**	**25.00**
Verve V-4058	*(M)*	**Ella Fitzgerald Sings The Harold Arlen Songbook, Vol. 2**	*1962*	**12.00**	**30.00**
Verve V6-4058	*(S)*	**Ella Fitzgerald Sings The Harold Arlen Songbook, Vol. 2**	*1962*	**10.00**	**25.00**
		(Verve 4057 and 4058 are reissues of 4046.)			
Verve V-4059	*(M)*	**Ella Sings Broadway**	*1963*	**12.00**	**30.00**
Verve V6-4059	*(S)*	**Ella Sings Broadway**	*1963*	**10.00**	**25.00**
Verve V-4060	*(M)*	**Ella Fitzgerald Sings The Jerome Kern Songbook**	*1963*	**12.00**	**30.00**
Verve V6-4060	*(S)*	**Ella Fitzgerald Sings The Jerome Kern Songbook**	*1963*	**10.00**	**25.00**
Verve V-4061	*(M)*	**Ella And Basie**	*1963*	**12.00**	**30.00**
Verve V6-4061	*(S)*	**Ella And Basie**	*1963*	**10.00**	**25.00**
Verve V-4062	*(M)*	**These Are The Blues**	*1963*	**12.00**	**30.00**
Verve V6-4062	*(S)*	**These Are The Blues**	*1963*	**10.00**	**25.00**
		(Verve 4062 features cover art by David Stone Martin.)			
Verve V-4063	*(M)*	**The Best Of Ella Fitzgerald**	*1964*	**6.00**	**15.00**
Verve V6-4063	*(S)*	**The Best Of Ella Fitzgerald**	*1964*	**5.00**	**12.00**
Verve V-4064	*(M)*	**Hello, Dolly!**	*1964*	**10.00**	**25.00**
Verve V6-4064	*(S)*	**Hello, Dolly!**	*1964*	**8.00**	**20.00**
Verve V-4065	*(M)*	**Ella At Juan Les Pins**	*1964*	**10.00**	**25.00**
Verve V6-4065	*(S)*	**Ella At Juan Les Pins**	*1964*	**8.00**	**20.00**
Verve V-4066	*(M)*	**A Tribute To Cole Porter**	*1964*	**10.00**	**25.00**
Verve V6-4066	*(S)*	**A Tribute To Cole Porter**	*1964*	**8.00**	**20.00**
Verve V-4067	*(M)*	**Ella Fitzgerald Sings The Johnny Mercer Songbook**	*1965*	**10.00**	**25.00**
Verve V6-4067	*(S)*	**Ella Fitzgerald Sings The Johnny Mercer Songbook**	*1965*	**8.00**	**20.00**
Verve V-4068	*(M)*	**Porgy & Bess**	*1965*	**10.00**	**25.00**
Verve V6-4068	*(S)*	**Porgy & Bess**	*1965*	**8.00**	**20.00**
Verve V-4069	*(M)*	**Ella In Hamburg**	*1966*	**10.00**	**25.00**
Verve V6-4069	*(S)*	**Ella In Hamburg**	*1966*	**8.00**	**20.00**
		(Verve 4069 also features Louis Armstrong.)			
Verve V-4070	*(M)*	**Ella At Duke's Place**	*1966*	**10.00**	**25.00**
Verve V6-4070	*(S)*	**Ella At Duke's Place**	*1966*	**8.00**	**20.00**
		(Verve 4070 also features Duke Ellington.)			
Verve V-4071	*(M)*	**Whisper Not**	*1966*	**10.00**	**25.00**
Verve V6-4071	*(S)*	**Whisper Not**	*1966*	**8.00**	**20.00**
Verve V-4072	*(M)*	**Ella & Duke At Cote D'Azur**	*1967*	**10.00**	**25.00**
Verve V6-4072	*(S)*	**Ella & Duke At Cote D'Azur**	*1967*	**6.00**	**15.00**
		(Verve 4072 also features Duke Ellington.)			
Verve V-8670	*(M)*	**Ella Fitzgerald Sings The Jerome Kern Songbook**	*1967*	*Unreleased*	
Verve V-8720	*(M)*	**The Best Of Ella Fitzgerald**	*1967*	**6.00**	**15.00**
Verve V6-8720	*(S)*	**The Best Of Ella Fitzgerald**	*1967*	**4.00**	**10.00**
Verve V-8748	*(M)*	**Ella "Live"**	*1968*	**12.00**	**30.00**
Verve V6-8748	*(S)*	**Ella "Live"**	*1968*	**6.00**	**15.00**
Verve V6-8795	*(S)*	**The Best Of Ella Fitzgerald, Vol. 2**	*1969*	**5.00**	**12.00**
		— Verve albums above have black labels with "MGM Records" on the bottom.—			
Metro M-500	*(M)*	**Ella Fitzgerald**	*1965*	**5.00**	**12.00**
Metro MS-500	*(S)*	**Ella Fitzgerald**	*1965*	**4.00**	**10.00**
Metro M-567	*(M)*	**The World Of Ella Fitzgerald**	*1966*	**5.00**	**12.00**
Metro MS-567	*(S)*	**The World Of Ella Fitzgerald**	*1966*	**4.00**	**10.00**
Capitol T-2685	*(M)*	**Brighten The Corner**	*1967*	**8.00**	**20.00**
Capitol ST-2685	*(S)*	**Brighten The Corner**	*1967*	**5.00**	**12.00**
Capitol ST-2888	*(S)*	**Misty Blue**	*1968*	**5.00**	**12.00**
Reprise RS-6354	*(S)*	**Ella**	*1969*	**5.00**	**12.00**
Prestige PRLP-7685	*(S)*	**Sunshine Of Your Love**	*1969*	**4.00**	**10.00**
		— Prestige albums above have blue labels with a trident logo on top.—			

FITZGERALD, ELLA, & LOUIS ARMSTRONG

Verve MGV-4003	*(M)*	**Ella And Louis**	*1956*	**20.00**	**50.00**
Verve MGV-4006-2	*(M)*	**Ella And Louis Again** *(2 LPs)*	*1956*	**30.00**	**75.00**
Verve MGV-4011-2	*(M)*	**Porgy & Bess** *(2 LPs)*	*1957*	**30.00**	**75.00**
Verve MGVS-6040-2	*(S)*	**Porgy & Bess** *(2 LPs)*	*1960*	**24.00**	**60.00**
Verve MGV-4017	*(M)*	**Ella And Louis Again, Volume 1**	*1958*	**20.00**	**50.00**
Verve MGV-4018	*(M)*	**Ella And Louis Again, Volume 2**	*1958*	**20.00**	**50.00**
		(Verve 4017 and 4018 are reissues of Verve 4006.)			
		— Verve albums above have "Verve Record, Inc." on the bottom of the label.—			
Verve V-4003	*(M)*	**Ella And Louis**	*1961*	**10.00**	**25.00**

Label & Catalog #		Title	Year	VG+	NM
Verve V-4006-2	(M)	**Ella And Louis Again** *(2 LPs)*	1961	8.00	20.00
Verve V-4011-2	(M)	**Porgy & Bess** *(2 LPs)*	1961	10.00	25.00
Verve V6-4011-2	(S)	**Porgy & Bess** *(2 LPs)*	1961	8.00	20.00
Verve V-4017	(M)	**Ella And Louis Again, Volume 1**	1961	8.00	20.00
Verve V-4018	(M)	**Ella And Louis Again, Volume 2**	1961	6.00	15.00

— Verve albums above have black labels with "MGM Records" on the bottom.—

FITZGERALD, ELLA, & COUNT BASIE & JOE WILLIAMS

Verve MGV-8288	(M)	**One O' Clock Jump**	1958	20.00	50.00
— Verve albums above have black labels with "Verve Records, Inc." on the bottom.—					
Verve V-8288	(M)	**One O' Clock Jump**	1961	10.00	25.00

— Verve albums above have black labels with "MGM Records" on the bottom.—

FITZGERALD, ELLA, & BILLIE HOLIDAY

American Rec. Soc. G-433	(M)	**Ella Fitzgerald And Billie Holiday At Newport**	1957	16.00	40.00
Verve MGV-8234	(M)	**Ella Fitzgerald And Billie Holiday At Newport**	1958	20.00	50.00
Verve MGVS-6022	(S)	**Ella Fitzgerald And Billie Holiday At Newport**	1960	16.00	40.00
— Verve albums above have black labels with "Verve Records, Inc." on the bottom.—					
Verve V-8234	(M)	**Ella Fitzgerald And Billie Holiday At Newport**	1961	10.00	25.00
Verve V6-8234	(S)	**Ella Fitzgerald And Billie Holiday At Newport**	1961	6.00	15.00

— Verve albums above have black labels with "MGM Records" on the bottom.—

FITZGERALD, ELLA / LENA HORNE / BILLIE HOLIDAY / SARAH VAUGHAN

Columbia CL-2531	(10")	**Ella, Lena & Billie**	1955	60.00	150.00
Harmony HL-7125	(M)	**Ella, Lena, Billie & Sarah**	1958	10.00	25.00

(Harmony 7125 is a reissue of Columbia 2531 with tracks by Ms. Vaughan added.)

FITZGERALD, WARREN: ***Refer to*** **HAL STEIN & WARREN FITZGERALD**

FIVE, THE

The Five is Conte Candoli, Buddy Clark, Pete Jolly, Mel Lewis and Bill Perkins.

RCA Victor LPM-1121	(M)	**The Five**	1955	30.00	75.00

— RCA albums above have black labels with "Long Play" on the bottom.—

FIVE BROTHERS

The Five Brothers are Frank Capp, Bobby Enevoldsen, Herbie Harper, Red Mitchell, and Don Overburg.

Tampa TP-25	(M)	**Five Brothers** *(Colored vinyl)*	1957	60.00	150.00
Tampa TP-25	(M)	**Five Brothers**	1958	30.00	75.00

FLANAGAN, TOMMY

Thomas Flanagan is a modern jazz pianist. For additional listings refer to The New York Jazz Septet; and the Various Artists section under Bethlehem, New Jazz, and Savoy.

Prestige PRLP-7134	(M)	**Overseas**	1958	100.00	200.00
— Prestige albums above have yellow labels with a W. 50th Street, NYC address.—					
Regent MG-6055	(M)	**Jazz... It's Magic**	1958	30.00	75.00
Moodsville MVLP-9	(M)	**The Tommy Flanagan Trio** *(Moodsville 9 is a reissue of Prestige 7134.)*	1960	20.00	50.00
— Moodsville mono albums above have green labels with silver print.—					
Moodsville MVLP-9	(M)	**The Tommy Flanagan Trio**	1965	10.00	25.00
— Moodsville albums above have blue labels with a trident logo on the right side.—					
Prestige PRST-7632	(E)	**The Tommy Flanagan Trio** *(Prestige 7632 is a reissue of 7134.)*	1969	5.00	12.00

— Prestige albums above have blue labels with a trident logo on top.—

FLEMING, KING

King Fleming is a jazz-based pianist.

Argo LP-4004	(M)	**Misty Night**	1960	12.00	30.00
Argo LPS-4004	(S)	**Misty Night**	1960	10.00	25.00
Argo LP-4019	(M)	**Stand By**	1962	12.00	30.00
Argo LPS-4019	(S)	**Stand By**	1962	10.00	25.00
Cadet LP-4053	(M)	**The Weary Traveler**	1965	8.00	20.00
Cadet LSP-4053	(S)	**The Weary Traveler**	1965	6.00	15.00

FLORENCE, BOB

Robert Florence is a jazz-based pianist, vocalist and composer.

Era 20003	(M)	**The Bob Florence Trio**	1956	40.00	100.00
Carlton LP-12-115	(M)	**Name Band 1959**	1959	20.00	50.00
Carlton ST-12-115	(S)	**Name Band 1959**	1959	16.00	40.00

Label & Catalog #		Title	Year	VG+	NM
Liberty LRP-3380	(M)	**Here And Now**	1964	8.00	20.00
Liberty LST-7380	(S)	**Here And Now**	1964	6.00	15.00

FLOREY, MED

Meredith "Med" Flory is a West Coast jazz alto and tenor saxophone player, composer and composer.

Jubilee JLP-1066	(M)	**Jazzwave**	1958	20.00	50.00
Jubilee JGS-1066	(S)	**Jazzwave**	1958	16.00	40.00
Josie JJM-3506	(M)	**Med Flory Big Band**	1963	10.00	25.00
Josie JJS-3506	(S)	**Med Flory Big Band**	1963	8.00	20.00

(Josie 3506 is a reissue of Jubilee 1066.)

FOL, RAYMOND

Philips PHM-200-198	(M)	**Vivaldi's Four Seasons In Jazz**	1966	6.00	15.00
Philips PHS-600-198	(S)	**Vivaldi's Four Seasons In Jazz**	1966	5.00	12.00

FORREST, HELEN

Helen Forrest is a big band singer.

Capitol T-704	(M)	**Voice Of The Name Bands**	1956	20.00	50.00

—Capitol albums above have turquoise labels.—

FORREST, JIMMY

James Forrest is a modern jazz tenor saxophone player. For additional listings refer to Jack McDuff; Oliver Nelson; King Curtis & Jimmy Forrest; The Prestige Blues Swingers.

New Jazz NJLP-8250	(M)	**Forrest Fire**	1960	30.00	75.00
New Jazz NJLP-8293	(M)	**Soul Street**	1962	20.00	50.00

—New Jazz albums above have purple labels.—

New Jazz NJLP-8250	(M)	**Forrest Fire**	1965	12.00	30.00
New Jazz NJLP-8293	(M)	**Soul Street**	1965	10.00	25.00

—New Jazz albums above have blue labels with a trident logo on the right side.—

Prestige PRLP-7202	(M)	**Out Of The Forrest**	1961	20.00	50.00
Prestige PRLP-7218	(M)	**Most Much!**	1961	20.00	50.00
Prestige PRLP-7235	(M)	**Sit Down And Relax With Jimmy Forrest**	1962	20.00	50.00
Prestige PRST-7235	(S)	**Sit Down And Relax With Jimmy Forrest**	1962	20.00	50.00

—Prestige albums above have yellow mono or silver stereo labels with a Bergenfield, NJ address.—

Prestige PRST-7712	(S)	**The Best Of Jimmy Forrest**	1969	6.00	15.00

—Prestige albums above have blue labels with a trident logo on top.—

FORTUNE, SONNY: ***Refer to*** **STAN HUNTER & SONNY FORTUNE**

FOSTER, FRANK

Frank Foster is a modern jazz tenor saxophone player and composer. For additional listings refer to Sammy Davis Jr; Kenny Dorham; Elmo Hope; Joe Newman; Paul Quinichette & Frank Foster; and the Various Artists section under Prestige and Savoy.

Blue Note BLP-5043	(10")	**Frank Foster Quintet**	1954	300.00	500.00
Argo LP-717	(M)	**Basie Is Our Boss**	1963	12.00	30.00
Argo LPS-717	(S)	**Basie Is Our Boss**	1963	10.00	25.00
Prestige PRLP-7461	(M)	**Fearless Frank Foster**	1967	12.00	30.00
Prestige PRST-7461	(S)	**Fearless Frank Foster**	1967	10.00	25.00
Prestige PRLP-7479	(M)	**Soul Outing!**	1967	12.00	30.00
Prestige PRST-7479	(S)	**Soul Outing!**	1967	10.00	25.00

—Prestige albums above have blue labels with a trident logo on the right side.—

Blue Note BST-84278	(S)	**Manhattan Fever**	1968	12.00	30.00
Blue Note BST-84316	(S)	**Frank Foster**	1969	*Unreleased*	

—Blue Note albums above have blue on white labels with "A Division of Liberty Records."—

FOSTER, GARY

Revelation REV-5	(S)	**Subconsciously**	1969	6.00	15.00

FOSTER, HERMAN

Herman Foster is a jazz-based pianist.

Epic LA-16010	(M)	**Have You Heard?**	1960	10.00	25.00
Epic BA-17010	(S)	**Have You Heard?**	1960	8.00	20.00
Epic LA-16016	(M)	**The Explosive Piano Of Herman Foster**	1961	10.00	25.00
Epic BA-17016	(S)	**The Explosive Piano Of Herman Foster**	1961	8.00	20.00
Argo LP-727	(M)	**Ready And Willing**	1963	10.00	25.00
Argo LPS-727	(S)	**Ready And Willing**	1963	8.00	20.00

Label & Catalog #		Title	Year	VG+	NM

FOUR BROTHERS, THE

The Four Brothers, all ex-Hermanites, are Serge Chaloff, Al Cohn, Zoot Sims and Herbie Steward.

Vik LX-1096	(M)	**The Four Brothers—Together Again**	1957	30.00	75.00

FOUR MOST, THE

The seven members of The Four Most are Al Cohn, Hank Jones, Mundell Lowe, Mat Mathews, Oscar Pettiford, Joe Puma, and Gene Quill.

Dawn DLP-1111	(M)	**The Four Most**	1956	30.00	75.00

FRANCIS, PANAMA

David "Panama" Francis is a traditional jazz drummer.

Epic LN-3839	(M)	**Exploding Drums**	1959	16.00	40.00
Epic BN-629	(S)	**Exploding Drums**	1959	12.00	30.00
20th Cent. Fox TCF-510	(M)	**Tough Talk**	196?	14.00	35.00
20th Cent. Fox TCFS-510	(S)	**Tough Talk**	196?	12.00	30.00

FRANKLIN, ARETHA

Ms. Franklin's Columbia recordings are a potpourri of vocal jazz, blues, spirtuals and pop. With Atlantic in 1967, her recordings are firmly grounded in rhythm 'n' blues and rock 'n' roll and are not included here.

Columbia CL-1612	(M)	**Aretha**	1961	20.00	50.00
Columbia CS-8412	(S)	**Aretha**	1961	30.00	75.00
Columbia CL-1761	(M)	**The Electrifying Aretha Franklin**	1962	16.00	40.00
Columbia CS-8561	(S)	**The Electrifying Aretha Franklin**	1962	20.00	50.00
Columbia CL-1876	(M)	**The Tender... Swinging Aretha Franklin**	1962	16.00	40.00
Columbia CS-8676	(S)	**The Tender... Swinging Aretha Franklin**	1962	20.00	50.00
—Columbia albums above have three white "eye" logos on each side of the spindle hole.—					
Columbia CL-2079	(M)	**Laughing On The Outside**	1963	8.00	20.00
Columbia CS-8879	(S)	**Laughing On The Outside**	1963	10.00	25.00
Columbia CL-2163	(M)	**Unforgettable**	1964	8.00	20.00
Columbia CS-8963	(S)	**Unforgettable**	1964	10.00	25.00
Columbia CL-2281	(M)	**Runnin' Out Of Fools**	1964	8.00	20.00
Columbia CS-9081	(S)	**Runnin' Out Of Fools**	1964	10.00	25.00
Columbia CL-2351	(M)	**Yeah!!!**	1965	8.00	20.00
Columbia CS-9151	(S)	**Yeah!!!**	1965	10.00	25.00
—Columbia albums above have "Guaranteed High Fidelity" or "360 Sound Stereo" in black on the label.—					
Columbia CL-2521	(M)	**Soul Sister**	1966	8.00	20.00
Columbia CS-9321	(S)	**Soul Sister**	1966	10.00	25.00
Columbia CL-2629	(M)	**Take It Like You Give It**	1967	8.00	20.00
Columbia CS-9429	(S)	**Take It Like You Give It**	1967	10.00	25.00
Columbia CL-2673	(M)	**Aretha Franklin's Greatest Hits**	1967	8.00	20.00
Columbia CS-9473	(S)	**Aretha Franklin's Greatest Hits**	1967	10.00	25.00
Columbia CL-2754	(M)	**Take A Look**	1967	8.00	20.00
Columbia CS-9554	(S)	**Take A Look**	1967	10.00	25.00
Columbia CS-9601	(S)	**Aretha Franklin's Greatest Hits, Volume 2**	1968	8.00	20.00
Columbia CS-9776	(S)	**Soft And Beautiful**	1969	8.00	20.00
—Columbia albums above have "360 Sound" on the bottom of the label.—					

FREE MUSIC QUARTET, THE

ESP-Disk' 1083	(S)	**Free Music One And Two**	1969	8.00	20.00

FREEDMAN, BOB

Robert Freedman is a traditional jazz based piano and saxophone player and composer.

Savoy MG-15040	(10")	**Piano Moods**	1954	20.00	50.00

FREEMAN, BUD

Lawrence "Bud" Freeman is a traditional jazz tenor saxophone and clarinet player and composer. For additional listings refer to Bobby Byrne / Will Bradley / Bud Freeman; Joe Marsala / Bud Freeman.; the Jazzy Soundtracks section under Commentary; and the Various Artists section under Verve.

Decca DL-5213	(10")	**Wolverine Jazz**	1950	40.00	100.00
Columbia CL-6107	(10")	**Comes Jazz**	1950	40.00	100.00
Paramount PAL-105	(10")	**Bud Freeman And The Chicagoans**	1954	30.00	75.00
Capitol H-625	(10")	**Classics In Jazz**	1954	30.00	75.00
Capitol T-625	(M)	**Classics In Jazz**	1955	20.00	50.00
—Capitol albums above have turquoise labels.—					
Bethlehem BCP-29	(M)	**Nice And Easy**	1955	30.00	75.00
EmArcy MG-36013	(M)	**Midnight At Eddie Condon's**	1955	20.00	50.00
Columbia CL-2558	(10")	**Jazz—Chicago Style**	1955	30.00	75.00
Harmony HL-7046	(M)	**Bud Freeman & His All-Star Jazz**	1957	10.00	25.00

Label & Catalog #		Title	Year	VG+	NM
RCA Victor LPM-1508	(M)	**Chicago—Austin High School Jazz In Hi Fi**	1957	20.00	50.00
		—RCA albums above have black labels with "Long Play" on the bottom.—			
Dot DLP-3166	(M)	**Bud Freeman & His Summa Cum Laude Trio**	1959	16.00	40.00
Dot DLP-25166	(S)	**Bud Freeman & His Summa Cum Laude Trio**	1959	12.00	30.00
Dot DLP-3254	(M)	**Midnight Session**	1960	16.00	40.00
Dot DLP-25254	(S)	**Midnight Session**	1960	12.00	30.00
Swingville SVLP-2012	(M)	**Bud Freeman All Stars**	1960	20.00	50.00
		—Swingville albums above have purple mono or red stereo labels.—			
Swingville SVLP-2012	(M)	**Bud Freeman All Stars**	1965	10.00	25.00
		—Swingville albums above have blue labels with a trident logo on the right side.—			
United Arts. UAJ-14033	(M)	**Something Tender— Bud Freeman And Two Guitars**	1963	20.00	50.00
United Arts. UAJS-15033	(S)	**Something Tender— Bud Freeman And Two Guitars**	1963	16.00	40.00
		(United Artists 14033 also features George Barnes and Carl Krass)			

FREEMAN, RUSS

Russ Freeman is a West Coast jazz pianist. For additional listings refer to Chet Baker; Shelly Manne; Andre Previn & Russ Freeman.

Pacific Jazz PJLP-8	(10")	**The Russ Freeman Trio**	1953	60.00	150.00
Pacific Jazz PJ-1212	(M)	**Trio: Russ Freeman/Richard Twardzik**	1956	40.00	100.00
		(Side two of Pacific Jazz 1212 is a reissue of 8.)			
Pacific Jazz PJ-1232	(M)	**Quartet: Russ Freeman/Chet Baker**	1957	40.00	100.00
		(Pacific Jazz 1232 were issued in World Pacific 1232 covers.)			
World Pacific WP-1212	(M)	**Trio: Russ Freeman/Richard Twardzik**	1958	20.00	50.00
World Pacific WP-1232	(M)	**Quartet: Russ Freeman/Chet Baker**	1958	20.00	50.00

FREEMAN, STAN

Stanley Freeman is a modern jazz-based pianist, vocalist and composer.

Columbia CL-6158	(10")	**Piano Moods**	1951	20.00	50.00
Columbia CL-6193	(10")	**Come On-a Stan's House**	1951	20.00	50.00
Columbia CL-1120	(M)	**Stan Freeman Swings "The Music Man"**	1958	12.00	30.00
		—Columbia albums above have six white on black "eye" logos on each label.—			
Harmony HL-7067	(M)	**Stan Freeman Plays 30 All-Time Hits**	195?	6.00	15.00

FRIEDMAN, DON

Donald Friedman is a modern jazz pianist. For additional listings refer to Hank DeMano.

Riverside RLP-384	(M)	**A Day In The City**	1961	20.00	50.00
Riverside RS-9384	(S)	**A Day In The City**	1961	16.00	40.00
Riverside RLP-431	(M)	**Circle Waltz**	1962	16.00	40.00
Riverside RS-9431	(S)	**Circle Waltz**	1962	12.00	30.00
Riverside RLP-463	(M)	**Flashback**	1963	12.00	30.00
Riverside RS-9463	(S)	**Flashback**	1963	10.00	25.00
		—Riverside albums above have blue mono or black stereo labels with a reel & mike logo on top.—			
Riverside RLP-485	(M)	**Dreams And Explorations**	1965	10.00	25.00
Riverside RS-9485	(S)	**Dreams And Explorations**	1965	8.00	20.00
		—Riverside albums above blue labels with "Orpheum Productions" on the bottom.—			
Prestige PRLP-7488	(M)	**Metamorphosis**	1966	12.00	30.00
Prestige PRST-7488	(S)	**Metamorphosis**	1966	10.00	25.00
		—Prestige albums above have blue labels with a trident logo on the right side.—			

FRIGO, JOHNNY

Mercury MG-20285	(M)	**I Love Johnny Frigo, He Swings**	1957	12.00	30.00

FROEBA, FRANK

Frank Froeba is a traditional jazz pianist.

Decca DL-5043	(10")	**Back Room Piano**	1950	20.00	50.00
Decca DL-5048	(10")	**Old Time Piano**	1950	20.00	50.00
Varsity VLP-6031	(10")	**Boys In The Backroom**	1950	20.00	50.00
Royale 1818	(10")	**Old Time Piano**	1954	20.00	50.00

FRONTIERE, DOM

Liberty LJH-6002	(M)	**The Dom Frontiere Sextet**	1956	16.00	40.00

FRUSCELLA, TONY

Anthony Fuscella is a modern jazz trumpet player. For additional listings refer to Al Collins.

Atlantic 1220	(M)	**Tony Fruscella**	1955	30.00	75.00
		—Atlantic albums above have black mono or green stereo labels.—			

Label & Catalog #		Title	Year	VG+	NM

FULLER, CURTIS

Curtis Fuller is a modern jazz trombone player. For additional listings refer to Pepper Adams; Art Blakey & The Jazz Messengers; and the Various Artists section under Savoy.

Label & Catalog #		Title	Year	VG+	NM
Prestige PRLP-7107	(M)	**New Trombone**	1957	40.00	100.00
		—Prestige albums above have yellow labels with a W. 50th St, NYC address.—			
Regent MG-6055	(M)	**Jazz... It's Magic**	1957	30.00	75.00
Blue Note BLP-1567	(M)	**The Opener** *(Deep groove)*	1957	50.00	125.00
Blue Note BLP-1567	(M)	**The Opener**	1957	30.00	75.00
Blue Note BST-1567	(S)	**The Opener** *(Deep groove)*	1959	30.00	75.00
Blue Note BST-1567	(S)	**The Opener**	1959	20.00	50.00
Blue Note BLP-1572	(M)	**Bone & Bari** *(Deep groove)*	1957	50.00	125.00
Blue Note BLP-1572	(M)	**Bone & Bari**	1957	30.00	75.00
Blue Note BST-1572	(S)	**Bone & Bari** *(Deep groove)*	1959	30.00	75.00
Blue Note BST-1572	(S)	**Bone & Bari**	1959	20.00	50.00
Blue Note BLP-1583	(M)	**Curtis Fuller, Volume 3** *(Deep groove)*	1958	50.00	125.00
Blue Note BLP-1583	(M)	**Curtis Fuller, Volume 3**	1958	30.00	75.00
Blue Note BST-1583	(S)	**Curtis Fuller, Volume 3** *(Deep groove)*	1959	30.00	75.00
Blue Note BST-1583	(S)	**Curtis Fuller, Volume 3**	1959	20.00	50.00
		—Blue Note albums above have blue on white labels with a W. 63rd St, NYC address.—			
Blue Note BLP-1567	(M)	**The Opener**	1963	10.00	25.00
Blue Note BST-1567	(S)	**The Opener**	1963	8.00	20.00
Blue Note BLP-1572	(M)	**Bone & Bari**	1963	10.00	25.00
Blue Note BST-1572	(S)	**Bone & Bari**	1963	8.00	20.00
Blue Note BLP-1583	(M)	**Curtis Fuller, Volume 3**	1963	10.00	25.00
Blue Note BST-1583	(S)	**Curtis Fuller, Volume 3**	1963	8.00	20.00
		—Blue Note albums above have blue on white labels with a New York, USA address.—			
Blue Note BST-81567	(S)	**The Opener**	196?	5.00	12.00
Blue Note BST-81572	(S)	**Bone & Bari**	196?	5.00	12.00
Blue Note BST-81583	(S)	**Curtis Fuller, Volume 3**	196?	5.00	12.00
		—Blue Note albums above have blue on white labels with "A Division of Liberty Records."—			
Savoy MG-12141	(M)	**Blues-ette**	1959	20.00	50.00
Savoy SST-13006	(S)	**Blues-ette**	1959	16.00	40.00
		(Savoy 12141 also features Benny Golson.)			
Savoy MG-12143	(M)	**The Curtis Fuller Jazztet With Benny Golson**	1959	16.00	40.00
Savoy MG-12144	(M)	**Imagination**	1959	12.00	40.00
Savoy MG-12164	(M)	**Images Of Curtis Fuller**	1960	16.00	40.00
Savoy MG-12209	(M)	**Jazz... It's Magic**	196?	6.00	15.00
		(Savoy 12209 is a reissue of Regent 6055.)			
United Arts. UAL-4051	(M)	**Sliding Easy**	1959	20.00	50.00
United Arts. UAS-5051	(S)	**Sliding Easy**	1959	16.00	40.00
Warwick W-2038	(M)	**Boss Of The Soul Stream Trombone**	1961	14.00	35.00
Warwick W-2038ST	(S)	**Boss Of The Soul Stream Trombone**	1961	20.00	50.00
Epic LA-16013	(M)	**The Magnificent Trombone**	1961	16.00	40.00
Epic BA-17013	(S)	**The Magnificent Trombone**	1961	12.00	30.00
Epic LA-16020	(M)	**South American Cookin'**	1961	20.00	50.00
Epic BA-17020	(S)	**South American Cookin'**	1961	16.00	40.00
		(Epic 16020 also features Zoot Sims.)			
Impulse A-13	(M)	**Soul Trombone**	1962	12.00	30.00
Impulse AS-13	(S)	**Soul Trombone**	1962	10.00	25.00
Impulse A-22	(M)	**Cabin In The Sky**	1962	12.00	30.00
Impulse AS-22	(S)	**Cabin In The Sky**	1962	10.00	25.00
		—Impulse albums above have orange & black labels.—			
Impulse AS-22	(S)	**Cabin In The Sky**	1968	4.00	10.00
		—Impulse albums above have red & black labels with the "abc" logo on top.—			
Smash MGS-27034	(M)	**Jazz Conference Abroad**	1962	12.00	30.00
Smash SRS-67034	(S)	**Jazz Conference Abroad**	1962	10.00	25.00
New Jazz NJLP-8277	(M)	**Curtis Fuller With Red Garland**	1962	20.00	50.00
New Jazz NJLP-8305	(M)	**Curtis Fuller And Hampton Hawes With French Horns**	1963	*Unreleased*	
		—New Jazz albums above have purple labels.—			
New Jazz NJLP-8277	(M)	**Curtis Fuller With Red Garland**	1965	10.00	25.00
		—New Jazz albums above have blue labels with a trident logo on the right side.—			
Status ST-8305	(M)	**Curtis Fuller And Hampton Hawes With French Horns**	1965	16.00	40.00
		(Status 8305 is a reissue of one half of "Modern Jazz Survey 2," listed in the "Jazz At 16 2/3 RPM" article.)			

Label & Catalog #		Title	Year	VG+	NM
FULLER, GIL					
Gilbert Fuller is a West Coast jazz band leader and composer.					
Pacific Jazz PJ-93	*(M)*	**Gil Fuller & The Monterey Jazz Festival Orchestra With Dizzy Gillespie**	*1965*	**12.00**	**30.00**
Pacific Jazz ST-93	*(S)*	**Gil Fuller & The Monterey Jazz Festival Orchestra With Dizzy Gillespie**	*1965*	**10.00**	**25.00**
Pacific Jazz PJ-10101	*(M)*	**Night Flight**	*1966*	**10.00**	**25.00**
Pacific Jazz ST-20101	*(S)*	**Night Flight**	*1966*	**8.00**	**20.00**
FULLER, JERRY					
Gerald Fuller is a traditional jazz-based clarinet player.					
Andex A-3008	*(M)*	**Clarinet Portrait**	*1958*	**16.00**	**40.00**
Andex AS-3008	*(S)*	**Clarinet Portrait**	*1958*	**12.00**	**30.00**

Louis Bellson by David Stone Martin.

G.

GAILLARD, SLIM

"Slim" Bulee Gaillard is a traditional jazz guitar, piano, vibes and tenor saxophone player and vocalist.

Disc DLP-505	(10")	**Opera In Vout**	195?	100.00	200.00
		(Disc 505 features cover art by David Stone Martin.)			
Norgran MGN-13	(10")	**Slim Gaillard And His Musical Aggregation Wherever They May Be**	1954	60.00	150.00
Mercury MGC-126	(10")	**Mish Mash**	1953	Unreleased	
Clef MGC-126	(10")	**Mish Mash**	1953	40.00	100.00
		(Clef 126 features cover art by David Stone Martin.)			
Clef MGC-138	(10")	**Slim Gaillard Cavorts**	1953	40.00	100.00
		(Clef 138 is a reissue of Norgran 13.)			
Verve MGV-2013	(M)	**Smorgasboard, Help Yourself**	1956	20.00	50.00
		(Verve 2013 is a reissue of Clef 126 and 138.)			
		— Verve albums above have "Verve Record, Inc." on the bottom of the label.—			
Verve MGV-2013	(M)	**Smorgasboard, Help Yourself**	1961	8.00	20.00
		— Verve albums above have black labels with "MGM Records" on the bottom.—			
Dot DLP-3190	(M)	**Slim Gaillard Rides Again**	1959	16.00	40.00
Dot DLP-25190	(S)	**Slim Gaillard Rides Again**	1959	12.00	30.00

GAILLARD, SLIM / DIZZIE GILLESPIE

Ultraphonic ULP-50273	(M)	**Gaillard And Gillespie**	1958	20.00	50.00

GAILLARD, SLIM / MEADE LUX LEWIS

Mercury MGC-506	(10")	**Boogie Woogie At The Philharmonic**	1951	60.00	150.00
Clef MGC-506	(10")	**Boogie Woogie At The Philharmonic**	1954	50.00	125.00

GALBRAITH, BARRY

Joseph Barry Galbraith is a modern jazz guitar player. For addiional listings refer to Pia Beck; The Manhattan Jazz Septette.

Decca DL-9200	(M)	**Guitar And The Wind**	1958	20.00	50.00
Decca DL-79200	(S)	**Guitar And The Wind**	1958	16.00	40.00

GALE, EDDIE

Edward Gale is a modern jazz trumpet player and arranger.

Blue Note BST-84294	(S)	**Eddie Gale's Ghetto Music**	1968	8.00	20.00
Blue Note BST-84320	(S)	**Black Rhythm Happening**	1969	8.00	20.00
		— Blue Note albums above have blue on white labels with "A Division of Liberty Records."—			

GALLODORO, AL

Alphonse Gallodoro is a traditional jazz clarinet player.

Arco AL-3	(10")	**Al Gallodoro Concert**	1950	20.00	50.00
Columbia CL-6188	(10")	**Al Gallodoro**	1951	20.00	50.00

GAMBRELL, FREDDIE

Frederic Gambrell is a West Coast jazz pianist. For additional listings for Gambrell refer to Chico Hamilton.

World Pacific WP-1256	(M)	**Freddie Gambrell**	1959	20.00	50.00
		(World Pacific 1256 also features Ben Tucker.)			

GAMBRELL, FREDDIE, & PAUL HORN

World Pacific WP-1262	(M)	**Mikado**	1959	16.00	40.00
World Pacific ST-1023	(S)	**Mikado**	1959	12.00	30.00

GARCIA, DICK

Richard Garcia is a modern jazz guitar player.

Dawn DLP-1106	(M)	**A Message From Dick Garcia**	1956	24.00	60.00
Seeco SLP-428	(M)	**A Message From Dick Garcia**	1959	16.00	40.00
		(Seeco 428 is a reissue of Dawn 1106.)			

GARCIA, RUSS

Russell Garcia is a modern jazz guitar player. For additional listings refer to Louis Armstrong; Mel Torme.

Bethlehem BCP-1040	(10")	**Wigville**	1955	100.00	200.00

Label & Catalog #		Title	Year	VG+	NM
Bethlehem BCP-46	(M)	**Four Horns And A Lush Life**	1956	20.00	50.00
Dawn LP-	M)	**Jazzville USA, Vol. 2**	195?	30.00	75.00
ABC-Paramount ABC-147	(M)	**The Johnny Evergreens**	1956	20.00	50.00
Verve MGV-2088	(M)	**The Warm Feeling**	1957	20.00	50.00
		(Verve 2088 also features Roy Eldridge.)			
— Verve albums above have black labels with "Verve Records, Inc." on the bottom.—					
Verve V-2088	(M)	**The Warm Feeling**	1961	8.00	20.00
— Verve albums above have black labels with "MGM Records" on the bottom.—					
Kapp KL-1050	(M)	**Listen To The Music Of Russell Garcia**	1957	20.00	50.00

GARCIA, RUSS / MARTY PAICH

Bethlehem BCP-6039	(M)	**Music For Birds And The Hep Cats**	1959	20.00	50.00
Bethlehem SBCP-6039	(S)	**Music For Birds And The Hep Cats**	1959	20.00	50.00

GARI, RALPH

Ralph Garofalo, aka Ralph Gari, is a jazz-based alto sax, clarinet, flute, piccolo and English horn player.

EmArcy MG-36019	(M)	**Ralph Gari**	1955	20.00	50.00
— EmArcy albums above have blue labels with silver print.—					

GARLAND, HANK

Henry Garland is a modern jazz guitar player noted for his session work with Nashville's country singers.

SeSac SN-2301/2	(M)	**Subtle Swing**	196?	40.00	100.00
Columbia CL-2572	(M)	**Jazz Winds From A New Direction**	1961	16.00	40.00
Columbia CS-8372	(S)	**Jazz Winds From A New Direction**	1961	14.00	35.00
		(Columbia 2572 also features Gary Burton and Joe Morello.)			
Columbia CL-2913	(M)	**The Unforgettable Guitar Of Hank Garland**	1962	16.00	40.00
Columbia CS-8713	(S)	**The Unforgettable Guitar Of Hank Garland**	1962	14.00	35.00
— Columbia albums above have six white on black "eye" logos on each label.—					

GARLAND, RED

William "Red" Garland is a modern jazz pianist known for his work with the Miles Davis Quartet from 1954-58. For additional listings refer to John Coltrane; Curtis Fuller; Coleman Hawkins; Phil Woods.

Prestige PRLP-7064	(M)	**A Garland Of Red**	1956	30.00	75.00
Prestige PRLP-7086	(M)	**Red Garland's Piano**	1957	30.00	75.00
Prestige PRLP-7113	(M)	**Groovy**	1957	30.00	75.00
Prestige PRLP-7130	(M)	**All Morning Long**	1958	30.00	75.00
— Prestige albums above have a W. 50th St., NYC address on the label.—					
Prestige PRLP-7139	(M)	**Manteca**	1958	20.00	50.00
		(Prestige 7139 also features Ray Barretto.)			
Prestige PRLP-7148	(M)	**All Kinds Of Weather**	1958	20.00	50.00
Prestige PRLP-7157	(M)	**Red In Bluesville**	1959	20.00	50.00
Prestige PRLP-7170	(M)	**Red Garland At The Prelude**	1959	20.00	50.00
Prestige PRLP-7181	(M)	**Soul Junction**	1960	20.00	50.00
		(Prestige 7181 also features John Coltrane and Donald Byrd.)			
— Prestige albums above have yellow mono or silver stereo labels with a Bergenfield, NJ address.—					
Moodsville MVLP-1	(M)	**Red Garland + Eddie "Lockjaw" Davis**	1960	20.00	50.00
Moodsville MVLP-3	(M)	**Red Alone—Vol. 3**	1960	20.00	50.00
Moodsville MVLP-6	(M)	**The Red Garland Trio**	1960	20.00	50.00
Moodsville MVLP-10	(M)	**Alone With The Blues**	1960	20.00	50.00
— Moodsville mono albums above have green labels with silver print.—					
Moodsville MVLP-1	(M)	**Red Garland + Eddie "Lockjaw" Davis**	1965	10.00	25.00
Moodsville MVLP-3	(M)	**Red Alone—Vol. 3**	1965	10.00	25.00
Moodsville MVLP-6	(M)	**The Red Garland Trio**	1965	10.00	25.00
Moodsville MVLP-10	(M)	**Alone With The Blues**	1965	10.00	25.00
— Moodsville albums above have blue labels with a trident logo on the right side.—					
Prestige PRLP-7193	(M)	**Rojo**	1961	16.00	40.00
Prestige PRLP-7209	(M)	**High Pressure**	1961	20.00	50.00
		(Prestige 7209 also features John Coltrane.)			
Prestige PRLP-7229	(M)	**Dig It!**	1962	20.00	50.00
Prestige PRST-7229	(S)	**Dig It!**	1962	16.00	40.00
		(Prestige 7229 also features John Coltrane.)			
Prestige PRLP-7258	(M)	**When There Are Grey Skies**	1963	16.00	40.00
Prestige PRST-7258	(S)	**When There Are Grey Skies**	1963	12.00	30.00
Prestige PRLP-7276	(M)	**Can't See For Lookin'**	1963	16.00	40.00
Prestige PRST-7276	(S)	**Can't See For Lookin'**	1963	12.00	30.00
Prestige PRLP-7288	(M)	**Halleloo-Y'-All**	1964	16.00	40.00
Prestige PRST-7288	(S)	**Halleloo-Y'-All**	1964	12.00	30.00
— Prestige albums above have yellow mono or silver stereo labels with a Bergenfield, NJ address.—					

Red Garland worked with Hot Lips Page, Bird, Hawk, Roy Eldridge, Charlie Ventura, Billy Eckstine, Sonny Stitt, Ben Webster, Eddie Davis, Bennie Green, Lou Donaldson, before joining Miles Davis' legendary group with Prestige and Columbia (1956-58). He formed his own trio with Paul Chambers and Art Taylor in 1956, which enjoyed a successful relationship with Prestige, with two examples above. Aside from Davis, he has been a featured soloist with John Coltrane, Curtis Fuller, Coleman Hawkins, and Phil Woods. He has recorded as a sideman with Art Taylor on Prestige and Art Pepper on Contemporary.

Label & Catalog #		Title	Year	VG+	NM
New Jazz NJLP-8314	(M)	**Lil' Darlin'**	1963	Unreleased	
New Jazz NJLP-8325	(M)	**High Pressure**	1963	Unreleased	
New Jazz NJLP-8326	(M)	**Red Garland Live!**	1963	Unreleased	
Prestige PRLP-7307	(M)	**Soul Burnin'**	1964	12.00	30.00
Prestige PRST-7307	(S)	**Soul Burnin'**	1964	10.00	25.00
—Prestige albums above have blue labels with a trident logo on the right side.—					
Status ST-8314	(M)	**Lil' Darlin'**	1965	16.00	40.00
Status ST-8325	(M)	**High Pressure**	1965	16.00	40.00
		(Status 8325 is a reissue of Prestige 7209.)			
Status ST-8326	(M)	**Red Garland Live!**	1965	16.00	40.00
Prestige PRST-7658	(S)	**Red Garland Revisited!**	1969	6.00	15.00
—Prestige albums above have blue labels with a trident logo on top.—					
Jazzland JLP-48	(M)	**Bright And Breezy**	1961	16.00	40.00
Jazzland JLP-948	(S)	**Bright And Breezy**	1961	12.00	30.00
Jazzland JLP-62	(M)	**The Nearness Of You— Ballads Played By Red Garland**	1962	16.00	40.00
Jazzland JLP-962	(S)	**The Nearness Of You— Ballads Played By Red Garland**	1962	12.00	30.00
Jazzland JLP-73	(M)	**Solar**	1962	16.00	40.00
Jazzland JLP-973	(S)	**Solar**	1962	12.00	30.00
Jazzland JLP-87	(M)	**Red's Good Groove!**	1962	16.00	40.00
Jazzland JLP-987	(S)	**Red's Good Groove!**	1962	12.00	30.00

GARNER, ERROLL

Erroll Garner is a traditional jazz-based pianist. For additional listings refer to Woody Herman; Dodo Marmarosa / Erroll Garner; Kay Starr / Erroll Garner; Art Tatum / Erroll Garner; and the Jazzy Soundtracks section under Mercury.

Label & Catalog #		Title	Year	VG+	NM
Dial LP-902	(M)	**Free Piano Improvisations Recorded By Baron Timme Rosenkrantz At One Of His Famous Gaslight Jazz Sessions**	1949	150.00	300.00
Dial LP-205	(10")	**Erroll Garner, Volume 1**	1950	100.00	200.00
Savoy MG-15000	(10")	**Erroll Garner Playing Piano Solos, Volume 1**	1950	30.00	75.00
Savoy MG-15001	(10")	**Erroll Garner Playing Piano Solos, Volume 2**	1950	30.00	75.00
Savoy MG-15002	(10")	**Erroll Garner Playing Piano Solos, Volume 3**	1950	30.00	75.00
Savoy MG-15004	(10")	**Erroll Garner Playing Piano Solos, Volume 4**	1951	30.00	75.00
Savoy MG-15026	(10")	**Erroll Garner At The Piano**	1953	30.00	75.00
Mercury MG-25117	(10")	**Erroll Garner At The Piano**	1951	30.00	75.00
Mercury MG-25157	(10")	**Gone With Garner**	1951	30.00	75.00
Mercury MG-20009	(M)	**Erroll Garner At The Piano**	1953	20.00	50.00
Mercury MG-20055	(M)	**Mambo Moves Garner**	1954	20.00	50.00
Mercury MG-20063	(M)	**Solitaire**	1954	20.00	50.00
Mercury MG-20090	(M)	**Afternoon Of An Elf**	1955	20.00	50.00
—Mercury albums above have silver on black labels.—					
EmArcy MG-26016	(10")	**Garnering**	1954	30.00	75.00
EmArcy MG-26042	(10")	**Gone With Garner**	1954	30.00	75.00
EmArcy MG-36001	(M)	**Contrasts**	1954	12.00	30.00
EmArcy MG-36026	(M)	**Garnering**	1955	12.00	30.00
EmArcy MG-36069	(M)	**Erroll!**	1956	12.00	30.00
—EmArcy albums above have blue labels with silver print.—					
Savoy MG-12002	(M)	**Penthouse Serenade**	1955	12.00	30.00
Savoy MG-12003	(M)	**Serenade To "Laura"**	1955	12.00	30.00
Atlantic ALR-109	(10")	**Rhapsody**	1950	30.00	75.00
Atlantic ALR-112	(10")	**Erroll Garner At The Piano**	1951	30.00	75.00
Atlantic ALR-128	(10")	**Passport To Fame**	1952	40.00	100.00
Atlantic ALR-135	(10")	**Piano Solos, Volume 2**	1952	30.00	75.00
Atlantic 1227	(M)	**The Greatest Garner**	1956	16.00	40.00
Atlantic 1315	(M)	**Perpetual Motion**	1959	16.00	40.00
—Atlantic albums above have black mono or green stereo labels.—					
Atlantic 1227	(M)	**The Greatest Garner**	1961	6.00	15.00
—Atlantic albums above have multi-color labels with a white fan logo.—					
Atlantic 1227	(M)	**The Greatest Garner**	196?	4.00	10.00
—Atlantic albums above have multi-color labels with a black fan logo.—					
King 265-17	(10")	**Piano Stylist**	1952	30.00	75.00
King 395-540	(M)	**Piano Variations**	1958	20.00	50.00
		(King 540 is a reissue of 17.)			
Blue Note BLP-5007	(10")	**Overture To Dawn, Volume 1**	1952	125.00	250.00
Blue Note BLP-5008	(10")	**Overture To Dawn, Volume 2**	1952	125.00	250.00
Blue Note BLP-5014	(10")	**Overture To Dawn, Volume 3**	1953	125.00	250.00

Label & Catalog #		Title	Year	VG+	NM
Blue Note BLP-5015	*(10")*	**Overture To Dawn, Volume 4**	*1953*	**125.00**	**250.00**
Blue Note BLP-5016	*(10")*	**Overture To Dawn, Volume 5**	*1953*	**125.00**	**250.00**
Columbia CL-6139	*(10")*	**Piano Moods**	*1950*	**30.00**	**75.00**
Columbia CL-6173	*(10")*	**Gems**	*1951*	**30.00**	**75.00**
Columbia CL-6209	*(10")*	**Solo Flight**	*1952*	**30.00**	**75.00**
Columbia CL-6259	*(10")*	**Erroll Garner Plays For Dancing**	*1953*	**30.00**	**75.00**
Columbia CL-2540	*(10")*	**Garnerland**	*1955*	**30.00**	**75.00**
Columbia CL-2606	*(10")*	**He's Here! He's Gone! He's Garner!**	*1956*	**30.00**	**75.00**
Columbia CL-535	*(M)*	**Erroll Garner At The Piano**	*1953*	**20.00**	**50.00**
Columbia CL-583	*(M)*	**Gems**	*1954*	**20.00**	**50.00**
Columbia CL-617	*(M)*	**Gone Garner Gonest**	*1955*	**20.00**	**50.00**
		—Columbia albums above have "Long Playing" on the bottom of the label.—			
Columbia CL-535	*(M)*	**Erroll Garner At The Piano**	*1955*	**12.00**	**30.00**
Columbia CL-583	*(M)*	**Gems**	*1955*	**12.00**	**30.00**
Columbia CL-617	*(M)*	**Gone Garner Gonest**	*1955*	**12.00**	**30.00**
Columbia CL-667	*(M)*	**Erroll Garner Plays For Dancing**	*1955*	**12.00**	**30.00**
Columbia CL-883	*(M)*	**Concert By The Sea**	*1956*	**12.00**	**30.00**
Columbia CL-939	*(M)*	**Most Happy Piano**	*1957*	**12.00**	**30.00**
Columbia CL-1014	*(M)*	**Other Voices**	*1957*	**12.00**	**30.00**
Columbia CL-1060	*(M)*	**Soliloquy**	*1957*	**12.00**	**30.00**
Columbia CL-1141	*(M)*	**Encores In Hi Fi**	*1958*	**12.00**	**30.00**
Columbia C2L-9	*(M)*	**Paris Impressions** *(2 LPs)*	*1958*	**16.00**	**40.00**
Columbia CL-1216	*(M)*	**Paris Impressions, Volume 1**	*1958*	**8.00**	**20.00**
Columbia CL-1217	*(M)*	**Paris Impressions, Volume 2**	*1958*	**8.00**	**20.00**
Columbia CL-1452	*(M)*	**The One And Only Erroll Garner**	*1960*	**8.00**	**20.00**
Columbia CS-8252	*(S)*	**The One And Only Erroll Garner**	*1960*	**6.00**	**15.00**
Columbia CL-1512	*(M)*	**Swinging Solos**	*1960*	**8.00**	**20.00**
Columbia CS-8312	*(S)*	**Swinging Solos**	*1960*	**6.00**	**15.00**
Columbia CL-1587	*(M)*	**The Provocative Erroll Garner**	*1961*	**8.00**	**20.00**
Columbia CS-8387	*(S)*	**The Provocative Erroll Garner**	*1961*	**6.00**	**15.00**
		—Columbia albums above have six white on black "eye" logos on each label.—			
Jazztone J-1269	*(M)*	**Early Erroll**	*1957*	**16.00**	**40.00**
		(Jazztone 1269 is a reissue of Dial 902.)			
Ron-lette A-15	*(M)*	**Erroll Garner**	*1958*	**10.00**	**25.00**
ABC-Paramount ABC-365	*(M)*	**Dreamstreet**	*1961*	**8.00**	**20.00**
ABC-Paramount ABCS-365	*(S)*	**Dreamstreet**	*1961*	**6.00**	**15.00**
ABC-Paramount ABC-395	*(M)*	**Closeup In Swing**	*1961*	**8.00**	**20.00**
ABC-Paramount ABCS-395	*(S)*	**Closeup In Swing**	*1961*	**6.00**	**15.00**
Baronet B-109	*(M)*	**Informal Piano Improvisations**	*1962*	**4.00**	**10.00**
Baronet BS-109	*(E)*	**Informal Piano Improvisations**	*1962*	**1.00**	**5.00**
		(Baronet 109 is a reissue of Dial 902.)			
Mercury MG-20662	*(M)*	**Misty**	*1962*	**8.00**	**20.00**
Mercury SR-60662	*(S)*	**Misty**	*1962*	**6.00**	**15.00**
Mercury MG-21308	*(S)*	**Seeing Is Believing**	*1964*	**8.00**	**20.00**
Mercury SR-61308	*(S)*	**Seeing Is Believing**	*1964*	**6.00**	**15.00**
		—Mercury albums above have silver on black labels.—			
Reprise R-6080	*(M)*	**One World Concert**	*1964*	**8.00**	**20.00**
Reprise RS-6080	*(S)*	**One World Concert**	*1964*	**6.00**	**15.00**
MGM E-4345	*(M)*	**Now Playing**	*1966*	**6.00**	**15.00**
MGM SE-4345	*(S)*	**Now Playing**	*1966*	**5.00**	**12.00**
MGM E-4361	*(M)*	**Campus Concert**	*1966*	**6.00**	**15.00**
MGM SE-4361	*(S)*	**Campus Concert**	*1966*	**5.00**	**12.00**
MGM E-4463	*(M)*	**That's My Kick**	*1967*	**6.00**	**15.00**
MGM SE-4463	*(S)*	**That's My Kick**	*1967*	**5.00**	**12.00**
MGM E-4520	*(M)*	**Up In Erroll's Room**	*1967*	**6.00**	**15.00**
MGM SE-4520	*(S)*	**Up In Erroll's Room**	*1967*	**5.00**	**12.00**

GARNER, ERROLL / PETE JOHNSON

Grand Award GA-33-321	*(M)*	**Jazz Piano**	*1956*	**30.00**	**75.00**
		(G.A. 321 was issued with a removable "second" cover of a David Stone Martin painting that could be peeled off and framed.)			
Grand Award GA-33-321	*(M)*	**Jazz Piano**	*1956*	**12.00**	**30.00**
		(Without the second removable cover.)			

GARNER, ERROLL / SLAM STEWART

Savoy MG-1500?	*(10")*	**Erroll Garner & Slam Stewart**	*195?*	**30.00**	**75.00**

Label & Catalog #		Title	Year	VG+	NM

GARNER, ERROLL / BILLY TAYLOR

Savoy MG-12008	(M)	**Erroll Garner-Billy Taylor**	1955	20.00	50.00

(Savoy 12008 reissues early Garner plus 9035, "Billy Taylor Piano.")

GARNER, MORRIS

Thunderbird TH-1958	(M)	**The Worst Of Morris Garner**	196?	10.00	25.00

GASKIN, LEONARD

Leonard Gaskin is a traditional jazz bass player.

Swingville SVLP-2031	(M)	**At The Jazz Band Ball**	1962	20.00	50.00
Swingville SVST-2031	(S)	**At The Jazz Band Ball**	1962	16.00	40.00
Swingville SVLP-2033	(M)	**At The Darktown Strutter's Ball**	1962	20.00	50.00
Swingville SVST-2033	(S)	**At The Darktown Strutter's Ball**	1962	16.00	40.00

— Swingville albums above have purple mono or red stereo labels.—

Swingville SVLP-2031	(M)	**At The Jazz Band Ball**	1965	10.00	25.00
Swingville SVST-2031	(S)	**At The Jazz Band Ball**	1965	8.00	20.00
Swingville SVLP-2033	(M)	**At The Darktown Strutter's Ball**	1965	10.00	25.00
Swingville SVST-2033	(S)	**At The Darktown Strutter's Ball**	1965	8.00	20.00

— Swingville albums above have blue labels with a trident logo on the right side.—

GAVIN, KEVIN

Kevin Gavin is a jazz-based vocalist.

Charlie Parker PLP-810	(M)	**Hey! This Is Kevin Gavin**	1962	16.00	40.00
Charlie Parker PLP-810S	(S)	**Hey! This Is Kevin Gavin**	1962	16.00	40.00

GAYLE, ROZELLE

Mercury MG-20374	(M)	**Like, Be My Guest**	1958	12.00	30.00

GEE, MATTHEW

Matthew Gee Jr. is a modern jazz trombone player. For additional listings refer to Johnny Griffin & Matthew Gee.

Riverside RLP-12-221	(M)	**Jazz By Gee!**	1956	30.00	75.00

— Riverside albums above have blue on white labels.—

Riverside RLP-12-221	(M)	**Jazz By Gee!**	195?	16.00	40.00

— Riverside albums above have blue mono or black stereo labels with a reel & mike logo on top.—

GELLER, HERB

Herbert Geller, husband to Lorraine, is a West Coast jazz also saxophone player. For additional listings refer to John Graas; and the Various Artists section under EmArcy.

EmArcy MG-26045	(10")	**Herb Geller Plays**	1954	60.00	150.00
EmArcy MG-36024	(M)	**The Gellers**	1955	40.00	100.00
		(EmArcy 36024 also features Lorraine Geller.)			
EmArcy MG-36040	(M)	**The Herb Geller Sextette**	1955	40.00	100.00
		(EmArcy 36040 is a reissue of 26045.)			
EmArcy MG-36045	(M)	**Herb Geller Plays**	1955	30.00	75.00

— EmArcy albums above have blue labels with silver print.—

Jubilee JLP-1044	(M)	**Fire In The West**	1957	20.00	50.00
Jubilee JFS-1044	(S)	**Fire In The West**	1958	16.00	40.00
Jubilee JLP-1094	(M)	**Stax Of Sax**	1958	16.00	40.00
Jubilee JGS-1094	(S)	**Stax Of Sax**	1958	12.00	30.00
Atco 33-109	(M)	**Gypsy**	1959	16.00	40.00

— Atco albums above have yellow labels with a harp logo on top.—

Josie JLPM-3502	(M)	**Herb Geller Alto Saxophone**	1963	10.00	25.00
Josie JLPS-3502	(S)	**Herb Geller Alto Saxophone**	1963	8.00	20.00

(Josie 3502 is a reissue of Jubilee 1044.)

GELLER, LORRAINE

Lorraine Geller, wife to Herb, is a West Coast jazz pianist.

Dot DLP-3174	(M)	**Lorraine Geller**	1959	500.00	750.00
Dot DLP-25174	(S)	**Lorraine Geller**	1959	360.00	600.00

GETZ, EDDIE

Edward Getz is a modern jazz alto saxophone player.

MGM E-3462	(M)	**The Eddie Getz Quintette**	1957	20.00	50.00

GETZ, STAN / RED RODNEY / KAI WINDING

Savoy MG-12105	(M)	**Lestorian Mode**	1957	24.00	60.00

— Savoy albums above have silver on red labels.—

Label & Catalog #		Title	Year	VG+	NM
GETZ, STAN / SONNY STITT / FATS NAVARRO					
Savoy MG-12114	(M)	**Opus De Bop**	1957	24.00	60.00
		—Savoy albums above have silver on red labels.—			
GETZ, STAN					
Stanley Getz is a modern jazz saxophone player and band leader. For additional listings refer to Bob Brookmeyer; Lionel Hampton & Stan Getz; Dizzy Gillespie; Billie Holiday; The Modern Jazz Society; Gerry Mulligan; Charlie Parker; Johnny Smith; Cal Tjader; the Jazzy Soundtracks section under Decca and MGM; and the Various Artists section under Verve.					
New Jazz NJLP-102	(10")	**Stan Getz And The Tenor Sax Stars**	1950	125.00	250.00
New Jazz NJLP-104	(10")	**Stan Getz, Volume 2**	1950	125.00	250.00
Prestige PRLP-102	(10")	**Stan Getz And The Tenor Sax Stars**	1951	100.00	200.00
Prestige PRLP-104	(10")	**Stan Getz, Volume 2**	1951	100.00	200.00
Prestige PRLP-108	(10")	**Stan Getz-Lee Konitz**	1951	100.00	200.00
Prestige PRLP-7002	(M)	**Stan Getz Quartets**	1955	40.00	100.00
		(Prestige 7002 is a reissue of 104.)			
		—Prestige albums above have yellow labels with a W. 50th Street, NYC address.—			
New Jazz NJLP-8214	(M)	**Long Island Sound**	1959	24.00	60.00
		(New Jazz 8214 is a reissue of Prestige 7002)			
		—New Jazz albums above have purple labels.—			
New Jazz NJLP-8214	(M)	**Long Island Sound**	1965	10.00	25.00
		—New Jazz albums above have blue labels with a trident logo on the right side.—			
Prestige PRLP-7255	(M)	**Early Stan**	1963	16.00	40.00
Prestige PRST-7255	(E)	**Early Stan**	1963	10.00	25.00
Prestige PRLP-7256	(M)	**Stan Getz' Greatest Hits**	1963	16.00	40.00
Prestige PRST-7256	(E)	**Stan Getz' Greatest Hits**	1963	10.00	25.00
		—Prestige albums above have yellow mono or silver stereo labels with a Bergenfield, NJ address.—			
Prestige PRLP-7337	(M)	**Stan Getz' Greatest Hits**	1964	10.00	25.00
Prestige PRST-7337	(E)	**Stan Getz' Greatest Hits**	1964	8.00	20.00
		(Prestige 7337 is a reissue of 7256.)			
Prestige PRLP-7434	(M)	**Getz Plays Jazz Classics**	1967	10.00	25.00
Prestige PRST-7434	(E)	**Getz Plays Jazz Classics**	1967	8.00	20.00
		(Prestige 7434 is a reissue of 7255.)			
Prestige PRLP-7516	(S)	**Preservation**	1967	10.00	25.00
Prestige PRST-7516	(E)	**Preservation**	1967	8.00	20.00
		(Prestige 7516 also features Al Haig.)			
		—Prestige albums above have blue labels with a trident logo on the right side.—			
Roost R-402	(10")	**Stan Getz**	1950	100.00	200.00
Roost R-404	(10")	**Stan Getz & The Swedish All Stars**	1951	100.00	200.00
Roost R-407	(10")	**Jazz At Storyville**	1952	100.00	200.00
Roost R-411	(10")	**Jazz At Storyville, Volume 2**	1953	100.00	200.00
Roost R-417	(10")	**Chamber Music**	1953	100.00	200.00
Roost R-420	(10")	**Jazz At Storyville, Volume 3**	1954	100.00	200.00
Roost R-423	(10")	**Split Kick**	1954	100.00	200.00
Roost LP-2207	(M)	**The Sounds Of Stan Getz**	1956	30.00	75.00
		(Roost 2207 is a reissue of 402.)			
Roost LP-2209	(M)	**Storyville**	1956	30.00	75.00
		(Roost 2209 is a reissue of 407 and half of 411.)			
Roost LP-2225	(M)	**Storyville, Volume 2**	1957	30.00	75.00
		(Roost 2225 is a reissue of 420 and half of 411.)			
Roost LP-2249	(M)	**The Greatest Of Stan Getz**	1963	12.00	30.00
Roost SLP-2249	(E)	**The Greatest Of Stan Getz**	1963	8.00	20.00
Roost LP-2251	(M)	**Moonlight In Vermont**	1963	12.00	30.00
Roost SLP-2251	(E)	**Moonlight In Vermont**	1963	8.00	20.00
Roost LP-2255	(M)	**Modern World**	1963	12.00	30.00
Roost SLP-2255	(E)	**Modern World**	1963	8.00	20.00
Roost LP-2258	(M)	**Getz Age**	1963	12.00	30.00
Roost SLP-2258	(E)	**Getz Age**	1963	8.00	20.00
Roost RK-103	(M)	**The Stan Getz Years** *(2 LP box)*	1964	12.00	30.00
Roost SRK-103	(E)	**The Stan Getz Years** *(2 LP box)*	1964	12.00	30.00
Dale 21	(10")	**In Retrospect**	1951	150.00	300.00
Dale 25	(10")	**Billie And Stan**	1951	240.00	400.00
		(Dial 25 also features Billie Holiday.)			
Savoy MG-9004	(10")	**New Sounds In Modern Music**	1951	150.00	300.00
Clef MGC-137	(10")	**Stan Getz Plays**	1953	100.00	200.00
		(Clef 137 features cover art by David Stone Martin.)			
Clef MGC-143	(10")	**The Artistry Of Stan Getz**	1953	100.00	200.00

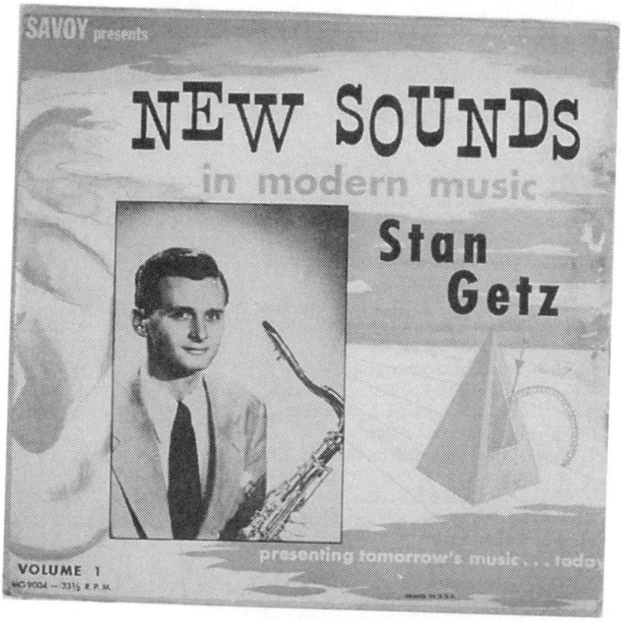

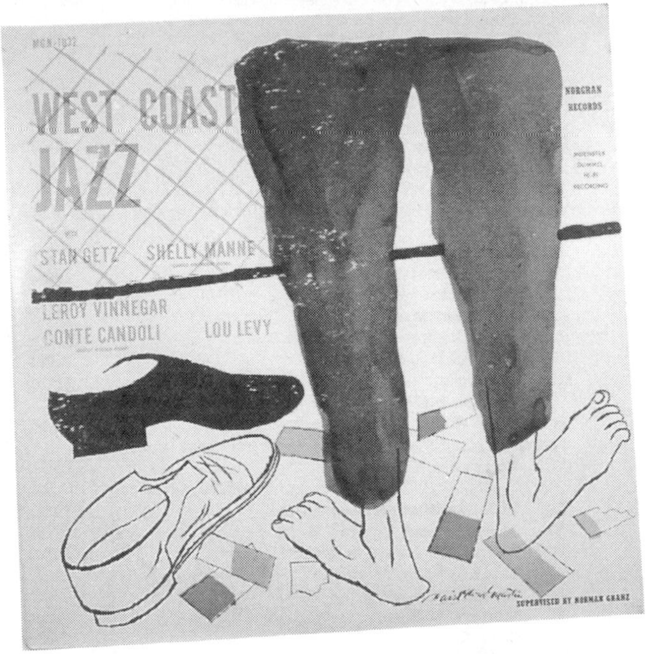

At the age of sixteen Stan Getz was playing with Jack Teagarden before moving into Stan Kenton's band in 1944-45. He then played with Jimmy Dorsey, Benny Goodman, Randy Brooks, Buddy Morrow, Herbie Fields and Butch Stone before making his mark with Woody Herman as one of the "Four Brothers" in 1947-49. Forming his own quintet, he immediately made a national reputation as a mover in the cool school with his Savoy (the rare 10" LP from these sessions is pictured above), Prestige and Roost recordings before beginning a lengthy and mutually profitable association with Norman Granz's Clef, Norgran and Verve labels. He has also recorded with Lionel Hampton, as a member of The Modern Jazz Society, and, as a featured soloist, on albums by Bob Brookmeyer, Billie Holiday, Gerry Mulligan, Charlie Parker, Johnny Smith, and Cal Tjader. He can be heard as a sideman with Herman on Columbia, Harmony and Capitol, Oscar Peterson on Verve, and Kai Winding on Savoy.

Label & Catalog #		Title	Year	VG+	NM
Norgran MGN-1000	*(M)*	**Interpretations By The Stan Getz Quintet #1**	*1954*	**50.00**	**125.00**
Norgran MGN-1008	*(M)*	**Interpretations By The Stan Getz Quintet #2**	*1954*	**50.00**	**125.00**
Norgran MGN-1029	*(M)*	**Interpretations By The Stan Getz Quintet #3**	*1955*	**60.00**	**150.00**
		(Norgran 1029 features cover art by David Stone Martin.)			
Norgran MGN-2000-2	*(M)*	**Stan Getz At The Shrine**	*1955*	**100.00**	**200.00**
		(Boxed set of two LPs with booklet. Cover art by David Stone Martin.)			
Norgran MGN-1032	*(M)*	**West Coast Jazz**	*1955*	**60.00**	**150.00**
		(Norgran 1032 features cover art by David Stone Martin.)			
Norgran MGN-1042	*(M)*	**Stan Getz Plays**	*1955*	**40.00**	**100.00**
		(Norgran 1042 is a reissue of Clef 137 and 143.)			
Norgran MGN-1087	*(M)*	**Stan Getz '56**	*1956*	**40.00**	**100.00**
Norgran MGN-1088	*(M)*	**More West Coast Jazz With Stan Getz**	*1956*	**40.00**	**100.00**
		(Norgran 1087 and 1088 reissue the material from 1000 and 1008.)			
American Rec. Soc. G-407	*(M)*	**Stan Getz**	*1956*	**16.00**	**40.00**
American Rec. Soc. G-428	*(M)*	**Intimate Portrait**	*1957*	**16.00**	**40.00**
American Rec. Soc. G-443	*(M)*	**Stan Getz**	*1957*	**16.00**	**40.00**
Verve MGV-8028	*(M)*	**West Coast Jazz**	*1957*	**20.00**	**50.00**
		(Verve 8028 is a reissue of Norgran 1032.)			
Verve MGV-8029	*(M)*	**Stan Getz '57**	*1957*	**20.00**	**50.00**
		(Verve 8029 is a reissue of Norgran 1087.)			
Verve MGV-8122	*(M)*	**Interpretations By The Stan Getz Quintet #3**	*1957*	**20.00**	**50.00**
		(Verve 8122 is a reissue of Norgran 1029 with the DSM cover.)			
Verve MGV-8133	*(M)*	**Stan Getz Plays**	*1957*	**20.00**	**50.00**
		(Verve 8133 is a reissue of Norgran 1042.)			
Verve MGV-8177	*(M)*	**More West Coast Jazz With Stan Getz**	*1957*	**20.00**	**50.00**
		(Verve 8177 is a reissue of Norgran 1088.)			
Verve MGV-8188-2	*(M)*	**Stan Getz At The Shrine** *(2 LPs)*	*1957*	**40.00**	**100.00**
		(Verve 8188 is a reissue of Norgran 2000.)			
Verve MGV-8200	*(M)*	**Stan Getz And The Cool Sounds**	*1957*	**20.00**	**50.00**
		(Verve 8200 is a reissue of A.R.S. 407.)			
Verve MGV-8213	*(M)*	**Stan Getz In Stockholm**	*1958*	**20.00**	**50.00**
		(Verve 8213 is a reissue of A.R.S. 428.)			
Verve MGV-8251	*(M)*	**Stan Getz And The Oscar Peterson Trio**	*1958*	**20.00**	**50.00**
Verve MGV-8263	*(M)*	**Stan Meets Chet**	*1958*	**30.00**	**75.00**
		(Verve 8263 also features Chet Baker.)			
Verve MGV-8294	*(M)*	**The Steamer**	*1959*	**20.00**	**50.00**
Verve MGV-8296	*(M)*	**Award Winner**	*1959*	**20.00**	**50.00**
Verve MGV-8321	*(M)*	**The Soft Swing**	*1959*	**20.00**	**50.00**
Verve MGV-8331	*(M)*	**Imported From Europe**	*1959*	**20.00**	**50.00**
Verve MGV-8348	*(M)*	**Stan Getz With Gerry Mulligan & The Oscar Peterson Trio**	*1959*	**20.00**	**50.00**
Verve MGV-8356	*(M)*	**Stan Getz Quintet**	*1960*	*Unreleased*	
Verve MGV-8379	*(M)*	**Cool Velvet—Stan Getz And Strings**	*1960*	**20.00**	**50.00**
Verve MGVS-6160	*(S)*	**Cool Velvet—Stan Getz And Strings**	*1960*	*Unreleased*	
Verve MGV-8393-2	*(M)*	**Stan Getz At Large** *(2 LPs)*	*1960*	**24.00**	**60.00**
Verve MGV-8401	*(M)*	**Stan Getz At Large, Volume 1**	*1960*	*Unreleased*	
Verve MGV-8402	*(M)*	**Stan Getz At Large, Volume 1**	*1960*	*Unreleased*	
		— Verve albums above have black labels with "Verve Records, Inc." on the bottom.—			
Verve V-8028	*(M)*	**West Coast Jazz**	*1961*	**8.00**	**20.00**
Verve V-8029	*(M)*	**Stan Getz '57**	*1961*	**8.00**	**20.00**
Verve V-8122	*(M)*	**Interpretations By The Stan Getz Quintet #3**	*1961*	**8.00**	**20.00**
Verve V-8133	*(M)*	**Stan Getz Plays**	*1961*	**8.00**	**20.00**
Verve V-8177	*(M)*	**More West Coast Jazz With Stan Getz**	*1961*	**8.00**	**20.00**
Verve V-8188-2	*(M)*	**Stan Getz At The Shrine** *(2 LPs)*	*1961*	**10.00**	**25.00**
Verve V-8200	*(M)*	**Stan Getz And The Cool Sounds**	*1961*	**8.00**	**20.00**
Verve V-8213	*(M)*	**Stan Getz In Stockholm**	*1961*	**8.00**	**20.00**
Verve V-8251	*(M)*	**Stan Getz And The Oscar Peterson Trio**	*1961*	**8.00**	**20.00**
Verve V-8263	*(M)*	**Stan Meets Chet**	*1961*	**8.00**	**20.00**
Verve V-8294	*(M)*	**The Steamer**	*1961*	**8.00**	**20.00**
Verve V-8296	*(M)*	**Award Winner**	*1961*	**8.00**	**20.00**
Verve V-8321	*(M)*	**The Soft Swing**	*1961*	**8.00**	**20.00**
Verve V-8331	*(M)*	**Imported From Europe**	*1961*	**8.00**	**20.00**
Verve V-8348	*(M)*	**Stan Getz With Gerry Mulligan & The Oscar Peterson Trio**	*1961*	**8.00**	**20.00**
Verve V-8379	*(M)*	**Cool Velvet—Stan Getz And Strings**	*1961*	**8.00**	**20.00**
Verve V-8393-2	*(M)*	**Stan Getz At Large** *(2 LPs)*	*1961*	**10.00**	**25.00**
Verve V-8412	*(M)*	**Focus**	*1961*	**10.00**	**25.00**
Verve V6-8412	*(S)*	**Focus**	*1961*	**8.00**	**20.00**

Label & Catalog #		Title	Year	VG+	NM
Verve V-8432	(M)	**Jazz Samba**	1962	10.00	25.00
Verve V6-8432	(S)	**Jazz Samba**	1962	8.00	20.00
		(Verve 8263 also features Charlie Byrd.)			
Verve V-8494	(M)	**Big Band Bossa Nova**	1962	10.00	25.00
Verve V6-8494	(S)	**Big Band Bossa Nova**	1962	8.00	20.00
		(Verve 8263 also features Gary McFarland.)			
Verve V-8523	(M)	**Jazz Samba Encore!**	1963	10.00	25.00
Verve V6-8523	(S)	**Jazz Samba Encore!**	1963	8.00	20.00
		(Verve 8263 also features Luiz Bonfa.)			
Verve V-8554	(M)	**Reflections**	1963	8.00	20.00
Verve V6-8554	(S)	**Reflections**	1963	6.00	15.00
Verve V-8600	(M)	**Getz Au Go Go**	1965	8.00	20.00
Verve V6-8600	(S)	**Getz Au Go Go**	1965	6.00	15.00
		(Verve 8600 also features Astrud Gilberto.)			
Verve V-8665	(M)	**Stan Getz With Guest Artist Laurindo Almeida**	1966	8.00	20.00
Verve V6-8665	(S)	**Stan Getz With Guest Artist Laurindo Almeida**	1966	6.00	15.00
Verve VSP-2	(M)	**Eloquence**	1966	6.00	15.00
Verve VSPS-2	(E)	**Eloquence**	1966	4.00	10.00
Verve VSP-22	(M)	**Another Time, Another Place**	1966	6.00	15.00
Verve VSPS-22	(E)	**Another Time, Another Place**	1966	4.00	10.00
Verve VSP-31	(M)	**Stan Getz Plays Blues**	1966	6.00	15.00
Verve VSPS-31	(E)	**Stan Getz Plays Blues**	1966	4.00	10.00
Verve V-8693	(M)	**Sweet Rain**	1967	10.00	25.00
Verve V6-8693	(S)	**Sweet Rain**	1967	6.00	15.00
Verve V-8707	(M)	**Voices**	1967	10.00	25.00
Verve V6-8707	(S)	**Voices**	1967	6.00	15.00
Verve V-8719	(M)	**The Best Of Stan Getz**	1967	10.00	25.00
Verve V6-8719	(S)	**The Best Of Stan Getz**	1967	6.00	15.00
Verve V-8752	(M)	**What The World Needs Now— Stan Getz Plays Bacharach And David**	1968	12.00	30.00
Verve V6-8752	(S)	**What The World Needs Now— Stan Getz Plays Bacharach And David**	1968	6.00	15.00
Verve V6-8780	(S)	**Didn't We**	1969	6.00	15.00
		— Verve albums above have black labels with "MGM Records" on the bottom.—			
Modern MLP-1202	(M)	**Groovin' High**	1956	60.00	150.00
Crown CLP-5002	(M)	**Groovin' High**	1957	16.00	40.00
		(Crown 5022 is a reissue of Modern 1202.)			
Jazztone J-1230	(M)	**Stan Getz' Most Famous**	1956	16.00	40.00
Metronome BLP-6	(M)	**The Sound**	1956	20.00	50.00
Blue Ribbon BR-8012	(M)	**Rhythms**	1961	8.00	20.00
Blue Ribbon BS-8012	(E)	**Rhythms**	1961	4.00	10.00
Metro M-501	(M)	**The Melodic Stan Getz**	1965	5.00	12.00
Metro MS-501	(S)	**The Melodic Stan Getz**	1965	4.00	10.00
RCA Victor LM-2925	(M)	**A Song After Sundown— Stan Getz & Arthur Fiedler At Tanglewood**	1967	10.00	25.00
RCA Victor LSC-2925	(S)	**A Song After Sundown— Stan Getz & Arthur Fiedler At Tanglewood**	1967	6.00	15.00
		—RCA albums above have black labels with "Monaural" or "Stereo" on the bottom.—			
MGM SE-4696	(S)	**Marakesh Express**	1969	5.00	12.00

GETZ, STAN, & BOB BROOKMEYER

Verve V-8418	(M)	**Stan Getz & Bob Brookmeyer Recorded Fall 1961**	1961	10.00	25.00
Verve V6-8418	(S)	**Stan Getz & Bob Brookmeyer Recorded Fall 1961**	1961	8.00	20.00
		— Verve albums above have black labels with "MGM Records" on the bottom.—			

GETZ, STAN, & JOAO GILBERTO

Verve V-8545	(M)	**Getz/Gilberto**	1963	8.00	20.00
Verve V6-8545	(S)	**Getz/Gilberto**	1963	6.00	15.00
		(Verve 8545 also features Antonio Carlos Jobim.)			

GETZ, STAN / JOAO GILBERTO

Verve V-8623	(M)	**Getz/Gilberto #2**	1964	8.00	20.00
Verve V6-8623	(S)	**Getz/Gilberto #2**	1964	6.00	15.00
		— Verve albums above have black labels with "MGM Records" on the bottom.—			

Label & Catalog #		Title	Year	VG+	NM
GETZ, STAN, & DIZZY GILLESPIE & SONNY STITT					
Verve MGV-8198	*(M)*	**For Musicians Only**	*1958*	**30.00**	**75.00**
		—Verve albums above have black labels with "Verve Records, Inc." on the bottom.—			
Verve V-8198	*(M)*	**For Musicians Only**	*1961*	**10.00**	**25.00**
		—Verve albums above have black labels with "MGM Records" on the bottom.—			
GETZ, STAN / WARDELL GRAY					
Seeco SLP-7	*(10")*	**Highlights In Modern Jazz**	*1954*	**100.00**	**200.00**
Dawn DLP-1126	*(M)*	**Tenors Anyone?**	*1958*	**30.00**	**75.00**
		(Dawn 1126 is a reissue of Seeco 7.)			
GETZ, STAN, & J.J. JOHNSON					
Verve MGV-8265	*(M)*	**Stan Getz & J.J. Johnson At The Opera House**	*1958*	**20.00**	**50.00**
Verve MGVS-6027	*(S)*	**Stan Getz & J.J. Johnson At The Opera House**	*1960*	**16.00**	**40.00**
Verve MGV-8405	*(M)*	**Stan Getz & J.J. Johnson**	*1960*	*Unreleased*	
		—Verve albums above have black labels with "Verve Records, Inc." on the bottom.—			
Verve V-8490	*(M)*	**Stan Getz & J.J. Johnson At The Opera House**	*1962*	**8.00**	**20.00**
Verve V6-8490	*(S)*	**Stan Getz & J.J. Johnson At The Opera House**	*1962*	**6.00**	**15.00**
		(Verve 8490 is a reissue of 8265.)			
		—Verve albums above have black labels with "MGM Records" on the bottom.—			
GETZ, STAN, & HORACE SILVER					
Baronet B-102	*(M)*	**Pair Of Kings**	*1962*	**6.00**	**15.00**
Baronet BS-102	*(E)*	**Pair Of Kings**	*1962*	**3.00**	**7.50**
		(Baronet 102 reissues Roost recordings.)			
GETZ, STAN / ZOOT SIMS					
Prestige PRLP-7022	*(M)*	**The Brothers**	*1956*	**60.00**	**150.00**
		(Prestige 7022 is a reissue of 102, "Stan Getz," and 138, "Zoot Sims.")			
		—Prestige albums above have yellow labels with a W. 50th St, NYC address.—			
Prestige PRLP-7252	*(M)*	**The Brothers**	*1963*	**20.00**	**50.00**
Prestige PRST-7252	*(E)*	**The Brothers**	*1963*	**14.00**	**35.00**
		—Prestige albums above have yellow mono or silver stereo labels with a Bergenfield, NJ address.—			

GIBBS, TERRY

Julius Gubenko, aka Terry Gibbs, is a modern jazz vibraphone and percussion player, band leader and composer. For additional listings refer to Harry Babasin / Terry Gibbs; Dinah Washington / Terry Gibbs & Max Roach & Don Elliott.

Label & Catalog #		Title	Year	VG+	NM
Brunswick BL-58055	*(10")*	**Terry Gibbs Quartet**	*1954*	**40.00**	**100.00**
Brunswick BL-54009	*(M)*	**Terry**	*1955*	**20.00**	**50.00**
EmArcy MG-36047	*(M)*	**Terry Gibbs**	*1956*	**20.00**	**50.00**
EmArcy MG-36064	*(M)*	**Vibes On Velvet**	*1956*	**20.00**	**50.00**
EmArcy MG-36075	*(M)*	**Mallets A-Plenty**	*1956*	**20.00**	**50.00**
EmArcy MG-36103	*(M)*	**Swingin' Terry Gibbs**	*1956*	**20.00**	**50.00**
EmArcy MG-36148	*(M)*	**More Vibes On Velvet**	*1956*	**20.00**	**50.00**
EmArcy MG-36128	*(M)*	**Terry Plays The Duke**	*1958*	**20.00**	**50.00**
EmArcy MG-36138	*(M)*	**Steve Allen's All Stars**	*1958*	**20.00**	**50.00**
EmArcy SR-80004	*(S)*	**Steve Allen's All Stars**	*1959*	**16.00**	**40.00**
EmArcy MG-36148	*(M)*	**More Vibes On Velvet**	*1958*	**20.00**	**50.00**
		—EmArcy albums above have blue labels with silver print.—			
Mode LP-123	*(M)*	**A Jazz Band Ball**	*1957*	**30.00**	**75.00**
Interlude MO-506	*(M)*	**Vibrations**	*1959*	**16.00**	**40.00**
Interlude ST-1006	*(S)*	**Vibrations**	*1959*	**12.00**	**30.00**
		(Interlude 506 is a reissue of Mode 123.)			
Mercury MG-20440	*(M)*	**Launching A New Sound In Music**	*1959*	**16.00**	**40.00**
Mercury SR-60112	*(S)*	**Launching A New Sound In Music**	*1959*	**12.00**	**30.00**
Mercury MG-20518	*(M)*	**Steve Allen's All Stars**	*1960*	**12.00**	**30.00**
Mercury SR-60195	*(S)*	**Steve Allen's All Stars**	*1960*	**10.00**	**25.00**
		(Mercury 20518 is a reissue of EmArcy 36138.)			
Mercury MG-20704	*(M)*	**Explosion!**	*1962*	**8.00**	**20.00**
Mercury SR-60704	*(S)*	**Explosion!**	*1962*	**6.00**	**15.00**
Mercury MG-20812	*(M)*	**Jewish Melodies In Jazztime**	*1963*	**8.00**	**20.00**
Mercury SR-60812	*(S)*	**Jewish Melodies In Jazztime**	*1963*	**6.00**	**15.00**
		—Mercury albums above have silver on black labels.—			
Verve MGV-2134	*(M)*	**Swing Is Here!**	*1960*	**20.00**	**50.00**
Verve MGVS-6140	*(S)*	**Swing Is Here!**	*1960*	**16.00**	**40.00**
Verve MGV-2151	*(M)*	**The Exciting Terry Gibbs Big Band**	*1960*	**20.00**	**50.00**

Label & Catalog #		Title	Year	VG+	NM
Verve MGV-2136	(M)	**Music From Cole Porter's "Can Can"**	1960	20.00	50.00
Verve MGVS-6145	(S)	**Music From Cole Porter's "Can Can"**	1960	16.00	40.00
		—Verve albums above have "Verve Record, Inc." on the bottom of the label.—			
Verve V-2134	(M)	**Swing Is Here!**	1961	8.00	20.00
Verve V6-2134	(S)	**Swing Is Here!**	1961	6.00	15.00
Verve V-2151	(M)	**The Exciting Terry Gibbs Big Band**	1961	8.00	20.00
Verve V6-2151	(S)	**The Exciting Terry Gibbs Big Band**	1961	6.00	15.00
Verve V-2136	(M)	**Music From Cole Porter's "Can Can"**	1961	8.00	20.00
Verve V6-2136	(S)	**Music From Cole Porter's "Can Can"**	1961	6.00	15.00
Verve V-8447	(M)	**That Swing Thing**	1962	10.00	25.00
Verve V6-8447	(S)	**That Swing Thing**	1962	8.00	20.00
Verve V-8496	(M)	**Straight Ahead**	1962	10.00	25.00
Verve V6-8496	(S)	**Straight Ahead**	1962	8.00	20.00
		—Verve albums above have black labels with "MGM Records" on the bottom.—			
Time 52105	(M)	**Hootenanny My Way**	1963	12.00	30.00
Time S-2105	(S)	**Hootenanny My Way**	1963	10.00	25.00
Limelight LM-82005	(M)	**El Nutto**	1964	10.00	25.00
Limelight LS-86005	(S)	**El Nutto**	1964	8.00	20.00
Impulse A-58	(M)	**Take It From Me**	1964	12.00	30.00
Impulse AS-58	(S)	**Take It From Me**	1964	10.00	25.00
		—Impulse albums above have orange & black labels.—			
Impulse AS-58	(S)	**Take It From Me**	1968	4.00	10.00
		—Impulse albums above have red & black labels with the "abc" logo on top.—			
Roost LP-2260	(M)	**Latino**	1965	8.00	20.00
Roost RS-2260	(S)	**Latino**	1965	6.00	15.00
Mainstream 56048	(M)	**It's Time We Met**	1965	8.00	20.00
Mainstream S-6048	(S)	**It's Time We Met**	1965	6.00	15.00
		(Mainstream 56048 is a reissue of Time 2105.)			
Dot DLP-3726	(M)	**Reza**	1966	8.00	20.00
Dot DLP-25726	(S)	**Reza**	1966	6.00	15.00

GIBBS, TERRY, & BILL HARRIS

Mode LP-129	(M)	**The Ex-Hermanites**	1957	30.00	75.00
Premier PM-2006	(M)	**Woodchoppers' Ball**	1963	6.00	15.00
Premier PS-2006	(E)	**Woodchoppers' Ball**	1963	3.00	7.50
		(Premier 2006 is a reissue of Mode 129.)			

GILBERT, ANN

Ann Gilbert is a jazz-based vocalist.

Groove LG-1004	(M)	**The Many Moods Of Ann**	1956	20.00	50.00

GILBERT & SULLIVAN JAZZ WORKSHOP, THE

Andex A-27101	(M)	**The Coolest Mikado**	1961	10.00	25.00
Andex AS-27101	(S)	**The Coolest Mikado**	1961	8.00	20.00

GILBERTO, ASTRUD

Brazilian born Astrud Gilberto, the wife of Joao Gilberto, is a Latin jazz-based vocalist. For additional listings refer to Stan Getz; the Jazzy Soundtracks section.

Verve V-8608	(M)	**The Astrud Gilberto Album**	1965	5.00	12.00
Verve V6-8608	(S)	**The Astrud Gilberto Album**	1965	6.00	15.00
Verve V-8629	(M)	**The Shadow Of Your Smile**	1965	5.00	12.00
Verve V6-8629	(S)	**The Shadow Of Your Smile**	1965	6.00	15.00
Verve V-8643	(M)	**Look To The Rainbow**	1965	5.00	12.00
Verve V6-8643	(S)	**Look To The Rainbow**	1965	6.00	15.00
Verve V-8673	(M)	**A Certain Smile, A Certain Sadness**	1966	5.00	12.00
Verve V6-8673	(S)	**A Certain Smile, A Certain Sadness**	1966	6.00	15.00
Verve V-8708	(M)	**Beach Samba**	1967	5.00	12.00
Verve V6-8708	(S)	**Beach Samba**	1967	6.00	15.00
Verve V6-8754	(S)	**Windy**	1968	5.00	12.00
Verve V6-8776	(S)	**I Haven't Got Anything Better To Do**	1969	5.00	12.00
Verve V6-8754	(S)	**Astrud Gilberto-September 17, 1969**	1969	5.00	12.00
		—Verve albums above have black labels with "MGM Records" on the bottom.—			

GILBERTO, JOAO

Brazilian born Joao Gilberto is a Latin-jazz guitar player and vocalist. For additional listings refer to Stan Getz; Herbie Mann & Joao Gilberto; the Jazzy Soundtracks section.

Atlantic 8070	(M)	**The Boss Of The Bossa Nova**	1963	8.00	20.00
Atlantic SD-8070	(S)	**The Boss Of The Bossa Nova**	1963	6.00	15.00

Label & Catalog #		Title	Year	VG+	NM
Atlantic 8076	(M)	**The Warm World Of Astrud Gilberto**	1964	8.00	20.00
Atlantic SD-8076	(S)	**The Warm World Of Astrud Gilberto**	1964	6.00	15.00
		—Atlantic albums above have multi-color labels with a black fan logo.—			

GILLESPIE, DIZZY

John "Dizzy" Gillespie is a traditional jazz-based trumpet player, vocalist and composer. For further listings refer to Count Basie / Dizzie Gillespie; Clifford Brown & Max Roach; Benny Carter; Miles Davis / Dizzie Gillespie / Fats Navarro; Roy Eldridge & Dizzy Gillespie; Roy Eldridge & Dizzy Gillespie & Harry Edison; Gil Fuller; Slim Gaillard / Dizzie Gillespie; Coleman Hawkins; The Modern Jazz Sextet; Kati Bell Nubin; Charlie Parker; The Quintet; Stuff Smith; Sonny Stitt; the Jazzy Soundtracks section under Philips; and the Various Artists section under Verve.

Dial LP-212	(10")	**Modern Trumpets**	1950	300.00	500.00
Discovery DL-3013	(10")	**Dizzy Gillespie Plays/ Johnny Richards Conducts**	1950	150.00	300.00
Dee Gee LP-1000	(10")	**Dizzy Gillespie**	1952	150.00	300.00
Atlantic ALR-138	(10")	**Dizzy Gillespie, Volume 1**	1952	150.00	300.00
Atlantic ALR-142	(10")	**Dizzy Gillespie, Volume 2**	1952	150.00	300.00
Atlantic 1257	(M)	**Dizzy At Home And Abroad**	1957	40.00	100.00
		(Atlantic 1257 is a reissue of 138 and 142.)			
		—Atlantic albums above have black mono or green stereo labels.—			
Atlantic 1257	(M)	**Dizzy At Home And Abroad**	1961	12.00	30.00
		—Atlantic albums above have multi-color labels with a white fan logo.—			
Atlantic 1257	(M)	**Dizzy At Home And Abroad**	196?	6.00	15.00
		—Atlantic albums above have multi-color labels with a black fan logo.—			
Allegro 4023	(10")	**Dizzy Gillespie Orchestra**	1954	100.00	200.00
Allegro 4108	(10")	**Dizzy Gillespie Plays**	1954	100.00	200.00
Allegro 3017	(M)	**Dizzy Gillespie Plays**	1955	60.00	150.00
		(Allegro 13017 is a reissue of 4108.)			
Allegro 3083	(M)	**Dizzy Gillespie**	1955	60.00	150.00
Allegro ALL-1593	(M)	**Dizzy Gillespie**	1955	40.00	100.00
		(Allegro 1593 is a reissue of 3083.)			
Blue Note BLP-5017	(10")	**Horn Of Plenty**	1953	150.00	300.00
Contemporary C-2504	(10")	**Dizzy In Paris**	1953	100.00	200.00
Roost R-414	(10")	**Dizzy Over Paris**	1953	100.00	250.00
Roost LP-2214	(M)	**Concert In Paris**	1956	60.00	150.00
		(Roost 2214 is a reissue of 414.)			
Roost LP-2234	(M)	**Diz 'N' Bird In Concert**	1959	30.00	75.00
Roost SK-106	(M)	**The Beginning: Diz And Bird** *(2 LP box)*	196?	20.00	50.00
Esoteric ESJ-4	(10")	**Dizzy Gillespie With Charlie Christian**	1953	100.00	200.00
Gene Norman GNP-4	(10")	**Dizzy Gillespie And His Original Big Band**	1954	60.00	150.00
RCA Victor LJM-1009	(M)	**Dizzier And Dizzier**	1954	50.00	125.00
Clef MGC-136	(10")	**Dizzy Gillespie With Strings**	1953	100.00	200.00
Norgran MGN-2	(10")	**The Dizzy Gillespie-Stan Getz Sextet #1**	1954	125.00	250.00
Norgran MGN-18	(10")	**The Dizzy Gillespie-Stan Getz Sextet #2**	1954	125.00	250.00
Norgran MGN-1003	(M)	**Afro**	1954	60.00	150.00
		(Norgran 1003 features cover art by David Stone Martin.)			
Norgran MGN-1023	(M)	**Dizzy And Strings**	1955	60.00	150.00
		(Norgran 1023 features cover art by David Stone Martin.)			
Norgran MGN-1050	(M)	**Diz And Getz**	1955	50.00	125.00
		(Norgran 1050 is a reissue of 2 and 18.)			
Norgran MGN-1083	(M)	**Dizzy Gillespie And His Orchestra**	1956	50.00	125.00
Norgran MGN-1084	(M)	**World Statesman**	1956	50.00	125.00
Norgran MGN-1090	(M)	**Diz Big Band**	1956	50.00	125.00
		(Norgran 1090 is a reissue of 1023.)			
American Rec. Soc. G-405	(M)	**Dizzy Gillespie**	1956	16.00	40.00
American Rec. Soc. G-423	(M)	**Big Band Jazz**	1956	16.00	40.00
Verve MGV-8017	(M)	**Dizzy In Greece**	1957	24.00	60.00
Verve MGV-8141	(M)	**Diz And Getz**	1957	30.00	75.00
		(Verve 8141 is a reissue of Norgran 1050.)			
Verve MGV-8173	(M)	**Jazz Recital**	1957	24.00	60.00
		(Verve 8173 is a reissue of Norgran 1083.)			
Verve MGV-8174	(M)	**World Statesman**	1957	24.00	60.00
		(Verve 8174 is a reissue of Norgran 1084.)			
Verve MGV-8178	(M)	**Diz Big Band**	1957	30.00	75.00
		(Verve 8178 is a reissue of Norgran 1090 with the DSM cover.)			
Verve MGV-8191	(M)	**Afro**	1957	*Unreleased*	
Verve MGV-8208	(M)	**Manteca**	1958	24.00	60.00
Verve MGV-8214	(M)	**Dizzy Gillespie And Stuff Smith**	1958	24.00	60.00

Label & Catalog #		Title	Year	VG+	NM
Verve MGV-8222	(M)	Birk's Works	1958	24.00	60.00
Verve MGV-8242	(M)	Dizzy Gillespie At Newport	1958	24.00	60.00
Verve MGVS-6023	(S)	Dizzy Gillespie At Newport	1960	20.00	50.00
Verve MGV-8260	(M)	Duets	1958	30.00	75.00
		(Verve 8260 also features Sonny Rollins and Sonny Stitt.)			
Verve MGV-8313	(M)	Have Trumpet, Will Excite!	1959	24.00	60.00
Verve MGVS-6047	(S)	Have Trumpet, Will Excite!	1960	20.00	50.00
Verve MGV-8328	(M)	The Ebullient Mr. Gillespie	1959	24.00	60.00
Verve MGVS-6068	(S)	The Ebullient Mr. Gillespie	1960	20.00	50.00
Verve MGV-8352	(M)	Greatest Trumpet Of Them All	1959	24.00	60.00
Verve MGVS-6117	(S)	Greatest Trumpet Of Them All	1960	20.00	50.00
Verve MGV-8357	(M)	The Dizzy Gillespie Big Band	1960	Unreleased	
Verve MGV-8386	(M)	A Portrait Of Duke Ellington	1960	24.00	60.00
Verve MGV-8394	(M)	Gillespiana	1960	24.00	60.00
		—Verve albums above have black labels with "Verve Records, Inc." on the bottom.—			
Verve V-8017	(M)	Dizzy In Greece	1961	10.00	25.00
Verve V-8141	(M)	Diz And Getz	1961	10.00	25.00
Verve V-8173	(M)	Jazz Recital	1961	10.00	25.00
Verve V-8174	(M)	World Statesman	1961	10.00	25.00
Verve V-8178	(M)	Diz Big Band	1961	10.00	25.00
Verve V-8214	(M)	Dizzy Gillespie And Stuff Smith	1961	10.00	25.00
Verve V-8222	(M)	Birk's Works	1961	10.00	25.00
Verve V-8242	(M)	Dizzy Gillespie At Newport	1961	10.00	25.00
Verve V6-8242	(S)	Dizzy Gillespie At Newport	1961	8.00	20.00
Verve V-8313	(M)	Have Trumpet, Will Excite!	1961	10.00	25.00
Verve V6-8313	(S)	Have Trumpet, Will Excite!	1961	8.00	20.00
Verve V-8328	(M)	The Ebullient Mr. Gillespie	1961	10.00	25.00
Verve V6-8328	(S)	The Ebullient Mr. Gillespie	1961	8.00	20.00
Verve V-8352	(M)	Greatest Trumpet Of Them All	1961	10.00	25.00
Verve V6-8352	(S)	Greatest Trumpet Of Them All	1961	8.00	20.00
Verve V-8386	(M)	A Portrait Of Duke Ellington	1961	20.00	25.00
Verve V-8394	(M)	Gillespiana	1961	10.00	25.00
Verve V-8401	(M)	An Electrifying Evening With The Dizzy Gillespie Quintet	1961	12.00	30.00
Verve V6-8401	(S)	An Electrifying Evening With The Dizzy Gillespie Quintet	1961	10.00	25.00
Verve V-8411	(M)	Perceptions	1961	12.00	30.00
Verve V6-8411	(S)	Perceptions	1961	10.00	25.00
Verve V-8423	(M)	Carnegie Hall Concert	1962	12.00	30.00
Verve V6-8423	(S)	Carnegie Hall Concert	1962	10.00	25.00
Verve V-8477	(M)	Dizzy, Rollins & Stitt	1962	12.00	30.00
Verve V6-8477	(S)	Dizzy, Rollins & Stitt	1962	10.00	25.00
		(Verve 8477 is a reissue of 8260.)			
Verve V-8566	(M)	The Essential Dizzy Gillespie	1964	6.00	15.00
Verve V6-8566	(S)	The Essential Dizzy Gillespie	1964	5.00	12.00
		—Verve albums above have black labels with "MGM Records" on the bottom.—			
Savoy MG-12020	(M)	Groovin' High	1955	40.00	100.00
Savoy MG-12047	(M)	The Champ	1956	40.00	100.00
Savoy MG-12110	(M)	The Dizzy Gillespie Story	1957	40.00	100.00
Regent MG-6043	(M)	School Days	1957	40.00	100.00
		(Regent 6043 is a reissue of Dee Gee 1000.)			
Gene Norman GNP-23	(M)	Dizzy Gillespie And His Big Band	1957	30.00	75.00
Ron-lette A-11	(M)	Dizzy Gillespie	1958	12.00	30.00
		(Ron-lette 11 is a reissue of Allegro 3083.)			
RCA Victor LPM-2398	(M)	The Greatest	1961	16.00	40.00
RCA Victor LSP-2398	(E)	The Greatest	1961	8.00	20.00
		—RCA albums above have black labels with "Long Play" or "Reprocessed Stereo" on the bottom.—			
Philips PHM-200-048	(M)	Jazz On The French Riviera	1962	10.00	25.00
Philips PHS-600-048	(S)	Jazz On The French Riviera	1962	8.00	20.00
Philips PHM-200-070	(M)	New Wave!	1963	10.00	25.00
Philips PHS-600-070	(S)	New Wave!	1963	8.00	20.00
Philips PHM-200-091	(M)	Something Old, Something New	1963	10.00	25.00
Philips PHS-600-091	(S)	Something Old, Something New	1963	8.00	20.00
Philips PHM-200-106	(M)	Dizzy Gillespie And The Double Six Of Paris	1963	10.00	25.00
Philips PHS-600-106	(S)	Dizzy Gillespie And The Double Six Of Paris	1963	8.00	20.00
Philips PHM-200-123	(M)	Dizzy Gillespie Goes Hollywood	1964	10.00	25.00
Philips PHS-600-123	(S)	Dizzy Gillespie Goes Hollywood	1964	8.00	20.00

Label & Catalog #		Title	Year	VG+	NM
Reprise R-6072	(M)	**Dateline Europe**	1963	10.00	25.00
Reprise RS-6072	(S)	**Dateline Europe**	1963	8.00	20.00
Limelight LM-82007	(M)	**Jambo Caribe**	1964	10.00	25.00
Limelight LS-86007	(S)	**Jambo Caribe**	1964	8.00	20.00
Limelight LM-82022	(M)	**The New Continent**	1965	10.00	25.00
Limelight LS-86022	(S)	**The New Continent**	1965	8.00	20.00
RCA Victor LPV-530	(M)	**Dizzy Gillespie**	1965	8.00	20.00
Verve VSP-7	(M)	**Night In Tunisia**	1966	6.00	15.00
Verve VSPS-7	(S)	**Night In Tunisia**	1966	4.00	10.00
Savoy MG-12204	(M)	**School Days**	1969	8.00	20.00
		(Savoy 12204 is a reissue of Regent 6043.)			
Solid State SS-18034	(S)	**Live At The Village Vanguard**	1969	6.00	15.00
Solid State SS-18054	(S)	**My Way**	1969	6.00	15.00
Solid State SS-18061	(S)	**Cornucopia**	1969	6.00	15.00

GILLESPIE, DIZZY / COUNT BASIE

Verve MGV-8244	(M)	**Dizzy Gillespie And Count Basie At Newport**	1958	20.00	50.00
Verve MGVS-6025	(S)	**Dizzy Gillespie And Count Basie At Newport**	1960	16.00	40.00
		—Verve albums above have black labels with "Verve Records, Inc." on the bottom.—			
Verve V-8244	(M)	**Dizzy Gillespie And Count Basie At Newport**	1961	8.00	20.00
Verve V6-8244	(S)	**Dizzy Gillespie And Count Basie At Newport**	1961	6.00	15.00
		—Verve albums above have black labels with "MGM Records" on the bottom.—			

GILLESPIE, DIZZY / JIMMY McPARTLAND

MGM E-3286	(M)	**Hot Vs. Cool**	1955	30.00	75.00

GILLESPIE, DIZZY / DJANGO REINHARDT

Clef MGC-747	(M)	**Jazz From Paris**	1956	*Unreleased*	
Verve MGV-8015	(M)	**Jazz From Paris**	1957	20.00	50.00
		(Verve 8015 is a reissue of Clef 136 and 516.)			
		—Verve albums above have black labels with "Verve Records, Inc." on the bottom.—			
Verve V-8015	(M)	**Jazz From Paris**	1961	8.00	20.00
		—Verve albums above have black labels with "MGM Records" on the bottom.—			

GIN BOTTLE SEVEN, THE: *Refer to* CARL HALEN

GINSBERG, ALLEN

Allen Ginsburg is a beat-based poet.

Fantasy 7006	(M)	**"Howl" And Other Poems**	1957	150.00	300.00
		—Fantasy albums above have red labels on dark red, non-flexible vinyl.—			
Fantasy 7006	(M)	**"Howl" And Other Poems**	195?	60.00	150.00
		—Fantasy albums above have red labels on non-flexible vinyl.—			

GIRARD, GEORGE

George Girard is a traditional jazz trumpeteer. For additional listings refer to Jack Delaney / George Girard.

Vik LX-1058	(M)	**Jam Session On Bourbon Street**	1957	16.00	40.00
Vik LX-1063	(M)	**Stompin' At The Famous Door**	1957	16.00	40.00

GIUFFRE, JIMMY

James Giuffre is a modern jazz clarinet and woodwinds player and composer. For additional listings refer to Teddy Charles; Herb Ellis; Lee Konitz; Shelly Manne; The Modern Jazz Quartet.

Capitol H-549	(10")	**Jimmy Giuffre**	1954	50.00	125.00
Capitol T-549	(M)	**Jimmy Giuffre**	1954	30.00	75.00
Capitol T-634	(M)	**Tangents In Jazz**	1955	30.00	75.00
Atlantic 1238	(M)	**The Jimmy Giuffre Clarinet**	1956	20.00	50.00
Atlantic 1254	(M)	**The Jimmy Giuffre 3**	1957	20.00	50.00
Atlantic 1276	(M)	**Music Man**	1958	20.00	50.00
Atlantic SD-1276	(S)	**Music Man**	1958	20.00	50.00
Atlantic 1282	(M)	**Trav'lin' Light**	1958	20.00	50.00
Atlantic SD-1282	(S)	**Trav'lin' Light**	1958	20.00	50.00
Atlantic 1295	(M)	**Four Brothers Sound**	1958	20.00	50.00
Atlantic SD-1295	(S)	**Four Brothers Sound**	1958	16.00	40.00
		—Atlantic albums above have black mono or green stereo labels.—			
Atlantic 1238	(M)	**The Jimmy Giuffre Clarinet**	1960	8.00	20.00
Atlantic 1254	(M)	**The Jimmy Giuffre 3**	1960	8.00	20.00
Atlantic 1276	(M)	**Music Man**	1960	8.00	20.00
Atlantic SD-1276	(S)	**Music Man**	1960	6.00	15.00

Label & Catalog #		Title	Year	VG+	NM
Atlantic 1282	(M)	**Trav'lin' Light**	1960	8.00	20.00
Atlantic SD-1282	(S)	**Trav'lin' Light**	1960	6.00	15.00
Atlantic 1295	(M)	**Four Brothers Sound**	1960	8.00	20.00
Atlantic SD-1295	(S)	**Four Brothers Sound**	1960	6.00	15.00
Atlantic 1330	(M)	**Western Suite**	1960	12.00	30.00
Atlantic SD-1330	(S)	**Western Suite**	1960	10.00	25.00
—Atlantic albums above have multi-color labels with a white fan logo.—					
Atlantic 1238	(M)	**The Jimmy Giuffre Clarinet**	196?	5.00	12.00
Atlantic 1254	(M)	**The Jimmy Giuffre 3**	196?	5.00	12.00
Atlantic 1282	(M)	**Trav'lin' Light**	196?	5.00	12.00
Atlantic SD-1282	(S)	**Trav'lin' Light**	196?	4.00	10.00
Atlantic 1330	(M)	**Western Suite**	196?	5.00	12.00
Atlantic SD-1330	(S)	**Western Suite**	196?	4.00	10.00
—Atlantic albums above have multi-color labels with a black fan logo.—					
Verve MGV-8307	(M)	**Seven Pieces**	1959	16.00	40.00
Verve MGVS-6039	(S)	**Seven Pieces**	1960	12.00	30.00
Verve MGV-8337	(M)	**The Easy Way**	1959	16.00	40.00
Verve MGVS-6095	(S)	**The Easy Way**	1960	12.00	30.00
Verve MGV-8361	(M)	**Ad Lib**	1960	16.00	40.00
Verve MGVS-6130	(S)	**Ad Lib**	1960	12.00	30.00
Verve MGV-8387	(M)	**The Jimmy Giuffre Quartet In Person**	1960	16.00	40.00
Verve MGV-8395	(M)	**Piece For Clarinet And String Orchestra**	1961	16.00	40.00
Verve MGV-8397	(M)	**Fusion**	1961	16.00	40.00
Verve MGV-8402	(M)	**Thesis**	1961	16.00	40.00
—Verve albums above have black labels with "Verve Records, Inc." on the bottom.—					
Verve V-8307	(M)	**Seven Pieces**	1961	8.00	20.00
Verve V6-8307	(S)	**Seven Pieces**	1961	6.00	15.00
Verve V-8337	(M)	**The Easy Way**	1961	8.00	20.00
Verve V6-8337	(S)	**The Easy Way**	1961	6.00	15.00
Verve V-8361	(M)	**Ad Lib**	1961	8.00	20.00
Verve V6-8361	(S)	**Ad Lib**	1961	6.00	15.00
Verve V-8387	(M)	**The Jimmy Giuffre Quartet In Person**	1961	8.00	20.00
Verve V6-8387	(S)	**The Jimmy Giuffre Quartet In Person**	1961	6.00	15.00
Verve V-8395	(M)	**Piece For Clarinet And String Orchestra**	1961	8.00	20.00
Verve V6-8395	(S)	**Piece For Clarinet And String Orchestra**	1961	6.00	15.00
Verve V-8397	(M)	**Fusion**	1961	8.00	20.00
Verve V6-8397	(S)	**Fusion**	1961	6.00	15.00
Verve V-8402	(M)	**Thesis**	1961	8.00	20.00
Verve V6-8402	(S)	**Thesis**	1961	6.00	15.00
—Verve albums above have black labels with "MGM Records" on the bottom.—					
Columbia CL-1964	(M)	**Free Fall**	1963	8.00	20.00
Columbia CS-8764	(S)	**Free Fall**	1963	6.00	15.00
—Columbia albums above have "Guaranteed High Fidelity" or "360 Sound Stereo" in black on the label.—					

GLASEL, JOHN

John Glasel is a modern jazz trumpet player.

ABC-Paramount ABC-165	(M)	**Jazz Session**	1957	20.00	50.00
Jazz Unlimited 1002	(M)	**Brasstet**	1960	12.00	30.00

GOLD, SANFORD

Sanford Gold is a modern jazz pianist.

Prestige PRLP-7019	(M)	**Piano D'or**	1956	24.00	60.00
—Prestige albums above have yellow labels with a W. 50th Street, NYC address.—					

GOLDIE, DON

Donald Gold is a modern jazz trumpet player.

Argo LP-4010	(M)	**Brilliant**	1960	12.00	30.00
Argo LPS-4010	(S)	**Brilliant**	1960	10.00	25.00
Argo LP-708	(M)	**Trumpet Caliente**	1962	12.00	30.00
Argo LPS-708	(S)	**Trumpet Caliente**	1962	10.00	25.00
Verve V-8475	(M)	**Trumpet Exodus**	1962	12.00	30.00
Verve V6-8475	(S)	**Trumpet Exodus**	1962	10.00	25.00
—Verve albums above have black labels with "MGM Records" on the bottom.—					

GOLDKETTE, JEAN

French born Jean Goldkette is a traditional jazz pianist and band leader.

"X" LVA-3017	(10")	**Jean Goldkette And His Orchestra Featuring Bix Beiderbecke**	1954	20.00	50.00

Benny Golson started with Bull Moose Jackson's band in 1951, which included Tadd Dameron. When Dameron started his own group in '53, Benny signed on. He then played with Lionel Hampton (1953), Johnny Hodges (1954), Earl Bostic (1954-56), Dizzy Gillespie (1956-58) and joined Art Blakey's Jazz Messengers (1958-59). In 1959 he formed The Jazztet with Art Farmer. Aside from his career with his own group (examples from his early '60s output on Argo and Mercury are shown here) and with The Jazztet, he has recorded as a featured soloist with Curtis Fuller, Roland Kirk and Lem Winchester, and can be found as a sideman on LPs by Blakey and Lee Morgan, both on Blue Note, Gillespie on Verve, James Moody on Argo, Jimmy Cleveland on EmArcy, Sahib Shibab on Savoy, Philly Joe Jones on Riverside, George Russell on Decca, and Clifford Brown on Prestige.

Label & Catalog #		Title	Year	VG+	NM

GOLSON, BENNY

Benjamin Golson is a modern jazz tenor saxophone player and composer. For additional listings refer to Curtis Fuller; The Jazztet; Roland Kirk; Lem Winchester.

Riverside RLP-12-256	(M)	**The Modern Touch Of Benny Golson**	1957	24.00	60.00
Riverside RLP-12-290	(M)	**The Other Side Of Benny Golson**	1958	24.00	60.00
		—Riverside albums above have blue mono or black stereo labels with a reel & mike logo on top.—			
Contemporary C-3552	(M)	**Benny Golson's New York Scene**	1958	20.00	50.00
United Arts. UAL-4020	(M)	**Benny Golson And The Philadelphians**	1959	20.00	50.00
United Arts. UAS-5020	(S)	**Benny Golson And The Philadelphians**	1959	16.00	40.00
New Jazz NJLP-8220	(M)	**Groovin' With Golson**	1959	20.00	50.00
New Jazz NJLP-8235	(M)	**Gone With Golson**	1960	20.00	50.00
New Jazz NJLP-8248	(M)	**Gettin' With It**	1960	20.00	50.00
		—New Jazz albums above have purple labels.—			
New Jazz NJLP-8220	(M)	**Groovin' With Golson**	1965	10.00	25.00
New Jazz NJLP-8235	(M)	**Gone With Golson**	1965	10.00	25.00
New Jazz NJLP-8248	(M)	**Gettin' With It**	1965	10.00	25.00
		—New Jazz albums above have blue labels with a trident logo on the right side.—			
Argo LP-681	(M)	**Take A Number From 1 To 10**	1961	16.00	40.00
Argo LPS-681	(S)	**Take A Number From 1 To 10**	1961	12.00	30.00
Argo LP-716	(M)	**Free: Benny Golson Quartet**	1963	16.00	40.00
Argo LPS-716	(S)	**Free: Benny Golson Quartet**	1963	12.00	30.00
Jazzland JLP-85	(M)	**Reunion**	1962	16.00	40.00
Jazzland JLP-985	(S)	**Reunion**	1962	12.00	30.00
		(Jazzland 85 is a reissue of Riverside 256.)			
Audio Fidelity AFLP-1978	(M)	**Pop + Jazz = Swing**	1962	8.00	20.00
Audio Fidelity AFSD-5978	(S)	**Pop + Jazz = Swing**	1962	6.00	15.00
Audio Fidelity AFLP-2150	(M)	**Just Jazz**	1963	8.00	20.00
Audio Fidelity AFSD-6150	(S)	**Just Jazz**	1963	6.00	15.00
Mercury MG-20801	(M)	**Turning Point**	1963	8.00	20.00
Mercury SR-60801	(S)	**Turning Point**	1963	6.00	15.00
Prestige PRLP-7361	(M)	**Stockholm Sojourn**	1965	10.00	25.00
Prestige PRST-7361	(S)	**Stockholm Sojourn**	1965	8.00	20.00
		—Prestige albums above have blue labels with a trident logo on the right side.—			
Verve V-8710	(M)	**Turn In, Turn On**	1967	8.00	20.00
Verve V6-8710	(S)	**Turn In, Turn On**	1967	6.00	15.00
		—Verve albums above have black labels with "MGM Records" on the bottom.—			

GONSALVES, PAUL

Paul Gonsalves is a big band-based tenor saxophone player associated with Duke Ellington from the '50s through the '70s.

Argo LP-626	(M)	**Cookin'**	1958	20.00	50.00
Argo LPS-626	(S)	**Cookin'**	1958	16.00	40.00
Jazzland JLP-36	(M)	**Gettin' Together**	1961	16.00	40.00
Jazzland JLP-936	(S)	**Gettin' Together**	1961	12.00	30.00
Impulse A-41	(M)	**Cleopatra Feelin' Jazzy**	1963	12.00	30.00
Impulse AS-41	(S)	**Cleopatra Feelin' Jazzy**	1963	10.00	25.00
Impulse A-52	(M)	**Salt And Pepper**	1963	12.00	30.00
Impulse AS-52	(S)	**Salt And Pepper**	1963	10.00	25.00
		(Impulse 52 also features Sonny Stitt.)			
Impulse A-55	(M)	**Tell It The Way It Is**	1963	12.00	30.00
Impulse AS-55	(S)	**Tell It The Way It Is**	1963	10.00	25.00
		—Impulse albums above have orange & black labels.—			
Impulse AS-41	(S)	**Cleopatra Feelin' Jazzy**	1968	4.00	10.00
Impulse AS-52	(S)	**Salt And Pepper**	1968	4.00	10.00
Impulse AS-55	(S)	**Tell It The Way It Is**	1968	4.00	10.00
		—Impulse albums above have red & black labels with the "abc" logo on top.—			

GONZALES, BABS

Babs Gonzales is a jazz-based vocalist.

Hope 001	(M)	**Voila!**	1958	50.00	125.00
Jaro 5000	(M)	**Tales Of Manhattan**	1959	40.00	100.00
Jaro 8000	(S)	**Tales Of Manhattan**	1959	30.00	75.00
Dauntless DM-4311	(M)	**Sunday Afternoon At Small's Paradise**	1963	20.00	50.00
Dauntless DS-6311	(S)	**Sunday Afternoon At Small's Paradise**	1963	16.00	40.00

GONSALVES, VIRGIL

Virgil Gonsalves is a West Coast jazz baritone saxophone and clarinet player.

Nocturne NLP-8	(10")	**Virgil Gonsalves**	1954	40.00	100.00

Label & Catalog #		Title	Year	VG+	NM
Liberty LJH-6010	*(M)*	**Jazz San Francisco Style**	*1955*	**20.00**	**50.00**
Omega OML-1047	*(M)*	**Jazz At Monterey**	*1959*	**16.00**	**40.00**

GOODMAN, BENNY

Benjamin Goodman is a traditional jazz clarinet player and band leader. For additional listings refer to Steve Allen; Buck Clayton; Rosemary Clooney; Ben Pollack; and the Jazzy Soundtracks section under Decca.

Label & Catalog #		Title	Year	VG+	NM
Columbia CL-6033	*(10")*	**Benny Goodman And Peggy Lee**	*1949*	**30.00**	**75.00**
Columbia CL-6048	*(10")*	**Dance Parade**	*1949*	**20.00**	**50.00**
Columbia CL-6052	*(10")*	**Goodman Sextet Session**	*1949*	**20.00**	**50.00**
Columbia GL-102	*(10")*	**Let's Hear The Melody**	*1950*	**24.00**	**60.00**
Columbia CL-6100	*(10")*	**Dance Parade, Volume 2**	*1950*	**20.00**	**50.00**
Columbia CL-6302	*(10")*	**Let's Hear The Melody**	*1951*	**20.00**	**50.00**
Columbia SL-160	*(M)*	**Carnegie Hall Jazz Concert** *(2 LPs)*	*1950*	**40.00**	**100.00**
Columbia ML-4358	*(M)*	**Carnegie Hall Concert, Volume 1**	*1950*	**16.00**	**40.00**
Columbia ML-4359	*(M)*	**Carnegie Hall Concert, Volume 2**	*1950*	**16.00**	**40.00**
Columbia SL-176	*(M)*	**King Of Swing** *(6 LP box)*	*1950*	**60.00**	**150.00**
		(The six LPs in this box were issued separately as 4358, 4359, 180, 500 and 534.)			
Columbia SL-180	*(M)*	**1937/38 Jazz Concert No. 2** *(2 LPs)*	*1952*	**30.00**	**75.00**
		(The two LPs in this set were issued separately as 4590 and 4591.)			
Columbia ML-4590	*(M)*	**1937/38 Jazz Concert No. 2—Volume 1**	*1950*	**16.00**	**40.00**
Columbia ML-4591	*(M)*	**1937/38 Jazz Concert No. 2—Volume 2**	*1950*	**16.00**	**40.00**
Columbia ML-4613	*(M)*	**King Of Swing—Volume 1**	*1950*	**16.00**	**40.00**
Columbia ML-4614	*(M)*	**King Of Swing—Volume 2**	*1950*	**16.00**	**40.00**
Martin Block MB-1000	*(M)*	**Benny Goodman Trio Plays For The Fletcher Henderson Fund**	*1951*	**20.00**	**50.00**
		(Limited Edition reissued as Columbia 516.)			
Columbia GL-500	*(M)*	**The Golden Era: Combos**	*195?*	**20.00**	**50.00**
Columbia GL-501	*(M)*	**The Golden Era: Bands**	*195?*	**20.00**	**50.00**
Columbia GL-516	*(M)*	**Benny Goodman Trio Plays For The Fletcher Henderson Fund**	*195?*	**20.00**	**50.00**
Columbia GL-523	*(M)*	**Benny Goodman Presents Eddie Sauter Arrangements**	*195?*	**20.00**	**50.00**
Columbia GL-524	*(M)*	**Benny Goodman Presents Fletcher Henderson Arrangements**	*195?*	**20.00**	**50.00**
Columbia CL-500	*(M)*	**The Golden Era: Combos**	*1954*	**16.00**	**40.00**
Columbia CL-501	*(M)*	**The Golden Era: Bands**	*1954*	**16.00**	**40.00**
Columbia CL-516	*(M)*	**Benny Goodman Trio Plays For The Fletcher Henderson Fund**	*1954*	**16.00**	**40.00**
Columbia CL-523	*(M)*	**Benny Goodman Presents Eddie Sauter Arrangements**	*1954*	**16.00**	**40.00**
Columbia CL-524	*(M)*	**Benny Goodman Presents Fletcher Henderson Arrangements**	*1954*	**16.00**	**40.00**
Columbia CL-534	*(M)*	**Benny Goodman And His Orchestra**	*1954*	**16.00**	**40.00**
Columbia CL-552	*(M)*	**The New Benny Goodman Sextet**	*1954*	**16.00**	**40.00**
		—Columbia albums above have "Long Playing" on the bottom of the label.—			
Columbia CL-500	*(M)*	**The Golden Era: Combos**	*1955*	**12.00**	**30.00**
Columbia CL-501	*(M)*	**The Golden Era: Bands**	*1955*	**12.00**	**30.00**
Columbia CL-516	*(M)*	**Benny Goodman Trio Plays For The Fletcher Henderson Fund**	*1955*	**12.00**	**30.00**
Columbia CL-523	*(M)*	**Benny Goodman Presents Eddie Sauter Arrangements**	*1955*	**12.00**	**30.00**
Columbia CL-524	*(M)*	**Benny Goodman Presents Fletcher Henderson Arrangements**	*1955*	**12.00**	**30.00**
Columbia CL-534	*(M)*	**Benny Goodman And His Orchestra**	*1955*	**12.00**	**30.00**
Columbia CL-552	*(M)*	**The New Benny Goodman Sextet**	*1955*	**12.00**	**30.00**
Columbia CL-652	*(M)*	**Benny Goodman Sextet And Orchestra With Charlie Christian**	*1955*	**12.00**	**30.00**
Columbia OSL-160	*(M)*	**Carnegie Hall Jazz Concert** *(2 LPs)*	*1956*	**30.00**	**75.00**
		(Columbia OSL-160 is a reissue of SL-160.)			
Columbia CL-814	*(M)*	**Carnegie Hall Concert, Volume 1**	*1956*	**12.00**	**30.00**
Columbia CL-815	*(M)*	**Carnegie Hall Concert, Volume 2**	*1956*	**12.00**	**30.00**
Columbia CL-816	*(M)*	**Carnegie Hall Concert, Volume 3**	*1956*	**12.00**	**30.00**
		(Columbia 814-816 are reissues of 4358 and 4359.)			
Columbia OSL-180	*(M)*	**The King Of Swing** *(2 LPs)*	*1956*	**30.00**	**75.00**
		(Columbia OSL-180 is a reissue of SL-150.)			
Columbia CL-817	*(M)*	**The King Of Swing, Volume 1**	*1956*	**12.00**	**30.00**
Columbia CL-818	*(M)*	**The King Of Swing, Volume 2**	*1956*	**12.00**	**30.00**

Label & Catalog #		Title	Year	VG+	NM
Columbia CL-819	*(M)*	**The King Of Swing, Volume 3**	*1956*	**12.00**	**30.00**
Columbia CL-820	*(M)*	**The Great Benny Goodman**	*1956*	**12.00**	**30.00**
Columbia CL-821	*(M)*	**The Vintage Benny Goodman**	*1956*	**12.00**	**30.00**
Columbia CL-2533	*(10")*	**Benny At The Ballroom**	*1956*	**16.00**	**40.00**
		(Columbia 2533 is a reissue of 6100.)			
Columbia CL-2564	*(10")*	**The Benny Goodman Six**	*1956*	**16.00**	**40.00**
		(Columbia 2564 is a reissue of 6052.)			
Westinghouse *(No number)*	*(M)*	**Benny Goodman Plays World Favorites In High Fidelity**	*1958*	**12.00**	**30.00**
Westinghouse *(No number)*	*(M)*	**Benny In Brussels** *(5 LPs)*	*1958*	**40.00**	**100.00**
Columbia CL-1247	*(M)*	**Benny Goodman In Brussels—Volume 1**	*1958*	**12.00**	**30.00**
Columbia CL-1248	*(M)*	**Benny Goodman In Brussels—Volume 2**	*1958*	**12.00**	**30.00**
		(Columbia 1247 and 1248 reissue material from the Westinghouse box.)			
Columbia CS-8075	*(S)*	**Benny Goodman In Brussels** *(2 LPs)*	*1959*	**16.00**	**40.00**
		(Columbia 8075 is a 2-LP stereo reissue of 1247 and 1248.)			
Columbia XTV-28995	*(M)*	**Swing Into Spring**	*1959*	**8.00**	**20.00**
		(Promo made for Texaco using the early red & gold label.)			
Columbia CL-1324	*(M)*	**Happy Session**	*1959*	**12.00**	**30.00**
Columbia CS-8129	*(S)*	**Happy Session**	*1959*	**10.00**	**25.00**
Columbia CL-1579	*(M)*	**Benny Goodman Swings Again**	*1960*	**12.00**	**30.00**
Columbia CS-8379	*(S)*	**Benny Goodman Swings Again**	*1960*	**10.00**	**25.00**
—Columbia albums above have six white on black "eye" logos on each label.—					
Columbia CL-2483	*(M)*	**Benny Goodman's Greatest Hits**	*1966*	**6.00**	**15.00**
Columbia CS-9283	*(P)*	**Benny Goodman's Greatest Hits**	*1966*	**5.00**	**12.00**
—Columbia albums above have "360 Sound" in white on the bottom of the label.—					
Harmony HL-7005	*(M)*	**Peggy Lee Sings With Benny Goodman**	*1957*	**8.00**	**20.00**
Harmony HL-7190	*(M)*	**Swing With Benny Goodman In High Fidelity**	*196?*	**6.00**	**15.00**
Harmony HS-11090	*(E)*	**Swing With Benny Goodman In High Fidelity**	*196?*	**3.00**	**7.50**
Harmony HL-7225	*(M)*	**Swing Time**	*196?*	**6.00**	**15.00**
Harmony HL-7278	*(M)*	**Swingin' Benny Goodman Sextet**	*196?*	**6.00**	**15.00**
Capitol H-202	*(10")*	**Session For Six**	*1950*	**20.00**	**50.00**
Capitol H-295	*(10")*	**Easy Does It**	*1952*	**20.00**	**50.00**
Capitol H-343	*(10")*	**The Benny Goodman Trio**	*1952*	**20.00**	**50.00**
Capitol H-409	*(10")*	**The Benny Goodman Band**	*1953*	**20.00**	**50.00**
Capitol H-441	*(10")*	**The Goodman Touch**	*1953*	**20.00**	**50.00**
Capitol H-479	*(10")*	**Small Combo-1947**	*1954*	**20.00**	**50.00**
Capitol H1-565	*(10")*	**B.G. In Hi-Fi (Volume 1)**	*1954*	**12.00**	**30.00**
Capitol H2-565	*(10")*	**B.G. In Hi-Fi (Volume 2)**	*1954*	**12.00**	**30.00**
		(Capitol H1 and H2 565 are the 12" album 565 split into two 10" LPs.)			
Capitol T-395	*(M)*	**Session For Six**	*1953*	**16.00**	**40.00**
Capitol T-409	*(M)*	**The Benny Goodman Band**	*1953*	**16.00**	**40.00**
Capitol T-441	*(M)*	**The Benny Goodman Touch**	*1954*	**16.00**	**40.00**
Capitol W-565	*(M)*	**B.G. In Hi Fi**	*1955*	**16.00**	**40.00**
Capitol T-668	*(M)*	**Mostly Sextets**	*1956*	**12.00**	**30.00**
Capitol T-669	*(M)*	**Benny Goodman Combos**	*1956*	**12.00**	**30.00**
Capitol S-706	*(M)*	**Selections Featured In "The Benny Goodman Story"**	*1956*	**12.00**	**30.00**
—Capitol albums above have turquoise labels.—					
Capitol T-395	*(M)*	**Session For Six**	*195?*	**8.00**	**20.00**
Capitol T-409	*(M)*	**The Benny Goodman Band**	*195?*	**8.00**	**20.00**
Capitol T-441	*(M)*	**The Benny Goodman Touch**	*195?*	**8.00**	**20.00**
Capitol W-565	*(M)*	**B.G. In Hi Fi**	*195?*	**8.00**	**20.00**
Capitol T-668	*(M)*	**Mostly Sextets**	*195?*	**8.00**	**20.00**
Capitol T-669	*(M)*	**Benny Goodman Combos**	*195?*	**8.00**	**20.00**
Capitol S-706	*(M)*	**Selections Featured In "The Benny Goodman Story"**	*195?*	**8.00**	**20.00**
Capitol T-1514	*(M)*	**The Hits Of Benny Goodman**	*1961*	**8.00**	**20.00**
Capitol DT-1514	*(E)*	**The Hits Of Benny Goodman**	*1961*	**5.00**	**12.00**
—Capitol albums above have black "rainbow" labels with the logo on the left side.—					
Capitol T-2157	*(M)*	**Hello Benny!**	*1964*	**5.00**	**12.00**
Capitol ST-2157	*(S)*	**Hello Benny!**	*1964*	**6.00**	**15.00**
Capitol T-2282	*(M)*	**Made In Japan**	*1964*	**5.00**	**12.00**
Capitol ST-2282	*(S)*	**Made In Japan**	*1964*	**6.00**	**15.00**
Brunswick BL-58015	*(10")*	**Chicago Jazz Classics**	*1950*	**20.00**	**50.00**
Brunswick BL-54010	*(M)*	**Benny Goodman 1927-1934**	*1954*	**12.00**	**30.00**
RCA Victor WPT-12	*(10")*	**Benny Goodman**	*1951*	**20.00**	**50.00**
RCA Victor WPT-26	*(10")*	**Immortal Performances**	*1952*	**20.00**	**50.00**

Label & Catalog #		Title	Year	VG+	NM
RCA Victor LPT-3004	(10")	**Benny Goodman Quartet**	1952	20.00	50.00
RCA Victor LPT-3056	(10")	**Benny Goodman 1937-39**	1954	20.00	50.00
RCA Victor LPT-1005	(M)	**Benny Goodman**	1954	16.00	40.00
RCA Victor LPM-1099	(M)	**The Golden Age Of Benny Goodman**	1955	16.00	40.00
RCA Victor LPM-1226	(M)	**The Benny Goodman Trio, Quartet, Quintet**	1956	16.00	40.00
RCA Victor LPM-1239	(M)	**This Is Benny Goodman**	1956	16.00	40.00
RCA Victor LPT-6703	(M)	**The Golden Age Of Swing**	1956	*See below*	
		(Deluxe five album set in a plush white binder with booklet. Rare as a zoot suit with no way to reasonably suggest a value.)			
RCA Victor LPM-2247	(M)	**The Kingdom Of Swing**	1960	8.00	20.00
RCA Victor LST-2247	(S)	**The Kingdom Of Swing**	1960	10.00	25.00
RCA Victor LOC-6008	(M)	**Benny Goodman In Moscow** *(2 LPs)*	1962	10.00	25.00
RCA Victor LSO-6008	(S)	**Benny Goodman In Moscow** *(2 LPs)*	1962	8.00	20.00
		—RCA albums above have black labels with "Long Play" or "Living Stereo" on the bottom.—			
RCA Victor LPM-2968	(M)	**Together Again**	1964	8.00	20.00
RCA Victor LSP-2968	(S)	**Together Again**	1964	6.00	15.00
		(BG is joined by Lionel Hampton, Gene Krupa and Teddy Wilson.)			
		—RCA albums above have black labels with "Mono" or "Stereo" on the bottom.—			
RCA Victor LPV-521	(M)	**B.G., The Small Groups**	1965	8.00	20.00
Camden CAL-624	(M)	**Swing, Swing, Swing**	1960	6.00	15.00
Camden CAS-624	(E)	**Swing, Swing, Swing**	1960	5.00	12.00
Camden CAL-872	(M)	**Benny Goodman & His Orchestra Featuring Great Vocalists Of Our Time**	1965	5.00	12.00
Camden CAS-872	(E)	**Benny Goodman & His Orchestra Featuring Great Vocalists Of Our Time**	1965	4.00	10.00
Verve MGV-4013	(M)	**The Superlative Goodman, Volume 1**	1958	*Unreleased*	
Verve MGV-4014	(M)	**The Superlative Goodman, Volume 2**	1958	*Unreleased*	
Verve MGV-4015-2	(M)	**The Superlative Goodman** *(2 LPs)*	1958	*Unreleased*	
		—Verve albums above have black labels with "Verve Records, Inc" on the bottom.—			
Verve V-8582	(M)	**The Essential Benny Goodman**	1964	6.00	15.00
Verve V6-8582	(E)	**The Essential Benny Goodman**	1964	5.00	12.00
		(Verve 8582 is a reissue of material from the MGM albums.)			
		—Verve albums above have black labels with "MGM Records" on the bottom.—			
MGM 3E-9	(M)	**The Benny Goodman Treasure Chest** *(3 LP box)*	1959	60.00	150.00
		(The LPs in this box were issued separately as 3788, 3789 and 3790.)			
MGM E-3788	(M)	**Performance Recordings—Volume 1**	1959	10.00	25.00
MGM E-3789	(M)	**Performance Recordings—Volume 2**	1959	10.00	25.00
MGM E-3790	(M)	**Performance Recordings—Volume 3**	1959	10.00	25.00
MGM E-3810	(M)	**The Sound Of Music**	1960	8.00	20.00
MGM SE-3810	(S)	**The Sound Of Music**	1960	10.00	25.00
		—MGM albums above have yellow labels.—			
MGM E-3788	(M)	**Performance Recordings—Volume 1**	197?	4.00	10.00
MGM E-3789	(M)	**Performance Recordings—Volume 2**	197?	4.00	10.00
MGM E-3790	(M)	**Performance Recordings—Volume 3**	197?	4.00	10.00
		—MGM albums above have blue & gold swirl labels.—			
Chess LP-1440	(DJ)	**Benny Rides Again** *(Multi-color vinyl)*	1960	40.00	100.00
Chess LP-1440	(M)	**Benny Rides Again**	1960	20.00	50.00
Command RS-921	(S)	**Benny Goodman & Paris: Listen To The Magic**	1967	5.00	12.00
Classics Rec. Lib. RL-7673	(M)	**An Album Of Swing Classics** *(3 LPs)*	1967	20.00	50.00
Classics Rec. Lib. SRL-7673	(E)	**An Album Of Swing Classics** *(3 LPs)*	1967	16.00	40.00
		(A collection of 1955 sides packaged by the Book Of The Month Club.)			
Epic EE-22025	(M)	**Clarinet A La King**	1969	5.00	12.00
Prestige PRST-7644	(S)	**Benny Goodman And The Giants Of Swing**	1969	6.00	15.00
		—Prestige albums above have blue labels with a trident logo on top.—			

GOODMAN, BENNY, & JACK TEADARDEN

Jazz Panorama 1807	(10")	**Goodman & Teagarden**	1951	20.00	50.00
Jolly Rogers 5023	(10")	**Benny Goodman Featuring Jack Teagarden**	1954	20.00	50.00

GORDON, BOB

Robert Gordon is a West Coast jazz baritone saxophone player. For additional listings refer to Herbie Harper; Jack Montrose.

Pacific Jazz PJLP-12	(10")	**Meet Mr. Gordon**	1954	50.00	125.00
Tampa TP-26	(M)	**Jazz Impressions** *(Colored vinyl)*	1957	40.00	100.00
Tampa TP-26	(M)	**Jazz Impressions**	1958	20.00	50.00
		(Tampa 26 is a reissue of Skylark 20, "The George Redman Group.")			

Dexter Gordon kicked off his career with Lionel Hampton in 1940-43, eventually playing with Lee Young, Jessie Price, and Louis Armstrong (1944) and Billy Eckstine and Charlie Parker during the war years. He bounced back and forth between the East and West Coast scenes before enjoying a bit of a renaissance in the early '60s when signed by Blue Note's new head of talent, contemporary Ike Quebec. He can be found on albums by Eckstine on EmArcy, Fats Navarro on Savoy, Stan Levey on Bethlehem, and Wardell Gray on Prestige and Regent.

Label & Catalog #		Title	Year	VG+	NM
GORDON, BOB / CLIFFORD BROWN					
Pacific Jazz PJ-1214	*(M)*	**The Bob Gordon Quintet/ The Clifford Brown Ensemble**	*1956*	**40.00**	**100.00**
		(Pacific Jazz 1214 is a reissue of 12 and 19.)			
Pacific Jazz PJ-3	*(M)*	**Jazz Immortal**	*1960*	**20.00**	**50.00**
		(Pacific Jazz 3 is a reissue of 1214.)			
GORDON, BOBBY					
Robert Gordon is a clarinet player with an easy-listening jazz flavor.					
Decca DL-4394	*(M)*	**Warm And Sentimental**	*1963*	**6.00**	**15.00**
Decca DL-74394	*(S)*	**Warm And Sentimental**	*1963*	**5.00**	**12.00**
GORDON, DEXTER					
Dexter Gordon is a modern jazz tenor saxophone player pivotal to the early bebop movement. For additional listings refer to Booker Ervin; Wardell Gray & Dexter Gordon; and the Various Artists section under Savoy.					
Dial LP-204	*(10")*	**Dexter Gordon Quintet**	*1950*	**150.00**	**300.00**
Savoy MG-9003	*(10")*	**All Star Series—Dexter Gordon**	*1951*	**125.00**	**250.00**
Savoy MG-9016	*(10")*	**New Trends In Modern Jazz, Volume 3**	*1952*	**125.00**	**250.00**
Bethlehem BCP-36	*(M)*	**Daddy Plays The Horn**	*1955*	**50.00**	**125.00**
Dootone DL-207	*(M)*	**Dexter Blows Hot & Cool** *(Red vinyl)*	*1956*	**100.00**	**200.00**
Dootone DL-207	*(M)*	**Dexter Blows Hot & Cool**	*1957*	**40.00**	**100.00**
Savoy MG-12130	*(M)*	**Dexter Rides Again**	*1958*	**40.00**	**100.00**
Jazzland JLP-29	*(M)*	**The Resurgence of Dexter Gordon**	*1960*	**30.00**	**75.00**
Jazzland JLP-929	*(S)*	**The Resurgence of Dexter Gordon**	*1960*	**20.00**	**50.00**
Blue Note BLP-4077	*(M)*	**Doin' Allright**	*1961*	**100.00**	**200.00**
Blue Note BST-84077	*(S)*	**Doin' Allright**	*1961*	**60.00**	**150.00**
—Blue Note albums above have blue on white labels with a W. 63rd St, NYC address.—					
Blue Note BLP-4083	*(M)*	**Dexter Calling**	*1961*	**30.00**	**75.00**
Blue Note BST-84083	*(S)*	**Dexter Calling**	*1961*	**20.00**	**50.00**
—Blue Note albums above have blue on white labels with a 61st St, NYC address.—					
Blue Note BLP-4077	*(M)*	**Doin' Allright**	*1963*	**10.00**	**25.00**
Blue Note BST-84077	*(S)*	**Doin' Allright**	*1963*	**8.00**	**20.00**
Blue Note BLP-4083	*(M)*	**Dexter Calling**	*1963*	**10.00**	**25.00**
Blue Note BST-84083	*(S)*	**Dexter Calling**	*1963*	**8.00**	**20.00**
Blue Note BLP-4112	*(M)*	**Go!**	*1962*	**16.00**	**40.00**
Blue Note BST-84112	*(S)*	**Go!**	*1962*	**12.00**	**30.00**
Blue Note BLP-4133	*(M)*	**A Swingin' Affair**	*1963*	**16.00**	**40.00**
Blue Note BST-84133	*(S)*	**A Swingin' Affair**	*1963*	**12.00**	**30.00**
Blue Note BLP-4146	*(M)*	**Our Man In Paris**	*1963*	**16.00**	**40.00**
Blue Note BST-84146	*(S)*	**Our Man In Paris**	*1963*	**12.00**	**30.00**
Blue Note BLP-4176	*(M)*	**One Flight Up**	*1964*	**16.00**	**40.00**
Blue Note BST-84176	*(S)*	**One Flight Up**	*1964*	**12.00**	**30.00**
Blue Note BLP-4204	*(M)*	**Gettin' Around**	*1965*	**16.00**	**40.00**
Blue Note BST-84204	*(S)*	**Gettin' Around**	*1965*	**12.00**	**30.00**
—Blue Note albums above have blue on white labels with a New York, USA address.—					
Blue Note BST-84077	*(S)*	**Doin' Allright**	*196?*	**5.00**	**12.00**
Blue Note BST-84083	*(S)*	**Dexter Calling**	*196?*	**5.00**	**12.00**
Blue Note BST-84112	*(S)*	**Go!**	*196?*	**5.00**	**12.00**
Blue Note BST-84133	*(S)*	**A Swingin' Affair**	*196?*	**5.00**	**12.00**
Blue Note BST-84146	*(S)*	**Our Man In Paris**	*196?*	**5.00**	**12.00**
Blue Note BST-84176	*(S)*	**One Flight Up**	*196?*	**5.00**	**12.00**
Blue Note BST-84204	*(S)*	**Gettin' Around**	*196?*	**5.00**	**12.00**
—Blue Note albums above have blue on white labels with "A Division of Liberty Records."—					
Prestige PRST-7623	*(S)*	**The Tower Of Power**	*1969*	**6.00**	**15.00**
Prestige PRST-7680	*(S)*	**More Power**	*1969*	**6.00**	**15.00**
—Prestige albums above have blue labels.—					
GORDON, DEXTER / HOWARD McGHEE					
Jazztone J-1235	*(M)*	**The Chase**	*1956*	**16.00**	**40.00**
GORDON, HONI					
Honi Gordon is a jazz-based vocalist.					
Prestige PRLP-7230	*(M)*	**Honi—Honi Gordon Sings**	*1962*	**20.00**	**50.00**
Prestige PRST-7230	*(S)*	**Honi—Honi Gordon Sings**	*1962*	**16.00**	**40.00**
—Prestige albums above have yellow mono or silver stereo labels with a Bergenfield, NJ address.—					

Classically trained John Graas began his jazz career with Claude Thornhill in 1942. After the war he toured with Tex Beneke (1947-48) and Stan Kenton (1948-50). Through the '50s he worked for both television and the movies, and toured as a member of Liberace's orchestra! While the bulk of his solo outings have been with Decca, his first album was issued by Trend and reissued by Kapp (pictured above). As a sideman he has recorded with Kenton, Shorty Rogers and Bob Cooper, all on Capitol, and Pete Rugolo on Columbia.

Label & Catalog #		Title	Year	VG+	NM
GORDON, JOE					
Joseph Gordon is a West Coast jazz trumpet player.					
EmArcy MG-26046	(10")	**Introducing Joe Gordon**	1954	**50.00**	**125.00**
EmArcy MG-36025	(M)	**Introducing Joe Gordon**	1955	**40.00**	**100.00**
		—EmArcy albums above have blue labels with silver print.—			
Contemporary M-3597	(M)	**Lookin' Good**	1961	**16.00**	**40.00**
Contemporary S-7597	(S)	**Lookin' Good**	1961	**12.00**	**30.00**
		—Contemporary stereo albums have gold & black labels.—			
GOWANS, BRAD					
Arthur Bradford Gowans is a traditional jazz valve trombone, clarinet, cornet and saxophone(s) player.					
RCA Victor LJM-3000	(10")	**Brad Gowans' New York Nine**	1954	**20.00**	**50.00**
GOZZO, CONRAD					
Conrad Gozzo is a West Coast jazz trumpet player.					
RCA Victor LPM-1124	(M)	**Goz The Great**	1955	**20.00**	**50.00**
		—RCA albums above have black labels with "Long Play" on the bottom.—			
GRAAS, JOHN					
John Graas is a West Coast jazz French horn player.					
Trend TL-1005	(10")	**French Horn Jazz**	1954	**20.00**	**100.00**
Decca DL-8079	(M)	**Jazz Studio 2**	1954	**20.00**	**50.00**
		(Decca 8079 also features Herb Geller.)			
Decca DL-8104	(M)	**Jazz Studio 3**	1955	**20.00**	**50.00**
		(Decca 8104 also features Gerry Mulligan.)			
Decca DL-8343	(M)	**Jazz Lab 1**	1956	**20.00**	**50.00**
Decca DL-8478	(M)	**Jazz Lab 2**	1957	**20.00**	**50.00**
Decca DL-8677	(M)	**Jazzmantics**	1958	**20.00**	**50.00**
Kapp KL-1046	(M)	**French Horn Jazz**	1957	**20.00**	**50.00**
		(Kapp 1046 is a reissue of Trend 1005.)			
Andex A-3003	(M)	**Premiere In Jazz**	1958	**20.00**	**50.00**
Andex AS-3003	(S)	**Premiere In Jazz**	1958	**16.00**	**40.00**
EmArcy MG-36117	(M)	**Coup De Graas**	1958	**20.00**	**50.00**
Mercury SR-80020	(S)	**Coup De Graas**	1959	**16.00**	**40.00**
		(Mercury 80020 is a stereo reissue of EmArcy 36117.)			
GRACEN, THELMA					
Thelma Gracen is a jazz-based vocalist.					
EmArcy MG-36096	(M)	**Thelma Gracen**	1956	**100.00**	**200.00**
		—EmArcy albums above have blue labels with silver print.—			
Wing MGW-60005	(M)	**Thelma Gracen**	1956	**60.00**	**150.00**
		(Wing 60005 is a reissue of EmArcy 36096.)			
GRANT, EARL					
Decca DL-4299	(M)	**Earl Grant At Basin Street East**	1962	**6.00**	**15.00**
Decca DL7-4299	(S)	**Earl Grant At Basin Street East**	1962	**5.00**	**12.00**
GRAPPELLI, STEPHANE					
Stephane Grapelly, aka Stephane Grapelli, is a traditional-jazz based violin player. For additional listings refer to Stuff Smith.					
EmArcy MG-36120	(M)	**Improvisations**	1957	**20.00**	**50.00**
		—EmArcy albums above have blue labels with silver print.—			
Atlantic 1391	(M)	**Feeling + Finesse = Jazz**	1962	**8.00**	**20.00**
Atlantic SD-1391	(S)	**Feeling + Finesse = Jazz**	1962	**6.00**	**15.00**
		—Atlantic albums above have multi-color labels with a black fan logo.—			
GRAVES, CONLEY					
Conley Graves is a jazz-based pianist.					
Nocturne NLP-4	(10")	**Piano Artistry**	1954	**40.00**	**100.00**
Decca DL-8220	(M)	**Genius At Work**	1956	**16.00**	**40.00**
Decca DL-8412	(M)	**Piano Dynamics**	1957	**16.00**	**40.00**
Decca DL-8475	(M)	**Rendezvous In Paris**	1957	**16.00**	**40.00**
GRAVES, JOE					
Joseph Graves is a modern jazz trumpet player.					
Capitol T-1977	(M)	**The Great New Swingers**	1963	**12.00**	**30.00**
Capitol ST-1977	(S)	**The Great New Swingers**	1963	**10.00**	**25.00**

Label & Catalog #		Title	Year	VG+	NM

GRAVES, MILFORD

Milford Graves is a modern jazz drummer. For additional listings refer to The New York Art Quintet.

ESP-Disk' 1015	(M)	**Milford Graves Percussion Ensemble**	1966	10.00	25.00
ESP-Disk' 1015	(S)	**Milford Graves Percussion Ensemble**	1966	8.00	20.00

GRAY, GLEN

Glen Gray Knoblaugh is a traditional jazz and big band saxophone(s) player and band leader. For additional listings refer to Jonah Jones.

Coral CRL-56006	(10")	**Hoagy Carmichael Songs**	1950	20.00	50.00
Coral CRL-56009	(10")	**Glen Gray Souvenirs**	1950	20.00	50.00
Decca DL-5089	(10")	**Musical Smoke Rings**	1950	20.00	50.00
Decca DL-5397	(10")	**No Name Jive**	1952	20.00	50.00
Capitol W-747	(M)	**Casa Loma In Hi-Fi**	1956	12.00	30.00
Harmony HL-7045	(M)	**The Great Recordings Of Glen Gray**	1957	8.00	20.00

GRAY, JERRY

Jerry Gray is a traditional jazz-based composer and big band leader who took over Glenn Miller's orchestra in the wake of Miller's death during WWII.

Decca DL-5266	(10")	**Dance To The Music Of Gray**	1950	20.00	50.00
Decca DL-5375	(10")	**A Tribute To Glen Miller**	1951	20.00	50.00
Decca DL-5478	(10")	**Dance Time**	1952	20.00	50.00
Decca DL-8101	(M)	**Jerry Gray & His Orchestra**	1955	16.00	40.00
Liberty LRP-3???	(M)	**Hi Fi Shades Of Gray**	195?	16.00	40.00
Liberty LST-7002	(S)	**Hi Fi Shades Of Gray**	1958	12.00	30.00
Liberty LRP-3089	(M)	**Jerry Gray At The Hollywood Palladium**	1957	16.00	40.00
Liberty LST-7013	(S)	**Jerry Gray At The Hollywood Palladium**	1958	12.00	30.00
Tops L-1627	(M)	**A Salute To Glenn Miller**	1958	8.00	20.00
Tops L-1640	(M)	**Glenn Miller Greats**	1958	8.00	20.00
Craftsman 8035	(M)	**More Miller Hits**	195?	8.00	20.00
Vocalion L-3602	(M)	**A Tribute To Glenn Miller**	195?	8.00	20.00
Warner Bros. W-1446	(M)	**Singin' & Swingin'**	1962	10.00	25.00
Warner Bros. WS-1446	(S)	**Singin' & Swingin'**	1962	8.00	20.00

GRAY, WARDELL

Wardell Gray is a modern jazz tenor saxophone player. For additional listings refer to Louis Bellson; Stan Getz / Wardell Gray; and the Various Artists section under Savoy.

Prestige PRLP-115	(10")	**Wardell Gray Tenor Sax**	1951	125.00	250.00
Prestige PRLP-128	(10")	**Jazz Concert**	1952	125.00	250.00
Prestige PRLP-147	(10")	**Wardell Gray's Los Angeles Stars**	1953	125.00	250.00
Prestige PRLP-7008	(M)	**Wardell Gray Memorial, Volume 1**	1955	40.00	100.00
		(Prestige 7008 is a reissue of 115.)			
Prestige PRLP-7009	(M)	**Wardell Gray Memorial, Volume 2**	1955	40.00	100.00
		(Prestige 7009 is a reissue of 128 and 147.)			
		—Prestige albums above have yellow labels with a W. 50th Street, NYC address.—			
Modern MLP-1204	(M)	**Way Out Wardell**	1956	60.00	150.00
Crown CLP-5004	(M)	**Way Out Wardell**	1957	16.00	40.00
		(Crown 5004 is a reissue of Modern 1204.)			
Prestige PRLP-7343	(M)	**Wardell Gray Memorial Album** *(2 LPs)*	1964	16.00	40.00
Prestige PRST-7343	(E)	**Wardell Gray Memorial Album** *(2 LPs)*	1964	12.00	30.00
		(Prestige 7343 is a reissue of 7008 and 7009.).			
		—Prestige albums above have blue labels with a trident logo on the right side.—			

GRAY, WARDELL, & DEXTER GORDON

Decca DL-7025	(10")	**The Chase And Steeplechase**	1952	125.00	250.00
Jazztone J-1235	(M)	**The Chase And Steeplechase**	1956	20.00	50.00
		(Jazztone 1235 is a reissue of Decca 7025.)			

GREEN, BENNIE

Benjamin Green is a modern jazz trombone player. For additional listings refer to J.J. Johnson / Bennie Green; J.J. Johnson & Kai Winding / Bennie Green; Paul Quinichette / Bennie Green; Sonny Stitt..

Prestige PRLP-210	(10")	**Bennie Blows His Horn**	1955	60.00	150.00
Prestige PRLP-7041	(M)	**Bennie Green And Art Farmer**	1956	40.00	100.00
Prestige PRLP-7049	(M)	**Walking Down**	1956	40.00	100.00
Prestige PRLP-7052	(M)	**Bennie Green Blows His Horn**	1956	40.00	100.00
		—Prestige albums above have yellow labels with a W. 50th Street, NYC address.—			
Prestige PRLP-7160	(M)	**Bennie Green Blows His Horn**	1959	30.00	75.00
		(Prestige 7160 is a reissue of 7052.)			
		—Prestige albums above have yellow mono or silver stereo labels with a Bergenfield, NJ address.—			

Label & Catalog #		Title	Year	VG+	NM
Blue Note BLP-1587	*(M)*	**Back On The Scene** *(Deep groove)*	1958	50.00	125.00
Blue Note BLP-1587	*(M)*	**Back On The Scene**	1958	30.00	75.00
Blue Note BST-1587	*(S)*	**Back On The Scene** *(Deep groove)*	1959	30.00	75.00
Blue Note BST-1587	*(S)*	**Back On The Scene**	1959	20.00	50.00
Blue Note BLP-1599	*(M)*	**Soul Stirrin'** *(Deep groove)*	1958	50.00	125.00
Blue Note BLP-1599	*(M)*	**Soul Stirrin'**	1958	30.00	75.00
Blue Note BST-1599	*(S)*	**Soul Stirrin'** *(Deep groove)*	1959	30.00	75.00
Blue Note BST-1599	*(S)*	**Soul Stirrin'**	1959	20.00	50.00
Blue Note BLP-4010	*(M)*	**Walkin' And Talkin'** *(Deep groove)*	1959	50.00	125.00
Blue Note BLP-4010	*(M)*	**Walkin' And Talkin'**	1959	30.00	75.00
Blue Note BST-4010	*(S)*	**Walkin' And Talkin'** *(Deep groove)*	1959	30.00	75.00
Blue Note BST-4010	*(S)*	**Walkin' And Talkin'**	1959	20.00	50.00
		—Blue Note albums above have blue on white labels with a W. 63rd St, NYC address.—			
Blue Note BLP-1587	*(M)*	**Back On The Scene**	1963	10.00	25.00
Blue Note BST-81587	*(S)*	**Back On The Scene**	1963	8.00	20.00
Blue Note BLP-1599	*(M)*	**Soul Stirrin'**	1963	10.00	25.00
Blue Note BST-81599	*(S)*	**Soul Stirrin'**	1963	8.00	20.00
Blue Note BLP-4010	*(M)*	**Walkin' And Talkin'**	1963	10.00	25.00
Blue Note BST-84010	*(S)*	**Walkin' And Talkin'**	1963	8.00	20.00
		—Blue Note albums above have blue on white labels with a New York, USAaddress.—			
Blue Note BST-81587	*(S)*	**Back On The Scene**	196?	5.00	12.00
Blue Note BST-81599	*(S)*	**Soul Stirrin'**	196?	5.00	12.00
Blue Note BST-84010	*(S)*	**Walkin' And Talkin'**	196?	5.00	12.00
		—Blue Note albums above have blue on white labels with "A Division of Liberty Records."—			
Vee Jay LP-1005	*(M)*	**The Swingin'est**	1960	20.00	50.00
Vee Jay LPS-1005	*(S)*	**The Swingin'est**	1960	16.00	40.00
		(V.J. 1005 was reissued as 3024, Gene Ammons' "Juggin' Around.")			
		—Vee Jay albums above have silver on maroon labels.—			
Time 52021	*(M)*	**Bennie Green**	1960	20.00	50.00
Time S-2021	*(S)*	**Bennie Green**	1960	16.00	40.00
Enrica 2002	*(M)*	**Bennie Green Swings The Blues**	1960	16.00	40.00
Enrica 2002	*(S)*	**Bennie Green Swings The Blues**	1960	12.00	30.00
Bethlehem BCP-6054	*(M)*	**Hornful Of Soul**	1961	12.00	30.00
RCA Victor LPM-2376	*(M)*	**Futura**	1961	12.00	30.00
RCA Victor LSP-2376	*(S)*	**Futura**	1961	10.00	25.00
		—RCA albums above have black labels with "Long Play" or "Living Stereo" on the bottom.—			
Jazzland JLP-43	*(M)*	**Glidin' Along**	1961	12.00	30.00
Jazzland JLP-943	*(S)*	**Glidin' Along**	1961	10.00	25.00

GREEN, BENNIE / PAUL QUINICHETTE

Decca DL-8176	*(M)*	**Blow Your Horn**	1955	20.00	50.00

GREEN, BUNKY

Bunky Green is a modern jazz alto and tenor saxophone player.

Argo LP-753	*(M)*	**Testifyin' Time**	1965	12.00	30.00
Argo LPS-753	*(S)*	**Testifyin' Time**	1965	10.00	25.00
Cadet LP-766	*(M)*	**Playin' For Keeps**	1965	12.00	30.00
Cadet LPS-766	*(S)*	**Playin' For Keeps**	1965	10.00	25.00

GREEN, FREDDIE

Frederick Green is a traditional jazz guitar player. For additional listings refer to the Various Artists section under Savoy and United Artists.

RCA Victor LPM-1210	*(M)*	**Mr. Rhythm**	1956	20.00	50.00
		—RCA albums above have black labels with "Long Play" on the bottom.—			

GREEN, GRANT

Grant Green is a modern jazz guitar player. For additional listings refer to Sonny Red.

Blue Note BLP-4064	*(M)*	**Grant's First Stand**	1961	30.00	75.00
Blue Note BST-84064	*(S)*	**Grant's First Stand**	1961	20.00	50.00
Blue Note BLP-4071	*(M)*	**Green Street**	1962	30.00	75.00
Blue Note BST-84071	*(S)*	**Green Street**	1962	20.00	50.00
		—Blue Note albums above have blue on white labels with a W. 63rd St, NYC address.—			
Blue Note BLP-4086	*(M)*	**Grant Stand**	1961	30.00	75.00
Blue Note BST-84086	*(S)*	**Grant Stand**	1961	20.00	50.00
Blue Note BLP-4099	*(M)*	**Sunday Mornin'**	1962	30.00	75.00
Blue Note BST-84099	*(S)*	**Sunday Mornin'**	1962	20.00	50.00
		—Blue Note albums above have blue on white labels with a 61st St, NYC address.—			

Label & Catalog #		Title	Year	VG+	NM
Blue Note BLP-4064	(M)	**Grant's First Stand**	1963	10.00	25.00
Blue Note BST-84064	(S)	**Grant's First Stand**	1963	8.00	20.00
Blue Note BLP-4071	(M)	**Green Street**	1963	10.00	25.00
Blue Note BST-84071	(S)	**Green Street**	1963	8.00	20.00
Blue Note BLP-4086	(M)	**Grant Stand**	1963	10.00	25.00
Blue Note BST-84086	(S)	**Grant Stand**	1963	8.00	20.00
Blue Note BLP-4099	(M)	**Sunday Mornin'**	1963	10.00	25.00
Blue Note BST-84099	(S)	**Sunday Mornin'**	1963	8.00	20.00
Blue Note BLP-4111	(M)	**The Latin Bit**	1962	20.00	50.00
Blue Note BST-84111	(S)	**The Latin Bit**	1962	16.00	40.00
Blue Note BLP-4132	(M)	**Feelin' The Spirit**	1963	20.00	50.00
Blue Note BST-84132	(S)	**Feelin' The Spirit**	1963	16.00	40.00
Blue Note BLP-4139	(M)	**Am I Blue**	1963	20.00	50.00
Blue Note BST-84139	(S)	**Am I Blue**	1963	16.00	40.00
Blue Note BLP-4154	(M)	**Idle Moments**	1964	20.00	50.00
Blue Note BST-84154	(S)	**Idle Moments**	1964	16.00	40.00
Blue Note BLP-4183	(M)	**Talkin' About!**	1964	20.00	50.00
Blue Note BST-84183	(S)	**Talkin' About!**	1964	16.00	40.00
Blue Note BLP-4202	(M)	**I Want To Hold Your Hand**	1964	20.00	50.00
Blue Note BST-84202	(S)	**I Want To Hold Your Hand**	1964	16.00	40.00
—Blue Note albums above have blue on white labels with a New York, USA address.—					
Blue Note BST-84064	(S)	**Grant's First Stand**	196?	5.00	12.00
Blue Note BST-84071	(S)	**Green Street**	196?	5.00	12.00
Blue Note BST-84086	(S)	**Grant Stand**	196?	5.00	12.00
Blue Note BST-84099	(S)	**Sunday Mornin'**	196?	5.00	12.00
Blue Note BST-84111	(S)	**The Latin Bit**	196?	5.00	12.00
Blue Note BST-84132	(S)	**Feelin' The Spirit**	196?	5.00	12.00
Blue Note BST-84139	(S)	**Am I Blue**	196?	5.00	12.00
Blue Note BST-84154	(S)	**Idle Moments**	196?	5.00	12.00
Blue Note BST-84183	(S)	**Talkin' About!**	196?	5.00	12.00
Blue Note BST-84202	(S)	**I Want To Hold Your Hand**	196?	5.00	12.00
Blue Note BLP-4253	(M)	**Street Of Dreams**	1967	20.00	50.00
Blue Note BST-84253	(S)	**Street Of Dreams**	1967	16.00	40.00
Blue Note BST-84310	(S)	**Goin' West**	1969	16.00	40.00
Blue Note BST-84327	(S)	**Carryin' On**	1969	16.00	40.00
—Blue Note albums above have blue on white labels with "A Division of Liberty Records."—					
Verve V-8627	(M)	**His Majesty, King Funk**	1965	16.00	40.00
Verve V6-8627	(S)	**His Majesty, King Funk**	1965	12.00	30.00
—Verve albums above have black labels with "MGM Records" on the bottom.—					
Delmark DL-404	(M)	**All The Gin Is Gone**	1967	12.00	30.00
Delmark DS-404	(S)	**All The Gin Is Gone**	1967	10.00	25.00
Delmark DL-427	(M)	**Black Forrest**	1967	12.00	30.00
Delmark DS-427	(S)	**Black Forrest**	1967	10.00	25.00

GREEN, PHIL

London LPB-17	(10")	**Rhythm On Reeds**	1950	20.00	50.00

GREEN, URBIE

Urbie Green is a modern jazz trombone player. For additional listings refer to The Manhattan Jazz Septette; and The Brass Ensemble of The Jazz & Classical Music Society.

Blue Note BLP-5036	(10")	**Urbie Green Septet**	1954	125.00	250.00
Vanguard VRS-8010	(10")	**Urbie Green And His Band**	1954	40.00	100.00
"X" LXA-3026	(10")	**A Cool Yuletide**	1954	40.00	100.00
Bethlehem BCP-14	(M)	**East Coast Jazz/6**	1955	30.00	75.00
ABC-Paramount ABC-101	(M)	**Blues And Other Shades Of Green**	1956	20.00	50.00
ABC-Paramount ABC-137	(M)	**All About Urbie Green**	1956	20.00	50.00
RCA Victor LPM-1667	(M)	**Let's Face The Music And Dance**	1958	16.00	40.00
RCA Victor LSP-1667	(S)	**Let's Face The Music And Dance**	1958	12.00	30.00
RCA Victor LPM-1969	(M)	**Best Of The New Broadway Show Hits**	1959	16.00	40.00
RCA Victor LSP-1969	(S)	**Best Of The New Broadway Show Hits**	1959	12.00	30.00
—RCA albums above have black labels with "Long Play" or "Living Stereo" on the bottom.—					
Command 33-815	(M)	**The Persuasive Trombone Of Urbie Green**	1963	5.00	12.00
Command CS-815	(S)	**The Persuasive Trombone Of Urbie Green**	1963	4.00	10.00
Command 33-838	(M)	**Urbie Green, Volume 2**	1963	5.00	12.00
Command CS-838	(S)	**Urbie Green, Volume 2**	1963	4.00	10.00
Command 33-857	(M)	**Urbie Green 6-Tet**	1964	5.00	12.00
Command CS-857	(S)	**Urbie Green 6-Tet**	1964	4.00	10.00

Label & Catalog #		Title	Year	VG+	NM

GREEN, URBIE / VIC DICKENSON

Jazztone J-1259	(M)	**Urbie Green Octet/Slidin' Swing**	1957	16.00	40.00

GREEN, WILLIAM

William Green is a modern jazz alto and tenor saxophone and flute player. For additional listings refer to the Various Artists section under Tampa.

Everest LPBR-5213	(M)	**Shades Of Green**	1963	8.00	20.00
Everest SDBR-1213	(S)	**Shades Of Green**	1963	6.00	15.00

GREENE, BURTON

Burton Greene is a modern jazz pianist.

ESP-Disk' 1024	(M)	**Burton Greene**	1966	10.00	25.00
ESP-Disk' 1024	(S)	**Burton Greene**	1966	8.00	20.00
ESP-Disk' 1074	(S)	**Burton Greene Concert Tour**	1969	10.00	25.00
Columbia CS-9784	(S)	**Presenting Burton Greene**	1969	6.00	15.00

—Columbia albums above have red labels with "360 Sound" on the bottom.—

GREENE, DODO

Dodo Greene is a modern jazz vocalist.

Blue Note BLP-9001	(M)	**My Hour Of Need**	1962	20.00	50.00

—Blue Note albums above have blue on white labels with a W. 63rd Street, NYC address.—

Blue Note BLP-9001	(M)	**My Hour Of Need**	196?	10.00	25.00

—Blue Note albums above have blue on white labels with a New York, USA address.—

Blue Note BST-89001	(E)	**My Hour Of Need**	196?	4.00	10.00

—Blue Note albums above have blue on white labels with a "A Division of Liberty Records."—

GREY, AL, & BILLY MITCHELL

Specialty SP-2110	(M)	**Dizzy Atmosphere**	1959	30.00	75.00

GREY, AL

Albert Grey is a traditional jazz big band trombone player.

Argo LP-653	(M)	**The Last Of The Big Plungers**	1959	12.00	30.00
Argo LPS-653	(S)	**The Last Of The Big Plungers**	1959	10.00	25.00
Argo LP-677	(M)	**The Thinking Man's Trombone**	1961	10.00	25.00
Argo LPS-677	(S)	**The Thinking Man's Trombone**	1961	8.00	20.00
Argo LP-689	(M)	**The Al Grey-Billy Mitchell Sextet**	1961	10.00	25.00
Argo LPS-689	(S)	**The Al Grey-Billy Mitchell Sextet**	1961	8.00	20.00
Argo LP-700	(M)	**Snap Your Fingers**	1962	10.00	25.00
Argo LPS-700	(S)	**Snap Your Fingers**	1962	8.00	20.00
Argo LP-711	(M)	**Night Song**	1962	10.00	25.00
Argo LPS-711	(S)	**Night Song**	1962	8.00	20.00
Argo LP-718	(M)	**Having A Ball**	1963	10.00	25.00
Argo LPS-718	(S)	**Having A Ball**	1963	8.00	20.00
Argo LP-731	(M)	**Boss Bones**	1964	10.00	25.00
Argo LPS-731	(S)	**Boss Bones**	1964	8.00	20.00
Tangerine TT-1504	(M)	**Shades Of Grey**	1965	6.00	15.00
Tangerine TTS-1504	(S)	**Shades Of Grey**	1965	5.00	12.00

GRIFFIN, JOHNNY

John "Little Giant" Griffin is a modern jazz tenor saxophone player. For additional listings refer to Ahmed Abdul-Malik; Nat Adderley; Thelonious Monk; Wilbur Ware & Johnny Griffin & Junior Mance.

Blue Note BLP-1533	(M)	**Introducing Johnny Griffin** *(Deep groove)*	1956	100.00	200.00
Blue Note BLP-1533	(M)	**Introducing Johnny Griffin**	1956	60.00	150.00

—Blue Note albums above have blue on white labels with a Lexington Ave, NYC address.—

Blue Note BLP-1533	(M)	**Introducing Johnny Griffin**	1957	20.00	50.00
Blue Note BLP-1559	(M)	**A Blowing Session** *(Deep groove)*	1957	60.00	150.00
Blue Note BLP-1559	(M)	**A Blowing Session**	1957	40.00	100.00
Blue Note BLP-1580	(M)	**The Congregation** *(Deep groove)*	1958	50.00	125.00
Blue Note BLP-1580	(M)	**The Congregation**	1958	30.00	75.00
Blue Note BST-1580	(S)	**The Congregation** *(Deep groove)*	1959	30.00	75.00
Blue Note BST-1580	(S)	**The Congregation**	1959	20.00	50.00

(Blue Note 1580 features cover art by Andy Warhol.)

—Blue Note albums above have blue on white labels with a W. 63rd Street, NYC address.—

Blue Note BLP-1533	(M)	**Introducing Johnny Griffin**	1963	10.00	25.00
Blue Note BLP-1559	(M)	**A Blowing Session**	1963	10.00	25.00
Blue Note BLP-1580	(M)	**The Congregation**	1963	10.00	25.00
Blue Note BST-1580	(S)	**The Congregation**	1963	8.00	20.00

—Blue Note albums above have blue on white labels with a New York, USA address.—

Label & Catalog #		Title	Year	VG+	NM
Blue Note BST-81533	(E)	**Introducing Johnny Griffin**	1967?	4.00	10.00
Blue Note BST-81559	(E)	**A Blowing Session**	1967?	4.00	10.00
Blue Note BST-1580	(S)	**The Congregation**	1967?	5.00	12.00

—Blue Note albums above have blue on white labels with "A Division of Liberty Records."—

Label & Catalog #		Title	Year	VG+	NM
Argo LP-624	(M)	**Johnny Griffin**	1958	20.00	50.00
Argo LPS-624	(S)	**Johnny Griffin**	1958	16.00	40.00
Riverside RLP-12-264	(M)	**Johnny Griffin Sextet**	1958	20.00	50.00
Riverside RLP-12-274	(M)	**Way Out!**	1958	20.00	50.00
Riverside RLP-12-304	(M)	**The Little Giant**	1959	20.00	50.00
Riverside RLP-1149	(S)	**The Little Giant**	1959	16.00	40.00
Riverside RLP-12-331	(M)	**The Big Soul-Band**	1960	16.00	40.00
Riverside RLP-1179	(S)	**The Big Soul-Band**	1960	12.00	30.00
Riverside RLP-338	(M)	**Studio Jazz Party**	1960	16.00	40.00
Riverside RS-9338	(S)	**Studio Jazz Party**	1960	12.00	30.00
Riverside RLP-368	(M)	**Change Of Pace**	1961	16.00	40.00
Riverside RS-9368	(S)	**Change Of Pace**	1961	12.00	30.00
Riverside RLP-387	(M)	**White Gardenia**	1961	16.00	40.00
Riverside RS-9387	(S)	**White Gardenia**	1961	12.00	30.00
Riverside RLP-420	(M)	**The Kerry Dancers**	1962	12.00	30.00
Riverside RS-9420	(S)	**The Kerry Dancers**	1962	10.00	25.00
Riverside RLP-437	(M)	**Grab This!**	1962	12.00	30.00
Riverside RS-9437	(S)	**Grab This!**	1962	10.00	25.00
		(Riverside 437 also features Paul Bryant.)			
Riverside RLP-462	(M)	**Do Nothing 'Til You Hear From Me**	1963	12.00	30.00
Riverside RS-9462	(S)	**Do Nothing 'Til You Hear From Me**	1963	10.00	25.00
		(Riverside 462 also features Buddy Montgomery)			

—Riverside albums above have blue mono or black stereo labels with a reel & mike logo on top.—

Label & Catalog #		Title	Year	VG+	NM
Riverside RLP-479	(M)	**Wade In The Water**	1964	10.00	25.00
Riverside RS-9479	(S)	**Wade In The Water**	1964	8.00	20.00

—Riverside albums above blue labels with "Orpheum Productions" on the bottom.—

Label & Catalog #		Title	Year	VG+	NM
Jazzland JLP-93	(M)	**The Little Giant**	1961	16.00	40.00
Jazzland JLP-993	(S)	**The Little Giant**	1961	12.00	30.00
		(Jazzland 93 is a reissue of Riverside 304.)			
EmArcy MG-26001	(M)	**Night Lady**	1967	16.00	40.00
EmArcy SR-66001	(S)	**Night Lady**	1967	12.00	30.00

GRIFFIN-DAVIS QUINTET, THE: ***Refer to*** **EDDIE DAVIS & JOHNNY GRIFFIN**

GRIFFIN, JOHNNY, & MATHEW GEE

Label & Catalog #		Title	Year	VG+	NM
Atlantic 1431	(M)	**Soul Groove**	1965	10.00	25.00
Atlantic SD-1431	(S)	**Soul Groove**	1965	8.00	20.00

—Atlantic albums above have multi-color labels with a black fan logo.—

GRIMES, HENRY

Henry Grimes is a modern jazz bass player.

Label & Catalog #		Title	Year	VG+	NM
ESP-Disk' 1027	(M)	**Henry Grimes Trio**	1966	10.00	25.00
ESP-Disk' 1027	(S)	**Henry Grimes Trio**	1966	8.00	20.00

GRIMES, TINY

Lloyd "Tiny" Grimes is a traditional jazz guitarist and vocalist. For additional listings refer to Kenny Burrell / Tiny Grimes / Bill Jennings; The Prestige Blues Swingers.

Label & Catalog #		Title	Year	VG+	NM
Prestige PRLP-7138	(M)	**Blues Groove**	1958	40.00	100.00
		(Prestige 7138 also features Coleman Hawkins.)			
Prestige PRLP-7144	(M)	**Callin' The Blues**	1958	40.00	100.00
		(Prestige 7144 also features J. C. Higginbotham.)			

—Prestige albums above have yellow labels with a W. 50th Street, NYC address.—

Label & Catalog #		Title	Year	VG+	NM
Swingville SVLP-2002	(M)	**Tiny In Swingville**	1960	20.00	50.00
Swingville SVLP-2004	(M)	**Callin' The Blues**	1960	20.00	50.00
		(Swingville 2004 is a reissue of Prestige 7144.)			

—Swingville albums above have purple mono or red stereo labels.—

Label & Catalog #		Title	Year	VG+	NM
Swingville SVLP-2002	(M)	**Tiny In Swingville**	1965	10.00	25.00
Swingville SVLP-2004	(M)	**Callin' The Blues**	1965	10.00	25.00

—Swingville albums above have blue labels with a trident logo on the right side.—

Label & Catalog #		Title	Year	VG+	NM
United Arts. UAL-3232	(M)	**Big Time Guitar**	1962	12.00	30.00
United Arts. UAS-6232	(S)	**Big Time Guitar**	1962	10.00	25.00

Label & Catalog #		Title	Year	VG+	NM
GRISSOM, JIMMY					
James Grissom is a jazz-based vocalist.					
Argo LP-729	(M)	**World Of Trouble**	1963	10.00	25.00
Argo LPS-729	(S)	**World Of Trouble**	1963	12.00	30.00
GROSZ, MARTY					
Riverside RLP-12-268	(M)	**Hurrah For Bix**	1958	16.00	40.00
Riverside RLP-1109	(S)	**Hurrah For Bix**	1959	12.00	30.00
—Riverside albums above have blue mono or black stereo labels with a reel & mike logo on top.—					
GROUP, THE					
The Group is a jazz vocal ensemble consisting of Larry Benson, Anne Gable and Tom Kampman.					
RCA Victor LPM-2663	(M)	**The Group**	1963	12.00	30.00
RCA Victor LSP-2663	(S)	**The Group**	1963	16.00	40.00
—RCA albums above have black labels with "Long Play" or "Living Stereo" on the bottom.—					
GROVE, DICK					
Pacific Jazz PJ-74	(M)	**Little Bird Suite**	1963	10.00	25.00
Pacific Jazz ST-74	(S)	**Little Bird Suite**	1963	8.00	20.00
GRUNTZ, GEORGE					
Philips PHM-200-162	(M)	**Bach Humbug**	1964	8.00	20.00
Philips PHS-600-162	(S)	**Bach Humbug**	1964	6.00	15.00
GRUSIN, DAVE					
David Grusin is a pianist and composer who specializes in Hollywood soundtrack work.					
Epic LN-3829	(M)	**Subways Are For Sleeping**	1962	8.00	20.00
Epic BN-622	(S)	**Subways Are For Sleeping**	1962	6.00	15.00
Columbia CL-2344	(M)	**Kaleidoscope**	1965	8.00	20.00
Columbia CS-9144	(S)	**Kaleidoscope**	1965	6.00	15.00
—Columbia albums above have "360 Sound" in white on the bottom of the label.—					
GRYCE, GIG, & CLIFFORD BROWN					
Blue Note BLP-5048	(10")	**Gigi Gryce-Clifford Brown Sextet**	1954	240.00	400.00
GRYCE, GIGI					
Gigi Gryce is a modern jazz alto saxophone and flute player and composer. For additional listings refer to Art Farmer.					
Blue Note BLP-5049	(10")	**Gigi Gryce's Jazztime Paris**	1954	150.00	300.00
Blue Note BLP-5050	(10")	**Gigi Gryce And His Little Band, Volume 2**	1954	150.00	300.00
Blue Note BLP-5051	(10")	**Gigi Gryce Quintet/Sextet, Volume 3**	1954	150.00	300.00
Signal S-1201	(M)	**Gigi Gryce Quartet**	1955	150.00	300.00
—Signal albums above have an arrow & ear logo on the label.—					
Savoy MG-12137	(M)	**Nica's Tempo**	1958	30.00	75.00
		(Savoy 12137 is a reissue of Signal 1201.)			
Metrojazz E-1006	(M)	**Gigi Gryce**	1958	30.00	75.00
Metrojazz SE-1006	(S)	**Gigi Gryce**	1958	20.00	50.00
New Jazz NJLP-8230	(M)	**Sayin' Somethin'!**	1959	20.00	50.00
New Jazz NJLP-8246	(M)	**The Hap'nin's**	1960	20.00	50.00
New Jazz NJLP-8262	(M)	**The Rat Race Blues**	1961	20.00	50.00
—New Jazz albums above have purple labels.—					
New Jazz NJLP-8230	(M)	**Sayin' Somethin'!**	1965	10.00	25.00
New Jazz NJLP-8246	(M)	**The Hap'nin's**	1965	10.00	25.00
New Jazz NJLP-8262	(M)	**The Rat Race Blues**	1965	10.00	25.00
—New Jazz albums above have blue labels with a trident logo on the right side.—					
Mercury MG-20628	(M)	**Reminiscin'**	1961	16.00	40.00
Mercury SR-60628	(S)	**Reminiscin'**	1961	12.00	30.00
GRYCE, GIGI, & DONALD BYRD (THE JAZZ LAB)					
Jubilee JLP-1059	(M)	**Jazz Lab**	1957	40.00	100.00
Columbia CL-998	(M)	**Jazz Lab**	1957	30.00	75.00
Columbia CL-1058	(M)	**Modern Jazz Perspective/Jazz Lab, Volume 2**	1957	30.00	75.00
—Columbia albums above have six white on black "eye" logos on each label.—					
Riverside RLP-12-229	(M)	**Gigi Gryce And The Jazz Lab Quintet**	1957	40.00	100.00
—Riverside albums above have blue on white labels.—					
Riverside RLP-12-229	(M)	**Gigi Gryce And The Jazz Lab Quintet**	1959	20.00	50.00
Riverside RLP-1110	(S)	**Gigi Gryce And The Jazz Lab Quintet**	1959	20.00	50.00
—Riverside albums above have blue mono or black stereo labels with a reel & mike logo on top.—					

Gigi Gryce started with such groups as Max Roach, Howard McGhee, Tadd Dameron, and Lionel Hampton before starring with Donald Byrd in the Jazz Lab Quintet in 1955-58, after which he formed his own group. Aside from albums with Byrd (above), he has recorded as a featured soloist on albums by Clifford Brown and Art Farmer (also above). As a sideman he has recorded with Lee Morgan and Thad Jones, both on Blue Note, Oscar Pettiford on Bethlehem and ABC-Paramount, Mal Waldron on Prestige, Thelonious Monk on Riverside, and Teddy Charles on Atlantic.

Label & Catalog #		Title	Year	VG+	NM
Jazzland JLP-1	(M)	**Jazz Lab**	1960	16.00	40.00
Jazzland JLP-91	(S)	**Jazz Lab**	1960	12.00	30.00
		(Jazzland 1 is a reissue of Riverside 229.)			
Josie JLPM-3500	(M)	**Gigi Gryce/Donald Byrd**	1963	16.00	40.00
Josie JLPS-3500	(E)	**Gigi Gryce/Donald Byrd**	1963	10.00	25.00
		(Jose 3500 is a reissue of Jubilee 1059.)			

GUARALDI, VINCE

Vincente Guaraldi is a jazz-based pianist. For additional listings refer to the Jazzy Soundtracks section under Warner Bros.

Label & Catalog #		Title	Year	VG+	NM
Fantasy 3213	(M)	**Modern Music From San Francisco** *(Dark red vinyl)*	1956	20.00	50.00
Fantasy 3225	(M)	**Vince Guaraldi Trio** *(Dark red vinyl)*	1956	20.00	50.00
		—Fantasy albums above are pressed on dark red, non-flexible vinyl.—			
Fantasy 3213	(M)	**Modern Music From San Francisco**	195?	4.00	20.00
Fantasy 3225	(M)	**Vince Guaraldi Trio**	195?	4.00	20.00
Fantasy 3257	(M)	**A Flower Is A Lovesome Thing** *(Red vinyl)*	1958	12.00	30.00
Fantasy 3257	(M)	**A Flower Is A Lovesome Thing**	195?	4.00	20.00
Fantasy 3337	(M)	**Cast Your Fate To The Wind—Jazz Impressions Of "Black Orpheus"** *(Red vinyl)*	1962	12.00	30.00
Fantasy 3337	(M)	**Cast Your Fate To The Wind—Jazz Impressions Of "Black Orpheus"**	1962	4.00	20.00
Fantasy 8089	(S)	**Cast Your Fate To The Wind—Jazz Impressions Of "Black Orpheus"** *(Blue vinyl)*	1962	8.00	20.00
Fantasy 8089	(S)	**Cast Your Fate To The Wind—Jazz Impressions Of "Black Orpheus"**	1962	6.00	15.00
		—Fantasy albums above have red mono or blue stereo labels on non-flexible vinyl.—			
Fantasy 3225	(M)	**Vince Guaraldi Trio**	196?	5.00	12.00
Fantasy 3257	(M)	**A Flower Is A Lovesome Thing**	196?	5.00	12.00
Fantasy 3337	(M)	**Cast Your Fate To The Wind—Jazz Impressions Of "Black Orpheus"**	196?	5.00	12.00
Fantasy 8089	(S)	**Cast Your Fate To The Wind—Jazz Impressions Of "Black Orpheus"**	196?	4.00	10.00
Fantasy 3352	(M)	**Vince Guaraldi In Person** *(Red vinyl)*	1963	8.00	20.00
Fantasy 3352	(M)	**Vince Guaraldi In Person**	1963	6.00	15.00
Fantasy 8352	(S)	**Vince Guaraldi In Person** *(Blue vinyl)*	1963	6.00	15.00
Fantasy 8352	(S)	**Vince Guaraldi In Person**	1963	5.00	12.00
Fantasy 3356	(M)	**Vince Guaraldi And Bola Sete And Friends** *(Red vinyl)*	1963	8.00	20.00
Fantasy 3356	(M)	**Vince Guaraldi And Bola Sete And Friends**	1963	6.00	15.00
Fantasy 8356	(S)	**Vince Guaraldi And Bola Sete And Friends** *(Blue vinyl)*	1963	6.00	15.00
Fantasy 8356	(S)	**Vince Guaraldi And Bola Sete And Friends**	1963	5.00	12.00
Fantasy 3358	(M)	**Tour De Force** *(Red vinyl)*	1963	8.00	20.00
Fantasy 3358	(M)	**Tour De Force**	1963	6.00	15.00
Fantasy 8358	(S)	**Tour De Force** *(Blue vinyl)*	1963	6.00	15.00
Fantasy 8358	(S)	**Tour De Force**	1963	4.00	10.00
Fantasy 5017	(M)	**Jazz Impressions Of "Charlie Brown"** *(Red vinyl)*	1964	8.00	20.00
Fantasy 5017	(M)	**Jazz Impressions Of "Charlie Brown"**	1964	6.00	15.00
Fantasy 85017	(S)	**Jazz Impressions Of "Charlie Brown"** *(Blue vinyl)*	1964	6.00	15.00
Fantasy 85017	(S)	**Jazz Impressions Of "Charlie Brown"**	1964	4.00	10.00
Fantasy 3359	(M)	**Jazz Impressions** *(Red vinyl)*	1964	8.00	20.00
Fantasy 3359	(M)	**Jazz Impressions**	1964	6.00	15.00
Fantasy 8359	(S)	**Jazz Impressions** *(Blue vinyl)*	1964	6.00	15.00
Fantasy 8359	(S)	**Jazz Impressions**	1964	4.00	10.00
Fantasy 3360	(M)	**The Latin Side Of Vince Guaraldi** *(Red vinyl)*	1964	8.00	20.00
Fantasy 3360	(M)	**The Latin Side Of Vince Guaraldi**	1964	6.00	15.00
Fantasy 8360	(S)	**The Latin Side Of Vince Guaraldi** *(Blue vinyl)*	1964	6.00	15.00
Fantasy 8360	(S)	**The Latin Side Of Vince Guaraldi**	1964	4.00	10.00
Fantasy 3362	(M)	**From All Sides** *(Red vinyl)*	1965	8.00	20.00
Fantasy 3362	(M)	**From All Sides**	1965	6.00	15.00
Fantasy 8362	(S)	**From All Sides** *(Blue vinyl)*	1965	6.00	15.00
Fantasy 8362	(S)	**From All Sides**	1965	4.00	10.00
Fantasy 3367	(M)	**Vince Guaraldi At Grace Cathedral** *(Red vinyl)*	1966	8.00	20.00
Fantasy 3367	(M)	**Vince Guaraldi At Grace Cathedral**	1966	6.00	15.00

Label & Catalog #		Title	Year	VG+	NM
Fantasy 8367	(S)	**Vince Guaraldi At Grace Cathedral** *(Blue vinyl)*	1966	6.00	15.00
Fantasy 8367	(S)	**Vince Guaraldi At Grace Cathedral**	1966	4.00	10.00
Fantasy 3371	(M)	**Live At The El Matador** *(Red vinyl)*	1966	8.00	20.00
Fantasy 3371	(M)	**Live At The El Matador**	1966	6.00	15.00
Fantasy 8371	(S)	**Live At The El Matador** *(Blue vinyl)*	1966	6.00	15.00
Fantasy 8371	(S)	**Live At The El Matador**	1966	4.00	10.00

GUARALDI, VINCE / CONTE CANDOLI

Crown CLP-5417	(M)	**Vince Guaraldi And The Conte Candoli All Stars**	196?	6.00	15.00
Crown CST-417	(E)	**Vince Guaraldi And The Conte Candoli All Stars**	196?	3.00	7.50
Premier PM-2009	(M)	**Vince Guaraldi / Conte Candoli Quartet**	1963	6.00	15.00
Premier PS-2009	(E)	**Vince Guaraldi / Conte Candoli Quartet**	1963	3.00	7.50

GUARALDI, VINCE / FRANK ROSOLINO

Premier PM-2014	(M)	**Vince Guaraldi / Frank Rosolino Quintet**	1963	6.00	15.00
Premier PS-2014	(E)	**Vince Guaraldi / Frank Rosolino Quintet**	1963	3.00	7.50

(Side 2 of Premier 2104 is a reissue of Mode 107.)

GUARNIERI, JOHNNY

John Guarnieri is a traditional jazz pianist and composer. For additional listings refer to Bernie Leighton / Johnny Guarnieri.

Savoy MG-15007	(10")	**Hot Piano**	1951	30.00	75.00
Coral CRL-57085	(M)	**Songs Of Hudson And DeLange**	1957	16.00	40.00
Coral CRL-57086	(M)	**The Duke Again**	1957	16.00	40.00
Golden Crest GC-3020	(M)	**Johnny Guarnieri Plays Johnny Guarnieri**	1958	16.00	40.00
Camden CAL-345	(M)	**Cheerful Little Earful**	1958	6.00	15.00
Camden CAL-391	(M)	**Side By Side**	1958	6.00	15.00

GULDA, FRIEDRICH

Austrian born Friedrich Gulda is a classically trained jazz pianist.

RCA Victor LPM-1355	(M)	**Friedrich Gulda At Birdland**	1957	20.00	50.00

—RCA albums above have black labels with "Long Play" on the bottom.—

Columbia CL-2251	(M)	**From Vienna With Jazz**	1964	6.00	15.00
Columbia CS-9051	(S)	**From Vienna With Jazz**	1964	5.00	12.00
Columbia CL-2346	(M)	**The Ineffable Friedrich Gulda**	1965	6.00	15.00
Columbia CS-9146	(S)	**The Ineffable Friedrich Gulda**	1965	5.00	12.00

—Columbia albums above have "360 Sound " in white on the bottom of the label.—

GULLIN, LARS

Swedish born Lars Gullin is a modern jazz baritone saxophone player. For additional listings refer to Arne Domnerus / Lars Gullin; Bengt Hallberg / Lars Gullin.

Prestige PRLP-144	(10")	**New Sounds From Sweden, Volume 5**	1953	125.00	250.00
Prestige PRLP-151	(10")	**New Sounds From Sweden, Volume 7**	1953	125.00	250.00
Contemporary C-2505	(10")	**Modern Sounds**	1953	100.00	200.00
EmArcy MG-26041	(10")	**Lars Gullin Quartet**	1954	100.00	200.00
EmArcy MG-26044	(10")	**Gullin's Garden**	1954	100.00	200.00
EmArcy MG-36012	(M)	**Lars Gullin**	1955	50.00	125.00
EmArcy MG-36059	(M)	**Lars Gullin With The Moretone Singers**	1955	40.00	100.00

—EmArcy albums above have blue labels with silver print.—

Atlantic 1246	(M)	**Baritone Sax**	1956	50.00	125.00

—Atlantic albums above have black mono or green stereo labels.—

Atlantic 1246	(M)	**Baritone Sax**	1961	20.00	50.00

—Atlantic albums above have multi-color labels with a white fan logo.—

East-West 4003	(M)	**Lars Gullin Swings**	196?	12.00	30.00

GUMINA, TOMMY: ***Refer to*** **BUDDY DeFRANCO & TOMMY GUMINA**

GWALTNEY, TOMMY

Riverside RLP-353	(M)	**Goin' To Kansas City With Buck Clayton**	1960	16.00	40.00
Riverside RS-9353	(S)	**Goin' To Kansas City With Buck Clayton**	1960	12.00	30.00

—Riverside albums above have blue mono or black stereo labels with a reel & mike logo on top.—

H.

HACKETT, BOBBY

Robert Hackett is a traditional jazz trumpet, cornet and guitar player. For additional listings refer to Jack Teagarden / Bobby Hackett.

Brunswick BL-58014	*(10")*	**Trumpet Solos**	*1950*	**20.00**	**50.00**
Columbia CL-6156	*(10")*	**Jazz Session**	*1951*	**20.00**	**50.00**
Commodore FL-20016	*(10")*	**Horn A Plenty**	*1951*	**20.00**	**50.00**
Capitol H-458	*(10")*	**Soft Lights**	*1954*	**20.00**	**50.00**
Capitol T-458	*(M)*	**Soft Lights**	*1955*	**16.00**	**40.00**
Capitol T-575	*(M)*	**In A Mellow Mood**	*1955*	**16.00**	**40.00**
Capitol T-692	*(M)*	**Coast Concert**	*1956*	**16.00**	**40.00**
Capitol T-719	*(M)*	**Rendezvous**	*1956*	**16.00**	**40.00**
Capitol T-857	*(M)*	**Gotham Jazz Scene**	*1957*	**16.00**	**40.00**
Capitol T-933	*(M)*	**Jazz Ultimate**	*1958*	**16.00**	**40.00**
		(Capitol 933 also features Jack Teagarden.)			
Capitol T-1002	*(M)*	**Don't Take Your Love From Me**	*1958*	**16.00**	**40.00**
		— Capitol albums above have turquoise labels.—			
Capitol T-458	*(M)*	**Soft Lights**	*1958*	**10.00**	**25.00**
Capitol T-575	*(M)*	**In A Mellow Mood**	*1958*	**10.00**	**25.00**
Capitol T-692	*(M)*	**Coast Concert**	*1958*	**10.00**	**25.00**
Capitol T-719	*(M)*	**Rendezvous**	*1958*	**10.00**	**25.00**
Capitol T-857	*(M)*	**Gotham Jazz Scene**	*1958*	**10.00**	**25.00**
Capitol T-933	*(M)*	**Jazz Ultimate**	*1958*	**10.00**	**25.00**
Capitol ST-933	*(S)*	**Jazz Ultimate**	*1959*	**10.00**	**25.00**
Capitol T-1002	*(M)*	**Don't Take Your Love From Me**	*1958*	**10.00**	**25.00**
Capitol T-1077	*(M)*	**Bobby Hackett At The Embers**	*1958*	**10.00**	**25.00**
Capitol ST-1077	*(S)*	**Bobby Hackett At The Embers**	*1958*	**8.00**	**20.00**
Capitol T-1172	*(M)*	**Blues With A Kick**	*1959*	**10.00**	**25.00**
Capitol ST-1172	*(S)*	**Blues With A Kick**	*1959*	**8.00**	**20.00**
Capitol T-1235	*(M)*	**Bobby Hackett Quartet**	*1959*	**10.00**	**25.00**
Capitol ST-1235	*(S)*	**Bobby Hackett Quartet**	*1959*	**8.00**	**20.00**
Capitol T-1413	*(M)*	**Easy Beat**	*1960*	**10.00**	**25.00**
Capitol ST-1413	*(S)*	**Easy Beat**	*1960*	**8.00**	**20.00**
		— Capitol albums above have black "rainbow" labels with the logo on the left side.—			
Epic LN-3106	*(M)*	**The Hackett Horn**	*1955*	**16.00**	**40.00**
Columbia CL-2566	*(10")*	**The Bobby Hackett Horn**	*1956*	**20.00**	**50.00**
SeSac N-4101	*(M)*	**The Spirit Swings Me**	*1960*	**12.00**	**30.00**
SeSac SN-4101	*(S)*	**The Spirit Swings Me**	*1960*	**10.00**	**25.00**
SeSac N-4105	*(M)*	**Candlelight And Romance**	*1960*	**12.00**	**30.00**
SeSac SN-4105	*(S)*	**Candlelight And Romance**	*1960*	**10.00**	**25.00**
Columbia CL-1602	*(M)*	**Dream Awhile**	*1961*	**10.00**	**25.00**
Columbia CS-8402	*(S)*	**Dream Awhile**	*1961*	**8.00**	**20.00**
Columbia CL-1729	*(M)*	**The Most Beautiful Horn In The World**	*1962*	**10.00**	**25.00**
Columbia CS-8529	*(S)*	**The Most Beautiful Horn In The World**	*1962*	**8.00**	**20.00**
		— Columbia albums above have six eye logos on the label.—			
Columbia CL-1895	*(M)*	**Night Love**	*1962*	**8.00**	**20.00**
Columbia CS-8695	*(S)*	**Night Love**	*1962*	**6.00**	**15.00**
		— Columbia albums above have "Guaranteed High Fidelity" or "360 Sound Stereo" in black on the label.—			
Epic LA-16037	*(M)*	**Oliver**	*1963*	**6.00**	**15.00**
Epic BA-17037	*(S)*	**Oliver**	*1963*	**5.00**	**12.00**
Epic LN-24080	*(M)*	**The Music Of Bert Kaempfert**	*1964*	**6.00**	**15.00**
Epic BN-26080	*(S)*	**The Music Of Bert Kaempfert**	*1964*	**5.00**	**12.00**
Epic LN-24099	*(M)*	**Hello, Louis!**	*1964*	**6.00**	**15.00**
Epic BN-26099	*(S)*	**Hello, Louis!**	*1964*	**5.00**	**12.00**
Epic LN-24155	*(M)*	**Trumpet's Greatest Hits**	*1965*	**6.00**	**15.00**
Epic BN-26155	*(S)*	**Trumpet's Greatest Hits**	*1965*	**5.00**	**12.00**
Verve V-8698	*(M)*	**Creole Cookin'**	*1967*	**5.00**	**12.00**
Verve V6-8698	*(S)*	**Creole Cookin'**	*1967*	**4.00**	**10.00**
		— Verve albums above have black labels with "MGM Records" on the bottom.—			

Label & Catalog #		Title	Year	VG+	NM
HACKETT, BOBBY, & BILLY BUTTERFIELD & LUIZ HENRIQUE					
Verve V-8723	(M)	**Brazil**	1967	6.00	15.00
Verve V6-8723	(S)	**Brazil**	1967	5.00	12.00
—Verve albums above have black labels with "MGM Records" on the bottom.—					
HACKETT, BOBBY / MAX KAMINSKY					
Brunswick BL-58043	(10")	**Battle Of Jazz, Vol. 5**	1953	20.00	50.00
HADEN, CHARLIE					
Charles Haden is a modern jazz bass player.					
Impulse AS-9183	(S)	**Liberation Music Orchestra**	1969	8.00	20.00
—Impulse albums above have orange & black labels.—					
HAGGART, BOB: ***Refer to*** **THE LAWSON-HAGGART JAZZ BAND**					
HAHN, JERRY					
Changes LP-7001	(S)	**Arabein**	1968	6.00	15.00
HAIG, AL / MARY LOU WILLIAMS					
Prestige PRLP-175	(10")	**Piano Moderns**	1953	70.00	175.00
HAIG, AL					
Alan Haig is a modern jazz pianist.					
Esoteric ESJ-7	(10")	**Al Haig Trio**	1954	60.00	150.00
Period SPL-1104	(10")	**Al Haig Quartet**	1954	60.00	150.00
Pacific Jazz PJLP-18	(10")	**Al Haig Trio**	1955	60.00	150.00
Seeco SLP-7	(10")	**Highlights In Modern Jazz**	195?	40.00	100.00
Counterpoint C-551	(M)	**Jazz-Will-O-The-Wisp**	1957	40.00	100.00
		(Counterpoint 551 is a reissue of Esoteric 7.)			
Mint AL-711	(M)	**Al Haig Today**	1964	60.00	150.00
HALE, CORKY					
Merrilyn Hechy, aka Corky Hale, is a traditional jazz piano and harp player and singer.					
Gene Norman GNP-17	(M)	**Corky Hale**	1956	20.00	50.00
HALEN, CARL (CARL HALEN'S GIN BOTTLE SEVEN)					
Carl Halen is a traditional jazz cornet and trumpet player.					
Empirical LP-101	(10")	**Gin Bottle Seven**	1957	20.00	50.00
Riverside RLP-12-231	(M)	**Gin Bottle Jazz**	1958	24.00	60.00
—Riverside albums above have blue on white labels.—					
Riverside RLP-12-231	(M)	**Gin Bottle Jazz**	1958	12.00	30.00
Riverside RLP-12-261	(M)	**Whoopee Makers' Jazz**	1958	16.00	40.00
Riverside RLP-1103	(S)	**Whoopee Makers' Jazz**	1959	12.00	30.00
—Riverside albums above have blue mono or black stereo labels with a reel & mike logo on top.—					
HALL, BECKY					
Rebecca Hall is a jazz-based vocalist.					
Aamco ALP-324	(M)	**A Tribute To Bessie Smith**	1958	12.00	30.00
HALL, EDMOND					
Edmond Hall is a traditional jazz clarinet and baritone saxophone player. For additional listings refer to Miff Mole / Edmond Hall; The Street Swingers.					
United Arts. UAL-4028	(M)	**Petite Fleur**	1959	16.00	40.00
United Arts. UAS-5028	(S)	**Petite Fleur**	1959	12.00	30.00
Blue Note B-6505	(M)	**Celestial Express**	1969	8.00	20.00
HALL, EDMOND / SIDNEY DePARIS					
Blue Note BLP-7007	(10")	**Jamming In Jazz Hall**	1951	100.00	200.00
HALL, EDMOND / ART HODES					
Blue Note B-6504	(M)	**Original Blue Note Jazz, Volume 1**	1969	8.00	20.00
HALL, JIM					
James Hall is a West Coast jazz guitar player. For additional listings refer to Bob Brookmeyer & Jim Hall & Jim Raney; Bill Evans; The Modern Jazz Trio; Zoot Sims & Jimmy Raney & Jim Hall.					
Pacific Jazz PJ-1227	(M)	**Jazz Guitar**	1957	30.00	75.00
World Pacific WP-1227	(M)	**Jazz Guitar**	1958	20.00	50.00

Label & Catalog #		Title	Year	VG+	NM
Pacific Jazz PJ-10	(M)	**Good Friday Blues**	1960	16.00	40.00
		(Pacific Jazz 10 also features Red Mitchell.)			
Pacific Jazz PJ-79	(M)	**Jazz Guitar**	1963	12.00	30.00
Pacific Jazz ST-79	(S)	**Jazz Guitar**	1963	10.00	25.00
		(Pacific Jazz 79 is a reissue of World Pacific 1227.)			

HALLBERG, BENGT / LARS GULLIN

Prestige PRLP-121	(10")	**New Sounds From Sweden, Volume 2**	1952	120.00	200.00

HALLBERG, BENGT / ARNE DOMNERUS

Prestige PRLP-145	(10")	**New Sounds From Sweden, Volume 6**	1953	120.00	200.00

HALLBERG, BENGT

Swedish born Bengt Hallberg is a modern jazz piano player. For additional listings refer to Reinhold Svensson / Bengt Hallberg.

Prestige PRLP-176	(10")	**Bengt Hallberg's Swedish All Stars**	1953	70.00	175.00
Epic LN-3375	(M)	**Bengt Hallberg**	1957	40.00	100.00

HAMBRO, LENNY

Leonard Hambro is a traditional jazz alto saxophone player.

Savoy MG-15031	(10")	**Mambo Hambro**	1954	20.00	50.00
Columbia CL-757	(M)	**Message From Hambro**	1956	16.00	40.00
		—Columbia albums above have six white on black "eye" logos on each label.—			
Epic LN-3361	(M)	**The Nature Of Things**	1956	16.00	40.00

HAMILTON, CHICO

Foreststorn "Chico" Hamilton is a West Coast jazz drummer and band leader. For additional listings refer to Laurindo Almeida / Chico Hamilton; and the Jazzy Soundtracks section under Decca.

Pacific Jazz PJLP-17	(10")	**Chico Hamilton Trio**	1955	40.00	100.00
Pacific Jazz PJ-1209	(M)	**Chico Hamilton Quintet**	1955	30.00	75.00
		(Pacific Jazz 1209 also features Buddy Collette.)			
Pacific Jazz PJ-1216	(M)	**Chico Hamilton Quintet In Hi-Fi**	1956	30.00	75.00
Pacific Jazz PJ-1220	(M)	**Chico Hamilton Trio**	1956	30.00	75.00
Pacific Jazz PJ-1225	(M)	**Chico Hamilton Quintet**	1957	30.00	75.00
		(Pacific Jazz 1225 is a reissue of 17.)			
Pacific Jazz PJ-1231	(M)	**Chico Hamilton Plays The Music Of Fred Katz**	1957	30.00	75.00
World Pacific WP-1216	(M)	**Chico Hamilton Quintet In Hi-Fi**	1958	20.00	50.00
World Pacific WP-1225	(M)	**Chico Hamilton Quintet**	1958	20.00	50.00
World Pacific ST-1005	(S)	**Chico Hamilton Quintet**	1958	16.00	40.00
World Pacific WP-1231	(M)	**Chico Hamilton Plays The Music Of Fred Katz**	1958	20.00	50.00
World Pacific PJ-1238	(M)	**South Pacific In Hi-Fi**	1957	20.00	50.00
World Pacific WP-1238	(M)	**South Pacific In Hi-Fi**	1958	16.00	40.00
World Pacific ST-1003	(S)	**South Pacific In Hi-Fi**	1958	16.00	40.00
World Pacific PJ-1242	(M)	**The Chico Hamilton Trio Introduces Freddie Gambrell**	1957	20.00	50.00
World Pacific WP-1242	(M)	**The Chico Hamilton Trio Introduces Freddie Gambrell**	1958	16.00	40.00
World Pacific ST-1008	(S)	**The Chico Hamilton Trio Introduces Freddie Gambrell**	1958	16.00	40.00
World Pacific WP-1258	(M)	**Ellington Suite**	1959	20.00	50.00
World Pacific ST-1016	(S)	**Ellington Suite**	1959	16.00	40.00
World Pacific WP-1287	(M)	**The Original Hamilton Quintet**	1960	20.00	50.00
Kimberly 2019	(M)	**Meet Chico Hamilton**	1960	12.00	30.00
Kimberly 11019	(S)	**Meet Chico Hamilton**	1960	10.00	25.00
		(Kimberly 2019 is a reissue of World Pacific 1242.)			
Pacific Jazz PJ-39	(M)	**Spectacular**	1962	10.00	25.00
		(Pacific Jazz 39 is a reissue of 1209.)			
Warner Bros. W-1245	(M)	**Chico Hamilton Quintet With Strings Attached**	1958	20.00	50.00
Warner Bros. WS-1245	(M)	**Chico Hamilton Quintet With Strings Attached**	1958	16.00	40.00
Warner Bros. W-1271	(M)	**Gongs East!**	1958	20.00	50.00
Warner Bros. WS-1271	(S)	**Gongs East!**	1958	16.00	40.00
Warner Bros. W-1344	(M)	**The Three Faces Of Chico**	1959	20.00	50.00
Warner Bros. WS-1344	(S)	**The Three Faces Of Chico**	1959	16.00	40.00
SeSac N-2901	(M)	**That Hamilton Man**	1959	20.00	50.00
SeSac SN-2901	(S)	**That Hamilton Man**	1959	16.00	40.00
Columbia CL-1590	(M)	**Selections From "Bye Bye Birdie"**	1961	10.00	25.00
Columbia CS-8390	(S)	**Selections From "Bye Bye Birdie"**	1961	8.00	20.00

Label & Catalog #		Title	Year	VG+	NM
Columbia CL-1619	(M)	**Chico Hamilton Special**	1961	10.00	25.00
Columbia CS-8419	(S)	**Chico Hamilton Special**	1961	8.00	20.00
		— Columbia albums above have six white on black "eye" logos on each label.—			
Columbia CL-1807	(M)	**Drumfusion**	1962	8.00	20.00
Columbia CS-8607	(S)	**Drumfusion**	1962	6.00	15.00
		— Columbia albums above have "Guaranteed High Fidelity" or "360 Sound Stereo" in black on the label.—			
Reprise R-6078	(M)	**A Different Journey**	1963	16.00	40.00
Reprise R9-6078	(S)	**A Different Journey**	1963	12.00	30.00
Crown CLP-5310	(M)	**Chico Hamilton With Paul Horn**	196?	6.00	15.00
Crown CST-310	(E)	**Chico Hamilton With Paul Horn**	196?	3.00	7.50
		(Crown 5310 reissues material from Pacific Jazz 1220 and 1231.)			
Crown CLP-53??	(M)	**The Great Chico Hamilton Featuring Paul Horn**	196?	6.00	15.00
Crown CST-3??	(E)	**The Great Chico Hamilton Featuring Paul Horn**	196?	3.00	7.50
		(Crown 5310 reissues material from Pacific Jazz 1220 and 1231.)			
Impulse A-29	(M)	**Passin' Thru**	1963	12.00	30.00
Impulse AS-29	(S)	**Passin' Thru**	1963	10.00	25.00
Impulse A-59	(M)	**Man From Two Worlds**	1964	12.00	30.00
Impulse AS-59	(S)	**Man From Two Worlds**	1964	10.00	25.00
Impulse A-82	(M)	**Chic Chic Chico**	1965	12.00	30.00
Impulse AS-82	(S)	**Chic Chic Chico**	1965	10.00	25.00
Impulse A-9102	(M)	**El Chico**	1965	12.00	30.00
Impulse AS-9102	(S)	**El Chico**	1965	10.00	25.00
Impulse A-9114	(M)	**The Further Adventures Of El Chico**	1966	10.00	25.00
Impulse AS-9114	(S)	**The Further Adventures Of El Chico**	1966	8.00	20.00
Impulse A-9130	(M)	**The Dealer**	1966	10.00	25.00
Impulse AS-9130	(S)	**The Dealer**	1966	8.00	20.00
Impulse A-9174	(M)	**The Best Of Chico Hamilton**	1967	10.00	25.00
Impulse AS-9174	(S)	**The Best Of Chico Hamilton**	1967	8.00	20.00
Impulse A-9212	(M)	**Chico Hamilton-His Greatest Hits**	1967	10.00	25.00
Impulse AS-9212	(S)	**Chico Hamilton-His Greatest Hits**	1967	8.00	20.00
		—Impulse albums above have orange & black labels.—			
Impulse AS-29	(S)	**Passin' Thru**	1968	4.00	10.00
Impulse AS-59	(S)	**Man From Two Worlds**	1968	4.00	10.00
Impulse AS-82	(S)	**Chic Chic Chico**	1968	4.00	10.00
Impulse AS-9102	(S)	**El Chico**	1968	4.00	10.00
Impulse AS-9114	(S)	**The Further Adventures Of El Chico**	1968	4.00	10.00
Impulse AS-9130	(S)	**The Dealer**	1968	4.00	10.00
Impulse AS-9174	(S)	**The Best Of Chico Hamilton**	1968	4.00	10.00
Impulse AS-9212	(S)	**Chico Hamilton-His Greatest Hits**	1968	4.00	10.00
		—Impulse albums above have red & black labels with the "abc" logo on top.—			
Solid State SS-18043	(S)	**The Gamut**	1969	6.00	15.00
Solid State SS-18050	(S)	**The Headhunters**	1969	6.00	15.00
Sunset SUS-5215	(S)	**Easy Living**	1969	4.00	10.00
		(Sunset 5215 reissues Pacific Jazz/Wolrd Pacific material.)			

HAMILTON, DAVE

David Hamilston is a modern jazz vibraphone player.

Jazz Workshop JWS-206	(M)	**Blue Vibrations**	1963	20.00	50.00

HAMILTON, JIMMY

James Hamilton is a traditional jazz clarinet and tenor saxophone player, arranger and composer.

Urania UJLP-1003	(10")	**Clarinet In Hi-Fi**	1954	50.00	125.00
Urania UJLP-1204	(M)	**Accent On Clarinet**	1955	20.00	50.00
Urania UJLP-1208	(M)	**Clarinet In Hi-Fi**	1955	20.00	50.00
Everest LPBR-5100	(M)	**Swing Low, Sweet Clarinet**	1960	12.00	30.00
Everest SDBR-1100	(S)	**Swing Low, Sweet Clarinet**	1960	10.00	25.00
Swingville SVLP-2022	(M)	**It's About Time**	1961	20.00	50.00
Swingville SVLP-2028	(M)	**Can't Help Swingin'**	1961	20.00	50.00
		— Swingville mono albums above have purple mono or red stereo labels.—			
Swingville SVLP-2022	(M)	**It's About Time**	1965	10.00	25.00
Swingville SVLP-2028	(M)	**Can't Help Swingin'**	1965	10.00	25.00
		— Swingville albums above have blue labels with a trident logo on the right side.—			

HAMILTON, VICKI: ***Refer to*** **DAVID MacKAY & VICKI HAMILTON**

HAMLIN, JOHNNY

Argo LP-4001	(M)	**Johnny Hamlin Quintet**	1960	12.00	30.00
Argo LPS-4001	(S)	**Johnny Hamlin Quintet**	1960	10.00	25.00

Label & Catalog #		Title	Year	VG+	NM
HAMMER, BOB					
Robert Hammer is a modern jazz pianist and composer.					
ABC-Paramount ABC-497	*(M)*	**Beatle Jazz**	*1964*	**12.00**	**30.00**
ABC-Paramount ABCS-497	*(S)*	**Beatle Jazz**	*1964*	**10.00**	**25.00**
HAMPEL, GUNTER					
ESP-Disk' 1042	*(M)*	**Music From Europe**	*1967*	**10.00**	**25.00**
ESP-Disk' 1042	*(S)*	**Music From Europe**	*1967*	**8.00**	**20.00**
HAMPTON, LIONEL					
Lionel "Hamp" Hampton is a traditional jazz vibraphone and piano player, drummer, vocalist and big band leader. For additional listings refer to Benny Goodman; and the Jazzy Soundtracks section under Decca.					
Decca DL-5230	*(10")*	**Boogie Woogie**	*1950*	**30.00**	**75.00**
Decca DL-5297	*(10")*	**Moonglow**	*1951*	**30.00**	**75.00**
Decca DL-7013	*(10")*	**Just Jazz**	*1952*	**30.00**	**75.00**
Decca DL-8088	*(M)*	**All-American Award Concert At Carnegie Hall**	*1955*	**20.00**	**50.00**
Decca DL-8230	*(M)*	**Moonglow**	*1956*	**20.00**	**50.00**
Decca DL-9055	*(M)*	**Just Jazz**	*1958*	**20.00**	**50.00**
Clef MGC-142	*(10")*	**The Lionel Hampton Quartet**	*1953*	**50.00**	**125.00**
		(Clef 142 features cover art by David Stone Martin.)			
Clef MGC-611	*(M)*	**The Lionel Hampton Quartet**	*1954*	**30.00**	**75.00**
Clef MGC-628	*(M)*	**The Lionel Hampton Quintet**	*1954*	**30.00**	**75.00**
Clef MGC-642	*(M)*	**The Lionel Hampton Quintet, Volume 2**	*1955*	**40.00**	**100.00**
		(Clef 642 features cover art by David Stone Martin.)			
Clef MGC-667	*(M)*	**The Lionel Hampton Quartet/Quintet**	*1955*	**40.00**	**100.00**
		(Clef 667 features cover art by David Stone Martin.)			
Clef MGC-670	*(M)*	**Lionel Hampton Big Band**	*1955*	**40.00**	**100.00**
		(Clef 670 features cover art by David Stone Martin.)			
Clef MGC-673	*(M)*	**The Lionel Hampton Quartet**	*1955*	**30.00**	**75.00**
		(Clef 673 is a reissue of 142.)			
Clef MGC-714	*(M)*	**Lionel Hampton Plays Love Songs**	*1956*	**30.00**	**75.00**
Clef MGC-726	*(M)*	**King Of The Vibes**	*1956*	**30.00**	**75.00**
Clef MGC-727	*(M)*	**Air Mail Special**	*1956*	**30.00**	**75.00**
Clef MGC-735	*(M)*	**Flying Home**	*1956*	**30.00**	**75.00**
Clef MGC-736	*(M)*	**Swingin' With Hamp**	*1956*	**30.00**	**75.00**
Clef MGC-737	*(M)*	**Hamp Roars Again**	*1956*	*Unreleased*	
Clef MGC-738	*(M)*	**Hamp!**	*1956*	**30.00**	**75.00**
		(Clef 738 is a reissue of 673.)			
Clef MGC-744	*(M)*	**Hamp's Big Four**	*1956*	**30.00**	**75.00**
Norgran MGN-1080	*(M)*	**Lionel Hampton And His Giants**	*1956*	**40.00**	**100.00**
American Rec. Soc. G-403	*(M)*	**The Swinging Jazz Of Lionel Hampton**	*1956*	**16.00**	**40.00**
Verve MGV-2018	*(M)*	**Lionel Hampton Plays Love Songs**	*1956*	**20.00**	**50.00**
		(Verve 2018 is a reissue of Clef 714.)			
Verve MGV-8019	*(M)*	**Travelin' Band**	*1957*	**20.00**	**50.00**
		(Verve 8019 is a reissue of Clef 670.)			
Verve MGV-8105	*(M)*	**King Of The Vibes**	*1957*	**20.00**	**50.00**
		(Verve 8105 is a reissue of Clef 726.)			
Verve MGV-8106	*(M)*	**Air Mail Special**	*1957*	**20.00**	**50.00**
		(Verve 8106 is a reissue of Clef 727.)			
Verve MGV-8112	*(M)*	**Flying Home**	*1957*	**20.00**	**50.00**
		(Verve 8112 is a reissue of Clef 735.)			
Verve MGV-8113	*(M)*	**Swingin' With Hamp**	*1957*	**20.00**	**50.00**
		(Verve 8113 is a reissue of Clef 736.)			
Verve MGV-8114	*(M)*	**Hamp!**	*1957*	**20.00**	**50.00**
		(Verve 8114 is a reissue of Clef 738.)			
Verve MGV-8117	*(M)*	**Hamp's Big Four**	*1957*	**20.00**	**50.00**
		(Verve 8117 is a reissue of Clef 744.)			
Verve MGV-8170	*(M)*	**Lionel Hampton And His Giants**	*1957*	**20.00**	**50.00**
		(Verve 8170 is a reissue of Norgran 1080.)			
Verve MGV-8215	*(M)*	**The Genius Of Lionel Hampton**	*1958*	**20.00**	**50.00**
Verve MGV-8223	*(M)*	**Lionel Hampton '58**	*1958*	**20.00**	**50.00**
Verve MGV-8226	*(M)*	**Hallelujah Hamp**	*1958*	**20.00**	**50.00**
Verve MGV-8228	*(M)*	**The High And The Mighty**	*1958*	**20.00**	**50.00**
Verve MGV-8275	*(M)*	**Lionel Hampton**	*1958*	*Unreleased*	
—Verve albums above have black labels with "Verve Records, Inc." on the bottom.—					
Verve V-2018	*(M)*	**Lionel Hampton Plays Love Songs**	*1961*	**6.00**	**15.00**
Verve V-8019	*(M)*	**Travelin' Band**	*1961*	**6.00**	**15.00**
Verve V-8105	*(M)*	**The King Of The Vibes**	*1961*	**6.00**	**15.00**

Label & Catalog #		Title	Year	VG+	NM
Verve V-8106	(M)	**Air Mail Special**	1961	6.00	15.00
Verve V-8112	(M)	**Flying Home**	1961	6.00	15.00
Verve V-8113	(M)	**Swingin' With Hamp**	1961	6.00	15.00
Verve V-8114	(M)	**Hamp**	1961	6.00	15.00
Verve V-8117	(M)	**Hamp's Big Four**	1961	6.00	15.00
Verve V-8170	(M)	**Lionel Hampton And His Giants**	1961	6.00	15.00
Verve V-8215	(M)	**The Genius Of Lionel Hampton**	1961	6.00	15.00
Verve V-8223	(M)	**Lionel Hampton '58**	1961	6.00	15.00
Verve V-8226	(M)	**Hallelujah Hamp**	1961	6.00	15.00
Verve V-8228	(M)	**The High And The Mighty**	1961	6.00	15.00
		—Verve albums above have black labels with "MGM Records" on the bottom.—			
Blue Note BLP-5046	(10")	**Rockin' And Groovin'**	1954	150.00	300.00
MGM E-285	(10")	**Oh, Rock**	1954	40.00	100.00
MGM E-3386	(M)	**Oh, Rock**	1956	20.00	50.00
EmArcy MG-27537	(10")	**Hamp In Paris**	1954	40.00	100.00
EmArcy MG-27538	(10")	**Crazy Hamp**	1954	40.00	100.00
EmArcy MG-36032	(M)	**Hamp In Paris**	1955	20.00	50.00
		(EmArcy 36032 is a reissue of 26037 and 26038.)			
EmArcy MG-36034	(M)	**Crazy Rhythm**	1955	20.00	50.00
EmArcy MG-36035	(M)	**Jam Session In Paris**	1955	20.00	50.00
		—EmArcy albums above have blue labels with silver print.—			
RCA Victor LJM-1000	(M)	**Hot Mallets**	1954	20.00	50.00
RCA Victor LPM-1422	(M)	**Jazz Flamenco**	1957	20.00	50.00
RCA Victor LPM-2318	(M)	**Swing Classics**	1961	10.00	25.00
RCA Victor LSP-2318	(S)	**Swing Classics**	1961	8.00	20.00
		—RCA albums above have black labels with "Long Play" or "Living Stereo" on the bottom.—			
Epic LN-3190	(M)	**Apollo Hall Concert 1954**	1955	20.00	50.00
Contemporary C-3502	(M)	**Hampton In Paris**	1955	20.00	50.00
Columbia CL-711	(M)	**Wailin' At The Trianon**	1955	16.00	40.00
Columbia CL-1304	(M)	**Golden Vibes**	1959	10.00	25.00
Columbia CS-8110	(S)	**Golden Vibes**	1959	8.00	20.00
Columbia CL-1486	(M)	**Silver Vibes**	1960	10.00	25.00
Columbia CS-8277	(S)	**Silver Vibes**	1960	8.00	20.00
Columbia CL-1661	(M)	**Soft Vibes**	1961	10.00	25.00
Columbia CS-8461	(S)	**Soft Vibes**	1961	8.00	20.00
		—Columbia albums above have six white on black "eye" logos on each label.—			
Gene Norman GNP-15	(M)	**Lionel Hampton With The Just Jazz All Stars**	1956	20.00	50.00
Jazztone J-1040	(10")	**Visist On A Skyscraper**	195?	20.00	50.00
Jazztone J-1238	(M)	**The Fabulous Lionel Hampton & His All Stars**	1957	16.00	40.00
Jazztone J-1246	(M)	**Lionel Hampton's All Star Groups**	1957	16.00	40.00
Audio Fidelity AFLP-1849	(M)	**Lionel**	1957	16.00	40.00
Audio Fidelity AFSD-5849	(S)	**Lionel**	1958	12.00	30.00
Audio Fidelity AFLP-1913	(M)	**Hamp's Big Band**	1958	16.00	40.00
Audio Fidelity AFSD-5913	(S)	**Hamp's Big Band**	1958	12.00	30.00
Camden CAL-317	(M)	**Open House**	1957	8.00	20.00
Camden CAL-402	(M)	**Jivin' The Vibes**	1958	8.00	20.00
Lion L-70064	(M)	**Lionel Hampton & His Orchestra**	1958	8.00	20.00
Harmony HL-7115	(M)	**Hamp In Hi Fi**	1958	8.00	20.00
Harmony HL-7281	(M)	**The One And Only Lionel Hampton**	1961	6.00	15.00
Perfect 12002	(M)	**Lionel Hampton Swings**	1959	12.00	30.00
Perfect 14002	(S)	**Lionel Hampton Swings**	1959	12.00	30.00
Glad Hamp GHLP-1001	(M)	**The Many Sides Of Lionel Hampton**	1961	12.00	30.00
Glad Hamp GHLP-1003	(M)	**The Exciting Hamp In Europe**	1962	12.00	30.00
Glad Hamp GHLP-3050	(M)	**All That Twistin' Jazz**	1962	12.00	30.00
Glad Hamp GHLP-1004	(M)	**Bossa Nova Jazz**	1963	12.00	30.00
Glad Hamp GHLP-1005	(M)	**Lionel Hampton On Tour**	1963	12.00	30.00
Glad Hamp GHLP-1006	(M)	**Lionel Hampton In Japan**	1964	12.00	30.00
Glad Hamp GHLP-1007	(M)	**East Meets West**	1965	12.00	30.00
Glad Hamp GHLP-1009	(M)	**A Taste Of Hamp**	1965	12.00	30.00
Decca DL-4194	(M)	**Original Star Dust**	1962	8.00	20.00
Decca DL-74194	(S)	**Original Star Dust**	1962	6.00	15.00
Decca DL-4296	(M)	**Hamp's Golden Favorites**	1962	8.00	20.00
Decca DL-74296	(S)	**Hamp's Golden Favorites**	1962	6.00	15.00
Impulse A-78	(M)	**You Better Know It**	1965	12.00	30.00
Impulse AS-78	(M)	**You Better Know It**	1965	10.00	25.00
		—Impulse albums above have orange & black labels.—			
Impulse AS-78	(M)	**You Better Know It**	1968	4.00	10.00
		—Impulse albums above have red & black labels with the "abc" logo on top.—			

Label & Catalog #		Title	Year	VG+	NM

HAMPTON, LIONEL, & STAN GETZ

Norgran MGN-1037	(M)	**Hamp And Getz**	1955	40.00	100.00
		(Norgran 1037 features cover art by David Stone Martin.)			
Verve MGV-8128	(M)	**Hamp And Getz**	1957	20.00	50.00
		—Verve albums above have black labels with "Verve Records, Inc." on the bottom.—			
Verve V-8128	(M)	**Hamp And Getz**	1961	6.00	15.00
		—Verve albums above have black labels with "MGM Records" on the bottom.—			

HAMPTON, LIONEL, & ART TATUM & BUDDY RICH

Clef MGC-709	(M)	**The Hampton-Tatum-Rich Trio**	1956	30.00	75.00
Verve MGV-8093	(M)	**The Hampton-Tatum-Rich Trio**	1957	20.00	50.00
		—Verve albums above have black labels with "Verve Records, Inc." on the bottom.—			
Verve V-8093	(M)	**The Hampton-Tatum-Rich Trio**	1961	6.00	15.00
		—Verve albums above have black labels with "MGM Records" on the bottom.—			

HAMPTON, LIONEL, & CHARLIE TEAGARDEN

Coral CRL-57438	(M)	**The Great Hamp And Little T.**	1963	10.00	25.00
Coral CRL-757438	(S)	**The Great Hamp And Little T.**	1963	8.00	20.00

HAMPTON, SLIDE

Locksley "Slide" Hampton is a modern jazz trombone and tuba player, arranger and composer. For additional listings refer to Harold Betters.

Strand 1006	(M)	**His Horn Of Plenty**	1959	20.00	50.00
Strand S-1006	(S)	**His Horn Of Plenty**	1959	16.00	40.00
Atlantic 1339	(M)	**Sister Salvation**	1960	16.00	40.00
Atlantic SD-1339	(S)	**Sister Salvation**	1960	12.00	30.00
Atlantic 1362	(M)	**Somethin' Sanctified**	1961	16.00	40.00
Atlantic SD-1362	(S)	**Somethin' Sanctified**	1961	12.00	30.00
		—Atlantic albums above have multi-color labels with a white fan logo.—			
Atlantic 1339	(M)	**Sister Salvation**	196?	8.00	20.00
Atlantic SD-1339	(S)	**Sister Salvation**	196?	6.00	15.00
Atlantic 1362	(M)	**Somethin' Sanctified**	196?	8.00	20.00
Atlantic SD-1362	(S)	**Somethin' Sanctified**	196?	6.00	15.00
Atlantic 1379	(M)	**Jazz With A Twist**	1962	12.00	30.00
Atlantic SD-1379	(S)	**Jazz With A Twist**	1962	10.00	25.00
Atlantic 1396	(M)	**Explosion!**	1962	10.00	25.00
Atlantic SD-1396	(S)	**Explosion!**	1962	8.00	20.00
		—Atlantic albums above have multi-color labels with a black fan logo.—			
Charlie Parker PLP-803	(M)	**Two Sides Of Slide**	1962	12.00	30.00
Charlie Parker PLP-803S	(S)	**Two Sides Of Slide**	1962	10.00	25.00
Epic LA-16030	(M)	**Drum Suite**	1962	10.00	25.00
Epic BA-17030	(S)	**Drum Suite**	1962	8.00	20.00

HANCOCK, HERBIE

Herbert Hancock is a modern jazz piano and electric keyboards player and composer. For additional listings refer to the Jazzy Soundtracks section under MGM.

Blue Note BLP-4109	(M)	**Takin' Off**	1962	20.00	50.00
Blue Note BST-84109	(S)	**Takin' Off**	1962	16.00	40.00
Blue Note BLP-4126	(M)	**My Point Of View**	1963	16.00	40.00
Blue Note BST-84126	(S)	**My Point Of View**	1963	12.00	30.00
Blue Note BLP-4147	(M)	**Inventions And Dimensions**	1963	16.00	40.00
Blue Note BST-84147	(S)	**Inventions And Dimensions**	1963	12.00	30.00
Blue Note BLP-4175	(M)	**Empyrean Isles**	1964	16.00	40.00
Blue Note BST-84175	(S)	**Empyrean Isles**	1964	12.00	30.00
Blue Note BLP-4195	(M)	**Maiden Voyage**	1965	16.00	40.00
Blue Note BST-84195	(S)	**Maiden Voyage**	1965	12.00	30.00
		—Blue Note albums above have blue on white labels with a New York, NY address.—			
Blue Note BST-84109	(S)	**Takin' Off**	196?	5.00	12.00
Blue Note BST-84126	(S)	**My Point Of View**	196?	5.00	12.00
Blue Note BST-84147	(S)	**Inventions And Dimensions**	196?	5.00	12.00
Blue Note BST-84175	(S)	**Empyrean Isles**	196?	5.00	12.00
Blue Note BST-84195	(S)	**Maiden Voyage**	196?	5.00	12.00
Blue Note BST-84279	(S)	**Speak Like A Child**	1968	5.00	12.00
Blue Note BST-84321	(S)	**The Prisoner**	1969	5.00	12.00
		—Blue Note albums above have blue on white labels with "A Division of Liberty Records."—			

Label & Catalog #		Title	Year	VG+	NM

HANDY, GEORGE

George Hendleman, aka George Handy, is a West Coast jazz pianist and arranger.

"X" LXA-1004	(M)	**Handyland, U.S.A.**	1954	24.00	60.00
"X" LXA-1032	(M)	**By George! Handy Of Course**	1954	24.00	60.00

HANDY, JOHN

John Handy III is a modern jazz soprano, alto, baritone and tenor saxophone player.

Roulette R-52042	(M)	**In The Ver-nac'u-lar**	1960	10.00	25.00
Roulette SR-52042	(S)	**In The Ver-nac'u-lar**	1960	8.00	20.00
Roulette R-52088	(M)	**No Coast Jazz**	1962	10.00	25.00
Roulette SR-52088	(S)	**No Coast Jazz**	1962	8.00	20.00
Roulette R-52121	(M)	**John Handy Jazz**	1964	8.00	20.00
Roulette SR-52121	(S)	**John Handy Jazz**	1964	6.00	15.00
Roulette R-52124	(M)	**Quote, Unquote**	1964	8.00	20.00
Roulette SR-52124	(S)	**Quote, Unquote**	1964	6.00	15.00
Columbia CL-2462	(M)	**Recorded Live At The Monterey Jazz Festival**	1966	6.00	15.00
Columbia CS-9262	(S)	**Recorded Live At The Monterey Jazz Festival**	1966	5.00	12.00
Columbia CL-2567	(M)	**The Second John Handy Album**	1966	6.00	15.00
Columbia CS-9367	(S)	**The Second John Handy Album**	1966	5.00	12.00
Columbia CL-2697	(M)	**New View**	1967	6.00	15.00
Columbia CS-9497	(S)	**New View**	1967	5.00	12.00
Columbia CL-2889	(M)	**Projections**	1968	8.00	20.00
Columbia CS-9689	(S)	**Projections**	1968	5.00	12.00

—Columbia albums above have "360 Sound" in white on the bottom of the label.—

HANDY, W.C.

William Christopher Handy is a traditional jazz cornet player, vocalist and composer.

Heritage 0052	(10")	**Blues Revisited**	195?	40.00	100.00

HANNA, KEN

Kenneth Hanna is a traditional jazz-based trumpet player, composer and band leader.

Capitol T-6512	(M)	**Jazz For Dancers**	1955	16.00	40.00

HANNA, ROLAND

Roland Hanna is a jazz-based pianist.

Atco 33-108	(M)	**Destry Rides Again**	1959	16.00	40.00
Atco SD-33-108	(S)	**Destry Rides Again**	1959	16.00	40.00
Atco 33-121	(M)	**Easy To Love**	1960	16.00	40.00
Atco SD-33-121	(S)	**Easy To Love**	1960	16.00	40.00

—Atco albums above have yellow labels with a harp logo on top.—

HANSON, OLA: *Refer to* CHEZ ALFRED & OLA HANSON & CHUCK LEE

HARDAWAY, BOB

Robert Hardaway is a West Coast jazz tenor saxophone player and arranger. For additional listings refer to Art Blakey & The Jazz Messengers; Eddie Shu / Bob Hardaway.

Bethlehem BCP-1026	(10")	**Bob Hardaway**	1955	40.00	100.00

HARDEN, WILBUR

Wilbur Harden is a modern jazz flugel horn and trumpet player.

Savoy MG-12127	(M)	**Mainstream 1958/The East Coast Jazz Scene Featuring John Coltrane**	1958	24.00	60.00
Savoy MG-12131	(M)	**Jazz Way Out**	1958	20.00	50.00
Savoy SST-13004	(S)	**Jazz Way Out**	1958	16.00	40.00
		(Savoy 12131 also features John Coltrane.)			
Savoy MG-12134	(M)	**The King And I**	1958	16.00	40.00
Savoy SST-13002	(S)	**The King And I**	1958	12.00	30.00
Savoy MG-12136	(M)	**Tanganyika Suite**	1958	20.00	50.00
Savoy SST-13005	(S)	**Tanganyika Suite**	1958	16.00	40.00
		(Savoy 12136 also features John Coltrane.)			

HARDMAN, BILL

William Hardman is a modern jazz trumpet player. For additional listings refer to Jackie McLean.

Savoy MG-12170	(M)	**Bill Hardman Quintet**	1961	24.00	60.00

HARIAN, KENT

Kent Harian's orchestra includes Al Cohn and Nick Travis.

Caravan LP-15611	(M)	**Echoes Of Joy**	1956	125.00	250.00

Label & Catalog #		Title	Year	VG+	NM

HARNELL, JOE

Jo Harnell is a jazz-based vocalist.

Jubilee JLP-1015	(M)	**Jo Harnell**	1956	20.00	50.00

HARPER, HERBIE

Herbert Harper is a West Coast jazz trombone player.

Nocturne NLP-1	(10")	**Herbie Harper Quintet**	1954	60.00	150.00
		(Nocturne 1 also features Bob Gordon.)			
Nocturne NLP-7	(10")	**Herbie Harper**	1954	60.00	150.00
Liberty LRS-6003	(M)	**Herbie Harper**	1955	30.00	75.00
		(Liberty 6003 is a reissue of Nocturne 7.)			
Bethlehem BCP-1025	(10")	**Herbie Harper**	1955	50.00	125.00
Mode LP-100	(M)	**Herbie Harper Sextet**	1957	40.00	100.00
Tampa TP-11	(M)	**Herbie Harper Quintet** *(Colored vinyl)*	1957	40.00	100.00
Tampa TP-11	(M)	**Herbie Harper Quintet**	1958	20.00	50.00

HARPER, TONI

Rocquelle Toni Harper is a jazz vocalist.

Verve MGV-2001	(M)	**Toni Harper Sings**	1956	30.00	75.00
		(Verve 2001 also features Oscar Peterson.)			
		—Verve albums above have "Verve Records, Inc." on the bottom of the label.—			
Verve V-2001	(M)	**Toni Harper Sings**	1961	12.00	30.00
		—Verve albums above have black labels with "MGM Records" on the bottom.—			
RCA Victor LPM-2092	(M)	**Lady Lonely**	1960	10.00	25.00
RCA Victor LSP-2092	(S)	**Lady Lonely**	1960	12.00	30.00
RCA Victor LPM-2253	(M)	**Night Mood**	1960	10.00	25.00
RCA Victor LSP-2253	(S)	**Night Mood**	1960	12.00	30.00
		(RCA 2092 and 2253 also feature Marty Paich with Art Pepper.)			
		—RCA albums above have black labels with "Long Play" or "Living Stereo" on the bottom.—			

HARRIOTT, JOE

Arthurlin "Joe" Harriott is a modern jazz alto, baritone and tenor saxophone player.

Jazzland JLP-37	(M)	**Southern Horizons**	1961	12.00	30.00
Jazzland JLP-937	(S)	**Southern Horizons**	1961	10.00	25.00
Jazzland JLP-49	(M)	**Free Form**	1961	12.00	30.00
Jazzland JLP-949	(S)	**Free Form**	1961	10.00	25.00
Capitol T-10351	(M)	**Abstract**	1962	8.00	20.00
Capitol DT-10351	(E)	**Abstract**	1962	4.00	10.00
Atlantic 1465	(M)	**Indo-Jazz Suite**	1966	6.00	15.00
Atlantic SD-1465	(S)	**Indo-Jazz Suite**	1966	5.00	12.00
Atlantic 1482	(M)	**Indo-Jazz Fusions**	1967	6.00	15.00
Atlantic SD-1482	(S)	**Indo-Jazz Fusions**	1967	5.00	12.00
		—Atlantic albums above have multi-color labels with a black fan logo.—			

HARRIS, ART

Arthur Harris is a traditional jazz-based pianist and composer.

Kapp KL-1015	(M)	**Jazz Goes To Post Graduate School**	1956	16.00	40.00

HARRIS, ART, & MITCH LEIGH (THE HARRIS-LEIGH GROUP)

Epic LG-1010	(10")	**Modern Woodwind Expressions**	1954	20.00	50.00
Kapp KL-1011	(M)	**Baroque Band And Brass Choir—Jazz 1775**	1956	16.00	40.00
Epic LN-3200	(M)	**New Jazz In Hi-Fi**	1956	16.00	40.00

HARRIS, BARRY

Barry Harris is a modern jazz pianist. For additional listings refer to Charles McPherson; Sonny Red.

Argo LP-644	(M)	**Breakin' It Up**	1959	16.00	40.00
Argo LPS-644	(S)	**Breakin' It Up**	1959	12.00	30.00
Riverside RLP-12-326	(M)	**Barry Harris At The Jazz Workshop**	1960	16.00	40.00
Riverside RLP-1177	(S)	**Barry Harris At The Jazz Workshop**	1960	12.00	30.00
Riverside RLP-354	(M)	**Preminado**	1961	16.00	40.00
Riverside RS-9354	(S)	**Preminado**	1961	12.00	30.00
Riverside RLP-392	(M)	**Listen To Barry Harris**	1961	16.00	40.00
Riverside RS-9392	(S)	**Listen To Barry Harris**	1961	12.00	30.00
Riverside RLP-413	(M)	**Newer Than New**	1962	16.00	40.00
Riverside RS-9413	(S)	**Newer Than New**	1962	12.00	30.00
Riverside RLP-435	(M)	**Chasin' The Bird**	1962	12.00	30.00
Riverside RS-9435	(S)	**Chasin' The Bird**	1962	10.00	25.00
		—Riverside albums above have blue mono or black stereo labels with a reel & mike logo on top.—			

Label & Catalog #		Title	Year	VG+	NM
Prestige PRLP-7498	(M)	**Luminescence**	1967	12.00	30.00
Prestige PRST-7498	(S)	**Luminescence**	1967	8.00	20.00

—Prestige albums above have blue labels with a trident logo on the right side.—

Prestige PRST-7600	(S)	**Bull's Eye**	1969	6.00	15.00

—Prestige albums above have blue labels with a trident logo on top.—

HARRIS, BILL

Willard "Bill" Harris is a traditional jazz trombonist. For additional listings refer to Terry Gibbs & Bill Harris; Benny Carter; Chubby Jackson & Bill Harris.

Mercury MGC-125	(10")	**Bill Harris Collates**	1953	*Unreleased*	
Clef MGC-125	(10")	**Bill Harris Collates**	1953	60.00	150.00
		(Clef 125 features cover art by David Stone Martin.)			
Norgran MGN-1062	(M)	**The Bill Harris Herd**	1956	40.00	100.00
Verve MGV-8152	(M)	**The Bill Harris Herd**	1957	*See below*	
		(The existence of this record, both as an MGV-8152 original and an MGM V-8152 reissue, is in doubt. . .)			

—Verve albums above have black labels with "Verve Records, Inc." on the bottom.—

Fantasy 3263	(M)	**Bill Harris And Friends** *(Red vinyl)*	1958	16.00	40.00
Fantasy 3263	(M)	**Bill Harris And Frienda**	195?	8.00	20.00

—Fantasy albums above are pressed on non-flexible vinyl.—

HARRIS, BILL

William Harris is a jazz-based guitarist.

EmArcy MG-36097	(M)	**Bill Harris**	1956	16.00	40.00
EmArcy MG-36113	(M)	**The Harris Touch**	1957	16.00	40.00

—EmArcy albums above have blue labels with silver print.—

Mercury MG-20552	(M)	**The Harris Touch**	1960	12.00	30.00
Mercury SR-60552	(S)	**The Harris Touch**	1960	10.00	25.00
		(Mercury 20552 is a reissue of EmArcy 36113.)			
Wing MGW-12220	(M)	**Great Guitar Sounds**	1963	8.00	20.00
Wing MGS-16220	(S)	**Great Guitar Sounds**	1963	6.00	15.00
		(Wing 12220 is a reissue of Mercury 20552.)			

HARRIS, EDDIE

Edward Harris is a modern jazz tenor sax player and composer. For additional listings refer to Les McCann.

Exodus EX-6002	(M)	**For Bird And Bags**	196?	10.00	25.00
Exodus EXS-6002	(S)	**For Bird And Bags**	196?	6.00	20.00
Vee Jay LP-3016	(M)	**Exodus To Jazz**	1961	10.00	25.00
Vee Jay LPS-3016	(S)	**Exodus To Jazz**	1961	8.00	20.00
Vee Jay LP-3025	(M)	**Mighty Like A Rose**	1961	10.00	25.00
Vee Jay LPS-3025	(S)	**Mighty Like A Rose**	1961	8.00	20.00
Vee Jay LP-3027	(M)	**Jazz For "Breakfast At Tiffany's"**	1961	8.00	20.00
Vee Jay LPS-3027	(S)	**Jazz For "Breakfast At Tiffany's"**	1961	6.00	15.00
Vee Jay LP-3028	(M)	**A Study In Jazz**	1962	8.00	20.00
Vee Jay LPS-3028	(S)	**A Study In Jazz**	1962	6.00	15.00
Vee Jay LP-3031	(M)	**Eddie Harris Goes To The Movies**	1962	8.00	20.00
Vee Jay LPS-3031	(S)	**Eddie Harris Goes To The Movies**	1962	6.00	15.00
Vee Jay LP-3034	(M)	**Bossa Nova**	1963	8.00	20.00
Vee Jay LPS-3034	(S)	**Bossa Nova**	1963	6.00	15.00
Columbia CL-2168	(M)	**Cool Sax, Warm Heart**	1964	6.00	15.00
Columbia CS-8968	(S)	**Cool Sax, Warm Heart**	1964	5.00	12.00
Columbia CL-2295	(M)	**Cool Sax From Hollywood To Broadway**	1965	6.00	15.00
Columbia CS-9095	(S)	**Cool Sax From Hollywood To Broadway**	1965	5.00	12.00

—Columbia albums above have "Guaranteed High Fidelity" or "360 Sound Stereo" in black on the label.—

Atlantic 1448	(M)	**The In Sound**	1966	6.00	15.00
Atlantic SD-1448	(S)	**The In Sound**	1966	5.00	12.00
Atlantic 1453	(M)	**Means Greens**	1966	6.00	15.00
Atlantic SD-1453	(S)	**Means Greens**	1966	5.00	12.00
Atlantic 1478	(M)	**The Tender Storm**	1967	6.00	15.00
Atlantic SD-1478	(S)	**The Tender Storm**	1967	5.00	12.00
Atlantic 1495	(M)	**The Electrifying Eddie Harris**	1968	6.00	15.00
Atlantic SD-1495	(S)	**The Electrifying Eddie Harris**	1968	5.00	12.00
Atlantic SD-1517	(S)	**Silver Cycles**	1969	5.00	12.00
Atlantic SD-1529	(S)	**High Voltage**	1969	5.00	12.00

—Atlantic albums above have multi-color labels with a black fan logo.—

Label & Catalog #		Title	Year	VG+	NM
HARRIS, GENE					
Gene Harris is a modern jazz pianist.					
Jubilee JLP-1005	*(M)*	**Gene Harris Trio**	*1955*	**20.00**	**50.00**
Jubilee JLP-1115	*(M)*	**Genie In My Soul**	*1959*	**16.00**	**40.00**
Jubilee JGS-1115	*(S)*	**Genie In My Soul**	*1959*	**12.00**	**30.00**
HARRIS, HAROLD					
Harold Harris is a jazz-based pianist.					
Vee Jay LP-3018	*(M)*	**Here's Harold**	*1961*	**12.00**	**30.00**
Vee Jay LPS-3018	*(S)*	**Here's Harold**	*1961*	**10.00**	**25.00**
Vee Jay LP-3036	*(M)*	**Harold Harris At The Playboy Club**	*1963*	**12.00**	**30.00**
Vee Jay LPS-3036	*(S)*	**Harold Harris At The Playboy Club**	*1963*	**10.00**	**25.00**
HARRISON, CASS					
MGM E-3388	*(M)*	**The Duke And I**	*1956*	**16.00**	**40.00**
MGM E-3495	*(M)*	**Wrappin' It Up**	*1957*	**16.00**	**40.00**
HARROW, NANCY					
Nancy Harrow is a modern jazz vocalist.					
Candid CD-8008	*(M)*	**Wild Women Don't Have The Blues**	*1962*	**12.00**	**30.00**
Candid CS-9008	*(S)*	**Wild Women Don't Have The Blues**	*1962*	**16.00**	**40.00**
Atlantic 8075	*(M)*	**You Never Know**	*1963*	**10.00**	**25.00**
Atlantic SD-8075	*(S)*	**You Never Know**	*1963*	**12.00**	**30.00**
—Atlantic albums above have multi-color lables with a black fan logo.—					
HARTMAN, GEORGE: ***Refer to*** **IRVING FAZOLA / GEORGE HARTMAN**					
HARTMAN, JOHNNY					
Johnny Hartman is a modern jazz vocalist. For additional listings refer to John Coltrane.					
Regent MG-6014	*(M)*	**Just You, Just Me**	*1956*	**30.00**	**75.00**
Bethlehem BCP-43	*(M)*	**Songs From The Heart**	*1956*	**30.00**	**75.00**
Bethlehem BCP-6014	*(M)*	**All Of Me**	*1957*	**30.00**	**75.00**
Impulse A-57	*(M)*	**Dropped By To Say Hello**	*1964*	**16.00**	**40.00**
Impulse AS-57	*(S)*	**Dropped By To Say Hello**	*1964*	**14.00**	**35.00**
Impulse A-74	*(M)*	**The Voice That Is**	*1965*	**16.00**	**40.00**
Impulse AS-74	*(S)*	**The Voice That Is**	*1965*	**14.00**	**35.00**
—Impulse albums above have orange & black labels.—					
Impulse AS-57	*(S)*	**Dropped By To Say Hello**	*1968*	**4.00**	**10.00**
Impulse AS-74	*(S)*	**The Voice That Is**	*1968*	**4.00**	**10.00**
—Impulse albums above have red & black labels with the "abc" logo on top.—					
ABC-Paramount ABC-574	*(M)*	**The Unforgettable Johnny Hartman**	*1966*	**14.00**	**35.00**
ABC-Paramount ABCS-574	*(S)*	**The Unforgettable Johnny Hartman**	*1966*	**12.00**	**30.00**
HARVEY, LAURENCE					
Atlantic 1367	*(M)*	**This Is My Beloved**	*1961*	**8.00**	**20.00**
Atlantic SD-1367	*(M)*	**This Is My Beloved**	*1961*	**6.00**	**15.00**
—Atlantic albums above have multi-color labels with a black fan logo.—					
HATZA, GREG					
Gregory Hatza is a jazzy organist.					
Coral CRL-57493	*(M)*	**The Wizardry Of Greg Hatza**	*1962*	**6.00**	**15.00**
Coral CRL-757493	*(S)*	**The Wizardry Of Greg Hatza**	*1962*	**5.00**	**12.00**
Coral CRL-57495	*(M)*	**Organized Jazz**	*1962*	**6.00**	**15.00**
Coral CRL-757495	*(S)*	**Organized Jazz**	*1962*	**5.00**	**12.00**
HAWES, HAMPTON					
Hampton "Hamp" Hawes is a West Coast jazz pianist. For additional listings refer to Curtis Fuller; Freddie Redd & Hampton Hawes; and the Various Artists section under Savoy.					
Vantage VLP-1	*(10")*	**Hamp Hawes**	*1954*	**40.00**	**100.00**
Prestige PRLP-212	*(10")*	**Hampton Hawes Quartet**	*1955*	**40.00**	**100.00**
Contemporary C-3505	*(M)*	**Hampton Hawes**	*1955*	**20.00**	**50.00**
Contemporary C-3515	*(M)*	**This Is Hampton Hawes**	*1956*	**20.00**	**50.00**
Contemporary C-3523	*(M)*	**Everybody Likes Hampton Hawes**	*1956*	**20.00**	**50.00**
Contemporary C-3545	*(M)*	**All Night Session! Volume 1**	*1958*	**20.00**	**50.00**
Contemporary S-7545	*(S)*	**All Night Session! Volume 1**	*1959*	**16.00**	**40.00**
Contemporary C-3546	*(M)*	**All Night Session! Volume 2**	*1958*	**20.00**	**50.00**
Contemporary S-7546	*(S)*	**All Night Session! Volume 2**	*1959*	**16.00**	**40.00**

Label & Catalog #		Title	Year	VG+	NM
Contemporary C-3547	(M)	**All Night Session! Volume 3**	1958	20.00	50.00
Contemporary S-7547	(S)	**All Night Session! Volume 3**	1959	16.00	40.00
Contemporary C-3553	(M)	**Four! Hampton Hawes!!!!**	1958	20.00	50.00
Stereo Records S-7026	(S)	**Four! Hampton Hawes!!!!**	1958	18.00	45.00
Contemporary S-7553	(S)	**Four! Hampton Hawes!!!!**	1959	16.00	40.00
Contemporary M-3589	(M)	**For Real!**	1961	16.00	40.00
Contemporary S-7589	(S)	**For Real!**	1961	12.00	30.00
		(Cont. 3589 also features Harold Land, Scott LaFaro & Frank Butler)			
Contemporary M-3614	(M)	**The Green Leaves Of Summer**	1964	20.00	50.00
Contemporary S-7614	(S)	**The Green Leaves Of Summer**	1964	14.00	35.00
Contemporary M-3616	(M)	**Here And Now**	1965	10.00	25.00
Contemporary S-7616	(S)	**Here And Now**	1965	8.00	20.00
Contemporary M-3621	(M)	**The Seance**	1966	10.00	25.00
Contemporary S-7621	(S)	**The Seance**	1966	8.00	20.00
Contemporary M-3631	(M)	**I'm All Smiles**	1967	10.00	25.00
Contemporary S-7631	(S)	**I'm All Smiles**	1967	8.00	20.00
		—Contemporary stereo albums above have black & gold labels.—			
Vault LPS-9009	(S)	**Hampton Hawes Plays Movie Musicals**	1969	6.00	15.00
Prestige PRST-7695	(S)	**Hampton Hawes In Europe**	1969	5.00	12.00
		—Prestige albums above have blue labels with a trident logo on top.—			

HAWES, HAMPTON / JOHN MEHEGAN / HERBIE NICHOLS / PAUL SMITH

Label & Catalog #		Title	Year	VG+	NM
Savoy MG-12100	(M)	**I Just Love Jazz Piano!**	1957	20.00	50.00
		—Savoy albums above have maroon labels.—			

HAWKINS, COLEMAN

Coleman Hawkins, aka "Hawk" or "Bean," is a traditional jazz-based tenor sax player. For additional listings refer to Kenny Burrell; Al Collins; Ida Cox; Tiny Grimes; Earl Hines & Coleman Hawkins; Milt Jackson; Katy Bell Nubin; Sonny Rollins; Clark Terry / Coleman Hawkins; and the Various Artists section under Prestige and Verve.

Label & Catalog #		Title	Year	VG+	NM
Stinson SLP-22	(10")	**Originals With Hawkins**	1950	150.00	300.00
		(Stinson 22 features cover art by David Stone Martin.)			
Apollo LAP-101	(10")	**Coleman Hawkins All Stars**	1951	150.00	300.00
		(The All Stars were the first be-bop unit assembled for recording purposes and featured Dizzy Gillespie and Max Roach.)			
Advance LSP-9	(10")	**Coleman Hawkins Favorites**	1951	150.00	300.00
Commodore FL-20025	(10")	**King Of The Tenor Sax**	1952	150.00	300.00
Capitol H-327	(10")	**Classics In Jazz**	1952	100.00	200.00
Brunswick BL-58030	(10")	**Tenor Sax**	1953	100.00	200.00
Savoy MG-15039	(10")	**The Hawk Talks**	1954	100.00	200.00
Savoy MG-12013	(M)	**The Hawk Returns**	1955	40.00	100.00
EmArcy MG-26013	(10")	**The Bean**	1954	100.00	200.00
Concert Hall Jazz 1201	(M)	**Improvisations Unlimited**	1955	20.00	50.00
Jazztone J-1201	(M)	**Timeless Jazz**	1955	20.00	50.00
		(CHJ 1201 and Jazztone 1201 are the same album.)			
Urania UJLP-1201	(M)	**Accent On Tenor Sax**	1955	40.00	100.00
RCA Victor LJM-1017	(M)	**Hawk In Flight**	1955	30.00	75.00
RCA Victor LPM-1281	(M)	**Hawk In Hi Fi**	1956	30.00	75.00
		—RCA albums above have black labels with "Long Play" on the bottom.—			
Decca DL-8127	(M)	**The Hawk Talks**	1955	30.00	75.00
Vik LX-1059	(M)	**The Hawk In Paris**	1957	30.00	75.00
American Rec. Soc. G-316	(M)	**Coleman Hawkins And His Orchestra**	1956	16.00	40.00
Riverside RLP-12-117/8	(M)	**Coleman Hawkins—A Documentary** *(2 LPs)*	1956	50.00	125.00
Riverside RLP-12-233	(M)	**The Hawk Flies High**	1957	40.00	100.00
		—Riverside albums above have blue on white labels.—			
Riverside RLP-12-233	(M)	**The Hawk Flies High**	195?	16.00	40.00
		—Riverside albums above have blue mono or black stereo labels with a reel & mike logo on top.—			
Capitol T-819	(M)	**Gilded Hawk**	1957	30.00	75.00
		—Capitol albums above have turquoise labels.—			
Verve MGV-8261	(M)	**The Genius Of Coleman Hawkins**	1958	20.00	50.00
Verve MGVS-6033	(S)	**The Genius Of Coleman Hawkins**	1960	16.00	40.00
Verve MGV-8327	(M)	**Coleman Hawkins Encounters Ben Webster**	1959	20.00	50.00
Verve MGVS-6066	(S)	**Coleman Hawkins Encounters Ben Webster**	1959	16.00	40.00
Verve MGV-8346	(M)	**Coleman Hawkins And His Confreres With The Oscar Peterson Trio**	1959	20.00	50.00
Verve MGVS-6110	(S)	**Coleman Hawkins And His Confreres With The Oscar Peterson Trio**	1960	16.00	40.00
		—Verve albums above have black labels with "Verve Records, Inc." on the bottom.—			

Label & Catalog #		Title	Year	VG+	NM
Verve V-8261	(M)	**The Genius Of Coleman Hawkins**	1961	10.00	25.00
Verve V6-8261	(S)	**The Genius Of Coleman Hawkins**	1961	8.00	20.00
Verve V-8327	(M)	**Coleman Hawkins Encounters Ben Webster**	1961	10.00	25.00
Verve V6-8327	(S)	**Coleman Hawkins Encounters Ben Webster**	1961	8.00	20.00
Verve V-8346	(M)	**Coleman Hawkins And His Confreres With The Oscar Peterson Trio**	1961	10.00	25.00
Verve V6-8346	(S)	**Coleman Hawkins And His Confreres With The Oscar Peterson Trio**	1961	8.00	20.00
Verve V-8509	(M)	**Hawkins! Alive! At The Village Gate**	1963	12.00	30.00
Verve V6-8509	(S)	**Hawkins! Alive! At The Village Gate**	1963	10.00	25.00
Verve V-8568	(M)	**The Essential Coleman Hawkins**	1964	10.00	25.00
Verve V6-8568	(S)	**The Essential Coleman Hawkins**	1964	8.00	20.00
		—Verve albums above have black labels with "MGM Records" on the bottom.—			
World Wide MGS-20001	(S)	**Coleman Hawkins With The Basie Sax Section**	1958	20.00	50.00
Felsted FM-7005	(M)	**The High And The Mighty Hawk**	1958	30.00	75.00
Felsted FS-2005	(S)	**The High And The Mighty Hawk**	1958	24.00	60.00
Prestige PRLP-7149	(M)	**Soul**	1958	30.00	75.00
		(Prestige 7149 also features Kenny Burrell.)			
Prestige PRLP-7156	(M)	**Hawk Eyes**	1959	30.00	75.00
		—Prestige albums above have yellow mono or silver stereo labels with a Bergenfield, NJ address.—			
Crown CLP-5181	(M)	**Coleman Hawkins & His Orchestra**	1960	6.00	15.00
Crown CST-206	(E)	**Coleman Hawkins & His Orchestra**	1960	3.00	7.50
Crown CLP-5207	(M)	**The Hawk Swings**	1961	6.00	15.00
Crown CST-224	(E)	**The Hawk Swings**	1961	3.00	7.50
Swingville SVLP-2001	(M)	**Coleman Hawkins Plus The Red Garland Trio**	1960	20.00	50.00
Swingville SVLP-2005	(M)	**The Coleman Hawkins All Stars**	1960	20.00	50.00
Swingville SVLP-2016	(M)	**Night Hawk**	1961	20.00	50.00
		(Swingville 2016 also features Eddie Davis.)			
Swingville SVLP-2024	(M)	**Things Ain't What They Used To Be**	1961	20.00	50.00
Swingville SVST-2024	(S)	**Things Ain't What They Used To Be**	1961	16.00	40.00
Swingville SVLP-2025	(M)	**Years Ago**	1961	20.00	50.00
Swingville SVST-2025	(S)	**Years Ago**	1961	16.00	40.00
Swingville SVLP-2035	(M)	**Blues Groove**	1962	20.00	50.00
Swingville SVST-2035	(S)	**Blues Groove**	1962	16.00	40.00
		(Swingville 2035 is a reissue of Prestige 7138, Tiny Grimes' "Blues Groove.")			
Swingville SVLP-2038	(M)	**Soul**	1962	20.00	50.00
Swingville SVST-2038	(S)	**Soul**	1962	16.00	40.00
		(Swingville 2038 is a reissue of Prestige 7149.)			
Swingville SVLP-2039	(M)	**Hawk Eyes**	1962	20.00	50.00
Swingville SVST-2039	(S)	**Hawk Eyes**	1962	16.00	40.00
		(Swingville 2039 is a reissue of Prestige 7156.)			
		—Swingville mono albums above have purple mono or red stereo labels.—			
Swingville SVLP-2001	(M)	**Coleman Hawkins Plus The Red Garland Trio**	1965	10.00	25.00
Swingville SVLP-2005	(M)	**The Coleman Hawkins All Stars**	1965	10.00	25.00
Swingville SVLP-2016	(M)	**Night Hawk**	1965	10.00	25.00
Swingville SVLP-2024	(M)	**Things Ain't What They Used To Be**	1965	10.00	25.00
Swingville SVST-2024	(S)	**Things Ain't What They Used To Be**	1965	8.00	20.00
Swingville SVLP-2025	(M)	**Years Ago**	1965	10.00	25.00
Swingville SVST-2025	(S)	**Years Ago**	1965	8.00	20.00
Swingville SVLP-2035	(M)	**Blues Groove**	1965	10.00	25.00
Swingville SVST-2035	(S)	**Blues Groove**	1965	8.00	20.00
Swingville SVLP-2038	(M)	**Soul**	1965	10.00	25.00
Swingville SVST-2038	(S)	**Soul**	1965	8.00	20.00
Swingville SVLP-2039	(M)	**Hawk Eyes**	1965	10.00	25.00
Swingville SVST-2039	(S)	**Hawk Eyes**	1965	8.00	20.00
		—Swingville albums above have blue labels with a trident logo on the right side.—			
Moodsville MVLP-7	(M)	**At Ease With Coleman Hawkins**	1960	20.00	50.00
Moodsville MVLP-15	(M)	**The Hawk Relaxes**	1961	20.00	50.00
Moodsville MVLP-23	(M)	**Good Old Broadway**	1962	20.00	50.00
Moodsville MVST-23	(S)	**Good Old Broadway**	1962	16.00	40.00
Moodsville MVLP-25	(M)	**The Jazz Version Of No Strings**	1962	20.00	50.00
Moodsville MVST-25	(S)	**The Jazz Version Of No Strings**	1962	16.00	40.00
Moodsville MVLP-31	(M)	**Make Someone Happy**	1963	20.00	50.00
Moodsville MVST-31	(S)	**Make Someone Happy**	1963	16.00	40.00
		—Moodsville mono albums above have green labels with silver print.—			
Moodsville MVLP-7	(M)	**At Ease With Coleman Hawkins**	1965	10.00	25.00
Moodsville MVLP-15	(M)	**The Hawk Relaxes**	1965	10.00	25.00

Label & Catalog #		Title	Year	VG+	NM
Moodsville MVLP-23	(M)	**Good Old Broadway**	1965	10.00	25.00
Moodsville MVST-23	(S)	**Good Old Broadway**	1965	8.00	20.00
Moodsville MVLP-25	(M)	**The Jazz Version Of No Strings**	1965	10.00	25.00
Moodsville MVST-25	(S)	**The Jazz Version Of No Strings**	1965	8.00	20.00
Moodsville MVLP-31	(M)	**Make Someone Happy**	1965	10.00	25.00
Moodsville MVST-31	(S)	**Make Someone Happy**	1965	8.00	20.00
		—Moodsville albums above have blue labels with a trident logo on the right side.—			
Decca DL-4081	(M)	**The Hawk Blows At Midnight**	1961	16.00	40.00
Decca DL-74081	(S)	**The Hawk Blows At Midnight**	1961	12.00	30.00
Continental 16006	(M)	**On The Bean**	1962	12.00	30.00
Continental 16006	(S)	**On The Bean**	1962	10.00	25.00
Philips PHM-200-022	(M)	**Jazz At The Metropole**	1962	10.00	25.00
Philips PHS-600-022	(S)	**Jazz At The Metropole**	1962	8.00	20.00
Impulse A-26	(M)	**Duke Ellington Meets Coleman Hawkins**	1962	12.00	30.00
Impulse AS-26	(S)	**Duke Ellington Meets Coleman Hawkins**	1962	10.00	25.00
Impulse A-28	(M)	**Desafinado: Bossa Nova & Jazz Samba**	1963	12.00	30.00
Impulse AS-28	(S)	**Desafinado: Bossa Nova & Jazz Samba**	1963	10.00	25.00
Impulse A-34	(M)	**Today And Now**	1963	16.00	40.00
Impulse AS-34	(S)	**Today And Now**	1963	12.00	30.00
Impulse A-87	(M)	**Wrapped Tight**	1965	16.00	40.00
Impulse AS-87	(S)	**Wrapped Tight**	1965	12.00	30.00
		—Impulse albums above have orange & black labels.—			
Impulse AS-26	(S)	**Duke Ellington Meets Coleman Hawkins**	1968	4.00	10.00
Impulse AS-28	(S)	**Desafinado: Bossa Nova & Jazz Samba**	1968	4.00	10.00
Impulse AS-34	(S)	**Today And Now**	1968	4.00	10.00
Impulse AS-87	(S)	**Wrapped Tight**	1968	4.00	10.00
		—Impulse albums above have red & black labels with the "abc" logo on top.—			
RCA Victor LPV-501	(M)	**Body And Soul**	1965	8.00	20.00
Mainstream 56037	(M)	**Meditations**	1965	10.00	25.00
Mainstream S-6037	(E)	**Meditations**	1965	5.00	12.00
		(Mainstream 56037 is a reissue of Commodore 20025.)			
Prestige PRST-7671	(E)	**Night Hawk**	1969	6.00	15.00
		(Prestige 7671 is a reissue of Swingville 2016.)			
		—Prestige albums above have blue labels with a trident logo on top.—			

HAWKINS, COLEMAN / GEORGE AULD

Grand Award GA-33-316	(M)	**Jazz Concert**	1955	30.00	75.00
		(Grand Award 316 is a reissue of Apollo 101 and 102. This album was issued with a removable "second" cover of a David Stone Martin painting that could be peeled off and framed.)			
Grand Award GA-33-316	(M)	**Jazz Concert**	1955	16.00	40.00
		(Without the removable second cover.)			

HAWKINS, COLEMAN, & ROY ELDRIDGE

Verve MGV-8266	(M)	**At The Opera House**	1958	20.00	50.00
Verve MGVS-6028	(S)	**At The Opera House**	1960	16.00	40.00
		—Verve albums above have black labels with "Verve Records, Inc." on the bottom.—			
Verve V-8266	(M)	**At The Opera House**	1961	10.00	25.00
Verve V6-8266	(S)	**At The Opera House**	1961	8.00	20.00
		—Verve albums above have black labels with "MGM Records" on the bottom.—			

HAWKINS, COLEMAN, & ROY ELDRIDGE & PETE BROWN & JO JONES

Verve MGV-8240	(M)	**Coleman Hawkins-Roy Eldridge-Pete Brown-Jo Jones All Stars At Newport**	1958	20.00	50.00
		—Verve albums above have black labels with "Verve Records, Inc." on the bottom.—			
Verve V-8240	(M)	**Coleman Hawkins-Roy Eldridge-Pete Brown-Jo Jones All Stars At Newport**	1961	8.00	20.00
		—Verve albums above have black labels with "MGM Records" on the bottom.—			

HAWKINS, COLEMAN, & ROY ELDRIDGE & JOHNNY HODGES

Verve V-8504	(M)	**Alive At The Village Gate**	1963	12.00	30.00
Verve V6-8504	(S)	**Alive At The Village Gate**	1963	10.00	25.00
		—Verve albums above have black labels with "MGM Records" on the bottom.—			

HAWKINS, COLEMAN, & FRANK HUNTER

Mira M-3003	(M)	**The Hawk And The Hunter**	1965	10.00	25.00
Mira MS-3003	(S)	**The Hawk And The Hunter**	1965	8.00	20.00

Label & Catalog #		Title	Year	VG+	NM
HAWKINS, COLEMAN / HOWARD McGHEE / LESTER YOUNG					
Imperial LP-9188	(M)	**A Date With Greatness**	1962	20.00	50.00
Imperial LP-12188	(E)	**A Date With Greatness**	1962	10.00	25.00
HAWKINS, COLEMAN, & PEE WEE RUSSELL					
Candid CD-8020	(M)	**Jazz Reunion**	1960	20.00	50.00
Candid CS-9020	(S)	**Jazz Reunion**	1960	16.00	40.00
HAWKINS, COLEMAN, & CLARK TERRY					
Columbia CL-1991	(M)	**Back In Bean's Bag**	1963	8.00	20.00
Columbia CS-8791	(S)	**Back In Bean's Bag**	1963	6.00	15.00
—Columbia albums above have "Guaranteed High Fidelity" or "360 Sound Stereo" in black on the label.—					
HAWKINS, COLEMAN / BEN WEBSTER					
Brunswick BL-54016	(M)	**The Big Sounds Of Coleman Hawkins And Ben Webster** *(BL 54016 is a reissue of 58030 and 58031, Webster's "Tenor Sax.")*	1956	30.00	75.00
HAWKINS, ERSKINE					
Ersdkine Hawkins is a traditional jazz trumpet player and band leader.					
Coral CRL-56061	(10")	**After Hours**	1952	40.00	100.00
RCA Victor LPM-2227	(M)	**After Hours**	1966	8.00	20.00
RCA Victor LSP-2227	(S)	**After Hours**	1966	6.00	15.00
HAWKS, BILLY					
Prestige PRLP-7501	(M)	**New Genius Of The Blues**	1967	12.00	30.00
Prestige PRST-7501	(S)	**New Genius Of The Blues**	1967	4.00	20.00
—Prestige albums above have blue labels with a trident logo on the right side.—					
Prestige PRST-7556	(S)	**More Heavy Soul**	1968	6.00	15.00
—Prestige albums above have blue labels with a trident logo on top.—					
HAYES, CLANCY					
Clancy Hayes is a traditional jazz banjo player and vocalist. For additional listings refer to Bob Scobey.					
Down Home MGD-3	(M)	**Clancy Hayes Sings** *(Down Home 3 features cover art by David Stone Martin. Hayes is backed by Lu Watters.)*	1956	20.00	50.00
Verve MGV-1003	(M)	**Clancy Hayes Sings**	1956	16.00	40.00
—Verve albums above have "Verve Records, Inc." on the bottom of the label.—					
Good Time Jazz L-12050	(M)	**Swingin' Minstrel**	195?	12.00	30.00
Good Time Jazz S-10050	(S)	**Swingin' Minstrel**	195?	16.00	40.00
HAYES, LOUIS					
Louis Hayes is a modern jazz drummer. For additional listings refer to The Young Lions; and the Various Artists section under Bethlehem and Prestige.					
Vee Jay LP-3010	(M)	**Louis Hayes**	1960	16.00	40.00
Vee Jay LPS-3010	(S)	**Louis Hayes**	1960	16.00	40.00
HAYES, MARTHA					
Martha Hayes is a jazz-based vocalist.					
Jubilee JLP-1023	(M)	**A Hayes Named Martha**	1956	20.00	50.00
HAYES, TUBBY					
English born Edward "Tubby" Hayes is a modern jazz alto, tenor and baritone saxophone and flute player. For additional listings refer to The Jazz Couriers; Dizzy Reece & Tubby Hayes.					
Imperial LP-9046	(M)	**Little Giant Of Jazz**	1957	30.00	75.00
Epic LA-16019	(M)	**Introducing Tubbs**	1961	20.00	50.00
Epic BA-17019	(S)	**Introducing Tubbs**	1961	16.00	40.00
Epic LA-16023	(M)	**Tubby The Tenor**	1962	20.00	50.00
Epic BA-17023	(S)	**Tubby The Tenor**	1962	16.00	40.00
Smash MGS-27026	(M)	**Tubby's Back In Town**	1962	20.00	50.00
Smash SRS-67026	(S)	**Tubby's Back In Town**	1962	16.00	40.00
HAYNES, ROY					
Roy Haynes is a modern jazz drummer.					
EmArcy MG-26048	(10")	**Bushman's Holiday**	1954	60.00	150.00
New Jazz NJLP-8245	(M)	**Just Us**	1960	30.00	75.00
New Jazz NJLP-8286	(M)	**Cracklin'** *(New Jazz 8286 also features Booker Ervin.)*	1962	30.00	75.00

Label & Catalog #		Title	Year	VG+	NM
New Jazz NJLP-8287	(M)	**Cymbalism**	1962	30.00	75.00
		—New Jazz albums above have purple labels.—			
New Jazz NJLP-8245	(M)	**Just Us**	1965	12.00	30.00
New Jazz NJLP-8286	(M)	**Cracklin'**	1965	12.00	30.00
New Jazz NJLP-8287	(M)	**Cymbalism**	1965	12.00	30.00
		—New Jazz albums above have blue labels with a trident logo on the right side.—			
Impulse A-23	(M)	**Out Of The Afternoon**	1962	16.00	40.00
Impulse AS-23	(S)	**Out Of The Afternoon**	1962	12.00	30.00
		—Impulse albums above have orange & black labels.—			
Impulse AS-23	(S)	**Out Of The Afternoon**	1968	4.00	10.00
		—Impulse albums above have red & black labels with the "abc" logo on top.—			
Pacific Jazz PJ-82	(M)	**People**	1964	16.00	40.00
Pacific Jazz ST-82	(S)	**People**	1964	12.00	30.00

HAYNES, ROY / QUINCY JONES

EmArcy MG-36083	(M)	**Jazz Abroad**	1956	30.00	75.00
		—EmArcy albums above have blue labels with silver print.—			

HAYNES, ROY, & PHINEAS NEWBORN & PAUL CHAMBERS

New Jazz NJLP-8210	(M)	**We Three**	1958	40.00	100.00

HAZEL, MONK

Arthur "Monk" Hazel is a traditional jazz drummer, mellophone and cornet player.

Southland SLP-217	(M)	**Monk Hazel**	1956	16.00	40.00

HEALY, PAT

Pat Healy is a jazz vocalist.

World Pacific WPM-409	(M)	**Just Before Dawn**	1958	30.00	75.00

HEARD, J.C.

James Charles Heard is a traditional jazz drummer and vocalist. For additional listings refer to the Various Artists section under Verve.

Argo LP-633	(M)	**This Is Me, J.C.**	1958	16.00	40.00
Argo LPS-633	(S)	**This Is Me, J.C.**	1958	12.00	30.00

HEATH, JIMMY

James "Little Bird" Heath is a modern jazz alto and tenor saxophone player and composer. For additional listings refer to The Riverside Jazz Stars.

Riverside RLP-12-314	(M)	**The Thumper**	1960	20.00	50.00
Riverside RLP-1160	(S)	**The Thumper**	1960	16.00	40.00
Riverside RLP-12-333	(M)	**Really Big**	1960	16.00	40.00
Riverside RLP-1188	(S)	**Really Big**	1960	12.00	30.00
Riverside RLP-372	(M)	**The Quota**	1961	16.00	40.00
Riverside RS-9372	(S)	**The Quota**	1961	12.00	30.00
Riverside RLP-400	(M)	**Triple Threat**	1962	16.00	40.00
Riverside RS-9400	(S)	**Triple Threat**	1962	12.00	30.00
Riverside RLP-465	(M)	**Swamp Seed**	1963	16.00	40.00
Riverside RS-9465	(S)	**Swamp Seed**	1963	12.00	30.00
		—Riverside albums above have blue mono or black stereo labels with a reel & mike logo on top.—			
Riverside RLP-486	(M)	**On The Trail**	1966	10.00	25.00
Riverside RS-9486	(S)	**On The Trail**	1965	8.00	20.00
		—Riverside albums above blue labels with "Orpheum Productions" on the bottom.—			

HEATH, TED

English born Edward "Ted" Heath is a traditional jazz trombone player, composer and band leader. For additional listings refer to Winifred Atwell.

London LPB-340	(10")	**Tempo For Dancing**	195?	16.00	40.00
London LPB-374	(10")	**Ted Heat And His Orchestra**	195?	16.00	40.00
London LB-511	(10")	**Listen To My Music**	195?	16.00	40.00
London LB-732	(10")	**Black And White Magic**	195?	16.00	40.00
		(London 732 also features Winifred Atwell.)			
London LL-750	(M)	**Ted Heath Strikes Up The Band**	1953	10.00	25.00
London LL-802	(M)	**Jazz Concert At The London Palladium**	1953	10.00	25.00
London LL-978	(M)	**Ted Heath Plays The Music Of Fats Waller**	1954	10.00	25.00
London LL-1000	(M)	**100th London Palladium Concert**	1955	10.00	25.00
London LL-1211	(M)	**Jazz Concert At The London Palladium, Vol. 3**	1955	10.00	25.00
London LL-1217	(M)	**Gershwin For Moderns**	1956	10.00	25.00
London LL-1279	(M)	**Kern For Moderns**	1956	10.00	25.00

Label & Catalog #		Title	Year	VG+	NM
London LL-1379	(M)	**Jazz Concert At The London Palladium, Vol. 4**	1956	10.00	25.00
London LL-1475	(M)	**Heath Swings In H-Fi**	1956	10.00	25.00
London LL-1500	(M)	**Rodgers For Moderns**	1956	10.00	25.00
London LL-1564	(M)	**Ted Heath At Carnegie Hall**	1956	10.00	25.00
London LL-1676	(M)	**A Yank In Europe**	1956	10.00	25.00
London LL-1716	(M)	**All Time Top Twelve**	1957	10.00	25.00
London PS-117	(S)	**All Time Top Twelve**	1961	6.00	15.00
London LL-1721	(M)	**Spotlight On Sidemen**	1957	10.00	25.00
London LL-1737	(M)	**Showcase**	1957	10.00	25.00
London LL-1743	(M)	**Tribute To The Fabulous Dorseys**	1957	10.00	25.00
London LL-1749	(M)	**Rhapsody In Blue**	1957	10.00	25.00
		(London 1749 also features Winifred Atwell.)			
London LL-3047	(M)	**Things To Come**	1958	10.00	25.00
London LL-3057	(M)	**Hits I Missed**	1958	10.00	25.00
London PS-116	(S)	**Hits I Missed**	1961	6.00	15.00
London LL-3058	(M)	**Old English**	1958	10.00	25.00
London PS-138	(S)	**Swing Session**	1961	6.00	15.00
London PS-140	(S)	**Ted Heath Swings In High Stereo**	1961	6.00	15.00
London LL-3062	(M)	**Shall We Dance?**	1959	10.00	25.00
London PS-148	(S)	**Shall We Dance?**	1961	6.00	15.00
London LL-3106	(M)	**The Great Film Hits**	1959	10.00	25.00
London PS-159	(S)	**The Great Film Hits**	1961	6.00	15.00
London LL-3124	(M)	**Pop Hits From The Classics**	1959	10.00	25.00
London PS-171	(S)	**Pop Hits From The Classics**	1961	6.00	15.00
London LL-3125	(M)	**Big Band Blues**	1959	10.00	25.00
London PS-172	(S)	**Big Band Blues**	1961	6.00	15.00
London LL-3127	(M)	**My Very Good Friends, The Band Leaders**	1959	10.00	25.00
London PS-174	(S)	**My Very Good Friends, The Band Leaders**	1961	6.00	15.00
London LL-3128	(M)	**The Hits Of The Twenties**	1960	10.00	25.00
London PS-175	(S)	**The Hits Of The Twenties**	1961	6.00	15.00
London LL-3138	(M)	**The Big Band Dixie Sound**	1960	10.00	25.00
London PS-184	(S)	**The Big Band Dixie Sound**	1961	6.00	15.00
London LL-3143	(M)	**Ted Heath In Concert**	1960	10.00	25.00
London PS-187	(S)	**Ted Heath In Concert**	1961	6.00	15.00
London LL-3146	(M)	**Songs For The Young At Heart**	1960	10.00	25.00
London PS-190	(S)	**Songs For The Young At Heart**	1961	6.00	15.00
London LL-3192	(M)	**The Hits Of The '30s**	1960	8.00	20.00
London PS-216	(S)	**The Hits Of The '30s**	1961	6.00	15.00
London LL-3195	(M)	**Latin Swingers**	1961	8.00	20.00
London PS-219	(S)	**Latin Swingers**	1961	6.00	15.00
Richmond B-20034	(M)	**Big Band Beat**	196?	4.00	10.00
Richmond B-20037	(M)	**Ted Heath Plays Gershwin**	196?	4.00	10.00
		(Richmond 20037 also features Winifred Atwell.)			
Richmond B-20082	(M)	**Ted Heath Plays The Music Of Fats Waller**	196?	4.00	10.00
Richmond B-20096	(M)	**Big Band Gershwin**	196?	4.00	10.00
Richmond B-20097	(M)	**Big Band Kern**	196?	4.00	10.00
Richmond B-20098	(M)	**Big Band Rogers**	196?	4.00	10.00

HECKMAN, DON

Ictus 101	(S)	**Summerlin Improvisational Jazz Workshop**	1967	20.00	50.00

HEFTI, NEAL

Neal Hefti is a West Coast piano and trumpet player, arranger and composer primarily associated with television and movie scores. For additional listings refer to Frances Wayne.

Coral CRL-56083	(10")	**Swingin' On A Coral Reef**	1953	20.00	50.00
"X" LXA-3021	(10")	**Music Of Rudolf Frimi**	1954	20.00	50.00
Columbia CL-1516	(M)	**Light And Right!!**	1960	12.00	30.00
Columbia CS-8316	(S)	**Light And Right!!**	1960	10.00	25.00

— Columbia albums above have six white on black "eye" logos on each label.—

HELM, BOB

Robert Helm is a traditional jazz clarinet player.

Riverside RLP-2510	(10")	**Bob Helm**	1954	30.00	75.00

HELM, BOB / LU WATTERS

Riverside RLP-12-213	(M)	**San Francisco Style**	1956	24.00	60.00

— Riverside albums above have blue on white labels.—

Label & Catalog #		Title	Year	VG+	NM

HENDERSON, BILL

William Henderson is a modern jazz vocalist.

Vee Jay LP-1015	(M)	**Bill Henderson**	1960	10.00	25.00
Vee Jay LP-1031	(M)	**Bill Henderson**	1960	14.00	35.00
MGM E-4128	(M)	**Bill Henderson With The Oscar Peterson Trio**	1963	10.00	25.00
MGM SE-4128	(S)	**Bill Henderson With The Oscar Peterson Trio**	1963	12.00	30.00
Verve V-8619	(M)	**When My Dreamboat Comes Home**	1965	8.00	20.00
Verve V6-8619	(S)	**When My Dreamboat Comes Home**	1965	12.00	25.00

—Verve albums above have black labels with "MGM Records" on the bottom.—

HENDERSON, BOBBY

Robert Henderson is a traditional jazz pianist, trumpet player and vocalist. For additional listings refer to Ruby Braff & Pee Wee Russell / Bobby Henderson.

Vanguard VRS-8511	(M)	**Handful Of Keys**	1955	16.00	40.00

HENDERSON, FLETCHER

James Fletcher "Smack" Henderson is a traditional big band leader and arranger known for his work with Benny Goodman's Orchestra. For additional listings refer to Rex Stewart.

Decca DL-6025	(10")	**Fletcher Henderson Memorial Album**	1952	50.00	125.00
Decca DL-9228	(M)	**Fletcher Henderson Memorial Album, Vol. 2**	1958	20.00	50.00
"X" LVA-3013	(10")	**Fletcher Henderson And His Connie's Inn Orchestra**	1954	50.00	125.00
Riverside RLP-1055	(10")	**Fletcher Henderson**	1954	50.00	125.00
Columbia C4L-19	(M)	**The Fletcher Henderson Story** *(4 LP box with booklet)*	196?	30.00	75.00

—Columbia albums above have six white on black "eye" logos on each label.—

HENDERSON, JOE

Joseph Henderson is a modern jazz tenor and soprano saxophone and flute player and composer.

Blue Note BLP-4140	(M)	**Page One**	1963	12.00	30.00
Blue Note BST-84140	(S)	**Page One**	1963	10.00	25.00
Blue Note BLP-4152	(M)	**Our Thing**	1963	12.00	30.00
Blue Note BST-84152	(S)	**Our Thing**	1963	10.00	25.00
Blue Note BLP-4166	(M)	**In 'N Out**	1964	12.00	30.00
Blue Note BST-84166	(S)	**In 'N Out**	1964	10.00	25.00
Blue Note BLP-4189	(M)	**Inner Urge**	1965	12.00	30.00
Blue Note BST-84189	(S)	**Inner Urge**	1965	10.00	25.00
Blue Note BLP-4227	(M)	**Mode For Joe**	1966	12.00	30.00
Blue Note BST-84227	(S)	**Mode For Joe**	1966	10.00	25.00

—Blue Note albums above have blue on white labels with a New York, NY address.—

Blue Note BST-84140	(S)	**Page One**	196?	5.00	12.00
Blue Note BST-84152	(S)	**Our Thing**	196?	5.00	12.00
Blue Note BST-84166	(S)	**In 'N Out**	196?	5.00	12.00
Blue Note BST-84189	(S)	**Inner Urge**	196?	5.00	12.00
Blue Note BST-84227	(S)	**Mode For Joe**	196?	5.00	12.00

—Blue Note albums above have blue on white labels with "A Division of Liberty Records."—

Milestone MSP-9017	(S)	**Tetragon**	1969	8.00	20.00

HENDRICKS, JON

John "Jon" Hendricks is a modern jazz vocalist and lyricist. For additional listings refer to Lambert, Hendricks & Ross; Lambert, Hendricks & Bavan.

World Pacific WP-1283	(M)	**A Good Git-Together**	1959	30.00	75.00
Columbia CL-1583	(M)	**Evolution Of The Blues**	1961	12.00	30.00
Columbia CS-8383	(S)	**Evolution Of The Blues**	1961	14.00	35.00
Columbia CL-1805	(M)	**Fast Livin' Blues**	1962	12.00	30.00
Columbia CS-8605	(S)	**Fast Livin' Blues**	1962	14.00	35.00

—Columbia albums above have six white on black "eye" logos on each label.—

Smash MGS-27069	(M)	**Recorded In Person At The Trident**	1963	10.00	25.00
Smash SRS-67069	(S)	**Recorded In Person At The Trident**	1963	12.00	30.00
Reprise R-6089	(M)	**Salud!**	1964	10.00	25.00
Reprise RS-6089	(S)	**Salud!**	1964	12.00	30.00

HENKE, MEL

Melvin Henke is a traditional jazz pianist.

Contemporary C-5001	(M)	**Dig Mel Henke**	1955	20.00	50.00
Contemporary C-5003	(M)	**Now Spin This**	1956	20.00	50.00

Label & Catalog #		Title	Year	VG+	NM

HENRY, ERNIE

Ernest Henry is a modern jazz alto saxophone player. For additional listings refer to Kenny Dorham.

Riverside RLP-12-222	(M)	**Presenting Ernie Henry**	1956	60.00	150.00
—Riverside albums above have blue on white labels.—					
Riverside RLP-12-248	(M)	**Seven Standards And A Blues**	1957	40.00	100.00
Riverside RLP-12-266	(M)	**Last Chorus**	1958	30.00	75.00
—Riverside albums above have blue mono or black stereo labels with a reel & mike logo on top.—					

HERBERT, MORT

Morton Herbert Pelovitz is a modern jazz bass player and composer.

Savoy MG-12073	(M)	**Night People**	1956	16.00	40.00

HERDSMEN, THE

The Herdsmen are Ralph Burns, Jerry Coker, Dick Collins, Chuck Flores, Dick Hafner, Red Kelly, Bill Perkins and Cy Touff— all members of Woody Herman's Herd. For additional listings refer to Nat Pierce.

Fantasy 3201	(M)	**The Herdsmen Play Paris** *(Green vinyl)*	1955	30.00	75.00
—Fantasy albums above have red labels on dark red, non-flexible vinyl.—					
Fantasy 3201	(M)	**The Herdsmen Play Paris**	195?	16.00	40.00
—Fantasy albums above have red labels on non-flexible vinyl.—					

HERMAN, WOODY

Woodrow Herman is a traditional jazz clarinet and alto saxophone player, vocalist and big band leader. For additional listings refer to The Ex-Hermanites; The Four Brothers; The Herdsmen; The Small Herd.

Columbia CL-6026	(10")	**Sequence In Jazz**	1949	30.00	75.00
Columbia CL-6049	(10")	**Dance Parade**	1949	30.00	75.00
Columbia CL-6092	(10")	**Woody Herman And His Woodchoppers**	1950	30.00	75.00
Columbia CL-592	(M)	**The Three Herds**	1954	20.00	50.00
—Columbia albums above have "Long Playing" on the bottom of the label.—					
Columbia CL-592	(M)	**The Three Herds**	195?	16.00	40.00
Columbia CL-651	(M)	**Music For Tired Lovers**	1955	16.00	40.00
		(Columbia 651 also features Erroll Garner.)			
Columbia CL-683	(M)	**Twelve Shades Of Blue**	1955	16.00	40.00
Columbia CL-2509	(10")	**Ridin' Herd**	1955	20.00	50.00
Columbia CL-2563	(10")	**Woody!**	1956	20.00	50.00
—Columbia albums above have six white on black "eye" logos on each label.—					
Columbia C3L-25	(M)	**The Thundering Herds** *(3 LP box)*	1963	20.00	50.00
Columbia C3S-825	(S)	**The Thundering Herds** *(3 LP box)*	1963	16.00	40.00
Columbia CL-2357	(M)	**My Kind Of Broadway**	1965	6.00	15.00
Columbia CS-9157	(S)	**My Kind Of Broadway**	1965	5.00	12.00
—Columbia albums above have "Guaranteed High Fidelity" or "360 Sound Stereo" in black on the label.—					
Columbia CL-2436	(M)	**Woody's Winners**	1966	6.00	15.00
Columbia CS-9236	(S)	**Woody's Winners**	1966	5.00	12.00
Columbia CL-2491	(M)	**Woody Herman's Greatest Hits**	1966	6.00	15.00
Columbia CS-9291	(S)	**Woody Herman's Greatest Hits**	1966	5.00	12.00
Columbia CL-2552	(M)	**The Jazz Swinger**	1966	6.00	15.00
Columbia CS-9352	(S)	**The Jazz Swinger**	1966	5.00	12.00
Columbia CL-2693	(M)	**Woody Live-East & West**	1967	6.00	15.00
Columbia CS-9493	(S)	**Woody Live-East & West**	1967	5.00	12.00
—Columbia albums above have "360 Sound" in white on the bottom of the label.—					
Harmony HL-7013	(M)	**Bijou**	1957	8.00	20.00
Harmony HL-7093	(M)	**Summer Sequence**	1958	8.00	20.00
Dial LP-210	(10")	**Swinging With The Woodchoppers**	1950	60.00	150.00
Coral CRL-56005	(10")	**Blue Prelude**	1950	30.00	75.00
Coral CRL-56010	(10")	**Woody Herman Souvenirs**	1950	30.00	75.00
Coral CRL-56090	(10")	**Woody's Best**	1953	30.00	75.00
Capitol H-324	(10")	**Classics In Jazz**	1952	30.00	75.00
Capitol T-324	(M)	**Classics In Jazz**	1955	16.00	40.00
Capitol T-560	(M)	**The Woody Herman Band**	1955	16.00	40.00
Capitol T-658	(M)	**Road Band**	1955	16.00	40.00
Capitol T-748	(M)	**Jackpot!**	1956	16.00	40.00
Capitol T-784	(M)	**Blues Groove**	1956	16.00	40.00
—Capitol albums above have turquoise labels.—					
Capitol T-1554	(M)	**The Hits Of Woody Herman**	1961	6.00	15.00
Capitol ST-1554	(S)	**The Hits Of Woody Herman**	1961	5.00	12.00
Mars MRX-1	(10")	**Dance Date On Mars**	1952	60.00	150.00
Mars MRX-2	(10")	**Woody Herman Goes Native**	1953	60.00	150.00
MGM E-158	(10")	**Woody Herman At Carnegie Hall, 1946, Vol. 1**	1952	30.00	75.00
MGM E-159	(10")	**Woody Herman At Carnegie Hall, 1946, Vol. 2**	1952	30.00	75.00

Woody Herman began his career with such Dixieland bands as Harry Sosnick, Gus Arnheim, and Isham Jones before forming his own in 1936 out of the remains of Jones'. By the '40s Herman's band had switched to modern swing arrangements. The 1947-49 version of the band, known as The Herd, featured the famous "Four Bothers" sax section of Serge Chaloff, Stan Getz, Zoot Sims and Herb Steward. His various groups, large and small, have featured many name players, some of whom have recorded as The Herdsmen and The Small Herd. His ten year stay with Verve records allowed him to blow *and* sing! As a sideman he has appeared on albums by Erroll Garner and Buck Clayton, both on Columbia, and backing Jimmy Witherspoon on Hifijazz.

Label & Catalog #		Title	Year	VG+	NM
MGM E-192	(10")	**The Third Herd**	1953	30.00	75.00
MGM E-284	(10")	**Blue Flame**	1955	30.00	75.00
MGM E-3043	(M)	**Carnegie Hall 1946**	1953	20.00	50.00
		(MGM 3043 is a reissue of 158 and 159.)			
MGM E-3385	(M)	**Hi-Fi-ing Herd**	1956	16.00	40.00
Lion L-70059	(M)	**The Herman Herd At Carnegie Hall**	1958	10.00	25.00
		(Lion 70059 is a reissue of MGM 3043.)			
Metro M-514	(M)	**Woody Herman**	1965	6.00	15.00
Metro MS-514	(E)	**Woody Herman**	1965	3.00	7.50
Decca DL-8133	(M)	**Woodchopper's Ball**	1955	16.00	40.00
Decca DL-4484	(M)	**Woody Herman's Golden Hits**	1964	6.00	15.00
Decca DL-74484	(E)	**Woody Herman's Golden Hits**	1964	4.00	10.00
		(Decca 4484 is a reissue of 8133.)			
Decca DL-9229	(M)	**The Turning Point—1943-44**	1967	5.00	12.00
Decca DL-79229	(E)	**The Turning Point—1943-44**	1967	4.00	10.00
American Rec. Soc. G-410	(M)	**The Progressive Big Band Sound**	1956	16.00	40.00
Clef MGC-745	(M)	**Jazz, The Utmost!**	1956	30.00	75.00
Verve MGV-2030	(M)	**Early Autumn**	1957	16.00	40.00
Verve MGV-2069	(M)	**Songs For Hip Lovers**	1957	16.00	40.00
Verve MGV-2096	(M)	**Love Is The Sweetest Thing—Sometimes**	1958	16.00	40.00
		—Verve albums above have "Verve Records, Inc." on the bottom of the label.—			
Verve MGV-8014	(M)	**Jazz, The Utmost!**	1957	16.00	40.00
		(Verve 8014 is a reissue of Clef 745.)			
Verve MGV-8216	(M)	**Men From Mars**	1958	16.00	40.00
Verve MGV-8255	(M)	**Woody Herman '58**	1958	16.00	40.00
		—Verve albums above have black labels with "Verve Records, Inc." on the bottom.—			
Verve V-2030	(M)	**Early Autumn**	196?	6.00	15.00
Verve V-2069	(M)	**Songs For Hip Lovers**	196?	6.00	15.00
Verve V-2096	(M)	**Love Is The Sweetest Thing—Sometimes**	196?	6.00	15.00
Verve V-8014	(M)	**Jazz, The Utmost!**	196?	6.00	15.00
Verve V-8255	(M)	**Woody Herman '58**	196?	6.00	15.00
Verve V-8558	(M)	**Hey! Heard The Herd?**	1963	8.00	20.00
Verve V6-8558	(S)	**Hey! Heard The Herd?**	1963	6.00	15.00
		(Verve 8558 is a reissue of 8216.)			
		—Verve albums above have silver on black labels.—			
Verve VSP-1	(M)	**The First Herd At Carnegie Hall**	1966	6.00	15.00
Verve VSPS-1	(E)	**The First Herd At Carnegie Hall**	1966	3.00	7.50
Verve VSP-26	(M)	**Woody Herman's Woodchoppers & The First Herd Live At Carnegie Hall**	1966	6.00	15.00
Verve VSPS-26	(E)	**Woody Herman's Woodchoppers & The First Herd Live At Carnegie Hall**	1966	3.00	7.50
Verve V6-8764	(S)	**Concerto For Herd**	1968	4.00	20.00
		—Verve albums above have black labels with "MGM Records" on the bottom.—			
Brunswick BL-54024	(M)	**The Swinging Herman Herd**	1957	16.00	40.00
Everest SDBR-1003	(S)	**The Herd Rides Again... In Stereo**	1958	16.00	40.00
Everest LPBR-5032	(M)	**Moody Woody**	1958	12.00	30.00
Everest SDBR-1032	(E)	**Moody Woody**	1958	8.00	20.00
Everest EV-5222	(M)	**The Best Of Woody Herman**	1963	8.00	20.00
Everest EV-1222	(E)	**The Best Of Woody Herman**	1963	6.00	15.00
Roulette R-25067	(M)	**Woody Herman Sextet At The Round Table**	1959	16.00	40.00
Roulette SR-25067	(S)	**Woody Herman Sextet At The Round Table**	1959	12.00	30.00
Forum F-9016	(M)	**Woody Herman Sextet At The Round Table**	196?	10.00	25.00
Forum FS-9016	(S)	**Woody Herman Sextet At The Round Table**	196?	8.00	20.00
		(Forum 9016 is a reissue of Roulette 25067.)			
Crown CLP-5180	(M)	**The New Swingin' Herman Herd**	1960	8.00	20.00
Atlantic 1328	(M)	**Woody Herman At The Monterey Jazz Festival**	1960	16.00	40.00
Atlantic SD-1328	(S)	**Woody Herman At The Monterey Jazz Festival**	1960	12.00	30.00
		—Atlantic albums above have black mono or green stereo labels.—			
Jazzland JLP-17	(M)	**The Fourth Herd**	1960	12.00	30.00
Jazzland JLP-917	(S)	**The Fourth Herd**	1960	10.00	25.00
Philips PHM-200-004	(M)	**Swing Low, Sweet Chariot**	1962	8.00	20.00
Philips PHS-600-004	(S)	**Swing Low, Sweet Chariot**	1962	6.00	15.00
Philips PHM-200-065	(M)	**Woody Herman 1963**	1963	8.00	20.00
Philips PHS-600-065	(S)	**Woody Herman 1963**	1963	6.00	15.00
Philips PHM-200-092	(M)	**Encore: Woody Herman 1963**	1963	8.00	20.00
Philips PHS-600-092	(S)	**Encore: Woody Herman 1963**	1963	6.00	15.00
Philips PHM-200-118	(M)	**Woody Herman 1964**	1964	8.00	20.00
Philips PHS-600-118	(S)	**Woody Herman 1964**	1964	6.00	15.00

Label & Catalog #		Title	Year	VG+	NM
Philips PHM-200-131	(M)	**The Swinging Herman Herd Recorded Live**	1964	8.00	20.00
Philips PHS-600-131	(S)	**The Swinging Herman Herd Recorded Live**	1964	6.00	15.00
Philips PHM-200-171	(M)	**Woody's Big Band Goodies**	1965	8.00	20.00
Philips PHS-600-171	(S)	**Woody's Big Band Goodies**	1965	6.00	15.00
Wing MGW-12329	(M)	**Woody's Big Band Goodies**	1966	5.00	12.00
Wing SRW-16329	(S)	**Woody's Big Band Goodies**	1966	4.00	10.00
		(Wing 12329 is a reissue of Philips 171.)			
Sunset SUM-1139	(M)	**Blowin' Up A Storm**	1966	5.00	12.00
Sunset SUS-5139	(S)	**Blowin' Up A Storm**	1966	4.00	10.00
Cadet LPS-819	(S)	**Light My Fire**	1969	4.00	10.00
Cadet LPS-845	(S)	**Woody**	1969	4.00	10.00

HERMAN, WOODY / TITO PUENTE

Everest LPBR-5010	(M)	**Herman's Beat And Puente's Beat**	1958	16.00	40.00
Everest SDBR-1010	(S)	**Herman's Beat And Puente's Beat**	1958	12.00	30.00

HEYWOOD, EDDIE

Edward Heywood Jr. is a traditional jazz pianist, arranger and composer.

Commodore FL-20007	(10")	**Eight Selections**	1950	30.00	75.00
Columbia CL-6157	(10")	**Piano Moods**	1951	20.00	50.00
MGM E-135	(10")	**It's Easy To Remember**	1952	20.00	50.00
MGM E-3093	(M)	**Pianorama**	1955	16.00	40.00
MGM E-3260	(M)	**Eddie Heywood**	1955	16.00	40.00
Brunswick BL-58036	(10")	**Eddie Heywood '45**	1953	20.00	50.00
EmArcy MG-36042	(M)	**Eddie Heywood**	1955	16.00	40.00
		—EmArcy albums above have blue labels with silver print.—			
Epic LN-3327	(M)	**Eddie Heywood At Twilight**	1956	16.00	40.00
Decca DL-8202	(M)	**Lightly And Politely**	1956	16.00	40.00
Decca DL-8270	(M)	**Swing Low Sweet Heywood**	1956	16.00	40.00
Coral CRL-57095	(M)	**Featuring Eddie Heywood**	1957	20.00	50.00
RCA Victor LPM-1466	(M)	**The Touch Of Eddie Heywood**	1957	16.00	40.00
RCA Victor LPM-1529	(M)	**Canadian Sunset**	1957	16.00	40.00
RCA Victor LPM-1900	(M)	**The Keys And I**	1958	16.00	40.00
		—RCA albums above have black labels with "Long Play" on the bottom.—			
Mercury MG-20445	(M)	**Breezin' Along With The Breeze**	1959	12.00	30.00
Mercury SR-60115	(S)	**Breezin' Along With The Breeze**	1959	10.00	25.00
Mercury MG-20590	(M)	**Eddie Heywood At The Piano**	1960	12.00	30.00
Mercury SR-60248	(S)	**Eddie Heywood At The Piano**	1960	10.00	25.00
Mercury MG-20632	(M)	**One For My Baby**	1960	10.00	25.00
Mercury SR-60632	(S)	**One For My Baby**	1960	8.00	20.00
Wing MGW-12137	(M)	**Eddie Heywood**	1963	6.00	15.00
Wing SRW-16137	(E)	**Eddie Heywood**	1963	5.00	12.00
Liberty LRP-3313	(M)	**Canadian Sunset Bossa Nova**	1963	6.00	15.00
Liberty LST-7313	(S)	**Canadian Sunset Bossa Nova**	1963	5.00	12.00
Vocalion VL-3748	(M)	**The Piano Stylings Of Eddie Heywood**	196?	6.00	15.00
Vocalion VL-73748	(E)	**The Piano Stylings Of Eddie Heywood**	196?	5.00	12.00
Capitol T-2833	(M)	**With Love And Strings**	1967	6.00	15.00
Capitol ST-2833	(S)	**With Love And Strings**	1967	4.00	10.00

HI-LO'S, THE

The Hi-Lo's are a jazz-oriented vocal quartet consisting of Clark Burroughs, Bob Morse, Gene Puerling and Don Shelton. For additional listings refer to Rosemary Clooney & The Hi-Lo's.

Starlite 6004	(10")	**Listen!**	1955	30.00	75.00
Starlite 6005	(10")	**The Hi-Lo's, I Presume**	1955	30.00	75.00
Starlite 7005	(M)	**Under Glass**	1956	20.00	50.00
Starlite 7006	(M)	**Listen!**	1956	20.00	50.00
Starlite 7007	(M)	**The Hi-Lo's, I Presume**	1956	20.00	50.00
Starlite 7008	(M)	**On Hand**	1956	20.00	50.00
Kapp KL-1027	(M)	**The Hi-Lo's And The Jerry Fielding Band**	1956	16.00	40.00
Kapp KL-1184	(M)	**Under Glass**	1959	12.00	30.00
Kapp KL-1194	(M)	**On Hand**	1960	12.00	30.00
Omega OSL-11	(S)	**The Hi-Lo's In Stereo**	195?	12.00	30.00
Columbia CL-952	(M)	**Suddenly It's The Hi-Lo's**	1957	16.00	40.00
Columbia CL-1023	(M)	**Now Hear This**	1957	16.00	40.00
Columbia CL-1259	(M)	**The Hi-Lo's And All That Jazz**	1959	12.00	30.00
Columbia CS-8077	(S)	**The Hi-Lo's And All That Jazz**	1959	16.00	40.00
		(Columbia 1259 also features Marty Paich.)			

Label & Catalog #		Title	Year	VG+	NM
Columbia CL-1416	(M)	**Broadway Playbill**	1959	12.00	30.00
Columbia CS-8213	(S)	**Broadway Playbill**	1959	16.00	40.00
Columbia CL-1509	(M)	**All Over The Place**	1960	10.00	25.00
Columbia CS-8300	(S)	**All Over The Place**	1960	12.00	30.00
Columbia CL-1723	(M)	**This Time It's Love**	1962	10.00	25.00
Columbia CS-8523	(S)	**This Time It's Love**	1962	12.00	30.00
— Columbia albums above have six white on black "eye" logos on each label.—					
Reprise R-6066	(M)	**The Hi-Lo's Happen To Bossa Nova**	1963	8.00	20.00
Reprise RS-6066	(S)	**The Hi-Lo's Happen To Bossa Nova**	1963	8.00	20.00

HIBBLER, AL

Albert Hibbler is a jazz/big band-based vocalist. For additional listings refer to Duke Ellington; The Ellingtonians; Billie Holiday / Al Hibbler.

Label & Catalog #		Title	Year	VG+	NM
Norgran MGN-4	(10")	**Al Hibbler Favorites**	1954	60.00	150.00
Norgran MGN-15	(10")	**Al Hibbler Sings Duke Ellington**	1954	60.00	150.00
Verve MGV-4000	(M)	**Al Hibbler Sings Love Songs**	1956	24.00	60.00
— Verve albums above have "Verve Records, Inc." on the bottom of the label.—					
Verve V-4000	(M)	**Al Hibbler Sings Love Songs**	1961	10.00	25.00
— Verve albums above have black labels with "MGM Records" on the bottom.—					
Marterry LP-601	(M)	**Melodies By Al Hibbler**	1956	30.00	75.00
Argo LP-601	(M)	**Melodies By Al Hibbler**	1956	20.00	50.00
		(Argo 601 is a reissue of Marterry 601.)			
Decca DL-8328	(M)	**Starring Al Hibbler**	1956	20.00	50.00
Decca DL-8420	(M)	**Here's Hibbler**	1957	20.00	50.00
Decca DL-8697	(M)	**Torchy And Blue**	1958	20.00	50.00
Decca DL-8757	(M)	**Hits By Hibbler**	1958	20.00	50.00
Decca DL-8862	(M)	**Al Hibbler Remembers The Big Songs Of The Big Bands**	1958	16.00	40.00
Decca DL-78862	(S)	**Al Hibbler Remembers The Big Songs Of The Big Bands**	1958	20.00	50.00
— Decca albums above have black labels with silver print.—					
Score SLP-4013	(M)	**I Surrender, Dear**	1957	40.00	100.00
Brunswick BL-54036	(M)	**Al Hibbler With The Ellingtonians**	1957	24.00	60.00
Atlantic 1251	(M)	**After The Lights Go Down Low**	1957	24.00	60.00
— Atlantic albums above have black mono or green stereo labels.—					
Atlantic 1251	(M)	**After The Lights Go Down Low**	1961	10.00	25.00
— Atlantic albums above have multi-color labels with a white fan logo.—					
Atlantic 1251	(M)	**After The Lights Go Down Low**	196?	6.00	15.00
— Atlantic albums above have multi-color labels with a black fan logo.—					
Reprise R-2005	(M)	**Monday Every Day**	1961	12.00	30.00
Reprise R9-2005	(S)	**Monday Every Day**	1961	16.00	40.00
LMI 10001	(M)	**Early One Morning**	1964	12.00	30.00

HIGGINS, EDDIE

Haydn "Ed" Higgins is a modern jazz piano, clarinet and bass player.

Label & Catalog #		Title	Year	VG+	NM
Vee Jay LP-3017	(M)	**Eddie Higgins**	1961	16.00	40.00
Vee Jay LPS-3017	(S)	**Eddie Higgins**	1961	12.00	30.00
Atlantic 1446	(M)	**Soulero**	1966	8.00	20.00
Atlantic SD-1446	(S)	**Soulero**	1966	6.00	15.00
— Atlantic albums above have multi-color labels with a black fan logo.—					

HIGHTOWER, DONNA

Donna Hightower is a jazz-based vocalist.

Label & Catalog #		Title	Year	VG+	NM
Capitol T-1133	(M)	**Take One**	1959	12.00	30.00
Capitol ST-1133	(S)	**Take One**	1959	16.00	40.00
Capitol T-1273	(M)	**Gee Baby, Ain't I Good To You?**	1959	12.00	30.00
Capitol ST-1273	(S)	**Gee Baby, Ain't I Good To You?**	1959	16.00	40.00
— Capitol albums above have black "rainbow" labels with the logo on the left side.—					

HILDINGER, DAVE

David Hildinger is a jazz-based pianist.

Label & Catalog #		Title	Year	VG+	NM
Baton 1204	(M)	**The Young Moderns**	1957	16.00	40.00

HILL, ANDREW

Andrew Hill is a modern jazz pianist and composer.

Label & Catalog #		Title	Year	VG+	NM
Warwick W-2002	(M)	**So In Love**	1960	24.00	60.00
Warwick W-2002ST	(S)	**So In Love**	1960	30.00	75.00

Label & Catalog #		Title	Year	VG+	NM
Blue Note BLP-4151	(M)	**Black Fire**	1963	16.00	40.00
Blue Note BST-84151	(S)	**Black Fire**	1963	12.00	30.00
Blue Note BLP-4159	(M)	**Judgment!**	1964	16.00	40.00
Blue Note BST-84159	(S)	**Judgment!**	1964	12.00	30.00
Blue Note BLP-4160	(M)	**Smoke Stack**	1964	16.00	40.00
Blue Note BST-84160	(S)	**Smoke Stack**	1964	12.00	30.00
Blue Note BLP-4167	(M)	**Point Of Departure**	1964	16.00	40.00
Blue Note BST-84167	(S)	**Point Of Departure**	1964	12.00	30.00
Blue Note BLP-4203	(M)	**Andrew!!!—The Music Of Andrew Hill**	1965	*Unreleased*	
Blue Note BST-84203	(S)	**Andrew!!!—The Music Of Andrew Hill**	1965	*Unreleased*	
Blue Note BLP-4217	(M)	**Compulsion**	1965	12.00	30.00
Blue Note BST-84217	(S)	**Compulsion**	1965	10.00	25.00
Blue Note BLP-4233	(M)	**One For One**	1966	*Unreleased*	
Blue Note BST-84233	(S)	**One For One**	1966	*Unreleased*	
—Blue Note albums above have blue on white labels with a New York, NY address.—					
Blue Note BST-84151	(S)	**Black Fire**	196?	5.00	12.00
Blue Note BST-84159	(S)	**Judgment!**	196?	5.00	12.00
Blue Note BST-84160	(S)	**Smoke Stack**	196?	5.00	12.00
Blue Note BST-84167	(S)	**Point Of Departure**	196?	5.00	12.00
Blue Note BST-84203	(S)	**Andrew!!!—The Music Of Andrew Hill**	196?	8.00	20.00
Blue Note BST-84217	(S)	**Compulsion**	196?	5.00	12.00
Blue Note BST-84303	(S)	**Grass Roots**	1968	8.00	20.00
Blue Note BST-84330	(S)	**Lift Every Voice**	1969	8.00	20.00
—Blue Note albums above have blue on white labels with "A Division of Liberty Records."—					

HILL, VINSON

Savoy MG-12187	(M)	**The Vinson Hill Trio**	1966	12.00	30.00

HINES, EARL "FATHA"

Earl "Fatha" Hines is a traditional jazz pianist, vocalist and composer. For additional listings refer to Louis Armstrong; Count Basie; Benny Carter; Cozy Cole / Earl Hines; Johnny Hodges & Earl Hines.

Mercury MG-25018	(10")	**Earl Hines And The All Stars**	1950	125.00	250.00
Columbia CL-6171	(10")	**Piano Moods**	1951	50.00	125.00
Advance 4	(10")	**Fats Waller Memorial Set**	1951	50.00	125.00
Atlantic ALS-120	(10")	**Earl Hines: QRS Solos**	1952	100.00	200.00
Dial LP-303	(10")	**Earl Hines Trio**	1952	125.00	250.00
Dial LP-306	(10")	**Earl Hines All Stars**	1953	125.00	250.00
RCA Victor LPT-20	(10")	**Earl Hines With Billy Eckstine**	1953	50.00	125.00
Brunswick BL-58035	(10")	**Earl Hines Plays Fats Waller**	1953	50.00	125.00
Nocturne NLP-5	(10")	**Earl "Fatha" Hines**	1954	50.00	125.00
"X" LVA-3023	(10")	**Piano Solos**	1954	50.00	125.00
Royale 18166	(10")	**Earl "Fatha" Hines—Great Piano Solos**	195?	50.00	125.00
Fantasy 3217	(M)	**"Fatha" Plays "Fats"** *(Dark red vinyl)*	1956	30.00	75.00
Fantasy 3238	(M)	**Earl "Fatha" Hines Solo** *(Dark red vinyl)*	1956	30.00	75.00
—Fantasy albums above have red labels on dark red, non-flexible vinyl.—					
Fantasy 3217	(M)	**"Fatha" Plays "Fats"**	195?	16.00	40.00
Fantasy 3238	(M)	**Earl "Fatha" Hines Solo**	195?	16.00	40.00
—Fantasy albums above have red labels on non-flexible vinyl.—					
Epic LN-3223	(M)	**Oh, Father!**	1956	20.00	50.00
Epic LN-3501	(M)	**Earl "Fatha" Hines**	1958	20.00	50.00
Tops L-1599	(M)	**"Fatha"**	1958	10.00	25.00
Craftsmen 8041	(M)	**Swingin' And Singin'**	1960	8.00	20.00
		(Craftsmen 8041 is a reissue of Tops 1599.)			
MGM E-3832	(M)	**Earl's Pearls**	1960	12.00	30.00
MGM SE-3832	(S)	**Earl's Pearls**	1960	10.00	25.00
Jazz Panorama 7	(M)	**All Stars**	1961	16.00	40.00
Riverside RLP-398	(M)	**A Monday Date**	1961	12.00	30.00
Riverside RS-9398	(E)	**A Monday Date**	1961	6.00	15.00
—Riverside albums above have blue mono or black stereo labels with a reel & mike logo on top.—					
Capitol T-1971	(M)	**Earl "Fatha" Hines**	1963	12.00	30.00
Capitol ST-1971	(S)	**Earl "Fatha" Hines**	1963	10.00	25.00
Contact 2	(M)	**Spontaneous Explorations**	1964	12.00	30.00
Contact 2	(S)	**Spontaneous Explorations**	1964	10.00	25.00
Focus FM-335	(M)	**The Real Earl Hines In Concert**	1965	12.00	30.00
Focus FS-335	(S)	**The Real Earl Hines In Concert**	1965	10.00	25.00
Columbia CL-2320	(M)	**The New Earl Hines Trio**	1965	8.00	20.00
Columbia CS-9120	(S)	**The New Earl Hines Trio**	1965	6.00	15.00
—Columbia albums above have "Guaranteed High Fidelity" or "360 Sound Stereo" in black on the label.—					

Label & Catalog #		Title	Year	VG+	NM
RCA Victor LPV-512	(M)	**The Grand Terrace Band**	1965	10.00	25.00
RCA Victor LPM-3380	(M)	**Up To Date**	1965	10.00	25.00
RCA Victor LSP-3380	(S)	**Up To Date**	1965	8.00	20.00
		—RCA albums above have black labels with "Monaural" or "Stereo" on the bottom.—			
Impulse AS-9108	(M)	**Once Upon A Time**	1966	14.00	35.00
Impulse A-9108	(S)	**Once Upon A Time**	1966	10.00	25.00
		—Impulse albums above have orange & black labels.—			
Impulse A-9108	(S)	**Once Upon A Time**	1968	4.00	10.00
		—Impulse albums above have red & black labels with the "abc" logo on top.—			
Verve VSP-35	(M)	**Life With Fatha**	1966	6.00	15.00
Verve VSPS-35	(E)	**Life With Fatha**	1966	3.00	7.50

HINES, EARL, & COLEMAN HAWKINS

Limelight LM-82020	(M)	**Grand Reunion**	1965	10.00	25.00
Limelight LS-86020	(S)	**Grand Reunion**	1965	8.00	20.00

HINES, EARL, & ROY ELDRIDGE

Limelight LM-82028	(M)	**Grand Reunion, Volume 2**	1965	10.00	25.00
Limelight LS-86028	(S)	**Grand Reunion, Volume 2**	1965	8.00	20.00

HINTON, MILT

Milton Hinton is a traditional jazz bass player. For additional listings refer to Charlene Bartley; Pia Beck.

Bethlehem BCP-1020	(M)	**Milt Hinton Quartet**	1955	30.00	75.00
Epic LN-3271	(M)	**The Rhythm Section**	1956	20.00	50.00
Bethlehem BCP-10	(M)	**East Coast Jazz Series #5**	1957	20.00	50.00

HINTON, MILT, & WENDELL MARSHALL & BULL RUTHER

RCA Victor LPM-1107	(M)	**Basses Loaded!**	1955	30.00	75.00
		—RCA albums above have black labels with "Long Play" on the bottom.—			

HIPP, JUTTA

German born Jutta Hipp is a modern jazz pianist.

MGM E-3157	(M)	**Cool Europe**	1955	60.00	150.00
		—MGM albums above have black labels.—			
Blue Note BLP-5056	(10")	**New Faces-New Sounds From Germany**	1955	150.00	300.00
Blue Note BLP-1515	(M)	**At The Hickory House, Volume 1** *(Deep groove)*	1956	125.00	250.00
Blue Note BLP-1515	(M)	**At The Hickory House, Volume 1**	1956	100.00	200.00
Blue Note BLP-1516	(M)	**At The Hickory House, Volume 2** *(Deep groove)*	1956	125.00	250.00
Blue Note BLP-1516	(M)	**At The Hickory House, Volume 2**	1956	100.00	200.00
Blue Note BLP-1530	(M)	**Jutta Hipp With Zoot Sims** *(Deep groove)*	1956	125.00	250.00
Blue Note BLP-1530	(M)	**Jutta Hipp With Zoot Sims**	1956	100.00	200.00
		—Blue Note albums above have blue on white labels with a Lexington Ave address.—			
Blue Note BLP-1515	(M)	**At The Hickory House, Volume 1**	1963	12.00	30.00
Blue Note BLP-1516	(M)	**At The Hickory House, Volume 2**	1963	12.00	30.00
Blue Note BLP-1530	(M)	**Jutta Hipp With Zoot Sims**	1963	12.00	30.00
		—Blue Note albums above have blue on white labels with a New York, USA address.—			

HIRT, AL

New Orleans-based trumpet player Al Hirt's recordings, especially for RCA, are primarily of pop music.

Verve MGV-1012	(M)	**Swinging Dixie From Dan's Pier 600**	1957	20.00	50.00
Verve MGV-1028	(M)	**Blockbustin' Dixie!**	1957	16.00	40.00
		(Verve 1028 is a reissue of Verve 1012.)			
		—Verve albums above have "Verve Records, Inc." on the bottom of the label.—			
Verve MGV-1028	(M)	**Blockbustin' Dixie!**	1961	6.00	15.00
		—Verve albums above have black labels with "MGM Records" on the bottom.—			
Audio Fidelity AFLP-1878	(M)	**Swingin' Dixie**	1959	6.00	15.00
Audio Fidelity AFSD-5878	(S)	**Swingin' Dixie**	1959	8.00	20.00
Coral CRL-57402	(M)	**Al Hirt In New Orleans**	1961	6.00	15.00
Coral CRL-757402	(S)	**Al Hirt In New Orleans**	1961	5.00	12.00
Crown CLP-5457	(M)	**Al Hirt And The Dawn Busters**	196?	5.00	12.00
Crown CST-457	(S)	**Al Hirt And The Dawn Busters**	196?	4.00	10.00
Metro M-517	(M)	**Al Hirt**	1965	5.00	12.00
Metro MS-517	(S)	**Al Hirt**	1965	4.00	10.00

HODEIR, ANDRE

French born Andre Hodeir is a modern jazz composer and conductor.

Savoy MG-12104	(M)	**American Jazzmen Play Andre Hodeir**	1957	20.00	50.00

Label & Catalog #		Title	Year	VG+	NM
Savoy MG-12113	(M)	**Andre Hodeir Presents The Paris Scene**	1957	20.00	50.00
		—Savoy albums above have silver on red labels.—			
Philips PHM-200-073	(M)	**Jazz Et All**	1963	12.00	30.00
Philips PHS-600-073	(S)	**Jazz Et All**	1963	10.00	25.00

HODES, ART

Arthur Hodes is a traditional jazz pianist. For additional listings refer to Edmond Hall / Art Hodes.

Blue Note BLP-7004	(10")	**The Best In Two Beat**	1950	125.00	250.00
Blue Note BLP-7005	(10")	**Art Hodes' Hot Five**	1950	125.00	250.00
		(Blue Note 7005 was reissued as part of 1203, Sidney Bechet's "Giant Of Jazz, Volume 2.")			
Blue Note BLP-7006	(10")	**Dixieland Jubilee**	1950	125.00	250.00
Blue Note BLP-7015	(10")	**Dixieland Clambake**	1951	125.00	250.00
Blue Note BLP-7021	(10")	**Out Of The Backroom**	1952	125.00	250.00
Riverside RLP-1012	(10")	**Chicago Rhythm Kings**	1953	30.00	75.00
EmArcy MG-26104	(10")	**Jazz Chicago Style**	1954	30.00	75.00
Paramount LP-113	(M)	**The Trios**	1955	30.00	75.00
Mercury MG-20185	(M)	**Chicago Style Jazz**	1957	16.00	40.00
Dotted-Eighth 1000	(M)	**Art For Art's Sake**	195?	20.00	50.00
Jazzology 46	(M)	**For Art's Sake**	196?	6.00	15.00
Blue Note B-6502	(M)	**The Funky Piano Of Art Hodes**	1969	6.00	15.00
		(Blue Note 6502 is a reissue of material from 7006 and 7021.)			
Blue Note B-6508	(M)	**Sittin' In**	1969	6.00	15.00
		(Blue Note 6508 is a reissue of material from 7004, 7006 and 7021.)			

HODGES, JOHNNY

John Hodges, aka "Rabbit" or "Jeep," is a traditional jazz alto and soprano saxophone player and composer. For additional listings refer to Coleman Hawkins; Gerry Mulligan; Jo Stafford.

Mercer LP-1000	(10")	**Johnny Hodges, Vol. 1**	1951	60.00	150.00
Mercer LP-1006	(10")	**Johnny Hodges, Vol. 2**	1951	60.00	150.00
Jazz Panorama 1806	(10")	**Johnny Hodges, Vol. 1**	1951	60.00	150.00
RCA Victor LPT-3000	(10")	**Alto Sax**	1952	60.00	150.00
Mercury MGC-111	(10")	**Johnny Hodges Collates**	1952	125.00	250.00
		(Mercury 111 features cover art by David Stone Martin.)			
Mercury MGC-128	(10")	**Johnny Hodges Collates #2**	1953	*Unreleased*	
Clef MGC-111	(10")	**Johnny Hodges Collates**	1953	70.00	175.00
Clef MGC-128	(10")	**Johnny Hodges Collates #2**	1953	70.00	175.00
Clef MGC-151	(10")	**Swing With Johnny Hodges**	1954	*Unreleased*	
Norgran MGN-1	(10")	**Swing With Johnny Hodges**	1954	100.00	200.00
Norgran MGN-1004	(M)	**Memories Of Ellington**	1954	60.00	150.00
Norgran MGN-1009	(M)	**More Of Johnny Hodges**	1954	60.00	150.00
Norgran MGN-1024	(M)	**Johnny Hodges Dance Bash**	1955	60.00	150.00
		(Norgran 1024 features cover art by David Stone Martin.)			
Norgran MGN-1045	(M)	**Creamy**	1955	60.00	150.00
		(Norgran 1045 features cover art by David Stone Martin.)			
Norgran MGN-1048	(M)	**Castle Rock**	1955	40.00	100.00
Norgran MGN-1055	(M)	**Ellingtonia '56**	1956	40.00	100.00
Norgran MGN-1059	(M)	**In A Tender Mood**	1956	40.00	100.00
Norgran MGN-1060	(M)	**Used To Be Duke**	1956	40.00	100.00
Norgran MGN-1061	(M)	**The Blues**	1956	40.00	100.00
Norgran MGN-1091	(M)	**Perdido**	1956	40.00	100.00
		(Norgran 1091 is a reissue of 1024 with the DSM cover.)			
Norgran MGN-1092	(M)	**In A Mellow Tone**	1956	40.00	100.00
		(Norgran 1092 is a reissue of 1004.)			
Epic LN-3105	(M)	**Hodge Podge**	1955	20.00	50.00
Verve MGV-8136	(M)	**Creamy**	1957	20.00	50.00
		(Verve 8136 is a reissue of Norgran 1045 with the DSM cover.)			
Verve MGV-8139	(M)	**Castle Rock**	1957	20.00	50.00
		(Verve 8139 is a reissue of Norgran 1048.)			
Verve MGV-8145	(M)	**Ellingtonia '56**	1957	20.00	50.00
		(Verve 8145 is a reissue of Norgran 1055.)			
Verve MGV-8149	(M)	**In A Tender Mood**	1957	20.00	50.00
		(Verve 8149 is a reissue of Norgran 1059.)			
Verve MGV-8150	(M)	**Used To Be Duke**	1957	20.00	50.00
		(Verve 8150 is a reissue of Norgran 1060.)			
Verve MGV-8151	(M)	**The Blues**	1957	20.00	50.00
		(Verve 8151 is a reissue of Norgran 1061.)			

Label & Catalog #		Title	Year	VG+	NM
Verve MGV-8179	(M)	**Perdido**	1957	20.00	50.00
		(Verve 8179 is a reissue of Norgran 1091.)			
Verve MGV-8180	(M)	**In A Mellow Tone**	1957	20.00	50.00
		(Verve 8180 is a reissue of Norgran 1092.)			
Verve MGV-8203	(M)	**Duke's In Bed**	1957	20.00	50.00
American Rec. Soc. G-421	(M)	**Johnny Hodges And The Ellington All Stars**	1957	16.00	40.00
		(A.R.S. 421 is a reissue of Verve 8203.)			
Verve MGV-8271	(M)	**The Big Sound**	1958	20.00	50.00
Verve MGVS-6017	(S)	**The Big Sound**	1960	16.00	40.00
		(Verve 8271 also features The Ellington Men.)			
Verve MGV-8314	(M)	**The Prettiest Gershwin**	1959	20.00	50.00
Verve MGVS-6048	(S)	**The Prettiest Gershwin**	1960	16.00	40.00
Verve MGV-8317	(M)	**Back To Back—Duke Ellington & Johnny Hodges Play The Blues**	1959	20.00	50.00
Verve MGVS-6055	(S)	**Back To Back—Duke Ellington & Johnny Hodges Play The Blues**	1960	16.00	40.00
Verve MGV-8345	(M)	**Side By Side**	1959	20.00	50.00
Verve MGVS-6109	(S)	**Side By Side**	1960	16.00	40.00
		(Verve 8345 also features Duke Ellington.)			
Verve MGV-8350	(M)	**The Smooth One**	1960	*Unreleased*	
Verve MGVS-6115	(S)	**The Smooth One**	1960	*Unreleased*	
Verve MGV-8355	(M)	**Not So Dukish**	1960	20.00	50.00
Verve MGVS-6120	(S)	**Not So Dukish**	1960	*Unreleased*	
Verve MGV-8358	(M)	**Blues-A-Plenty**	1960	20.00	50.00
Verve MGVS-6123	(S)	**Blues-A-Plenty**	1960	*Unreleased*	
Verve MGV-8391	(M)	**Johnny Hodges**	1960	*Unreleased*	
—Verve albums above have black labels with "Verve Records, Inc." on the bottom.—					
Verve V-8136	(M)	**Creamy**	1961	8.00	20.00
Verve V-8139	(M)	**Castle Rock**	1961	8.00	20.00
Verve V-8145	(M)	**Ellingtonia '56**	1961	8.00	20.00
Verve V-8149	(M)	**In A Tender Mood**	1961	8.00	20.00
Verve V-8150	(M)	**Used To Be Duke**	1961	8.00	20.00
Verve V-8151	(M)	**The Blues**	1961	8.00	20.00
Verve V-8179	(M)	**Perdido**	1961	8.00	20.00
Verve V-8180	(M)	**In A Mellow Tone**	1961	8.00	20.00
Verve V-8203	(M)	**Duke's In Bed**	1961	8.00	20.00
Verve V-8271	(M)	**The Big Sound**	1961	8.00	20.00
Verve V6-8271	(S)	**The Big Sound**	1961	6.00	15.00
Verve V-8314	(M)	**The Prettiest Gershwin**	1961	8.00	20.00
Verve V6-8314	(S)	**The Prettiest Gershwin**	1961	6.00	15.00
Verve V-8317	(M)	**Back To Back—Duke Ellington & Johnny Hodges Play The Blues**	1961	8.00	20.00
Verve V6-8317	(S)	**Back To Back—Duke Ellington & Johnny Hodges Play The Blues**	1961	6.00	15.00
Verve V-8345	(M)	**Side By Side**	1961	8.00	20.00
Verve V6-8345	(S)	**Side By Side**	1961	6.00	15.00
Verve V-8355	(M)	**Not So Dukish**	1961	8.00	20.00
Verve V-8358	(M)	**Blues-A-Plenty**	1961	8.00	20.00
Verve V6-8358	(S)	**Blues-A-Plenty**	1961	6.00	15.00
Verve V-8452	(M)	**Johnny Hodges With Billy Strayhorn**	1962	12.00	30.00
Verve V6-8452	(S)	**Johnny Hodges With Billy Strayhorn**	1962	10.00	25.00
Verve V-8492	(M)	**The Eleventh Hour**	1962	12.00	30.00
Verve V6-8492	(S)	**The Eleventh Hour**	1962	10.00	25.00
Verve V-8546	(M)	**Johnny Hodges**	1963	*Unreleased*	
Verve V6-8546	(S)	**Johnny Hodges**	1963	*Unreleased*	
Verve V-8561	(M)	**Sandy's Gone**	1963	12.00	30.00
Verve V6-8561	(S)	**Sandy's Gone**	1963	10.00	25.00
—Verve albums above have black labels with "MGM Records" on the bottom.—					
Dot DLP-3682	(M)	**Johnny Hodges With Lawrence Welk's Orchestra**	1965	8.00	20.00
Dot DLP-25682	(S)	**Johnny Hodges With Lawrence Welk's Orchestra**	1965	6.00	15.00
Verve VSP-3	(M)	**Johnny Hodges And All The Dukesmen**	1966	4.00	10.00
Verve VSPS-3	(E)	**Johnny Hodges And All The Dukesmen**	1966	1.00	5.00
Verve VSP-20	(M)	**Alto Blue**	1966	4.00	10.00
Verve VSPS-20	(E)	**Alto Blue**	1966	1.00	5.00
RCA Victor LPV-533	(M)	**Things Ain't What They Used To Be**	1966	8.00	20.00
—RCA albums above have purple labels.—					

Label & Catalog #		Title	Year	VG+	NM
RCA Victor LPM-3867	(M)	**Triple Play**	1967	12.00	30.00
RCA Victor LSP-3867	(S)	**Triple Play**	1967	8.00	20.00
		—RCA albums above have black labels with "Monaural" or "Stereo" on the bottom.—			
Verve V-8680	(M)	**Blue Notes**	1966	8.00	20.00
Verve V6-8680	(S)	**Blue Notes**	1966	6.00	15.00
Verve V-8726	(M)	**Don't Sleep In The Subway**	1967	8.00	20.00
Verve V6-8726	(S)	**Don't Sleep In The Subway**	1967	6.00	15.00
Verve V6-8753	(S)	**Rippin' And Runnin'**	1968	6.00	15.00
		—Verve albums above have black labels with "MGM Records" on the bottom.—			

HODGES, JOHNNY, & "WILD" BILL DAVIS

Verve V-8406	(M)	**Blue Hodges**	1961	10.00	25.00
Verve V6-8406	(S)	**Blue Hodges**	1961	8.00	20.00
Verve V-8570	(M)	**Mess Of Blues**	1964	10.00	25.00
Verve V6-8570	(S)	**Mess Of Blues**	1964	8.00	20.00
Verve V-8599	(M)	**Blue Rabbit**	1964	10.00	25.00
Verve V6-8599	(S)	**Blue Rabbit**	1964	8.00	20.00
Verve V-8617	(M)	**Joe's Blues**	1965	10.00	25.00
Verve V6-8617	(S)	**Joe's Blues**	1965	8.00	20.00
Verve V-8630	(M)	**Wings And Things**	1965	10.00	25.00
Verve V6-8630	(S)	**Wings And Things**	1965	8.00	20.00
Verve V-8635	(M)	**Blue Pyramid**	1965	10.00	25.00
Verve V6-8635	(S)	**Blue Pyramid**	1965	8.00	20.00
		—Verve albums above have black labels with "MGM Records" on the bottom.—			

HODGES, JOHNNY, & EARL "FATHA" HINES

Verve V-8647	(M)	**Stride Right**	1965	10.00	25.00
Verve V6-8647	(S)	**Stride Right**	1965	8.00	20.00
Verve V-8732	(M)	**Swing's Our Thing**	1967	8.00	20.00
Verve V6-8732	(S)	**Swing's Our Thing**	1967	6.00	15.00
		—Verve albums above have black labels with "MGM Records" on the bottom.—			

HOLIDAY, BILLIE

Eleanora McKay, aka Billie "Lady Day" Holiday, is a traditional jazz-based vocalist and the single most noted jazz singer ever recorded. For additional listings refer to Ralph Burns / Billie Holiday; Ella Fitzgerald & Billie Holiday; Stan Getz; Teddy Wilson.

Commodore FL-20005	(10")	**Billie Holiday, Volume 1**	1950	125.00	250.00
Commodore FL-20006	(10")	**Billie Holiday, Volume 2**	1950	125.00	250.00
Columbia CL-6129	(10")	**Billie Holiday Sings**	1950	60.00	150.00
Columbia CL-6163	(10")	**Favorites**	1951	60.00	150.00
Columbia CL-637	(M)	**Lady Day**	1955	20.00	50.00
		(CL 637 is a reissue of 6040, "Teddy Wilson Featuring Billie Holiday.")			
		—Columbia albums above have "Long Playing" on the bottom of the label.—			
Columbia CL-637	(M)	**Lady Day**	195?	12.00	30.00
Columbia CL-1157	(M)	**Lady In Satin**	1958	16.00	40.00
Columbia CS-8048	(S)	**Lady In Satin**	1959	16.00	40.00
Columbia C3L-21	(M)	**The Golden Years** *(3 LPs)*	1962	16.00	40.00
Columbia C3S-821	(E)	**The Golden Years** *(3 LPs)*	1962	10.00	25.00
		—Columbia albums above have six white on black "eye" logos on each label.—			
Columbia CL-637	(M)	**Lady Day**	196?	6.00	15.00
Columbia CL-1157	(M)	**Lady In Satin**	196?	6.00	15.00
Columbia CS-8048	(S)	**Lady In Satin**	196?	8.00	20.00
Columbia C3L-21	(M)	**The Golden Years** *(3 LPs)*	196?	8.00	20.00
Columbia C3S-821	(E)	**The Golden Years** *(3 LPs)*	1962	5.00	12.00
Columbia C3L-40	(M)	**The Golden Years, Volume 2**	1966	8.00	20.00
Columbia C3S-840	(E)	**The Golden Years, Volume 2**	1966	5.00	12.00
Columbia CL-2666	(M)	**Billie Holiday's Greatest Hits**	1967	6.00	15.00
Columbia CS-9466	(E)	**Billie Holiday's Greatest Hits**	1967	4.00	10.00
		—Columbia albums above have "360 Sound" on the bottom of the label.—			
Decca DL-5345	(10")	**Lover Man**	1951	100.00	200.00
Decca DL-8215	(M)	**The Lady Sings**	1956	20.00	50.00
Decca DL-8701	(M)	**The Blues Are Brewin'**	1958	20.00	50.00
Decca DL-8702	(M)	**Lover Man**	1958	20.00	50.00
Jolly Roger 5020	(10")	**Billie Holiday, Volume 1**	1954	30.00	75.00
Jolly Roger 5021	(10")	**Billie Holiday, Volume 2**	1954	30.00	75.00
Jolly Roger 5022	(10")	**Billie Holiday, Volume 3**	1954	30.00	75.00
Mercury MGC-118	(10")	**Billie Holiday Sings**	1952	125.00	250.00
		(Mercury 118 features cover art by David Stone Martin.)			

Billie Holiday began singing in clubs in Harlem in 1930, was "discovered" by John Hammond, signed to Columbia, and had her recording debut with Benny Goodman in 1933. Whether recording as the vocal soloist for Teddy Wilson's orchestra or leading her own sessions, from 1935 through her death in 1959 she was the most widely known, listened to, and respected of all jazz vocalists, a heritage that continues in the '90s.

Label & Catalog #		Title	Year	VG+	NM
Clef MGC-118	(10")	**Billie Holiday Sings**	1953	70.00	175.00
Clef MGC-144	(10")	**An Evening With Billie Holiday**	1953	70.00	175.00
		(Clef 144 features cover art by David Stone Martin.)			
Clef MGC-161	(10")	**Billie Holiday**	1954	70.00	175.00
		(Clef 161 features cover art by David Stone Martin.)			
Clef MGC-169	(10")	**Billie Holiday At Jazz At The Philharmonic**	1954	70.00	175.00
		(Clef 169 features cover art by David Stone Martin.)			
Clef MGC-669	(M)	**Music For Torching**	1955	50.00	125.00
		(Clef 669 features cover art by David Stone Martin.)			
Clef MGC-686	(M)	**A Recital By Billie Holiday**	1956	50.00	125.00
		(Clef 686 is a reissue of 144 and 161 with cover art by David Stone Martin.)			
Clef MGC-690	(M)	**Solitude—Songs By Billie Holiday**	1956	40.00	100.00
		(Clef 690 is a reissue of Clef 118.)			
Clef MGC-713	(M)	**Velvet Mood**	1956	40.00	100.00
Clef MGC-721	(M)	**Lady Sings The Blues**	1956	40.00	100.00
American Rec. Soc. G-409	(M)	**Billie Holiday Sings**	1956	16.00	40.00
		(A.R.S. 409 is a reissue of Clef 713.)			
American Rec. Soc. G-431	(M)	**Lady Sings The Blues**	1957	16.00	40.00
		(A.R.S. 431 is a reissue of Clef 721.)			
Verve MGV-8026	(M)	**Music For Torching**	1957	24.00	60.00
		(Verve 8026 is a reissue of Clef 699 with the DSM cover.)			
Verve MGV-8027	(M)	**A Recital By Billie Holiday**	1957	24.00	60.00
		(Verve 8027 is a reissue of Clef 686 with the DSM cover.)			
Verve MGV-8074	(M)	**Solitude—Songs By Billie Holiday**	1957	24.00	60.00
		(Verve 8074 is a reissue of Clef 690.)			
Verve MGV-8096	(M)	**Velvet Mood**	1957	24.00	60.00
		(Verve 8096 is a reissue of Clef 713.)			
Verve MGV-8099	(M)	**Lady Sings The Blues**	1957	24.00	60.00
		(Verve 8099 is a reissue of Clef 721.)			
Verve MGV-8197	(M)	**Body And Soul**	1957	24.00	60.00
Verve MGV-8257	(M)	**Songs For Distingue' Lovers**	1958	24.00	60.00
Verve MGVS-6021	(S)	**Songs For Distingue' Lovers**	1960	24.00	60.00
Verve MGV-8302	(M)	**Stay With Me**	1959	20.00	50.00
Verve MGV-8329	(M)	**All Or Nothing At All**	1959	24.00	60.00
		(Verve 8329 features cover art by David Stone Martin.)			
Verve MGV-8338-2	(M)	**The Unforgettable Lady Day** *(2 LPs)*	1959	30.00	75.00
		—Verve albums above have black labels with "Verve Records, Inc." on the bottom.—			
Verve V-8026	(M)	**Music For Torching**	1961	8.00	20.00
Verve V-8027	(M)	**A Recital By Billie Holiday**	1961	8.00	20.00
Verve V-8074	(M)	**Solitude—Songs By Billie Holiday**	1961	8.00	20.00
Verve V-8096	(M)	**Velvet Mood**	1961	8.00	20.00
Verve V-8099	(M)	**Lady Sings The Blues**	1961	8.00	20.00
Verve V-8197	(M)	**Body And Soul**	1961	8.00	20.00
Verve V-8257	(M)	**Songs For Distingue' Lovers**	1961	8.00	20.00
Verve V6-8257	(S)	**Songs For Distingue' Lovers**	1961	6.00	15.00
Verve V-8302	(M)	**Stay With Me**	1961	8.00	20.00
Verve V-8329	(M)	**All Or Nothing At All**	1961	8.00	20.00
Verve V-8338-2	(M)	**The Unforgettable Lady Day** *(2 LPs)*	1961	10.00	25.00
Verve V-8410	(M)	**The Essential Billie Holiday**	1961	8.00	20.00
Verve V6-8410	(S)	**The Essential Billie Holiday**	1961	6.00	15.00
		—Verve albums above have black labels with "MGM Records" on the bottom.—			
Jazztone J-1209	(M)	**Billie Holiday Sings**	1955	20.00	50.00
		(Jazztone 1209 is a reissue of Commodore 20005.)			
Score SLP-4014	(M)	**Billie Holiday Sings The Blues**	1957	70.00	175.00
MGM E-3764	(M)	**Billie Holiday**	1959	16.00	40.00
MGM SE-3764	(S)	**Billie Holiday**	1959	20.00	50.00
Commodore DL-30008	(M)	**Billie Holiday**	1959	20.00	50.00
		(Commodore 30008 is a reissue of 20006.)			
Commodore DL-30011	(M)	**Billie Holiday**	1959	20.00	50.00
		(Commodore 30011 is a reissue of 20005.)			
United Arts. UAJ-14014	(M)	**Billie's Blues**	1962	16.00	40.00
United Arts. UAJS-15014	(S)	**Billie's Blues**	1962	20.00	50.00
Ric R-2001	(M)	**Rare Live Recordings**	1964	10.00	25.00
Metro M-515	(M)	**Billie Holiday**	1965	6.00	15.00
Metro MS-515	(E)	**Billie Holiday**	1965	4.00	10.00
Mainstream 56000	(M)	**The Commodore Recordings**	1965	10.00	25.00
Mainstream S-6000	(E)	**The Commodore Recordings**	1965	4.00	10.00

Label & Catalog #		Title	Year	VG+	NM
Mainstream 56022	(M)	**Once Upon A Time**	1965	10.00	25.00
Mainstream S-6022	(E)	**Once Upon A Time**	1965	4.00	10.00
		(Mainstream 56022 also features Teddy Wilson.)			
Verve VSP-5	(M)	**Lady**	1966	6.00	15.00
Verve VSPS-5	(E)	**Lady**	1966	3.00	7.50
Decca DXB-161	(M)	**The Billie Holiday Story** *(2 LPs)*	196?	8.00	20.00
Decca DXSB-161	(E)	**The Billie Holiday Story** *(2 LPs)*	196?	6.00	15.00
Decca DL-75040	(S)	**Billie Holiday's Greatest Hits**	1968	4.00	10.00

HOLIDAY, BILLIE / AL HIBBLER

Imperial LP-9185	(M)	**Billie Holiday, Al Hibbler And The Blues**	1962	20.00	50.00
Imperial LP-12185	(E)	**Billie Holiday, Al Hibbler And The Blues**	1962	12.00	30.00

HOLIDAY, JOE

Joseph Befumo, aka Joe Holiday, is a modern jazz tenor saxophone player.

Prestige PRLP-131	(10")	**Joe Holiday**	1952	100.00	200.00
Decca DL-8487	(M)	**Holiday For Jazz**	1957	30.00	75.00

HOLIDAY, JOE / BILLY TAYLOR

Prestige PRLP-171	(10")	**Mambo Jazz**	1953	60.00	150.00

HOLLOWAY, RED

Red Holloway is a modern jazz tenor saxophone player.

Prestige PRLP-7299	(M)	**Burner**	1964	20.00	50.00
Prestige PRST-7299	(S)	**Burner**	1964	20.00	50.00
		—Prestige albums above have yellow mono or silver stereo labels with a Bergenfield, NJ address.—			
Prestige PRLP-7325	(M)	**Cookin' Together**	1964	16.00	40.00
Prestige PRST-7325	(S)	**Cookin' Together**	1964	12.00	30.00
		(Prestige 7325 also features Jack McDuff.)			
Prestige PRLP-7390	(M)	**Sax, Strings & Soul**	1965	10.00	25.00
Prestige PRST-7390	(S)	**Sax, Strings & Soul**	1965	8.00	20.00
Prestige PRLP-7473	(M)	**Red Soul**	1966	10.00	25.00
Prestige PRST-7473	(S)	**Red Soul**	1966	8.00	20.00
		—Prestige albums above have blue labels with a trident logo on the right side.—			

HOLLYWOOD SAXOPHONE QUARTET, THE

Liberty LJH-6005	(M)	**The Hollywood Saxophone Quartet**	1955	16.00	40.00
Liberty LRP-3047	(M)	**Warm Winds**	1957	16.00	40.00

HOLMAN, BILL

Willis Holman is a West Coast jazz tenor saxophone player, arranger and composer. For additional listings refer to Richie Kamuca.

Capitol H-6500	(10")	**The Bill Holman Octet**	1954	40.00	100.00
Capitol T-1464	(M)	**Great Big Band**	1960	12.00	30.00
Capitol ST-1464	(S)	**Great Big Band**	1960	10.00	25.00
		—Capitol albums above have black "rainbow" labels with the logo on the left side.—			
Coral CRL-57188	(M)	**The Fabulous Bill Holman**	1958	30.00	75.00
Andex A-3004	(M)	**In A Jazz Orbit**	1958	16.00	40.00
Andex AS-3004	(S)	**In A Jazz Orbit**	1958	12.00	30.00
Andex A-3005	(M)	**Jive For Five**	1958	16.00	40.00
Andex AS-3005	(S)	**Jive For Five**	1958	12.00	30.00

HOLMES, RICHARD "GROOVE"

Richard "Groove" Holmes is a modern jazz organ player. For additional listings refer to Gerald Wilcox; Jimmy Witherspoon & Groove Holmes.

Pacific Jazz PJ-23	(M)	**Richard "Groove" Holmes**	1961	12.00	30.00
Pacific Jazz ST-23	(S)	**Richard "Groove" Holmes**	1961	10.00	25.00
		(Pacific Jazz 51 also features Les McCann and Ben Webster.)			
Pacific Jazz PJ-32	(M)	**Groovin' With Jug**	1961	16.00	40.00
Pacific Jazz ST-32	(S)	**Groovin' With Jug**	1961	12.00	30.00
		(Pacific Jazz 51 also features Gene Ammons.)			
Pacific Jazz PJ-51	(M)	**Somethin' Special**	1962	10.00	25.00
Pacific Jazz ST-51	(S)	**Somethin' Special**	1962	8.00	20.00
		(Pacific Jazz 51 also features Les McCann.)			
Pacific Jazz PJ-59	(M)	**After Hours**	1962	10.00	25.00
Pacific Jazz ST-59	(S)	**After Hours**	1962	8.00	20.00
Warner Bros. W-1553	(M)	**Book Of The Blues**	1964	10.00	25.00
Warner Bros. WS-1553	(S)	**Book Of The Blues**	1964	8.00	20.00

Label & Catalog #		Title	Year	VG+	NM
Pacific Jazz PJ-10105	(M)	**Tell It Like It is**	1966	12.00	30.00
Pacific Jazz ST-20105	(S)	**Tell It Like It is**	1966	10.00	25.00
Prestige PRLP-7435	(M)	**Soul Message**	1967	12.00	30.00
Prestige PRST-7435	(S)	**Soul Message**	1967	10.00	25.00
Prestige PRLP-7468	(M)	**Living Soul**	1967	12.00	30.00
Prestige PRST-7468	(S)	**Living Soul**	1967	10.00	25.00
Prestige PRLP-7485	(M)	**Misty**	1967	12.00	30.00
Prestige PRST-7485	(S)	**Misty**	1967	10.00	25.00
Prestige PRLP-7493	(M)	**Spicy**	1967	12.00	30.00
Prestige PRST-7493	(S)	**Spicy**	1967	10.00	25.00
Prestige PRLP-7497	(M)	**Super Cool**	1967	12.00	30.00
Prestige PRST-7497	(S)	**Super Cool**	1967	10.00	25.00
Prestige PRLP-7514	(M)	**Get Up And Get It**	1967	12.00	30.00
Prestige PRST-7514	(S)	**Get Up And Get It**	1967	10.00	25.00

—Prestige albums above have blue labels with a trident logo on the right side.—

Prestige PRST-7543	(S)	**Soul Power**	1968	10.00	25.00
Prestige PRST-7570	(S)	**The Groover**	1968	10.00	25.00
Prestige PRST-7601	(S)	**That Healin' Feelin'**	1969	10.00	25.00
Prestige PRST-7700	(S)	**The Best Of Richard "Groove" Holmes**	1969	8.00	20.00

—Prestige albums above have blue labels with a trident logo on top.—

HOLT, RED

Issac "Red" Holt is a modern jazz drummer.

Argo LP-696	(M)	**Look Out, Look Out**	1962	10.00	25.00
Argo LPS-696	(S)	**Look Out, Look Out**	1962	8.00	20.00

HONEY DREAMERS, THE (WITH ELLIOT LAWRENCE)

Fantasy 3207	(M)	**The Honey Dreamers Sing Gershwin**	1956	30.00	75.00

—Fantasy albums above have red labels on dark red, non-flexible vinyl.—

Fantasy 3207	(M)	**The Honey Dreamers Sing Gershwin**	195?	16.00	40.00

—Fantasy albums above have red labels on non-flexible vinyl.—

HOPE, ELMO

Elmo Hope is a modern jazz pianist and composer. For additional listings refer to Art Blakey & The Jazz Messengers / Elmo Hope; Jackie McLean.

Blue Note BLP-5029	(10")	**Elmo Hope Trio**	1953	150.00	300.00
Blue Note BLP-5044	(10")	**Elmo Hope Quintet, Volume 2**	1954	150.00	300.00
Prestige PRLP-7010	(M)	**Meditations**	1956	50.00	125.00
Prestige PRLP-7021	(M)	**Hope Meets Foster**	1956	50.00	125.00
		(Prestige 7021 also features Frank Foster.)			
Prestige PRLP-7021	(M)	**Wail Frank, Wail**	1957	30.00	75.00
		("Wail Frank, Wail" is a retitled reissue of "Hope Meets Foster.")			
Prestige PRLP-7043	(M)	**Informal Jazz**	1956	50.00	125.00

—Prestige albums above have yellow labels with a W. 50th Street, NYC address.—

Hifijazz J-616	(M)	**Elmo Hope**	1960	20.00	50.00
Hifijazz JS-616	(S)	**Elmo Hope**	1960	16.00	40.00
Beacon B-401	(M)	**High Hopes**	1961	16.00	40.00
Beacon BS-401	(S)	**High Hopes**	1961	12.00	30.00
Riverside RLP-381	(M)	**Homecoming!**	1961	20.00	50.00
Riverside RS-9381	(S)	**Homecoming!**	1961	16.00	40.00
Riverside RLP-408	(M)	**Hope-Full**	1962	12.00	30.00
Riverside RS-9408	(S)	**Hope-Full**	1962	10.00	25.00
		(Riverside 408 also features Bertha Hope.)			

—Riverside albums above have blue mono or black stereo labels with a reel & mike logo on top.—

Celebrity 209	(M)	**Elmo Hope Trio**	1962	12.00	30.00
Celebrity 209	(S)	**Elmo Hope Trio**	1962	10.00	25.00
Audio Fidelity AFLP-2119	(M)	**Sounds From Riker's Island**	1963	16.00	40.00
Audio Fidelity AFSD-6119	(S)	**Sounds From Riker's Island**	1963	12.00	30.00
Contemporary M-3620	(M)	**The Elmo Hope Trio**	1966	12.00	30.00
Contemporary S-7620	(S)	**The Elmo Hope Trio**	1966	10.00	25.00
		(Contemporary 3620 is a reissue of Hifijazz 616.)			
Prestige PRST-7675	(E)	**The Elmo Hope Memorial Album**	1969	5.00	12.00
		(Prestige 7675 is a reissue of Prestige 7010.)			

—Prestige albums above have blue labels with a trident logo on top.—

HOPKINS, CLAUDE

Claude Hopkins is a traditional jazz pianist, arranger, composer and band leader.

Swingville SVLP-2009	(M)	**Yes Indeed**	1960	20.00	50.00

Label & Catalog #		Title	Year	VG+	NM
Swingville SVLP-2020	(M)	**Let's Jam**	1961	20.00	50.00
Swingville SVLP-2041	(M)	**Swing Time**	1962	20.00	50.00

—Swingville mono albums above have purple mono or red stereo labels.—

Swingville SVLP-2009	(M)	**Yes Indeed**	1965	10.00	25.00
Swingville SVLP-2020	(M)	**Let's Jam**	1965	10.00	25.00
Swingville SVLP-2041	(M)	**Swing Time**	1965	10.00	25.00

—Swingville albums above have blue labels with a trident logo on the right side.—

HOPKINS, KENYON

Kenyon Hopkins is a modern jazz-based composer the bulk of whose work can be found in the Jazzy Soundtracks section under Columbia, Coral, RCA Victor, United Artists and Verve.

Verve V-8694	(M)	**Dream Songs**	1967	6.00	15.00
Verve V6-8694	(S)	**Dream Songs**	1967	5.00	12.00

—Verve albums above have black labels with "MGM Records" on the bottom.—

HORN, PAUL

Paul Horn is a West Coast jazz alto saxophone, clarinet and flute player. For additional listings refer to Chico Hamilton; Freddie Gambrell & Paul Horn.

Dot DLP-3091	(M)	**House Of Horn**	1957	20.00	50.00
Dot DLP-9002	(M)	**Plenty Of Horn**	1958	20.00	50.00
Dot DLP-25002	(S)	**Plenty Of Horn**	1958	16.00	40.00
World Pacific WP-1266	(M)	**Impressions**	1959	20.00	50.00
Hifijazz J-615	(M)	**Something Blue**	1960	16.00	40.00
Hifijazz JS-615	(S)	**Something Blue**	1960	12.00	30.00
Columbia CL-1677	(M)	**The Sound Of Paul Horn**	1961	12.00	30.00
Columbia CS-8477	(S)	**The Sound Of Paul Horn**	1961	10.00	25.00

—Columbia albums above have six white on black "eye" logos on each label.—

Columbia CL-1922	(M)	**Profile Of A Jazz Musician**	1962	8.00	20.00
Columbia CS-8722	(S)	**Profile Of A Jazz Musician**	1962	6.00	15.00
Columbia CL-2050	(M)	**Impressions Of "Cleopatra"**	1963	8.00	20.00
Columbia CS-8850	(S)	**Impressions Of "Cleopatra"**	1963	6.00	15.00

—Columbia albums above have "Guaranteed High Fidelity" or "360 Sound Stereo" in black on the label.—

RCA Victor LPM-3386	(M)	**Cycle**	1965	8.00	20.00
RCA Victor LSP-3386	(S)	**Cycle**	1965	6.00	15.00
RCA Victor LPM-3414	(M)	**Jazz Suite On The Mass Texts**	1965	8.00	20.00
RCA Victor LSP-3414	(S)	**Jazz Suite On The Mass Texts**	1965	6.00	15.00
RCA Victor LPM-3519	(M)	**Here's That Rainy Day**	1966	8.00	20.00
RCA Victor LSP-3519	(S)	**Here's That Rainy Day**	1966	6.00	15.00
RCA Victor LPM-3613	(M)	**Monday, Monday**	1966	8.00	20.00
RCA Victor LSP-3613	(S)	**Monday, Monday**	1966	6.00	15.00

—RCA albums above have black labels with "Monaural" or "Stereo" on the bottom.—

HORN, SHIRLEY

Shirley Horn is a jazz-based pianist and vocalist.

Stereo-Craft RTN-16	(M)	**Embers And Ashes**	1961	24.00	60.00
Stereo-Craft RTS-16	(S)	**Embers And Ashes**	1961	30.00	75.00
Mercury MG-20761	(M)	**Loads Of Love**	1963	20.00	50.00
Mercury SR-60761	(S)	**Loads Of Love**	1963	24.00	60.00
Mercury MG-20835	(M)	**Shirley Horn With Horns**	1963	20.00	50.00
Mercury SR-60835	(S)	**Shirley Horn With Horns**	1963	24.00	60.00
ABC-Paramount ABC-538	(M)	**Travelin' Light**	1965	16.00	40.00
ABC-Paramount ABCS-538	(S)	**Travelin' Light**	1965	20.00	50.00

HOWARD, DAVE

David Howard is a jazz-based vocalist.

Choreo 5	(M)	**I Love Everybody**	1961	10.00	25.00
Choreo 5	(S)	**I Love Everybody**	1961	12.00	30.00

HOWARD, JOE

Francis "Joe" Howard is a traditional jazz trombone player.

Sunset SU-3001	(M)	**Patterns For Trombone**	1955	16.00	40.00
King 661	(M)	**The Golden Sound Of Joe Howard**	1959	20.00	50.00

HOWARD, NOAH

Noah Howard is a modern jazz alto saxophone player.

ESP-Disk' 1031	(M)	**Noah Howard Quartet**	1966	10.00	25.00
ESP-Disk' 1031	(S)	**Noah Howard Quartet**	1966	8.00	20.00

Label & Catalog #		Title	Year	VG+	NM
ESP-Disk' 1064	*(M)*	**Live At Judson Hall**	*1967*	**10.00**	**25.00**
ESP-Disk' 1064	*(S)*	**Live At Judson Hall**	*1967*	**8.00**	**20.00**
ESP-Disk' 1073	*(S)*	**Noah Howard**	*1969*	*Unreleased*	

HUBBARD, FREDDIE

Frederick Hubbard is a modern jazz trumpet player and composer. For additional listings refer to Art Blakey & The Jazz Messengers; Ronnie Mathews.

Label & Catalog #		Title	Year	VG+	NM
Blue Note BLP-4040	*(M)*	**Open Sesame** *(Deep groove)*	*1960*	**50.00**	**125.00**
Blue Note BLP-4040	*(M)*	**Open Sesame**	*1960*	**30.00**	**75.00**
Blue Note BST-84040	*(S)*	**Open Sesame**	*1960*	**20.00**	**50.00**
Blue Note BLP-4056	*(M)*	**Goin' Up**	*1960*	**30.00**	**75.00**
Blue Note BST-84056	*(S)*	**Goin' Up**	*1960*	**20.00**	**50.00**
Blue Note BLP-4073	*(M)*	**Hub Cap**	*1961*	**30.00**	**75.00**
Blue Note BST-84073	*(S)*	**Hub Cap**	*1961*	**20.00**	**50.00**

—Blue Note albums above have blue on white labels with a W. 63rd St, NYC address.—

Label & Catalog #		Title	Year	VG+	NM
Blue Note BLP-4085	*(M)*	**Ready For Freddie**	*1961*	**30.00**	**75.00**
Blue Note BST-84085	*(S)*	**Ready For Freddie**	*1961*	**20.00**	**50.00**

—Blue Note albums above have blue on white labels with a 61st St, NYC address.—

Label & Catalog #		Title	Year	VG+	NM
Blue Note BLP-4040	*(M)*	**Open Sesame**	*1963*	**10.00**	**25.00**
Blue Note BST-84040	*(S)*	**Open Sesame**	*1963*	**8.00**	**20.00**
Blue Note BLP-4056	*(M)*	**Goin' Up**	*1963*	**10.00**	**25.00**
Blue Note BST-84056	*(S)*	**Goin' Up**	*1963*	**8.00**	**20.00**
Blue Note BLP-4073	*(M)*	**Hub Cap**	*1963*	**10.00**	**25.00**
Blue Note BST-84073	*(S)*	**Hub Cap**	*1963*	**8.00**	**20.00**
Blue Note BLP-4085	*(M)*	**Ready For Freddie**	*1963*	**10.00**	**25.00**
Blue Note BST-84085	*(S)*	**Ready For Freddie**	*1963*	**8.00**	**20.00**
Blue Note BLP-4115	*(M)*	**Hub Tones**	*1962*	**12.00**	**30.00**
Blue Note BST-84115	*(S)*	**Hub Tones**	*1962*	**10.00**	**25.00**
Blue Note BLP-4135	*(M)*	**Here To Stay**	*1963*	*Unreleased*	
Blue Note BST-84135	*(S)*	**Here To Stay**	*1963*	*Unreleased*	
Blue Note BLP-4172	*(M)*	**Breaking Point**	*1964*	**12.00**	**30.00**
Blue Note BST-84172	*(S)*	**Breaking Point**	*1964*	**10.00**	**25.00**
Blue Note BLP-4196	*(M)*	**Blue Spirits**	*1965*	**12.00**	**30.00**
Blue Note BST-84196	*(S)*	**Blue Spirits**	*1965*	**10.00**	**25.00**
Blue Note BLP-4207	*(M)*	**The Night Of The Cookers— Live At Club La Marchal, Vol. 1**	*1965*	**12.00**	**30.00**
Blue Note BST-84207	*(S)*	**The Night Of The Cookers— Live At Club La Marchal, Vol. 1**	*1965*	**10.00**	**25.00**
Blue Note BLP-4208	*(M)*	**The Night Of The Cookers— Live At Club La Marchal, Vol. 2**	*1965*	**12.00**	**30.00**
Blue Note BST-84208	*(S)*	**The Night Of The Cookers— Live At Club La Marchal, Vol. 2**	*1965*	**10.00**	**25.00**

—Blue Note albums above have blue on white labels with a New York, NY address.—

Label & Catalog #		Title	Year	VG+	NM
Blue Note BST-84040	*(S)*	**Open Sesame**	*196?*	**5.00**	**12.00**
Blue Note BST-84056	*(S)*	**Goin' Up**	*196?*	**5.00**	**12.00**
Blue Note BST-84073	*(S)*	**Hub Cap**	*196?*	**5.00**	**12.00**
Blue Note BST-84085	*(S)*	**Ready For Freddie**	*196?*	**5.00**	**12.00**
Blue Note BST-84115	*(S)*	**Hub Tones**	*196?*	**5.00**	**12.00**
Blue Note BST-84172	*(S)*	**Breaking Point**	*196?*	**5.00**	**12.00**
Blue Note BST-84196	*(S)*	**Blue Spirits**	*196?*	**5.00**	**12.00**
Blue Note BST-84207	*(S)*	**The Night Of The Cookers— Live At Club La Marchal, Vol. 1**	*196?*	**5.00**	**12.00**
Blue Note BST-84208	*(S)*	**The Night Of The Cookers— Live At Club La Marchal, Vol. 2**	*196?*	**5.00**	**12.00**

—Blue Note albums above have blue on white labels with "A Division of Liberty Records."—

Label & Catalog #		Title	Year	VG+	NM
Impulse A-27	*(M)*	**The Artistry Of Freddie Hubbard**	*1962*	**12.00**	**30.00**
Impulse AS-27	*(S)*	**The Artistry Of Freddie Hubbard**	*1962*	**10.00**	**25.00**
Impulse A-38	*(M)*	**The Body And Soul Of Freddie Hubbard**	*1963*	**12.00**	**30.00**
Impulse AS-38	*(S)*	**The Body And Soul Of Freddie Hubbard**	*1963*	**10.00**	**25.00**

—Impulse albums above have orange & black labels.—

Label & Catalog #		Title	Year	VG+	NM
Impulse AS-27	*(S)*	**The Artistry Of Freddie Hubbard**	*1968*	**4.00**	**10.00**
Impulse AS-38	*(S)*	**The Body And Soul Of Freddie Hubbard**	*1968*	**4.00**	**10.00**

—Impulse albums above have red & black labels with the "abc" logo on top.—

Label & Catalog #		Title	Year	VG+	NM
Atlantic 1477	*(M)*	**Backlash**	*1967*	**10.00**	**25.00**
Atlantic SD-1477	*(S)*	**Backlash**	*1967*	**6.00**	**15.00**
Atlantic SD-1501	*(S)*	**High Pressure Blues**	*1969*	**6.00**	**15.00**

—Atlantic albums above have multi-color labels with a black fan logo.—

Label & Catalog #		Title	Year	VG+	NM
HUCKO, PEANUTS					
Michael "Peanuts" Hucko is a traditional jazz clarinet and tenor saxophone player.					
Grand Award GA-33-331	(M)	**Tribute To Benny Goodman**	1956	16.00	40.00
HUCKO, PEANUTS / RAY McKINLEY					
Grand Award GA-33-333	(M)	**The Swingin' Thirties**	1956	16.00	40.00
HUG, ARMAND					
Armand Hug is a traditional jazz pianist.					
Circle L-411	(10")	**New Orleans 88**	1951	20.00	50.00
Paramount LP-114	(10")	**Armand Hug Plays Armand Piron**	1954	20.00	50.00
HUGHES, LANGSTON					
Langston Hughes narrates the records listed below. For additional listings refer to Big Miller.					
Folkways FA-7312	(10")	**The Story Of Jazz** *(With booklet)*	1954	20.00	50.00
Folkways FA-7312	(10")	**The Story Of Jazz For Children** *(With booklet)*	1954	20.00	50.00
MGM E-3697	(M)	**The Weary Blues**	1958	20.00	50.00
		(On MGM 3697 Hughes is backed by Leonard Feather's group on side 1 and Charles Mingus' on side 2.)			
Verve VSP-36	(M)	**The Weary Blues**	1966	6.00	15.00
Verve VSPS-36	(E)	**The Weary Blues**	1966	3.00	7.50
		(Verve 36 is a reissue of MGM 3697.)			
HUGHES, RHETA					
Rheta Hughes is a jazz-based vocalist.					
Columbia CL-2385	(M)	**Introducing An Electrifying New Star**	1965	12.00	30.00
Columbia CL-2385	(M)	**Introducing An Electrifying New Star**	1965	16.00	40.00
—Columbia albums above have "Guaranteed High Fidelity" or "360 Sound Stereo" in black on the label.—					
HUGHES, SPIKE					
English born Patrick "Spike" Hughes is a traditional jazz bass player and composer.					
London LL-1387	(M)	**Spike Hughes And His All-American Orchestra**	1956	16.00	40.00
HUMES, HELEN					
Helen Humes is a traditional jazz-based vocalist associated with West Coast jazz.					
Contemporary M-3571	(M)	**Helen Humes**	1960	16.00	40.00
Contemporary S-7571	(S)	**Helen Humes**	1960	14.00	35.00
Contemporary M-3582	(M)	**Songs I Like To Sing!**	1960	16.00	40.00
Contemporary S-7582	(S)	**Songs I Like To Sing!**	1960	14.00	35.00
Contemporary M-3598	(M)	**Swingin' With Humes**	1961	16.00	40.00
Contemporary S-7598	(S)	**Swingin' With Humes**	1961	14.00	35.00
—Contemporary stereo albums have gold & black labels.—					
HUMPHREY, PERCY					
Percy Humphrey is a traditional jass trumpet player.					
Riverside RLP-378	(M)	**Percy Humphrey's Crescent City Joymakers**	1961	12.00	30.00
Riverside RS-9378	(E)	**Percy Humphrey's Crescent City Joymakers**	1961	6.00	15.00
—Riverside albums above have blue mono or black stereo labels with a reel & mike logo on top.—					
HUNT, PEE WEE					
Walter "Pee Wee" Hunt is a traditional jazz trombone player and vocalist.					
Royale 18153	(10")	**Pee Wee Hunt And His Dixieland Band**	195?	16.00	40.00
Capitol H-203	(10")	**Straight From Dixie**	1950	12.00	30.00
Capitol H-312	(10")	**Dixieland Detour**	1952	12.00	30.00
Capitol H-492	(10")	**Swingin' Around**	1954	12.00	30.00
Capitol T-573	(M)	**Dixieland Classics**	1955	10.00	25.00
Capitol T-783	(M)	**Pee Wee And Fingers**	1956	10.00	25.00
—Capitol albums above have turquoise labels.—					
Allegro 1633	(M)	**Dixieland**	1956	10.00	25.00
HUNT, PEE WEE / PEE WEE RUSSELL					
Rondo-lette A-9	(M)	**Pee Wee Hunt & Pee Wee Russell**	195?	10.00	25.00
HUNTER, ALBERTA					
Alberta Hunter is a traditional jazz-based vocalist.					
Riverside RLP-418	(M)	**Alberta Hunter With Lovie Austin's Blues Serenaders**	1962	12.00	30.00

Label & Catalog #		Title	Year	VG+	NM
Riverside RS-9418	(E)	**Alberta Hunter With Lovie Austin's Blues Serenaders**	1962	6.00	15.00

—Riverside albums above have blue mono or black stereo labels with a reel & mike logo on top.—

HUNTER, LURLEAN

Lurlean Hunter is a jazz-based vocalist.

RCA Victor LPM-1151	(M)	**Lonesome Gal**	1955	40.00	100.00

—RCA albums above have black labels with "Long Play" on the bottom.—

Vik LX-1061	(M)	**Night Life**	1956	40.00	100.00
Vik LX-1116	(M)	**Stepping Out**	1958	40.00	100.00
Atlantic 1344	(M)	**Blue And Sentimental**	1960	20.00	50.00
Atlantic SD-1344	(S)	**Blue And Sentimental**	1960	24.00	60.00

—Atlantic albums above have multi-color labels with a white fan logo.—

HUNTER, STAN, & SONNY FORTUNE

Prestige PRLP-7458	(M)	**Trip On The Strip**	1967	12.00	30.00
Prestige PRST-7458	(S)	**Trip On The Strip**	1967	10.00	25.00

—Prestige albums above have blue labels with a trident logo on the right side.—

HUTCHERSON, BOBBY

Robert Hutcherson is a modern jazz vibraphone player.

Blue Note BLP-4198	(M)	**Dialogue**	1965	12.00	30.00
Blue Note BST-84198	(S)	**Dialogue**	1965	10.00	25.00
Blue Note BLP-4213	(M)	**Components**	1965	12.00	30.00
Blue Note BST-84213	(S)	**Components**	1965	10.00	25.00
Blue Note BLP-4231	(M)	**Happenings**	1965	12.00	30.00
Blue Note BST-84231	(S)	**Happenings**	1965	10.00	25.00
Blue Note BLP-4244	(M)	**Stick-Up!**	1966	*Unreleased*	
Blue Note BST-84244	(S)	**Stick-Up!**	1966	*Unreleased*	

—Blue Note albums above have blue on white labels with a New York, USA address.—

Blue Note BST-84198	(S)	**Dialogue**	196?	5.00	12.00
Blue Note BST-84213	(S)	**Components**	196?	5.00	12.00
Blue Note BST-84231	(S)	**Happenings**	196?	5.00	12.00
Blue Note BST-84244	(S)	**Stick-Up!**	1968	8.00	20.00
Blue Note BST-84291	(S)	**Total Eclipse**	1968	8.00	20.00
Blue Note BST-84333	(S)	**Bobby Hutcherson Now**	1969	8.00	20.00

—Blue Note albums above have blue on white labels with "A Division of Liberty Records."—

I.

ILORI, SOLOMON

Nigerian born Solomon Ilori is a jazz-based guitar player, percussionist and vocalist.

Blue Note BLP-4136	(M)	**African High Life**	1963	30.00	75.00
Blue Note BST-84136	(S)	**African High Life**	1963	20.00	50.00

—Blue Note albums above have blue on white labels with a New York, USA address.—

Blue Note BST-84136	(S)	**African High Life**	196?	5.00	12.00

—Blue Note albums above have blue on white labels with "A Division of Liberty Records.".—

IND, PETER

Wave W-1	(M)	**Looking Out**	1961	12.00	30.00
WaveWS- 1	(S)	**Looking Out**	1961	10.00	25.00

IRVIN, BOOKER

Bethlehem BCP-6048	(M)	**The Book Cooks**	1960	16.00	40.00

J.

"J F.K." QUINTET, THE

Riverside RLP-396	*(M)*	**New Frontiers From Washington**	*1961*	**15.00**	**40.00**
Riverside RS-9396	*(S)*	**New Frontiers From Washington**	*1961*	**12.00**	**30.00**
Riverside RLP-424	*(M)*	**Young Ideas**	*1962*	**15.00**	**40.00**
Riverside RS-9424	*(S)*	**Young Ideas**	*1962*	**12.00**	**30.00**

—Riverside albums above have blue mono or black stereo labels with a reel & mike logo on top.—

JACKIE & ROY: *Refer to* JACKIE CAIN & ROY KRAL

JACKSON, CALVIN

Calvin Jackson is a traditional jazz-based pianist and composer.

"X" LXA-1005	*(M)*	**Calvin Jackson At The Plaza**	*1954*	**20.00**	**50.00**
Columbia CL-756	*(M)*	**Calvin Jackson & The All Stars Quartet**	*1956*	**20.00**	**50.00**
Columbia CL-824	*(M)*	**Rave Notice**	*1956*	**20.00**	**50.00**
		—Columbia albums above have six white on black "eye" logos on each label.—			
Ray Note SM-3001	*(M)*	**Cal-Essence**	*1959*	**20.00**	**50.00**

JACKSON, CHUBBY, & BILL HARRIS (THE CHUBBY JACKSON & BILL HARRIS ALL STARS)

Mercury MG-25076	*(10")*	**Jazz Journey**	*1950*	**125.00**	**250.00**
		(Mercury 25076 is a compilation of 78s issued under the names of various members of Woody Herman's band.)			
EmArcy MG-26003	*(10")*	**The Small Herd**	*1954*	**40.00**	**100.00**
		(EmArcy 26003 is an abridged reissue Mercury 25076.)			
EmArcy MGE-26012	*(M)*	**Out Of The Herd**	*1965*	**8.00**	**20.00**
EmArcy SRE-66012	*(E)*	**Out Of The Herd**	*1965*	**4.00**	**10.00**
		(EmArcy 26012 is a reissue of Mercury 25076 plus four tracks)			

JACKSON, CHUBBY

Graig "Chubby" Jackson is a traditional jazz string bassist and composer.

New Jazz NJLP-105	*(10")*	**Chubby Jackson And His All Star Band**	*1950*	**240.00**	**400.00**
Prestige PRLP-105	*(10")*	**Chubby Jackson And His All Star Band**	*1951*	**150.00**	**300.00**
Rainbow 708	*(10")*	**Chubby Jackson**	*1951*	**60.00**	**150.00**
Stereo-Craft RTN-108	*(M)*	**The Big Three**	*195?*	**20.00**	**50.00**
Stereo-Craft RTS-108	*(S)*	**The Big Three**	*195?*	**16.00**	**40.00**
Argo LP-614	*(M)*	**Chubby's Back**	*1958*	**20.00**	**50.00**
Argo LP-625	*(M)*	**I'm Entitled To You**	*1958*	**20.00**	**50.00**
Argo LPS-625	*(S)*	**I'm Entitled To You**	*1958*	**16.00**	**40.00**
Everest LPBR-5009	*(M)*	**Chubby Takes Over**	*1959*	**16.00**	**40.00**
Everest SDBR-1009	*(S)*	**Chubby Takes Over**	*1959*	**12.00**	**30.00**
Everest LPBR-5029	*(M)*	**The Big Three**	*1959*	**16.00**	**40.00**
Everest SDBR-1029	*(S)*	**The Big Three**	*1959*	**12.00**	**30.00**
Everest LPBR-5041	*(M)*	**Jazz Then Till Now**	*1960*	**16.00**	**40.00**
Everest SDBR-1041	*(S)*	**Jazz Then Till Now**	*1960*	**12.00**	**30.00**
Laurie LLP-2011	*(M)*	**Twist Calling**	*1962*	**12.00**	**30.00**
Laurie LLPS-2011	*(S)*	**Twist Calling**	*1962*	**10.00**	**25.00**
Prestige PRST-7641	*(E)*	**Chubby Jackson Sextet And Big Band**	*1969*	**6.00**	**15.00**
		(Prestige 7641 is a reissue of 105.)			

—Prestige albums above have blue labels with a trident logo on top.—

JACKSON, FRANZ

Franz Jackson is a traditional jazz tenor saxophone and clarinet player and arranger.

Riverside RLP-406	*(M)*	**Franz Jackson & The Original Jass All-Stars**	*1962*	**12.00**	**30.00**
Riverside RS-9406	*(E)*	**Franz Jackson & The Original Jass All-Stars**	*1962*	**6.00**	**15.00**

—Riverside albums above have blue mono or black stereo labels with a reel & mike logo on top.—

JACKSON, FRED

Fred Jackson is a modern jazz tenor saxophone player.

Blue Note BLP-4094	*(M)*	**Hootin' 'N Tootin'**	*1962*	**30.00**	**75.00**
Blue Note BST-84094	*(S)*	**Hootin' 'N Tootin'**	*1962*	**20.00**	**50.00**

—Blue Note albums above have blue on white labels with a 61st St, NYC address.—

Label & Catalog #		Title	Year	VG+	NM
Blue Note BLP-4094	(M)	**Hootin' 'N Tootin'**	1963	**10.00**	**25.00**
Blue Note BST-84094	(S)	**Hootin' 'N Tootin'**	1963	**8.00**	**20.00**
		—Blue Note albums above have blue on white labels with a New York, USA address.—			
Blue Note BST-84094	(S)	**Hootin' 'N Tootin'**	196?	**5.00**	**12.00**
		—Blue Note albums above have blue on white labels with "A Division of Liberty Records."—			

JACKSON, MARY ANNE

Hanover HM-8009 is a spoof of modern jazz and bop by that master of the idiom, Steve Allen, who wrote the music and the liner notes and played the piano. The cover features Allen's maid posing as Ms Jackson. . .

Label & Catalog #		Title	Year	VG+	NM
Hanover HM-8009	(M)	**The Wild Piano Of Mary Anne Jackson**	1959	**30.00**	**75.00**

JACKSON, MILT

Milton "Bags" Jackson is a modern jazz vibraphone player and co-founder of The Modern Jazz Quartet. For additional listings refer to Cannonball Adderley; Ray Brown; Miles Davis; Howard McGhee; Oscar Peterson; the "Jazz At 16 2/3 RPM" article; and the Various Artists section under Savoy.

Label & Catalog #		Title	Year	VG+	NM
Dee Gee 1002	(10")	**Milt Jackson**	1952	**150.00**	**300.00**
Blue Note BLP-5011	(10")	**Wizard Of The Vibes**	1952	**150.00**	**300.00**
Blue Note BLP-1509	(M)	**Milt Jackson** *(Deep groove)*	1956	**60.00**	**150.00**
Blue Note BLP-1509	(M)	**Milt Jackson**	1956	**40.00**	**100.00**
		(Blue Note 1509 is a reissue of 5011.)			
		—Blue Note albums above have blue on white labels with a Lexington Ave, NYC address.—			
Blue Note BLP-1509	(M)	**Milt Jackson**	1963	**10.00**	**25.00**
		—Blue Note albums above have blue on white labels with a New York, USA address.—			
Blue Note BST-81509	(E)	**Milt Jackson**	196?	**4.00**	**10.00**
		—Blue Note albums above have blue on white labels with a Lexington Ave, NYC address.—			
Savoy MG-15058	(10")	**Milt Jackson**	1954	**60.00**	**150.00**
Prestige PRLP-183	(10")	**Milt Jackson Quintet**	1954	**100.00**	**200.00**
Prestige PRLP-7003	(M)	**Milt Jackson**	1955	**40.00**	**100.00**
		—Prestige albums above have a W. 50th Street, NYC address on the label.—			
Savoy MG-12042	(M)	**Roll Em Bags**	1955	**30.00**	**75.00**
Savoy MG-12061	(M)	**Meet Milt Jackson**	1956	**20.00**	**50.00**
		(Savoy 12061 is a reissue of Savoy 15058.)			
Savoy MG-12070	(M)	**The Jazz Skyline**	1956	**20.00**	**50.00**
Savoy MG-12080	(M)	**Jackson's-ville**	1956	**20.00**	**50.00**
Atlantic 1242	(M)	**Ballads & Blues**	1956	**16.00**	**40.00**
Atlantic 1269	(M)	**Plenty, Plenty Soul**	1957	**16.00**	**40.00**
Atlantic SD-1269	(S)	**Plenty, Plenty Soul**	1958	**12.00**	**30.00**
Atlantic 1294	(M)	**Bags & Flutes**	1958	**16.00**	**40.00**
Atlantic SD-1294	(S)	**Bags & Flutes**	1958	**12.00**	**30.00**
Atlantic 1316	(M)	**Bean Bags**	1959	**16.00**	**40.00**
Atlantic SD-1316	(S)	**Bean Bags**	1959	**12.00**	**30.00**
		(Atlantic 1316 also features Coleman Hawkins.)			
		—Atlantic albums above have black mono or green stereo labels.—			
Atlantic 1242	(M)	**Ballads & Blues**	1961	**6.00**	**15.00**
Atlantic 1269	(M)	**Plenty, Plenty Soul**	1961	**6.00**	**15.00**
Atlantic SD-1269	(M)	**Plenty, Plenty Soul**	1961	**5.00**	**12.00**
Atlantic 1294	(M)	**Bags & Flutes**	1961	**6.00**	**15.00**
Atlantic SD-1294	(M)	**Bags & Flutes**	1961	**5.00**	**12.00**
Atlantic 1316	(M)	**Bean Bags**	1961	**6.00**	**15.00**
Atlantic SD-1316	(S)	**Bean Bags**	1961	**5.00**	**12.00**
Atlantic 1342	(M)	**Ballad Artistry**	1960	**10.00**	**25.00**
Atlantic SD-1342	(S)	**Ballad Artistry**	1960	**8.00**	**20.00**
		—Atlantic albums above have multi-color labels with a white fan logo.—			
Atlantic 1242	(M)	**Ballads & Blues**	196?	**5.00**	**12.00**
Atlantic 1269	(M)	**Plenty, Plenty Soul**	196?	**5.00**	**12.00**
Atlantic SD-1269	(M)	**Plenty, Plenty Soul**	196?	**4.00**	**10.00**
Atlantic 1294	(M)	**Bags & Flutes**	196?	**5.00**	**12.00**
Atlantic SD-1294	(M)	**Bags & Flutes**	196?	**4.00**	**10.00**
Atlantic 1316	(M)	**Bean Bags**	196?	**5.00**	**12.00**
Atlantic SD-1316	(S)	**Bean Bags**	196?	**4.00**	**10.00**
Atlantic 1342	(M)	**Ballad Artistry**	196?	**5.00**	**12.00**
Atlantic SD-1342	(S)	**Ballad Artistry**	196?	**4.00**	**10.00**
Atlantic 1417	(M)	**Vibrations**	1964	**8.00**	**20.00**
Atlantic SD-1417	(S)	**Vibrations**	1964	**6.00**	**15.00**
		—Atlantic albums above have multi-color labels with a black fan logo.—			
United Arts. UAL-4022	(M)	**Bags' Opus**	1959	**16.00**	**40.00**
United Arts. UAS-5022	(S)	**Bags' Opus**	1959	**12.00**	**30.00**

Milt Jackson moved from his native Detroit to New York with Dizzy Gillespie's band in 1945. He proceeded to establish himself as the first bop vibraphones player with Howard McGhee, Tadd Dameron, and Thelonious Monk's groups before finding a spot with Woody Herman's Herd (1949-50) and then rejoined Diz in 1950-52. In 1953 he helped form the most enduring of modern jazz ensembles, the Modern Jazz Quartet. He has recorded projects with Ray Charles, John Coltrane and Wes Montgomery; been featured as a soloist with Cannonball Adderley, Ray Brown, Miles Davis, and Oscar Peterson; and served as a sideman for albums by Hank Mobley, Thelonious Monk, and Fats Navarro, each on Blue Note, Sonny Rollins on Prestige, Kenny Clarke and Dizzy, both on Savoy, and Dinah Washington on Grand Award.

Label & Catalog #		Title	Year	VG+	NM
Prestige PRLP-7224	(M)	**Soul Pioneers**	1962	16.00	40.00
		(Prestige 7224 is a reissue of 7003.)			
—Prestige albums above have yellow mono or silver stereo labels with a Bergenfield, NJ address.—					
Impulse A-14	(M)	**Statements**	1962	12.00	30.00
Impulse AS-14	(S)	**Statements**	1962	10.00	25.00
Impulse A-70	(M)	**Jazz n' Samba**	1964	10.00	25.00
Impulse AS-70	(S)	**Jazz n' Samba**	1964	8.00	20.00
Impulse A-9193	(M)	**Memphis Jackson**	1967	10.00	25.00
Impulse AS-9193	(S)	**Memphis Jackson**	1967	8.00	20.00
—Impulse albums above have orange & black labels.—					
Impulse AS-14	(S)	**Statements**	1968	4.00	10.00
Impulse AS-70	(S)	**Jazz n' Samba**	1968	4.00	10.00
Impulse AS-9193	(S)	**Memphis Jackson**	1968	4.00	10.00
—Impulse albums above have red & black labels with the "abc" logo on top.—					
Riverside RLP-429	(M)	**Big Bags**	1962	10.00	25.00
Riverside RS-9429	(S)	**Big Bags**	1962	8.00	20.00
Riverside RLP-446	(M)	**Invitation**	1963	10.00	25.00
Riverside RS-9446	(S)	**Invitation**	1963	8.00	20.00
—Riverside albums above have blue mono or black stereo labels with a reel & mike logo on top.—					
Limelight LM-82006	(M)	**In A New Setting**	1964	8.00	20.00
Limelight LS-86006	(S)	**In A New Setting**	1964	6.00	15.00
Limelight LM-82024	(M)	**At The Museum Of Modern Art**	1965	8.00	20.00
Limelight LS-86024	(S)	**At The Museum Of Modern Art**	1965	6.00	15.00
Limelight LM-82045	(M)	**Born Free**	1966	8.00	20.00
Limelight LS-86045	(S)	**Born Free**	1966	6.00	15.00
Riverside RLP-478	(M)	**For Someone I Love**	1966	8.00	20.00
Riverside RS-9478	(S)	**For Someone I Love**	1966	6.00	15.00
Riverside RLP-495	(M)	**'Live' At The Village Gate**	1967	10.00	25.00
Riverside RS-9495	(S)	**'Live' At The Village Gate**	1967	6.00	15.00
—Riverside albums above blue labels with "Orpheum Productions" on the bottom.—					
Riverside RS-3021	(S)	**Bags And Brass**	1968	6.00	15.00
Verve V6-8761	(S)	**Milt Jackson And The Hip String Quartet**	1969	5.00	12.00
—Verve albums above have black labels with "MGM Records" on the bottom.—					
Prestige PRST-7655	(E)	**The Complete Milt Jackson**	1969	4.00	10.00
—Prestige albums above have blue labels with a trident logo on top.—					

JACKSON, MILT, & RAY CHARLES

Atlantic 1279	(M)	**Soul Brothers**	1958	20.00	50.00
Atlantic SD-1279	(S)	**Soul Brothers**	1958	16.00	40.00
—Atlantic albums above have black mono or green stereo labels.—					
Atlantic 1279	(M)	**Soul Brothers**	1961	6.00	15.00
Atlantic SD-1279	(S)	**Soul Brothers**	1961	8.00	12.00
Atlantic 1360	(M)	**Soul Meeting**	1961	12.00	30.00
Atlantic SD-1360	(S)	**Soul Meeting**	1961	10.00	25.00
—Atlantic albums abiove have multi-color labels with a white fan logo on the right side.—					

JACKSON, MILT, & JOHN COLTRANE

Atlantic 1368	(M)	**Bags And Trane**	1961	16.00	40.00
Atlantic SD-1368	(S)	**Bags And Trane**	1961	12.00	30.00
—Atlantic albums above have multi-color labels with a white fan logo.—					
Atlantic 1368	(M)	**Bags And Trane**	196?	6.00	15.00
Atlantic SD-1368	(S)	**Bags And Trane**	196?	5.00	12.00
—Atlantic albums above have multi-color labels with a black fan logo.—					

JACKSON, MILT, & WES MONTGOMERY

Riverside RLP-407	(M)	**Bags Meets Wes**	1962	10.00	25.00
Riverside RS-9407	(S)	**Bags Meets Wes**	1962	8.00	20.00
—Riverside albums above have blue mono or black stereo labels with a reel & mike logo on top.—					

JACKSON, WILLIS

Willis "Gator Tail" Jackson is a modern jazz tenor saxophone player. For additional listings refer to Johnny "Hammond" Smith & Willis Jackson.

Prestige PRLP-7162	(M)	**Please, Mr. Jackson**	1959	20.00	50.00
Prestige PRLP-7172	(M)	**Cool Gator**	1959	20.00	50.00
Prestige PRLP-7183	(M)	**Blue Gator**	1960	20.00	50.00
Prestige PRLP-7196	(M)	**Really Groovin'**	1961	20.00	50.00
Moodsville MVLP-17	(M)	**In My Solitude**	1961	20.00	50.00
—Moodsville mono albums above have green labels with silver print.—					

Label & Catalog #		Title	Year	VG+	NM
Moodsville MVLP-17	(M)	**In My Solitude**	1965	10.00	25.00

—Moodsville albums above have blue labels with a trident logo on the right side.—

Prestige PRLP-7211	(M)	**Cookin' Sherry**	1961	16.00	40.00
Prestige PRST-7211	(S)	**Cookin' Sherry**	1961	12.00	30.00
Prestige PRLP-7232	(M)	**Thunderbird**	1962	16.00	40.00
Prestige PRST-7232	(S)	**Thunderbird**	1962	12.00	30.00
Prestige PRLP-7260	(M)	**Bossa Nova Plus**	1963	16.00	40.00
Prestige PRST-7260	(S)	**Bossa Nova Plus**	1963	12.00	30.00
Prestige PRLP-7264	(M)	**Neapolitan Nights**	1963	16.00	40.00
Prestige PRST-7264	(S)	**Neapolitan Nights**	1963	12.00	30.00
Prestige PRLP-7273	(M)	**Loose...**	1963	16.00	40.00
Prestige PRST-7273	(S)	**Loose...**	1963	12.00	30.00
Prestige PRLP-7285	(M)	**Grease 'n' Gravy**	1963	16.00	40.00
Prestige PRST-7285	(S)	**Grease 'n' Gravy**	1963	12.00	30.00
Prestige PRLP-7296	(M)	**The Good Life**	1964	16.00	40.00
Prestige PRST-7296	(S)	**The Good Life**	1964	12.00	30.00
Prestige PRLP-7317	(M)	**More Gravy**	1964	16.00	40.00
Prestige PRST-7317	(S)	**More Gravy**	1964	12.00	30.00

—Prestige albums above have yellow mono or silver stereo labels with a Bergenfield, NJ address.—

Prestige PRLP-7329	(M)	**Boss Shoutin'**	1964	12.00	30.00
Prestige PRST-7329	(S)	**Boss Shoutin'**	1964	10.00	25.00
Prestige PRLP-7348	(M)	**Live! Jackson's Action**	1965	12.00	30.00
Prestige PRST-7348	(S)	**Live! Jackson's Action**	1965	10.00	25.00
Prestige PRLP-7364	(M)	**Together Again**	1965	12.00	30.00
Prestige PRST-7364	(S)	**Together Again**	1965	10.00	25.00
		(Prestige 7364 also features Jack McDuff.)			
Prestige PRLP-7380	(M)	**Live! Action**	1965	10.00	25.00
Prestige PRST-7380	(S)	**Live! Action**	1965	8.00	20.00
Prestige PRLP-7396	(M)	**Soul Night—Live!**	1965	10.00	25.00
Prestige PRST-7396	(S)	**Soul Night—Live!**	1965	8.00	20.00
Prestige PRLP-7412	(M)	**Tell It...**	1966	10.00	25.00
Prestige PRST-7412	(S)	**Tell It...**	1966	8.00	20.00
Prestige PRLP-7428	(M)	**Together Again, Again**	1966	10.00	25.00
Prestige PRST-7428	(S)	**Together Again, Again**	1966	8.00	20.00
		(Prestige 7364 also features Jack McDuff.)			

—Prestige albums above have blue labels with a trident logo on the right side.—

Prestige PRST-7551	(S)	**Soul Grabber**	1968	8.00	20.00
Prestige PRST-7571	(S)	**Star Bag**	1968	8.00	20.00
Prestige PRST-7602	(S)	**Swivel Hips**	1969	8.00	20.00
Prestige PRST-7648	(S)	**Gator's Groove**	1969	8.00	20.00
Prestige PRST-7702	(S)	**The Best Of Willis Jackson With Brother Jack McDuff**	1969	5.00	12.00

—Prestige albums above have blue labels with a trident logo on top.—

Verve V-8589	(M)	**'Gator Tails**	1964	8.00	20.00
Verve V6-8589	(S)	**'Gator Tails**	1964	6.00	15.00

—Verve albums above have black labels with "MGM Records" on the bottom.—

Cadet LP-763	(M)	**Smoking With Willis**	1965	8.00	20.00
Cadet LPS-763	(S)	**Smoking With Willis**	1965	6.00	15.00
Verve V6-8782	(S)	**Willis Jackson**	1969	4.00	10.00
		(Verve 8782 is a reissue of 8589.)			

—Verve albums above have black labels with "MGM Records" on the bottom.—

JACOBY, DON

Decca DL-4241	(M)	**Swinging Big Sound**	1963	8.00	20.00
Decca DL-74241	(S)	**Swinging Big Sound**	1963	6.00	15.00

JACQUET, ILLINOIS

Jean Battiste "Illinois" Jacquet is a modern jazz tenor saxophone player. For additional listings refer to Rex Stewart / Illinois Jacquet; Ben Webster; Lester Young / Illinois Jacquet.

Apollo LP-104	(10")	**Illinois Jacquet Jam Session**	1951	150.00	300.00
RCA Victor LPM-3236	(10")	**Black Velvet**	195?	100.00	200.00
Savoy MG-15024	(10")	**Tenor Sax**	1953	100.00	200.00
Aladdin LP-708	(10")	**Illinois Jacquet And His Tenor Sax**	1954	125.00	250.00
Aladdin LP-803	(M)	**Illinois Jacquet And His Tenor Sax**	1956	60.00	150.00
		(Aladdin 803 is a reissue of 708.)			
Mercury MGC-112	(10")	**Illinois Jacquet Collates**	1952	125.00	250.00
		(Mercury 112 features cover art by David Stone Martin.)			
Mercury MGC-129	(10")	**Illinois Jacquet Collates #2**	1953	*Unreleased*	

Illinois Jacquet's career began in the late '30s with the bands of Lionel Proctor, Bob Cooper and Milt Larkins. After moving to the West Coast he joined Floyd Ray in 1941 and then Lionel Hampton, Cab Calloway (1943-44), Count Basie (1945-46) and the Jazz at the Philharmonic tours. Aside from sharing an LP apiece with Rex Stewart and Lester Young (shown here), he can be found as a featured guest with Ben Webster and as a sideman on albums by Basie on Columbia, Gene Krupa on Verve, and many of the JATP releases.

Label & Catalog #		Title	Year	VG+	NM
Clef MGC-112	(10")	**Illinois Jacquet Collates**	1953	60.00	150.00
Clef MGC-129	(10")	**Illinois Jacquet Collates #2**	1953	60.00	150.00
Clef MGC-167	(10")	**Jazz By Jacquet**	1954	60.00	150.00
Clef MGC-676	(M)	**Illinois Jacquet Septet**	1955	50.00	125.00
		(Clef 676 features cover art by David Stone Martin.)			
Clef MGC-700	(M)	**Jazz Moods By Illinois Jacquet**	1956	40.00	100.00
Clef MGC-701	(M)	**Port Of Rico**	1956	40.00	100.00
Clef MGC-702	(M)	**Groovin' With Jacquet**	1956	50.00	125.00
		(Clef 702 features cover art by David Stone Martin.)			
Clef MGC-750	(M)	**Swing's The Thing**	1956	40.00	100.00
Verve MGV-8023	(M)	**Swing's The Thing**	1957	20.00	50.00
		(Verve 8023 is a reissue of Clef 750.)			
Verve MGV-8061	(M)	**Illinois Jacquet And His Orchestra**	1957	20.00	50.00
		(Verve 8061 is a reissue of Clef 676 with the DSM cover.)			
Verve MGV-8086	(M)	**Groovin'**	1957	20.00	50.00
Verve MGV-8084	(M)	**Jazz Moods By Illinois Jacquet**	1957	20.00	50.00
		(Verve 8084 is a reissue of Clef 700.)			
Verve MGV-8085	(M)	**Port Of Rico**	1957	20.00	50.00
		(Verve 8085 is a reissue of Clef 701.)			
Verve MGV-8086	(M)	**Groovin' With Jacquet**	1957	20.00	50.00
		(Verve 8086 is a reissue of Clef 702 with the DSM cover.)			
		—Verve albums above have black labels with "Verve Records, Inc." on the bottom.—			
Verve MGV-8023	(M)	**Swing's The Thing**	1961	8.00	20.00
Verve MGV-8061	(M)	**Illinois Jacquet And His Orchestra**	1961	8.00	20.00
Verve MGV-8086	(M)	**Groovin'**	1961	8.00	20.00
Verve MGV-8084	(M)	**Jazz Moods**	1961	8.00	20.00
Verve MGV-8085	(M)	**Port Of Rico**	1961	8.00	20.00
Verve MGV-8086	(M)	**Groovin' With Jacquet**	1961	8.00	20.00
		—Verve albums above have black labels with "MGM Records" on the bottom.—			
Roulette R-52035	(M)	**Illinois Jacquet Flies Again**	1959	20.00	50.00
Roulette SR-52035	(S)	**Illinois Jacquet Flies Again**	1959	16.00	40.00
Epic LA-16033	(M)	**Illinois Jacquet**	1962	16.00	40.00
Epic BA-17033	(S)	**Illinois Jacquet**	1962	12.00	30.00
Imperial LP-9184	(M)	**Flying Home**	1962	16.00	40.00
Imperial LP-12184	(S)	**Flying Home**	1962	12.00	30.00
Argo LP-722	(M)	**Message**	1963	12.00	30.00
Argo LPS-722	(S)	**Message**	1963	10.00	25.00
Argo LP-735	(M)	**Desert Winds**	1964	12.00	30.00
Argo LPS-735	(S)	**Desert Winds**	1964	10.00	25.00
Argo LP-746	(M)	**Illinois Jacquet Plays Cole Porter**	1964	12.00	30.00
Argo LPS-746	(S)	**Illinois Jacquet Plays Cole Porter**	1964	10.00	25.00
Argo LP-754	(M)	**Spectrum**	1965	12.00	30.00
Argo LPS-754	(S)	**Spectrum**	1965	10.00	25.00
Cadet LP-773	(M)	**Go Power**	1965	10.00	25.00
Cadet LPS-773	(S)	**Go Power**	1965	8.00	20.00
Prestige PRST-7575	(S)	**Illinois Jacquet On Prestige! Bottoms Up**	1968	10.00	25.00
Prestige PRST-7597	(S)	**The King!**	1968	10.00	25.00
Prestige PRST-7629	(S)	**The Soul Explosion**	1969	10.00	25.00
Prestige PRTS-7731	(S)	**The Blues—That's Me**	1969	10.00	25.00
		—Prestige albums above have blue labels with a trident logo on top.—			

JACQUET, ILLINOIS, & BEN WEBSTER

Clef MGC-680	(M)	**"The Kid" And "The Brute"**	1955	50.00	125.00
		(Clef 680 features cover art by David Stone Martin.)			
Verve MGV-8065	(M)	**"The Kid" And "The Brute"**	1957	20.00	50.00
		—Verve albums above have black labels with "Verve Records, Inc." on the bottom.—			
Verve V-8065	(M)	**"The Kid" And "The Brute"**	1961	8.00	20.00
		—Verve albums above have black labels with "MGM Records" on the bottom.—			

JACQUET, RUSSELL

Robert Russell Jacquet is a modern jazz trumpet player and vocalist.

King 295-??	(10")	**Russell Jacquet**	1954	100.00	200.00

JAMAL, AHMAD

Ahmad Jamal is a modern jazz pianist.

Epic LN-3212	(M)	**Ahmad Jamal Trio**	1956	20.00	50.00
Epic BN-627	(E)	**Ahmad Jamal Trio**	1959	8.00	20.00

Label & Catalog #		Title	Year	VG+	NM
Epic LN-3631	(M)	**Ahmad Jamal Trio**	1959	12.00	30.00
Epic BN-634	(S)	**Ahmad Jamal Trio**	1959	10.00	25.00
Creative LP-602	(M)	**Chamber Music Of New Jazz**	1956	20.00	50.00
Argo LP-602	(M)	**Chamber Music Of New Jazz** *(Argo 602 is a reissue of Creative 602.)*	1956	12.00	30.00
Argo LP-610	(M)	**Count 'Em 88**	1956	12.00	30.00
Argo LP-628	(M)	**Ahmad Jamal At The Pershing**	1958	12.00	30.00
Argo LPS-628	(S)	**Ahmad Jamal At The Pershing**	1958	8.00	20.00
Argo LP-636	(M)	**Ahmad Jamal Trio—Volume 4**	1958	12.00	30.00
Argo LPS-636	(S)	**Ahmad Jamal Trio—Volume 4**	1958	8.00	20.00
Argo LP-638	(M)	**Portfolio Of Ahmad Jamal** *(2 LPs)*	1958	12.00	30.00
Argo LPS-638	(S)	**Portfolio Of Ahmad Jamal** *(2 LPs)*	1958	12.00	30.00
Argo LP-646	(M)	**Ahmad Jamal At The Penthouse**	1959	8.00	20.00
Argo LPS-646	(S)	**Ahmad Jamal At The Penthouse**	1959	8.00	20.00
Argo LP-662	(M)	**Happy Mood**	1960	8.00	20.00
Argo LPS-662	(S)	**Happy Mood**	1960	8.00	20.00
Argo LP-667	(M)	**Ahmad Jamal At The Pershing, Volume 2**	1961	8.00	20.00
Argo LPS-667	(S)	**Ahmad Jamal At The Pershing, Volume 2**	1961	6.00	15.00
Argo LP-673	(M)	**Listen To Ahmad Jamal**	1961	8.00	20.00
Argo LPS-673	(S)	**Listen To Ahmad Jamal**	1961	6.00	15.00
Argo LP-685	(M)	**Alhambra**	1961	8.00	20.00
Argo LPS-685	(S)	**Alhambra**	1961	6.00	15.00
Argo LP-691	(M)	**All Of You**	1962	8.00	20.00
Argo LPS-691	(S)	**All Of You**	1962	6.00	15.00
Argo LP-703	(M)	**Ahmad Jamal At The Blackhawk**	1962	8.00	20.00
Argo LPS-703	(S)	**Ahmad Jamal At The Blackhawk**	1962	6.00	15.00
Argo LP-712	(M)	**Macanudo**	1962	8.00	20.00
Argo LPS-712	(S)	**Macanudo**	1962	6.00	15.00
Argo LP-719	(M)	**Poin'ci-an'a**	1963	8.00	20.00
Argo LPS-719	(S)	**Poin'ci-an'a**	1963	6.00	15.00
Argo LP-733	(M)	**"Naked City" Theme**	1964	8.00	20.00
Argo LPS-733	(S)	**"Naked City" Theme**	1964	6.00	15.00
Argo LP-751	(M)	**The Roar Of The Greasepaint**	1965	8.00	20.00
Argo LPS-751	(S)	**The Roar Of The Greasepaint**	1965	6.00	15.00
Argo LP-758	(M)	**Extensions**	1965	8.00	20.00
Argo LPS-758	(S)	**Extensions**	1965	6.00	15.00
Cadet LP-764	(M)	**Rhapsody**	1966	6.00	15.00
Cadet LPS-764	(S)	**Rhapsody**	1966	5.00	12.00
Cadet LP-777	(M)	**Heat Wave**	1966	6.00	15.00
Cadet LPS-777	(S)	**Heat Wave**	1966	5.00	12.00
Cadet LP-786	(M)	**Standard Eyes**	1967	6.00	15.00
Cadet LPS-786	(S)	**Standard Eyes**	1967	5.00	12.00
Cadet LP-792	(M)	**Cry Young**	1967	6.00	15.00
Cadet LPS-792	(S)	**Cry Young**	1967	5.00	12.00
Cadet LPS-807	(S)	**The Bright, The Blue And The Beautiful**	1968	5.00	12.00
ABC S-660	(S)	**Tranquility**	1968	5.00	12.00
Impulse AS-9176	(S)	**At The Top—Poinciana Revisited**	1969	6.00	15.00

—Impulse albums above have orange & black labels.—

JAMES, BOB

Robert James is a modern jazz pianist and composer.

Mercury MG-20768	(M)	**Bold Conceptions**	1963	8.00	20.00
Mercury SR-60768	(S)	**Bold Conceptions**	1963	6.00	15.00
ESP-Disk' 1009	(M)	**Explosions**	1965	8.00	20.00
ESP-Disk' 1009	(S)	**Explosions**	1965	6.00	15.00

JAMES, HARRY

Harry James is a traditional jazz trumpet player and big band leader. For additional listings refer to Rosemary Clooney; and the Jazzy Soundtracks section under Columbia.

Columbia CL-6009	(10")	**All-Time Favorites**	1950	20.00	50.00
Columbia CL-6044	(10")	**Trumpet Time**	1950	20.00	50.00
Columbia CL-6088	(10")	**Dance Parade**	1950	20.00	50.00
Columbia CL-6138	(10")	**Your Dance Date**	1950	20.00	50.00
Columbia CL-6207	(10")	**Soft Lights And Sweet Trumpet**	1952	20.00	50.00
Columbia GL-522	(M)	**One Night Stand**	1953	16.00	40.00
Columbia GL-562	(M)	**Harry James At The Hollywood Palladium**	1954	16.00	40.00
Columbia GL-553	(M)	**Trumpet After Midnight**	1954	16.00	40.00
Columbia GL-581	(M)	**Soft Lights And Sweet Trumpet**	1954	16.00	40.00

Label & Catalog #		Title	Year	VG+	NM
Columbia GL-615	(M)	**Juke Box Jamboree**	1955	16.00	40.00
Columbia CL-2527	(10")	**Man With The Horn**	1955	20.00	50.00
		—Columbia albums above have "Long Playing" on the bottom of the label.—			
Columbia CL-522	(M)	**One Night Stand**	195?	12.00	30.00
Columbia CL-562	(M)	**Harry James At The Hollywood Palladium**	195?	12.00	30.00
Columbia CL-553	(M)	**Trumpet After Midnight**	195?	12.00	30.00
Columbia CL-581	(M)	**Soft Lights And Sweet Trumpet**	195?	12.00	30.00
Columbia CL-615	(M)	**Juke Box Jamboree**	195?	12.00	30.00
		—Columbia albums above have three white on black "eye" logos on each abel.—			
Capitol W-654	(M)	**Harry James In Hi-Fi**	1955	12.00	30.00
Capitol W-712	(M)	**More Harry James In Hi-Fi**	1956	12.00	30.00
Capitol T-874	(M)	**Wild About Harry**	1957	12.00	30.00
Capitol T-1093	(M)	**Harry's Choice**	1958	12.00	30.00
		—Capitol albums above have turquoise labels.—			
MGM E-3848	(M)	**Harry James Today**	1960	10.00	25.00
MGM SE-3848	(S)	**Harry James Today**	1960	8.00	20..00

JANIS, CONRAD

Conrad Janis is a traditional jazz-based trombone player and band leader.

Circle L-404	(10")	**Conrad Janis' Tailgate Jazz Band**	1951	20.00	50.00
Jubilee JLP-7	(10")	**Conrad Janis And His Tailgaters**	1954	20.00	50.00
Jubilee JLP-1010	(M)	**Conrad Janis And His Tailgate Five**	1955	16.00	40.00
Riverside RLP-12-215	(M)	**Dixieland Jam Session**	1956	24.00	60.00
		—Riverside albums above have blue on white labels.—			
Riverside RLP-12-215	(M)	**Dixieland Jam Session**	195?	12.00	30.00
		—Riverside albums above have blue mono or black stereo labels with a reel & mike logo on top.—			

JARMAN, JOSEPH

Delmark DS-410	(S)	**Song For**	1968	8.00	20.00
Delmark DS-417	(S)	**As If It Were The Seasons**	1969	8.00	20.00

JARRETT, JEITH

Vortex 2006	(S)	**Life Between The Exit Signs**	1969	6.00	15.00
Vortex 2008	(S)	**Restoration Ruin**	1969	6.00	15.00

JASPAR, BOBBY

Robert Jaspar is a modern jazz tenor saxophone, flute and clarinet player. For additional listings refer to Herbie Mann; The Nutty Squirrels; and the Various Artists section under Prestige.

EmArcy MG-36105	(M)	**Bobby Jaspar And His All Stars**	1957	30.00	75.00
		—EmArcy albums above have blue labels with silver print.—			
Riverside RLP-12-240	(M)	**Bobby Jaspar**	1957	30.00	75.00
		(Riverside 240 also features George Wallington and Idrees Sulieman.)			
		—Riverside albums above have blue on white labels.—			
Riverside RLP-12-240	(M)	**Bobby Jaspar**	195?	16.00	40.00
		—Riverside albums above have blue mono or black stereo labels with a reel & mike logo on top.—			

JAZZ ARTISTS GUILD, THE

The J.A.G. includes Eric Dolphy, Kenny Dorham, Roy Eldridge, Jo Jones, Abbey Lincoln, Charles Mingus and Max Roach.

Candid CD-8022	(M)	**Newport Rebels**	1960	20.00	50.00
Candid CS-9022	(S)	**Newport Rebels**	1960	16.00	40.00

JAZZ BROTHERS, THE

The Jazz Brothers are Chuck and Gap Mangione.

Riverside RLP-335	(M)	**Jazz Brothers**	1960	10.00	25.00
Riverside RS-9335	(S)	**Jazz Brothers**	1960	8.00	20.00
Riverside RLP-371	(M)	**Hey, Baby!**	1961	10.00	25.00
Riverside RS-9371	(S)	**Hey, Baby!**	1961	8.00	20.00
Riverside RLP-405	(M)	**Spring Fever**	1962	10.00	25.00
Riverside RS-9405	(S)	**Spring Fever**	1962	8.00	20.00
		—Riverside albums above have blue mono or black stereo labels with a reel & mike logo on top.—			

JAZZ CITY ALL STARS, THE

Bethlehem BCP-79	(M)	**Jazz City Presents**	1957	20.00	50.00

JAZZ COMPOSERS ORCHESTRA

The JCO includes Gato Barbieri, Don Cherry, Larry Coryell, Pharoah Sanders and Cecil Taylor.

J.C.O.A. LP-1001/2	(S)	**Jazz Composers Orchestra** *(2 LPs with booklet)*	1968	20.00	50.00

Label & Catalog #		Title	Year	VG+	NM
JAZZ CORDS, THE					
Pacific Jazz PJ-10116	(M)	**The Jazz Cords Under The Direction Of Tommy Peltier**	1967	10.00	25.00
Pacific Jazz ST-20116	(M)	**The Jazz Cords Under The Direction Of Tommy Peltier**	1967	6.00	15.00
		(Pacific Jazz 10116 also features Roland Kirk.)			
JAZZ COURIERS, THE					
Britain's Jazz Couriers are Tubby Hayes, Kenny Nepper, Ronnie Scott, Phil Seamen and Terry Shannon.					
Whippet WLP-700	(M)	**The Jazz Couriers**	1956	40.00	100.00
Carlton LP-12-116	(M)	**The Couriers Of Jazz**	1959	20.00	50.00
Carlton ST-12-116	(S)	**The Couriers Of Jazz**	1959	16.00	40.00
Jazzland JLP-34	(M)	**The Message Is From Britain**	1961	12.00	30.00
Jazzland JLP-934	(S)	**Message From Britain**	1961	10.00	25.00
JAZZ CRUSADERS, THE					
The Jazz Crusaders are Wilton Fedler, Wayne Henderson, Nesbert Hooper and Joseph Sample. For additional listings refer to Les McCann.					
Pacific Jazz PJ-27	(M)	**Freedom Sound**	1961	12.00	30.00
Pacific Jazz ST-27	(S)	**Freedom Sound**	1961	10.00	25.00
Pacific Jazz PJ-43	(M)	**Lookin' Ahead**	1962	12.00	30.00
Pacific Jazz ST-43	(S)	**Lookin' Ahead**	1962	10.00	25.00
Pacific Jazz PJ-57	(M)	**The Jazz Crusaders At The Lighthouse**	1962	12.00	30.00
Pacific Jazz ST-57	(S)	**The Jazz Crusaders At The Lighthouse**	1962	10.00	25.00
Pacific Jazz PJ-68	(M)	**Tough Talk**	1963	12.00	30.00
Pacific Jazz ST-68	(S)	**Tough Talk**	1963	10.00	25.00
Pacific Jazz PJ-76	(M)	**Heat Wave**	1963	12.00	30.00
Pacific Jazz ST-76	(S)	**Heat Wave**	1963	10.00	25.00
Pacific Jazz PJ-83	(M)	**Stretchin' Out**	1964	12.00	30.00
Pacific Jazz ST-83	(S)	**Stretchin' Out**	1964	10.00	25.00
Pacific Jazz PJ-87	(M)	**The Thing**	1964	12.00	30.00
Pacific Jazz ST-87	(S)	**The Thing**	1964	10.00	25.00
Pacific Jazz PJ-10092	(M)	**Chile Con Soul**	1965	8.00	20.00
Pacific Jazz ST-20092	(S)	**Chile Con Soul**	1965	6.00	15.00
Pacific Jazz PJ-10098	(M)	**The Jazz Crusaders At Lighthouse '66**	1966	8.00	20.00
Pacific Jazz ST-20098	(S)	**The Jazz Crusaders At Lighthouse '66**	1966	6.00	15.00
Pacific Jazz PJ-10106	(M)	**Talk That Talk**	1966	8.00	20.00
Pacific Jazz ST-20106	(S)	**Talk That Talk**	1966	6.00	15.00
Pacific Jazz PJ-10115	(M)	**The Festival Album**	1967	8.00	20.00
Pacific Jazz ST-20115	(S)	**The Festival Album**	1967	6.00	15.00
Pacific Jazz PJ-10131	(M)	**The Jazz Crusaders At Lighthouse '68**	1968	8.00	20.00
Pacific Jazz ST-20131	(S)	**The Jazz Crusaders At Lighthouse '68**	1968	6.00	15.00
Pacific Jazz ST-20136	(S)	**Powerhouse**	1969	6.00	15.00
Pacific Jazz ST-20165	(S)	**The Jazz Crusaders At Lighthouse '69**	1969	6.00	15.00
Pacific Jazz ST-20175	(S)	**Uh Huh**	1969	6.00	15.00
JAZZ EXPONENTS, THE					
The Jazz Exponents are Norm Diamond, Bill Elliott, Jack Gridley and Dick Riorda.					
Argo LP-622	(M)	**The Jazz Exponents**	1958	16.00	40.00
Argo LPS-622	(S)	**The Jazz Exponents**	1958	12.00	30.00
JAZZ FIVE, THE					
The Jazz Five are Vic Arch, Malcolm Cecil, Brian Dee, Bill Eyden and Barry Klein.					
Riverside RLP-361	(M)	**The Hooter**	1961	12.00	30.00
Riverside RS-9361	(S)	**The Hooter**	1961	10.00	25.00
		—Riverside albums above have blue mono or black stereo labels with a reel & mike logo on top.—			
JAZZ INTERACTIONS ORCHESTRA, THE					
Verve V-8731	(M)	**Jazzhattan Suite**	1967	6.00	15.00
Verve V6-8731	(S)	**Jazzhattan Suite**	1967	5.00	12.00
		—Verve albums above have black labels with "MGM Records" on the bottom.—			
JAZZ MESSENGERS, THE: *Refer to* **ART BLAKEY (& THE JAZZ MESSENGERS)**					
JAZZ MODES, THE (LES JAZZ MODES)					
Les Jazz Modes are Paul Chambers, Ron Jefferson, Gildo Mahones, Oscar Pettiford, Charlie Rouse, Art Taylor and Julius Watkins.					
Dawn DLP-1101	(M)	**Jazzville**	1956	40.00	100.00

The Jazztet was formed by Art Farmer and Benny Golson in 1959 to further the development of Golson's composing and arranging skills. They recorded a mere half dozen albums for Argo and Mercury, each represented here.

Label & Catalog #		Title	Year	VG+	NM
Dawn DLP-1108	(M)	**Les Jazz Modes**	1956	40.00	100.00
Dawn DLP-1117	(M)	**Mood In Scarlet**	1957	40.00	100.00
Seeco SLP-466	(M)	**Smart Jazz For The Smart Set**	1960	12.00	30.00

(Seeco 466 is a reissue of Dawn 1117.)

Label & Catalog #		Title	Year	VG+	NM
Atlantic 1280	(M)	**The Most Happy Fella**	1958	30.00	75.00
Atlantic 1306	(M)	**Les Jazz Modes**	1959	20.00	50.00
Atlantic SD-1306	(S)	**Les Jazz Modes**	1959	20.00	50.00

—Atlantic albums above have black mono or green stereo labels.—

Label & Catalog #		Title	Year	VG+	NM
Atlantic 1280	(M)	**The Most Happy Fella**	1961	12.00	30.00
Atlantic 1306	(M)	**Les Jazz Modes**	1961	12.00	30.00
Atlantic SD-1306	(S)	**Les Jazz Modes**	1961	10.00	25.00

—Atlantic albums above have multi-color labels with a white fan logo.—

JAZZ SYMPHONICS

Label & Catalog #		Title	Year	VG+	NM
Renfro LP-12369	(S)	**The Beginning**	1968	20.00	50.00

JAZZPICKERS, THE

The Jazzpickers feature Red Norvo and Harry Babasin.

Label & Catalog #		Title	Year	VG+	NM
EmArcy MG-36111	(M)	**Jazzpickers**	1957	20.00	50.00
EmArcy MG-36123	(M)	**Command Performance**	1958	20.00	50.00

—EmArcy albums above have blue labels with silver print.—

JAZZTET, THE (THE ART FARMER-BENNY GOLSON JAZZTET)

Label & Catalog #		Title	Year	VG+	NM
Argo LP-664	(M)	**Meet The Jazztet**	1960	16.00	40.00
Argo LPS-664	(S)	**Meet The Jazztet**	1960	12.00	30.00
Argo LP-672	(M)	**Big City Sounds**	1961	12.00	30.00
Argo LPS-672	(S)	**Big City Sounds**	1961	10.00	25.00
Argo LP-684	(M)	**The Jazztet And John Lewis**	1961	12.00	30.00
Argo LPS-684	(S)	**The Jazztet And John Lewis**	1961	10.00	25.00
Argo LP-688	(M)	**The Jazztet At Birdhouse**	1961	12.00	30.00
Argo LPS-688	(S)	**The Jazztet At Birdhouse**	1961	10.00	25.00
Mercury MG-20698	(M)	**Here And Now**	1962	12.00	30.00
Mercury SR-60698	(S)	**Here And Now**	1962	10.00	25.00
Mercury MG-20737	(M)	**Another Git Together**	1962	12.00	30.00
Mercury SR-60737	(S)	**Another Git Together**	1962	10.00	25.00

JEFFERSON, EDDIE

Vocalist Edgar Jefferson is credited with establishing—not inventing—the "vocalese" style of jazz singing.

Label & Catalog #		Title	Year	VG+	NM
Riverside RLP-411	(M)	**Letter From Home**	1962	12.00	30.00
Riverside RS-9411	(S)	**Letter From Home**	1962	16.00	40.00

—Riverside albums above have blue mono or black stereo labels with a reel & mike logo on top.—

Label & Catalog #		Title	Year	VG+	NM
Prestige PRST-7619	(S)	**Body And Soul**	1969	8.00	20.00
Prestige PRST-7698	(S)	**Come Along With Me**	1969	8.00	20.00

—Prestige albums above have blue labels with a trident logo on top.—

JEFFERSON, RON

Roland "Ron" Jefferson is a modern jazz drummer. For additional listings refer to The Jazz Modes.

Label & Catalog #		Title	Year	VG+	NM
Pacific Jazz PJ-36	(M)	**Love Lifted Me**	1962	16.00	40.00
Pacific Jazz ST-36	(S)	**Love Lifted Me**	1962	12.00	30.00

JEFFRIES, FRAN

Fran Jeffries is a jazz-based vocalist backed by Ralph Burns.

Label & Catalog #		Title	Year	VG+	NM
Warwick W-2020	(M)	**Fran Can Really Hang You Up The Most**	1960	16.00	40.00
Warwick W-2020ST	(S)	**Fran Can Really Hang You Up The Most**	1960	20.00	50.00

JEFFRIES, HERB

Herbert Jeffries is a jazz-based vocalist.

Label & Catalog #		Title	Year	VG+	NM
Mercury MG-25089	(10")	**Magenta Moods**	1950	40.00	100.00
Mercury MG-25091	(10")	**Just Jeffries**	1951	40.00	100.00
Coral CRL-56044	(10")	**Time On My Hands**	1951	40.00	100.00
Bethlehem BCP-72	(M)	**Say It Isn't So**	1957	20.00	50.00

JEFFREY, PAUL

Label & Catalog #		Title	Year	VG+	NM
Savoy MG-12192	(S)	**Electrifying Sounds**	1968	6.00	15.00

Label & Catalog #		Title	Year	VG+	NM

JENKINS, JOHN

John Jenkins is a modern jazz alto saxophone player. For additional listings refer to Jackie McLean; Phil Woods & Gene Quill; Phil Woods & Gene Quill / Jackie McLean & John Jenkins / Hal McKusick; and the Various Artists section under New Jazz.

Regent MG-6056	(M)	**Jazz Eyes**	1957	40.00	100.00
Blue Note BLP-1573	(M)	**John Jenkins With Kenny Burrell** *(Deep groove)*	1958	50.00	125.00
Blue Note BLP-1573	(M)	**John Jenkins With Kenny Burrell**	1958	30.00	75.00
Blue Note BST-1573	(S)	**John Jenkins With Kenny Burrell** *(Deep groove)*	1959	30.00	75.00
Blue Note BST-1573	(S)	**John Jenkins With Kenny Burrell**	1959	20.00	50.00

—Blue Note albums above have blue on white labels with a W. 63rd St, NYC address.—

Blue Note BLP-1573	(M)	**John Jenkins With Kenny Burrell**	1963	10.00	25.00
Blue Note BST-1573	(S)	**John Jenkins With Kenny Burrell**	1963	8.00	20.00

—Blue Note albums above have blue on white labels with a New York, USA address.—

Blue Note BST-1573	(S)	**John Jenkins With Kenny Burrell**	196?	5.00	12.00

—Blue Note albums above have blue on white labels with "A Division of Liberty."—

Savoy MG-12201	(M)	**Jazz Eyes**	196?	8.00	20.00

(Savoy 12201 is a reissue of Regent 6056.)

JENKINS, JOHN, & CLIFF JORDAN & BOBBY TIMMONS

New Jazz NJLP-8232	(M)	**Jenkins, Jordan & Timmons**	1960	24.00	60.00

—New Jazz albums above have purple labels.—

New Jazz NJLP-8232	(M)	**Jenkins, Jordan & Timmons**	1965	10.00	25.00

—New Jazz albums above have blue labels with a trident logo on the right side.—

JENKINS, MARV

Orovox 1001	(M)	**Marv Jenkins Arrives**	196?	20.00	50.00
Orovox 1001	(S)	**Marv Jenkins Arrives**	196?	16.00	40.00
Reprise R-6077	(M)	**Good Little Man At The Rubaiyat Room**	1963	10.00	25.00
Reprise R9-6077	(S)	**Good Little Man At The Rubaiyat Room**	1963	8.00	20.00

JENNEY, JACK

Truman "Jack" Jenney is a traditional jazz trombone player.

Columbia GL-100	(10")	**The Golden Era**	1949	20.00	50.00
Columbia ML-4803	(M)	**Jack Jenney**	195?	40.00	100.00

JENNINGS, BILL

William Jennings is a modern jazz guitarist. For additional listings refer to Kenny Burrell / Tiny Grimes / Bill Jennings; Jack McDuff.

King 395-527	(M)	**Billy In The Lion's Den**	1956	40.00	100.00

—King albums above have black labels without a crown on top.—

Audio Lab AL-1514	(M)	**Guitar, Vibes**	1959	40.00	100.00
Prestige PRLP-7164	(M)	**Enough Said!**	1959	20.00	50.00
Prestige PRLP-7177	(M)	**Glide On**	1960	20.00	50.00

—Prestige albums above have yellow mono or silver stereo labels with a Bergenfield, NJ address.—

JOBIM, ANTONIO CARLOS

Brazilian born Antonio Jobim is a Latin jazz guitar and piano player and composer. For additional listings refer to Stan Getz & Joao Gilberto; Herbie Mann & Joao Gilberto; Frank Sinatra; and the Jazzy Soundtracks section under Epic.

Verve V-8547	(M)	**The Composer Of "Desafinado" Plays**	1963	6.00	15.00
Verve V6-8547	(S)	**The Composer Of "Desafinado" Plays**	1963	5.00	12.00

—Verve albums above have black labels with "MGM Records" on the bottom.—

JOHANNSON, JAN

Dot DLP-3416	(M)	**Jan Johannson Trio**	1962	10.00	25.00
Dot DLP-32516	(S)	**Jan Johannson Trio**	1962	8.00	20.00

JOHNSON, BUDD

Albert "Budd" Johnson is a traditional jazz saxophone(s) and clarinet player, vocalist and arranger.

Felsted 2007	(M)	**Blues A La Mode**	1958	30.00	75.00
Felsted 7007	(S)	**Blues A La Mode**	1958	24.00	60.00
Riverside RLP-343	(M)	**Budd Johnson & The Four Brass Giants**	1960	20.00	50.00
Riverside RS-9343	(S)	**Budd Johnson & The Four Brass Giants**	1960	16.00	40.00

(Riverside 343 also features Nat Adderley, Harry Edison, Ray Nance and Clark Terry.)

—Riverside albums above have blue mono or black stereo labels with a reel & mike logo on top.—

Swingville SVLP-2015	(M)	**Let's Swing**	1961	20.00	50.00

—Swingville albums above have purple mono or red stereo labels.—

Label & Catalog #		Title	Year	VG+	NM
Swingville SVLP-2015	(M)	**Let's Swing**	1965	10.00	25.00

—Swingville albums above have blue labels with a trident logo on the right side.—

Argo LP-721	(M)	**French Cookin'**	1963	12.00	30.00
Argo LPS-721	(S)	**French Cookin'**	1963	10.00	25.00
Argo LP-736	(M)	**Ya! Ya!**	1964	12.00	30.00
Argo LPS-736	(S)	**Ya! Ya!**	1964	10.00	25.00
Argo LP-748	(M)	**Off The Wall**	1965	12.00	30.00
Argo LPS-748	(S)	**Off The Wall**	1965	10.00	25.00

JOHNSON, BUDDY (BUDDY & ELLA JOHSON)

Woodrow Wilson "Buddy" Johnson is a traditional jazz and R&B-based pianist, singer, arranger, composer and big band leader. Sister Ella Johnson is a modern blues-based vocalist.

Wing MGW-12005	(M)	**Rock 'N' Roll Stage Show**	1956	40.00	100.00
Mercury MG-20072	(M)	**Buddy Johnson Wails**	1958	30.00	75.00
Mercury MG-20209	(M)	**Rock 'N' Roll**	1958	30.00	75.00
Mercury MG-20322	(M)	**Walkin'**	1958	30.00	75.00
Mercury MG-20347	(M)	**Swing Me**	1958	30.00	75.00
		(Mercury 20347 also features Ella Johnson.)			
Roulette R-25085	(M)	**Go Ahead And Rock And Roll**	1959	30.00	75.00
Roulette SR-25085	(S)	**Go Ahead And Rock And Roll**	1959	50.00	125.00
		(Roulette 25085 also features Ella Johnson.)			

JOHNSON, BUNK

William "Bunk" Johnson is a traditional jazz trumpet, clarinet, piano and saxophone player. For additional listings refer to Sidney Bechet; Ernestine Washington.

Columbia ML-4802	(M)	**The Last Testament Of A Great New Orleans Jazzman**	1950	30.00	75.00
American Music 638	(10")	**Bunk Plays The Blues—The Spirituals**	1951	20.00	50.00
American Music 644	(10")	**Bunk Johnson Talking**	1952	20.00	50.00
Commodore DL-30007	(M)	**The Bunk Johnson Band**	1952	20.00	50.00
Good Time Jazz L-17	(10")	**Bunk Johnson & The Yerba Buena Jazz Band**	1953	20.00	50.00
Columbia GL-520	(M)	**The Last Testament Of A Great New Orleans Jazzman**	1953	20.00	50.00

—Columbia albums above have "Long Playing" on the bottom of the label.—

Columbia CL-520	(M)	**The Last Testament Of A Great New Orleans Jazzman**	1955	16.00	40.00
Columbia CL-829	(M)	**Bunk Johnson**	1955	16.00	40.00

—Columbia albums above have six white on black "eye" logos on each label.—

Good Time Jazz M-12048	(M)	**Bunk Johnson & His Superior Jazz Band**	1962	12.00	30.00
Mainstream 56039	(M)	**Bunk Johnson—A Legend**	1965	8.00	20.00
Mainstream S-6039	(E)	**Bunk Johnson—A Legend**	1965	4.00	10.00

JOHNSON, BUNK, & LU WATTERS

Good Time Jazz L-12024	(M)	**Bunk And Lu**	1955	16.00	40.00

JOHNSON, CHARLIE

Charles Johnson is a traditional jazz pianist.

"X" LVA-3026	(10")	**Harlem In The Twenties, Vol. 2**	1954	20.00	50.00

JOHNSON, DICK

Richard Johnson is a modern jazz alto saxophone and clarinet player. For additional listings refer to Eddie Costa / Mat mathews & Don Elliott.

EmArcy MG-36081	(M)	**Music For Swinging Moderns**	1956	30.00	75.00

—EmArcy albums above have blue labels with silver print.—

Riverside RLP-12-253	(M)	**Most Likely...**	1957	20.00	50.00

—Riverside albums above have blue mono or black stereo labels with a reel & mike logo on top.—

JOHNSON, JAMES P.

James Price Johnson is a traditional jazz pianist, arranger and composer. For additional listings refer to Sidney DeParis / James P. Johnson; Oscar Simeon.

Stinson SLP-21	(10")	**New York Jazz**	1950	50.00	125.00
		(Stinson 21 features cover art by David Stone Martin.)			
Decca DL-5190	(10")	**The Daddy Of The Piano**	1950	40.00	100.00
Decca DL-5228	(10")	**James P. Johnson Plays Fats Waller Favorites**	1950	40.00	100.00
Blue Note BLP-7011	(10")	**Stomps, Rags And Blues**	1951	125.00	250.00
Blue Note BLP-7012	(10")	**Jazz Band Ball**	1951	125.00	250.00
Riverside RLP-1011	(10")	**Rent Party**	1953	40.00	100.00
Riverside RLP-1046	(10")	**Early Harlem Piano, Vol. 2**	1954	40.00	100.00

Label & Catalog #		Title	Year	VG+	NM
Riverside RLP-1056	*(10")*	**Harlem Rent Party**	*1955*	**40.00**	**100.00**
Riverside RLP-12-105	*(M)*	**Rediscovered Early Solos**	*1955*	**24.00**	**60.00**
Riverside RLP-12-151	*(M)*	**Backwater Blues**	*1955*	**24.00**	**60.00**
		—Riverside albums above have blue on white labels.—			
Riverside RLP-12-105	*(M)*	**Rediscovered Early Solos**	*195?*	**12.00**	**30.00**
Riverside RLP-12-151	*(M)*	**Backwater Blues**	*195?*	**12.00**	**30.00**
		—Riverside albums above have blue mono or black stereo labels with a reel & mike logo on top.—			

JOHNSON, JAY JAY (J.J. JOHNSON)

James Louis "Jay Jay" or "J.J." Johnson is a modern jazz trombone player, arranger and composer. For additional listings refer to The Brass Ensemble Of The Jazz & Classical Music Society; Stan Getz & J.J. Johnson; Bennie Green; Andre Previn & J.J. Johnson; Sonny Stitt.

Label & Catalog #		Title	Year	VG+	NM
Blue Note BLP-5028	*(10")*	**Jay Jay Johnson All Stars**	*1953*	**150.00**	**300.00**
Blue Note BLP-5057	*(10")*	**The Eminent Jay Jay Johnson, Volume 2**	*1955*	**150.00**	**300.00**
Blue Note BLP-5070	*(10")*	**Jay Jay Johnson, Volume 3**	*1955*	**150.00**	**300.00**
Blue Note BLP-1505	*(M)*	**The Eminent Jay Jay Johnson, Volume 1** *(Deep groove)*	*1955*	**60.00**	**150.00**
Blue Note BLP-1505	*(M)*	**The Eminent Jay Jay Johnson, Volume 1**	*1955*	**40.00**	**100.00**
Blue Note BLP-1506	*(M)*	**The Eminent Jay Jay Johnson, Volume 2** *(Deep groove)*	*1956*	**60.00**	**150.00**
Blue Note BLP-1506	*(M)*	**The Eminent Jay Jay Johnson, Volume 2** *(Blue Note 1505 and 1506 collect 5028, 5057 and 5070.)*	*1956*	**40.00**	**100.00**
		—Blue Note albums above have blue on white labels with a Lexington Ave, NYC address.—			
Blue Note BLP-1505	*(M)*	**The Eminent Jay Jay Johnson, Volume 1**	*1963*	**10.00**	**25.00**
Blue Note BLP-1506	*(M)*	**The Eminent Jay Jay Johnson, Volume 2**	*1963*	**10.00**	**25.00**
		—Blue Note albums above have blue on white labels with a New York, USA address.—			
Blue Note BST-81505	*(E)*	**The Eminent Jay Jay Johnson, Volume 1**	*196?*	**4.00**	**10.00**
Blue Note BST-81506	*(E)*	**The Eminent Jay Jay Johnson, Volume 2**	*196?*	**4.00**	**10.00**
		—Blue Note albums above have blue on white labels with "A Division of Liberty Records."—			
Columbia CL-935	*(M)*	**"J" Is For Jazz**	*1956*	**20.00**	**50.00**
Columbia CL-1030	*(M)*	**First Place**	*1957*	**20.00**	**50.00**
Columbia CL-1084	*(M)*	**Dial J.J. 5**	*1957*	**20.00**	**50.00**
Columbia CL-1161	*(M)*	**J.J. In Person**	*1958*	**20.00**	**50.00**
Columbia CS-8009	*(S)*	**J.J. In Person**	*1959*	**16.00**	**40.00**
Columbia CL-1303	*(M)*	**Blue Trombone**	*1959*	**20.00**	**50.00**
Columbia CS-8109	*(S)*	**Blue Trombone**	*1959*	**16.00**	**40.00**
Columbia CL-1383	*(M)*	**Really Livin'**	*1959*	**20.00**	**50.00**
Columbia CS-8178	*(S)*	**Really Livin'**	*1959*	**16.00**	**40.00**
Columbia CL-1547	*(M)*	**Trombone & Voices**	*1960*	**14.00**	**35.00**
Columbia CS-8347	*(S)*	**Trombone & Voices**	*1960*	**12.00**	**30.00**
Columbia CL-1606	*(M)*	**J.J., Inc.**	*1961*	**14.00**	**35.00**
Columbia CS-8406	*(S)*	**J.J., Inc.**	*1961*	**12.00**	**30.00**
Columbia CL-1737	*(M)*	**A Touch Of Satin**	*1962*	**14.00**	**35.00**
Columbia CS-8537	*(S)*	**A Touch Of Satin**	*1962*	**12.00**	**30.00**
		—Columbia albums above have six white on black "eye" logos on each label.—			
Columbia CL-935	*(M)*	**"J" Is For Jazz**	*196?*	**5.00**	**12.00**
Columbia CL-1030	*(M)*	**First Place**	*196?*	**5.00**	**12.00**
Columbia CL-1084	*(M)*	**Dial J.J. 5**	*196?*	**5.00**	**12.00**
Columbia CL-1161	*(M)*	**J.J. In Person**	*196?*	**5.00**	**12.00**
Columbia CS-8009	*(S)*	**J.J. In Person**	*196?*	**4.00**	**10.00**
Columbia CL-1303	*(M)*	**Blue Trombone**	*196?*	**5.00**	**12.00**
Columbia CS-8109	*(S)*	**Blue Trombone**	*196?*	**4.00**	**10.00**
Columbia CL-1383	*(M)*	**Really Livin'**	*196?*	**5.00**	**12.00**
Columbia CS-8178	*(S)*	**Really Livin'**	*196?*	**4.00**	**10.00**
Columbia CL-1547	*(M)*	**Trombone & Voices**	*196?*	**5.00**	**12.00**
Columbia CS-8347	*(S)*	**Trombone & Voices**	*196?*	**4.00**	**10.00**
Columbia CL-1606	*(M)*	**J.J., Inc.**	*196?*	**5.00**	**12.00**
Columbia CS-8406	*(S)*	**J.J., Inc.**	*196?*	**4.00**	**10.00**
Columbia CL-1737	*(M)*	**A Touch Of Satin**	*196?*	**5.00**	**12.00**
Columbia CS-8537	*(S)*	**A Touch Of Satin**	*196?*	**4.00**	**10.00**
		—Columbia albums above have "360 Sound" in white on the bottom of the label.—			
Verve V-8530	*(M)*	**J.J.'s Broadway**	*1963*	**10.00**	**25.00**
Verve V6-8530	*(S)*	**J.J.'s Broadway**	*1963*	**8.00**	**20.00**
		—Verve albums above have black labels with "MGM Records" on the bottom.—			
Impulse A-68	*(M)*	**Proof Positive**	*1965*	**12.00**	**30.00**
Impulse AS-68	*(S)*	**Proof Positive**	*1965*	**10.00**	**25.00**
		—Impulse albums above have orange & black labels.—			

J.J. Johnson began touring with the bands of Clarence Love (1941-42), Snookum Russell (1942), Benny Carter (1942-45), Count Basie (1945-46), Illinois Jacquet (1947-49), Woody Herman, Dizzy Gillespie and Oscar Pettiford (1951-52). After retiring for nearly two years, he formed a group with Kai Winding (the Jay & Kay Quartet), a pairing that was artistically and commercially successful for years, then extended that into the "trombone by three" setting that included Bennie Green. He established himself as the primary bop trombonist *and* a capable modern composer and has recorded with Stan Getz and as a member of The Brass Ensemble Of The Jazz & Classical Music Society. He has been a featured soloist with Benny Green and Sonny Stitt, and a sideman on LPs with Miles Davis on Capitol, Blue Note and Prestige, and Coleman Hawkins on Riverside.

Label & Catalog #		Title	Year	VG+	NM
Impulse AS-68	(S)	**Proof Positive**	1968	4.00	10.00
		—Impulse albums above have red & black labels with the "abc" logo on top.—			
RCA Victor LPM-3350	(M)	**J.J.!**	1965	10.00	25.00
RCA Victor LSP-3350	(S)	**J.J.!**	1965	8.00	20.00
RCA Victor LPM-3458	(M)	**Goodies**	1965	10.00	25.00
RCA Victor LSP-3458	(S)	**Goodies**	1965	8.00	20.00
RCA Victor LPM-3544	(M)	**Broadway Express**	1966	10.00	25.00
RCA Victor LSP-3544	(S)	**Broadway Express**	1966	8.00	20.00
RCA Victor LPM-3833	(M)	**The Total J.J. Johnson**	1967	12.00	30.00
RCA Victor LSP-3833	(S)	**The Total J.J. Johnson**	1967	8.00	20.00
		—RCA albums above have black labels with "Monaural" or "Stereo" on the bottom.—			
A&M SP-3008	(S)	**Israel**	1968	4.00	10.00

JOHNSON, JAY JAY / BENNIE GREEN

Label & Catalog #		Title	Year	VG+	NM
Prestige PRLP-123	(10")	**Modern Jazz Trombones, Volume 2**	1952	100.00	200.00

JOHNSON, JAY JAY, & KAI WINDING

Label & Catalog #		Title	Year	VG+	NM
Prestige PRLP-109	(10")	**Modern Jazz Trombones**	1951	100.00	200.00
Prestige PRLP-195	(10")	**Jay And Kai**	1954	100.00	200.00
Prestige PRLP-7253	(M)	**Looking Back**	1963	20.00	50.00
Prestige PRST-7253	(E)	**Looking Back**	1963	14.00	35.00
		—Prestige albums above have yellow mono or silver stereo labels with a Bergenfield, NJ address.—			
Savoy MG-15038	(10")	**Jay And Kai**	1954	40.00	100.00
Savoy MG-15048	(10")	**Jay And Kai, Volume 2**	1955	40.00	100.00
Savoy MG-15049	(10")	**Jay And Kai, Volume 3**	1955	40.00	100.00
Savoy MG-12010	(M)	**Jay & Kai**	1955	30.00	75.00
		(Savoy 12010 is a reissue of 15038 and 15048.)			
Savoy MG-12106	(M)	**J.J. Johnson's Jazz Quintets**	1957	30.00	75.00
		(Savoy 12106 is a reissue of 15049.)			
Vik LXA-1040	(M)	**An Afternoon At Birdland**	1955	30.00	75.00
Bethlehem BCP-13	(M)	**Kai Winding & J.J. Johnson**	1955	30.00	75.00
Bethlehem BCP-6001	(M)	**East Coast Jazz 7**	1956	20.00	50.00
		(Bethlehem 6001 is a reissue of 13.)			
Columbia CL-2573	(10")	**Kai + J.J.**	1956	30.00	75.00
Columbia CL-742	(M)	**Trombone For Two**	1956	20.00	50.00
Columbia CL-892	(M)	**J.J. Johnson/Kai Winding + Six**	1956	20.00	50.00
Columbia CL-973	(M)	**Jay And Kai**	1957	20.00	50.00
		(Columbia 973 is a reissue of 2573.)			
		—Columbia albums above have six white on black "eye" logos on each label.—			
Columbia CL-742	(M)	**Trombone For Two**	196?	8.00	20.00
Columbia CL-892	(M)	**J.J. Johnson/Kai Winding + Six**	196?	8.00	20.00
Columbia CL-973	(M)	**Jay And Kai**	196?	8.00	20.00
		—Columbia albums above have "360 Sound" in white on the bottom of the label.—			
Impulse A-1	(M)	**The Great Kai & J.J.**	1961	12.00	30.00
Impulse AS-1	(S)	**The Great Kai & J.J.**	1961	10.00	25.00
		—Impulse albums above have orange & black labels.—			
Impulse AS-1	(S)	**The Great Kai & J.J.**	1968	4.00	10.00
		—Impulse albums above have red & black labels with the "abc" logo on top.—			

JOHNSON, JAY JAY, & KAI WINDING / BENNIE GREEN

For additional listings refer to Dave Brubeck / J.J. Johnson & Kai Winding; the "Jazz At 16 2/3 RPM" article.

Label & Catalog #		Title	Year	VG+	NM
Debut DLP-5	(10")	**Jazz Workshop, Vol. 1**	1953	100.00	200.00
Debut DLP-14	(10")	**Jazz Workshop, Vol. 2**	1955	100.00	200.00
Prestige PRLP-7023	(M)	**Trombone By Three**	1956	30.00	75.00
Prestige PRLP-7030	(M)	**J.J. Johnson, Kai Winding, Bennie Green**	1956	30.00	75.00
		—Prestige albums above have yellow labels with a W. 50th Street, NYC address.—			
Debut DEB-126	(M)	**Four Trombones**	1958	40.00	100.00
		(Debut 125 is a reissue of 5 and 14.)			
Fantasy 6005	(M)	**Four Trombones** *(Red vinyl)*	1963	20.00	50.00
Fantasy 6005	(M)	**Four Trombones**	1963	12.00	30.00
Fantasy 86005	(E)	**Four Trombones** *(Blue vinyl)*	1963	12.00	30.00
Fantasy 86005	(E)	**Four Trombones**	1963	6.00	15.00
		(Fantasy 6005 is a reissue of Debut 125.)			

JOHNSON, OSIE

James Osie Johnson is a traditional jazz drummer, vocalist and composer. For additional listings refer to Pia Beck; The Brass Ensemble Of The Jazz & Classical Music Society; The Manhattan Jazz Septette.

Label & Catalog #		Title	Year	VG+	NM
Period SPL-1108	(10")	**Osie's Oasis**	1955	30.00	75.00

Label & Catalog #		Title	Year	VG+	NM
Period SPL-1112	(10")	**Johnson's Whacks**	1955	30.00	75.00
Jazztone J-1234	(M)	**Swingin' Sounds**	1956	16.00	40.00
		(Jazztone 1234 reissues Period 1108 and 1112.)			
Bethlehem BCP-66	(M)	**The Happy Jazz Of Osie Johnson**	1957	20.00	50.00
RCA Victor LPM-1369	(M)	**A Bit Of The Blues**	1957	20.00	50.00
		—RCA albums above have black labels with "Long Play" on the bottom.—			

JOHNSON, PETE

Pete Johnson is a traditional jazz pianist. For additional listings refer to Albert Ammons / Pete Johnson; Erroll Garner / Pete Johnson; Joe Turner / Pete Johnson.

Label & Catalog #		Title	Year	VG+	NM
Blue Note BLP-7019	(10")	**Boogie Woogie Blues And Skiffle**	1952	125.00	250.00
RCA Victor LPT-9	(10")	**Eight To The Bar**	195?	40.00	100.00
Brunswick BL-58041	(10")	**Boogie Woogie Mood**	1953	30.00	75.00
Riverside RLP-1056	(10")	**Jumpin' With Pete Johnson**	1955	30.00	75.00
Savoy MG-14018	(M)	**Pete's Blues**	1958	50.00	125.00

JOHNSON, PLAS

Plas Johnson is a jazz-based saxophone player. For additional listings refer to the Jazzy Soundtracks section under RCA Victor.

Label & Catalog #		Title	Year	VG+	NM
Tampa TP-24	(M)	**Bop Me, Daddy** *(Colored vinyl)*	1957	40.00	100.00
Tampa TP-24	(M)	**Bop Me, Daddy**	1958	16.00	40.00
Capitol T-1281	(M)	**This Must Be The Plas!**	1960	12.00	30.00
Capitol ST-1281	(S)	**This Must Be The Plas!**	1960	10.00	25.00
Capitol T-1503	(M)	**Mood For The Blues**	1961	10.00	25.00
Capitol ST-1503	(S)	**Mood For The Blues**	1961	8.00	20.00

JOLLY, PETE

Peter Ceragioli, aka Pete Jolly, is a West Coast jazz pianist. For additional listings refer to The Five.

Label & Catalog #		Title	Year	VG+	NM
RCA Victor LPM-1105	(M)	**Jolly Jumps In**	1955	20.00	50.00
RCA Victor LPM-1125	(M)	**Duo, Trio, Quartet**	1955	20.00	50.00
RCA Victor LPM-1367	(M)	**When Lights Are Low**	1957	20.00	50.00
		—RCA albums above have black labels with "Long Play" on the bottom.—			
Metrojazz E-1014	(M)	**Impossible**	1958	16.00	40.00
Metrojazz SE-1014	(S)	**Impossible**	1958	12.00	30.00
Stereo Fidelity SF-11000	(M)	**Continental Jazz**	1960	10.00	25.00
Stereo Fidelity SFS-11000	(S)	**Continental Jazz**	1960	8.00	20.00
Charlie Parker PLP-825	(M)	**Pete Jolly Gasses Everybody**	1962	10.00	25.00
Charlie Parker PLP-825S	(S)	**Pete Jolly Gasses Everybody**	1962	8.00	20.00
Ava A-22	(M)	**Little Bird**	1963	10.00	25.00
Ava AS-22	(S)	**Little Bird**	1963	8.00	20.00
Ava A-39	(M)	**Sweet September**	1963	10.00	25.00
Ava AS-39	(S)	**Sweet September**	1963	8.00	20.00
MGM E-4127	(M)	**5 O' Clock Shadows**	1963	10.00	25.00
MGM SE-4127	(S)	**5 O' Clock Shadows**	1963	8.00	20.00
Columbia CL-2397	(M)	**Too Much, Baby**	1965	12.00	30.00
Columbia CS-9197	(S)	**Too Much, Baby**	1965	8.00	20.00
		—Columbia albums above have "360 Sound " in white on the bottom of the label.—			
A&M SP-4145	(S)	**Herb Alpert Presents Pete Jolly**	1968	4.00	10.00
A&M SP-3033	(S)	**Seasons**	1969	4.00	10.00

JONES, CARMELL

Carmell Jones is a West Coast jazz trumpet player. For additional listings refer to Tricky Lofton & Carmell Jones; Charles McPherson; Bud Shank; and the Jazzy Soundtracks section under Pacific Jazz.

Label & Catalog #		Title	Year	VG+	NM
Pacific Jazz PJ-29	(M)	**The Remarkable Carmell Jones**	1961	20.00	50.00
Pacific Jazz ST-29	(S)	**The Remarkable Carmell Jones**	1961	16.00	40.00
		(Pacific Jazz 29 also features Harold Land)			
Pacific Jazz PJ-53	(M)	**Business Meetin'**	1962	20.00	50.00
Pacific Jazz ST-53	(S)	**Business Meetin'**	1962	16.00	40.00
Pacific Jazz ST-53	(S)	**Business Meetin'** *(Colored vinyl)*	1962	30.00	75.00
		(Pacific Jazz 53 also features Gerald Wilson.)			
Prestige PRLP-7401	(M)	**Jay Hawk Talk**	1965	16.00	40.00
Prestige PRST-7401	(S)	**Jay Hawk Talk**	1965	12.00	30.00
		—Prestige albums above have blue labels with a trident logo on the right side.—			
Prestige PRST-7669	(S)	**Carmell Jones In Europe**	1969	6.00	15.00
		—Prestige albums above have blue labels with a trident logo on top.—			

Label & Catalog #		Title	Year	VG+	NM

JONES, ELVIN

Elvin Jones is a modern jazz drummer. For additional listings refer to Jaki Byard; Philly Joe & Elvin Jones; The Jones Brothers; Roland Kirk; Jimmy Woods; and the Various Artists section under Prestige.

Riverside RLP-409	(M)	**Elvin!**	1962	12.00	30.00
Riverside RS-9409	(S)	**Elvin!**	1962	10.00	25.00
—Riverside albums above have blue mono or black stereo labels with a reel & mike logo on top.—					
Impulse A-88	(M)	**Dear John C.**	1965	12.00	30.00
Impulse AS-88	(S)	**Dear John C.**	1965	10.00	25.00
Impulse A-9160	(M)	**Heavy Sounds**	1967	10.00	25.00
Impulse AS-9160	(S)	**Heavy Sounds**	1967	8.00	20.00
—Impulse albums above have orange & black labels.—					
Impulse AS-88	(S)	**Dear John C.**	1968	4.00	10.00
Impulse AS-9160	(S)	**Heavy Sounds**	1968	4.00	10.00
—Impulse albums above have red & black labels with the "abc" logo on top.—					
Atlantic 1443	(M)	**And Then Again**	1965	10.00	25.00
Atlantic SD-1443	(S)	**And Then Again**	1965	8.00	20.00
Atlantic 1485	(M)	**Midnight Walk**	1967	10.00	25.00
Atlantic SD-1485	(S)	**Midnight Walk**	1967	8.00	20.00
—Atlantic albums above have multi-color labels with a black fan logo.—					
Blue Note BST-84282	(S)	**Puttin' It Together**	1968	10.00	25.00
Blue Note BST-84305	(S)	**The Ultimate Elvin Jones**	1969	10.00	25.00
Blue Note BST-84331	(S)	**Poly-Currents**	1969	10.00	25.00
— Blue Note albums above have blue on white labels with "A Division of Liberty Records."—					

JONES, ELVIN, & JIMMY GARRISON SEXTETTE (FEATURING McCOY TYNER)

Impulse A-49	(M)	**Illumination**	1963	12.00	30.00
Impulse AS-49	(S)	**Illumination**	1963	10.00	25.00
—Impulse albums above have orange & black labels.—					

JONES, ETTA

Etta Jones is a modern jazz vocalist. For additional listings refer to Gene Ammons.

King 395-544	(M)	**The Jones Girl... Etta**	1958	60.00	150.00
King 707	(M)	**Etta Jones Sings**	1960	30.00	75.00
		(King 707 is a reissue of 544.)			
Prestige PRLP-7186	(M)	**Don't Go To Strangers**	1960	20.00	50.00
Prestige PRST-7186	(S)	**Don't Go To Strangers**	1960	16.00	40.00
Prestige PRLP-7194	(M)	**Something Nice**	1961	20.00	50.00
Prestige PRLP-7204	(M)	**So Warm—Etta Jones & Strings**	1961	20.00	50.00
Prestige PRST-7204	(S)	**So Warm—Etta Jones & Strings**	1961	16.00	40.00
Prestige PRLP-7214	(M)	**From The Heart**	1961	20.00	50.00
Prestige PRST-7214	(S)	**From The Heart**	1961	16.00	40.00
Prestige PRLP-7241	(M)	**Lonely And Blue**	1962	20.00	50.00
Prestige PRST-7241	(S)	**Lonely And Blue**	1962	16.00	40.00
Prestige PRLP-7272	(M)	**Love Shout**	1963	20.00	50.00
Prestige PRST-7272	(S)	**Love Shout**	1963	16.00	40.00
Prestige PRLP-7284	(M)	**Hollar!**	1963	20.00	50.00
Prestige PRST-7284	(S)	**Hollar!**	1963	16.00	40.00
—Prestige albums above have yellow mono or silver stereo labels with a Bergenfield, NJ address.—					
Prestige PRLP-7186	(M)	**Don't Go To Strangers**	196?	10.00	25.00
Prestige PRST-7186	(S)	**Don't Go To Strangers**	196?	8.00	20.00
Prestige PRLP-7194	(M)	**Something Nice**	196?	10.00	25.00
Prestige PRLP-7204	(M)	**So Warm—Etta Jones & Strings**	196?	10.00	25.00
Prestige PRST-7204	(S)	**So Warm—Etta Jones & Strings**	196?	8.00	20.00
Prestige PRLP-7214	(M)	**From The Heart**	196?	10.00	25.00
Prestige PRST-7214	(S)	**From The Heart**	196?	8.00	20.00
Prestige PRLP-7241	(M)	**Lonely And Blue**	196?	10.00	25.00
Prestige PRST-7241	(S)	**Lonely And Blue**	196?	8.00	20.00
Prestige PRLP-7272	(M)	**Love Shout**	196?	10.00	25.00
Prestige PRST-7272	(S)	**Love Shout**	196?	8.00	20.00
Prestige PRLP-7284	(M)	**Hollar!**	196?	10.00	25.00
Prestige PRST-7284	(S)	**Hollar!**	196?	8.00	20.00
Prestige PRLP-7443	(M)	**Etta Jones' Greatest Hits**	1967	10.00	25.00
Prestige PRST-7443	(E)	**Etta Jones' Greatest Hits**	1967	6.00	15.00
—Prestige albums above have blue labels with a trident logo on the right side.—					
Roulette R-25329	(M)	**Etta Jones Sings**	1965	10.00	25.00
Roulette SR-25329	(S)	**Etta Jones Sings**	1965	8.00	20.00

Singer Etta Jones began her career as a singer for the almost exclusively rhythm 'n' blues-based King Records. She moved to Prestige, where she recorded seven albums accompanied by some of the finest musicians jazz had to offer.

Label & Catalog #		Title	Year	VG+	NM

JONES, HANK

Henry Jones is a traditional jazz pianist. For additional listings refer to The Four Most; The Jones Brothers; The Trio; and the Various Artists section under Savoy.

Label & Catalog #		Title	Year	VG+	NM
Mercury MG-25022	(10")	**Hank Jones Piano**	1950	100.00	200.00
Mercury MG-35014	(10")	**Hank Jones Piano**	1950	100.00	200.00
Mercury MGC-100	(10")	**Hank Jones Piano**	1950	60.00	150.00
		(Mercury 100 features cover art by David Stone Martin.)			
Clef MGC-100	(10")	**Hank Jones Piano**	1953	40.00	100.00
Clef MGC-707	(M)	**Urbanity—Piano Solos By Hank Jones**	1956	40.00	100.00
		(Clef 707 is a reissue of 100 with cover art by David Stone Martin.)			
Verve MGV-8091	(M)	**Urbanity—Piano Solos By Hank Jones**	1957	30.00	75.00
		(Verve 8091 is a reissue of Clef 707 with the DSM cover.)			
		—Verve albums above have black labels with "Verve Records, Inc." on the bottom.—			
Verve V-8091	(M)	**Urbanity—Piano Solos By Hank Jones**	1961	10.00	25.00
		—Verve albums above have black labels with "MGM Records" on the bottom.—			
Savoy MG-12037	(M)	**Hank Jones Quartet-Quintet**	1955	30.00	75.00
Savoy MG-12053	(M)	**The Trio**	1956	30.00	75.00
Savoy MG-12084	(M)	**Have You Met Hank Jones**	1956	30.00	75.00
Savoy MG-12087	(M)	**Hank Jones Trio**	1956	30.00	75.00
Golden Crest GC-3042	(M)	**Hank Jones Swings "Gigi"**	1958	20.00	50.00
Golden Crest GC-5002	(S)	**Hank Jones Swings "Gigi"**	1959	16.00	40.00
Capitol T-1044	(M)	**The Talented Touch Of Hank Jones**	1958	16.00	40.00
Capitol ST-1044	(S)	**The Talented Touch Of Hank Jones**	1958	12.00	30.00
Capitol T-1175	(M)	**Porgy & Bess**	1959	16.00	40.00
Capitol ST-1175	(S)	**Porgy & Bess**	1959	12.00	30.00
		—Capitol albums above have black "rainbow" labels with the logo on the left side.—			
RCA Victor LPM-2570	(M)	**Arrival Time**	1962	12.00	30.00
RCA Victor LSP-2570	(S)	**Arrival Time**	1962	10.00	25.00
		—RCA albums above have black labels with "Long Play" or "Living Stereo" on the bottom.—			
Argo LP-728	(M)	**Here's Love**	1963	10.00	25.00
Argo LPS-728	(S)	**Here's Love**	1963	8.00	20.00
ABC-Paramount ABC-496	(M)	**This Is Ragtime Now**	1964	8.00	20.00
ABC-Paramount ABCS-496	(S)	**This Is Ragtime Now**	1964	6.00	15.00

JONES, JO

Jonathon Jones is a traditional jazz-based drummer. For additional listings refer to Blossom Dearie; Coleman Hawkins; Roy Eldridge, Pete Brown & Jo Jones; Jazz Artists Guild; Jones Boys; Oscar Peterson.

Label & Catalog #		Title	Year	VG+	NM
Vanguard VRS-8503	(M)	**Jo Jones Special**	1955	24.00	60.00
Jazztone J-1242	(M)	**Jo Jones Special**	1956	16.00	40.00
		(Jazztone 1242 is a reissue of Vanguard 8503.)			
Vanguard VRS-8525	(M)	**Jo Jones Plus Two**	1959	16.00	40.00
Vanguard VSD-2031	(S)	**Jo Jones Plus Two**	1959	12.00	30.00
Everest LPBR-5023	(M)	**Jo Jones Trio**	1959	12.00	30.00
Everest SDBR-1023	(S)	**Jo Jones Trio**	1959	10.00	25.00
Everest LPBR-5099	(M)	**Vamp Till Ready**	1960	12.00	30.00
Everest SDBR-1099	(S)	**Vamp Till Ready**	1960	10.00	25.00
Everest LPBR-5110	(M)	**Percussion & Bass**	1960	12.00	30.00
Everest SDBR-1110	(S)	**Percussion & Bass**	1960	10.00	25.00

JONES, JOE

Joseph Jones is a modern jazz-influenced guitar player.

Label & Catalog #		Title	Year	VG+	NM
Prestige PRST-7557	(S)	**Mindbender**	1968	6.00	15.00
Prestige PRST-7617	(S)	**My Fire**	1969	6.00	15.00
Prestige PRST-7697	(S)	**Boogaloo Jones**	1969	6.00	15.00
		—Prestige albums above have blue labels with a trident logo on top.—			

JONES, JONAH

Robert "Jonah" Jones is a traditional jazz trumpet player and vocalist. For additional listings refer to Pete Brown / Jonah Jones; Jack Teagarden / Jonah Jones.

Label & Catalog #		Title	Year	VG+	NM
Bethlehem BCP-1014	(10")	**Jonah Jones Sextet**	1954	40.00	100.00
Angel ANG-60005	(10")	**Jonah Wails—1st Blast**	1954	30.00	75.00
Angel ANG-60006	(10")	**Jonah Wails—2nd Wind**	1954	30.00	75.00
Groove LG-1001	(M)	**Jonah Jones At The Embers**	1956	20.00	50.00
Vik LXA-1135	(M)	**Jonah Jones At The Embers**	1958	16.00	40.00
		(Vik 1135 is a reissue of Groove 1001.)			
RCA Victor LPM-2004	(M)	**Jonah Jones At The Embers**	1959	16.00	40.00
		(RCA Victor 2004 is a reissue of Vik 1135.)			
		—RCA albums above have black labels with "Long Play" on the bottom.—			

Label & Catalog #		Title	Year	VG+	NM
Capitol T-839	(M)	**Muted Jazz**	1957	16.00	40.00
Capitol T-963	(M)	**Swingin' On Broadway**	1958	16.00	40.00

—Capitol albums above have turquoise labels.—

Capitol T-1039	(M)	**Jumpin' With Jonah**	1958	12.00	30.00
Capitol ST-1039	(S)	**Jumpin' With Jonah**	1958	10.00	25.00
Capitol T-1083	(M)	**Swingin' At The Cinema**	1958	12.00	30.00
Capitol ST-1083	(S)	**Swingin' At The Cinema**	1958	10.00	25.00
Capitol T-1115	(M)	**Jonah Jumps Again**	1959	12.00	30.00
Capitol ST-1115	(S)	**Jonah Jumps Again**	1959	10.00	25.00
Capitol T-1193	(M)	**I Dig Chicks**	1959	10.00	25.00
Capitol ST-1193	(S)	**I Dig Chicks**	1959	8.00	20.00
Capitol T-1237	(M)	**Swingin' 'Round The World**	1959	10.00	25.00
Capitol ST-1237	(S)	**Swingin' 'Round The World**	1959	8.00	20.00
Capitol T-1375	(M)	**Hit Me Again!**	1960	10.00	25.00
Capitol ST-1375	(S)	**Hit Me Again!**	1960	8.00	20.00
Capitol T-1405	(M)	**A Touch Of Blue**	1960	10.00	25.00
Capitol ST-1405	(S)	**A Touch Of Blue**	1960	8.00	20.00
Capitol T-1532	(M)	**The Unsinkable Molly Brown**	1961	10.00	25.00
Capitol ST-1532	(S)	**The Unsinkable Molly Brown**	1961	8.00	20.00
Capitol T-1557	(M)	**Great Instrumental Hits Styled By Jonah Jones**	1961	10.00	25.00
Capitol ST-1557	(S)	**Great Instrumental Hits Styled By Jonah Jones**	1961	8.00	20.00
Capitol T-1641	(M)	**Broadway Swings Again**	1961	10.00	25.00
Capitol ST-1641	(S)	**Broadway Swings Again**	1961	8.00	20.00
Capitol T-1660	(M)	**Jonah Jones/Glenn Gray**	1961	10.00	25.00
Capitol ST-1660	(S)	**Jonah Jones/Glenn Gray**	1961	8.00	20.00

—Capitol albums above have black labels with the logo on the left side.—

Capitol T-1773	(M)	**Jazz Bonus**	1962	6.00	15.00
Capitol ST-1773	(S)	**Jazz Bonus**	1962	5.00	12.00
Capitol T-1948	(M)	**And Now, In Person—Jonah Jones**	1963	6.00	15.00
Capitol ST-1948	(S)	**And Now, In Person—Jonah Jones**	1963	5.00	12.00
Capitol T-2087	(M)	**Blowin' Up A Storm**	1964	6.00	15.00
Capitol ST-2087	(S)	**Blowin' Up A Storm**	1964	5.00	12.00

—Capitol albums above have black "rainbow" labels with the logo on top.—

Decca DL-4638	(M)	**Hello Broadway**	1965	6.00	15.00
Decca DL-74638	(S)	**Hello Broadway**	1965	5.00	12.00
Decca DL-4688	(M)	**On The Sunny Side Of The Street**	1966	6.00	15.00
Decca DL-74688	(S)	**On The Sunny Side Of The Street**	1966	5.00	12.00

JONES, JONAH / CHARLIE SHAVERS

Bethlehem BCP-6034	(M)	**Sounds Of The Trumpets**	1959	16.00	40.00

JONES, PHILLY JOE

Joseph "Philly Joe" Jones is a modern jazz drummer. For additional listings refer to Kenny Drew & Paul Chambers & Philly Joe Jones

Riverside RLP-12-282	(M)	**Blues For Dracula**	1958	20.00	50.00
Riverside RLP-12-302	(M)	**Drums Around The World**	1959	20.00	50.00
Riverside RLP-1147	(M)	**Drums Around The World**	1959	16.00	40.00
Riverside RLP-12-313	(M)	**Showcase**	1959	20.00	50.00
Riverside RLP-1159	(M)	**Showcase**	1959	16.00	40.00

—Riverside albums above have blue mono or black stereo labels with a reel & mike logo on top.—

Atlantic 1340	(M)	**Philly Joe's Beat**	1960	12.00	30.00
Atlantic SD-1340	(S)	**Philly Joe's Beat**	1960	10.00	25.00

—Atlantic albums above have multi-color labels with a white fan logo.—

Atlantic 1340	(M)	**Philly Joe's Beat**	196?	5.00	12.00
Atlantic SD-1340	(S)	**Philly Joe's Beat**	196?	4.00	10.00

—Atlantic albums above have multi-color labels with a black fan logo.—

JONES, PHILLY JOE, & ELVIN JONES

Atlantic 1428	(M)	**Together**	1964	12.00	30.00
Atlantic SD-1428	(S)	**Together**	1964	10.00	25.00

—Atlantic albums above have multi-color labels with a black fan logo.—

JONES, QUINCY

Quincy Jones Jr. is a modern jazz trumpet player, arranger and composer who is known for his soundtrack work and pop productions. For additional listing s refer to Billy Eckstine; Astrud Gilberto; Roy Haynes / Quincy Jones; The Jones Boys; Dinah Washington; and the Jazzy Soundtracks section under Verve.

Prestige PRLP-172	(10")	**Quincy Jones With The Swedish/U.S. All Stars**	1953	60.00	150.00
ABC-Paramount ABC-149	(M)	**This Is How I Feel About Jazz**	1957	30.00	75.00

Label & Catalog #		Title	Year	VG+	NM
ABC-Paramount ABC-186	(M)	**Go West, Man!**	1957	30.00	75.00
Mercury MG-20444	(M)	**Birth Of A Band**	1959	16.00	40.00
Mercury SR-60129	(S)	**Birth Of A Band**	1959	12.00	30.00
Mercury MG-20561	(M)	**The Great Wide World Of Quincy Jones**	1960	12.00	30.00
Mercury SR-60221	(S)	**The Great Wide World Of Quincy Jones**	1960	10.00	25.00
Mercury MG-20612	(M)	**I Dig Dancers**	1961	10.00	25.00
Mercury SR-60612	(S)	**I Dig Dancers**	1961	8.00	20.00
Mercury MG-20614	(M)	**Around The World**	1961	10.00	25.00
Mercury SR-60614	(S)	**Around The World**	1961	8.00	20.00
Mercury MG-20653	(M)	**Quincy Jones At Newport '61**	1961	10.00	25.00
Mercury SR-60653	(S)	**Quincy Jones At Newport '61**	1961	8.00	20.00
Impulse A-11	(M)	**The Quintessence**	1961	14.00	35.00
Impulse AS-11	(S)	**The Quintessence**	1961	10.00	25.00
		—Impulse albums above have orange & black labels.—			
Impulse AS-11	(S)	**The Quintessence**	1968	4.00	10.00
		—Impulse albums above have red & black labels with the "abc" logo on top.—			
Mercury MG-20751	(M)	**Bossa Nova**	1962	8.00	20.00
Mercury SR-60751	(S)	**Bossa Nova**	1962	6.00	15.00
Mercury MG-20799	(M)	**Quincy Jones Plays Hip Hits**	1963	8.00	20.00
Mercury SR-60799	(S)	**Quincy Jones Plays Hip Hits**	1963	6.00	15.00
Mercury MG-20863	(M)	**Quincy Jones Explores The Music Of Henry Mancini**	1964	8.00	20.00
Mercury SR-60863	(S)	**Quincy Jones Explores The Music Of Henry Mancini**	1964	6.00	15.00
Mercury MG-20938	(M)	**Golden Boy**	1964	8.00	20.00
Mercury SR-60938	(S)	**Golden Boy**	1964	6.00	15.00
Mercury MG-21011	(M)	**The Pawnbroker**	1964	8.00	20.00
Mercury SR-61011	(S)	**The Pawnbroker**	1964	6.00	15.00
Mercury MG-21050	(M)	**Quincy Jones Plays For Pussycats**	1965	8.00	20.00
Mercury SR-61050	(S)	**Quincy Jones Plays For Pussycats**	1965	6.00	15.00
Mercury MG-21063	(M)	**Quincy's Got A Brand New Bag**	1964	8.00	20.00
Mercury SR-61063	(S)	**Quincy's Got A Brand New Bag**	1964	6.00	15.00
Liberty LM-16004	(M)	**Enter Laughing**	1967	6.00	15.00
Liberty LS-17004	(S)	**Enter Laughing**	1967	6.00	15.00
Mercury 16398	(S)	**Around The World**	1969	4.00	10.00
A&M SP-3023	(S)	**Walking In Space**	1969	4.00	10.00

JONES, RICHARD

Richard Jones is a traditional jazz pianist and composer.

Pax 6010	(10")	**New Orleans Style** *(Pax 6010 also features Punch Miller.)*	1954	30.00	75.00
Riverside RLP-1017	(10")	**Richard P. Jones And Clarence Williams**	1953	30.00	75.00

JONES, RUFUS

Rufus Jones is a modern jazz drummer.

Cameo C-1076	(M)	**Five On Eight**	1964	12.00	30.00
Cameo CS-1076	(S)	**Five On Eight**	1964	16.00	40.00

JONES, SAM

Samuel Jones is a modern jazz bass player.

Riverside RLP-12-324	(M)	**The Soul Society**	1960	18.00	45.00
Riverside RLP-1172	(S)	**The Soul Society**	1960	14.00	35.00
Riverside RLP-358	(M)	**The Chant!**	1961	16.00	40.00
Riverside RS-9358	(S)	**The Chant!**	1961	12.00	30.00
Riverside RLP-432	(M)	**Down Home**	1962	16.00	40.00
Riverside RS-9432	(S)	**Down Home**	1962	12.00	30.00
		—Riverside albums above have blue mono or black stereo labels with a reel & mike logo on top.—			

JONES, THAD

Thaddeus Jones is a "modern big band" jazz cornet and flugel horn player, composer and band leader. For additional listings refer to Sammy Davis Jr; The Jones Boys; The Jones Brothers; Charles Mingus; Sonny Rollins; Frank Wess & Thad Jones; and the Various Artists section under Prestige and Savoy.

Debut DLP-12	(10")	**The Fabulous Thad Jones**	1954	125.00	250.00
Debut DLP-17	(10")	**Jazz Collaborations** *(Debut 17 also features Charles Mingus.)*	1954	125.00	250.00
Debut DEB-127	(M)	**Thad Jones** *(Debut 127 is a reissue of 12 plus two tracks.)*	1958	100.00	200.00
Period SPL-1208	(M)	**Mad Thad**	1956	50.00	125.00

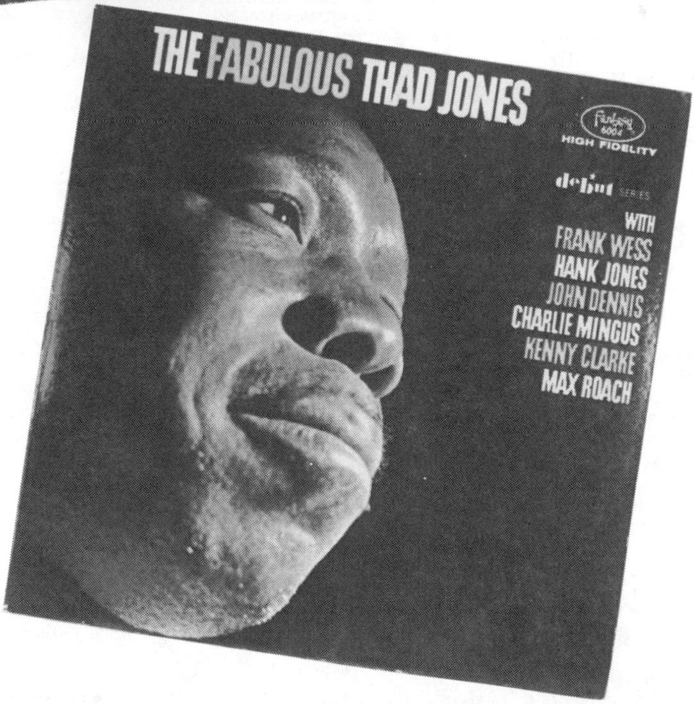

Thad Jones, brother to Hank, had a combo with a third Jones, Elvin, in the late '30s before joining Sonny Stitt in 1942. After the war he played with Billy Mitchell, Larry Steele, and Count Basie. He was given his debut as a solo artist on Mingus and Roach's Debut Records (illustrated here with the Fantasy reissue) before recording a trio of albums for Blue Note. He also recorded an album with Frank Wess, as a member of the Jones Boys, and as a featured soloist with Charles Mingus. He has recorded as a sideman with Basie on Verve and Roulette, Stitt on Roost, Thelonious Monk on Riverside, and backing Sammy Davis Jr. on Decca.

Label & Catalog #		Title	Year	VG+	NM
Blue Note BLP-1513	(M)	**Detroit-New York Junction** *(Deep groove)*	1956	100.00	200.00
Blue Note BLP-1513	(M)	**Detroit-New York Junction**	1956	60.00	150.00
Blue Note BLP-1527	(M)	**The Magnificent Thad Jones** *(Deep groove)*	1956	100.00	200.00
Blue Note BLP-1527	(M)	**The Magnificent Thad Jones**	1956	60.00	150.00
		—Blue Note albums above have blue on white labels with a Lexington Ave, NYC address.—			
Blue Note BLP-1546	(M)	**The Magnificent Thad Jones, Volume 3** *(Deep groove)*	1957	60.00	150.00
Blue Note BLP-1546	(M)	**The Magnificent Thad Jones, Volume 3**	1957	40.00	100.00
		—Blue Note albums above have blue on white labels with a W. 63rd St, NYC address.—			
Blue Note BLP-1513	(M)	**Detroit-New York Junction**	1963	10.00	25.00
Blue Note BLP-1527	(M)	**The Magnificent Thad Jones**	1963	10.00	25.00
Blue Note BLP-1546	(M)	**The Magnificent Thad Jones, Volume 3**	1963	10.00	25.00
		—Blue Note albums above have blue on white labels with a New York, USA address.—			
Blue Note BST-81513	(E)	**Detroit-New York Junction**	196?	4.00	10.00
Blue Note BST-81527	(E)	**The Magnificent Thad Jones**	196?	4.00	10.00
Blue Note BST-81546	(E)	**The Magnificent Thad Jones, Volume 3**	196?	4.00	10.00
		—Blue Note albums above have blue on white labels with "A Division of Liberty Records."—			
Prestige PRLP-7118	(M)	**After Hours**	1957	30.00	75.00
		—Prestige albums above have yellow labels with a W. 50th Street, NYC address.—			
United Arts. UAL-4025	(M)	**Motor City Scene**	1959	30.00	75.00
United Arts. UAS-5025	(S)	**Motor City Scene**	1959	24.00	60.00
Fantasy 6004	(M)	**The Fabulous Thad Jones** *(Red vinyl)*	1962	20.00	50.00
Fantasy 6004	(M)	**The Fabulous Thad Jones**	196?	10.00	25.00
Fantasy 86004	(E)	**The Fabulous Thad Jones** *(Blue vinyl)*	1962	12.00	30.00
Fantasy 86004	(E)	**The Fabulous Thad Jones**	196?	6.00	15.00
		(Fantasy 6004 is a reissue of Debut 17 and part of 12.)			

JONES, THAD, & PEPPER ADAMS

Milestone MLP-1001	(M)	**Mean What You Say**	1966	10.00	25.00
Milestone MSP-9001	(S)	**Mean What You Say**	1966	8.00	20.00

JONES, THAD, & MEL LEWIS

Solid State SM-17003	(M)	**Presenting Thad Jones-Mel Lewis & The Jazz Orchestra**	1966	8.00	20.00
Solid State SS-18003	(S)	**Presenting Thad Jones-Mel Lewis & The Jazz Orchestra**	1966	6.00	15.00
Solid State SM-17016	(M)	**Thad Jones Live At The Village Vanguard**	1967	8.00	20.00
Solid State SS-18016	(S)	**Thad Jones Live At The Village Vanguard**	1967	6.00	15.00
Solid State SS-180??	(S)	**The Big Band Sound Of Thad Jones & Mel Lewis**	1968	6.00	15.00
Solid State SS-18041	(S)	**Thad Jones & Mel Lewis Featuring Miss Ruth Brown**	1969	6.00	15.00
Solid State SS-18048	(S)	**Monday Night**	1969	6.00	15.00
Solid State SS-18058	(S)	**Central Park North**	1969	6.00	15.00

JONES BOYS, THE

The Jones Boys are Eddie, Jimmy, Jo, Quincy, Reunald and Thad.

Period SPL-1210	(M)	**The Jones Bash**	1954	30.00	75.00

JONES BROTHERS, THE

The Jones Brothers are Eddie, Elvin, Hank and Thad.

Metrojazz E-1003	(M)	**Keepin' Up With The Joneses**	1958	30.00	75.00
Metrojazz SE-1003	(S)	**Keepin' Up With The Joneses**	1958	24.00	60.00

JORDAN, CLIFFORD

Clifford Jones is a modern jazz tenor saxophone player. For additional listings refer to John Jenkins & Cliff Jordan & Bobby Timmons.

Blue Note BLP-1549	(M)	**Blowing In From Chicago** *(Deep groove)*	1957	50.00	125.00
Blue Note BLP-1549	(M)	**Blowing In From Chicago**	1957	30.00	75.00
		(Blue Note 1549 also features John Gilmore.)			
Blue Note BLP-1565	(M)	**Cliff Jordan** *(Deep groove)*	1957	50.00	125.00
Blue Note BLP-1565	(M)	**Cliff Jordan**	1957	30.00	75.00
Blue Note BST-1565	(S)	**Cliff Jordan** *(Deep groove)*	1959	30.00	75.00
Blue Note BST-1565	(S)	**Cliff Jordan**	1959	20.00	50.00
Blue Note BLP-1582	(M)	**Cliff Craft** *(Deep groove)*	1958	50.00	125.00
Blue Note BLP-1582	(M)	**Cliff Craft**	1958	30.00	75.00
Blue Note BST-1582	(S)	**Cliff Craft** *(Deep groove)*	1959	30.00	75.00
Blue Note BST-1582	(S)	**Cliff Craft**	1959	20.00	50.00
		—Blue Note albums above have blue on white labels with a W. 63rd St, NYC address.—			

Label & Catalog #		Title	Year	VG+	NM
Blue Note BLP-1549	(M)	**Blowing In From Chicago**	1963	10.00	25.00
Blue Note BLP-1565	(M)	**Cliff Jordan**	1963	10.00	25.00
Blue Note BST-1565	(S)	**Cliff Jordan**	1963	8.00	20.00
Blue Note BLP-1582	(M)	**Cliff Craft**	1963	10.00	25.00
Blue Note BST-1582	(S)	**Cliff Craft**	1963	8.00	20.00
		—Blue Note albums above have blue on white labels with a New York, USA address.—			
Blue Note BST-81549	(E)	**Blowing In From Chicago**	1967	4.00	10.00
Blue Note BST-81565	(S)	**Cliff Jordan**	196?	5.00	12.00
Blue Note BST-81582	(S)	**Cliff Craft**	196?	5.00	12.00
		—Blue Note albums above have blue on white labels with "A Division of Liberty Records."—			
Riverside RLP-340	(M)	**Spellbound**	1960	16.00	40.00
Riverside RS-9340	(S)	**Spellbound**	1960	12.00	30.00
		—Riverside albums above have blue mono or black stereo labels with a reel & mike logo on top.—			
Jazzland JLP-40	(M)	**A Story Tale**	1961	16.00	40.00
Jazzland JLP-940	(S)	**A Story Tale**	1961	12.00	30.00
		(Jazzland 40 also features Sonny Red.)			
Jazzland JLP-52	(M)	**Starting Time**	1961	16.00	40.00
Jazzland JLP-952	(S)	**Starting Time**	1961	12.00	30.00
Jazzland JLP-69	(M)	**Bearcat**	1962	16.00	40.00
Jazzland JLP-969	(S)	**Bearcat**	1962	12.00	30.00
Atlantic 1444	(M)	**These Are My Roots**	1965	10.00	25.00
Atlantic SD-1444	(S)	**These Are My Roots**	1965	8.00	20.00
		—Atlantic albums above have multi-color labels with a black fan logo.—			

JORDAN, DUKE

Irving "Duke" Jordan is a modern jazz pianist. For additional listings refer to Hall Overton; the Jazzy Soundtracks section under Charlie Parker; and the Various Artists section under Signal.

New Jazz NJ-810	(10")	**Jordu**	195?	100.00	200.00
Signal S-1202	(M)	**Duke Jordan**	1955	125.00	250.00
		—Signal albums above have an arrow & ear logo on the label.—			
Savoy MG-12149	(M)	**Duke Jordan**	1959	30.00	75.00
		(Savoy 12149 is a reissue of Signal 1202.)			
Blue Note BLP-4046	(M)	**Flight To Jordan**	1960	30.00	75.00
Blue Note BST-84046	(S)	**Flight To Jordan**	1960	20.00	50.00
		—Blue Note albums above have blue on white labels with a W. 63rd St, NYC address.—			
Blue Note BLP-4046	(M)	**Flight To Jordan**	1963	10.00	25.00
Blue Note BST-84046	(S)	**Flight To Jordan**	1963	8.00	20.00
		—Blue Note albums above have blue on white labels with a New York, USA address.—			
Blue Note BST-84046	(S)	**Flight To Jordan**	196?	5.00	12.00
		—Blue Note albums above have blue on white labels with "A Division of Liberty Records."—			
Charlie Parker PLP-805	(M)	**East And West Of Jazz**	1962	12.00	30.00
Charlie Parker PLP-805S	(S)	**East And West Of Jazz**	1962	10.00	25.00
		(Charlie Parker 805 also features Sadik Hakim.)			

JORDAN, DUKE / HALL OVERTON

Signal S-101/2	(M)	**Jazz Laboratory Series**	1955	100.00	200.00
		(Issued with a four page "Musical Analysis" booklet by Overton, worth an additional $25.)			
Savoy MG-12145	(M)	**Do It Yourself Jazz**	1959	40.00	100.00
		(Savoy 12145 is a reissue of Signal 101/2.)			
Savoy MG-12146	(M)	**Jazz Laboratory Series**	1959	40.00	100.00

JORDAN, LUIS

Louis Jordan is a traditional jazz and R&B-based alto saxophone player, vocalist and big band leader.

Score SLP-4007	(M)	**Go Blow Your Horn**	1957	100.00	200.00
Mercury MG-20242	(M)	**Somebody Up There Digs Me**	1957	50.00	125.00
Mercury MG-20331	(M)	**Man, We're Wailin'**	1958	50.00	125.00
Decca DL-8551	(M)	**Let The Good Times Roll**	1958	40.00	100.00

JORDAN, SHEILA

Sheila Jordan is a jazz-based vocalist.

Wave W-1	(M)	**Looking Out**	1961	30.00	75.00
Wave WS-1	(S)	**Looking Out**	1961	20.00	50.00
Blue Note BLP-9002	(M)	**Portrait Of Sheila Jordan**	1962	60.00	150.00
		—Blue Note albums above have blue on white labels with a W. 63rd St., NY address.—			
Blue Note BLP-9002	(M)	**Portrait Of Sheila Jordan**	1963	10.00	25.00
		—Blue Note albums above have blue on white labels with a New York, USA address.—			

Label & Catalog #		Title	Year	VG+	NM
Blue Note BST-89002	(E)	**Portrait Of Sheila Jordan**	196?	4.00	10.00
		—Blue Note albums above have blue on white labels with "A Division of Liberty Records."—			

JORDAN, TAFT

James Taft Jordan is a traditional jazz trumpet player and vocalist.

Label & Catalog #		Title	Year	VG+	NM
Mercury MG-20429	(M)	**The Moods Of Taft Jordan**	1959	16.00	40.00
Mercury SR-60101	(S)	**The Moods Of Taft Jordan**	1959	12.00	30.00
		—Mercury albums above have silver on black labels.—			
Moodsville MVLP-21	(M)	**Mood Indigo—Taft Jordan Plays Duke Ellington**	1961	20.00	50.00
		—Moodsville mono albums above have green labels with silver print.—			
Moodsville MVLP-21	(M)	**Mood Indigo—Taft Jordan Plays Duke Ellington**	1965	10.00	25.00
		—Moodsville albums above have blue labels with a trident logo on the right side.—			

Illustrations done for a Jazz at the Philharmonic collection by David Stone Martin.

Richie Kamuca worked through the '50s with Stan Kenton (1951-52), Woody Herman (1954-55), Chet Baker and Maynard Ferguson (1957), the Lighthouse All Stars (1957-58), and Shorty Rogers and Shelly Manne (1959). He also recorded albums with Al Cohn and Bill Perkins. As a sideman he can be found on many LPs, including Kenton and Herman, both on Capitol, Rogers on RCA Victor, Cy Touff on Pacific Jazz, Manny Albam on Coral, and Stan Levey and Johnny Richards, both on Bethlehem.

K.

KALLAO, ALEX
Alexander Kallao is a jazz-based pianist.

RCA Victor LJM-1011	*(M)*	**Evening At The Embers**	*1954*	**20.00**	**50.00**

KAMINSKY, MAX
Max Kaminsky is a traditional jazz trumpet player. For additional listings refer to Buddy Hackett / Max Kaminsky.

Commodore FL-20019	*(10")*	**Max Kaminsky**	*1952*	**20.00**	**50.00**
MGM E-261	*(10")*	**When The Saints Go Marching In**	*1954*	**20.00**	**50.00**
RCA Victor LJM-3003	*(10")*	**Jazz On The Campus, Ltd.**	*1954*	**20.00**	**50.00**
Concert Hall Jazz 1009	*(10")*	**Windy City Jazz**	*1955*	**20.00**	**50.00**
Jazztone J-1208	*(M)*	**Windy City Six**	*1955*	**16.00**	**40.00**
		(Jazztone 1208 is a reissue of Concert Hall 1009.)			
United Arts. UAL-3174	*(M)*	**Max Goes East**	*1961*	**10.00**	**25.00**
United Arts. UAS-6174	*(S)*	**Max Goes East**	*1961*	**8.00**	**20.00**

KAMUCA, RICHIE
Richard Kamuca is a West Coast jazz tenor saxophone player. For additional listings refer to Al Cohn & Rich Kamuca & Bill Perkins; Bill Perkins & Richie Kamuca; Bill Perkins & Art Pepper & Richie Kamuca; Cy Touff.

Mode LP-102	*(M)*	**Richie Kamuca Quartet**	*1957*	**30.00**	**75.00**
Interlude 50?	*(M)*	**Richie Kamuca Quartet**	*1959*	**16.00**	**40.00**
Interlude 100?	*(S)*	**Richie Kamuca Quartet**	*1959*	**12.00**	**30.00**
		(Interlude 50? is a reissue of Mode 102.)			
Hifijazz J-604	*(M)*	**Jazz Erotica**	*1959*	**24.00**	**60.00**
Hifijazz JS-604	*(S)*	**Jazz Erotica**	*1959*	**20.00**	**50.00**
Hifijazz J-609	*(M)*	**West Coast Jazz In Hifi**	*1959*	**16.00**	**40.00**
Hifijazz JS-609	*(S)*	**West Coast Jazz In Hifi**	*1959*	**12.00**	**30.00**
		(Hifijazz 609 is a reissue of 604.)			

KATZ, DICK / DEREK SMITH / RENE URTREGER

Atlantic 1287	*(M)*	**John Lewis Presents Jazz Piano International**	*1958*	**16.00**	**40.00**
		—Atlantic albums above have black mono or green stereo labels.—			
Atlantic 1287	*(M)*	**John Lewis Presents Jazz Piano International**	*1961*	**8.00**	**20.00**
		—Atlantic albums above have multi-color labels with a white fan logo.—			

KATZ, DICK
Richard Katz is a jazz-based pianist and composer.

Atlantic 1314	*(M)*	**Piano And Pin**	*1959*	**16.00**	**40.00**
Atlantic SD-1314	*(S)*	**Piano And Pin**	*1959*	**12.00**	**30.00**
		—Atlantic albums above have black mono or green stereo labels.—			
Atlantic 1314	*(M)*	**Piano And Pin**	*1961*	**8.00**	**20.00**
Atlantic SD-1314	*(S)*	**Piano And Pin**	*1961*	**6.00**	**15.00**
		—Atlantic albums above have multi-color labels with a white fan logo.—			

KATZ, FRED
Classically trained Frederick Katz is a modern jazz cellist and pianist. For additional listings refer to the Jazzy Soundtracks section under Decca.

Decca DL-9213	*(M)*	**4-5-6 Trio**	*1958*	**16.00**	**40.00**
Decca DL-79213	*(S)*	**4-5-6 Trio**	*1958*	**12.00**	**30.00**
Decca DL-9217	*(M)*	**Fred Katz And Jammers**	*1958*	**16.00**	**40.00**
Decca DL-79217	*(S)*	**Fred Katz And Jammers**	*1958*	**12.00**	**30.00**
Decca DL-9202	*(M)*	**Soulo Cello**	*1958*	**16.00**	**40.00**
Decca DL-79202	*(S)*	**Soulo Cello**	*1958*	**12.00**	**30.00**
Warner Bros. W-1277	*(M)*	**Folk Songs For Far Out Folks**	*1959*	**12.00**	**30.00**
Warner Bros. WS-1277	*(S)*	**Folk Songs For Far Out Folks**	*1959*	**10.00**	**25.00**

KAZ, FRED
Frederick Kaz is a modern jazz pianist.

Atlantic 1335	*(M)*	**Eastern Exposure**	*1960*	**12.00**	**30.00**
Atlantic SD-1335	*(M)*	**Eastern Exposure**	*1960*	**10.00**	**25.00**
		—Atlantic albums above have multi-color labels with a white fan logo.—			

Label & Catalog #		Title	Year	VG+	NM

KEATING, JOHNNY

Scottish born John Keating is a traditional jazz-based trombone player, arranger and composer.

Bally BAL-12001	(M)	**English Jazz**	1956	20.00	50.00
Dot DLP-3066	(M)	**Swinging Scots**	1957	16.00	40.00

KEENE, BOB

Robert Kuhn, aka Bob Keene, is a traditional jazz clarinet player and band leader.

Gene Norman GNP-149	(10")	**Bob Keene**	1954	20.00	50.00

KELLAWAY, ROGER

Roger Kellaway is a jazz-based pianist and composer.

Regina R-298	(M)	**Portraits**	1964	10.00	25.00
Regina RS-298	(S)	**Portraits**	1964	8.00	20.00
Prestige PRLP-7399	(M)	**The Roger Kellaway Trio**	1965	12.00	30.00
Prestige PRST-7399	(S)	**The Roger Kellaway Trio**	1965	10.00	25.00

—Prestige albums above have blue labels with a trident logo on the right side.—

World Pacific WP-21861	(M)	**Stride**	1967	8.00	20.00
World Pacific ST-21861	(S)	**Stride**	1967	6.00	15.00
Pacific Jazz PJ-10122	(M)	**Spirit Feel**	1967	8.00	20.00
Pacific Jazz ST-20122	(S)	**Spirit Feel**	1967	6.00	15.00

KELLER, ALLEN

Allan Keller is a jazz-based vocalist.

Charlie Parker PLP-817	(M)	**A New Look At The World**	1962	10.00	25.00
Charlie Parker PLP-817S	(S)	**A New Look At The World**	1962	10.00	25.00

KELLER, HAL

Harold Keller is a modern jazz-based pianist.

Sand 7	(M)	**Hal Keller Debut**	1957	20.00	50.00
Sound 602	(M)	**Hal Keller Debut**	1959	16.00	40.00

(Sound 602 is a reissue of Sand 7.)

KELLY, BEVERLY

Beverly Kelly is a jazz-based vocalist.

Audio Fidelity AFLP-1874	(M)	**Beverly Kelly Sings**	1958	12.00	30.00
Audio Fidelity AFSD-5874	(S)	**Beverly Kelly Sings**	1958	16.00	40.00
Riverside RLP-328	(M)	**Love Locked Out**	1960	10.00	25.00
Riverside RS-9328	(S)	**Love Locked Out**	1960	12.00	30.00
Riverside RLP-345	(M)	**Bev Kelly In Person**	1960	10.00	25.00
Riverside RS-9345	(S)	**Bev Kelly In Person**	1960	12.00	30.00

—Riverside albums above have blue mono or black stereo labels with a reel & mike logo on top.—

KELLY, JACK

Jubilee JLP-21	(10")	**Jack Kelly's Badinage**	1955	20.00	50.00

KELLY, WYNTON

Wynton Kelly is a modern jazz pianist and composer. For additional listings refer to Cannonball Adderley; Donna Drake; Steve Lacy; and the Various Artists section under Verve.

Blue Note BLP-5025	(10")	**Piano Interpretations By Wynton Kelly**	1953	150.00	300.00
Riverside RLP-12-254	(M)	**Wynton Kelly Piano**	1957	20.00	50.00
Riverside RLP-12-298	(M)	**Kelly Blue**	1959	20.00	50.00
Riverside RLP-1142	(S)	**Kelly Blue**	1959	16.00	40.00

—Riverside albums above have blue mono or black stereo labels with a reel & mike logo on top.—

Vee Jay LP-1016	(M)	**Kelly Great**	1960	16.00	40.00
Vee Jay LPS-1016	(S)	**Kelly Great**	1960	12.00	30.00
Vee Jay LP-3011	(M)	**Kelly At Midnight**	1960	12.00	30.00
Vee Jay LPS-3011	(S)	**Kelly At Midnight**	1960	10.00	25.00
Vee Jay LP-3022	(M)	**Wynton Kelly**	1961	12.00	30.00
Vee Jay LPS-3022	(S)	**Wynton Kelly**	1961	10.00	25.00
Vee Jay LP-1086	(M)	**The Best Of Wynton Kelly**	1963	10.00	25.00
Vee Jay LPS-1086	(S)	**The Best Of Wynton Kelly**	1963	8.00	20.00
Jazzland JLP-83	(M)	**Whisper Not**	1962	12.00	30.00
Jazzland JLP-983	(S)	**Whisper Not**	1962	10.00	25.00

(Jazzland 83 is a reissue of Riverside 254.)

Verve V-8576	(M)	**Comin' In The Back Door**	1964	8.00	20.00
Verve V6-8576	(S)	**Comin' In The Back Door**	1964	6.00	15.00
Verve V-8588	(M)	**It's All Right**	1964	8.00	20.00
Verve V6-8588	(S)	**It's All Right**	1964	6.00	15.00

Label & Catalog #		Title	Year	VG+	NM
Verve V-8622	(M)	**Undiluted**	1965	8.00	20.00
Verve V6-8622	(S)	**Undiluted**	1965	6.00	15.00
Verve V-8633	(M)	**Smokin' At The Half Note**	1965	8.00	20.00
Verve V6-8633	(S)	**Smokin' At The Half Note**	1965	6.00	15.00
		(Verve 8633 also features Wes Montgomery)			
		— Verve albums above have black labels with "MGM Records" on the bottom.—			
Milestone MSP-9004	(S)	**Full View**	1968	6.00	15.00

KENNEDY, GEORGE: ***Refer to*** **CHARLIE VENTURA / GEORGE KENNEDY**

KENNEY, BEVERLY

Beverly Kenney is a modern jazz-based vocalist.

Roost LP-2206	(M)	**Beverly Kenney Sings For Jimmy Smith**	1956	60.00	150.00
Roost LP-2212	(M)	**Come Swing With Me**	1956	60.00	150.00
		(Roost 2212 also features Ralph Burns.)			
Roost LP-2218	(M)	**Beverly Kenney With Jimmy Jones And The Basie-ites**	1956	60.00	150.00
Decca DL-8743	(M)	**Beverly Kenney Sings For Playboys**	1958	100.00	200.00
Decca DL-8850	(M)	**Born To Be Blue**	1959	100.00	200.00
Decca DL-8948	(M)	**Like Yesterday**	1960	60.00	150.00
Decca DL-78948	(S)	**Like Yesterday**	1960	100.00	200.00

KENTON, STAN

Pianist, composer, arranger and leader Stanley Kenton is the originator of the progressive jazz movement of the '50s. For additional listings refer to June Christy; Ann Richards; Dakota Staton.

Capitol H-155	(10")	**Encores**	1950	20.00	50.00
Capitol H-167	(10")	**Artistry In Rhythm**	1950	20.00	50.00
Capitol H-172	(10")	**A Presentation Of Progressive Jazz**	1950	20.00	50.00
Capitol P-189	(10")	**Innovations In Modern Music**	1950	20.00	50.00
Capitol H-190	(10")	**Milestones**	1950	20.00	50.00
Capitol L-248	(10")	**Stan Kenton Presents**	1950	20.00	50.00
Capitol H-353	(10")	**City Of Glass**	1952	20.00	50.00
Capitol H-358	(10")	**Classics**	1952	20.00	50.00
Capitol H-383	(10")	**New Concepts Of Artistry In Rhythm**	1953	20.00	50.00
Capitol H-386	(10")	**Prologue: This Is An Orchestra**	1953	20.00	50.00
Capitol H-421	(10")	**Popular Favorites**	1953	20.00	50.00
Capitol H-426	(10")	**Sketches On Standards**	1953	20.00	50.00
Capitol H-460	(10")	**This Modern World**	1953	20.00	50.00
Capitol H-462	(10")	**Portraits Of Standards**	1953	20.00	50.00
Capitol H-525	(10")	**Kenton Showcase—The Music Of Bill Russo**	1954	20.00	50.00
Capitol H-526	(10")	**Kenton Showcase—The Music Of Bill Holman**	1954	20.00	50.00
MacGregor LP-201 (10")	M)	**Stan Kenton Radio Transcriptions**	1953	30.00	75.00
MacGregor LP-202 (10")	M)	**Stan Kenton Radio Transcriptions**	1953	30.00	75.00
Capitol T-155	(M)	**Encores**	1955	16.00	40.00
Capitol T-167	(M)	**Artistry In Rhythm**	1955	16.00	40.00
Capitol T-172	(M)	**A Presentation Of Progressive Jazz**	1955	16.00	40.00
Capitol T-189	(M)	**Innovations In Modern Music**	1955	16.00	40.00
Capitol T-190	(M)	**Milestones**	1955	16.00	40.00
Capitol T-248	(M)	**Stan Kenton Presents**	1955	16.00	40.00
Capitol T-358	(M)	**Classics**	1955	16.00	40.00
Capitol T-383	(M)	**New Concepts Of Artistry In Rhythm**	1955	16.00	40.00
Capitol T-421	(M)	**Popular Favorites**	1955	16.00	40.00
Capitol T-426	(M)	**Sketches On Standards**	1955	16.00	40.00
Capitol T-462	(M)	**Portraits Of Standards**	1955	16.00	40.00
Capitol W-524	(M)	**Kenton Showcase**	1955	16.00	40.00
		(Capitol W-524 is a reissue of H-525 and 526.)			
Capitol T-569	(M)	**The Kenton Era**	1955	30.00	75.00
		(Limited Edition boxed set of 4 LPs with 44 page book.)			
Capitol T-666	(M)	**Contemporary Concepts**	1955	16.00	40.00
Capitol W-724	(M)	**Stan Kenton In Hi Fi**	1956	16.00	40.00
Capitol T-731	(M)	**Cuban Fire**	1956	16.00	40.00
Capitol T-736	(M)	**City Of Glass/This Modern World**	1956	16.00	40.00
		(Capitol 736 s a reissue of H 353 and 450.)			
Capitol T-810	(M)	**Kenton With Voices**	1957	16.00	40.00
Capitol T-932	(M)	**Rendezvous With Kenton**	1957	16.00	40.00
Capitol T-995	(M)	**Back To Balboa**	1958	16.00	40.00
		— Capitol albums above have turquoise labels.—			
Capitol T-155	(M)	**Encores**	196?	6.00	15.00

Label & Catalog #		Title	Year	VG+	NM
Capitol T-167	(M)	**Artistry In Rhythm**	*196?*	**6.00**	**15.00**
Capitol T-172	(M)	**A Presentation Of Progressive Jazz**	*196?*	**6.00**	**15.00**
Capitol T-189	(M)	**Innovations In Modern Music**	*196?*	**6.00**	**15.00**
Capitol T-190	(M)	**Milestones**	*196?*	**6.00**	**15.00**
Capitol T-248	(M)	**Stan Kenton Presents**	*196?*	**6.00**	**15.00**
Capitol T-358	(M)	**Classics**	*196?*	**6.00**	**15.00**
Capitol T-383	(M)	**New Concepts Of Artistry In Rhythm**	*196?*	**6.00**	**15.00**
Capitol T-421	(M)	**Popular Favorites**	*196?*	**6.00**	**15.00**
Capitol T-426	(M)	**Sketches On Standards**	*196?*	**6.00**	**15.00**
Capitol T-462	(M)	**Portraits Of Standards**	*196?*	**6.00**	**15.00**
Capitol W-524	(M)	**Kenton Showcase**	*196?*	**6.00**	**15.00**
Capitol T-666	(M)	**Contemporary Concepts**	*196?*	**6.00**	**15.00**
Capitol W-724	(M)	**Stan Kenton In Hi Fi**	*196?*	**6.00**	**15.00**
Capitol T-731	(M)	**Cuban Fire**	*196?*	**6.00**	**15.00**
Capitol T-736	(M)	**City Of Glass/This Modern World**	*196?*	**6.00**	**15.00**
Capitol T-810	(M)	**Kenton With Voices**	*196?*	**6.00**	**15.00**
Capitol T-995	(M)	**Back To Balboa**	*196?*	**6.00**	**15.00**
Capitol T-1068	(M)	**The Ballad Style Of Stan Kenton**	*1959*	**10.00**	**25.00**
Capitol ST-1068	(S)	**The Ballad Style Of Stan Kenton**	*1959*	**8.00**	**20.00**
Capitol T-1130	(M)	**Lush Interlude**	*1959*	**10.00**	**25.00**
Capitol ST-1130	(S)	**Lush Interlude**	*1959*	**8.00**	**20.00**
Capitol T-1166	(M)	**The Stage Door Swings**	*1959*	**10.00**	**25.00**
Capitol ST-1166	(S)	**The Stage Door Swings**	*1959*	**8.00**	**20.00**
Capitol T-1276	(M)	**The Kenton Touch**	*1960*	**10.00**	**25.00**
Capitol ST-1276	(S)	**The Kenton Touch**	*1960*	**8.00**	**20.00**
Capitol W-1305	(M)	**Viva Kenton**	*1960*	**10.00**	**25.00**
Capitol SW-1305	(S)	**Viva Kenton**	*1960*	**8.00**	**20.00**
Capitol T-1327	(M)	**Road Show**	*1960*	**10.00**	**25.00**
Capitol ST-1327	(S)	**Road Show**	*1960*	**8.00**	**20.00**
Capitol T-1394	(M)	**Standards In Silhouette**	*1960*	**10.00**	**25.00**
Capitol ST-1394	(S)	**Standards In Silhouette**	*1960*	**8.00**	**20.00**
Capitol T-1460	(M)	**Kenton At The Las Vegas, Tropicana**	*1961*	**8.00**	**20.00**
Capitol ST-1460	(S)	**Kenton At The Las Vegas, Tropicana**	*1961*	**6.00**	**15.00**
Capitol T-1533	(M)	**The Romantic Approach**	*1961*	**8.00**	**20.00**
Capitol ST-1533	(S)	**The Romantic Approach**	*1961*	**6.00**	**15.00**
Capitol T-1609	(M)	**Stan Kenton's "West Side Story"**	*1961*	**8.00**	**20.00**
Capitol ST-1609	(S)	**Stan Kenton's "West Side Story"**	*1961*	**6.00**	**15.00**
—Capitol albums above have black "rainbow" labels with the logo on the left side.—					
Capitol T-155	(M)	**Encores**	*196?*	**5.00**	**12.00**
Capitol T-167	(M)	**Artistry In Rhythm**	*196?*	**5.00**	**12.00**
Capitol T-172	(M)	**A Presentation Of Progressive Jazz**	*196?*	**5.00**	**12.00**
Capitol T-189	(M)	**Innovations In Modern Music**	*196?*	**5.00**	**12.00**
Capitol T-190	(M)	**Milestones**	*196?*	**5.00**	**12.00**
Capitol T-248	(M)	**Stan Kenton Presents**	*196?*	**5.00**	**12.00**
Capitol T-358	(M)	**Classics**	*196?*	**5.00**	**12.00**
Capitol T-383	(M)	**New Concepts Of Artistry In Rhythm**	*196?*	**5.00**	**12.00**
Capitol T-421	(M)	**Popular Favorites**	*196?*	**5.00**	**12.00**
Capitol T-426	(M)	**Sketches On Standards**	*196?*	**5.00**	**12.00**
Capitol T-462	(M)	**Portraits Of Standards**	*196?*	**5.00**	**12.00**
Capitol W-524	(M)	**Kenton Showcase**	*196?*	**5.00**	**12.00**
Capitol T-666	(M)	**Contemporary Concepts**	*196?*	**5.00**	**12.00**
Capitol W-724	(M)	**Stan Kenton In Hi Fi**	*196?*	**5.00**	**12.00**
Capitol T-731	(M)	**Cuban Fire**	*196?*	**5.00**	**12.00**
Capitol T-736	(M)	**City Of Glass/This Modern World**	*196?*	**5.00**	**12.00**
Capitol T-810	(M)	**Kenton With Voices**	*196?*	**5.00**	**12.00**
Capitol T-995	(M)	**Back To Balboa**	*196?*	**5.00**	**12.00**
Capitol T-1130	(M)	**Lush Interlude**	*196?*	**5.00**	**12.00**
Capitol ST-1130	(S)	**Lush Interlude**	*196?*	**4.00**	**10.00**
Capitol T-1166	(M)	**The Stage Door Swings**	*196?*	**5.00**	**12.00**
Capitol ST-1166	(S)	**The Stage Door Swings**	*196?*	**4.00**	**10.00**
Capitol T-1276	(M)	**The Kenton Touch**	*196?*	**5.00**	**12.00**
Capitol ST-1276	(S)	**The Kenton Touch**	*196?*	**4.00**	**10.00**
Capitol T-1305	(M)	**Viva Kenton**	*196?*	**5.00**	**12.00**
Capitol ST-1305	(S)	**Viva Kenton**	*196?*	**4.00**	**10.00**
Capitol T-1327	(M)	**Road Show**	*196?*	**5.00**	**12.00**
Capitol ST-1327	(S)	**Road Show**	*196?*	**4.00**	**10.00**
Capitol T-1394	(M)	**Standards In Silhouette**	*196?*	**5.00**	**12.00**
Capitol ST-1394	(S)	**Standards In Silhouette**	*196?*	**4.00**	**10.00**

Label & Catalog #		Title	Year	VG+	NM
Capitol T-1533	(M)	**The Romantic Approach**	196?	5.00	12.00
Capitol ST-1533	(S)	**The Romantic Approach**	196?	4.00	10.00
Capitol T-1609	(M)	**Stan Kenton's "West Side Story"**	196?	5.00	12.00
Capitol ST-1609	(S)	**Stan Kenton's "West Side Story"**	196?	4.00	10.00
Capitol T-1796	(M)	**Adventures In Jazz**	1963	6.00	15.00
Capitol ST-1796	(S)	**Adventures In Jazz**	1963	5.00	12.00
Capitol T-1844	(M)	**Adventures In Time**	1963	6.00	15.00
Capitol ST-1844	(S)	**Adventures In Time**	1963	5.00	12.00
Capitol T-2327	(M)	**Stan Kenton's Greatest Hits**	1965	5.00	12.00
Capitol ST-2327	(S)	**Stan Kenton's Greatest Hits**	1965	4.00	10.00
Capitol T-2424	(M)	**Stan Kenton Conducts The Los Angeles Neophonic Orchestra**	1966	6.00	15.00
Capitol ST-2424	(S)	**Stan Kenton Conducts The Los Angeles Neophonic Orchestra**	1966	5.00	12.00
Capitol ST-2932	(S)	**The Compositions Of Dee Barton**	1968	5.00	12.00

— Capitol albums above have black "rainbow" labels with the logo on top.—

KENYATA, ROBIN

Vortex 2005	(S)	**Until**	1968	8.00	20.00

KEROUAC, JACK

Poet and novelist Jack Kerouac is the pivotal figure in the blues and jazz-based poetry of the Beat movement.

Dot DLP-3154	(M)	**Poetry For The Beat Generation** *(Kerouac "blows" verse accompanied by Steve Allen on piano. Pressed in a run of less than 150 copies and then deleted. Rare with a suggested Near Mint value of $2,000-5,000.)*	1959		*See below*
Hanover HML-5000	(M)	**Poetry For The Beat Generation** *(Hanover 5000 is a reissue of Dot 3154.)*	1959	150.00	300.00
Hanover HML-5006	(M)	**Blues And Haikus** *(Kerouac reads while Al Cohn and Zoot Sims honk in bewilderment.)*	1959	150.00	300.00
Verve MGV-15005	(M)	**Readings On The Beat Generation**	1959	125.00	250.00

KESSEL, BARNEY

Barney Kessel is a West Coast jazz guitar player noted for his session work on Holywood soundtracks. For additional listings refer to Fred Astaire; The Poll Winners; and the Various Artists section under Savoy.

Contemporary C-2508	(10")	**Barney Kessel, Volume 1**	1953	40.00	100.00
Contemporary C-2514	(10")	**Barney Kessel, Volume 2**	1954	40.00	100.00
Contemporary C-3511	(M)	**Easy Like** *(Contemporary 3511 is a reissue of 2508.)*	1956	30.00	75.00
Contemporary C-3512	(M)	**Kessel Plays Standards** *(Contemporary 3512 is a reissue of 2514.)*	1956	30.00	75.00
Contemporary C-3513	(M)	**To Swing Or Not To Swing**	1956	24.00	60.00
Contemporary C-3521	(M)	**Music To Listen To Barney Kessel By**	1956	24.00	60.00
Stereo Records S-7001	(S)	**Music To Listen To Barney Kessel By**	1958	20.00	50.00
Contemporary S-7521	(S)	**Music To Listen To Barney Kessel By**	1959	16.00	40.00
Contemporary M-3563	(M)	**Barney Kessel Plays "Carmen"**	1959	16.00	40.00
Contemporary S-7563	(S)	**Barney Kessel Plays "Carmen"**	1959	12.00	30.00
Contemporary M-3565	(M)	**Some Like It Hot**	1959	16.00	40.00
Contemporary S-7565	(S)	**Some Like It Hot**	1959	12.00	30.00
Contemporary M-3585	(M)	**Workin' Out!**	1960	16.00	40.00
Contemporary S-7585	(S)	**Workin' Out!**	1960	12.00	30.00
Contemporary M-3603	(M)	**Let's Cook!**	1962	12.00	30.00
Contemporary S-7603	(S)	**Let's Cook!**	1962	10.00	25.00
Contemporary M-3613	(M)	**Swingin' Party**	1963	12.00	30.00
Contemporary S-7613	(S)	**Swingin' Party**	1963	10.00	25.00
Contemporary M-3618	(M)	**Feeling Free**	1965	12.00	30.00
Contemporary S-7618	(S)	**Feeling Free**	1965	10.00	25.00

— Contemporary stereo albums have gold & black labels.—

Reprise R-6019	(M)	**Breakfast At Tiffany's**	1961	8.00	20.00
Reprise R9-6019	(S)	**Breakfast At Tiffany's**	1961	6.00	15.00
Reprise R-6049	(M)	**Bossa Nova Plus Big Band**	1962	8.00	20.00
Reprise R9-6049	(S)	**Bossa Nova Plus Big Band**	1962	6.00	15.00
Reprise R-6073	(M)	**Kessel/Jazz**	1963	8.00	20.00
Reprise R9-6073	(S)	**Kessel/Jazz**	1963	6.00	15.00
Emerald 1401	(M)	**On Fire**	1965	8.00	20.00
Emerald 2401	(S)	**On Fire**	1965	6.00	15.00

KID ORY: ***Refer to* ORY, KID**

Morgana King started in Basin Street and related New York clubs in the '50s. Her background allowed her to record jazz and pop for a variety of labels through the '50s and '60s. While her recordings veered from jazzy to poppish to folkie, searching for a market, she nonetheless maintained a degree of credibility with fans of jazz vocals, who are very accepting of female singers' need to stray afield.

Label & Catalog #		Title	Year	VG+	NM

KID RENA: *Refer to* RENA, KID

KID THOMAS

Kid Thomas is a traditional jazz trumpet player.

American Music 642	(10")	**Kid Thomas**	1952	20.00	50.00
Riverside RLP-365	(M)	**Kid Thomas And His Algiers Stompers**	1961	12.00	30.00
Riverside RS-9365	(E)	**Kid Thomas And His Algiers Stompers**	1961	6.00	15.00
Riverside RLP-385	(M)	**Kid Thomas And His Algiers Stompers**	1961	12.00	30.00
Riverside RS-9385	(E)	**Kid Thomas And His Algiers Stompers**	1961	6.00	15.00

—Riverside albums above have blue mono or black stereo labels with a reel & mike logo on top.—

KINCAIDE, DEAN

Dean Kincaide is a traditional jazz saxophone, clarinet, trombone and flute player, arranger and composer.

Weathers 5610	(M)	**Arranged For You**	1954	20.00	50.00

KING, MORGANA

Morgana King is a folk and jazz-based vocalist

EmArcy MG-36079	(M)	**For You, For Me, For Evermore**	1956	24.00	60.00
—EmArcy albums above have blue labels with silver print.—					
Mercury MG-20231	(M)	**Morgana King Sings The Blues**	1958	20.00	50.00
—Mercury albums above have silver on black labels.—					
United Arts. UAL-40020	(M)	**Let Me Love You**	1958	20.00	50.00
United Arts. UAL-30020S	(S)	**Let Me Love You**	1958	20.00	50.00
—U.A. albums above have red & black mono or gold & black stereo labels.—					
United Arts. UAL-3028	(M)	**Folk Songs a la King**	1959	16.00	40.00
United Arts. UAS-6028	(S)	**Folk Songs a la King**	1959	16.00	40.00
Camden CAL-543	(M)	**The Greatest Songs Ever Swung**	1959	8.00	20.00
Camden CAS-543	(S)	**The Greatest Songs Ever Swung**	1959	10.00	25.00
Ascot ALM-13014	(M)	**The Winter Of My Discontent**	1965	8.00	20.00
Ascot ALS-16014	(S)	**The Winter Of My Discontent**	1965	10.00	25.00
Ascot ALM-13019	(M)	**The End Of A Love Affair**	1965	8.00	20.00
Ascot ALS-16019	(S)	**The End Of A Love Affair**	1965	10.00	25.00
(Ascot 13019 is a reissue of U.A. 40020.)					
Ascot ALM-13020	(M)	**Everybody Loves Saturday Night**	1965	8.00	20.00
Ascot ALS-16020	(S)	**Everybody Loves Saturday Night**	1965	10.00	25.00
Ascot ALM-13025	(M)	**More Morgana**	1965	8.00	20.00
Ascot ALS-16025	(S)	**More Morgana**	1965	10.00	25.00
Mainstream 56015	(M)	**With A Taste Of Honey**	1965	8.00	20.00
Mainstream S-6015	(S)	**With A Taste Of Honey**	1965	10.00	25.00
Wing MRW-12307	(M)	**More Morgana King**	1965	6.00	15.00
Wing SRW-16307	(E)	**More Morgana King**	1965	5.00	12.00
(Wing 12307 is a reissue of Mercury 20231.)					
Reprise R-6192	(M)	**It's A Quiet Thing**	1965	8.00	20.00
Reprise RS-6192	(S)	**It's A Quiet Thing**	1965	10.00	25.00
Reprise R-6205	(M)	**Wild Is Love**	1966	8.00	20.00
Reprise RS-6205	(S)	**Wild Is Love**	1966	10.00	25.00
Reprise R-6257	(M)	**Gemini Changes**	1967	8.00	20.00
Reprise RS-6257	(S)	**Gemini Changes**	1967	8.00	20.00

KING, TEDDI

Teddi King is a modern jazz-based vocalist.

Storyville STLP-302	(10")	**'Round Midnight**	1954	100.00	200.00
Storyville STLP-314	(10")	**Storyville Presents Teddi King**	1954	100.00	200.00
Storyville STLP-903	(M)	**Now In Vogue**	1956	50.00	125.00
RCA Victor LPM-1147	(M)	**Bidin' My Time**	1955	30.00	75.00
RCA Victor LPM-1313	(M)	**To You From Teddi King**	1956	20.00	50.00
RCA Victor LPM-1454	(M)	**A Girl And Her Songs**	1957	20.00	50.00
—RCA albums above have black labels with "Long Play" on the bottom.—					
Coral CRL-57278	(M)	**All The King's Songs**	1959	16.00	40.00
Coral CRL-757278	(S)	**All The King's Songs**	1959	20.00	50.00

KING CURTIS

King Curtis is a modern jazz tenor saxophone player known for his work is in '50s and '60s R&B and soul. For additional listings refer to Oliver Nelson, King Curtis & Jimmy Forrest.

New Jazz NJLP-8237	(M)	**The New Scene Of King Curtis**	1960	30.00	75.00
—New Jazz albums above have purple labels.—					
New Jazz NJLP-8237	(M)	**The New Scene Of King Curtis**	1965	120.00	30.00

—New Jazz albums above have blue labels with a trident logo on the right side.—

Label & Catalog #		Title	Year	VG+	NM
Everest LPBR-5121	(M)	**Azsure**	1961	20.00	50.00
Everest SDBR-1121	(S)	**Azsure**	1961	30.00	75.00
Tru-Sound TRU-15001	(M)	**Trouble In Mind**	1961	20.00	50.00
Tru-Sound TRU-15008	(M)	**It's Party Time**	1962	20.00	50.00
Tru-Sound TRU-15009	(M)	**Doin' The Dixie Twist**	1962	20.00	50.00
Prestige PRLP-7222	(M)	**Soul Meeting**	1962	20.00	50.00
Prestige PRST-7222	(S)	**Soul Meeting**	1962	30.00	75.00

(Prestige 7222 also features Nat Adderley.)

—Prestige albums above have yellow mono or silver stereo labels with a Bergenfield, NJ address.—

Prestige PRST-7709	(S)	**The Best Of King Curtis**	1969	6.00	15.00
Prestige PRST-7789	(S)	**Soul**	1969	6.00	15.00
Prestige PRST-7833	(S)	**Soul Meeting**	1969	6.00	15.00

(Prestige 7833 is a reissue of 7222.)

Prestige PRST-8237	(S)	**The New Scene**	1969	6.00	15.00

—Prestige albums above have blue labels with a trident logo on top.—

KING OLIVER: *Refer to* OLIVER, KING

KING PLEASURE

Clarence Beeks, aka King Pleasure, is a jazz composer and the inventor of jazz "vocalese" singing.

Prestige PRLP-208	(10")	**King Pleasure Sings**	1955	100.00	200.00
Hifijazz J-425	(M)	**Golden Days**	1959	20.00	50.00
Hifijazz JS-425	(S)	**Golden Days**	1959	16.00	40.00
United Arts. UAJ-14031	(M)	**Mr. Jazz**	1962	20.00	50.00
United Arts. UAJS-15031	(S)	**Mr. Jazz**	1962	16.00	40.00
Prestige PRST-7586	(E)	**The Original Moody's Mood**	1968	6.00	15.00

(Prestige 7568 is a reissue of 208.)

—Prestige albums above have blue labels with a trident logo on top.—

KING PLEASURE / ANNIE ROSS

Prestige PRLP-7128	(M)	**King Pleasure Sings/Annie Ross Sings**	1957	40.00	100.00

(Prestige 7128 is a reissue of 208 plus four tracks by Ms. Ross)

—Prestige albums above have yellow labels with a W. 50th Street, NYC address.—

KINSEY, TONY

English born Anthony Kinsey is a modern jazz drummer and pianist.

London LL-1672	(M)	**Kinsey Comes On**	1957	20.00	50.00

KIRBY, JOHN

John Kirby is a traditional jazz string bass and tuba player and arranger. For additional listings refer to Sarah Vaughan.

Columbia ML-4801	(M)	**John Kirby And His Orchestra**	195?	16.00	40.00
Columbia GL-502	(M)	**John Kirby 1938-41**	1951	16.00	40.00

—Columbia albums above have "Long Playing" on the bottom of the label.—

Harmony HL-7124	(M)	**Intimate Swing**	1958	6.00	15.00

KIRK, ANDY

Andrew Kirk is a traditional jazz bass and baritone saxophone and tuba player.

Coral CRL-56019	(10")	**Andy Kirk Souvenir Album—Vol. 1**	1951	40.00	100.00
RCA Victor LPM-1302	(M)	**A Mellow Bit Of Rhythm**	1956	16.00	40.00

—RCA albums above have black labels with "Long Play" on the bottom.—

KIRK, ROLAND (RAHSAAN ROLAND KIRK)

Rahsaan Roland Kirk is a modern jazz tenor saxophone and clarinet player—along with a variety of other reed instruments. For additional listings refer to The Jazz Cords.

King 395-539	(M)	**Triple Threat**	1956	100.00	200.00
Bethlehem BCP-6064	(M)	**Third Dimension**	1961	60.00	150.00

(Bethlehem 6064 is a reissue of King 539.)

Argo LP-669	(M)	**Introducing Roland Kirk**	1961	16.00	40.00
Argo LPS-669	(S)	**Introducing Roland Kirk**	1961	12.00	30.00
Prestige PRLP-7210	(M)	**Kirk's Work**	1961	16.00	40.00

(Prestige 7210 also features Jack McDuff.)

—Prestige albums above have yellow mono or silver stereo labels with a Bergenfield, NJ address.—

Mercury MG-20679	(M)	**We Free Kings**	1962	12.00	30.00
Mercury SR-60679	(S)	**We Free Kings**	1962	10.00	25.00
Mercury MG-20748	(M)	**Domino**	1962	12.00	30.00
Mercury SR-60748	(S)	**Domino**	1962	10.00	25.00

Label & Catalog #		Title	Year	VG+	NM
Mercury MG-20800	(M)	**Reeds And Deeds**	1963	12.00	30.00
Mercury SR-60800	(S)	**Reeds And Deeds**	1963	10.00	25.00
Mercury MG-20844	(M)	**Roland Kirk Meets The Benny Golson Orchestra**	1963	12.00	30.00
Mercury SR-60844	(S)	**Roland Kirk Meets The Benny Golson Orchestra**	1963	10.00	25.00
Mercury MG-20894	(M)	**Kirk In Copenhagen**	1963	12.00	30.00
Mercury SR-60894	(S)	**Kirk In Copenhagen**	1963	10.00	25.00
Mercury MG-20939	(M)	**Gifts And Messages**	1964	12.00	30.00
Mercury SR-60939	(S)	**Gifts And Messages**	1964	10.00	25.00
Limelight LM-82008	(M)	**I Talk With The Spirits**	1964	10.00	25.00
Limelight LS-86008	(S)	**I Talk With The Spirits**	1964	8.00	20.00
Limelight LM-82027	(M)	**Rip, Rig And Panic**	1965	10.00	25.00
Limelight LS-86027	(S)	**Rip, Rig And Panic**	1965	8.00	20.00
		(Limelight 82027 also features Elvin Jones.)			
Limelight LM-82033	(M)	**Slightly Latin**	1966	10.00	25.00
Limelight LS-86033	(S)	**Slightly Latin**	1966	8.00	20.00
Verve V-8709	(M)	**Now Please Don't You Cry, Beautiful Edith**	1967	8.00	20.00
Verve V6-8709	(S)	**Now Please Don't You Cry, Beautiful Edith**	1967	6.00	15.00
		—Verve albums above have black labels with "MGM Records" on the bottom.—			
Prestige PRLP-7450	(M)	**Funk Underneath**	1967	10.00	25.00
Prestige PRST-7450	(E)	**Funk Underneath**	1967	6.00	15.00
		(Prestige 7450 is a reissue of 7210.)			
		—Prestige albums above have blue labels with a trident logo on the right side.—			
Atlantic 3007	(M)	**Here Comes The Whistle Man**	1967	8.00	20.00
Atlantic SD-3007	(S)	**Here Comes The Whistle Man**	1967	6.00	15.00
Atlantic SC-1502	(M)	**The Inflated Tear**	1968	10.00	25.00
Atlantic CSG-1502	(S)	**The Inflated Tear**	1968	6.00	15.00
Atlantic SD-1518	(S)	**Left And Right**	1969	4.00	10.00
Atlantic SD-1534	(S)	**Volunteer Slavery**	1969	4.00	10.00
		—Atlantic albums above have multi-color labels with a black fan logo.—			

KLEMMER, JOHN

Cadet LP-797	(M)	**Involvement**	1967	10.00	25.00
Cadet LPS-797	(S)	**Involvement**	1967	6.00	15.00
Cadet LPS-808	(S)	**John Klemmer Quartet And Strings**	1968	6.00	15.00

KLINK, AL / BOB ALEXANDER

Albert Klink is a traditional jazz-based saxophone(s) player.

Grand Award GA-33-525	(M)	**Progressive Jazz**	1956	30.00	75.00
		(G.A. 321 was issued with a removable "second" cover of a David Stone Martin painting that could be peeled off and framed.)			
Grand Award GA-33-525	(M)	**Progressive Jazz**	1956	12.00	30.00
		(Without the second removable cover.)			

KLOSS, ERIC

Eric Kloss is a modern jazz alto and tenor saxophone player.

Prestige PRLP-7442	(M)	**Introducing Eric Kloss**	1967	10.00	25.00
Prestige PRST-7442	(S)	**Introducing Eric Kloss**	1967	8.00	20.00
Prestige PRLP-7469	(M)	**Love And All That Jazz**	1967	10.00	25.00
Prestige PRST-7469	(S)	**Love And All That Jazz**	1967	8.00	20.00
		(Prestige 7469 also features Don Patterson and Groove Holmes)			
Prestige PRLP-7486	(M)	**Grits & Gravy**	1967	10.00	25.00
Prestige PRST-7486	(S)	**Grits & Gravy**	1967	8.00	20.00
Prestige PRLP-7520	(M)	**First Class Kloss**	1967	10.00	25.00
Prestige PRST-7520	(S)	**First Class Kloss**	1967	8.00	20.00
Prestige PRLP-7535	(M)	**Life Force**	1967	10.00	25.00
Prestige PRST-7535	(S)	**Life Force**	1967	8.00	20.00
		—Prestige albums above have blue labels with a trident logo on the right side.—			
Prestige PRST-7565	(S)	**We're Goin' Up**	1968	5.00	12.00
Prestige PRST-7594	(S)	**Sky Shadows**	1968	5.00	12.00
Prestige PRST-7627	(S)	**In The Land Of Giants**	1969	5.00	12.00
Prestige PRST-7689	(S)	**To Hear Is To See**	1969	5.00	12.00
		—Prestige albums above have blue labels with a trident logo on top.—			

KNEPPER, JIMMY

James Knepper is a modern jazz trombone player. For additional listings refer to Pepper Adams & Jimmy Knepper; Tony Scott & Jimmy Knepper.

Debut DEB-129	(M)	**New Faces**	1956	Unreleased	
Bethlehem BCP-77	(M)	**A Swinging Introduction To Jimmy Knepper**	1957	20.00	50.00

Label & Catalog #		Title	Year	VG+	NM
KNOPF, PAUL					
Paul Knopf is a modern jazz pianist.					
Playback PLP-500	(M)	**The Outcat**	1959	20.00	50.00
Playback PLP-500ST	(S)	**The Outcat**	1959	16.00	40.00
Playback PLP-501	(M)	**Enigma Of A Day**	1959	20.00	50.00
Playback PLP-501ST	(S)	**Enigma Of A Day**	1959	16.00	40.00
Playback PLP-502	(M)	**And The Walls Came Tumbling Down**	1960	20.00	50.00
Playback PLP-502ST	(S)	**And The Walls Came Tumbling Down**	1960	16.00	40.00
Playback PLP-503	(M)	**Paul Knopf Trio**	1960	20.00	50.00
Playback PLP-503ST	(S)	**Paul Knopf Trio**	1960	16.00	40.00
Playback PLP-600	(M)	**Music From The Morgue**	1961	20.00	50.00
Playback PLP-600ST	(S)	**Music From The Morgue**	1961	16.00	40.00
KOFFMAN, MOE					
Canadian born Moe Koffman is a traditional jazz-based flute and alto saxophone player and composer.					
Jubilee JLP-1037	(M)	**Cool And Hot Sax**	1957	16.00	40.00
Jubilee JLP-1074	(M)	**The Shepherd Swings Again**	1958	16.00	40.00
Jubilee JGS-1074	(S)	**The Shepherd Swings Again**	1958	12.00	30.00
United Arts. UAJ-14029	(M)	**Tales Of Koffman**	1963	12.00	30.00
United Arts. UAJS-15029	(S)	**Tales Of Koffman**	1963	10.00	25.00
KOHLMAN, FREDDIE					
MGM E-297	(10")	**New Orleans Now—New Orleans Then**	1955	30.00	75.00
KOLLER, HANS					
Austrian born Hans Koller is a modern jazz tenor and baritone saxophone and clarinet player.					
Discovery DL-2005	(10")	**Hans Koller**	1954	30.00	75.00
Vanguard VRS-8509	(M)	**Hans Across The Sea**	1956	20.00	50.00
KONITZ, LEE					
Lee Konitz is a modern jazz alto saxophone player. For additional listings refer to Stan Getz ; Gerry Mulligan; Lennie Tristano.					
Prestige PRLP-116	(10")	**Lee Konitz-The New Sounds**	1951	100.00	200.00
Prestige PRLP-7004	(M)	**Lee Konitz Groups**	1955	50.00	125.00
		(Prestige 7004 is a reissue of 101, "Lennie Tristano With Lee Konitz," and 108, "Stan Getz-Lee Konitz.")			
		—Prestige albums above have yellow labels with a W. 50th Street, NYC address.—			
Roost LP-416	(10")	**Originalee**	1953	100.00	200.00
Storyville STLP-304	(10")	**Lee Konitz At Storyville**	1954	70.00	175.00
Storyville STLP-313	(10")	**Konitz**	1954	70.00	175.00
Storyville STLP-323	(10")	**Lee Konitz In Harvard Square**	1955	70.00	175.00
Storyville STLP-901	(M)	**Lee Konitz At Storyville**	1956	50.00	125.00
Jazztone J-1275	(M)	**Jazz At Storyville**	1957	16.00	40.00
		(Jazztone 1275 is a reissue of Storyville 901.)			
Atlantic 1217	(M)	**Lee Konitz With Warne Marsh**	1955	35.00	75.00
Atlantic 1258	(M)	**Inside Hi-Fi**	1957	24.00	60.00
Atlantic SD-1258	(S)	**Inside Hi-Fi**	1958	20.00	50.00
Atlantic 1273	(M)	**The Real Lee Konitz**	1958	20.00	50.00
		—Atlantic albums above have black mono or green stereo labels.—			
Atlantic 1217	(M)	**Lee Konitz With Warne Marsh**	1961	10.00	25.00
Atlantic 1258	(M)	**Inside Hi-Fi**	1961	8.00	20.00
Atlantic SD-1258	(S)	**Inside Hi-Fi**	1961	10.00	25.00
Atlantic 1273	(M)	**The Real Lee Konitz**	1961	8.00	20.00
		—Atlantic albums above have multi-color labels with a white fan logo.—			
Verve MGV-8209	(M)	**Very Cool**	1958	20.00	50.00
Verve MGV-8281	(M)	**Tranquility**	1958	20.00	50.00
Verve MGV-8286	(M)	**An Image—Lee Konitz With Strings**	1958	16.00	40.00
Verve MGVS-6035	(S)	**An Image—Lee Konitz With Strings**	1959	12.00	30.00
Verve MGV-8335	(M)	**Lee Konitz Meets Jimmy Giuffre**	1959	16.00	40.00
Verve MGVS-6073	(S)	**Lee Konitz Meets Jimmy Giuffre**	1959	12.00	30.00
Verve MGV-8362	(M)	**You And Lee**	1960	16.00	40.00
Verve MGVS-6131	(S)	**You And Lee**	1960	12.00	30.00
		—Verve albums above have black labels with "Verve Records, Inc." on the bottom.—			
Verve V-8209	(M)	**Very Cool**	1961	8.00	20.00
Verve V-8281	(M)	**Tranquility**	1961	8.00	20.00
Verve V-8286	(M)	**An Image—Lee Konitz With Strings**	1961	8.00	20.00
Verve V6-8286	(S)	**An Image—Lee Konitz With Strings**	1961	6.00	15.00

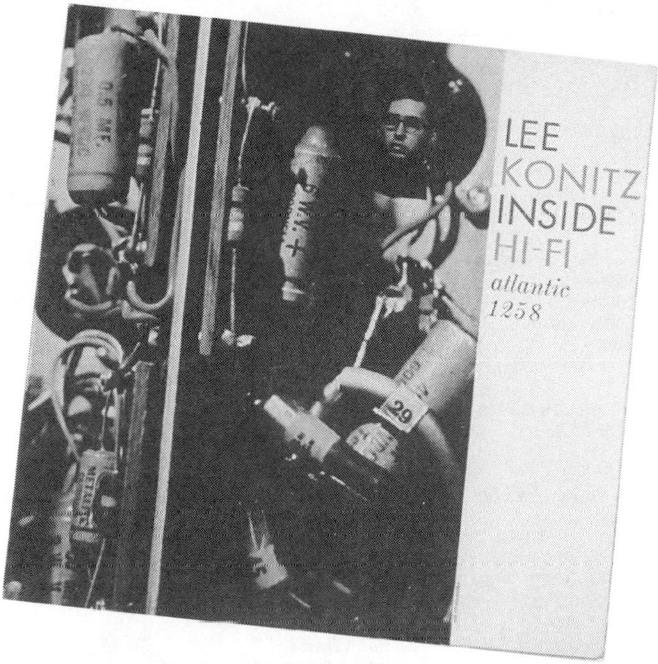

Lee Konitz entered the jazz world with Jerry Wald and Claude Thornhill before finding his way to Miles Davis in 1948-50, where he participated in the "birth of the cool" sessions. He then worked with Lennie Tristano and Stan Kenton (1952-53) before forming his own group. Always in demand, he has played as a feature soloist with Gerry Mulligan and as a sideman on albums by Davis on Capitol, Thornhill on Harmony, Tristano on Atlantic, and Ralph Burns on Verve.

Label & Catalog #		Title	Year	VG+	NM
Verve V-8335	(M)	**Lee Konitz Meets Jimmy Giuffre**	1961	8.00	20.00
Verve V6-8335	(S)	**Lee Konitz Meets Jimmy Giuffre**	1961	6.00	15.00
Verve V-8362	(M)	**You And Lee**	1961	8.00	20.00
Verve V6-8362	(S)	**You And Lee**	1961	6.00	15.00
Verve V-8399	(M)	**Motion**	1961	10.00	25.00
Verve V6-8399	(S)	**Motion**	1961	8.00	20.00

—Verve albums above have black labels with "MGM Records" on the bottom.—

Prestige PRLP-7250	(M)	**Subconsciouslee**	1962	20.00	50.00

(Prestige 7250 is a reissue of 7004.)

—Prestige albums above have yellow mono or silver stereo labels with a Bergenfield, NJ address.—

Milestone MSP-9013	(S)	**Duets**	1968	6.00	15.00
Milestone MSP-9025	(S)	**Peacemeal**	1969	6.00	15.00
Milestone MSP-9038	(S)	**Spirits**	1969	6.00	15.00
Atlantic SD-8235	(S)	**Duets**	1969	6.00	15.00

— —Atlantic albums above have multi-color labels with a black fan logo.—

KONITZ, LEE / MILES DAVIS / TEDDY CHARLES

New Jazz NJLP-8295	(M)	**Ezz-Thetic**	1962	20.00	50.00

—New Jazz albums above have purple labels.—

New Jazz NJLP-8295	(M)	**Ezz-Thetic**	1965	10.00	25.00

—New Jazz albums above have blue labels with a trident logo on the right side.—

KRAL, IRENE

Irene Kral is a big band-based vocalist. For additional listings refer to Maynard Ferguson.

United Arts. UAL-3052	(M)	**Steve Irene O!**	1959	40.00	100.00
United Arts. UAS-6052	(S)	**Steve Irene O!**	1959	50.00	125.00
United Arts. UAL-4016	(M)	**The Band And I**	1959	40.00	100.00
United Arts. UAS-5016	(S)	**The Band And I**	1959	50.00	125.00

(United Artists 4016 also features Herb Pomeroy.)

Ava A-33	(M)	**Better Than Anything**	1963	16.00	40.00
Ava AS-33	(S)	**Better Than Anything**	1963	20.00	50.00
Mainstream 56058	(M)	**Wonderful Life**	1965	14.00	35.00
Mainstream S-6058	(S)	**Wonderful Life**	1965	16.00	40.00

KRESS, CARL

Carl Kress is a traditional jazz guitar player.

Capitol H-368	(10")	**Classics In Jazz**	1953	20.00	50.00

KRUPA, GENE

Gene Krupa is a traditional jazz drummer and big band leader. For additional listings refer to Louis Bellson; Buck Clayton, Gene Krupa & Mel Powell; Benny Goodman; Buddy Rich; and the Jazzy Soundtracks section under Decca and Verve.

Columbia CL-6017	(10")	**Gene Krupa**	1949	30.00	75.00
Columbia CL-6066	(10")	**Dance Parade**	1949	30.00	75.00
Columbia CL-641	(M)	**Gene Krupa's Sidekicks**	1955	16.00	40.00

—Columbia albums above have "Long Playing" on the bottom of the label.—

Columbia CL-641	(M)	**Gene Krupa's Sidekicks**	195?	12.00	30.00
Columbia CL-2515	(10")	**Drummin' Man**	1955	20.00	50.00
Columbia CL-735	(M)	**Gene Krupa**	1956	12.00	30.00
Columbia C2L-29	(M)	**Drummer Man** *(2 LP box with booklet)*	1962	16.00	40.00

—Columbia albums above have six white on black "eye" logos on each label.—

Columbia CL-641	(M)	**Gene Krupa's Sidekicks**	196?	6.00	15.00
Columbia CL-735	(M)	**Gene Krupa**	196?	6.00	15.00
Columbia C2L-29	(M)	**Drummer Man** *(2 LP box with booklet)*	196?	8.00	20.00

—Columbia albums above have "360 Sound" in white on the bottom of the label.—

Mercury MGC-514	(10")	**Gene Krupa Trio**	1953	40.00	100.00
Mercury MGC-121	(10")	**The Gene Krupa Trio Collates**	1953	*Unreleased*	

(Jackets of Mercury 121 apparently contain copies of Clef 121.)

Mercury MGC-600	(M)	**The Gene Krupa Trio At JATP**	1953	30.00	75.00
Clef MGC-121	(10")	**The Gene Krupa Trio Collates**	1953	30.00	75.00

(Clef 121 features cover art by David Stone Martin.)

Clef MGC-147	(10")	**The Gene Krupa Sextet #1**	1954	30.00	75.00
Clef MGC-152	(10")	**The Gene Krupa Sextet #2**	1954	30.00	75.00

(Clef 152 features cover art by David Stone Martin.)

Clef MGC-514	(10")	**Gene Krupa Trio**	1953	30.00	75.00

(Clef 514 is a reissue of Mercury 514.)

Clef MGC-600	(M)	**The Gene Krupa Trio At JATP**	1953	24.00	60.00

(Clef 600 is a reissue of Mercury 600.)

Label & Catalog #		Title	Year	VG+	NM
Clef MGC-607	(M)	**Gene Krupa**	1954	Unreleased	
Clef MGC-627	(M)	**Sing, Sing, Sing— The Rocking Mr. Krupa And His Orchestra**	1954	24.00	60.00
Clef MGC-631	(M)	**The Gene Krupa Sextet #3**	1954	24.00	60.00
Clef MGC-668	(M)	**The Gene Krupa Quartet**	1955	24.00	60.00
		(Clef 668 features cover art by David Stone Martin.)			
Clef MGC-684	(M)	**Krupa And Rich**	1956	24.00	60.00
Clef MGC-687	(M)	**The Exciting Gene Krupa And His Quartet**	1956	24.00	60.00
		(Clef 687 is a reissue of 147.)			
Clef MGC-703	(M)	**Drum Boogie**	1956	24.00	60.00
		(Clef 703 is a reissue of 121.)			
Clef MGC-710	(M)	**Krupa's Wail**	1956	Unreleased	
Clef MGC-728	(M)	**The Driving Gene Krupa Plays With His Sextet**	1956	24.00	60.00
		(Clef 728 is a reissue of 631.)			
Verve MGV-2008	(M)	**Drummer Man—Gene Krupa In Highest-Fi**	1956	20.00	50.00
		(Verve 2008 also features Anita O' Day and Roy Eldridge.)			
— Verve albums above have "Verve Records, Inc." on the bottom of the label.—					
Verve MGV-8031	(M)	**The Gene Krupa Trio**	1957	20.00	50.00
		(Verve 8031 is a reissue of Clef 600.)			
Verve MGV-8069	(M)	**Krupa And Rich**	1957	20.00	50.00
		(Verve 8069 is a reissue of Clef 684.)			
Verve MGV-8071	(M)	**The Exciting Gene Krupa**	1957	20.00	50.00
		(Verve 8071 is a reissue of Clef 687.)			
Verve MGV-8087	(M)	**Drum Boogie**	1957	20.00	50.00
		(Verve 8087 is a reissue of Clef 703.)			
Verve MGV-8107	(M)	**The Driving Gene Krupa**	1957	20.00	50.00
		(Verve 8107 is a reissue of Clef 631.)			
American Rec. Soc. L-411	(M)	**Gene Krupa Quartet**	1956	16.00	40.00
American Rec. Soc. L-427	(M)	**Drummer Man**	1957	16.00	40.00
		(A.R.S. 427 is a reissue of Verve 2008.)			
Verve MGV-8190	(M)	**Sing, Sing, Sing**	1957	20.00	50.00
		(Verve 8190 is a reissue of Clef 627.)			
Verve MGV-8204	(M)	**The Jazz Rhythms Of Gene Krupa**	1957	20.00	50.00
		(Verve 8204 is a reissue of A.R.S. 411.)			
Verve MGV-4016	(M)	**The Gene Krupa Plays The Classics**	1958	Unreleased	
Verve MGV-8276	(M)	**Krupa Rocks**	1958	20.00	50.00
Verve MGV-8292	(M)	**Gene Krupa Plays Gerry Mulligan Arrangements**	1958	20.00	50.00
Verve MGVS-6008	(S)	**Gene Krupa Plays Gerry Mulligan Arrangements**	1960	16.00	40.00
Verve MGV-8300	(M)	**Hey! Here's Gene Krupa**	1959	20.00	50.00
Verve MGV-8310	(M)	**Big Noise From Winnetka— Gene Krupa At The London House**	1959	20.00	50.00
Verve MGVS-6042	(S)	**Big Noise From Winnetka— Gene Krupa At The London House**	1959	16.00	40.00
Verve MGV-8369	(M)	**The Drum Battle**	1960	20.00	50.00
		(Verve 8369 also features Buddy Rich.)			
Verve MGV-8373	(M)	**Gene Krupa**	1960	Unreleased	
Verve MGVS-6148	(S)	**Gene Krupa**	1960	Unreleased	
— Verve albums above have black labels with "Verve Records, Inc." on the bottom.—					
Verve V-2008	(M)	**Drummer Man—Gene Krupa In Highest-Fi**	1961	8.00	20.00
Verve V-8031	(M)	**The Gene Krupa Trio**	1961	8.00	20.00
Verve V-8069	(M)	**Krupa And Rich**	1961	8.00	20.00
Verve V-8071	(M)	**The Exciting Gene Krupa**	1961	8.00	20.00
Verve V-8087	(M)	**Drum Boogie**	1961	8.00	20.00
Verve V-8107	(M)	**The Driving Gene Krupa**	1961	8.00	20.00
Verve V-8190	(M)	**Sing, Sing, Sing**	1961	8.00	20.00
Verve V-8204	(M)	**The Jazz Rhythms Of Gene Krupa**	1961	8.00	20.00
Verve V-8276	(M)	**Krupa Rocks**	1961	8.00	20.00
Verve V-8292	(M)	**Gene Krupa Plays Gerry Mulligan Arrangements**	1961	8.00	20.00
Verve V6-8292	(S)	**Gene Krupa Plays Gerry Mulligan Arrangements**	1961	6.00	15.00
Verve V-8300	(M)	**Hey! Here's Gene Krupa**	1961	8.00	20.00
Verve V-8310	(M)	**Big Noise From Winnetka— Gene Krupa At The London House**	1961	8.00	20.00
Verve V6-8310	(S)	**Big Noise From Winnetka— Gene Krupa At The London House**	1961	6.00	15.00

Label & Catalog #		Title	Year	VG+	NM
Verve V-8400	(M)	**Krupa And Rich**	1961	8.00	20.00
Verve V6-8400	(S)	**Krupa And Rich**	1961	6.00	15.00
		(Verve 8400 is a reissue of Verve 8369.)			
Verve V-8414	(M)	**Percussion King**	1961	8.00	20.00
Verve V6-8414	(M)	**Percussion King**	1961	6.00	15.00
Verve V-8450	(M)	**Classics In Percussion**	1962	8.00	20.00
Verve V6-8450	(S)	**Classics In Percussion**	1962	6.00	15.00
		(Verve 8450 is a reissue of 8414.)			
Verve V-8484	(M)	**The Original Drum Battle**	1962	6.00	15.00
Verve V6-8484	(E)	**The Original Drum Battle**	1962	4.00	10.00
		(Verve 8484 is a reissue of Clef 684.)			
Verve V-8571	(M)	**Let Me Off Uptown—The Essential Gene Krupa**	1964	6.00	15.00
Verve V6-8571	(S)	**Let Me Off Uptown—The Essential Gene Krupa**	1964	5.00	12.00
Verve V-8584	(M)	**The Great New Gene Krupa Quartet Featuring Charlie Ventura**	1964	8.00	20.00
Verve V6-8584	(M)	**The Great New Gene Krupa Quartet Featuring Charlie Ventura**	1964	6.00	15.00
Verve V-8594	(M)	**Verve's Choice—The Best Of Gene Krupa**	1964	5.00	12.00
Verve V6-8594	(S)	**Verve's Choice—The Best Of Gene Krupa**	1964	4.00	10.00
		—Verve albums above have black labels with "MGM Records" on the bottom.—			
Verve VSP-4	(M)	**That Drummer's Band**	1966	5.00	12.00
Verve VSPS-4	(E)	**That Drummer's Band**	1966	4.00	10.00
Metro M-518	(M)	**Gene Krupa**	1965	5.00	12.00
Metro MS-518	(S)	**Gene Krupa**	1965	4.00	10.00
Camden CAL-340	(M)	**Swingin' With Krupa**	1958	8.00	20.00
Harmony HL-7252	(M)	**The Gene Krupa Story In Music**	1960	6.00	15.00

KRUPA, GENE, & LIONEL HAMPTON & TEDDY WILSON

Clef MGC-681	(M)	**Selections From "The Benny Goodman Story"**	1956	30.00	75.00
Verve MGV-8066	(M)	**Gene Krupa-Lionel Hampton-Teddy Wilson With Red Callender**	1957	20.00	50.00
		(Verve 8066 is a reissue of Clef 681.)			
		—Verve albums above have black labels with "Verve Records, Inc." on the bottom.—			
Verve V-8066	(M)	**Gene Krupa-Lionel Hampton-Teddy Wilson With Red Callender**	1961	10.00	25.00
		—Verve albums above have black labels with "MGM Records" on the bottom.—			

KRUPA, GENE, & CHARLIE VENTURA

Commodore FL-20028	(10")	**The Krupa-Ventura Trio**	1950	30.00	75.00

KUHN, ROLF

Vanguard VRS-8510	(M)	**Streamline**	1955	16.00	40.00
Urania US-1220	(M)	**Sound Of Jazz**	1962	12.00	30.00
Urania US-41220	(S)	**Sound Of Jazz**	1962	10.00	25.00

KUHN, ROLF & JOACHIM

Impulse S-9150	(S)	**Impressions Of New York**	1968	8.00	20.00
		—Impulse albums above have orange & black labels.—			

KUHN, STEVE

Steve Kuhn is a modern jazz pianist.

Contact CM-5	(M)	**Steve Kuhn Trio Featuring Steve Swallow & Pete PaRoca**	1965	10.00	25.00
Contact CS-5	(S)	**Steve Kuhn Trio Featuring Steve Swallow & Pete PaRoca**	1965	8.00	20.00
Impulse A-9136	(M)	**The October Suite**	1967	10.00	25.00
Impulse AS-9136	(S)	**The October Suite**	1967	6.00	15.00
		—Impulse albums above have orange & black labels.—			
Prestige PRST-7694	(S)	**Steve Kuhn In Europe**	1969	6.00	15.00
		—Prestige albums above have blue labels with a trident logo on top.—			

KUHN, STEVE, & TOSHIKO AKIYOSHI

Dauntless DM-4308	(M)	**The Country & Western Sound For Jazz Pianos**	1963	10.00	25.00
Dauntless DS-6308	(S)	**The Country & Western Sound For Jazz Pianos**	1963	8.00	20.00

Label & Catalog #		Title	Year	VG+	NM
KYNARD, CHARLES					
Charles Kynard is a modern jazz organ and piano player and composer.					
Pacific Jazz PJ-72	(M)	**Where It's At**	1963	**16.00**	**40.00**
Pacific Jazz ST-72	(S)	**Where It's At**	1963	**12.00**	**30.00**
World Pacific WP-1823	(M)	**Charles Kynard**	1964	**12.00**	**30.00**
World Pacific ST-1823	(S)	**Charles Kynard**	1964	**10.00**	**25.00**
Prestige PRST-7599	(S)	**Professor Soul**	1968	**6.00**	**15.00**
Prestige PRST-7630	(S)	**The Soul Brotherhood**	1969	**6.00**	**15.00**
Prestige PRST-7688	(S)	**Reelin' With The Feelin'**	1969	**6.00**	**15.00**

—Prestige albums above have blue labels with a trident logo on top.—

Illustrations done for a Jazz at the Philharmonic collection by David Stone Martin.

L

LACY, STEVE

Stephen Lackritz, aka Steve Lacy, is a modern jazz soprano saxophone player.

Prestige PRLP-7125	*(M)*	**Steve Lacy Soprano Sax**	*1956*	**40.00**	**100.00**

—Prestige albums above have yellow labels with a W. 50th Street, NYC address.—

New Jazz NJLP-8206	*(M)*	**Reflections—Steve Lacy Plays The Music Of Thelonious Monk**	*1958*	**40.00**	**100.00**
Candid CD-8007	*(M)*	**The Straight Horn Of Steve Lacy**	*1960*	**20.00**	**50.00**
Candid CS-9007	*(S)*	**The Straight Horn Of Steve Lacy**	*1960*	**16.00**	**40.00**
New Jazz NJLP-8271	*(M)*	**Evidence**	*1962*	**30.00**	**75.00**

(New Jazz 8271 also features Don Cherry.)

New Jazz NJLP-8308	*(M)*	**Wynton Kelly With Steve Lacy**	*1963*	*Unreleased*	

—New Jazz albums above have purple labels.—

New Jazz NJLP-8206	*(M)*	**Reflections—Steve Lacy Plays The Music Of Thelonious Monk**	*1965*	**10.00**	**25.00**
New Jazz NJLP-8271	*(M)*	**Evidence**	*1965*	**10.00**	**25.00**

—New Jazz albums above have blue labels with a trident logo on the right side.—

Status ST-8308	*(M)*	**Wynton Kelly With Steve Lacy**	*1965*	**16.00**	**40.00**

(Status 8308 is a reissue of Prestige 7125.)

ESP-Disk' 1060	*(M)*	**The Forest And The Zoo**	*1967*	**10.00**	**25.00**
ESP-Disk' 1060	*(S)*	**The Forest And The Zoo**	*1967*	**8.00**	**20.00**

LADNIER, TOMMY

Thomas Ladnier is a traditional jazz trumpet player.

Riverside RLP-1019	*(10")*	**Ida Cox With Tommy Ladnier**	*1953*	**40.00**	**100.00**
Riverside RLP-1026	*(10")*	**Early Ladnier**	*1954*	**40.00**	**100.00**
Riverside RLP-1044	*(10")*	**Tommy Ladnier Plays The Blues**	*1954*	**40.00**	**100.00**
"X" LVA-3027	*(M)*	**Tommy Ladnier**	*1954*	**20.00**	**50.00**

LaFORCE, JACK

Regina R-282	*(M)*	**I Remember You**	*196?*	**10.00**	**25.00**
Regina RS-282	*(S)*	**I Remember You**	*196?*	**8.00**	**20.00**
Regina R-288	*(M)*	**Unchain My Heart**	*196?*	**10.00**	**25.00**
Regina RS-288	*(S)*	**Unchain My Heart**	*196?*	**8.00**	**20.00**
Regina R-301	*(M)*	**You Fascinate Me So**	*196?*	**10.00**	**25.00**
Regina RS-301	*(S)*	**You Fascinate Me So**	*196?*	**8.00**	**20.00**
Regina R-309	*(M)*	**Comin' Home, Baby**	*196?*	**10.00**	**25.00**
Regina RS-309	*(S)*	**Comin' Home, Baby**	*196?*	**8.00**	**20.00**
Regina R-314	*(M)*	**Jazz Portrait Of Jack LaForce**	*196?*	**10.00**	**25.00**
Regina RS-314	*(S)*	**Jazz Portrait Of Jack LaForce**	*196?*	**8.00**	**20.00**

LAMBERT, DAVE

David Lambert is a modern jazz vocalist and arranger.

United Arts. UAL-3084	*(M)*	**Dave Lambert Sings And Swings Alone**	*1959*	**20.00**	**50.00**
United Arts. UAS-6084	*(S)*	**Dave Lambert Sings And Swings Alone**	*1959*	**16.00**	**40.00**

LAMBERT, HENDRICKS & ROSS

Dave Lambert, Jon Hendricks and Annie Ross are the most successful jazz vocalese practitioners.

ABC-Paramount ABC-223	*(M)*	**Sing A Song Of Basie**	*1958*	**20.00**	**50.00**
ABC-Paramount ABCS-223	*(S)*	**Sing A Song Of Basie**	*1958*	**16.00**	**40.00**
Roulette R-52018	*(M)*	**Sing Along With Basie**	*1958*	**20.00**	**50.00**
Roulette SR-52018	*(S)*	**Sing Along With Basie**	*1958*	**16.00**	**40.00**
World Pacific WP-1264	*(M)*	**The Swingers!**	*1959*	**20.00**	**50.00**
World Pacific ST-1025	*(S)*	**The Swingers!**	*1959*	**16.00**	**40.00**

(World Pacific 1264 also features Zoot Sims.)

Columbia CL-1403	*(M)*	**The Hottest New Group In Jazz**	*1959*	**14.00**	**35.00**
Columbia CS-8198	*(S)*	**The Hottest New Group In Jazz**	*1959*	**12.00**	**30.00**
Columbia CL-1510	*(M)*	**Lambert, Hendricks & Ross Sing Ellington**	*1960*	**14.00**	**35.00**
Columbia CS-8310	*(S)*	**Lambert, Hendricks & Ross Sing Ellington**	*1960*	**12.00**	**30.00**
Columbia CL-1675	*(M)*	**High Flying**	*1961*	**14.00**	**35.00**
Columbia CS-8475	*(S)*	**High Flying**	*1961*	**12.00**	**30.00**

—Columbia albums above have six white on black "eye" logos on each label.—

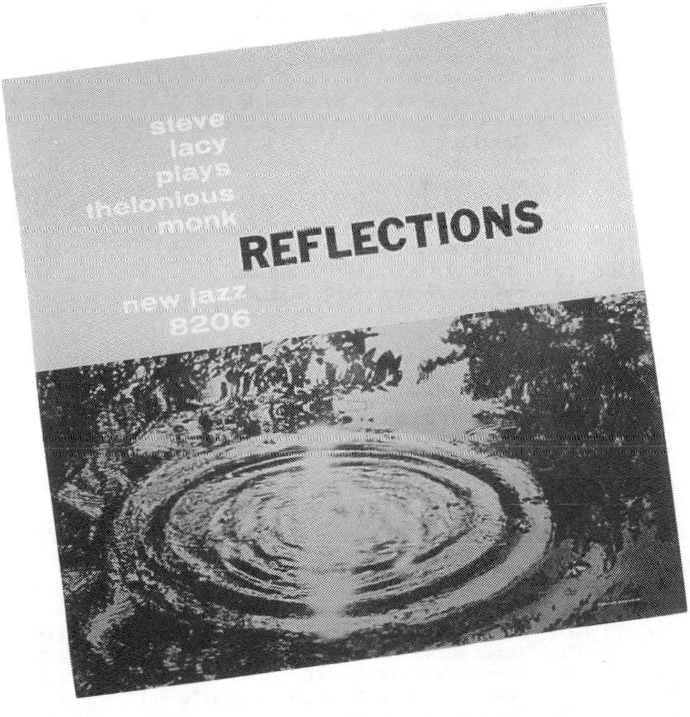

Steve Lacy opened his career with various Dixieland groups, including those of Maz Kaminsky, Jimmy McPartland, Rex Stewart, Buck Clayton, Charlie Shavers, Zutty Singleton and Hot Lips Page before stepping into modern jazz with Cecil Taylor (1956-57) and Gil Evans (1958-59). His playing can also be found on LPs by Taylor on Transition and Verve, Evans on New Jazz and World Pacific, and Whitey Mitchell and Tom Stewart, both on ABC-Paramount.

Label & Catalog #		Title	Year	VG+	NM
Columbia CL-1403	(M)	**The Hottest New Group In Jazz**	195?	6.00	15.00
Columbia CS-8198	(S)	**The Hottest New Group In Jazz**	195?	5.00	12.00
Columbia CL-1510	(M)	**Lambert, Hendricks & Ross Sing Ellington**	196?	6.00	15.00
Columbia CS-8310	(S)	**Lambert, Hendricks & Ross Sing Ellington**	196?	5.00	12.00
Columbia CL-1675	(M)	**High Flying**	196?	6.00	15.00
Columbia CS-8475	(S)	**High Flying**	196?	5.00	12.00
		—Columbia albums above have "360 Sound" on the bottom of the label.—			
Impulse A-83	(M)	**Sing A Song Of Basie**	1965	12.00	30.00
Impulse AS-83	(S)	**Sing A Song Of Basie**	1965	10.00	25.00
		(Impulse 83 is a reissue of ABC-Paramount 223.)			
		—Impulse albums above have orange & black labels.—			
Impulse AS-83	(S)	**Sing A Song Of Basie**	1968	4.00	10.00
		—Impulse albums above have red & black labels with the "abc" logo on top.—			

LAMBERT, HENDRICKS & BAVAN

Dave Lambert, Jon Hendricks and Yolanda Bavan are a jazz vocal group.

RCA Victor LPM-2635	(M)	**Live At Basin Street East**	1963	14.00	35.00
RCA Victor LSP-2635	(S)	**Live At Basin Street East**	1963	12.00	30.00
RCA Victor LPM-2747	(M)	**Lambert, Hendricks & Bavan At Newport**	1963	14.00	35.00
RCA Victor LSP-2747	(S)	**Lambert, Hendricks & Bavan At Newport**	1963	12.00	30.00
		—RCA albums above have black labels with "Long Play" or "Living Stereo" on the bottom.—			
RCA Victor LPM-2861	(M)	**Lambert, Hendricks & Bavan At The Village Gate**	1964	12.00	30.00
RCA Victor LSP-2861	(S)	**Lambert, Hendricks & Bavan At The Village Gate**	1964	10.00	25.00
		—RCA albums above have black labels with "Mono" or "Stereo" on the bottom.—			

LANCASTER, BYARD

Vortex 2003	(S)	**It's Not Up To Us**	1968	8.00	20.00

LAND, HAROLD

Harold Land is a West Coast jazz tenor saxophone player. For additional listings refer to Art Blakey & The Jass Messengers / Elmo Hope; Hampton Hawes; Carmell Jones; Red Mitchell & Harold Land.

Contemporary C-3550	(M)	**Harold In The Land Of Hi Fi**	1958	30.00	75.00
Contemporary M-3550	(M)	**Grooveyard**	1959	20.00	50.00
Contemporary S-7550	(S)	**Grooveyard**	1959	16.00	40.00
		("Grooveyard" is a retitled reissue of "In The Land Of Hi Fi.")			
		—Contemporary stereo albums have gold & black labels.—			
Hifijazz J-612	(M)	**The Fox**	1959	30.00	75.00
Hifijazz JS-612	(S)	**The Fox**	1959	20.00	50.00
Jazzland JLP-20	(M)	**West Coast Blues!**	1960	20.00	50.00
Jazzland JLP-920	(S)	**West Coast Blues!**	1960	16.00	40.00
Jazzland JLP-33	(M)	**Eastward Ho! Harold Land In New York**	1961	20.00	50.00
Jazzland JLP-933	(S)	**Eastward Ho! Harold Land In New York**	1961	16.00	40.00
Imperial LP-9247	(M)	**Jazz Impressions Of Folk Music**	1963	12.00	30.00
Imperial LP-12247	(S)	**Jazz Impressions Of Folk Music**	1963	10.00	25.00
Contemporary M-3619	(M)	**The Fox**	1965	10.00	25.00
Contemporary S-7619	(S)	**The Fox**	1965	8.00	20.00
		(Contemporary 7619 is a reissue of Hifijazz 612.)			
Cadet LPS-813	(S)	**The Peace-Maker**	1968	6.00	15.00

LANG, EDDIE: ***Refer to*** **JOE VENUTI / EDDIE LANG**

LANG, RONNIE

Ronald Langinger, aka Ronnie Lang, is a traditional jazz saxophone and flute player. For additional listings refer to Les Brown.

Tops L-1521	(M)	**Modern Jazz**	1958	10.00	25.00

LaPORTA, JOHN

John LaPorta is a modern jazz clarinet and saxophone player and composer. For additional listings refer to Kenny Clarke.

Debut DLP-10	(10")	**The John LaPorta Quintet**	1954	100.00	200.00
Debut DEB-122	(M)	**Three Moods**	1955	60.00	150.00
Fantasy 3228	(M)	**Conceptions** *(Dark red vinyl)*	1956	24.00	60.00
Fantasy 3237	(M)	**South American Brothers** *(Dark red vinyl)*	1956	24.00	60.00
Fantasy 3248	(M)	**The Clarinet Artistry Of John LaPorta** *(Dark red vinyl)*	1956	24.00	60.00
		—Fantasy albums above have red labels on dark red, non-flexible vinyl.—			
Fantasy 3228	(M)	**Conceptions**	195?	12.00	30.00
Fantasy 3237	(M)	**South American Brothers**	195?	12.00	30.00

Label & Catalog #		*Title*	*Year*	*VG+*	*NM*
Fantasy 3248	*(M)*	**The Clarinet Artistry Of John LaPorta**	*195?*	**12.00**	**30.00**
		—Fantasy albums above have red labels on non-flexible vinyl.—			
Everest LPBR-5037	*(M)*	**The Most Minor**	*1959*	**16.00**	**40.00**
Everest SDBR-1037	*(S)*	**The Most Minor**	*1959*	**12.00**	**30.00**
Music Minus One 4003	*(M)*	**8 Men In Search Of A Drummer**	*1961*	**8.00**	**20.00**

LARKIN, BILLY

William Larkin is a modern jazz pianist. For additional listings refer to The Delegates.

World Pacific WP-1843	*(M)*	**Ain't That A Groove?**	*1966*	**8.00**	**20.00**
World Pacific ST-1843	*(S)*	**Ain't That A Groove?**	*1966*	**6.00**	**15.00**
World Pacific WP-1850	*(M)*	**Hold On!**	*1966*	**8.00**	**20.00**
World Pacific ST-1850	*(S)*	**Hold On!**	*1966*	**6.00**	**15.00**

LARKINS, ELLIS

Ellis Larkins is a traditional jazz-based pianist. For additional listings refer to Ruby Braff & Ellis Larkins.

Decca DL-5391	*(10")*	**Blues In The Night**	*1952*	**20.00**	**50.00**
Storyville STLP-316	*(10")*	**Perfume And Rain**	*1955*	**30.00**	**75.00**
Storyville STLP-913	*(M)*	**Do Nothin' Till You Hear From Me**	*1956*	**20.00**	**50.00**
Decca DL-8303	*(M)*	**Manhattan At Midnight**	*1956*	**16.00**	**40.00**
Decca DL-9205	*(M)*	**The Soft Touch**	*1958*	**12.00**	**30.00**
Decca DL-79205	*(S)*	**The Soft Touch**	*1958*	**10.00**	**25.00**
Decca DL-9211	*(M)*	**Blue And Sentimental**	*1958*	**12.00**	**30.00**
Decca DL-79211	*(S)*	**Blue And Sentimental**	*1958*	**10.00**	**25.00**

LARKINS, ELLIS / LEE WILEY

Storyville STLP-911	*(M)*	**Duologue**	*1956*	**30.00**	**60.00**

LaROCA, PETE

Peter Sims, aka Pete LaRoca, is a modern jazz drummer and composer.

Blue Note BLP-4205	*(M)*	**Basra**	*1965*	**16.00**	**40.00**
Blue Note BST-84205	*(S)*	**Basra**	*1965*	**12.00**	**30.00**
		—Blue Note albums above have blue on white labels with a New York, NY address.—			
Blue Note BST-84205	*(S)*	**Basra**	*196?*	**5.00**	**12.00**
		—Blue Note albums above have blue on white labels with "A Division of Liberty Records."—			
Douglas SD-782	*(S)*	**Turkish Women At The Bath**	*1969*	**5.00**	**12.00**

LASHA, PRINCE

Prince Lasha is a modern jazz flautist and composer.

Contemporary M-3610	*(M)*	**The Cry**	*1963*	**12.00**	**30.00**
Contemporary S-7610	*(S)*	**The Cry**	*1963*	**10.00**	**25.00**
Contemporary S-7617	*(S)*	**Firebirds**	*1968*	**8.00**	**20.00**
		(Contemporary 3510 and 3617 also feature Sonny Simmons.)			
		—Contemporary stereo albums have gold & black labels.—			

LATEEF, YUSEF

Yusef Lateef, formerly William Evans, is a modern jazz flute, tenor saxophone and oboe player, composer and band leader. For additionasl listings refer to Cannonball Adderley.

Prestige PRLP-7122	*(M)*	**The Sounds Of Yusef**	*1957*	**30.00**	**75.00**
		—Prestige albums above have yellow labels with a W. 50th Street, NYC address.—			
Savoy MG-12103	*(M)*	**Jazz Mood**	*1957*	**20.00**	**50.00**
Savoy MG-12109	*(M)*	**Jazz For The Thinker**	*1957*	**20.00**	**50.00**
Savoy MG-12117	*(M)*	**Prayer To The East**	*1957*	**20.00**	**50.00**
Savoy MG-12120	*(M)*	**Jazz And The Sounds Of Nature**	*1957*	**20.00**	**50.00**
Savoy MG-12139	*(M)*	**The Dreamer**	*1958*	**20.00**	**50.00**
Savoy SR-13007	*(S)*	**The Dreamer**	*1959*	**16.00**	**40.00**
Savoy MG-12140	*(M)*	**The Fabric Of Jazz**	*1958*	**20.00**	**50.00**
Savoy SR-13008	*(S)*	**The Fabric Of Jazz**	*1959*	**16.00**	**40.00**
Verve MGV-8217	*(M)*	**Before Dawn**	*1958*	**30.00**	**75.00**
		—Verve albums above have black labels with "Verve Records, Inc" on the bottom.—			
Verve V-8217	*(M)*	**Before Dawn**	*1961*	**10.00**	**25.00**
		—Verve albums above have black labels with "MGM Records" on the bottom.—			
Argo LP-634	*(M)*	**Live At Cranbrook**	*1959*	**12.00**	**30.00**
New Jazz NJLP-8218	*(M)*	**Other Sounds**	*1959*	**20.00**	**50.00**
New Jazz NJLP-8234	*(M)*	**Cry! Tender**	*1960*	**20.00**	**50.00**
New Jazz NJLP-8261	*(M)*	**The Sounds Of Yusef**	*1961*	**20.00**	**50.00**
		(New Jazz 8261 is a reissue of Prestige 7122.)			
New Jazz NJLP-8272	*(M)*	**Into Something**	*1962*	**20.00**	**50.00**
		—New Jazz albums above have purple labels.—			

Label & Catalog #		Title	Year	VG+	NM
New Jazz NJLP-8218	(M)	**Other Sounds**	1965	10.00	25.00
New Jazz NJLP-8234	(M)	**Cry! Tender**	1965	10.00	25.00
New Jazz NJLP-8261	(M)	**The Sounds Of Yusef**	1965	10.00	25.00
New Jazz NJLP-8272	(M)	**Into Something**	1965	10.00	25.00
		—New Jazz albums above have blue labels with a trident logo on the right side.—			
Riverside RLP-12-325	(M)	**Three Faces Of Yusef Lateef**	1960	18.00	45.00
Riverside RLP-1176	(S)	**Three Faces Of Yusef Lateef**	1960	14.00	35.00
Riverside RLP-337	(M)	**The Centaur And The Phoenix**	1960	16.00	40.00
Riverside RS-9337	(S)	**The Centaur And The Phoenix**	1960	12.00	30.00
		—Riverside albums above have blue mono or black stereo labels with a reel & mike logo on top.—			
Moodsville MVLP-22	(M)	**Eastern Sounds**	1961	20.00	50.00
Moodsville MVST-22	(S)	**Eastern Sounds**	1961	16.00	40.00
		—Moodsville mono albums above have green labels with silver print.—			
Moodsville MVLP-22	(M)	**Eastern Sounds**	1965	10.00	25.00
Moodsville MVST-22	(S)	**Eastern Sounds**	1965	8.00	20.00
		—Moodsville albums above have blue labels with a trident logo on the right side.—			
Charlie Parker PLP-814	(M)	**Lost In Sound**	1962	12.00	30.00
Charlie Parker PLP-814S	(S)	**Lost In Sound**	1962	10.00	25.00
Impulse A-56	(M)	**Jazz Around The World**	1963	12.00	30.00
Impulse AS-56	(S)	**Jazz Around The World**	1963	10.00	25.00
Impulse A-69	(M)	**Live At Pep's**	1964	12.00	30.00
Impulse AS-69	(S)	**Live At Pep's**	1964	10.00	25.00
Impulse A-84	(M)	**1984**	1965	12.00	30.00
Impulse AS-84	(S)	**1984**	1965	10.00	25.00
Impulse A-92	(M)	**Psychicemotus**	1966	12.00	30.00
Impulse AS-92	(S)	**Psychicemotus**	1966	10.00	25.00
Impulse A-9117	(M)	**A Flat, G Flat And C**	1966	12.00	30.00
Impulse AS-9117	(S)	**A Flat, G Flat And C**	1966	10.00	25.00
Impulse A-9125	(M)	**The Golden Flute**	1966	12.00	30.00
Impulse AS-9125	(S)	**The Golden Flute**	1966	10.00	25.00
		—Impulse albums above have orange & black labels.—			
Impulse AS-56	(S)	**Jazz Around The World**	1968	4.00	10.00
Impulse AS-69	(S)	**Live At Pep's**	1968	4.00	10.00
Impulse AS-84	(S)	**1984**	1968	4.00	10.00
Impulse AS-92	(S)	**Psychicemotus**	1968	4.00	10.00
Impulse AS-9117	(S)	**A Flat, G Flat And C**	1968	4.00	10.00
Impulse AS-9125	(S)	**The Golden Flute**	1968	4.00	10.00
		—Impulse albums above have red & black labels with the "abc" logo on top.—			
Prestige PRLP-7319	(M)	**Eastern Sounds**	1964	12.00	30.00
Prestige PRST-7319	(S)	**Eastern Sounds**	1964	10.00	25.00
		(Prestige 7319 is a reissue of Moodsville 22.)			
Delmark DL-407	(M)	**Yusef!**	1965	12.00	30.00
Delmark DS-407	(S)	**Yusef!**	1965	10.00	25.00
Prestige PRLP-7398	(M)	**The Sounds Of Yusef Lateef**	1966	10.00	25.00
Prestige PRST-7398	(S)	**The Sounds Of Yusef Lateef**	1966	8.00	20.00
		(Prestige 7398 is a reissue of 7122.)			
Prestige PRLP-7447	(M)	**Yusef Lateef Plays For Lovers**	1967	10.00	25.00
Prestige PRST-7447	(S)	**Yusef Lateef Plays For Lovers**	1967	8.00	20.00
		—Prestige albums above have blue labels with a trident logo on the right side.—			
Prestige PRST-7637	(E)	**Into Something**	1969	6.00	15.00
		(Prestige 7637 is a reissue of New Jazz 8272.)			
Prestige PRST-7653	(E)	**Expressions**	1969	6.00	15.00
		(Prestige 7653 is a reissue of New Jazz 8218.)			
		—Prestige albums above have blue labels with a trident logo on top.—			
Riverside RS-3011	(S)	**Three Faces Of Yusef Lateef**	1968	6.00	15.00
		(Riverside 3011 is a reisue of 1176.)			
Atlantic SD-1499	(S)	**The Complete Lateef**	1968	6.00	15.00
Atlantic SD-1508	(S)	**The Blue Lateef**	1969	6.00	15.00
		—Atlantic albums above have multi-color labels with a black fan logo.—			
Cadet LPS-816	(E)	**Live At Cranbrook**	1969	4.00	10.00
		(Cadet 816 is a reissue of Argo 634.)			

LATIN JAZZ QUINTET, THE

New Jazz NJLP-8251	(M)	**Caribe**	1960	20.00	50.00
		(New Jazz 8251 also features Eric Dolphy.)			
United Arts. UAL-4071	(M)	**The Latin Jazz Quintet**	1960	16.00	40.00
United Arts. UAS-5071	(S)	**The Latin Jazz Quintet**	1960	12.00	30.00
Tru-Sound TRU-15003	(M)	**Hot Sauce**	1962	16.00	40.00

Elliot Lawrence started his own band in 1947, often incorporating Gerry Mulligan's arrangements. Aside from recording for several labels and taking part in the Dan Drew & His Daredevils spoof on Groove, he worked throughout the '50s on radio and television, broadening jazz's exposure. His LP for Top Rank features one of the most [delightfully] outrageous sexist covers of the time and is pictured here with one of his Fantasy outings.

Label & Catalog #		Title	Year	VG+	NM
Tru-Sound TRU-15012	(M)	**The Latin Jazz Quintet**	1962	16.00	40.00
New Jazz NJLP-8321	(M)	**Latin Soul**	1963	Unreleased	
		—New Jazz albums above have purple labels.—			
New Jazz NJLP-8251	(M)	**Caribe**	1965	10.00	25.00
		—New Jazz albums above have blue labels with a trident logo on the right side.—			
Status ST-8321	(M)	**Latin Soul**	1965	16.00	40.00

LAWRENCE, ARNIE

Project PR-5028	(S)	**Look Toward A Dream**	1968	8.00	20.00

LAWRENCE, ELLIOT

Elliot Lawrence Broza is a modern jazz pianist, composer and band leader. For additional listings refer to Boots Brown.

Decca DL-5274	(10")	**College Prom**	1950	20.00	50.00
Decca DL-5353	(10")	**Moonlight On The Campus**	1951	20.00	50.00
Fantasy 3206	(M)	**Elliott Lawrence Plays Gerry Mulligan Arrangements** *(Dark red vinyl)*	1956	20.00	50.00
Fantasy 3219	(M)	**Elliott Lawrence Plays Tiny Kahn & Johnny Mandel Arrangements** *(Dark red vinyl)*	1956	20.00	50.00
Fantasy 3226	(M)	**Dream** *(Dark red vinyl)*	1956	20.00	50.00
Fantasy 3236	(M)	**Swinging At The Steel Pier** *(Dark red vinyl)*	1956	20.00	50.00
		—Fantasy albums have red labels on dark red, non-flexible vinyl.—			
Fantasy 3206	(M)	**Elliott Lawrence Plays Gerry Mulligan Arrangements**	195?	12.00	30.00
Fantasy 3219	(M)	**Elliott Lawrence Plays Tiny Kahn & Johnny Mandel Arrangements**	195?	12.00	30.00
Fantasy 3226	(M)	**Dream**	195?	12.00	30.00
Fantasy 3236	(M)	**Swinging At The Steel Pier**	195?	12.00	30.00
		—Fantasy albums have red labels on non-flexible vinyl.—			
Fantasy 3206	(M)	**Elliott Lawrence Plays Gerry Mulligan Arrangements**	195?	6.00	15.00
Fantasy 3219	(M)	**Elliott Lawrence Plays Tiny Kahn & Johnny Mandel Arrangements**	195?	6.00	15.00
Fantasy 3226	(M)	**Dream**	195?	6.00	15.00
Fantasy 3236	(M)	**Swinging At The Steel Pier**	195?	6.00	15.00
Fantasy 3246	(M)	**Elliott Lawrence Plays For Swinging Dancers** *(Red vinyl)*	1957	16.00	40.00
Fantasy 3246	(M)	**Elliott Lawrence Plays For Swinging Dancers**	195?	10.00	25.00
Fantasy 8021	(S)	**Elliott Lawrence Plays For Swinging Dancers** *(Blue vinyl)*	1962	10.00	25.00
Fantasy 8021	(S)	**Elliott Lawrence Plays For Swinging Dancers**	196?	6.00	15.00
Fantasy 3261	(M)	**Dream On... Dance On** *(Red vinyl)*	1958	16.00	40.00
Fantasy 3261	(M)	**Dream On... Dance On**	195?	10.00	25.00
Fantasy 8002	(S)	**Dream On... Dance On** *(Blue vinyl)*	1962	10.00	25.00
Fantasy 8002	(S)	**Dream On... Dance On**	196?	6.00	15.00
Fantasy 3290	(M)	**Big Band Sound** *(Red vinyl)*	1959	16.00	40.00
Fantasy 3290	(M)	**Big Band Sound**	195?	10.00	25.00
Fantasy 8031	(S)	**Big Band Sound** *(Blue vinyl)*	1962	10.00	25.00
Fantasy 8031	(S)	**Big Band Sound**	196?	6.00	15.00
		—Fantasy albums have red mono or blue stereo labels on flexible vinyl.—			
Jazztone J-1279	(M)	**Big Band Modern**	1958	16.00	40.00
Vik LX-1113	(M)	**Jazz Goes Broadway**	1958	16.00	40.00
Top Rank RM-304	(M)	**Music For Trapping—Tender, That Is**	1959	20.00	50.00
Top Rank RS-604	(S)	**Music For Trapping—Tender, That Is**	1959	16.00	40.00
SeSac N-1153	(M)	**Jump Steady**	1960	16.00	40.00
SeSac SN-1153	(S)	**Jump Steady**	1960	12.00	30.00

LAWS, HUBERT

Hubert Laws is a modern jazz pianist, flautist and composer.

Atlantic 1432	(M)	**The Laws Of Jazz**	1965	6.00	15.00
Atlantic SD-1432	(S)	**The Laws Of Jazz**	1965	5.00	12.00
Atlantic 1452	(M)	**Flute By-Laws**	1966	6.00	15.00
Atlantic SD-1452	(S)	**Flute By-Laws**	1966	5.00	12.00
Atlantic SD-1509	(S)	**Laws Cause**	1969	5.00	12.00
		—Atlantic albums above have multi-color labels with a black fan logo.—			

Label & Catalog #		Title	Year	VG+	NM

LAWSON, DEE

Dee Lawson is a modern jazz-based vocalist.

Roulette R-52017	(M)	**'Round Midnight**	1958	12.00	30.00
Roulette SR-52017	(S)	**'Round Midnight**	1958	16.00	40.00

LAWSON, YANK

Riverside RLP-2509	(10")	**Yank Lawson's Dixieland Jazz**	1954	30.00	75.00

LAWSON, YANK, & HAGGART, BOB (THE LAWSON-HAGGART JAZZ BAND)

John Lausen, aka Yank Lawson, is a traditional jazz trumpet player. Robert Haggart is a traditional jazz string bass player, arranger and composer. For additional listings for Haggart refer to the Various Artists section under Verve.

Decca DL-5368	(10")	**Lawson-Haggart Band Play Jelly Roll's Jazz**	1951	24.00	60.00
Decca DL-5427	(10")	**College Fight Songs**	1952	24.00	60.00
Decca DL-5437	(10")	**Lawson-Haggart Band Play King Oliver's Jazz**	1952	24.00	60.00
Decca DL-5439	(10")	**Lawson-Haggart Band**	1952	24.00	60.00
Decca DL-5456	(10")	**Blues On The River**	1952	24.00	60.00
Decca DL-5502	(10")	**Windy City Jazz**	1953	24.00	60.00
Decca DL-5529	(10")	**South Of The Mason-Dixon Line**	1954	24.00	60.00
Decca DL-5533	(10")	**Louis' Hot 5's And 7's**	1954	24.00	60.00
Decca DL-8182	(M)	**Lawson-Haggart Band Play Jelly Roll's Jazz**	1955	16.00	40.00
Decca DL-8195	(M)	**Lawson-Haggart Band Play King Oliver's Jazz**	1955	16.00	40.00
Decca DL-8196	(M)	**Blues On The River**	1955	16.00	40.00
Decca DL-8197	(M)	**South Of The Mason-Dixon Line**	1955	16.00	40.00
Decca DL-8198	(M)	**Windy City Jazz**	1955	16.00	40.00
Decca DL-8200	(M)	**Louis' Hot 5's And 7's**	1955	16.00	40.00
Decca DL-8453	(M)	**Hold That Tiger**	1956	12.00	30.00
Decca DL-8801	(M)	**Boppin' At The Hop**	1959	12.00	30.00
Decca DL-78801	(S)	**Boppin' At The Hop**	1959	10.00	25.00
Stinson SLP-59	(10")	**Lawson-Haggart With Jerry Jerome & His Orchestra**	195?	12.00	30.00
Everest LPBR-5040	(M)	**Junior Prom**	1959	10.00	25.00
Everest SDBR-1040	(S)	**Junior Prom**	1959	8.00	20.00
Everest LPBR-5084	(M)	**Dixieland Goes West**	1960	10.00	25.00
Everest SDBR-1084	(S)	**Dixieland Goes West**	1960	8.00	20.00
Project-3 PR-5039	(M)	**Extra**	196?	8.00	20.00
Project-3 PR-5039	(S)	**Extra**	196?	6.00	15.00
Atlantic SD-1570	(S)	**Live At The Roosevelt Grill**	1969	4.00	10.00
Atlantic SD-1582	(S)	**What's New?**	1969	4.00	10.00

LAZAR, SAM

Samuel Lazar is a modern jazz organist.

Argo LP-4002	(M)	**Space Flight**	1960	16.00	40.00
Argo LPS-4002	(S)	**Space Flight**	1960	12.00	30.00
Argo LP-4015	(M)	**Playback**	1961	16.00	40.00
Argo LPS-4015	(S)	**Playback**	1961	12.00	30.00
Argo LP-714	(M)	**Soul Merchant**	1963	12.00	30.00
Argo LPS-714	(S)	**Soul Merchant**	1963	10.00	25.00

LEA, BARBARA

Barbara Lea is a jazz-based vocalist.

Riverside RLP-2518	(10")	**A Woman In Love**	1955	100.00	200.00
Prestige PRLP-7065	(M)	**Barbara Lea**	1956	60.00	150.00
Prestige PRLP-7100	(M)	**Lea In Love**	1957	60.00	150.00

—Prestige albums above have yellow labels with a W. 50th Street, NYC address.—

LEADBELLY

Guitar player, singer and composer Huddie Ledbetter, aka Leadbelly, is a founder of American folk music.

Capitol H-369	(10")	**Classics In Jazz**	1953	60.00	150.00

LEE, CHUCK: ***Refer to*** **CHEZ ALFRED & OLA HANSON & CHUCK LEE**

LEE, JEANNE, & RAN BLAKE

Jeanne Lee is a modern jazz-based vocalist.

RCA Victor LPM-2500	(M)	**The Newest Sound Around**	1962	16.00	40.00
RCA Victor LSP-2500	(S)	**The Newest Sound Around**	1962	14.00	35.00

—RCA albums above have black labels with "Long Play" or "Living Stereo" on the bottom.—

Label & Catalog #		Title	Year	VG+	NM

LEE, JULIA

Julia Lee is a traditional jazz-based pianist, vocalist and composer.

Capitol H-228	(10")	**Party Time**	1955	**50.00**	**125.00**
Capitol T-228	(M)	**Party Time**	1955	**30.00**	**75.00**

LEE, PEGGY

Norma Egstrom, aka Peggy Lee, is a jazz/big band-based vocalist. For additional listings refer to Benny Goodman & Peggy Lee; and the Jazzy Soundtracks section under Decca.

Capitol H-151	(10")	**Rendezvous With Peggy Lee**	1952	**30.00**	**75.00**
Capitol H-204	(10")	**My Best To You**	1952	**30.00**	**75.00**
Decca DL-5482	(10")	**Black Coffee**	1953	**40.00**	**100.00**
Decca DL-5539	(10")	**Song In Intimate Style**	1954	**30.00**	**75.00**
Decca DL-8358	(M)	**Black Coffee**	1957	**30.00**	**75.00**
Decca DL-8411	(M)	**Dream Street**	1957	**20.00**	**50.00**
Decca DL-8591	(M)	**Sea Shells**	1958	**20.00**	**50.00**
Decca DL-8816	(M)	**Miss Wonderful**	1959	**20.00**	**50.00**
		—Decca albums above have silver on black labels.—			
Decca DL-4458	(M)	**Lover**	1964	**10.00**	**25.00**
Decca DL-74458	(E)	**Lover**	1964	**5.00**	**12.00**
Decca DL-4461	(M)	**The Fabulous Peggy Lee**	1964	**10.00**	**25.00**
Decca DL-74461	(E)	**The Fabulous Peggy Lee**	1964	**5.00**	**12.00**
Decca DXB-164	(M)	**The Best Of Peggy Lee** *(2 LPs)*	1964	**12.00**	**30.00**
Decca DXSB-164	(E)	**The Best Of Peggy Lee** *(2 LPs)*	1964	**6.00**	**15.00**
Capitol T-151	(M)	**Rendezvous With Peggy Lee**	1954	**20.00**	**50.00**
Capitol T-204	(M)	**My Best To You**	1954	**20.00**	**50.00**
Capitol T-864	(M)	**The Man I Love**	1957	**12.00**	**40.00**
Capitol T-975	(M)	**Jump For Joy**	1958	**12.00**	**40.00**
		—Capitol albums above have turquoise labels.—			
Capitol T-151	(M)	**Rendezvous With Peggy Lee**	1958	**10.00**	**25.00**
Capitol T-204	(M)	**My Best To You**	1958	**10.00**	**25.00**
Capitol T-864	(M)	**The Man I Love**	1958	**10.00**	**25.00**
Capitol T-975	(M)	**Jump For Joy**	1958	**10.00**	**25.00**
Capitol T-1049	(M)	**Things Are Swingin'**	1958	**10.00**	**25.00**
Capitol ST-1049	(S)	**Things Are Swingin'**	1958	**12.00**	**30.00**
Capitol T-1131	(M)	**I Like Men**	1959	**10.00**	**25.00**
Capitol ST-1131	(S)	**I Like Men**	1959	**12.00**	**30.00**
Capitol T-1219	(M)	**Beauty And The Beat**	1959	**10.00**	**25.00**
Capitol ST-1219	(S)	**Beauty And The Beat**	1959	**12.00**	**30.00**
		(Capitol 1219 also features backing by George Shearing.)			
		—Capitol albums above have black "rainbow" labels with the logo on the left side.—			
Capitol T-151	(M)	**Rendezvous With Peggy Lee**	196?	**5.00**	**12.00**
Capitol T-204	(M)	**My Best To You**	196?	**5.00**	**12.00**
Capitol T-864	(M)	**The Man I Love**	196?	**5.00**	**12.00**
Capitol T-975	(M)	**Jump For Joy**	196?	**5.00**	**12.00**
Capitol T-1049	(M)	**Things Are Swingin'**	196?	**5.00**	**12.00**
Capitol ST-1049	(S)	**Things Are Swingin'**	196?	**6.00**	**15.00**
Capitol T-1131	(M)	**I Like Men**	196?	**5.00**	**12.00**
Capitol ST-1131	(S)	**I Like Men**	196?	**6.00**	**15.00**
Capitol T-1219	(M)	**Beauty And The Beat**	196?	**5.00**	**12.00**
Capitol ST-1219	(S)	**Beauty And The Beat**	196?	**6.00**	**15.00**
Capitol T-1290	(M)	**Latin Ala Lee!**	1960	**8.00**	**20.00**
Capitol ST-1290	(S)	**Latin Ala Lee!**	1960	**10.00**	**25.00**
Capitol T-1366	(M)	**All Aglow Again**	1960	**8.00**	**20.00**
Capitol ST-1366	(S)	**All Aglow Again**	1960	**10.00**	**25.00**
Capitol T-1401	(M)	**Pretty Eyes**	1960	**8.00**	**20.00**
Capitol ST-1401	(S)	**Pretty Eyes**	1960	**10.00**	**25.00**
Capitol T-1475	(M)	**Ole' A La Lee**	1961	**8.00**	**20.00**
Capitol ST-1475	(S)	**Ole' A La Lee**	1961	**10.00**	**25.00**
Capitol T-1520	(M)	**Basin Street East**	1961	**8.00**	**20.00**
Capitol ST-1520	(S)	**Basin Street East**	1961	**10.00**	**25.00**
Capitol T-1630	(M)	**If You Go**	1961	**8.00**	**20.00**
Capitol ST-1630	(S)	**If You Go**	1961	**10.00**	**25.00**
Capitol T-1671	(M)	**Blue Cross Country**	1961	**8.00**	**20.00**
Capitol ST-1671	(S)	**Blue Cross Country**	1961	**10.00**	**25.00**
Capitol T-1743	(M)	**Bewitching Lee**	1962	**10.00**	**25.00**
Capitol DT-1743	(E)	**Bewitching Lee**	1962	**6.00**	**15.00**
		(Capitol 1743 is a reissue of 151 and 204.)			

Peggy Lee hit the big time as a vocalist with the Benny Goodman Orchestra in 1941 before "retiring" briefly after marrying BG's guitarist, Dave Barbour. She then signed as a solo with Capitol and Decca. Her first albums for each label are illustrated above, although in each case, the 12" reissue is pictured. *Black Coffee* on Decca is her most highly regarded album among jazz collectors although her *Rendezvous* album on Capitol is a close second, especially with its lovely cover.

Label & Catalog #		Title	Year	VG+	NM
Capitol T-1772	(M)	**Sugar 'N' Spice**	1962	8.00	20.00
Capitol ST-1772	(S)	**Sugar 'N' Spice**	1962	10.00	25.00
Capitol T-1850	(M)	**Mink Jazz**	1963	10.00	25.00
Capitol ST-1850	(S)	**Mink Jazz**	1963	12.00	30.00
Capitol T-1857	(M)	**I'm A Woman**	1963	6.00	15.00
Capitol ST-1857	(S)	**I'm A Woman**	1963	8.00	20.00
Capitol T-1969	(M)	**In Love Again**	1963	6.00	15.00
Capitol ST-1969	(S)	**In Love Again**	1963	8.00	20.00
Capitol T-2096	(M)	**In The Name Of Love**	1964	6.00	15.00
Capitol ST-2096	(S)	**In The Name Of Love**	1964	8.00	20.00
Capitol T-2320	(M)	**Pass Me By**	1965	6.00	15.00
Capitol ST-2320	(S)	**Pass Me By**	1965	8.00	20.00
Capitol T-2388	(M)	**Then Was Then Now Is Now**	1965	6.00	15.00
Capitol ST-2388	(S)	**Then Was Then Now Is Now**	1965	8.00	20.00
Capitol T-2475	(M)	**Big Spender**	1966	5.00	12.00
Capitol ST-2475	(S)	**Big Spender**	1966	6.00	15.00
Capitol T-2781	(M)	**Something Groovy**	1967	5.00	12.00
Capitol ST-2781	(S)	**Something Groovy**	1967	6.00	15.00
Capitol ST-2887	(S)	**The Hits Of Peggy Lee**	1968	6.00	15.00
Capitol ST-108	(S)	**Two Shows Nightly**	1968	*See below*	
		(Capitol 108 wulled shortly after release and is preposterously rare.)			
Capitol ST-386	(S)	**Is That All There Is?**	1969	6.00	15.00

— Capitol albums above have black "rainbow" labels with the logo on top.—

LEE, PERRI

Perri Lee is a jazz-based organ player.

Roulette R-52080	(M)	**A Night At Count Basie's**	1962	8.00	20.00
Roulette SR-52080	(S)	**A Night At Count Basie's**	1962	6.00	15.00

LEGGE, WADE

Wade Legge is a modern jazz pianist.

Blue Note BLP-5031	(10")	**Wade Legge Trio**	1953	300.00	500.00

LEGRAND, MICHEL

Paris born Michel Legrand is a modern jazz pianist, composer and band leader.

Columbia CL-555	(M)	**I Love Paris**	1954	16.00	40.00
		— Columbia albums above have "Long Playing" on the bottom of the label.—			
Columbia CL-1115	(M)	**Michel Legrand Plays Cole Porter**	1957	12.00	30.00
Columbia CL-1139	(M)	**Legrand In Rio**	1958	12.00	30.00
Columbia CL-1250	(M)	**Legrand Jazz**	1958	16.00	40.00
Columbia CS-8079	(S)	**Legrand Jazz**	1960	12.00	30.00
		(Columbia 1250 also features Miles Davis.)			
Columbia CL-1437	(M)	**I Love Paris**	1960	10.00	25.00
Columbia CS-8237	(E)	**I Love Paris**	1960	5.00	12.00
		(Columbia 1437 is a reissue of 555.)			
		— Columbia albums above have six white on black "eye" logos on each label.—			
Philips PHM-200-074	(M)	**The Michel Legrand Big Band Plays Richard Rogers**	1963	10.00	25.00
Philips PHS-600-074	(S)	**The Michel Legrand Big Band Plays Richard Rogers**	1963	8.00	20.00
Verve V6-8760	(S)	**Michel Legrand At Shelly Manne's Hole**	1969	4.00	10.00

— Verve albums above have black labels with "MGM Records" on the bottom.—

LEIGHTON, BERNIE

Bernard Leighton is a traditional jazz pianist. For additional listings refer to The First Jazz Piano Quartet.

Columbia CL-6112	(10")	**East Side Rendezvous**	1950	30.00	75.00
Cameo C-1005	(M)	**Dizzy Fingers**	1959	10.00	25.00

LEIGHTON, BERNIE / JOHNNY GUARNIERI

EmArcy MG-26018	(10")	**Piano Stylings**	1954	30.00	75.00

LEMER, PETER

Peter Lemer is a modern jazz pianist.

ESP-Disk' 1057	(S)	**Local Colour**	1968	8.00	20.00

LEONARD, HARLAN

Harlan "Mike" Leonard is a traditional jazz alto, soprano and tenor saxophone player.

RCA Victor LPV-531	(M)	**Harlan Leonard And His Rockets**	1965	10.00	25.00

Label & Catalog #		Title	Year	VG+	NM

LEONARD, HARVEY
Harvey Leonard is a traditional jazz pianist.

Keynote 1102	(M)	**Jazz Ecstasy**	1955	20.00	50.00

LES JAZZ MODES: *Refer to* THE JAZZ MODES

LESLIE, BILL
William Leslie is a modern jazz tenor saxophone player.

Argo LP-710	(M)	**Diggin' The Chicks**	1962	12.00	30.00
Argo LPS-710	(S)	**Diggin' The Chicks**	1962	10.00	25.00

LETMAN, JOHN
John Letman is a traditional jazz trumpet player and vocalist.

Bethlehem BCP-6053	(M)	**The Many Angles Of John Letman**	1961	12.00	30.00
Bethlehem SBCP-6053	(S)	**The Many Angles Of John Letman**	1961	12.00	30.00

LEVEY, STAN
Stanley Levey is a modern jazz drummwer. For additional listings refer to Conte Candoli / Stan Levey; Max Roach / Stan Levey.

Bethlehem BCP-1017	(10")	**Stan Levey Plays**	1954	40.00	100.00
Bethlehem BCP-37	(M)	**This Time The Drums On Me**	1955	20.00	50.00
Bethlehem BCP-71	(M)	**Grand Stan**	1957	20.00	50.00
Mode LP-101	(M)	**Stan Levey Quartet**	1957	30.00	75.00
Liberty LRP-3067	(M)	**Drummin' The Blues**	1957	20.00	50.00

LEVIN, MARC

Savoy MG-12190	(S)	**The Dragon Suite**	1967	8.00	20.00

LEVINE, HENRY
Henry "Hot Lips" Levine is a traditional jazz trumpet player.

RCA Victor LPM-1283	(M)	**Dixieland Jazz Band**	1956	20.00	50.00
—RCA albums above have black labels with "Long Play" on the bottom.—					
Camden CAL-321	(M)	**Lower Basin Street**	1958	8.00	20.00

LEVISTER, ALONZO
Alonzo Levister is a modern jazz-based pianist and composer.

Debut DEB-125	(M)	**Manhattan Monodrama**	1956	60.00	150.00

LEVITT, ROD
Rod Levitt is a modern jazz trombone player and composer.

Riverside RLP-471	(M)	**The Dynamic Sound Patterns Of The Rod Levitt Orchestra**	1964	8.00	20.00
Riverside RS-9471	(S)	**The Dynamic Sound Patterns Of The Rod Levitt Orchestra**	1964	6.00	15.00
—Riverside albums above have blue mono or black stereo labels with a reel & mike logo on top.—					
RCA Victor LPM-3372	(M)	**Insight**	1965	8.00	20.00
RCA Victor LSP-3372	(S)	**Insight**	1965	6.00	15.00
RCA Victor LPM-3448	(M)	**Solid Ground**	1965	8.00	20.00
RCA Victor LSP-3448	(S)	**Solid Ground**	1965	6.00	15.00
RCA Victor LPM-3615	(M)	**42nd Street**	1966	8.00	20.00
RCA Victor LSP-3615	(S)	**42nd Street**	1966	6.00	15.00
—RCA albums above have black labels with "Monaural" or "Stereo" on the bottom.—					

LEVY, LOU
Louis Levy is a West Coast jazz pianist.

Nocturne NLP-10	(10")	**Lou Levy Trio**	1954	40.00	100.00
RCA Victor LPM-1267	(M)	**Solo Scene**	1956	20.00	50.00
RCA Victor LPM-1319	(M)	**Jazz In Four Colors**	1956	20.00	50.00
RCA Victor LPM-1491	(M)	**A Most Musical Fella**	1957	20.00	50.00
—RCA albums above have black labels with "Long Play" on the bottom.—					
Jubilee JLP-1101	(M)	**Baby Grand Jazz**	1959	16.00	40.00
Jubilee JGS-1101	(S)	**Baby Grand Jazz**	1959	12.00	30.00
Philips PHM-200-056	(M)	**The Hymn**	1962	8.00	20.00
Philips PHS-600-056	(S)	**The Hymn**	1962	6.00	15.00

LEVY, LOU / CONTE CANDOLI

Atlantic 1268	(M)	**West Coast Wailers**	1957	20.00	50.00
—Atlantic albums above have black mono or green stereo labels.—					

Label & Catalog #		Title	Year	VG+	NM
Atlantic 1268	(M)	**West Coast Wailers**	1961	10.00	25.00
		—Atlantic albums above have multi-color labels with a white fan logo.—			
LEWES, WILSON					
Diplomat D-2369	(M)	**The "In" Crowd**	1966	4.00	10.00
Diplomat DS-2369	(S)	**The "In" Crowd**	1966	3.20	8.00
Diplomat D-2378	(M)	**The Shadow Of Your Smile**	1966	4.00	10.00
Diplomat DS-2378	(S)	**The Shadow Of Your Smile**	1966	3.20	8.00
LEWIS-FARBERMAN-SCHULLER-SMITH					
Cambridge 820	(S)	**Pieces By Lewis, Farberman, Schuller & Smith**	1967	20.00	50.00
LEWIS, GEORGE					
George Louis Zeno, aka George Lewis, is a traditional jazz clarinet and alto saxophone player.					
Disc Jockey DDL-100	(M)	**Jazz At Ohio Union** *(2 LP box with insert)*	195?	660.00	1,000.00
Blue Note BLP-7010	(10")	**George Lewis' New Orleans Stompers, Vol. 1**	1951	125.00	250.00
Blue Note BLP-7013	(10")	**George Lewis' New Orleans Stompers, Vol. 2**	1951	125.00	250.00
Blue Note BLP-7027	(10")	**George Lewis' New Orleans Stompers, Vol. 3**	1954	125.00	250.00
Blue Note BLP-7028	(10")	**George Lewis' New Orleans Stompers, Vol. 4**	1954	125.00	250.00
Blue Note BLP-1205	(M)	**George Lewis & His New Orleans Stompers, Volume 1** *(Deep groove)*	1955	60.00	150.00
Blue Note BLP-1205	(M)	**George Lewis & His New Orleans Stompers, Voume 1** *(Blue Note 1205 is a reissue of 7027 and 7023.)*	1955	40.00	100.00
Blue Note BLP-1206	(M)	**George Lewis & His New Orleans Stompers, Volume 2** *(Deep groove)*	1955	60.00	150.00
Blue Note BLP-1206	(M)	**George Lewis & His New Orleans Stompers, Volume 2** *(Blue Note 1206 is a reissue of 7010 and 7013.)*	1955	40.00	100.00
Blue Note BLP-1208	(M)	**George Lewis Concert!** *(Deep groove)*	1955	60.00	150.00
Blue Note BLP-1208	(M)	**George Lewis Concert!**	1955	40.00	100.00
		—Blue Note albums above have blue on white labels with a Lexington Ave, NYC address.—			
Blue Note BLP-1205	(M)	**George Lewis & His New Orleans Stompers, Volume 1**	1963	10.00	25.00
Blue Note BLP-1206	(M)	**George Lewis & His New Orleans Stompers, Volume 2**	1963	10.00	25.00
Blue Note BLP-1208	(M)	**George Lewis Concert!**	1963	10.00	25.00
		—Blue Note albums above have blue on white labels with a New York, USA address.—			
Blue Note BST-81205	(E)	**George Lewis & His New Orleans Stompers, Volume 1**	196?	4.00	10.00
Blue Note BST-81206	(E)	**George Lewis & His New Orleans Stompers, Volume 2**	196?	4.00	10.00
Blue Note BST-81208	(E)	**George Lewis Concert!**	196?	4.00	10.00
		—Blue Note albums above have blue on white labels with a "A Division of Liberty Records."—			
Circle L-421	(10")	**George Lewis And His New Orleans All Stars**	1951	30.00	75.00
Paradox LP-6001	(10")	**George Lewis**	1951	30.00	75.00
American Music 639	(10")	**The George Lewis Band In The French Quarter**	1951	30.00	75.00
American Music 645	(10")	**George Lewis With Kid Shots Madison**	1952	30.00	75.00
Jazzman LJ-331	(10")	**New Orleans Music**	1954	30.00	75.00
Southland SLP-208	(10")	**George Lewis**	1955	30.00	75.00
Cavalier CVLP-6004	(M)	**George Lewis In Hi Fi**	1956	20.00	50.00
Empirical EM-107	(10")	**Spirituals In Ragtime**	1956	30.00	75.00
Riverside RLP-2507	(10")	**George Lewis**	1954	30.00	75.00
Riverside RLP-2512	(10")	**George Lewis With Guest Artist Red Allen**	1955	30.00	75.00
Riverside RLP-12-207	(M)	**Jazz In The Classic New Orleans Tradition**	1956	20.00	50.00
Riverside RLP-12-230	(M)	**Jazz At Vespers**	1957	20.00	50.00
		—Riverside albums above have blue on white labels.—			
Riverside RLP-12-207	(M)	**Jazz In The Classic New Orleans Tradition**	195?	12.00	30.00
Riverside RLP-12-230	(M)	**Jazz At Vespers**	195?	12.00	30.00
Riverside RLP-12-283	(M)	**George Lewis Of New Orleans**	1958	16.00	40.00
		—Riverside albums above have blue mono or black stereo labels with a reel & mike logo on top.—			
Verve MGV-1019	(M)	**Blues From The Bayou**	1957	20.00	50.00
Verve MGVS-6113	(S)	**Blues From The Bayou**	1960	16.00	40.00
Verve MGV-1021	(M)	**Doctor Jazz**	1957	20.00	50.00
Verve MGVS-6122	(S)	**Doctor Jazz**	1960	16.00	40.00
Verve MGV-1024	(M)	**Hot Time In The Old Town Tonight**	1957	20.00	50.00
Verve MGV-1027	(M)	**George Lewis' Dixieland Band**	1957	20.00	50.00
		—Verve albums above have "Verve Records, Inc." on the bottom of the label.—			

Label & Catalog #		Title	Year	VG+	NM
Verve MGV-8232	(M)	**George Lewis And Turk Murphy At Newport**	195?	20.00	50.00
Verve MGV-8277	(M)	**The Perennial George Lewis**	1958	20.00	50.00
Verve MGV-8303	(M)	**On Stage—George Lewis Concert, Volume 1**	1959	20.00	50.00
Verve MGV-8304	(M)	**On Stage—George Lewis Concert, Volume 2**	1959	20.00	50.00
Verve MGV-8325	(M)	**Oh, Didn't He Ramble**	1959	20.00	50.00
Verve MGVS-6064	(S)	**Oh, Didn't He Ramble**	1960	16.00	40.00
—Verve albums above have black labels with "Verve Records, Inc." on the bottom.—					
Verve V-1019	(M)	**Blues From The Bayou**	1961	8.00	20.00
Verve V6-1019	(S)	**Blues From The Bayou**	1961	6.00	15.00
Verve V-1021	(M)	**Doctor Jazz**	1961	8.00	20.00
Verve V6-1021	(S)	**Doctor Jazz**	1961	6.00	15.00
Verve V-1024	(M)	**Hot Time In The Old Town Tonight**	1961	8.00	20.00
Verve V6-1024	(S)	**Hot Time In The Old Town Tonight**	1961	6.00	15.00
Verve V-1027	(M)	**George Lewis' Dixieland Band**	1961	8.00	20.00
Verve V-8232	(M)	**George Lewis And Turk Murphy At Newport**	1961	8.00	20.00
Verve V-8277	(M)	**The Perennial George Lewis**	1961	8.00	20.00
Verve V-8303	(M)	**On Stage—George Lewis Concert, Volume 1**	1961	8.00	20.00
Verve V-8304	(M)	**On Stage—George Lewis Concert, Volume 2**	1961	8.00	20.00
Verve V-8325	(M)	**Oh, Didn't He Ramble**	1961	8.00	20.00
Verve V6-8325	(S)	**Oh, Didn't He Ramble**	1961	6.00	15.00
—Verve albums above have black labels with "MGM Records" on the bottom.—					
Delmar DL-201	(M)	**Doctor Jazz**	195?	16.00	40.00
Atlantic 1411	(M)	**The George Lewis Band**	1963	8.00	20.00
Atlantic SD-1411	(S)	**The George Lewis Band**	1963	6.00	15.00
—Atlantic albums above have multi-color labels a black fan logo.—					
LEWIS, JOHN, & BILL PERKINS					
Pacific Jazz PJ-1217	(M)	**Grand Encounter: 2° East 3° West**	1956	60.00	150.00
World Pacific WP-1217	(M)	**Grand Encounter: 2° East 3° West**	1958	40.00	100.00
Pacific Jazz PJ-44	(M)	**Grand Encounter: 2° East 3° West**	1962	16.00	40.00
LEWIS, JOHN, & SACHA DISTEL					
Atlantic 1267	(M)	**Afternoon In Paris**	1957	16.00	40.00
—Atlantic albums above have black mono or green stereo labels.—					
Atlantic 1267	(M)	**Afternoon In Paris**	1961	6.00	15.00
—Atlantic albums above have multi-color labels with a white fan logo.—					
Atlantic 1267	(M)	**Afternoon In Paris**	196?	4.00	10.00
—Atlantic albums above have multi-color labels with a white fan logo.—					

LEWIS, JOHN

John Lewis is a modern jazz pianist and composer best known as the leader of The Modern Jazz Quarte. For additional listings refer to The Jazz Combo / John Lewis; The Modern Jazz Sextet; Orchestra USA; and the Jazzy Soundtracks section under Atlantic and United Artists.

Label & Catalog #		Title	Year	VG+	NM
RCA Victor LPM-1742	(M)	**European Windows**	1958	20.00	50.00
—RCA albums above have black labels with "Long Play" on the bottom.—					
Atlantic 1272	(M)	**The John Lewis Piano**	1958	16.00	40.00
Atlantic 1313	(M)	**Improvised Meditations & Excursions**	1959	16.00	40.00
Atlantic SD-1313	(S)	**Improvised Meditations & Excursions**	1959	16.00	40.00
—Atlantic albums above have black mono or green stereo labels.—					
Atlantic 1272	(M)	**The John Lewis Piano**	1960	8.00	20.00
Atlantic 1313	(M)	**Improvised Meditations & Excursions**	1960	8.00	20.00
Atlantic SD-1313	(S)	**Improvised Meditations & Excursions**	1960	6.00	15.00
Atlantic 1334	(M)	**The Golden Striker**	1960	10.00	25.00
Atlantic SD-1334	(S)	**The Golden Striker**	1960	8.00	20.00
Atlantic 1365	(M)	**John Lewis Presents Jazz Abstractions**	1961	12.00	30.00
Atlantic SD-1365	(S)	**John Lewis Presents Jazz Abstractions**	1961	10.00	25.00
Atlantic 1370	(M)	**Original Sin**	1961	10.00	25.00
Atlantic SD-1370	(S)	**Original Sin**	1961	8.00	20.00
Atlantic 1375	(M)	**The Wonderful World Of Jazz**	1961	12.00	30.00
Atlantic SD-1375	(S)	**The Wonderful World Of Jazz**	1961	10.00	25.00
—Atlantic albums above have multi-color labels with a white fan logo.—					
Atlantic 1272	(M)	**The John Lewis Piano**	1960	6.00	15.00
Atlantic 1313	(M)	**Improvised Meditations & Excursions**	1960	6.00	15.00
Atlantic SD-1313	(S)	**Improvised Meditations & Excursions**	1960	5.00	12.00
Atlantic 1334	(M)	**The Golden Striker**	1960	6.00	15.00
Atlantic SD-1334	(S)	**The Golden Striker**	1960	5.00	12.00
Atlantic 1365	(M)	**John Lewis Presents Jazz Abstractions**	1961	6.00	15.00
Atlantic SD-1365	(S)	**John Lewis Presents Jazz Abstractions**	1961	5.00	12.00

Label & Catalog #		Title	Year	VG+	NM
Atlantic 1370	(M)	**Original Sin**	1961	6.00	15.00
Atlantic SD-1370	(S)	**Original Sin**	1961	5.00	12.00
Atlantic 1375	(M)	**The Wonderful World Of Jazz**	1961	6.00	15.00
Atlantic SD-1375	(S)	**The Wonderful World Of Jazz**	1961	5.00	12.00
Atlantic 1392	(M)	**European Encounter**	1962	8.00	20.00
Atlantic SD-1392	(S)	**European Encounter**	1962	6.00	15.00
Atlantic 1402	(M)	**Animal Dance**	1963	8.00	20.00
Atlantic SD-1402	(S)	**Animal Dance**	1963	6.00	15.00
Atlantic 1425	(M)	**Essence**	1964	8.00	20.00
Atlantic SD-1425	(S)	**Essence**	1964	6.00	15.00

—Atlantic albums above have multi-color labels with a white fan logo.—

LEWIS, MEADE LUX

Meade Lux Lewis is a traditional jazz pianist and composer. For additional listings refer to Slim Gaillard / Meade Lux Lewis.

Label & Catalog #		Title	Year	VG+	NM
Mercury MG-25158	(10")	**Meade Lux Lewis**	1951	60.00	150.00
Disc DLP-352	(10")	**Meade Lux Lewis At The Philharmonic**	195?	50.00	125.00
		(Disc 352 features cover art by David Stone Martin.)			
Down Home MGD-6	(M)	**Cat House Piano**	1955	*Unreleased*	
Down Home MGD-7	(M)	**Yancey's Last Ride**	1956	20.00	50.00
		(Down Home 7 features cover art by David Stone Martin.)			
Verve MGV-1006	(M)	**Cat House Piano**	1956	20.00	50.00
		(Verve 1066 features cover art by David Stone Martin.)			
Verve MGV-1007	(M)	**Meade Lux Lewis**	1956	20.00	50.00
		—Verve albums above have "Verve Records, Inc." on the bottom of the label.—			
Verve V-1006	(M)	**Cat House Piano**	1961	6.00	15.00
Verve V-1007	(M)	**Meade Lux Lewis**	1961	6.00	15.00
		—Verve albums above have black labels with "MGM Records" on the bottom.—			
Blue Note BLP-7018	(10")	**Boogie Woogie Classics**	1952	100.00	25.00
Atlantic ALS-133	(10")	**Boogie-Woogie Interpretations**	1952	30.00	75.00
ABC-Paramount ABC-164	(M)	**Out Of The Roaring 20's**	1957	16.00	40.00
Riverside RLP-402	(M)	**The Blues Piano Artistry Of Meade Lux Lewis**	1962	12.00	30.00
Riverside RLP-9402	(S)	**The Blues Piano Artistry Of Meade Lux Lewis**	1962	10.00	25.00

—Riverside albums above have blue mono or black stereo labels with a reel & mike logo on top.—

LEWIS, MEADE LUX, & LOUIS BELLSON

Label & Catalog #		Title	Year	VG+	NM
Clef MGC-632	(M)	**Boogie Woogie Piano And Drums**	1954	20.00	50.00
		(Clef 632 features cover art by David Stone Martin.)			

LEWIS, MEL

Melvin Sokoloff, aka Mel Lewis, is a West Coast jazz drummer. For additional listings refer to Pepper Adams; The Five; Thad Jones & Mel Lewis.

Label & Catalog #		Title	Year	VG+	NM
San Francisco 2	(M)	**Got 'Cha**	1957	30.00	75.00
Mode LP-103	(M)	**Mel Lewis Sextet**	1957	30.00	75.00
Vee Jay LP-3062	(M)	**Gettin' Together**	1963	12.00	30.00
Vee Jay LPS-3062	(S)	**Gettin' Together**	1963	12.00	30.00

LEWIS, RAMSEY (THE RAMSEY LEWIS TRIO)

Ramsey Lewis Jr. is a modern jazz pianist and composer. For additional listings refer to Lorez Alexandria; Lem Winchester.

Label & Catalog #		Title	Year	VG+	NM
EmArcy MG-36150	(M)	**Down To Earth**	1958	16.00	40.00
EmArcy SR-80029	(S)	**Down To Earth**	1958	12.00	30.00
		—EmArcy albums above have blue labels with silver print.—			
Mercury MG-20536	(M)	**Down To Earth**	1960	8.00	20.00
Mercury SR-60536	(S)	**Down To Earth**	1960	6.00	15.00
		(Mercury 20536 is a reissue of EmArcy 36150.)			
		—Mercury albums above have silver on black labels.—			
Argo LP-611	(M)	**Gentleman Of Swing**	1958	12.00	30.00
Argo LPS-611	(S)	**Gentleman Of Swing**	1958	10.00	25.00
Argo LP-627	(M)	**Gentleman Of Jazz**	1958	12.00	30.00
Argo LSP-627	(S)	**Gentleman Of Jazz**	1958	10.00	25.00
Argo LP-645	(M)	**An Hour With The Ramsey Lewis Trio**	1959	12.00	30.00
Argo LPS-645	(S)	**An Hour With The Ramsey Lewis Trio**	1959	10.00	25.00
Argo LP-665	(M)	**Stretching Out**	1960	10.00	25.00
Argo LPS-665	(S)	**Stretching Out**	1960	8.00	20.00
Argo LP-671	(M)	**The Ramsey Lewis Trio In Chicago**	1961	10.00	25.00
Argo LPS-671	(S)	**The Ramsey Lewis Trio In Chicago**	1961	8.00	20.00

Label & Catalog #		Title	Year	VG+	NM
Argo LP-680	(M)	**More Music From The Soil**	1961	10.00	25.00
Argo LPS-680	(S)	**More Music From The Soil**	1961	8.00	20.00
Argo LP-687	(M)	**The Sound Of Christmas**	1961	10.00	25.00
Argo LPS-687	(S)	**The Sound Of Christmas**	1961	8.00	20.00
Argo LP-693	(M)	**The Sound Of Spring**	1962	8.00	20.00
Argo LPS-693	(S)	**The Sound Of Spring**	1962	6.00	15.00
Argo LP-701	(M)	**Country Meets The Blues**	1962	10.00	25.00
Argo LPS-701	(S)	**Country Meets The Blues**	1962	8.00	20.00
Argo LP-705	(M)	**Bossa Nova**	1962	8.00	20.00
Argo LPS-705	(S)	**Bossa Nova**	1962	6.00	15.00
Argo LP-715	(M)	**Pot Luck**	1962	8.00	20.00
Argo LPS-715	(S)	**Pot Luck**	1962	6.00	15.00
Argo LP-723	(M)	**Barefoot Sunday Blues**	1963	8.00	20.00
Argo LPS-723	(S)	**Barefoot Sunday Blues**	1963	6.00	15.00
Argo LP-732	(M)	**Bach To The Blues**	1964	8.00	20.00
Argo LPS-732	(S)	**Bach To The Blues**	1964	6.00	15.00
Argo LP-741	(M)	**Ramsey Lewis Trio At The Bohemian Caverns**	1964	8.00	20.00
Argo LPS-741	(S)	**Ramsey Lewis Trio At The Bohemian Caverns**	1964	6.00	15.00
Argo LP-745	(M)	**More Sound Of Christmas**	1964	10.00	25.00
Argo LPS-745	(S)	**More Sound Of Christmas**	1964	8.00	20.00
Argo LP-750	(M)	**You Better Believe It**	1965	8.00	20.00
Argo LPS-750	(S)	**You Better Believe It**	1965	6.00	15.00
Argo LP-757	(M)	**The In Crowd**	1965	8.00	20.00
Argo LPS-757	(S)	**The In Crowd**	1965	10.00	25.00
Cadet LP-755	(M)	**Choice! The Best Of The Ramsey Lewis Trio**	1965	8.00	20.00
Cadet LPS-755	(S)	**Choice! The Best Of The Ramsey Lewis Trio**	1965	6.00	15.00
Cadet LP-761	(M)	**Hang On, Ramsey!**	1966	6.00	15.00
Cadet LPS-761	(S)	**Hang On, Ramsey!**	1966	5.00	12.00
Cadet LP-771	(M)	**Swingin'**	1966	6.00	15.00
Cadet LPS-771	(S)	**Swingin'**	1966	5.00	12.00
Cadet LP-774	(M)	**Wade In The Water**	1966	6.00	15.00
Cadet LPS-774	(S)	**Wade In The Water**	1966	5.00	12.00
Cadet LP-782	(M)	**The Movie Album**	1967	6.00	15.00
Cadet LPS-782	(S)	**The Movie Album**	1967	5.00	12.00
Cadet LP-790	(M)	**Goin' Latin**	1967	6.00	15.00
Cadet LPS-790	(S)	**Goin' Latin**	1967	5.00	12.00
Cadet LPS-794	(S)	**Dancing In The Street**	1968	5.00	12.00
Cadet LPS-799	(S)	**Up Pops Ramsey Lewis**	1969	5.00	12.00
Cadet LPS-821	(S)	**Mother Nature's Son**	1969	5.00	12.00
Cadet LPS-827	(S)	**Another Voyage**	1969	5.00	12.00

LEWIS, TED

Theodore Friedman, aka Ted Lewis, is a traditional jazz clarinet player and vocalist.

Columbia CL-6127	(10")	**Classic Jazz**	1950	20.00	50.00
Epic LN-3170	(M)	**Everybody's Happy!**	1955	16.00	40.00
Decca DL-8322	(M)	**The Medicine Man For The Blues**	1956	16.00	40.00

LIBBY, JERRY

Sabrina SA-100	(M)	**Live? At Wilkins**	1964	8.00	20.00

LIDSTROM, JACK (THE JACK LIDTROM STOMPERS)

World Pacific PJ-1235	(M)	**Look, Dad! They're Comin' Down Our Street In Hi-Fi**	1957	16.00	40.00

LIGHTHOUSE ALL-STARS, THE: ***Refer to*** **HOWARD RUMSEY**

LINCOLN, ABBEY

Anna Woolridge, aka Abbey Lincoln, is a West Coast jazz-based vocalist. For additional listings refer to Jazz Artists Guild; Max Roach.

Liberty LRP-3025	(M)	**Abbey Lincoln's Affair:... A Story Of A Girl In Love**	1957	20.00	50.00
Riverside RLP-12-251	(M)	**That's Him!**	1957	20.00	50.00
Riverside RLP-1107	(S)	**That's Him!**	1958	16.00	40.00
Riverside RLP-12-277	(M)	**It's Magic**	1958	20.00	50.00
Riverside RLP-12-308	(M)	**Abbey Is Blue**	1959	20.00	50.00
Riverside RLP-1153	(S)	**Abbey Is Blue**	1959	16.00	40.00

—Riverside albums above have blue mono or black stereo labels with a reel & mike logo on top.—

Candid 8015	(M)	**Straight Ahead**	1960	20.00	50.00
Candid 9015	(S)	**Straight Ahead**	1960	16.00	40.00

Label & Catalog #		Title	Year	VG+	NM
LINDBERG, NILS					
Capitol T-10367	(M)	**Trisection**	196?	10.00	25.00
Capitol ST-10367	(S)	**Trisection**	196?	8.00	20.00
LISTON, MELBA					
Melba Liston is a modern jazz trombone player and composer.					
Metrojazz E-1013	(M)	**Melba Liston And Her Bones**	1958	30.00	75.00
Metrojazz SE-1013	(S)	**Melba Liston And Her Bones**	1958	24.00	60.00
LITTLE, BOOKER					
Booker Little is a modern jazz trumpet player. For additional listings refer to Eric Dolphy; Young Men From Memphis.					
United Arts. UAL-4034	(M)	**Booker Little 4**	1959	30.00	75.00
United Arts. UAS-5034	(S)	**Booker Little 4**	1959	24.00	60.00
Time 52011	(M)	**Booker Little**	1960	30.00	75.00
Time S-2011	(S)	**Booker Little**	1960	24.00	60.00
Candid CD-8027	(M)	**Out Front**	1961	20.00	50.00
Candid CS-9027	(S)	**Out Front**	1961	16.00	40.00
		(Candid 8027 also features Max Roach.)			
Bethlehem BCP-6061	(M)	**Booker Little And Friend**	1961	20.00	50.00
LLOYD, CHARLES					
Charles Lloyd is a modern jazz-based tenor saxophone and flute player and composer.					
Columbia CL-2267	(M)	**Discovery!**	1965	8.00	20.00
Columbia CS-9067	(S)	**Discovery!**	1965	6.00	15.00
—Columbia albums above have "Guaranteed High Fidelity" or "360 Sound Stereo" in black on the label.—					
Columbia CL-2412	(M)	**Of Course, Of Course**	1965	6.00	15.00
Columbia CS-9212	(S)	**Of Course, Of Course**	1965	5.00	12.00
Columbia CL-2809	(M)	**Nirvana**	1968	6.00	15.00
Columbia CS-9609	(S)	**Nirvana**	1968	5.00	12.00
—Columbia albums above have "360 Sound" in white on the bottom of the label.—					
Atlantic 1459	(M)	**Dream Weaver**	1966	5.00	12.00
Atlantic SD-1459	(S)	**Dream Weaver**	1966	4.00	10.00
Atlantic 1473	(M)	**Forest Flower**	1967	5.00	12.00
Atlantic SD-1473	(S)	**Forest Flower**	1967	4.00	10.00
Atlantic 1481	(M)	**Love In At The Fillmore In San Francisco**	1967	5.00	12.00
Atlantic SD-1481	(S)	**Love In At The Fillmore In San Francisco**	1967	4.00	10.00
Atlantic 1493	(M)	**Journey Within**	1968	5.00	12.00
Atlantic SD-1493	(S)	**Journey Within**	1968	4.00	10.00
Atlantic SD-1500	(S)	**Charles Lloyd In Europe**	1969	4.00	10.00
—Atlantic albums above have multi-color labels with a black fan logo.—					
LOFTON, CLARENCE					
"Cripple Clarence" Lofton is a traditional jazz pianist and vocalist.					
Riverside RLP-1037	(10")	**Honky-Tonk And Boogie-Woogie Piano**	1954	30.00	75.00
LOFTON, TRICKY, & CARMELL JONES					
Pacific Jazz PJ-49	(M)	**Brass Bag**	1962	20.00	50.00
Pacific Jazz ST-49	(S)	**Brass Bag**	1962	16.00	40.00
		(Pacific Jazz 49 also features Gerald Wilson.)			
LOGAN, GIUSEPPI					
Giuseppi Logan is a modern jazz tenor and alto saxophone player and composer.					
ESP-Disk' 1007	(M)	**Giuseppi Logan Quartet**	1965	8.00	20.00
ESP-Disk' 1007	(S)	**Giuseppi Logan Quartet**	1965	6.00	15.00
ESP-Disk' 1013	(M)	**More Giuseppi Logan**	1966	8.00	20.00
ESP-Disk' 1013	(S)	**More Giuseppi Logan**	1966	6.00	15.00
LONDON, JULIE					
Julie London is a jazz/big band-based pop vocalist. For additional listings refer to Chris Connor / Carmen McRae / Julie London.					
Liberty LRP-3006	(M)	**Julie Is Her Name**	1956	20.00	50.00
Liberty LRP-3012	(M)	**Lonely Girl**	1956	20.00	50.00
Liberty SL-9002	(M)	**Calendar Girl** *(Gatefold cover)*	1956	40.00	100.00
Liberty LRP-3027	(M)	**Julie Is Her Name**	1957	20.00	50.00
Liberty LST-7027	(S)	**Julie Is Her Name**	1958	20.00	50.00
Liberty LST-7027	(S)	**Julie Is Her Name** *(Blue vinyl)*	1958	40.00	100.00
Liberty LST-7027	(S)	**Julie Is Her Name** *(Red vinyl)*	1958	40.00	100.00

Label & Catalog #		Title	Year	VG+	NM
Liberty LRP-3043	(M)	**About The Blues**	1957	16.00	40.00
Liberty LRP-3060	(M)	**Make Love To Me**	1957	16.00	40.00
Liberty LRP-3096	(M)	**Julie**	1957	16.00	40.00
Liberty LRP-3100	(M)	**Julie Is Her Name, Volume 2**	1958	12.00	30.00
Liberty LST-7100	(S)	**Julie Is Her Name, Volume 2**	1958	16.00	40.00
Liberty LRP-3105	(M)	**London By Night**	1958	12.00	30.00
Liberty LST-7105	(S)	**London By Night**	1958	16.00	40.00
Liberty LRP-3119	(M)	**Swing Me An Old Song**	1959	12.00	30.00
Liberty LST-7119	(S)	**Swing Me An Old Song**	1959	16.00	40.00
Liberty LRP-3130	(M)	**Your Number Please**	1959	12.00	30.00
Liberty LST-7130	(S)	**Your Number Please**	1959	16.00	40.00
—Liberty albums above have turquoise mono or silver on black stereo labels.—					
Liberty LRP-3006	(M)	**Julie Is Her Name**	1960	6.00	15.00
Liberty LRP-3012	(M)	**Lonely Girl**	1960	6.00	15.00
Liberty LRP-3027	(M)	**Julie Is Her Name**	1960	6.00	15.00
Liberty LST-7027	(S)	**Julie Is Her Name**	1960	6.00	15.00
Liberty LRP-3043	(M)	**About The Blues**	1960	6.00	15.00
Liberty LRP-3060	(M)	**Make Love To Me**	1960	6.00	15.00
Liberty LRP-3096	(M)	**Julie**	1960	6.00	15.00
Liberty LRP-3100	(M)	**Julie Is Her Name, Volume 2**	1960	5.00	12.00
Liberty LST-7100	(S)	**Julie Is Her Name, Volume 2**	1960	6.00	15.00
Liberty LRP-3105	(M)	**London By Night**	1960	5.00	12.00
Liberty LST-7105	(S)	**London By Night**	1960	6.00	15.00
Liberty LRP-3119	(M)	**Swing Me An Old Song**	1960	5.00	12.00
Liberty LST-7119	(S)	**Swing Me An Old Song**	1960	6.00	15.00
Liberty LRP-3130	(M)	**Your Number Please**	1960	5.00	12.00
Liberty LST-7130	(S)	**Your Number Please**	1960	6.00	15.00
Liberty LRP-3152	(M)	**Julie London At Home**	1960	10.00	25.00
Liberty LST-7152	(S)	**Julie London At Home**	1960	12.00	30.00
Liberty LRP-3164	(M)	**Around Midnight**	1960	10.00	25.00
Liberty LST-7164	(S)	**Around Midnight**	1960	12.00	30.00
Liberty LRP-3171	(M)	**Send For Me**	1960	10.00	25.00
Liberty LST-7171	(S)	**Send For Me**	1960	12.00	30.00
Liberty LRP-3192	(M)	**Whatever Julie Wants**	1961	10.00	25.00
Liberty LST-7192	(S)	**Whatever Julie Wants**	1961	12.00	30.00
Liberty LRP-3203	(M)	**Sophisticated Lady**	1962	10.00	25.00
Liberty LST-7203	(S)	**Sophisticated Lady**	1962	12.00	30.00
Liberty LRP-3231	(M)	**Love Letters**	1962	10.00	25.00
Liberty LST-7231	(S)	**Love Letters**	1962	12.00	30.00
Liberty LRP-3278	(M)	**Latin In A Satin Mood**	1963	10.00	25.00
Liberty LST-7278	(S)	**Latin In A Satin Mood**	1963	12.00	30.00
Liberty LRP-3291	(M)	**Golden Greats**	1963	8.00	20.00
Liberty LST-7291	(S)	**Golden Greats**	1963	10.00	25.00
Liberty LRP-3300	(M)	**The End Of The World**	1963	8.00	20.00
Liberty LST-7300	(S)	**The End Of The World**	1963	10.00	25.00
Liberty LRP-3324	(M)	**The Wonderful World Of Julie London**	1963	8.00	20.00
Liberty LST-7324	(S)	**The Wonderful World Of Julie London**	1963	10.00	25.00
Liberty LRP-3342	(M)	**Julie London**	1964	8.00	20.00
Liberty LST-7342	(S)	**Julie London**	1964	10.00	25.00
Liberty LRP-3375	(M)	**Julie London In Person At The Americana**	1964	8.00	20.00
Liberty LST-7375	(S)	**Julie London In Person At The Americana**	1964	10.00	25.00
Liberty LRP-3392	(M)	**Our Fair Lady**	1965	8.00	20.00
Liberty LST-7392	(S)	**Our Fair Lady**	1965	10.00	25.00
Liberty LRP-3434	(M)	**All Through The Night**	1965	8.00	20.00
Liberty LST-7434	(S)	**All Through The Night**	1965	10.00	25.00
Liberty LRP-3478	(M)	**For The Night People**	1966	8.00	20.00
Liberty LST-7478	(S)	**For The Night People**	1966	10.00	25.00
—Liberty albums above have black labels with a gold & white logo on the side.—					

LONG, BARBARA

Savoy MG-12161	(M)	**Soul**	1960	12.00	30.00

LONG, DANNY

Daniel Long is a modern jazz-based pianist.

Capitol T-1988	(M)	**Jazz Furlough**	1963	8.00	20.00
Capitol ST-1988	(S)	**Jazz Furlough**	1963	6.00	15.00

Mundell Lowe began his jazz career on New Orleans' famed Bourbon Street with such combos as Abbie Brunis and Sid DeVilla before spending part of 1939 with Pee Wee King on the Grand Ole Opry! After the war he worked with Ray McKinley (1945-47) before hitting the Big Apple and playing with Dave Martin, Ellis Larkins, Red Norvo, Sauter-Finnegan, Billy Taylor, and his own group. He spent most of the '50s with NBC, eventually moving into television and movie scores; his work on the *Satan In High Heels* soundtrack is classic. . . Illustrated here are two of his solo albums (Riverside and Offbeat) that display his skill as a musician and composer. He also assisted a pair of Columbia's pop artists, Johnnies Ray and Mathis, in making their sole jazz-tinged albums.

Label & Catalog #		Title	Year	VG+	NM
LOOKOFSKY, HARRY					
Harold Lookofsky is a modern jazz violin and viola player.					
Atlantic 1319	(M)	**Stringsville**	1959	16.00	40.00
Atlantic SD-1319	(S)	**Stringsville**	1959	16.00	40.00
		—Atlantic albums above have black mono or green stereo labels.—			
Atlantic 1319	(M)	**Stringsville**	1961	8.00	20.00
Atlantic SD-1319	(S)	**Stringsville**	1961	6.00	15.00
		—Atlantic albums above have multi-color labels with a white fan logo.—			
Atlantic 1319	(M)	**Stringsville**	196?	5.00	12.00
Atlantic SD-1319	(S)	**Stringsville**	196?	4.00	10.00
		—Atlantic albums above have multi-color labels with a black fan logo.—			
LORD BUCKLEY					
RCA Victor LPM-3246	(10")	**Hipsters, Flipsters And Finger Poppin' Daddies, Knock Me Your Lobes**	1955	150.00	300.00
Vaya 101	(10")	**Euphoria** *(Colored vinyl)*	1955	100.00	200.00
Vaya 101/2	(M)	**Euphoria, Volume 1**	1957	40.00	100.00
Vaya 107/8	(M)	**Euphoria, Volume 2**	1957	40.00	100.00
World Pacific WP-1279	(M)	**The Way Out Humor Of Lord Buckley**	1959	40.00	100.00
Crestview CRV-801	(M)	**The Best Of Lord Buckley**	1963	16.00	40.00
Crestview CRV7-801	(E)	**The Best Of Lord Buckley**	1963	12.00	30.00
		(Crestview 801 is a reissue of the Vaya material.)			
World Pacific WP-1815	(M)	**Lord Buckley In Concert**	1964	16.00	40.00
World Pacific WP-1849	(M)	**Blowing His Mind And Yours, Too**	1966	16.00	40.00
World Pacific WPS-21879	(E)	**Buckley's Best**	1968	16.00	40.00
World Pacific WPS-21889	(E)	**Bad Rapping The Marquis De Sade**	1969	12.00	30.00
Elcktra EKS-74047	(E)	**The Best Of Lord Buckley**	1969	12.00	30.00
		(Elektra 74047 is a reissue of the Vaya material.)			
Straight STS-1054	(S)	**A Most Immaculately Hip Autocrat**	1969	16.00	40.00
Reprise RS-6389	(S)	**A Most Immaculately Hip Autocrat**	1970	20.00	50.00
		(Reprise 6389 is a rare reissue of Straight 1054.)			
LOUSSIER, JACQUES					
London LL-3287	(M)	**Jacques Loussier Plays Back Jazz Vol. 1**	1964	6.00	15.00
London PS-287	(S)	**Jacques Loussier Plays Back Jazz Vol. 1**	1964	5.00	12.00
London LL-3288	(M)	**Jacques Loussier Plays Back Jazz Vol. 2**	1964	6.00	15.00
London PS-288	(S)	**Jacques Loussier Plays Back Jazz Vol. 2**	1964	5.00	12.00
London PS-524	(S)	**Jacques Loussier, Vol. 5**	1968	5.00	12.00
LOVETT, LEE					
Leroy Lovett is a modern jazz pianist and arranger.					
Strand 1055	(M)	**Jazz Dance Party**	1960	12.00	30.00
Strand S-1055	(S)	**Jazz Dance Party**	1960	10.00	25.00
Strand 1059	(M)	**Misty**	1960	12.00	30.00
Strand S-1059	(S)	**Misty**	1960	10.00	25.00
LOWE, MUNDELL					
Mundell Lowe is a modern jazz guitarist, arranger and composer. For additional listings refer to Sammy Davis Jr; Blossom Dearie; The Four Most; Johnnie Ray; and the Jazzy Soundtracks section under Charlie Parker.					
RCA Victor LJM-3002	(10")	**The Mundell Lowe Quintet**	1954	40.00	100.00
Riverside RLP-12-204	(M)	**The Mundell Lowe Quartet**	1956	24.00	60.00
Riverside RLP-12-208	(M)	**Guitar Moods**	1956	24.00	60.00
Riverside RLP-12-219	(M)	**New Music Of Alec Wilder**	1956	24.00	60.00
Riverside RLP-12-238	(M)	**A Grand Night For Swinging**	1957	24.00	60.00
		—Riverside albums above have blue on white labels.—			
Riverside RLP-12-204	(M)	**The Mundell Lowe Quartet**	195?	16.00	40.00
Riverside RLP-12-208	(M)	**Guitar Moods**	195?	16.00	40.00
Riverside RLP-12-219	(M)	**New Music Of Alec Wilder**	195?	16.00	40.00
Riverside RLP-12-238	(M)	**A Grand Night For Swinging**	195?	16.00	40.00
		—Riverside albums above have blue mono or black stereo labels with a reel & mike logo on top.—			
Camden CAL-490	(M)	**Porgy And Bess**	1959	10.00	25.00
Camden CAS-490	(S)	**Porgy And Bess**	1959	8.00	20.00
Camden CAL-522	(M)	**TV Action Jazz!**	1959	10.00	25.00
Camden CAS-522	(S)	**TV Action Jazz!**	1959	8.00	20.00
Camden CAL-627	(M)	**TV Action Jazz!—Volume 2**	1960	10.00	25.00
Camden CAS-627	(S)	**TV Action Jazz!—Volume 2**	1960	8.00	20.00
		—Camden albums above have purple & blue labels.—			

Label & Catalog #		Title	Year	VG+	NM
Offbeat OLP-3010	(M)	**Tacit For Neurotics**	1960	16.00	40.00
Offbeat OS-93010	(S)	**Tacit For Neurotics**	1960	12.00	30.00
		(Offbeat 3010 is a reissue of Riverside 219.)			
Charlie Parker PLP-822	(M)	**Blues For A Stripper**	1962	12.00	30.00
Charlie Parker PLP-822S	(S)	**Blues For A Stripper**	1962	10.00	25.00

LOWE, MUNDELL, & BILLY TAYLOR & GENE QUILL

Jazzland JLP-8	(M)	**Low-Down Guitar**	1960	14.00	35.00
		(Jazzland 8 is a reissue of Riverside 238.)			

LUCRAFT, HOWARD

Howard Lucraft is a traditional jazz guitarist and composer.

Decca DL-8679	(M)	**Showcase For Modern Jazz**	1958	12.00	30.00

LUNA

Arhoolie ST-8001	(S)	**Space Swell**	1968	6.00	15.00

LUNCEFORD, JIMMIE

James Lunceford is a traditional jazz multi-instrumentalist, arranger and big band leader.

Columbia GL-104	(10")	**Lunceford Special**	1950	30.00	75.00
Columbia ML-4804	(M)	**Lunceford Special**	195?	20.00	50.00
Columbia CL-2715	(10")	**Lunceford Special**	1955	20.00	50.00
Columbia CL-634	(M)	**Lunceford Special**	1955	16.00	40.00
Decca DL-5393	(10")	**For Dancer's Only**	1952	20.00	50.00
		—Columbia albums above have "Long Playing" on the bottom of the label.—			
Decca DL-8050	(M)	**Jimmie Lunceford And Orchestra**	1954	16.00	40.00
Decca DL-9237	(M)	**Rhythm Is Our Business**	1958	16.00	40.00
Decca DL-79237	(S)	**Rhythm Is Our Business**	1958	12.00	30.00
Decca DL-9238	(M)	**Harlem Shout**	1958	16.00	40.00
Decca DL-79238	(S)	**Harlem Shout**	1958	12.00	30.00
Decca "X" LX-3002	(M)	**Jimmie Lunceford & His Chicksaw Syncopaters**	1954	20.00	50.00

LYMAN, ARTHUR

Arthur Lyman is a vibraphone player with this sole jazz-based outing.

Hifijazz J-607	(M)	**Leis Of Jazz**	1959	12.00	30.00
Hifijazz JS-607	(S)	**Leis Of Jazz**	1959	10.00	25.00

LYNNE, GLORIA

Gloria Lynne is a jazz-based vocalist.

Everett E-5001	(M)	**Gloria Lynne Live! Take: 1**	1959	10.00	25.00
Everett ES-1001	(S)	**Gloria Lynne Live! Take: 1**	1959	12.00	30.00
Everest LPBR-5022	(M)	**Miss Gloria Lynne**	1959	8.00	20.00
Everest SDBR-1022	(S)	**Miss Gloria Lynne**	1959	10.00	25.00
Everest LPBR-5063	(M)	**Lonely And Sentimental**	1959	8.00	20.00
Everest SDBR-1063	(S)	**Lonely And Sentimental**	1959	10.00	25.00
Everest LPBR-5090	(M)	**Try A Little Tenderness**	1960	8.00	20.00
Everest SDBR-1090	(S)	**Try A Little Tenderness**	1960	10.00	25.00
Everest LPBR-5101	(M)	**Day In, Day Out**	1960	8.00	20.00
Everest SDBR-1101	(S)	**Day In, Day Out**	1960	10.00	25.00
Everest LPBR-5126	(M)	**I Am Glad There's You**	1961	8.00	20.00
Everest SDBR-1126	(S)	**I Am Glad There's You**	1961	10.00	25.00
Everest LPBR-5128	(M)	**He Needs Me**	1961	8.00	20.00
Everest SDBR-1128	(S)	**He Needs Me**	1961	10.00	25.00
Everest LPBR-5131	(M)	**This Little Boy Of Mine**	1961	8.00	20.00
Everest SDBR-1131	(S)	**This Little Boy Of Mine**	1961	10.00	25.00
Everest LPBR-5132	(M)	**Gloria Lynne At Basin Street**	1962	8.00	20.00
Everest SDBR-1132	(S)	**Gloria Lynne At Basin Street**	1962	10.00	25.00
Everest LPBR-5203	(M)	**Gloria Blue**	1962	8.00	20.00
Everest SDBR-1203	(S)	**Gloria Blue**	1962	10.00	25.00
Everest LPBR-5208	(M)	**At The Las Vegas Thunderbird**	1962	6.00	15.00
Everest SDBR-1208	(S)	**At The Las Vegas Thunderbird**	1962	8.00	20.00
Everest EV-5220	(M)	**Gloria, Marty And Strings**	1963	6.00	15.00
Everest EV-1220	(S)	**Gloria, Marty And Strings**	1963	8.00	20.00
Everest EV-5226	(M)	**I Wish You Love**	1964	6.00	15.00
Everest EV-1226	(S)	**I Wish You Love**	1964	8.00	20.00
Everest EV-5228	(M)	**Glorious Gloria Lynne**	1964	6.00	15.00
Everest EV-1228	(S)	**Glorious Gloria Lynne**	1964	8.00	20.00

Label & Catalog #		Title	Year	VG+	NM
Fontana MGF-27528	(M)	**Intimate Moments**	1964	6.00	15.00
Fontana SGF-67528	(S)	**Intimate Moments**	1964	8.00	20.00
Fontana MGF-27541	(M)	**Soul Serenade**	1965	6.00	15.00
Fontana SGF-67541	(S)	**Soul Serenade**	1965	8.00	20.00
Sunset SUM-1145	(M)	**Gloria Lynne**	1967	4.00	10.00
Sunset SUS-5145	(S)	**Gloria Lynne**	1967	5.00	12.00

LYTLE, JOHNNY

John Lyttle is a modern jazz vibraphone player.

Label & Catalog #		Title	Year	VG+	NM
Jazzland JLP-22	(M)	**Blue Vibes**	1960	12.00	30.00
Jazzland JLP-922	(S)	**Blue Vibes**	1960	10.00	25.00
Jazzland JLP-44	(M)	**Happy Ground**	1961	12.00	30.00
Jazzland JLP-944	(S)	**Happy Ground**	1961	10.00	25.00
Jazzland JLP-67	(M)	**Nice And Easy**	1962	12.00	30.00
Jazzland JLP-967	(S)	**Nice And Easy**	1962	10.00	25.00
Jazzland JLP-81	(M)	**Moon Child**	1962	12.00	30.00
Jazzland JLP-981	(S)	**Moon Child**	1962	10.00	25.00
Riverside RLP-456	(M)	**Got That Feeling**	1963	12.00	30.00
Riverside RS-9456	(S)	**Got That Feeling**	1964	10.00	25.00
Riverside RLP-470	(M)	**Happy Ground**	1964	12.00	30.00
Riverside RS-9470	(S)	**Happy Ground**	1963	10.00	25.00
—Riverside albums above have blue mono or black stereo labels with a reel & mike logo on top.—					
Riverside RLP-480	(M)	**The Village Caller**	1965	10.00	25.00
Riverside RS-9480	(S)	**The Village Caller**	1965	8.00	20.00
—Riverside albums above blue labels with "Orpheum Productions" on the bottom.—					
Riverside RM-3003	(M)	**A Groove**	1967	10.00	25.00
Riverside RS-3003	(S)	**A Groove**	1967	6.00	15.00
Riverside RS-3017	(S)	**Moon Child**	1968	6.00	15.00
Solid State SS-18044	(S)	**Be Proud**	1969	6.00	15.00

LYTTELTON, HUMPHREY

English born Humphrey Lyttelton is a traditional jazz trumpet player and band leader.

Label & Catalog #		Title	Year	VG+	NM
Angel ANG-60008	(10")	**Some Like It Hot**	1955	20.00	50.00
London LL-3101	(M)	**I Play As I Please**	195?	12.00	30.00
London LL-3132	(M)	**Humph Dedicates**	195?	12.00	30.00
London PS-178	(S)	**Humph Dedicates**	195?	10.00	25.00
Bethlehem BCP-6063	(M)	**Humph Plays Standards**	1961	12.00	30.00

M.

MACERO, TEO

Attilio "Teo" Macero is a modern jazz sax player, composer and producer. For additional listings refer to The Manhattan Jazz All-Stars.; Charlie Mingus & Teo Macero.

Debut DLP-6	*(10")*	**Explorations By Teo Macero**	*1954*	**100.00**	**200.00**
Prestige PRLP-7104	*(M)*	**Teo Macero With The Prestige Jazz Quartet**	*1957*	**30.00**	**75.00**

—Prestige albums above have yellow labels with a W. 50th Street, NYC address.—

MACERO, TEO, & BOB PRINCE

Columbia CL-842	*(M)*	**What's New?**	*1956*	**20.00**	**50.00**

—Columbia albums above have six white on black "eye" logos on each label.—

MACHITO

Frank Grillo, aka Machito, is an Afro-Cuban jazz band leader. For additional listings refer to Herbie Mann.

Decca DL-5157	*(10")*	**Machito's Afro-Cuban**	*1950*	**60.00**	**150.00**
Mercury MG-25009	*(10")*	**Jungle Drums**	*1950*	**60.00**	**150.00**
Mercury MG-25020	*(10")*	**Rhumbas**	*1950*	**60.00**	**150.00**
Mercury MGC-505	*(10")*	**Afro-Cuban Jazz Suite**	*1951*	**60.00**	**150.00**
Mercury MGC-511	*(10")*	**Machito Jazz With Flip & Bird**	*1952*	**60.00**	**150.00**
Clef MGC-505	*(10")*	**Afro-Cuban Jazz Suite**	*1953*	**50.00**	**125.00**
Clef MGC-511	*(10")*	**Machito Jazz With Flip & Bird**	*1953*	**50.00**	**125.00**
Clef MGC-689	*(M)*	**Afro-Cuban Jazz**	*1956*	**40.00**	**100.00**
		(Clef 689 features cover art by David Stone Martin.)			
Verve MGV-8073	*(M)*	**Afro-Cuban Jazz**	*1957*	**20.00**	**50.00**
		(Verve 8073 is a reissue of Clef 689 with the DSM cover.)			
		—Verve albums above have black labels with "Verve Records, Inc." on the bottom.—			
Verve V-8073	*(M)*	**Afro-Cuban Jazz**	*1961*	**8.00**	**20.00**
		—Verve albums above have black labels with "MGM Records" on the bottom.—			
Roulette R-52006	*(M)*	**Kenya**	*1958*	**16.00**	**40.00**
Roulette SR-52006	*(S)*	**Kenya**	*1958*	**12.00**	**30.00**
Roulette R-52026	*(M)*	**With Flute To Boot**	*1959*	**16.00**	**40.00**
Roulette SR-52026	*(S)*	**With Flute To Boot**	*1959*	**12.00**	**30.00**
Coral CRL-57258	*(M)*	**Vacation At The Concord**	*1959*	**16.00**	**40.00**
Coral CRL-757258	*(S)*	**Vacation At The Concord**	*1959*	**12.00**	**30.00**
Verve VSP-19	*(M)*	**Soul Source**	*1966*	**6.00**	**15.00**
Verve VSPS-19	*(E)*	**Soul Source**	*1966*	**3.00**	**7.50**

MACK, DAVID

Serenus SRE-1009	*(M)*	**New Directions**	*1965*	**10.00**	**25.00**
Serenus SRS-1009	*(S)*	**New Directions**	*1965*	**8.00**	**20.00**

MacKAY, DAVID, & VICKI HAMILTON

Impulse AS-9184	*(S)*	**David Mac Kay & Vicki Hamilton**	*1969*	**6.00**	**15.00**

—Impulse albums above have orange & black labels.—

MADIGAN, BETTY

MGM E-3448	*(M)*	**Am I Blue?**	*1956*	**16.00**	**40.00**

MAHONES, GILDO

Gildo Mahones is a modern jazz pianist. For additional listings refer to Les Jazz Modes.

New Jazz NJLP-8299	*(M)*	**Shooting High**	*1963*	*Unreleased*	
Prestige PRLP-16004	*(M)*	**Shooting High**	*1964*	**16.00**	**40.00**
Prestige PRLP-7339	*(M)*	**The Soulful Piano Of Gildo Mahones** *(2 LPs)*	*1964*	**14.00**	**35.00**
Prestige PRST-7339	*(S)*	**The Soulful Piano Of Gildo Mahones** *(2 LPs)*	*1964*	**12.00**	**30.00**

—Prestige albums above have blue labels with a trident logo on the right side.—

MAINERI, MIKE

Michael Maineri is a modern jazz vibraphone player.

Argo LP-706	*(M)*	**Blues On The Other Side**	*1962*	**12.00**	**30.00**
Argo LPS-706	*(S)*	**Blues On The Other Side**	*1962*	**10.00**	**25.00**
Solid State SS-18029	*(S)*	**Insight**	*1968*	**6.00**	**15.00**
Solid State SS-18049	*(S)*	**Journey Thru An Electric Tube**	*1969*	**6.00**	**15.00**

Label & Catalog #		Title	Year	VG+	NM

MANCE, JUNIOR

Julian Mance Jr. is a modern jazz pianist. For additional listings refer to Billie Poole; Wilbur Ware & Johnny Griffin & Junior Mance.

Label & Catalog #		Title	Year	VG+	NM
Verve MGV-8319	(M)	**Junior**	1959	16.00	40.00
Verve MGVS-6057	(S)	**Junior**	1960	12.00	30.00
—Verve albums above have black labels with "Verve Records, Inc." on the bottom.—					
Verve V-8319	(M)	**Junior**	1961	8.00	20.00
Verve V6-8319	(S)	**Junior**	1961	6.00	15.00
—Verve albums above have black labels with "MGM Records" on the bottom.—					
Jazzland JLP-30	(M)	**The Soulful Piano Of Junior Mance**	1960	12.00	30.00
Jazzland JLP-930	(S)	**The Soulful Piano Of Junior Mance**	1960	10.00	25.00
Jazzland JLP-41	(M)	**Junior Mance Trio At The Village Vanguard**	1961	12.00	30.00
Jazzland JLP-941	(S)	**Junior Mance Trio At The Village Vanguard**	1961	10.00	25.00
Jazzland JLP-53	(M)	**Big Chief!**	1961	12.00	30.00
Jazzland JLP-953	(S)	**Big Chief!**	1962	10.00	25.00
Jazzland JLP-63	(M)	**The Jazz Soul Of Hollywood**	1961	12.00	30.00
Jazzland JLP-963	(S)	**The Jazz Soul Of Hollywood**	1962	10.00	25.00
Jazzland JLP-77	(M)	**Happy Time**	1962	12.00	30.00
Jazzland JLP-977	(S)	**Happy Time**	1962	10.00	25.00
Riverside RLP-447	(M)	**Junior's Blues**	1963	12.00	30.00
Riverside RS-9447	(S)	**Junior's Blues**	1963	10.00	25.00
—Riverside albums above have blue mono or black stereo labels with a reel & mike logo on top.—					
Capitol T-2092	(M)	**Get Ready, Set, Jump!**	1964	10.00	25.00
Capitol ST-2092	(S)	**Get Ready, Set, Jump!**	1964	8.00	20.00
Capitol T-2218	(M)	**Straight Ahead**	1965	6.00	15.00
Capitol ST-2218	(S)	**Straight Ahead**	1965	5.00	12.00
Capitol T-2393	(M)	**That's Where It Is**	1965	6.00	15.00
Capitol ST-2393	(S)	**That's Where It Is**	1965	5.00	12.00
Atlantic 1496	(M)	**I Believe To My Soul**	1968	6.00	15.00
Atlantic SD-1496	(S)	**I Believe To My Soul**	1968	5.00	12.00
Atlantic SD-1521	(S)	**At The Top**	1969	5.00	12.00
—Atlantic albums above have multi-color labels with a black fan logo.—					

MANCINI, HENRY

Henry Mancini's jazz entries feature a small combo that in-cludes Pete Candoli, Shelly Manne and Art Pepper. For additional listings refer to the Jazzy Soundtracks section under Decca and RCA Victor.

Label & Catalog #		Title	Year	VG+	NM
RCA Victor LPM-1956	(M)	**The Music From "Peter Gunn"**	1959	16.00	40.00
RCA Victor LSP-1956	(S)	**The Music From "Peter Gunn"**	1959	20.00	50.00
		(First pressings of RCA 1956 feature cover art by Jason Kirby.)			
RCA Victor LPM-1956	(M)	**The Music From "Peter Gunn"**	196?	8.00	20.00
RCA Victor LSP-1956	(S)	**The Music From "Peter Gunn"**	196?	10.00	25.00
		(Later pressings of RCA 1956 feature cover art by Fritz Miller)			
RCA Victor LPM-2040	(M)	**More Music From "Peter Gunn"**	1959	8.00	20.00
RCA Victor LSP-2040	(S)	**More Music From "Peter Gunn"**	1959	10.00	25.00
RCA Victor LPM-2147	(M)	**The Blues And The Beat**	1960	10.00	25.00
RCA Victor LSP-2147	(S)	**The Blues And The Beat**	1960	12.00	30.00
RCA Victor LPM-2198	(M)	**Music From "Mr. Lucky"**	1960	10.00	25.00
RCA Victor LSP-2198	(S)	**Music From "Mr. Lucky"**	1960	10.00	25.00
RCA Victor LPM-2258	(M)	**Henry Mancini Combo!**	1960	10.00	25.00
RCA Victor LSP-2258	(S)	**Henry Mancini Combo!**	1960	12.00	30.00
RCA Victor LPM-2360	(M)	**Mr. Lucky Goes Latin**	1961	10.00	25.00
RCA Victor LSP-2360	(S)	**Mr. Lucky Goes Latin**	1961	12.00	30.00
—RCA albums above have black labels with "Long Play" or "Living Stereo" on the bottom.—					
RCA Victor LPM-1956	(M)	**The Music From "Peter Gunn"**	196?	4.00	10.00
RCA Victor LSP-1956	(S)	**The Music From "Peter Gunn"**	196?	5.00	12.00
RCA Victor LPM-2040	(M)	**More Music From "Peter Gunn"**	196?	4.00	10.00
RCA Victor LSP-2040	(S)	**More Music From "Peter Gunn"**	196?	5.00	12.00
RCA Victor LPM-2147	(M)	**The Blues And The Beat**	196?	4.00	10.00
RCA Victor LSP-2147	(S)	**The Blues And The Beat**	196?	5.00	12.00
RCA Victor LPM-2198	(M)	**Music From "Mr. Lucky"**	196?	4.00	10.00
RCA Victor LSP-2198	(S)	**Music From "Mr. Lucky"**	196?	5.00	12.00
RCA Victor LPM-2258	(M)	**Henry Mancini Combo!**	196?	4.00	10.00
RCA Victor LSP-2258	(S)	**Henry Mancini Combo!**	196?	5.00	12.00
RCA Victor LPM-2360	(M)	**Mr. Lucky Goes Latin**	196?	4.00	10.00
RCA Victor LSP-2360	(S)	**Mr. Lucky Goes Latin**	196?	5.00	12.00
—RCA albums above have black labels with "Monaural" or "Stereo" on the bottom.—					

Label & Catalog #		Title	Year	VG+	NM
RCA Victor LPM-3694	(M)	**Mancini '67**	1967	5.00	12.00
RCA Victor LSP-3694	(S)	**Mancini '67**	1967	6.00	15.00
—RCA albums above have black labels with "Mono Dynagroove" or "Stereo Dynagroove" on the bottom.—					
MANCUSO, GUS					
Ronald "Gus" Mancuso is a modern jazz baritone horn player.					
Fantasy 3223	(M)	**Introducing Gus Mancuso** *(Dark red vinyl)*	1956	24.00	60.00
—Fantasy albums above have red labels on dark red, non-flexible vinyl.—					
Fantasy 3223	(M)	**Introducing Gus Mancuso**	195?	16.00	40.00
Fantasy 3282	(M)	**Music From New Faces** *(Red vinyl)*	1958	16.00	40.00
Fantasy 3282	(M)	**Music From New Faces**	195?	10.00	25.00
Fantasy 8025	(S)	**Music From New Faces** *(Blue vinyl)*	1962	10.00	25.00
Fantasy 8025	(S)	**Music From New Faces**	196?	6.00	15.00
—Fantasy albums above have red mono or blue stereo labels on non-flexible vinyl.—					
MANGELSDORF, ALBERT					
German born Albert Mangelsdorf is a modern jazz trombone player and composer.					
Pacific Jazz PJ-10095	(M)	**Now, Jazz Ramwong**	1966	6.00	15.00
Pacific Jazz ST-20095	(S)	**Now, Jazz Ramwong**	1966	5.00	12.00
MANGIONE, CHUCK					
Charles Mangione is a modern jazz trumpet player. For additional list-ings refer to The Jazz Brothers.					
Jazzland JLP-84	(M)	**Recuerdo**	1962	10.00	25.00
Jazzland JLP-984	(S)	**Recuerdo**	1962	8.00	20.00
MANHATTAN JAZZ ALL-STARS, THE					
The All-Stars are Mose Allison, Aaron Bell, Bob Brookmeyer, Teddy Charles, Addison Farmer, Teo Macero, Dave McKenna, Jimmy Raney, Ed Shaughnessy, Zoot Sims, Sir Charles Thompson, Nick Travis, Julius Watkins, and Phil Woods.					
Columbia CL-1426	(M)	**Swinging Guys And Dolls**	1960	12.00	30.00
Columbia CS-8223	(S)	**Swinging Guys And Dolls**	1960	10.00	25.00
—Columbia albums above have six white on black "eye" logos on each label.—					
MANHATTAN JAZZ SEPTETTE, THE					
The Septette is Eddie Costa, Barry Galbraith, Urbie Green, Osie Johnson, Herbie Mann, Hal McKusick and Oscar Pettiford.					
Coral CRL-57090	(M)	**The Manhattan Jazz Septette**	1956	30.00	75.00
MANN, HERBIE					
Herbert Solomon, aka Herbie Mann, is a modern jazz-based flute and tenor saxophone and composer. For additional listings refer to LaVern Baker / Chris Connor / Herbie Mann / Bobby Short; The Manhattan Jazz Septette; The New York Jazz Quartet; Sahib Shibab / Herbie Mann.					
Bethlehem BCP-1018	(10")	**East Coast Jazz 4**	1954	35.00	75.00
Bethlehem BCP-24	(M)	**Flamingo, My Goodness—Four Flutes, Vol. 2**	1955	20.00	50.00
Bethlehem BCP-58	(M)	**Herbie Mann Plays**	1956	20.00	50.00
Bethlehem BCP-63	(M)	**Love And The Weather**	1956	20.00	50.00
Bethlehem BCP-6020	(M)	**The Mann With The Most**	1958	12.00	30.00
Bethlehem BCP-6067	(M)	**Epitome Of Jazz**	1961	12.00	30.00
Bethlehem SBCP-6067	(S)	**Epitome Of Jazz**	1961	12.00	30.00
Savoy MG-12102	(M)	**Flute Suite**	1957	20.00	50.00
		(Savoy 12102 also features Frank Wess.)			
Savoy MG-12107	(M)	**Mann Alone**	1957	20.00	50.00
Savoy MG-12108	(M)	**Yardbird Suite**	1957	20.00	50.00
—Savoy albums above have maroon labels.—					
Riverside RLP-12-234	(M)	**Sultry Serenade**	1957	24.00	60.00
—Riverside albums above have blue on white labels.—					
Riverside RLP-12-234	(M)	**Sultry Serenade**	195?	12.00	30.00
Riverside RLP-12-245	(M)	**Great Ideas Of Western Mann**	1957	16.00	40.00
—Riverside albums above have blue mono or black stereo labels with a reel & mike logo on top.—					
Prestige PRLP-7101	(M)	**Flute Souffle**	1957	30.00	75.00
		(Prestige 7101 also features Bobby Jaspar.)			
Prestige PRLP-7124	(M)	**Flute Flight**	1957	30.00	75.00
		(Prestige 7124 also features Bobby Jaspar.)			
Prestige PRLP-7136	(M)	**Mann In The Morning**	1958	30.00	75.00
—Prestige albums above have yellow labels with a W. 50th Street, NYC address.—					
Epic LN-3395	(M)	**Salute To The Flute**	1957	16.00	40.00
Epic LN-3499	(M)	**Herbie Mann With The Ilcken Trio**	1958	16.00	40.00

Herbie Mann began recording with Mat Mathews' quintet in 1953 and toured with Pete Rugolo in '54 before forming his Afro Jazz Sextet in '59. In between he worked for television, toured Europe and took part in the West Coast scene for a summer. He has recorded prolifically on his own and while his early work on Bethlehem, Riverside (examples from these labels are shown above) and Prestige, his stay with Atlantic through the '60s is of less interest to jazz collectors, due in part to his eclecticism that included Latin jazz and various forms of popular music. He has also recorded as a member of The Manhattan Jazz Septette and The New York Jazz Quartet and as a sideman on albums by Mathews on Dawn, Billy Taylor and Philly Joe Jones, both on Riverside, Art Blakey on Blue Note, A.K. Salim on Savoy, and Buddy DeFranco on Verve.

Label & Catalog #		Title	Year	VG+	NM
New Jazz NJLP-8211	(M)	**Just Wailin'**	1958	20.00	50.00
		—New Jazz albums above have purple labels.—			
New Jazz NJLP-8211	(M)	**Just Wailin'**	1964	10.00	25.00
		—New Jazz albums above have blue labels with a trident logo on the right side.—			
Verve MGV-8247	(M)	**The Magic Flute Of Herbie Mann**	1958	16.00	40.00
Verve MGV-8336	(M)	**Flautista!—Herbie Mann Plays Afro-Cuban Jazz**	1959	16.00	40.00
Verve MGVS-6074	(S)	**Flautista!—Herbie Mann Plays Afro-Cuban Jazz**	1960	12.00	30.00
Verve MGV-8392	(M)	**Flute, Brass, Vibes And Percussion**	1960	12.00	30.00
		—Verve albums above have black labels with "Verve Records, Inc." on the bottom.—			
Verve V-8247	(M)	**The Magic Flute Of Herbie Mann**	1961	6.00	15.00
Verve V-8336	(M)	**Flautista!—Herbie Mann Plays Afro-Cuban Jazz**	1961	6.00	15.00
Verve V6-8336	(S)	**Flautista!—Herbie Mann Plays Afro-Cuban Jazz**	1961	5.00	12.00
Verve V-8392	(M)	**Flute, Brass, Vibes And Percussion**	1961	6.00	15.00
Verve V-8527	(M)	**Sound Of Herbie**	1963	6.00	15.00
Verve V6-8527	(S)	**Sound Of Herbie**	1963	5.00	12.00
		—Verve albums above have black labels with "MGM Records" on the bottom.—			
United Arts. UAL-4042	(M)	**African Suite**	1959	10.00	25.00
United Arts. UAS-5042	(S)	**African Suite**	1959	8.00	20.00
Jazzland JLP-5	(M)	**Herbie Mann Quintet**	1960	12.00	30.00
Jazzland JLP-95	(S)	**Herbie Mann Quintet**	1960	10.00	25.00
		(Jazzland 5 is a reissue of Riverside 245.)			
United Arts. UAJ-14009	(M)	**Brasil, Bossa Nova And Blue**	1962	12.00	30.00
United Arts. UAJS-15009	(S)	**Brasil, Bossa Nova And Blue**	1962	10.00	25.00
United Arts. UAJ-14022	(M)	**St. Thomas**	1962	12.00	30.00
United Arts. UAJS-15022	(S)	**St. Thomas**	1962	10.00	25.00
Atlantic 1343	(M)	**The Common Ground**	1960	6.00	15.00
Atlantic SD-1343	(S)	**The Common Ground**	1960	5.00	12.00
Atlantic 1371	(M)	**The Family Of Mann**	1961	6.00	15.00
Atlantic SD-1371	(S)	**The Family Of Mann**	1961	5.00	12.00
Atlantic 1380	(M)	**Herbie Mann At The Village Gate**	1962	6.00	15.00
Atlantic SD-1380	(S)	**Herbie Mann At The Village Gate**	1962	5.00	12.00
Atlantic 1384	(M)	**Right Now**	1962	6.00	15.00
Atlantic SD-1384	(S)	**Right Now**	1962	5.00	12.00
Atlantic 1397	(M)	**Do The Bossa Nova With Herbie Mann**	1962	6.00	15.00
Atlantic SD-1397	(S)	**Do The Bossa Nova With Herbie Mann**	1962	5.00	12.00
Atlantic 1407	(M)	**Herbie Mann Returns To The Village Gate**	1963	6.00	15.00
Atlantic SD-1407	(S)	**Herbie Mann Returns To The Village Gate**	1963	5.00	12.00
Atlantic 1413	(M)	**Herbie Mann "Live" At Newport**	1963	6.00	15.00
Atlantic SD-1413	(S)	**Herbie Mann "Live" At Newport**	1963	5.00	12.00
Atlantic 1422	(M)	**Latin Fever**	1964	6.00	15.00
Atlantic SD-1422	(S)	**Latin Fever**	1964	5.00	12.00
Atlantic 1426	(M)	**Nirvana**	1964	6.00	15.00
Atlantic SD-1426	(S)	**Nirvana**	1964	5.00	12.00
		(Atlantic 1426 also features Bill Evans.)			
Atlantic 1433	(M)	**My Kinda Groove**	1965	6.00	15.00
Atlantic SD-1433	(S)	**My Kinda Groove**	1965	5.00	12.00
Atlantic 1437	(M)	**The Roar Of The Greasepaint-The Smell Of The Crowd**	1965	5.00	12.00
Atlantic SD-1437	(S)	**The Roar Of The Greasepaint-The Smell Of The Crowd**	1965	4.00	10.00
Atlantic 1445	(M)	**Standing Ovation At Newport**	1966	5.00	12.00
Atlantic SD-1445	(S)	**Standing Ovation At Newport**	1966	4.00	10.00
Atlantic 1454	(M)	**Herbie Mann Today**	1966	5.00	12.00
Atlantic SD-1454	(S)	**Herbie Mann Today**	1966	4.00	10.00
Atlantic 1462	(M)	**Monday Night At The Village Gate**	1966	5.00	12.00
Atlantic SD-1462	(S)	**Monday Night At The Village Gate**	1966	4.00	10.00
Atlantic 1464	(M)	**Our Man Flute**	1966	5.00	12.00
Atlantic SD-1464	(S)	**Our Man Flute**	1966	4.00	10.00
Atlantic 1471	(M)	**New Mann At Newport**	1967	6.00	15.00
Atlantic SD-1471	(S)	**New Mann At Newport**	1967	4.00	10.00
Atlantic 1475	(M)	**Impressions Of The Middle East**	1967	6.00	15.00
Atlantic SD-1475	(S)	**Impressions Of The Middle East**	1967	4.00	10.00
Atlantic 1483	(M)	**The Beat Goes On**	1967	6.00	15.00
Atlantic SD-1483	(S)	**The Beat Goes On**	1967	4.00	10.00
Atlantic 8105	(M)	**Mann And A Woman**	1967	6.00	15.00
Atlantic SD-8105	(S)	**Mann And A Woman**	1967	4.00	10.00
Atlantic 1490	(M)	**The Herbie Mann String Album**	1968	8.00	20.00
Atlantic SD-1490	(S)	**The Herbie Mann String Album**	1968	4.00	10.00

Label & Catalog #		Title	Year	VG+	NM
Atlantic 1497	(M)	**Wailing Dervishes**	1968	8.00	20.00
Atlantic SD-1497	(S)	**Wailing Dervishes**	1968	4.00	10.00
Atlantic SD-1507	(S)	**Windows Open**	1969	4.00	10.00
Atlantic SD-1522	(S)	**Memphis Underground**	1969	4.00	10.00
Atlantic SD-1540	(S)	**Concerto Grosso In D Blues**	1969	4.00	10.00
—Atlantic albums above have multi-color labels with a black fan logo.—					
Columbia CL-2388	(M)	**Latin Mann**	1965	6.00	15.00
Columbia CS-9188	(S)	**Latin Mann**	1965	5.00	12.00
—Columbia albums above have "360 Sound" in white on the bottom of the label.—					
Prestige PRLP-7432	(M)	**The Best Of Herbie Mann**	1965	6.00	15.00
Prestige PRST-7432	(E)	**The Best Of Herbie Mann**	1965	5.00	12.00
—Prestige albums above have blue labels with a trident logo on the right side.—					
Prestige PRST-7659	(E)	**Herbie Mann In Sweden**	1969	4.00	10.00
		(Prestige 7659 is a reissue of 7136.)			
—Prestige albums above have blue labels with a trident logo on top.—					
Surrey S-1015	(M)	**Big Band**	1966	8.00	20.00
Surrey SS-1015	(S)	**Big Band**	1966	6.00	15.00
Verve VSP-8	(M)	**Bongo, Conga & Flute**	1966	5.00	12.00
Verve VSPS-8	(E)	**Bongo, Conga & Flute**	1966	4.00	10.00
Verve VSP-19	(M)	**Big Band Mann**	1966	5.00	12.00
Verve VSPS-19	(E)	**Big Band Mann**	1966	4.00	10.00
Verve V6-8784	(S)	**The Great Mann**	1969	*Unreleased*	
A&M LP-3003	(M)	**Glory Of Love**	1967	6.00	15.00
A&M SP-3003	(S)	**Glory Of Love**	1967	4.00	10.00
Riverside RS-3029	(S)	**Moody Mann**	1968	4.00	10.00
Solid State SS-18020	(S)	**Jazz Impressions Of Brazil**	1968	4.00	10.00
		(Solid State 18020 is a reissue of U.A. 15009.)			
Solid State SS-18023	(S)	**St. Thomas**	1968	4.00	10.00
		(Solid State 18043 is a reissue of U.A. 15022.)			
MANN, HERBIE, & BUDDY COLETTE					
Mode LP-114	(M)	**Flute Fraternity**	1957	30.00	75.00
Interlude MO-503	(M)	**Flute Fraternity**	1959	16.00	40.00
Interlude ST-1103	(S)	**Flute Fraternity**	1959	12.00	30.00
		(Interlude 503 is a reissue of Mode 114.)			
MANN, HERBIE, & JOAO GILBERTO					
Atlantic 8105	(M)	**Herbie Mann And Joao Gilberto With Antonio Carlos Jobim**	1965	6.00	15.00
Atlantic SD-8105	(S)	**Herbie Mann And Joao Gilberto With Antonio Carlos Jobim**	1965	5.00	12.00
—Atlantic albums above have multi-color labels with a black fan logo.—					
MANN, HERBIE, & MACHITO					
Roulette R-52122	(M)	**Afro-Jazziac**	1963	8.00	20.00
Roulette SR-52122	(S)	**Afro-Jazziac**	1963	6.00	15.00
MANN, HERBIE, & SAM MOST					
Bethlehem BCP-40	(M)	**The Herbie Mann-Sam Most Quintet**	1956	20.00	50.00

MANNE, SHELLY

Drummer Sheldon Manne was a nucleus of the West Coast jazz establishment. For additional listings refer to Boots Brown; Bill Evans; Henry Mancini; Jack Marshall & Shelly Manne; Art Pepper & Shelly Manne; The Poll Winners; Andre Previn & Herb Ellis & Shelly Manne & Ray Brown; Ruth Price; The Video All Stars; and the Jazzy Soundtracks section under Chancellor, Colpix, Contemporary, Decca, MGM, Pacific Jazz, RCA Victor, United Artists, and Verve.

Label & Catalog #		Title	Year	VG+	NM
Dee Gee 1003	(10")	**Here's That Manne**	1952	125.00	250.00
Contemporary C-2503	(10")	**Shelly Manne And His Men**	1953	50.00	125.00
Contemporary C-2511	(10")	**Shelly Manne And His Men, Volume 2**	1954	50.00	125.00
Contemporary C-2516	(10")	**The Three**	1954	50.00	125.00
		(Contemporary 2516 also features Jimmy Giuffre and Shorty Rogers.)			
Contemporary C-2518	(10")	**The Two**	1954	50.00	125.00
		(Contemporary 2518 also features Russ freeman.)			
Contemporary C-3507	(M)	**The West Coast Sound**	1955	24.00	60.00
Contemporary C-3516	(M)	**Swinging Sounds, Vol. 4**	1956	24.00	60.00
Contemporary C-3519	(M)	**More Swinging Sounds, Vol. 5**	1957	24.00	60.00
Stereo Records S-7007	(S)	**Swinging Sounds In Stereo**	1958	20.00	50.00
Contemporary S-7007	(S)	**Swinging Sounds In Stereo**	1959	16.00	40.00

Label & Catalog #		Title	Year	VG+	NM
Contemporary C-3525	(M)	**Shelly Manne And His Friends**	1956	20.00	50.00
		(Contemporary 3525 also features Andre Previn and Leroy Vinegar.)			
Contemporary C-3527	(M)	**Modern Jazz Performances Of Songs From "My Fair Lady"**	1957	20.00	50.00
Stereo Records S-7002	(S)	**Modern Jazz Performances Of Songs From "My Fair Lady"**	1958	18.00	45.00
Contemporary S-7527	(S)	**Modern Jazz Performances Of Songs From "My Fair Lady"**	1959	16.00	40.00
		(Contemporary 3527 also features Andre Previn and Leroy Vinegar.)			
Contemporary C-3533	(M)	**Lil' Abner**	1957	20.00	50.00
Stereo Records S-7019	(S)	**Lil' Abner**	1958	18.00	45.00
Contemporary S-7533	(S)	**Lil' Abner**	1959	16.00	40.00
		(Contemporary 3533 also features Andre Previn and Leroy Vinegar.)			
Contemporary C-3536	(M)	**Concerto For Clarinet And Combo**	1957	20.00	50.00
Contemporary C-3557	(M)	**The Gambit**	1958	20.00	50.00
Stereo Records S-7030	(S)	**The Gambit**	1958	18.00	45.00
Contemporary S-7030	(S)	**The Gambit**	1959	16.00	40.00
Contemporary C-3559	(M)	**Bells Are Ringing**	1958	16.00	40.00
Contemporary S-7559	(S)	**Bells Are Ringing**	1959	12.00	30.00
Contemporary C-3560	(M)	**Shelly Manne Plays "Peter Gunn"**	1958	20.00	50.00
Stereo Records S-7025	(S)	**Shelly Manne Plays "Peter Gunn"**	1958	18.00	45.00
Contemporary S-7025	(S)	**Shelly Manne Plays "Peter Gunn"**	1959	16.00	40.00
Contemporary M-3566	(M)	**Son Of Gunn**	1959	16.00	40.00
Contemporary S-7566	(S)	**Son Of Gunn**	1959	12.00	30.00
Contemporary M-3577	(M)	**Shelly Manne & His Men At The Blackhawk, Vol. 1**	1960	16.00	40.00
Contemporary S-7577	(S)	**Shelly Manne & His Men At The Blackhawk, Vol. 1**	1960	12.00	30.00
Contemporary M-3578	(M)	**Shelly Manne & His Men At The Blackhawk, Vol. 2**	1960	16.00	40.00
Contemporary S-7578	(S)	**Shelly Manne & His Men At The Blackhawk, Vol. 2**	1960	12.00	30.00
Contemporary M-3579	(M)	**Shelly Manne & His Men At The Blackhawk, Vol. 3**	1960	16.00	40.00
Contemporary S-7579	(S)	**Shelly Manne & His Men At The Blackhawk, Vol. 3**	1960	12.00	30.00
Contemporary M-3580	(M)	**Shelly Manne & His Men At The Blackhawk, Vol. 4**	1960	16.00	40.00
Contemporary S-7580	(S)	**Shelly Manne & His Men At The Blackhawk, Vol. 4**	1960	12.00	30.00
Contemporary M-3584	(M)	**The Three And The Two**	1960	12.00	30.00
		(Contemporary 3584 is a reissue of 2516 and 2518.)			
Contemporary M-3593/4	(M)	**Live! Shelly Manne & His Men At The Manne-hole** *(2 LPs)*	1961	16.00	40.00
Contemporary S-7593/4	(S)	**Live! Shelly Manne & His Men At The Manne-hole** *(2 LPs)*	1961	12.00	30.00
Contemporary M-3599	(M)	**Checkmate**	1961	12.00	30.00
Contemporary S-7599	(S)	**Checkmate**	1961	10.00	25.00
Contemporary M-3609	(M)	**My Son, The Jazz Drummer!**	1962	12.00	30.00
Contemporary S-7609	(S)	**My Son, The Jazz Drummer!**	1962	10.00	25.00
Contemporary M-5006	(M)	**Sounds Unheard Of**	1962	12.00	30.00
Contemporary S-6006	(S)	**Sounds Unheard Of**	1962	10.00	25.00
		(Contemporary 5006 also features Jack Marshall.)			
Contemporary M-3624	(M)	**Outside**	1966	12.00	30.00
Contemporary S-7624	(S)	**Outside**	1966	10.00	25.00
		— Contemporary stereo albums have gold & black labels.—			
Impulse A-20	(M)	**2 3 4**	1962	12.00	30.00
Impulse AS-20	(S)	**2 3 4**	1962	10.00	25.00
		—Impulse albums above have orange & black labels.—			
Impulse AS-20	(S)	**2 3 4**	1968	4.00	10.00
		—Impulse albums above have red & black labels with the "abc" logo on top.—			
Capitol T-2173	(M)	**"My Fair Lady" With Un-Original Cast**	1964	6.00	15.00
Capitol ST-2173	(S)	**"My Fair Lady" With Un-Original Cast**	1964	5.00	12.00
Capitol T-2313	(M)	**Manne, That's Gershwin**	1965	6.00	15.00
Capitol ST-2313	(S)	**Manne, That's Gershwin**	1965	5.00	12.00
Capitol T-2610	(M)	**Shelly Manne Sounds**	1966	6.00	15.00
Capitol ST-2610	(S)	**Shelly Manne Sounds**	1966	5.00	12.00

Shelly Manne cut his teeth with Bobby Byrne in 1939 before joining Joe Marsala (1940), Bob Astor (1941), Ray Scott (1941-42), Will Bradley (1942) and Les Brown (1942). After the war he worked with Stan Kenton (1946-48), Charlie Ventura (1947). the JATP (1948-49), Woody Herman (1949) and Kenton again (1950-51). After moving to California in 1952 he played with Howard Rumsey (1953) and Shorty Rogers (1954) before becoming the most prolific jazz drummer of the '50s, backing virtually every artist who recorded in Los Angeles, while both composing and acting in television and movies. He has recorded album projects with Art Pepper, and Andre Previn, Herb Ellis and Ray Brown and as a member of Boots Brown's Daredevils, Henry Mancini's jazz combo, The Poll Winners, and the Video All Stars. As a featured guest he has recorded with Teddy Charles, Bill Evans, Stan Getz, and Ruth Price.. His successful solo career includes the LP shown here, first issued in mono in 1956 as *More Swinging Sounds: Shelly Manne & His Men, Vol. 5* . When Stereo Records released Manne's first stereo album in 1958, the catty cover art was retained but the album was titled *Swinging Sounds In Stereo.*

Label & Catalog #		Title	Year	VG+	NM
Atlantic 1469	(M)	**Boss Sounds!**	1967	6.00	15.00
Atlantic SD-1469	(S)	**Boss Sounds!**	1967	5.00	12.00
Atlantic 1487	(M)	**Jazz Gunn**	1967	6.00	15.00
Atlantic SD-1487	(S)	**Jazz Gunn**	1967	5.00	12.00
Atlantic 8157	(M)	**Daktari**	1968	10.00	25.00
Atlantic SD-8157	(S)	**Daktari**	1968	5.00	12.00

—Atlantic albums above have multi-color labels with a black fan logo.—

MANNE, SHELLY / BILL RUSSO

Savoy MG-12045	(M)	**Deep People**	1955	20.00	50.00

—Savoy albums above have maroon labels.—

MANONE, WINGY

Joseph "Wingy" Manone is a traditional jazz trumpet player and vocalist. For additional listings refer to Bunny Berigan & Wingy Manone.

"X" LVA-3014	(10")	**Wingy Manone, Vol. 1**	1954	20.00	50.00
Decca DL-8473	(M)	**Trumpet On The Wing**	1957	16.00	40.00

MARABLE, LAWRENCE

Lawrence Marable is a West Coast jazz drummer.

Jazz: West JWLP-	(M)	**Tenorman**	1956	125.00	250.00

MARCUS, LEW

Lewis Marcus is a traditional jazz-based pianist.

Savoy MG-15006	(10")	**Back Room Piano**	1951	20.00	50.00

MARCUS, STEVE

Vortex 2001	(S)	**Tomorrow Never Knows**	1968	8.00	20.00
Vortex 2009	(S)	**Count's Rock Band**	1969	8.00	20.00
Vortex 2013	(S)	**The Lord's Prayer**	1969	8.00	20.00

MARIACHI BRASS, THE

The Mariachi Brass is a pop ensemble (ala The Tijuana Brass) that features Chet Baker.

World Pacific WP-1825	(M)	**A Taste Of Tequila**	1964	8.00	20.00
World Pacific ST-1825	(S)	**A Taste Of Tequila**	1964	6.00	15.00
World Pacific WP-1842	(M)	**Hats Off!!!**	1965	8.00	20.00
World Pacific ST-1842	(S)	**Hats Off!!!**	1965	6.00	15.00
World Pacific WP-1852	(M)	**Double Shot**	1966	8.00	20.00
World Pacific ST-1852	(S)	**Double Shot**	1966	6.00	15.00
World Pacific WP-1859	(M)	**In The Mood**	1966	8.00	20.00
World Pacific ST-1859	(S)	**In The Mood**	1966	6.00	15.00

MARIANO, CHARLIE

Charles Mariano is a West Coast jazz alto saxophone player. For additional listings refer to John Coltrane / Charlie Mariano; Nat Pierce & Dick Collins / Charlie Mariano; Toshiko-Mariano.

Prestige PRLP-130	(10")	**Charlie Mariano**	1952	70.00	175.00
Prestige PRLP-153	(10")	**Charlie Mariano Boston All Stars**	1953	70.00	175.00
Fantasy 3-10	(10")	**Charlie Mariano Sextet**	1953	70.00	175.00
Imperial IM-3006	(10")	**Charlie Mariano, Volume 1**	1953	70.00	175.00
Imperial IM-3007	(10")	**Charlie Mariano, Volume 2**	1953	70.00	175.00
Bethlehem BCP-1022	(10")	**Charlie Mariano Sextet**	1955	60.00	150.00
Bethlehem BCP-25	(M)	**Alto Sax For Young Moderns**	1957	40.00	100.00
Bethlehem BCP-49	(M)	**Charlie Mariano Plays**	1957	40.00	100.00
Regina R-286	(M)	**A Jazz Portrait Of Charlie Mariano**	1963	12.00	30.00
Regina RS-286	(S)	**A Jazz Portrait Of Charlie Mariano**	1963	10.00	25.00

MARIANO, CHARLIE, & JERRY DODGION

World Pacific WP-1245	(M)	**Beauties Of 1918**	1958	20.00	50.00

MARIANO, TOSHIKO: ***Refer to*** **TOSHIKO**

MARKEWICH, REESE

Modern Age MA-134	(M)	**New Designs In Jazz**	1958	20.00	50.00

MARLENE

Savoy MG-12058	(M)	**I Think Of You With Every Breath I Take**	1956	20.00	50.00

Label & Catalog #		Title	Year	VG+	NM

MARMAROSA, DODO / ERROLL GARNER

Dial LP-208	*(10")*	**Piano Contrasts**	*1950*	**100.00**	**200.00**
Concert Hall Jazz 1001	*(10")*	**Piano Contrasts**	*1955*	**20.00**	**50.00**

MARMAROSA, DODO

Michael "Dodo" Marmarosa is a West Coast jazz pianist.

Argo LP-4012	*(M)*	**Dodo's Back**	*1961*	**12.00**	**30.00**
Argo LPS-4012	*(S)*	**Dodo's Back**	*1961*	**10.00**	**25.00**

MARR, HANK

Henry Marr is a jazz-based pianist.

King 899	*(M)*	**Live At The Club 502**	*1964*	**16.00**	**40.00**

MARSALA, JOE / BUD FREEMAN

Joseph Marsala is a traditional jazz clarinet and sax player and composer. For additional listings refer to Ray McKinley / Joe Marsala.

Brunswick BL-58037	*(10")*	**Battle Of Jazz, Vol. 1**	*1953*	**20.00**	**50.00**

MARSH, WARNE

Warne Marsh is a West Coast jazz tenor sax player. For additional listings refer to Joe Albany; Lee Konitz.

Imperial LP-9013	*(M)*	**Winds Of Marsh**	*1956*	**30.00**	**75.00**
Imperial LP-9027	*(M)*	**Jazz Of Two Cities**	*1956*	**30.00**	**75.00**
Imperial LP-12013	*(E)*	**Jazz Of Two Cities**	*1958*	**20.00**	**50.00**
Mode LP-125	*(M)*	**Music For Prancing**	*1957*	**30.00**	**75.00**
Atlantic 1291	*(M)*	**Warne Marsh**	*1958*	**20.00**	**50.00**
Atlantic SD-1291	*(S)*	**Warne Marsh**	*1958*	**20.00**	**50.00**
		—Atlantic albums above have black mono or green stereo labels.—			
Atlantic 1291	*(M)*	**Warne Marsh**	*1961*	**10.00**	**25.00**
Atlantic SD-1291	*(S)*	**Warne Marsh**	*1961*	**8.00**	**20.00**
		—Atlantic albums above have multi-color labels with a white fan logo.—			

MARSHALL, JACK

Jack Marshall is a traditional jazz-based guitarist, composer and big band leader. For additional listings refer to Shelly Manne.

Capitol T-1108	*(M)*	**18th Century Jazz**	*1959*	**10.00**	**25.00**
Capitol ST-1108	*(S)*	**18th Century Jazz**	*1959*	**8.00**	**20.00**
Capitol T-1194	*(M)*	**Soundsville!**	*1959*	**10.00**	**25.00**
Capitol ST-1194	*(S)*	**Soundsville!**	*1959*	**8.00**	**20.00**
Capitol T-1351	*(M)*	**Jack Marshall Swings**	*1960*	**10.00**	**25.00**
Capitol ST-1351	*(S)*	**Jack Marshall Swings**	*1960*	**8.00**	**20.00**
Capitol T-1601	*(M)*	**Songs Without Words**	*1961*	**10.00**	**25.00**
Capitol ST-1601	*(S)*	**Songs Without Words**	*1961*	**8.00**	**20.00**
Capitol T-2610	*(M)*	**Sounds!**	*1966*	**8.00**	**20.00**
Capitol ST-2610	*(S)*	**Sounds!**	*1966*	**6.00**	**15.00**

MARSHALL, WEMDELL: ***Refer to*** **MILT HINTON & WENDELL MARSHALL & BULL RUTGHER; THE TRIO;** ***and the Various Artists section under Signal and Verve***

MARTIN, ARCH

Martin Arch is a modern jazz trombone player.

Zephyr 12009	*(M)*	**Arch Martin Quintet**	*1959*	**12.00**	**30.00**

MARX, BILL

William Marx—Harpoo's son—is a modern jazz pianist.

Vee Jay LP-3032	*(M)*	**Jazz Kaleidoscope**	*1962*	**10.00**	**25.00**
Vee Jay LPS-3032	*(S)*	**Jazz Kaleidoscope**	*1962*	**8.00**	**20.00**
Vee Jay LP-3035	*(M)*	**My Son, The Folk Swinger**	*1963*	**10.00**	**25.00**
Vee Jay LPS-3035	*(S)*	**My Son, The Folk Swinger**	*1963*	**8.00**	**20.00**

MARX, DICK

Popular pianist Richard Marx is backed by Buddy Collette and Howard Roberts on this jazzy outing.

Omega OML-1002	*(M)*	**Marx Makes Broadway**	*1958*	**16.00**	**40.00**
Omega OSP-2	*(S)*	**Marx Makes Broadway**	*1958*	**12.00**	**30.00**

MARX, DICK, & JOHN FRIGO

Brunswick BL-54006	*(M)*	**Two Much Piano**	*1955*	**16.00**	**40.00**

Label & Catalog #		Title	Year	VG+	NM

MARZETTE WATTS ENSEMBLE, THE

Savoy MGS-12193	(S)	**The Marzette Watts Ensemble**	1968	6.00	15.00

MASTERSOUNDS, THE

The Mastersounds are a West Coast jazz ensemble that features Benny Barth, Richie Crabtree with Buddy and Monk Montgomery. For additional listings refer to The Montgomery Brothers.

World Pacific PJM-403	(M)	**Introducing The Mastersounds**	1957	20.00	50.00
World Pacific PJM-405	(M)	**The King And I**	1958	20.00	50.00
World Pacific WP-1243	(M)	**Kismet**	1958	16.00	40.00
World Pacific ST-1010	(S)	**Kismet**	1958	12.00	30.00
		(World Pacific 1243 also featues Wes Montgomery.)			
World Pacific WP-1252	(M)	**Flower Drum Song**	1958	16.00	40.00
World Pacific ST-1012	(S)	**Flower Drum Song**	1958	12.00	30.00
World Pacific WP-1260	(M)	**Ballads And Blues**	1959	16.00	40.00
World Pacific ST-1019	(S)	**Ballads And Blues**	1959	12.00	30.00
World Pacific WP-1269	(M)	**The Mastersounds In Concert**	1959	16.00	40.00
World Pacific ST-1026	(S)	**The Mastersounds In Concert**	1959	12.00	30.00
World Pacific WP-1271	(M)	**Jazz Showcase**	1959	16.00	40.00
		(World Pacific 1271 is a reissue of Pacific Jazz 403.)			
World Pacific WP-1272	(M)	**The King And I**	1959	16.00	40.00
World Pacific ST-1017	(E)	**The King And I**	1959	12.00	30.00
		(World Pacific 1272 is a reissue of Pacific Jazz 405.)			
World Pacific WP-1280	(M)	**Happy Holidays From Many Lands**	1959	16.00	40.00
World Pacific ST-1030	(S)	**Happy Holidays From Many Lands**	1959	12.00	30.00
World Pacific WP-1284	(M)	**The Mastersounds Play Horace Silver**	1960	16.00	40.00
World Pacific ST-1284	(S)	**The Mastersounds Play Horace Silver**	1960	12.00	30.00
Fantasy 3305	(M)	**Swingin' With The Mastersounds** *(Red vinyl)*	1960	16.00	40.00
Fantasy 3305	(M)	**Swingin' With The Mastersounds**	1962	12.00	30.00
Fantasy 8050	(S)	**Swingin' With The Mastersounds** *(Blue vinyl)*	1962	12.00	30.00
Fantasy 8050	(S)	**Swingin' With The Mastersounds**	196?	8.00	20.00
Fantasy 3316	(M)	**A Date With The Mastersounds** *(Red vinyl)*	1961	16.00	40.00
Fantasy 3316	(M)	**A Date With The Mastersounds**	196?	12.00	30.00
Fantasy 8062	(S)	**A Date With The Mastersounds** *(Blue vinyl)*	1962	12.00	30.00
Fantasy 8062	(S)	**A Date With The Mastersounds**	196?	8.00	20.00
Fantasy 3327	(M)	**The Mastersounds On Tour** *(Red vinyl)*	1961	14.00	35.00
Fantasy 3327	(M)	**The Mastersounds On Tour**	196?	10.00	25.00
Fantasy 8066	(S)	**The Mastersounds On Tour** *(Blue vinyl)*	1962	10.00	25.00
Fantasy 8066	(S)	**The Mastersounds On Tour**	196?	6.00	15.00

MATHEWS, MAT

Mat Mathews is a modern jazz accordionist. For additional listings refer to Eddie Costa; The Four Most; The New York Jazz Quartet; Bob Stewart.

Brunswick BL-54013	(M)	**Accordion Solos**	1956	20.00	50.00
Dawn DLP-1104	(M)	**The Modern Art Of Jazz By Mat Mathews**	1956	30.00	75.00

MATHEWS, RONNIE

Ronald Matthews is a modern jazz pianist.

Prestige PRLP-7303	(M)	**Doin' The Thang**	1964	16.00	40.00
Prestige PRST-7303	(S)	**Doin' The Thang**	1964	12.00	30.00
		(Prestige 7303 also features Freddie Hubbard.)			

— Prestige albums above have yellow mono or silver stereo labels with a Bergenfield, NJ address.—

MATHIS, JOHNNY

On his jazzy debut, pop vocalist Johnny Mathis is backed by Art Farmer, Hal McKusick and Nick Travis.

Columbia CL-887	(M)	**Johnny Mathis**	1956	16.00	40.00
		— Columbia albums above have six white on black "eye" logos on each label.—			
Columbia CL-887	(M)	**Johnny Mathis**	196?	6.00	15.00
		— Columbia albums above have "Guaranteed High Fidelity" in black on the label.—			
Columbia CL-887	(M)	**Johnny Mathis**	196?	4.00	10.00
		— Columbia albums above have "360 Sound" on the bottom of the label.—			

MATLOCK, MATTY

Julian "Matty" Matlock is a traditional jazz clarinet player. For additional listings refer to Rampart Street Paraders; the Jazzy Soundtracks section under Columbia and RCA Victor.

"X" LXA-3035	(10")	**Sports Parade**	1955	20.00	50.00
RCA Victor LPM-1413	(M)	**Pete Kelly At Home**	1957	16.00	40.00

— RCA mono albums above have black labels with "Long Play" on the bottom.—

Label & Catalog #		Title	Year	VG+	NM
MATTHEWS, ONZY					
For additional listings refer to Lou Rawls.					
Capitol T-2099	(M)	**Blues With A Touch Of Elegance**	1964	8.00	20.00
Capitol ST-2099	(S)	**Blues With A Touch Of Elegance**	1964	6.00	15.00
MAXTED, BILLY					
William Maxted is a traditional jazz pianist and composer.					
Cadence CLP-1005	(M)	**Billy Maxted Plays Hi Fi Keyboard**	1955	16.00	40.00
Cadence CLP-1012	(M)	**Jazz At Nick's**	1955	16.00	40.00
Cadence CLP-1013	(M)	**Dixieland Manhattan Style**	1955	16.00	40.00
McBROWNE, LENNY					
Leonard McBrowne is a modern jazz drummer.					
Pacific Jazz PJ-1	(M)	**The Four Souls**	1960	16.00	40.00
Pacific Jazz ST-1	(S)	**The Four Souls**	1960	12.00	30.00
Riverside RLP-346	(M)	**Eastern Lights**	1960	16.00	40.00
Riverside RS-9346	(S)	**Eastern Lights**	1960	12.00	30.00
		—Riverside albums above have blue mono or black stereo labels with a reel & mike logo on top.—			
McCALL, MARY ANN					
Mary Ann McCall is a jazz vocalist. For additional listings refer to Charlie Ventura & Mary Ann McCall.					
Discovery DL-3011	(10")	**Mary Ann McCall Sings**	1950	100.00	200.00
Regent MG-6040	(M)	**Easy Living**	1957	16.00	40.00
Jubilee JLP-1078	(M)	**Detour To The Moon**	1958	16.00	40.00
Jubilee JGS-1078	(S)	**Detour To The Moon**	1958	20.00	50.00
Coral CRL-57276	(M)	**Melancholy Baby**	1959	16.00	40.00
Coral CRL-757276	(S)	**Melancholy Baby**	1959	20.00	50.00
McCANN, LES					
Lester McCann is a modern jazz pianist, vocalist and composer. For additional listings refer to Teddy Edwards; Richard Holmes; Lou Rawls; Clifford Scott & Les McCann.					
Pacific Jazz PJ-2	(M)	**The Truth**	1960	12.00	30.00
Pacific Jazz ST-2	(S)	**The Truth**	1960	10.00	25.00
Pacific Jazz PJ-7	(M)	**The Shout**	1960	12.00	30.00
Pacific Jazz ST-7	(S)	**The Shout**	1960	10.00	25.00
Pacific Jazz PJ-16	(M)	**Les McCann In San Francisco**	1961	12.00	30.00
Pacific Jazz ST-16	(S)	**Les McCann In San Francisco**	1961	10.00	25.00
Pacific Jazz PJ-25	(M)	**Pretty Lady**	1961	10.00	25.00
Pacific Jazz ST-25	(S)	**Pretty Lady**	1961	8.00	20.00
Pacific Jazz PJ-31	(M)	**Les McCann Sings**	1961	10.00	25.00
Pacific Jazz ST-31	(S)	**Les McCann Sings**	1961	8.00	20.00
Pacific Jazz PJ-45	(M)	**Les McCann In New York— Recorded "Live" At The Village Gate**	1962	10.00	25.00
Pacific Jazz ST-45	(S)	**Les McCann In New York— Recorded "Live" At The Village Gate**	1962	8.00	20.00
		(Pacific Jazz 45 also features Blue Mitchell and Stanley Turrentine.)			
Pacific Jazz PJ-56	(M)	**Les McCann On Time** *(Yellow vinyl)*	1962	20.00	50.00
Pacific Jazz PJ-56	(M)	**Les McCann On Time**	1962	10.00	25.00
Pacific Jazz ST-56	(S)	**Les McCann On Time** *(Yellow vinyl)*	1962	16.00	40.00
Pacific Jazz ST-56	(S)	**Les McCann On Time**	1962	8.00	20.00
Pacific Jazz PJ-63	(M)	**Les McCann Plays The Shampoo At The Village**	1962	8.00	20.00
Pacific Jazz ST-63	(S)	**Les McCann Plays The Shampoo At The Village**	1962	6.00	15.00
Pacific Jazz PJ-69	(M)	**The Gospel Truth**	1963	8.00	20.00
Pacific Jazz ST-69	(S)	**The Gospel Truth**	1963	6.00	15.00
Pacific Jazz PJ-78	(M)	**Soul Hits**	1963	8.00	20.00
Pacific Jazz ST-78	(S)	**Soul Hits**	1963	6.00	15.00
Pacific Jazz PJ-81	(M)	**Jazz Waltz**	1964	8.00	20.00
Pacific Jazz ST-81	(S)	**Jazz Waltz**	1964	6.00	15.00
		(Pacific Jazz 45 also features The Jazz Crusaders.)			
Pacific Jazz PJ-84	(M)	**McCanna**	1964	8.00	20.00
Pacific Jazz ST-84	(S)	**McCanna**	1964	6.00	15.00
Pacific Jazz PJ-91	(M)	**McCann/Wilson**	1965	8.00	20.00
Pacific Jazz ST-91	(S)	**McCann/Wilson**	1965	6.00	15.00
		(Pacific Jazz 45 also features Gerald Wilson.)			
Pacific Jazz PJ-10097	(M)	**Spanish Onions**	1966	8.00	20.00
Pacific Jazz ST-20097	(S)	**Spanish Onions**	1966	6.00	15.00
World Pacific WP-10166	(M)	**More Or Les McCann**	1967	6.00	15.00
World Pacific ST-20166	(S)	**More Or Les McCann**	1967	5.00	12.00

Label & Catalog #		Title	Year	VG+	NM
Limelight LM-82016	(M)	**But Not Really**	1965	8.00	20.00
Limelight LS-86016	(S)	**But Not Really**	1965	6.00	15.00
Limelight LM-82025	(M)	**Poo Boo**	1965	8.00	20.00
Limelight LS-86025	(S)	**Poo Boo**	1965	6.00	15.00
Limelight LM-82031	(M)	**Beaux J. Pooboo**	1966	8.00	20.00
Limelight LS-86031	(S)	**Beaux J. Pooboo**	1966	6.00	15.00
Limelight LM-82036	(M)	**Live At Shelly's Manne-Hole**	1966	8.00	20.00
Limelight LS-86036	(S)	**Live At Shelly's Manne-Hole**	1966	6.00	15.00
Limelight LM-82041	(M)	**Les McCann Plays The Hits**	1966	8.00	20.00
Limelight LS-86041	(S)	**Les McCann Plays The Hits**	1966	6.00	15.00
Limelight LM-82043	(M)	**Bucket Of Grease**	1967	8.00	20.00
Limelight LS-86043	(S)	**Bucket Of Grease**	1967	6.00	15.00
Limelight LM-82046	(M)	**Les McCann Live At The Bohemian Caverns**	1967	8.00	20.00
Limelight LS-86046	(S)	**Les McCann Live At The Bohemian Caverns**	1967	6.00	15.00
Atlantic SD-1516	(S)	**Much Les**	1969	4.00	10.00
Atlantic SD-1537	(S)	**Swiss Movement**	1969	4.00	10.00
		(Atlantic 1537 also features Eddie Harris.)			
		—Atlantic albums above have multi-color labels with a black fan logo.—			
Sunset SUS-5214	(S)	**Django**	1969	4.00	10.00

McCOY, FREDDIE

Frederick McCoy is a modern jazz vibraphone player.

Prestige PRLP-7395	(M)	**Lonely Avenue**	1965	10.00	25.00
Prestige PRST-7395	(S)	**Lonely Avenue**	1965	8.00	20.00
Prestige PRLP-7444	(M)	**Spider Man**	1967	10.00	25.00
Prestige PRST-7444	(S)	**Spider Man**	1967	8.00	20.00
Prestige PRLP-7470	(M)	**Funk Drops**	1967	10.00	25.00
Prestige PRST-7470	(S)	**Funk Drops**	1967	8.00	20.00
Prestige PRLP-7487	(M)	**Peas 'N' Rice**	1967	10.00	25.00
Prestige PRST-7487	(S)	**Peas 'N' Rice**	1967	8.00	20.00
		—Prestige albums above have blue labels with a trident logo on the right side.—			
Prestige PRST-7542	(S)	**Beans And Greens**	1968	8.00	20.00
Prestige PRST-7561	(S)	**Soul Yogi**	1968	8.00	20.00
Prestige PRST-7582	(S)	**Listen Here**	1968	8.00	20.00
Prestige PRST-7706	(S)	**The Best Of Freddie McCoy**	1969	6.00	15.00
		—Prestige albums above have blue labels with a trident logo on top.—			

McDUFF, JACK

"Brother" Jack McDuff is a modern jazz organist and composer. For additional listings refer to Gene Ammons; George Benson; Kenny Burrell; Joe Dukes & Jack McDuff; Red Holloway; Willis Jackson; Roland Kirk; Sonny Stitt; Sonny Stitt & Gene Ammons.

Prestige PRLP-7174	(M)	**Brother Jack**	1960	20.00	50.00
		(Prestige 7174 also features Bill Jennings.)			
Prestige PRLP-7185	(M)	**Tough 'Duff**	1960	20.00	50.00
		(Prestige 7185 also features Jimmy Forrest.)			
Prestige PRLP-7199	(M)	**The Honeydripper**	1961	20.00	50.00
Prestige PRLP-7220	(M)	**Goodnight, It's Time To Go**	1961	16.00	40.00
Prestige PRST-7220	(S)	**Goodnight, It's Time To Go**	1961	16.00	40.00
Prestige PRLP-7228	(M)	**Mellow Gravy—Brother Jack Meets The Boss**	1962	16.00	40.00
Prestige PRST-7228	(S)	**Mellow Gravy—Brother Jack Meets The Boss**	1962	16.00	40.00
		(Prestige 7228 also features Gene Ammons.)			
Prestige PRLP-7259	(M)	**Screamin'**	1963	16.00	40.00
Prestige PRST-7259	(S)	**Screamin'**	1963	16.00	40.00
Prestige PRLP-7265	(M)	**Somethin' Slick!**	1963	16.00	40.00
Prestige PRST-7265	(S)	**Somethin' Slick!**	1963	16.00	40.00
Prestige PRLP-7274	(M)	**Brother Jack McDuff Live!**	1963	16.00	40.00
Prestige PRST-7274	(S)	**Brother Jack McDuff Live!**	1963	16.00	40.00
Prestige PRLP-7286	(M)	**Live! At The Jazz Workshop**	1963	16.00	40.00
Prestige PRST-7286	(S)	**Live! At The Jazz Workshop**	1963	16.00	40.00
Prestige PRLP-7323	(M)	**Dynamic!**	1964	16.00	40.00
Prestige PRST-7323	(S)	**Dynamic!**	1964	16.00	40.00
		—Prestige albums above have yellow mono or silver stereo labels with a Bergenfield, NJ address.—			
Prestige PRLP-7333	(M)	**Prelude**	1964	12.00	30.00
Prestige PRST-7333	(S)	**Prelude**	1964	10.00	25.00
Prestige PRLP-7362	(M)	**The Concert McDuff Recorded Live!**	1965	12.00	30.00
Prestige PRST-7362	(S)	**The Concert McDuff Recorded Live!**	1965	10.00	25.00
Prestige PRLP-7404	(M)	**Silk And Soul**	1965	12.00	30.00
Prestige PRST-7404	(S)	**Silk And Soul**	1965	10.00	25.00

Label & Catalog #		Title	Year	VG+	NM
Prestige PRLP-7422	(M)	**Hot Barbeque**	1966	10.00	25.00
Prestige PRST-7422	(S)	**Hot Barbeque**	1966	8.00	20.00
Prestige PRLP-7476	(M)	**Walk On By**	1967	10.00	25.00
Prestige PRST-7476	(S)	**Walk On By**	1967	8.00	20.00
Prestige PRLP-7481	(M)	**Brother Jack McDuff's Greatest Hits**	1967	10.00	25.00
Prestige PRST-7481	(S)	**Brother Jack McDuff's Greatest Hits**	1967	8.00	20.00
Prestige PRLP-7492	(M)	**Hallelujah Time!**	1967	10.00	25.00
Prestige PRST-7492	(S)	**Hallelujah Time!**	1967	8.00	20.00
Prestige PRLP-7529	(S)	**The Midnight Sun**	1967	10.00	25.00
Prestige PRST-7529	(S)	**The Midnight Sun**	1967	8.00	20.00
—Prestige albums above have blue labels with a trident logo on the right side.—					
Prestige PRST-7567	(S)	**Soul Circle**	1968	8.00	20.00
Prestige PRST-7596	(S)	**Jack McDuff Plays For Beautiful People**	1969	8.00	20.00
Prestige PRST-7642	(S)	**I Got A Woman**	1969	8.00	20.00
Prestige PRST-7666	(S)	**Steppin' Out**	1969	8.00	20.00
Prestige PRST-7703	(S)	**Live! The Best Of Brother Jack McDuff**	1969	8.00	20.00
—Prestige albums above have blue labels with a trident logo on top.—					
Atlantic 1463	(M)	**A Change Is Gonna Come**	1966	8.00	20.00
Atlantic SD-1463	(S)	**A Change Is Gonna Come**	1966	6.00	15.00
Atlantic 1472	(M)	**Tobacco Road**	1967	8.00	20.00
Atlantic SD-1472	(S)	**Tobacco Road**	1967	6.00	15.00
—Atlantic albums above have multi-color labels with a black fan logo.—					
Blue Note BST-84322	(S)	**Down Home Style**	1969	6.00	15.00
Blue Note BST-84334	(S)	**Moon Rappin'**	1969	6.00	15.00
—Blue Note albums above have blue on white labels with "A Division of Liberty Records."—					

McFARLAND, GARY

For additional listings refer to Stan Getz; Orchestra USA; Archie Shepp.

Label & Catalog #		Title	Year	VG+	NM
Verve V-8443	(M)	**How To Succeed In Business Without Really Trying**	1962	8.00	20.00
Verve V6-8443	(S)	**How To Succeed In Business Without Really Trying**	1962	6.00	15.00
Verve V-8518	(M)	**The Gary McFarland Orchestra With Special Guest Soloist Bill Evans**	1963	8.00	20.00
Verve V6-8518	(S)	**The Gary McFarland Orchestra With Special Guest Soloist Bill Evans**	1963	6.00	15.00
Verve V-8603	(M)	**Soft Samba**	1964	6.00	15.00
Verve V6-8603	(S)	**Soft Samba**	1964	5.00	12.00
Verve V-8632	(M)	**The "In" Sound**	1965	6.00	15.00
Verve V6-8632	(S)	**The "In" Sound**	1965	5.00	12.00
Verve V-8674	(M)	**Gary McFarland**	1965	*Unreleased*	
Verve V6-8674	(S)	**Gary McFarland**	1965	*Unreleased*	
Verve V-8682	(M)	**Soft Samba Strings**	1966	6.00	15.00
Verve V6-8682	(S)	**Soft Samba Strings**	1966	5.00	12.00
Verve V-8738	(M)	**Scorpio & Other Signs**	1967	6.00	15.00
Verve V6-8738	(S)	**Scorpio & Other Signs**	1967	5.00	12.00
Verve V6-8786	(S)	**Sympathetic Vibrations**	1969	4.00	10.00
—Verve albums above have black labels with "MGM Records" on the bottom.—					
Impulse A-46	(M)	**Points Of Departure**	1963	10.00	25.00
Impulse AS-46	(S)	**Points Of Departure**	1963	8.00	20.00
Impulse A-9104	(M)	**Tijuana Jazz**	1966	10.00	25.00
Impulse AS-9104	(S)	**Tijuana Jazz**	1966	8.00	20.00
Impulse A-9112	(M)	**Profiles**	1966	10.00	25.00
Impulse AS-9112	(S)	**Profiles**	1966	8.00	20.00
Impulse A-9122	(M)	**Simpatico**	1966	10.00	25.00
Impulse AS-9122	(S)	**Simpatico**	1966	8.00	20.00
		(Impulse 9122 also features Archie Shepp.)			
—Impulse albums above have orange & black labels.—					
Impulse AS-46	(S)	**Points Of Departure**	1968	4.00	10.00
Impulse AS-9104	(S)	**Tijuana Jazz**	1968	4.00	10.00
Impulse AS-9112	(S)	**Profiles**	1968	4.00	10.00
Impulse AS-9122	(S)	**Simpatico**	1968	4.00	10.00
—Impulse albums above have red & black labels with the "abc" logo on top.—					

McGARRITY, LOU

Robert Louis McGarrity is a traditional jazz trombone and violin player and vocalist.

Label & Catalog #		Title	Year	VG+	NM
Jubilee JLP-1108	(M)	**Some Like It Hot**	1959	20.00	50.00
Jubilee JGS-1108	(S)	**Some Like It Hot**	1959	16.00	40.00

Label & Catalog #		Title	Year	VG+	NM
Argo LP-654	(M)	**Blue Lou**	1959	16.00	40.00
Argo LPS-654	(S)	**Blue Lou**	1959	12.00	30.00

McGHEE, HOWARD

Howard McGhee is a traditional jazz trumpet player and composer. For additional listings refer to Teddy Edwards; Dexter Gordon / Howard McGhee; Coleman Hawkins / Howard McGhee / Lester Young; the Jazzy Soundtracks section under Felsted; and the Various Artists section under Savoy.

Label & Catalog #		Title	Year	VG+	NM
Dial LP-217	(10")	**Night Music**	1951	125.00	250.00
Hi Lo HL-6001	(10")	**Jazz Goes To The Battlefront, Volume 1**	1952	100.00	200.00
Hi Lo HL-6002	(10")	**Jazz Goes To The Battlefront, Volume 2**	1952	100.00	200.00
Blue Note BLP-5012	(10")	**Howard McGhee's All Stars/ Howard McGhee-Fats Navarro Sextet**	1952	150.00	300.00
Blue Note BLP-5024	(10")	**Howard McGhee, Volume 2**	1953	150.00	300.00
Savoy MG-12026	(M)	**Howard McGhee And Milt Jackson**	1955	30.00	75.00
Bethlehem BCP-42	(M)	**The Return Of Howard McGhee**	1956	30.00	75.00
Bethlehem BCP-61	(M)	**Life Is Just A Bowl Of Cherries**	1956	30.00	75.00
Bethlehem BCP-6055	(M)	**Dusty Blue**	1961	20.00	50.00
Bethlehem SBCP-6055	(S)	**Dusty Blue**	1961	20.00	50.00
Contemporary M-3596	(M)	**Maggie's Back In Town**	1961	20.00	50.00
Contemporary S-7596	(S)	**Maggie's Back In Town**	1961	16.00	40.00
		—Contemporary stereo albums have gold & black labels.—			
Argo LP-4020	(M)	**House Warmin'!**	1962	12.00	30.00
Argo LPS-4020	(S)	**House Warmin'!**	1962	10.00	25.00
United Arts. UAJ-14028	(M)	**Nobody Knows You When You're Down & Out**	1963	16.00	40.00
United Arts. UAJS-15028	(S)	**Nobody Knows You When You're Down & Out**	1963	12.00	30.00

McGOVERN, PATTY, & THOMAS TALBERT

Label & Catalog #		Title	Year	VG+	NM
Atlantic 1245	(M)	**Wednesday's Child**	1956	20.00	50.00
		—Atlantic albums above have black mono or green stereo labels.—			
Atlantic 1245	(M)	**Wednesday's Child**	1961	10.00	25.00
		—Atlantic albums above have multi-color labels with a white fan logo.—			

McGRIFF, JIMMY

James McGriff is a modern jazz organist.

Label & Catalog #		Title	Year	VG+	NM
Sue LP-1012	(M)	**I've Got A Woman**	1962	16.00	40.00
Sue SLP-1012	(S)	**I've Got A Woman**	1962	16.00	40.00
Sue LP-1017	(M)	**Jimmy McGriff At The Apollo**	1963	16.00	40.00
Sue SLP-1017	(S)	**Jimmy McGriff At The Apollo**	1963	16.00	40.00
Sue LP-1020	(M)	**Jimmy McGriff At The Organ**	1963	16.00	40.00
Sue SLP-1020	(S)	**Jimmy McGriff At The Organ**	1963	16.00	40.00
Sue LP-1033	(M)	**Topkapi**	1964	16.00	40.00
Sue SLP-1033	(S)	**Topkapi**	1964	16.00	40.00
Sue LP-1039	(M)	**Blues For Mister Jimmy**	1965	16.00	40.00
Sue SLP-1039	(S)	**Blues For Mister Jimmy**	1965	16.00	40.00
Solid State SM-17001	(M)	**The Big Band Of Jimmy McGriff**	1966	6.00	15.00
Solid State SS-18001	(S)	**The Big Band Of Jimmy McGriff**	1966	5.00	12.00
Solid State SM-17002	(M)	**A Bag Full Of Soul**	1966	6.00	15.00
Solid State SS-18002	(S)	**A Bag Full Of Soul**	1966	5.00	12.00
Solid State SM-17006	(M)	**Cherry**	1967	6.00	15.00
Solid State SS-18006	(S)	**Cherry**	1967	5.00	12.00
Solid State SS-18036	(S)	**Honey**	1968	5.00	12.00
Solid State SS-18045	(S)	**The Worm**	1969	5.00	12.00
Solid State SS-18060	(S)	**A Thing To Come By**	1969	5.00	12.00

McHARGUE, ROSY

James "Rosy" McHargue is a traditional jazz clarinet and saxophone(s) player.

Label & Catalog #		Title	Year	VG+	NM
Jump JL-8	(10")	**Dixie Combo**	1955	20.00	50.00

McHUGH, JIMMY

Label & Catalog #		Title	Year	VG+	NM
RCA Victor LPM-1741	(M)	**Jimmy McHugh In Hi Fi**	1958	20.00	50.00
		—RCA albums above have black labels with "Long Play" on the bottom.—			

McINTYRE, HAL

Label & Catalog #		Title	Year	VG+	NM
Columbia CL-6124	(10")	**Dance Date**	1950	20.00	50.00

Label & Catalog #		Title	Year	VG+	NM
McINTYRE, KEN					
Kenneth McIntyre is a modern jazz alto saxophone and flute player.					
New Jazz NJLP-8247	(M)	**Looking Ahead**	1960	20.00	50.00
		(New Jazz 8247 also features Eric Dolphy.)			
New Jazz NJLP-8259	(M)	**Stone Blues**	1961	20.00	50.00
		—New Jazz albums above have purple labels.—			
New Jazz NJLP-8247	(M)	**Looking Ahead**	1965	10.00	25.00
New Jazz NJLP-8259	(M)	**Stone Blues**	1965	10.00	25.00
		—New Jazz albums above have blue labels with a trident logo on the right side.—			
United Arts. UAJ-14015	(M)	**Year Of The Iron Sheep**	1962	16.00	40.00
United Arts. UAJS-15015	(S)	**Year Of The Iron Sheep**	1962	12.00	30.00
United Arts. UAL-3336	(M)	**Way Way Out**	1964	12.00	30.00
United Arts. UAS-6336	(S)	**Way Way Out**	1964	10.00	25.00
McINTYRE, MAURICE					
Delmark DS-419	(S)	**Humility**	1969	8.00	20.00
McKAY, STUART					
RCA Victor LJM-1021	(M)	**Stuart McKay And His Woods**	1955	16.00	40.00
McKENNA, DAVE					
David McKenna is a traditional jazz pianist. For additional listings refer to Ruby Braff; The Manhattan Jazz All-Stars..					
ABC Paramount ABC-104	(M)	**Solo Piano**	1956	16.00	40.00
Epic LN-3558	(M)	**Dave McKenna**	1959	12.00	30.00
Epic BN-527	(S)	**Dave McKenna**	1959	10.00	25.00
McKENNA, DAVE, & HALL OVERTON					
Bethlehem BCP-6049	(M)	**Dual Piano Jazz**	1960	12.00	30.00
Bethlehem SBCP-6049	(S)	**Dual Piano Jazz**	1960	12.00	30.00
McKINLEY, RAY					
Ray McKinley is a traditional jazz drummer and vocalist. For additional listings for Ray McKinley refer to Will Bradley; Peanuts Hucko./ Ray McKinley.					
Allegro Elite 4129	(10")	**Ray McKinley & His Famous Orchestra**	195?	40.00	100.00
McKINLEY, RAY / JOE MARSALA					
Decca DL-5262	(10")	**Dixieland Jazz Battle, Vol. 2**	1950	20.00	50.00
McKINLEY, RAY, & EDDIE SAUTER					
Savoy MG-12024	(M)	**Borderline**	1955	20.00	50.00
McKINNEY'S COTTON PICKERS, BILL					
William McKinney is a traditional jazz drummer and big band leader.					
RCA Victor WPT-24	(10")	**McKinney's Cotton Pickers**	1952	20.00	50.00
"X" LVA-3031	(10")	**McKinney's Cotton Pickers**	1955	20.00	50.00
McKUSICK, HAL					
Harold McKusick is a modern jazz alto saxophone and clarinet player. For additional listings refer to Charlene Bartley; The Manhattan Jazz Septette; Johnny Mathis; Nutty Squirrels; Betty St. Claire; Phil Woods & Gene Quill / Jackie McLean & John Jenkins / Hal McKusick; and the Various Artists section under Prestige.					
Bethlehem BCP-16	(M)	**East Coast Jazz 8**	1955	50.00	125.00
RCA Victor LPM-1164	(M)	**In The 20th Century Drawing Room**	1956	24.00	60.00
RCA Victor LPM-1366	(M)	**The Jazz Workshop**	1957	30.00	75.00
		—RCA albums above have black labels with "Long Play" on the bottom.—			
Prestige PRLP-7135	(M)	**Triple Exposure**	1957	30.00	75.00
		—Prestige albums above have yellow labels with a W. 50th Street, NYC address.—			
Coral CRL-57116	(M)	**Jazz At The Academy**	1957	30.00	75.00
Coral CRL-57131	(M)	**Quintet**	1957	30.00	75.00
Decca DL-9209	(M)	**Cross Section Saxes**	1958	20.00	50.00
Decca DL-79209	(S)	**Cross Section Saxes**	1958	16.00	40.00
McLEAN, JACKIE					
John "Jackie" McLean is a modern jazz alto sax player. For additional listings refer to Art Blakey & The Jazz Messengers; Kenny Dorham; Phil Woods & Gene Quill / Jackie McLean & John Jenkins / Hal McKusick.					
Adlib ADL-6601	(M)	**The Jackie McLean Quintet**	1955	800.00	1,200.00
Prestige PRLP-7035	(M)	**Lights Out!**	1956	60.00	150.00
		(Prestige 7035 also features Donald Byrd and Elmo Hope.)			

Label & Catalog #		Title	Year	VG+	NM
Prestige PRLP-7048	(M)	**4, 5 And 6**	1956	60.00	150.00
Prestige PRLP-7068	(M)	**Jackie's Pal—Introducing Bill Hardman**	1956	60.00	150.00
Prestige PRLP-7087	(M)	**Jackie McLean & Co.**	1957	40.00	100.00
Prestige PRLP-7114	(M)	**Alto Madness**	1957	40.00	100.00
		(Prestige 7114 also features John Jenkins.)			
		—Prestige albums above have a W. 50th Street, NYC address on the label.—			
Jubilee JLP-1064	(M)	**The Jackie McLean Quintet**	1958	30.00	75.00
Jubilee JGS-1064	(E)	**The Jackie McLean Quintet**	1959	16.00	40.00
		(Jubilee 1064 is a reissue of Adlib 6601.)			
Jubilee JLP-1093	(M)	**Jackie McLean Plays Fat Jazz**	1958	30.00	75.00
Jubilee JGS-1093	(S)	**Jackie McLean Plays Fat Jazz**	1959	20.00	50.00
New Jazz NJLP-8212	(M)	**McLean's Scene**	1958	40.00	100.00
New Jazz NJLP-8231	(M)	**Makin' The Changes**	1960	40.00	100.00
New Jazz NJLP-8253	(M)	**A Long Drink Of The Blues**	1961	40.00	100.00
New Jazz NJLP-8263	(M)	**Lights Out**	1961	20.00	50.00
		(New Jazz 8263 is a reissue of Prestige 7035.)			
New Jazz NJLP-8279	(M)	**4, 5 And 6**	1962	20.00	50.00
		(New Jazz 8279 is a reissue of Prestige 7048.)			
New Jazz NJLP-8290	(M)	**Steeplechase**	1962	20.00	50.00
		(New Jazz 8290 is a reissue of Prestige 7068.)			
New Jazz NJLP-8312	(M)	**Alto Madness**	1963	*Unreleased*	
New Jazz NJLP-8323	(M)	**Jackie McLean & Co.**	1963	*Unreleased*	
		—New Jazz albums above have purple labels.—			
New Jazz NJLP-8212	(M)	**McLean's Scene**	1965	10.00	25.00
New Jazz NJLP-8231	(M)	**Makin' The Changes**	1965	10.00	25.00
New Jazz NJLP-8253	(M)	**A Long Drink Of The Blues**	1965	10.00	25.00
New Jazz NJLP-8263	(M)	**Lights Out**	1965	10.00	25.00
New Jazz NJLP-8279	(M)	**4, 5 And 6**	1965	10.00	25.00
New Jazz NJLP-8290	(M)	**Steeplechase**	1965	10.00	25.00
		—New Jazz albums above have blue labels with a trident logo on the right side.—			
Status ST-8312	(M)	**Alto Madness**	1965	16.00	40.00
		(Status 8312 is a reissue of Prestige 7114.)			
Status ST-8323	(M)	**Jackie McLean & Co.**	1965	16.00	40.00
		(Status 8323 is a reissue of Prestige 7087.)			
Blue Note BLP-4013	(M)	**New Soil** *(Deep groove)*	1959	100.00	200.00
Blue Note BLP-4013	(M)	**New Soil**	1959	60.00	150.00
Blue Note BST-4013	(S)	**New Soil** *(Deep groove)*	1959	60.00	150.00
Blue Note BST-4013	(S)	**New Soil**	1959	40.00	100.00
Blue Note BLP-4024	(M)	**Swing, Swang, Swingin'** *(Deep groove)*	1959	200.00	400.00
Blue Note BLP-4024	(M)	**Swing, Swang, Swingin'**	1959	150.00	300.00
Blue Note BST-84024	(S)	**Swing, Swang, Swingin'**	1959	100.00	200.00
Blue Note BLP-4038	(M)	**Capuchin Swing** *(Deep groove)*	1960	100.00	200.00
Blue Note BLP-4038	(M)	**Capuchin Swing**	1960	60.00	150.00
Blue Note BST-84038	(S)	**Capuchin Swing**	1960	40.00	100.00
Blue Note BLP-4051	(M)	**Jackie's Bag**	1960	40.00	100.00
Blue Note BST-84051	(S)	**Jackie's Bag**	1960	30.00	75.00
Blue Note BLP-4067	(M)	**Bluesnik**	1961	40.00	100.00
Blue Note BST-84067	(S)	**Bluesnik**	1961	30.00	75.00
		—Blue Note albums above have blue on white labels with a W. 63rd St, NYC address.—			
Blue Note BLP-4089	(M)	**A Fickle Sonance**	1961	30.00	75.00
Blue Note BST-84089	(S)	**A Fickle Sonance**	1961	20.00	50.00
		—Blue Note albums above have blue on white labels with a 61st St, NYC address.—			
Blue Note BLP-4013	(M)	**New Soil**	1963	10.00	25.00
Blue Note BST-4013	(S)	**New Soil**	1963	8.00	20.00
Blue Note BLP-4024	(M)	**Swing, Swang, Swingin'**	1963	10.00	25.00
Blue Note BST-84024	(S)	**Swing, Swang, Swingin'**	1963	8.00	20.00
Blue Note BLP-4038	(M)	**Capuchin Swing**	1963	10.00	25.00
Blue Note BST-84038	(S)	**Capuchin Swing**	1963	8.00	20.00
Blue Note BLP-4051	(M)	**Jackie's Bag**	1963	10.00	25.00
Blue Note BST-84051	(S)	**Jackie's Bag**	1963	8.00	20.00
Blue Note BLP-4067	(M)	**Bluesnik**	1963	10.00	25.00
Blue Note BST-84067	(S)	**Bluesnik**	1963	8.00	20.00
Blue Note BLP-4089	(M)	**A Fickle Sonance**	1963	10.00	25.00
Blue Note BST-84089	(S)	**A Fickle Sonance**	1963	8.00	20.00
Blue Note BLP-4106	(M)	**Let Freedom Ring**	1962	16.00	40.00
Blue Note BST-84106	(S)	**Let Freedom Ring**	1962	12.00	30.00
Blue Note BLP-4116	(M)	**Jackie McLean Quintet**	1962	*Unreleased*	
Blue Note BST-84116	(S)	**Jackie McLean Quintet**	1962	*Unreleased*	

Jackie McLean began his jazz career playing guitar for Tiny Bradshaw before moving working with Paul Bley, George Wallington and Charlie Mingus in the early '50s. From 1956-58 he was a member of Art Blakey's Jazz Messengers. Meanwhile he had his own quintet (with Ray Draper) and quartet, recording his first album for the small Adlib label, now one of the rarest of all jazz albums. His career as a leader has been primarily with Prestige and Blue Note, from which the examples here are taken. As a featured artist, he recorded with Kenny Dorham, as a sideman he can be found on albums by Blakey on World Pacific, Columbia and Elektra, Mingus on Atlantic, Miles Davis on Prestige and Blue Note, and Gene Ammons, Hank Mobley and Mal Waldron, all on Prestige.

Label & Catalog #		Title	Year	VG+	NM
Blue Note BLP-4137	(M)	**One Step Beyond**	1963	16.00	40.00
Blue Note BST-84137	(S)	**One Step Beyond**	1963	12.00	30.00
Blue Note BLP-4165	(M)	**Destination... Out!**	1964	16.00	40.00
Blue Note BST-84165	(S)	**Destination... Out!**	1964	12.00	30.00
Blue Note BLP-4179	(M)	**It's Time!**	1964	16.00	40.00
Blue Note BST-84179	(S)	**It's Time!**	1964	12.00	30.00
Blue Note BLP-4215	(M)	**Right Now!**	1965	16.00	40.00
Blue Note BST-84215	(S)	**Right Now!**	1965	12.00	30.00
Blue Note BLP-4218	(M)	**Action Action Action**	1965	16.00	40.00
Blue Note BST-84218	(S)	**Action Action Action**	1965	12.00	30.00
Blue Note BLP-4223	(M)	**Jackknife**	1965	*Unreleased*	
Blue Note BST-84223	(S)	**Jackknife**	1965	*Unreleased*	
Blue Note BLP-4236	(M)	**High Frequency**	1966	*Unreleased*	
Blue Note BST-84236	(S)	**High Frequency**	1966	*Unreleased*	
—Blue Note albums above have blue on white labels with a New York., USA address.—					
Blue Note BST-84013	(S)	**New Soil**	196?	5.00	12.00
Blue Note BST-84024	(S)	**Swing, Swang, Swingin'**	196?	5.00	12.00
Blue Note BST-84038	(S)	**Capuchin Swing**	196?	5.00	12.00
Blue Note BST-84051	(S)	**Jackie's Bag**	196?	5.00	12.00
Blue Note BST-84067	(S)	**Bluesnik**	196?	5.00	12.00
Blue Note BST-84089	(S)	**A Fickle Sonance**	196?	5.00	12.00
Blue Note BST-84106	(S)	**Let Freedom Ring**	196?	5.00	12.00
Blue Note BST-84137	(S)	**One Step Beyond**	196?	5.00	12.00
Blue Note BST-84165	(S)	**Destination... Out!**	196?	5.00	12.00
Blue Note BST-84179	(S)	**It's Time!**	196?	5.00	12.00
Blue Note BST-84215	(S)	**Right Now!**	196?	5.00	12.00
Blue Note BST-84218	(S)	**Action Action Action**	196?	5.00	12.00
Blue Note BLP-4262	(M)	**New And Old Gospel**	1967	12.00	30.00
Blue Note BST-84262	(S)	**New And Old Gospel**	1967	8.00	20.00
Blue Note BST-84284	(S)	**'Bout Soul**	1968	8.00	20.00
Blue Note BST-84345	(S)	**Demon's Dance**	1969	8.00	20.00
—Blue Note albums above have blue on white labels with "A Division of Liberty Records."—					
Josie JLPM-3503	(M)	**Jackie McLean Sextet**	1963	12.00	30.00
Josie JLPS-3503	(S)	**Jackie McLean Sextet**	1963	10.00	25.00
		(Josie 3503 reissues Jubilee material.)			
RCA Victor LPM-3230	(M)	**Alto Madness**	1965	10.00	25.00
RCA Victor LSP-3230	(S)	**Alto Madness**	1965	8.00	20.00
—RCA albums above have black labels with "Monaural" or "Stereo" on the bottom.—					
Prestige PRLP-7500	(M)	**Strange Blues**	1967	10.00	25.00
Prestige PRST-7500	(S)	**Strange Blues**	1967	8.00	20.00
—Prestige albums above have blue labels with a trident logo on the right side.—					

McNABB, TED

Theodore McNabb is a band leader whose "company" includes Al Cohn and Zoot Sims.

Epic LN-3663	(M)	**Ted McNabb And Company**	1959	20.00	50.00
Epic BN-558	(S)	**Ted McNabb And Company**	1959	16.00	40.00

McPARTLAND, JIMMY

James McPartland is a traditional jazz trumpet player. For additional listings refer to Dizzy Gillespie / Jimmy McPartland; and the Various Artists section under Verve.

Brunswick BL-58049	(10")	**Shades Of Bix**	1953	30.00	75.00
Brunswick BL-54018	(M)	**Dixieland Band**	1956	20.00	50.00
Jazztone J-1227	(M)	**The Middle Road**	1956	16.00	40.00
Epic LN-3371	(M)	**Jimmy McPartland's Dixieland**	1956	16.00	40.00
Epic LN-3463	(M)	**Jimmy McPartland & His Dixieland**	1958	16.00	40.00
Epic BN-506	(S)	**Jimmy McPartland & His Dixieland**	1959	12.00	30.00
Jazzology 16	(M)	**Jimmy McPartland On Stage**	196?	6.00	15.00
RCA Victor LPV-549	(M)	**That Happy Dixieland Jazz**	1965	8.00	20.00

McPARTLAND, MARIAN

Margaret Marian Turner, aka Marian McPartland through her marriage to Jimmy (above), is a traditional jazz pianist. For additional listings refer to Adelaide Robbins / Marian McPartland / Barbara Carroll.; Lennie Tristano / Joe Bushkin / Bobby Scott / Marian McPartland.

Savoy MG-15019	(10")	**Jazz At Storyville, Volume 3**	1952	30.00	75.00
Savoy MG-15021	(10")	**Piano Moods**	1952	30.00	75.00
Savoy MG-15027	(10")	**Marian McPartland**	1953	30.00	75.00
Savoy MG-15032	(10")	**Jazz At The Hickory House**	1953	30.00	75.00
Savoy MG-12004	(M)	**Marian McPartland In Concert**	1955	20.00	50.00

Label & Catalog #		Title	Year	VG+	NM
Savoy MG-12005	(M)	**Lullaby Of Birdland**	1955	20.00	50.00
Capitol T-574	(M)	**Marian McPartland At The Hickory House**	1955	16.00	40.00
Capitol T-699	(M)	**After Dark**	1956	16.00	40.00
Capitol T-785	(M)	**Marian McPartland Trio**	1956	16.00	40.00
		—Capitol albums above have turquoise labels.—			
Argo LP-640	(M)	**Marian McPartland At The London House**	1958	16.00	40.00
Argo LPS-640	(S)	**Marian McPartland At The London House**	1958	12.00	30.00
Time 52073	(M)	**Bossa Nova Plus Soul**	1960	12.00	30.00
Time S-2073	(S)	**Bossa Nova Plus Soul**	1960	10.00	25.00
Time 52199	(M)	**West Side Story**	1965	12.00	30.00
Time S-2199	(S)	**West Side Story**	1965	10.00	25.00

McPARTLAND, MARIAN / GEORGE SHEARING

Savoy MG-12016	(M)	**Great Britain's Marian McPartland And George Shearing**	1955	16.00	40.00
		(Savoy 12015 is a reissue of 15021 and 15003.)			

McPHERSON, CHARLES

Charles McPherson is a modern jazz alto saxophone player.

Prestige PRLP-7359	(M)	**Bebop Revisited!**	1965	14.00	35.00
Prestige PRST-7359	(S)	**Bebop Revisited!**	1965	12.00	30.00
		(Prestige 7359 also features Carmell Jones and Barry Harris)			
Prestige PRLP-7427	(M)	**Con Alma!**	1966	14.00	35.00
Prestige PRST-7427	(S)	**Con Alma!**	1966	12.00	30.00
Prestige PRLP-7480	(M)	**The Charles McPherson Quintet Live!**	1967	14.00	35.00
Prestige PRST-7480	(S)	**The Charles McPherson Quintet Live!**	1967	12.00	30.00
		—Prestige albums above have blue labels with a trident logo on the right side.—			
Prestige PRST-7559	(S)	**From This Moment On**	1968	12.00	30.00
Prestige PRST-7603	(S)	**Horizons**	1969	10.00	25.00
		—Prestige albums above have blue labels with a trident logo on top.—			

McRAE, CARMEN

Carmen McRae is a modern jazz vocalist. For additional listings refer to Dave Brubeck; Chris Connor / Carmen McRae / Julie London; and the Jazzy Soundtracks section under MGM.

Bethlehem BCP-1023	(10")	**Carmen McRae**	1955	30.00	75.00
Decca DL-8173	(M)	**By Special Request**	1955	20.00	50.00
Decca DL-8267	(M)	**Torchy!**	1956	20.00	50.00
Decca DL-8347	(M)	**Blue Moon**	1957	20.00	50.00
Decca DL-8583	(M)	**After Glow**	1957	20.00	50.00
Decca DL-8662	(M)	**Mad About The Man**	1958	20.00	50.00
Decca DL-8738	(M)	**Carmen For Cool Ones**	1958	20.00	50.00
Decca DL-8815	(M)	**Birds Of A Feather**	1958	20.00	50.00
		—Decca albums above have silver on black labels.—			
Kapp KL-1117	(M)	**Book Of Ballads**	1958	10.00	25.00
Kapp KS-3001	(S)	**Book Of Ballads**	1960	10.00	25.00
Kapp KL-1135	(M)	**When You're Away**	1959	10.00	25.00
Kapp KS-3018	(S)	**When You're Away**	1960	10.00	25.00
Kapp KL-1169	(M)	**Something To Swing About**	1959	10.00	25.00
Kapp KS-3053	(S)	**Something To Swing About**	1960	10.00	25.00
Time 52104	(M)	**Live At Sugar Hill**	1960	8.00	20.00
Time S-2104	(S)	**Live At Sugar Hill**	1960	10.00	25.00
Columbia CL-1730	(M)	**Lover Man**	1962	8.00	20.00
Columbia CS-8530	(S)	**Lover Man**	1962	10.00	25.00
Columbia CL-1943	(M)	**Something Wonderful**	1962	8.00	20.00
Columbia CS-8743	(S)	**Something Wonderful**	1962	10.00	25.00
		—Columbia albums above have "Guaranteed High Fidelity" or "360 Sound Stereo" in black on the label.—			
Vocalion VL-3697	(M)	**Carmen McRae**	1963	6.00	15.00
Focus FL-334	(M)	**Bittersweet**	1964	6.00	15.00
Focus FS-334	(S)	**Bittersweet**	1964	8.00	20.00
Mainstream 56028	(M)	**Second To None**	1965	6.00	15.00
Mainstream S-6028	(S)	**Second To None**	1965	8.00	20.00
Mainstream 56044	(M)	**Haven't We Met?**	1965	6.00	15.00
Mainstream S-6044	(S)	**Haven't We Met?**	1965	8.00	20.00
Mainstream 56065	(M)	**Woman Talk**	1966	6.00	15.00
Mainstream S-6065	(S)	**Woman Talk**	1966	8.00	20.00
Mainstream 56084	(M)	**Alfie**	1966	6.00	15.00
Mainstream S-6084	(S)	**Alfie**	1966	8.00	20.00

Label & Catalog #		Title	Year	VG+	NM
Kapp KL-1541	(M)	**This Is Carmen McRae**	1967	8.00	20.00
Kapp KS-3541	(S)	**This Is Carmen McRae**	1967	6.00	15.00
Atlantic SD-8143	(S)	**For Once In My Life**	1967	8.00	20.00
Atlantic SD-8143	(S)	**For Once In My Life**	1967	6.00	15.00
Atlantic SD-8165	(S)	**Portrait**	1968	6.00	15.00
Harmony HL-7452	(M)	**Yesterday**	1968	8.00	20.00
Harmony HS-11252	(S)	**Yesterday**	1968	5.00	12.00

McRITCHIE, GREIG

Greig McRitchie is a modern jazz arranger.

Zephyr 12005	(M)	**Easy Jazz On A Fish Beat Bass**	1959	20.00	50.00

McSHANN, JAY

Jay "Hootie" McShann is a traditional jazz-based pianist, vocalist and band leader. The sessions below features early Charlie Parker.

Decca DL-5503	(10")	**Kansas City Memories**	1954	300.00	500.00
Decca DL-9236	(M)	**Kansas City Memories**	1958	125.00	250.00
Decca DL-79236	(E)	**Kansas City Memories**	1958	100.00	100.00

MECCA, LOU

Louis Mecca is a modern jazz guitarist.

Blue Note BLP-5067	(10")	**Lou Mecca Quartet**	1955	150.00	300.00

MEHEGAN, JOHN

John Mehegan is a modern jazz pianist and composer. For additional listings refer to Hampton Hawes / John Mehegan / Herbie Nichols / Paul Smith.

Savoy MG-15054	(10")	**The Last Mehegan**	1955	20.00	50.00
Savoy MG-12028	(M)	**Reflections**	1955	16.00	40.00
Savoy MG-12076	(M)	**How I Play Jazz Piano**	1956	16.00	40.00
Perspective PR-1	(M)	**From Barrelhouse To Bop**	195?	20.00	50.00
"TJ" LP-1	(M)	**Casual Affair**	1959	16.00	40.00
Epic LA-16007	(M)	**Act Of Jazz**	1960	10.00	25.00
Epic BA-17007	(S)	**Act Of Jazz**	1960	8.00	20.00

MEHEGAN, JOHN, & EDDIE COSTA

Savoy MG-12049	(M)	**A Pair Of Pianos**	1956	16.00	40.00

MELLE, GIL

Gilbert Melle is a modern jazz saxophone(s) player.

Blue Note BLP-5020	(10")	**Gil Melle Quintet/Sextet**	1953	150.00	300.00
Blue Note BLP-5033	(10")	**Gil Melle Quintet, Volume 2**	1953	150.00	300.00
Blue Note BLP-5054	(10")	**Gil Melle Quartet, Volume 3**	1954	150.00	300.00
Blue Note BLP-5063	(10")	**Gil Melle Quintet, Volume 4— Five Impressions Of Color**	1955	150.00	300.00
Blue Note BLP-1517	(M)	**Patterns In Jazz** *(Deep groove)*	1956	100.00	200.00
Blue Note BLP-1517	(M)	**Patterns In Jazz**	1956	60.00	150.00

—Blue Note albums above have blue on white labels with a Lexington Ave, NYC address.—

Prestige PRLP-7040	(M)	**Melle Plays Primitive Modern**	1956	30.00	75.00
Prestige PRLP-7063	(M)	**Gil's Guests**	1956	30.00	75.00
Prestige PRLP-7097	(M)	**Quadrama**	1957	30.00	75.00

—Prestige albums above have yellow labels with a W. 50th Street, NYC address.—

Verve V6-8744	(S)	**Tome VI**	1968	6.00	15.00

—Verve albums above have black labels with "MGM Records" on the bottom.—

MELLO-LARKS, THE

The Mello-Larks are a jazz vocal group consisting of Adele Castle, Joseph Eich, Thomas Hamm and Robert Wollter.

Camden CAL-530	(M)	**Just For A Lark**	1959	16.00	40.00

MELROSE, FRANK

Franklyn Melrose is a traditional jazz pianist and composer.

ABC-Paramount ABC-10?	(M)	**Kansas City Frank Melrose**	1956	16.00	40.00

MENDEZ, SERGIO

Brazilian born Sergio Mendez is a Latin jazz pianist who achieved fame with his pop group, Brasil '66.

Atlantic 1434	(M)	**The Swinger From Rio**	1965	6.00	15.00
Atlantic SD-1434	(S)	**The Swinger From Rio**	1965	5.00	12.00

Helen Merrill first toured with the Reggie Childs Orchestra in 1946-47 before taking time off for marriage. She gigged occasionally with Jerry Wald during this time and toured with Earl Hines in 1952 before embarking on a career as a solo singer. Her earliest albums are on the EmArcy label (a trio of which are pictured here) and are the ones usually sought by jazz aficionados.

Label & Catalog #		Title	Year	VG+	NM
Atlantic 8112	(M)	**Sergio Mendes In Person At The El Matador**	1967	6.00	15.00
Atlantic SD-8112	(S)	**Sergio Mendes In Person At The El Matador**	1967	4.00	10.00
Atlantic SD-8177	(S)	**Sergio Mendes' Favorite Things**	1968	4.00	10.00

—Atlantic albums above have multi-color labels with a black fan logo.—

MERCER, MABEL

Mabel Mercer is a jazz-based vocalist.

Atlantic ALS-402	(10")	**Songs By Mable Mercer, Volume 1**	1954	30.00	75.00
Atlantic 1213	(M)	**Mable Mercer Sings Cole Porter**	1955	16.00	40.00
Atlantic 1244	(M)	**Midnight At Mable Mercer's**	1956	16.00	40.00
Atlantic 1301	(M)	**Once In A Blue Moon**	1958	16.00	40.00
Atlantic SD-1301	(S)	**Once In A Blue Moon**	1958	20.00	50.00
Atlantic 2-602	(M)	**The Art Of Mabel Mercer** *(2 LPs)*	1958	24.00	60.00
Atlantic 1322	(M)	**Merely Marvelous Mable Mercer**	1960	16.00	40.00
Atlantic SD-1322	(S)	**Merely Marvelous Mable Mercer**	1960	20.00	50.00

—Atlantic albums above have black mono or green stereo labels.—

Atlantic 1213	(M)	**Mable Mercer Sings Cole Porter**	1961	6.00	15.00
Atlantic 1244	(M)	**Midnight At Mable Mercer's**	1961	6.00	15.00
Atlantic 1301	(M)	**Once In A Blue Moon**	1961	6.00	15.00
Atlantic SD-1301	(S)	**Once In A Blue Moon**	1961	8.00	20.00
Atlantic 2-602	(M)	**The Art Of Mabel Mercer** *(2 LPs)*	1961	10.00	25.00
Atlantic 1322	(M)	**Merely Marvelous Mable Mercer**	1961	6.00	15.00
Atlantic SD-1322	(S)	**Merely Marvelous Mable Mercer**	1961	8.00	20.00

—Atlantic albums above have multi-color labels with a white fan logo.—

Atlantic 1213	(M)	**Mable Mercer Sings Cole Porter**	196?	4.00	10.00
Atlantic 1244	(M)	**Midnight At Mable Mercer's**	196?	4.00	10.00
Atlantic 1301	(M)	**Once In A Blue Moon**	196?	4.00	10.00
Atlantic SD-1301	(S)	**Once In A Blue Moon**	196?	5.00	12.00
Atlantic 2-602	(M)	**The Art Of Mabel Mercer** *(2 LPs)*	196?	6.00	15.00
Atlantic 1322	(M)	**Merely Marvelous Mable Mercer**	196?	4.00	10.00
Atlantic SD-1322	(S)	**Merely Marvelous Mable Mercer**	196?	5.00	12.00

—Atlantic albums above have multi-color labels with a black fan logo.—

MERRILL, HELEN

Helen Milcetic Merrill is a modern jazz-based vocalist.

EmArcy MG-36006	(M)	**Helen Merrill**	1955	30.00	75.00
EmArcy MG-36057	(M)	**Helen Merrill With Strings**	1955	30.00	75.00
EmArcy MG-36078	(M)	**Dream Of You**	1956	20.00	50.00
EmArcy MG-36107	(M)	**Merrill At Midnight**	1957	20.00	50.00
EmArcy MG-36134	(M)	**The Nearness Of You**	1958	20.00	50.00

—EmArcy albums above have silver on blue labels.—

Metrojazz E-1010	(M)	**You've Got A Date With The Blues**	1958	20.00	50.00
Metrojazz SE-1010	(S)	**You've Got A Date With The Blues**	1958	16.00	40.00
Atco 33-112	(M)	**American Country Songs**	1959	16.00	40.00

—Atco albums above have yellow labels with a harp logo on top.—

Mainstream 56014	(M)	**The Artistry Of Helen Merrill**	1965	12.00	30.00
Mainstream S-6014	(S)	**The Artistry Of Helen Merrill**	1965	10.00	25.00
Milestone MLP-1003	(M)	**The Feeling Is Mutual**	1967	10.00	25.00
Milestone MLSP-9003	(S)	**The Feeling Is Mutual**	1967	8.00	20.00

MEZZROW, MEZZ

Milton Mesirow, aka Mezz Mezzrow, is a traditional jazz clarinet and saxophone(s) player.

Blue Note BLP-7023	(10")	**Mezz Mezzrow And His Band**	1952	125.00	250.00
"X" LVA-3015	(10")	**Mezz Mezzrow's Swing Session**	1954	30.00	75.00
"X" LVA-3027	(10")	**Mezz Mezzrow**	1954	30.00	75.00
RCA Victor LJM-1006	(M)	**Mezzin' Around**	1954	20.00	50.00

—RCA albums above have black labels with "Long Play" on the bottom.—

London TKL-93092	(10")	**A La Schola Cantorum**	1956	20.00	50.00

MIGLIORI, JAY

Transition TRLP-18	(M)	**Jay Migliori Quintet**	1956	*Unreleased*	

MIL-COMBO, THE

The Mil-Combo is a modern jazz group featuring Don Mamblow; Connie Milano; and Ziggy Millonzi.

Capitol T-579	(M)	**The Mil-Combo**	1955	16.00	40.00

—Capitol albums above have turquoise labels.—

Label & Catalog #		Title	Year	VG+	NM

MILES, BARRY

Barry Miles is a modern jazz vibraphone and piano player and drummer.

Charlie Parker PLP-804	(M)	**Miles Of Genius**	1962	12.00	30.00
Charlie Parker PLP-804S	(S)	**Miles Of Genius**	1962	10.00	25.00

MILES, LIZZIE

Elizabeth Landreaux, aka Lizzie Miles, is a traditional jazz vocalist. For additional listings refer to Sharkey Bonano & Lizzie Miles; Bob Scobey.

Cook 1181	(10")	**Queen Mother Of The Rue Royale**	1955	20.00	50.00
Cook 1182	(M)	**Moans And Blues**	1955	16.00	40.00
Cook 1183	(M)	**Hot Songs My Mother Taught Me**	1955	16.00	40.00
Cook 1184	(M)	**Torchy Lullabies My Mother Sang Me**	1955	16.00	40.00

MILLER, BIG

Clarence"Big" Miller is a traditional jazz and rhythm 'n' blues vocalist.

United Arts. UAL-3047	(M)	**Did You Ever Hear The Blues?**	1959	16.00	40.00
United Arts. UAS-6047	(S)	**Did You Ever Hear The Blues?**	1959	20.00	50.00
		(United Artists 3047 also features Langston Hughes.)			
Columbia CL-1611	(M)	**Revelation And The Blues**	1961	12.00	30.00
Columbia CS-8411	(S)	**Revelation And The Blues**	1961	16.00	40.00

—Columbia albums above have six black on white "eye" logos on each label.—

Columbia CL-1808	(M)	**Big Miller Sings, Twists, Shouts And Preaches**	1962	10.00	25.00
Columbia CS-8608	(S)	**Big Miller Sings, Twists, Shouts And Preaches**	1962	12.00	30.00

—Columbia albums above have "Guaranteed High Fidelity" or "360 Sound Stereo" in black on the label.—

MILLER, EDDIE

Edward Miller is a traditional jazz tenor saxophone and clarinet player and vocalist.

Capitol T-614	(10")	**Classics In Jazz**	1955	20.00	50.00

MILLER, EDDIE / GEORGE VAN EPS

Jump JL-5	(10")	**Eddie Miller-George Van Eps**	1953	20.00	50.00

MILLER, DON

Donald Miller is a modern jazz guitarist.

King 712	(M)	**The Don Miller Quartet**	1960	20.00	50.00

—King albums above have silver on black labels.—

MILLER, GLENN (THE GLENN MILLER ORCHESTRA)

Alton Glenn Miller is a traditional jazz trombone player, arranger, composer and big band leader. For additional listings refer to the Jazzy Soundtracks section under Decca, RCA Victor, and 20th Century Fox..

RCA Victor LPT-16	(10")	**Glenn Miller Concert—Volume 1**	1951	24.00	60.00
RCA Victor LPT-30	(10")	**Glenn Miller Concert—Volume 2**	1951	24.00	60.00
RCA Victor LPT-31	(10")	**Glenn Miller**	1951	24.00	60.00
RCA Victor LPT-3001	(10")	**Glenn Miller Concert—Volume 3**	1951	24.00	60.00
RCA Victor LPT-3002	(10")	**This Is Glenn Miller**	1951	24.00	60.00
RCA Victor LPT-3036	(10")	**This Is Glenn Miller—Volume 2**	1951	24.00	60.00
RCA Victor LPT-3057	(10")	**Selections From The Film "The Glenn Miller Story"**	1951	24.00	60.00
RCA Victor LPT-3067	(10")	**Sunrise Serenade**	1951	24.00	60.00

—RCA albums above have silver labels with red print.—

RCA Victor LPT-6700	(M)	**Glenn Miller & His Orchestra/Limited Edition** *(5 LPs with red on silver labels. Issued in a spiral-bound binder with a booklet that has a blank first page that is sequentially numbered.)*	1953	100.00	200.00
RCA Victor LPT-6700	(M)	**Glenn Miller & His Orchestra/Limited Edition—Second Pressing** *(5 LPs with black labels with "Long Play" on the bottom. Issued in in a spiral-bound binder.)*	195?	30.00	75.00
RCA Victor LPT-6701	(M)	**Glenn Miller & His Orchestra-Limited Edition Vol. 2** *(5 LPs with black "Long Play" labels in a spiral-bound binder with a booklet that has a blank first page that is sequentially numbered.)*	1954	60.00	150.00
RCA Victor LPT-6701	(M)	**Glenn Miller & His Orchestra-Limited Edition Vol. 2** *(5 LPs with black labeels that read "Second Pressing." Issued in a spiral-bound binder with a booklet.)*	195?	30.00	75.00
RCA Victor LPT-6702	(M)	**Glenn Miller Army Air Force Band** *(5 LPs with black labels with "Long Play" on the bottom. Issued in in a spiral-bound binder.)*	1955	60.00	150.00

Label & Catalog #		Title	Year	VG+	NM
RCA Victor LPM-6700	(M)	**Glenn Miller Army Air Force Band**	195?	20.00	50.00
		(Boxed set of 5 LPs. This is a budget version of LPT-6702 with identical discs and booklet.)			
RCA Victor LPM-6100	(M)	**For The Very First Time...**	195?	20.00	50.00
		(3 LPs with black labels with "Long Play" on the bottom. Issued in in a spiral-bound binder.)			
RCA Victor LOP-1005	(M)	**The Marvelous Miller Medleys**	1955	16.00	40.00
RCA Victor LPT-1016	(M)	**Juke Box Saturday Night**	1955	16.00	40.00
RCA Victor LPT-1031	(M)	**The Nearness Of You**	1955	16.00	40.00
RCA Victor LPM-1189	(M)	**The Sound Of Glenn Miller**	1956	16.00	40.00
RCA Victor LPM-1190	(M)	**This Is Glenn Miller**	1956	16.00	40.00
RCA Victor LPM-1192	(M)	**Selections From "The Glenn Miller Story" & Other Hits**	1956	16.00	40.00
RCA Victor LSP-1192	(E)	**Selections From "The Glenn Miller Story" & Other Hits**	196?	6.00	15.00
RCA Victor LPM-1193	(M)	**Glenn Miller Concert**	1956	16.00	40.00
		(RCA 1189-1193 repackage material from the earlier 10" releases.)			
RCA Victor LPM-1494	(M)	**Marvelous Miller Moods**	1957	16.00	40.00
RCA Victor LPM-1506	(M)	**The Glenn Miller Carnegie Hall Concert**	1957	16.00	40.00
RCA Victor LPM-1522	(M)	**The New Glenn Miller Orchestra In Hi-Fi**	1958	16.00	40.00
RCA Victor LPM-1522	(S)	**The New Glenn Miller Orchestra In Hi-Fi**	1958	12.00	30.00
RCA Victor LPM-1678	(M)	**Something Old, New, Borrowed and Blue**	1958	16.00	40.00
RCA Victor LPM-1678	(S)	**Something Old, New, Borrowed and Blue**	1958	12.00	30.00
RCA Victor LPM-1852	(M)	**The Miller Sound**	1959	16.00	40.00
RCA Victor LPM-1852	(S)	**The Miller Sound**	1959	12.00	30.00
RCA Victor LPM-1948	(M)	**On Tour With The New Glenn Miller Orchestra**	1959	16.00	40.00
RCA Victor LPM-1948	(S)	**On Tour With The New Glenn Miller Orchestra**	1959	12.00	30.00
RCA Victor LPM-1973	(M)	**The Marvelous Miller Medleys**	1959	12.00	30.00
RCA Victor LSP-1973	(E)	**The Marvelous Miller Medleys**	1959	6.00	15.00
RCA Victor LPM-2080	(M)	**The Great Dance Bands Of The '30s And '40s**	1959	12.00	30.00
RCA Victor LSP-2080	(S)	**The Great Dance Bands Of The '30s And '40s**	1959	10.00	25.00
RCA Victor LPM-2193	(M)	**Dance, Anyone?**	1960	12.00	30.00
RCA Victor LPM-2193	(S)	**Dance, Anyone?**	1960	10.00	25.00
RCA Victor LPM-2270	(M)	**The Authentic Sound Of The New Glenn Miller Orchestra—Today**	1961	12.00	30.00
RCA Victor LPM-2270	(S)	**The Authentic Sound Of The New Glenn Miller Orchestra—Today**	1961	10.00	25.00
RCA Victor LPM-2436	(M)	**Glenn Miller Time**	1961	12.00	30.00
RCA Victor LPM-2436	(S)	**Glenn Miller Time**	1961	10.00	25.00
RCA Victor LPM-2519	(M)	**Echoes Of Glenn Miller**	1962	12.00	30.00
RCA Victor LPM-2519	(S)	**Echoes Of Glenn Miller**	1962	10.00	25.00
		—RCA albums above have black labels with "Long Play" or "Living Stereo" on the bottom.—			
RCA Victor SP-33-90	(DJ)	**The Authentic Sound Of Glenn Miller**	1960	12.00	30.00
RCA Victor LPM-6101	(M)	**Glenn Miller On The Air**	1963	10.00	25.00
RCA Victor LSP-6101	(E)	**Glenn Miller On The Air**	1963	6.00	15.00
		(The 3 LPs in this box were issued individually and are listed below.)			
RCA Victor LPM-2767	(M)	**Glenn Miller On The Air, Volume 1**	1963	6.00	15.00
RCA Victor LSP-2767	(E)	**Glenn Miller On The Air, Volume 1**	1963	4.00	10.00
RCA Victor LPM-2768	(M)	**Glenn Miller On The Air, Volume 2**	1963	6.00	15.00
RCA Victor LSP-2768	(E)	**Glenn Miller On The Air, Volume 2**	1963	4.00	10.00
RCA Victor LPM-2769	(M)	**Glenn Miller On The Air, Volume 3**	1963	6.00	15.00
RCA Victor LSP-2769	(E)	**Glenn Miller On The Air, Volume 3**	1963	4.00	10.00
RCA Victor LPM-3377	(M)	**The Best Of Glenn Miller—Volume 1**	1965	6.00	15.00
RCA Victor LSP-3377	(E)	**The Best Of Glenn Miller—Volume 1**	1965	4.00	10.00
RCA Victor LPM-3564	(M)	**The Best Of Glenn Miller—Volume 2**	1966	6.00	15.00
RCA Victor LSP-3564	(E)	**The Best Of Glenn Miller—Volume 2**	1966	4.00	10.00
RCA Victor LPM-3657	(M)	**Blue Moonlight**	1966	5.00	12.00
RCA Victor LSP-3657	(E)	**Blue Moonlight**	1966	4.00	10.00
RCA Victor LPM-3819	(M)	**In The Mood**	1967	10.00	25.00
RCA Victor LPM-3819	(S)	**In The Mood**	1967	6.00	15.00
RCA Victor LPM-3873	(M)	**The Chesterfield Broadcasts, Volume 1**	1967	6.00	15.00
RCA Victor LSP-3873	(E)	**The Chesterfield Broadcasts, Volume 1**	1967	4.00	10.00
RCA Victor LPM-3880	(M)	**The Glenn Miller Orchestra Under The Direction Of Buddy DeFranco Returns To The Glen Island Casino**	1967	10.00	25.00
RCA Victor LPM-3880	(S)	**The Glenn Miller Orchestra Under The Direction Of Buddy DeFranco Returns To The Glen Island Casino**	1967	6.00	15.00

Label & Catalog #		Title	Year	VG+	NM
RCA Victor LSP-3981	(E)	**The Chesterfield Broadcasts, Volume 2**	1968	6.00	15.00
RCA Victor LSP-4125	(E)	**The Best Of Glenn Miller—Volume 3**	1969	4.00	10.00
RCA Victor VPM-6019	(M)	**Glenn Miller: A Memorial 1944-1969** *(2 LPs)*	1969	6.00	15.00
Camden CAL-751	(M)	**The Great Glenn Miller & His Orchestra**	1963	5.00	12.00
Camden CAS-751	(E)	**The Great Glenn Miller & His Orchestra**	1963	4.00	10.00
Camden CAL-829	(M)	**The Original Recordings By Glenn Miller & His Orchestra**	1964	5.00	12.00
Camden CAS-829	(E)	**The Original Recordings By Glenn Miller & His Orchestra**	1964	4.00	10.00
Camden CAL-2128	(M)	**The Nearness Of You**	1967	5.00	12.00
Camden CAS-2128	(E)	**The Nearness Of You**	1967	4.00	10.00
Camden CAS-2267	(E)	**The One And Only Glenn Miller**	1968	4.00	10.00
Reader's Digest RD3-64	(M)	**The Unforgettable Glenn Miller** *(6 LP box)*	196?	20.00	50.00
Reader's Digest RD4-64	(E)	**The Unforgettable Glenn Miller** *(6 LP box)*	196?	12.00	30.00

MILLER, PUNCH / MUTT CAREY

Ernest Burden, aka Punch Miller, is a traditional jazz trumpet player and vocalist. For additional listings refer to Paul Barbarin & Punch Miller; Richard Jones.

Savoy MG-12038	(M)	**Jazz: New Orleans, Volume 1**	1955	20.00	50.00
Savoy MG-12050	(M)	**Jazz: New Orleans, Volume 2**	1955	20.00	50.00

MILLMAN, JACK

Jack Millman is a modern jazz trumpet and flugel horn player.

Decca DL-8156	(M)	**Jazz Studio 4**	1955	20.00	50.00
Era EL-20005	(M)	**Blowing Up A Storm** *(Red vinyl)*	1956	20.00	50.00
Liberty LJH-6007	(M)	**Shades Of Things To Come**	1956	20.00	50.00

MINGUS, CHARLES

Charles Mingus is a modern jazz bass player, arranger, composer and band leader. For additional listings refer to Paul Bley; Duke Ellington & Charles Mingus & Max Roach; Langston Hughes; Jazz Artists Guild; Thad Jones; Red Norvo; The Quintet; and the Jazzy Soundtracks section under Epic.

Debut DLP-1	(10")	**Strings And Keys**	1953	240.00	400.00
Debut DEB-123	(M)	**Mingus At The Bohemia**	1956	100.00	200.00
Debut DEB-139	(M)	**The Charlie Mingus Quintet + Max Roach**	1956	*Unreleased*	
Savoy MG-15050	(10")	**Charlie Mingus**	1955	100.00	200.00
Savoy MG-12059	(M)	**Jazz Composers Workshop** *(Savoy 12059 is a reissue of 15050.)*	1956	40.00	100.00
Period SPL-1107	(10")	**Jazzical Moods, Volume 1**	1955	100.00	200.00
Period SPL-1111	(10")	**Jazzical Moods, Volume 2**	1955	100.00	200.00
Bethlehem BCP-65	(M)	**The Jazz Experiment Of Charlie Mingus** *(Bethlehem 65 is a reissue of Period 1107 and 1111.)*	1956	40.00	100.00
Jazztone J-1226	(M)	**Jazz Experiment** *(Jazztone 1226 is a reissue of Period 1107 and 1111.)*	1956	20.00	50.00
Jazztone J-1271	(M)	**The Jazz Experiments Of Charlie Mingus** *(Jazztone 1271 is a reissue of Bethlehem 65.)*	1957	20.00	50.00
Bethlehem BCP-6019	(M)	**East Coasting**	1958	40.00	100.00
Bethlehem SBCP-6019	(S)	**East Coasting**	1958	40.00	100.00
Bethlehem BCP-6026	(M)	**A Modern Jazz Symposium Of Music & Poetry**	1958	40.00	100.00
Bethlehem SBCP-6026	(S)	**A Modern Jazz Symposium Of Music & Poetry**	1958	40.00	100.00
Jubilee JLP-1054	(M)	**Mingus Three**	1957	30.00	75.00
Atlantic 1237	(M)	**Pithecanthropus Erectus**	1956	30.00	75.00
Atlantic 1260	(M)	**The Clown**	1957	20.00	50.00
		—Atlantic albums above have black mono or green stereo labels.—			
Atlantic 1305	(M)	**Blues & Roots**	1959	20.00	50.00
Atlantic SD-1305	(S)	**Blues & Roots**	1959	16.00	40.00
		—Atlantic albums above have white "bullseye" labels.—			
Atlantic 1237	(M)	**Pithecanthropus Erectus**	1961	8.00	20.00
Atlantic 1260	(M)	**The Clown**	1961	8.00	20.00
Atlantic 1305	(M)	**Blues & Roots**	1961	8.00	20.00
Atlantic SD-1305	(S)	**Blues & Roots**	1961	6.00	15.00
Atlantic 1377	(M)	**Oh, Yeah**	1961	12.00	30.00
Atlantic SD-1377	(S)	**Oh, Yeah**	1961	10.00	25.00
		—Atlantic albums above have multi-color labels with a white fan logo.—			
Atlantic 1237	(M)	**Pithecanthropus Erectus**	196?	5.00	12.00
Atlantic 1260	(M)	**The Clown**	196?	5.00	12.00
Atlantic 1305	(M)	**Blues & Roots**	196?	5.00	12.00
Atlantic SD-1305	(S)	**Blues & Roots**	196?	4.00	10.00

Label & Catalog #		Title	Year	VG+	NM
Atlantic 1377	(M)	**Oh, Yeah**	196?	5.00	12.00
Atlantic SD-1377	(S)	**Oh, Yeah**	196?	4.00	10.00
Atlantic 1416	(M)	**Tonight At Noon**	1964	12.00	30.00
Atlantic SD-1416	(S)	**Tonight At Noon**	1964	10.00	25.00
		—Atlantic albums above have multi-color labels with a black fan logo.—			
United Arts. UAL-4036	(M)	**Jazz Portraits**	1959	20.00	50.00
United Arts. UAS-5036	(S)	**Jazz Portraits**	1959	16.00	40.00
United Arts. UAJ-14005	(M)	**Wonderland**	1962	20.00	50.00
United Arts. UAJS-15005	(S)	**Wonderland**	1962	16.00	40.00
United Arts. UAJ-14024	(M)	**Town Hall Concert**	1963	20.00	50.00
United Arts. UAJS-15024	(S)	**Town Hall Concert**	1963	16.00	40.00
Columbia CL-1370	(M)	**Mingus Ah Um**	1959	16.00	40.00
Columbia CS-8171	(S)	**Mingus Ah Um**	1959	12.00	30.00
Columbia CL-1440	(M)	**Mingus Dynasty**	1960	16.00	40.00
Columbia CS-8236	(S)	**Mingus Dynasty**	1960	12.00	30.00
		—Columbia albums above have six white on black "eye" logos on each label.—			
Candid CD-8005	(M)	**Charles Mingus Presents Charles Mingus**	1960	20.00	50.00
Candid CS-9005	(S)	**Charles Mingus Presents Charles Mingus**	1960	16.00	40.00
Candid CD-8021	(M)	**Mingus**	1960	20.00	50.00
Candid CS-9021	(S)	**Mingus**	1960	16.00	40.00
Mercury MG-20627	(M)	**Pre Bird**	1961	16.00	40.00
Mercury SR-60627	(S)	**Pre Bird**	1961	12.00	30.00
RCA Victor LPM-2533	(M)	**Tijuana Moods** *(Dancer with jukebox cover)*	1962	20.00	50.00
RCA Victor LSP-2533	(S)	**Tijuana Moods** *(Dancer with jukebox cover)*	1962	16.00	40.00
		—RCA albums above have black labels with "Long Play" or "Living Stereo" on the bottom.—			
Fantasy 6002	(M)	**Chazz!** *(Red vinyl)*	1962	20.00	50.00
Fantasy 6002	(M)	**Chazz!**	1962	12.00	30.00
Fantasy 86002	(E)	**Chazz!** *(Blue vinyl)*	1962	10.00	25.00
Fantasy 86002	(E)	**Chazz!**	1962	6.00	15.00
		(Fantasy 6002 is a reissue of Debut 123.)			
Fantasy 6009	(M)	**The Charlie Mingus Quintet + Max Roach**	1963	12.00	30.00
Fantasy 86009	(E)	**The Charlie Mingus Quintet + Max Roach**	1963	6.00	15.00
		(Fantasy 6009 is a "reissue" of the unreleased Debut 139.)			
Fantasy 6017	(M)	**Right Now—Live At The Jazz Workshop**	1966	12.00	30.00
Fantasy 86017	(S)	**Right Now—Live At The Jazz Workshop**	1966	10.00	25.00
Josie JLPM-3508	(M)	**Mingus Three**	1963	12.00	30.00
Josie JLPS-3508	(S)	**Mingus Three**	1963	10.00	25.00
		(Josie 3508 is a reissue of Jubilee 1054.)			
Impulse A-35	(M)	**Black Saint And Sinner Lady**	1963	16.00	40.00
Impulse AS-35	(S)	**Black Saint And Sinner Lady**	1963	12.00	30.00
Impulse A-54	(M)	**Mingus, Mingus, Mingus, Mingus, Mingus**	1963	16.00	40.00
Impulse AS-54	(S)	**Mingus, Mingus, Mingus, Mingus, Mingus**	1963	12.00	30.00
Impulse A-60	(M)	**Charlie Mingus Plays Piano**	1964	16.00	40.00
Impulse AS-60	(S)	**Charlie Mingus Plays Piano**	1964	12.00	30.00
		—Impulse albums above have orange & black labels.—			
Impulse AS-35	(S)	**Black Saint And Sinner Lady**	1968	6.00	15.00
Impulse AS-54	(S)	**Mingus, Mingus, Mingus, Mingus, Mingus**	1968	6.00	15.00
Impulse AS-60	(S)	**Charlie Mingus Plays Piano**	1968	6.00	15.00
		—Impulse albums above have red & black labels with the "abc" logo on top.—			
Limelight LM-82015	(M)	**Mingus Revisited**	1965	12.00	30.00
Limelight LS-86015	(S)	**Mingus Revisited**	1965	10.00	25.00
Char. Mingus JWS-001/2	(S)	**Mingus At Monterey** *(2 LPs)*	1968	300.00	600.00
		(First pressings of JWS-001/002 have black labels with silver print and were issued in a single-pocket jacket with a black & white, sepia-toned "fisheye" photo of the California coast on the cover.)			
Char. Mingus JWS-001/2	(S)	**Mingus At Monterey** *(2 LPs)*	1968	150.00	300.00
		(Second pressings of JWS-001/002 have black labels with silver print were issued in a gatefold jacket with a color "fish eye" photo of the California coast on the cover. A note on the back reads "This album can be purchased only by mail.")			
Char. Mingus JWS-001/2	(S)	**Mingus At Monterey** *(2 LPs)*	1968	20.00	50.00
		(Later pressings of JWS-001/002 have black labels with silver print were issued in a gatefold jacket with a color photo of the California coast on the cover. A note on the back reads "Exclusively distributed by Saul Zaentz and Fantasy Records.")			
Char. Mingus JWS-005	(S)	**Town Hall Concert, 1964, Vol. 1**	1966	150.00	300.00
		(JWS-005 has black labels with silver print and a note on the back cover that reads "This album can be purchased only by mail.")			

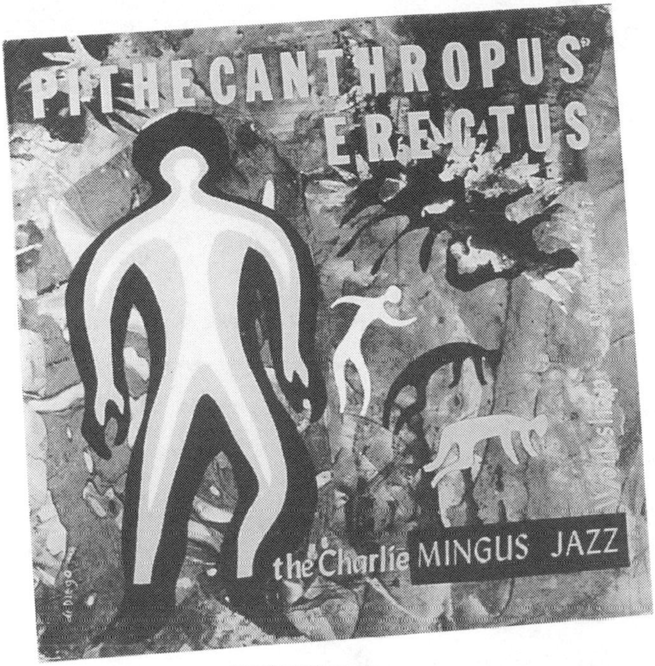

Charles Mingus first played jazz professionally at the age of sixteen with Red Callender. He then played with Lee Young (1940), Louis Armstrong (1941-43), Kid Ory, Lionel Hampton (1946-48), Red Norvo (1950-51) and Billy Taylor (1952-53). He started his own record company, Debut, in 1952, and followed that with the Jazz Workshop label in the '60s. While he has recorded with many labels, perhaps his most enduring achievements as a composer, arranger, leader and musician occurred with Atlantic between 1956 and 1961, from which the two examples here were chosen. He has recorded as a featured artist with Red Norvo. As a sideman he can be found on albums by Langston Hughes on MGM, Teddy Charles on Atlantic and Prestige, John Mehegan on Savoy, with The Quintet on Debut, and The Jazz Artists Guild.

Label & Catalog #		Title	Year	VG+	NM
Char. Mingus JWS-009	(S)	**My Favorite Quintet** *(JWS-009 has black labels with silver print and a note on the back cover that reads "This album can be purchased only by mail.")*	1966	150.00	300.00
Char. Mingus JWS-013/14	(S)	**Special Music Written For (And Not Heard At) Monterey** *(2 LPs)* *(JWS-013/014 was issued in a single-pocket jacket with a note on the back cover reads "This album can be purchased only by mail.")*	1966	500.00	1,000.00
Solid State SS-18019	(S)	**Wonderland** *(Solid State 18109 is a reissue of U.A. 15005.)*	1968	6.00	15.00
Solid State SS-18024	(S)	**Town Hall Concert** *(Solid State 18204 is a reissue of U.A. 15024.)*	1968	6.00	15.00
Fantasy JWS-001/002	(S)	**Mingus At Monterey** *(2 LPs)* *(Fantasy 001/002 is a reissue of Charles Mingus 001/002.)*	1969	8.00	20.00
Fantasy JWS-005	(S)	**My Favorite Quintet** *(Fantasy 005 is a reissue of Charles Mingus 009.)*	1969	6.00	15.00
Fantasy JWS-009	(S)	**Town Hall Concert, 1964, Vol. 1** *(Fantasy 009 is a reissue of Charles Mingus 005.)*	1969	6.00	15.00
Archive Of Folk & Jazz 235	(M)	**Charlie Mingus** *(AOFJ 235 is a reissue of period 1107 and 1111.)*	1969	4.00	10.00

MINION, FRANK

Bethlehem BCP-6033	(M)	**The Forward Sound**	1959	16.00	40.00
Bethlehem BCP-6052	(M)	**The Soft Land Of Make Believe**	1960	16.00	40.00
Bethlehem SBCP-6052	(S)	**The Soft Land Of Make Believe**	1960	16.00	40.00

MISSOURIANS, THE

"X" LVA-3020	(10")	**Harlem In The Twenties, Volume 1**	1954	20.00	50.00

MITCHELL, BILLY

William Mitchell is a modern jazz tenor saxophone player. For additional listings refer to Al Grey; Al Grey & Billy Mitchell.

Smash MGS-27027	(M)	**This Is Billy Mitchell**	1962	12.00	30.00
Smash SRS-67027	(S)	**This Is Billy Mitchell**	1962	10.00	25.00
Smash MGS-27042	(M)	**A Little Juicy**	1962	12.00	30.00
Smash SRS-67042	(S)	**A Little Juicy**	1962	10.00	25.00

MITCHELL, BLUE

Richard "Blue" Mitchell is a modern jazz trumpet player. For additional listings refer to Les McCann; The Mitchells; The Riverside Jazz Stars.

Riverside RLP-12-273	(M)	**Big 6**	1958	20.00	50.00
Riverside RLP-12-293	(M)	**Out Of The Blue**	1958	20.00	50.00
Riverside RLP-1131	(S)	**Out Of The Blue**	1958	16.00	40.00
Riverside RLP-12-309	(M)	**Blue Soul**	1959	20.00	50.00
Riverside RLP-1155	(S)	**Blue Soul**	1959	16.00	40.00
Riverside RLP-336	(M)	**Blue's Moods**	1960	20.00	50.00
Riverside RS-9336	(S)	**Blue's Moods**	1960	16.00	40.00
Riverside RLP-367	(M)	**Smooth As The Wind**	1961	20.00	50.00
Riverside RS-9367	(S)	**Smooth As The Wind**	1961	16.00	40.00
Riverside RLP-414	(M)	**A Sure Thing**	1962	20.00	50.00
Riverside RS-9414	(S)	**A Sure Thing**	1962	16.00	40.00
Riverside RLP-439	(M)	**The Cup Bearers**	1963	20.00	50.00
Riverside RS-9439	(S)	**The Cup Bearers**	1963	16.00	40.00
—Riverside albums above have blue mono or black stereo labels with a reel & mike logo on top.—					
Blue Note BLP-4142	(M)	**Step Lightly**	1963	*Unreleased*	
Blue Note BST-84142	(S)	**Step Lightly**	1963	*Unreleased*	
Blue Note BLP-4178	(M)	**The Thing To Do**	1964	12.00	30.00
Blue Note BST-84178	(S)	**The Thing To Do**	1964	10.00	25.00
Blue Note BLP-4214	(M)	**Down With It**	1965	12.00	30.00
Blue Note BST-84214	(S)	**Down With It**	1965	10.00	25.00
Blue Note BLP-4228	(M)	**Bring It Home To Me**	1966	16.00	40.00
Blue Note BST-84228	(S)	**Bring It Home To Me**	1966	12.00	30.00
—Blue Note albums above have blue on white labels with a New York, USA address.—					
Blue Note BST-84178	(S)	**The Thing To Do**	196?	5.00	12.00
Blue Note BST-84214	(S)	**Down With It**	196?	5.00	12.00
Blue Note BST-84228	(S)	**Bring It Home To Me**	196?	5.00	12.00
Blue Note BLP-4257	(M)	**Boss Horn**	1967	12.00	30.00
Blue Note BST-84257	(S)	**Boss Horn**	1967	10.00	25.00
Blue Note BST-84272	(S)	**Heads Up!**	1968	12.00	30.00

Label & Catalog #		Title	Year	VG+	NM
Blue Note BST-84300	(S)	**Collision In Black**	1968	8.00	20.00
Blue Note BST-84324	(S)	**Bantu Village**	1969	8.00	20.00

—Blue Note albums above have blue on white labels with "A Division of Liberty Records."—

Atlantic 1458	(M)	**After This Message**	1966	10.00	25.00
Atlantic SD-1458	(S)	**After This Message**	1966	8.00	20.00

—Atlantic albums above have multi-color labels with a black fan logo.—

MITCHELL, PAUL

Verve V-8713	(M)	**Live At The Atlanta Playboy Club**	1967	5.00	12.00
Verve V6-8713	(S)	**Live At The Atlanta Playboy Club**	1967	4.00	10.00

—Verve albums above have black labels with "MGM Records" on the bottom.—

MITCHELL, RED

Keith "Red" Mitchell is a West Coast jazz bass player. For additional listings refer to Jim Hall; The Mitchell-Land Quintet; The Mitchells; The Modern Jazz Trio; Red Norvo; Oscar Pettiford; The Video All Stars.

Bethlehem BCP-1033	(10")	**Happy Minors**	1955	240.00	400.00
Bethlehem BCP-38	(M)	**Some Hot, Some Sweet, Some Wild**	1957	30.00	75.00
Contemporary C-3538	(M)	**Presenting Red Mitchell**	1957	30.00	75.00
Pacific Jazz PJ-22	(M)	**Rejoice**	1961	16.00	40.00
Pacific Jazz ST-22	(S)	**Rejoice**	1961	12.00	30.00

(Pacific Jazz 22 also features Frank Butler.)

MITCHELL, ROSCOE

Delmark DL-408	(M)	**Roscoe Mitchell Sextet**	1966	10.00	25.00
Delmark DS-9408	(S)	**Roscoe Mitchell Sextet**	1966	8.00	20.00
Nessa 2	(S)	**Conglipitous**	1968	8.00	20.00

MITCHELL, WHITEY

Gordon "Whitey" Mitchell is a modern jazz bass player. For additional listings refer to The Mitchells; The New York Jazz Quartet.

ABC-Paramount ABC-126	(M)	**Whitey Mitchell Sextette**	1956	20.00	50.00

MITCHELL, RED, & HAROLD LAND (THE MITCHELL-LAND QUINTET)

Atlantic 1376	(M)	**Hear Ye!**	1961	16.00	40.00
Atlantic SD-1376	(S)	**Hear Ye!**	1961	12.00	30.00

—Atlantic albums above have multi-color labels with a white fan logo.—

Atlantic 1376	(M)	**Hear Ye!**	196?	6.00	15.00
Atlantic SD-1376	(S)	**Hear Ye!**	196?	5.00	12.00

—Atlantic albums above have multi-color labels with a black fan logo.—

MITCHELL, DWIKE, & WILLIE RUFF (THE MITCHELL-RUFF DUO)

Dwike Mitchell is a modern jazz pianist; Willie Ruff, a bass and french horn player..

Epic LN-3221	(M)	**The Mitchell-Ruff Duo**	1956	16.00	40.00
Epic LN-3318	(M)	**Campus Concert**	1956	16.00	40.00
Roulette R-52002	(M)	**Appearing Nightly**	1958	16.00	40.00
Roulette SR-52002	(S)	**Appearing Nightly**	1958	12.00	30.00
Roulette R-52013	(M)	**The Mitchell-Ruff Duo Plus Strings & Brass**	1958	16.00	40.00
Roulette SR-52013	(S)	**The Mitchell-Ruff Duo Plus Strings & Brass**	1958	12.00	30.00
Roulette R-52025	(M)	**Jazz For Juniors**	1959	12.00	30.00
Roulette SR-52025	(S)	**Jazz For Juniors**	1959	10.00	25.00
Roulette R-52034	(M)	**Jazz Mission To Moscow**	1959	12.00	30.00
Roulette SR-52034	(S)	**Jazz Mission To Moscow**	1959	10.00	25.00
Roulette R-52037	(M)	**The Sound Of Music**	1960	10.00	25.00
Roulette SR-52037	(S)	**The Sound Of Music**	1960	8.00	20.00
Atlantic 1374	(M)	**The Catbird Seat**	1961	10.00	25.00
Atlantic SD-1374	(S)	**The Catbird Seat**	1961	8.00	20.00

—Atlantic albums above have multi-color labels with a white fan logo.—

Atlantic 1374	(M)	**The Catbird Seat**	196?	6.00	15.00
Atlantic SD-1374	(S)	**The Catbird Seat**	196?	5.00	12.00
Atlantic 1458	(M)	**After This Message**	1966	6.00	15.00
Atlantic SD-1458	(S)	**After This Message**	1966	5.00	12.00

—Atlantic albums above have multi-color labels with a black fan logo.—

MITCHELLS, THE

The Mitchells are Blue, Red and Whitey with Andre Previn.

Metrojazz E-1012	(M)	**"Get Those Elephants Out'a Here"**	1958	30.00	75.00
Metrojazz SE-1012	(S)	**"Get Those Elephants Out'a Here"**	1958	20.00	50.00

Label & Catalog #		Title	Year	VG+	NM

MOBLEY, HANK

Henry Mobley is a modern jazz tenor saxophone player. For additional listings refer to Art Blakey & The Jazz Messengers; Donald Byrd & Hank Mobley & Kenny Burrell; Kenny Drew & Donald Byrd & Hank Mobley; Max Roach; and the Various Artists section under Prestige.

Label & Catalog #		Title	Year	VG+	NM
Blue Note BLP-5066	(10")	**Hank Mobley Quartet**	1955	240.00	400.00
Blue Note BLP-1540	(M)	**Hank Mobley With Donald Byrd & Lee Morgan** *(Deep groove)*	1957	150.00	300.00
Blue Note BLP-1540	(M)	**Hank Mobley With Donald Byrd & Lee Morgan**	1957	125.00	250.00
		—Blue Note albums above have blue on white labels with a Lexington Ave, NYC address.—			
Blue Note BLP-1544	(M)	**Hank Mobley And His All Stars** *(Deep groove)*	1957	100.00	200.00
Blue Note BLP-1544	(M)	**Hank Mobley And His All Stars**	1957	60.00	150.00
Blue Note BLP-1550	(M)	**Hank Mobley** *(Deep groove)*	1957	100.00	200.00
Blue Note BLP-1550	(M)	**Hank Mobley**	1957	60.00	150.00
Blue Note BLP-1560	(M)	**Hank** *(Deep groove)*	1957	100.00	200.00
Blue Note BLP-1560	(M)	**Hank**	1957	60.00	150.00
Blue Note BLP-1568	(M)	**Hank Mobley** *(Deep groove)*	1957	100.00	200.00
Blue Note BLP-1568	(M)	**Hank Mobley**	1957	60.00	150.00
Blue Note BST-1568	(S)	**Hank Mobley** *(Deep groove)*	1959	60.00	150.00
Blue Note BST-1568	(S)	**Hank Mobley**	1959	40.00	100.00
Blue Note BLP-1574	(M)	**Peckin' Time** *(Deep groove)*	1958	100.00	200.00
Blue Note BLP-1574	(M)	**Peckin' Time**	1958	60.00	150.00
Blue Note BST-1574	(S)	**Peckin' Time**	1958	*Unreleased*	
Blue Note BLP-4031	(M)	**Soul Station** *(Deep groove)*	1960	50.00	125.00
Blue Note BLP-4031	(M)	**Soul Station**	1960	30.00	75.00
Blue Note BST-84031	(S)	**Soul Station**	1960	20.00	50.00
Blue Note BLP-4058	(M)	**Roll Call**	1961	30.00	75.00
Blue Note BST-84058	(S)	**Roll Call**	1961	20.00	50.00
		—Blue Note albums above have blue on white labels with a W. 63rd St, NYC address.—			
Blue Note BLP-4080	(M)	**Workout**	1961	20.00	50.00
Blue Note BST-84080	(S)	**Workout**	1961	16.00	40.00
		—Blue Note albums above have blue on white labels with a 61st St, NYC address.—			
Blue Note BLP-1540	(M)	**Hank Mobley With Donald Byrd & Lee Morgan**	1963	10.00	25.00
Blue Note BLP-1544	(M)	**Hank Mobley And His All Stars**	1963	10.00	25.00
Blue Note BLP-1550	(M)	**Hank Mobley**	1963	10.00	25.00
Blue Note BLP-1560	(M)	**Hank**	1963	10.00	25.00
Blue Note BLP-1568	(M)	**Hank Mobley**	1963	10.00	25.00
Blue Note BST-1568	(S)	**Hank Mobley**	1963	8.00	20.00
Blue Note BLP-1574	(M)	**Peckin' Time**	1963	10.00	25.00
Blue Note BLP-4031	(M)	**Soul Station**	1963	10.00	25.00
Blue Note BST-84031	(S)	**Soul Station**	1963	8.00	20.00
Blue Note BLP-4058	(M)	**Roll Call**	1963	10.00	25.00
Blue Note BST-84058	(S)	**Roll Call**	1963	8.00	20.00
Blue Note BLP-4080	(M)	**Workout**	1963	10.00	25.00
Blue Note BST-84080	(S)	**Workout**	1963	8.00	20.00
Blue Note BLP-4149	(M)	**No Room For Squares**	1963	16.00	40.00
Blue Note BST-84149	(S)	**No Room For Squares**	1963	12.00	30.00
Blue Note BLP-4186	(M)	**The Turnaround!**	1964	16.00	40.00
Blue Note BST-84186	(S)	**The Turnaround!**	1964	12.00	30.00
Blue Note BLP-4209	(M)	**Dippin'**	1965	16.00	40.00
Blue Note BST-84209	(S)	**Dippin'**	1965	12.00	30.00
Blue Note BLP-4230	(M)	**A Caddy For Daddy**	1966	16.00	40.00
Blue Note BST-84230	(S)	**A Caddy For Daddy**	1966	12.00	30.00
Blue Note BLP-4241	(M)	**Hank Mobley**	1966	*Unreleased*	
Blue Note BST-84241	(S)	**Hank Mobley**	1966	*Unreleased*	
		—Blue Note albums above have blue on white labels with a New York, USA address.—			
Blue Note BST-1540	(E)	**Hank Mobley With Donald Byrd & Lee Morgan**	196?	4.00	10.00
Blue Note BST-81544	(E)	**Hank Mobley And His All Stars**	196?	4.00	10.00
Blue Note BST-81550	(E)	**Hank Mobley**	196?	4.00	10.00
Blue Note BST-81560	(E)	**Hank**	196?	4.00	10.00
Blue Note BST-81568	(S)	**Hank Mobley**	196?	5.00	12.00
Blue Note BST-81574	(E)	**Peckin' Time**	196?	4.00	10.00
Blue Note BST-84031	(S)	**Soul Station**	196?	5.00	12.00
Blue Note BST-84058	(S)	**Roll Call**	196?	5.00	12.00
Blue Note BST-84080	(S)	**Workout**	196?	5.00	12.00
Blue Note BST-84149	(S)	**No Room For Squares**	196?	5.00	12.00
Blue Note BST-84186	(S)	**The Turnaround!**	196?	5.00	12.00
Blue Note BST-84209	(S)	**Dippin'**	196?	5.00	12.00
Blue Note BST-84230	(S)	**A Caddy For Daddy**	196?	5.00	12.00

Hank Mobley worked with Paul Gayten (1950), Max Roach (1951-53), Dizzy Gillespie, and Horace Silver (1954) and then as one of Art Blakey's original Jazz Messengers (1955-56). He can be experienced on albums by Roach on Mercury and Argo, Silver on Blue Note and Epic, Blakey on Blue Note and Columbia, Kenny Dorham, Johnny Griffin, Dizzy Reece, and Jimmy Smith, all on Blue Note, Curtis Fuller on Blue Note and United Artists, Art Farmer on New Jazz, Kenny Drew on Riverside, and Lee Morgan on Savoy.

Label & Catalog #		Title	Year	VG+	NM
Blue Note BLP-4273	(M)	**Hi Voltage**	1968	40.00	100.00
Blue Note BST-84273	(S)	**Hi Voltage**	1968	10.00	25.00
Blue Note BST-84288	(S)	**Reach Out!**	1968	10.00	25.00
Blue Note BST-84329	(S)	**The Flip**	1969	8.00	20.00
		—Blue Note albums above have blue on white labels with "A Division of Liberty Records."—			
Savoy MG-12092	(M)	**Jazz Message #2**	1956	50.00	150.00
Prestige PRLP-7061	(M)	**Mobley's Message**	1956	50.00	150.00
Prestige PRLP-7082	(M)	**Mobley's 2nd Message**	1957	50.00	150.00
		—Prestige albums above have yellow labels with a W. 50th Street, NYC address.—			
New Jazz NJLP-8311	(M)	**52nd Street Theme**	1963	Unreleased	
Status ST-8311	(M)	**52nd Street Theme**	1965	16.00	40.00
		(Status 8311 is a reissue of Prestige 7061.)			
Prestige PRST-7661	(E)	**Hank Mobley's Message**	1969	5.00	12.00
		(Prestige 7661 is a reissue of Prestige 7061.)			
Prestige PRST-7667	(E)	**Mobley's 2nd Message**	1969	5.00	12.00
		(Prestige 7667 is a reissue of Prestige 7082.)			
		—Prestige albums above have blue labels with a trident logo on top.—			

MODERN JAZZ DISCIPLES, THE

The MJD are Bill Brown, Mike Kelly, Roy McCurdy, Curtis Peagler, Lee Tucker and Wilbur Jackson.

Label & Catalog #		Title	Year	VG+	NM
New Jazz NJLP-8222	(M)	**Modern Jazz Disciples**	1959	20.00	50.00
New Jazz NJLP-8240	(M)	**Right Down Front**	1960	20.00	50.00
		—New Jazz albums above have purple labels.—			
New Jazz NJLP-8222	(M)	**Modern Jazz Disciples**	1965	10.00	25.00
New Jazz NJLP-8240	(M)	**Right Down Front**	1965	10.00	25.00
		—New Jazz albums above have blue labels with a trident logo on the right side.—			

MODERN JAZZ ENSEMBLE, THE: *Refer to* THE MODERN JAZZ SOCIETY

MODERN JAZZ QUARTET, THE [MJQ]

MJQ is Milt Jackson, John Lewis, Percy Heath and Kenny Clarke on Prestige and Savoy. Clarke was replaced by Connie Kay in 1955. For additional listings refer to Oscar Peterson; Sonny Rollins; The Swingle Singers; the "Jazz At 16 2/3 RPM" article; and the Jazzy Soundtracks section under United Artists.

Label & Catalog #		Title	Year	VG+	NM
Prestige PRLP-160	(10")	**Modern Jazz Quartet With Milt Jackson**	1953	60.00	150.00
Prestige PRLP-170	(10")	**Modern Jazz Quartet, Volume 2**	1953	60.00	150.00
Prestige PRLP-7005	(M)	**Concorde**	1955	30.00	75.00
Prestige PRLP-7057	(M)	**Django**	1956	30.00	75.00
		(Prestige 7057 reissues 170 and half of 160.)			
Prestige PRLP-7059	(M)	**Modern Jazz Quartet/Milt Jackson Quintet**	1956	30.00	75.00
		(Prestige 7059 reissues 183, "Milt Jackson Quintet," and half of 160.)			
		—Prestige albums above have yellow labels with a W. 50th Street, NYC address.—			
Savoy MG-12046	(M)	**Modern Jazz Quartet**	1955	20.00	50.00
Atlantic 1231	(M)	**Fontessa**	1956	16.00	40.00
Atlantic SD-1231	(S)	**Fontessa**	1958	12.00	30.00
Atlantic 1247	(M)	**The Modern Jazz Quartet At The Music Inn**	1956	16.00	40.00
		(Atlantic 1247 also features Jimmy Giuffre.)			
Atlantic 1265	(M)	**The Modern Jazz Quartet**	1957	16.00	40.00
Atlantic 1299	(M)	**The Modern Jazz Quartet At Music Inn, Vol. 2**	1958	16.00	40.00
Atlantic SD-1299	(S)	**The Modern Jazz Quartet At Music Inn, Vol. 2**	1958	12.00	30.00
		(Atlantic 1299 also features Sonny Rollins.)			
Atlantic 1325	(M)	**Pyramid**	1960	16.00	40.00
Atlantic SD-1325	(S)	**Pyramid**	1960	12.00	30.00
		—Atlantic albums above have black mono or green stereo labels.—			
Atlantic 1231	(M)	**Fontessa**	196?	6.00	15.00
Atlantic SD-1231	(S)	**Fontessa**	196?	5.00	12.00
Atlantic 1247	(M)	**The Modern Jazz Quartet At The Music Inn**	196?	6.00	15.00
Atlantic 1265	(M)	**The Modern Jazz Quartet**	196?	6.00	15.00
Atlantic 1299	(M)	**The Modern Jazz Quartet At Music Inn, Vol. 2**	196?	6.00	15.00
Atlantic SD-1299	(S)	**The Modern Jazz Quartet At Music Inn, Vol. 2**	196?	5.00	12.00
Atlantic 1325	(M)	**Pyramid**	196?	6.00	15.00
Atlantic SD-1325	(S)	**Pyramid**	196?	5.00	12.00
Atlantic 1345	(M)	**The MJQ & Guests—Third Stream Music**	1960	10.00	25.00
Atlantic SD-1345	(S)	**The MJQ & Guests—Third Stream Music**	1960	8.00	20.00
Atlantic 2-603	(M)	**The European Concert** *(2 LPs)*	1961	12.00	30.00
Atlantic SD-2-603	(S)	**The European Concert** *(2 LPs)*	1961	10.00	25.00
Atlantic 1359	(M)	**The MJQ And Orchestra**	1961	10.00	25.00
Atlantic SD-1359	(S)	**The MJQ And Orchestra**	1961	8.00	20.00
		—Atlantic albums above have multi-color labels with a white fan logo.—			

The Modern Jazz Quartet was formed by Kenny Clarke, Percy Heath, Milt Jackson and John Lewis in 1951 but did not record until 1952 and did not become a full-time group until 1954. When Clarke left in 1955 he was replaced by Connie Kay at which time the MJQ began an acclaimed twelve year stay with Atlantic, from which the two examples here were chosen. Both Lewis and Jackson also carried on successful solo careers at the same time. MJQ can be found as featured guests on LPs by Oscar Peterson, Sonny Rollins, and The Swingle Singers.

Label & Catalog #		Title	Year	VG+	NM
Atlantic 1231	*(M)*	**Fontessa**	*196?*	**5.00**	**12.00**
Atlantic SD-1231	*(S)*	**Fontessa**	*196?*	**4.00**	**10.00**
Atlantic 1247	*(M)*	**The Modern Jazz Quartet At The Music Inn**	*196?*	**5.00**	**12.00**
Atlantic 1265	*(M)*	**The Modern Jazz Quartet**	*196?*	**5.00**	**12.00**
Atlantic 1299	*(M)*	**The Modern Jazz Quartet At Music Inn, Vol. 2**	*196?*	**5.00**	**12.00**
Atlantic SD-1299	*(S)*	**The Modern Jazz Quartet At Music Inn, Vol. 2**	*196?*	**4.00**	**10.00**
Atlantic 1325	*(M)*	**Pyramid**	*196?*	**5.00**	**12.00**
Atlantic SD-1325	*(S)*	**Pyramid**	*196?*	**4.00**	**10.00**
Atlantic 1345	*(M)*	**The MJQ & Guests—Third Stream Music**	*1960*	**5.00**	**12.00**
Atlantic SD-1345	*(S)*	**The MJQ & Guests—Third Stream Music**	*1960*	**4.00**	**10.00**
Atlantic 2-603	*(M)*	**The European Concert** *(2 LPs)*	*196?*	**6.00**	**15.00**
Atlantic SD-2-603	*(S)*	**The European Concert** *(2 LPs)*	*196?*	**5.00**	**12.00**
Atlantic 1359	*(M)*	**The MJQ And Orchestra**	*196?*	**5.00**	**12.00**
Atlantic SD-1359	*(S)*	**The MJQ And Orchestra**	*196?*	**4.00**	**10.00**
Atlantic 1381	*(M)*	**Lonely Woman**	*1962*	**8.00**	**20.00**
Atlantic SD-1381	*(S)*	**Lonely Woman**	*1962*	**6.00**	**15.00**
Atlantic 1385	*(M)*	**European Concert, Volume 1**	*1962*	**8.00**	**20.00**
Atlantic SD-1385	*(S)*	**European Concert, Volume 1**	*1962*	**6.00**	**15.00**
Atlantic 1386	*(M)*	**European Concert, Volume 2**	*1962*	**8.00**	**20.00**
Atlantic SD-1386	*(S)*	**European Concert, Volume 2**	*1962*	**6.00**	**15.00**
		(Atlantic 1385 and 1386 are reissues of 603.)			
Atlantic 1390	*(M)*	**The Comedy**	*1962*	**8.00**	**20.00**
Atlantic SD-1390	*(S)*	**The Comedy**	*1962*	**6.00**	**15.00**
Atlantic 1414	*(M)*	**The Sheriff**	*1964*	**8.00**	**20.00**
Atlantic SD-1414	*(S)*	**The Sheriff**	*1964*	**6.00**	**15.00**
Atlantic 1420	*(M)*	**A Quartet Is A Quartet Is A Quartet**	*1964*	**8.00**	**20.00**
Atlantic SD-1420	*(S)*	**A Quartet Is A Quartet Is A Quartet**	*1964*	**6.00**	**15.00**
Atlantic 1429	*(M)*	**Collaboration—The Modern Jazz Quartet With Laurindo Almeida**	*1964*	**5.00**	**12.00**
Atlantic SD-1429	*(S)*	**Collaboration—The Modern Jazz Quartet With Laurindo Almeida**	*1964*	**6.00**	**15.00**
Atlantic 1440	*(M)*	**The MJQ Plays Gershwin's "Porgy And Bess"**	*1965*	**5.00**	**12.00**
Atlantic SD-1440	*(S)*	**The MJQ Plays Gershwin's "Porgy And Bess"**	*1965*	**6.00**	**15.00**
Atlantic 1449	*(M)*	**Jazz Dialogue**	*1966*	**6.00**	**15.00**
Atlantic SD-1449	*(S)*	**Jazz Dialogue**	*1966*	**5.00**	**12.00**
Atlantic 1468	*(M)*	**Blues At Carnegie Hall**	*1967*	**6.00**	**15.00**
Atlantic SD-1468	*(S)*	**Blues At Carnegie Hall**	*1967*	**5.00**	**12.00**
Atlantic 1486	*(M)*	**Live At The Lighthouse**	*1967*	**6.00**	**15.00**
Atlantic SD-1486	*(S)*	**Live At The Lighthouse**	*1967*	**5.00**	**12.00**
		—Atlantic albums above have multi-color labels with a black fan logo.—			
United Arts. UAL-4072	*(M)*	**Patterns**	*1960*	**10.00**	**25.00**
United Arts. UAS-5072	*(S)*	**Patterns**	*1960*	**8.00**	**20.00**
Prestige PRLP-7421	*(M)*	**The Modern Jazz Quartet Play For Lovers**	*1966*	**8.00**	**20.00**
Prestige PRST-7421	*(E)*	**The Modern Jazz Quartet Play For Lovers**	*1966*	**5.00**	**12.00**
Prestige PRLP-7425	*(M)*	**The Modern Jazz Quartet Plays Jazz Classics**	*1966*	**8.00**	**20.00**
Prestige PRST-7425	*(E)*	**The Modern Jazz Quartet Plays Jazz Classics**	*1966*	**5.00**	**12.00**
		—Prestige albums above have blue labels with a trident logo on the right side.—			
Solid State SS-18035	*(S)*	**The Modern Jazz Quartet On Tour**	*1968*	**4.00**	**10.00**
		(Solid State 18035 is a reissue of U.A. 5072.)			
Apple ST-3353	*(S)*	**Under The Jasmine Tree**	*1968*	**8.00**	**20.00**
Apple STAO-3360	*(S)*	**Space** *(Gatefold cover)*	*1969*	**10.00**	**25.00**
		—Apple albums above have "Mfd. by Apple Records" on the bottom of the label.—			
Apple ST-5-3353	*(S)*	**Under The Jasmine Tree** *(Capitol Record Club)*	*1968*	**16.00**	**40.00**
Apple STAO-5-3360	*(S)*	**Space** *(Capitol Record Club)*	*1969*	**16.00**	**40.00**

MODERN JAZZ QUINTET, THE

Surrey S-1030	*(M)*	**Q.T. Hush**	*1966*	**12.00**	**30.00**
Surrey SS-1030	*(S)*	**Q.T. Hush**	*1966*	**10.00**	**25.00**

MODERN JAZZ SEXTET, THE

The Sextet is Skeeter Best, Dizzy Gillespie, Percy Heath, John Lewis, Charlie Persip and Sonny Stitt.

Norgran MGN-1076	*(M)*	**The Modern Jazz Sextet**	*1956*	**40.00**	**100.00**
American Rec. Soc. G-429	*(M)*	**The Modern Jazz Sextet**	*1957*	**16.00**	**40.00**
Verve MGV-8166	*(M)*	**The Modern Jazz Sextet**	*1957*	**30.00**	**75.00**
		(A.R.S. 429 and Verve 8166 are reissues of Norgran 1076.)			
		—Verve albums above have black labels with "Verve Records, Inc." on the bottom.—			
Verve V-8166	*(M)*	**The Modern Jazz Sextet**	*1961*	**10.00**	**25.00**
		—Verve albums above have black labels with "MGM Records" on the bottom.—			

Label & Catalog #		Title	Year	VG+	NM
MODERN JAZZ SOCIETY, THE (THE MODERN JAZZ ENSEMBLE)					
The MJS is Stan Getz, Percy Heath, J.J. Johnson, Connie Kay, James Politis, Jim Poole, Janet Putnam, Lucky Thompson, Aaron Sachs, Gunther Schuller, Tony Scott and Manny Ziegler.					
Norgran MGN-1040	(M)	**A Concert Of Contemporary Music**	1955	50.00	100.00
		(Norgran 1040 features cover art by David Stone Martin.)			
Verve MGV-8131	(M)	**A Concert Of Contemporary Music**	1957	30.00	75.00
— Verve albums above have black labels with "Verve Records, Inc." on the bottom.—					
American Rec. Soc. G-432	(M)	**A Concert Of Contemporary Music**	1957	16.00	40.00
Verve V-8131	(M)	**A Concert Of Contemporary Music**	1961	10.00	25.00
— Verve albums above have black labels with "MGM Records" on the bottom.—					
Verve VSP-18	(M)	**Little David's Fugue**	1966	6.00	15.00
Verve VSPS-18	(E)	**Little David's Fugue**	1966	3.00	7.50
		(Verve 18 is a reissue of 8131 but credits The Modern Jazz Ensemble.)			
MODERN JAZZ TRIO, THE (THE M.J.T. + 3)					
The MJT is Jim Hall, Red Kelly and Red Mitchell.					
Argo LP-621	(M)	**Daddy-O Presents MJT + 3**	1957	16.00	40.00
Vee Jay LP-1013	(M)	**M.J.T. Plus 3**	1960	12.00	30.00
Vee Jay LPS-1013	(S)	**M.J.T. Plus 3**	1960	10.00	25.00
— Vee Jay albums above have silver on maroon labels.—					
Vee Jay LP-3008	(M)	**Make Everybody Happy**	1960	10.00	25.00
Vee Jay LPS-3008	(S)	**Make Everybody Happy**	1960	8.00	20.00
Vee Jay LP-3014	(M)	**M.J.T. Plus 3**	1960	10.00	25.00
Vee Jay LPS-3014	(S)	**M.J.T. Plus 3**	1960	8.00	20.00
MOER, PAUL					
Del Fi DFLP-1212	(M)	**The Contemporary Jazz Classics**	1962	10.00	25.00
Del Fi DFST-1212	(S)	**The Contemporary Jazz Classics**	1962	8.00	20.00
MOFFETT, CHARLES					
Savoy MG-12194	(S)	**The Gift**	1969	6.00	15.00
MOLE, MIFF / EDMOND HALL					
Irving "Miff" Mole is a traditional jazz trombone player. For additional listings refer to Miff Mole.					
Brunswick BL-58042	(10")	**Battle Of Jazz, Vol. 4**	1953	20.00	50.00
MONCUR, GRACHAN					
Grachan Moncur is a traditional jazz string bass player.					
Blue Note BLP-4153	(M)	**Evolution**	1963	12.00	30.00
Blue Note BST-84153	(S)	**Evolution**	1963	10.00	25.00
Blue Note BLP-4177	(M)	**Some Other Stuff**	1964	12.00	30.00
Blue Note BST-84177	(S)	**Some Other Stuff**	1964	10.00	25.00
— Blue Note albums above have blue on white labels with a New York., NY address.—					
Blue Note BST-84153	(S)	**Evolution**	196?	6.00	12.00
Blue Note BST-84177	(S)	**Some Other Stuff**	196?	6.00	12.00
— Blue Note albums above have blue on white labels with "A Division of Liberty Records."—					
MONK, THELONIOUS					
Thelonious Monk is a modern jazz pianist and composer and one of the prime movers of modern jazz. For additional listings refer to Art Blakey & Thelonious Monk; Miles Davis / Thelonious Monk; Clark Terry.					
Blue Note BLP-5002	(10")	**Genius Of Modern Music, Vol. 1**	1951	300.00	500.00
Blue Note BLP-5009	(10")	**Genius Of Modern Music, Vol. 2**	1952	200.00	400.00
Blue Note BLP-1510	(M)	**Genius Of Modern Music, Vol. 1** *(Deep groove)*	1956	125.00	250.00
Blue Note BLP-1510	(M)	**Genius Of Modern Music, Vol. 1**	1956	100.00	200.00
Blue Note BLP-1511	(M)	**Genius Of Modern Music, Vol. 2** *(Deep groove)*	1956	125.00	250.00
Blue Note BLP-1511	(M)	**Genius Of Modern Music, Vol. 2**	1956	100.00	200.00
		(Blue Note 1510 and 1511 are reissues of 5002 and 5009.)			
— Blue Note albums above have blue on white labels with a Lexington Ave, NYC address.—					
Blue Note BLP-1510	(M)	**Genius Of Modern Music, Vol. 1**	196?	10.00	25.00
Blue Note BLP-1511	(M)	**Genius Of Modern Music, Vol. 2**	196?	10.00	25.00
— Blue Note albums above have blue on white labels with a New York, USA address.—					
Blue Note BST-81510	(E)	**Genius Of Modern Music, Vol. 1**	196?	4.00	10.00
Blue Note BST-81511	(E)	**Genius Of Modern Music, Vol. 2**	196?	4.00	10.00
— Blue Note albums above have blue on white labels with "A Division of Liberty Records."—					
Prestige PRLP-142	(10")	**Thelonious Monk Trio**	1953	150.00	300.00
Prestige PRLP-166	(10")	**Thelonious Monk Quintet With Sonny Rollins And Julius Watkins**	1953	150.00	300.00
Prestige PRLP-180	(10")	**Thelonious Monk Quintet**	1954	150.00	300.00

Label & Catalog #		Title	Year	VG+	NM
Prestige PRLP-189	(10")	**Thelonious Monk Trio**	1954	150.00	300.00
Prestige PRLP-7027	(M)	**Thelonious Monk**	1956	50.00	125.00
		(Prestige 7027 is a reissue of 142 and 189.)			
Prestige PRLP-7053	(M)	**Monk**	1956	50.00	125.00
		(Prestige 7053 is a reissue of 150.)			
Prestige PRLP-7075	(M)	**Thelonious Monk/Sonny Rollins**	1957	50.00	125.00
		(Prestige 7075 is a reissue of Prestige 166.)			
—Prestige albums above have yellow labels with a W. 50th Street, NYC address on the label.—					
Prestige PRLP-7159	(M)	**Monk's Moods**	1959	40.00	100.00
		(Prestige 7159 is a reissue of 7027.)			
Prestige PRLP-7169	(M)	**Work**	1959	40.00	100.00
		(Prestige 7169 is a reissue of 7075.)			
Prestige PRLP-7245	(M)	**We See**	1962	30.00	75.00
Prestige PRST-7245	(E)	**We See**	1962	20.00	50.00
		(Prestige 7245 is a reissue of 7053.)			
—Prestige albums above have yellow mono or silver stereo labels with a Bergenfield, NJ address.—					
Prestige PRLP-7363	(M)	**The Golden Monk**	1965	12.00	30.00
Prestige PRST-7363	(E)	**The Golden Monk**	1965	8.00	20.00
		(Prestige 7363 is a reissue of 7245.)			
Prestige PRLP-7508	(M)	**The High Priest**	1967	12.00	30.00
Prestige PRST-7508	(E)	**The High Priest**	1967	8.00	20.00
		(Prestige 7508 is a reissue of 7027.)			
—Prestige albums above have blue labels with a trident logo on the right side.—					
Prestige PRST-7656	(E)	**The Genius Of Thelonious Monk**	1969	6.00	15.00
		(Prestige 7656 is a reissue of 7075.)			
—Prestige albums above have blue labels with a trident logo on top.—					
Riverside RLP-12-201	(M)	**Thelonious Monk Plays Duke Ellington** *(Photo cover)*	1955	200.00	400.00
Riverside RLP-12-209	(M)	**The Unique Thelonious Monk**	1956	40.00	100.00
Riverside RLP-12-226	(M)	**Brilliant Corners**	1957	40.00	100.00
Riverside RLP-12-235	(M)	**Thelonious Himself**	1957	40.00	100.00
Riverside RLP-12-242	(M)	**Monk's Music**	1957	40.00	100.00
Riverside RLP-12-247	(M)	**Mulligan Meets Monk**	1957	40.00	100.00
—Riverside albums above have blue on white labels.—					
Riverside RLP-12-201	(M)	**Thelonious Monk Plays Duke Ellington**	1958	16.00	40.00
Riverside RLP-12-209	(M)	**The Unique Thelonious Monk**	1958	16.00	40.00
Riverside RLP-12-226	(M)	**Brilliant Corners**	1958	16.00	40.00
Riverside RLP-12-235	(M)	**Thelonious Himself**	1958	16.00	40.00
Riverside RLP-12-242	(M)	**Monk's Music**	1958	16.00	40.00
Riverside RLP-1102	(S)	**Monk's Music**	1958	16.00	40.00
Riverside RLP-12-247	(M)	**Mulligan Meets Monk**	1958	16.00	40.00
Riverside RLP-1106	(S)	**Mulligan Meets Monk**	1958	16.00	40.00
Riverside RLP-12-262	(M)	**Thelonious In Action Recorded At The Five Spot Cafe, New York With Johnny Griffin**	1958	20.00	50.00
Riverside RLP-1190	(S)	**Thelonious In Action Recorded At The Five Spot Cafe, New York With Johnny Griffin**	1958	16.00	40.00
Riverside RLP-12-279	(M)	**Misterioso**	1958	20.00	50.00
Riverside RLP-1133	(S)	**Misterioso**	1958	16.00	40.00
Riverside RLP-12-300	(M)	**The Thelonious Monk Orchestra At Town Hall**	1959	20.00	50.00
Riverside RLP-1138	(S)	**The Thelonious Monk Orchestra At Town Hall**	1959	16.00	40.00
Riverside RLP-12-305	(M)	**5 By Monk By 5**	1959	20.00	50.00
Riverside RLP-1150	(S)	**5 By Monk By 5**	1959	16.00	40.00
Riverside RLP-12-312	(M)	**Thelonious Alone In San Francisco**	1959	20.00	50.00
Riverside RLP-1158	(S)	**Thelonious Alone In San Francisco**	1959	16.00	40.00
Riverside RLP-12-323	(M)	**Thelonious Monk Quartet Plus Two At The Blackhawk**	1960	20.00	50.00
Riverside RLP-1171	(S)	**Thelonious Monk Quartet Plus Two At The Blackhawk**	1960	16.00	40.00
Jazzland JLP-46	(M)	**Thelonious Monk With John Coltrane**	1961	20.00	50.00
Jazzland JLP-946	(S)	**Thelonious Monk With John Coltrane**	1961	16.00	40.00
Riverside RLP-421	(M)	**Thelonious Monk's Greatest Hits**	1962	10.00	25.00
Riverside RS-9421	(S)	**Thelonious Monk's Greatest Hits**	1962	8.00	20.00
Riverside RLP-443	(M)	**Thelonious Monk In Italy**	1963	12.00	30.00
Riverside RS-9443	(S)	**Thelonious Monk In Italy**	1963	10.00	25.00
Riverside RLP-460/461	(M)	**April In Paris** *(2 LPs)*	1963	20.00	50.00
Riverside RS-9460/461	(S)	**April In Paris** *(2 LPs)*	1963	16.00	40.00
		(Riverside 460 reissues 443 as one of its discs.)			
—Riverside albums above have blue mono or black stereo labels with a reel & mike logo on top.—					

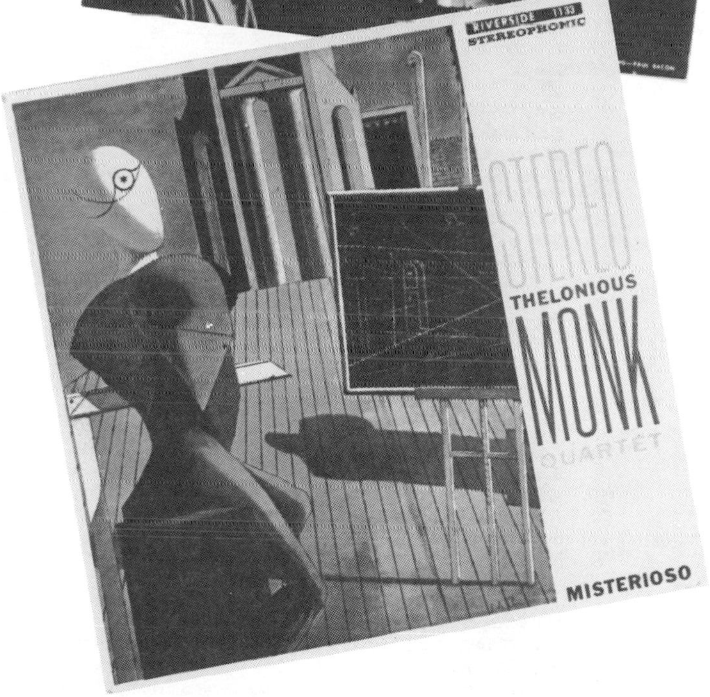

Monk started with Lucky Millinder in 1942 at the same time Dizzy Gillespie was a part of the band. He also worked briefly with Coleman Hawkins and Diz's combos but basically kept his own small group that allowed him to experiment rhythmically, harmonically and compositionally on patterns that would lead to the development of bop as a major style. After years of being all but ignored, he developed a reputation as one of jazz's real visionaries. Aside from his work with Blue Note, Prestige, Riverside (from which the examples above were chosen) and Columbia, he can also be found on LPs with Art Blakey, Miles Davis, and Clark Terry and as a sideman on albums by Milt Jackson on Blue Note, and Sonny Rollins, both on Prestige, Gerry Mulligan on Riverside, Gigi Gryce on Signal, and Dizzy on Contemporary.

Label & Catalog #		Title	Year	VG+	NM
Riverside RLP-483	(M)	**The Thelonious Monk Story, Volume 1**	1965	10.00	25.00
Riverside RS-9483	(S)	**The Thelonious Monk Story, Volume 1**	1965	8.00	20.00
Riverside RLP-484	(M)	**The Thelonious Monk Story, Volume 2**	1965	10.00	25.00
Riverside RS-9484	(S)	**The Thelonious Monk Story, Volume 2**	1965	8.00	20.00
Riverside RLP-490	(M)	**Thelonious Monk With John Coltrane**	1965	12.00	30.00
Riverside RS-9490	(S)	**Thelonious Monk With John Coltrane**	1965	10.00	25.00
Riverside RLP-491	(M)	**Monk In France**	1965	10.00	25.00
Riverside RS-9491	(S)	**Monk In France**	1965	8.00	20.00
		(Riverside 491 is a reissue of half of 460/461.)			
—Riverside albums above blue labels with "Orpheum Productions" on the bottom.—					
Riverside RM-3000	(M)	**Mighty Monk** *(Compilation)*	1967	10.00	25.00
Riverside RS-3000	(S)	**Mighty Monk** *(Compilation)*	1967	6.00	15.00
Riverside RM-3004	(M)	**Monk's Music**	1967	10.00	25.00
Riverside RS-3004	(S)	**Monk's Music**	1967	6.00	15.00
		(Riverside 3004 is a reissue of 1102.)			
Riverside RS-3015	(E)	**Monk Plays Duke**	1968	5.00	12.00
		(Riverside 3015 is a reissue of 201.)			
Riverside RS-3020	(E)	**Two Hours With Thelonious Monk** *(2 LPs)*	1968	8.00	20.00
		(Riverside 3020 is a reissue of 460 and 461.)			
Riverside RS-3037	(S)	**Best Of Thelonoius Monk**	1969	5.00	12.00
Columbia CL-1965	(M)	**Monk's Dream**	1963	10.00	25.00
Columbia CS-8765	(S)	**Monk's Dream**	1963	8.00	20.00
Columbia CL-2038	(M)	**Criss-Cross**	1963	10.00	25.00
Columbia CS-8838	(S)	**Criss-Cross**	1963	8.00	20.00
Columbia CL-2164	(M)	**Monk Big Band And Quartet In Concert**	1964	10.00	25.00
Columbia CS-8964	(S)	**Monk Big Band And Quartet In Concert**	1964	8.00	20.00
Columbia CL-2184	(M)	**It's Monk's Time**	1964	10.00	25.00
Columbia CS-8984	(S)	**It's Monk's Time**	1964	8.00	20.00
Columbia CL-2291	(M)	**Monk**	1965	10.00	25.00
Columbia CS-9091	(S)	**Monk**	1965	8.00	20.00
Columbia CL-2349	(M)	**Solo Monk**	1965	10.00	25.00
Columbia CS-9149	(S)	**Solo Monk**	1965	8.00	20.00
—Columbia albums above have "Guaranteed High Fidelity" or "360 Sound Stereo" in black on the label.—					
Columbia CL-2416	(M)	**Misterioso**	1965	10.00	25.00
Columbia CS-9216	(S)	**Misterioso**	1965	8.00	20.00
Columbia CL-2651	(M)	**Straight, No Chaser**	1967	12.00	30.00
Columbia CS-9451	(S)	**Straight, No Chaser**	1967	8.00	20.00
Columbia DS-338	(S)	**Monk's Miracles**	1967	10.00	25.00
		(Columbia Record Club compilation.)			
Columbia CL-2832	(M)	**Underground**	1968	20.00	50.00
Columbia CS-9632	(S)	**Underground**	1968	10.00	25.00
Columbia CS-9806	(S)	**Monk's Blues**	1969	8.00	20.00
—Columbia albums above have "360 Sound" in white on the bottom of the label.—					

MONTEGO, JOE

Jamaican born Montego Joe is a Latin jazz-based percussionist.

Prestige PRLP-7336	(M)	**Arriba Con Montego Joe**	1964	12.00	30.00
Prestige PRST-7336	(S)	**Arriba Con Montego Joe**	1964	10.00	25.00
Prestige PRLP-7413	(M)	**Wild And Warm**	1966	12.00	30.00
Prestige PRST-7413	(S)	**Wild And Warm**	1966	10.00	25.00
—Prestige albums above have blue labels with a trident logo on the right side.—					
ESP-Disk' 1067	(S)	**Montego Joe's HARYOU Percussion Ensemble**	1968	8.00	20.00

MONTEROSE, J.R.

J.R. Monterose is a modern jazz tenor saxophone player.

Blue Note BLP-1536	(M)	**J. R. Monterose** *(Deep groove)*	1956	100.00	200.00
Blue Note BLP-1536	(M)	**J. R. Monterose**	1956	60.00	150.00
—Blue Note albums above have blue on white labels with a Lexington Ave, NYC address.—					
Blue Note BLP-1536	(M)	**J. R. Monterose**	1963	10.00	25.00
—Blue Note albums above have blue on white labels with a New York, USA address.—					
Blue Note BST-81536	(E)	**J. R. Monterose**	196?	4.00	10.00
—Blue Note albums above have blue on white labels with "A Division of Liberty Records."—					
Studio-4 100	(M)	**J. R. Monterose In Action**	195?	360.00	600.00
		(Privately pressed limited edition.)			
Jaro 5004	(M)	**The Message**	1959	300.00	500.00
Jaro 8004	(S)	**The Message**	1959	150.00	300.00

Label & Catalog #		Title	Year	VG+	NM

MONTGOMERY, BUDDY

Buddy Montgomery is a modern jazz piano and vibraphone player. For additional listings refer to Montgomery Brothers.

Milestone MLS-9015	(S)	**Two-Sided Album**	1969	6.00	15.00

MONTGOMERY, MARIAN

Marian Montgomery is a modern jazz vocalist.

Capitol T-1884	(M)	**Marian Montgomery Swings For Winners And Losers**	1963	10.00	25.00
Capitol ST-1884	(S)	**Marian Montgomery Swings For Winners And Losers**	1963	12.00	30.00
Capitol T-1982	(M)	**Let There Be Love, Let There Be Swing, Let There Be Marian Montgomery**	1963	10.00	25.00
Capitol ST-1982	(S)	**Let There Be Love, Let There Be Swing, Let There Be Marian Montgomery**	1963	12.00	30.00
Decca DL-4773	(M)	**What's New?**	1965	8.00	20.00
Decca DL-74773	(S)	**What's New?**	1965	10.00	25.00

MONTGOMERY, WES

John "Wes" Montgomery is a modern jazz guitar player. For additional listings refer to Milt Jackson & Wes Montgomery; Wynton Kelly; The Montgomery Brothers; Jimmy Smith & Wes Montgomery.

Riverside RLP-12-310	(M)	**New Concepts In Jazz Guitar**	1959	16.00	40.00
Riverside RLP-1156	(S)	**New Concepts In Jazz Guitar**	1959	12.00	30.00
Riverside RLP-12-320	(M)	**Incredible Jazz Guitar Of Wes Montgomery**	1960	16.00	40.00
Riverside RLP-1169	(S)	**Incredible Jazz Guitar Of Wes Montgomery**	1960	12.00	30.00
Riverside RLP-342	(M)	**Movin' Along**	1960	12.00	30.00
Riverside RS-9342	(S)	**Movin' Along**	1960	10.00	25.00
Riverside RLP-382	(M)	**So Much Guitar!**	1961	12.00	30.00
Riverside RS-9382	(S)	**So Much Guitar!**	1961	10.00	25.00
Riverside RLP-434	(M)	**Full House Recorded 'Live' At Tsubo-Berkeley, California**	1962	14.00	35.00
Riverside RS-9434	(S)	**Full House Recorded 'Live' At Tsubo-Berkeley, California**	1962	12.00	30.00
Riverside RLP-459	(M)	**Boss Guitar**	1963	10.00	25.00
Riverside RS-9459	(S)	**Boss Guitar**	1963	8.00	20.00
Riverside RLP-472	(M)	**Fusion! Wes Montgomery With Strings**	1964	10.00	25.00
Riverside RS-9472	(S)	**Fusion! Wes Montgomery With Strings**	1964	8.00	20.00
—Riverside albums above have blue mono or black stereo labels with a reel & mike logo on top.—					
Riverside RLP-492	(M)	**Portrait Of Wes**	1965	8.00	20.00
Riverside RS-9492	(S)	**Portrait Of Wes**	1965	6.00	15.00
Riverside RLP-494	(M)	**Guitar On The Go**	1965	8.00	20.00
Riverside RS-9494	(S)	**Guitar On The Go**	1965	6.00	15.00
—Riverside albums above blue labels with "Orpheum Productions" on the bottom.—					
Riverside RSM3002	(M)	**In The Wee Small Hours**	1967	6.00	15.00
Riverside RS-3002	(S)	**In The Wee Small Hours** *(Riverside 3002 is a reissue of 9472.)*	1967	4.00	10.00
Riverside RS-3012	(S)	**This Is Wes Montgomery** *(Riverside 3002 is a reissue of 9459.)*	1968	4.00	10.00
Riverside RS-3014	(S)	**Round Midnight** *(Riverside 3002 is a reissue of 91156)*	1968	4.00	10.00
Riverside RS-3036	(S)	**March 6, 1925 - June 15, 1968** *(Compilation)*	1968	4.00	10.00
Riverside RS-3039	(S)	**The Best Of Wes Montgomery**	1968	4.00	10.00
Riverside RS-3046	(S)	**Panorama** *(Compilation)*	1969	4.00	10.00
Pacific Jazz PJ-10104	(M)	**Easy Groove**	1966	8.00	20.00
Pacific Jazz ST-20104	(S)	**Easy Groove**	1966	6.00	15.00
Pacific Jazz PJ-10130	(M)	**Kismet**	1968	8.00	20.00
Pacific Jazz ST-20130	(S)	**Kismet**	1968	6.00	15.00
Pacific Jazz ST-20137	(S)	**Portrait** *(Compilation)*	1968	6.00	15.00
Verve V-8610	(M)	**Movin' Wes**	1965	6.00	15.00
Verve V6-8610	(S)	**Movin' Wes**	1965	5.00	12.00
Verve V-8625	(M)	**Bumpin'**	1965	6.00	15.00
Verve V6-8625	(S)	**Bumpin'**	1965	5.00	12.00
Verve V-8642	(M)	**Goin' Out Of My Head**	1965	6.00	15.00
Verve V6-8642	(S)	**Goin' Out Of My Head**	1965	5.00	12.00
Verve V-8653	(M)	**Tequila**	1966	6.00	15.00
Verve V6-8653	(S)	**Tequila**	1966	5.00	12.00
Verve V-8672	(M)	**California Dreaming**	1966	6.00	15.00
Verve V6-8672	(S)	**California Dreaming**	1966	5.00	12.00

Label & Catalog #		Title	Year	VG+	NM
Verve V-8714	(M)	**The Best Of Wes Montgomery**	1967	5.00	12.00
Verve V6-8714	(S)	**The Best Of Wes Montgomery**	1967	4.00	10.00
Verve V6-8757	(S)	**The Best Of Wes Montgomery, Volume 2**	1969	4.00	10.00
Verve V6-8765	(S)	**Willow Weep For Me**	1969	4.00	10.00
Verve V6-8796	(S)	**Eulogy**	1969	4.00	10.00
		—Verve albums above have black labels with "MGM Records" on the bottom.—			
A&M LP-3001	(M)	**A Day In The Life**	1967	5.00	12.00
A&M SP-3001	(S)	**A Day In The Life**	1967	4.00	10.00
A&M LP-3006	(M)	**Down Here On The Ground**	1968	5.00	12.00
A&M SP-3006	(S)	**Down Here On The Ground**	1968	4.00	10.00
A&M SP-3012	(S)	**Road Songs**	1968	4.00	10.00
Sunset SUS-21008	(S)	**Mood I'm In**	1969	4.00	10.00

MONTGOMERY BROTHERS, THE

The brothers are Buddy, Monk and Wes. For additional listings refer to The Mastersounds; George Shearing & The Montgomery Brothers.

World Pacific PJ-1240	(M)	**The Montgomery Brothers And Five Others**	1957	30.00	75.00
World Pacific WP-1240	(M)	**The Montgomery Brothers And Five Others**	1958	20.00	50.00
Pacific Jazz PJ-5	(M)	**Montgomeryland**	1960	12.00	30.00
Pacific Jazz ST-5	(S)	**Montgomeryland**	1960	10.00	25.00
Pacific Jazz PJ-17	(M)	**Wes, Buddy & Monk Montgomery**	1961	12.00	30.00
		(Pacific Jazz 17 is a reissue of World Pacific 1240.)			
Fantasy 3308	(M)	**The Montgomery Brothers** *(Red vinyl)*	1960	20.00	50.00
Fantasy 3308	(M)	**The Montgomery Brothers**	1960	12.00	30.00
Fantasy 8052	(S)	**The Montgomery Brothers** *(Blue vinyl)*	1960	16.00	40.00
Fantasy 8052	(S)	**The Montgomery Brothers**	1960	10.00	25.00
Fantasy 3323	(M)	**The Montgomery Brothers In Canada** *(Red vinyl)*	1961	20.00	50.00
Fantasy 3323	(M)	**The Montgomery Brothers In Canada**	1961	12.00	30.00
Fantasy 8066	(S)	**The Montgomery Brothers In Canada** *(Blue vinyl)*	1961	16.00	40.00
Fantasy 8066	(S)	**The Montgomery Brothers In Canada**	1961	10.00	25.00
Riverside RLP-362	(M)	**Groove Yard**	1961	12.00	30.00
Riverside RS-9362	(S)	**Groove Yard**	1961	10.00	25.00
		—Riverside albums above have blue mono or black stereo labels with a reel & mike logo on top.—			
Fantasy 3376	(S)	**Wes' Best**	1967	6.00	15.00
Fantasy 8376	(S)	**Wes' Best**	1967	5.00	12.00
		(Fantasy 3376 reissues material from 3308 and 3323.)			

MONTROSE, JACK

Jack Montrose is a West Coast jazz tenor saxophone player and composer.

Pacific Jazz PJ-1208	(M)	**Jack Montrose Sextet** *(Red vinyl)*	1955	50.00	125.00
Pacific Jazz PJ-1208	(M)	**Jack Montrose Sextet**	1955	30.00	75.00
World Pacific WP-1208	(M)	**Jack Montrose Sextet**	1958	20.00	50.00
Atlantic 1223	(M)	**Arranged Played Composed By Jack Montrose With Bob Gordon**	1956	30.00	75.00
		—Atlantic albums above have black mono or green stereo labels.—			
Atlantic 1223	(M)	**Arranged Played Composed By Jack Montrose With Bob Gordon**	1961	8.00	20.00
		—Atlantic albums above have multi-color labels with a white fan logo.—			
Atlantic 1223	(M)	**Arranged Played Composed By Jack Montrose With Bob Gordon**	196?	4.00	10.00
		—Atlantic albums above have multi-color labels with a black fan logo.—			
RCA Victor LPM-1451	(M)	**Blues And Vanilla**	1957	20.00	50.00
RCA Victor LPM-1572	(M)	**The Horns Full**	1957	20.00	50.00
		(RCA 1451 and 1572 also feature Red Norvo.)			
		—RCA albums above have black labels with "Long Play" on the bottom.—			

MOODY, JAMES

James Moody is a modern jazz tenor and alto sax and flute player and composer. For additional listings refer to Art Blakey / James Moody; The New York Jazz Sextet.

Dial LP-209	(10")	**James Moody-His Saxophone And His Band**	1950	240.00	400.00
Roost LP-405	(10")	**James Moody In France**	1951	150.00	300.00
Blue Note BLP-5005	(10")	**James Moody With Strings**	1952	150.00	300.00
Blue Note BLP-5006	(10")	**James Moody And His Modernists**	1952	150.00	300.00
Prestige PRLP-110	(10")	**James Moody Favorites, No. 1**	1951	70.00	175.00
Prestige PRLP-125	(10")	**James Moody Favorites, No. 2**	1952	70.00	175.00
Prestige PRLP-146	(10")	**James Moody, Volume 3**	1953	70.00	175.00

Label & Catalog #		Title	Year	VG+	NM
Prestige PRLP-157	(10")	**Moody In France**	1953	60.00	150.00
Prestige PRLP-192	(10")	**Moody's Mood**	1954	60.00	150.00
Prestige PRLP-198	(10")	**James Moody And His Band**	1954	60.00	150.00
Prestige PRLP-7011	(M)	**Hi-Fi Party**	1955	40.00	100.00
Prestige PRLP-7036	(M)	**Wail Moody Wail**	1956	40.00	100.00
Prestige PRLP-7056	(M)	**James Moody's Moods**	1956	40.00	100.00
		(Prestige 7056 is a reissue of 198.)			
Prestige PRLP-7072	(M)	**Moody**	1956	40.00	100.00
		(Prestige 7072 is a reissue of 192.)			
		—Prestige albums above have yellow labels with a W. 50th Street, NYC address.—			
Prestige PRLP-7179	(M)	**Moody's Workshop**	1960	20.00	50.00
		(Prestige 7179 is a reissue of 192 and 198.)			
		—Prestige albums above have yellow mono or silver stereo labels with a Bergenfield, NJ address.—			
EmArcy MG-26004	(10")	**The Moody Story**	1954	60.00	150.00
EmArcy MG-26040	(10")	**Moodsville**	1954	60.00	150.00
EmArcy MG-36031	(M)	**The Moody Story**	1955	40.00	100.00
		(EmArcy 36031 is a reissue of 26004.)			
		—EmArcy albums above have blue labels with silver print.—			
Creative LP-603	(M)	**Flute 'N Blues**	1956	50.00	125.00
Argo LP-603	(M)	**Flute 'N Blues**	1956	16.00	40.00
		(Argo 603 is a reissue of Creative 603.)			
Argo LP-613	(M)	**Moody's Mood For Love**	1957	16.00	40.00
Argo LP-637	(M)	**Last Train From Overbrook**	1958	16.00	40.00
Argo LPS-637	(S)	**Last Train From Overbrook**	1958	12.00	30.00
Argo LP-648	(M)	**James Moody**	1959	16.00	40.00
Argo LPS-648	(S)	**James Moody**	1959	12.00	30.00
Argo LP-666	(M)	**Hey! It's James Moody**	1960	16.00	40.00
Argo LPS-666	(S)	**Hey! It's James Moody**	1960	12.00	30.00
Argo LP-679	(M)	**Moody With Strings**	1961	16.00	40.00
Argo LPS-679	(S)	**Moody With Strings**	1961	12.00	30.00
Argo LP-695	(M)	**Another Bag**	1962	16.00	40.00
Argo LPS-695	(S)	**Another Bag**	1962	12.00	30.00
Argo LP-725	(M)	**Great Day**	1963	12.00	30.00
Argo LPS-725	(S)	**Great Day**	1963	10.00	25.00
Argo LP 740	(M)	**Comin' On Strong**	1964	12.00	30.00
Argo LPS-740	(S)	**Comin' On Strong**	1964	10.00	25.00
Argo LP-756	(M)	**Cookin' The Blues**	1965	12.00	30.00
Argo LPS-756	(S)	**Cookin' The Blues**	1965	10.00	25.00
Scepter S-525	(M)	**Runnin' The Gamut**	1964	10.00	25.00
Scepter SS-525	(S)	**Runnin' The Gamut**	1964	8.00	20.00
Prestige PRLP-7431	(M)	**James Moody's Greatest Hits**	1967	10.00	25.00
Prestige PRST-7431	(E)	**James Moody's Greatest Hits**	1967	6.00	15.00
Prestige PRLP-7441	(M)	**James Moody's Greatest Hits, Volume 2**	1967	10.00	25.00
Prestige PRST-7441	(E)	**James Moody's Greatest Hits, Volume 2**	1967	6.00	15.00
		—Prestige albums above have blue labels wih a trident logo on the right side.—			
Prestige PRST-7554	(E)	**Moody's Moods**	1968	5.00	12.00
		(Prestige 7554 is a reissue of 7056.)			
Prestige PRST-7625	(S)	**Don't Look Away Now!**	1969	6.00	15.00
Prestige PRST-7663	(S)	**Moody's Workshop**	1969	6.00	15.00
		(Prestige 7663 is a reissue of 7179.)			
		—Prestige albums above have blue labels wih a trident logo on top.—			
Milestone MLS-9015	(S)	**Brass Figures**	1968	6.00	15.00

MOODY, JAMES / GEORGE WALLINGTON

Blue Note B-6503	(M)	**The Beginning And End Of Bop**	1969	10.00	25.00
		(Blue Note 6503 is a reissue of 5006 and 5045.)			

MOODY, PHIL

Philip Moody is a jazz-based pianist.

Somerset P-1-10400	(M)	**Intimate Jazz**	1959	12.00	30.00

MOONDOG

Louis Thomas Hardin, aka Moondog, is a "primitive modern" musician and composer..

Epic LG-1002	(10")	**Moondog And His Friends**	1954	100.00	200.00
Prestige PRLP-7042	(M)	**Moondog**	1956	40.00	100.00
Prestige PRLP-7069	(M)	**More Moondog**	1956	40.00	100.00
Prestige PRLP-7099	(M)	**The Story Of Moondog**	1957	40.00	100.00
		—Prestige albums above have yellow labels with a W. 50th Street, NYC address.—			

Label & Catalog #		Title	Year	VG+	NM
Columbia MS-7335	(S)	**Moondog**	1969	10.00	25.00
		—Columbia albums above have gray labels with "Mastersound" in white on the bottom.—			

MOONEY, JOE

Joseph Mooney is a traditional jazz-based piano, Hammond organ and accordion player and singer.

Decca DL-5555	(10")	**You Go To My Head**	1955	20.00	50.00
Decca DL-8468	(M)	**On The Rocks**	1957	16.00	40.00
Atlantic 1255	(M)	**Lush Life**	1959	16.00	40.00
		—Atlantic albums above have black mono or green stereo labels.—			
Atlantic 1255	(M)	**Lush Life**	1959	8.00	20.00
		—Atlantic albums above have multi-color labels with a white fan logo—			
Columbia CL-2186	(M)	**The Greatness Of Joe Mooney**	1964	6.00	15.00
Columbia CS-8986	(S)	**The Greatness Of Joe Mooney**	1964	5.00	12.00

MOORE, ADA

Ada Moore is a jazz-based vocalist. For additional listings refer to Jimmy Rushing.

Debut DLP-15	(10")	**Jazz Workshop**	1955	125.00	250.00

MOORE, "WILD" BILL

William Moore is a modern jazz tenor saxophone player.

Jazzland JLP-38	(M)	**Wild Bill's Beat**	1961	16.00	40.00
Jazzland JLP-938	(S)	**Wild Bill's Beat**	1961	12.00	30.00
Jazzland JLP-54	(M)	**Bottom Groove**	1961	16.00	40.00
Jazzland JLP-954	(S)	**Bottom Groove**	1961	12.00	30.00

MOORE, BREW

Milton "Brew" Moore Jr. is a modern jazz tenor saxophone player. For additional listings refer to Fats Navarro / Kai Winding / Brew Moore.

Savoy MG-9028	(10")	**Tenor Sax**	1953	60.00	150.00
Fantasy 3222	(M)	**The Brew Moore Quintet** *(Dark red vinyl)*	1956	30.00	75.00
		—Fantasy albums above have red labels on dark red, non-flexible vinyl.—			
Fantasy 3222	(M)	**The Brew Moore Quintet**	195?	16.00	40.00
Fantasy 3264	(M)	**Brew Moore** *(Red vinyl)*	1958	20.00	50.00
Fantasy 3264	(M)	**Brew Moore**	195?	12.00	30.00
Fantasy 6013	(M)	**Brew Moore In Europe** *(Red vinyl)*	1962	16.00	40.00
Fantasy 6013	(M)	**Brew Moore In Europe**	1962	12.00	30.00
Fantasy 86013	(S)	**Brew Moore In Europe** *(Blue vinyl)*	1962	12.00	30.00
Fantasy 86013	(S)	**Brew Moore In Europe**	1962	10.00	25.00
		—Fantasy albums above have red mono or blue stereo labels on non-flexible vinyl.—			

MOORE, DEBBY

Deborah Moore is a modern jazz guitarist and vocalist.

Top Rank LP-12-301	(M)	**Debby Moore**	1959	20.00	50.00
Top Rank ST-12-301	(S)	**Debby Moore**	1959	24.00	60.00

MOORE, DUDLEY

Comedic actor Dudley Moore is an accomplished pianist with this jazzy outing to his credit.

London PS-558	(S)	**Dudley Moore Trio**	1969	8.00	20.00

MOORE, MARILYN

Marilyn Moore big band-based vocalist.

Bethlehem BCP-73	(M)	**Moody**	1957	30.00	75.00

MOORE, OSCAR

Oscar Moore is a traditional jazz-based guitar player.

Skylark SKLP-19	(M)	**Oscar Moore Trio**	1954	40.00	100.00
Tampa TP-16	(M)	**Oscar Moore Trio** *(Colored vinyl)*	1957	40.00	100.00
Tampa TP-16	(M)	**Oscar Moore Trio**	1958	20.00	50.00
		(Tampa 16 is a reissue of Skylark 19.)			
Tampa TP-22	(M)	**Galivantin' Guitar** *(Colored vinyl)*	1957	40.00	100.00
Tampa TP-22	(M)	**Galivantin' Guitar**	1958	20.00	50.00
Charlie Parker PLP-830	(M)	**The Fabulous Oscar Moore Guitar**	1962	12.00	30.00
Charlie Parker PLP-830S	(S)	**The Fabulous Oscar Moore Guitar**	1962	10.00	25.00

MOORE, PHIL

Philip Moore is a traditional jazz-based pianist, singer and composer.

Clef MGC-635	(M)	**Music For Moderns**	1954	30.00	75.00
		(Clef 635 features cover art by David Stone Martin.)			

MOORE, SHELLY

Shelly Moore is a jazz-based vocalist.

Label & Catalog #		Title	Year	VG+	NM
Argo LP-4016	(M)	**For The First Time**	1962	10.00	25.00
Argo LPS-4016	(S)	**For The First Time**	1962	12.00	30.00

MORAN, PAT

Helen Mudgett, aka Pat Moran, is a jazz vocalist.

Label & Catalog #		Title	Year	VG+	NM
Bethlehem BCP-6007	(M)	**Pat Moran Quartet**	1956	20.00	50.00
Audio Fidelity AFLP-1875	(M)	**This Is Pat Moran**	1958	16.00	40.00
Audio Fidelity AFST-5875	(S)	**This Is Pat Moran**	1958	16.00	40.00

MOREL, TERRY

Terry Morel is a jazz-based vocalist.

Label & Catalog #		Title	Year	VG+	NM
Bethlehem BCP-47	(M)	**Songs Of A Woman In Love**	1956	60.00	150.00

MORELLO, JOE

Joseph Morello is a modern jazz drummer. For additional listings refer to Hank Garland.

Label & Catalog #		Title	Year	VG+	NM
Intro 608	(M)	**Joe Morello Sextet** *(Intro 608 was reissued as Score 4031, "Art Pepper-Red Norvo Collections.")*	1957	60.00	150.00
RCA Victor LPM-2486	(M)	**It's About Time**	1961	12.00	30.00
RCA Victor LSP-2486	(S)	**It's About Time**	1961	10.00	25.00

—RCA albums above have black labels with "Long Play" or "Living Stereo" on the bottom.—

MORGAN, DICK

Richard Morgan is a jazz-based pianist.

Label & Catalog #		Title	Year	VG+	NM
Riverside RLP-12-329	(M)	**Dick Morgan At The Showboat**	1960	16.00	40.00
Riverside RLP-1183	(S)	**Dick Morgan At The Showboat**	1960	12.00	30.00
Riverside RLP-347	(M)	**See What I Mean?**	1960	16.00	40.00
Riverside RS-9347	(S)	**See What I Mean?**	1960	12.00	30.00
Riverside RLP-383	(M)	**Settin' In**	1961	16.00	40.00
Riverside RS-9383	(S)	**Settin' In**	1961	12.00	30.00

—Riverside albums above have blue mono or black stereo labels with a reel & mike logo on top.—

MORGAN FRANK

Frank Morgan is a West Coast jazz alto sexophone player.

Label & Catalog #		Title	Year	VG+	NM
Gene Norman GNP-12	(M)	**Frank Morgan** *(Red vinyl)*	1955	50.00	125.00
Whippet WLP-704	(M)	**Frank Morgan** *(Whippet 704 is a reissue of Gene Norman 12.)*	1956	40.00	100.00

MORGAN, LEE

Lee Morgan is a modern jazz trumpet player. For additional listings refer to Art Blakey & The Jazz Messengers; John Coltrane / Lee Morgan; Hank Mobley; The Young Lions.

Label & Catalog #		Title	Year	VG+	NM
Savoy MG-12091	(M)	**Introducing Lee Morgan**	1956	100.00	200.00
Blue Note BLP-1538	(M)	**Lee Morgan Indeed!** *(Deep groove)*	1957	125.00	250.00
Blue Note BLP-1538	(M)	**Lee Morgan Indeed!**	1957	100.00	200.00
Blue Note BLP-1541	(M)	**Lee Morgan, Volume 2** *(Deep groove)*	1957	125.00	250.00
Blue Note BLP-1541	(M)	**Lee Morgan, Volume 2**	195?	100.00	200.00
—Blue Note albums above have blue on white labels with a Lexington Ave., NYC address.—					
Blue Note BLP-1557	(M)	**Lee Morgan, Volume 3** *(Deep groove)*	1957	60.00	150.00
Blue Note BLP-1557	(M)	**Lee Morgan, Volume 3**	1957	40.00	100.00
Blue Note BLP-1575	(M)	**City Lights** *(Deep groove)*	1958	60.00	150.00
Blue Note BLP-1575	(M)	**City Lights**	1958	40.00	100.00
Blue Note BST-1575	(S)	**City Lights** *(Deep groove)*	1959	40.00	100.00
Blue Note BST-1575	(S)	**City Lights**	1959	30.00	75.00
Blue Note BLP-1578	(M)	**The Cooker** *(Deep groove)*	1958	60.00	150.00
Blue Note BLP-1578	(M)	**The Cooker**	1958	40.00	100.00
Blue Note BST-1578	(S)	**The Cooker** *(Deep groove)*	1959	40.00	100.00
Blue Note BST-1578	(S)	**The Cooker**	1959	30.00	75.00
Blue Note BLP-1590	(M)	**Candy** *(Deep groove)*	1958	60.00	150.00
Blue Note BLP-1590	(M)	**Candy**	1958	40.00	100.00
Blue Note BST-1590	(S)	**Candy** *(Deep groove)*	1959	40.00	100.00
Blue Note BST-1590	(S)	**Candy**	1959	30.00	75.00
Blue Note BLP-4034	(M)	**Lee-Way** *(Deep groove)*	1960	50.00	125.00
Blue Note BLP-4034	(M)	**Lee-Way**	1960	30.00	75.00
Blue Note BST-84034	(S)	**Lee-Way**	1960	20.00	50.00

—Blue Note albums above have blue on white labels with a W. 63rd St, NYC address.—

Label & Catalog #		Title	Year	VG+	NM
Blue Note BLP-1538	(M)	**Lee Morgan Indeed!**	1963	10.00	25.00
Blue Note BLP-1541	(M)	**Lee Morgan, Volume 2**	1963	10.00	25.00
Blue Note BLP-1557	(M)	**Lee Morgan, Volume 3**	1963	10.00	25.00
Blue Note BLP-1575	(M)	**City Lights**	1963	10.00	25.00
Blue Note BST-1575	(S)	**City Lights**	1963	8.00	20.00
Blue Note BLP-1578	(M)	**The Cooker**	1963	10.00	25.00
Blue Note BST-1578	(S)	**The Cooker**	1963	8.00	20.00
Blue Note BLP-1590	(M)	**Candy**	1963	10.00	25.00
Blue Note BST-1590	(S)	**Candy**	1963	8.00	20.00
Blue Note BLP-4034	(M)	**Lee-Way**	1963	10.00	25.00
Blue Note BST-84034	(S)	**Lee-Way**	1963	8.00	20.00
Blue Note BLP-4157	(M)	**The Sidewinder**	1963	16.00	40.00
Blue Note BST-84157	(S)	**The Sidewinder**	1963	12.00	30.00
Blue Note BLP-4169	(M)	**Search For The New Land**	1964	16.00	40.00
Blue Note BST-84169	(S)	**Search For The New Land**	1964	12.00	30.00
Blue Note BLP-4199	(M)	**The Rumproller**	1965	16.00	40.00
Blue Note BST-84199	(S)	**The Rumproller**	1965	12.00	30.00
Blue Note BLP-4212	(M)	**The Gigolo**	1965	16.00	40.00
Blue Note BST-84212	(S)	**The Gigolo**	1965	12.00	30.00
Blue Note BLP-4222	(M)	**Cornbread**	1965	16.00	40.00
Blue Note BST-84222	(S)	**Cornbread**	1965	12.00	30.00
Blue Note BLP-4243	(M)	**Delightfulee Morgan**	1966	16.00	40.00
Blue Note BST-84243	(S)	**Delightfulee Morgan**	1966	12.00	30.00
—Blue Note albums above have blue on white labels with a New York, USA address.—					
Blue Note BST-81538	(E)	**Lee Morgan Indeed!**	196?	4.00	10.00
Blue Note BST-81541	(E)	**Lee Morgan, Volume 2**	196?	4.00	10.00
Blue Note BST-81557	(E)	**Lee Morgan, Volume 3**	196?	4.00	10.00
Blue Note BST-81575	(S)	**City Lights**	196?	5.00	12.00
Blue Note BST-81578	(S)	**The Cooker**	196?	5.00	12.00
Blue Note BST-81590	(S)	**Candy**	196?	5.00	12.00
Blue Note BST-84034	(S)	**Lee-Way**	196?	5.00	12.00
Blue Note BST-84157	(S)	**The Sidewinder**	196?	5.00	12.00
Blue Note BST-84169	(S)	**Search For The New Land**	196?	5.00	12.00
Blue Note BST-84199	(S)	**The Rumproller**	196?	5.00	12.00
Blue Note BST-84222	(S)	**Cornbread**	196?	5.00	12.00
Blue Note BST-84212	(S)	**The Gigolo**	196?	5.00	12.00
Blue Note BST-84243	(S)	**Delightfulee Morgan**	196?	5.00	12.00
Blue Note BST-84312	(S)	**Charisma**	1969	10.00	25.00
Blue Note BST-84335	(S)	**The Sixth Sense**	1969	10.00	25.00
— OBlue Note albums above have blue on white labels with "A Division of Liberty Records."—					
Vee Jay LP-3007	(M)	**Here's Lee Morgan**	1960	16.00	40.00
Vee Jay SR-3007	(S)	**Here's Lee Morgan**	1960	12.00	30.00
Vee Jay LP-3015	(M)	**Expoobident**	1960	16.00	40.00
Vee Jay SR-3015	(S)	**Expoobident**	1960	20.00	50.00
Vee Jay LP-2508	(M)	**Lee Morgan Quintet**	1965	16.00	40.00
Vee Jay LPS-2508	(S)	**Lee Morgan Quintet**	1965	12.00	30.00
Jazzland JLP-80	(M)	**Take Twelve**	1962	16.00	40.00
Jazzland JLP-980	(S)	**Take Twelve**	1962	12.00	30.00

MORRIS, AUDREY

Audrey Morris is a modern jazz vocalist.

Bethlehem BCP-6010	(M)	**The Voice Of Audrey Morris**	1956	50.00	125.00

MORRIS, MARLOWE

Marlowe Morris is a traditional jazz-based piano and organ player.

Columbia CL-1819	(M)	**Play The Thing**	1962	10.00	25.00
Columbia CS-8619	(S)	**Play The Thing**	1962	8.00	20.00
—Columbia albums above have six white on black "eye" logos on each label.—					

MORRISEY, PAT

Mercury MG-20197	(M)	**I'm Pat Morrisey, I Sing**	1956	30.00	75.00

MORROW, BUDDY

RCA Victor LPM-2042	(M)	**Impact**	1959	12.00	30.00
RCA Victor LSP-2042	(S)	**Impact**	1959	16.00	40.00
RCA Victor LPM-2180	(M)	**Double Impact**	1960	12.00	30.00
RCA Victor LSP-2180	(S)	**Double Impact**	1960	16.00	40.00
—RCA albums above have black labels with "Long Play" or "Living Stereo" on the bottom.—					

Label & Catalog #		Title	Year	VG+	NM

MORTON, JELLY ROLL

Ferdinand Le Menthe Jr., aka Jelly Roll Morton, is a traditional jazz pianist, vocalist, arranger and composer. For additional listings refer to Sidney Bechet; The New Orleans Rhythm Kings; Pine Top Smith.

Label & Catalog #		Title	Year	VG+	NM
Commodore DL-30000	*(M)*	**New Orleans Memories**	*1950*	**40.00**	**100.00**
Jazz Panorama 1804	*(10")*	**Peppers**	*1951*	**40.00**	**100.00**
Jazz Panorama 1810	*(10")*	**Peppers**	*1951*	**40.00**	**100.00**
Circle L-14001	*(M)*	**The Saga Of Mr. Jelly Lord, Volume 1— Jazz Started In New Orleans**	*1951*	**50.00**	**125.00**
Circle L-14002	*(M)*	**The Saga Of Mr. Jelly Lord, Volume 2— Way Down Yonder**	*1951*	**50.00**	**125.00**
Circle L-14003	*(M)*	**The Saga Of Mr. Jelly Lord, Volume 3— Jazz Is Strictly Music**	*1951*	**50.00**	**125.00**
Circle L-14004	*(M)*	**The Saga Of Mr. Jelly Lord, Volume 4— The Spanish Tinge**	*1951*	**50.00**	**125.00**
Circle L-14005	*(M)*	**The Saga Of Mr. Jelly Lord, Volume 5— Bad Man Ballads**	*1951*	**50.00**	**125.00**
Circle L-14006	*(M)*	**The Saga Of Mr. Jelly Lord, Volume 6— Jazz Piano Soloist #1**	*1951*	**50.00**	**125.00**
Circle L-14007	*(M)*	**The Saga Of Mr. Jelly Lord, Volume 7— Everyone Had His Style**	*1951*	**50.00**	**125.00**
Circle L-14008	*(M)*	**The Saga Of Mr. Jelly Lord, Volume 8— Jelly And The Blues**	*1951*	**50.00**	**125.00**
Circle L-14009	*(M)*	**The Saga Of Mr. Jelly Lord, Volume 9— Alabama Bound**	*1951*	**50.00**	**125.00**
Circle L-14010	*(M)*	**The Saga Of Mr. Jelly Lord, Volume 10— Jazz Piano Soloist #2**	*1951*	**50.00**	**125.00**
Circle L-14011	*(M)*	**The Saga Of Mr. Jelly Lord, Volume 11— The Saga Of Mr. Jelly Lord In New Orleans**	*1951*	**50.00**	**125.00**
Circle L-14012	*(M)*	**The Saga Of Mr. Jelly Lord, Volume 12— I'm The Winin' Boy**	*1951*	**50.00**	**125.00**
		(Circle 14001-14012 consist of Morton talking and playing to Alan Lomax for the Library Of Congress.)			
Riverside RLP-1018	*(10")*	**Jelly Roll Morton: Rediscovered Solos**	*1953*	**40.00**	**100.00**
Riverside RLP-27	*(10")*	**First Recordings**	*1954*	**40.00**	**100.00**
Riverside RLP-1038	*(10")*	**Classic Jazz Piano, Volume 1**	*1954*	**40.00**	**100.00**
Riverside RLP-1041	*(10")*	**Classic Jazz Piano, Volume 2**	*1954*	**40.00**	**100.00**
Riverside RLP-12-102	*(M)*	**The New Orleans Rhyhtm Kings With Jelly Roll Morton**	*1955*	**20.00**	**50.00**
Riverside RLP-12-111	*(M)*	**Classic Piano Solos**	*1955*	**20.00**	**50.00**
Riverside RLP-12-128	*(M)*	**The Incomparable Jelly Roll Morton**	*1956*	**20.00**	**50.00**
Riverside RLP-12-132	*(M)*	**Mr. Jelly Lord**	*1956*	**20.00**	**50.00**
Riverside RLP-12-133	*(M)*	**Jelly Roll Morton Plays And Sings**	*1956*	**20.00**	**50.00**
Riverside RLP-12-140	*(M)*	**Rags And Blues**	*1956*	**20.00**	**50.00**
Riverside RLP-9001	*(M*	**Library Of Congress Recordings—Volume 1**	*1955*	**20.00**	**50.00**
Riverside RLP-9002	*(M*	**Library Of Congress Recordings—Volume 2**	*1955*	**20.00**	**50.00**
Riverside RLP-9003	*(M*	**Library Of Congress Recordings—Volume 3**	*1955*	**20.00**	**50.00**
Riverside RLP-9004	*(M*	**Library Of Congress Recordings—Volume 4**	*1955*	**20.00**	**50.00**
Riverside RLP-9005	*(M*	**Library Of Congress Recordings—Volume 5**	*1955*	**20.00**	**50.00**
Riverside RLP-9006	*(M*	**Library Of Congress Recordings—Volume 6**	*1955*	**20.00**	**50.00**
Riverside RLP-9007	*(M*	**Library Of Congress Recordings—Volume 7**	*1955*	**20.00**	**50.00**
Riverside RLP-9008	*(M*	**Library Of Congress Recordings—Volume 8**	*1955*	**20.00**	**50.00**
Riverside RLP-9009	*(M*	**Library Of Congress Recordings—Volume 9**	*1955*	**20.00**	**50.00**
Riverside RLP-9010	*(M*	**Library Of Congress Recordings—Volume 10**	*1955*	**20.00**	**50.00**
Riverside RLP-9011	*(M*	**Library Of Congress Recordings—Volume 11**	*1955*	**20.00**	**50.00**
Riverside RLP-9012	*(M*	**Library Of Congress Recordings—Volume 12**	*1955*	**20.00**	**50.00**
		(Riverside 9001-12 are reissues of Circle's "Saga Of Mr. Jelly Lord.")			
		—Riverside albums above have blue on white labels.—			
RCA Victor WPT-32	*(10")*	**Immortal Performances**	*1952*	**40.00**	**100.00**
"X" LX-3008	*(10")*	**Red Hot Peppers, Volume 1**	*1954*	**40.00**	**100.00**
"X" LVA-3028	*(10")*	**Red Hot Peppers, Volume 2**	*1954*	**40.00**	**100.00**
RCA Victor LPM-1649	*(M)*	**The King Of New Orleans Jazz**	*1957*	**20.00**	**50.00**
		—RCA albums above have black labels with "Long Play" on the bottom.—			
RCA Victor LPV-508	*(M)*	**Stomps And Joys**	*1965*	**8.00**	**20.00**
RCA Victor LPV-524	*(M)*	**Hot Jazz, Pop Jazz, Hokum And Hilarity**	*1965*	**8.00**	**20.00**
RCA Victor LPV-546	*(M)*	**Mr. Jelly Lord**	*1966*	**8.00**	**20.00**
RCA Victor LPV-559	*(M)*	**I Thought I Heard Buddy Bolden Say...**	*1966*	**8.00**	**20.00**
Mainstream 56020	*(M)*	**Jelly Roll Morton**	*1965*	**10.00**	**25.00**
Mainstream S-6020	*(E)*	**Jelly Roll Morton**	*1965*	**5.00**	**12.00**

Label & Catalog #		Title	Year	VG+	NM

MOSSE, SANDY

Sandy Mosse is a modern jazz tenor and alto saxophone player.

Argo LP-609	(M)	**Chicago Scene**	1956	16.00	40.00
Argo LP-639	(M)	**Relaxin' With Sandy Mosse**	1958	16.00	40.00
Argo LPS-639	(S)	**Relaxin' With Sandy Mosse**	1958	12.00	30.00

MOST, ABE

Abraham Most is a modern jazz clarinet player.

Liberty LJH-6004	(M)	**Mister Clarinet**	1955	20.00	50.00

MOST, SAM

Samuel Most is a modern jazz flute, clarinet and alto saxophone player. For additional listings refer to Don Elliott / Sam Most; Herbie Mann & Sam Most; The Nutty Squirrels.

Debut DLP-11	(10")	**Sam Most Sextet**	1954	125.00	250.00
Vanguard VRS-8014	(10")	**Sam Most Sextet**	1954	30.00	75.00
Bethlehem BCP-18	(M)	**I'm Nuts About The Most—East Coast Jazz 8**	1955	20.00	50.00
Bethlehem BCP-6008	(M)	**Musically Yours**	1956	20.00	50.00
Bethlehem BCP-75	(M)	**Sam Most Plays Bird, Bud, Monk And Miles**	1957	20.00	50.00
Bethlehem BCP-78	(M)	**The Amazing Mr. Sam Most**	1957	20.00	50.00

MOTEN, BENNIE

Benjamin Moten is a traditional jazz pianist, composer and band leader.

"X" LX-3004	(10")	**Kansas City Jazz, Volume 1**	1954	20.00	50.00
"X" LVA-3025	(10")	**Kansas City Jazz, Volume 2**	1954	20.00	50.00
"X" LVA-3038	(10")	**Kansas City Jazz, Volume 3**	1955	20.00	50.00
RCA Victor LPV-514	(M)	**Bennie Moten's Great Band Of 1930-32**	1965	8.00	20.00

MOULE, KEN

English born Kenneth Moule is a modern jazz pianist and arranger.

London LL-1673	(M)	**Ken Moule Arranges**	1957	20.00	50.00

MOZIAN, ROGER KING

Roger King Mozian is a traditonal jazz trumpet player, arranger and big band leader.

Clef MGC-166	(10")	**The Colorful Music Of Roger King Mozian**	1954	40.00	100.00

MULLIGAN, GERRY

Baritone saxophone and piano player, arranger and band leader Gerald "Jeru" Mulligan is an innovator of the "cool jazz" that influenced the West Coast sound of the '50s. For additional listings refer to Chet Baker & Gerry Mulligan; Boots Brown; Paul Desmond; Stan Getz; John Graas; Thelonious Monk; Oscar Peterson / Gerry Mulligan; Andre Previn; Shorty Rogers / Gerry Mulligan; Annie Ross; Phil Sunkel; Teddy Wilson / Gerry Mulligan; and the Jazzy Soundtracks section under MGM, United Artists, and Verve.

Prestige PRLP-120	(10")	**Gerry Mulligan**	1951	125.00	250.00
Prestige PRLP-7006	(M)	**Mulligan Plays Mulligan**	1955	40.00	100.00
		(Prestige 7006 is a reissue of 120 and 141.)			
		—Prestige albums above have a W. 50th Street, NYC address on the label.—			
Prestige PRLP-7251	(M)	**Historically Speaking**	1963	16.00	40.00
Prestige PRST-7251	(E)	**Historically Speaking**	1963	12.00	30.00
		(Prestige 7251 is a reissue of 7006.)			
		—Prestige albums above have yellow mono or silver stereo labels with a Bergenfield, NJ address.—			
Pacific Jazz PJLP-1	(10")	**Gerry Mulligan Quartet**	1952	100.00	200.00
Pacific Jazz PJLP-2	(10")	**Lee Konitz Plays With The Gerry Mulligan Quartet**	1953	100.00	200.00
Pacific Jazz PJLP-5	(10")	**Gerry Mulligan Quartet**	1953	100.00	200.00
Pacific Jazz PJLP-10	(10")	**Lee Konitz And The Gerry Mulligan Quartet**	1954	100.00	200.00
Pacific Jazz PJ-1201	(M)	**California Concerts**	1955	40.00	100.00
Pacific Jazz PJ-1207	(M)	**The Original Mulligan Quartet**	1955	40.00	100.00
Pacific Jazz PJ-1210	(M)	**Paris Concert**	1956	40.00	100.00
Pacific Jazz PJM-406	(M)	**Lee Konitz With The Gerry Mulligan Quartet**	1956	40.00	100.00
Pacific Jazz PJ-1228	(M)	**Gerry Mulligan At Storyville**	1957	40.00	100.00
World Pacific PJM-406	(M)	**Lee Konitz Plays With The Gerry Mulligan Quartet**	1958	30.00	75.00
World Pacific WP-1201	(M)	**California Concerts**	1958	30.00	75.00
World Pacific WP-1207	(M)	**The Original Mulligan Quartet**	1958	30.00	75.00
World Pacific WP-1210	(M)	**Gerry Mulligan Quartet Paris Concert**	1958	30.00	75.00
World Pacific WP-1228	(M)	**Gerry Mulligan Quartet Recorded In Boston At Storyville**	1958	30.00	75.00
World Pacific ST-1006	(S)	**Gerry Mulligan Quartet Recorded In Boston At Storyville**	1958	30.00	75.00

Gerry Mulligan joined Gene Krupa's band in 1947, Miles Davis' group in 1948, in time for the "birth of the cool" sessions for Capitol, followed by stints with Elliot Lawrence and Claude Thornhill. After moving to California in 1952, Gerry began experimenting with a piano-less quartet and, after a couple of sessions with Prestige, became the bread and butter of Richard Bock's Pacific Jazz label through 1958, when he signed with Verve. Aside from his solo career as one of the primary exponents of West Coast jazz, he can be found sharing LP space with Oscar Peterson, Shorty Rogers, and Teddy Wilson. He also recorded with Chet Baker, as a member of Boots Brown's Blockbusters, and as a featured guest with Paul Desmond, Stan Getz, John Graas, Thelonious Monk, Andre Previn and Annie Ross. As a sideman he can be found on LPs by Miles on Capitol, Manny Albam on Coral, and Phil Sunkel on ABC-Paramount.

Label & Catalog #		Title	Year	VG+	NM
World Pacific PJ-1237	(M)	**The Mulligan Songbook**	1957	40.00	100.00
World Pacific WP-1237	(M)	**The Mulligan Songbook**	1958	30.00	75.00
World Pacific ST-1001	(S)	**The Mulligan Songbook**	1958	30.00	75.00
World Pacific PJ-1241	(M)	**Reunion With Chet Baker**	1957	40.00	100.00
World Pacific WP-1241	(M)	**Reunion With Chet Baker**	1958	30.00	75.00
World Pacific ST-1007	(S)	**Reunion With Chet Baker**	1958	30.00	75.00
World Pacific WP-1273	(M)	**Lee Konitz Plays With The Gerry Mulligan Quartet**	1959	30.00	75.00
		(World Pacific 1273 is a reissue of 406.)			
Pacific Jazz PJ-8	(M)	**The Genius Of Gerry Mulligan**	1960	16.00	40.00
Pacific Jazz PJ-38	(M)	**Konitz Meets Mulligan**	1962	12.00	30.00
		(Pacific Jazz 38 is a reissue of World Pacific 1273.)			
Pacific Jazz PJ-47	(M)	**Reunion With Chet Baker**	1962	12.00	30.00
Pacific Jazz ST-47	(S)	**Reunion With Chet Baker**	1962	10.00	25.00
		(Pacific Jazz 47 is a reissue of World Pacific 1241.)			
Pacific Jazz PJ-50	(M)	**California Concerts**	1962	12.00	30.00
		(Pacific Jazz 50 is a reissue of World Pacific 1201.)			
Pacific Jazz PJ-75	(M)	**Timeless**	1963	12.00	30.00
		(Pacific Jazz 75 also features Chet Baker.)			
Pacific Jazz PJ-10102	(M)	**Paris Concert**	1966	8.00	20.00
Pacific Jazz ST-20102	(S)	**Paris Concert**	1966	6.00	15.00
		(Pacific Jazz 10120 is a reissue of World Pacific 1210.)			
Pacific Jazz PJ-10140	(M)	**The Genius Of Gerry Mulligan**	1968	10.00	25.00
Pacific Jazz ST-20140	(E)	**The Genius Of Gerry Mulligan**	1968	5.00	12.00
		(Pacific Jazz 10140 is a reissue of 8.)			
Capitol H-439	(10")	**Gerry Mulligan And His Ten-tette**	1953	60.00	150.00
Fantasy 3-6	(10")	**Gerry Mulligan Quartet**	1953	60.00	150.00
Gene Norman GNP-3	(10")	**Gerry Mulligan Quartet**	1954	60.00	150.00
		(Gene Norman 3 also features Chet Baker.)			
EmArcy MG-36056	(M)	**Presenting The Gerry Mulligan Sextet**	1955	30.00	75.00
EmArcy MG-36101	(M)	**Mainstream Of Jazz**	1956	30.00	75.00
		—EmArcy albums above have blue labels with silver print.—			
Jazztone J-1253	(M)	**Gerry Mulligan & Chet Baker**	195?	16.00	40.00
Verve MGV-8246	(M)	**The Gerry Mulligan-Paul Desmond Quartet**	1958	20.00	50.00
Verve MGV-8249	(M)	**Getz Meets Mulligan In Hi-Fi**	1958	20.00	50.00
Verve MGVS-6003	(S)	**Getz Meets Mulligan In Hi-Fi**	1960	16.00	40.00
Verve MGV-8343	(M)	**Gerry Mulligan Meets Ben Webster**	1959	20.00	50.00
Verve MGVS-6104	(S)	**Gerry Mulligan Meets Ben Webster**	1960	16.00	40.00
Verve MGV-8367	(M)	**Gerry Mulligan Meets Johnny Hodges**	1960	20.00	50.00
Verve MGVS-6137	(S)	**Gerry Mulligan Meets Johnny Hodges**	1960	*Unreleased*	
Verve MGV-8388	(M)	**Gerry Mulligan And The Concert Jazz Band**	1960	20.00	50.00
Verve MGV-8396	(M)	**Gerry Mulligan And The Concert Jazz Band At The Village Vanguard**	1960	20.00	50.00
		—Verve albums above have black labels with "Verve Records, Inc." on the bottom.—			
Verve V-8246	(M)	**The Gerry Mulligan-Paul Desmond Quartet**	1961	8.00	20.00
Verve V-8249	(M)	**Getz Meets Mulligan In Hi-Fi**	1961	8.00	20.00
Verve V6-8249	(S)	**Getz Meets Mulligan In Hi-Fi**	1961	6.00	15.00
Verve V-8343	(M)	**Gerry Mulligan Meets Ben Webster**	1961	8.00	20.00
Verve V6-8343	(S)	**Gerry Mulligan Meets Ben Webster**	1961	6.00	15.00
Verve V-8367	(M)	**Gerry Mulligan Meets Johnny Hodges**	1961	8.00	20.00
Verve V6-8367	(S)	**Gerry Mulligan Meets Johnny Hodges**	1961	8.00	20.00
Verve V-8388	(M)	**Gerry Mulligan And The Concert Jazz Band**	1961	8.00	20.00
Verve V6-8388	(S)	**Gerry Mulligan And The Concert Jazz Band**	1961	6.00	15.00
Verve V-8396	(M)	**Gerry Mulligan And The Concert Jazz Band At The Village Vanguard**	1961	8.00	20.00
Verve V-8415	(M)	**Gerry Mulligan And The Concert Jazz Band Presents A Concert In Jazz**	1961	12.00	30.00
Verve V6-8415	(S)	**Gerry Mulligan And The Concert Jazz Band Presents A Concert In Jazz**	1961	10.00	25.00
Verve V-8438	(M)	**The Gerry Mulligan Concert Jazz Band On Tour With Guest Soloist Zoot Sims**	1962	12.00	30.00
Verve V6-8438	(S)	**The Gerry Mulligan Concert Jazz Band On Tour With Guest Soloist Zoot Sims**	1962	10.00	25.00
Verve V-8466	(M)	**The Gerry Mulligan Quartet**	1962	12.00	30.00
Verve V6-8466	(S)	**The Gerry Mulligan Quartet**	1962	10.00	25.00
Verve V-8478	(M)	**Blues In Time**	1962	12.00	30.00
Verve V6-8478	(S)	**Blues In Time**	1962	10.00	25.00
		(Verve 8478 is a reissue of 8246.)			

Label & Catalog #		Title	Year	VG+	NM
Verve V-8515	(M)	**Gerry Mulligan '63-The Concert Jazz Band**	1963	8.00	20.00
Verve V6-8515	(S)	**Gerry Mulligan '63-The Concert Jazz Band**	1963	6.00	15.00
Verve V-8534	(M)	**Gerry Mulligan Meets Ben Webster**	1963	8.00	20.00
Verve V6-8534	(S)	**Gerry Mulligan Meets Ben Webster**	1963	6.00	15.00
		(Verve 8534 is a reissue of 8343.)			
Verve V-8535	(S)	**Gerry Mulligan Meets Stan Getz**	1963	8.00	20.00
Verve V6-8535	(S)	**Gerry Mulligan Meets Stan Getz**	1963	6.00	15.00
		(Verve 8535 is a reissue of 8249.)			
Verve V-8536	(M)	**Gerry Mulligan Meets Johnny Hodges**	1963	8.00	20.00
Verve V6-8536	(S)	**Gerry Mulligan Meets Johnny Hodges**	1963	6.00	15.00
		(Verve 8536 is a reissue of 8367.)			
Verve V-8567	(M)	**The Essential Gerry Mulligan**	1964	6.00	15.00
Verve V6-8567	(S)	**The Essential Gerry Mulligan**	1964	5.00	12.00
		—Verve albums above have black labels with "MGM Records" on the bottom.—			
Verve VSP-6	(M)	**Gerry's Time**	1966	6.00	15.00
Verve VSPS-6	(E)	**Gerry's Time**	1966	3.00	7.50
Mercury MG-20453	(M)	**A Profile Of Gerry Mulligan**	1959	16.00	40.00
Mercury SR-60???	(S)	**A Profile Of Gerry Mulligan**	1959	12.00	30.00
		—Mercury albums above have silver on black labels.—			
United Arts. UAL-4085	(M)	**Nightwatch**	1960	20.00	50.00
United Arts. UAS-5085	(S)	**Nightwatch**	1960	16.00	40.00
Columbia CL-1307	(M)	**What Is There To Say?**	1959	16.00	40.00
Columbia CS-8116	(S)	**What Is There To Say?**	1960	12.00	30.00
		—Columbia albums above have six white on black "eye" logos on each label.—			
Columbia CL-1932	(M)	**Jeru**	1963	12.00	30.00
Columbia CS-8732	(S)	**Jeru**	1963	10.00	25.00
		—Columbia albums above have "Guaranteed High Fidelity" or "360 Sound Stereo" in black on the label.—			
Columbia CL-1307	(M)	**What Is There To Say?**	196?	6.00	15.00
Columbia CS-8116	(S)	**What Is There To Say?**	196?	5.00	12.00
Columbia CL-1932	(M)	**Jeru**	196?	6.00	15.00
Columbia CS-8732	(S)	**Jeru**	196?	5.00	12.00
		—Columbia albums above have "360 Sound" on the bottom of the label.—			
Philips PHM-200-077	(M)	**Spring Is Sprung**	1963	8.00	20.00
Philips PHS-600-077	(S)	**Spring Is Sprung**	1963	6.00	15.00
Philips PHM-200-108	(M)	**Night Lights**	1963	8.00	20.00
Philips PHS-600-108	(S)	**Night Lights**	1963	6.00	15.00
Wing MGW-12335	(M)	**Night Lights**	1964	6.00	15.00
Wing SRW-16335	(S)	**Night Lights**	1964	5.00	12.00
Limelight LM-82004	(M)	**Butterfly With Hiccups**	1964	8.00	20.00
Limelight LS-86004	(S)	**Butterfly With Hiccups**	1964	6.00	15.00
Limelight LM-82021	(M)	**If You Can't Beat 'Em, Join 'Em**	1965	8.00	20.00
Limelight LS-86021	(S)	**If You Can't Beat 'Em, Join 'Em**	1965	6.00	15.00
Limelight LM-82030	(M)	**Feelin' Good**	1965	8.00	20.00
Limelight LS-86030	(S)	**Feelin' Good**	1965	6.00	15.00
Limelight LM-82040	(M)	**Something Borrowed, Something Blue**	1966	8.00	20.00
Limelight LS-86040	(S)	**Something Borrowed, Something Blue**	1966	6.00	15.00
Sunset SUM-1117	(M)	**Concert Days**	1966	6.00	15.00
Sunset SUS-5117	(S)	**Concert Days**	1966	5.00	12.00
Odyssey 32160258	(S)	**What Is There To Say?**	1968	4.00	10.00
		(Odyssey 32160258 is a reissue of Columbia 8116.)			
Odyssey 32160290	(S)	**Jeru**	1968	4.00	10.00
		(Odyssey 32160290 is a reissue of Columbia 8732.)			

MULLIGAN, GERRY / BUDDY DeFRANCO

Label & Catalog #		Title	Year	VG+	NM
Gene Norman GNP-26	(M)	**Gerry Mulligan Quartet With Chet Baker/ Buddy DeFranco Quartet**	1957	30.00	75.00
		(Gene Norman 26 is a reissue of 8 and 2, "Buddy DeFranco Takes You To The Stars.")			
Gene Norman GNP-56	(M)	**Gerry Mulligan Quartet With Chet Baker/ Buddy DeFranco Quartet**	196?	16.00	40.00
Gene Norman GNP-56S	(S)	**Gerry Mulligan Quartet With Chet Baker/ Buddy DeFranco Quartet**	196?	12.00	30.00
		(Gene Norman 56 is a reissue of 26.)			

MULLIGAN, GERRY, & PAUL DESMOND

Label & Catalog #		Title	Year	VG+	NM
Fantasy 3220	(M)	**Gerry Mulligan Quartet/Paul Desmond Quintet**	1956	30.00	75.00
		(Fantasy 220 is a reissue of 6 and 21, "Paul Desmond.")			
		—Fanasy albums above have red labels on dark red, non-flexible vinyl.—			

Label & Catalog #		Title	Year	VG+	NM
Fantasy 3220	(M)	**Gerry Mulligan Quartet/Paul Desmond Quintet**	195?	16.00	40.00

—Fanasy albums above have red labels on non-flexible vinyl.—

RCA Victor LPM-2624	(M)	**Two Of A Kind**	1962	10.00	25.00
RCA Victor LSP-2624	(S)	**Two Of A Kind**	1962	8.00	20.00

—RCA albums above have black labels with "Long Play" or "Living Stereo" on the bottom.—

MULLIGAN, GERRY & KAI WINDING / RED RODNEY

New Jazz NJLP-8306	(M)	**Broadway**	1963	*Unreleased*	
Status ST-8306	(M)	**Broadway**	1965	16.00	40.00

MURPHY, LYLE

Lyle "Spud" Murphy is a traditional jazz saxophone(s) and clarinet player, arranger and composer later associated with the West Coast jazz scene.

Gene Norman GNP-9	(10")	**Four Saxophones In Twelve Tones**	1954	50.00	125.00
Gene Norman GNP-152	(M)	**Four Saxophones In Twelve Tones**	1955	20.00	50.00
Gene Norman GNP-33	(M)	**New Orbits In Sound**	1957	20.00	50.00
Contemporary C-3506	(M)	**12-Tone Compositions & Arrangements**	1955	20.00	50.00

MURPHY, MARK

Mark Murphy is a modern jazz vocalist.

Decca DL-8390	(M)	**Meet Mark Murphy**	1957	20.00	50.00
Decca DL-8632	(M)	**Let Yourself Go**	1958	16.00	40.00
Capitol T-1177	(M)	**This Could Be The Start Of Something**	1959	12.00	30.00
Capitol ST-1177	(S)	**This Could Be The Start Of Something**	1959	10.00	25.00
Capitol T-1299	(M)	**Hip Parade**	1960	12.00	30.00
Capitol ST-1299	(S)	**Hip Parade**	1960	10.00	25.00
Capitol T-1458	(M)	**Playing The Field**	1960	12.00	30.00
Capitol ST-1458	(S)	**Playing The Field**	1960	10.00	25.00

—Capitol albums above have black "rainbow" labels with the logo on the left side.—

Riverside RLP-395	(M)	**Rah**	1961	12.00	30.00
Riverside RS-9395	(S)	**Rah**	1961	10.00	25.00
Riverside RLP-441	(M)	**That's How I Love The Blues!**	1963	12.00	30.00
Riverside RS-9441	(S)	**That's How I Love The Blues!**	1963	10.00	25.00

—Riverside albums above have blue mono or black stereo labels with a reel & mike logo on top.—

Fontana MGF-27537	(M)	**A Swingin' Singin' Affair**	1965	10.00	25.00
Fontana SRF-67537	(S)	**A Swingin' Singin' Affair**	1965	8.00	20.00

MURPHY, ROSE

Rose Murphy is a jazz-based vocalist.

Verve MGV-2070	(M)	**Not Cha-Cha But Chi-Chi**	1957	16.00	40.00

—Verve albums above have "Verve Records, Inc" on the bottom.—

Verve V-2070	(M)	**Not Cha-Cha But Chi-Chi**	1961	8.00	20.00

—Verve albums above have black labels with "MGM Records" on the bottom.—

United Arts. UAJ-14025	(M)	**Jazz, Joy And Happiness**	1962	16.00	40.00
United Arts. UAJS-15025	(S)	**Jazz, Joy And Happiness**	1962	16.00	40.00

MURPHY, TURK

Melvin "Turk" Murphy is a traditional jazz trombone player and composer. For additional listings refer to George Lewis.

Good Time Jazz L-7	(10")	**Turk Murphy With Claire Austin**	1952	20.00	50.00
Columbia CL-6257	(10")	**Barrelhouse Jazz**	1953	20.00	50.00
Good Time Jazz L-12026	(M)	**San Francisco Jazz, Volume 1**	1955	16.00	40.00
Good Time Jazz L-12027	(M)	**San Francisco Jazz, Volume 2**	1955	16.00	40.00
Columbia CL-546	(M)	**When The Saints Go Marching In**	1954	16.00	40.00
Columbia CL-559	(M)	**Music Of Jelly Roll Morton**	1954	16.00	40.00
Columbia CL-595	(M)	**Barrelhouse Jazz**	1954	16.00	40.00
Columbia CL-650	(M)	**Dancing Jazz**	1955	16.00	40.00

—Columbia albums above have "Long Playing" on the bottom of the label.—

Columbia CL-546	(M)	**When The Saints Go Marching In**	1956	12.00	30.00
Columbia CL-559	(M)	**Music Of Jelly Roll Morton**	1956	12.00	30.00
Columbia CL-595	(M)	**Barrelhouse Jazz**	1956	12.00	30.00
Columbia CL-650	(M)	**Dancing Jazz**	1956	12.00	30.00
Columbia CL-793	(M)	**New Orleans Jazz Festival**	1956	12.00	30.00
Columbia CL-927	(M)	**New Orleans Shuffle**	1957	12.00	30.00

—Columbia albums above have six white on black "eye" logos on each label.—

Verve MGV-1013	(M)	**Music For Losers**	1957	16.00	40.00
Verve MGV-1015	(M)	**Turk Murphy At Easy Street**	1957	16.00	40.00

—Verve albums above have "Verve Records, Inc." on the bottom of the label.—

Label & Catalog #		Title	Year	VG+	NM
Verve V-1013	(M)	**Music For Losers**	1961	6.00	15.00
Verve V-1015	(M)	**Turk Murphy At Easy Street**	1961	6.00	15.00
—Verve albums above have black labels with "MGM Records" on the bottom.—					
Roulette R-25076	(M)	**Turk Murphy At The Round Table**	1960	10.00	25.00
Roulette SR-25076	(S)	**Turk Murphy At The Round Table**	1960	8.00	20.00
RCA Victor LPM-2501	(M)	**Let The Good Times Roll**	1962	10.00	25.00
RCA Victor LSP-2501	(S)	**Let The Good Times Roll**	1962	8.00	20.00
—RCA albums above have black labels with "Long Play" or "Living Stereo" on the bottom.—					

MURRAY, SUNNY

Sunny Murray is a modern jazz drummer.

ESP-Disk' 1032	(M)	**Sunny Murray**	1966	10.00	25.00
ESP-Disk' 1032	(S)	**Sunny Murray**	1966	8.00	20.00
Jihad 663	(S)	**Sunny's Time Now**	1967	60.00	150.00
		(Jihad 663 also features readings by poet Leroi Jones.)			

MUSSO, VIDO

Vido Musso is a traditional jazz tenor saxophone and clarinet player.

Modern LMP-1207	(M)	**The Swingin'st**	1956	40.00	100.00
Crown CRP-5007	(M)	**The Swingin'st**	1957	20.00	50.00
		(Crown 5007 is a reissue of Modern 1207.)			
Crown CRP-5029	(M)	**Teenage Dance Party**	1957	16.00	40.00

MUSSULLI, BOOTS

Henry "Boots" Mussulli is a traditional jazz saxophone(s) player. For additional listings refer to Serge Chaloff.

Capitol H-6506	(10")	**Boots Mussulli**	1955	40.00	100.00
Capitol T-6506	(M)	**Boots Mussulli**	1955	20.00	50.00

N.

NANCE, RAY

Solid State SS-18062	*(S)*	**Body And Soul**	*1969*	**6.00**	**15.00**

NANTON, MORRIS

Morris Nanton is a modern jazz-based pianist. For additional listings refer to The First Jazz Piano Quartet.

Warner Bros. W-1256	*(M)*	**Flower Drum Song**	*1958*	**12.00**	**30.00**
Warner Bros. WS-1256	*(S)*	**Flower Drum Song**	*1958*	**10.00**	**25.00**
Warner Bros. W-1279	*(M)*	**The Original Jazz Performance Of "Roberta"**	*1959*	**12.00**	**30.00**
Warner Bros. WS-1279	*(S)*	**The Original Jazz Performance Of "Roberta"**	*1959*	**10.00**	**25.00**
Prestige PRLP-7345	*(M)*	**Preface**	*1964*	**10.00**	**25.00**
Prestige PRST-7345	*(S)*	**Preface**	*1964*	**8.00**	**20.00**
Prestige PRLP-7409	*(M)*	**Something We've Got**	*1965*	**10.00**	**25.00**
Prestige PRST-7409	*(S)*	**Something We've Got**	*1965*	**8.00**	**20.00**
Prestige PRLP-7467	*(M)*	**Soul Fingers**	*1966*	**10.00**	**25.00**
Prestige PRST-7467	*(S)*	**Soul Fingers**	*1966*	**8.00**	**20.00**

—Prestige albums above have blue labels with a trident logo on the right side.—

NAPOLEON, PHIL

Filippo Napoli, aka Phil Napoleon, is a traditional jazz trumpet player. For additional listings refer to Pete Daily / Phil Napoleon.

Mercury MG-25079	*(10")*	**Dixieland Classics**	*1953*	**20.00**	**50.00**
EmArcy MG-26008	*(10")*	**Dixieland Classics #1**	*1954*	**20.00**	**50.00**
EmArcy MG-26009	*(10")*	**Dixieland Classics #2**	*1954*	**20.00**	**50.00**
EmArcy MG-36033	*(M)*	**Dixieland Classics**	*1955*	**20.00**	**50.00**

(EmArcy 36033 is a reissue of 26008 and 26009.)

—EmArcy albums above have blue labels with silver print.—

Jolly Roger 5006	*(10")*	**Dixieland By Phil Napoleon**	*1954*	**20.00**	**50.00**
Columbia CL-2505	*(10")*	**Two-Beat**	*1955*	**20.00**	**50.00**
Capitol T-1344	*(M)*	**Phil Napoleon And The Memphis Five**	*1960*	**10.00**	**25.00**
Capitol ST-1344	*(S)*	**Phil Napoleon And The Memphis Five**	*1960*	**8.00**	**20.00**

—Capitol albums above have black "rainbow" labels with the logo on the left side.—

NASH, TED

Starlite LP-6001	*(10")*	**Ted Nash**	*1954*	**20.00**	**50.00**
Columbia CL-989	*(M)*	**Star Eyes**	*1957*	**16.00**	**40.00**

—Columbia albums above have six white on black "eye" logos on each label.—

NASH, TED & DICK

Theodore Nash is a modern jazz saxophone and flute player; Theodore Nash is a tenor saxophone, flute and piccolo player.

Liberty LJH-6011	*(M)*	**The Brothers Nash**	*1956*	**20.00**	**50.00**

NAVARRO, FATS

Theodore "Fats" Navarro is a modern jazz trumpet player. For additional listings refer to Tadd Dameron; Miles Davis / Dizzie Gillespie / Fats Navarro; Stan Getz / Sonny Stitt / Fats Navarro; Howard McGhee.

Savoy MG-9005	*(10")*	**New Sounds Of Modern Music**	*1952*	**150.00**	**300.00**
Savoy MG-9019	*(10")*	**New Trends Of Jazz**	*1952*	**150.00**	**300.00**
Savoy MG-12011	*(M)*	**Fats Navarro Memorial**	*1955*	**60.00**	**150.00**
Savoy MG-12133	*(M)*	**Nostalgia**	*1958*	**40.00**	**100.00**
Blue Note BLP-5004	*(10")*	**Fats Navarro Memorial Album**	*1952*	**240.00**	**400.00**
Blue Note BLP-1531	*(M)*	**The Fabulous Fats Navarro, Vol. 1** *(Deep groove)*	*1956*	**125.00**	**250.00**
Blue Note BLP-1531	*(M)*	**The Fabulous Fats Navarro, Vol. 1**	*1956*	**100.00**	**200.00**
Blue Note BLP-1532	*(M)*	**The Fabulous Fats Navarro, Vol. 2** *(Deep groove)*	*1956*	**125.00**	**250.00**
Blue Note BLP-1532	*(M)*	**The Fabulous Fats Navarro, Vol. 2**	*1956*	**100.00**	**200.00**

—Blue Note albums above have blue on white labels with a Lexington Ave, NYC address.—

Blue Note BLP-1531	*(M)*	**The Fabulous Fats Navarro, Vol. 1**	*1963*	**10.00**	**25.00**
Blue Note BLP-1532	*(M)*	**The Fabulous Fats Navarro, Vol. 2**	*1963*	**10.00**	**25.00**

—Blue Note albums above have blue on white labels with a New York, USA address.—

Blue Note BST-81531	*(E)*	**The Fabulous Fats Navarro, Vol. 1**	*196?*	**4.00**	**10.00**
Blue Note BST-81532	*(E)*	**The Fabulous Fats Navarro, Vol. 2**	*196?*	**4.00**	**10.00**

—Blue Note albums above have blue on white labels with "A Division of Liberty Records."—

Label & Catalog #		Title	Year	VG+	NM
NAVARRO, FATS / KAIE WINDING / BREW MOORE					
Savoy MG-12119	*(M)*	**In The Beginning... Bebop**	*1957*	**24.00**	**60.00**
		—Savoy albums above have silver on red labels.—			
NEELY, JIMMY					
James Neely is a modern jazz-based pianist.					
Tru-Sound TRU-15002	*(M)*	**Misirlou**	*1962*	**16.00**	**40.00**
NELSON, OLIVER					
Oliver Nelson is a modern jazz alto saxophone player and composer. For additional listings refer to the Jazzy Soundtracks section under Impulse.					
New Jazz NJLP-8224	*(M)*	**Meet Oliver Nelson**	*1959*	**20.00**	**50.00**
New Jazz NJLP-8233	*(M)*	**Takin' Care Of Business**	*1960*	**20.00**	**50.00**
New Jazz NJLP-8243	*(M)*	**Screamin' The Blues**	*1960*	**20.00**	**50.00**
New Jazz NJLP-8255	*(M)*	**Straight Ahead**	*1961*	**20.00**	**50.00**
		(Status 8255 also features Eric Dolphy.)			
New Jazz NJLP-8324	*(M)*	**Screamin' The Blues**	*1963*	*Unreleased*	
		—New Jazz albums above have purple labels.—			
New Jazz NJLP-8224	*(M)*	**Meet Oliver Nelson**	*1965*	**10.00**	**25.00**
New Jazz NJLP-8233	*(M)*	**Takin' Care Of Business**	*1965*	**10.00**	**25.00**
New Jazz NJLP-8243	*(M)*	**Screamin' The Blues**	*1965*	**10.00**	**25.00**
New Jazz NJLP-8255	*(M)*	**Straight Ahead**	*1965*	**10.00**	**25.00**
		—New Jazz albums above have blue labels with a trident logo on the right side.—			
Moodsville MVLP-13	*(M)*	**Nocturne**	*1960*	**20.00**	**50.00**
		—Moodsville mono albums above have green labels with silver print.—			
Moodsville MVLP-13	*(M)*	**Nocturne**	*1965*	**10.00**	**25.00**
		—Moodsville albums above have blue labels with a trident logo on the right side.—			
Prestige PRLP-7225	*(M)*	**Afro/American Sketches**	*1962*	**20.00**	**50.00**
Prestige PRST-7225	*(S)*	**Afro/American Sketches**	*1962*	**16.00**	**40.00**
Prestige PRLP-7236	*(M)*	**Main Stem**	*1962*	**20.00**	**50.00**
Prestige PRST-7236	*(S)*	**Main Stem**	*1962*	**16.00**	**40.00**
		(Prestige 7236 also features Joe Newman.)			
		—Prestige albums above have yellow mono or silver stereo labels with a Bergenfield, NJ address.—			
Status ST-8324	*(M)*	**Screamin' The Blues**	*1965*	**16.00**	**40.00**
		(Status 8324 also features Eric Dolphy.)			
Impulse A-5	*(M)*	**The Blues And The Abstract Truth** *(Art cover)*	*1961*	**20.00**	**50.00**
Impulse AS-5	*(S)*	**The Blues And The Abstract Truth** *(Art cover)*	*1961*	**20.00**	**50.00**
		(Impulse AS-5 may be worth $75-100 in the audiophile market.)			
Impulse A-5	*(M)*	**The Blues And The Abstract Truth** *(Photo cover)*	*196?*	**10.00**	**25.00**
Impulse AS-5	*(S)*	**The Blues And The Abstract Truth** *(Photo cover)*	*196?*	**8.00**	**20.00**
Impulse A-75	*(M)*	**More Blues And The Abstract Truth**	*1964*	**12.00**	**30.00**
Impulse AS-75	*(S)*	**More Blues And The Abstract Truth**	*1964*	**10.00**	**25.00**
Impulse A-9113	*(M)*	**Michelle**	*1966*	**10.00**	**25.00**
Impulse AS-9113	*(S)*	**Michelle**	*1966*	**8.00**	**20.00**
Impulse A-9129	*(M)*	**Sound Pieces**	*1966*	**10.00**	**25.00**
Impulse AS-9129	*(S)*	**Sound Pieces**	*1966*	**8.00**	**20.00**
Impulse A-9132	*(M)*	**Happenings**	*1967*	**10.00**	**25.00**
Impulse AS-9132	*(S)*	**Happenings**	*1967*	**8.00**	**20.00**
Impulse A-9144	*(M)*	**The Kennedy Dream**	*1967*	**10.00**	**25.00**
Impulse AS-9144	*(S)*	**The Kennedy Dream**	*1967*	**8.00**	**20.00**
Impulse A-9147	*(M)*	**The Spirit Of '67**	*1967*	**10.00**	**25.00**
Impulse AS-9147	*(S)*	**The Spirit Of '67**	*1967*	**8.00**	**20.00**
Impulse A-9153	*(M)*	**Live From Los Angeles**	*1967*	**10.00**	**25.00**
Impulse AS-9153	*(S)*	**Live From Los Angeles**	*1967*	**8.00**	**20.00**
		—Impulse albums above have orange & black labels.—			
Impulse AS-5	*(S)*	**The Blues And The Abstract Truth**	*1968*	**4.00**	**10.00**
Impulse AS-75	*(S)*	**More Blues And The Abstract Truth**	*1968*	**4.00**	**10.00**
Impulse AS-9113	*(S)*	**Michelle**	*1968*	**4.00**	**10.00**
Impulse AS-9129	*(S)*	**Sound Pieces**	*1968*	**4.00**	**10.00**
Impulse AS-9132	*(S)*	**Happenings**	*1968*	**4.00**	**10.00**
Impulse AS-9144	*(S)*	**The Kennedy Dream**	*1968*	**4.00**	**10.00**
Impulse AS-9147	*(S)*	**The Spirit Of '67**	*1968*	**4.00**	**10.00**
Impulse AS-9153	*(S)*	**Live From Los Angeles**	*1968*	**4.00**	**10.00**
Impulse S-9168	*(S)*	**Soulful Brass**	*1968*	**6.00**	**15.00**
		—Impulse albums above have red & black labels with the "abc" logo on top.—			
United Arts. UAJ-14019	*(M)*	**Impressions Of Phaedra**	*1962*	**16.00**	**40.00**
United Arts. UAJS-15019	*(S)*	**Impressions Of Phaedra**	*1962*	**12.00**	**30.00**

Label & Catalog #		Title	Year	VG+	NM
Verve V-8508	(M)	**Full Nelson**	1963	12.00	30.00
Verve V6-8508	(S)	**Full Nelson**	1963	10.00	25.00

— Verve albums above have black labels with "MGM Records" on the bottom.—

Label & Catalog #		Title	Year	VG+	NM
Argo LP-737	(M)	**Fantabulous**	1964	10.00	25.00
Argo LPS-737	(S)	**Fantabulous**	1964	8.00	20.00
Verve V6-8743	(S)	**Leonard Feather Presents The Sound Of Feeling And The Sound Of Oliver Nelson**	1968	6.00	15.00

— Verve albums above have black labels with "MGM Records" on the bottom.—

NELSON, OLIVER, & KING CURTIS & JIMMY FORREST

Label & Catalog #		Title	Year	VG+	NM
Prestige PRLP-7223	(M)	**Soul Battle**	1962	16.00	40.00
Prestige PRST-7223	(S)	**Soul Battle**	1962	16.00	40.00

— Prestige albums above have yellow mono or silver stereo labels with a Bergenfield, NJ address .—

NERO, PAUL

German born Kurt Paul Nero is a traditional jazz violin player and composer.

Label & Catalog #		Title	Year	VG+	NM
Sunset LP-303	(M)	**Play The Music Of Paul Nero & His Hi-Fiddles**	1956	20.00	50.00

NEROW, BERNIE

Bernie Nerow, aka Peter Nero, is a classically trained pop pianist with this sole jazz outing.

Label & Catalog #		Title	Year	VG+	NM
Mode LP-117	(M)	**Bernie Nerow Trio**	1957	30.00	75.00
Premier PM-2011	(M)	**Just For You**	1963	6.00	15.00
Premier PS-2011	(E)	**Just For You**	1963	3.00	7.50

(Credited to Peter Nero, Premier 2011 is a reissue of Mode 117.)

NEW ART JAZZ ENSEMBLE, THE

Label & Catalog #		Title	Year	VG+	NM
Revelation REV-9	(S)	**Seeking**	1969	8.00	20.00

NEW ORLEANS RHYTHM KINGS, THE: *Refer to* GEORG BRUNIS; JELLY ROLL MORTON

NEW ORLEANS SHUFFLERS, THE

Label & Catalog #		Title	Year	VG+	NM
Kingsway KL-700	(M)	**The New Orleans Shufflers**	1955	16.00	40.00

NEW YORK ART QUINTET, THE

The NYAQ includes Milford Graves, Roswell Rudd, John Tchicai and Lewis Worrell.

Label & Catalog #		Title	Year	VG+	NM
ESP-Disk' 1004	(M)	**The New York Art Quintet**	1965	8.00	20.00
ESP-Disk' 1004	(S)	**The New York Art Quintet**	1965	6.00	15.00

NEW YORK JAZZ QUARTET, THE

The New York Jazz Quartet is Herbie Mann, Mat Mathews, Whitey Mitchell and Joe Puma.

Label & Catalog #		Title	Year	VG+	NM
Elektra EKL-115	(M)	**The New York Jazz Quartet**	1957	20.00	50.00
Elektra EKL-118	(M)	**Gone Native**	1957	20.00	50.00
Coral CRL-57136	(M)	**Music For Suburban Living**	1958	16.00	40.00
Coral CRL-757136	(S)	**Music For Suburban Living**	1958	12.00	30.00
Savoy MG-12172	(M)	**Adam's Theme**	1960	12.00	30.00
Savoy SR-16172	(S)	**Adam's Theme**	1960	10.00	25.00
Savoy MG-12175	(M)	**Gone Native**	1961	12.00	30.00
Savoy SR-16175	(S)	**Gone Native**	1961	10.00	25.00

(Savoy 12175 is a reissue of Elektra 115.)

NEW YORK JAZZ SEXTET, THE

The New York Jazz Sextet includes Art Farmer, Tommy Flanagan and James Moody.

Label & Catalog #		Title	Year	VG+	NM
Scepter S-526	(M)	**New York Jazz Sextet**	1964	10.00	25.00
Scepter SS-526	(S)	**New York Jazz Sextet**	1964	8.00	20.00

NEW YORK ORIGINATORS, THE

Label & Catalog #		Title	Year	VG+	NM
Paramount RS-201	(10")	**The New York Style**	1952	20.00	50.00

NEW YORK SAXOPHONE QUARTET, THE

Label & Catalog #		Title	Year	VG+	NM
20th Cent. Fox TFM-3150	(M)	**The New York Saxophone Quartet**	1964	10.00	25.00
20th Cent. Fox TFS-3150	(S)	**The New York Saxophone Quartet**	1964	8.00	20.00

NEWBORN, PHINEAS

Phineas Newborn is a modern jazz pianist and trumpet, tenor sax vibraphone and Flugel horn player. For additional listings refer to Roy Haynes & Phineas Newborn & Paul Chambers; Young Men From Memphis.

Label & Catalog #		Title	Year	VG+	NM
Atlantic 1235	(M)	**Here Is Phineas**	1956	20.00	50.00
Atlantic SD-1235	(S)	**Here Is Phineas**	1958	20.00	50.00

— Atlantic albums above have black mono or green stereo labels.—

Label & Catalog #		Title	Year	VG+	NM
Atlantic 1235	(M)	**Here Is Phineas**	1961	8.00	20.00
Atlantic SD-1235	(S)	**Here Is Phineas**	1961	6.00	15.00
		—Atlantic albums above have multi-color labels with a white fan logo.—			
Atlantic 1235	(M)	**Here Is Phineas**	196?	5.00	12.00
Atlantic SD-1235	(S)	**Here Is Phineas**	196?	4.00	10.00
		—Atlantic albums above have multi-color labels with a black fan logo.—			
RCA Victor LPM-1421	(M)	**Phineas' Rainbow**	1957	20.00	50.00
RCA Victor LPM-1474	(M)	**While The Lady Sleeps**	1957	20.00	50.00
RCA Victor LPM-1589	(M)	**Phineas Newborn Plays Jamaica**	1957	20.00	50.00
RCA Victor LPM-1873	(M)	**Fabulous Phineas**	1958	20.00	50.00
RCA Victor LSP-1873	(S)	**Fabulous Phineas**	1958	16.00	40.00
		—RCA albums above have black labels with "Long Play" or "Living Stereo" on the bottom.—			
Roulette R-52031	(M)	**Piano Portraits**	1959	12.00	30.00
Roulette SR-52031	(S)	**Piano Portraits**	1959	10.00	25.00
Roulette R-52043	(M)	**I Love A Piano**	1960	12.00	30.00
Roulette SR-52043	(S)	**I Love A Piano**	1960	10.00	25.00
Contemporary M-3600	(M)	**The World Of Piano!**	1961	10.00	25.00
Contemporary S-7600	(S)	**The World Of Piano!**	1961	8.00	20.00
Contemporary M-3611	(M)	**Great Jazz Piano**	1962	10.00	25.00
Contemporary S-7611	(S)	**Great Jazz Piano**	1962	8.00	20.00
Contemporary M-3615	(M)	**The Newborn Touch**	1964	10.00	25.00
Contemporary S-7615	(S)	**The Newborn Touch**	1964	8.00	20.00
Contemporary S-7622	(S)	**Please Send Me Someone To Love**	1969	8.00	20.00
		— Contemporary stereo albums have gold & black labels.—			

NEWMAN, DAVID "FATHEAD"

David Newman is a modern jazz alto and tenor saxophone and flute player. For additional listings refer to James Clay & David "Fathead" Newman; Don Patterson.

Atlantic 1304	(M)	**Ray Charles Presents David "Fathead" Newman**	1959	20.00	50.00
Atlantic SD-1304	(S)	**Ray Charles Presents David "Fathead" Newman**	1959	16.00	40.00
		—Atlantic albums above have black mono or green stereo labels.—			
Atlantic 1304	(M)	**Ray Charles Presents David "Fathead" Newman**	1961	8.00	20.00
Atlantic SD-1304	(S)	**Ray Charles Presents David "Fathead" Newman**	1961	6.00	15.00
Atlantic 1366	(M)	**Straight Ahead**	1961	10.00	25.00
Atlantic SD-1366	(S)	**Straight Ahead**	1961	8.00	20.00
		—Atlantic albums above have multi-color labels with a white fan logo.—			
Atlantic 1304	(M)	**Ray Charles Presents David "Fathead" Newman**	196?	5.00	12.00
Atlantic SD-1304	(S)	**Ray Charles Presents David "Fathead" Newman**	196?	4.00	10.00
Atlantic 1366	(M)	**Straight Ahead**	196?	5.00	12.00
Atlantic SD-1366	(S)	**Straight Ahead**	196?	4.00	10.00
Atlantic 1399	(M)	**Fathead Comes On**	1962	10.00	25.00
Atlantic SD-1399	(S)	**Fathead Comes On**	1962	8.00	20.00
Atlantic SD-1489	(S)	**House Of David**	1968	6.00	15.00
		—Atlantic albums above have multi-color labels with a black fan logo.—			

NEWMAN, JOE

Joseph Newman is a traditional jazz-based trumpet player. For additional listings refer to Eddie Bert / Billy Byers & Joe Newman; Oliver Nelson.

Vanguard VRS-8007	(10")	**Joe Newman And His Band**	1954	60.00	150.00
Storyville STLP-318	(10")	**Joe Newman And The Boys In The Band**	1955	60.00	150.00
Storyville STLP-905	(M)	**I Feel Like A Newman**	1956	40.00	100.00
RCA Victor LPM-1118	(M)	**All I Want To Do Is Swing**	1955	40.00	100.00
RCA Victor LPM-1198	(M)	**I'm Still Swinging**	1956	40.00	100.00
RCA Victor LPM-1324	(M)	**Salute To Satch**	1956	30.00	75.00
		—RCA albums above have black labels with "Long Play" on the bottom.—			
Jazztone J-1217	(M)	**New Sounds In Swing**	1956	16.00	40.00
Jazztone J-1220	(M)	**The Count's Men**	1956	16.00	40.00
Jazztone J-1265	(M)	**Swing Lightly**	1957	16.00	40.00
		(Jazztone 1265 also features Ruby Braff.)			
Vik LX-1060	(M)	**Midgets**	1957	30.00	75.00
Rama LP-1003	(M)	**Locking Horns**	1957	40.00	100.00
Roulette R-52009	(M)	**Locking Horns**	1958	16.00	40.00
Roulette SR-52009	(S)	**Locking Horns**	1958	12.00	30.00
		(Roulette 52009 is a reissue of Rama 1003.)			
Roulette R-52014	(M)	**Joe Newman With Woodwinds**	1958	16.00	40.00
Roulette SR-52014	(S)	**Joe Newman With Woodwinds**	1958	12.00	30.00
Coral CRL-57121	(M)	**The Happy Cats**	1957	20.00	50.00
Coral CRL-57208	(M)	**Soft Swingin' Jazz**	1958	20.00	50.00

Label & Catalog #		Title	Year	VG+	NM
American Rec. Soc. G-447	(M)	**Basically Swing**	1958	16.00	40.00
		(A.R.S. 447 is a reissue of Vanguard 8007.)			
American Rec. Soc. G-451	(M)	**New Sounds In Swing**	1958	16.00	40.00
		(A.R.S. 451 is a reissue of Jazztone 1217.)			
World Pacific WP-1288	(M)	**Countin'**	1960	16.00	40.00
World Pacific ST-1288	(S)	**Countin'**	1960	16.00	40.00
Swingville SVLP-2011	(M)	**Jive At Five**	1961	20.00	50.00
Swingville SVLP-2019	(M)	**Good 'N Groovy**	1961	20.00	50.00
		(Swingville 2019 also features Frank Foster.)			
Swingville SVLP-2027	(M)	**Joe's Hap'nin's**	1961	20.00	50.00
Swingville SVST-2027	(S)	**Joe's Hap'nin's**	1961	16.00	40.00
		—Swingville mono albums above have purple mono or red stereo labels.—			
Swingville SVLP-2011	(M)	**Jive At Five**	1965	10.00	25.00
Swingville SVLP-2019	(M)	**Good 'N Groovy**	1965	10.00	25.00
Swingville SVLP-2027	(M)	**Joe's Hap'nin's**	1965	10.00	25.00
Swingville SVST-2027	(S)	**Joe's Hap'nin's**	1965	8.00	20.00
		—Swingville albums above have blue labels with a trident logo on the right side.—			
Mercury MG-20696	(M)	**Joe Newman At Count Basie's**	1962	12.00	30.00
Mercury SR-60696	(S)	**Joe Newman At Count Basie's**	1962	10.00	25.00

NICHOLAS, ALBERT / SIDNEY BECHET

Albert Nicholas is a traditional jazz clarinet and saxophone(s) player.

Riverside RLP-12-216	(M)	**Creole Reeds**	1956	30.00	75.00
		—Riverside albums above have blue on white labels.—			
Riverside RLP-12-216	(M)	**Creole Reeds**	195?	16.00	40.00
		—Riverside albums above have blue mono or black stereo labels with a reel & mike logo on top.—			

NICHOLAS, JOSEPH "WOODEN JOE"

America Music 640	(10")	**A Nite At Artesian Hall With Wooden Joe**	1951	20.00	50.00

NICHOLS, HERBIE

Herbert Nichols is a traditional jazz pianist and composer. For additional listings refer to Hampton Hawes / John Mehegan / Herbie Nichols / Paul Smith.

Blue Note BLP-5068	(10")	**The Prophetic Herbie Nichols, Volume 1**	1955	150.00	300.00
Blue Note BLP-5069	(10")	**The Prophetic Herbie Nichols, Volume 2**	1955	150.00	300.00
Blue Note BLP-1519	(M)	**Herbie Nichols Trio** *(Deep groove)*	1956	60.00	150.00
Blue Note BLP-1519	(M)	**Herbie Nichols Trio**	1956	40.00	100.00
		—Blue Note albums above have blue on white labels with a Lexington Ave, NYC address.—			
Blue Note BLP-1519	(M)	**Herbie Nichols Trio**	1963	10.00	25.00
		—Blue Note albums above have blue on white labels with a New York, USA address.—			
Blue Note BST-81519	(E)	**Herbie Nichols Trio**	196?	4.00	10.00
		—Blue Note albums above have blue on white labels with "A Division of Liberty Records."—			
Bethlehem BCP-81	(M)	**Love Gloom Cash And Love**	1957	40.00	100.00

NICHOLS, NAT

Najo LPS-001	(S)	**Nat Nichols Trio**	1967	8.00	20.00
Najo LPS-002	(S)	**Spring Play**	1967	8.00	20.00

NICHOLS, RED

Ernest "Red" Nichols is a traditional jazz cornet player. For additional listings refer to the Jazzy Soundtracks section under Dot and Verve..

Brunswick BL-58008	(10")	**Red Nichols, Vol. 1**	1950	30.00	75.00
Brunswick BL-58009	(10")	**Red Nichols, Vol. 2**	1950	30.00	75.00
Brunswick BL-58027	(10")	**Red Nichols, Vol. 3**	1951	30.00	75.00
Brunswick BL-54008	(M)	**For Collectors Only**	1954	20.00	50.00
Brunswick BL-54047	(M)	**The Red Nichols Story**	1955	20.00	50.00
Capitol H-215	(10")	**Jazz Time**	1950	30.00	75.00
Capitol T-775	(M)	**Hot Pennies**	1956	20.00	50.00
Audiophile AP-1	(M)	**Red Nichols & Band**	1953	20.00	50.00
Audiophile AP-7	(M)	**Syncopated Chamber Music, Volume 1**	1953	20.00	50.00
Audiophile AP-8	(M)	**Syncopated Chamber Music, Volume 2**	1953	20.00	50.00

NIEHAUS, LENNIE

Leneord Niehaus is a West Coast jazz alto saxophone player and arranger.

Contemporary C-2513	(10")	**Lennie Niehaus, Vol. 1—The Quintet**	1954	50.00	125.00
Contemporary C-2517	(10")	**Lennie Niehaus, Vol. 2—The Octet**	1954	50.00	125.00
Contemporary C-3503	(M)	**Lennie Niehaus, Vol. 3—The Octet No. 2**	1955	30.00	75.00
Contemporary C-3510	(M)	**Lennie Niehaus, Vol. 4—The Quintets & Strings**	1956	30.00	75.00

Label & Catalog #		Title	Year	VG+	NM
Contemporary C-3518	(M)	**The Lennie Niehaus Quintet**	1956	30.00	75.00
		(Contemporary 3518 is a reissue of 2513 plus four tracks.)			
Contemporary C-3524	(M)	**Lennie Niehaus, Vol. 5—The Sextet**	1956	30.00	75.00
Contemporary C-3540	(M)	**Zounds! Lennie Niehaus, Vol. 2—The Octet**	1957	30.00	75.00
		(Contemporary 3540 is a reissue of 2517 plus four tracks.)			
EmArcy MG-36118	(M)	**I Swing For You**	1957	20.00	50.00
		—EmArcy albums above have blue labels with silver print.—			
Mercury MG-20555	(M)	**I Swing For You**	1960	12.00	30.00
Mercury SR-60123	(S)	**I Swing For You**	1960	10.00	25.00
		(Mercury 20555 is a reissue of EmArcy 36118.)			
		—Mercury albums above have black labels with silver print.—			

NIMMONS, PHIL

Canadian born Phillip Nimmons is a modern jazz alto saxophone and clarinet player.

Label & Catalog #		Title	Year	VG+	NM
Clef MGC-753	(M)	**The Canadian Scene Via Phil Nimmons**	1955	*Unreleased*	
		(Clef 753 was issued as Verve 8025.)			
Verve MGV-8025	(M)	**The Canadian Scene Via Phil Nimmons**	1957	20.00	50.00
Verve MGV-8376	(M)	**Nimmons 'n' Nine**	1960	20.00	50.00
Verve MGVS-6153	(S)	**Nimmons 'n' Nine**	1960	*Unreleased*	
		—Verve albums above have black labels with "Verve Records, Inc." on the bottom.—			
Verve V-8025	(M)	**The Canadian Scene Via Phil Nimmons**	1961	6.00	20.00
Verve V-8376	(M)	**Nimmons 'n' Nine**	1961	6.00	20.00
		—Verve albums above have black labels with "MGM Records" on the bottom.—			

NISTICO, SAL

Salvadore Nistico is a modern jazz tenor saxophone player.

Label & Catalog #		Title	Year	VG+	NM
Jazzland JLP-66	(M)	**Heavyweights**	1962	16.00	40.00
Jazzland JLP-966	(S)	**Heavyweights**	1962	12.00	30.00
Riverside RLP-457	(M)	**Comin' On Up**	1963	16.00	40.00
Riverside RS-9457	(S)	**Comin' On Up**	1963	12.00	30.00
		—Riverside albums above have blue mono or black stereo labels with a reel & mike logo on top.—			

NOONE, JIMMIE

James Noone is a traditional jazz clarinet, alto and soprano saxophone player. For additional listings refer to Johnny Dodds / Jimmy Noone.

Label & Catalog #		Title	Year	VG+	NM
Brunswick BL-58006	(10")	**The Apex Club Orchestra**	1950	20.00	50.00

NORDINE, KEN

Ken Nordine's spoken word recordings are a surreal blend of jazz, beat amd '50s television commercials.

Label & Catalog #		Title	Year	VG+	NM
Decca DL-8550	(M)	**Concert In The Sky**	1957	30.00	75.00
Dot DLP-3075	(M)	**Word Jazz**	1957	20.00	50.00
Dot DLP-25075	(E)	**Word Jazz**	1957	12.00	30.00
Dot DLP-3096	(M)	**Son Of Word Jazz**	1958	16.00	40.00
Dot DLP-25096	(S)	**Son Of Word Jazz**	1958	20.00	50.00
Dot DLP-3115	(M)	**Love Words**	1958	12.00	30.00
Dot DLP-25115	(S)	**Love Words**	1958	16.00	40.00
Dot DLP-3142	(M)	**My Baby**	1958	12.00	30.00
Dot DLP-25142	(S)	**My Baby**	1958	16.00	40.00
Dot DLP-3196	(M)	**Next!**	1959	12.00	30.00
Dot DLP-25196	(S)	**Next!**	1959	16.00	40.00
Dot DLP-3301	(M)	**Word Jazz, Volume 2**	1960	12.00	30.00
Dot DLP-25301	(S)	**Word Jazz, Volume 2**	1960	16.00	40.00
FM 304	(M)	**Passion In The Desert**	1963	12.00	30.00
FM 304	(S)	**Passion In The Desert**	1963	16.00	40.00
Hamilton HL-12102	(M)	**The Voice Of Love**	1964	6.00	15.00
Hamilton HS-12102	(S)	**The Voice Of Love**	1964	8.00	20.00
Philips PHM-200-224	(M)	**Colors**	1966	8.00	20.00
Philips PHS-600-224	(S)	**Colors**	1966	10.00	25.00
Philips PHM-200-258	(M)	**Ken Nordine Does Robert Shure's "Twink"**	1967	8.00	20.00
Philips PHS-600-258	(S)	**Ken Nordine Does Robert Shure's "Twink"**	1967	10.00	25.00
Dot DLP-25880	(S)	**Classic Collection—Best Of Word Jazz**	1968	6.00	15.00

NORVO, RED

Kenneth Norville, aka Red Norvo, is a traditional jazz vibraphone and piano player. For additional listings refer to Red Allen / Red Norvo; The Jazz Pickers; Jack Montrose; Charlie Parker, Dizzie Gillespie & Red Norvo; Art Pepper & Red Norvo; Mavis Rivers; George Shearing / Red Norvo; Dinah Shore & Red Norvo.

Label & Catalog #		Title	Year	VG+	NM
Discovery DL-3012	(10")	**Red Norvo Trio**	1950	50.00	125.00
Discovery DL-3018	(10")	**Red Norvo Trio**	1952	50.00	125.00

Label & Catalog #		Title	Year	VG+	NM
Discovery DL-4005	(M)	**Red Norvo Trio, Volume 1**	1951	50.00	125.00
Dial LP-903	(M)	**Fabulous Jazz Session**	1951	100.00	200.00
Commodore FL-20023	(10")	**Town Hall Concert, Volume 1**	1952	50.00	125.00
Commodore FL-20027	(10")	**Town Hall Concert, Volume 2**	1952	50.00	125.00
Decca DL-5501	(10")	**Dancing On The Ceiling**	1953	50.00	125.00
Fantasy 3-12	(10")	**Red Norvo Trio** *(Colored vinyl)*	1953	60.00	150.00
Fantasy 3-12	(10")	**Red Norvo Trio**	1953	40.00	100.00
Fantasy 3-19	(M)	**Red Norvo Trio** *(Dark red vinyl)*	1955	30.00	75.00
		(Although this has a 10" number, this was Fantasy's first 12" album.)			
Fantasy 3218	(M)	**Red Norvo With Strings** *(Dark red vinyl)*	1956	30.00	75.00
		(Fantasy 3218 also features Tal Farlow and Red Mitchell.)			
Fantasy 3244	(M)	**The Red Norvo Trios** *(Dark red vinyl)*	1957	30.00	75.00
		(Fantasy 3244 is a reissue of 12.)			
		— Fantasy albums above have red labels on dark red, non-flexible vinyl. —			
Fantasy 3-19	(M)	**Red Norvo Trio**	195?	16.00	40.00
Fantasy 3218	(M)	**Red Norvo With Strings**	195?	16.00	40.00
Fantasy 3244	(M)	**The Red Norvo Trios**	195?	16.00	40.00
		— Fantasy albums above have red labels on non-flexible vinyl. —			
EmArcy MG-26002	(10")	**Improvisation**	1954	50.00	125.00
"X" LXA-3034	(M)	**Red's Blue Room**	1955	60.00	150.00
Capitol T-616	(M)	**Classics In Jazz**	1955	30.00	75.00
Epic LN-3128	(M)	**Red Norvo And His All Stars**	1955	20.00	50.00
Rave 101	(M)	**Red Norvo Quintet**	1956	30.00	75.00
Savoy MG-12088	(M)	**Move!**	1956	30.00	75.00
		(Savoy 12088 also features Tal Farlow and Charles Mingus.)			
Savoy MG-12093	(M)	**Midnight On Cloud 69**	1956	30.00	75.00
		(Savoy 12093 also features George Shearing.)			
Liberty LJH-6012	(M)	**Vibe-rations In Hi-Fi**	1956	20.00	50.00
Liberty LRP-3035	(M)	**Ad Lib**	1957	20.00	50.00
Tampa TP-35	(M)	**Norvo Naturally** *(Colored vinyl)*	1957	40.00	100.00
Tampa TP-35	(M)	**Norvo Naturally**	1958	20.00	50.00
		(Tampa 35 is a reissue of Rave 101.)			
Contemporary C-3534	(M)	**Music To Listen To Red Norvo By**	1957	20.00	50.00
Stereo Records S-7009	(S)	**Music To Listen To Red Norvo By**	1958	18.00	45.00
Contemporary S-7009	(S)	**Music To Listen To Red Norvo By**	1959	16.00	40.00
		— Contemporary stereo albums have gold & black labels. —			
RCA Victor LPM-1420	(M)	**Hi Five**	1957	16.00	40.00
RCA Victor LPM-1449	(M)	**Some Of My Favorites**	1957	16.00	40.00
RCA Victor LSP-1711	(S)	**Red Norvo In Stereo**	1958	16.00	40.00
RCA Victor LPM-1729	(M)	**Red Plays The Blues**	1958	16.00	40.00
RCA Victor LSP-1729	(S)	**Red Plays The Blues**	1958	12.00	30.00
		— RCA albums above have black labels with "Long Play" or "Living Stereo" on the bottom. —			
Rondo-lette A-28	(M)	**Red Norvo Trio**	1958	10.00	25.00
Dot DLP-3126	(M)	**Windjammer City Style**	1958	16.00	40.00
Dot DLP-25126	(S)	**Windjammer City Style**	1958	12.00	30.00
Continental C-16005	(M)	**Mainstream Jazz**	1962	8.00	20.00
Continental CS-16005	(S)	**Mainstream Jazz**	1962	6.00	15.00
Charlie Parker PLP-833	(M)	**Pretty Is The Only Way To Fly**	1962	10.00	25.00
Charlie Parker PLP-833S	(S)	**Pretty Is The Only Way To Fly**	1962	10.00	25.00

NOTHING, CHARLIE

Charles Nothing (?) is a modern jazz-influenced saxophone player.

Takoma C-1015	(S)	**The Psychedelic Saxophone Of Charlie Nothing**	1967	16.00	40.00

NOW CREATIVE ARTS JAZZ ENSEMBLE, THE

Arhoolie 8002	(S)	**Now**	1969	6.00	15.00

NUBIN, KATI BELL

Vocalist Kati Bell is backed by a small jazz group featuring Dizzy Gillespie and Coleman Hawkins.

Verve MGV-8372	(M)	**Soul, Soul Searchin'**	1960	*Unreleased*	
Verve MGV-3004	(M)	**Soul, Soul Searchin'**	1960	30.00	75.00
Verve MGVS-6147	(S)	**Soul, Soul Searchin'**	1960	*Unreleased*	
		— Verve albums above have "Verve Records, Inc." on the bottom of the label. —			
Verve V-3004	(M)	**Soul, Soul Searchin'**	1961	16.00	40.00
Verve V6-3004	(S)	**Soul, Soul Searchin'**	1961	16.00	40.00
		— Verve albums above have black labels with "MGM Records" on the bottom. —			

Label & Catalog #		Title	Year	VG+	NM

NUTTY SQUIRRELS, THE

The Nutty Squirrels were a pair of beatnik rodents with their own cartoon TV show in the '50s. The music on this album was provided by a Don Elliott band featuring Cannonball Adderley, Bobby Jaspar, Hal McKusick, Sam Most, Romeo Penque and Sol Schlinger with Sacha Burland's vocals.

Columbia CL-1589	*(M)*	**Bird Watching**	*1961*	**12.00**	**30.00**
Columbia CS-8389	*(S)*	**Bird Watching**	*1961*	**16.00**	**40.00**

—Columbia albums above have six white on black "eye" logos on each label.—

Django Reinhardt by David Stone Martin.

O

O'DAY, ANITA

Anita Belle Colton, aka Anita O'Day, is a traditional jazz and big band vocalist. For additional listings refer to Gene Krupa; the Jazzy Soundtracks section under Verve.

Advance LSP-8	*(10")*	**Anita O'Day Specials**	*1951*	**100.00**	**200.00**
Coral CRL-56073	*(10")*	**Singin' And Swingin'**	*1953*	**60.00**	**150.00**
		(Coral 56073 is a reissue of Advance 8.)			
Clef MGC-130	*(10")*	**Anita O'Day Collates**	*1953*	**60.00**	**150.00**
Norgran MGN-30	*(10")*	**Songs By Anita O'Day**	*1954*	**60.00**	**150.00**
Norgran MGN-1049	*(M)*	**Anita O'Day**	*1955*	**50.00**	**125.00**
		(Norgran 1049 is a reissue of Clef 130 with cover art by David Stone Martin.)			
Norgran MGN-1057	*(M)*	**An Evening With Anita O'Day**	*1956*	**40.00**	**100.00**
		(Norgran 1057 is a reissue of 30.)			
Verve MGV-2000	*(M)*	**Anita**	*1956*	**30.00**	**75.00**
Verve MGV-2043	*(M)*	**Pick Yourself Up With Anita O'Day**	*1957*	**30.00**	**75.00**
Verve MGV-8140	*(M)*	**The Lady Is A Tramp**	*1957*	*Unreleased*	
Verve MGV-2049	*(M)*	**The Lady Is A Tramp**	*1957*	**24.00**	**60.00**
		(Verve 2049 is a reissue of Norgran 1049.)			
Verve MGV-8147	*(M)*	**An Evening With Anita O'Day**	*1957*	*Unreleased*	
Verve MGV-2050	*(M)*	**An Evening With Anita O'Day**	*1957*	**24.00**	**60.00**
		(Verve 2050 is a reissue of Norgran 1057.)			
Verve MGV-2086	*(M)*	**'S Wonderful**	*1957*	*Unreleased*	
American Rec. Soc. G-426	*(M)*	**For Oscar**	*1957*	**16.00**	**40.00**
Verve MGV-2113	*(M)*	**Anita O'Day At Mr. Kelly's**	*1958*	**20.00**	**50.00**
Verve MGVS-6043	*(S)*	**Anita O'Day At Mr. Kelly's**	*1960*	**24.00**	**60.00**
Verve MGV-2118	*(M)*	**Anita O'Day Swings Cole Porter**	*1959*	**20.00**	**50.00**
Verve MGVS-6059	*(S)*	**Anita O'Day Swings Cole Porter**	*1960*	**24.00**	**60.00**
Verve MGV-2141	*(M)*	**Anita O'Day And Billy May Swing Rodgers And Hart**	*1960*	**24.00**	**60.00**
Verve MGV-2145	*(M)*	**Waiter, Make Mine Blues**	*1960*	**24.00**	**60.00**
Verve MGV-2154	*(M)*	**I Remember Billie Holiday**	*1960*	*Unreleased*	
Verve MGV-2157	*(M)*	**Trav'lin' Light**	*1960*	**20.00**	**50.00**
Verve MGV-8259	*(M)*	**Anita Sings The Most**	*1958*	**20.00**	**50.00**
Verve MGV-8283	*(M)*	**Anita O'Day Sings The Winners**	*1958*	**20.00**	**50.00**
Verve MGVS-6002	*(S)*	**Anita O'Day Sings The Winners**	*1960*	**24.00**	**60.00**
Verve MGV-8312	*(M)*	**Cool Heat—Anita O'Day Sings Jimmy Giuffre Arrangements**	*1959*	**20.00**	**50.00**
Verve MGVS-6046	*(S)*	**Cool Heat—Anita O'Day Sings Jimmy Giuffre Arrangements**	*1960*	**24.00**	**60.00**
		—Verve albums above have "Verve Records, Inc." on the bottom of the label.—			
Verve V-2000	*(M)*	**Anita**	*1961*	**8.00**	**20.00**
Verve V-2043	*(M)*	**Pick Yourself Up With Anita O'Day**	*1961*	**8.00**	**20.00**
Verve V-2049	*(M)*	**The Lady Is A Tramp**	*1961*	**8.00**	**20.00**
Verve V-2050	*(M)*	**An Evening With Anita O'Day**	*1961*	**8.00**	**20.00**
Verve V-2113	*(M)*	**Anita O'Day At Mr. Kelly's**	*1961*	**8.00**	**20.00**
Verve V6-2113	*(S)*	**Anita O'Day At Mr. Kelly's**	*1961*	**10.00**	**25.00**
Verve V-2118	*(M)*	**Anita O'Day Swings Cole Porter**	*1961*	**0.00**	**20.00**
Verve V6-2118	*(S)*	**Anita O'Day Swings Cole Porter**	*1961*	**10.00**	**25.00**
Verve V-2141	*(M)*	**Anita O'Day And Billy May Swing Rodgers And Hart**	*1961*	**8.00**	**20.00**
Verve V6-2141	*(S)*	**Anita O'Day And Billy May Swing Rodgers And Hart**	*1961*	**10.00**	**25.00**
Verve V-2145	*(M)*	**Waiter, Make Mine Blues**	*1961*	**8.00**	**20.00**
Verve V6-2145	*(S)*	**Waiter, Make Mine Blues**	*1961*	**10.00**	**25.00**
Verve V-2157	*(M)*	**Trav'lin' Light**	*1961*	**8.00**	**20.00**
Verve V6-2157	*(S)*	**Trav'lin' Light**	*1961*	**10.00**	**25.00**
Verve V-8259	*(M)*	**Anita Sings The Most**	*1961*	**8.00**	**20.00**
Verve V-8283	*(M)*	**Anita O'Day Sings The Winners**	*1961*	**10.00**	**25.00**
Verve V6-8283	*(S)*	**Anita O'Day Sings The Winners**	*1961*	**12.00**	**30.00**

Label & Catalog #		Title	Year	VG+	NM
Verve V-8312	(M)	**Cool Heat—Anita O'Day Sings Jimmy Giuffre Arrangements**	1961	8.00	20.00
Verve V6-8312	(S)	**Cool Heat—Anita O'Day Sings Jimmy Giuffre Arrangements**	1961	10.00	25.00
Verve V-8442	(M)	**All The Sad Young Men**	1962	12.00	30.00
Verve V6-8442	(S)	**All The Sad Young Men**	1962	16.00	40.00
Verve V-8472	(M)	**Time For Two**	1962	12.00	30.00
Verve V6-8472	(S)	**Time For Two**	1962	16.00	40.00
		(Verve 8472 also features Cal Tjader.)			
Verve V-8483	(M)	**This Is Anita**	1962	12.00	30.00
Verve V6-8483	(E)	**This Is Anita**	1962	6.00	15.00
		(Verve 8483 is a reissue of 2000.)			
Verve V-8485	(M)	**Anita O'Day Sings The Winners**	1962	8.00	20.00
Verve 6-8485	(S)	**Anita O'Day Sings The Winners**	1962	10.00	25.00
		(Verve 8485 is a reissue of 8283.)			
Verve V-8514	(M)	**Anita O'Day & The Three Sounds**	1963	10.00	25.00
Verve V6-8514	(S)	**Anita O'Day & The Three Sounds**	1963	12.00	30.00
Verve V-8572	(M)	**Incomparable! Anita O'Day**	1964	10.00	25.00
Verve V6-8572	(S)	**Incomparable! Anita O'Day**	1964	12.00	30.00

—Verve albums above have black labels with "MGM Records" on the bottom.—

O'FARRILL, CHICO

Cuban born Arturo "Chico" O'Farrill is a Latin jazz composer and band leader.

Clef MGC-131	(10")	**Afro-Cuban**	1953	100.00	200.00
		(Clef 131 features cover art by David Stone Martin.)			
Clef MGC-132	(10")	**Chico O'Farrill Jazz**	1953	100.00	200.00
		(Clef 132 features cover art by David Stone Martin.)			
Norgran MGN-9	(10")	**The Second Afro-Cuban Jazz Suite**	1954	60.00	150.00
Norgran MGN-27	(10")	**Mambo Dance Sessions**	1954	30.00	75.00
Norgran MGN-28	(10")	**Latino Dance Sessions**	1954	30.00	75.00
Norgran MGN-31	(10")	**Chico O'Farrill**	1954	30.00	75.00
Clef MGC-699	(M)	**Chico O'Farrill Jazz**	1956	30.00	75.00
		(Clef 699 is a reissue of 132 with the DSM cover.)			
Verve MGV-2003	(M)	**Mambo/Latino Dances**	1956	20.00	50.00
		(Verve 2003 is a reissue of Norgran 27 and 28.)			
Verve MGV-2024	(M)	**Music From South America**	1956	20.00	50.00
Verve MGV-8083	(M)	**Jazz North Of The Border And South Of The Border**	1957	20.00	50.00
		(Verve 8083 is a reissue of Clef 699.)			

—Verve albums above have "Verve Records, Inc." on the bottom of the label.—

Verve V-2003	(M)	**Mambo/Latino Dances**	1961	8.00	20.00
Verve V-2024	(M)	**Music From South America**	1961	8.00	20.00
Verve V-8083	(M)	**Jazz North Of The Border And South Of The Border**	1961	8.00	20.00

—Verve albums above have black labels with "MGM Records" on the bottom.—

ODETTA

Odetta Felious Gordon is a blues-based folk singer; her sole jazz outing features backing by Abdul Ahmed-Malik, Buck Clayton and Vic Dickerson.

Riverside RLP-417	(M)	**Odetta And The Blues**	1962	10.00	25.00
Riverside RS-9417	(S)	**Odetta And The Blues**	1962	12.00	30.00

—Riverside albums above have blue mono or black stereo labels with a reel & mike logo on top.—

OLAY, RUTH

Ruth Olay is a modern jazz-based vocalist.

EmArcy MG-36125	(M)	**Olay! The New Sound Of Ruth Olay**	1958	20.00	50.00

—EmArcy albums above have blue labels with silver print.—

Mercury MG-20390	(M)	**Easy Living**	1959	16.00	40.00
Mercury SR-60069	(S)	**Easy Living**	1959	20.00	50.00

—Mercury albums above have black labels with silver print.—

United Arts. UAL-3115	(M)	**Ruth Olay In Person**	1960	12.00	30.00
United Arts. UAS-4115	(S)	**Ruth Olay In Person**	1960	16.00	40.00
ABC-Paramount ABC-???	(M)	**Soul In The Night**	196?	10.00	25.00
ABC-Paramount ABCS-???	(S)	**Soul In The Night**	196?	12.00	30.00
Everest LPBR-5218	(M)	**Olay! OK**	1963	10.00	25.00
Everest SDBR-1218	(S)	**Olay! OK**	1963	12.00	30.00

Label & Catalog #		Title	Year	VG+	NM

OLIPHANT, GRASELLA

Atlantic 1438	(M)	**The Grass Roots**	1965	8.00	20.00
Atlantic SD-1438	(S)	**The Grass Roots**	1965	6.00	15.00

OLIVER, KING

Joseph "King" Oliver, aka "Papa Joe," is a traditional jazz cornet player and composer. For additional listings refer to Louis Armstrong.

Brunswick BL-58020	(10")	**King Oliver**	1950	50.00	125.00
Riverside RLP-1007	(10")	**King Oliver Plays The Blues**	1953	30.00	75.00
"X" LVA-3018	(10")	**King Oliver's Uptown Jazz**	1954	30.00	75.00
Epic LN-3208	(M)	**King Oliver Featuring Louis Armstrong**	1956	20.00	50.00
Epic LA-16003	(M)	**King Oliver And His Orchestra**	1960	12.00	30.00
Epic BA-17003	(S)	**King Oliver And His Orchestra**	1960	10.00	25.00
RCA Victor LPV-529	(M)	**King Oliver In New York**	1965	8.00	20.00

ORCHESTRA U.S.A.

Orchestra U.S.A. features John Lewis with Eric Dolphy, Gary McFarland, Zoot Sims and Phil Woods.

Columbia CL-2247	(M)	**Jazz Journey**	1963	12.00	30.00
Columbia CS-9047	(S)	**Jazz Journey**	1963	10.00	25.00

—Columbia albums above have "Guaranteed High Fidelity" or "360 Sound Stereo" in black on the label.—

Colpix CP-448	(M)	**Orchestra U.S.A. Debut**	1964	12.00	30.00
Colpix SCP-448	(S)	**Orchestra U.S.A. Debut**	1964	16.00	40.00
RCA Victor LPM-3498	(M)	**The Sextet Of Orchestra U.S.A.**	1965	10.00	25.00
RCA Victor LSP-3498	(S)	**The Sextet Of Orchestra U.S.A.**	1965	8.00	20.00

—RCA albums above have black labels with "Mono" or "Stereo" on the bottom.—

ORIGINAL DIXIELAND JASS BAND, THE

"X" LX-3007	(M)	**The Original Dixieland Jass Band**	1954	20.00	50.00
RCA Victor LPV-547	(M)	**The Original Dixieland Jass Band**	1965	8.00	20.00

ORTEGA, ANTHONY

Anthony Ortega is a West Coast jazz alto saxophone and clarinet player. For additional listings refer to Nat Pierce.

Vantage VLP-2	(10")	**Anthony Ortega**	1954	50.00	125.00
Herald HLP-0101	(M)	**A Man And His Horn**	1956	20.00	50.00
Bethlehem BCP-79	(M)	**Jazz For Young Moderns**	1957	20.00	50.00
Revelation REV-M3	(M)	**New Dance**	1968	10.00	25.00
Revelation REV-3	(S)	**New Dance**	1968	8.00	20.00

ORTEGA-DOMANICO-WEST-GOODWIN

Revelation REV-7	(S)	**Permutations**	1969	8.00	20.00

ORTEGA, FRANKIE

Frank Ortega is a jazz-based pianist.

Jubilee JLP-1106	(M)	**77 Sunset Strip**	1959	10.00	25.00
Jubilee JGS-1106	(S)	**77 Sunset Strip**	1959	12.00	30.00

(Jazz-oriented interpretations of the TV show's themes.)

ORY, KID

Edward "Kid" Ory is a traditional jazz trombone, string bass, cornet and alto saxophone player and vocalist. For additional listings refer to Red Allen & Kid Ory; Johnny Dodds & Kid Ory.

Columbia CL-6145	(10")	**Kid Ory & His Creole Dixieland Band**	1950	30.00	75.00
Columbia CL-835	(M)	**Kid Ory**	1955	20.00	50.00

—Columbia albums above have six eye logos on the label.—

Good Time Jazz L-21	(10")	**Kid Ory's Creole Jazz Band, 1953**	1954	20.00	50.00
Good Time Jazz LTJ-12004	(M)	**Kid Ory's Creole Jazz Band, 1954**	1954	16.00	40.00
Good Time Jazz L-12008	(M)	**Kid Ory's Creole Jazz Band, 1955**	1955	16.00	40.00
Good Time Jazz L-12016	(M)	**The Legendary Kid**	1955	16.00	40.00
Good Time Jazz L-12022	(M)	**Kid Ory's Creole Jazz Band, 1944-45**	1955	16.00	40.00
Good Time Jazz L-12041/2	(M)	**Kid Ory's Favorites!**	195?	16.00	40.00
Good Time Jazz S-10041/2	(S)	**Kid Ory's Favorites!**	195?	12.00	30.00
Good Time Jazz M-12045	(M)	**This Kid's The Greatest!**	195?	16.00	40.00
Verve MGV-1014	(M)	**Song Of The Wanderer**	1957	20.00	50.00
Verve MGVS-6011	(S)	**Song Of The Wanderer**	1960	16.00	40.00
Verve MGV-1016	(M)	**The Kid From New Orleans**	1957	20.00	50.00
Verve MGV-1017	(M)	**Kid Ory Plays W.C. Handy**	1957	20.00	50.00
Verve MGVS-6061	(S)	**Kid Ory Plays W.C. Handy**	1960	16.00	40.00

(Verve 1017 features cover art by David Stone Martin.)

Label & Catalog #		Title	Year	VG+	NM
Verve MGV-1022	*(M)*	**Dance With Kid Ory or Just Listen**	*1957*	**20.00**	**50.00**
Verve MGVS-6125	*(S)*	**Dance With Kid Ory or Just Listen**	*1960*	**16.00**	**40.00**
		(Verve 1022 features cover art by David Stone Martin.)			
Verve MGV-1023	*(M)*	**The Original Jazz**	*1957*	**20.00**	**50.00**
Verve MGVS-6126	*(S)*	**The Original Jazz**	*1960*	*Unreleased*	
Verve MGV-1026	*(M)*	**Dixieland Marching Songs**	*1957*	**20.00**	**50.00**
Verve MGV-1030	*(M)*	**Kid Ory Sings French Traditional Songs**	*1957*	*Unreleased*	
Verve MGV-8254	*(M)*	**Kid Ory In Europe**	*1958*	**20.00**	**50.00**
		— Verve albums above have "Verve Records, Inc." on the bottom of the label.—			
Verve V-1014	*(M)*	**Song Of The Wanderer**	*1961*	**8.00**	**20.00**
Verve V6-1014	*(S)*	**Song Of The Wanderer**	*1961*	**6.00**	**15.00**
Verve V-1016	*(M)*	**The Kid From New Orleans**	*1961*	**8.00**	**20.00**
Verve V-1017	*(M)*	**Kid Ory Plays W.C. Handy**	*1961*	**8.00**	**20.00**
Verve V6-1017	*(S)*	**Kid Ory Plays W.C. Handy**	*1961*	**6.00**	**15.00**
Verve V-1022	*(M)*	**Dance With Kid Ory or Just Listen**	*1961*	**8.00**	**20.00**
Verve V6-1022	*(S)*	**Dance With Kid Ory or Just Listen**	*1961*	**6.00**	**15.00**
Verve V-1023	*(M)*	**The Original Jazz**	*1961*	**8.00**	**20.00**
Verve V6-1023	*(S)*	**The Original Jazz**	*1961*	**6.00**	**15.00**
Verve V-1026	*(M)*	**Dixieland Marching Songs**	*1961*	**8.00**	**20.00**
Verve V6-1026	*(S)*	**Dixieland Marching Songs**	*1961*	**6.00**	**15.00**
Verve V-8254	*(M)*	**Kid Ory In Europe**	*1961*	**8.00**	**20.00**
		— Verve albums above have black labels with "MGM Records" on the bottom.—			
Verve V-8456	*(M)*	**Storyville Nights**	*1962*	**10.00**	**25.00**
Verve V6-8456	*(S)*	**Storyville Nights**	*1962*	**8.00**	**20.00**
		— Verve albums above have silver on black labels.—			

KID ORY / JOHNNY WITTWER

Jazz Man LP-2	*(10")*	**Kid Ory's Creole Band/Johnny Wittwer Trio**	*1954*	**20.00**	**50.00**

OSBORNE, MARY

Mary Osborne is a modern jazz-based guitarist and vocalist.

Warwick W-2004	*(M)*	**A Girl And Her Guitar**	*1960*	**50.00**	**125.00**
Warwick W-2004ST	*(S)*	**A Girl And Her Guitar**	*1960*	**40.00**	**100.00**

OSTERWALD, HAZY

Bally BAL-12004	*(M)*	**Swiss Jazz**	*1956*	**16.00**	**40.00**

OUSLEY, HAROLD

Harold Ousley is a modern jazz tenor saxophone player.

Bethlehem BCP-6059	*(M)*	**Tenor Sax**	*1961*	**12.00**	**30.00**
Bethlehem SBCP-6059	*(S)*	**Tenor Sax**	*1961*	**12.00**	**30.00**

OVERTON, HALL: ***Refer to*** **DUKE JORDAN / HALL OVERTON; DAVE McKENNA & HALL OVERTON; JIMMY RANEY**

P.

PACE, JOHNNY
John Pace is a modern jazz vocalist.

Riverside RLP-12-292	(M)	**Chet Baker Introduces Johnny Pace**	1958	20.00	50.00
Riverside RLP-1130	(S)	**Chet Baker Introduces Johnny Pace**	1959	20.00	50.00

—Riverside albums above have blue mono or black stereo labels with a reel & mike logo on top.—

PACHECO, MIKE
Michael Pacheco is a jazz-based bongos player.

Tampa TP-10	(M)	**Bongo Skins** *(Colored vinyl)*	1957	40.00	100.00
Tampa TP-10	(M)	**Bongo Skins**	1958	20.00	50.00
Tampa TP-21	(M)	**Bongo Session** *(Colored vinyl)*	1957	40.00	100.00
Tampa TP-21	(M)	**Bongo Session**	1958	20.00	50.00
Tampa TP-30	(M)	**Bongo Date** *(Colored vinyl)*	1957	40.00	100.00
Tampa TP-30	(M)	**Bongo Date**	1958	20.00	50.00
Interlude MO-513	(M)	**Hot Skins**	1959	16.00	40.00
Interlude ST-1013	(S)	**Hot Skins**	1959	12.00	30.00

(Interlude 513 reissues Tampa material.)

PAGE, HOT LIPS
Oran "Hot Lips" Page is a traditional jazz trumpet and mellophone player and vocalist.

Continental 16007	(M)	**Hot And Cozy**	1962	12.00	30.00

(Continental 16007 also features Cozy Cole.)

PAGE, PATTI
Pop singer Patti Page is backed by Pete Rugolo's orchestra on these three jazzy outings.

EmArcy MG-36074	(M)	**In The Land Of Hi-Fi**	1956	20.00	50.00
EmArcy MG-36116	(M)	**The East Side**	1957	20.00	50.00
EmArcy MG-36136	(M)	**The West Side**	1958	20.00	50.00

—EmArcy albums above have silver on blue labels.—

PAICH, MARTY
Martin Paich is a West Coast jazz pianist, arranger and band leader. His groups usually featured Art Pepper. For additional listings refer to Ethel Azama; Jesse Belvin; Russ Garcia / Marty Paich; Toni Harper; Joannie Sommers; Mel Torme.

Gene Norman GNP-10	(10")	**Marty Paich Octet** *(Red vinyl)*	1955	50.00	125.00
Gene Norman GNP-21	(M)	**Marty Paich Octet**	1956	30.00	75.00
		(Gene Norman 21 is a reissue of 10 plus four tracks.)			
Bethlehem BCP-44	(M)	**Jazz City Workshop**	1956	30.00	75.00
Tampa TP-23	(M)	**Jazz For Relaxation** *(Colored vinyl)*	1957	100.00	200.00
Tampa TP-23	(M)	**Jazz For Relaxation**	1958	40.00	100.00
Tampa TP-28	(M)	**Marty Paich Quintet Featuring Art Pepper** *(Colored vinyl)*	1957	250.00	500.00
Tampa TP-28	(M)	**Marty Paich Quintet Featuring Art Pepper**	1958	100.00	200.00
Mode LP-105	(M)	**Marty Paich Trio**	1957	30.00	75.00
Mode LP-110	(M)	**Jazz Band Ball**	1957	30.00	75.00
Cadence CLP-3010	(M)	**Marty Paich Big Band**	1958	20.00	50.00
Warner Bros. W-1296	(M)	**The Broadway Bit**	1959	10.00	25.00
Warner Bros. WS-1296	(S)	**The Broadway Bit**	1959	8.00	20.00
Warner Bros. W-1349	(M)	**I Get A Boot Out Of You**	1959	10.00	25.00
Warner Bros. WS-1349	(S)	**I Get A Boot Out Of You**	1959	8.00	20.00
Interlude MO-509	(M)	**Revel Without Pause**	1959	12.00	30.00
Interlude ST-1009	(S)	**Revel Without Pause**	1959	10.00	25.00
		(Interlude 509 is a reissue of Mode 110.)			
Interlude MO-514	(M)	**Like Wow—Jazz 1960**	1960	12.00	30.00
Interlude ST-1014	(S)	**Like Wow—Jazz 1960**	1960	10.00	25.00
		(Interlude 514 is a reissue of Tampa 28.)			
RCA Victor LPM-2164	(M)	**Piano Quartet**	1960	10.00	25.00
RCA Victor LSP-2164	(S)	**Piano Quartet**	1960	8.00	20.00
RCA Victor LPM-2259	(M)	**Piano Quartet**	1960	10.00	25.00
RCA Victor LSP-2259	(S)	**Piano Quartet**	1960	8.00	20.00

—RCA albums above have black labels with "Long Play" or "Living Stereo" on the bottom.—

Label & Catalog #		Title	Year	VG+	NM

PALMER, ROY

Roy Palmer is a traditional jazz trombone player.

Riverside RLP-1020	(10")	**Roy Palmer's State Street Ramblers**	1953	30.00	75.00

PARENTI, TONY

Anthony Parenti is a traditional jazz clarinet and saxophone(s) player.

Riverside RLP-12-205	(M)	**Ragtime**	1956	24.00	60.00
		—Riverside albums above blue on white labels.—			
Riverside RLP-12-205	(M)	**Ragtime**	195?	12.00	30.00
		—Riverside albums above have blue mono or black stereo labels with a reel & mike logo on top.—			
Jazzology JCE-1	(10")	**Tony Parenti & His New Orleanians**	1962	6.00	15.00
Jazzology J-1	(M)	**Tony Parenti**	1962	6.00	15.00
Jazzology J-21	(M)	**Ragtime Jubilee**	196?	6.00	15.00
Jazzology J-31	(M)	**Night At Jimmy Ryan's**	196?	6.00	15.00

PARENTI, TONY / THE DIXIELAND RHYTHM KINGS

Jazztone J-1273	(M)	**Two Beat Bash**	195?	16.00	40.00

PARHAM, TINY

Hartzell "Tiny" Parham is a traditional jazz piano and organ player, arranger and composer.

"X" LVA-3039	(10")	**Tiny Parham's South Side Jazz**	1955	20.00	50.00

PARIS, JACKIE

Jackie Paris is a jazz-based vocalist.

Coral CRL-56118	(10")	**That Paris Mood**	195?	30.00	75.00
EmArcy MG-36095	(M)	**Songs By Jackie Paris**	1956	40.00	100.00
		—EmArcy albums above have blue labels with silver print.—			
Wing WGW-60004	(M)	**Songs By Jackie Paris**	1956	30.00	75.00
		(Wing 60004 is a reissue of EmArcy 36095.)			
Brunswick BL-54019	(M)	**Skylark**	1957	40.00	100.00
East West 4002	(M)	**The Jackie Paris Sound**	1958	30.00	75.00
Time T-70009	(M)	**Jackie Paris Sings The Lyrics Of Ira Gershwin**	1959	16.00	40.00
Time ST-70009	(S)	**Jackie Paris Sings The Lyrics Of Ira Gershwin**	1959	20.00	50.00
Impulse A-17	(M)	**The Song Is Paris**	1962	16.00	40.00
Impulse AS-17	(S)	**The Song Is Paris**	1962	14.00	35.00
		—Impulse albums above have orange & black labels.—			
Impulse AS-17	(S)	**The Song Is Paris**	1968	4.00	10.00
		—Impulse albums above have red & black labels with the "abc" logo on top.—			

PARKER, CHARLIE

Charles Parker, aka "Yardbird" or "Bird," is a modern jazz alto saxophone player and composer. For additional listings refer to Stan Getz & Charlie Parker; Dizzy Gillespie; Woody Herman; Machito; The Quintet.

Dial LP-1	(M)	**The Bird Blows The Blues**	1949		See below
		(Dial LP-1 was sold through the mail via ads in trade publications. Rare with a suggested Near Mint vlaue of $3,000-6,000.)			
Dial LP-201	(10")	**Charlie Parker Quintet**	1949	500.00	750.00
Dial LP-202	(10")	**Charlie Parker Quintet**	1949	500.00	750.00
Dial LP-203	(10")	**Charlie Parker Quintet**	1949	500.00	750.00
Dial LP-207	(10")	**Charlie Parker Sextet**	1950	500.00	750.00
Dial LP-901	(M)	**The Bird Blows The Blues**	1950	300.00	500.00
		(Dial 901 is a reissue of 1.)			
Dial LP-904	(M)	**Alternate Masters**	1951	300.00	500.00
Dial LP-905	(M)	**Alternate Masters**	1951	300.00	500.00
Roost LP-2210	(M)	**All Star Sextet**	1958	40.00	100.00
		(Roost 2210 is a reissue of Dial material.)			
Roost LP-2257	(M)	**The World Of Charlie Parker**	1963	12.00	30.00
		(Roost 2257 is a reissue of Dial material.)			
Savoy MG-9000	(10")	**Charlie Parker, Volume 1**	1950	240.00	400.00
Savoy MG-9001	(10")	**Charlie Parker, Volume 2**	1951	240.00	400.00
Savoy MG-9010	(10")	**Charlie Parker, Volume 3**	1952	240.00	400.00
Savoy MG-9011	(10")	**Charlie Parker, Volume 4**	1952	240.00	400.00
Savoy MG-12000	(M)	**Charlie Parker Memorial, Volume 1**	1955	50.00	125.00
Savoy MG-12001	(M)	**The Immortal Charlie Parker**	1955	50.00	125.00
Savoy MG-12009	(M)	**Charlie Parker Memorial, Volume 2**	1955	50.00	125.00
		(Savoy 12009 is a reissue of 9001.)			
Savoy MG-12014	(M)	**The Genius Of Charlie Parker**	1955	50.00	125.00
		(Savoy 12014 is a reissue of 9000.)			

Label & Catalog #		Title	Year	VG+	NM
Savoy MG-12079	(M)	**The Charlie Parker Story**	1956	40.00	100.00
		(Savoy 12079 is a reissue of Savoy LP material.)			
Savoy MG-12152	(M)	**An Evening At Home With The Bird**	1959	16.00	40.00
Savoy MG-12179	(M)	**The 'Bird' Returns**	1962	12.00	30.00
Savoy MG-12186	(M)	**Newly Discovered Sides By The Immortal Charlie Parker**	1964	12.00	30.00
		—Savoy albums above have maroon labels.—			
Mercury MG-35010	(10")	**Charlie Parker With Strings**	1950	300.00	500.00
Mercury MGC-101	(10")	**Charlie Parker With Strings**	1950	300.00	500.00
		(Mercury 101 is a reissue of 35010.)			
Mercury MGC-109	(10")	**Charlie Parker With Strings, Volume 2**	1950	300.00	500.00
Mercury MGC-501	(10")	**Charlie Parker With Strings**	1951	300.00	500.00
		(Mercury 501 is a reissue of 101 with cover art by David Stone Martin.)			
Mercury MGC-509	(10")	**Charlie Parker With Strings, Volume 2**	1952	300.00	500.00
		(Mercury 509 is a reissue of 109 with cover art by David Stone Martin.)			
Mercury MGC-512	(10")	**Bird And Diz**	1952	300.00	500.00
		(Mercury 512 features cover art by David Stone Martin.)			
Mercury MGC-513	(10")	**South Of The Border**	1952	300.00	500.00
		(Mercury 513 features cover art by David Stone Martin.)			
Clef MGC-101	(10")	**Charlie Parker With Strings**	1958	*Unreleased*	
Clef MGC-501	(10")	**Charlie Parker With Strings**	1954	240.00	400.00
Clef MGC-509	(10")	**Charlie Parker With Strings, No. 2**	1954	240.00	400.00
Clef MGC-512	(10")	**Bird And Diz**	1954	240.00	400.00
Clef MGC-513	(10")	**South Of The Border**	1954	240.00	400.00
Clef MGC-157	(10")	**Charlie Parker**	1954	240.00	400.00
		(Clef 157 features cover art by David Stone Martin.)			
Clef MGC-609	(M)	**Charlie Parker Big Band**	1954	240.00	400.00
		(Clef 609 features cover art by David Stone Martin.)			
Clef MGC-646	(M)	**The Magnificent Charlie Parker**	1955	240.00	400.00
		(Clef 646 features cover art by David Stone Martin.)			
Clef MGC-675	(M)	**Charlie Parker With Strings**	1955	240.00	400.00
		(Clef 675 is a reissue of 501 and 509 with the DSM cover.)			
Clef MGC-725	(M)	**Night And Day**	1956	50.00	125.00
		(Clef 725 is a reissue of 609.)			
Clef MGC-733	(M)	**Yardbird**	1955	*Unreleased*	
Verve MGV-8000	(M)	**Charlie Parker Story, Volume 1**	1957	30.00	75.00
Verve MGV-8001	(M)	**Charlie Parker Story, Volume 2**	1957	30.00	75.00
Verve MGV-8002	(M)	**Charlie Parker Story, Volume 3**	1957	30.00	75.00
Verve MGV-8003	(M)	**The Genius Of Charlie Parker #1—Night And Day**	1957	30.00	75.00
		(Verve 8003 is a reissue of Clef 609.)			
Verve MGV-8004	(M)	**The Genius Of Charlie Parker #2—April In Paris**	1957	30.00	75.00
Verve MGV-8005	(M)	**The Genius Of Charlie Parker #3—Now's The Time**	1957	30.00	75.00
		(Verve 8005 is a reissue of Clef 157.)			
Verve MGV-8006	(M)	**The Genius Of Charlie Parker #4—Bird & Diz**	1957	30.00	75.00
		(Verve 8006 is a reissue of Clef 512.)			
Verve MGV-8007	(M)	**The Genius Of Charlie Parker #5—Charlie Parker Plays Cole Porter**	1957	30.00	75.00
Verve MGV-8008	(M)	**The Genius Of Charlie Parker #6—Fiesta**	1957	30.00	75.00
Verve MGV-8009	(M)	**The Genius Of Charlie Parker #7—Jazz Perennial**	1957	30.00	75.00
Verve MGV-8010	(M)	**The Genius Of Charlie Parker #8—S wedish Schnapps**	1957	30.00	75.00
Verve MGV-8100-3	(M)	**The Charlie Parker Story**	1957	50.00	125.00
		(Boxed three record set reissues Verve 8000-8002.)			
		—Verve albums above have black labels with "Verve Records, Inc." on the bottom.—			
Verve V-8000	(M)	**Charlie Parker Story, Volume 1**	1961	10.00	25.00
Verve V-8001	(M)	**Charlie Parker Story, Volume 2**	1961	10.00	25.00
Verve V-8002	(M)	**Charlie Parker Story, Volume 3**	1961	10.00	25.00
Verve V-8003	(M)	**The Genius Of Charlie Parker #1—Night And Day**	1961	10.00	25.00
Verve V-8004	(M)	**The Genius Of Charlie Parker #2—April In Paris**	1961	10.00	25.00
Verve V-8005	(M)	**The Genius Of Charlie Parker #3—Now's The Time**	1961	10.00	25.00
Verve V-8006	(M)	**The Genius Of Charlie Parker #4—Bird & Diz**	1961	10.00	25.00
Verve V-8007	(M)	**The Genius Of Charlie Parker #5—Charlie Parker Plays Cole Porter**	1961	10.00	25.00

Charlie Parker started as a professional under the aegis of Jay McShann, Lawrence Keys, and Harlan Leonard during 1937-39. Residing in New York, he played with groups led by Noble Sissle (1942) and Earl Hines (1943), then playing with Cootie Williams, Andy Kirk, and Billy Eckstine. He began recording in 1941 with McShann, again with Tiny Grimes in 1944 and then, in 1945, with Dizzy Gillespie he recorded the first real bebop sides. Established in New York's coterie of clubs on 52nd Street among musicians, Bird was damned by the critics. Taking to the more open minds of the West Coast, he took the new music to California in 1945. . . to more hostility. Aside from his own recordings, he was featured on albums by Stan Getz, Gillespie, and Machito, and as a member of The Quintet. He can also be found as a sideman on albums by McShann on Decca, Miles Davis on Prestige, and on several of Norman Granz' *Jam Session* and *the JATP* albums.

Label & Catalog #		Title	Year	VG+	NM
Verve V-8008	(M)	**The Genius Of Charlie Parker #6—Fiesta**	1961	10.00	25.00
Verve V-8009	(M)	**The Genius Of Charlie Parker #7— Jazz Perennial**	1961	10.00	25.00
Verve V-8010	(M)	**The Genius Of Charlie Parker #8— Swedish Schnapps**	1961	10.00	25.00
Verve V-8100-3	(M)	**The Charlie Parker Story** *(3 LPs)*	1961	20.00	50.00
Verve V-8409	(M)	**The Essential Charlie Parker**	1961	10.00	25.00
Verve V6-8787	(E)	**Bird Set**	1969	6.00	15.00
—Verve albums above have black labels with "MGM Records" on the bottom.—					
Vogue LAE-12002	M)	**Memorial Album**	1955	50.00	125.00
Concert Hall Jazz 1004	(10")	**The Fabulous Bird**	1955	20.00	50.00
Concert Hall Jazz 1017	(10")	**The Art Of Charlie Parker, Vol. 2**	1955	20.00	50.00
Jazztone J-1204	(M)	**Giants Of Modern Jazz**	1955	20.00	50.00
		(Jazztobe 1204 also features Dizzy Gillespie.)			
Jazztone J-1214	(M)	**The Fabulous Bird**	1955	20.00	50.00
Jazztone J-12??	(M)	**The Art Of Charlie Parker, Vol. 2**	1955	20.00	50.00
Jazztone J-1240	(M)	**The Saxes Of Stan Getz And Charlie Parker**	1957	20.00	50.00
		(The Concert Hall and Jazztone albums above repackage Dial material.)			
Birdland 425	(10")	**A Night At Carnegie Hall**	1956	150.00	300.00
Jazz Workshop JWS-500	(M)	**Bird At St. Nick's**	1958	50.00	125.00
Jazz Workshop JWS-501	(M)	**Bird On 52nd Street**	1958	50.00	125.00
Debut DEB-611	(M)	**Bird On 52nd Street**	196?	20.00	50.00
		(Debut 611 is a reissue of Jazz Workshop 501.)			
Les Jazz Cool 101	(M)	**Les Jazz Cool, Volume 1**	1960	20.00	50.00
Les Jazz Cool 102	(M)	**Les Jazz Cool, Volume 2**	1960	20.00	50.00
Les Jazz Cool 103	(M)	**Les Jazz Cool, Volume 3**	1960	20.00	50.00
Charlie Parker CP-2-502	(M)	**Live At Rockland Palace September 26, 1952** *(2 LPs)*	196?	20.00	50.00
Charlie Parker CP-513	(M)	**Charlie Parker Plus Strings**	196?	16.00	40.00
Charlie Parker PLP-401	(M)	**Bird Is Free**	1961	16.00	40.00
Charlie Parker PLP-404	(M)	**The Happy Bird**	1961	16.00	40.00
Charlie Parker PLP-406	(M)	**Charlie Parker**	1961	16.00	40.00
Charlie Parker PLP-407	(M)	**Bird Symbols**	1961	16.00	40.00
Charlie Parker PLP-408	(M)	**Once There Was Bird**	1961	16.00	40.00
Continental 16004	(M)	**Bird Lives**	1962	16.00	40.00
Baronet B-105	(M)	**A Handful Of Modern Jazz**	1962	8.00	20.00
Baronet BS-105	(E)	**A Handful Of Modern Jazz**	1962	3.00	7.50
		(Baronet 105 is a reissue of Jazztone 1204.)			
Baronet B-107	(M)	**The Early Bird**	1962	8.00	20.00
Baronet BS-107	(E)	**The Early Bird**	1962	3.00	7.50
Blue Ribbon 8011	(M)	**The Early Bird**	1962	8.00	20.00
Blue Ribbon 8011	(E)	**The Early Bird**	1962	3.00	7.50
Fantasy 6011	(M)	**Bird On 52nd Street**	1964	12.00	30.00
Fantasy 86011	(E)	**Bird On 52nd Street**	1964	4.00	10.00
		(Fantasy 6011 is a reissue of Jazz Workshop 501.)			
Fantasy 6012	(M)	**Bird At St. Nick's**	1964	12.00	30.00
Fantasy 86012	(E)	**Bird At St. Nick's**	1964	4.00	10.00
		(Fantasy 6012 is a reissue of Jazz Workshop 500.)			
Verve VSP-23	(M)	**Bird Wings**	1966	6.00	15.00
Verve VSPS-23	(E)	**Bird Wings**	1966	3.00	7.50
Archive Of Folk & Jazz 214	(E)	**Charlie Parker**	1969	4.00	10.00

PARKER, CHARLIE, & DIZZY GILLESPIE & RED NORVO

Dial LP-903	(M)	**Fabulous Jam Session**	1951	300.00	500.00

PARKER, CHARLIE, & DIZZY GILLESPIE & BUD POWELL & MAX ROACH

Savoy MG-9034	(10")	**Bird, Diz, Bud, Max**	1953	300.00	500.00

PARKER, JACY

Jacy Parker is a modern jazz pianist and vocalist.

Verve V-8424	(M)	**Spotlight On Jacy Parker**	1962	20.00	50.00
Verve V6-8424	(S)	**Spotlight On Jacy Parker**	1962	16.00	40.00
—Verve albums above have black labels with "MGM Records" on the bottom.—					

PARKER, KNOCKY

John "Knocky" Parker is a traditional jazz pianist.

Progressive PLP-1	(10")	**New Orleans Stomps**	1954	20.00	50.00
Audiophile AP-28	(M)	**Boogie Woogie Maxixe**	1956	20.00	50.00

Label & Catalog #		Title	Year	VG+	NM
PARKER, LEO					
Leo Parker is a modern jazz baritone saxophone player.					
Savoy MG-9009	(10")	**Leo Parker**	1952	125.00	250.00
Savoy MG-9018	(10")	**New Trends In Modern Music**	1952	125.00	250.00
Blue Note BLP-4087	(M)	**Let Me Tell You 'Bout It**	1961	30.00	75.00
Blue Note BST-84087	(S)	**Let Me Tell You 'Bout It**	1961	20.00	50.00
Blue Note BLP-4095	(M)	**Rollin' With Leo**	1961	Unreleased	
Blue Note BST-84095	(S)	**Rollin' With Leo**	1961	Unreleased	
—Blue Note albums above have blue on white labels with a 61st St, NYC address.—					
Blue Note BLP-4087	(M)	**Let Me Tell You 'Bout It**	1963	10.00	25.00
Blue Note BST-84087	(S)	**Let Me Tell You 'Bout It**	1963	8.00	20.00
—Blue Note albums above have blue on white labels with a New York, USA address.—					
Blue Note BST-84087	(S)	**Let Me Tell You 'Bout It**	196?	5.00	12.00
—Blue Note albums above have blue on white labels with "A Division of Liberty Records."—					
PARKINS, LeROY					
Bethlehem BCP-6047	(M)	**LeRoy Parkins And His Yazoo River Band**	1960	12.00	30.00
Bethlehem SBCP-6047	(S)	**LeRoy Parkins And His Yazoo River Band**	1960	12.00	30.00
PARLAN, HORACE					
Horace Parlan is a modern jazz pianist.					
Blue Note BLP-4028	(M)	**Movin' & Groovin'** *(Deep groove)*	1960	40.00	100.00
Blue Note BLP-4028	(M)	**Movin' & Groovin'**	1960	30.00	75.00
Blue Note BST-84028	(S)	**Movin' & Groovin'**	1960	20.00	50.00
Blue Note BLP-4037	(M)	**Us Three** *(Deep groove)*	1960	40.00	100.00
Blue Note BLP-4037	(M)	**Us Three**	1960	30.00	75.00
Blue Note BST-84037	(S)	**Us Three**	1960	20.00	50.00
		(Blue Note 4037 also features George Tucker and Al Harewood.)			
Blue Note BLP-4043	(M)	**Speakin' My Piece** *(Deep groove)*	1960	40.00	100.00
Blue Note BLP-4043	(M)	**Speakin' My Piece**	1960	30.00	75.00
Blue Note BST-84043	(S)	**Speakin' My Piece**	1960	20.00	50.00
Blue Note BLP-4062	(M)	**Headin' South**	1961	30.00	75.00
Blue Note BST-84062	(S)	**Headin' South**	1961	20.00	50.00
Blue Note BLP-4074	(M)	**On The Spur Of The Moment**	1961	100.00	200.00
Blue Note BST-84074	(S)	**On The Spur Of The Moment**	1961	60.00	150.00
—Blue Note albums above have blue on white labels with a W. 63rd Street, NYC address.—					
Blue Note BLP-4074	(M)	**On The Spur Of The Moment**	1961	30.00	75.00
Blue Note BST-84074	(S)	**On The Spur Of The Moment**	1961	20.00	50.00
Blue Note BLP-4082	(M)	**Up & Down**	1961	30.00	75.00
Blue Note BST-84082	(S)	**Up & Down**	1961	20.00	50.00
—Blue Note albums above have blue on white labels with a 61st St, NYC address.—					
Blue Note BLP-4028	(M)	**Movin' & Groovin'**	1963	10.00	25.00
Blue Note BST-84028	(S)	**Movin' & Groovin'**	1963	8.00	20.00
Blue Note BLP-4037	(M)	**Us Three**	1963	10.00	25.00
Blue Note BST-84037	(S)	**Us Three**	1963	8.00	20.00
Blue Note BLP-4043	(M)	**Speakin' My Piece**	1963	10.00	25.00
Blue Note BST-84043	(S)	**Speakin' My Piece**	1963	8.00	20.00
Blue Note BLP-4062	(M)	**Headin' South**	1963	10.00	25.00
Blue Note BST-84062	(S)	**Headin' South**	1963	8.00	20.00
Blue Note BLP-4074	(M)	**On The Spur Of The Moment**	1963	10.00	25.00
Blue Note BST-84074	(S)	**On The Spur Of The Moment**	1963	8.00	20.00
Blue Note BLP-4082	(M)	**Up & Down**	1963	10.00	25.00
Blue Note BST-84082	(S)	**Up & Down**	1963	8.00	20.00
—Blue Note albums above have blue on white labels with a New York, USA,address.—					
Blue Note BST-84028	(S)	**Movin' & Groovin'**	196?	5.00	12.00
Blue Note BST-84037	(S)	**Us Three**	196?	5.00	12.00
Blue Note BST-84043	(S)	**Speakin' My Piece**	196?	5.00	12.00
Blue Note BST-84062	(S)	**Headin' South**	196?	5.00	12.00
Blue Note BST-84074	(S)	**On The Spur Of The Moment**	196?	5.00	12.00
Blue Note BST-84082	(S)	**Up & Down**	196?	5.00	12.00
—Blue Note albums above have blue on white labels with "A Division of Liberty Records."—					
PASS, JOE					
Joseph Passalaqua, aka Joe Pass, is a modern jazz guitarist. For additional listings refer to Bud Shank.					
Pacific Jazz PJ-73	(M)	**Catch Me!**	1963	12.00	30.00
Pacific Jazz ST-73	(S)	**Catch Me!**	1963	10.00	25.00
Pacific Jazz PJ-85	(M)	**For Django**	1963	12.00	30.00
Pacific Jazz ST-85	(S)	**For Django**	1963	10.00	25.00

Label & Catalog #		Title	Year	VG+	NM
World Pacific WP-11844	(M)	**A Sign Of The Times**	1966	8.00	20.00
World Pacific ST-21844	(S)	**A Sign Of The Times**	1966	6.00	15.00
World Pacific WP-11854	(M)	**The Stones Jazz**	1967	10.00	25.00
World Pacific ST-21854	(S)	**The Stones Jazz**	1967	6.00	15.00
World Pacific WP-11865	(M)	**Simplicity**	1967	10.00	25.00
World Pacific ST-21865	(S)	**Simplicity**	1967	6.00	15.00

PASS, JOE, & ARNOLD ROSS

Pacific Jazz PJ-48	(M)	**Sounds Of Synanon**	1962	12.00	30.00
Pacific Jazz ST-48	(S)	**Sounds Of Synanon**	1962	10.00	25.00

PATE, JOHNNY

John Pate is a modern jazz bassist.

Talisman TLP-1	(10")	**Johnny Pate Trio**	1956	50.00	125.00
Gig GLP-100	(M)	**Subtle Sounds**	1956	40.00	100.00
Stepheny 4002	(M)	**Johnny Pate At The Blue Note**	1957	40.00	100.00
King 395-561	(M)	**Jazz Goes Ivy League**	1958	30.00	75.00
King 395-584	(M)	**Swingin' Flute**	1958	30.00	75.00
King 395-611	(M)	**A Date With Johnny Pate**	1959	30.00	75.00

—King albums above have silver on black labels.—

PATTERSON, DON

Donald Patterson is a modern jazz organ player. For additional listings refer to Sonny Stitt.

Prestige PRLP-7331	(M)	**The Exciting New Organ Of Don Patterson**	1964	12.00	30.00
Prestige PRST-7331	(S)	**The Exciting New Organ Of Don Patterson**	1964	10.00	25.00
Prestige PRLP-7349	(M)	**Hip Cake Walk**	1965	12.00	30.00
Prestige PRST-7349	(S)	**Hip Cake Walk**	1965	10.00	25.00
		(Prestige 7331 and 7349 also feature Booker Ervin.)			
Prestige PRLP-7381	(M)	**Patterson's People**	1965	12.00	30.00
Prestige PRST-7381	(S)	**Patterson's People**	1965	10.00	25.00
		(Prestige 7381 also features Booker Ervin and Sonny Stitt.)			
Prestige PRLP-7415	(M)	**Holiday Soul**	1966	12.00	30.00
Prestige PRST-7415	(S)	**Holiday Soul**	1966	10.00	25.00
Prestige PRLP-7430	(M)	**Satisfaction**	1966	12.00	30.00
Prestige PRST-7430	(S)	**Satisfaction**	1966	10.00	25.00
Prestige PRLP-7466	(M)	**The Boss Men**	1967	12.00	30.00
Prestige PRST-7466	(S)	**The Boss Men**	1967	10.00	25.00
		(Prestige 7466 also features Sonny Stitt.)			
Prestige PRLP-7484	(M)	**Soul Happening!**	1967	10.00	25.00
Prestige PRST-7484	(S)	**Soul Happening!**	1967	8.00	20.00
Prestige PRLP-7510	(M)	**Mellow Soul**	1967	10.00	25.00
Prestige PRST-7510	(S)	**Mellow Soul**	1967	8.00	20.00
		(Prestige 7510 also features David Newman.)			
Prestige PRLP-7533	(M)	**Four Dimensions**	1967	10.00	25.00
Prestige PRST-7533	(S)	**Four Dimensions**	1967	8.00	20.00

—Prestige albums above have blue labels with a trident logo on the right side.—

Prestige PRST-7563	(S)	**Boppin' And Burnin'**	1968	6.00	15.00
Prestige PRST-7577	(S)	**Opus De Don**	1968	6.00	15.00
Prestige PRST-7613	(S)	**Funk You**	1969	6.00	15.00
Prestige PRST-7640	(S)	**Oh, Happy Day!**	1969	6.00	15.00
Prestige PRST-7704	(S)	**The Best Of Don Patterson**	1969	6.00	15.00

—Prestige albums above have blue labels with a trident logo on top.—

PATTON, "BIG" JOHN

John Patton is a modern jazz organ player.

Blue Note BLP-4130	(M)	**Along Came John**	1963	16.00	40.00
Blue Note BST-84130	(S)	**Along Came John**	1963	12.00	30.00
Blue Note BLP-4143	(M)	**Blue John**	1963	*Unreleased*	
Blue Note BST-84143	(S)	**Blue John**	1963	*Unreleased*	
Blue Note BLP-4174	(M)	**The Way I Feel**	1964	12.00	30.00
Blue Note BST-84174	(S)	**The Way I Feel**	1964	10.00	25.00
Blue Note BLP-4192	(M)	**Oh Baby!**	1964	12.00	30.00
Blue Note BST-84192	(S)	**Oh Baby!**	1964	10.00	25.00
Blue Note BLP-4229	(M)	**Got A Good Thing Goin'**	1966	12.00	30.00
Blue Note BST-84229	(S)	**Got A Good Thing Goin'**	1966	10.00	25.00
Blue Note BLP-4239	(M)	**Let 'Em Roll**	1966	12.00	30.00
Blue Note BST-84239	(S)	**Let 'Em Roll**	1966	10.00	25.00

—Blue Note albums above have blue on white labels with a New York, NY address.—

Label & Catalog #		Title	Year	VG+	NM
Blue Note BST-84130	(S)	**Along Came John**	196?	5.00	12.00
Blue Note BST-84174	(S)	**The Way I Feel**	196?	5.00	12.00
Blue Note BST-84192	(S)	**Oh Baby!**	196?	5.00	12.00
Blue Note BST-84229	(S)	**Got A Good Thing Goin'**	196?	5.00	12.00
Blue Note BST-84239	(S)	**Let 'Em Roll**	196?	5.00	12.00
Blue Note BST-84281	(S)	**That Certain Feeling**	1968	10.00	25.00
Blue Note BST-84306	(S)	**Understanding**	1968	10.00	25.00
Blue Note BST-84340	(S)	**Accent On The Blues**	1969	10.00	25.00

— Blue Note albums above have blue on white labels with "A Division of Liberty Records."—

PAYNE, BENNIE

Benjamin Payne is a traditional jazz pianist and vocalist.

Kapp KL-1004	(M)	**Bennie Payne Plays And Sings**	1955	30.00	75.00

PAYNE, CECIL

Cecil Payne is a modern jazz baritone and alto sax player. For additional listings refer to Eandy Weston & Cecil Payne; the Jazzy Soundtracks section under Charlie Parker; and Various Artists sunder Signal.

Signal S-1203	(M)	**Cecil Payne Quintet & Quartet**	1955	100.00	200.00
Savoy MG-12147	(M)	**Patterns Of Jazz**	1959	30.00	75.00
		(Savoy 12147 is a reissue of Signal 1203.)			
Charlie Parker PLP-801	(M)	**Cecil Payne Performing Charlie Parker's Music**	1962	20.00	50.00
Charlie Parker PLP-801S	(S)	**Cecil Payne Performing Charlie Parker's Music**	1962	16.00	40.00
Charlie Parker PLP-506	(M)	**Shaw Nuff**	1962	12.00	30.00
Charlie Parker PLP-506S	(S)	**Shaw Nuff**	1962	10.00	25.00

PAYNE, FREDA

Rhythm 'n' blues-based pop vocalist Freda Payne's first album is a jazz outing.

Impulse A-53	(M)	**After The Lights Go Down**	1963	12.00	30.00
Impulse AS-53	(S)	**After The Lights Go Down**	1963	10.00	25.00
		—Impulse albums above have orange & black labels.—			
Impulse AS-53	(S)	**After The Lights Go Down**	1968	4.00	10.00

—Impulse albums above have red & black labels with the "abc" logo on top.—

PEARSON, DUKE

Columbus "Duke" Pearson Jr. is a modern jazz pianist.

Blue Note BLP-4022	(M)	**Profile—Duke Pearson** *(Deep groove)*	1959	50.00	125.00
Blue Note BLP-4022	(M)	**Profile—Duke Pearson**	1959	30.00	75.00
Blue Note BST-84022	(S)	**Profile—Duke Pearson**	1959	20.00	50.00
Blue Note BLP-4035	(M)	**Tender Feelin's** *(Deep groove)*	1960	50.00	125.00
Blue Note BLP-4035	(M)	**Tender Feelin's**	1960	30.00	75.00
Blue Note BST-84035	(S)	**Tender Feelin's**	1960	20.00	50.00
		—Blue Note albums above have blue on white labels with a W. 63rd St, NYC address.—			
Blue Note BLP-4022	(M)	**Profile—Duke Pearson**	1963	10.00	25.00
Blue Note BST-84022	(S)	**Profile—Duke Pearson**	1963	8.00	20.00
Blue Note BLP-4035	(M)	**Tender Feelin's**	1963	10.00	25.00
Blue Note BST-84035	(S)	**Tender Feelin's**	1963	8.00	20.00
Blue Note BLP-4191	(M)	**Wahoo!**	1965	12.00	30.00
Blue Note BST-84191	(S)	**Wahoo!**	1965	10.00	25.00
Blue Note BLP-4252	(M)	**Sweet Honey Bee**	1966	12.00	30.00
Blue Note BST-84252	(S)	**Sweet Honey Bee**	1966	10.00	25.00
		—Blue Note albums above have blue on white labels with a New York, NY address.—			
Blue Note BST-84022	(S)	**Profile:—Duke Pearson**	196?	5.00	12.00
Blue Note BST-84035	(S)	**Tender Feelin's**	196?	5.00	12.00
Blue Note BST-84191	(S)	**Wahoo!**	196?	5.00	12.00
Blue Note BST-84252	(S)	**Sweet Honey Bee**	196?	5.00	12.00
Blue Note BST-84267	(S)	**The Right Touch**	1968	10.00	25.00
Blue Note BST-84276	(S)	**Introducing Duke Pearson's Big Band**	1968	10.00	25.00
Blue Note BST-84293	(S)	**The Phantom**	1968	10.00	25.00
Blue Note BST-84308	(S)	**Now Hear This**	1969	10.00	25.00
Blue Note BST-84323	(S)	**Merry Ole Soul**	1969	10.00	25.00
		— Blue Note albums above have blue on white labels with "A Division of Liberty Records."—			
Jazztime 33-02	(M)	**Hush!**	1962	16.00	40.00

PECORA, SANTO

Santo Pecoraro, aka Santo Pecora, is a traditional jazz trombone player. For additional listings refer to Lu Watters / Santo Pecora.

Mercury MGC-123	(10")	**Dixieland Jazz Band**	1953	*Unreleased*	
		(Jackets of Mercury 123 apparently contain copies of Clef 123.)			

Label & Catalog #		Title	Year	VG+	NM
Clef MGC-123	(10")	**Santo Pecora Collates**	1953	40.00	100.00
		(Clef 123 features cover art by David Stone Martin.)			
Southland SLP-213	(M)	**Santo Pecora**	1955	20.00	50.00
Vik XLA-1081	(M)	**Dixieland Mardi Gras**	1957	20.00	50.00

PEIFFER, BERNARD

French born Bernard Peiffer is a modern jazz pianist and composer. For additional listings refer to Don Byas / Bernard Peiffer.

Norgran MGN-11	(10")	**Bernard Peiffer Et Son Trio**	1954	30.00	75.00
EmArcy MG-26036	(10")	**Le Most**	1954	30.00	75.00
EmArcy MG-36080	(M)	**Bernie's Tunes**	1956	20.00	50.00
		—EmArcy albums above have blue labels with silver print.—			
Decca DL-8626	(M)	**The Astounding Bernard Peiffer**	1958	20.00	50.00
Decca DL-9203	(M)	**Piano Ala Mood**	1958	16.00	40.00
Decca DL-79203	(S)	**Piano Ala Mood**	1958	12.00	30.00
Decca DL-9218	(M)	**The Pied Peiffer Of The Piano**	1959	16.00	40.00
Decca DL-79218	(S)	**The Pied Peiffer Of The Piano**	1959	12.00	30.00
Laurie LLP-1006	(M)	**Modern Jazz For People Who Like Original Music**	1960	12.00	30.00
Laurie LLPS-1006	(S)	**Modern Jazz For People Who Like Original Music**	1960	10.00	25.00
Laurie LLP-1008	(M)	**Cole Porter's "Can Can"**	1960	12.00	30.00
Laurie LLPS-1008	(S)	**Cole Porter's "Can Can"**	1960	10.00	25.00

PELL, DAVE

David Pell is a modern jazz saxophone(s) and clarinet player. For additional listings refer to Boots Brown; Les Brown; Scooby Doo; Lucy Ann Polk.

Trend TL-1003	(10")	**Dave Pell Plays Irving Berlin**	1953	50.00	125.00
Trend TL-1501	(M)	**Dave Pell Plays Rodgers & Hart**	1954	40.00	100.00
Atlantic 1216	(M)	**Jazz And Romantic Places**	1955	40.00	100.00
Atlantic 1249	(M)	**Love Story**	1956	30.00	75.00
		—Atlantic albums above have black mono or green stereo labels.—			
Atlantic 1216	(M)	**Jazz And Romantic Places**	1961	12.00	30.00
Atlantic 1249	(M)	**Love Story**	1961	12.00	30.00
		—Atlantic albums above have multi-color labels with a white fan logo.—			
RCA Victor LPM-1320	(M)	**Jazz Goes Dancing**	1956	20.00	50.00
RCA Victor LPM-1394	(M)	**Swingin' In The Ol' Corral**	1957	20.00	50.00
RCA Victor LPM-1524	(M)	**Pell Of A Time**	1957	20.00	50.00
RCA Victor LPM-1662	(M)	**Campus Hop**	1957	20.00	50.00
		—RCA albums above have black labels with "Long Play" on the bottom.—			
Kapp KL-1025	(M)	**Dave Pell Plays Rodgers & Hart**	1956	12.00	30.00
		(Kapp 1025 is a reissue of Trend 1501.)			
Kapp KL-1034	(M)	**Dave Pell Plays Burke & Van Heusen**	1956	16.00	40.00
Kapp KL-1036	(M)	**Dave Pell Plays Irving Berlin**	1957	16.00	40.00
		(Kapp 1036 is a reissue of Trend 1003.)			
Coral CRL-57248	(M)	**Swingin' School Songs**	1958	12.00	30.00
Coral CRL-757248	(S)	**Swingin' School Songs**	1958	10.00	25.00
Capitol T-925	(M)	**I Had The Craziest Dream**	1958	12.00	30.00
		—Capitol albums above have turquoise labels.—			
Capitol T-1309	(M)	**The Big Small Bands**	1960	10.00	25.00
Capitol ST-1309	(S)	**The Big Small Bands**	1960	8.00	20.00
Capitol T-1512	(M)	**Old South Wails**	1961	8.00	20.00
Capitol ST-1512	(S)	**Old South Wails**	1961	6.00	15.00
Capitol T-1687	(M)	**I Remember John Kirby**	1962	8.00	20.00
Capitol ST-1687	(S)	**I Remember John Kirby**	1962	6.00	15.00
Liberty LRP-3298	(M)	**Today's Hits In Jazz**	1961	8.00	20.00
Liberty LST-7298	(S)	**Today's Hits In Jazz**	1961	6.00	15.00
Liberty LRP-3321	(M)	**Jazz Voices In Video**	1963	8.00	20.00
Liberty LST-7321	(S)	**Jazz Voices In Video**	1963	6.00	15.00
PRI 3002	(M)	**Dave Pell Plays Harry James' Big Band Sounds**	196?	8.00	20.00
PRI 3003	(M)	**Dave Pell Plays Artie James' Big Band Sounds**	196?	8.00	20.00
PRI 3004	(M)	**Dave Pell Plays Benny Goodman's Big Band Sounds**	196?	8.00	20.00
PRI 3005	(M)	**Dave Pell Plays Lawrence Welk's Big Band Sounds**	196?	8.00	20.00
PRI 3006	(M)	**Dave Pell Plays Prez Prado's Big Band Sounds**	196?	8.00	20.00
PRI 3007	(M)	**Dave Pell Plays Duke Ellington's Big Band Sounds**	196?	8.00	20.00
PRI 3009	(M)	**Dave Pell Plays Mantovani's Big Band Sounds**	196?	8.00	20.00

Art Pepper began his career in Los Angeles in 1943 gigging with the bands of Gus Arnheim, Benny Carter, Lee Young, and Stan Kenton. After the war he was back with Kenton through 1952 before embarking on a series of solo projects. An important part of the West Coast jazz scene, he has recorded projects with Bill Perkins and Richie Kamuca; been a featured guest on albums by Chet Baker and Andre Previn; played as a member of Henry Mancini's combo and Marty Paich's Orchestra backing singers such as Ethel Azama, Heleyne Stewart and Mel Torme. As a sideman he can be found on LPs by Kenton on Capitol, Shorty Rogers and Capitol and RCA Victor, Ted Brown on Vanguard, John Graas on Mercury and Decca, Howard Lucraft on Decca, and Shelly Manne on Contemporary. Collectors should note the ludicrous attempt to cash in on the all but unknown sport of surfing on the Savoy album pictured here. . . Is this the first "surfing" album?

Label & Catalog #		Title	Year	VG+	NM
PRI 3010	(M)	**Dave Pell Plays The Dorsey Brothers' Big Band Sounds**	196?	8.00	20.00
PRI 3011	(M)	**Dave Pell Plays The Big Band Sounds**	196?	8.00	20.00
Liberty LST-7631	(S)	**Man-Ha-Man-Ha**	1969	4.00	10.00

PEPPER, ART

Arthur Pepper is a West Coast jazz alto and tenor saxophone and clarinet player. For additional listings refer to Ethel Azama; Chet Baker & Art Pepper; Toni Harper; Henry Mancini; Marty Paich; Bill Perkins, Art Pepper & Richie Kamuca; Andre Previn; Heleyne Stewart; and the Jazzy Soundtracks section under MGM and RCA Victor.

Label & Catalog #		Title	Year	VG+	NM
Discovery 3019	(10")	**Art Pepper Quartet**	1952	125.00	250.00
Discovery 3023	(10")	**Art Pepper Quintet**	1954	125.00	250.00
Savoy MG-12089	(M)	**Surf Ride**	1956	40.00	100.00
		(Savoy 12089 is a reissue of Discovery 3023.)			
Jazz: West JLP-10	(M)	**The Return Of Art Pepper**	1956	300.00	500.00
Intro 606	(M)	**Modern Art**	1957	300.00	500.00
Tampa TP-20	(M)	**Art Pepper Quartet** *(Colored vinyl)*	1957	100.00	200.00
Tampa TP-20	(M)	**Art Pepper Quartet**	1958	40.00	100.00
Tampa TS-1001	(S)	**Art Pepper Quartet**	1959	30.00	75.00
Score SLP-4030	(M)	**Modern Art**	1958	40.00	100.00
		(Score 4030 is a reissue of Intro 606.)			
Score SLP-4031	(M)	**The Art Pepper-Red Norvo Sextet**	1958	40.00	100.00
		(Score 4031 is a reissue of Intro 608, "Joe Morello Sextet.")			
Score SLP-4032	(M)	**The Return Of Art Pepper**	1958	40.00	100.00
		(Score 4032 is a reissue of Jazz: West 10.)			
Interlude 512	(M)	**Art Pepper Quartet**	1959	20.00	50.00
Interlude 1012	(S)	**Art Pepper Quartet**	1959	16.00	40.00
		(Interlude 512 is a reissue of Tampa 20.)			
Contemporary C-3532	(M)	**Art Pepper Meets The Rhythm Section**	1957	40.00	100.00
Stereo Records S-7018	(S)	**Art Pepper Meets The Rhythm Section**	1958	24.00	60.00
Contemporary S-7532	(S)	**Art Pepper Meets The Rhythm Section**	1959	20.00	50.00
Contemporary M-3568	(M)	**Art Pepper + Eleven: Modern Jazz Classics**	1959	30.00	75.00
Contemporary S-7568	(S)	**Art Pepper + Eleven: Modern Jazz Classics**	1959	20.00	50.00
Contemporary M-3573	(M)	**Gettin' Together!**	1960	24.00	60.00
Contemporary S-7573	(S)	**Gettin' Together!**	1960	20.00	50.00
Contemporary M-3602	(M)	**Smack Up!**	1961	20.00	50.00
Contemporary S-7602	(S)	**Smack Up!**	1961	16.00	40.00
Contemporary M-3607	(M)	**Intensity**	1963	16.00	40.00
Contemporary S-7607	(S)	**Intensity**	1963	12.00	30.00
Contemporary M-3630	(M)	**The Way It Was!**	1966	12.00	30.00
Contemporary S-7630	(S)	**The Way It Was!**	1966	10.00	25.00
		—Contemporary stereo albums have gold & black labels.—			
Pacific Jazz PJ-60	(M)	**The Artistry Of Pepper**	1962	16.00	40.00

PEPPER, ART / SHELLY MANNE

Label & Catalog #		Title	Year	VG+	NM
Charlie Parker PLP-836	(M)	**Pepper/Manne**	1963	12.00	30.00
Charlie Parker PLP-836S	(S)	**Pepper/Manne**	1963	10.00	25.00

PEPPER, ART / SONNY REDD

Red's name is spelled with one "d" on the Regent album and two on the Savoy.

Label & Catalog #		Title	Year	VG+	NM
Regent MG-6069	(M)	**Two Altos**	1959	20.00	50.00
		—EmArcy albums above have blue labels with silver print.—			
Savoy MG-12215	(M)	**Art Pepper—Sonny Redd**	1969	8.00	20.00
		(Savoy 12215 is a reissue of Regent 6069.)			

PERKINS, BILL

William Perkins is a West Coast jazz tenor saxophone player. For additional listings refer to Al Cohn & Rich Kamuca & Bill Perkins; The Five; John Lewis & Bill Perkins; Mavis Rivers.

Label & Catalog #		Title	Year	VG+	NM
Pacific Jazz PJ-1221	(M)	**The Bill Perkins Octet On Stage**	1956	40.00	100.00
World Pacific WP-1221	(M)	**The Bill Perkins Octet On Stage**	1958	30.00	75.00
Liberty LRP-3293	(M)	**Bossa Nova**	1963	10.00	25.00
Liberty LST-7293	(S)	**Bossa Nova**	1963	8.00	20.00
Riverside RS-3052	(S)	**Quietly There**	1969	10.00	25.00
		—Riverside albums above have black on brown labels.—			

PERKINS, BILL, & RICHIE KAMUCA

Label & Catalog #		Title	Year	VG+	NM
Liberty LRP-3051	(M)	**Tenors Head On**	1957	20.00	50.00

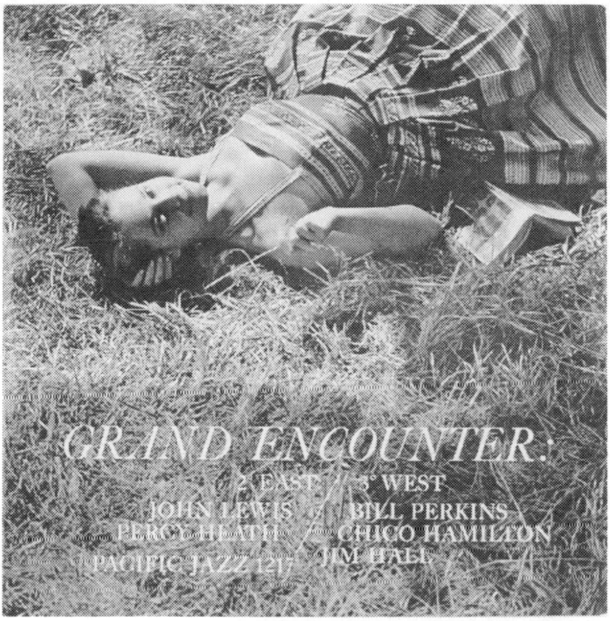

Bill Perkins started with Jerry Wald in 1950 and then played with Woody Herman, Stan Kenton, and Marty Paich (1952-59) before taking a gig as an engineer with World Pacific. Perkins can also be found as a sideman on albums by Paich on Tampa and Warner Bros. and backing vocalists Ethel Azama, Jessie Belvin, and Joannie Sommers, Herman on Capitol and Verve, Kenton on Capitol, Barney Kessel on Contemporary and Mercury, Lennie Niehaus on Contemporary and Mercury, Art Pepper on Contemporary, Bud Shank on World Pacific, Max Roach & Stan Levey on Liberty, and Tal Farlow on Verve. The two albums here illustrate some of the problems with assigning listings in a jazz discography: The Pacific Jazz album would appear to be a John Lewis effort, his name is first, when in fact it's another of owner Richard Bock's attempt to feature his star sax player in a novel setting. The album was eventually reissued credited to Lewis & Perkins, under whom it is listed in this book. The Liberty album has Perkins' name first but is also listed as a joint session (the album's title *is* plural).

Label & Catalog #		Title	Year	VG+	NM
PERKINS, BILL, & ART PEPPER & RICHIE KAMUCA					
Pacific Jazz PJM-401	*(M)*	**Just Friends**	*1956*	**50.00**	**125.00**
World Pacific PJM-401	*(M)*	**Just Friends**	*1958*	**30.00**	**75.00**
PERKINS, CARL					
Carl Perkins is a West Coast jazz pianist.					
Dootone DL-211	*(M)*	**Introducing Carl Perkins** *(Red vinyl)*	*1956*	**100.00**	**200.00**
Dootone DL-211	*(M)*	**Introducing Carl Perkins**	*1956*	**50.00**	**125.00**
PERSIP, CHARLIE					
Charles Persip is a modern jazz drummer. For additional listings refer to The Modern Jazz Sextet.					
Bethlehem BCP-6046	*(M)*	**Charlie Persip & The Jazz Statesmen**	*1960*	**16.00**	**40.00**
Bethlehem SBCP-6046	*(S)*	**Charlie Persip & The Jazz Statesmen**	*1960*	**16.00**	**40.00**
PERSON, HOUSTON					
Houston Person is a modern jazz tenor saxophone player.					
Prestige PRLP-7491	*(M)*	**Underground Soul**	*1967*	**10.00**	**25.00**
Prestige PRST-7491	*(S)*	**Underground Soul**	*1967*	**8.00**	**20.00**
		—Prestige albums above have blue labels with a trident logo on the right side.—			
PERSSON, AAKE / ARNE DOMNERUS					
Prestige PRLP-173	*(10")*	**Aake Persson Swedish All Stars**	*1953*	**125.00**	**250.00**
PERSSON, AAKE					
Swedish born Aake Persson is a modern jazz trombone player.					
EmArcy MG-26039	*(10")*	**Swedish Modern**	*1954*	**100.00**	**200.00**
PETERSON, OSCAR					
Oscar Peterson is a modern jazz pianist and band leader. For additional listings refer to Louis Armstrong; Fred Astaire; Benny Carter; Buddy DeFranco; Stan Getz; Coleman Hawkins; Bill Henderson; Sonny Stitt; Ben Webster; Lester Young; and the Various Artists section under Verve.					
RCA Victor LPT-3006	*(10")*	**This Is Oscar Peterson**	*1952*	**50.00**	**125.00**
Mercury MG-25024	*(10")*	**Oscar Peterson Piano Solos**	*1950*	**60.00**	**150.00**
Mercury MGC-106	*(10")*	**Oscar Peterson Piano Solos**	*1951*	**40.00**	**100.00**
		(Mercury 106 is a reissue of 25024 with cover by David Stone Martin.)			
Mercury MGC-107	*(10")*	**Oscar Peterson At Carnegie Hall**	*1951*	**40.00**	**100.00**
		(Mercury 107 features cover art by David Stone Martin.)			
Mercury MGC-110	*(10")*	**Oscar Peterson Collates**	*1952*	**40.00**	**100.00**
Mercury MGC-116	*(10")*	**The Oscar Peterson Quartet**	*1952*	**40.00**	**100.00**
Mercury MGC-119	*(10")*	**Oscar Peterson Plays Pretty**	*1952*	**40.00**	**100.00**
		(Mercury 119 features cover art by David Stone Martin.)			
Mercury MGC-603	*(M)*	**Oscar Peterson Plays Cole Porter**	*1953*	**30.00**	**75.00**
		(Mercury 603 features cover art by David Stone Martin.)			
Mercury MGC-604	*(M)*	**Oscar Peterson Plays Irving Berlin**	*1953*	**30.00**	**75.00**
		(Mercury 604 features cover art by David Stone Martin.)			
Mercury MGC-605	*(M)*	**Oscar Peterson Plays George Gershwin**	*1953*	**30.00**	**75.00**
		(Mercury 605 features cover art by David Stone Martin.)			
Mercury MGC-606	*(M)*	**Oscar Peterson Plays Duke Ellington**	*1953*	**30.00**	**75.00**
		(Mercury 606 features cover art by David Stone Martin.)			
Clef MGC-106	*(10")*	**Oscar Peterson Piano Solos**	*1953*	**30.00**	**75.00**
Clef MGC-107	*(10")*	**Oscar Peterson At Carnegie Hall**	*1953*	**30.00**	**75.00**
Clef MGC-110	*(10")*	**Oscar Peterson Collates**	*1953*	**30.00**	**75.00**
Clef MGC-116	*(10")*	**The Oscar Peterson Quartet**	*1953*	**30.00**	**75.00**
Clef MGC-119	*(10")*	**Oscar Peterson Plays Pretty**	*1953*	**30.00**	**75.00**
Clef MGC-127	*(10")*	**Oscar Peterson Collates No. 2**	*1953*	**30.00**	**75.00**
Clef MGC-145	*(10")*	**Oscar Peterson Sings**	*1954*	**30.00**	**75.00**
Clef MGC-155	*(10")*	**Oscar Peterson Plays Pretty No. 2**	*1954*	**30.00**	**75.00**
Clef MGC-168	*(10")*	**The Oscar Peterson Quartet No. 2**	*1954*	**30.00**	**75.00**
		(Clef 168 features cover art by David Stone Martin.)			
Clef MGC-603	*(M)*	**Oscar Peterson Plays Cole Porter**	*1953*	**20.00**	**50.00**
Clef MGC-604	*(M)*	**Oscar Peterson Plays Irving Berlin**	*1953*	**20.00**	**50.00**
Clef MGC-605	*(M)*	**Oscar Peterson Plays George Gershwin**	*1953*	**20.00**	**50.00**
Clef MGC-606	*(M)*	**Oscar Peterson Plays Duke Ellington**	*1953*	**20.00**	**50.00**
Clef MGC-623	*(M)*	**Oscar Peterson Plays Jerome Kern**	*1954*	**20.00**	**50.00**
		(Clef 623 features cover art by David Stone Martin.)			
Clef MGC-624	*(M)*	**Oscar Peterson Plays Richard Rogers**	*1954*	**20.00**	**50.00**
		(Clef 624 features cover art by David Stone Martin.)			

Label & Catalog #		Title	Year	VG+	NM
Clef MGC-625	(M)	**Oscar Peterson Plays Vincent Youmans**	1954	20.00	50.00
		(Clef 625 features cover art by David Stone Martin.)			
Clef MGC-648	(M)	**Oscar Peterson Plays Harry Warren**	1955	20.00	50.00
		(Clef 648 features cover art by David Stone Martin.)			
Clef MGC-649	(M)	**Oscar Peterson Plays Harold Arlen**	1955	20.00	50.00
		(Clef 649 features cover art by David Stone Martin.)			
Clef MGC-650	(M)	**Oscar Peterson Plays Jimmy McHugh**	1955	20.00	50.00
		(Clef 650 features cover art by David Stone Martin.)			
Clef MGC-688	(M)	**Oscar Peterson Quartet**	1956	20.00	50.00
		(Clef 688 is a reissue of 116 with cover art by David Stone Martin.)			
Clef MGC-694	(M)	**Recital By Oscar Peterson**	1956	20.00	50.00
Clef MGC-695	(M)	**Nostalgic Memories By Oscar Peterson**	1956	20.00	50.00
Clef MGC-696	(M)	**Tenderly—Music By Oscar Peterson**	1956	20.00	50.00
		(Clef 696 is a reissue of 106 and 127.)			
Clef MGC-697	(M)	**Keyboard—Music By Oscar Peterson**	1956	20.00	50.00
		(Clef 697 is a reissue of 110.)			
Clef MGC-698	(M)	**An Evening With Oscar Peterson Duo/Quartet**	1956	20.00	50.00
Clef MGC-708	(M)	**Oscar Peterson Plays Count Basie**	1956	20.00	50.00
Clef MGC-751	(M)	**The Oscar Peterson Trio At The Stratford Shakesperean Festival, Volume 1**	1955	*Unreleased*	
Clef MGC-752	(M)	**The Oscar Peterson Trio At The Stratford Shakesperean Festival, Volume 2**	1955	*Unreleased*	
Verve MGV-2002	(M)	**In A Romantic Mood— Oscar Peterson With Strings**	1956	16.00	40.00
Verve MGV-2004	(M)	**Pastel Moods By Oscar Peterson**	1956	16.00	40.00
		(Verve 2004 is a reissue of Clef 119.)			
Verve MGV-2012	(M)	**Romance—The Vocal Styling Of Oscar Peterson**	1956	16.00	40.00
		(Verve 2012 is a reissue of Clef 145.)			
Verve MGV-2044	(M)	**Recital By Oscar Peterson**	1957	16.00	40.00
		(Verve 2044 is a reissue of Clef 694.)			
Verve MGV-2045	(M)	**Nostalgic Memories By Oscar Peterson**	1957	16.00	40.00
		(Verve 2045 is a reissue of Clef 695.)			
Verve MGV-2046	(M)	**Tenderly—Music By Oscar Peterson**	1957	16.00	40.00
		(Verve 2046 is a reissue of Clef 696.)			
Verve MGV-2047	(M)	**Keyboard Music By Oscar Peterson**	1957	16.00	40.00
		(Verve 2047 is a reissue of Clef 697.)			
Verve MGV-2048	(M)	**An Evening With Oscar Peterson**	1957	16.00	40.00
		(Verve 2048 is a reissue of Clef 698.)			
Verve MGV-2052	(M)	**Oscar Peterson Plays The Cole Porter Songbook**	1957	16.00	40.00
Verve MGVS-6083	(S)	**Oscar Peterson Plays The Cole Porter Songbook**	1960	12.00	30.00
Verve MGV-2053	(M)	**Oscar Peterson Plays The Irving Berlin Songbook**	1957	16.00	40.00
Verve MGVS-6084	(S)	**Oscar Peterson Plays The Irving Berlin Songbook**	1960	12.00	30.00
Verve MGV-2054	(M)	**Oscar Peterson Plays The George Gershwin Songbook**	1957	16.00	40.00
Verve MGVS-6085	(S)	**Oscar Peterson Plays The George Gershwin Songbook**	1960	12.00	30.00
Verve MGV-2055	(M)	**Oscar Peterson Plays The Duke Ellington Songbook**	1957	16.00	40.00
Verve MGVS-6086	(S)	**Oscar Peterson Plays The Duke Ellington Songbook**	1960	12.00	30.00
Verve MGV-2056	(M)	**Oscar Peterson Plays The Jerome Kern Songbook**	1957	16.00	40.00
Verve MGVS-6087	(S)	**Oscar Peterson Plays The Jerome Kern Songbook**	1960	12.00	30.00
Verve MGV-2057	(M)	**Oscar Peterson Plays The Richard Rodgers Songbook**	1957	16.00	40.00
Verve MGVS-6088	(S)	**Oscar Peterson Plays The Richard Rodgers Songbook**	1960	12.00	30.00
Verve MGV-2058	(M)	**Oscar Peterson Plays The Vincent Youmans Songbook**	1957	*Unreleased*	
Verve MGVS-6089	(S)	**Oscar Peterson Plays The Vincent Youmans Songbook**	1960	*Unreleased*	

Label & Catalog #		Title	Year	VG+	NM
Verve MGV-2059	(M)	**Oscar Peterson Plays The Harry Warren Songbook**	1957	16.00	40.00
Verve MGVS-6090	(S)	**Oscar Peterson Plays The Harry Warren Songbook**	1960	12.00	30.00
Verve MGV-2060	(M)	**Oscar Peterson Plays The Harold Arlen Songbook**	1957	16.00	40.00
Verve MGVS-6091	(S)	**Oscar Peterson Plays The Harold Arlen Songbook**	1960	12.00	30.00
Verve MGV-2061	(M)	**Oscar Peterson Plays The Jimmy McHugh Songbook**	1957	16.00	40.00
Verve MGVS-6092	(S)	**Oscar Peterson Plays The Jimmy McHugh Songbook**	1960	12.00	30.00
Verve MGV-2079	(M)	**Soft Sands**	1957	16.00	40.00
Verve MGV-2119	(M)	**Oscar Peterson Plays "My Fair Lady"**	1958	16.00	40.00
Verve MGVS-6060	(S)	**Oscar Peterson Plays "My Fair Lady"**	1960	12.00	30.00
Verve MGV-2156	(M)	**The Oscar Peterson Trio With David Rose**	1958	*Unreleased*	
		—Verve albums above have "Verve Records, Inc." on the bottom of the label.—			
Verve MGV-8024	(M)	**The Oscar Peterson Trio At The Stratford Shakesperean Festival**	1957	16.00	40.00
Verve MGV-8072	(M)	**The Oscar Peterson Quartet No. 1**	1957	16.00	40.00
		(Verve 8072 is a reissue of Clef 688 with the DSM cover.)			
Verve MGV-8078	(M)	**Recital By Oscar Peterson**	1957	*Unreleased*	
Verve MGV-8079	(M)	**Nostalgic Memories By Oscar Peterson**	1957	*Unreleased*	
Verve MGV-8080	(M)	**Tenderly—Music By Oscar Peterson**	1957	*Unreleased*	
Verve MGV-8081	(M)	**Keyboard Music By Oscar Peterson**	1957	*Unreleased*	
Verve MGV-8082	(M)	**An Evening With Oscar Peterson**	1957	*Unreleased*	
Verve MGV-8092	(M)	**Oscar Peterson Plays Count Basie**	1957	16.00	40.00
		(Verve 8092 is a reissue of Clef 708.)			
Verve MGV-8239	(M)	**Oscar Peterson Trio With Sonny Stitt, Roy Eldridge And Jo Jones At Newport**	1958	16.00	40.00
Verve MGV-8268	(M)	**Oscar Peterson Trio At The Concertgebouw**	1958	16.00	40.00
Verve MGV-8269	(M)	**Oscar Peterson Trio With The Modern Jazz Quartet At The Opera House**	1958	16.00	40.00
Verve MGVS-6069	(S)	**Oscar Peterson Trio With The Modern Jazz Quartet At The Opera House**	1960	12.00	30.00
Verve MGV-8287	(M)	**A Night On The Town**	1958	16.00	40.00
Verve MGVS-6036	(S)	**A Night On The Town**	1960	*Unreleased*	
Verve MGV-8334	(M)	**Songs For A Swinging Affair—A Jazz Portrait Of Sinatra**	1959	16.00	40.00
Verve MGVS-6071	(S)	**Songs For A Swinging Affair—A Jazz Portrait Of Sinatra**	1960	12.00	30.00
Verve MGV-8340	(M)	**Porgy & Bess**	1959	16.00	40.00
Verve MGVS-6098	(S)	**Porgy & Bess**	1960	*Unreleased*	
Verve MGV-8351	(M)	**The Jazz Soul Of Oscar Peterson**	1959	16.00	40.00
Verve MGVS-6116	(S)	**The Jazz Soul Of Oscar Peterson**	1960	*Unreleased*	
Verve MGV-8364	(M)	**Swinging Brass With The Oscar Peterson Trio**	1959	16.00	40.00
Verve MGVS-6119	(S)	**Swinging Brass With The Oscar Peterson Trio**	1960	12.00	30.00
Verve MGV-8366	(M)	**The Music From "Fiorello!"**	1960	16.00	40.00
Verve MGVS-6134	(S)	**The Music From "Fiorello!"**	1960	*Unreleased*	
Verve MGV-8368	(M)	**The Oscar Peterson Trio At J.A.T.P.**	1960	16.00	40.00
Verve MGV-8399	(M)	**Carnival**	1960	*Unreleased*	
		—Verve albums above have black labels with "Verve Records, Inc." on the bottom.—			
Verve V-2002	(M)	**In A Romantic Mood—Oscar Peterson With Strings**	1961	6.00	15.00
Verve V-2004	(M)	**Pastel Moods By Oscar Peterson**	1961	6.00	15.00
Verve V-2012	(M)	**Romance—The Vocal Styling Of Oscar Peterson**	1961	6.00	15.00
Verve V-2044	(M)	**Recital By Oscar Peterson**	1961	6.00	15.00
Verve V-2045	(M)	**Nostalgic Memories By Oscar Peterson**	1961	6.00	15.00
Verve V-2046	(M)	**Tenderly—Music By Oscar Peterson**	1961	6.00	15.00
Verve V-2047	(M)	**Keyboard Music By Oscar Peterson**	1961	6.00	15.00
Verve V-2048	(M)	**An Evening With Oscar Peterson**	1961	6.00	15.00
Verve V-2052	(M)	**Oscar Peterson Plays The Cole Porter Songbook**	1961	6.00	15.00
Verve V6-2052	(S)	**Oscar Peterson Plays The Cole Porter Songbook**	1961	5.00	12.00
Verve V-2053	(M)	**Oscar Peterson Plays The Irving Berlin Songbook**	1961	6.00	15.00

Label & Catalog #		*Title*	*Year*	*VG+*	*NM*
Verve V6-2053	*(S)*	**Oscar Peterson Plays The Irving Berlin Songbook**	*1961*	**5.00**	**12.00**
Verve V-2054	*(M)*	**Oscar Peterson Plays The George Gershwin Songbook**	*1961*	**6.00**	**15.00**
Verve V6-2054	*(S)*	**Oscar Peterson Plays The George Gershwin Songbook**	*1961*	**5.00**	**12.00**
Verve V-2055	*(M)*	**Oscar Peterson Plays The Duke Ellington Songbook**	*1961*	**6.00**	**15.00**
Verve V6-2055	*(S)*	**Oscar Peterson Plays The Duke Ellington Songbook**	*1961*	**5.00**	**12.00**
Verve V-2056	*(M)*	**Oscar Peterson Plays The Jerome Kern Songbook**	*1961*	**6.00**	**15.00**
Verve V6-2056	*(S)*	**Oscar Peterson Plays The Jerome Kern Songbook**	*1961*	**5.00**	**12.00**
Verve V-2057	*(M)*	**Oscar Peterson Plays The Richard Rodgers Songbook**	*1961*	**6.00**	**15.00**
Verve V6-2057	*(S)*	**Oscar Peterson Plays The Richard Rodgers Songbook**	*1961*	**5.00**	**12.00**
Verve V-2059	*(M)*	**Oscar Peterson Plays The Harry Warren Songbook**	*1961*	**6.00**	**15.00**
Verve V6-2059	*(S)*	**Oscar Peterson Plays The Harry Warren Songbook**	*1961*	**5.00**	**12.00**
Verve V-2060	*(M)*	**Oscar Peterson Plays The Harold Arlen Songbook**	*1961*	**6.00**	**15.00**
Verve V6-2060	*(S)*	**Oscar Peterson Plays The Harold Arlen Songbook**	*1961*	**5.00**	**12.00**
Verve V-2061	*(M)*	**Oscar Peterson Plays The Jimmy McHugh Songbook**	*1961*	**6.00**	**15.00**
Verve V6-2061	*(S)*	**Oscar Peterson Plays The Jimmy McHugh Songbook**	*1961*	**5.00**	**12.00**
Verve V-2079	*(M)*	**Soft Sands**	*1961*	**6.00**	**15.00**
Verve V-2119	*(M)*	**Oscar Peterson Plays "My Fair Lady"**	*1961*	**6.00**	**15.00**
Verve V6-2119	*(S)*	**Oscar Peterson Plays "My Fair Lady"**	*1961*	**5.00**	**12.00**
Verve V-8024	*(M)*	**The Oscar Peterson Trio At The Stratford Shakesperean Festival**	*1961*	**6.00**	**15.00**
Verve V-8072	*(M)*	**The Oscar Peterson Quartet No. 1**	*1961*	**8.00**	**15.00**
Verve V-8092	*(M)*	**Oscar Peterson Plays Count Basie**	*1961*	**6.00**	**15.00**
Verve V-8239	*(M)*	**Oscar Peterson Trio With Sonny Stitt, Roy Eldridge And Jo Jones At Newport**	*1961*	**6.00**	**15.00**
Verve V-8268	*(M)*	**Oscar Peterson Trio At The Concertgebouw**	*1961*	**6.00**	**15.00**
Verve V-8269	*(M)*	**Oscar Peterson Trio With The Modern Jazz Quartet At The Opera House**	*1961*	**6.00**	**15.00**
Verve V6-8269	*(S)*	**Oscar Peterson Trio With The Modern Jazz Quartet At The Opera House**	*1961*	**5.00**	**12.00**
Verve V-8287	*(M)*	**A Night On The Town**	*1961*	**6.00**	**15.00**
Verve V-8322	*(M)*	**Louis Armstrong Meets Oscar Peterson**	*1961*	**6.00**	**15.00**
Verve V6-8322	*(S)*	**Louis Armstrong Meets Oscar Peterson**	*1961*	**5.00**	**12.00**
Verve V-8334	*(M)*	**Songs For A Swinging Affair— A Jazz Portrait Of Sinatra**	*1961*	**6.00**	**15.00**
Verve V6-8334	*(S)*	**Songs For A Swinging Affair— A Jazz Portrait Of Sinatra**	*1961*	**5.00**	**12.00**
Verve V-8340	*(M)*	**Porgy & Bess**	*1961*	**6.00**	**15.00**
Verve V6-8340	*(S)*	**Porgy & Bess**	*1961*	**5.00**	**12.00**
Verve V-8351	*(M)*	**The Jazz Soul Of Oscar Peterson**	*1961*	**6.00**	**15.00**
Verve V-8364	*(M)*	**Swinging Brass With The Oscar Peterson Trio**	*1961*	**6.00**	**15.00**
Verve V6-8364	*(S)*	**Swinging Brass With The Oscar Peterson Trio**	*1961*	**5.00**	**12.00**
Verve V-8366	*(M)*	**The Music From "Fiorello!"**	*1961*	**6.00**	**15.00**
Verve V-8368	*(M)*	**The Oscar Peterson Trio At J.A.T.P.**	*1961*	**6.00**	**15.00**
Verve V-8420	*(M)*	**The Trio-Live From Chicago**	*1961*	**10.00**	**25.00**
Verve V6-8420	*(S)*	**The Trio-Live From Chicago**	*1961*	**8.00**	**20.00**
Verve V-8429	*(M)*	**Very Tall**	*1962*	**10.00**	**25.00**
Verve V6-8429	*(S)*	**Very Tall** *(Verve 8429 also features Milt Jackson.)*	*1962*	**8.00**	**20.00**
Verve V-8454	*(M)*	**West Side Story**	*1962*	**8.00**	**20.00**
Verve V6-8454	*(S)*	**West Side Story**	*1962*	**6.00**	**15.00**
Verve V-8476	*(M)*	**Bursting Out With The All Star Big Band**	*1962*	**8.00**	**20.00**
Verve V6-8476	*(S)*	**Bursting Out With The All Star Big Band**	*1962*	**6.00**	**15.00**

Label & Catalog #		Title	Year	VG+	NM
Verve V-8480	(M)	**The Sound Of The Trio**	1962	8.00	20.00
Verve V6-8480	(S)	**The Sound Of The Trio**	1962	6.00	15.00
Verve V-8482	(M)	**The Modern Jazz Quartet & The Oscar Peterson Trio At The Opera House**	1962	8.00	20.00
Verve V6-8482	(S)	**The Modern Jazz Quartet & The Oscar Peterson Trio At The Opera House** *(Verve 8482 is a reissue of 8269.)*	1962	6.00	15.00
Verve V-8516	(M)	**Affinity**	1963	8.00	20.00
Verve V6-8516	(S)	**Affinity**	1963	6.00	15.00
Verve V-8538	(M)	**Night Train**	1963	8.00	20.00
Verve V6-8538	(S)	**Night Train**	1963	6.00	15.00
Verve V-8562	(M)	**The Oscar Peterson Trio With Nelson Riddle**	1963	6.00	15.00
Verve V6-8562	(S)	**The Oscar Peterson Trio With Nelson Riddle**	1963	5.00	12.00
Verve V-8581	(M)	**Oscar Peterson Plays "My Fair Lady"**	1964	6.00	15.00
Verve V6-8581	(S)	**Oscar Peterson Plays "My Fair Lady"**	1964	5.00	12.00
Verve V-8591	(M)	**The Oscar Peterson Trio Plays**	1964	6.00	15.00
Verve V6-8591	(S)	**The Oscar Peterson Trio Plays**	1964	5.00	12.00
Verve V-8606	(M)	**We Get Requests**	1965	6.00	15.00
Verve V6-8606	(S)	**We Get Requests**	1965	5.00	12.00
Verve V-8660	(M)	**Put On A Happy Face**	1966	6.00	15.00
Verve V6-8660	(S)	**Put On A Happy Face**	1966	5.00	12.00
Verve V-8681	(M)	**Something Warm**	1966	6.00	15.00
Verve V6-8681	(S)	**Something Warm**	1966	5.00	12.00
Verve VSP-11	(M)	**Stage Right**	1966	6.00	15.00
Verve VSPS-11	(S)	**Stage Right**	1966	5.00	12.00
Verve V-8700	(M)	**Thoroughly Modern '20s**	1967	6.00	15.00
Verve V6-8700	(S)	**Thoroughly Modern '20s**	1967	5.00	12.00
Verve V-8740	(M)	**Night Train, Volume 2**	1967	6.00	15.00
Verve V6-8740	(S)	**Night Train, Volume 2**	1967	5.00	12.00
Verve V6-8775	(S)	**Oscar's— Oscar Peterson Plays The Academy Awards**	1969	4.00	10.00
		—Verve albums above have black labels with "MGM Records" on the bottom.—			
Mercury MG-20975	(M)	**Oscar Peterson Trio + One**	1964	10.00	25.00
Mercury SR-60975	(S)	**Oscar Peterson Trio + One**	1964	8.00	20.00
		—Mercury albums above have silver on black labels.—			
Limelight LM-82010	(M)	**Canadian Suite**	1964	6.00	15.00
Limelight LS-86010	(S)	**Canadian Suite**	1964	5.00	12.00
Limelight LM-82023	(M)	**Eloquence**	1965	6.00	15.00
Limelight LS-86023	(S)	**Eloquence**	1965	5.00	12.00
Limelight LM-82029	(M)	**With Respect To Nat**	1965	6.00	15.00
Limelight LS-86029	(S)	**With Respect To Nat**	1965	5.00	12.00
Limelight LM-82039	(M)	**Blues Etude**	1966	6.00	15.00
Limelight LS-86039	(S)	**Blues Etude**	1966	5.00	12.00
Prestige PRST-7595	(S)	**Soul-O!**	1968	5.00	12.00
Prestige PRST-7620	(S)	**The Great Oscar Peterson On Prestige!**	1969	5.00	12.00
Prestige PRST-7649	(S)	**Oscar Peterson Plays For Lovers**	1969	5.00	12.00
Prestige PRST-7690	(S)	**Easy Walker**	1969	5.00	12.00
		—Prestige albums above have blue labels with a trident logo on top.—			

PETERSON, OSCAR / GERRY MULLIGAN

Verve V-8559	(M)	**The Oscar Peterson Trio And The Gerry Mulligan Four At Newport**	1963	12.00	30.00
Verve V6-8559	(S)	**The Oscar Peterson Trio And The Gerry Mulligan Four At Newport**	1963	10.00	25.00
		—Verve albums above have black labels with "MGM Records" on the bottom.—			

PETTERSTEIN, SHORTY

World Pacific WP-1274	(M)	**The Wide Weird World Of Shorty Petterstein**	1959	16.00	40.00

PETTIFORD, OSCAR

Oscar Pettiford is a modern jazz bass and cello player. For additional listings refer to Serge Chaloff / Oscar Pettiford; The Four Most; The Jazz Modes; The Manhattan Jazz Septette; Lucky Thompson.

Debut DLP-8	(10")	**Oscar Pettiford Sextet**	1954	125.00	250.00
Bethlehem BCP-1003	(10")	**Oscar Pettiford**	1954	60.00	150.00
Bethlehem BCP-1019	(10")	**Basically Duke**	1955	60.00	150.00
Bethlehem BCP-33	(M)	**Oscar Pettiford Sextet**	1955	40.00	100.00
ABC-Paramount ABC-135	(M)	**Oscar Pettiford Orchestra In Hi Fi**	1956	40.00	100.00

Oscar Pettiford hit the road with Charlie Barnett in 1943 before winding up the year with Dizzy Gillespie as co-leader of the first bebop group to play 52nd Street in New York. He then played with Boyd Raeburn, Coleman Hawkins (1945), Duke Ellington (1945-48), Woody Herman (1949), and the Louis Bellson-Charlie Shavers group (1950). He recorded as a member of Les Jazz Modes, shared half an album with Serge Chaloff, and was featured on a Lucky Thompson LP. As a sideman he can be heard on albums by Miles Davis on Blue Note and Prestige, Kenny Dorham, Coleman Hawkins, Thelonious Monk and Sonny Rollins, all on Riverside, Teddy Charles and Joe Puma, both on Jubilee, Art Blakey on Columbia, Duke Ellington on Rondo-lette and RCA Victor, Eddie Heywood on Coral, Urbie Green on Bethlehem, Jimmy Cleveland and Clark Terry, both on EmArcy, Joe Roland on Savoy, Lee Konitz on Atlantic, and Sonny Stitt on Roost. The 10" album here, Bethlehem 1003, was reissued as one side of the 12" album, Bethlehem 6, also shown, with Vinnie Burke's 10"-er on the other side.

Label & Catalog #		Title	Year	VG+	NM
ABC-Paramount ABC-227	(M)	**O.P.'s Jazz Men— Oscar Pettiford Orchestra In Hi Fi, Vol. 2**	1958	30.00	75.00
ABC-Paramount ABCS-227	(S)	**O.P.'s Jazz Men— Oscar Pettiford Orchestra In Hi Fi, Vol. 2**	1958	20.00	50.00
Jazzland JLP-64	(M)	**Last Recordings By The Late, Great Bassist**	1962	20.00	50.00
Jazzland JLP-964	(E)	**Last Recordings By The Late, Great Bassist**	1962	12.00	30.00
Fantasy 6010	(M)	**My Little Cello**	1964	12.00	30.00
Fantasy 86010	(E)	**My Little Cello**	1964	6.00	15.00
Fantasy 6015	(M)	**The Essen Jazz Festival**	1964	12.00	30.00
Fantasy 86015	(E)	**The Essen Jazz Festival**	1964	6.00	15.00
Atlantic 8111	(M)	**Live At Jilly's**	1965	10.00	25.00
Atlantic SD-8111	(S)	**Live At Jilly's**	1965	8.00	20.00

—Atlantic albums above have multi-color labels with a black fan logo.—

PETTIFORD, OSCAR / VINNIE BURKE

Label & Catalog #		Title	Year	VG+	NM
Bethlehem BCP-6	(M)	**Bass By Pettiford / Burke** *(Bethlehem 6 is a reissue of 1003 and 1010.)*	1957	40.00	100.00

PETTIFORD, OSCAR / RED MITCHELL

Label & Catalog #		Title	Year	VG+	NM
Bethlehem BCP-2	(M)	**Jazz Mainstream** *(Bethlehem 2 is a reissue of 1019 and 1033.)*	1957	40.00	100.00

PHILLIPS, FLIP

Joseph Filipelli, aka Flip Phillips, is a traditional jazz tenor saxophone and clarinet player. For additional listings refer to Fred Astaire; Machito.

Label & Catalog #		Title	Year	VG+	NM
Brunswick BL-58032	(10")	**Tenor Sax Stylings**	1953	60.00	150.00
Mercury MG-25023	(10")	**Flip Phillips Quartet**	1950	150.00	300.00
Mercury MGC-105	(10")	**Flip Phillips Quartet** *(Mercury 105 is a reissue of 25023 with cover art by David Stone Martin.)*	1951	125.00	250.00
Mercury MGC-109	(10")	**Flip Phillips Collates** *(Mercury 109 features cover art by David Stone Martin.)*	1952	100.00	200.00
Mercury MGC-133	(10")	**Flip Phillips Collates No. 2**	1953	*Unreleased*	
Clef MGC-105	(10")	**Flip Phillips Quartet**	1953	60.00	150.00
Clef MGC-109	(10")	**Flip Phillips Collates**	1953	60.00	150.00
Clef MGC-133	(10")	**Flip Phillips Collates No. 2** *(Clef 133 features cover art by David Stone Martin.)*	1953	60.00	150.00
Clef MGC-158	(10")	**Jumping Moods With Flip Phillips**	1954	60.00	150.00
Clef MGC-634	(M)	**The Flips Phillips-Buddy Rich Trio** *(Clef 634 is a reissue of 105.)*	1954	50.00	125.00
Clef MGC-637	(M)	**The Flip Phillips Quintet**	1954	50.00	125.00
Clef MGC-691	(M)	**Flip Wails** *(Clef 691 is a reissue of 133 with cover art by David Stone Martin.)*	1956	50.00	125.00
Clef MGC-692	(M)	**Swinging With Flip Phillips And His Orchestra** *(Clef 692 is a reissue of 158 with cover art by David Stone Martin.)*	1956	50.00	125.00
Clef MGC-693	(M)	**Flip** *(Clef 693 is a reissue of 109.)*	1956	40.00	100.00
Clef MGC-740	(M)	**Rock With Flip** *(Clef 740 is a reissue of 637.)*	1956	40.00	100.00
Verve MGV-8075	(M)	**Flip Wails** *(Verve 8075 is a reissue of Clef 691 with the DSM cover.)*	1957	40.00	100.00
Verve MGV-8076	(M)	**Swingin' With Flip** *(Verve 8076 is a reissue of Clef 692 with the DSM cover.)*	1957	40.00	100.00
Verve MGV-8077	(M)	**Flip** *(Verve 8077 is a reissue of Clef 693.)*	1957	40.00	100.00
Verve MGV-8116	(M)	**Rock With Flip** *(Verve 8116 is a reissue of Clef 740.)*	1957	40.00	100.00

—Verve albums above have black labels with "Verve Records, Inc." on the bottom.—

Label & Catalog #		Title	Year	VG+	NM
Verve V-8075	(M)	**Flip Wails**	1961	10.00	25.00
Verve V-8076	(M)	**Swingin' With Flip**	1961	10.00	25.00
Verve V-8077	(M)	**Flip**	1961	10.00	25.00
Verve V-8116	(M)	**Rock With Flip**	1961	10.00	25.00

—Verve albums above have black labels with "MGM Records" on the bottom.—

Label & Catalog #		Title	Year	VG+	NM
Sue LP-1035	(M)	**Flip Phillips Revisited**	1965	16.00	40.00

PHILLIPS, WOOLF

Label & Catalog #		Title	Year	VG+	NM
Coral CRL-56036	(10")	**Woolf Phillips Plays Duke Ellington Songs**	1951	20.00	50.00

PIANO RED

Label & Catalog #		Title	Year	VG+	NM
Groove LG-1001	(M)	**Jump Man, Jump**	1956	200.00	400.00
Groove LG-1002	(M)	**Piano Red In Concert**	1956	300.00	500.00

PIERCE, BILLE & DEDE

Joseph De Lacrois, trumpet, and Wilhelmina Goodson, piano, aka the wife/husband team of Billie & DeDe Pierce, are traditional jazz vocalists. For additional listings refer to Jim Robinson & Billie & Dede Pierce.

Riverside RLP-370	(M)	**Blues In The Classic Tradition**	1961	12.00	30.00
Riverside RS-9370	(E)	**Blues In The Classic Tradition**	1961	6.00	15.00
Riverside RLP-394	(M)	**Blues And Tonks From The Delta**	1961	12.00	30.00
Riverside RS-9394	(E)	**Blues And Tonks From The Delta**	1961	6.00	15.00

—Riverside albums above have blue mono or black stereo labels with a reel & mike logo on top.—

PIERCE, NAT

Nathaniel Pierce is a traditional jazz-based pianist and composer. For additional listings refer to the Various Artists section under United Artists.

Fantasy 3-14	(10")	**Nat Pierce And The Herdsmen Featuring Dick Collins**	1954	30.00	75.00
Vanguard VRS-8017	(10")	**Nat Pierce Bandstand**	1955	30.00	75.00
Keynote LP-1101	(M)	**Nat Pierce Octet And Tentette**	1955	30.00	75.00
Coral CRL-57091	(M)	**Kansas City Memories** (Coral 57091 also features Anthony Ortega.)	1957	20.00	50.00
Coral CRL-57128	(M)	**Chamber Music For Moderns**	1957	16.00	40.00
RCA Victor LPM-2543	(M)	**Big Band At The Savoy Ballroom**	1962	12.00	30.00
RCA Victor LSP-2543	(S)	**Big Band At The Savoy Ballroom** (RCA Victor 2543 also features Buck Clayton.)	1962	10.00	25.00

—RCA albums above have black labels with "Long Play" or "Living Stereo" on the bottom.—

PIERCE, NAT, & DICK COLLINS / CHARLIE MARIANO

Fantasy 3224	(M)	**Nat Pierce—Dick Collins Nonet/ Charlie Mariano Sextet** (Fantasy 3224 is a reissue of 14 and 10, "Charlie Mariano Sextet.")	1956	40.00	100.00

—Fantasy albums above have red labels on dark red, non-flexible vinyl.—

Fantasy 3224	(M)	**Nat Pierce—Dick Collins Nonet/ Charlie Mariano Sextet**	195?	20.00	50.00

—Fantasy albums above have red labels on non-flexible vinyl.—

PIERCE, NAT, & MILT HINTON & BARRY GALBRAITH & OSIE JOHNSON

Music Minus One Vol. 1	(M)	**Nat Pierce & Milt Hinton & Barry Galbraith & Osie Johnson** (Issued with 14 pages of sheet music glued and stapled into the spine.)	1956	12.00	30.00

PIKE, DAVID

David Pike is a modern jazz vibraphone player.

Riverside RLP-360	(M)	**It's Time For David Pike**	1961	12.00	30.00
Riverside RS-9360	(S)	**It's Time For David Pike**	1961	10.00	25.00

—Riverside albums above have blue mono or black stereo labels with a reel & mike logo on top.—

New Jazz NJLP-8281	(M)	**Bossa Nova Carnival**	1962	20.00	50.00
New Jazz NJLP-8284	(M)	**Limbo Carnival**	1962	20.00	50.00

—New Jazz albums above have purple labels.—

New Jazz NJLP-8281	(M)	**Bossa Nova Carnival**	1965	10.00	25.00
New Jazz NJLP-8284	(M)	**Limbo Carnival**	1965	10.00	25.00

—New Jazz albums above have blue labels with a trident logo on the right side.—

Epic LA-16025	(M)	**Pike's Peak**	1962	12.00	30.00
Epic BA-17025	(S)	**Pike's Peak**	1962	10.00	25.00
Moodsville MVLP-36	(M)	**Dave Pike Plays The Jazz Version Of "Oliver"**	1963	20.00	50.00

—Moodsville mono albums above have green labels with silver print.—

Moodsville MVLP-36	(M)	**Dave Pike Plays The Jazz Version Of "Oliver"**	1965	10.00	25.00

—Moodsville albums above have blue labels with a trident logo on the right side.—

Decca DL-4568	(M)	**Manhattan Latin**	1965	6.00	15.00
Decca DL-74568	(S)	**Manhattan Latin**	1965	5.00	12.00
Atlantic 1457	(M)	**Jazz For The Jet Set**	1966	6.00	15.00
Atlantic SD-1457	(S)	**Jazz For The Jet Set**	1966	5.00	12.00

—Atlantic albums above have multi-color labels with a black fan logo.—

PILHOFER, HERB

Herbert Pilhofer is a modern jazz pianist.

Zephyr ZP-12103-G	(M)	**Dick And Don Maw Present The Herb Pilhofer Octet— Jazz From The North Coast, Volume 2**	1959	20.00	50.00

Label & Catalog #		Title	Year	VG+	NM
Argo LP-657	(M)	**Jazz**	1960	12.00	30.00
Argo LPS-657	(S)	**Jazz**	1960	10.00	25.00

PISANO, JOHNNY, & BILLY BEAN

John Pisano and William Bean are modern jazz-based guitar players.

Decca DL-9206	(M)	**Makin' It**	1958	12.00	30.00
Decca DL-79206	(S)	**Makin' It**	1958	10.00	25.00
Decca DL-9219	(M)	**Take Your Pick**	1958	12.00	30.00
Decca DL-79219	(S)	**Take Your Pick**	1958	10.00	25.00

PIZZARELLI, BUCKY, & VINNIE BURKE

Savoy MG-12158	(M)	**Music Minus Many Men**	1960	12.00	30.00

PLONSKY, JOHN

Golden Crest GC-3014	(M)	**Cool Man, Cool**	1958	12.00	30.00

PLUMMER, BILL

Impulse A-9164	(M)	**Bill Plummer & The Cosmic Brotherhood**	1968	12.00	30.00
Impulse AS-9164	(S)	**Bill Plummer & The Cosmic Brotherhood**	1968	8.00	20.00
		—Impulse albums above have orange & black labels.—			
Impulse AS-9164	(S)	**Bill Plummer & The Cosmic Brotherhood**	1969	4.00	10.00
		—Impulse albums above have red & black labels with the "abc" logo on top.—			

POINDEXTER, PONY

Norwood "Pony" Poindexter is a West Coast jazz-based alto saxophone player.

Epic LA-16035	(M)	**Pony's Express**	1962	30.00	75.00
Epic BA-17035	(S)	**Pony's Express**	1962	24.00	60.00
New Jazz NJLP-8285	(M)	**Pony Poindexter Plays The Big Ones**	1962	30.00	75.00
New Jazz NJLP-8297	(M)	**Gumbo**	1963	*Unreleased*	
		—New Jazz albums above have purple labels.—			
New Jazz NJLP-8285	(M)	**Pony Poindexter Plays The Big Ones**	1965	10.00	25.00
		—New Jazz albums above have blue labels with a trident logo on the right side.—			
Prestige PRLP-16001	(M)	**Gumbo**	1964	16.00	40.00

POLK, LUCY ANN

Lucy Ann Polk is a jazz-based vocalist.

Trend TL-1008	(10")	**Lucy Ann Polk With Dave Pell**	1954	40.00	100.00
Mode LP-115	(M)	**Lucky Lucy Ann**	1957	50.00	125.00
Interlude MO-504	(M)	**Easy Livin'**	1959	20.00	50.00
Interlude ST-1004	(S)	**Easy Livin'**	1959	16.00	40.00
		(Interlude 504 is a reissue of Mode 115.)			

POLL WINNERS, THE

The Poll Winners are Barney Kessel, Shelly Manne and Ray Brown.

Contemporary C-3535	(M)	**The Poll Winners**	1957	20.00	50.00
Stereo Records S-7010	(S)	**The Poll Winners**	1958	18.00	45.00
Contemporary S-7535	(S)	**The Poll Winners**	1959	16.00	40.00
Contemporary C-3556	(M)	**The Poll Winners Ride Again**	1958	20.00	50.00
Stereo Records S-7029	(S)	**The Poll Winners Ride Again**	1958	18.00	45.00
Contemporary S-7556	(S)	**The Poll Winners Ride Again**	1959	16.00	40.00
Contemporary M-3576	(M)	**Poll Winners Three**	1960	16.00	40.00
Contemporary S-3576	(S)	**Poll Winners Three**	1960	12.00	30.00
Contemporary M-3581	(M)	**Exploring The Scene**	1960	16.00	40.00
Contemporary S-7581	(S)	**Exploring The Scene**	1960	12.00	30.00
		— Contemporary stereo albums have gold & black labels.—			

POLLACK, BEN

Ben Pollack is a traditional jazz drummer and band leader.

Brunswick BL-58025	(10")	**Ben Pollack**	1951	20.00	50.00
"X" LX-3003	(10")	**Ben Pollack And His Orchestra Featuring Benny Goodman**	1954	20.00	50.00
Savoy MG-12090	(M)	**Dixieland**	1956	20.00	50.00
Savoy MG-12207	(M)	**Dixieland Strut**	196?	6.00	15.00

POLLARD, TERRY

Terry Pollard is a modern jazz piano and vibraphone player.

Bethlehem BCP-1015	(10")	**Terry Pollard**	1954	40.00	100.00

Label & Catalog #		Title	Year	VG+	NM

POLLARD, TERRY / BOBBY SCOTT

Bethlehem BCP-1	(M)	**Young Moderns**	1957	20.00	50.00
		(Bethlehem 1 is a reissue of 1015 and 1004, "Great Scott.")			

POMEROY, HERB

Irving Herbert Pomeroy III is a modern jazz trumpet player and band leader.

Transition TRLP-1	(M)	**Jazz In A Stable**	1956	60.00	150.00
		(Transition 1 was issued with a booklet, worth an additional $25.)			
Roulette R-52001	(M)	**Life Is A Many Splendored Gig**	1958	30.00	75.00
Roulette SR-52001	(S)	**Life Is A Many Splendored Gig**	1958	24.00	60.00
United Arts. UAL-4015	(M)	**Band In Boston**	1959	30.00	75.00
United Arts. UAS-5015	(S)	**Band In Boston**	1959	24.00	60.00

PONTY, JEAN-LUC

Jean-Luc Ponty is a modern jazz violinist and composer.

Prestige PRST-7676	(S)	**Critic's Choice**	1969	6.00	15.00
		—Prestige albums above have blue labels with a trident logo on top.—			
World Pacific ST-20134	(S)	**More Than Meets The Ear**	1969	6.00	15.00
Pacific Jazz ST-20156	(S)	**Electric Connection**	1969	6.00	15.00
Pacific Jazz ST-20168	(S)	**Experience**	1969	6.00	15.00
Pacific Jazz ST-20172	(S)	**King Kong/Jean-Luc Ponty Plays The Music Of Frank Zappa**	1969	10.00	25.00
		(Pacific Jazz 20172 also features Frank Zappa.)			

POOLE, BILLIE

Billie Poole is a modern jazz vocalist.

Riverside RLP-425	(M)	**Sermonette**	1962	12.00	30.00
Riverside RS-9425	(S)	**Sermonette**	1962	12.00	30.00
Riverside RLP-458	(M)	**Confessin' The Blues**	1963	12.00	30.00
Riverside RS-9458	(S)	**Confessin' The Blues**	1963	12.00	30.00
		(Riverside 458 also features Kenny Burrell and Junior Mance.)			
		—Riverside albums above have blue mono or black stereo labels with a reel & mike logo on top.—			

POTTER, TOMMY

Charles Thomas Potter is a traditional jazz string bass player. For additional listings refer to the Various Artists section under Prestige.

East West 4001	(M)	**Tommy Potter's Hard Funk**	1958	16.00	40.00

POTTS, BILL

William Potts is a jazz-based pianist and composer.

United Arts. UAL-4032	(M)	**The Jazz Soul Of Porgy & Bess**	1959	16.00	40.00
United Arts. UAS-5032	(S)	**The Jazz Soul Of Porgy & Bess**	1959	12.00	30.00
Colpix CP-451	(M)	**Bye Bye Birdie**	1963	12.00	30.00
Colpix SCP-451	(S)	**Bye Bye Birdie**	1963	16.00	40.00

POWELL, BUD

Earl "Bud" Powell is a modern jazz piano player. For additional listings refer to Charlie Parker & Dizzie Gillespie & Bud Powell; The Quintet; Sonny Stitt.

Roost LP-401	(10")	**Bud Powell Trio**	1950	240.00	400.00
Roost LP-412	(10")	**Bud Powell Trio**	1953	150.00	300.00
Roost LP-2224	(M)	**Bud Powell Trio**	1957	40.00	100.00
		(Roost 2224 is a reissue of 401 and 412.)			
Debut DLP-3	(10")	**Jazz At Massey Hall, Volume 2**	1953	240.00	400.00
		(This is the second set of the famed May 15, 1953 performance with Powell backed by Charles Mingus and Max Roach.)			
Mercury MG-35012	(10")	**Bud Powell Piano**	1950	150.00	300.00
		(Mercury 35012 features cover art by David Stone Martin.)			
Mercury MGC-102	(10")	**Bud Powell Piano**	1950	125.00	250.00
Mercury MGC-502	(10")	**Bud Powell Piano Solos**	1951	125.00	250.00
		(Mercury 502 features cover art by David Stone Martin.)			
Mercury MGC-507	(10")	**Bud Powell Piano Solos, No. 2**	1951	125.00	250.00
		(Mercury 507 features cover art by David Stone Martin.)			
Mercury MGC-610	(M)	**Bud Powell's Moods**	1953	125.00	250.00
		(Mercury 610 features cover art by David Stone Martin.)			
Clef MGC-102	(10")	**Bud Powell Piano Solos**	1953	*Unreleased*	
Clef MGC-502	(10")	**Bud Powell Piano Solos**	1954	100.00	200.00
Clef MGC-507	(10")	**Bud Powell Piano Solos, No. 2**	1954	100.00	200.00

Label & Catalog #		Title	Year	VG+	NM
Clef MGC-610	(M)	**Bud Powell's Moods**	1954	100.00	200.00
Clef MGC-739	(M)	**The Genius Of Bud Powell**	1956	50.00	125.00
		(Clef 739 is a reissue of 610.)			
Norgran MGN-23	(10")	**Bud Powell Trio**	1954	125.00	250.00
Norgran MGN-1017	(M)	**Jazz Original**	1955	50.00	100.00
Norgran MGN-1063	(M)	**Jazz Giant**	1956	50.00	100.00
		(Norgran 1063 is a reissue of Clef 502 and 507 with cover art by David Stone Martin.)			
Norgran MGN-1064	(M)	**Bud Powell's Moods**	1956	50.00	100.00
		(Norgran 1064 is a reissue of 23 with cover art by David Stone Martin.)			
Norgran MGN-1077	(M)	**Piano Interpretations By Bud Powell**	1956	50.00	100.00
		(Norgran 1077 features cover art by David Stone Martin.)			
Norgran MGN-1098	(M)	**Bud Powell '57**	1957	50.00	100.00
		(Norgran 1098 is a reissue of 1017.)			
Verve MGV-8115	(M)	**The Genius Of Bud Powell**	1957	20.00	50.00
		(Verve 8115 is a reissue of Clef 739.)			
Verve MGV-8153	(M)	**Jazz Giant**	1957	24.00	60.00
		(Verve 8153 is a reissue of Norgran 1063 with the DSM cover.)			
Verve MGV-8154	(M)	**Bud Powell's Moods**	1957	24.00	60.00
		(Verve 8154 is a reissue of Norgran 1064 with the DSM cover.)			
Verve MGV-8167	(M)	**Piano Interpretations By Bud Powell**	1957	24.00	60.00
		(Verve 8167 is a reissue of Norgran 1077 with the DSM cover.)			
Verve MGV-8185	(M)	**Bud Powell '57**	1957	20.00	50.00
		(Verve 8185 is a reissue of Norgran 1098.)			
Verve MGV-8218	(M)	**Blues In The Closet**	1958	20.00	50.00
Verve MGV-8301	(M)	**The Lonely One...**	1959	20.00	50.00
		—Verve albums above have black labels with "Verve Records, Inc." on the bottom.—			
Verve V-8115	(M)	**The Genius Of Bud Powell**	1961	10.00	25.00
Verve V-8153	(M)	**Jazz Giant**	1961	10.00	25.00
Verve V-8154	(M)	**Bud Powell's Moods**	1961	10.00	25.00
Verve V-8167	(M)	**Piano Interpretations By Bud Powell**	1961	10.00	25.00
Verve V-8185	(M)	**Bud Powell '57**	1961	10.00	25.00
Verve V-8218	(M)	**Blues In The Closet**	1961	10.00	25.00
Verve V-8301	(M)	**The Lonely One...**	1961	10.00	25.00
		—Verve albums above have black labels with "MGM Records" on the bottom.—			
Verve VSP-35	(M)	**The Jazz Legacy Of Bud Powell**	1966	8.00	20.00
Verve VSPS-35	(E)	**The Jazz Legacy Of Bud Powell**	1966	4.00	10.00
Verve VSP-37	(M)	**This Was Bud Powell**	1966	8.00	20.00
Verve VSPS-37	(E)	**This Was Bud Powell**	1966	4.00	10.00
Blue Note BLP-5003	(10")	**The Amazing Bud Powell, Vol. 1**	1951	150.00	300.00
Blue Note BLP-5041	(10")	**The Amazing Bud Powell, Vol. 2**	1954	150.00	300.00
Blue Note BLP-1503	(M)	**The Amazing Bud Powell, Vol. 1** *(Deep groove)*	1955	100.00	200.00
Blue Note BLP-1503	(M)	**The Amazing Bud Powell, Vol. 1**	1955	60.00	150.00
Blue Note BLP-1504	(M)	**The Amazing Bud Powell, Vol. 2** *(Deep groove)*	1955	100.00	200.00
Blue Note BLP-1504	(M)	**The Amazing Bud Powell, Vol. 2**	1955	60.00	150.00
		—Blue Note albums above have blue on white labels with a Lexington Ave, NYC address.—			
Blue Note BLP-1571	(M)	**Bud!** *(Deep groove)*	1957	60.00	150.00
Blue Note BLP-1571	(M)	**Bud!**	1957	40.00	100.00
Blue Note BST-1571	(S)	**Bud!** *(Deep groove)*	1959	40.00	100.00
Blue Note BST-1571	(S)	**Bud!**	1959	30.00	75.00
Blue Note BLP-1598	(M)	**The Time Waits** *(Deep groove)*	1959	60.00	150.00
Blue Note BLP-1598	(M)	**The Time Waits**	1959	40.00	100.00
Blue Note BST-1598	(S)	**The Time Waits** *(Deep groove)*	1959	40.00	100.00
Blue Note BST-1598	(S)	**The Time Waits**	1959	30.00	75.00
Blue Note BLP-4009	(M)	**The Scene Changes** *(Deep groove)*	1959	60.00	150.00
Blue Note BLP-4009	(M)	**The Scene Changes**	1959	40.00	100.00
Blue Note BST-4009	(S)	**The Scene Changes** *(Deep groove)*	1959	40.00	100.00
Blue Note BST-4009	(S)	**The Scene Changes**	1959	30.00	75.00
		—Blue Note albums above have blue on white labels with a W. 63rd St, NYC address.—			
Blue Note BLP-1503	(M)	**The Amazing Bud Powell, Vol. 1**	1963	10.00	25.00
Blue Note BLP-1504	(M)	**The Amazing Bud Powell, Vol. 2**	1963	10.00	25.00
Blue Note BLP-1571	(M)	**Bud!**	1963	10.00	25.00
Blue Note BST-1571	(S)	**Bud!**	1963	8.00	20.00
Blue Note BLP-1598	(M)	**The Time Waits**	1963	10.00	25.00
Blue Note BST-1598	(S)	**The Time Waits**	1963	8.00	20.00
Blue Note BLP-4009	(M)	**The Scene Changes**	1963	10.00	25.00
Blue Note BST-4009	(S)	**The Scene Changes**	1963	8.00	20.00
		—Blue Note albums above have blue on white labels with a New York, USA address.—			

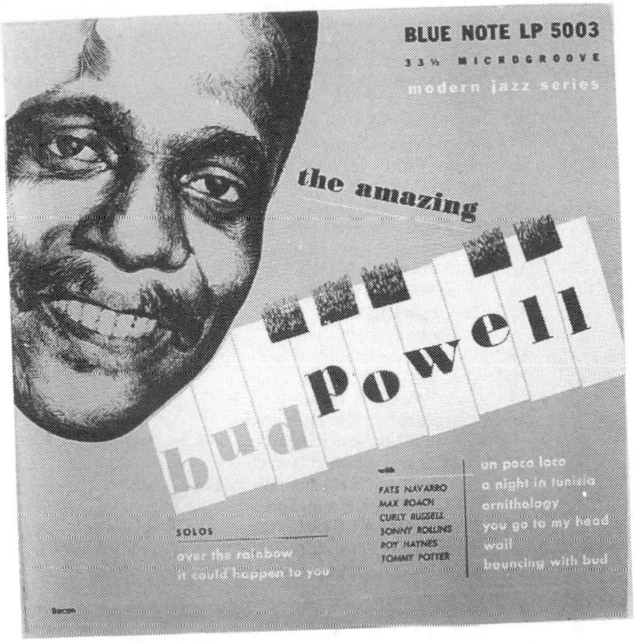

Bud Powell first played with Cootie Williams in 1943-44, moving on to John Kirby, Dizzy Gillespie, Allen Eager, Sid Catlett, and Don Byas. Through this time he gigged regularly with combos on the 52nd Street scene, easily gaining the reputation as bop's first piano stylist. He recorded with several Savoy session bands and cut a series of influential albums for Norman Granz' labels and Blue Note. As a sideman he has recorded with Sonny Stitt on Prestige, Fats Navarro on Blue Note and Savoy, Dexter Gordon, J.J. Johnson and Charlie Parker, all on Savoy, and as a member of The Quintet on Debut.

Label & Catalog #		Title	Year	VG+	NM
Blue Note BST-81503	*(E)*	**The Amazing Bud Powell, Vol. 1**	*196?*	**4.00**	**10.00**
Blue Note BST-81504	*(E)*	**The Amazing Bud Powell, Vol. 2**	*196?*	**4.00**	**10.00**
Blue Note BST-81571	*(S)*	**Bud!**	*196?*	**5.00**	**12.00**
Blue Note BST-81598	*(S)*	**The Time Waits**	*196?*	**5.00**	**12.00**
Blue Note BST-84009	*(S)*	**The Scene Changes**	*196?*	**5.00**	**12.00**
—Blue Note albums above have blue on white labels with a "A Division of Liberty Records."—					
RCA Victor LPM-1423	*(M)*	**Strictly Powell**	*1957*	**40.00**	**100.00**
RCA Victor LPM-1507	*(M)*	**Swingin' With Bud**	*1957*	**40.00**	**100.00**
—RCA albums above have black labels with "Long Play" on the bottom.—					
Fantasy 6006	*(M)*	**Bud Powell Trio** *(Red vinyl)*	*1962*	**20.00**	**50.00**
Fantasy 6006	*(M)*	**Bud Powell Trio**	*1962*	**12.00**	**30.00**
Fantasy 86006	*(E)*	**Bud Powell Trio** *(Blue vinyl)*	*1962*	**12.00**	**30.00**
Fantasy 86006	*(E)*	**Bud Powell Trio**	*1962*	**6.00**	**15.00**
		(Side 1 of Fantasy 6006 is a reissue of Debut 3 .)			
—Fantasy albums above have red mono or blue stereo labels on non-flexible vinyl.—					
Reprise R-6098	*(M)*	**Bud Powell In Paris**	*1964*	**16.00**	**40.00**
Reprise RS-6098	*(S)*	**Bud Powell In Paris**	*1964*	**12.00**	**30.00**
Roulette R-52115	*(M)*	**The Return Of Bud Powell— His First New Recordings Since 1958**	*1965*	**12.00**	**30.00**
Roulette SR-52115	*(S)*	**The Return Of Bud Powell— His First New Recordings Since 1958**	*1965*	**10.00**	**25.00**
Columbia CL-2292	*(M)*	**A Portrait Of Thelonious**	*1965*	**12.00**	**30.00**
Columbia CS-9092	*(S)*	**A Portrait Of Thelonious**	*1965*	**10.00**	**25.00**
—Columbia albums above have "Guaranteed High Fidelity" or "360 Sound Stereo" in black on the label.—					
Delmark DL-406	*(M)*	**Bouncing With Bud**	*1966*	**12.00**	**30.00**
Delmark DS-9406	*(S)*	**Bouncing With Bud**	*1966*	**10.00**	**25.00**
ESP-Disk' 1066	*(S)*	**Bud Powell At The Blue Note Cafe, Paris**	*1968*	**10.00**	**25.00**

POWELL, LOVEY

Lovey Powell is a jazzish vocalist.

Transition TRLP-1	*(M)*	**Lovelady**	*1956*	**30.00**	**75.00**
		(Transition 1 was issued with a booklet, worth an additional $25.)			

POWELL, MEL

Melvin Powell is a traditional jazz-based pianist and composer. For additional listings refer to Buck Clayton & Ruby Braff & Mel Powell; Buck Clayton & Gene Krupa.

Vanguard VRS-8004	*(10")*	**Mel Powell Septet**	*1953*	**30.00**	**75.00**
Vanguard VRS-8015	*(10")*	**Bandstand**	*1954*	**30.00**	**75.00**
Vanguard VRS-8501	*(M)*	**Borderline**	*1954*	**20.00**	**50.00**
Vanguard VRS-8503	*(M)*	**Thigamagig**	*1954*	**20.00**	**50.00**
Vanguard VRS-8506	*(M)*	**Out On A Limb**	*1955*	**20.00**	**50.00**
Vanguard VRS-8519	*(M)*	**Easy Swing**	*1955*	**20.00**	**50.00**
Capitol T-615	*(M)*	**Classics In Jazz**	*1955*	**16.00**	**40.00**
		—Capitol albums above have turquoise labels.—			

POWELL, SELDON

Shelson Powell is a modern tenor saxophone and flute player. For additional listings refer to Ahmed Abdul-Malik; Charlie Rouse; Johnny "Hammond" Smith; Teri Thornton.

Roost LP-2205	*(M)*	**Seldon Powell Plays**	*1956*	**20.00**	**50.00**
Roost LP-2220	*(M)*	**Seldon Powell Sextet**	*1956*	**20.00**	**50.00**

POWELL, SPECS

Gordon "Specs" Powell is a traditional jazz-based drummer.

Roulette R-52004	*(M)*	**Movin' In**	*1958*	**12.00**	**30.00**
Roulette SR-52004	*(S)*	**Movin' In**	*1958*	**10.00**	**25.00**

POZAR, ROBERT

Savoy MG-12189	*(M)*	**Good Golly, Miss Nancy**	*1967*	**8.00**	**20.00**
		—Savoy albums above have red labels with silver print.—			

PREACHER ROLLO

Preacher Rollo is a pseudonym for Rollo Laylan.

MGM E-95	*(10")*	**Preacher Rollo & The Five Saints**	*1951*	**30.00**	**75.00**
MGM E-217	*(10")*	**Preacher Rollo At The Jazz Band Ball**	*1953*	**30.00**	**75.00**
MGM E-3259	*(M)*	**Dixieland Favorites**	*1955*	**16.00**	**40.00**
MGM E-3403	*(M)*	**Swanee River Jazz**	*1956*	**16.00**	**40.00**
		—MGM albums above have black labels.—			

Label & Catalog #		Title	Year	VG+	NM

PRESTIGE BLUES SWINGERS, THE

The Prestige Blues Swingers are Pepper Adams, Ray Bryant, George Cooper, Art Farmer, Jimmy Forrest, Tiny Grimes, Osie Johnson, Wendell Marshall, Jerome Richardson, Idris Sulieman and Jerry Valentine.

Prestige PRLP-7145	(M)	**Outskirts Of Town**	1958	0.00	75.00
—Prestige albums above have yellow mono or silver stereo labels with a Bergenfield, NJ address .—					
Swingville SVLP-2013	(M)	**Stasch**	1960	20.00	50.00
—Swingville albums above have purple mono or red stereo labels.—					
Swingville SVLP-2013	(M)	**Stasch**	1965	10.00	25.00
—Swingville albums above have blue labels with a trident logo on the right side.—					

PRESTIGE JAZZ QUARTET, THE

The PJQ is Teddy Charles, Addison Farmer, Jerry Segal and Mal Waldron. For additional listings refer to Teo Macero.

Prestige PRLP-7108	(M)	**The Prestige Jazz Quartet**	1957	20.00	50.00
—Prestige albums above have yellow mono or silver stereo labels with a Bergenfield, NJ address .—					

PREVIN, ANDRE

Classically trained Andre Previn is a modern jazz pianist For additional listings refer to Shelly Manne; The Mitchells; Shorty Rogers & Andre Previn; and the Jazzy Soundtracks sec-tion under MGM.

Monarch 203	(10")	**All Star Jazz**	1952	30.00	75.00
Monarch 204	(10")	**Andre Previn Plays Duke**	1952	30.00	75.00
RCA Victor LPT-3002	(10")	**Andre Previn Plays Harry Warren**	1952	30.00	75.00
RCA Victor LPM-1011	(M)	**Gershwin**	1955	16.00	40.00
RCA Victor LPM-1356	(M)	**Three Little Words**	1957	16.00	40.00
(RCA Victor 1356 is a reissue of 3002.)					
—RCA albums above have black labels with "Long Play" on the bottom.—					
Decca DL-8131	(M)	**Let's Get Away From It All**	1955	16.00	40.00
Decca DL-8341	(M)	**Hollywood At Midnight**	1957	16.00	40.00
Contemporary C-3543	(M)	**Pal Joey**	1957	20.00	50.00
Stereo Records S-7004	(S)	**Pal Joey**	1958	18.00	45.00
Contemporary S-7543	(S)	**Pal Joey**	1959	16.00	40.00
Contemporary C-3548	(M)	**Gigi**	1958	20.00	50.00
Stereo Records S-7020	(S)	**Gigi**	1958	18.00	45.00
Contemporary S-7548	(S)	**Gigi**	1959	16.00	40.00
Contemporary M-3558	(M)	**Andre Previn Plays Vernon Duke**	1959	20.00	50.00
Contemporary S-7558	(S)	**Andre Previn Plays Vernon Duke**	1959	16.00	40.00
Contemporary M-3567	(M)	**Andre Previn Plays Jerome Kern**	1959	20.00	50.00
Contemporary S-7567	(S)	**Andre Previn Plays Jerome Kern**	1959	16.00	40.00
Contemporary M-3570	(M)	**Jazz: King Size**	1959	20.00	50.00
Contemporary S-7570	(S)	**Jazz: King Size**	1959	16.00	40.00
Contemporary M-3572	(M)	**West Side Story**	1960	16.00	40.00
Contemporary S-7572	(S)	**West Side Story**	1960	12.00	30.00
Contemporary M-3575	(M)	**Like Previn**	1960	16.00	40.00
Contemporary S-7575	(S)	**Like Previn**	1960	12.00	30.00
Contemporary M-3586	(M)	**Andre Previn Plays Harold Arlen**	1960	16.00	40.00
Contemporary S-7586	(S)	**Andre Previn Plays Harold Arlen**	1960	12.00	30.00
—Contemporary stereo albums have gold & black labels.—					
Columbia CL-1530	(M)	**Give My Regards To Broadway**	1960	10.00	25.00
Columbia CS-8330	(S)	**Give My Regards To Broadway**	1960	8.00	20.00
Columbia CL-1569	(M)	**Camelot**	1961	10.00	25.00
Columbia CL-1569	(S)	**Camelot**	1961	8.00	20.00
Columbia CL-1595	(M)	**Thinking Of You**	1961	10.00	25.00
Columbia CL-1595	(S)	**Thinking Of You**	1961	8.00	20.00
Columbia CL-1741	(M)	**Mack The Knife & Other Kurt Weill Music**	1962	10.00	25.00
Columbia CS-8541	(S)	**Mack The Knife & Other Kurt Weill Music**	1962	8.00	20.00
Columbia CL-1786	(M)	**Faraway Part Of Town**	1962	10.00	25.00
Columbia CL-1786	(S)	**Faraway Part Of Town**	1962	8.00	20.00
Columbia CL-1888	(M)	**The Light Fantastic**	1962	10.00	25.00
Columbia CL-1888	(S)	**The Light Fantastic**	1962	8.00	20.00
—Columbia albums above have six white on black "eye" logos on each label.—					
PRI 3026	(S)	**The World's Most Honored Pianist** *(Yellow vinyl)*	1962	10.00	25.00
Verve V-8565	(M)	**The Essential Andre Previn**	1963	5.00	12.00
Verve V6-8565	(S)	**The Essential Andre Previn**	1963	4.00	10.00
—Verve albums above have black labels with "MGM Records" on the bottom.—					
Harmony HL-7429	(M)	**Camelot**	1967	5.00	12.00
Harmony HS-11429	(S)	**Camelot**	1967	4.00	10.00

Label & Catalog #		Title	Year	VG+	NM
PREVIN, ANDRE, & HERB ELLIS & SHELLY MANNE & RAY BROWN					
Columbia CL-2018	(M)	**Four To Go**	1963	**8.00**	**20.00**
Columbia CS-8818	(S)	**Four To Go**	1963	**6.00**	**15.00**
— Columbia albums above have "Guaranteed High Fidelity" or "360 Sound Stereo" in black on the label.—					
PREVIN, ANDRE, & RUSS FREEMAN					
Contemporary C-3537	(M)	**Double Play!**	1957	**20.00**	**50.00**
Stereo Records S-7011	(S)	**Double Play!**	1958	**18.00**	**45.00**
Contemporary S-7011	(S)	**Double Play!**	1959	**16.00**	**40.00**
PREVIN, ANDRE, & J.J. JOHNSON					
Odyssey 32160260	(S)	**Mack The Knife**	1968	**4.00**	**10.00**
		(Odyssey 32160260 is a reissue of Columbia 8541.)			
PRICE, RUTH					
Ruth Price is a jazz vocalist.					
Roost LP-2217	(M)	**Ruth Price Sings**	1956	**50.00**	**125.00**
Kapp KL-1006	(M)	**My Name Is Ruth Price, I Sing**	1955	**50.00**	**125.00**
Kapp KL-1054	(M)	**The Party's Over**	1957	**50.00**	**125.00**
Contemporary M-3590	(M)	**Ruth Price With Shelly Manne At The Manne-Hole**	1961	**30.00**	**75.00**
Contemporary S-7590	(S)	**Ruth Price With Shelly Manne At The Manne-Hole**	1961	**20.00**	**50.00**
— Contemporary stereo albums have gold & black labels.—					
Ava A-54	(M)	**Live And Beautiful**	1963	**20.00**	**50.00**
Ava AS-54	(S)	**Live And Beautiful**	1963	**16.00**	**40.00**
PRICE, SAM					
Samuel Price is a traditional jazz pianist. For additional listings refer to Roy Eldridge / Sam Price.					
Concert Hall Jazz 1008	(10")	**Barrelhouse And Blues**	1955	**20.00**	**50.00**
Jazztone J-1207	(M)	**Barrelhouse And Blues**	1956	**16.00**	**40.00**
		(Jazztone 1207 is a reissue of C.H.J. 1008.)			
Jazztone J-1236	(M)	**Les Jeunesses Musicales**	1956	**16.00**	**40.00**
Jazztone J-1260	(M)	**The Price Is Right**	1957	**16.00**	**40.00**
PRICE, VITO					
Vito Pizzo, aka Vito Price, is a modern jazz tenor and alto saxophone player.					
Argo LP-631	(M)	**Swingin' The Loop**	1958	**16.00**	**40.00**
Argo LPS-631	(S)	**Swingin' The Loop**	1958	**12.00**	**30.00**
PRIESTER, JULIAN					
Julian Priester is a modern jazz trombone player.					
Jazzland JLP-25	(M)	**Spiritsville**	1960	**16.00**	**40.00**
Jazzland JLP-925	(S)	**Spiritsville**	1960	**12.00**	**30.00**
Riverside RLP-12-316	(M)	**Keep Swingin'**	1960	**16.00**	**40.00**
Riverside RLP-1163	(S)	**Keep Swingin'**	1960	**12.00**	**30.00**
— Riverside albums above have blue mono or black stereo labels with a reel & mike logo on top.—					
PRIMA, LOUIS					
Louis Prima is a traditional jazz and rhythm 'n' blues-based trumpet player, vocalist and big band leader.					
Mercury MG-25142	(10")	**Louis Prima Plays**	1953	**30.00**	**75.00**
Capitol T-755	(M)	**The Wildest**	1956	**20.00**	**50.00**
Capitol T-836	(M)	**Call Of The Wildest**	1957	**20.00**	**50.00**
Capitol T-908	(M)	**The Wildest Show At Tahoe**	1957	**20.00**	**50.00**
Capitol T-1010	(M)	**Las Vegas Prima Style**	1958	**14.00**	**35.00**
Capitol T-1132	(M)	**Strictly Prima**	1959	**14.00**	**35.00**
— Capitol albums abive have black "rainbow" labels with the logo on the left side.—					
Capitol T-1723	(M)	**The Wildest Comes Home**	1962	**10.00**	**25.00**
Capitol ST-1723	(S)	**The Wildest Comes Home**	1962	**12.00**	**30.00**
Capitol T-1797	(M)	**Lake Tahoe Prima Style**	1963	**8.00**	**20.00**
Capitol ST-1797	(S)	**Lake Tahoe Prima Style**	1963	**10.00**	**25.00**
— Capitol albums abive have black "rainbow" labels with the logo on top.—					
Columba CL-1206	(M)	**Breakin' It Up**	1958	**14.00**	**35.00**
— Columbia albums above have six white on black "eye" logos on each label.—					
Rondo-lette 8-9	(M)	**Louis Prima In All His Moods**	1959	**10.00**	**25.00**
Dot DLP-3262	(M)	**His Greatest Hits**	1960	**12.00**	**30.00**
Dot DLP-25262	(S)	**His Greatest Hits**	1960	**10.00**	**25.00**

Label & Catalog #		Title	Year	VG+	NM
Dot DLP-3264	(M)	**Pretty Music Prima Style**	1960	12.00	30.00
Dot DLP-25264	(S)	**Pretty Music Prima Style**	1960	10.00	25.00
Dot DLP-3352	(M)	**Wonderland By Night**	1961	12.00	30.00
Dot DLP-25352	(S)	**Wonderland By Night**	1961	10.00	25.00
Dot DLP-2385	(M)	**Blue Moon**	1961	12.00	30.00
Dot DLP-25385	(S)	**Blue Moon**	1961	10.00	25.00
Dot DLP-3410	(M)	**Doin' The Twist**	1961	12.00	30.00
Dot DLP-25410	(S)	**Doin' The Twist**	1961	10.00	25.00

PRIMA, LOUIS, & KEELY SMITH

For additional listings refer to the Jazzy Soundtracks section under Capitol.

Label & Catalog #		Title	Year	VG+	NM
Dot DLP-3210	(M)	**Louis And Keely**	1959	14.00	35.00
Dot DLP-25210	(S)	**Louis And Keely**	1959	16.00	40.00
Dot DLP-3263	(M)	**Together**	1960	10.00	25.00
Dot DLP-25263	(S)	**Together**	1960	12.00	30.00
Dot DLP-3266	(M)	**Louis And Keely On Stage**	1961	10.00	25.00
Dot DLP-25266	(S)	**Louis And Keely On Stage**	1961	12.00	30.00
Dot DLP-3392	(M)	**Return Of The Wildest**	1961	10.00	25.00
Dot DLP-25392	(S)	**Return Of The Wildest**	1961	12.00	30.00
Capitol T-1531	(M)	**The Hits Of Louis And Keely**	1961	10.00	25.00
Capitol ST-1531	(S)	**The Hits Of Louis And Keely**	1961	12.00	30.00

—Capitol albums abive have black "rainbow" labels with the logo on the left side.—

PRINCE, BOB

Robert Prince is a jazz-based composer and leador. For additional listings refer to Teo Macero & Bob Prince.

Label & Catalog #		Title	Year	VG+	NM
Warner Bros. W-1240	(M)	**Jazz Ballets From Broadway**	1958	10.00	25.00
Warner Bros. WS-1240	(S)	**Jazz Ballets From Broadway**	1958	8.00	20.00
Warner Bros. W-1276	(M)	**Charleston 1970**	1959	10.00	25.00
Warner Bros. WS-1276	(S)	**Charleston 1970**	1959	8.00	20.00
RCA Victor LPM-2435	(M)	**Opus Jazz**	1961	10.00	25.00
RCA Victor LSP-2435	(S)	**Opus Jazz**	1961	8.00	20.00

—RCA albums above have black labels with "Long Play" or "Living Stereo" on the bottom.—

PROCOPE, RUSSELL

Russell Procope is a traditional jazz alto saxophone and clarinet player.

Label & Catalog #		Title	Year	VG+	NM
Dot DLP-3010	(M)	**The Persuasive Sax Of Russell Procope**	1956	16.00	40.00

PRYSOCK, ARTHUR

Arthur Prysock is a big band-based vocalist. For additional listings refer to Count Basie.

Label & Catalog #		Title	Year	VG+	NM
Old Town LP-102	(M)	**I Worry About You**	1962	20.00	50.00
Old Town LP-2004	(M)	**Arthur Prysock Sings Only For You**	1962	20.00	50.00
Old Town LP-2005	(M)	**Coast To Coast**	1963	20.00	50.00
Old Town T-90604	(M)	**A Portrait Of Arthur Prysock** *(Capitol Record Club compilation)*	1963	12.00	30.00
Old Town LP-2006	(M)	**Portrait**	1963	16.00	40.00
Old Town LP-2007	(M)	**Everlasting Songs For Everlasting Lovers**	1964	16.00	40.00
Old Town LP-2008	(M)	**Intimately Yours**	1964	16.00	40.00
Old Town LP-2009	(M)	**Double Header**	1965	16.00	40.00
Old Town LP-2010	(M)	**In A Mood**	1965	16.00	40.00
Decca DL-4581	(M)	**Strictly Sentimental**	1965	6.00	15.00
Decca DL-74581	(S)	**Strictly Sentimental**	1965	8.00	20.00
Decca DL-4628	(M)	**Showcase**	1965	6.00	15.00
Decca DL-74628	(S)	**Showcase**	1965	8.00	20.00
Verve V-5009	(M)	**Art And Soul**	1966	6.00	15.00
Verve V6-5009	(S)	**Art And Soul**	1966	6.00	15.00
Verve V-5011	(M)	**The Best Of Arthur Prysock**	1967	5.00	12.00
Verve V6-5011	(S)	**The Best Of Arthur Prysock**	1967	6.00	15.00
Verve V-5012	(M)	**A Portrait Of Arthur Prysock**	1967	6.00	15.00
Verve V6-5012	(S)	**A Portrait Of Arthur Prysock**	1967	6.00	15.00
Verve V-5014	(M)	**Mister Prysock**	1967	6.00	15.00
Verve V6-5014	(S)	**Mister Prysock**	1967	6.00	15.00
Verve V-5029	(M)	**Love Me**	1968	6.00	15.00
Verve V6-5029	(S)	**Love Me**	1968	5.00	12.00
Verve V-5038	(M)	**The Best Of Arthur Prysock, Volume 2**	1968	6.00	15.00
Verve V6-5038	(S)	**The Best Of Arthur Prysock, Volume 2**	1968	5.00	12.00
Verve V-5048	(M)	**To Love Or Not To Love**	1968	6.00	15.00
Verve V6-5048	(S)	**To Love Or Not To Love**	1968	5.00	12.00

Label & Catalog #		Title	Year	VG+	NM
Verve V-5059	*(M)*	**I Must Be Doing Something Right**	*1968*	**6.00**	**15.00**
Verve V6-5059	*(S)*	**I Must Be Doing Something Right**	*1968*	**5.00**	**12.00**
Verve V6-5070	*(S)*	**This Is My Beloved**	*1969*	**5.00**	**12.00**
Verve V6-650	*(S)*	**24 Karat Hits** *(2 LPs)*	*1969*	**6.00**	**15.00**

— Verve albums above have black labels with "MGM Records" on the bottom.—

PUCHO & THE LATIN SOUL BROTHERS

Henry "Pucho" Brown is a Latin jazz percussionist.

Prestige PRLP-7471	*(M)*	**Pucho & The Latin Soul Brothers**	*1967*	**16.00**	**40.00**
Prestige PRST-7471	*(S)*	**Pucho & The Latin Soul Brothers**	*1967*	**12.00**	**30.00**
Prestige PRLP-7502	*(M)*	**Saffron & Soul**	*1967*	**16.00**	**40.00**
Prestige PRST-7502	*(S)*	**Saffron & Soul**	*1967*	**12.00**	**30.00**
Prestige PRLP-7528	*(M)*	**Shuckin' And Jivin'**	*1967*	**16.00**	**40.00**
Prestige PRST-7528	*(S)*	**Shuckin' And Jivin'**	*1967*	**12.00**	**30.00**

— Prestige albums above have blue labels with a trident logo on the right side.—

Prestige PRST-7555	*(S)*	**Big Stick**	*1968*	**12.00**	**30.00**
Prestige PRST-7572	*(S)*	**Heat!**	*1968*	**12.00**	**30.00**
Prestige PRST-7616	*(S)*	**Dateline**	*1969*	**12.00**	**30.00**
Prestige PRST-7679	*(S)*	**The Best Of Pucho & The Latin Soul Brothers**	*1969*	**12.00**	**30.00**

— Prestige albums above have blue labels with a trident logo on top.—

PUENTE, TITO: ***Refer to*** **CHARLENE BARTLEY; WOODY HERMAN / TITO PUENTE**

PULLEN, DON, & MILFORD GRAVES

Pullen-Graves Music	*(S)*	**Graves-Pullen Duo**	*1067*	**20.00**	**50.00**
S.R.P. LP-290	*(S)*	**Nommo**	*1968*	**16.00**	**40.00**

PUMA, JOE

Joseph Puma is a modern jazz guitarist. For additional listings refer to The Four Most; The New York Jazz Quartet.

Bethlehem BCP-1012	*(10")*	**East Coast Jazz 3**	*1954*	**100.00**	**200.00**
Dawn DLP-1118	*(M)*	**Wild Kitten**	*1957*	**40.00**	**100.00**
Jubilee JLP-1070	*(M)*	**Joe Puma Jazz**	*1958*	**30.00**	**75.00**
Columbia CL-1618	*(M)*	**Like Tweet**	*1961*	**16.00**	**40.00**
Columbia CS-8418	*(S)*	**Like Tweet**	*1961*	**12.00**	**30.00**

— Columbia albums above have six white on black "eye" logos on each label.—

Q

QUARTET, THE: *Refer to* THE MODERN JAZZ QUARTET

QUARTETTE TRES BIEN, THE

The Quartette Tres Bien is Percy James, Albert St. James, Richard Simmons and Jeter Thompson.

Gene Norman GNP-102	*(M)*	**Quartette Tres Bien**	*1962*	**10.00**	**25.00**
Gene Norman GNPS-102	*(S)*	**Quartette Tres Bien**	*1962*	**8.00**	**20.00**
Gene Norman GNP-107	*(M)*	**Kilimanjaro**	*1962*	**10.00**	**25.00**
Gene Norman GNPS-107	*(S)*	**Kilimanjaro**	*1962*	**8.00**	**20.00**
Decca DL-4547	*(M)*	**Boss Tres Bien**	*1964*	**6.00**	**15.00**
Decca DL-74547	*(S)*	**Boss Tres Bien**	*1964*	**5.00**	**12.00**
Decca DL-4548	*(M)*	**Kilimanjaro**	*1964*	**6.00**	**15.00**
Decca DL-74548	*(S)*	**Kilimanjaro**	*1964*	**5.00**	**12.00**
Decca DL-4617	*(M)*	**Spring Into Spring**	*1965*	**6.00**	**15.00**
Decca DL-74617	*(S)*	**Spring Into Spring**	*1965*	**5.00**	**12.00**
Decca DL-4675	*(M)*	**Stepping Out**	*1965*	**6.00**	**15.00**
Decca DL-74675	*(S)*	**Stepping Out**	*1965*	**5.00**	**12.00**
Atlantic 1461	*(M)*	**Bully!**	*1966*	**6.00**	**15.00**
Atlantic SD-1461	*(S)*	**Bully!**	*1966*	**5.00**	**12.00**

—Atlantic albums have multi-color labels with a black fan logo.—

QUEBEC, IKE

Ike Quebec is a traditional jazz-based tenor saxophone player and pianist.

Blue Note BLP-4093	*(M)*	**Heavy Soul**	*1961*	**30.00**	**75.00**
Blue Note BST-84093	*(S)*	**Heavy Soul**	*1961*	**20.00**	**50.00**
Blue Note BLP-4098	*(M)*	**Blue And Sentimental**	*1962*	**30.00**	**75.00**
Blue Note BST-84098	*(S)*	**Blue And Sentimental**	*1962*	**20.00**	**50.00**

—Blue Note albums above have blue on white labels with a 61st St, NYC address.—

Blue Note BLP-4093	*(M)*	**Heavy Soul**	*1961*	**10.00**	**25.00**
Blue Note BST-84093	*(S)*	**Heavy Soul**	*1961*	**8.00**	**20.00**
Blue Note BLP-4098	*(M)*	**Blue And Sentimental**	*1962*	**10.00**	**25.00**
Blue Note BST-84098	*(S)*	**Blue And Sentimental**	*1962*	**8.00**	**20.00**
Blue Note BLP-4105	*(M)*	**It Might As Well Be Spring**	*1962*	**16.00**	**40.00**
Blue Note BST-84105	*(S)*	**It Might As Well Be Spring**	*1962*	**12.00**	**30.00**
Blue Note BLP-4103	*(M)*	**Easy Livin'**	*1962*	*Unreleased*	
Blue Note BST-84103	*(S)*	**Easy Livin'**	*1962*	*Unreleased*	
Blue Note BLP-4114	*(M)*	**Bossa Nova Soul Samba**	*1962*	**16.00**	**40.00**
Blue Note BST-8114	*(S)*	**Bossa Nova Soul Samba**	*1962*	**12.00**	**30.00**

—Blue Note albums above have blue on white labels with a New York, USA address.—

Blue Note BST-84093	*(S)*	**Heavy Soul**	*196?*	**6.00**	**15.00**
Blue Note BST-84098	*(S)*	**Blue And Sentimental**	*196?*	**6.00**	**15.00**
Blue Note BST-84105	*(S)*	**It Might As Well Be Spring**	*196?*	**6.00**	**15.00**
Blue Note BST-8114	*(S)*	**Bossa Nova Soul Samba**	*196?*	**6.00**	**15.00**

—Blue Note albums above have blue on white labels with "A Division of Liberty Records."—

QUIGLEY, JACK

Sand C-28	*(M)*	**Jack Quigley In Hollywood** *(Red vinyl)*	*196?*	**12.00**	**30.00**
Sand CS-28	*(S)*	**Jack Quigley In Hollywood**	*196?*	**8.00**	**20.00**
Sand C-30	*(M)*	**Class In Session** *(Red vinyl)*	*196?*	**12.00**	**30.00**
Sand CS-30	*(S)*	**Class In Session**	*196?*	**8.00**	**20.00**
Sand C-32	*(M)*	**Listen! Quigley** *(Red vinyl)*	*196?*	**12.00**	**30.00**
Sand CS-32	*(S)*	**Listen! Quigley**	*196?*	**8.00**	**20.00**
Sand C-38	*(M)*	**D' Jever**	*196?*	**10.00**	**25.00**
Sand CS-38	*(S)*	**D' Jever**	*196?*	**8.00**	**20.00**

QUILL, GENE

Daniel Eugene Quill is a modern jazz alto saxophone and clarinet player. For additional listings refer to The Four Most; Mundell Lowe & Billy Taylor & Gene Quill; Phil Woods & Gene Quill; Phil Woods & Gene Quill / Jackie McLean & John Jenkins / Hal McKusick; and the Various Artists section under Prestige.

Roost LP-2229	*(M)*	**Three Bones And A Quill**	*1958*	**20.00**	**50.00**

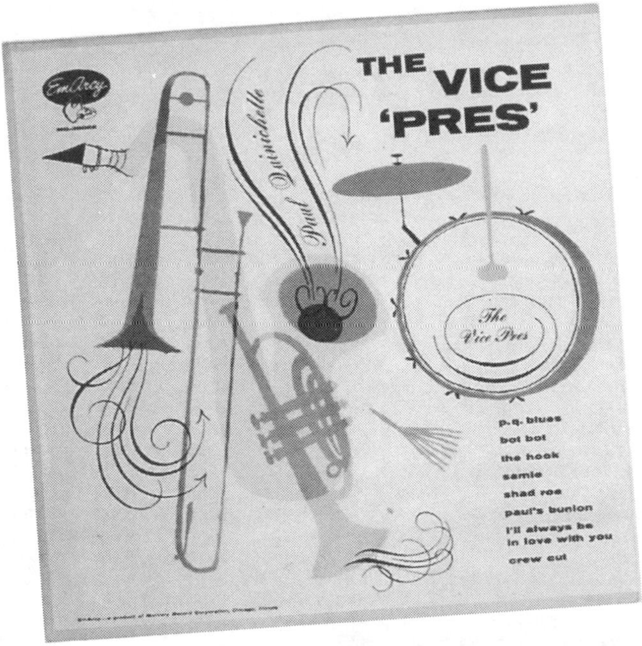

Paul Quinichette played with Jay McShann in 1942, Johnny Otis, Louis Jordan, Lucky Millinder, Eddie Wilcox, J.C. Heard and Hot Lips Page through 1951 and then joined Count Basie until 1953. He formed his own group but also gigged with Benny Goodman (1955) and Nat Pierce (1957-59). He has album projects with Charlie Rouse and Lester Young, shares an LP with Bennie Green, and was a featured guest with John Coltrane. As a sideman he can be looked up on albums by Bob Brookmeyer on United Artists, Mel Powell on Vanguard, Billie Holiday and Count Basie, both on Verve, and Woody Herman on Everest.

Label & Catalog #		Title	Year	VG+	NM

QUINICHETTE, PAUL

Paul "Vice Pres" Quinichette is a traditional jazz and big band tenor saxophone player. For additional listings refer to John Coltrane; Bennie Green / Paul Quinichette; Charlie Rouse & Paul Quinichette; Lester Young & Paul Quinichette; and the Various Artists section under Prestige.

EmArcy MG-26022	(10")	**The Vice 'Pres'**	1954	100.00	200.00
EmArcy MG-26035	(10")	**Sequel**	1954	100.00	200.00
EmArcy MG-36003	(M)	**Moods**	1955	40.00	100.00
EmArcy MG-36027	(M)	**The Vice 'Pres'**	1955	40.00	100.00
		(EmArcy 36027 is a reissue of 26022.)			
		—EmArcy albums above have blue labels with silver print.—			
Dawn DLP-1109	(M)	**The Kid From Denver**	1956	40.00	100.00
Prestige PRLP-7103	(M)	**On The Sunny Side**	1957	30.00	75.00
Prestige PRLP-7127	(M)	**For Basie**	1957	30.00	75.00
		—Prestige albums above have yellow labels with a W. 50th Street, NYC address.—			
Prestige PRLP-7147	(M)	**Basie Reunion**	1958	20.00	50.00
		—Prestige albums above have yellow mono or silver stereo labels with a Bergenfield, NJ address .—			
United Arts. UAL-4024	(M)	**Like Basie**	1959	20.00	50.00
United Arts. UAS-5024	(S)	**Like Basie**	1959	16.00	40.00
United Arts. UAL-4054	(M)	**Like Who?**	1959	16.00	40.00
United Arts. UAS-5054	(S)	**Like Who?**	1959	12.00	30.00
		(United Artists 4054 is a reissue of 4024.)			
United Arts. UAL-4077	(M)	**Paul Quinichette**	1960	20.00	50.00
United Arts. UAS-5077	(S)	**Paul Quinichette**	1960	16.00	40.00
Swingville SVLP-2036	(M)	**For Basie**	1962	20.00	50.00
Swingville SVLP-2037	(M)	**Basie Reunion**	1962	20.00	50.00
		(Swingville 2037 is a reissue of Prestige 7147.)			
		—Swingville mono albums above have purple mono or red stereo labels.—			
Swingville SVLP-2036	(M)	**For Basie**	1965	10.00	25.00
Swingville SVLP-2037	(M)	**Basie Reunion**	1965	10.00	25.00
		—Swingville albums above have blue labels with a trident logo on the right side.—			

QUINICHETTE, PAUL, & FRANK FOSTER

Decca DL-8058	(M)	**Jazz Studio 1**	1954	40.00	100.00

QUINICHETTE, PAUL / BENNIE GREEN

Decca DL-8176	(M)	**Blow Your Horn**	1955	40.00	100.00

QUINICHETTE, PAUL / GENE ROLAND

Dawn DLP-1112	(M)	**Jazzville**	1957	40.00	100.00

QUINTET, THE

The Quintet features the last public reunion of Dizzy Gillespie, Charles Mingus, "Charlie Chan" a.k.a. Charlie Parker, Bud Powell and Max Roach. Note that Volume 2 is listed under Powell's name.

Debut DLP-2	(10")	**Jazz At Massey Hall**	1953	240.00	400.00
Debut DLP-4	(10")	**Jazz At Massey Hall, Volume 3**	1953	240.00	400.00
Debut DEB-124	(M)	**Jazz At Massey Hall**	1956	150.00	300.00
		(Debut 124 is a reissue of 2 and 4.)			
Fantasy 6006	(M)	**Jazz At Massey Hall** *(Red vinyl)*	1962	20.00	50.00
Fantasy 6006	(E)	**Jazz At Massey Hall**	1962	12.00	30.00
Fantasy 86006	(M)	**Jazz At Massey Hall** *(Blue vinyl)*	1962	12.00	30.00
Fantasy 86006	(E)	**Jazz At Massey Hall**	1962	6.00	15.00
		(Fantasy 6006 is a reissue of Debut 124.)			

QUINTET OF THE HOT CLUB OF FRANCE, THE (*aka* THE HOT CLUB QUINTET)

The Quintet of the Hot Club of Paris features Django Reinhardt.

Dial LP-214	(10")	**Django Reinhardt And The Hot Club Quintet**	1951	125.00	250.00
Dial LP-218	(10")	**Django Reinhardt And The Quintet Of The Hot Club Of France**	1951	125.00	250.00
London 810	(10")	**Hot Club Quintet**	1954	50.00	125.00
London LL-1344	(M)	**Swing From Paris**	1956	30.00	75.00
		(London 1344 is a reissue of 810.)			
Capitol T-2045	(M)	**Hot Club Of France**	1964	12.00	30.00
Capitol DT-2045	(E)	**Hot Club Of France**	1964	8.00	20.00
Prestige PRST-7614	(E)	**First Recordings**	1969	6.00	15.00
		—Prestige albums above have blue labels with a trident logo on top.—			

R.

RAE, JOHN
John Rae is a modern jazz vibraphones player.

Savoy MG-12156	(M)	**Opus De Jazz, Volume 2**	1960	16.00	40.00

RAEBURN, BOYD
Boyd Raeburn is a traditional jazz-based saxophone(s) player, composer and big band leader.

Savoy MG-15010	(10")	**Innovations By Boyd Raeburn, Volume 1**	1951	30.00	75.00
Savoy MG-15011	(10")	**Innovations By Boyd Raeburn, Volume 2**	1951	30.00	75.00
Savoy MG-15012	(10")	**Innovations By Boyd Raeburn, Volume 3**	1951	30.00	75.00
Savoy MG-12025	(M)	**Man With The Horn**	1955	20.00	50.00
Savoy MG-12040	(M)	**Boyd Meets Stravinsky**	1955	16.00	40.00
Columbia CL-889	(M)	**Dance Spectacular**	1956	12.00	30.00

— Columbia albums above have six white on black "eye" logos on each label.—

RAINEY, MA
Gertrude Malissa Nix Pridgett, aka Ma Rainey, is a traditional jazz vocalist.

Riverside RLP-1003	(10")	**Ma Rainey, Vol. 1**	1953	40.00	100.00
Riverside RLP-1016	(10")	**Ma Rainey, Vol. 2**	1953	40.00	100.00
Riverside RLP-1045	(10")	**Ma Rainey, Vol. 3**	1953	40.00	100.00
Riverside RLP-12-108	(M)	**Ma Rainey**	1955	24.00	60.00
Riverside RLP-12-137	(M)	**Broken Hearted Blues**	1956	24.00	60.00

— Riverside albums above have blue on white labels.—

RALKE, DON
Donald Ralke is a jazz-based bongo player.

Crown CLP-5019	(M)	**Bongo Madness**	1957	10.00	25.00

RAMPART STREET PARADERS, THE
The Paraders include Clyde Hurley, Abe Lincoln, Matty Matlock, Eddie Miller and George Van Eps. For additional listings refer to Eddie Condon / The Rampart Street Paraders.

Columbia CL-648	(M)	**Rampart And Vine**	1955	16.00	40.00

— Columbia albums above have "Long Playing" on the bottom of the label.—

Columbia CL-648	(M)	**Rampart And Vine**	1956	12.00	30.00
Columbia CL-785	(M)	**Dixieland My Dixieland**	1956	12.00	30.00
Columbia CL-1061	(M)	**Texas! U.S.A.**	1957	12.00	30.00

— Columbia albums above have six white on black "eye" logos on each label.—

RANDI, DON
Donald Randi is a modern jazz pianist.

World Pacific WP-1297	(M)	**Feelin' Like Blues**	1960	14.00	35.00
World Pacific ST-1297	(S)	**Feelin' Like Blues**	1960	10.00	25.00
Verve V-8469	(M)	**Where Do We Go From Here?**	1962	6.00	15.00
Verve V6-8469	(S)	**Where Do We Go From Here?**	1962	5.00	12.00
Verve V-8524	(M)	**Last Night With The Don Randi Trio**	1963	6.00	15.00
Verve V6-8524	(S)	**Last Night With The Don Randi Trio**	1963	5.00	12.00

— Verve albums above have black labels with "MGM Records" on the bottom.—

Palomar 24002	(M)	**Don Randi**	1965	6.00	15.00
Palomar 34002	(S)	**Don Randi**	1965	5.00	12.00

RANEY, JIMMY
James Raney is a modern jazz guitarist and composer. For additional listings refer to Bob Brookmeyer; Bob Brookmeyer & Jim Hall & Jim Raney; Kenny Burrell & Jimmy Raney; The Manhattan Jazz All-Stars.; Zoot Sims & Jimmy Raney & Jim Hall.

New Jazz NJLP-1101	(10")	**Jimmy Raney Quartet Featuring Hall Overton**	1953	125.00	250.00
New Jazz NJLP-1103	(10")	**Jimmy Raney Ensemble Introducing Phil Woods**	1953	125.00	250.00
Prestige PRLP-156	(10")	**Jimmy Raney Plays**	1953	60.00	150.00
Prestige PRLP-179	(10")	**Jimmy Raney In Sweden**	1954	60.00	150.00
Prestige PRLP-199	(10")	**Jimmy Raney Quintet**	1954	60.00	150.00
Prestige PRLP-201	(10")	**Jimmy Raney Quartet**	1955	60.00	150.00

(Prestige 201 is a reissue of New Jazz 1101.)

Jimmy Raney began in 1944 with Jerry Wald's band before moving to Chicago and playing with local groups. He joined Woody Herman (1948), Al Haig, Buddy DeFranco, Artie Shaw (1949-50), Terry Gibbs, and then Stan Getz (1951-53). He followed with Red Norvo (1953-54), Les Elgart (1953), and Jimmy Lyons (1954-60). Aside from his handful of LPs under his own name, he has recorded album projects with Kenny Burrell, Zoot Sims and Jim Hall, and George Wallington (shown above). He has appeared as a featured guest with Teddy Charles, as a member of The Street Swingers, and has appeared as a sideman on albums by Getz on Verve and Roost, Norvo on Fantasy, DeFranco on MGM, and as "Sir Osbert Haberdasher" with Al Cohn on RCA Victor.

Label & Catalog #		Title	Year	VG+	NM
Prestige PRLP-203	(10")	**Jimmy Raney Ensemble**	1955	60.00	150.00
		(Prestige 203 is a reissue of New Jazz 1103.)			
Prestige PRLP-7089	(M)	**Jimmy Raney/A**	1957	30.00	75.00
—Prestige albums above have yellow labels with a W. 50th Street, NYC address.—					
ABC-Paramount ABC-129	(M)	**Jimmy Raney Featuring Bob Brookmeyer**	1956	24.00	60.00
ABC-Paramount ABC-167	(M)	**Jimmy Raney In Three Attitudes**	1957	24.00	60.00
Dawn DLP-1120	(M)	**Jimmy Raney Visits Paris**	1958	24.00	60.00

RANEY, JIMMY / GEORGE WALLINGTON

EmArcy MG-36121	(M)	**Swingin' In Sweden**	1958	24.00	60.00
—EmArcy albums above have blue labels with silver print.—					

RAWLS, LOU

Pop vocalist Lou Rawls' first few albums were jazz tinged: On Capitol 1714, Rawls is backed by Les McCann; on 1824 and 2042, by Onzy Matthews.

Capitol T-1714	(M)	**Stormy Monday**	1962	5.00	12.00
Capitol ST-1714	(S)	**Stormy Monday**	1962	6.00	15.00
Capitol T-1824	(M)	**Black And Blue**	1963	5.00	12.00
Capitol ST-1824	(S)	**Black And Blue**	1963	6.00	15.00
Capitol T-2042	(M)	**Tobacco Road**	1964	5.00	12.00
Capitol ST-2042	(S)	**Tobacco Road**	1964	6.00	15.00
—Capitol albums above have black "rainbow" labels with the logo on top.—					

RAY, JOHNNIE

Pop singer Johnny Ray is backed by a small jazz group featuring Mundell Lowe and Billy Taylor.

Columbia CL-1225	(M)	**'Til Morning**	1958	16.00	40.00
—Columbia albums above have six white on black "eye" logos on each label.—					
Columbia CL-1225	(M)	**'Til Morning**	196?	6.00	15.00
—Columbia albums above have "360 Sound" in white on the bottom of the label.—					

RED, SONNY

Sonny Red is a moden jazz alto saxophone player. For additional listings refer to Cliff Jordan; Art Pepper & Sonny Red.

Blue Note BLP-4032	(M)	**Out Of The Blue** *(Deep groove)*	1960	40.00	100.00
Blue Note BLP-4032	(M)	**Out Of The Blue**	1960	30.00	75.00
Blue Note ST-84032	(S)	**Out Of The Blue**	1960	20.00	50.00
—Blue Note albums above have blue on white labels with a W. 63rd St., NYC address.—					
Blue Note BLP-4032	(M)	**Out Of The Blue**	1963	10.00	25.00
Blue Note ST-84032	(S)	**Out Of The Blue**	1963	8.00	20.00
—Blue Note albums above have blue on white labels with a New York, USA address.—					
Blue Note ST-84032	(S)	**Out Of The Blue**	196?	5.00	12.00
—Blue Note albums above have blue on white labels with a "A Division of Liberty Records."—					
Jazzland JLP-32	(M)	**Breezin'**	1960	16.00	40.00
Jazzland JLP-932	(S)	**Breezin'**	1960	12.00	30.00
Jazzland JLP-59	(M)	**The Mode**	1961	16.00	40.00
Jazzland JLP-959	(S)	**The Mode**	1961	12.00	30.00
		(Jazzland 59 also features Grant Geen and Barry Harris.)			
Jazzland JLP-74	(M)	**Images**	1962	16.00	40.00
Jazzland JLP-974	(S)	**Images**	1962	12.00	30.00

RED ONION JAZZ BAND, THE

Riverside RLP-12-260	(M)	**Dance Off Both Your Shoes In Hi-Fi**	1958	16.00	40.00
—Riverside albums above have blue mono or black stereo labels with a reel & mike logo on top.—					

REDD, FREDDIE

Frederick Redd is a modern jazz pianist and composer.

Prestige PRLP-197	(10")	**Introducing The Freddie Redd Trio**	1954	60.00	150.00
Riverside RLP-12-250	(M)	**San Francisco Suite For Jazz Trio**	1957	20.00	50.00
—Riverside albums above have blue mono or black stereo labels with a reel & mike logo on top.—					
Blue Note BLP-4027	(M)	**Music From "The Connection"** *(Deep groove)*	1960	50.00	125.00
Blue Note BLP-4027	(M)	**Music From "The Connection"**	196?	30.00	75.00
Blue Note BST-84027	(S)	**Music From "The Connection"**	196?	20.00	50.00
		(B.N. 4027 features music composed for an off-Broadway production.)			
Blue Note BLP-4045	(M)	**Shades Of Redd** *(Deep groove)*	1960	50.00	125.00
Blue Note BLP-4045	(M)	**Shades Of Redd**	1960	30.00	75.00
Blue Note BST-84045	(S)	**Shades Of Redd**	1960	*Unreleased*	
—Blue Note albums above have blue on white labels with a W. 63rd St., NYC address.—					

Label & Catalog #		Title	Year	VG+	NM
Blue Note BLP-4027	*(M)*	**Music From "The Connection"**	*196?*	**10.00**	**25.00**
Blue Note BST-84027	*(S)*	**Music From "The Connection"**	*196?*	**8.00**	**20.00**
Blue Note BLP-4045	*(M)*	**Shades Of Redd**	*196?*	**10.00**	**25.00**
Blue Note BST-84045	*(S)*	**Shades Of Redd**	*196?*	*Unreleased*	

—Blue Note albums above have blue on white labels with a New York, USA address.—

Blue Note BST-84027	*(S)*	**Music From "The Connection"**	*196?*	**5.00**	**12.00**

—Blue Note albums above have blue on white labels with "A Division of Liberty Records."—

REDD, FREDDIE, & HAMPTON HAWES

Prestige PRLP-7067	*(M)*	**Piano East Piano West**	*1956*	**30.00**	**75.00**

—Prestige albums above have yellow labels with a W. 50th Street, NYC address.—

New Jazz NJLP-8307	*(M)*	**Movin'**	*1963*	*Unreleased*	
Status ST-8307	*(M)*	**Movin'**	*1965*	**16.00**	**40.00**

(Status 8307 is a reissue of Prestige 7067.)

REDD, VI

Vi Redd is a West Coast jazz vocalist and alto saxophone player.

United Arts. UAJ-14016	*(M)*	**Bird Call**	*1962*	**20.00**	**50.00**
United Arts. UAJS-15016	*(S)*	**Bird Call**	*1962*	**16.00**	**40.00**
Atco 33-157	*(M)*	**Lady Soul**	*1963*	**16.00**	**40.00**
Atco SD-33-157	*(S)*	**Lady Soul**	*1963*	**12.00**	**30.00**

—Atco albums above have a white stripe through the center of the label.—

REDMAN, DON

Donald Redman is a traditional jazz multi-instrumentalist, vocalist, arranger and composer. For additional listings refer to the Jazzy Soundtracks section under Revue.

Golden Crest GC-3017	*(M)*	**Park Avenue Patter**	*1958*	**16.00**	**40.00**
Roulette R-25070	*(M)*	**Dixieland In High Society**	*1960*	**10.00**	**25.00**
Roulette SR-25070	*(S)*	**Dixieland In High Society**	*1960*	**8.00**	**20.00**
RCA Victor LPV-520	*(M)*	**Master Of The Big Band**	*1965*	**8.00**	**20.00**

REDMAN, GEORGE

George Redman is a modern jazz drummer.

Skylark SKLP-20	*(10")*	**The George Redman Group**	*1954*	**60.00**	**150.00**

(Sky. 20 was reissued as Tampa 26, Bob Gordon's "Jazz Impressions.")

REDMOND, EDGAR

Disque-Phenom. 2696	*(10")*	**Edgar Redmond & The Modern String Ensemble**	*1965*	**12.00**	**30.00**

REECE, DIZZY, & TUBBY HAYES

Savoy MG-12111	*(M)*	**Changing The Jazz At Buckingham Palace**	*1957*	**40.00**	**100.00**

REECE, DIZZY

Jamaican born Alphonso "Dizzy" Reece is a modern jazz trumpet player.

Imperial LP-9043	*(M)*	**London Jazz**	*1957*	**30.00**	**75.00**
Blue Note BLP-4006	*(M)*	**Blues In Trinity** *(Deep groove)*	*1958*	**60.00**	**150.00**
Blue Note BLP-4006	*(M)*	**Blues In Trinity**	*1958*	**40.00**	**100.00**
Blue Note BST-4006	*(S)*	**Blues In Trinity** *(Deep groove)*	*1959*	**40.00**	**100.00**
Blue Note BST-4006	*(S)*	**Blues In Trinity**	*1959*	**30.00**	**75.00**
Blue Note BLP-4023	*(M)*	**Star Bright** *(Deep groove)*	*1959*	**50.00**	**125.00**
Blue Note BLP-4023	*(M)*	**Star Bright**	*1959*	**30.00**	**75.00**
Blue Note BST-84023	*(S)*	**Star Bright**	*1959*	**20.00**	**50.00**
Blue Note BLP-4033	*(M)*	**Soundin' Off** *(Deep groove)*	*1960*	**50.00**	**125.00**
Blue Note BLP-4033	*(M)*	**Soundin' Off**	*1960*	**30.00**	**75.00**
Blue Note BST-84033	*(S)*	**Soundin' Off**	*1960*	**20.00**	**50.00**

—Blue Note albums above have blue on white labels with a W. 63rd St., NYC address.—

Blue Note BLP-4006	*(M)*	**Blues In Trinity**	*1963*	**10.00**	**25.00**
Blue Note BST-4006	*(S)*	**Blues In Trinity**	*1963*	**8.00**	**20.00**
Blue Note BLP-4023	*(M)*	**Star Bright**	*1963*	**10.00**	**25.00**
Blue Note BST-84023	*(S)*	**Star Bright**	*1963*	**8.00**	**20.00**
Blue Note BLP-4033	*(M)*	**Soundin' Off**	*1963*	**10.00**	**25.00**
Blue Note BST-84033	*(S)*	**Soundin' Off**	*1963*	**8.00**	**20.00**

—Blue Note albums above have blue on white labels with a New York, USA address.—

Blue Note BST-4006	*(S)*	**Blues In Trinity**	*196?*	**5.00**	**12.00**
Blue Note BST-84023	*(S)*	**Star Bright**	*196?*	**5.00**	**12.00**
Blue Note BST-84033	*(S)*	**Soundin' Off**	*196?*	**5.00**	**12.00**

—Blue Note albums above have blue on white labels with "A Division of Liberty Records."—

Label & Catalog #		Title	Year	VG+	NM
New Jazz NJLP-8274	(M)	**Asia Minor**	1962	20.00	50.00
—New Jazz albums above have purple labels.—					
New Jazz NJLP-8274	(M)	**Asia Minor**	1965	10.00	25.00
—New Jazz albums above have blue labels with a trident logo on the right side.—					

REED, LUCY

Lucille Reed is a jazz-based vocalist.

Label & Catalog #		Title	Year	VG+	NM
Fantasy 3212	(M)	**The Singing Reed**	1956	60.00	150.00
Fantasy 3243	(M)	**This Is Lucy Reed**	1957	60.00	150.00
—Fantasy albums above have red labels on dark red, non-flexible vinyl.—					
Fantasy 3212	(M)	**The Singing Reed**	195?	30.00	75.00
Fantasy 3243	(M)	**This Is Lucy Reed**	195?	30.00	75.00
—Fantasy albums above have red labels on non-flexible vinyl.—					

REESE, DELLA

Dellareese Taliaferro, aka Della Reese, is a jazz-based popular vocalist.

Label & Catalog #		Title	Year	VG+	NM
Jubilee JLP-1026	(M)	**Melancholy Baby**	1957	12.00	30.00
Jubilee JLP-1071	(M)	**A Date With Della Reese**	1958	10.00	25.00
Jubilee JGS-1071	(S)	**A Date With Della Reese**	1959	12.00	30.00
Jubilee JLP-1083	(M)	**Amen**	1958	10.00	25.00
Jubilee JGS-1083	(S)	**Amen**	1959	12.00	30.00
Jubilee JLP-1095	(M)	**The Story Of The Blues**	1958	10.00	25.00
Jubilee JGS-1095	(S)	**The Story Of The Blues**	1959	12.00	30.00
Jubilee JLP-1109	(M)	**What Do You Know About Love?**	1959	10.00	25.00
Jubilee JGS-1109	(S)	**What Do You Know About Love?**	1959	12.00	30.00
Jubilee JLP-1116	(M)	**And That Reminds Me**	1959	10.00	25.00
Jubilee JGS-1116	(S)	**And That Reminds Me**	1959	12.00	30.00
RCA Victor LPM-2157	(M)	**Della**	1960	10.00	25.00
RCA Victor LSP-2157	(S)	**Della**	1960	12.00	30.00
RCA Victor LPM-2204	(M)	**Della By Starlight**	1960	10.00	25.00
RCA Victor LSP-2204	(S)	**Della By Starlight**	1960	12.00	30.00
RCA Victor LPM-2280	(M)	**Della Della Cha-Cha-Cha**	1960	10.00	25.00
RCA Victor LSP-2280	(S)	**Della Della Cha-Cha-Cha**	1960	12.00	30.00
RCA Victor LPM-2391	(M)	**Special Delivery**	1961	10.00	25.00
RCA Victor LSP-2391	(S)	**Special Delivery**	1961	12.00	30.00
RCA Victor LPM-2419	(M)	**Classic Della**	1961	10.00	25.00
RCA Victor LSP-2419	(S)	**Classic Della**	1961	12.00	30.00
RCA Victor LPM-2568	(M)	**Della Reese On Stage**	1962	10.00	25.00
RCA Victor LSP-2568	(S)	**Della Reese On Stage**	1962	12.00	30.00
RCA Victor LPM-2711	(M)	**Waltz With Me**	1963	4.00	20.00
RCA Victor LSP-2711	(S)	**Waltz With Me**	1963	10.00	25.00
—RCA albums above have black labels with "Long Play" or "Living Stereo" on the bottom.—					
RCA Victor LPM-2872	(M)	**Della Reese At Basin Street East**	1964	4.00	20.00
RCA Victor LSP-2872	(S)	**Della Reese At Basin Street East**	1964	10.00	25.00
—RCA albums above have black labels with "Mono" or "Living Stereo" on the bottom.—					
ABC-Paramount ABC-524	(M)	**C'mon And Hear**	1964	6.00	15.00
ABC-Paramount ABCS-524	(M)	**C'mon And Hear**	1964	4.00	20.00
ABC-Paramount ABC-540	(M)	**I Like It Like Dat!**	1965	6.00	15.00
ABC-Paramount ABCS-540	(M)	**I Like It Like Dat!**	1965	4.00	20.00
ABC-Paramount ABC-569	(M)	**Della Reese Live**	1965	6.00	15.00
ABC-Paramount ABCS-569	(S)	**Della Reese Live**	1965	4.00	20.00

REHAK, FRANK / ALEX SMITH

Frank Rehak is a modern jazz trombone player.

Label & Catalog #		Title	Year	VG+	NM
Dawn DLP-1107	(M)	**Jazzville, Vol. 2**	1956	40.00	100.00

REID, IRENE

Label & Catalog #		Title	Year	VG+	NM
MGM E-4159	(M)	**It's Only The Beginning For Irene Reid**	1963	8.00	20.00
MGM SE-4159	(S)	**It's Only The Beginning For Irene Reid**	1963	6.00	15.00
Verve V-8621	(M)	**Room For One More**	1965	8.00	20.00
Verve V6-8621	(S)	**Room For One More**	1965	6.00	15.00
—Verve albums above have black labels with "MGM Records" on the bottom.—					

REINHARDT, DJANGO

A French Gypsy by birth, Jean Baptiste "Django" Reinhardt's non-jazz guitar playing influenced jazz musicians worldwide. For additional listings refer to The Quintet; Dizzie Gillespie / Django Reinhardt.

Label & Catalog #		Title	Year	VG+	NM
Mercury MGC-516	(10")	**The Great Artistry Of Django Reinhardt**	1953	100.00	200.00
(Clef 516 features cover art by David Stone Martin.)					

Guitarist Django Reinhardt organized France's Quintet of The Hot Club with Stephane Grapelly (1934-39). By 1946 he was touring with the Ellington Orchestra. His style, based on his Gypsy background and affected by the paralysis of a portion of his left hand, while not truly jazz, nonetheless had an pronounced effect on jazz musicians worldwide.

Label & Catalog #		Title	Year	VG+	NM
Clef MGC-516	(10")	**The Great Artistry Of Django Reinhardt**	1954	60.00	150.00
Jay 3008	(10")	**Django Reinhardt**	1954	70.00	175.00
Angel ANG-60003	(10")	**Le Jazz Hot**	1954	60.00	150.00
Angel ANG-60011	(10")	**Django's Guitar**	1955	60.00	150.00
London LB-810	(10")	**Swing From Paris**	1955	50.00	125.00
Period SPL-1100	(10")	**Django Reinhardt Memorial, Volume 1**	1954	50.00	125.00
Period SPL-1101	(10")	**Django Reinhardt Memorial, Volume 2**	1954	50.00	125.00
Period SPL-1102	(10")	**Django Reinhardt Memorial, Volume 3**	1954	50.00	125.00
Period SPL-1201	(M)	**Django Reinhardt Memorial Album, Volume 1**	1956	20.00	50.00
Period SPL-1202	(M)	**Django Reinhardt Memorial Album, Volume 2**	1956	20.00	50.00
Period SPL-1203	(M)	**Django Reinhardt Memorial Album, Volume 3**	1956	20.00	50.00
Period SPL-1204	(M)	**The Best Of Django Reinhardt**	1956	20.00	50.00
Period SPL-2204	(E)	**The Best Of Django Reinhardt**	1959	10.00	25.00
RCA Victor LPM-1100	(M)	**Django Reinhardt**	1955	40.00	100.00
RCA Victor LPM-2319	(M)	**Djangology**	1961	16.00	40.00
RCA Victor LSP-2319	(E)	**Djangology**	1961	10.00	25.00
		—RCA albums above have black labels with "Long Play" or "Reprocessed Stereo" on the bottom.—			
Felsted 7005	(M)	**Django Reinhardt And His Rhythm**	1959	20.00	50.00
Felsted 2005	(E)	**Django Reinhardt And His Rhythm**	1959	12.00	30.00
		(Felsted 87005 is a reissue of Clef 516.)			
Capitol Int. T-10226	(M)	**The Best Of Django Reinhardt** *(2 LPs)*	1960	20.00	50.00
Reprise R-6075	(M)	**The Immortal Django Reinhardt**	1963	10.00	25.00
Reprise R9-6075	(E)	**The Immortal Django Reinhardt**	1963	6.00	15.00
Sutton SU-274	(M)	**Django Reinhardt And His Guitar**	1966	8.00	20.00
Sutton SSU-274	(E)	**Django Reinhardt And His Guitar**	1966	5.00	12.00
Archive Of Folk & Jazz 212	(E)	**Django Reinhardt**	1968	4.00	10.00
Archive Of Folk & Jazz 230	(E)	**Django Reinhardt, Vol. 2**	1969	4.00	10.00
Prestige PRST-7633	(E)	**Django Reinhardt And American Jazz Giants**	1969	5.00	12.00
		(Prestige 7633 also features Benny Carter, Garnet Clark and Coleman Hawkins)			
		—Prestige albums above have blue labels with a trident logo on top.—			

REMINGTON, DAVE

Jubilee JLP-1017	(M)	**Chicago Jazz Reborn**	1956	16.00	40.00

RENA, KID

Henry Rene, aka Kid Rena, is a traditional jazz trumpet player.

Circle L-409	(10")	**Kid Rena Delta Jazz Band**	1951	30.00	75.00

RENAUD, HENRI

French born Henri Renuad is a modern jazz pianist, composer and band leader.

Contemporary C-2502	(10")	**The Henri Renaud All Stars**	1953	50.00	125.00
Period SPL-1211	(M)	**The Birdlanders**	1954	30.00	75.00
Period SPL-1212	(M)	**The Birdlanders**	1954	30.00	75.00

RENDELL, DON

Donald Rendell is a modern jazz tenor saxophone and clarinet player.

Jazzland JLP-51	(M)	**Roarin'**	1961	16.00	40.00
Jazzland JLP-951	(S)	**Roarin'**	1961	12.00	30.00

RENE, HENRI

RCA Victor LPM-1947	(M)	**Compulsion To Swing**	1958	16.00	40.00
RCA Victor LSP-1947	(S)	**Compulsion To Swing**	1958	12.00	30.00
		—RCA albums above have black labels with "Long Play" or "Living Stereo" on the bottom.—			

REVELERS, THE

Rondo-lette A-50	(M)	**Jazz At The Downstairs Club**	1962	10.00	25.00
Rondo-lette SA-50	(S)	**Jazz At The Downstairs Club**	1962	8.00	20.00

REXROTH, KENNETH, & LAWRENCE FERLINGHETTI

Kenneth Rexroth and Lawrence Ferlenghetti are members of the San Francisco "beat" school of poetry and are backed by The Cellar Jazz Quintet.

Fantasy 7002	(M)	**Poetry Readings From The Cella** *(Dark red vinyl)*	1957	60.00	150.00
		—Fantasy albums above have red labels on dark red, non-flexible vinyl.—			
Fantasy 7002	(M)	**Poetry Readings From The Cellar**	195?	30.00	75.00
		—Fantasy albums above have red labels on non-flexible vinyl.—			

Label & Catalog #		Title	Year	VG+	NM
REXROTH, KENNETH					
Fantasy 7008	(M)	**Poetry And Jazz At The Blackhawk** *(Red vinyl)*	1958	40.00	100.00
Fantasy 7008	(M)	**Poetry And Jazz At The Blackhawk**	195?	20.00	50.00
		— Fantasy albums above have red labels on non-flexible vinyl. —			
REYS, RITA					
Rita Reys is a jazz-based vocalist.					
Columbia CL-903	(M)	**The Cool Voice Of Rita Reys With Art Blakey & The Jazz Messengers**	1956	40.00	100.00
		— Columbia albums above have six white on black "eye" logos on each label. —			
Epic LN-3522	(M)	**Her Name Is Rita Reys**	1957	30.00	75.00
REYNOLDS, TOMMY					
Thomas Reynolds is a traditional jazz clarinet player and band leader.					
Royale 18117	(10")	**Tommy Reynolds Orchestra With Bon Bon**	195?	30.00	75.00
King 395-510	(M)	**Jazz For Happy Feet**	1956	30.00	75.00
		— King albums above have silver on black labels. —			
Audio Lab AL-1509	(M)	**Dixieland All Stars**	1958	30.00	75.00
RHODES, GEORGE					
Groove LG-1005	(M)	**Real George!**	1956	16.00	40.00
RHYNE, MEL					
Melvin Rhyne is a modern jazz organist.					
Jazzland JLP-16	(M)	**Organizing**	1960	16.00	40.00
Jazzland JLP-916	(S)	**Organizing**	1960	12.00	30.00
RICH, BUDDY					
Bernard "Buddy" Rich is a traditional jazz drummer, vocalist and big band leader. For additional listings refer to Lionel Hampton & Art Tatum & Buddy Rich; Gene Krupa & Buddy Rich; Flip Phillips; Lester Young.					
Norgran MGN-26	(10")	**Buddy Rich Swinging**	1954	40.00	100.00
Norgran MGN-1031	(M)	**Sing And Swing With Buddy Rich**	1955	30.00	75.00
		(Norgran 1031 features cover art by David Stone Martin.)			
Norgran MGN-1052	(M)	**The Swingin' Buddy Rich**	1955	24.00	60.00
		(Norgran 1052 is a reissue of 26.)			
Norgran MGN-1078	(M)	**The Wailing Buddy Rich**	1956	24.00	60.00
Norgran MGN-1086	(M)	**This One's For Basie**	1956	24.00	60.00
Verve MGV-2009	(M)	**Buddy Rich Sings Johnny Mercer**	1956	16.00	40.00
Verve MGV-2075	(M)	**Buddy Rich Just Sings**	1957	16.00	40.00
Verve MGV-8142	(M)	**The Swingin' Buddy Rich**	1957	16.00	40.00
		(Verve 8142 is a reissue of Norgran 1052 with the DSM cover.)			
Verve MGV-8168	(M)	**The Wailing Buddy Rich**	1957	16.00	40.00
		(Verve 8186 is a reissue of Norgran 1078.)			
Verve MGV-8176	(M)	**This One's For Basie**	1957	16.00	40.00
		(Verve 8176 is a reissue of Norgran 1086.)			
Verve MGV-8285	(M)	**Buddy Rich In Miami**	1958	16.00	40.00
		— Verve albums above have black labels with "Verve Records, Inc." on the bottom. —			
Verve V-2009	(M)	**Buddy Rich Sings Johnny Mercer**	1961	6.00	15.00
Verve V-2075	(M)	**Buddy Rich Just Sings**	1961	6.00	15.00
Verve V-8142	(M)	**The Swingin' Buddy Rich**	1961	6.00	15.00
Verve V-8168	(M)	**The Wailing Buddy Rich**	1961	6.00	15.00
Verve V-8176	(M)	**This One's For Basie**	1961	6.00	15.00
Verve V-8285	(M)	**Buddy Rich In Miami**	1961	6.00	15.00
Verve V-8425	(M)	**Blues Caravan**	1962	10.00	25.00
Verve V6-8425	(S)	**Blues Caravan**	1962	8.00	20.00
Verve V-8471	(M)	**Burnin' Beat**	1962	10.00	25.00
Verve V6-8471	(S)	**Burnin' Beat**	1962	8.00	20.00
		(Verve 8471 also features Gene Krupa.)			
Verve V-8712	(M)	**Big Band Shout**	1967	6.00	15.00
Verve V6-8712	(S)	**Big Band Shout**	1967	5.00	12.00
		(Verve 8712 is a reissue of part of Norgran 1086.)			
Verve V6-8778	(S)	**Super Rich**	1969	4.00	10.00
		— Verve albums above have black labels with "MGM Records" on the bottom. —			
Mercury MG-20451	(M)	**Richcraft**	1959	12.00	30.00
Mercury SR-60136	(S)	**Richcraft**	1959	10.00	25.00
Mercury MG-20461	(M)	**The Voice Is Rich**	1959	12.00	30.00
Mercury SR-60144	(S)	**The Voice Is Rich**	1959	10.00	25.00
		— Mercury albums above have silver on black labels. —			

Ann Richards first hit the roads with Charlie Barnett followed by a stint with George Redman before touring with, and subsequently marrying, Stan Kenton. She then "retired" from touring although she continued to record on her own and with Kenton for Capitol.

Label & Catalog #		Title	Year	VG+	NM
Argo LP-676	(M)	**Playtime**	1961	10.00	25.00
Argo LPS-676	(S)	**Playtime**	1961	8.00	20.00
Pacific Jazz PJ-10113	(M)	**Swingin' New Band**	1967	8.00	20.00
Pacific Jazz ST-20113	(S)	**Swingin' New Band**	1967	6.00	15.00
Pacific Jazz PJ-10117	(M)	**Big Swing Face**	1967	8.00	20.00
Pacific Jazz ST-20117	(S)	**Big Swing Face**	1967	6.00	15.00
Pacific Jazz PJ-10126	(M)	**The New One**	1967	8.00	20.00
Pacific Jazz ST-20126	(S)	**The New One**	1967	6.00	15.00
World Pacific WPS-20113	(S)	**The Buddy Rich Big Band**	1968	6.00	15.00
World Pacific WPS-20133	(S)	**Mercy, Mercy**	1968	6.00	15.00
World Pacific WPS-20158	(S)	**Buddy & Soul**	1968	6.00	15.00
World Pacific WPS-21453	(S)	**Rich Ala Rahka**	1969	6.00	15.00

RICH, BUDDY, & SWEETS EDISON

Norgran MGN-1038	(M)	**Buddy And Sweets**	1955	30.00	75.00
		(Norgran 1038 features cover art by David Stone Martin.)			
Verve MGV-8129	(M)	**Buddy And Sweets**	1957	16.00	40.00
		(Verve 8129 is a reissue of Norgran 1038)			
		—Verve albums above have "Verve Records, Inc." on the bottom of the label.—			
Verve V-8129	(M)	**Buddy And Sweets**	1961	6.00	15.00
		—Verve albums above have black labels with "MGM Records" on the bottom.—			

RICH, BUDDY, & MAX ROACH

Mercury MG-20448	(M)	**Rich Versus Roach**	1959	20.00	50.00
Mercury SR-60133	(S)	**Rich Versus Roach**	1959	16.00	40.00
		—Mercury albums above have silver on black labels.—			

RICHARDS, ANN

Margaret Ann Borden, aka Ann Richards, is a West Coast jazz and big band vocalist (and the former Mrs. Stan Kenton).

Capitol T-1087	(M)	**I'm Shooting High**	1959	16.00	40.00
Capitol ST-1087	(S)	**I'm Shooting High**	1959	20.00	50.00
Capitol T-1406	(M)	**The Many Moods Of Ann Richards**	1960	16.00	40.00
Capitol ST-1406	(S)	**The Many Moods Of Ann Richards**	1960	20.00	50.00
Capitol T-1495	(M)	**Two Much!**	1961	16.00	40.00
Capitol ST-1495	(S)	**Two Much!**	1961	20.00	50.00
		(Capitol 1495 also features Stan Kenton.)			
		—Capitol albums above have black "rainbow" labels with the logo on the left side.—			
Atco 33-136	(M)	**Ann, Man!**	1961	20.00	50.00
Atco SD-33-136	(S)	**Ann, Man!**	1961	30.00	75.00
		—Atco albums above have a white stripe through the center of the label.—			

RICHARDS, EMIL

Uni 3003	(M)	**New Time Element**	1967	10.00	25.00
Uni 73003	(S)	**New Time Element**	1967	6.00	15.00
Uni 3008	(M)	**New Sound**	1967	10.00	25.00
Uni 73008	(S)	**New Sound**	1967	6.00	15.00
Impulse AS-9182	(S)	**Spirit Of '76**	1968	6.00	15.00
Impulse AS-9188	(S)	**Journey To Bliss**	1968	6.00	15.00
		—Impulse albums above have orange & black labels.—			
Impulse AS-9182	(S)	**Spirit Of '76**	1969	4.00	10.00
Impulse AS-9188	(S)	**Journey To Bliss**	1969	4.00	10.00
		—Impulse albums above have red & black labels with the "abc" logo on top.—			

RICHARDS, JOHNNY

John Richards is a modern jazz arranger, composer and band leader. For additional listings refer to Dizzy Gillespie.

Bethlehem BCP-6011	(M)	**Something Else By Johnny Richards**	1956	16.00	40.00
Capitol T-885	(M)	**Wide Range**	1957	16.00	40.00
Capitol T-981	(M)	**Experiments In Sound**	1958	16.00	40.00
		—Capitol albums above have turpuoise labels.—			
Roulette R-52008	(M)	**The Rites Of Diablo**	1958	12.00	30.00
Roulette SR-52008	(S)	**The Rites Of Diablo**	1958	10.00	25.00
Roulette R-52114	(M)	**My Fair Lady**	1964	6.00	15.00
Roulette SR-52114	(S)	**My Fair Lady**	1964	5.00	12.00
Coral CRL-57304	(M)	**Walk Softly/Run Wild**	1959	8.00	20.00
Coral CRL-757304	(S)	**Walk Softly/Run Wild**	1959	6.00	15.00

Label & Catalog #		Title	Year	VG+	NM

RICHARDSON, JEROME

Jerome Richardson is a modern jazz saxophone(s) and woodwinds player. For additional listings refer to The Prestige Blues Swingers; and the Various Artists section under Prestige.

New Jazz NJLP-8205	(M)	**Jerome Richardson Sextet**	1958	30.00	75.00
New Jazz NJLP-8226	(M)	**Roamin' With Richardson**	1959	30.00	75.00
		—New Jazz albums above have purple labels.—			
New Jazz NJLP-8205	(M)	**Jerome Richardson Sextet**	1965	10.00	25.00
New Jazz NJLP-8226	(M)	**Roamin' With Richardson**	1965	10.00	25.00
		—New Jazz albums above have blue labels with a trident logo on the right side.—			
United Arts. UAJ-14006	(M)	**Going To The Movies**	1962	16.00	40.00
United Arts. UAJS-15006	(S)	**Going To The Movies**	1962	12.00	30.00
Verve V-8729	(M)	**Groove Merchant**	1967	6.00	15.00
Verve V6-8729	(S)	**Groove Merchant**	1967	5.00	12.00
		—Verve albums above have black labels with "MGM Records" on the bottom.—			

RIEDEL, GEORGE

Philips PHM-200-140	(M)	**Jazz Ballet**	1964	8.00	20.00
Philips PHS-600-140	(S)	**Jazz Ballet**	1964	6.00	15.00

RITZ, LYLE

Lyle Ritz is a modern jazz bass, tuba, violin and ukelele platyer.

Verve MGV-2087	(M)	**How About Uke?**	1957	16.00	40.00
Verve MGV-8333	(M)	**50th State Jazz**	1959	16.00	40.00
Verve MGVS-6070	(S)	**50th State Jazz**	1960	12.00	30.00
		—Verve albums above have "Verve Records, Inc." on the bottom of the label.—			
Verve V-8333	(M)	**50th State Jazz**	1961	6.00	15.00
Verve V6-8333	(S)	**50th State Jazz**	1961	5.00	12.00
		—Verve albums above have black labels with "MGM Records" on the bottom.—			

RIVERS, MAVIS

Mavis Rivers is a jazz-based vocalist. For additional listings refer to Shorty Rogers.

Reprise R-2002	(M)	**Mavis**	1961	12.00	30.00
Reprise R9-2002	(S)	**Mavis**	1961	16.00	40.00
		(On Reprise 2002 Mavis is backed by Bill Perkins and Jack Sheldon.)			
Reprise R-6074	(M)	**Mavis Rivers Meets Shorty Rogers**	1963	10.00	25.00
Reprise RS-6074	(S)	**Mavis Rivers Meets Shorty Rogers**	1963	12.00	30.00
Vee Jay LP-1132	(M)	**We Remember Mildred Bailey**	1964	10.00	25.00
Vee Jay LPS-1132	(S)	**We Remember Mildred Bailey**	1964	16.00	40.00
		(On Vee Jay 1132 Mavis is backed by Red Norvo.)			

RIVERS, SAM

Samuel Rivers is a modern jazz saxophone(s), flute and piano player.

Blue Note BLP-4184	(M)	**Fuschia Swing Song**	1964	12.00	30.00
Blue Note BST-84184	(S)	**Fuschia Swing Song**	1964	10.00	25.00
Blue Note BLP-4206	(M)	**Contours**	1965	12.00	30.00
Blue Note BST-84206	(S)	**Contours**	1965	10.00	25.00
Blue Note BLP-4249	(M)	**A New Conception**	1966	12.00	30.00
Blue Note BST-84249	(S)	**A New Conception**	1966	10.00	25.00
Blue Note BLP-4261	(M)	**Dimensions & Extensions**	1966	*Unreleased*	
Blue Note BST-84261	(S)	**Dimensions & Extensions**	1966	*Unreleased*	
		—Blue Note albums above have blue on white labels with a New York, NY address.—			
Blue Note BST-84184	(S)	**Fuschia Swing Song**	196?	5.00	12.00
Blue Note BST-84206	(S)	**Contours**	196?	5.00	12.00
Blue Note BST-84249	(S)	**A New Conception**	196?	5.00	12.00
		—Blue Note albums above have blue on white labels with "A Division of Liberty Records."—			

RIVERSIDE JAZZ STARS, THE

The Riverside Jazz Stars are, primarily, Blue Mitchell, Jimmy Heath and the Bobby Timmons Trio with Clark Terry and Julius Watkins.

Riverside RLP-397	(M)	**A Jazz Version Of "Kean"**	1961	16.00	40.00
Riverside RS-9397	(S)	**A Jazz Version Of "Kean"**	1961	12.00	30.00
		—Riverside albums above have blue mono or black stereo labels with a reel & mike logo on top.—			

RIZZI, TONY

Anthony Rizzi is a jazz-based guitarist.

Starlite 6002	(10")	**Tony Rizzi Guitar**	1954	20.00	50.00

Label & Catalog #		Title	Year	VG+	NM

ROACH, FREDDIE

Frederick Roach is a modern jazz organ player and composer.

Blue Note BLP-4113	(M)	**Down To Earth**	1962	12.00	30.00
Blue Note BST-84113	(S)	**Down To Earth**	1962	10.00	25.00
Blue Note BLP-4128	(M)	**Mo' Greens, Please**	1963	12.00	30.00
Blue Note BST-84128	(S)	**Mo' Greens, Please**	1963	10.00	25.00
Blue Note BLP-4158	(M)	**Good Move**	1964	12.00	30.00
Blue Note BST-84158	(S)	**Good Move**	1964	10.00	25.00
Blue Note BLP-4168	(M)	**Brown Sugar**	1964	12.00	30.00
Blue Note BST-84168	(S)	**Brown Sugar**	1964	10.00	25.00
Blue Note BLP-4190	(M)	**All That's Good**	1965	12.00	30.00
Blue Note BST-84190	(S)	**All That's Good**	1965	10.00	25.00
—Blue Note albums above have blue on white labels with a New York, NY address.—					
Blue Note BST-84113	(S)	**Down To Earth**	196?	5.00	12.00
Blue Note BST-84128	(S)	**Mo' Greens, Please**	196?	5.00	12.00
Blue Note BST-84158	(S)	**Good Move**	196?	5.00	12.00
Blue Note BST-84168	(S)	**Brown Sugar**	196?	5.00	12.00
Blue Note BST-84190	(S)	**All That's Good**	196?	5.00	12.00
—Blue Note albums above have blue on white labels with "A Division of Liberty Records."—					
Prestige PRLP-7490	(M)	**The Soul Book**	1967	10.00	25.00
Prestige PRST-7490	(S)	**The Soul Book**	1967	8.00	20.00
Prestige PRLP-7507	(M)	**Mocha Motion**	1967	10.00	25.00
Prestige PRST-7507	(S)	**Mocha Motion**	1967	8.00	20.00
Prestige PRLP-7521	(M)	**My People—Soul People**	1967	10.00	25.00
Prestige PRST-7521	(S)	**My People—Soul People**	1967	8.00	20.00
—Prestige albums above have blue labels with a trident logo on the right side.—					

ROACH, MAX / ART BLAKEY

Blue Note BLP-5010	(10")	**Max Roach Quintet / Art Blakey & His Band**	1952	300.00	500.00

ROACH, MAX

Maxwell Roach is a modern jazz drummer. For additional listings refer to Duke Ellington & Charles Mingus & Max Roach; Coleman Hawkins; The Jazz Artists Guild; Booker Little; Charles Mingus; Charlie Parker, Dizzie Gillespie, Bud Powell & Max Roach; The Quintet; Buddy Rich & Max Roach; Sonny Rollins; Dinah Washington / Terry Gibbs & Max Roach & Don Elliott.; and the Various Artists section under EmArcy.

Debut DLP-13	(10")	**Max Roach Quartet Featuring Hank Mobley**	1954	150.00	300.00
EmArcy MG-36098	(M)	**Max Roach + 4**	1957	40.00	100.00
EmArcy SR-80000	(S)	**Max Roach + 4**	1959	30.00	75.00
EmArcy MG-36108	(M)	**Jazz In 3/4 Time**	1957	30.00	75.00
EmArcy SR-80002	(S)	**Jazz In 3/4 Time**	1959	24.00	60.00
EmArcy MG-36127	(M)	**The Max Roach 4 Plays Charlie Parker**	1958	30.00	75.00
EmArcy SR-80019	(S)	**The Max Roach 4 Plays Charlie Parker**	1959	24.00	60.00
EmArcy MG-36132	(M)	**Max Roach + 4 On The Chicago Scene**	1958	20.00	50.00
EmArcy SR-800??	(S)	**Max Roach + 4 On The Chicago Scene**	1959	16.00	40.00
EmArcy MG-36140	(M)	**Max Roach Plus Four At Newport**	1958	20.00	50.00
EmArcy SR-80010	(S)	**Max Roach Plus Four At Newport**	1959	16.00	40.00
EmArcy MG-36144	(M)	**Max Roach With The Boston Percussion Ensemble**	1958	20.00	50.00
EmArcy SR-80015	(S)	**Max Roach With The Boston Percussion Ensemble**	1959	16.00	40.00
—EmArcy albums above have blue labels with silver print.—					
Argo LP-623	(M)	**Max**	1958	20.00	50.00
Argo LPS-623	(S)	**Max**	1958	16.00	40.00
Riverside RLP-12-280	(M)	**Deeds, Not Words**	1958	20.00	50.00
Riverside RLP-1122	(S)	**Deeds, Not Words**	1959	16.00	40.00
—Riverside albums above have blue mono or black stereo labels with a reel & mike logo on top.—					
Mercury MG-20491	(M)	**Quiet As It's Kept**	1959	20.00	50.00
Mercury SR-60170	(S)	**Quiet As It's Kept**	1959	16.00	40.00
Mercury MG-20539	(M)	**Moon Faced And Starry-Eyed**	1960	20.00	50.00
Mercury SR-60215	(S)	**Moon Faced And Starry-Eyed**	1960	16.00	40.00
		(Mercury 20539 also features Abbey Lincoln.)			
—Mercury albums above have silver on black labels.—					
Time T-70003	(M)	**Award Winning Drummer**	1959	20.00	50.00
Time ST-70003	(S)	**Award Winning Drummer**	1959	16.00	40.00
Candid CD-8002	(M)	**We Insist—Freedom Now Suite**	1960	24.00	60.00
Candid CS-9002	(S)	**We Insist—Freedom Now Suite**	1960	20.00	50.00
Impulse A-8	(M)	**Percussion Bitter Sweet**	1961	14.00	35.00
Impulse AS-8	(S)	**Percussion Bitter Sweet**	1961	12.00	30.00

Max Roach checked in with Charlie Parker in 1942, although his first recording session was with Coleman Hawkins in 1944. He then worked with Dizzy Gillespie and Benny Carter (1944-45) before gigging with the smaller New York based combos of Parker and Miles Davis. In 1954 he played with Howard Rumsey's Lighthouse All Stars before touring with his own quintet featuring Clifford Brown. He has done album projects with Parker, Gillespie and Bud Powell, the Jazz Artists Guild, and with Buddy Rich, and as a member of The Quintet. He has appeared as a featured guest with Hawkins, Booker Little, and Charlie Mingus. As a sideman he can be heard on albums by Sonny Rollins on Prestige, Miles Davis on Capitol and Prestige, Thelonious Monk on Blue Note, prestige and Riverside, Bud Powell on Blue Note, Roost and Verve, and Charlie Parker on Savoy, Roost and Verve. The album illustrated above are the original issue (*Award-Winning Drummer*) and the reissue (*Max Roach*) of his sole release for Time Records

Label & Catalog #		Title	Year	VG+	NM
Impulse A-16	(M)	**It's Time**	1962	14.00	35.00
Impulse AS-16	(S)	**It's Time**	1962	12.00	30.00
		(Impulse 16 also features Abbey Lincoln.)			
		—Impulse albums above have orange & black labels.—			
Impulse AS-8	(S)	**Percussion Bitter Sweet**	1968	6.00	15.00
Impulse AS-16	(S)	**It's Time**	1968	6.00	15.00
		—Impulse albums above have red & black labels with the "abc" logo on top.—			
Jazzland JLP-79	(M)	**Conversation**	1962	12.00	30.00
Jazzland JLP-979	(S)	**Conversation**	1962	10.00	25.00
		(Jazzland 79 is a reissue of Riverside 2100.)			
Time 52087	(M)	**Max Roach**	1962	12.00	30.00
Time S-2087	(S)	**Max Roach**	1962	10.00	25.00
		(Time 2087 is a reissue of 70003.)			
Mercury MG-20760	(M)	**Parisian Sketches**	1962	16.00	40.00
Mercury SR-60760	(S)	**Parisian Sketches**	1962	12.00	30.00
Mercury MG-20911	(M)	**The Many Sides Of Max**	1964	12.00	30.00
Mercury SR-60911	(S)	**The Many Sides Of Max**	1964	10.00	25.00
		—Mercury albums above have silver on black labels.—			
Fantasy 6007	(M)	**Speak Brother, Speak**	1963	12.00	30.00
Fantasy 86007	(S)	**Speak Brother, Speak**	1963	10.00	25.00
Atlantic 1435	(M)	**Max Roach Trio Featuring The Legendary Hasaan**	1965	10.00	25.00
Atlantic SD-1435	(S)	**Max Roach Trio Featuring The Legendary Hasaan**	1965	8.00	20.00
Atlantic 1467	(M)	**Drums Unlimited**	1966	10.00	25.00
Atlantic SD-1467	(S)	**Drums Unlimited**	1966	8.00	20.00
Atlantic SD-1510	(S)	**Members Don't Get waey**	1968	8.00	20.00
		—Atlantic albums above have multi-color labels with a black fan logo.—			
Riverside RS-3018	(S)	**Deeds Not Words**	1968	6.00	15.00
		(Riverside 3018 is a reissue of 1122.)			

ROACH, MAX, & CLIFFORD BROWN: ***Refer to*** **CLIFFORD BROWN & MAX ROACH**

ROACH, MAX, & SONNY CLARK & GEORGE DUVIVIER

Time 52101	(M)	**Max Roach, Sonny Clark, George Duvivier**	1962	16.00	40.00
Time S-2101	(S)	**Max Roach, Sonny Clark, George Duvivier**	1962	12.00	30.00

ROACH, MAX, & STAN LEVEY

Liberty LRP-3064	(M)	**Drummin' The Blues**	1957	30.00	75.00
		—Liberty albums above have green labels with a lighthouse logo.—			

ROBBINS, ADELAIDE / MARIAN McPARTLAND / BARBARA CARROLL

Adelaide Robbins is a traditional jazz-based pianist.

Savoy MG-12097	(M)	**Lookin' For A Boy**	1957	20.00	50.00

ROBERTS, HOWARD

Howard Roberts is a West Coast jazz guitar player. For additional listings refer to Dick Marx.

Norgran MGN-1106	(M)	**Mr. Roberts Plays Guitar**	1955	*Unreleased*	
Verve MGV-8192	(M)	**Mr. Roberts Plays Guitar**	1957	20.00	50.00
Verve MGV-8305	(M)	**Good Pickin's**	1959	20.00	50.00
		—Verve albums above have black labels with "Verve Records, Inc." on the bottom.—			
Verve V-8192	(M)	**Mr. Roberts Plays Guitar**	1961	8.00	20.00
Verve V-8305	(M)	**Good Pickin's**	1961	8.00	20.00
Verve V-8662	(M)	**Velvet Groove**	1966	8.00	20.00
Verve V6-8662	(S)	**Velvet Groove**	1966	6.00	15.00
Verve VSP-29	(M)	**The Movin' Man**	1966	8.00	20.00
Verve VSPS-29	(E)	**The Movin' Man**	1966	4.00	10.00
		—Verve albums above have black labels with "MGM Records" on the bottom.—			
Capitol T-1887	(M)	**Color Him Funky**	1963	8.00	20.00
Capitol ST-1887	(S)	**Color Him Funky**	1963	6.00	15.00
Capitol T-1961	(M)	**H.R. Is A Dirty Guitar Player**	1963	8.00	20.00
Capitol ST-1961	(S)	**H.R. Is A Dirty Guitar Player**	1963	6.00	15.00
Capitol T-2214	(M)	**Something's Cookin'**	1965	8.00	20.00
Capitol ST-2214	(S)	**Something's Cookin'**	1965	6.00	15.00
Capitol T-2400	(M)	**Goodies**	1965	8.00	20.00
Capitol ST-2400	(S)	**Goodies**	1965	6.00	15.00
Capitol S-2478	(M)	**Whatever's Fair**	1966	8.00	20.00
Capitol ST-2478	(S)	**Whatever's Fair**	1966	6.00	15.00

Label & Catalog #		Title	Year	VG+	NM
Capitol S-2609	(M)	**All-Time Great Instrumental Hits**	1966	8.00	20.00
Capitol ST-2609	(S)	**All-Time Great Instrumental Hits**	1966	6.00	15.00
Capitol S-2716	(M)	**Jaunty—Jolly**	1967	10.00	25.00
Capitol ST-2716	(S)	**Jaunty—Jolly**	1967	6.00	15.00
Capitol T-2824	(M)	**Guilty**	1967	10.00	25.00
Capitol ST-2824	(S)	**Guilty**	1967	6.00	15.00
Capitol ST-2901	(S)	**Out Of Sight—But In Mind**	1968	6.00	15.00
Impulse AS-9207	(S)	**Antelope Freeway**	1969	6.00	15.00

—Impulse albums above have red & black labels with the "abc" logo on top.—

ROBERTS, LUCKEY

Charles Luckeyeth Roberts is a traditional jazz pianist and composer.

Period RL-1929	(M)	**Happy Go Luckey**	1956	16.00	40.00

ROBERTS, LUCKEY, & WILLIE "THE LION" SMITH

Good Time Jazz L-12035	(M)	**Harlem Piano Solos**	1958	16.00	40.00
Good Time Jazz S-10035	(S)	**Harlem Piano Solos**	1958	12.00	30.00

ROBERTS, POLA: ***Refer to*** **GLORIA COLEMAN & POLA ROBERTS**

ROBINSON, JIM

Nathan "Jim" Robinson is a traditional jazz trombone player.

Riverside RLP-369	(M)	**Jim Robinson's New Orleans Band**	1961	12.00	30.00
Riverside RS-9369	(E)	**Jim Robinson's New Orleans Band**	1961	6.00	15.00
Riverside RLP-393	(M)	**Jim Robinson Plays Spirituals And Blues**	1961	12.00	30.00
Riverside RS-9393	(E)	**Jim Robinson Plays Spirituals And Blues**	1961	6.00	15.00

—Riverside albums above have blue mono or black stereo labels with a reel & mike logo on top.—

ROBINSON, JIM, & BILLIE & DE DE PIERCE

Atlantic 1409	(M)	**Jim Robinson And Billie & DeDe Pierce**	1963	10.00	25.00
Atlantic SD-1409	(S)	**Jim Robinson And Billie & DeDe Pierce**	1963	8.00	20.00

—Atlantic albums above have multi-color labels with a black fan logo.—

ROBINSON, PERRY

Savoy MG-12177	(M)	**4-Funk Dumpling**	1962	12.00	30.00
Savoy MG-12202	(M)	**East Of Suez**	196?	6.00	15.00

ROBINSON, SUGAR CHILE

Capitol T-589	(M)	**Boogie Woogie**	1955	40.00	100.00

—Capitol albums above have turquoise labels.—

ROCHE, BETTY

Mary Elizabeth "Betty" Roche is a traditional jazz and big band vocalist.

Bethlehem BCP-64	(M)	**Take The 'A' Train**	1956	30.00	75.00
Prestige PRLP-7187	(M)	**Singin' & Swingin'**	1961	20.00	50.00
Prestige PRLP-7198	(M)	**Lightly And Politely**	1961	20.00	50.00

—Prestige albums above have yellow mono or silver stereo labels with a Bergenfield, NJ address .—

RODGERS, GENE

Eugene Rodgers is a traditional jazz pianist and arranger.

EmArcy MG-36145	(M)	**Jazz Comes To The Astor**	1958	16.00	40.00

—EmArcy albums above have blue labels with silver print.—

RODGERS, IKE

Ike Rodgers is a traditional jazz trombone player.

Riverside RLP-1013	(10")	**The Trombone Of Ike Rodgers**	1953	30.00	75.00

RODNEY, RED

Robert Chudnick, aka Red Rodney, is a modern jazz trumpet player. For additional listings refer to Stan Getz / Red Rodney / Kai Winding; Gerry Mulligan & Kai Winding / Red Rodney.

Prestige PRLP-122	(10")	**Red Rodney**	1952	100.00	200.00
Fantasy 3208	(M)	**Modern Music From Chicago**	1956	50.00	125.00

—Fantasy albums above have red labels on dark red, non-flexible vinyl.—

Fantasy 3208	(M)	**Modern Music From Chicago**	195?	30.00	75.00

—Fantasy albums above have red labels on non-flexible vinyl.—

Signal S-1206	(M)	**Red Rodney 1957**	1957	300.00	500.00

—Signal albums above have an arrow & ear logo on the label.—

Label & Catalog #		Title	Year	VG+	NM
Savoy MG-12148	(M)	**Fiery Red Rodney**	1959	40.00	100.00
		(Savoy 12148 is a reissue of Signal 1206.)			
Argo LP-643	(M)	**Red Rodney Returns**	1959	20.00	50.00
Argo LSP-643	(S)	**Red Rodney Returns**	1959	16.00	40.00

RODRIGUEZ, WILLIE

Willie Rodriguez is a traditional jazz drummer.

Riverside RLP-469	(M)	**Flatjacks**	1963	12.00	30.00
Riverside RS-9469	(S)	**Flatjacks**	1963	10.00	25.00

—Riverside albums above have blue mono or black stereo labels with a reel & mike logo on top.—

ROGERS, BOB

Robert Rogers is a modern jazz vibraphone player.

Indigo 1501	(M)	**All That And This, Too**	1961	12.00	30.00

ROGERS, SHORTY

Milton "Shorty" Rogers is a West Coast jazz trumpet player, arranger and composer. For additional listings refer to Boots Brown; Al Cohn / Shorty Rogers; Shelly Manne; Mavis Rivers; Bud Shank; Mel Torme; and the Jazzy Soundtracks section under Decca.

Capitol H-294	(10")	**Modern Sounds**	1952	100.00	200.00
RCA Victor LPM-3137	(10")	**Shorty Rogers' Giants**	1953	100.00	200.00
RCA Victor LPM-3138	(10")	**Cool And Crazy**	1953	125.00	250.00
RCA Victor LJM-1004	(M)	**Shorty Rogers Courts The Count**	1954	30.00	75.00
RCA Victor LPM-1195	(M)	**Shorty Rogers And His Giants**	1956	30.00	75.00
RCA Victor LPM-1326	(M)	**Wherever The Five Winds Blow**	1956	30.00	75.00
RCA Victor LPM-1334	(M)	**Collaboration**	1956	24.00	60.00
RCA Victor LPM-1350	(M)	**The Big Shorty Rogers Express**	1957	24.00	60.00
RCA Victor LPM-1428	(M)	**Shorty Rogers Plays Richard Rogers**	1957	24.00	60.00
RCA Victor LPM-1564	(M)	**Portrait Of Shorty**	1957	24.00	60.00
RCA Victor LPM-1696	(M)	**Gigi Goes Jazz**	1958	24.00	60.00
RCA Victor LSP-1696	(S)	**Gigi Goes Jazz**	1958	20.00	50.00
RCA Victor LPM-1763	(M)	**Afro-Cuban Influence**	1958	20.00	50.00
RCA Victor LSP-1763	(S)	**Afro-Cuban Influence**	1958	16.00	40.00
RCA Victor LPM-1975	(M)	**Chances Are It Swings**	1959	16.00	40.00
RCA Victor LSP-1975	(S)	**Chances Are It Swings**	1959	12.00	30.00
RCA Victor LPM-1997	(M)	**The Wizard Of Oz**	1959	16.00	40.00
RCA Victor LSP-1997	(S)	**The Wizard Of Oz**	1959	12.00	30.00
RCA Victor LPM-2110	(M)	**The Swingin' Nutcracker**	1960	16.00	40.00
RCA Victor LSP-2110	(S)	**The Swingin' Nutcracker**	1960	12.00	30.00
—RCA albums above have black labels with "Long Play" or "Living Stereo" on the bottom.—					
Atlantic 1212	(M)	**The Swinging Mr. Rogers**	1955	20.00	50.00
Atlantic 1232	(M)	**Martians, Come Back**	1956	20.00	50.00
Atlantic SD-1232	(S)	**Martians, Come Back**	1958	20.00	50.00
Atlantic 1270	(M)	**Way Up There**	1957	20.00	50.00
—Atlantic albums above have black mono or green stereo labels.—					
Atlantic 1212	(M)	**The Swinging Mr. Rogers**	1961	8.00	20.00
Atlantic 1232	(M)	**Martians, Come Back**	1961	8.00	20.00
Atlantic SD-1232	(S)	**Martians, Come Back**	1961	6.00	15.00
Atlantic 1270	(M)	**Way Up There**	1961	8.00	20.00
—Atlantic albums above have multi-color labels with a white fan logo.—					
Atlantic 1212	(M)	**The Swinging Mr. Rogers**	196?	5.00	12.00
Atlantic 1232	(M)	**Martians, Come Back**	196?	5.00	12.00
Atlantic SD-1232	(S)	**Martians, Come Back**	196?	4.00	10.00
Atlantic 1270	(M)	**Way Up There**	196?	5.00	12.00
—Atlantic albums above have multi-color labels with a black fan logo.—					
MGM E-3798	(M)	**Shorty Rogers Meets Tarzan**	1960	16.00	40.00
MGM SE-3798	(S)	**Shorty Rogers Meets Tarzan**	1960	12.00	30.00
Warner Bros. W-1443	(M)	**4th Dimension Jazz**	1961	12.00	30.00
Warner Bros. WS-1443	(S)	**4th Dimension Jazz**	1961	10.00	25.00
Reprise R-6050	(M)	**Bossa Nova**	1962	10.00	25.00
Reprise R9-6050	(S)	**Bossa Nova**	1962	8.00	20.00
Reprise R-6060	(M)	**Jazz Waltz**	1962	10.00	25.00
Reprise R9-6060	(S)	**Jazz Waltz**	1962	8.00	20.00
Capitol T-1960	(M)	**Gospel Mission**	1963	10.00	25.00
Capitol ST-1960	(S)	**Gospel Mission**	1963	8.00	20.00

—Capitol albums above have black "rainbow" labels with the logo on top.—

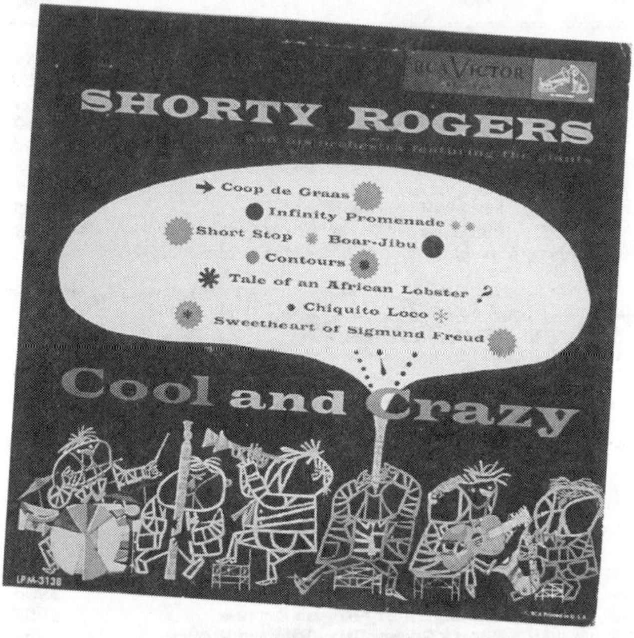

Shorty Rogers began his career with Will Bradley (1942) and Red Norvo (1942-43). After the war he worked on and off with Woody Herman from 1945 through 1951, also playing with Butch Stone and Charlie Barnett during the same time. He landed with Stan Kenton (1950-52) and Howard Rumsey (1953) before expanding into technical aspects of recording (musical director for Atlantic and A&R for RCA Victor) and film soundtracks. He was a member of the Boots Brown sessions and has been a featured guest on albums by Teddy Charles, Bud Shank and Shelly Manne. As a sideman he has recorded with Woody Herman on Capitol and Harmony, Kenton on Capitol, Johnny Richards on Bethlehem, Jimmy Giuffre on Atlantic, Rumsey on Contemporary, and Leith Stevens on Coral.

Label & Catalog #		Title	Year	VG+	NM

ROGERS, SHORTY / GERRY MULLIGAN

Capitol T-691	(M)	**Modern Sounds**	1956	30.00	75.00
		(Capitol 691 is a reissue of 294 and 439,.)			
Capitol T-2025	(M)	**Modern Sounds**	1963	8.00	20.00
Capitol DT-2025	(E)	**Modern Sounds**	1963	4.00	10.00

ROGERS, SHORTY, & ANDRE PREVIN

RCA Victor LPM-1018	(M)	**Collaboration**	1954	24.00	60.00

—RCA albums above have black labels with "Long Play" on the bottom.—

ROLAND, GENE

Gene Roland is a West Coast jazz trumpet and trombone player, arranger and composer. For additional listings refer to Paul Quinichette / Gene Roland.

Dawn DLP-1122	(M)	**Jazzville—Volume 4**	1958	30.00	75.00
Brunswick BL-54114	(M)	**Swingin' Friends**	1963	20.00	50.00
Brunswick BL-754114	(S)	**Swingin' Friends**	1963	16.00	40.00

ROLAND, JOE

Joseph Roland is a modern jazz vibraphone player. For additional listings refer to Eddie Shu / Joe Roland / Bill Davis.

Savoy MG-15034	(10")	**Joe Roland Quartet**	1954	50.00	125.00
Savoy MG-15047	(10")	**Joe Roland Quartet**	1954	50.00	125.00
Savoy MG-12039	(M)	**Joltin' Joe Roland**	1955	20.00	50.00
		(Savoy 12039 is a reissue of 15034 and 15047.)			
Bethlehem BCP-17	(M)	**Joe Roland Quintet**	1955	20.00	50.00

ROLLINI, ADRIAN

Adrian Rollini is a traditional jazz bass saxophone and vibraphone player.

Mercury MG-20011	(M)	**Chopsticks**	1953	16.00	40.00

ROLLINS, SONNY

Theodore "Sonny" or "Newk" Rollins is a modern jazz tenor saxophone player. For additional listings refer to Gary Burton / Sonny Rollins / Clark Terry; Miles Davis; Art Farmer; Dizzie Gillespie; The Modern Jazz Quartet; Thelonious Monk; Sonny Stitt; and the Jazzy Soundtracks section under Impulse.

Prestige PRLP-137	(10")	**Sonny Rollins Quartet**	1952	125.00	250.00
Prestige PRLP-186	(10")	**Sonny Rollins Quintet**	1954	125.00	250.00
Prestige PRLP-190	(10")	**Sonny Rollins**	1954	125.00	250.00
Prestige PRLP-7020	(M)	**Work Time**	1956	30.00	75.00
Prestige PRLP-7029	(M)	**Sonny Rollins With The Modern Jazz Quartet** *(Blue cover)*	1956	40.00	100.00
Prestige PRLP-7029	(M)	**Sonny Rollins With The Modern Jazz Quartet** *(Green cover)*	1956	40.00	100.00
Prestige PRLP-7029	(M)	**Sonny Rollins With The Modern Jazz Quartet** *(Yellow cover)*	1956	30.00	75.00
		(Prestige 7029 is a reissue of 137.)			
Prestige PRLP-7038	(M)	**Sonny Rollins Plus 4**	1956	30.00	75.00
Prestige PRLP-7047	(M)	**Tenor Madness**	1956	30.00	75.00
Prestige PRLP-7058	(M)	**Moving Out**	1956	30.00	75.00
		(Prestige 7058 is a reissue of 186 and 190.)			
Prestige PRLP-7079	(M)	**Saxophone Colossus**	1957	30.00	75.00
Prestige PRLP-7095	(M)	**Rollins Plays For Bird**	1957	30.00	75.00
Prestige PRLP-7126	(M)	**Tour De Force**	1957	30.00	75.00

—Prestige albums above have yellow labels with a W. 50th Street, NY address on the label.—

Prestige PRLP-7207	(M)	**Sonny Boy**	1961	16.00	40.00
Prestige PRLP-7246	(M)	**Work Time**	1962	16.00	40.00
Prestige PRST-7246	(E)	**Work Time**	1962	10.00	25.00
		(Prestige 7246 is a reissue of 7020.)			
Prestige PRLP-7269	(M)	**Sonny And The Stars**	1963	16.00	40.00
Prestige PRST-7269	(E)	**Sonny And The Stars**	1963	10.00	25.00
		(Prestige 7269 is a reissue of 7029.)			

—Prestige albums above have yellow mono or silver stereo labels with a Bergenfield, NJ address .—

Prestige PRLP-7326	(M)	**Saxophone Colossus**	1964	16.00	40.00
Prestige PRST-7326	(E)	**Saxophone Colossus**	1964	10.00	25.00
		(Prestige 7326 is a reissue of 7079.)			
Prestige PRLP-7433	(M)	**Sonny Rollins Plays Jazz Classics**	1967	12.00	30.00
Prestige PRST-7433	(E)	**Sonny Rollins Plays Jazz Classics**	1967	8.00	20.00
		(Prestige 7433 is a reissue of 7058.)			

—Prestige albums above have blue labels with a trident logo on the right side.—

Label & Catalog #		Title	Year	VG+	NM
Prestige PRST-7553	(E)	**Sonny Rollins Plays For Bird**	1968	5.00	12.00
		(Prestige 7553 is a reissue of 7095.)			
Prestige PRST-7657	(E)	**Tenor Madness**	1969	5.00	12.00
		(Prestige 7657 is a reissue of 7047.)			
		—Prestige albums above have blue labels with a trident logo on top.—			
Blue Note BLP-1542	(M)	**Sonny Rollins** *(Deep groove)*	1957	100.00	200.00
Blue Note BLP-1542	(M)	**Sonny Rollins**	1957	60.00	150.00
		—Blue Note albums above have blue on white labels with a Lexington Ave, NYC address.—			
Blue Note BLP-1558	(M)	**Sonny Rollins, Volume 2** *(Deep groove)*	1957	50.00	125.00
Blue Note BLP-1558	(M)	**Sonny Rollins, Volume 2**	1957	30.00	75.00
Blue Note BLP-1581	(M)	**A Night At The Village Vanguard** *(Deep groove)*	1958	50.00	125.00
Blue Note BLP-1581	(M)	**A Night At The Village Vanguard**	1958	30.00	75.00
Blue Note BLP-4001	(M)	**Newk's Time** *(Deep groove)*	1958	50.00	125.00
Blue Note BLP-4001	(M)	**Newk's Time**	1958	30.00	75.00
Blue Note BST-4001	(S)	**Newk's Time** *(Deep groove)*	1959	30.00	75.00
Blue Note BST-4001	(S)	**Newk's Time**	1959	20.00	50.00
		—Blue Note albums above have blue on white labels with a W. 63rd Street, NYC address.—			
Blue Note BLP-1542	(M)	**Sonny Rollins**	1963	10.00	25.00
Blue Note BLP-1558	(M)	**Sonny Rollins, Volume 2**	1963	10.00	25.00
Blue Note BLP-1581	(M)	**A Night At The Village Vanguard**	1963	10.00	25.00
Blue Note BLP-4001	(M)	**Newk's Time**	1963	10.00	25.00
Blue Note BST-4001	(S)	**Newk's Time**	1963	8.00	20.00
		—Blue Note albums above have blue on white labels with a New York, USA address.—			
Blue Note BST-81542	(E)	**Sonny Rollins**	196?	4.00	10.00
Blue Note BST-81558	(E)	**Sonny Rollins, Volume 2**	196?	4.00	10.00
Blue Note BST-81581	(E)	**A Night At The Village Vanguard**	196?	4.00	10.00
Blue Note BST-4001	(S)	**Newk's Time**	196?	5.00	12.00
		—Blue Note albums above have blue on white labels with "A Division of Liberty Records."—			
Contemporary C-3530	(M)	**Way Out West**	1957	40.00	100.00
Stereo Records S-7017	(S)	**Way Out West**	1958	30.00	75.00
Contemporary S-7530	(S)	**Way Out West**	1959	20.00	50.00
Contemporary M-3564	(M)	**Sonny Rollins & The Contemporary Leaders**	1959	30.00	75.00
Contemporary S-7564	(S)	**Sonny Rollins & The Contemporary Leaders**	1959	20.00	50.00
		—Contemporary stereo albums have gold & black labels.—			
Riverside RLP-12-241	(M)	**The Sound Of Sonny**	1957	40.00	100.00
		—Riverside albums above have white labels.—			
Riverside RLP-12-241	(M)	**The Sound Of Sonny**	1959	20.00	50.00
Riverside RLP-1124	(S)	**The Sound Of Sonny**	1959	20.00	50.00
Riverside RLP-258	(M)	**Freedom Suite**	1958	30.00	75.00
		—Riverside albums above have blue mono or black stereo labels with a reel & mike logo on top.—			
Metrojazz E-1002	(M)	**Sonny Rollins And The Big Brass**	1958	24.00	60.00
Metrojazz SE-1002	(S)	**Sonny Rollins And The Big Brass**	1958	20.00	50.00
Metrojazz E-1011	(M)	**Sonny Rollins At Music Inn**	1958	24.00	60.00
Metrojazz SE-1011	(S)	**Sonny Rollins At Music Inn**	1958	20.00	50.00
Jazzland JLP-72	(M)	**Sonny's Time**	1962	16.00	40.00
Jazzland JLP-972	(S)	**Sonny's Time**	1962	12.00	30.00
		(Jazzland 72 is a reissue of Riverside 241.)			
Jazzland JLP-86	(M)	**Shadow Waltz**	1962	16.00	40.00
Jazzland JLP-986	(S)	**Shadow Waltz**	1962	12.00	30.00
		(Jazzland 86 is a reissue of Riverside 258.)			
Verve V-8430	(M)	**Sonny Rollins/Brass, Sonny Rollins/Trio**	1962	12.00	30.00
Verve V6-8430	(S)	**Sonny Rollins/Brass, Sonny Rollins/Trio**	1962	10.00	25.00
		(Verve 8430 is a reissue of Metrojazz 1002.)			
		—Verve albums above have black labels with "MGM Records" on the bottom.—			
Verve VSP-32	(M)	**Tender Titan**	1966	6.00	15.00
Verve VSPS-32	(S)	**Tender Titan**	1966	5.00	12.00
		(Verve 32 is a reissue of Metrojazz 1011.)			
RCA Victor LPM-2527	(M)	**The Bridge**	1962	20.00	50.00
RCA Victor LSP-2527	(S)	**The Bridge**	1962	16.00	40.00
RCA Victor LPM-2572	(M)	**What's New?**	1962	16.00	40.00
RCA Victor LSP-2572	(S)	**What's New?**	1962	12.00	30.00
RCA Victor LPM-2612	(M)	**Our Man In Jazz**	1962	16.00	40.00
RCA Victor LSP-2612	(S)	**Our Man In Jazz**	1962	12.00	30.00
RCA Victor LPM-2712	(M)	**Sonny Meets Hawk!**	1963	20.00	50.00
RCA Victor LSP-2712	(S)	**Sonny Meets Hawk!**	1963	16.00	40.00
		(RCA Victor 2712 also features Coleman Hawkins.)			
		—RCA albums above have black labels with "Long Play" or "Living Stereo" on the bottom.—			

Sonny Rollins cut his first sides in 1948 on a Babs Gonzales session for Capitol. He then recorded with Bud Powell, Fats Navarro, and J.J. Johnson, played with Art Blakey (1949), Tadd Dameron, and Powell (1950), and Miles Davis (1951) and then led his own groups except for a brief stint with Max Roach in 1956-57. As a featured guest he has appeared on LPs with Davis, Dizzie Gillespie, Thelonious Monk, and Sonny Stitt. He has also appeared on albums by Powell on Blue Note, Roach on EmArcy, and Kenny Dorham on Riverside. As a focal point of the "hard bop" school, his protean creativity carries through to his recordings in the '90s!

Label & Catalog #		Title	Year	VG+	NM
RCA Victor LPM-2927	(M)	**Now's The Time**	1964	12.00	30.00
RCA Victor LSP-2927	(S)	**Now's The Time**	1964	10.00	25.00
RCA Victor LPM-3355	(M)	**The Standard Sonny Rollins**	1965	12.00	30.00
RCA Victor LSP-3355	(S)	**The Standard Sonny Rollins**	1965	10.00	25.00
		—RCA albums above have black labels with "Mono" or "Living Stereo" on the bottom.—			
Impulse S-91	(M)	**Sonny Rollins On Impulse!**	1966	12.00	30.00
Impulse AS-91	(S)	**Sonny Rollins On Impulse!**	1966	10.00	25.00
Impulse S-9121	(M)	**East Broadway Run Down**	1967	12.00	30.00
Impulse AS-9121	(S)	**East Broadway Run Down**	1967	10.00	25.00
		—Impulse albums above have orange & black labels.—			
Impulse AS-91	(S)	**Sonny Rollins On Impulse!**	1968	6.00	15.00
Impulse AS-9121	(S)	**East Broadway Run Down**	1968	6.00	15.00
		—Impulse albums above have red & black labels with the "abc" logo on top.—			
Riverside RS-3010	(S)	**The Freedom Suite**	1968	5.00	12.00
		(Riverside 3010 is a reissue of 258.)			
Archive Of Folk & Jazz 220	(E)	**Sonny Rollins With Guest Artist That Jones**	1968	4.00	10.00

ROLLINS, DONNY, SONNY, & CLIFFORD BROWN & MAX ROACH

Prestige PRLP-7291	(M)	**Three Giants**	1964	16.00	40.00
Prestige PRST-7291	(E)	**Three Giants**	1964	10.00	25.00
		(Prestige 7291 is a reissue of 7038.)			
		—Prestige albums above have yellow mono or silver stereo labels with a Bergenfield, NJ address .—			

ROLLINS, SONNY / JIMMY CLEVELAND

Period SPL-1204	(M)	**Sonny Rollins Plays/Jimmy Cleveland Plays**	1956	40.00	100.00

ROMAN NEW ORLEANS JAZZ BAND, THE

RCA Victor LPT-3033	(10")	**Around The World In Jazz—Italy**	1953	20.00	50.00

ROSE, WALLY

Walter Rose is a traditional jazz pianist.

Columbia CL-6260	(10")	**Wally Rose**	1953	20.00	50.00
Columbia CL-782	(M)	**Cake Walk To Lindy Hop**	1956	16.00	40.00
		—Columbia albums above have six white on black "eye" logos on each label.—			

ROSOLINO, FRANK

Frank Rosolino is a West Coast jazz trombone player. For additional listings refer to Vince Guaraldi & Frank Rosolino; The Video All Stars.

Capitol H-6507	(10")	**Frank Rosolino**	1954	30.00	75.00
Capitol T-6507	(M)	**Frank Rosolino**	1955	20.00	50.00
Capitol T-6509	(M)	**Frankly Speaking**	1955	20.00	50.00
Bethlehem BCP-26	(M)	**I Play Trombone**	1955	20.00	50.00
Mode LP-107	(M)	**Frank Rosolino Quintet**	1957	40.00	100.00
Interlude MO-500	(M)	**The Legend Of Frank Rosolino**	1959	16.00	40.00
Interlude ST-1000	(S)	**The Legend Of Frank Rosolino**	1959	12.00	30.00
		(Interlude 500 is a reissue of Mode 107.)			
Reprise R-6016	(M)	**Turn Me Loose**	1961	12.00	30.00
Reprise R9-6016	(S)	**Turn Me Loose**	1961	10.00	25.00

ROSS, ANNIE

Annabelle Short, aka Annie Ross, is a modern jazz vocalist. For additional listings refer to King Pleasure / Annie Ross; Lambert, Hendricks & Ross. .

World Pacific WP-1253	(M)	**Annie Ross Sings A Song With Mulligan!**	1959	20.00	50.00
World Pacific ST-1020	(S)	**Annie Ross Sings A Song With Mulligan!**	1959	16.00	40.00
		(World Pacific 1253 also features Gerry Mulliagn.)			
World Pacific WP-1808	(M)	**Gypsy**	1959	20.00	50.00
World Pacific ST-1028	(S)	**Gypsy**	1959	16.00	450.00
		(World Pacific 1808 also features Buddy Bregman.)			
World Pacific WP-1285	(M)	**A Gasser!**	1960	20.00	50.00
World Pacific ST-1285	(S)	**A Gasser!**	1960	16.00	40.00
		(World Pacific 1285 also features Zoot Sims.)			
Kimberly 2018	(M)	**Annie Ross Sings A Song With Mulligan!**	1963	16.00	30.00
Kimberly 11018	(S)	**Annie Ross Sings A Song With Mulligan!**	1963	10.00	25.00
		(Kimberly 2018 is a reissue of World Pacific 1253.)			
Decca DL-4922	(M)	**Fill My Heart With Song**	1967	10.00	25.00
Decca DL-74922	(S)	**Fill My Heart With Song**	1967	8.00	20.00

Annie Ross began as a child actor (including several *Our Gang* episodes!) before moving to Europe, where she sang with bands in France. Moving back and forth across the Atlantic, she cut her first solo sides for Prestige, which were finally gathered onto a 12" album to flesh out the reissue of a King Pleasure 10" (shown above), and Savoy in 1952. Teaming with Dave Lambert and Jon Hendricks, they recorded *Sing A Song Of Basie* in 1958, setting lyrics and vocal parts to both the instrumental ensemble and solo parts of the Basie band. She proceeded to successfully record as a member of the vocal trio and as a solo with World Pacific (also shown here).

Label & Catalog #		Title	Year	VG+	NM

ROSS, ANNIE / DOROTHY DUNN / SHELBY DAVIS
Like Annie Ross, both Ms. Dunn and Ms. Davis are modern jazz-based vocalists.

Savoy MG-12060	(M)	**Singin' 'N Swingin'**	1956	24.00	60.00

—Savoy albums above have silver on red labels.—

ROSS, ARNOLD
Arnold Ross is a modern jazz pianist, composer and band leader. For additional listings refer to Joe Pass & Arnold Ross; Lennie Tristano / Arnold Ross.

Mercury MGC-134	(10")	**Arnold Ross**	1952	50.00	125.00
Clef MGC-134	(10")	**Arnold Ross**	1953	Unreleased	
Discovery DL-2006	(M)	**Arnold Ross**	1954	20.00	50.00

ROSS, RONNIE
Indian born Ronald Ross is a modern jazz baritone saxophone player.

Atlantic 1333	(M)	**The Jazz Makers**	1960	16.00	40.00
Atlantic SD-1333	(S)	**The Jazz Makers**	1960	12.00	30.00

—Atlantic albums above have multi-color labels with a white fan logo.—

ROUSE, CHARLIE
Charles Rouse is a modern jazz tenor saxophone player. For additional listings refer to Les Jazz Modes.

Jazzland JLP-19	(M)	**Takin' Care Of Business**	1960	20.00	50.00
Jazzland JLP-919	(S)	**Takin' Care Of Business**	1960	16.00	40.00
Epic LA-16012	(M)	**Yeah!**	1960	20.00	50.00
Epic BA-17012	(S)	**Yeah!**	1960	16.00	40.00
Epic LA-16018	(M)	**We Paid Our Dues**	1961	20.00	50.00
Epic BA-17018	(S)	**We Paid Our Dues**	1961	16.00	40.00
		(Epic 16018 also features Seldon Powell.)			
Blue Note BLP-4119	(M)	**Bossa Nova Bacchanal**	1962	16.00	40.00
Blue Note BST-84119	(S)	**Bossa Nova Bacchanal**	1962	12.00	30.00
		—Blue Note albums above have blue on white labels with a New York, NY address.—			
Blue Note BST-84119	(S)	**Bossa Nova Bacchanal**	196?	5.00	12.00

—Blue Note albums above have blue on white labels with "A Division of Liberty Records."—

ROUSE, CHARLIE, & PAUL QUINICHETTE

Bethlehem BCP-6021	(M)	**The Chase Is On**	1958	20.00	50.00

ROWLES, JIMMY
James Rowles is a traditional jazz-based pianist. For additional listings refer to the Jazzy Soundtracks section under Chancellor.

Liberty LRP-3003	(M)	**Rare, But Well Done**	1955	24.00	60.00
Tampa TP-8	(M)	**Let's Get Acquainted With Jazz ... For People Who Hate Jazz** *(Colored vinyl)*	1957	60.00	150.00
Tampa TP-8	(M)	**Let's Get Acquainted With Jazz ...For People Who Hate Jazz**	1958	30.00	75.00
Tampa TP-8	(S)	**Let's Get Acquainted With Jazz ...For People Who Hate Jazz**	1958	20.00	50.00
Andex A-3007	(M)	**Weather In A Jazz Vane**	1958	16.00	40.00
Andex AS-3007	(S)	**Weather In A Jazz Vane**	1958	12.00	30.00
Interlude MO-515	(M)	**Upper Classmen**	1959	16.00	40.00
Interlude ST-1015	(S)	**Upper Classmen**	1959	12.00	30.00
		(Interlude 515 is a reissue of Tampa 8.)			
Signature SM-6011	(M)	**Fiorello Uptown, Mary Sunshine Downtown**	1960	30.00	75.00
Signature SS-6011	(S)	**Fiorello Uptown, Mary Sunshine Downtown**	1960	40.00	50.00
Capitol T-1831	(M)	**Kinda Groovy!**	1963	8.00	20.00
Capitol ST-1831	(S)	**Kinda Groovy!**	1963	6.00	15.00

ROYAL, ERNIE
Ernest Royal is a modern jazz trumpet player. For additional listings refer to Ernie Wilkin and the Various Artists section under Savoy.

Urania UJLP-1203	(M)	**Accent On Trumpet**	1955	20.00	50.00

ROYAL, MARSHALL

Everest LPBR-5087	(M)	**Gordon Jenkins Presents Marshall Royal**	1960	12.00	30.00
Everest SDBR-1087	(M)	**Gordon Jenkins Presents Marshall Royal**	1960	10.00	25.00

RUBIN, STAN (STAN RUBIN & THE COLLEGE ALL STARS)
Stanley Rubin is a traditional jazz-based clarinet and saxophone(s) player and band leader.

Princeton LP-102	(10")	**The Stan Rubin Tigertown Five**	1954	20.00	50.00

Label & Catalog #		Title	Year	VG+	NM
Jubilee JLP-4	(10")	**The Tigertown Five, Vol. 1**	1954	20.00	50.00
Jubilee JLP-5	(10")	**The Tigertown Five, Vol. 2**	1954	20.00	50.00
Jubilee JLP-6	(10")	**The Tigertown Five, Vol. 3**	1954	20.00	50.00
Jubilee JLP-1001	(M)	**The College All Stars At Carnegie Hall**	1955	16.00	40.00
Jubilee JLP-1003	(M)	**College Jazz Come To Carnegie Hall**	1955	16.00	40.00
Jubilee JLP-1016	(M)	**Tigertown Five**	1956	16.00	40.00
Jubilee JLP-1024	(M)	**Stan Rubin In Morocco**	1956	16.00	40.00
RCA Victor LPM-3277	(10")	**Stan Rubin's Dixieland Comes To Carnegie Hall**	1955	20.00	50.00
RCA Victor LPM-1200	(M)	**Dixieland Bash**	1956	16.00	40.00
		—RCA albums above have black labels with "Long Play" on the bottom.—			
Coral CRL-57185	(M)	**Dixieland Goes Broadway**	1959	12.00	30.00
Coral CRL-757185	(S)	**Dixieland Goes Broadway**	1959	10.00	25.00

RUDD, ROSWELL

Roswell Rudd is a modern jazz trombone player and composer.

Impulse A-9126	(M)	**Everywhere**	1967	12.00	30.00
Impulse AS-9126	(S)	**Everywhere**	1967	10.00	25.00
		—Impulse albums above have orange & black labels.—			
Impulse AS-9126	(S)	**Everywhere**	1968	4.00	10.00
		—Impulse albums above have red & black labels with the "abc" logo on top.—			

RUFF, WILLIE

For additional listings refer to Dwike Mitchell & Willie Ruff.

Columbia CS-9603	(S)	**The Smooth Side Of Willie Ruff**	1968	6.00	15.00
		—Columbia albums above have red labels with "360 Sound" on the bottom.—			

RUGOLO, PETE

Peter Rugolo is a modern jazz composer and band leader. For additional listings refer to June Christy; Patti Page; and the Jazzy Soundtracks section under EmArcy and Time..

Columbia CL-6289	(10")	**Introducing Pete Rugolo**	1954	20.00	50.00
Columbia CL-604	(M)	**Adventures In Rhythm**	1955	16.00	40.00
Columbia CL-635	(M)	**Introducing Pete Rugolo**	1955	16.00	40.00
		—Columbia albums above have "Long Playing" on the bottom of the label.—			
Columbia CL-604	(M)	**Adventures In Rhythm**	1956	12.00	30.00
Columbia CL-635	(M)	**Introducing Pete Rugolo**	1956	12.00	30.00
Columbia CL-689	(M)	**Rugolomania**	1956	12.00	30.00
		—Columbia albums above have six white on black "eye" logos on each label.—			
EmArcy MG-36082	(M)	**Music For Hi-Fi Bugs**	1956	16.00	40.00
EmArcy MG-36115	(M)	**Out On A Limb**	1957	16.00	40.00
EmArcy MG-36122	(M)	**Percussion At Work**	1958	16.00	40.00
EmArcy MG-36143	(M)	**Rugolo Plays Kenton**	1958	16.00	40.00
		—EmArcy albums above have blue labels with silver print.—			
Mercury MG-20118	(M)	**Music From Outer Space**	1957	20.00	50.00
Mercury MG-20???	(M)	**An Adventure In Sound—Reeds**	1958	16.00	40.00
Mercury SR-60039	(M)	**An Adventure In Sound—Reeds**	1959	12.00	30.00
Mercury MG-20260	(M)	**Reeds In Hi Fi**	1958	16.00	40.00
Mercury SR-60043	(S)	**Reeds In Hi Fi**	1959	12.00	30.00
Mercury MG-20261	(M)	**Brass In Hi Fi**	1958	16.00	40.00
Mercury SR-60044	(S)	**Brass In Hi Fi**	1959	12.00	30.00
		—Mercury albums above have silver on black labels.—			

RUMSEY, HOWARD (HOWARD RUMSEY'S LIGHTHOUSE ALL-STARS)

Howard Rumsey is a West Coast jazz bass player and band leader. The All-Stars originally consisted of Jimmy Giuffre, Shelly Manne, Frank Patchen, and Shorty Rogers but eventually included others, especially Bob Cooper and Bud Shank. For additional listings for Rumsey refer to Boots Brown.

Contemporary C-2501	(10")	**Sunday Jazz a la Lighthouse**	1953	50.00	125.00
Contemporary C-2506	(10")	**Howard Rumsey's Lighthouse All-Stars**	1953	50.00	125.00
Contemporary C-2510	(10")	**Howard Rumsey's Lighthouse All-Stars**	1954	50.00	125.00
Contemporary C-2513	(10")	**Howard Rumsey's Lighthouse All-Stars, Volume 1: The Quintet**	1954	50.00	125.00
Contemporary C-2515	(10")	**Howard Rumsey's Lighthouse All-Stars, Volume 2: The Octet**	1954	50.00	125.00
Contemporary C-3501	(M)	**Sunday Jazz a la Lighthouse**	1955	30.00	75.00
Contemporary C-3504	(M)	**Howard Rumsey's Lighthouse All-Stars, Vol. 2**	1955	30.00	75.00
Contemporary C-3508	(M)	**Howard Rumsey's Lighthouse All-Stars, Vol. 3**	1955	30.00	75.00
Contemporary C-3509	(M)	**Lighthouse At Laguna**	1955	30.00	75.00
Contemporary C-3517	(M)	**In The Solo Spotlight**	1956	30.00	75.00
		(Contemporary 3517 is a reissue of 2515.)			

Label & Catalog #		Title	Year	VG+	NM
Contemporary C-3520	(M)	**Howard Rumsey's Lighthouse All-Stars, Vol. 4: Oboe/Flute**	1956	30.00	75.00
		(Contemporary 3520 is a reissue of 2510.)			
Contemporary C-3528	(M)	**Music For Lighthousekeeping**	1957	30.00	75.00
Stereo Records S-7008	(S)	**Music For Lighthousekeeping**	1958	24.00	60.00
Contemporary S-7008	(S)	**Music For Lighthousekeeping**	1959	20.00	50.00
		— Contemporary stereo albums have gold & black labels.—			
Liberty LRP-3045	(M)	**Double Or Nothin'**	1957	20.00	50.00
Liberty LST-7014	(S)	**Double Or Nothin'**	1959	16.00	40.00
Lighthouse LP-300	(M)	**Jazz Rolls-Royce**	1958	16.00	40.00
Lighthouse LP-301	(M)	**Sunday Jazz a la Lighthouse** *(Red vinyl)*	1958	16.00	40.00
		(While Lighthouse 300 is a new recording, 301 is reissues early 78s.)			
Omega OML-5	(M)	**Jazz Rolls-Royce**	1960	12.00	30.00
Omega OSL-5	(S)	**Jazz Rolls-Royce**	1960	12.00	30.00
		(Omega 5 is a reissue of Lighthouse 300.)			
Philips PHM-200-012	(M)	**Jazz Structures**	1961	10.00	25.00
Philips PHS-600-012	(S)	**Jazz Structures**	1961	8.00	20.00

RUSHING, JIMMY

James Rushing is a traditional jazz/big band-based vocalist and piano player. For additional listings refer to Count Basie; Dave Brubeck.

Vanguard VRS-8011	(10")	**Jimmy Rushing Sings The Blues**	1954	30.00	75.00
Vanguard VRS-8505	(M)	**Listen To The Blues**	1955	20.00	50.00
Vanguard VRS-8513	(M)	**If This Ain't The Blues**	1957	20.00	50.00
Vanguard VDS-2008	(S)	**If This Ain't The Blues**	1958	20.00	50.00
Vanguard VRS-8518	(M)	**Going To Chicago**	1957	20.00	50.00
		(Vanguard 8518 is a reissue of 8011.)			
Jazztone J-1244	(M)	**Listen To The Blues**	1957	16.00	40.00
		(Jazztone 1244 is a reissue of Vanguard 8505.)			
Columbia CL-778	(M)	**Cat Meets Chick**	1956	16.00	40.00
		(Columbia 778 also features Ada Moore.)			
Columbia CL-963	(M)	**The Jazz Odyssey Of James Rushing, Esq.**	1957	16.00	40.00
Columbia CL-1152	(M)	**Little Jimmy Rushing And The Big Brass**	1958	12.00	30.00
Columbia CS-8060	(S)	**Little Jimmy Rushing And The Big Brass**	1959	16.00	40.00
Columbia CL-1401	(M)	**Rushing Lullabies**	1959	12.00	30.00
Columbia CS-8196	(S)	**Rushing Lullabies**	1959	16.00	40.00
Columbia CL-1605	(M)	**Jimmy Rushing And The Smith Girls**	1961	12.00	30.00
Columbia CS-8405	(S)	**Jimmy Rushing And The Smith Girls**	1961	16.00	40.00
		— Columbia albums above have six white on black "eye" logos on each label—			
Audio Lab AL-1512	(M)	**Two Shades Of Blue**	1959	40.00	100.00
Colpix CP-446	(M)	**Five Feet Of Soul**	1963	12.00	30.00
Colpix SCP-446	(S)	**Five Feet Of Soul**	1963	20.00	50.00
		— Colpix albums above have gold labels.—			
BluesWay BL-3005	(M)	**Everyday I Have The Blues**	1967	8.00	20.00
BluesWay BLS-6005	(S)	**Everyday I Have The Blues**	1967	6.00	15.00
BluesWay BLS-6107	(S)	**Livin' The Blues**	1968	6.00	15.00

RUSSELL, GEORGE

George Russell is a modern jazz pianist, composer and writer. His 1953 book "The Lydian Chromatic Concept Of Tonal Organization" is the first jazz-based music theory.

MGM E-3321	(M)	**George Russell Octets**	1955	30.00	75.00
RCA Victor LPM-1372	(M)	**Jazz Workshop**	1957	30.00	75.00
		— RCA albums above have black labels with "Long Play" on the bottom.—			
Decca DL-9216	(M)	**New York, N.Y**	1958	20.00	50.00
Decca DL-79216	(S)	**New York, N.Y.**	1958	16.00	40.00
Decca DL-9219	(M)	**Jazz In The Space Age**	1958	20.00	50.00
Decca DL-79219	(S)	**Jazz In The Space Age**	1958	16.00	40.00
Decca DL-9220	(M)	**George Russell At The Five Spot**	1958	20.00	50.00
Decca DL-79220	(S)	**George Russell At The Five Spot**	1958	16.00	40.00
Decca DL-4183	(M)	**George Russell In Kansas City**	1961	16.00	40.00
Decca DL-74183	(S)	**George Russell In Kansas City**	1961	12.00	30.00
Riverside RLP-341	(M)	**Stratusphunk**	1960	12.00	30.00
Riverside RS-9341	(S)	**Stratusphunk**	1960	10.00	25.00
Riverside RLP-375	(M)	**Ezz-thetics**	1961	16.00	40.00
Riverside RS-9375	(S)	**Ezz-thetics**	1961	12.00	30.00
		(Riverside 375 also features Eric Dolphy.)			
Riverside RLP-412	(M)	**The Stratus Seekers**	1962	12.00	30.00
Riverside RS-9412	(S)	**The Stratus Seekers**	1962	10.00	25.00

Label & Catalog #		Title	Year	VG+	NM
Riverside RLP-440	(M)	**The Outer View**	1963	12.00	30.00
Riverside RS-9440	(S)	**The Outer View**	1963	10.00	25.00
		—Riverside albums above have blue mono or black stereo labels with a reel & mike logo on top.—			
RCA Victor LPM-2534	(M)	**Jazz Workshop**	1962	12.00	30.00
RCA Victor LSP-2534	(E)	**Jazz Workshop**	1962	6.00	15.00
		(RCA Victor 2534 is a reissue of 1372.)			
		—RCA albums above have black labels with "Long Play" or "Reprocessed Stereo" on the bottom.—			
Riverside RS-3016	(S)	**The Outer View**	1968	6.00	15.00
		(Riverside 3016 is a reissue of 9440.)			

RUSSELL, PEE WEE / BILLY BANKS

Jazz Panorama 1808	(10")	**Pee Wee Russell / Billy Banks**	1951	30.00	75.00

RUSSELL, PEE WEE

Charles "Pee Wee" Russell is a traditional jazz clarinet and saxophone(s) player. For additional listings refer to Ruby Braff & Pee Wee Russell; Coleman Hawkins & Pee Wee Russell; Pee Wee Hunt / Pee Wee Russell; Jack Teagarden / Pee Wee Russell; and the Various Artists section under Verve.

Disc DLP-???	(10")	**Jazz Ensemble**	195?	50.00	125.00
		(Disc ??? features cover art by David Stone Martin.)			
Atlantic ALS-126	(10")	**Pee Wee Russell All Stars**	1952	30.00	75.00
Storyville STLP-308	(10")	**Pee Wee Russell**	1954	30.00	75.00
Riverside RLP-12-141	(M)	**Rhythmakers And Teagarden**	1955	20.00	50.00
		—Riverside albums above have blue on white labels.—			
Storyville STLP-909	(M)	**We're In The Money**	1956	20.00	50.00
Counterpoint 56?	(M)	**Portrait Of Pee Wee**	1957	20.00	50.00
Esoteric 565	(M)	**Pee Wee Russell All Stars**	1959	16.00	40.00
Esoteric 5565	(S)	**Pee Wee Russell All Stars**	1959	12.00	30.00
Swingville SVLP-2008	(M)	**Swingin' With Pee Wee**	1960	20.00	50.00
		—Swingville albums above have purple mono or red stereo labels.—			
Swingville SVLP-2008	(M)	**Swingin' With Pee Wee**	1965	10.00	25.00
		—Swingville albums above have blue labels with a trident logo on the right side.—			
Dot DLP-3253	(M)	**Pee Wee Russell Plays**	1960	10.00	25.00
Dot DLP-25253	(S)	**Pee Wee Russell Plays**	1960	8.00	20.00
Bell LP-42	(M)	**Pee Wee Russell Plays Pee Wee**	1961	12.00	30.00
Bell LPS-42	(S)	**Pee Wee Russell Plays Pee Wee**	1961	10.00	25.00
Stereo-Craft RTN-105	(M)	**Pee Wee Plays Pee Wee**	196?	10.00	25.00
Stereo-Craft RTS-105	(S)	**Pee Wee Plays Pee Wee**	196?	8.00	20.00
Columbia CL-1985	(M)	**New Groove**	1963	8.00	20.00
Columbia CS-8785	(S)	**New Groove**	1963	6.00	15.00
		—Columbia albums above have "Guaranteed High Fidelity" or "360 Sound Stereo" in black on the label.—			
Mainstream 56026	(M)	**A Legend**	1965	8.00	20.00
Mainstream S-6026	(S)	**A Legend**	1965	6.00	15.00
Impulse A-96	(M)	**Ask Me Now**	1966	12.00	30.00
Impulse AS-96	(S)	**Ask Me Now**	1966	10.00	25.00
Impulse A-9137	(M)	**College Concert Of Pee Wee Russell With Henry "Red" Allen**	1967	10.00	25.00
Impulse AS-9137	(S)	**College Concert Of Pee Wee Russell With Henry "Red" Allen**	1967	8.00	20.00
		—Impulse albums above have orange & black labels.—			
Impulse AS-96	(S)	**Ask Me Now**	1968	4.00	10.00
Impulse AS-9137	(S)	**College Concert Of Pee Wee Russell With Henry "Red" Allen**	1968	4.00	10.00
		—Impulse albums above have red & black labels with the "abc" logo on top.—			
Prestige PRST-7672	(E)	**The Pee Wee Russell Memorial Album**	1969	5.00	12.00
		(Prestige 7672 is a reissue of Swingville 2008.)			
		—Prestige albums above have blue labels with a trident logo on top.—			
Archive Of Folk & Jazz 233	(E)	**Pee Wee Russell**	1969	4.00	10.00

RUSSELL, PEE WEE, & RUBY BRAFF

Savoy MG-12034	(M)	**Jazz At Storyville, Volume 1**	1955	20.00	50.00
Savoy MG-12041	(M)	**Jazz At Storyville, Volume 2**	1955	20.00	50.00

RUSSIAN JAZZ QUARTET, THE

Impulse A-80	(M)	**Happiness**	1965	10.00	25.00
Impulse AS-80	(S)	**Happiness**	1965	8.00	20.00
		—Impulse albums above have orange & black labels.—			
Impulse AS-80	(S)	**Happiness**	1968	4.00	10.00
		—Impulse albums above have red & black labels with the "abc" logo on top.—			

Label & Catalog #		Title	Year	VG+	NM

RUSSIN, BABE

Irving "Babe" Russin is a traditional jazz tenor saxophone and clarinet player.

Dot DLP-3060	*(M)*	**To Soothe The Savage**	*1956*	**16.00**	**40.00**

RUSSO, BILL

William Russo is a modern jazz trombone player and composer. For additional listings refer to Shelly Manne / Bill Russo.

Dee Gee 1001	*(10")*	**A Recital In New American Music**	*1952*	**100.00**	**200.00**
Atlantic 1241	*(M)*	**The World Of Alcina**	*1956*	**30.00**	**75.00**
		—Atlantic albums above have black mono or green stereo labels.—			
Atlantic 1241	*(M)*	**The World Of Alcina**	*1961*	**12.00**	**30.00**
		—Atlantic albums above have multi-color labels with a white fan logo.—			
Roulette R-52045	*(M)*	**School Of Rebellion**	*1960*	**12.00**	**30.00**
Roulette SR-52045	*(S)*	**School Of Rebellion**	*1960*	**10.00**	**25.00**
Roulette R-52063	*(M)*	**Seven Deadly Sins**	*1960*	**12.00**	**30.00**
Roulette SR-52063	*(S)*	**Seven Deadly Sins**	*1960*	**10.00**	**25.00**
FM 302	*(M)*	**Stereophony**	*1963*	**12.00**	**30.00**
FM S-302	*(S)*	**Stereophony**	*1963*	**10.00**	**25.00**

RUTHER, BULL: ***Refer to*** **MILT HINTON & WENDELL MARSHALL & BULL RUTHER**

RYG, JORGEN

Danish born Jorgen Ryg is a traditional jazz-based trumpet player.

EmArcy MG-36099	*(M)*	**Jorgen Ryg Jazz Quartet**	*1956*	**20.00**	**50.00**
		—EmArcy albums above have blue labels with silver print.—			

S.

SABU

Cuban born Sabu martinez is a Latin jazz conga and bongos player and vocalist. For additional listings refer to Art Blakey / Sabu; Horace Silver / Art Blakey & Sabu.

Alegre 802	*(M)*	**Jazz Espagnole**	*195?*	**150.00**	**300.00**
Blue Note BLP-1561	*(M)*	**Palo Congo** *(Deep groove)*	*1957*	**60.00**	**150.00**
Blue Note BLP-1561	*(M)*	**Palo Congo**	*1957*	**40.00**	**100.00**

—Blue Note albums above have blue on white labels with a W. 63rd Street, NYC address.—

Blue Note BLP-1561	*(M)*	**Palo Congo**	*196?*	**10.00**	**25.00**

—Blue Note albums above have blue on white labels with a New York, USA address.—

Blue Note BST-81561	*(E)*	**Palo Congo**	*196?*	**4.00**	**10.00**

—Blue Note albums above have blue on white labels with "A Division of Liberty Records."—

SACHS, AARON

Aaron Sachs is a modern jazz clarinet and tenor saxophone player. For additional listings refer to Hank D' Amico / Aaron Sachs; The Modern Jazz Society.

Bethlehem BCP-1008	*(10")*	**Aaron Sachs Quintet**	*1954*	**50.00**	**125.00**
Dawn DLP-1114	*(M)*	**Jazzville, Volume 3**	*1957*	**30.00**	**75.00**
Rama LP-1004	*(M)*	**Clarinet & Co.**	*1957*	**30.00**	**75.00**

SADI, FATS

Belgium born Lallemand "Fats" Sadi is a traditional jazz-based vibraphone player.

Blue Note BLP-5061	*(10")*	**The Swinging Fats Sadi Combo**	*1955*	**150.00**	**300.00**

ST. CLAIRE, BETTY

Betty St. Claire is a jazz-based vocalist.

Jubilee JLP-15	*(10")*	**Hal McKusick Plays—Betty St. Clair Sings**	*1955*	**50.00**	**125.00**
Jubilee JLP-23	*(10")*	**Cool And Clearer**	*1955*	**40.00**	**100.00**
Jubilee JLP-1011	*(M)*	**What Is There To Say?**	*1956*	**20.00**	**50.00**
Seeco SLP-456	*(M)*	**Betty St. Claire At Basin Street**	*1960*	**16.00**	**40.00**

ST. CYR, JOHNNY: ***Refer to*** **PAUL BARBARIN / JOHNNY ST. CYR**

SALIM, A.K.

Ahmad Khatab Salim is a traditional jazz-based arranger, composer and band leader.

Savoy MG-12102	*(M)*	**The Flute Suite**	*1957*	**30.00**	**75.00**
Savoy MG-12118	*(M)*	**Pretty For The People**	*1957*	**30.00**	**75.00**
Savoy MG-12132	*(M)*	**Blues Suite**	*1958*	**20.00**	**50.00**
Savoy SST-13001	*(S)*	**Blues Suite**	*1959*	**16.00**	**40.00**
Prestige PRLP-7379	*(M)*	**Afro Soul Drum Orgy**	*1966*	**12.00**	**30.00**
Prestige PRST-7379	*(S)*	**Afro Soul Drum Orgy**	*1966*	**10.00**	**25.00**

—Prestige albums above have blue labels with a trident logo on the right side.—

SALT CITY FIVE, THE

Jubilee JLP-13	*(10")*	**Salt City Five**	*1955*	**20.00**	**50.00**
Jubilee JLP-1012	*(M)*	**Salt City Five**	*1956*	**16.00**	**40.00**

(Jubilee 1012 is a reissue of 13.)

SALVADOR, SAL

Sal Salvador is a big band-based guitarist and band leader.

Blue Note BLP-5035	*(10")*	**Sal Salvador Quintet**	*1954*	**125.00**	**250.00**
Capitol H-6505	*(10")*	**Sal Salvador**	*1954*	**50.00**	**125.00**
Capitol T-6505	*(M)*	**Sal Salvador**	*1955*	**30.00**	**75.00**
Bethlehem BCP-39	*(M)*	**Shades Of Sal Salvador**	*1956*	**20.00**	**50.00**
Bethlehem BCP-59	*(M)*	**Frivolous Sal**	*1956*	**20.00**	**50.00**
Bethlehem BCP-74	*(M)*	**Tribute To The Greats**	*1957*	**20.00**	**50.00**
Decca DL-9210	*(M)*	**Colors In Sound**	*1958*	**20.00**	**50.00**
Decca DL-79210	*(S)*	**Colors In Sound**	*1958*	**16.00**	**40.00**
Decca DL-4026	*(M)*	**Beat For This Generation**	*1959*	**20.00**	**50.00**
Decca DL-74026	*(S)*	**Beat For This Generation**	*1959*	**16.00**	**40.00**
Golden Crest GC-1001	*(M)*	**Sal Salvador Quartet**	*1961*	**12.00**	**30.00**
Golden Crest GCS-1001	*(S)*	**Sal Salvador Quartet**	*1961*	**10.00**	**25.00**

Label & Catalog #		Title	Year	VG+	NM
Dauntless DM-4307	(M)	**You Ain't Heard Nothin' Yet**	1963	16.00	40.00
Dauntless DS-6307	(S)	**You Ain't Heard Nothin' Yet**	1963	12.00	30.00
Roulette R-25262	(M)	**Music To Stop Smoking By**	1964	10.00	25.00
Roulette RS-25262	(S)	**Music To Stop Smoking By**	1964	8.00	20.00

SAMPSON, EDGAR

Edgar "The Lamb" Sampson is a traditional jazz saxophone(s) and violin player, arranger and composer.

Coral CRL-57049	(M)	**Swing Softly Sweet Sampson**	1957	16.00	40.00

SANDERS, PHAROAH

Farrell "Pharoah" Sanders is a modern jazz tenor saxophone player. For additional listings refer to The Jazz Composers Orchestra.

ESP-Disk' 1003	(M)	**Pharaohs's First** *(Black & white spiral cover)*	1965	12.00	30.00
ESP-Disk' 1003	(S)	**Pharaohs's First** *(Black & white spiral cover)*	1965	10.00	25.00
Impulse A-9138	(M)	**Tauhid**	1967	14.00	35.00
Impulse AS-9138	(S)	**Tauhid**	1967	10.00	25.00
Impulse AS-9181	(S)	**Karma**	1968	10.00	25.00
Impulse AS-9190	(S)	**Jewels Of Thought**	1969	10.00	25.00

—Impulse albums above have orange & black labels.—

SANDOLE, DENNIS

Dennis Sandole is a traditional jazz-based guitarist.

Fantasy 3251	(M)	**Compositions And Arrangements For Guitar**	1958	12.00	30.00

SANDOLE BROTHERS, THE

The Brothers Sandole are Adolphe, a traditional jazz-based piano, with Dennis.

Fantasy 3209	(M)	**Modern Music From Philadelphia**	1956	20.00	50.00

—Fantasy albums above have red labels on dark red, non-flexible vinyl.—

Fantasy 3209	(M)	**Modern Music From Philadelphia**	195?	12.00	30.00

—Fantasy albums above have red labels on non-flexible vinyl.—

SANTAMARIA, MONGO

Cuban born Mongo Santamaria is an Afro-Latin jazz conga player and band leader.

Fantasy 3267	(M)	**Yambu** *(Red vinyl)*	1958	16.00	40.00
Fantasy 3267	(M)	**Yambu**	1959	12.00	30.00
Fantasy 8012	(S)	**Yambu** *(Blue vinyl)*	1962	12.00	30.00
Fantasy 8012	(S)	**Yambu**	1962	8.00	20.00
Fantasy 3291	(M)	**Mongo** *(Red vinyl)*	1959	16.00	40.00
Fantasy 3291	(M)	**Mongo**	1959	12.00	30.00
Fantasy 8032	(S)	**Mongo** *(Blue vinyl)*	1962	12.00	30.00
Fantasy 8032	(S)	**Mongo**	1962	8.00	20.00
Fantasy 3302	(M)	**Our Man In Havana** *(Red vinyl)*	1960	16.00	40.00
Fantasy 3302	(M)	**Our Man In Havana**	1960	12.00	30.00
Fantasy 8045	(S)	**Our Man In Havana** *(Blue vinyl)*	1962	12.00	30.00
Fantasy 8045	(S)	**Our Man In Havana**	1962	8.00	20.00
Fantasy 3311	(M)	**Mongo In Havana** *(Red vinyl)*	1960	16.00	40.00
Fantasy 3311	(M)	**Mongo In Havana**	1960	12.00	30.00
Fantasy 8055	(S)	**Mongo In Havana** *(Blue vinyl)*	1962	12.00	30.00
Fantasy 8055	(S)	**Mongo In Havana**	1962	8.00	20.00
Fantasy 3314	(M)	**Sabroso** *(Red vinyl)*	1960	16.00	40.00
Fantasy 3314	(M)	**Sabroso**	1960	12.00	30.00
Fantasy 8058	(S)	**Sabroso** *(Blue vinyl)*	1962	12.00	30.00
Fantasy 8058	(S)	**Sabroso**	1962	8.00	20.00
Fantasy 3324	(M)	**Arriba!** *(Red vinyl)*	1961	16.00	40.00
Fantasy 3324	(M)	**Arriba!**	1961	12.00	30.00
Fantasy 8067	(S)	**Arriba!** *(Blue vinyl)*	1962	12.00	30.00
Fantasy 8067	(S)	**Arriba!**	1962	8.00	20.00
Fantasy 3328	(M)	**Mas Sabroso** *(Red vinyl)*	1961	16.00	40.00
Fantasy 3328	(M)	**Mas Sabroso**	1961	12.00	30.00
Fantasy 8071	(S)	**Mas Sabroso** *(Blue vinyl)*	1962	12.00	30.00
Fantasy 8071	(S)	**Mas Sabroso**	1962	8.00	20.00
Fantasy 3335	(M)	**Viva Mongo!** *(Red vinyl)*	1962	16.00	40.00
Fantasy 3335	(M)	**Viva Mongo!**	1962	10.00	25.00
Fantasy 8087	(S)	**Viva Mongo!** *(Blue vinyl)*	1962	12.00	30.00
Fantasy 8087	(S)	**Viva Mongo!**	1962	8.00	20.00

—Fantasy albums above have red mono and blue stereo labels on non-flexible vinyl.—

Label & Catalog #		Title	Year	VG+	NM
Riverside RLP-423	(M)	**Go, Mongo!**	1962	12.00	30.00
Riverside RS-9423	(S)	**Go, Mongo!**	1962	10.00	25.00
—Riverside albums above have blue mono or black stereo labels with a reel & mike logo on top.—					
Riverside RM-3523	(M)	**Mongo Introduces La Lupe**	1963	10.00	25.00
Riverside RS-95323	(S)	**Mongo Introduces La Lupe**	1963	8.00	20.00
Riverside RM-3529	(M)	**Mongo Santamaria At The Village Gate**	1963	10.00	25.00
Riverside RS-93529	(S)	**Mongo Santamaria At The Village Gate**	1963	8.00	20.00
Riverside RM-3530	(M)	**Mongo Santamaria Explodes**	1964	10.00	25.00
Riverside RS-93530	(S)	**Mongo Santamaria Explodes**	1964	8.00	20.00
Battle B-6129	(M)	**Mongo At The Village Gate**	1964	10.00	25.00
Battle BS-96129	(S)	**Mongo At The Village Gate**	1964	8.00	20.00
Columbia CL-2298	(M)	**El Pussy Cat**	1965	10.00	25.00
Columbia CS-9098	(S)	**El Pussy Cat**	1965	8.00	20.00
—Columbia albums above have "Guaranteed High Fidelity" or "360 Sound Stereo" in black on the label.—					
Columbia CL-2298	(M)	**El Pussy Cat**	1965	6.00	15.00
Columbia CS-9098	(S)	**El Pussy Cat**	1965	5.00	12.00
Columbia CL-2411	(M)	**Watermelon Man**	1965	6.00	15.00
Columbia CS-9211	(S)	**Watermelon Man**	1965	8.00	20.00
Columbia CL-2473	(M)	**Hey! Let's Party**	1966	6.00	15.00
Columbia CS-9273	(S)	**Hey! Let's Party**	1966	5.00	12.00
Columbia CL-2612	(M)	**Mongomania**	1967	6.00	15.00
Columbia CS-9412	(S)	**Mongomania**	1967	5.00	12.00
—Columbia albums above have "360 Sound" in white on the bottom of the label.—					
Riverside RS-3008	(M)	**Explosion**	1967	10.00	25.00
Riverside RS-3008	(S)	**Explosion**	1967	6.00	15.00
Riverside RS-3045	(S)	**Mongo Soul**	1969	6.00	15.00

SANTOS BROTHERS, THE

The Santos Brothers are modern jazz trumpet players.

Metrojazz E-1015	(M)	**Jazz For Two Trumpets**	1958	20.00	50.00
Metrojazz SE-1015	(S)	**Jazz For Two Trumpets**	1958	16.00	40.00

SASH, LEON

Leon Shash, aka Leon Sash, is a modern jazz accordion, vibraphone and guitar player. For additional listings refer to Toshiko / Leon Sash.

Storyville STLP-917	(M)	**Leon Sash Quartet**	1956	20.00	50.00

SAUNDERS, HERM

Vogue 101	(10")	**Music At The Bantam Cock**	1953	100.00	200.00

SAUSSY, TUPPER

Monument MLP-8004	(M)	**Discover Tupper Saussy**	1964	8.00	20.00
Monument SLP-18004	(S)	**Discover Tupper Saussy**	1964	6.00	15.00
Monument MLP-8027	(M)	**Said I To Shostakovitch**	1965	8.00	20.00
Monument SLP-18027	(S)	**Said I To Shostakovitch**	1965	6.00	15.00
Monument MLP-8034	(M)	**A Swinger's Guide To "Mary Poppins"**	1965	8.00	20.00
Monument SLP-18034	(S)	**A Swinger's Guide To "Mary Poppins"**	1965	6.00	15.00

SAUTER-FINEGAN

Edward Sauter is a traditional jazz trumpet player and arranger; William Finegan is a traditional jazz piano player, arranger and composer. For additional listings refer to Ray McKinley & Eddie Sauter.

RCA Victor LPM-3115	(10")	**New Directions In Music**	1953	50.00	125.00
—RCA mono albums above have black labels with "Long Play" on the bottom.—					
RCA Victor LJM-1003	(M)	**Inside Sauter-Finegan**	1954	30.00	75.00
—RCA mono albums above have silver labels.—					
RCA Victor LPM-1009	(M)	**The Sound Of Sauter-Finegan**	1954	30.00	75.00
RCA Victor LPM-1051	(M)	**Concert Jazz**	1955	20.00	50.00
RCA Victor LPM-1104	(M)	**Sons Of Sauter-Finegan**	1955	20.00	50.00
RCA Victor LPM-1227	(M)	**New Directions In Music**	1956	20.00	50.00
RCA Victor LPM-1240	(M)	**Adventure In Time**	1956	20.00	50.00
RCA Victor LPM-1341	(M)	**Under Analysis**	1957	20.00	50.00
RCA Victor LPM-1497	(M)	**Straight Down The Middle**	1957	20.00	50.00
RCA Victor LPM-2473	(M)	**Inside Sauter-Finegan Revisited**	1961	16.00	40.00
RCA Victor LSP-2473	(S)	**Inside Sauter-Finegan Revisited**	1961	12.00	30.00
—RCA albums above have black labels with "Long Play" or "Living Stereo" on the bottom.—					

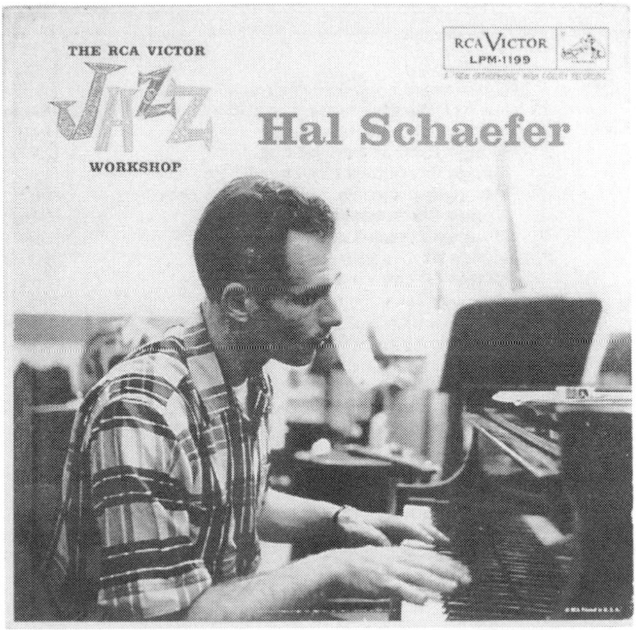

Hal Schaefer moved from high school to Lee Castle's band in 1940 and then onto Ina Ray Hutton (1941), Benny Carter, Harry James (1942), Boyd Raeburn (1943), Billy Eckstine (1944) and then as Peggy Lee's accompanist (1945-46). He recorded two LPs for RCA Victor (both shown here) before moving onto United Artists as a composer/conductor/producer, including albums with Benny Carter and his wife, Lee Schaefer.

Label & Catalog #		Title	Year	VG+	NM

SAYE, JOE

Scottish born Joseph Shulman, aka Joe Saye is a jazzy pianist.

EmArcy MG-36072	(M)	**Scotch On The Rocks**	1956	16.00	40.00
EmArcy MG-36112	(M)	**A Wee Bit Of Jazz**	1957	16.00	40.00
EmArcy MG-36147	(M)	**A Double Shot Of Saye**	1958	16.00	40.00
EmArcy SR-80022	(S)	**A Double Shot Of Saye**	1958	12.00	30.00

—EmArcy albums above have blue labels with silver print.—

Mercury SR-60052	(S)	**A Wee Bit Of Jazz**	1959	12.00	30.00

(Mercury 60052 is a stereo reissue of EmArcy 36112.)

—Mercury albums above have silver on black labels.—

SCALETTA, DON

Capitol T-2204	(M)	**Any Time, Any Groove**	1965	8.00	20.00
Capitol ST-2204	(S)	**Any Time, Any Groove**	1965	6.00	15.00
Capitol T-2328	(M)	**All In Good Time**	1965	8.00	20.00
Capitol ST-2328	(S)	**All In Good Time**	1965	6.00	15.00
Verve V-5027	(M)	**Sunday Afternoon At The Trident**	1967	8.00	20.00
Verve V6-5027	(S)	**Sunday Afternoon At The Trident**	1967	6.00	15.00

SCHAEFER, HAL

Harold Schaefer is a jazz-based pianist.

RCA Victor LPM-1106	(M)	**Just Too Much**	1955	20.00	50.00
RCA Victor LPM-1199	(M)	**The RCA Victor Jazz Workshop**	1956	20.00	50.00

—RCA albums above have black labels with "Long Play" on the bottom.—

United Arts. UAL-3021	(M)	**Ten Shades Of Blue**	1959	16.00	40.00
United Arts. UAS-5021	(S)	**Ten Shades Of Blue**	1959	12.00	30.00

SCHIFFRIN, LALO

Brazilian born Lalo Schiffri is a Latin-jazz composer and leader. For additional listings refer to Louis Bellson & Lalo Schifrin and the Jazzy Soundtracks section under Colpix, Dot, Paramount, Verve, and Warner Bros.

Audio Fidelity AFLP-1981	(M)	**Bossa Nova—New Brazilian Jazz**	1962	10.00	25.00
Audio Fidelity AFSD-5981	(S)	**Bossa Nova—New Brazilian Jazz**	1962	8.00	20.00
Verve V-8601	(M)	**New Fantasy**	1964	6.00	15.00
Verve V6-8601	(S)	**New Fantasy**	1964	5.00	12.00
Verve V-8654	(M)	**The Dissection And Reconstruction Of Music From The Past As Performed By The Inmates Of Lalo Schiffrin's Demented Ensemble As A Tribute To The Memory Of The Marquis De Sade**	1966	8.00	20.00
Verve V6-8654	(S)	**The Dissection And Reconstruction Of Music From The Past As Performed By The Inmates Of Lalo Schiffrin's Demented Ensemble As A Tribute To The Memory Of The Marquis De Sade**	1966	6.00	15.00
Verve V6-8785	(S)	**Insensatez**	1968	4.00	10.00

—Verve albums above have black labels with "MGM Records" on the bottom.—

SCHWARTZ, THORNEL

Thornel Schwartz jr. is a modern jazz guitarist.

Argo LP-704	(M)	**Soul Cookin'**	1962	12.00	30.00
Argo LPS-704	(S)	**Soul Cookin'**	1962	10.00	25.00

SCIANNI, JOSEPH

Savoy MG-12185	(M)	**New Concepts**	1964	12.00	30.00

SCOBEY, BOB

Robert Scobey is a traditional jazz trumpet player.

Good Time Jazz L-22	(10")	**Bob Scobey's Frisco Band**	1954	20.00	50.00
Down Home MGD-1	(M)	**Bob Scobey's Frisco Band With Clancy Hayes**	1954	16.00	40.00
Good Time Jazz L-12006	(M)	**Bob Scobey's Frisco Band With Clancy Hayes**	1955	16.00	40.00
Good Time Jazz L-12009	(M)	**Scobey And Clancy**	1955	16.00	40.00
Good Time Jazz L-12023	(M)	**Direct From San Francisco**	1955	16.00	40.00
Good Time Jazz L-12032	(M)	**Bob Scobey's Frisco Band, Volume 1**	1957	16.00	40.00
Good Time Jazz L-12033	(M)	**Bob Scobey's Frisco Band, Volume 2**	1957	16.00	40.00
American Rec. Soc. G-408	(M)	**Bob Scobey's Frisco Band**	1956	16.00	40.00
Verve MGV-1001	(M)	**Bob Scobey's Band**	1956	16.00	40.00
Verve MGV-1009	(M)	**Music From Bourbon Street**	1956	16.00	40.00

(Verve 1009 also features Lizzie Miles.)

Verve MGV-1011	(M)	**The San Francisco Jazz Of Bob Scobey**	1957	16.00	40.00

—Verve albums above have "Verve Records, Inc." on the bottom of the label.—

Label & Catalog #		Title	Year	VG+	NM
Verve V-1001	(M)	**Bob Scobey's Band**	1961	6.00	15.00
Verve V-1009	(M)	**Music From Bourbon Street**	1961	6.00	15.00
Verve V-1011	(M)	**The San Francisco Jazz Of Bob Scobey**	1961	6.00	15.00
		—Verve albums above have "MGM Records" on the bottom of the label.—			
RCA Victor LPM-1344	(M)	**Beauty And The Beat**	1957	16.00	40.00
RCA Victor LPM-1448	(M)	**Swingin' On The Golden Gate**	1957	16.00	40.00
RCA Victor LPM-1567	(M)	**Between 18th And 19th On Any Street**	1957	16.00	40.00
RCA Victor LPM-1700	(M)	**College Classics**	1958	16.00	40.00
RCA Victor LPM-1889	(M)	**Something Is Always Happening On The River**	1958	16.00	40.00
RCA Victor LPM-2086	(M)	**Rompin' And Stompin'**	1959	16.00	40.00
RCA Victor LSP-2086	(S)	**Rompin' And Stompin'**	1959	12.00	30.00
		—RCA albums above have black labels with "Long Play" on the bottom.—			

SCOOBY DOO

Scooby Doo is Ad Alshibrod, John Anderson, Irving Ashby, John Ewing, Ernie Freeman, Jewel Grant, Plas Johnson, Raymond Martinez and Dave Pell.

Zephyr ZMP-12002	(M)	**Jerry Leiber Presents Scooby Doo**	1959	16.00	40.00

SCOTT, BOBBY

Robert Scott is a modern jazz pianist, vocalist and composer. For additional listings refer to Willy Cirillo; Terry Pollard / Bobby Scott; Lennie Tristano / Joe Bushkin / Bobby Scott / Marian McPartland.

Bethlehem BCP-1004	(10")	**Great Scott**	1954	40.00	100.00
Bethlehem BCP-1009	(10")	**The Compositions Of Bobby Scott, Volume 1**	1954	40.00	100.00
Bethlehem BCP-1029	(10")	**The Compositions Of Bobby Scott, Volume 2**	1955	40.00	100.00
ABC-Paramount ABC-102	(M)	**Scott Free**	1956	20.00	50.00
ABC-Paramount ABC-148	(M)	**Bobby Scott And Two Horns**	1957	20.00	50.00
Bethlehem BCP-8	(M)	**The Compositions Of Bobby Scott** *(Bethlehem 8 is a reissue of 1009 and 1029.)*	1957	20.00	50.00
Verve MGV-2106	(M)	**Bobby Scott Sings The Best Of Lerner & Loewe**	1958	20.00	50.00
Verve MGVS-6030	(S)	**Bobby Scott Sings The Best Of Lerner & Loewe**	1960	16.00	40.00
Verve MGV-8297	(M)	**Serenate—Bobby Scott, Pianist**	1959	20.00	50.00
Verve MGVS-6031	(S)	**Serenate—Bobby Scott, Pianist**	1960	16.00	40.00
Verve MGV-8326	(M)	**Bobby Scott Plays The Music Of Leonard Bernstein**	1959	20.00	50.00
Verve MGVS-6065	(S)	**Bobby Scott Plays The Music Of Leonard Bernstein**	1960	16.00	40.00
		—Verve albums above have "Verve Records, Inc." on the bottom of the label.—			
Verve V-2106	(M)	**Bobby Scott Sings The Best Of Lerner & Loewe**	1961	8.00	20.00
Verve V6-2106	(S)	**Bobby Scott Sings The Best Of Lerner & Loewe**	1961	6.00	15.00
Verve V-8297	(M)	**Serenate—Bobby Scott, Pianist**	1961	8.00	20.00
Verve V6-8297	(S)	**Serenate—Bobby Scott, Pianist**	1961	6.00	15.00
Verve V-8326	(M)	**Bobby Scott Plays The Music Of Leonard Bernstein**	1961	8.00	20.00
Verve V6-8326	(S)	**Bobby Scott Plays The Music Of Leonard Bernstein**	1961	6.00	15.00
		—Verve albums above have black labels with "MGM Records" on the bottom.—			
Atlantic 1341	(M)	**The Compleat Musician**	1960	10.00	25.00
Atlantic SD-1341	(S)	**The Compleat Musician**	1960	8.00	20.00
Atlantic 1355	(M)	**A Taste Of Honey**	1960	10.00	25.00
Atlantic SD-1355	(S)	**A Taste Of Honey**	1960	8.00	20.00
		—Atlantic albums above have a white fan logo on the right side of the label.—			
Mercury MG-20701	(M)	**Joyful Noises**	1962	10.00	25.00
Mercury SR-60701	(S)	**Joyful Noises**	1962	8.00	20.00
Mercury MG-20767	(M)	**When The Feeling Hits You**	1963	10.00	25.00
Mercury SR-60767	(S)	**When The Feeling Hits You**	1963	8.00	20.00
Mercury MG-20854	(M)	**108 Pounds Of Heartache**	1963	10.00	25.00
Mercury SR-60854	(S)	**108 Pounds Of Heartache**	1963	8.00	20.00
Mercury MG-20995	(M)	**I Had A Ball**	1964	10.00	25.00
Mercury SR-60995	(S)	**I Had A Ball**	1964	8.00	20.00
		—Mercury albums above have silver on black labels.—			

SCOTT, CLIFFORD, & LES McCANN

Pacific Jazz PJ-66	(M)	**Out Front** *(Colored vinyl)*	1963	20.00	50.00
Pacific Jazz PJ-66	(M)	**Out Front**	1963	10.00	25.00
Pacific Jazz ST-66	(S)	**Out Front** *(Colored vinyl)*	1963	16.00	40.00
Pacific Jazz ST-66	(S)	**Out Front**	1963	8.00	20.00

Label & Catalog #		Title	Year	VG+	NM
SCOTT, CLIFFORD					
Clifford Scott is a West Coast jazz saxophone(s), flute and clarinet player.					
World Pacific WP-1811	(M)	**The Big Ones** *(Green vinyl)*	1964	20.00	50.00
World Pacific WP-1811	(M)	**The Big Ones**	1964	10.00	25.00
World Pacific ST-1811	(S)	**The Big Ones** *(Green vinyl)*	1964	16.00	40.00
World Pacific ST-1811	(S)	**The Big Ones**	1964	8.00	20.00
World Pacific WP-182?	(M)	**Lavender Sax**	1964	8.00	20.00
World Pacific ST-182?	(M)	**Lavender Sax**	1964	3.00	15.00
SCOTT, HAZEL					
Hazel Scott is a jazz-based pianist and vocalist.					
Columbia CL-6090	(10")	**Great Scott**	1950	30.00	75.00
Decca DL-5130	(10")	**Swinging The Classics**	195?	30.00	75.00
Coral CRL-56057	(10")	**Hazel Scott**	1952	30.00	75.00
Capitol H-364	(10")	**Late Show**	1953	30.00	75.00
Debut DLP-16	(10")	**Relaxed Piano Moods**	1955	125.00	250.00
Decca DL-8474	(M)	**'Round Midnight**	1957	16.00	40.00
SCOTT, JIMMY					
James Scott is a jazz-based vocalist.					
Savoy MG-12027	(M)	**Very Truly Yours**	1955	20.00	50.00
Savoy MG-12150	(M)	**The Fabulous Little Jimmy Scott**	1959	16.00	40.00
Savoy MG-12181	(M)	**If You Only Knew**	1963	16.00	40.00
Savoy MG-12300	(M)	**Very Truly Yours**	196?	6.00	15.00
		(Savoy 12301 is a reissue of 12027.)			
Savoy MG-12301	(M)	**The Fabulous Songs Of Jimmy Scott**	196?	6.00	15.00
		(Savoy 12301 is a reissue of 12150.)			
Savoy MG-12302	(M)	**The Fabulous Voice Of Jimmy Scott**	196?	6.00	15.00
SCOTT, SHIRLEY					
Shirley Scott is a modern jazz organist. Whether credited on the front cover or not, she is accompanied by Stanley Turrentine on many Prestige sessions. For additional listings refer to Eddie "Lockjaw" Davis.					
Prestige PRLP-7143	(M)	**Great Scott!**	1958	20.00	50.00
Prestige PRLP-7155	(M)	**Scottie**	1959	20.00	50.00
Prestige PRLP-7163	(M)	**Scottie Plays Duke**	1959	20.00	50.00
Prestige PRLP-7173	(M)	**Soul Searching**	1960	20.00	50.00
Prestige PRLP-7182	(M)	**Mucho, Mucho**	1960	20.00	50.00
Prestige PRLP-7195	(M)	**Shirley's Sounds**	1961	20.00	50.00
Prestige PRST-7195	(S)	**Shirley's Sounds**	1961	20.00	50.00
Moodsville MVLP-5	(M)	**Shirley Scott Trio**	1960	20.00	50.00
Moodsville MVLP-19	(M)	**Like Cozy**	1961	20.00	50.00
Moodsville MVST-19	(S)	**Like Cozy**	1961	16.00	40.00
—Moodsville mono albums above have green labels with silver print.—					
Moodsville MVLP-5	(M)	**Shirley Scott Trio**	1965	10.00	25.00
Moodsville MVLP-19	(M)	**Like Cozy**	1965	10.00	25.00
Moodsville MVST-19	(S)	**Like Cozy**	1965	8.00	20.00
—Moodsville albums above have blue labels with a trident logo on the right side.—					
Prestige PRLP-7205	(M)	**Hip Soul**	1961	20.00	50.00
Prestige PRLP-7226	(M)	**Hip Twist**	1962	20.00	50.00
Prestige PRST-7226	(S)	**Hip Twist**	1962	20.00	50.00
Prestige PRLP-7240	(M)	**Shirley Scott Plays Horace Silver**	1962	16.00	40.00
Prestige PRST-7240	(S)	**Shirley Scott Plays Horace Silver**	1962	16.00	40.00
Prestige PRLP-7262	(M)	**Happy Talk**	1963	16.00	40.00
Prestige PRST-7262	(S)	**Happy Talk**	1963	16.00	40.00
Prestige PRLP-7267	(M)	**The Soul Is Willing**	1963	16.00	40.00
Prestige PRST-7267	(S)	**The Soul Is Willing**	1963	16.00	40.00
Prestige PRLP-7283	(M)	**Satin Doll**	1963	16.00	40.00
Prestige PRST-7283	(S)	**Satin Doll**	1963	16.00	40.00
Prestige PRLP-7305	(M)	**Drag 'Em Out**	1964	16.00	40.00
Prestige PRST-7305	(S)	**Drag 'Em Out**	1964	16.00	40.00
Prestige PRLP-7312	(M)	**Soul Shoutin'**	1964	16.00	40.00
Prestige PRST-7312	(S)	**Soul Shoutin'**	1964	16.00	40.00
—Prestige albums above have yellow mono or silver stereo labels with a Bergenfield, NJ address .—					
Prestige PRLP-7205	(M)	**Hip Soul**	196?	10.00	25.00
Prestige PRLP-7226	(M)	**Hip Twist**	196?	10.00	25.00
Prestige PRST-7226	(S)	**Hip Twist**	196?	8.00	20.00
Prestige PRLP-7267	(M)	**The Soul Is Willing**	196?	10.00	25.00
Prestige PRST-7267	(S)	**The Soul Is Willing**	196?	8.00	20.00

Label & Catalog #		Title	Year	VG+	NM
Prestige PRLP-7312	(M)	**Soul Shoutin'**	196?	10.00	25.00
Prestige PRST-7312	(S)	**Soul Shoutin'**	196?	8.00	20.00
Prestige PRLP-7328	(M)	**Travelin' Light**	1964	10.00	25.00
Prestige PRST-7328	(S)	**Travelin' Light**	1964	8.00	20.00
		(Prestige 7328 also features Kenny Burrell.)			
Prestige PRLP-7338	(M)	**Blue Flames**	1965	10.00	25.00
Prestige PRST-7338	(S)	**Blue Flames**	1965	8.00	20.00
Prestige PRLP-7360	(M)	**Sweet Soul**	1965	10.00	25.00
Prestige PRST-7360	(S)	**Sweet Soul**	1965	8.00	20.00
		(Prestige 7360 is a reissue of 7262.)			
Prestige PRLP-7376	(M)	**Blue Seven**	1965	10.00	25.00
Prestige PRST-7376	(S)	**Blue Seven**	1965	8.00	20.00
Prestige PRLP-7392	(M)	**Soul Sisters**	1965	10.00	25.00
Prestige PRST-7392	(S)	**Soul Sisters**	1965	8.00	20.00
Prestige PRLP-7424	(M)	**Workin'**	1966	10.00	25.00
Prestige PRST-7424	(S)	**Workin'**	1966	8.00	20.00
Prestige PRLP-7440	(M)	**Now's The Time**	1967	10.00	25.00
Prestige PRST-7440	(S)	**Now's The Time**	1967	8.00	20.00
Prestige PRLP-7456	(M)	**Stompin'**	1967	10.00	25.00
Prestige PRST-7456	(S)	**Stompin'**	1967	8.00	20.00
		—Prestige albums above have blue labels with a trident logo on the right side.—			
Prestige PRST-7707	(S)	**The Best Of Shirley Scott & Stanley Turrentine**	1969	6.00	15.00
		—Prestige albums above have blue labels with a trident logo on top.—			
Impulse A-51	(M)	**For Members Only**	1963	10.00	25.00
Impulse AS-51	(S)	**For Members Only**	1963	8.00	20.00
Impulse A-67	(M)	**Great Scott!**	1964	10.00	25.00
Impulse AS-67	(S)	**Great Scott!**	1964	8.00	20.00
Impulse A-73	(M)	**Everybody Loves A Lover**	1964	10.00	25.00
Impulse AS-73	(S)	**Everybody Loves A Lover**	1964	8.00	20.00
Impulse A-81	(M)	**Queen Of The Organ**	1965	10.00	25.00
Impulse AS-81	(S)	**Queen Of The Organ**	1965	8.00	20.00
Impulse A-93	(M)	**Latin Shadows**	1965	10.00	25.00
Impulse AS-93	(S)	**Latin Shadows**	1965	8.00	20.00
		—Impulse albums above have orange & black labels.—			
Impulse AS-51	(S)	**For Members Only**	1968	4.00	10.00
Impulse AS-67	(S)	**Great Scott!**	1968	4.00	10.00
Impulse AS-73	(S)	**Everybody Loves A Lover**	1968	4.00	10.00
Impulse AS-81	(S)	**Queen Of The Organ**	1968	4.00	10.00
Impulse AS-93	(S)	**Latin Shadows**	1968	4.00	10.00
		—Impulse albums above have red & black labels with the "abc" logo on top.—			

SCOTT, SHIRLEY, & CLARK TERRY

Impulse A-9133	(M)	**Soul Duo**	1967	10.00	25.00
Impulse AS-9133	(S)	**Soul Duo**	1967	8.00	20.00
		—Impulse albums above have orange & black labels.—			
Impulse AS-9133	(S)	**Soul Duo**	1968	4.00	10.00
		—Impulse albums above have red & black labels with the "abc" logo on top.—			

SCOTT, TOM

Thomas Scott is a jazzy saxophone player.

Impulse AS-9171	(S)	**Fool On The Hill**	1969	6.00	15.00
		—Impulse albums above have red & black labels with the "abc" logo on top.—			
Flying Dutchman 106	(S)	**Hair**	1969	4.00	10.00

SCOTT, TONY

Anthony Sciacca, aka Tony Scott, is a modern jazz and big band clarinet, saxophone(s) and piano player and composer. For additional listings refer to The Modern Jazz Society; Zoot Sims & Tony Scott & Al Cohn..

Brunswick BL-58040	(10")	**Music After Midnight**	1953	50.00	125.00
Brunswick BL-58056	(10")	**Tony Scott Quartet**	1954	50.00	125.00
Brunswick BL-58057	(10")	**Jazz For GI's**	1954	50.00	125.00
Brunswick BL-54021	(M)	**Tony Scott In Hi Fi**	1957	30.00	75.00
		(Brunswick 54021 is a reissue of 58040 and 58056.)			
Brunswick BL-54056	(M)	**Tony Scott Quartet**	1957	50.00	125.00
RCA Victor LJM-1022	(M)	**Scott's Fling**	1955	30.00	75.00
RCA Victor LPM-1268	(M)	**Both Sides Of Tony Scott**	1956	30.00	75.00
RCA Victor LPM-1353	(M)	**The Touch Of Tony Scott**	1956	30.00	75.00
RCA Victor LPM-1452	(M)	**The Complete Tony Scott**	1957	30.00	75.00
		—RCA albums above have black labels with "Long Play" on the bottom.—			

Label & Catalog #		Title	Year	VG+	NM
Coral CRL-57239	(M)	**52nd Street Scene**	1958	20.00	50.00
Coral CRL-757239	(S)	**52nd Street Scene**	1958	16.00	40.00
Signature SM-6001	(M)	**Gypsy**	1959	20.00	50.00
Signature SS-6001	(S)	**Gypsy**	1959	16.00	40.00
ABC-Paramount ABC-235	(M)	**South Pacific**	1958	12.00	30.00
ABC-Paramount ABCS-235	(S)	**South Pacific**	1958	10.00	25.00
Seeco SLP-425	(M)	**The Modern Art Of Jazz**	1959	16.00	40.00
Seeco SLP-4250	(S)	**The Modern Art Of Jazz**	1959	12.00	30.00
Seeco SLP-42?	(M)	**Hi Fi Land Of Jazz**	1959	16.00	40.00
Seeco SLP-42?0	(S)	**Hi Fi Land Of Jazz**	1959	12.00	30.00
Perfect PL-12010	(M)	**My Kind Of Jazz**	1960	20.00	50.00
Perfect PL-14010	(S)	**My Kind Of Jazz**	1960	16.00	40.00
Verve V-8634	(M)	**Music For Zen Meditation**	1965	5.00	12.00
Verve V6-8634	(S)	**Music For Zen Meditation**	1965	4.00	10.00
Verve V-8742	(M)	**Music For Yoga Meditation & Other Joys**	1967	5.00	12.00
Verve V6-8742	(S)	**Music For Yoga Meditation & Other Joys**	1967	4.00	10.00
Verve V6-8788	(S)	**Homage To Lord Krishna**	1969	4.00	10.00

— Verve albums above have black labels with "MGM Records" on the bottom.—

SCOTT, TONY, & JIMMY KNEPPER

Carlton LP-12-113	(M)	**Free Blown Jazz**	1959	20.00	50.00
Carlton ST-12-113	(S)	**Free Blown Jazz**	1959	16.00	40.00

SEARS, AL

Albert Sears is a traditional jazz tenor saxophone player.

Audio Lab AL-1540	(M)	**Dance Music With A Swing Beat**	1959	40.00	100.00
Swingville SVLP-2018	(M)	**Swing's The Thing**	1961	20.00	50.00

— Swingville mono albums above have purple mono or red stereo labels.—

Swingville SVLP-2018	(M)	**Swing's The Thing**	1965	10.00	25.00

— Swingville albums above have blue labels with a trident logo on the right side.—

SEBESKY, DON

Donald Sebesky is a modern jazz trombone player and composer.

Verve V6-8756	(S)	**Don Sebesky & The Jazz-Rock Syndrome**	1968	4.00	10.00

— Verve albums above have black labels with "MGM Records" on the bottom.—

SERRANO, PAUL

Paul Serrano is a modern jazz trumpet player.

Riverside RLP-359	(M)	**Blues Holiday**	1961	12.00	30.00
Riverside RS-9359	(S)	**Blues Holiday**	1961	10.00	25.00

— Riverside albums above have blue mono or black stereo labels with a reel & mike logo on top.—

SETE, BOLA

Brazilian born Bola Sete is a Latin jazz guitarist. For additional listings refer to Vince Guaraldi & Bola Sete.

Fantasy 3349	(M)	**Bossa Nova**	1963	8.00	20.00
Fantasy 8349	(S)	**Bossa Nova**	1963	6.00	15.00
Fantasy 3364	(M)	**The Incomparable Bola Sete**	1965	8.00	20.00
Fantasy 8364	(S)	**The Incomparable Bola Sete**	1965	6.00	15.00
Fantasy 3368	(M)	**The Solo Guitar Of Bola Sete**	1966	8.00	20.00
Fantasy 8368	(S)	**The Solo Guitar Of Bola Sete**	1966	6.00	15.00
Fantasy 3375	(M)	**Autentico!**	1966	8.00	20.00
Fantasy 8375	(S)	**Autentico!**	1966	6.00	15.00
Verve V-8689	(M)	**Bola Sete At The Monterey Jazz Festival**	1967	8.00	20.00
Verve V6-8689	(S)	**Bola Sete At The Monterey Jazz Festival**	1967	6.00	15.00

— Verve albums above have black labels with "MGM Records" on the bottom.—

SEVERSON, PAUL

Academy MWJ-1	(M)	**Midwest Jazz**	1956	16.00	40.00

SEVILLA, JORGE

Verve MGV-8342	(M)	**The Incredible Guitar Of Jorge Sevilla**	1959	20.00	50.00
Verve MGVS-6103	(S)	**The Incredible Guitar Of Jorge Sevilla**	1960	16.00	40.00

— Verve albums above have black labels with "Verve Records, Inc." on the bottom.—

Verve V-8342	(M)	**The Incredible Guitar Of Jorge Sevilla**	1961	8.00	20.00
Verve V6-8342	(S)	**The Incredible Guitar Of Jorge Sevilla**	1961	6.00	15.00

— Verve albums above have black labels with "MGM Records" on the bottom.—

Label & Catalog #		Title	Year	VG+	NM

SHANK, BUD

Clifford "Bud" Shank is a West Coast jazz alto and baritone sax and clarinet player. For additional listings refer to Laurindo Almeida; Chet Baker; Boots Brown; and the Jazzy Soundtracks section under Chancellor, Decca, Pacific Jazz, and World Pacific.

Label & Catalog #		Title	Year	VG+	NM
Nocturne NLP-2	(10")	**Compositions Of Shorty Rogers**	1954	60.00	150.00
Pacific Jazz PJLP-14	(10")	**Bud Shank And Three Trombones**	1954	60.00	150.00
Pacific Jazz PJLP-20	(10")	**Bud Shank And Bob Brookmeyer**	1955	60.00	150.00
Pacific Jazz PJ-1205	(M)	**Bud Shank/Shorty Rogers**	1955	40.00	100.00
		(Pacific Jazz 1205 is a reissue of Nocturne 2 with additional material.)			
Pacific Jazz PJ-1213	(M)	**Strings And Trombones**	1956	40.00	100.00
		(Pacific Jazz 1213 is a reissue of 14 and 20.)			
Pacific Jazz PJ-1215	(M)	**The Bud Shank Quartet**	1956	40.00	100.00
		(Pacific Jazz 1215 also features Claude Williamson.)			
Pacific Jazz PJ-1219	(M)	**Jazz At Cal-Tech**	1956	30.00	75.00
		(Pacific Jazz 1219 also features Bob Cooper.)			
Pacific Jazz PJ-1226	(M)	**Flute 'N Oboe**	1957	30.00	75.00
		(Pacific Jazz 1226 also features Bob Cooper.)			
Pacific Jazz PJ-1230	(M)	**The Bud Shank Quartet**	1957	30.00	75.00
		(Pacific Jazz 1230 also features Claude Williamson.)			
Pacific Jazz PJM-411	(M)	**The Swing's To TV**	1957	30.00	75.00
		(Pacific Jazz 411 also features Bob Cooper.)			
World Pacific PJM-411	(M)	**The Swing's To TV**	1958	20.00	50.00
World Pacific ST-1002	(S)	**The Swing's To TV**	1959	16.00	40.00
World Pacific WP-1205	(M)	**Bud Shank/Shorty Rogers**	1958	20.00	50.00
World Pacific WP-1215	(M)	**The Bud Shank Quartet**	1958	20.00	50.00
World Pacific WP-1219	(M)	**Jazz At Cal-Tech**	1958	20.00	50.00
World Pacific WP-1226	(M)	**Flute 'N Oboe**	1958	16.00	40.00
World Pacific WP-1230	(M)	**The Bud Shank Quartet**	1958	16.00	40.00
World Pacific WP-1251	(M)	**I'll Take Romance**	1958	16.00	40.00
World Pacific WP-1259	(M)	**Holiday In Brazil**	1959	16.00	40.00
World Pacific ST-1018	(S)	**Holiday In Brazil**	1959	12.00	30.00
World Pacific WP-1281	(M)	**Latin Contrasts**	1959	16.00	40.00
World Pacific ST-1281	(S)	**Latin Contrasts**	1959	12.00	30.00
		(World Pacific 1281 also features Laurindo Almeida.)			
World Pacific WP-1286	(M)	**Flute 'N Alto**	1960	16.00	40.00
World Pacific ST-1286	(S)	**Flute 'N Alto**	1960	12.00	30.00
World Pacific WP-1299	(M)	**Koto 'N Flute**	1960	16.00	40.00
World Pacific ST-1299	(S)	**Koto 'N Flute**	1960	12.00	30.00
Pacific Jazz PJ-4	(M)	**Bud Shank Plays Tenor**	1960	12.00	30.00
Pacific Jazz ST-4	(S)	**Bud Shank Plays Tenor**	1960	10.00	25.00
Pacific Jazz PJ-21	(M)	**New Groove**	1961	12.00	30.00
Pacific Jazz ST-21	(S)	**New Groove**	1961	10.00	25.00
		(Pacific Jazz 21 also features Carmell Jones.)			
Pacific Jazz PJ-58	(M)	**Bossa Nova Jazz Samba**	1962	10.00	25.00
Pacific Jazz ST-58	(S)	**Bossa Nova Jazz Samba**	1962	8.00	20.00
		(Pacific Jazz 58 also features Clare Fischer.)			
Pacific Jazz PJ-64	(M)	**Brasamba Bossa Nova**	1963	10.00	25.00
Pacific Jazz ST-64	(S)	**Brasamba Bossa Nova**	1963	8.00	20.00
		(Pacific Jazz 64 also features Clare Fischer.)			
Pacific Jazz PJ-89	(M)	**Bud Shank And His Brazilian Friends**	1965	10.00	25.00
Pacific Jazz ST-89	(S)	**Bud Shank And His Brazilian Friends**	1965	8.00	20.00
Pacific Jazz PJ-10110	(M)	**Bud Shank And The Sax Section**	1966	8.00	20.00
Pacific Jazz ST-20110	(S)	**Bud Shank And The Sax Section**	1966	6.00	15.00
Crown CLP-5311	(M)	**Bud Shank**	1963	6.00	15.00
Crown CST-311	(E)	**Bud Shank**	1963	3.00	7.50
		(Crown 5311 reissues Pacific Jazz material.)			
Kimberly 2025	(M)	**The Talents Of Bud Shank**	1963	10.00	25.00
Kimberly 11025	(S)	**The Talents Of Bud Shank**	1963	8.00	20.00
		(Kimberly 2025 is a reissue of Pacific Jazz 1213.)			
World Pacific WP-1416	(M)	**Improvisations**	1962	10.00	25.00
		(World Pacific 1416 also features Ravi Shankar.)			
World Pacific WP-1424	(M)	**Koto And Flute**	1962	10.00	25.00
		(World Pacific 1424 also features Kimio Eto.)			
World Pacific WP-1819	(M)	**Folk 'N Flute**	1966	8.00	20.00
World Pacific ST-1819	(S)	**Folk 'N Flute**	1966	6.00	15.00
		(World Pacific 1819 also features Joe Pass.)			
World Pacific WP-1827	(M)	**Flute, Oboe And Strings**	1966	8.00	20.00
World Pacific ST-1827	(S)	**Flute, Oboe And Strings**	1966	6.00	15.00

Label & Catalog #		Title	Year	VG+	NM
World Pacific WP-1840	(M)	**Michelle**	1966	8.00	20.00
World Pacific ST-1840	(S)	**Michelle**	1966	6.00	15.00
World Pacific WP-1845	(M)	**California Dreaming**	1966	8.00	20.00
World Pacific ST-1845	(S)	**California Dreaming**	1966	6.00	15.00
World Pacific WP-1853	(M)	**Girl In Love**	1967	8.00	20.00
World Pacific ST-1853	(S)	**Girl In Love**	1967	6.00	15.00
World Pacific WP-1855	(M)	**Brazil! Brazil! Brazil!**	1967	8.00	20.00
World Pacific ST-1855	(S)	**Brazil! Brazil! Brazil!**	1967	6.00	15.00
World Pacific WP-1868	(M)	**A Spoonful Of Jazz**	1967	8.00	20.00
World Pacific ST-1868	(S)	**A Spoonful Of Jazz**	1967	6.00	15.00
World Pacific WP-1873	(M)	**Magical Mystery**	1967	8.00	20.00
World Pacific ST-1873	(S)	**Magical Mystery**	1967	6.00	15.00

SHARON, RALPH

English born Ralph Sharon is a jazz-based pianist and composer.

London LB-733	(10")	**Spring Fever**	1953	20.00	50.00
London LB-842	(10")	**Autumn Leaves**	1954	20.00	50.00
London LL-1339	(M)	**Autumn Leaves/Spring Fever**	1955	16.00	40.00
		(London 1339 is a reissue of 733 and 842.)			
London LL-1488	(M)	**Easy Jazz**	1956	16.00	40.00
Bethlehem BCP-13	(M)	**Mr. & Mrs. Jazz**	1955	16.00	40.00
		(Bethlehem 13 also features Sue Sharon.)			
Bethlehem BCP-41	(M)	**Ralph Sharon Trio**	1956	16.00	40.00
Rama LP-1001	(M)	**Jazz Around The World**	1957	20.00	50.00
Argo LP-635	(M)	**2:38 A.M.**	1958	16.00	40.00
Argo LPS-635	(S)	**2:38 A.M.**	1958	12.00	30.00
Columbia CL 2321	(M)	**Do I Hear A Waltz?**	1965	12.00	30.00
Columbia CS-9121	(S)	**Do I Hear A Waltz?**	1965	10.00	25.00

SHAVERS, CHARLIE

Charles Shavers is a traditional jazz trumpet player, vocalist, arranger and composer. For additional listings refer to Fred Astaire; Coleman Hawkins; Jonah Jones / Charlie Shavers; Hal Singer & Charlie Shavers; and the Various Artists section under Savoy.

Bethlehem BCP-1007	(10")	**Horn O' Plenty**	1954	40.00	100.00
Bethlehem BCP-1021	(10")	**The Most Intimate Charlie Shavers**	1955	40.00	100.00
Period SPL-1113	(10")	**Flow Gently, Sweet Rhythm**	1955	40.00	100.00
		(Period 1113 also features Maxine Sullivan.)			
Bethlehem BCP-5002	(M)	**The Most Intimate Charlie Shavers**	195?	30.00	75.00
Bethlehem BCP-27	(M)	**Gershwin, Shavers And Strings**	1955	30.00	75.00
Bethlehem BCP-67	(M)	**The Complete Charlie Shavers With Maxine Sullivan**	1957	30.00	75.00
		(Bethlehem 67 is a reissue of 1007 and Period 1113.)			
Jazztone J-1229	(M)	**Flow Gently, Sweet Rhythm**	1956	16.00	40.00
		(Jazztone 1229 is a reissue of Period 1113.)			
Aamco 310	(M)	**The Most Intimate Charlie Shavers**	1959	16.00	40.00
		(Aamco 310 is a reissue of Bethlehem 5002).			
MGM E-3765	(M)	**Charlie Digs Paree**	1959	12.00	30.00
MGM SE-3765	(S)	**Charlie Digs Paree**	1959	10.00	25.00
MGM E-3809	(M)	**Charlie Digs Dixie**	1960	12.00	30.00
MGM SE-3809	(S)	**Charlie Digs Dixie**	1960	10.00	25.00
Everest LPBR-5070	(M)	**Girl Of My Dreams**	1960	10.00	25.00
Everest SDBR-1070	(S)	**Girl Of My Dreams**	1960	8.00	20.00
Everest LPBR-5108	(M)	**Here Comes Charlie**	1960	10.00	25.00
Everest SDBR-108	(S)	**Here Comes Charlie**	1960	8.00	20.00
Everest LPBR-5127	(M)	**Like Charlie**	1961	10.00	25.00
Everest SDBR-1127	(S)	**Like Charlie**	1961	8.00	20.00
Capitol T-1883	(M)	**Excitement Unlimited**	1963	10.00	25.00
Capitol ST-1883	(S)	**Excitement Unlimited**	1963	8.00	20.00

SHAW, ARTIE

Arthur Arshawsky, aka Artie Shaw, is a traditional jazz clarinet and sax player, composer and band leader.

Columbia ML-4260	(M)	**Modern Music For Clarinet**	1950	20.00	50.00
MGM E-517	(10")	**Artie Shaw Plays Cole Porter**	1950	20.00	50.00
Decca DL-5286	(10")	**Artie Shaw Dance Program**	1950	20.00	50.00
Decca DL-5524	(10")	**Speak To Me Of Love**	1950	20.00	50.00
RCA Victor LPT-28	(10")	**Artie Shaw Favorites**	1952	20.00	50.00
RCA Victor LPM-30	(10")	**Four Star Favorites**	1952	20.00	50.00
RCA Victor LPT-3013	(10")	**This Is Artie Shaw**	1952	20.00	50.00

Label & Catalog #		Title	Year	VG+	NM
RCA Victor LPT-1020	(M)	**My Concerto**	1955	20.00	50.00
RCA Victor LPM-1201	(M)	**Both Feet In The Groove**	1956	16.00	40.00
RCA Victor LPM-1217	(M)	**Back Bay Shuffle**	1956	16.00	40.00
RCA Victor LPM-1241	(M)	**Artie Shaw And His Gramercy Five**	1956	16.00	40.00
RCA Victor LPM-1244	(M)	**Moonglow**	1956	16.00	40.00
RCA Victor LPM-1570	(M)	**Any Old Time**	1957	16.00	40.00
RCA Victor LPM-1648	(M)	**A Man And His Dream**	1957	16.00	40.00
		—RCA Victor albums above have black labels with "Long Play" on the bottom.—			
RCA Victor LPT-6000	(M)	**In The Blue Room/In The Cafe Rouge** *(2 LP box)*	195?	20.00	50.00
		—RCA Victor albums above have silver label with red print.—			
RCA Victor LPM-6701	(M)	**The Swingin' Mr. Shaw** *(5 LP box)*	196?	20.00	50.00
		—RCA Victor albums above have black labels with "Long Play" on the bottom.—			
Decca DL-8309	(M)	**Did Someone Say Party?**	1956	16.00	40.00
Epic LG-1006	(10")	**Artie Shaw With Strings**	1954	20.00	50.00
Epic LG-1017	(10")	**Non-Stop Flight**	1954	20.00	50.00
Epic LG-1102	(10")	**Artie Shaw**	1955	20.00	50.00
Epic LN-3112	(M)	**Artie Shaw With Strings**	1955	16.00	40.00
Epic LN-3150	(M)	**Artie Shaw And His Orchestra**	1955	16.00	40.00
Clef MGC-159	(10")	**Artie Shaw & His Gramercy Five, Volume 1**	1954	30.00	75.00
		(Clef 159 features cover art by David Stone Martin.)			
Clef MGC-160	(10")	**Artie Shaw & His Gramercy Five, Volume 2**	1954	30.00	75.00
		(Clef 160 features cover art by David Stone Martin.)			
Clef MGC-630	(M)	**Artie Shaw & His Gramercy Five, Volume 3**	1954	30.00	75.00
		(Clef 630 features cover art by David Stone Martin.)			
Clef MGC-645	(M)	**Artie Shaw & His Gramercy Five, Volume 4**	1955	30.00	75.00
		(Clef 645 features cover art by David Stone Martin.)			
Verve MGV-2014	(M)	**I Can't Get Started**	1956	20.00	50.00
		(Verve 2014 is a reissue of Clef 159 and 160.)			
Verve MGV-2015	(M)	**Sequence In Music**	1956	20.00	50.00
		—Verve albums above have "Verve Records, Inc" on the bottom of the label.—			
Verve V-2014	(M)	**I Can't Get Started**	1961	6.00	15.00
Verve V-2015	(M)	**Sequence In Music**	1961	6.00	15.00
		—Verve albums above have black labels with "MGM Records" on the bottom.—			
Allegro 1405	(M)	**An Hour With Artie Shaw**	1955	16.00	40.00
Allegro 1466	(M)	**Artie Shaw Hour**	1955	16.00	40.00
Lion L-70058	(M)	**Artie Shaw Plays Irving Berlin And Cole Porter**	1958	10.00	25.00
Camden CAL-584	(M)	**One Night Stand**	1959	8.00	20.00

SHAW, GENE

Eugene Shaw is a modern jazz trumpet player.

Argo LP-707	(M)	**Breakthrough**	1962	12.00	30.00
Argo LPS-707	(S)	**Breakthrough**	1962	10.00	25.00
Argo LP-726	(M)	**Debut In Blues**	1963	12.00	30.00
Argo LPS-726	(S)	**Debut In Blues**	1963	10.00	25.00
Argo LP-743	(M)	**Carnival Sketches**	1964	12.00	30.00
Argo LPS-743	(S)	**Carnival Sketches**	1964	10.00	25.00

SHEARING, GEORGE

English born George Shearing is a traditional jazz-based pianist, composer and band leader. For additional listings refer to Nat King Cole; Peggy Lee; Marian McPartland / George Shearing; Red Norvo; Dakota Staton; Nancy Wilson.

Discovery DL-3002	(10")	**George Shearing Quintet**	1949	20.00	50.00
Savoy MG-15003	(10")	**Piano Solo**	1950	20.00	50.00
London LL-295	(10")	**Souvenirs**	1951	16.00	40.00
MGM E-518	(10")	**You're Hearing The George Shearing Quartet**	1950	20.00	50.00
MGM E-90	(10")	**Touch Of Genius**	1951	16.00	40.00
MGM E-155	(10")	**I Hear Music**	1952	16.00	40.00
MGM E-226	(10")	**When Lights Are Low**	1953	16.00	40.00
MGM E-252	(10")	**An Evening With George Shearing**	1954	16.00	40.00
MGM E-3175	(M)	**Shearing Caravan**	1955	12.00	30.00
MGM E-3222	(M)	**An Evening With George Shearing**	1955	12.00	30.00
		(MGM 3222 is a reissue of 252.)			
MGM E-3264	(M)	**When Lights Are Low**	1955	12.00	30.00
		(MGM 3264 is a reissue of 226.)			
MGM E-3265	(M)	**Touch Of Genius**	1955	12.00	30.00
		(MGM 3265 is a reissue of 90.)			
MGM E-3266	(M)	**I Hear Music**	1955	12.00	30.00
		(MGM 3266 is a reissue of 155.)			

Label & Catalog #		Title	Year	VG+	NM
MGM E-3293	*(M)*	**Shearing In Hi Fi**	*1955*	**12.00**	**30.00**
London LL-1343	*(M)*	**By Request**	*1956*	**12.00**	**30.00**
Capitol T-648	*(M)*	**The Shearing Spell**	*1955*	**12.00**	**30.00**
Capitol T-720	*(M)*	**Velvet Carpet**	*1956*	**12.00**	**30.00**
Capitol T-737	*(M)*	**Latin Escapade**	*1956*	**12.00**	**30.00**
Capitol T-858	*(M)*	**Black Satin**	*1957*	**12.00**	**30.00**
Capitol T-909	*(M)*	**Shearing Piano**	*1957*	**12.00**	**30.00**
		—Capitol albums above have turquoise labels.—			
Capitol T-648	*(M)*	**The Shearing Spell**	*1958*	**6.00**	**15.00**
Capitol T-720	*(M)*	**Velvet Carpet**	*1958*	**6.00**	**15.00**
Capitol T-737	*(M)*	**Latin Escapade**	*1958*	**6.00**	**15.00**
Capitol T-858	*(M)*	**Black Satin**	*1958*	**6.00**	**15.00**
Capitol T-909	*(M)*	**Shearing Piano**	*1958*	**6.00**	**15.00**
Capitol T-1038	*(M)*	**Burnished Brass**	*1958*	**8.00**	**20.00**
Capitol ST-1038	*(S)*	**Burnished Brass**	*1958*	**6.00**	**15.00**
Capitol T-1082	*(M)*	**Latin Lace**	*1958*	**8.00**	**20.00**
Capitol ST-1082	*(S)*	**Latin Lace**	*1958*	**6.00**	**15.00**
Capitol T-1124	*(M)*	**Blue Chiffon**	*1959*	**8.00**	**20.00**
Capitol ST-1124	*(S)*	**Blue Chiffon**	*1959*	**6.00**	**15.00**
Capitol T-1187	*(M)*	**George Shearing On Stage**	*1959*	**8.00**	**20.00**
Capitol ST-1187	*(S)*	**George Shearing On Stage**	*1959*	**6.00**	**15.00**
Capitol T-1275	*(M)*	**Latin Affair**	*1959*	**8.00**	**20.00**
Capitol ST-1275	*(S)*	**Latin Affair**	*1959*	**6.00**	**15.00**
Capitol T-1334	*(M)*	**White Satin**	*1960*	**8.00**	**20.00**
Capitol ST-1334	*(S)*	**White Satin**	*1960*	**6.00**	**15.00**
Capitol T-1416	*(M)*	**On The Sunny Side Of The Strip**	*1960*	**8.00**	**20.00**
Capitol ST-1416	*(S)*	**On The Sunny Side Of The Strip**	*1960*	**6.00**	**15.00**
Capitol T-1472	*(M)*	**The Shearing Touch**	*1960*	**8.00**	**20.00**
Capitol ST-1472	*(S)*	**The Shearing Touch**	*1960*	**6.00**	**15.00**
Capitol T-1567	*(M)*	**Mood Latino**	*1961*	**8.00**	**20.00**
Capitol ST-1567	*(S)*	**Mood Latino**	*1961*	**6.00**	**15.00**
Capitol T-1628	*(M)*	**Satin Affair**	*1962*	**8.00**	**20.00**
Capitol ST-1628	*(S)*	**Satin Affair**	*1962*	**6.00**	**15.00**
		—Capitol albums above have black "rainbow" labels with the logo on the left side.—			
Capitol T-648	*(M)*	**The Shearing Spell**	*196?*	**4.00**	**10.00**
Capitol T-720	*(M)*	**Velvet Carpet**	*196?*	**4.00**	**10.00**
Capitol T-737	*(M)*	**Latin Escapade**	*196?*	**4.00**	**10.00**
Capitol T-858	*(M)*	**Black Satin**	*196?*	**4.00**	**10.00**
Capitol T-909	*(M)*	**Shearing Piano**	*196?*	**4.00**	**10.00**
Capitol T-1038	*(M)*	**Burnished Brass**	*196?*	**4.00**	**10.00**
Capitol ST-1038	*(S)*	**Burnished Brass**	*196?*	**3.20**	**8.00**
Capitol T-1082	*(M)*	**Latin Lace**	*196?*	**4.00**	**10.00**
Capitol ST-1082	*(S)*	**Latin Lace**	*196?*	**3.20**	**8.00**
Capitol T-1124	*(M)*	**Blue Chiffon**	*196?*	**4.00**	**10.00**
Capitol ST-1124	*(S)*	**Blue Chiffon**	*196?*	**3.20**	**8.00**
Capitol T-1187	*(M)*	**George Shearing On Stage**	*196?*	**4.00**	**10.00**
Capitol ST-1187	*(S)*	**George Shearing On Stage**	*196?*	**3.20**	**8.00**
Capitol T-1275	*(M)*	**Latin Affair**	*196?*	**4.00**	**10.00**
Capitol ST-1275	*(S)*	**Latin Affair**	*196?*	**3.20**	**8.00**
Capitol T-1334	*(M)*	**White Satin**	*196?*	**4.00**	**10.00**
Capitol ST-1334	*(S)*	**White Satin**	*196?*	**3.20**	**8.00**
Capitol T-1416	*(M)*	**On The Sunny Side Of The Strip**	*196?*	**4.00**	**10.00**
Capitol ST-1416	*(S)*	**On The Sunny Side Of The Strip**	*196?*	**3.20**	**8.00**
Capitol T-1472	*(M)*	**The Shearing Touch**	*196?*	**4.00**	**10.00**
Capitol ST-1472	*(S)*	**The Shearing Touch**	*196?*	**3.20**	**8.00**
Capitol T-1567	*(M)*	**Mood Latino**	*196?*	**4.00**	**10.00**
Capitol ST-1567	*(S)*	**Mood Latino**	*196?*	**3.20**	**8.00**
Capitol T-1628	*(M)*	**Satin Affair**	*196?*	**4.00**	**10.00**
Capitol ST-1628	*(S)*	**Satin Affair**	*196?*	**3.20**	**8.00**
Capitol T-1715	*(M)*	**San Francisco Scene**	*1962*	**5.00**	**12.00**
Capitol ST-1715	*(S)*	**San Francisco Scene**	*1962*	**4.00**	**10.00**
Capitol T-1827	*(M)*	**Jazz Moments**	*1963*	**5.00**	**12.00**
Capitol ST-1827	*(S)*	**Jazz Moments**	*1963*	**4.00**	**10.00**
Capitol T-1873	*(M)*	**Bossa Nova**	*1963*	**5.00**	**12.00**
Capitol ST-1873	*(S)*	**Bossa Nova**	*1963*	**4.00**	**10.00**
Capitol T-1992	*(M)*	**Jazz Concert**	*1963*	**5.00**	**12.00**
Capitol ST-1992	*(S)*	**Jazz Concert**	*1963*	**4.00**	**10.00**

Label & Catalog #		Title	Year	VG+	NM
Capitol T-2143	(M)	**Deep Velvet**	1964	5.00	12.00
Capitol ST-2143	(S)	**Deep Velvet**	1964	4.00	10.00
Capitol T-2247	(M)	**Rare Form**	1965	5.00	12.00
Capitol ST-2247	(S)	**Rare Form**	1965	4.00	10.00
Capitol T-2272	(M)	**Out Of The Woods**	1965	5.00	12.00
Capitol ST-2272	(S)	**Out Of The Woods**	1965	4.00	10.00
Capitol T-2447	(M)	**Rare Form**	1966	5.00	12.00
Capitol ST-2447	(S)	**Rare Form**	1966	4.00	10.00
Capitol T-2567	(M)	**That Fresh Feeling**	1966	5.00	12.00
Capitol ST-2567	(S)	**That Fresh Feeling**	1966	4.00	10.00
Capitol ST-2699	(S)	**George Shearing Today**	1968	4.00	10.00
Capitol ST-181	(S)	**Fool On The Hill**	1969	4.00	10.00
		— Capitol albums above have black "rainbow" labels with the logo on top.—			
MGM E-4042	(M)	**Soft And Silky**	1962	6.00	15.00
MGM SE-4042	(E)	**Soft And Silky**	1962	4.00	10.00
MGM E-4169	(M)	**The Very Best Of George Shearing**	1963	6.00	15.00
MGM SE-4169	(E)	**The Very Best Of George Shearing**	1963	4.00	10.00
Verve VSP-9	(M)	**Classic Shearing**	1966	6.00	15.00
Verve VSPS-9	(E)	**Classic Shearing**	1966	3.00	7.50
		(Verve 9 reissues MGM material.)			
Archive Of Folk & Jazz 223	(E)	**Young George Shearing**	1968	4.00	10.00
Archive Of Folk & Jazz 236	(E)	**The Early Years, Vol. 2**	1969	4.00	10.00

SHEARING, GEORGE, & THE MONTGOMERY BROTHERS

Jazzland JLP-55	(M)	**Love Walked In**	1961	16.00	40.00
Jazzland JLP-955	(S)	**Love Walked In**	1961	12.00	30.00
		(First pressing covers have a photo of Shearing and the brothers.)			
Jazzland JLP-55	(M)	**Love Walked In**	196?	10.00	25.00
Jazzland JLP-955	(S)	**Love Walked In**	196?	8.00	20.00
		(Later covers have a photo of an attractive woman.)			

SHEEN, MICKEY

Milton Scheinblum, aka Mickey Sheen, is a modern jazz drummer.

Herald HLP-0105	(M)	**Have Swing, Will Travel**	1956	16.00	40.00

SHELDON, JACK

Jack Sheldon is a West Coast jazz trumpet player. For additional listings refer to Heleyne Stewart.

Jazz: West JWLP-1	(10")	**Get Out Of Town**	1955	210.00	350.00
Jazz: West JWLP-2	(10")	**Jack Sheldon Quintet**	1955	210.00	350.00
Jazz: West JWLP-6	(M)	**The Quartet And The Quintet**	1956	125.00	250.00
		(Jazz: West 6 is a reissue of 1 and 2.)			
Gene Norman GNP-60	(M)	**Jack's Groove**	1961	24.00	60.00
Reprise R-2004	(M)	**A Jazz Profile Of Ray Charles**	1961	12.00	30.00
Reprise R9-2004	(S)	**A Jazz Profile Of Ray Charles**	1961	10.00	25.00
Capitol T-1851	(M)	**Out!**	1963	8.00	20.00
Capitol ST-1851	(S)	**Out!**	1963	6.00	15.00
Capitol T-2029	(M)	**Play Buddy, Play!**	1966	8.00	20.00
Capitol ST-2029	(S)	**Play Buddy, Play!**	1966	6.00	15.00

SHEPARD, TOMMY

Thomas Shepherd is a modern jazz trombone player.

Coral CRL-57110	(M)	**Shepard's Flock**	1957	30.00	75.00

SHEPP, ARCHIE, & BILL DIXON

Savoy MG-12178	(M)	**The Archie Shepp-Bill Dixon Quartet**	1962	12.00	30.00

SHEPP, ARCHIE / BILL DIXON

Savoy MG-12184	(M)	**Archie Shepp & The New Contemporary 5 / The Bill Dixon 7-Tette** *(White bordered cover)*	1964	20.00	50.00
Savoy MG-12184	(M)	**Archie Shepp & The New Contemporary 5 / The Bill Dixon 7-Tette** *(Purple bordered cover)*	1965	12.00	30.00

SHEPP, ARCHIE

Archie Shepp is a modern jazz tenor sax player and composer. For additional listings refer to John Coltrane.

Impulse A-71	(M)	**Archie Shepp**	1964	12.00	30.00
Impulse AS-71	(S)	**Archie Shepp**	1964	10.00	25.00
Impulse A-86	(M)	**Fire Music**	1965	12.00	30.00
Impulse AS-86	(S)	**Fire Music**	1965	10.00	25.00

Label & Catalog #		Title	Year	VG+	NM
Impulse A-97	(M)	**On This Night**	1966	12.00	30.00
Impulse AS-97	(S)	**On This Night**	1966	10.00	25.00
Impulse A-9118	(M)	**Live In San Francisco**	1967	12.00	30.00
Impulse AS-9118	(S)	**Live In San Francisco**	1967	10.00	25.00
Impulse A-9134	(M)	**Mama Too Tight**	1967	12.00	30.00
Impulse AS-9134	(S)	**Mama Too Tight**	1967	10.00	25.00

—Impulse albums above have orange & black labels.—

Label & Catalog #		Title	Year	VG+	NM
Impulse AS-71	(S)	**Archie Shepp**	1968	6.00	15.00
Impulse AS-86	(S)	**Fire Music**	1968	6.00	15.00
Impulse AS-97	(S)	**On This Night**	1968	6.00	15.00
Impulse AS-9118	(S)	**Live In San Francisco**	1968	6.00	15.00
Impulse AS-9134	(S)	**Mama Too Tight**	1968	6.00	15.00
Impulse AS-9154	(S)	**The Magic Of Ju Ju**	1968	8.00	20.00
Impulse AS-9162	(S)	**Three For A Quarter, One For A Dime**	1968	8.00	20.00
Impulse AS-9170	(S)	**The Way Ahead**	1969	8.00	20.00

—Impulse albums above have red & black labels with the "abc" logo on top.—

Label & Catalog #		Title	Year	VG+	NM
Delmark DEL-409	(M)	**Archie Shepp In Europe**	1968	12.00	30.00
Delmark DEL-9409	(S)	**Archie Shepp In Europe**	1968	8.00	20.00

SHERRILL, JOYA

Joya Sherrill is a traditional jazz vocalist and composer. For additional listings refer to the Jazzy Soundtracks section under Contact

Label & Catalog #		Title	Year	VG+	NM
Columbia CL-1378	(M)	**Sugar And Spice**	1959	12.00	30.00
Columbia CS-8178	(S)	**Sugar And Spice**	1960	10.00	25.00

—Columbia albums above have six white on black "eye" logos on each label.—

Label & Catalog #		Title	Year	VG+	NM
20th Cent. Fox TFL-3170	(M)	**Joya Sherrill Sings Duke Ellington**	196?	12.00	30.00
20th Cent. Fox TFS-4170	(S)	**Joya Sherrill Sings Duke Ellington**	196?	10.00	25.00

SHERWOOD, BOBBY

Robert Sherwood is a traditional jazz guitar and trumpet player, composer and band leader.

Label & Catalog #		Title	Year	VG+	NM
Capitol H-320	(10")	**Classics In Jazz**	1952	20.00	50.00
Capitol H-463	(10")	**Bobby Sherwood**	1954	20.00	50.00
Capitol T-320	(M)	**Classics In Jazz**	1955	16.00	40.00

SHIHAB, SAHIB

Edmund Gregory, aka Sahib Shibab, is a modern jazz alto and baritone saxophone and flute player. For additional listings refer to the Various Artists section under Prestige

Label & Catalog #		Title	Year	VG+	NM
Savoy MG-12124	(M)	**Jazz Sihab**	1957	20.00	50.00
Argo LP-742	(M)	**Summer Dawn**	1964	12.00	30.00
Argo LPS-742	(S)	**Summer Dawn**	1964	10.00	25.00

SHIBAB, SAHIB / HERBIE MANN

Label & Catalog #		Title	Year	VG+	NM
Savoy MG-12112	(M)	**The Jazz We Heard Last Summer**	1957	20.00	50.00

—Savoy albums above have silver on red labels.—

SHORE, DINAH, & RED NORVO

Dinah Shore is a pop vocalist vocalist.

Label & Catalog #		Title	Year	VG+	NM
Capitol T-1354	(M)	**Dinah Sings Some Blues With Red**	1960	8.00	20.00
Capitol ST-1354	(S)	**Dinah Sings Some Blues With Red**	1960	10.00	25.00

—Capitol albums above have black "rainbow" labels with the logo on the left side.—

SHORT, BOBBY

Robert Short is a jazz-based vocalist. For additional listings refer to LaVern Baker / Chris Connor / Herbie Mann / Bobby Short.

Label & Catalog #		Title	Year	VG+	NM
Atlantic ALS-606	(10")	**Bobby Short Loves Cole Porter**	1952	20.00	50.00
Atlantic 1214	(M)	**Songs By Bobby Short**	1955	12.00	30.00
Atlantic 1230	(M)	**Bobby Short**	1956	12.00	30.00
Atlantic 1262	(M)	**Speaking Of Love**	1958	12.00	30.00
Atlantic SD-1262	(S)	**Speaking Of Love**	1958	12.00	30.00
Atlantic 1285	(M)	**Sing Me A Swing Song**	1958	12.00	30.00
Atlantic 1302	(M)	**The Mad Twenties**	1959	12.00	30.00
Atlantic SD-1302	(S)	**The Mad Twenties**	1959	12.00	30.00
Atlantic 1321	(M)	**On The East Side**	1960	12.00	30.00
Atlantic SD-1321	(S)	**On The East Side**	1960	12.00	30.00

—Atlantic albums above have black mono or green stereo labels.—

Label & Catalog #		Title	Year	VG+	NM
Atlantic 1214	(M)	**Songs By Bobby Short**	1961	6.00	15.00
Atlantic 1230	(M)	**Bobby Short**	1961	6.00	15.00

Label & Catalog #		Title	Year	VG+	NM
Atlantic 1262	(M)	**Speaking Of Love**	1961	6.00	15.00
Atlantic SD-1262	(S)	**Speaking Of Love**	1961	5.00	12.00
Atlantic 1285	(M)	**Sing Me A Swing Song**	1961	6.00	15.00
Atlantic 1302	(M)	**The Mad Twenties**	1961	6.00	15.00
Atlantic SD-1302	(S)	**The Mad Twenties**	1961	5.00	12.00
Atlantic 1321	(M)	**On The East Side**	1961	6.00	15.00
Atlantic SD-1321	(S)	**On The East Side**	1961	5.00	12.00
		—Atlantic albums above have multi-color labels with a white fan logo.—			
Atlantic 1214	(M)	**Songs By Bobby Short**	196?	5.00	12.00
Atlantic 1230	(M)	**Bobby Short**	196?	5.00	12.00
Atlantic 1285	(M)	**Sing Me A Swing Song**	196?	5.00	12.00
Atlantic 1302	(M)	**The Mad Twenties**	196?	5.00	12.00
Atlantic SD-1302	(S)	**The Mad Twenties**	196?	4.00	10.00
Atlantic 1321	(M)	**On The East Side**	196?	5.00	12.00
Atlantic SD-1321	(S)	**On The East Side**	196?	4.00	10.00
		—Atlantic albums above have multi-color labels with a black fan logo.—			

SHORTER, ALAN

Verve V6-8769	(S)	**Orgasm**	1969	6.00	15.00
		—Verve albums above have black labels with "MGM Records" on the bottom.—			

SHORTER, WAYNE

Wayne Shorter is a modern jazz tenor and soprano saxophone player and composer. For additional listings refer to Art Blakey & The Jazz Messengers; The Young Lions.

Vee Jay VJ-3006	(M)	**Introducing Wayne Shorter**	1960	16.00	40.00
Vee Jay VJS-3006	(S)	**Introducing Wayne Shorter**	1960	16.00	40.00
Vee Jay VJ-3029	(M)	**Wayning Moments**	1962	16.00	40.00
Vee Jay VJS-3029	(S)	**Wayning Moments**	1962	16.00	40.00
Vee Jay VJ-3057	(M)	**Second Genesis**	1963	16.00	40.00
Vee Jay VJS-3057	(S)	**Second Genesis**	1963	16.00	40.00
Blue Note BLP-4173	(M)	**Night Dreamer**	1964	16.00	40.00
Blue Note BST-84173	(S)	**Night Dreamer**	1964	12.00	30.00
Blue Note BLP-4182	(M)	**Juju**	1964	16.00	40.00
Blue Note BST-84182	(S)	**Juju**	1964	12.00	30.00
Blue Note BLP-4194	(M)	**Speak No Evil**	1965	12.00	30.00
Blue Note BST-84194	(S)	**Speak No Evil**	1965	10.00	25.00
Blue Note BLP-4219	(M)	**The All Seeing Eye**	1965	12.00	30.00
Blue Note BST-84219	(S)	**The All Seeing Eye**	1965	10.00	25.00
Blue Note BLP-4232	(M)	**Adam's Apple**	1966	12.00	30.00
Blue Note BST-84232	(S)	**Adam's Apple**	1966	10.00	25.00
		—Blue Note albums above have blue on white labels with a New York, NY address.—			
Blue Note BST-84173	(S)	**Night Dreamer**	196?	5.00	12.00
Blue Note BST-84182	(S)	**Juju**	196?	5.00	12.00
Blue Note BST-84194	(S)	**Speak No Evil**	196?	5.00	12.00
Blue Note BST-84219	(S)	**The All Seeing Eye**	196?	5.00	12.00
Blue Note BST-84232	(S)	**Adam's Apple**	196?	5.00	12.00
Blue Note BST-84297	(S)	**Schizophrenia**	1968	8.00	20.00
Blue Note BST-84332	(S)	**Super Nova**	1969	8.00	20.00
		—Blue Note albums above have blue on white labels with "A Division of Liberty Records."—			

SHQ

ESP-Disk' 1080	(S)	**The Uhu Sleeps Only During The Day**	1969	8.00	20.00

SHU, EDDIE / JOE ROLAND / "WILD" BILL DAVIS

Mercer LP-1002	(10")	**New Stars-New Sounds, Volume 1**	1951	60.00	150.00

SHU, EDDIE

Edward Shulman, aka Eddie Shu, is a traditional jazz clarinet, sax and trumpet player and vocalist.

Bethlehem BCP-1013	(10")	**I Only Have Eyes For Shu**	1954	40.00	100.00

SHU, EDDIE / BOB HARDAWAY

Bethlehem BCP-3	(M)	**Jazz Practitioners**	1957	30.00	75.00
		(Bethlehem 3 is a reissue of 1013 and 1026.)			

SIGNATURES, THE

The Signatures are a jazz-based vocal group featuring Robert and Ruth Alcivar, Hal Curtis, Lee Humes and Bunny Phillips.

Whippet WLP-702	(M)	**The Signatures—Their Voices And Instruments**	1957	20.00	50.00

Label & Catalog #		Title	Year	VG+	NM
Warner Bros. W-1250	*(M)*	**The Signatures Sing In**	*1958*	**16.00**	**40.00**
Warner Bros. WS-1250	*(S)*	**The Signatures Sing In**	*1958*	**12.00**	**30.00**
Warner Bros. W-1353	*(M)*	**Prepare To Flip!**	*1959*	**16.00**	**40.00**
Warner Bros. WS-1353	*(S)*	**Prepare To Flip!**	*1959*	**12.00**	**30.00**

SIGNORELLI, FRANK

Frank Signoreli is a traditional jazz pianist and composer. For additional listings refer to George Wettling.

Label & Catalog #		Title	Year	VG+	NM
Davis JD-103	*(M)*	**Piano Moods**	*1951*	**16.00**	**40.00**

SILVA, ALAN

Alan Silva is a modern jazz bass and cello player.

Label & Catalog #		Title	Year	VG+	NM
ESP-Disk' 1091	*(S)*	**Alan Silva**	*1969*	**8.00**	**20.00**

SILVER, HORACE / ART BLAKEY & SABU

Label & Catalog #		Title	Year	VG+	NM
Blue Note BLP-5034	*(10")*	**Horace Silver Trio, Vol. 2 / Spotlight On Drums**	*1954*	**240.00**	**400.00**
Blue Note BLP-1520	*(M)*	**Horace Silver Trio, Vol. 2 / Spotlight On Drums** *(Deep groove)*	*1956*	**100.00**	**200.00**
Blue Note BLP-1520	*(M)*	**Horace Silver Trio, Vol. 2 / Spotlight On Drums**	*1956*	**60.00**	**150.00**
		—Blue Note albums above have blue on white labels with a Lexington Ave., NYC address.—			
Blue Note BLP-1520	*(M)*	**Horace Silver Trio, Vol. 2 / Spotlight On Drums**	*196?*	**10.00**	**25.00**
		—Blue Note albums above have blue on white labels with a New York, USA address.—			
Blue Note BST-81520	*(E)*	**Horace Silver Trio, Vol. 2 / Spotlight On Drums**	*196?*	**4.00**	**10.00**
		—Blue Note albums above have blue on white labels with "A Division of Liberty Records."—			

SILVER, HORACE

Horace Silver is a modern jazz pianist and composer. For additional listings refer to Art Blakey & The Jazz Messengers; Stan Getz & Horace Silver.

Label & Catalog #		Title	Year	VG+	NM
Blue Note BLP-5018	*(10")*	**Introducing The Horace Silver Trio**	*1953*	**240.00**	**400.00**
Blue Note BLP-5058	*(10")*	**Horace Silver Quintet**	*1955*	**210.00**	**350.00**
Blue Note BLP-5062	*(10")*	**Horace Silver Quintet**	*1955*	**210.00**	**350.00**
Blue Note BLP-1518	*(M)*	**Horace Silver And The Jazz Messengers** *(Deep groove)*	*1956*	**100.00**	**200.00**
Blue Note BLP-1518	*(M)*	**Horace Silver And The Jazz Messengers** *(Blue Note 1518 is a reissue of 5058 and 5062.)*	*1956*	**60.00**	**150.00**
Blue Note BLP-1539	*(M)*	**6 Pieces Of Silver** *(Deep groove)*	*1957*	**100.00**	**200.00**
Blue Note BLP-1539	*(M)*	**6 Pieces Of Silver**	*1957*	**60.00**	**150.00**
		—Blue Note albums above have blue on white labels with a Lexington Ave., NYC address.—			
Blue Note BLP-1562	*(M)*	**The Stylings Of Silver** *(Deep groove)*	*1957*	**60.00**	**150.00**
Blue Note BLP-1562	*(M)*	**The Stylings Of Silver**	*1957*	**40.00**	**100.00**
Blue Note BST-1562	*(S)*	**The Stylings Of Silver** *(Deep groove)*	*1959*	**40.00**	**100.00**
Blue Note BST-1562	*(S)*	**The Stylings Of Silver**	*1959*	**30.00**	**75.00**
Blue Note BLP-1589	*(M)*	**Further Explorations** *(Deep groove)*	*1958*	**60.00**	**150.00**
Blue Note BLP-1589	*(M)*	**Further Explorations**	*1958*	**40.00**	**100.00**
Blue Note BST-1589	*(S)*	**Further Explorations** *(Deep groove)*	*1959*	**40.00**	**100.00**
Blue Note BST-1589	*(S)*	**Further Explorations**	*1959*	**30.00**	**75.00**
Blue Note BLP-4008	*(M)*	**Finger Poppin'** *(Deep groove)*	*1959*	**60.00**	**150.00**
Blue Note BLP-4008	*(M)*	**Finger Poppin'**	*1959*	**40.00**	**100.00**
Blue Note BST-4008	*(S)*	**Finger Poppin'** *(Deep groove)*	*1959*	**40.00**	**100.00**
Blue Note BST-4008	*(S)*	**Finger Poppin'**	*1959*	**30.00**	**75.00**
Blue Note BLP-4017	*(M)*	**Blowin' The Blues Away** *(Deep groove)*	*1959*	**50.00**	**125.00**
Blue Note BLP-4017	*(M)*	**Blowin' The Blues Away**	*1959*	**30.00**	**75.00**
Blue Note BST-84017	*(S)*	**Blowin' The Blues Away**	*1959*	**20.00**	**50.00**
Blue Note BLP-4042	*(M)*	**Horace-Scope** *(Deep groove)*	*1960*	**50.00**	**125.00**
Blue Note BLP-4042	*(M)*	**Horace-Scope**	*1960*	**30.00**	**75.00**
Blue Note BST-84042	*(S)*	**Horace-Scope**	*1960*	**20.00**	**50.00**
		—Blue Note albums above have blue on white labels with a W. 63rd St, NYC address.—			
Blue Note BLP-4076	*(M)*	**Doin' The Thing At The Village Gate**	*1961*	**30.00**	**75.00**
Blue Note BST-84076	*(S)*	**Doin' The Thing At The Village Gate**	*1961*	**20.00**	**50.00**
		—Blue Note albums above have blue on white labels with a 61st St, NYC address.—			
Blue Note BLP-1518	*(M)*	**Horace Silver And The Jazz Messengers**	*1963*	**10.00**	**25.00**
Blue Note BLP-1539	*(M)*	**6 Pieces Of Silver**	*1963*	**10.00**	**25.00**
Blue Note BLP-1562	*(M)*	**The Stylings Of Silver**	*1963*	**10.00**	**25.00**
Blue Note BST-1562	*(S)*	**The Stylings Of Silver**	*1963*	**8.00**	**20.00**
Blue Note BLP-1589	*(M)*	**Further Explorations**	*1963*	**10.00**	**25.00**
Blue Note BST-1589	*(S)*	**Further Explorations**	*1963*	**8.00**	**20.00**
Blue Note BLP-4008	*(M)*	**Finger Poppin'**	*1963*	**10.00**	**25.00**
Blue Note BST-4008	*(S)*	**Finger Poppin'**	*1963*	**8.00**	**20.00**

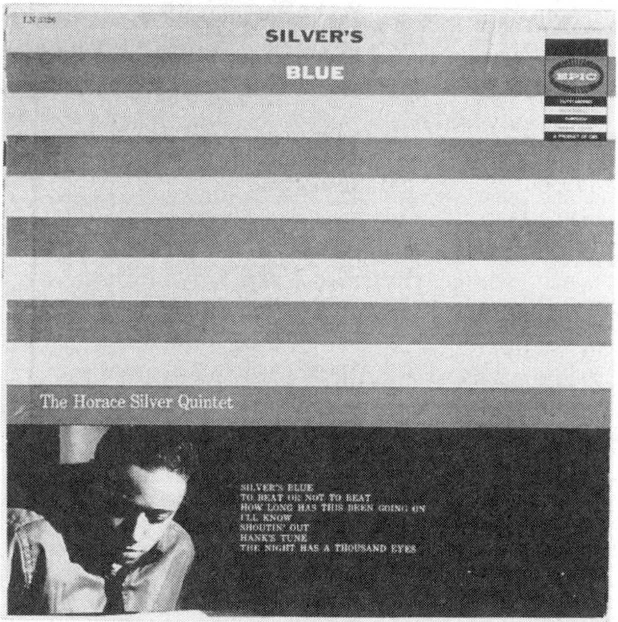

Horace Silver was hired by Stan Getz (1950-51) and then moved onto Art Blakey's (1951-52), Terry Gibbs, and Coleman Hawkins (1953), and Oscar Pettiford, Bill Harris, and Lester Young (1953). For a 1954 recording date with Blue Note, he requested Art Blakey, Kenny Dorham, Hank Mobley and Doug Watkins as his band, and the famed Jazz Messengers were born! While the bulk of his work during this time was with Blue Note (an example is shown above), he managed a lone album for Epic in 1956 (also above). He has completed album projects with Getz, Blakey and Milt Jackson and can be heard as a sideman on LPs by Miles Davis on Blue Note and Prestige, Paul Chambers, Lou Donaldson, Kenny Dorham, Hank Mobley, Lee Morgan, and Sonny Rollins, each on Blue Note, Art Farmer on Prestige, and Al Cohn, Gigi Gryce and Phil Urso, each on Savoy.

Label & Catalog #		Title	Year	VG+	NM
Blue Note BLP-4017	(M)	**Blowin' The Blues Away**	1963	10.00	25.00
Blue Note BST-84017	(S)	**Blowin' The Blues Away**	1963	8.00	20.00
Blue Note BLP-4042	(M)	**Horace-Scope**	1963	10.00	25.00
Blue Note BST-84042	(S)	**Horace-Scope**	1963	8.00	20.00
Blue Note BLP-4076	(M)	**Doin' The Thing At The Village Gate**	1963	10.00	25.00
Blue Note BST-84076	(S)	**Doin' The Thing At The Village Gate**	1963	8.00	20.00
Blue Note BLP-4110	(M)	**The Tokyo Blues**	1962	20.00	50.00
Blue Note BST-84110	(S)	**The Tokyo Blues**	1962	16.00	40.00
Blue Note BLP-4131	(M)	**Silver's Serenade**	1963	20.00	50.00
Blue Note BST-84131	(S)	**Silver's Serenade**	1963	16.00	40.00
Blue Note BLP-4185	(M)	**Song For My Father**	1964	20.00	50.00
Blue Note BST-84185	(S)	**Song For My Father**	1964	16.00	40.00
Blue Note BLP-4220	(M)	**The Cape Verdean Blues**	1965	16.00	40.00
Blue Note BST-84220	(S)	**The Cape Verdean Blues**	1965	12.00	30.00
Blue Note BLP-4250	(M)	**The Jody Grind**	1963	16.00	40.00
Blue Note BST-84250	(S)	**The Jody Grind**	1963	12.00	30.00
		— Blue Note albums above have blue on white labels with a New York, NY address.—			
Blue Note BST-81518	(E)	**Horace Silver And The Jazz Messengers**	196?	4.00	10.00
Blue Note BST-81539	(E)	**6 Pieces Of Silver**	196?	4.00	10.00
Blue Note BST-81562	(S)	**The Stylings Of Silver**	196?	5.00	12.00
Blue Note BST-81589	(S)	**Further Explorations**	196?	5.00	12.00
Blue Note BST-84008	(S)	**Finger Poppin'**	196?	5.00	12.00
Blue Note BST-84017	(S)	**Blowin' The Blues Away**	196?	5.00	12.00
Blue Note BST-84042	(S)	**Horace-Scope**	196?	5.00	12.00
Blue Note BST-84076	(S)	**Doin' The Thing At The Village Gate**	196?	5.00	12.00
Blue Note BST-84110	(S)	**The Tokyo Blues**	196?	5.00	12.00
Blue Note BST-84131	(S)	**Silver's Serenade**	196?	5.00	12.00
Blue Note BST-84185	(S)	**Song For My Father**	196?	5.00	12.00
Blue Note BST-84220	(S)	**The Cape Verdean Blues**	196?	5.00	12.00
Blue Note BST-84250	(S)	**The Jody Grind**	1966	10.00	25.00
Blue Note BST-84277	(S)	**Serenade To A Soul Sister**	1968	12.00	30.00
Blue Note BST-84309	(S)	**You Gotta Take A Little Love**	1969	10.00	25.00
Blue Note BST-84325	(S)	**The Best Of Horace Silver**	1969	8.00	20.00
		— Blue Note albums above have blue on white labels with "A Division of Liberty Records."—			
Epic LN-3326	(M)	**Silver's Blue**	1956	30.00	75.00
Epic LA-16006	(M)	**Silver's Blue**	1959	16.00	40.00
Epic BA-17006	(E)	**Silver's Blue**	1959	8.00	20.00

SIMEON, OMER

Omer Simeon is a traditional clarinet player. For additional listings refer to Sidney Bechet / Omer Simeon.

Disc DLP-748	(10")	**Omer Simeon Trio With James P. Johnson**	195?	70.00	175.00
		(Disc 748 features cover art by David Stone Martin.)			
Concert Hall Jazz 1014	(10")	**Clarinet A La Creole**	195?	20.00	50.00

SIMMONS, NORMAN

Norman Simmons is a modern jazz pianist and composer.

Creative LP-607	(M)	**Interpolations**	1956	30.00	75.00
Argo LP-607	(M)	**Norman Simmons Trio**	1956	16.00	40.00
		(Argo 607 is a reissue of Creative 607.)			

SIMMONS, SONNY

Sonny Simmons is a modern jazz alto sax player. For additional listings refer to Prince Lasha.

Contemporary M-3623	(M)	**Rumasuma**	1966	10.00	25.00
Contemporary S-7623	(S)	**Rumasuma**	1966	8.00	20.00
		— Contemporary stereo albums have gold & black labels.—			
ESP-Disk' 1030	(M)	**Sonny Simmons**	1966	10.00	25.00
ESP-Disk' 1030	(S)	**Sonny Simmons**	1966	8.00	20.00
ESP-Disk' 1043	(M)	**Music From The Spheres**	1967	10.00	25.00
ESP-Disk' 1043	(S)	**Music From The Spheres**	1967	8.00	20.00
Arhoolie 8003	(S)	**Manhattan Egos**	1969	6.00	15.00

SIMONE, NINA

Eunice Waymon, aka Nina Simone, is a jazz-based vocalist.

Bethlehem BCP-6028	(M)	**Little Girl Blue**	1959	20.00	50.00
Bethlehem SBCP-6028	(S)	**Little Girl Blue**	1959	30.00	75.00
Bethlehem BCP-6028	(M)	**The Original Nina Simone**	1961	12.00	30.00
Bethlehem SBCP-6028	(S)	**The Original Nina Simone**	1961	16.00	40.00
		("Original" is a retitled reissue of "Little Girl Blue.")			

Label & Catalog #		Title	Year	VG+	NM
Bethlehem BCP-6041	(M)	**Nina Simone And Her Friends**	1959	16.00	40.00
Bethlehem SBCP-6041	(S)	**Nina Simone And Her Friends**	1959	20.00	50.00
Colpix CP-407	(M)	**The Amazing Nina Simone**	1959	10.00	25.00
Colpix SCP-407	(S)	**The Amazing Nina Simone**	1959	12.00	30.00
Colpix CP-409	(M)	**Nina At Town Hall**	1959	10.00	25.00
Colpix SCP-409	(S)	**Nina At Town Hall**	1959	12.00	30.00
Colpix CP-412	(M)	**Nina Simone At Newport**	1960	10.00	25.00
Colpix SCP-412	(S)	**Nina Simone At Newport**	1960	12.00	30.00
Colpix CP-419	(M)	**Forbidden Fruit**	1961	10.00	25.00
Colpix SCP-419	(S)	**Forbidden Fruit**	1961	12.00	30.00
Colpix CP-421	(M)	**Nina Simone At The Village Gate**	1961	10.00	25.00
Colpix SCP-421	(S)	**Nina Simone At The Village Gate**	1961	12.00	30.00
Colpix CP-425	(M)	**Nina Simone Sings Ellington**	1962	10.00	25.00
Colpix SCP-425	(S)	**Nina Simone Sings Ellington**	1962	12.00	30.00
Colpix CP-443	(M)	**Nina's Choice**	1963	10.00	25.00
Colpix SCP-443	(S)	**Nina's Choice**	1963	12.00	30.00
Colpix CP-455	(M)	**Nina Simone At Carnegie Hall**	1963	10.00	25.00
Colpix SCP-455	(S)	**Nina Simone At Carnegie Hall**	1963	12.00	30.00
Colpix CP-465	(M)	**Folksy Nina**	1964	10.00	25.00
Colpix SCP-465	(S)	**Folksy Nina**	1964	12.00	30.00
Colpix CP-496	(M)	**Nina With Strings**	1966	10.00	25.00
Colpix SCP-496	(S)	**Nina With Strings**	1966	12.00	30.00
		– Colpix albums above have gold labels.–			
Philips PHM-200-135	(M)	**Nina Simone In Concert**	1964	6.00	15.00
Philips PHS-600-135	(S)	**Nina Simone In Concert**	1964	8.00	20.00
Philips PHM-200-148	(M)	**Broadway... Blues... Ballads**	1964	6.00	15.00
Philips PHS-600-148	(S)	**Broadway... Blues... Ballads**	1964	8.00	20.00
Philips PHM-200-172	(M)	**I Put A Spell On You**	1965	6.00	15.00
Philips PHS-600-172	(S)	**I Put A Spell On You**	1965	8.00	20.00
Philips PHM-200-187	(M)	**Pastel Blues**	1965	6.00	15.00
Philips PHS-600-187	(S)	**Pastel Blues**	1965	8.00	20.00
Philips PHM-200-202	(M)	**Let It All Out**	1966	6.00	15.00
Philips PHS-600-202	(S)	**Let It All Out**	1966	8.00	20.00
Philips PHM-200-207	(M)	**Wild Is The Wind**	1966	6.00	15.00
Philips PHS-600-207	(S)	**Wild Is The Wind**	1966	8.00	20.00
Philips PHM-200-219	(M)	**The High Priestess Of Soul**	1966	6.00	15.00
Philips PHS-600-219	(S)	**The High Priestess Of Soul**	1966	8.00	20.00
Philips PHM-200-298	(M)	**The Best Of Nina Simone**	1966	6.00	15.00
Philips PHS-600-298	(S)	**The Best Of Nina Simone**	1966	8.00	20.00
RCA Victor LPM-3789	(M)	**Nina Simone Sings The Blues**	1967	10.00	25.00
RCA Victor LSP-3789	(S)	**Nina Simone Sings The Blues**	1967	5.00	12.00
RCA Victor LPM-3837	(M)	**Silk And Soul**	1967	10.00	25.00
RCA Victor LSP-3837	(S)	**Silk And Soul**	1967	5.00	12.00
RCA Victor LSP-4065	(S)	**Nuff Said**	1968	5.00	12.00

– RCA albums above have black labels with "Monaural" or "Stereo" on the bottom.–

SIMPSON, CAROLE

Carole Simpson is a jazz-based vocalist.

Capitol T-878	(M)	**All About Carole**	1957	30.00	75.00
		– Capitol albums above have turquoise labels.–			
Tops L-1732	(M)	**Singin' And Swingin'**	1960	8.00	20.00

SIMPSON, CASS

Cassino Simpson is a traditional jazz pianist.

ABC-Paramount ABC-103	(M)	**Cass Simpson**	1956	16.00	40.00

SIMS, ZOOT

John "Zoot" Sims is a modern jazz tenor saxophone player. For additional listings refer to Pepper Adams & Zoot Sims; Bob Brookmeyer & Zoot Sims; Clifford Brown; Al Cohn & Zoot Sims; Roy Eldridge; The Four Brothers; Curtis Fuller; Stan Getz / Zoot Sims; Jutta Hipp; Jack Kerouac; Lambert, Hendricks & Ross; The Manhattan All Stars; Ted McNabb; Gerry Mulligan; Orchestra USA; Annie Ross; Sonny Stitt; and the Various Artists section under Prestige and United Artists.

Discovery DL-3015	(10")	**The Zoot Sims Quartet In Paris**	1951	100.00	200.00
Prestige PRLP-117	(10")	**Swingin' With Zoot Sims**	1951	100.00	200.00
Prestige PRLP-118	(10")	**Tenor Sax Favorites**	1951	100.00	200.00
Prestige PRLP-138	(10")	**Zoot Sims All Stars**	1953	100.00	200.00
		(Prestige 138 also features Kai Winding and Al Cohn.)			
New Jazz NJLP-1102	(10")	**Zoot Sims In Hollywood**	1954	100.00	200.00

Zoot Sims joined Kenny Baker in 1941, followed by Bobby Sherwood (1942-43), Sonny Dunham and Bob Astor (1943), Benny Goodman, and Sid Catlett (1944). After the war he was back with Goodman, then Bill Harris (1946) before achieving national prominence as one of Woody Herman's "Four Brothers" sax section in 1947-49. While maintaining a busy career in the studio with his own group and teamed with Al Cohn, he played in the '50s with Goodman, Kenton, Herman, and Mulligan. Aside from Cohn, he has recorded as a team with Bob Brookmeyer, as a member of The Manhattan All Stars and Orchestra USA, and as a featured guest with Clifford Brown, Roy Eldridge. Curtis Fuller, Jutta Hipp, Ted McNabb, Mulligan, and Sonny Stitt. He has backed vocalists as diverse as Jack Kerouac, Lambert Hendricks & Ross, and Annie Ross. As a sideman he has appeared on LP with Herman on Capitol and Columbia, Kenton on Capitol, Goodman and Chet Baker on Columbia, Trigger Alpert on Riverside, Mulligan on EmArcy and World Pacific, Ralph Burns on Decca, Miles Davis on Prestige, Elliot Lawrence on Top Rank and Fantasy, and Joe Newman on Roulette.

Label & Catalog #		Title	Year	VG+	NM
Prestige PRLP-202	(10")	**Zoot Sims Quintet**	1955	60.00	150.00
		(Prestige 202 is a reissue of New Jazz 1102.)			
Prestige PRLP-7026	(M)	**Zoot Sims Quartets**	1956	40.00	100.00
		—Prestige albums above have yellow labels with a W. 50th Street, NYC address.—			
Argo LP-608	(M)	**Zoot** *(Color cover)*	1956	30.00	75.00
Argo LP-608	(M)	**Zoot** *(Black & white cover)*	1957	20.00	50.00
Dawn DLP-1102	(M)	**The Modern Art Of Jazz**	1956	40.00	100.00
Dawn DLP-1115	(M)	**Zoot Sims Goes To Jazzville**	1957	40.00	100.00
Riverside RLP-12-228	(M)	**Zoot!**	1957	30.00	75.00
		—Riverside albums above have blue on white labels.—			
ABC-Paramount ABC-155	(M)	**Zoot Sims Plays Alto, Tenor And Baritone**	1957	30.00	75.00
ABC-Paramount ABC-198	(M)	**Zoot Sims Plays Four Altos**	1957	30.00	75.00
United Arts. UAL-4040	(M)	**A Night At The Half Note**	1959	20.00	50.00
United Arts. UAS-5040	(S)	**A Night At The Half Note**	1959	16.00	40.00
		(United Artists 4040 also features Al Cohn.)			
Seeco SLP-4520	(M)	**The Modern Art Of Jazz**	1960	16.00	40.00
		(Seeco 4520 is a reissue of Dawn 1102.)			
Jazzland JLP-2	(M)	**Zoot Sims Quintet**	1960	16.00	40.00
Jazzland JLP-92	(S)	**Zoot Sims Quintet**	1960	12.00	30.00
		(Jazzland 2 is a reissue of Riverside 228.)			
Bethlehem BCP-6051	(M)	**Down Home**	1960	16.00	40.00
Bethlehem SBCP-6051	(S)	**Down Home**	1960	16.00	40.00
Pacific Jazz PJ-20	(M)	**Choice**	1961	16.00	40.00
Fontana FJL-123	(M)	**Cookin'** *(UK pressing)*	1961	40.00	100.00
Fontana FJS-123	(S)	**Cookin'** *(UK pressing)*	1961	30.00	75.00
United Arts. UAJ-14013	(M)	**Zoot Sims In Paris**	1962	20.00	50.00
United Arts. UAJS-15013	(S)	**Zoot Sims In Paris**	1962	16.00	40.00
Colpix CP-435	(M)	**New Beat Bossa Nova**	1962	16.00	40.00
Colpix SCP-435	(S)	**New Beat Bossa Nova**	1962	20.00	50.00
Colpix CP-437	(M)	**New Beat Bossa Nova, Volume 2**	1962	16.00	40.00
Colpix SCP-437	(S)	**New Beat Bossa Nova, Volume 2**	1962	20.00	50.00
		—Colpix albums above have gold labels.—			
New Jazz NJLP-8280	(M)	**Good Old Zoot**	1962	20.00	50.00
		(New Jazz 8280 is a reissue of 1102.)			
New Jazz NJLP-8302	(M)	**Trotting**	1963	*Unreleased*	
New Jazz NJLP-8309	(M)	**Koo Koo**	1963	*Unreleased*	
		—New Jazz albums above have purple labels.—			
Prestige PRLP-16009	(M)	**Trotting**	1963	16.00	40.00
Status ST-8280	(M)	**Good Old Zoot**	1965	16.00	40.00
		(Status 8280 is a reissue of New Jazz 8210.)			
Status ST-8309	(M)	**Koo Koo**	1965	16.00	40.00
		(Status 8309 also features Phil Woods.)			
Impulse A-9131	(M)	**The Waiting Game**	1967	10.00	25.00
Impulse AS-9131	(S)	**The Waiting Game**	1967	8.00	20.00
		—Impulse albums above have orange & black labels.—			
Impulse AS-9131	(S)	**The Waiting Game**	1968	4.00	10.00
		—Impulse albums above have red & black labels with the "abc" logo on top.—			

SIMS, ZOOT, & JIMMY RANEY & JIM HALL

Mainstream 56013	(M)	**Two Jims And Zoot**	1965	10.00	25.00
Mainstream S-6013	(S)	**Two Jims And Zoot**	1965	8.00	20.00

SIMS, ZOOT, & TONY SCOTT & AL COHN

Jazzland JLP-11	(M)	**East Coast Sounds**	1960	16.00	40.00
Jazzland JLP-911	(S)	**East Coast Sounds**	1960	114.00	35.00
		(Jazzland 11 is a reissue of Riverside 225, Trigger Alpert's "Trigger Happy!")			

SINATRA, FRANK

Francis Sinatra's couplings with jazz figures are all that are listed in this volume from his vast catalog. For additional listings refer to Tommy Dorsey; Alec Wilder.

Columbia ML-4271	(M)	**Frank Sinatra Conducts Music Of Alec Wilder**	1955	30.00	75.00
		(Columbia 4271 also features Alec Wilder.)			
Columbia CL-884	(M)	**Frank Sinatra Conducts Music Of Alec Wilder**	1956	20.00	50.00
		(Columbia 884 is a reissue of 4271.)			
Reprise F-1008	(M)	**Sinatra-Basie**	1963	10.00	25.00
Reprise FS-1008	(S)	**Sinatra-Basie**	1963	6.00	15.00

Label & Catalog #		Title	Year	VG+	NM
Reprise F-1012	(M)	**It Might As Well Be Swing**	1964	10.00	25.00
Reprise FS-1012	(S)	**It Might As Well Be Swing**	1964	6.00	15.00
		(Reprise 1012 also features Count Basie.)			
Reprise F-1019	(M)	**Sinatra At The Sands** *(2 LPs)*	1966	12.00	30.00
Reprise FS-1019	(S)	**Sinatra At The Sands** *(2 LPs)*	1966	8.00	20.00
		(Reprise 1019 also features Count Basie.)			
Reprise F-1021	(M)	**Francis Albert Sinatra And Antonio Carlos Jobim**	1967	10.00	25.00
Reprise FS-1021	(S)	**Francis Albert Sinatra And Antonio Carlos Jobim**	1967	6.00	15.00
Reprise F-1024	(M)	**Francis A. And Edward K.**	1968	10.00	25.00
Reprise FS-1024	(S)	**Francis A. And Edward K.**	1968	6.00	15.00
		(Reprise 1024 also features Duke Ellington.)			

SINGER, HAL, & CHARLIE SHAVERS

Harold Singer is a traditional jazz tenor saxophone player.

Prestige PRLP-7153	(M)	**Blue Stompin'**	1959	30.00	75.00
		— Prestige albums above have yellow mono or silver stereo labels with a Bergenfield, NJ address .—			
Swingville SVLP-2023	(M)	**Blue Stompin'**	1961	20.00	50.00
		(Swingville 2023 is a reissue of Prestige 7153.)			
		— Swingville mono albums above have purple mono ore red stereo labels.—			
Swingville SVLP-2023	(M)	**Blue Stompin'**	1965	10.00	25.00
		— Swingville albums above have blue labels with a trident logo on the right side.—			

SINGLETON, ZUTTY / ART TATUM

Arthur "Zutty" Singleton is a traditional jazz drummer.

Brunswick BL-58038	(10")	**Battle Of Jazz, Vol. 2**	1953	20.00	50.00

SIRAVO, GEORGE

Columbia CL-6146	(10")	**Your Dance Date With George Siravo**	1951	16.00	40.00
Kapp KL-1016	(M)	**Polite Jazz**	1956	12.00	30.00
Decca DL-8464	(M)	**Portraits In Hi-Fi**	1957	12.00	30.00
Vik LX-1091	(M)	**Old But New**	1957	12.00	30.00
Vik LX-1125	(M)	**Swing Hi, Swing Fi**	1958	12.00	30.00
Mercury MG-20327	(M)	**Darling, Please Forgive Me**	1958	12.00	30.00
RCA Victor LPM-1970	(M)	**Swingin' In Hi-Fi In Studio A**	1959	12.00	30.00
RCA Victor LSP-1970	(S)	**Swingin' In Hi-Fi In Studio A**	1959	10.00	25.00
Camden CAL-505	(M)	**Siravo Swing Session**	1959	8.00	20.00
Camden CAS-505	(S)	**Siravo Swing Session**	1959	6.00	15.00
Epic LN-3803	(M)	**Everything Goes**	1961	8.00	20.00
Epic BN-6??	(S)	**Everything Goes**	1961	6.00	15.00
Ad-Lib 226	(M)	**Out On A Limb**	196?	8.00	20.00
Ad-Lib S-226	(S)	**Out On A Limb**	196?	6.00	15.00

SIX, THE

The Six are Bill Britto, Johnny Glasel, Bob Hammer, Eddie Phyfe, Sonny Truit and Bob Wilber.

Bethlehem BCP-28	(M)	**The Six**	1955	30.00	75.00
Bethlehem BCP-57	(M)	**The View From Jazzbo's Head**	1956	30.00	75.00

SIX & SEVEN-EIGHTHS STRING BAND, THE

Folkways FP-671	(M)	**The Six & Seven-Eighths String Band**	1951	16.00	40.00

SLACK, FREDDIE

Frederick Slack is a traditional jazz piano player, composer and band leader.

EmArcy MG-36094	(M)	**Boogie-Woogie On The 88**	1956	16.00	40.00
		— EmArcy albums above have blue labels with silver print.—			

SLEET, DON

Donald Sleet is a modern jazz trumpet player.

Jazzland JLP-45	(M)	**All Members**	1961	12.00	30.00
Jazzland JLP-945	(S)	**All Members**	1961	10.00	25.00

SLOANE, CAROL

Carol Sloane is a jazz-based vocalist.

Columbia CL-1766	(M)	**Out Of The Blue**	1962	24.00	60.00
Columbia CS-8566	(S)	**Out Of The Blue**	1962	30.00	75.00
Columbia CL-1923	(M)	**Carol Sloane Live At 30th Street**	1963	24.00	60.00
Columbia CS-8723	(S)	**Carol Sloane Live At 30th Street**	1963	30.00	75.00
		— Columbia albums above have "Guaranteed High Fidelity" or "360 Sound Stereo" in black on the label.—			

Label & Catalog #		Title	Year	VG+	NM
SMALL HERD, THE: *Refer to* CHUBBY JACKSON & BILL HARRIS					
SMART SET, THE					
The Smart Set is a jazz vocal group.					
Warner Bros. W-1203	(M)	**A New Experience In Vocal Styles**	1958	12.00	30.00
Warner Bros. WS-1203	(S)	**A New Experience In Vocal Styles**	1958	16.00	40.00
SMITH, BESSIE					
Bessie "Empress of the Blues" Smith is a traditional blues-based vocalist and composer.					
Columbia ML-4801	(M)	**The Bessie Smith Story, Volume 1**	1950	24.00	60.00
Columbia ML-4802	(M)	**The Bessie Smith Story, Volume 2**	1950	24.00	60.00
Columbia ML-4809	(M)	**The Bessie Smith Story, Volume 3**	1950	24.00	60.00
Columbia ML-4810	(M)	**The Bessie Smith Story, Volume 4**	1950	24.00	60.00
Columbia GL-503	(M)	**The Bessie Smith Story, Volume 1**	1951	12.00	30.00
Columbia GL-504	(M)	**The Bessie Smith Story, Volume 2**	1951	12.00	30.00
Columbia GL-505	(M)	**The Bessie Smith Story, Volume 3**	1951	12.00	30.00
Columbia GL-506	(M)	**The Bessie Smith Story, Volume 4**	1951	12.00	30.00
— Columbia albums above have "Long Playing" on the bottom of the label.—					
Columbia CL-855	(M)	**The Bessie Smith Story, Volume 1**	1956	10.00	25.00
Columbia CL-856	(M)	**The Bessie Smith Story, Volume 2**	1956	10.00	25.00
Columbia CL-857	(M)	**The Bessie Smith Story, Volume 3**	1956	10.00	25.00
Columbia CL-858	(M)	**The Bessie Smith Story, Volume 4**	1956	10.00	25.00
— Columbia albums above have six white on black "eye" logos on each label.—					
Columbia CL-855	(M)	**The Bessie Smith Story, Volume 1**	196?	6.00	15.00
Columbia CL-856	(M)	**The Bessie Smith Story, Volume 2**	196?	6.00	15.00
Columbia CL-857	(M)	**The Bessie Smith Story, Volume 3**	196?	6.00	15.00
Columbia CL-858	(M)	**The Bessie Smith Story, Volume 4**	196?	6.00	15.00
— Columbia albums above have "360 Sound" on the bottom of the label.—					
SMITH, BILL					
William Smith is a jazz-based clarinet player and composer.					
Contemporary M-3591	(M)	**Folk Jazz**	1961	10.00	25.00
Contemporary S-7591	(S)	**Folk Jazz**	1961	8.00	20.00
— Contemporary stereo albums have gold & black labels.—					
SMITH, BUSTER					
Henry "Buster" Smith is a traditional jazz alto saxophone, clarinet and guitar player and arranger.					
Atlantic 1323	(M)	**The Legendary Buster Smith**	1960	20.00	50.00
Atlantic SD-1323	(S)	**The Legendary Buster Smith**	1960	20.00	50.00
		(Atlantic 1323 was issued with a booklet, worth an additional $10.)			
— Atlantic albums above have black mono or green stereo labels.—					
Atlantic 1323	(M)	**The Legendary Buster Smith**	196?	10.00	25.00
Atlantic SD-1323	(S)	**The Legendary Buster Smith**	196?	8.00	20.00
— Atlantic albums above have multi-color labels with a white fan logo.—					
SMITH, DEREK: *Refer to* DICK KATZ / DEREK SMITH / RENE URTREGER					
SMITH, JIMMY					
James Oscar Smith is a modern jazz organ player. For additional listings refer to Kenny Burrell; Beverly Kenny.					
Blue Note BLP-1512	(M)	**Jimmy Smith At The Organ, Vol. 1** *(Deep groove)*	1956	60.00	150.00
Blue Note BLP-1512	(M)	**Jimmy Smith At The Organ, Vol. 1**	1956	40.00	100.00
Blue Note BLP-1514	(M)	**Jimmy Smith At The Organ, Vol. 2** *(Deep groove)*	1956	60.00	150.00
Blue Note BLP-1514	(M)	**Jimmy Smith At The Organ, Vol. 2**	1956	40.00	100.00
Blue Note BLP-1525	(M)	**The Incredible Jimmy Smith At The Organ, Vol. 3** *(Deep groove)*	1956	60.00	150.00
Blue Note BLP-1525	(M)	**The Incredible Jimmy Smith At The Organ, Vol. 3**	1956	40.00	100.00
Blue Note BLP-1528	(M)	**The Incredible Jimmy Smith At Club Baby Grand, Wilmington, Delaware, Vol. 1** *(Deep groove)*	1956	60.00	150.00
Blue Note BLP-1528	(M)	**The Incredible Jimmy Smith At Club Baby Grand, Wilmington, Delaware, Vol. 1**	1956	40.00	100.00
Blue Note BLP-1529	(M)	**The Incredible Jimmy Smith At Club Baby Grand, Wilmington, Delaware, Vol. 2** *(Deep groove)*	1956	60.00	150.00
Blue Note BLP-1529	(M)	**The Incredible Jimmy Smith At Club Baby Grand, Wilmington, Delaware, Vol. 2**	1956	40.00	100.00
— Blue Note albums above have blue on white labels with a Lexington Ave, NYC address.—					

Label & Catalog #		Title	Year	VG+	NM
Blue Note BLP-1547	(M)	**A Date With Jimmy Smith, Vol. 1** *(Deep groove)*	1957	50.00	125.00
Blue Note BLP-1547	(M)	**A Date With Jimmy Smith, Vol. 1**	1957	30.00	75.00
Blue Note BLP-1548	(M)	**A Date With Jimmy Smith, Vol. 2** *(Deep groove)*	1957	50.00	125.00
Blue Note BLP-1548	(M)	**A Date With Jimmy Smith, Vol. 2**	1957	30.00	75.00
Blue Note BLP-1551	(M)	**Jimmy Smith At The Organ, Vol. 1** *(Deep groove)*	1957	50.00	125.00
Blue Note BLP-1551	(M)	**Jimmy Smith At The Organ, Vol. 1**	1957	30.00	75.00
Blue Note BLP-1552	(M)	**Jimmy Smith At The Organ, Vol. 2** *(Deep groove)*	1957	50.00	125.00
Blue Note BLP-1552	(M)	**Jimmy Smith At The Organ, Vol. 2**	1957	30.00	75.00
Blue Note BLP-1556	(M)	**The Sounds Of Jimmy Smith** *(Deep groove)*	1957	50.00	125.00
Blue Note BLP-1556	(M)	**The Sounds Of Jimmy Smith**	1957	30.00	75.00
Blue Note BLP-1563	(M)	**Jimmy Smith Plays Pretty Just For You** *(Deep groove)*	1957	50.00	125.00
Blue Note BLP-1563	(M)	**Jimmy Smith Plays Pretty Just For You**	1957	30.00	75.00
Blue Note BST-1563	(S)	**Jimmy Smith Plays Pretty Just For You** *(Deep groove)*	1959	30.00	75.00
Blue Note BST-1563	(S)	**Jimmy Smith Plays Pretty Just For You**	1959	20.00	50.00
Blue Note BLP-1585	(M)	**Groovin' At Small's Paradise, Vol. 1** *(Deep groove)*	1958	50.00	125.00
Blue Note BLP-1585	(M)	**Groovin' At Small's Paradise, Vol. 1**	1958	30.00	75.00
Blue Note BST-1585	(S)	**Groovin' At Small's Paradise, Vol. 1** *(Deep groove)*	1959	30.00	75.00
Blue Note BST-1585	(S)	**Groovin' At Small's Paradise, Vol. 1**	1959	20.00	50.00
Blue Note BLP-1586	(M)	**Groovin' At Small's Paradise, Vol. 2** *(Deep groove)*	1958	50.00	125.00
Blue Note BLP-1586	(M)	**Groovin' At Small's Paradise, Vol. 2**	1958	30.00	75.00
Blue Note BST-1586	(S)	**Groovin' At Small's Paradise, Vol. 2** *(Deep groove)*	1959	30.00	75.00
Blue Note BST-1586	(S)	**Groovin' At Small's Paradise, Vol. 2**	1959	20.00	50.00
Blue Note BLP-4002	(M)	**House Party** *(Deep groove)*	1959	50.00	125.00
Blue Note BLP-4002	(M)	**House Party**	1959	30.00	75.00
Blue Note BST-4002	(S)	**House Party** *(Deep groove)*	1959	30.00	75.00
Blue Note BST-4002	(S)	**House Party**	1959	20.00	50.00
Blue Note BLP-4011	(M)	**The Sermon** *(Deep groove)*	1959	50.00	125.00
Blue Note BLP-4011	(M)	**The Sermon**	1959	30.00	75.00
Blue Note BST-4011	(S)	**The Sermon** *(Deep groove)*	1959	30.00	75.00
Blue Note BST-4011	(S)	**The Sermon**	1959	20.00	50.00
Blue Note BLP-4030	(M)	**Crazy Baby** *(Deep groove)*	1960	50.00	125.00
Blue Note BLP-4030	(M)	**Crazy Baby**	1960	30.00	75.00
Blue Note BST-84030	(S)	**Crazy Baby**	1960	20.00	50.00
Blue Note BLP-4050	(M)	**Home Cookin'**	1961	30.00	75.00
Blue Note BST-84050	(S)	**Home Cookin'**	1961	20.00	50.00
		—Blue Note albums above have blue on white labels with a W. 63rd St, NYC address.—			
Blue Note BLP-4078	(M)	**Midnight Special**	196?	30.00	75.00
Blue Note BST-84078	(S)	**Midnight Special**	196?	20.00	50.00
Blue Note BLP-4100	(M)	**Jimmy Smith Plays Fats Waller**	1962	30.00	75.00
Blue Note BST-84100	(S)	**Jimmy Smith Plays Fats Waller**	1962	20.00	50.00
		—Blue Note albums above have blue on white labels with a 61st St, NYC address.—			
Blue Note BLP-1512	(M)	**Jimmy Smith At The Organ, Vol. 1**	1963	10.00	25.00
Blue Note BLP-1514	(M)	**Jimmy Smith At The Organ, Vol. 2**	1963	10.00	25.00
Blue Note BLP-1525	(M)	**The Incredible Jimmy Smith At The Organ, Vol. 3**	1963	10.00	25.00
Blue Note BLP-1528	(M)	**The Incredible Jimmy Smith At Club Baby Grand, Wilmington, Delaware, Vol. 1**	1963	10.00	25.00
Blue Note BLP-1529	(M)	**The Incredible Jimmy Smith At Club Baby Grand, Wilmington, Delaware, Vol. 2**	1963	10.00	25.00
Blue Note BLP-1547	(M)	**A Date With Jimmy Smith, Vol. 1**	1963	10.00	25.00
Blue Note BLP-1548	(M)	**A Date With Jimmy Smith, Vol. 2**	1963	10.00	25.00
Blue Note BLP-1551	(M)	**Jimmy Smith At The Organ, Vol. 1**	1963	10.00	25.00
Blue Note BLP-1552	(M)	**Jimmy Smith At The Organ, Vol. 2**	1963	10.00	25.00
Blue Note BLP-1556	(M)	**The Sounds Of Jimmy Smith**	1963	10.00	25.00
Blue Note BLP-1563	(M)	**Jimmy Smith Plays Pretty Just For You**	1963	10.00	25.00
Blue Note BST-1563	(S)	**Jimmy Smith Plays Pretty Just For You**	1963	8.00	20.00
Blue Note BLP-1585	(M)	**Groovin' At Small's Paradise, Vol. 1**	1963	10.00	25.00
Blue Note BST-1585	(S)	**Groovin' At Small's Paradise, Vol. 1**	1963	8.00	20.00
Blue Note BLP-1586	(M)	**Groovin' At Small's Paradise, Vol. 2**	1963	10.00	25.00
Blue Note BST-1586	(S)	**Groovin' At Small's Paradise, Vol. 2**	1963	8.00	20.00
Blue Note BLP-4002	(M)	**House Party**	1963	10.00	25.00
Blue Note BST-4002	(S)	**House Party**	1963	8.00	20.00

Label & Catalog #		Title	Year	VG+	NM
Blue Note BLP-4011	(M)	**The Sermon**	1963	10.00	25.00
Blue Note BST-4011	(S)	**The Sermon**	1963	8.00	20.00
Blue Note BLP-4030	(M)	**Crazy Baby**	1963	10.00	25.00
Blue Note BST-84030	(S)	**Crazy Baby**	1963	8.00	20.00
Blue Note BLP-4050	(M)	**Home Cookin'**	1963	10.00	25.00
Blue Note BST-84050	(S)	**Home Cookin'**	1963	8.00	20.00
Blue Note BLP-4078	(M)	**Midnight Special**	1963	10.00	25.00
Blue Note BST-84078	(S)	**Midnight Special**	1963	8.00	20.00
Blue Note BLP-4100	(M)	**Jimmy Smith Plays Fats Waller**	1963	10.00	25.00
Blue Note BST-84100	(S)	**Jimmy Smith Plays Fats Waller**	1963	8.00	20.00
Blue Note BLP-4117	(M)	**Back At The Chicken Shack**	1962	16.00	40.00
Blue Note BST-84117	(S)	**Back At The Chicken Shack**	1962	12.00	30.00
Blue Note BLP-4141	(M)	**Rockin' The Boat**	1963	12.00	30.00
Blue Note BST-84141	(S)	**Rockin' The Boat**	1963	10.00	25.00
Blue Note BLP-4164	(M)	**Prayer Meetin'**	1964	16.00	40.00
Blue Note BST-84164	(S)	**Prayer Meetin'**	1964	12.00	30.00
		(Blue Note 4164 also features Stanley Turrentine.)			
Blue Note BLP-4200	(M)	**Softly As A Summer Breeze**	1965	12.00	30.00
Blue Note BST-84200	(S)	**Softly As A Summer Breeze**	1965	10.00	25.00
Blue Note BLP-4235	(M)	**Bucket!**	1966	12.00	30.00
Blue Note BST-84235	(S)	**Bucket!**	1966	10.00	25.00
— Blue Note albums above have blue on white labels with a New York, USA address.—					
Blue Note BST-81512	(E)	**Jimmy Smith At The Organ, Vol. 1**	196?	4.00	10.00
Blue Note BST-81514	(E)	**Jimmy Smith At The Organ, Vol. 2**	196?	4.00	10.00
Blue Note BST-81525	(E)	**The Incredible Jimmy Smith At The Organ, Vol. 3**	196?	4.00	10.00
Blue Note BST-81528	(E)	**The Incredible Jimmy Smith At Club Baby Grand, Wilmington, Delaware, Vol. 1**	196?	4.00	10.00
Blue Note BST-81529	(E)	**The Incredible Jimmy Smith At Club Baby Grand, Wilmington, Delaware, Vol. 2**	196?	4.00	10.00
Blue Note BST-81547	(E)	**A Date With Jimmy Smith, Vol. 1**	196?	4.00	10.00
Blue Note BST-81548	(E)	**A Date With Jimmy Smith, Vol. 2**	196?	4.00	10.00
Blue Note BST-81551	(E)	**Jimmy Smith At The Organ, Vol. 1**	196?	4.00	10.00
Blue Note BST-81552	(E)	**Jimmy Smith At The Organ, Vol. 2**	196?	4.00	10.00
Blue Note BST-81556	(E)	**The Sounds Of Jimmy Smith**	196?	4.00	10.00
Blue Note BST-1563	(S)	**Jimmy Smith Plays Pretty Just For You**	196?	5.00	12.00
Blue Note BST-1585	(S)	**Groovin' At Small's Paradise, Vol. 1**	196?	5.00	12.00
Blue Note BST-1586	(S)	**Groovin' At Small's Paradise, Vol. 2**	196?	5.00	12.00
Blue Note BST-4002	(S)	**House Party**	196?	5.00	12.00
Blue Note BST-4011	(S)	**The Sermon**	196?	5.00	12.00
Blue Note BST-84030	(S)	**Crazy Baby**	196?	5.00	12.00
Blue Note BST-84050	(S)	**Home Cookin'**	196?	5.00	12.00
Blue Note BST-84078	(S)	**Midnight Special**	196?	5.00	12.00
Blue Note BST-84100	(S)	**Jimmy Smith Plays Fats Waller**	196?	5.00	12.00
Blue Note BST-84117	(S)	**Back At The Chicken Shack**	196?	5.00	12.00
Blue Note BST-84141	(S)	**Rockin' The Boat**	196?	5.00	12.00
Blue Note BST-84164	(S)	**Prayer Meetin'**	196?	5.00	12.00
Blue Note BST-84200	(S)	**Softly As A Summer Breeze**	196?	5.00	12.00
Blue Note BST-84235	(S)	**Bucket!**	196?	5.00	12.00
Blue Note BLP-4255	(M)	**I'm Movin' On**	1967	12.00	30.00
Blue Note BST-84255	(S)	**I'm Movin' On**	1967	8.00	20.00
Blue Note BST-84269	(S)	**Open House**	1968	8.00	20.00
Blue Note BST-84296	(S)	**Plain Talk**	1968	8.00	20.00
— Blue Note albums above have blue on white labels with "A Division of Liberty Records."—					
Verve V-8474	(M)	**Bashin'**	1962	6.00	15.00
Verve V6-8474	(S)	**Bashin'**	1962	5.00	12.00
Verve V-8544	(M)	**Hobo Flats**	1963	6.00	15.00
Verve V6-8544	(S)	**Hobo Flats**	1963	5.00	12.00
Verve V-8552	(M)	**Any Number Can Win**	1963	6.00	15.00
Verve V6-8552	(S)	**Any Number Can Win**	1963	5.00	12.00
Verve V-8583	(M)	**Who's Afraid Of Virginia Woolf?**	1964	6.00	15.00
Verve V6-8583	(S)	**Who's Afraid Of Virginia Woolf?**	1964	5.00	12.00
Verve V-8587	(M)	**The Cat**	1964	6.00	15.00
Verve V6-8587	(S)	**The Cat**	1964	5.00	12.00
Verve V-8604	(M)	**Christmas '64**	1964	8.00	20.00
Verve V6-8604	(S)	**Christmas '64**	1964	6.00	15.00
Verve V-8618	(M)	**The Monster**	1965	6.00	15.00
Verve V6-8618	(S)	**The Monster**	1965	5.00	12.00

Label & Catalog #		Title	Year	VG+	NM
Verve V-8628	(M)	**Organ Grinder Swing**	1965	6.00	15.00
Verve V6-8628	(S)	**Organ Grinder Swing**	1965	5.00	12.00
Verve V-8641	(M)	**Got My Mojo Workin'**	1965	6.00	15.00
Verve V6-8641	(S)	**Got My Mojo Workin'**	1965	5.00	12.00
Verve V-8652	(M)	**Peter And The Wolf**	1966	5.00	12.00
Verve V6-8652	(S)	**Peter And The Wolf**	1966	4.00	10.00
Verve V-8666	(M)	**Christmas Cookin'**	1966	6.00	15.00
Verve V6-8666	(S)	**Christmas Cookin'**	1966	5.00	12.00
Verve V-8667	(M)	**Hoochie Coochie Man**	1966	6.00	15.00
Verve V6-8667	(S)	**Hoochie Coochie Man**	1966	5.00	12.00
Verve V-8705	(M)	**Respect**	1967	5.00	12.00
Verve V6-8705	(S)	**Respect**	1967	4.00	10.00
Verve V-8721	(M)	**The Best Of Jimmy Smith**	1967	5.00	12.00
Verve V6-8721	(S)	**The Best Of Jimmy Smith**	1967	4.00	10.00
Verve V-8745	(M)	**Stay Loose**	1968	6.00	15.00
Verve V6-8745	(S)	**Stay Loose**	1968	4.00	10.00
Verve V-8750	(M)	**Livin' It Up**	1968	6.00	15.00
Verve V6-8750	(S)	**Livin' It Up**	1968	4.00	10.00
Verve V6-8770	(S)	**The Boss**	1969	4.00	10.00
Verve V6-8794	(S)	**Groove Drops**	1969	4.00	10.00

— Verve albums above have black labels with "MGM Records" on the bottom.—

SMITH, JIMMY, & WES MONTGOMERY

Verve V-8678	(M)	**The Dynamic Duo**	1966	6.00	15.00
Verve V6-8678	(S)	**The Dynamic Duo**	1966	5.00	12.00
Verve V6-8766	(S)	**The Further Adventures Of Jimmy Smith And Wes Montgomery**	1969	4.00	10.00

— Verve albums above have black labels with "MGM Records" on the bottom.—

SMITH, JOHNNY

John Smith is a modern jazz guitar player. For additional listings refer to Jeri Southern.

Roost R-410	(10")	**A Three-Dimension Sound Recording Of Jazz At NBC With The Johnny Smith Quintet**	1953	50.00	125.00
Roost R-413	(10")	**Johnny Smith Quintet**	1953	50.00	125.00
		(Roost 410 and 413 also features Stan Getz.)			
Roost R-421	(10")	**In A Mellow Mood**	1954	40.00	100.00
Roost R-424	(10")	**In A Sentimental Mood**	1954	40.00	100.00
Legende 1401	(10")	**Annotations Of The Muses**	1955	40.00	100.00
Roost LP-2201	(M)	**Johnny Smith Plays Jimmy Van Heusen**	1955	30.00	75.00
Roost LP-2203	(M)	**Johnny Smith Quartet**	1955	30.00	75.00
Roost LP-2211	(M)	**Moonlight In Vermont**	1956	30.00	75.00
		(Roost 2211 is a reissue of 410 and 413.)			
Roost LP-2215	(M)	**Moods**	1956	20.00	50.00
		(Roost 2215 is a reissue of 421.)			
Roost LP-2216	(M)	**New Quartet**	1956	20.00	50.00
Roost LP-2223	(M)	**Johnny Smith Foursome, Volume 1**	1956	20.00	50.00
Roost LP-2228	(M)	**Johnny Smith Foursome, Volume 2**	1957	20.00	50.00
Roost LP-2231	(M)	**Flower Drum Song**	1958	16.00	40.00
Roost SLP-2231	(S)	**Flower Drum Song**	1958	12.00	30.00
Roost LP-2233	(M)	**Easy Listening**	1959	16.00	40.00
Roost SLP-2233	(S)	**Easy Listening**	1959	12.00	30.00
Roost LP-2237	(M)	**Favorites**	1959	16.00	40.00
Roost SLP-2237	(S)	**Favorites**	1959	12.00	30.00
Roost LP-2238	(M)	**Designed For You**	1960	16.00	40.00
Roost SLP-2238	(S)	**Designed For You**	1960	12.00	30.00
Roost LP-2239	(M)	**Dear Little Sweetheart**	1960	16.00	40.00
Roost SLP-2239	(S)	**Dear Little Sweetheart**	1960	12.00	30.00
Roost LP-2242	(M)	**Guitar And Strings**	1960	16.00	40.00
Roost SLP-2242	(S)	**Guitar And Strings**	1960	12.00	30.00
Roost LP-2243	(M)	**Johnny Smith Plus The Trio**	1960	16.00	40.00
Roost SLP-2243	(S)	**Johnny Smith Plus The Trio**	1960	12.00	30.00
Roost LP-2246	(M)	**The Sound Of The Johnny Smith Guitar**	1961	16.00	40.00
Roost SLP-2246	(S)	**The Sound Of The Johnny Smith Guitar**	1961	12.00	30.00
Roost LP-2248	(M)	**Man With The Blue Guitar**	1962	16.00	40.00
Roost SLP-2248	(S)	**Man With The Blue Guitar**	1962	12.00	30.00
Roost LP-2250	(M)	**Johnny Smith Plays Jimmy Van Heusen**	1963	12.00	30.00
Roost SLP-2250	(S)	**Johnny Smith Plays Jimmy Van Heusen**	1963	10.00	25.00

Label & Catalog #		Title	Year	VG+	NM
Roost LP-2254	(M)	**Guitar World**	1963	12.00	30.00
Roost SLP-2254	(S)	**Guitar World**	1963	10.00	25.00
Roost LP-2259	(M)	**Reminiscing**	1965	12.00	30.00
Roost SLP-2259	(S)	**Reminiscing**	1965	10.00	25.00
Verve V-8692	(M)	**Johnny Smith**	1967	10.00	25.00
Verve V6-8692	(S)	**Johnny Smith**	1967	8.00	20.00
Verve V-8737	(M)	**Johnny Smith's Kaleidoscope**	1967	10.00	25.00
Verve V6-8737	(S)	**Johnny Smith's Kaleidoscope**	1967	8.00	20.00
Verve V6-8767	(S)	**Phase It**	1969	8.00	20.00
		— Verve albums above have black labels with "MGM Records" on the bottom.—			

SMITH, JOHNNY "HAMMOND"

John Smith is a modern jazz organ player.

Label & Catalog #		Title	Year	VG+	NM
New Jazz NJLP-8221	(M)	**All Soul**	1959	20.00	50.00
New Jazz NJLP-8229	(M)	**That Good Feelin'**	1959	20.00	50.00
New Jazz NJLP-8241	(M)	**Talk That Talk**	1960	20.00	50.00
New Jazz NJLP-8288	(M)	**Look Out!**	1962	20.00	50.00
		(New Jazz 8288 also features Seldon Powell.)			
		— New Jazz albums above have purple labels.—			
New Jazz NJLP-8221	(M)	**All Soul**	1965	10.00	25.00
New Jazz NJLP-8229	(M)	**That Good Feelin'**	1965	10.00	25.00
New Jazz NJLP-8241	(M)	**Talk That Talk**	1965	10.00	25.00
New Jazz NJLP-8288	(M)	**Look Out!**	1965	10.00	25.00
		— New Jazz albums above have blue labels with a trident logo on the right side.—			
Prestige PRLP-7203	(M)	**Stimulation**	1961	16.00	40.00
Prestige PRLP-7217	(M)	**Gettin' The Message**	1961	16.00	40.00
		— Prestige albums above have yellow mono or silver stereo labels with a Bergenfield, NJ address .—			
Prestige PRLP-7203	(M)	**Stimulation**	196?	10.00	25.00
Prestige PRLP-7217	(M)	**Gettin' The Message**	196?	10.00	25.00
		— Prestige albums above have blue labels with a trident logo on the right side.—			
Riverside RLP-442	(M)	**Black Coffee**	1963	14.00	35.00
Riverside RS-9442	(S)	**Black Coffee**	1963	12.00	30.00
		(Riverside 442 also features Seldon Powell.)			
Riverside RLP-466	(M)	**Mr. Wonderful**	1963	14.00	35.00
Riverside RS-9466	(S)	**Mr. Wonderful**	1963	12.00	30.00
		— Riverside albums above have blue mono or black stereo labels with a reel & mike logo on top.—			
Riverside RLP-482	(M)	**Open House!**	1965	12.00	30.00
Riverside RS-9482	(S)	**Open House!**	1965	10.00	25.00
Riverside RLP-496	(M)	**A Little Taste**	1965	12.00	30.00
Riverside RS-9496	(S)	**A Little Taste**	1965	10.00	25.00
		— Riverside albums above blue labels with "Orpheum Productions" on the bottom.—			
Prestige PRLP-7408	(M)	**The Stinger**	1965	12.00	30.00
Prestige PRST-7408	(S)	**The Stinger**	1965	10.00	25.00
Prestige PRLP-7420	(M)	**Opus De Funk**	1966	12.00	30.00
Prestige PRST-7420	(S)	**Opus De Funk**	1966	10.00	25.00
Prestige PRLP-7464	(M)	**The Stinger Meets The Golden Thrush**	1967	12.00	30.00
Prestige PRST-7464	(S)	**The Stinger Meets The Golden Thrush**	1967	10.00	25.00
		(Prestige 7464 also features Byrdie Green.)			
Prestige PRLP-7482	(M)	**Love Potion #9**	1967	12.00	30.00
Prestige PRLST-7482	(S)	**Love Potion #9**	1967	10.00	25.00
Prestige PRLP-7494	(M)	**Ebb Tide**	1967	12.00	30.00
Prestige PRST-7494	(S)	**Ebb Tide**	1967	10.00	25.00
		— Prestige albums above have blue labels with a trident logo on the right side.—			
Prestige PRST-7549	(S)	**Soul Flowers**	1968	8.00	20.00
Prestige PRST-7564	(S)	**Dirty Grape**	1968	8.00	20.00
Prestige PRST-7588	(S)	**Nasty**	1968	8.00	20.00
Prestige PRST-7681	(S)	**Soul Talk**	1969	8.00	20.00
Prestige PRST-7705	(S)	**The Best Of Johnny "Hammond" Smith**	1969	6.00	15.00
		— Prestige albums above have blue labels with a trident logo on top.—			

SMITH, JOHNNY "HAMMOND," & WILLIS "GATOR TAIL" JACKSON

Label & Catalog #		Title	Year	VG+	NM
Prestige PRLP-7239	(M)	**Johnny "Hammond" Cooks With Gator Tail**	1962	16.00	40.00
Prestige PRST-7239	(S)	**Johnny "Hammond" Cooks With Gator Tail**	1962	16.00	40.00
		— Prestige albums above have yellow mono or silver stereo labels with a Bergenfield, NJ address .—			
Prestige PRLP-7239	(M)	**Johnny "Hammond" Cooks With Gator Tail**	196?	10.00	25.00
Prestige PRST-7239	(S)	**Johnny "Hammond" Cooks With Gator Tail**	196?	8.00	20.00
		— Prestige albums above have blue labels with a trident logo on the right side.—			

Label & Catalog #		Title	Year	VG+	NM

SMITH, KEELY

Dorothy Jacqueline Keely Smith is a jazz-based vocalist who also recorded with husband Luis Prima.

Capitol W-914	(M)	**I Wish You Love**	1957	20.00	50.00
— Capitol albums above have turquoise labels.—					
Capitol W-914	(M)	**I Wish You Love**	195?	12.00	30.00
Capitol T-1073	(M)	**Politely**	1958	16.00	40.00
Capitol ST-1073	(S)	**Politely**	1958	20.00	50.00
Capitol T-1145	(M)	**Swingin' Pretty**	1959	16.00	40.00
Capitol ST-1145	(S)	**Swingin' Pretty**	1959	20.00	50.00
— Capitol albums above have black "rainbow" labels with the logo on the left side.—					
Dot DLP-3241	(M)	**Be My Love**	1960	10.00	25.00
Dot DLP-25241	(S)	**Be My Love**	1960	12.00	30.00
Dot DLP-3265	(M)	**Swing, You Lovers**	1960	10.00	25.00
Dot DLP-25265	(S)	**Swing, You Lovers**	1960	12.00	30.00
Dot DLP-3387	(M)	**Dearly Beloved**	1961	10.00	25.00
Dot DLP-25387	(S)	**Dearly Beloved**	1961	12.00	30.00
Dot DLP-3345	(M)	**A Keely Christmas**	1961	10.00	25.00
Dot DLP-25345	(S)	**A Keely Christmas**	1961	12.00	30.00
Dot DLP-3415	(M)	**Because You're Mine**	1962	10.00	25.00
Dot DLP-25415	(S)	**Because You're Mine**	1962	12.00	30.00
Dot DLP-3423	(M)	**Twist With Keely Smith**	1962	10.00	25.00
Dot DLP-25423	(S)	**Twist With Keely Smith**	1962	12.00	30.00
Dot DLP-3460	(M)	**Cherokeely Swings**	1962	10.00	25.00
Dot DLP-25460	(S)	**Cherokeely Swings**	1962	12.00	30.00
Dot DLP-3461	(M)	**What Kind Of Fool Am I**	1962	10.00	25.00
Dot DLP-25461	(S)	**What Kind Of Fool Am I**	1962	12.00	30.00
Reprise R-6086	(M)	**Little Girl Blue, Little Girl New**	1963	10.00	25.00
Reprise R-96086	(S)	**Little Girl Blue, Little Girl New**	1963	12.00	30.00
Reprise R-6132	(M)	**The Intimate**	1964	10.00	25.00
Reprise RS-6132	(S)	**The Intimate**	1964	12.00	30.00
Reprise R-6142	(M)	**The Lennon-McCartney Songbook**	1964	10.00	25.00
Reprise RS-6142	(S)	**The Lennon-McCartney Songbook**	1964	12.00	30.00
Reprise R-6175	(M)	**That Old Black Magic**	1965	10.00	25.00
Reprise RS-6175	(S)	**That Old Black Magic**	1965	12.00	30.00

SMITH, LA VERGNE

LaVergne Smith is a traditional jazz vocalist.

Cook LP-1081	(10")	**Angel In The Absinthe House**	1955	50.00	125.00
Savoy MG-12031	(M)	**New Orleans Nightingale**	1955	20.00	50.00
Vik LX-1056	(M)	**La Vergne Smith**	1956	20.00	50.00

SMITH, LONNIE

Lonnie Smith is a modern jazz organ player.

Blue Note BST-84290	(S)	**Think!**	1968	12.00	30.00
Blue Note BST-84313	(S)	**Turning Point**	1969	10.00	25.00
Blue Note BST-84326	(S)	**Move Your Hand**	1969	10.00	25.00
— Blue Note albums above have blue on white labels with "A Division of Liberty Records."—					

SMITH, LOUIS

Louis Smith is a modern jazz trumpet player.

Blue Note BLP-1584	(M)	**Here Comes Louis Smith** *(Deep groove)*	1958	60.00	150.00
Blue Note BLP-1584	(M)	**Here Comes Louis Smith**	1958	40.00	100.00
Blue Note BST-1584	(S)	**Here Comes Louis Smith** *(Deep groove)*	1959	40.00	100.00
Blue Note BST-1584	(S)	**Here Comes Louis Smith**	1959	30.00	75.00
Blue Note BLP-1594	(M)	**Smithville** *(Deep groove)*	1958	60.00	150.00
Blue Note BLP-1594	(M)	**Smithville**	1958	40.00	100.00
Blue Note BST-1594	(S)	**Smithville** *(Deep groove)*	1959	40.00	100.00
Blue Note BST-1594	(S)	**Smithville**	1959	30.00	75.00
— Blue Note albums above have blue on white labels with a W. 63rd St, NYC address.—					
Blue Note BST-1584	(S)	**Here Comes Louis Smith**	196?	5.00	12.00
Blue Note BST-1594	(S)	**Smithville**	196?	5.00	12.00
— Blue Note albums above have blue on white labels with "A Division of Liberty Records."—					

SMITH, OSBORNE

Osborne Smith is a modern jazz vocalist.

Argo LP-4000	(M)	**Eyes Of Love**	1960	16.00	40.00
Argo LPS-4000	(S)	**Eyes Of Love**	1960	12.00	30.00

Label & Catalog #		Title	Year	VG+	NM

SMITH, PAUL

Paul Smith is a traditional jazz piano and organ player. For additional listings refer to Hampton Hawes / John Mehegan / Herbie Nichols / Paul Smith and the Jazzy Soundtracks section under Verve.

Discovery DL-3009	(10")	**Paul Smith**	1950	30.00	75.00
Discovery DL-3017	(10")	**Paul Smith Trio**	1952	30.00	75.00
Skylark SKLP-13	(10")	**Paul Smith Quartet**	1954	40.00	100.00
Capitol H-493	(10")	**Liquid Sounds**	1954	30.00	75.00
Capitol T-665	(M)	**Cascades**	1955	16.00	40.00
Capitol T-757	(M)	**Cool And Sparkling**	1956	16.00	40.00
Capitol T-829	(M)	**Softly, Baby**	1957	16.00	40.00
		—Capitol albums above have turquoise labels.—			
Capitol T-1017	(M)	**Delicate Jazz**	1958	12.00	30.00
Capitol ST-1017	(S)	**Delicate Jazz**	1958	10.00	25.00
Savoy MG-12094	(M)	**By The Fireside**	1956	20.00	50.00
Tampa TP-9	(M)	**Fine, Sweet And Tasty** *(Colored vinyl)*	1957	40.00	100.00
Tampa TP-9	(M)	**Fine, Sweet And Tasty**	1958	20.00	50.00
		(Tampa 9 is a reissue of Skylark 13.)			
Verve MGV-2128	(M)	**The Sound Of Music**	1960	16.00	40.00
Verve MGVS-6128	(S)	**The Sound Of Music**	1960	12.00	30.00
Verve MGV-2130	(M)	**The Big Men**	1960	16.00	40.00
Verve MGVS-6135	(S)	**The Big Men**	1960	12.00	30.00
Verve MGV-2148	(M)	**Latin Keyboards And Percussion**	1960	16.00	40.00
Verve MGV-4051	(M)	**Carnival! In Prcussion**	1961	16.00	40.00
		—Verve albums above have "Verve Records, Inc." on the bottom of the label.—			
Verve V-2128	(M)	**The Sound Of Music**	1961	6.00	15.00
Verve V6-2128	(S)	**The Sound Of Music**	1961	5.00	12.00
Verve V-2130	(M)	**The Big Men**	1961	6.00	15.00
Verve V6-2130	(S)	**The Big Men**	1961	5.00	12.00
Verve V-2148	(M)	**Latin Keyboards And Percussion**	1961	6.00	15.00
Verve V6-2148	(S)	**Latin Keyboards And Percussion**	1961	5.00	12.00
Verve V-4051	(M)	**Carnival! In Prcussion**	1961	6.00	15.00
Verve V6-4051	(S)	**Carnival! In Prcussion**	1961	5.00	12.00
		—Verve albums above have black labels with "MGM Records" on the bottom.—			
MGM E-4057	(M)	**Memories Of Paris**	1962	10.00	25.00
MGM SE-4057	(S)	**Memories Of Paris**	1962	8.00	20.00

SMITH, PINE TOP

Clarence "Pine Top" Smith is a traditional jazz pianist and vocalist.

Brunswick BL-58003	(10")	**Pine Top Smith**	1950	40.00	100.00
		(Brunswick 58003 also features Jelly Roll Morton.)			

SMITH, STUFF

Hezekiah "Stuff" Smith is a traditional jazz violin player and vocalist. For additional listings refer to Herb Ellis; Dizzie Gillespie; Gene Krupa & Ventura / Stuff Smith.

Verve MGV-2041	(M)	**Stuff Smith**	1957	*Unreleased*	
Verve MGV-8206	(M)	**Soft Winds**	1958	20.00	50.00
Verve MGV-8270	(M)	**Stephane Grappelli With Stuff Smith**	1958	*Unreleased*	
Verve MGV-8282	(M)	**Have Violin, Will Swing**	1958	20.00	50.00
Verve MGV-8339	(M)	**Cat On A Hot Fiddle**	1959	20.00	50.00
Verve MGVS-6097	(S)	**Cat On A Hot Fiddle**	1960	16.00	40.00
		—Verve albums above have black labels with "Verve Records, Inc." on the bottom.—			
Verve V-8206	(M)	**Soft Winds**	1961	6.00	15.00
Verve V-8282	(M)	**Have Violin, Will Swing**	1961	6.00	15.00
Verve V-8339	(M)	**Cat On A Hot Fiddle**	1961	6.00	15.00
Verve V6-8339	(S)	**Cat On A Hot Fiddle**	1961	5.00	12.00
		—Verve albums above have black labels with "MGM Records" on the bottom.—			
20th Century FTM-3008	(M)	**Sweet Singin' Stuff**	1959	12.00	30.00
20th Century FTS-3008	(S)	**Sweet Singin' Stuff**	1959	10.00	25.00
Prestige PRST-7691	(E)	**The Stuff Smith Memorial Album**	1969	5.00	12.00
		—Prestige albums above have blue labels with a trident logo on top.—			

SMITH, WILLIE

William McLeish Smith is a traditional jazz alto and baritone saxophone and clarinet player and vocalist.

Mercury MG-25075	(10")	**Alto Sax Artistry**	1950	100.00	200.00
EmArcy MG-26000	(10")	**Relaxin' After Hours**	1954	60.00	150.00
		(EmArcy 26000 is a reissue of Mercury 25075.)			

Label & Catalog #		Title	Year	VG+	NM

SMITH, WILLIE "THE LION"

William Bertholoff, aka Willie "The Lion" Smith, is a traditional jazz pianist, vocalist and composer. For additional listings refer to Lucky Roberts & Willie Smith.

Label & Catalog #		Title	Year	VG+	NM
Commodore DL-30004	(M)	**The Lion Of The Piano**	1951	40.00	100.00
Blue Circle 1500-33	(10")	**Willie "The Lion" Smith**	1952	30.00	75.00
Dial LP-305	(10")	**Harlem Memories**	1953	125.00	250.00
Urania UJLP-1207	(M)	**Accent On Piano**	1955	20.00	50.00
Grand Award GA-33-368	(M)	**The Legend Of Willie Smith**	1956	20.00	50.00
Dot DLP-3094	(M)	**The Lion Roars**	1958	20.00	50.00
Mainstream 56027	(M)	**A Legend**	1965	8.00	20.00
Mainstream S-6027	(E)	**A Legend**	1965	4.00	10.00

SMITH-GLAMANN

Label & Catalog #		Title	Year	VG+	NM
Bethlehem BCP-22	(M)	**Smith-Glamann Quintet**	1955	20.00	50.00

SNOWDEM, ELMER

Elmer "Pops" Snowdem is a traditional jazz guitar, banjo and saxophone(s) player.

Label & Catalog #		Title	Year	VG+	NM
Riverside RLP-348	(M)	**Harlem Banjo**	1960	10.00	25.00
Riverside RS-9348	(S)	**Harlem Banjo**	1960	8.00	20.00

—Riverside albums above have blue mono or black stereo labels with a reel & mike logo on top.—

SOCOLOW, FRANK

Frank Socolow is a modern jazz tenor saxophone player. For additional listings refer to the Various Artists section under Signal.

Label & Catalog #		Title	Year	VG+	NM
Bethlehem BCP-70	(M)	**Sounds By Socolow**	1957	30.00	75.00

SOLAL, MARTIAL

South African born Martial Solal is a modern jazz piano, clarinet and sax player and composer. For additional listings refer to Sidney Bechet & Martial Solal.

Label & Catalog #		Title	Year	VG+	NM
Contemporary C-2512	(10")	**French Modern Sounds**	1954	30.00	75.00
Capitol Int. T-10261	(M)	**Martial Solal**	1960	12.00	30.00
Capitol Int. ST-10261	(S)	**Martial Solal**	1960	10.00	25.00
Capitol Int. ST-10354	(M)	**Vive La France! Viva La Jazz! Vive Solal!**	1961	10.00	25.00
Capitol Int. ST-10354	(S)	**Vive La France! Viva La Jazz! Vive Solal!**	1961	8.00	20.00
		(Capitol 10354 is a reissue of 10261.)			
Liberty LRP-3335	(M)	**Martial Solal In Concert**	1963	8.00	20.00
Liberty LST-7335	(S)	**Martial Solal In Concert**	1963	6.00	15.00
RCA Victor LPM-2777	(M)	**Martial Solal At Newport '63**	1963	8.00	20.00
RCA Victor LSP-2777	(S)	**Martial Solal At Newport '63**	1963	6.00	15.00
		—RCA albums above have black labels with "Mono" or "Living Stereo" on the bottom.—			
Milestone MLP-1001	(M)	**Solal!**	1967	10.00	25.00
Milestone MSP-9001	(S)	**Solal!**	1967	6.00	15.00
Milestone MSP-9014	(S)	**On Home Ground**	1969	6.00	15.00

SOMMERS, JOANIE

Pop singer Joanie Sommers is backed by Marty Paich's Orchestra featuring Art Pepper.

Label & Catalog #		Title	Year	VG+	NM
Warner Bros. W-1346	(M)	**Positively The Most**	1959	12.00	30.00
Warner Bros. WS-1346	(S)	**Positively The Most**	1959	16.00	40.00

SONDHEIM, ALAN

Label & Catalog #		Title	Year	VG+	NM
ESP-Disk' 1048	(S)	**Ritual-All-7-70**	1969	6.00	15.00
ESP-Disk' 1082	(S)	**T'Other Little Tune**	1969	6.00	15.00

SONN, LARRY

Lawrence Sonn is a Latin jazz piano and trumpet player. For additional listings refer to Al Collins.

Label & Catalog #		Title	Year	VG+	NM
Coral CRL-57057	(M)	**The Sound Of Sonn**	1956	16.00	40.00
Dot DLP-9005	(M)	**Jazz Band Having A Ball**	1958	12.00	30.00
Dot DLP-29005	(S)	**Jazz Band Having A Ball**	1958	10.00	25.00

SOUND OF FEELING

Label & Catalog #		Title	Year	VG+	NM
Limelight LS-86063	(S)	**Spleen**	1969	6.00	15.00

SOUNDSTAGE ALL-STARS, THE

The All-Stars were arranged by Pete Candoli.

Label & Catalog #		Title	Year	VG+	NM
Dot DLP-3204	(M)	**More "Peter Gunn"**	1959	12.00	30.00
Dot DLP-25204	(S)	**More "Peter Gunn"**	1959	10.00	25.00

SOUTER, EDDIE: *Refer to* **RAY McKINLEY & EDDIE SOUTER**

Label & Catalog #		Title	Year	VG+	NM
SOUTH, EDDIE					
Edward South is a traditional jazz violin player.					
Mercury MG-20401	(M)	**The Distinguished Violin Of Eddie South**	1959	12.00	30.00
Mercury SR-60070	(S)	**The Distinguished Violin Of Eddie South**	1959	10.00	25.00
SOUTHERN, JERI					
Jeri Southern is a jazz-based vocalist and pianist.					
Decca DL-5531	(10")	**Intimate Songs**	1954	30.00	75.00
Decca DL-8055	(M)	**Southern Style**	1955	20.00	50.00
Decca DL-8214	(M)	**You Better Go Now**	1956	20.00	50.00
Decca DL-8394	(M)	**When Your Heart's On Fire**	1956	20.00	50.00
Decca DL 8472	(M)	**Jeri Southern Gently Jumps**	1957	20.00	50.00
Decca DL-8745	(M)	**Prelude To A Kiss**	1958	20.00	50.00
Decca DL-8761	(M)	**Southern Hospitality**	1958	20.00	50.00
		—Decca albums above have silver on black labels.—			
Roulette R-52010	(M)	**Southern Breeze**	1958	16.00	40.00
Roulette S-52010	(S)	**Southern Breeze**	1958	20.00	50.00
Roulette R-52016	(M)	**Jeri Southern Meets Johnny Smith**	1958	16.00	40.00
Roulette RS-52016	(S)	**Jeri Southern Meets Johnny Smith**	1958	20.00	50.00
Capitol T-1173	(M)	**Jeri Southern Meets Cole Porter**	1959	12.00	30.00
Capitol ST-1173	(S)	**Jeri Southern Meets Cole Porter**	1959	16.00	40.00
Capitol T-1278	(M)	**Jeri Southern At The Crescendo**	1960	12.00	30.00
Capitol ST-1278	(S)	**Jeri Southern At The Crescendo**	1960	16.00	40.00
		—Capitol albums above have black "rainbow" labels with the logo on the left side.—			
Capitol T-1173	(M)	**Jeri Southern Meets Cole Porter**	196?	6.00	15.00
Capitol ST-1173	(S)	**Jeri Southern Meets Cole Porter**	196?	8.00	20.00
Capitol T-1278	(M)	**Jeri Southern At The Crescendo**	196?	6.00	15.00
Capitol ST-1278	(S)	**Jeri Southern At The Crescendo**	196?	8.00	20.00
		—Capitol albums above have black "rainbow" labels with the logo on top.—			
SPANIER, MUGGSY					
Francis "Muggsy" Spanier is a traditional jazz cornet player. For additional listings refer to Sidney Bechet.					
Commodore FL-20009	(10")	**Spanier's Ragtimers**	1950	40.00	100.00
Zee Gee 101	(10")	**Muggsy Spanier's Ragtimers—Vol. 1**	195?	40.00	100.00
Zee Gee 102	(10")	**Muggsy Spanier's Ragtimers—Vol. 2**	195?	40.00	100.00
Mercury MG-25095	(10")	**Muggsy Spanier And His Dixieland Band**	1953	40.00	100.00
Riverside RLP-1004	(10")	**Muggsy Spanier And Frank Teschemacher**	1953	40.00	100.00
Riverside RLP-1035	(10")	**Muggsy Spanier And His Bucktown Five**	1954	40.00	100.00
Riverside RLP-12-107	(M)	**Classic Early Recordings**	1955	24.00	60.00
		(Riverside 107 is a reissue of 1004 and 1035.)			
		—Riverside albums above have blue on white labels.—			
EmArcy MG-26011	(10")	**Muggsy Spanier And His Dixieland Band**	1954	20.00	50.00
Weathers Indus. W-5401	(M)	**Dynamic Dixie**	1954	20.00	50.00
Decca DL-5552	(10")	**Hot Horn**	1955	20.00	50.00
RCA Victor LPM-3043	(10")	**Ragtime Favorites**	1956	40.00	100.00
RCA Victor LPM-1295	(M)	**The Great 16**	1956	20.00	50.00
		—RCA albums above have black labels with "Long Play" on the bottom.—			
Mercury MG-20171	(M)	**Muggsy Spanier And His Dixieland Band**	1956	20.00	50.00
		(Mercury 20171 is a reissue of 25095.)			
		—Mercury albums above have silver on black labels.—			
Commodore FL-30016	(M)	**Chicago Jazz**	1957	20.00	50.00
		(Commodore 30016 is a reissue of 200009.)			
London LL-3528	(M)	**Muggsy Spanier And The Bucktown Five**	1959	16.00	40.00
Ava S-12	(M)	**Columbia, The Gem Of The Ocean**	1963	6.00	15.00
Ava AS-12	(S)	**Columbia, The Gem Of The Ocean**	1963	5.00	12.00
SPANN, LES					
Leslie Spann is a modern jazz guitarist.					
Jazzland JLP-35	(M)	**Gemini**	1961	12.00	30.00
Jazzland JLP-935	(S)	**Gemini**	1961	10.00	25.00
SPRING STREET STOMPERS, THE					
Jubilee JLP-1002	(M)	**The Spring Street Stompers At Carnegie Hall**	1955	16.00	40.00
Jubilee JLP-1004	(M)	**I Go, Hook, Line And Sinker**	1955	16.00	40.00
STACY, JESS					
Jess Stacy is a traditional jazz pianist.					
Columbia CL-6147	(10")	**Piano Moods**	1950	30.00	75.00

Label & Catalog #		Title	Year	VG+	NM
Brunswick BL-58029	(10")	**Piano Solos**	1951	30.00	75.00
Brunswick BL-54017	(M)	**Piano Solos**	1956	20.00	50.00
		(Brunswick 54017 is a reissue of 58029.)			
Atlantic 1225	(M)	**A Tribute To Benny Goodman**	1956	20.00	50.00
		—Atlantic albums above have black mono or green stereo labels.—			
Hanover HL-8010	(M)	**The Return Of Jess Stacy**	1964	8.00	20.00
Hanover HS-8010	(S)	**The Return Of Jess Stacy**	1964	6.00	15.00
STAETER, TED					
Atlantic 1218	(M)	**Ted Staeter's New York**	1955	20.00	50.00
		—Atlantic albums above have black mono or green stereo labels.—			
Atlantic 1218	(M)	**Ted Staeter's New York**	1961	10.00	25.00
		—Atlantic albums above have multi-color labels with a white fan logo.—			
STAFFORD, JO					
Jo Stafford is a jazz/big band-based vocalist.					
Capitol H-75	(10")	**American Folk Songs**	1950	30.00	75.00
Capitol H-9014	(10")	**Songs Of Faith**	1950	30.00	75.00
Capitol H-197	(10")	**Autumn In New York**	1950	30.00	75.00
Capitol H-247	(10")	**Songs For Sunday Evening**	1950	30.00	75.00
Capitol H-435	(10")	**Starring Jo Stafford**	1953	30.00	75.00
Capitol T-197	(M)	**Autumn In New York**	1954	24.00	60.00
Capitol T-423	(M)	**Memory Songs**	1954	24.00	60.00
Capitol T-428	(M)	**Memory Songs**	1955	24.00	60.00
Capitol T-435	(M)	**Starring Jo Stafford**	1955	24.00	60.00
		— Capitol albums above have turquoise labels.—			
Capitol T-197	(M)	**Autumn In New York**	195?	12.00	30.00
Capitol T-423	(M)	**Memory Songs**	195?	12.00	30.00
Capitol T-428	(M)	**Memory Songs**	195?	12.00	30.00
Capitol T-435	(M)	**Starring Jo Stafford**	195?	12.00	30.00
		—Capitol albums above have black "rainbow" labels with the logo on the left side.—			
Columbia CL-6210	(10")	**As You Desire Me**	1952	24.00	60.00
Columbia CL-6238	(10")	**Broadway's Best**	1953	24.00	60.00
Columbia CL-6268	(10")	**New Orleans**	1954	24.00	60.00
Columbia CL-6274	(10")	**My Heart's In The Highland**	1954	24.00	60.00
Columbia CL-6286	(10")	**Garden Of Prayers**	1954	24.00	60.00
Columbia CL-578	(M)	**New Orleans**	1954	20.00	50.00
		(Columbia 578 is a reissue of 6268 plus four tracks.)			
Columbia CL-584	(M)	**Broadway's Best**	1954	20.00	50.00
		(Columbia 584 is a reissue of 6238 plus four tracks.)			
		— Columbia albums above have "Long Playing" on the bottom of the label.—			
Columbia CL-2501	(10")	**Soft And Sentimental**	1955	20.00	50.00
Columbia CL-2591	(10")	**A Gal Named Jo**	1956	20.00	50.00
Columbia CL-578	(M)	**New Orleans**	195?	12.00	30.00
Columbia CL-584	(M)	**Broadway's Best**	195?	12.00	30.00
Columbia CL-691	(M)	**Happy Holiday**	1955	20.00	50.00
Columbia CL-910	(M)	**Ski Trails**	1956	16.00	40.00
Columbia CL-968	(M)	**Once Over Lightly**	1957	16.00	40.00
		(Columbia 968 also features Art Van Damme.)			
Columbia CL-1043	(M)	**Songs Of Scotland**	1957	16.00	40.00
Columbia CL-1124	(M)	**Swingin' Down Broadway**	1958	16.00	40.00
Columbia CL-1228	(M)	**Jo Stafford's Greatest Hits**	1958	12.00	30.00
Columbia CL-1262	(M)	**I'll Be Seeing You**	1959	12.00	30.00
Columbia CS-8080	(S)	**I'll Be Seeing You**	1959	16.00	40.00
Columbia CL-1339	(M)	**Ballad Of The Blues**	1959	12.00	30.00
Columbia CS-8139	(S)	**Ballad Of The Blues**	1959	16.00	40.00
Columbia CL-1561	(M)	**Jo + Jazz**	1960	16.00	40.00
Columbia CS-8361	(S)	**Jo + Jazz**	1960	20.00	50.00
		(Columbia 1561 also features Johnny Hodges and Ben Webster.)			
		— Columbia albums above have six white on black "eye" logos on each label.—			
Reprise R-6090	(M)	**Getting Sentimental Over Tommy Dorsey**	1964	8.00	20.00
Reprise R9-6090	(S)	**Getting Sentimental Over Tommy Dorsey**	1964	10.00	25.00
Dot DLP-3673	(M)	**Do I Hear A Waltz?**	1965	8.00	20.00
Dot DLP-25673	(S)	**Do I Hear A Waltz?**	1965	10.00	25.00
Dot DLP-3745	(M)	**This Is Jo Stafford**	1966	8.00	20.00
Dot DLP-25745	(S)	**This Is Jo Stafford**	1966	10.00	25.00

Label & Catalog #		Title	Year	VG+	NM

STALLINGS, MARY, & CAL TJADER

Label & Catalog #		Title	Year	VG+	NM
Fantasy 3325	*(M)*	**Cal Tjader Plays, Mary Stallings Sings** *(Red vinyl)*	*1962*	**20.00**	**50.00**
Fantasy 3325	*(M)*	**Cal Tjader Plays, Mary Stallings Sings**	*1962*	**12.00**	**30.00**
Fantasy 8068	*(S)*	**Cal Tjader Plays, Mary Stallings Sings** *(Blue vinyl)*	*1962*	**16.00**	**40.00**
Fantasy 8068	*(S)*	**Cal Tjader Plays, Mary Stallings Sings**	*1962*	**10.00**	**25.00**

—Fantasy albums above have red mono and blue stereo labels on non-flexible vinyl.—

STAMM, MARVIN

Label & Catalog #		Title	Year	VG+	NM
Verve V6-8759	*(S)*	**Machinations**	*1968*	**6.00**	**15.00**

—Verve albums above have black labels with "MGM Records" on the bottom.—

STARR, KAY

Kathryn Starks, aka Kay Starr, is a jazz/big band-based vocalist.

Label & Catalog #		Title	Year	VG+	NM
Capitol H-211	*(10")*	**Songs By Starr**	*1950*	**30.00**	**75.00**
Capitol H-363	*(10")*	**Kay Starr Style**	*1953*	**30.00**	**75.00**
Capitol H-415	*(10")*	**The Hits Of Kay Starr**	*1953*	**30.00**	**75.00**
Capitol T-211	*(M)*	**Songs By Starr**	*1955*	**20.00**	**50.00**
Capitol T-363	*(M)*	**Kay Starr Style**	*1955*	**20.00**	**50.00**
Capitol T-415	*(M)*	**The Hits Of Kay Starr**	*1955*	**20.00**	**50.00**
Capitol T-580	*(M)*	**In A Blue Mood**	*1955*	**20.00**	**50.00**

—Capitol albums above have turquoise labels.—

Label & Catalog #		Title	Year	VG+	NM
Capitol T-211	*(M)*	**Songs By Starr**	*195?*	**10.00**	**25.00**
Capitol T-363	*(M)*	**Kay Starr Style**	*195?*	**10.00**	**25.00**
Capitol T-415	*(M)*	**The Hits Of Kay Starr**	*195?*	**10.00**	**25.00**
Capitol T-580	*(M)*	**In A Blue Mood**	*195?*	**10.00**	**25.00**
Capitol T-1254	*(M)*	**Movin'**	*1959*	**10.00**	**25.00**
Capitol ST-1254	*(S)*	**Movin'**	*1959*	**12.00**	**30.00**
Capitol T-1303	*(M)*	**Losers, Weepers**	*1960*	**10.00**	**25.00**
Capitol ST-1303	*(S)*	**Losers, Weepers**	*1960*	**12.00**	**30.00**
Capitol T-1358	*(M)*	**One More Time**	*1960*	**10.00**	**25.00**
Capitol ST-1358	*(S)*	**One More Time**	*1960*	**12.00**	**30.00**
Capitol T-1374	*(M)*	**Movin' On Broadway**	*1960*	**10.00**	**25.00**
Capitol ST-1374	*(S)*	**Movin' On Broadway**	*1960*	**12.00**	**30.00**
Capitol T-1438	*(M)*	**Jazz Singer**	*1960*	**10.00**	**25.00**
Capitol ST-1438	*(S)*	**Jazz Singer**	*1960*	**12.00**	**30.00**
Capitol T-1468	*(M)*	**All Starr Hits**	*1961*	**8.00**	**20.00**
Capitol ST-1468	*(S)*	**All Starr Hits**	*1961*	**10.00**	**25.00**
Capitol T-1681	*(M)*	**I Cry By Night**	*1962*	**8.00**	**20.00**
Capitol ST-1681	*(S)*	**I Cry By Night**	*1962*	**10.00**	**25.00**

—Capitol albums above have black "rainbow" labels with the logo on the left side.—

Label & Catalog #		Title	Year	VG+	NM
Capitol T-211	*(M)*	**Songs By Starr**	*196?*	**6.00**	**15.00**
Capitol T-363	*(M)*	**Kay Starr Style**	*196?*	**6.00**	**15.00**
Capitol T-415	*(M)*	**The Hits Of Kay Starr**	*196?*	**6.00**	**15.00**
Capitol T-580	*(M)*	**In A Blue Mood**	*196?*	**6.00**	**15.00**
Capitol T-1254	*(M)*	**Movin'**	*196?*	**5.00**	**12.00**
Capitol ST-1254	*(S)*	**Movin'**	*196?*	**6.00**	**15.00**
Capitol T-1303	*(M)*	**Losers, Weepers**	*196?*	**5.00**	**12.00**
Capitol ST-1303	*(S)*	**Losers, Weepers**	*196?*	**6.00**	**15.00**
Capitol T-1358	*(M)*	**One More Time**	*196?*	**5.00**	**12.00**
Capitol ST-1358	*(S)*	**One More Time**	*196?*	**6.00**	**15.00**
Capitol T-1374	*(M)*	**Movin' On Broadway**	*196?*	**5.00**	**12.00**
Capitol ST-1374	*(S)*	**Movin' On Broadway**	*196?*	**6.00**	**15.00**
Capitol T-1438	*(M)*	**Jazz Singer**	*196?*	**5.00**	**12.00**
Capitol ST-1438	*(S)*	**Jazz Singer**	*196?*	**6.00**	**15.00**
Capitol T-1468	*(M)*	**All Starr Hits**	*196?*	**5.00**	**12.00**
Capitol ST-1468	*(S)*	**All Starr Hits**	*196?*	**6.00**	**15.00**
Capitol T-1681	*(M)*	**I Cry By Night**	*196?*	**5.00**	**12.00**
Capitol ST-1681	*(S)*	**I Cry By Night**	*196?*	**6.00**	**15.00**
Capitol T-2106	*(M)*	**Fabulous Favorites**	*1964*	**5.00**	**12.00**
Capitol ST-2106	*(S)*	**Fabulous Favorites**	*1964*	**6.00**	**15.00**
Capitol T-2550	*(M)*	**Tears And Heartaches**	*1966*	**5.00**	**12.00**
Capitol ST-2550	*(S)*	**Tears And Heartaches**	*1966*	**6.00**	**15.00**

—Capitol albums above have black "rainbow" labels with the logo on top.—

Label & Catalog #		Title	Year	VG+	NM
Liberty LRP-9001	*(M)*	**Swingin' With The Starr**	*1956*	**12.00**	**30.00**
Rondo-lette A-3	*(M)*	**Them There Eyes**	*1958*	**10.00**	**25.00**
RCA Victor LPM-1149	*(M)*	**The One And Only Kay Starr**	*1955*	**12.00**	**30.00**

Label & Catalog #		Title	Year	VG+	NM
RCA Victor LPM-1549	(M)	**Blue Starr**	1957	12.00	30.00
RCA Victor LPM-1720	(M)	**Rockin' With Kay**	1958	20.00	50.00
RCA Victor LPM-2055	(M)	**I Hear The Word**	1959	10.00	25.00
RCA Victor LSP-2055	(S)	**I Hear The Word**	1959	12.00	30.00
		—RCA albums above have black labels with "Long Play" or "Living Stereo" on the bottom.—			
ABC ABCS-631	(S)	**When The Lights Go On Again**	1968	4.00	10.00
Paramount PAS-5001	(S)	**How About This**	1969	4.00	10.00
		(Paramount 5001 also features Count Basie.)			

STARR, KAY / ERROLL GARNER

Modern LMP-1203	(M)	**Singin' Kay Starr, Swingin' Erroll Garner**	1956	30.00	75.00
Crown CLP-5003	(M)	**Singin' Kay Starr, Swingin' Erroll Garner**	1957	12.00	30.00
		(Crown 5003 is a reissue of Modern 1203.)			

STATON, DAKOTA

Aliyah Rabia, aka Dakota Staton, is a jazz-based vocalist.

Capitol T-876	(M)	**The Late, Late Show**	1957	20.00	50.00
Capitol T-1003	(M)	**In The Night**	1958	20.00	50.00
		(Capitol 1003 also features George Shearing.)			
		—Capitol albums above have turquoise labels.—			
Capitol T-876	(M)	**The Late, Late Show**	1957	12.00	30.00
Capitol T-1003	(M)	**In The Night**	1958	12.00	30.00
Capitol T-1054	(M)	**Dynamic!**	1958	12.00	30.00
Capitol ST-1054	(S)	**Dynamic!**	1958	16.00	40.00
Capitol T-1170	(M)	**Crazy He Calls Me**	1959	12.00	30.00
Capitol ST-1170	(S)	**Crazy He Calls Me**	1959	16.00	40.00
Capitol T-1241	(M)	**Time To Swing**	1959	12.00	30.00
Capitol ST-1241	(S)	**Time To Swing**	1959	16.00	40.00
Capitol T-1325	(M)	**More Than The Most**	1959	12.00	30.00
Capitol ST-1325	(S)	**More Than The Most**	1959	16.00	40.00
Capitol T-1387	(M)	**Ballads And The Blues**	1960	12.00	30.00
Capitol ST-1387	(S)	**Ballads And The Blues**	1960	16.00	40.00
Capitol T-1427	(M)	**Softly**	1960	12.00	30.00
Capitol ST-1427	(S)	**Softly**	1960	16.00	40.00
Capitol T-1490	(M)	**Dakota**	1961	12.00	30.00
Capitol ST-1490	(S)	**Dakota**	1961	16.00	40.00
Capitol T-1597	(M)	**Round Midnight**	1961	12.00	30.00
Capitol ST-1597	(S)	**Round Midnight**	1961	16.00	40.00
Capitol T-1649	(M)	**Dakota At Storyville**	1961	12.00	30.00
Capitol ST-1649	(S)	**Dakota At Storyville**	1961	16.00	40.00
		—Capitol albums above have black "rainbow" labels with the logo on the left side.—			
Capitol T-876	(M)	**The Late, Late Show**	196?	6.00	15.00
Capitol T-1003	(M)	**In The Night**	196?	6.00	15.00
Capitol T-1054	(M)	**Dynamic!**	196?	5.00	12.00
Capitol ST-1054	(S)	**Dynamic!**	196?	6.00	15.00
Capitol T-1170	(M)	**Crazy He Calls Me**	196?	5.00	12.00
Capitol ST-1170	(S)	**Crazy He Calls Me**	196?	6.00	15.00
Capitol T-1241	(M)	**Time To Swing**	196?	5.00	12.00
Capitol ST-1241	(S)	**Time To Swing**	196?	6.00	15.00
Capitol T-1325	(M)	**More Than The Most**	196?	5.00	12.00
Capitol ST-1325	(S)	**More Than The Most**	196?	6.00	15.00
Capitol T-1387	(M)	**Ballads And The Blues**	196?	5.00	12.00
Capitol ST-1387	(S)	**Ballads And The Blues**	196?	6.00	15.00
Capitol T-1427	(M)	**Softly**	196?	5.00	12.00
Capitol ST-1427	(S)	**Softly**	196?	6.00	15.00
Capitol T-1490	(M)	**Dakota**	196?	5.00	12.00
Capitol ST-1490	(S)	**Dakota**	196?	6.00	15.00
Capitol T-1597	(M)	**Round Midnight**	196?	5.00	12.00
Capitol ST-1597	(S)	**Round Midnight**	196?	6.00	15.00
Capitol T-1649	(M)	**Dakota At Storyville**	196?	5.00	12.00
Capitol ST-1649	(S)	**Dakota At Storyville**	196?	6.00	15.00
		—Capitol albums above have black "rainbow" labels with the logo on top.—			
United Arts. UAL-3292	(M)	**From Dakota With Love**	1963	8.00	20.00
United Arts. UAS-6292	(S)	**From Dakota With Love**	1963	10.00	25.00
United Arts. UAL-3312	(M)	**Live And Swinging**	1963	8.00	20.00
United Arts. UAS-6312	(S)	**Live And Swinging**	1963	10.00	25.00
United Arts. UAL-3355	(M)	**Dakota Staton With Strings**	1964	8.00	20.00
United Arts. UAS-6355	(S)	**Dakota Staton With Strings**	1964	10.00	25.00

Label & Catalog #		Title	Year	VG+	NM

STEIG, JEREMY

Jeremy Steig is a jazz-based flautist. For additional listings refer to Bill Evans.

Columbia CL-2136	(M)	**Flute Fever**	1964	5.00	12.00
Columbia CS-8936	(S)	**Flute Fever**	1964	4.00	10.00

— Columbia albums above have "Guaranteed High Fidelity" or "360 Sound Stereo" in black on the label.—

Solid State SS-18059	(S)	**This Is Jeremy Steig**	1969	5.00	12.00

STEIN, HAL, & WARREN FITZGERALD

Harold Stein is a modern jazz alto and tenor saxophone player. For additional listings refer to the Various Artists section under Prestige.

Progressive PLP-1002	(M)	**Hal Stein-Warren Fitzgerald Quintet**	1955	300.00	500.00

STEIN, LOU

Louis Stein is a traditional jazz-based pianist.

Brunswick BL-58053	(10")	**Lou Stein**	1953	20.00	50.00
Jubilee JLP-8	(10")	**Six For Kicks**	1954	20.00	50.00
Epic LG-3101	(M)	**House Hop**	1955	16.00	40.00
Epic LN-3148	(M)	**Three, Four And Five**	1955	16.00	40.00
Epic LN-3186	(M)	**From Broadway To Paris**	1955	16.00	40.00
Jubilee JLP-1019	(M)	**Eight For Kicks, Four For Laughs**	1956	16.00	40.00

STEVENS, LEITH

Leith Stevens is a traditional jazz composer and conductor. For additional listings refer to the Jazzy Soundtracks section under Capitol, Colpix, Columbia, Coral, Decca, Mercury, Omega, and Warwick.

Decca DL-5515	(10")	**Jazz Themes In "The Wild One"**	1954	30.00	75.00
Coral-57283	(M)	**Jazz Themes For Cops & Robbers**	1958	20.00	50.00

STEWARD, HERBIE

Herbert Steward is a West Coast jazz alto, tenor and baritone saxophone player. For additional listings refer to The Four Brothers.

Ava A-9	(M)	**So Pretty**	1962	12.00	30.00
Ava AS-9	(S)	**So Pretty**	1962	10.00	25.00

STEWART, BOB

Dawn DLP-1103	(M)	**Let's Talk About Love**	1956	20.00	50.00

(Dawn 1103 also features Mat Mathews.)

STEWART, HELYNE

Vocalist Helene Stweart is accompanied by Teddy Edwards, Art Pepper and Jack Sheldon.

Contemporary M-3601	(M)	**Love Moods**	1961	14.00	35.00
Contemporary S-7601	(S)	**Love Moods**	1961	16.00	40.00

— Contemporary stereo albums have gold & black labels.—

STEWART, REX

Rex Stewart is a traditional jazz cornet player.

Dial LP-215	(10")	**Ellingtonia**	1951	100.00	200.00
"X" LX-3001	(10")	**Rex Stewart & His Orchestra**	1954	30.00	75.00
Urania UJLP-2012	(M)	**Cool Fever**	1955	20.00	50.00
Concert Hall Jazz 1202	(M)	**Dixieland On Location**	1954	20.00	50.00
Atlantic 1209	(M)	**Big Jazz**	1956	20.00	50.00

(Atlantic 1209 also features Jack Teagarden.)

—Atlantic albums above have black mono or green stereo labels.—

Jazztone J-1202	(M)	**Dixieland Free-For-All**	1956	16.00	40.00
Jazztone J-1250	(M)	**Dedicated To Jazz**	1957	16.00	40.00
Jazztone J-1268	(M)	**The Big Challenge**	1957	16.00	40.00

(Jazztone 1268 also features Cootie Williams.)

Jazztone J-1285	(M)	**The Big Reunion**	1957	16.00	40.00

(Jazztone 1285 also features Fletcher Henderson.)

American Rec. Soc. G-448	(M)	**The Big Challenge**	1958	16.00	40.00

(A.R.S. 448 is a reissue of Jazztone 1268.)

Felsted 7001	(M)	**Rendezvous With Rex**	1958	16.00	40.00
Felsted 2001	(S)	**Rendezvous With Rex**	1958	12.00	30.00
Warner Bros. W-1260	(M)	**Porgy And Bess Revisited**	1958	16.00	40.00
Warner Bros. WS-1260	(S)	**Porgy And Bess Revisited**	1958	12.00	30.00
United Arts. UAL-4009	(M)	**Henderson Homecoming**	1959	16.00	40.00
United Arts. UAS-5009	(S)	**Henderson Homecoming**	1959	12.00	30.00
Swingville SVLP-2006	(M)	**The Happy Jazz Of Rex Stewart**	1960	20.00	50.00

— Swingville mono albums above have purple mono or red stereo labels.—

Label & Catalog #		Title	Year	VG+	NM
Swingville SVLP-2006	(M)	**The Happy Jazz Of Rex Stewart**	1965	10.00	25.00

—Swingville albums above have blue labels with a trident logo on the right side.—

STEWART, REX / ILLINOIS JACQUET

Grand Award GA-33-315	(M)	**Rex Stewart Plays Duke/Uptown Jazz**	1955	16.00	40.00

STEWART, REX, & DICKIE WELLS

RCA Vivtor LPM-2024	(M)	**Chatter Jazz**	1959	12.00	30.00
RCA Vivtor LSP-2024	(S)	**Chatter Jazz**	1959	10.00	25.00

—RCA albums above have black labels with "Long Play" or "Living Stereo" on the bottom.—

STEWART, SLAM

Leroy "Slam" Stewart is a traditional jazz string bass player and vocalist. For additional listings refer to Erroll Garner / Slam Stewart.

Savoy MG-12067	(M)	**Bowin' Singin' Slam**	1956	16.00	40.00

STEWART, TOM

Thomas Stewart is a modern jazz tenor saxophone and trumpet player.

ABC-Paramount ABC-117	(M)	**Tom Stewart Sextette/Quintet**	1956	20.00	50.00

STITT, SONNY

Edward "Sonny" Stitt is a modern jazz alto and tenor saxophone player. For additional listings refer to Gene Ammons; Stan Getz, Dizzie Gillespie & Sonny Stitt; Stan Getz / Sonny Stitt / Fats Navarro; Dizzie Gillespie; Paul Gonsalves; The Modern Jazz Sextet; Don Patterson; Oscar Peterson.

New Jazz NJLP-103	(10")	**Sonny Stitt And Bud Powell**	1950	150.00	300.00
Prestige PRLP-103	(10")	**Sonny Stitt And Bud Powell**	1951	125.00	250.00
Prestige PRLP-111	(10")	**Mr. Saxophone**	1951	125.00	250.00
Prestige PRLP-126	(10")	**Sonny Stitt, Volume 1—Favorites**	1952	125.00	250.00
Prestige PRLP-148	(10")	**Sonny Stitt, Volume 2—Tenor Sax**	1953	125.00	250.00
Savoy MG-9006	(10")	**All Star Series: Sonny Stitt**	1952	125.00	250.00
Savoy MG-9012	(10")	**New Sounds In Modern Music**	1952	100.00	200.00
Savoy MG-9014	(10")	**New Trends Of Jazz**	1952	100.00	200.00
Jazztone J-1231	(M)	**Early Modern**	1956	16.00	40.00
Jazztone J-1263	(M)	**Early Modern**	1957	16.00	40.00
		(Jazztone 1263 is a reissue of 1231.)			
Prestige PRLP-7024	(M)	**Sonny Stitt With Bud Powell & J. J. Johnson**	1956	50.00	125.00
		(Prestige 7024 is a reissue of 103.)			
Prestige PRLP-7077	(M)	**Kaleidoscope**	1957	50.00	125.00
		(Prestige 7077 is a reissue of 111 and 148.)			
Prestige PRLP-7133	(M)	**Stitt's Bits**	1958	50.00	125.00
		(Prestige 7133 is a reissue of 126.)			

—Prestige albums above have yellow labels with a W. 50th Street, NYC address.—

Prestige PRLP-7244	(M)	**Stitt Meets Brother Jack**	1962	20.00	50.00
Prestige PRST-7244	(S)	**Stitt Meets Brother Jack**	1962	20.00	50.00
		(Prestige 7244 also features Jack McDuff.)			
Prestige PRLP-7248	(M)	**All God's Chillun Got Rhythm**	1962	20.00	50.00
Prestige PRST-7248	(E)	**All God's Chillun Got Rhythm**	1962	16.00	40.00
		(Prestige 7248 is a reissue of 7024.)			
Prestige PRLP-7297	(M)	**Soul Shack**	1964	20.00	50.00
Prestige PRST-7297	(S)	**Soul Shack**	1964	20.00	50.00
		(Prestige 7297 also features Jack McDuff.)			
Prestige PRLP-7302	(M)	**Primitivo Soul!**	1964	16.00	40.00
Prestige PRST-7302	(S)	**Primitivo Soul!**	1964	16.00	40.00

—Prestige albums above have yellow mono or silver stereo labels with a Bergenfield, NJ address .—

Prestige PRLP-7332	(M)	**Shangri-La**	1964	12.00	30.00
Prestige PRST-7332	(S)	**Shangri-La**	1964	10.00	25.00
		(Prestige 7332 also features Don Patterson.)			
Prestige PRLP-7372	(M)	**Soul People**	1965	12.00	30.00
Prestige PRST-7372	(S)	**Soul People**	1965	10.00	25.00
Prestige PRLP-7436	(M)	**Night Crawler**	1967	12.00	30.00
Prestige PRST-7436	(S)	**Night Crawler**	1967	10.00	25.00
		(Prestige 7436 also features Don Patterson.)			
Prestige PRLP-7452	(M)	**Nuther Fu'ther**	1967	10.00	25.00
Prestige PRST-7452	(S)	**Nuther Fu'ther**	1967	8.00	20.00
		(Prestige 7452 is a reissue of 7244.)			
Prestige PRLP-7459	(M)	**Sonny Stitt... Pow!**	1967	10.00	25.00
Prestige PRST-7459	(S)	**Sonny Stitt... Pow!**	1967	8.00	20.00

—Prestige albums above have blue label with a trident logo on the right sides—

Sonny Stitt toured with Tiny Bradshaw prior to establishing himself in the New York scene with Dizzy Gillespie in 1945-46. After a few years off he returned fronting a group with Gene Ammons in 1949, then with his own combo with a few months spent with Gillespie and the JATP in 1958-59. He has recorded as a featured artists with Stan Getz, Paul Gonsalves, Don Patterson, and as a member of The Modern Jazz Sextet. He can be found on LPs by Ammons on Prestige and Roy Eldridge on Verve.

Label & Catalog #		Title	Year	VG+	NM
Prestige PRST-7585	(S)	**Stitt's Bits, Volume 1**	1968	6.00	15.00
Prestige PRST-7612	(S)	**Stitt's Bits, Volume 2**	1969	6.00	15.00
Prestige PRST-7635	(S)	**Soul Electricity**	1969	6.00	15.00
Prestige PRST-7701	(S)	**The Best Of Sonny Stitt With Brother Jack McDuff**	1969	5.00	12.00
		—Prestige albums above have blue label with a trident logo on top.—			
Roost LP-415	(10")	**Sonny Stitt Plays Arrangements From The Pen Of Johnny Richards**	1953	150.00	300.00
Roost LP-418	(10")	**Jazz At The Hi Hat**	1954	150.00	300.00
Roost LP-1203	(M)	**Battle Of Birdland**	1955	40.00	100.00
		(Roost 1203 also features Eddie Davis.)			
Roost LP-1208	(M)	**Sonny Stitt**	1956	40.00	100.00
Roost LP-2204	(M)	**Sonny Stitt Plays Arrangements Of Quincy Jones**	1956	20.00	50.00
Roost LP-2208	(M)	**Sonny Stitt**	1956	20.00	50.00
Roost LP-2219	(M)	**37 Minutes And 48 Seconds**	1956	20.00	50.00
Roost LP-2226	(M)	**Sonny Stitt With The New Yorkers**	1957	20.00	50.00
Roost LP-2230	(M)	**The Saxophone Of Sonny Stitt**	1959	16.00	40.00
Roost SLP-2230	(S)	**The Saxophone Of Sonny Stitt**	1959	12.00	30.00
Roost LP-2235	(M)	**Little Bit Of Stitt**	1959	16.00	40.00
Roost SLP-2235	(S)	**Little Bit Of Stitt**	1959	12.00	30.00
Roost LP-2240	(M)	**Sonny Side Of Stitt**	1960	16.00	40.00
Roost SLP-2240	(S)	**Sonny Side Of Stitt**	1960	12.00	30.00
Roost LP-2244	(M)	**Stittsville**	1960	16.00	40.00
Roost SLP-2244	(S)	**Stittsville**	1960	12.00	30.00
Roost LP-2245	(M)	**Sonny Side Up**	1960	16.00	40.00
Roost SLP-2245	(S)	**Sonny Side Up**	1960	12.00	30.00
Roost LP-2247	(M)	**Feelin's**	1962	12.00	30.00
Roost SLP-2247	(S)	**Feelin's**	1962	10.00	25.00
Roost LP-2252	(M)	**Sonny Stitt In Orbit**	1963	12.00	30.00
Roost SLP-2252	(S)	**Sonny Stitt In Orbit**	1963	10.00	25.00
Roost LP-2253	(M)	**Sonny Stitt Goes Latin**	1963	12.00	30.00
Roost SLP-2253	(S)	**Sonny Stitt Goes Latin**	1963	10.00	25.00
Verve MGV-8219	(M)	**New York Jazz**	1958	24.00	60.00
Verve MGV-8250	(M)	**Only The Blues**	1958	24.00	60.00
Verve MGV-8262	(M)	**Sonny Side Up**	1958	30.00	75.00
		(Verve 8262 also features Dizzy Gillespie and Sonny Rollins.)			
Verve MGV-8306	(M)	**The Hard Swing**	1959	24.00	60.00
Verve MGVS-6038	(S)	**The Hard Swing**	1960	20.00	50.00
Verve MGV-8309	(M)	**Sonny Stitt Plays Jimmy Giuffre Arrangements**	1959	24.00	60.00
Verve MGVS-6041	(S)	**Sonny Stitt Plays Jimmy Giuffre Arrangements**	1960	20.00	50.00
Verve MGV-8324	(M)	**Personal Appearance**	1959	24.00	60.00
Verve MGV-8344	(M)	**Sonny Stitt Sits In With The Oscar Peterson Trio**	1959	24.00	60.00
Verve MGVS-6108	(S)	**Sonny Stitt Sits In With The Oscar Peterson Trio**	1960	20.00	50.00
Verve MGV-8374	(M)	**Sonny Stitt Blows The Blues**	1960	24.00	60.00
Verve MGVS-6149	(S)	**Sonny Stitt Blows The Blues**	1960	20.00	50.00
Verve MGV-8377	(M)	**Saxophone Supremacy**	1960	24.00	60.00
Verve MGVS-6154	(S)	**Saxophone Supremacy**	1960	*Unreleased*	
Verve MGV-8380	(M)	**Sonny Stitt Swings The Most**	1960	24.00	60.00
Verve MGVS-6162	(S)	**Sonny Stitt Swings The Most**	1960	*Unreleased*	
Verve MGV-8403	(S)	**Sonny Stitt**	1960	*Unreleased*	
		—Verve albums above have black labels with "Verve Records, Inc." on the bottom.—			
Verve V-8219	(M)	**New York Jazz**	1961	10.00	25.00
Verve V-8250	(M)	**Only The Blues**	1961	10.00	25.00
Verve V-8262	(M)	**Sonny Side Up**	1961	12.00	30.00
Verve V-8306	(M)	**The Hard Swing**	1961	10.00	25.00
Verve V6-6038	(S)	**The Hard Swing**	1961	8.00	20.00
Verve V-8309	(M)	**Sonny Stitt Plays Jimmy Giuffre Arrangements**	1961	10.00	25.00
Verve V6-6041	(S)	**Sonny Stitt Plays Jimmy Giuffre Arrangements**	1961	8.00	20.00
Verve V-8324	(M)	**Personal Appearance**	1961	10.00	25.00
Verve V-8344	(M)	**Sonny Stitt Sits In With The Oscar Peterson Trio**	1961	10.00	25.00
Verve V6-6108	(S)	**Sonny Stitt Sits In With The Oscar Peterson Trio**	1961	8.00	20.00
Verve V-8374	(M)	**Sonny Stitt Blows The Blues**	1961	10.00	25.00
Verve V6-6149	(S)	**Sonny Stitt Blows The Blues**	1961	8.00	20.00

Label & Catalog #		Title	Year	VG+	NM
Verve V-8377	(M)	**Saxophone Supremacy**	1961	10.00	25.00
Verve V-8380	(M)	**Sonny Stitt Swings The Most**	1961	10.00	25.00
Verve V-8451	(M)	**The Sensual Sound Of Sonny Stitt**	1962	12.00	30.00
Verve V6-8451	(S)	**The Sensual Sound Of Sonny Stitt**	1962	10.00	25.00
		(Verve 8451 also features Ralph Burns.)			
		—Verve albums above have black labels with "MGM Records" on the bottom.—			
Argo LP-629	(M)	**Sonny Stitt**	1958	16.00	40.00
Argo LPS-629	(S)	**Sonny Stitt**	1958	12.00	30.00
Argo LP-661	(M)	**Burnin'**	1960	12.00	30.00
Argo LPS-661	(S)	**Burnin'**	1960	10.00	25.00
Argo LP-683	(M)	**Sonny Stitt At The D.J. Lounge**	1961	12.00	30.00
Argo LPS-683	(S)	**Sonny Stitt At The D.J. Lounge**	1961	10.00	25.00
Argo LP-709	(M)	**Rearin' Back**	1962	12.00	30.00
Argo LPS-709	(S)	**Rearin' Back**	1962	10.00	25.00
Argo LP-730	(M)	**Move On Over**	1964	12.00	30.00
Argo LPS-730	(S)	**Move On Over**	1964	10.00	25.00
Argo LP-744	(M)	**My Main Man**	1965	12.00	30.00
Argo LPS-744	(S)	**My Main Man**	1965	10.00	25.00
		(Argo 744 also features Bennie Green.)			
Cadet LP-760	(M)	**Inter Action**	1965	8.00	20.00
Cadet LPS-760	(S)	**Inter Action**	1965	6.00	15.00
		(Cadet 760 also features Zoot Sims.)			
Cadet LP-770	(M)	**Soul In The Night**	1965	8.00	20.00
Cadet LPS-770	(S)	**Soul In The Night**	1965	6.00	15.00
Atlantic 1395	(M)	**Sonny Stitt And The Top Brass**	1962	12.00	30.00
Atlantic SD-1395	(S)	**Sonny Stitt And The Top Brass**	1962	10.00	25.00
Atlantic 1418	(M)	**Stitt Plays Bird**	1964	16.00	40.00
Atlantic SD-1418	(S)	**Stitt Plays Bird**	1964	12.00	30.00
		—Atlantic albums above have multi-color labels with a black fan logo.—			
Jazzland JLP-71	(M)	**Low Flame**	1962	12.00	30.00
Jazzland JLP-971	(S)	**Low Flame**	1962	10.00	25.00
Pacific Jazz PJ-71	(M)	**My Mother's Eyes**	1963	12.00	30.00
Pacific Jazz ST-71	(S)	**My Mother's Eyes**	1963	10.00	25.00
Impulse A-43	(M)	**Sonny Stitt Now!**	1963	12.00	30.00
Impulse AS-43	(S)	**Sonny Stitt Now!**	1963	10.00	25.00
		—Impulse albums above have orange & black labels.—			
Impulse AS-43	(S)	**Sonny Stitt Now!**	1968	4.00	10.00
		—Impulse albums above have red & black labels with the "abc" logo on top.—			
Colpix CP-499	(M)	**Broadway Soul**	1964	12.00	30.00
Colpix SCP-499	(S)	**Broadway Soul**	1964	12.00	30.00
Roulette R-25339	(M)	**The Matadors Meet The Bull**	1965	10.00	25.00
Roulette RS-25339	(S)	**The Matadors Meet The Bull**	1965	8.00	20.00
Roulette R-25343	(M)	**What's New?**	1966	8.00	20.00
Roulette RS-25343	(S)	**What's New?**	1966	6.00	15.00
Roulette R-25348	(M)	**I Keep Comin' Back**	1966	8.00	20.00
Roulette RS-25348	(S)	**I Keep Comin' Back**	1966	6.00	15.00
Solid State SS-18047	(S)	**Little Green Apples**	1969	6.00	15.00
Solid State SS-18057	(S)	**Come Together**	1969	6.00	15.00

STITT, SONNY, & GENE AMMONS

Label & Catalog #		Title	Year	VG+	NM
Prestige PRLP-107	(10")	**Battle Of The Saxes: Ammons Vs. Stitt**	1951	125.00	250.00
Prestige PRLP-7234	(M)	**Soul Summit**	1962	20.00	50.00
Prestige PRST-7234	(S)	**Soul Summit**	1962	16.00	40.00
		(Prestige 7244 also features Jack McDuff.)			
		—Prestige albums above have yellow mono or silver stereo labels with a Bergenfield, NJ address .—			
Prestige PRLP-7454	(M)	**Soul Summit**	1967	10.00	25.00
Prestige PRST-7454	(S)	**Soul Summit**	1967	8.00	20.00
		(Prestige 7454 is a reissue of 7234.)			
		—Prestige albums above have blue labels with a trident logo on the right side.—			
Verve V-8426	(M)	**Boss Tenors**	1962	10.00	25.00
Verve V6-8426	(S)	**Boss Tenors**	1962	8.00	20.00
Verve V-8468	(M)	**Boss Tenors In Orbit**	1962	10.00	25.00
Verve V6-8468	(S)	**Boss Tenors In Orbit**	1962	8.00	20.00
		—Verve albums above have black labels with "MGM Records" on the bottom.—			
Cadet LP-785	(M)	**Jug And Sonny**	1967	10.00	25.00
Cadet LPS-785	(S)	**Jug And Sonny**	1967	6.00	15.00
Prestige PRST-7606	(S)	**We'll Be Together Again**	1969	6.00	15.00
		—Prestige albums above have blue labels with a trident logo on top.—			

Label & Catalog #		Title	Year	VG+	NM
STORYVILLE STOMPERS, THE					
Tropicana 1204	(M)	**New Orleans Jazz**	195?	16.00	40.00
STOVER, SMOKEY					
Argo LP-652	(DJ)	**Smokey Stover's Original Firemen** (Multi-color vinyl)	1960	20.00	50.00
Argo LP-652	(M)	**Smokey Stover's Original Firemen**	1960	10.00	25.00
Argo LPS-652	(S)	**Smokey Stover's Original Firemen**	1960	8.00	20.00
STRAND, LES					
Leslie Strandt, aka Les Strand, is a modern jazz organ and piano player.					
Fantasy 3231	(M)	**Les Strand On The Baldwin Organ**	1956	20.00	50.00
Fantasy 3242	(M)	**Jazz Classics On The Baldwin Organ**	1956	20.00	50.00
—Fantasy albums above have red labels on dark red, non-flexible vinyl.—					
Fantasy 3231	(M)	**Les Strand On The Baldwin Organ**	195?	8.00	20.00
Fantasy 3242	(M)	**Jazz Classics On The Baldwin Organ**	195?	8.00	20.00
—Fantasy albums above have red labels on non-flexible vinyl.—					
STRATTON, DON					
Donald Stratton is a traditional jazz-based trumpet player.					
ABC-Paramount ABC-118	(M)	**Modern Jazz With Dixieland Roots**	1956	16.00	40.00
STRAYHORN, BILLY					
William "Swee' Pea" Strayhorn is a traditional jazz pianist, arranger and composer who worked almost exclusively with Duke Ellington. For additional listings refer to Duke Ellington; Johnny Hodges.					
Mercer LP-1001	(10")	**Billy Strayhorn Trio**	1951	100.00	200.00
Mercer LP-1005	(10")	**Billy Strayhorn And All Stars**	1951	100.00	200.00
Felsted 7008	(M)	**Billy Strayhorn Septet**	1958	30.00	75.00
Felsted 2008	(S)	**Billy Strayhorn Septet**	1958	24.00	60.00
United Arts. UAJ-14010	(M)	**The Peaceful Side Of Billy Strayhorn**	1962	20.00	50.00
United Arts. UAJS-15010	(S)	**The Peaceful Side Of Billy Strayhorn**	1962	16.00	40.00
Solid State SS-18031	(S)	**The Peaceful Side Of Billy Strayhorn** (Solid State 18031 is a reissue of U.A. 15010.)	1968	6.00	15.00
STRAZZERI, FRANK					
Frank Starzzeri is a jazz-based pianist.					
Revelation REV-10	(S)	**That's Him And This Is New**	1969	8.00	20.00
STROZIER, FRANK					
Frank Strozier is a modern jazz alto saxophone player. For additional listings refer to Young Lions; Young Men From Memphis.					
Vee Jay LP-3005	(M)	**Fantastic Frank Strozier**	1960	16.00	40.00
Vee Jay LPS-3005	(S)	**Fantastic Frank Strozier**	1960	16.00	40.00
Jazzland JLP-56	(M)	**Long Night**	1961	12.00	30.00
Jazzland JLP-956	(S)	**Long Night**	1961	10.00	25.00
Jazzland JLP-70	(M)	**March Of The Siamese Children**	1962	12.00	30.00
Jazzland JLP-970	(S)	**March Of The Siamese Children**	1962	10.00	25.00
SULIEMAN, IDREES					
Idrees Sulieman is a modern jazz trumpet player. For additional listings refer to Bobby Jaspar; The Prestige Blues Swingers; and the Various Artists section under New Jazz.					
New Jazz NJLP-8202	(M)	**Roots** (New Jazz 8202 features two all-star groups, both led by Sulieman.)	1958	40.00	100.00
—New Jazz albums above have yellow Prestige labels.—					
New Jazz NJLP-8202	(M)	**Roots**	1958	24.00	60.00
—New Jazz albums above have purple labels.—					
New Jazz NJLP-8202	(M)	**Roots**	1965	10.00	25.00
—New Jazz albums above have blue labels with a trident logo on the right side.—					
SULLIVAN, IRA					
Ira Sullivan Jr. is a modern jazz trumpet player. For additional listings refer to Billy Taylor.					
Vee Jay LP-3003	(M)	**Bird Lives!**	1960	16.00	40.00
Vee Jay LPS-3003	(S)	**Bird Lives!**	1960	16.00	40.00
Delmar DL-402	(M)	**Blue Stroll**	1961	16.00	40.00
Delmar DS-402	(S)	**Blue Stroll**	1961	12.00	30.00
Atlantic 1476	(M)	**Horizons**	1967	8.00	20.00
Atlantic SD-1476	(S)	**Horizons**	1967	6.00	15.00
—Atlantic albums above have multi-color labels with a black fan logo.—					

Label & Catalog #		Title	Year	VG+	NM

SULLIVAN, JOE

Dennis Patrick Terence Joseph O'Sullivan, aka Joe Sullivan, is a traditional jazz pianist. For additional listings refer to the Various Artists section under Verve.

Label & Catalog #		Title	Year	VG+	NM
Epic LG-1003	*(10")*	**Joe Sullivan Plays Fats Waller Compositions**	*1954*	**30.00**	**75.00**
Riverside RLP-12-202	*(M)*	**New Solos By An Old Master**	*1955*	**24.00**	**60.00**
		—Riverside albums above have blue on white labels.—			
Capitol T-636	*(M)*	**Classics In Jazz**	*1955*	**16.00**	**40.00**
		— Capitol albums above have turquoise labels.—			
Down Home MGD-2	*(M)*	**Mr. Piano Man—The Music Of Joe Sullivan**	*1956*	**20.00**	**50.00**
		(Down Home 2 features cover art by David Stone Martin.)			
Verve MGV-1002	*(M)*	**Mr. Piano Man—The Music Of Joe Sullivan**	*1957*	**16.00**	**40.00**
		—Verve albums above have "Verve Records, Inc." on the bottom of the label.—			
Verve V-1002	*(M)*	**Mr. Piano Man—The Music Of Joe Sullivan**	*1961*	**6.00**	**15.00**
		— Verve albums above have black labels with "MGM Records" on the bottom.—			

SULLIVAN, MAXINE

Marietta Williams, aka Maxine Sullivan, is a traditional jazz valve trombone and fluegel horn player and vocalist. For additional listings refer to Charlie Shavers.

Label & Catalog #		Title	Year	VG+	NM
Period RL-1909	*(M)*	**Maxine Sullivan 1956**	*1956*	**20.00**	**50.00**
Period SPL-1207	*(M)*	**Maxine Sullivan, Volume 2**	*1956*	**20.00**	**50.00**

SUMMERLIN, ED

Label & Catalog #		Title	Year	VG+	NM
Ecclesia ER-101	*(M)*	**Liturgical Jazz**	*1959*	**20.00**	**50.00**

SUN RA

Herman "Sonny" Blount, who changed his name to Le Sony'r Ra (Sun Ra), is a modern jazz pianist, composer, and leader of various "Arkestras." Although he also recorded for Transition, Savoy, ESP-Disk' and Jihad, the bulk of his early output was released on his own Saturn label. Saturn reflected the personality of its founder: The original serial numbers are unfathomable to those not versed in numerology. In 1967, however, after LP issues had begun to proliferate, a three-digit series of catalog numbers was instituted to simplify ordering. These three-digit numbers are given for releases from 1967 onward but the old numbers were retained on the label or the jacket. Pressing runs could be extremely small— as few as 75 at a time! Certain Saturns, however, received wider distribution through Royal Disc between 1971 and 1973, and were produced in larger quantities.

The original Saturn label (from 1956 through 1964) was yellow or gold with red or black print. The Saturn logo was displayed in block letters across the top or in script letters down the left side. Matrix numbers were stamped in the trail-off vinyl instead of being incised or etched. From 1965 to 1967, Saturn used a red label with silver lettering with the Saturn logo in block letters across the top. In 1968 a green label with black print appeared (sometimes with a Minneapolis address). From 1969 though the early '70s, many Saturn labels bore the motto "Thoth Intergalactic." These Thoth labels were black with silver print, or blue and white with black print. Labels that read "El Saturn" down the left side and include an ankh over an animated sun were used from 1969 until the shutdown of the Chicago label in 1985.

All Saturns prior to 1974 were issued by the Chicago Saturn operation, run by Alton Abraham. Most of these carried the address PO Box 7124, Chicago 7, Illinois (later Chicago, Illinois 60607) on the label. Saturn albums were issued in a confusing variety of covers; many early LPs were sent out in blank covers, often hand-decorated. This information on Sun Ra, along with the discography below, was provided by Robert Campbell, who is near completion on a sessionography for the late Arkestra leader. Tentatively titled "The Earthly Recordings Of Sun Ra," this book is due from Cadence Jazz Books in the summer of '94. Readers in possession of cover or label variations not listed below, or any other obscure data, may contact Mr. Campbell c/o PO Box 40116, Bellevue, WA 98015.

Label & Catalog #		Title	Year	VG+	NM
		— Saturn/Thoth Intergalactic releases—			
Saturn SRLP-0216	*(M)*	**Super-Sonic Jazz** *(Blank cover)*	*1957*	**60.00**	**150.00**
Saturn SRLP-0216	*(M)*	**Super-Sonic Jazz** *(Silk-screened cover)*	*1957*	**150.00**	**300.00**
Saturn SRLP-0216	*(M)*	**Super-Sonic Jazz** *(Purple "keyboard" cover)*	*1958*	**60.00**	**150.00**
Saturn LP-5786	*(M)*	**Jazz In Silhouette**	*1958*	**60.00**	**150.00**
Saturn LP-2066	*(M)*	**When Sun Comes Out** *(Blank cover)*	*1963*	**100.00**	**200.00**
Saturn LP-2066	*(M)*	**When Sun Comes Out** *(Green cover with yellow sun)*	*1963*	**150.00**	**300.00**
Saturn LP-2066	*(M)*	**When Sun Comes Out** *(Black ameboid figure on cover)*	*1963*	**150.00**	**300.00**
		— Saturn albums above have yellow labels.—			
Saturn SRLP-0216	*(M)*	**Super-Sonic Jazz** *(Blue or green cover)*	*1965*	**20.00**	**50.00**
Saturn LP-205	*(M)*	**Jazz In Silhouette**	*1967*	**20.00**	**50.00**
Saturn LP-2066	*(M)*	**When Sun Comes Out** *(Spaceman at piano cover)*	*1967*	**80.00**	**200.00**

Label & Catalog #		Title	Year	VG+	NM
Saturn LP-9956	(M)	**Art Forms Of Dimensions Tomorrow**	1965	20.00	50.00
Saturn GH-9954-E/F	(M)	**Secrets Of The Sun**	1965	40.00	100.00
Saturn LP-9956-2/A/B	(M)	**Fate In A Pleasant Mood**	1965	30.00	75.00
Saturn LP-9956-2/O/P	(M)	**Angels And Demons At Play** *(Metallic gold cover)*	1965	30.00	75.00
Saturn KH-98766	(M)	**Other Planes Of There**	1966	30.00	75.00
Saturn LP-9956-2-M/N	(M)	**Rocket #9 Take Off For The Planet Venus**	1966	150.00	300.00
		(Cover has Sun Ra logo with a burning candle.)			
Saturn LP-9956-11E/F	(M)	**The Lady With The Golden Stockings**	1966	150.00	300.00
		(Issued with a generic "Tonal View Of Times Tomorrow" cover.)			
Saturn HK-5445	(M)	**We Travel The Spaceways**	1966	24.00	60.00
Saturn LP-9956-11A/B	(M)	**Sun Ra Visits Planet Earth**	1966	30.00	75.00
Saturn LPB-711	(M)	**The Magic City**	1966	30.00	75.00
Saturn LP-1966	(M)	**When Angels Speak Of Love**	1966	150.00	300.00
		(Original covers are red with an image of Sun Ra pulled sideways.)			
Saturn LP-502	(S)	**Strange Strings**	1967	20.00	50.00
Saturn LP-408	(S)	**Cosmic Tones For Mental Therapy**	1967	150.00	300.00
		(Cover features doodle art by Sun Ra.)			
		—Saturn albums above have red labels.—			
Saturn LP-205	(M)	**Jazz In Silhouette**	1967	20.00	50.00
		—Saturn albums above have green labels.—			
Saturn LP-207	(M)	**Sun Ra Visits Planet Earth**	1968	20.00	50.00
		—Saturn albums above have green labels with a Minneapolis address.—			
Saturn LP-202	(M)	**Fate In A Pleasant Mood**	196?	14.00	35.00
Saturn LP-203	(M)	**Interstellar Low Ways**	1969	20.00	50.00
		(Saturn 203 is a reissue of 9956-2-M/N with a red & white cover.)			
Saturn LP-204	(M)	**Super-Sonic Jazz** *(Blue or green cover)*	1968	20.00	50.00
Saturn LP-206	(M)	**Other Planes Of There**	1967	16.00	40.00
Saturn LP-208	(M)	**Secrets Of The Sun**	196?	20.00	50.00
Saturn LP-403	(M)	**The Magic City**	196?	8.00	20.00
		(Although copies of Saturn 403 are stamped "Stereo," all are in mono.)			
Saturn LP-404	(M)	**Art Forms Of Dimensions Tomorrow**	1969	8.00	20.00
Saturn LP-406	(M)	**The Nubians Of Plutonia**	1969	20.00	50.00
		(Cover art by R. Pedreguera. Saturn 406 is a reissue of 9956-2-M/N.)			
Saturn LP-407	(M)	**Angels And Demons At Play**	196?	14.00	35.00
Saturn KH-2772	(S)	**Cosmic Tones For Mental Therapy** *(Blue cover)*	196?	8.00	20.00
		—Saturn albums above have labels with a Chicago address.—			
Saturn LP-207	(M)	**Sun Ra Visits Planet Earth**	196?	10.00	25.00
Saturn LP-409	(M)	**We Travel The Spaceways**	196?	12.00	30.00
Saturn LP-509	(M)	**Monorails And Satellites**	1968	20.00	50.00
Saturn ESR-507	(S)	**Atlantis**	1969	12.00	30.00
Saturn LP-519	(S)	**Monorails And Satellites, Vol. II**	1969	20.00	50.00
		—Saturn albums above have El Saturn labels.—			
Thoth Inter. KH-98766	(M)	**Other Planes Of There**	1969	16.00	40.00
Thoth Inter. KH-5472	(M)	**Strange Strings**	196?	16.00	40.00
Thoth Inter. LPB-711	(M)	**The Magic City**	1969	14.00	35.00
Thoth Inter. HK-2772	(S)	**Cosmic Tones For Mental Therapy**	1969	12.00	30.00
		(Cover art by R. Pedreguera)			
		—Thoth Intergalactic albums above have black labels.—			
		—Non-Ra releases—			
Transition TRLP-10	(M)	**Jazz By Sun Ra**	1957	70.00	175.00
		(Transition 10 was issued with a booklet, worth an additional $25)			
Savoy MG-12169	(M)	**The Futuristic Sounds Of Sun Ra**	1961	30.00	75.00
ESP-Disk' 1014	(M)	**The Heliocentric Worlds Of Sun Ra, Volume 1**	1966	16.00	40.00
ESP-Disk' 1014	(S)	**The Heliocentric Worlds Of Sun Ra, Volume 1**	1966	12.00	30.00
ESP-Disk' 1017	(M)	**The Heliocentric Worlds Of Sun Ra, Volume 2**	1966	16.00	40.00
ESP-Disk' 1017	(S)	**The Heliocentric Worlds Of Sun Ra, Volume 2**	1966	12.00	30.00
		(Some pressings of 1017 do not have voices on "The Sun Myth.")			
ESP-Disk' 1017	(M)	**The Heliocentric Worlds Of Sun Ra, Volume 2**	1966	8.00	20.00
ESP-Disk' 1017	(S)	**The Heliocentric Worlds Of Sun Ra, Volume 2**	1966	6.00	15.00
		(Most copies of 1017 have African voices dubbed onto "The Sun Myth.")			
ESP-Disk' 1045	(S)	**Nothing Is**	1969	6.00	15.00
Delmark DL-411	(M)	**Sun Song**	1967	12.00	30.00
Delmark DS-411	(E)	**Sun Song**	1967	6.00	15.00
		(Delmark 411 is a reissue of Transition 10.)			
Delmark DS-414	(E)	**Sound Of Joy**	1968	4.00	10.00
Jihad 1968	(S)	**A Black Mass** *(Black & white cover)*	1968	60.00	150.00
Jihad 1968	(S)	**A Black Mass** *(Color cover)*	1968	40.00	100.00

Label & Catalog #		Title	Year	VG+	NM
SUNKEL, PHIL					
Phillip Sunkel Jr. is a modern jazz trumpet and cornet player and composer.					
ABC-Paramount ABC-136	*(M)*	**Jazz Band**	*1956*	**30.00**	**75.00**
ABC-Paramount ABC-225	*(M)*	**Gerry Mulligan & Bob Brookmeyer Play Phil Sunkel's Jazz Concerto Grosso**	*1958*	**20.00**	**50.00**
ABC-Paramount ABCS-225	*(S)*	**Gerry Mulligan & Bob Brookmeyer Play Phil Sunkel's Jazz Concerto Grosso**	*1958*	**16.00**	**40.00**
SUTTON, DICK					
Richard Schwart, aka Dick Sutton, is a traditional jazz trumpet player, composer and band leader.					
Jaguar JP-802	*(10")*	**Jazz Idiom**	*1954*	**30.00**	**75.00**
Jaguar JP-804	*(10")*	**Progressive Dixieland**	*1954*	**30.00**	**75.00**
SUTTON, RALPH					
Ralph Sutton is a traditional jazz-based pianist.					
Columbia CL-6140	*(10")*	**Piano Moods**	*1950*	**30.00**	**75.00**
Commodore FL-30001	*(M)*	**Ralph Sutton**	*1951*	**30.00**	**75.00**
Circle L-413	*(10")*	**Ralph Sutton**	*1951*	**30.00**	**75.00**
Decca DL-5498	*(10")*	**I Got Rhythm**	*1953*	**30.00**	**75.00**
Down Home DH-1003	*(10")*	**Ragtime Piano Solos**	*1953*	**30.00**	**75.00**
Down Home MGD-4	*(M)*	**Backroom Piano— The Ragtime Piano Of Ralph Sutton**	*1955*	**24.00**	**60.00**
Verve MGV-1004	*(M)*	**Backroom Piano— The Ragtime Piano Of Ralph Sutton**	*1956*	**20.00**	**50.00**
—Verve albums above have "Verve Records, Inc." on the bottom of the label.—					
Riverside RLP-12-212	*(M)*	**Classic Jazz Piano**	*1956*	**24.00**	**60.00**
—Riverside albums above have blue on white labels.—					
Harmony HL-7109	*(M)*	**A Salute To Fats**	*1958*	**6.00**	**15.00**
Omega OML-51	*(M)*	**Jazz At The Olympics**	*196?*	**8.00**	**20.00**
Omega OSL-51	*(S)*	**Jazz At The Olympics**	*196?*	**6.00**	**15.00**
Roulette R-25232	*(M)*	**Ragtime, U.S.A.**	*1963*	**8.00**	**20.00**
Roulette RS-25232	*(S)*	**Ragtime, U.S.A.**	*1963*	**6.00**	**15.00**
SVENSSON, REINHOLD / BENGT HALLBERG					
Prestige PRLP-174	*(10")*	**Piano Moderns**	*1953*	**100.00**	**200.00**
SVENSSON, REINHOLD					
Swedish born Reinhold Svensson is a traditional jazz-based piano and organ player.					
Prestige PRLP-106	*(10")*	**Rheinhold Svensson Piano**	*1951*	**100.00**	**200.00**
Prestige PRLP-129	*(10")*	**Rheinhold Svensson, Volume 2—Favorites**	*1952*	**100.00**	**200.00**
Prestige PRLP-155	*(10")*	**New Sounds From Sweden, Volume 8**	*1953*	**100.00**	**200.00**
SWEDES FROM JAZZVILLE					
Epic LN-3309	*(M)*	**Swedes From Jazzville**	*195?*	**20.00**	**50.00**
SWEET EMMA: ***Refer to*** **EMMA BARRETT**					
SWINGING SWEDES, THE / THE COOL BRITONS					
Blue Note BLP-5019	*(10")*	**New Sounds From The Olde World**	*1951*	**150.00**	**300.00**
SWINGING SWEDES, THE					
Telefunken LGX-66050	*(M)*	**The Swinging Swedes**	*195?*	**20.00**	**50.00**
SWINGLE SINGERS, THE					
The Swingle Singers, a basically baroque band of pop vocalists, are backed by The Modern Jazz Quartet.					
Philips PHM-200-225	*(M)*	**Place Vendome**	*1966*	**8.00**	**20.00**
Philips PHS-600-225	*(S)*	**Place Vendome**	*1966*	**6.00**	**15.00**
SYMS, SYLVIA					
Sylvia Syms is a traditional jazz and big band vocalist.					
Atlantic ALS-137	*(10")*	**Songs By Sylvia Syms**	*1952*	**40.00**	**100.00**
Atlantic 1243	*(M)*	**Songs By Sylvia Syms**	*1956*	**20.00**	**50.00**
—Atlantic albums above have black mono or green stereo labels.—					
Atlantic 1243	*(M)*	**Songs By Sylvia Syms**	*1961*	**10.00**	**25.00**
—Atlantic albums above have multi-color labels with a white fan logo.—					
Version VLP-103	*(10")*	**After Dark**	*1955*	**30.00**	**75.00**
Decca DL-8188	*(M)*	**Sylvia Syms Sings**	*1955*	**20.00**	**50.00**
Decca DL-8639	*(M)*	**Songs Of Love**	*1958*	**16.00**	**40.00**

Label & Catalog #		Title	Year	VG+	NM
Columbia CL-1447	(M)	**Torch Song**	1960	12.00	30.00
Columbia CS-8243	(S)	**Torch Song**	1960	16.00	40.00
		—Columbia albums above have six white on black "eye" logos on each label.—			
Kapp KL-1236	(M)	**That Man—Love Songs To Frank Sinatra**	1961	12.00	30.00
Kapp KS-3236	(S)	**That Man—Love Songs To Frank Sinatra**	1961	16.00	40.00
20th Cent. Fox TFM-4123	(M)	**The Fabulous Sylvia Syms**	1963	10.00	25.00
20th Cent. Fox TFS-4123	(S)	**The Fabulous Sylvia Syms**	1963	12.00	30.00
Prestige PRLP-7439	(M)	**Sylvia Is!**	1967	12.00	30.00
Prestige PRST-7439	(S)	**Sylvia Is!**	1967	10.00	25.00
Prestige PRLP-7489	(M)	**For Once In My Life**	1967	12.00	30.00
Prestige PRST-7489	(S)	**For Once In My Life**	1967	10.00	25.00
		—Prestige albums above have blue labels with a trident logo on the right side.—			

SZABO, GABOR

Hungarian Gabor Szabo is a traditional jazz guitar player. For additional listings refer to Gary McFarland.

Impulse A-9105	(M)	**Gypsy 66**	1966	10.00	25.00
Impulse AS-9105	(M)	**Gypsy 66**	1966	8.00	20.00
		(Impulse 9105 also features Gary McFarland.)			
Impulse A-9123	(M)	**Spellbinder**	1966	10.00	25.00
Impulse AS-9123	(S)	**Spellbinder**	1966	8.00	20.00
Impulse A-9128	(M)	**Jazz Raga**	1967	12.00	30.00
Impulse AS-9128	(S)	**Jazz Raga**	1967	8.00	20.00
Impulse A-9146	(M)	**The Sorcerer**	1967	12.00	30.00
Impulse AS-9146	(S)	**The Sorcerer**	1967	8.00	20.00
		—Impulse albums above have orange & black labels.—			
Impulse AS-9105	(M)	**Gypsy 66**	1968	4.00	10.00
Impulse AS-9123	(S)	**Spellbinder**	1968	4.00	10.00
Impulse AS-9128	(S)	**Jazz Raga**	1968	4.00	10.00
Impulse AS-9146	(S)	**The Sorcerer**	1968	4.00	10.00
Impulse AS-9151	(S)	**Wind, Sky And Diamonds**	1968	6.00	15.00
Impulse AS-9159	(S)	**Light My Fire**	1968	6.00	15.00
Impulse AS-9167	(S)	**More Sorcery**	1968	6.00	15.00
Impulse AS-9173	(S)	**The Best Of Gabor Szabo**	1968	4.00	10.00
		—Impulse albums above have red & black labels with the "abc" logo on top.—			
Skye SK-3	(S)	**Bacchanal**	1968	6.00	15.00
Skye SK-7	(S)	**Dreams**	1969	6.00	15.00

T.

TALBERT, THOMAS

Thomas Talbert is a traditional jazz pianist and composer. For additional listings refer to Patty McGovern & Thomas Talbert.

Atlantic 1250	(M)	**Bix Fats Duke Interpreted By Thomas Talbert**	1957	16.00	40.00
Atlantic SD-1250	(S)	**Bix Fats Duke Interpreted By Thomas Talbert**	1958	16.00	40.00

—Atlantic albums above have black mono or green stereo labels.—

Atlantic 1250	(M)	**Bix Fats Duke Interpreted By Thomas Talbert**	1961	8.00	20.00
Atlantic SD-1250	(S)	**Bix Fats Duke Interpreted By Thomas Talbert**	1961	6.00	15.00

—Atlantic albums above have multi-color labels with a white fan logo.—

TAPSCOTT, HORACE

Flying Dutchman FDS-107	(S)	**the Giant Is Awakened**	1969	6.00	15.00

TATE, BUDDY

George "Buddy" Tate is a traditional jazz tenor saxophone and clarinet player. For additional listings refer to Buck Clayton & Buddy Tate and the Various Artists section under Prestige.

Felsted 7004	(M)	**Swinging Like Tate**	1958	30.00	75.00
Felsted 2004	(S)	**Swinging Like Tate**	1958	20.00	50.00
Swingville SVLP-2003	(M)	**Tate's Date**	1960	20.00	50.00
Swingville SVLP-2014	(M)	**Tate-A-Tate**	1960	20.00	50.00
Swingville SVLP-2029	(M)	**Groovin' With Buddy Tate**	1961	20.00	50.00

—Swingville mono albums above have purple mono or red stereo labels.—

Swingville SVLP-2003	(M)	**Tate's Date**	1965	10.00	25.00
Swingville SVLP-2014	(M)	**Tate-A-Tate**	1965	10.00	25.00
Swingville SVLP-2029	(M)	**Groovin' With Buddy Tate**	1965	10.00	25.00

—Swingville albums above have blue labels with a trident logo on the right side.—

TATRO, DUANE

Duane Tatro is a West Coast jazz saxophone player, arranger and composer.

Contemporary C-3514	(M)	**Jazz For Moderns**	1956	30.00	75.00

TATUM, ART

Arthur Tatum is a traditional jazz pianist. For additional listings refer to Lionel Hampton, Art Tatum & Buddy Rich. For additional listings refer to Zutty Singleton / Art Tatum.

Dial LP-206	(10")	**Art Tatum Trio**	1950	125.00	250.00
Asch ALP-356	(10")	**Art Tatum**	1950	50.00	125.00
		(Asch 356 features cover art by David Stone Martin.)			
Stinson SLP-40	(10")	**Art Tatum Trio**	1950	50.00	125.00
		(Stinson 40 features cover art by David Stone Martin.)			
Brunswick BL-58013	(10")	**Art Tatum Trio**	1950	40.00	100.00
Brunswick BL-58023	(10")	**Art Tatum Piano Solos**	1950	40.00	100.00
Brunswick BL-54004	(M)	**Here's Art Tatum**	1954	30.00	75.00
Decca DL-5086	(10")	**Art Tatum Piano Solos**	1950	40.00	100.00
Remington 2	(10")	**Tatum Piano**	1950	40.00	100.00
Capitol H-216	(10")	**Art Tatum**	1950	40.00	100.00
Capitol H-269	(10")	**Art Tatum Encores**	1951	40.00	100.00
Capitol H-408	(10")	**Art Tatum Trio**	1953	40.00	100.00
Capitol T-216	(M)	**Art Tatum**	1955	30.00	75.00

—Capitol albums above have turquoise labels.—

Folkways FL-33	(10")	**Art Tatum Trio**	1951	30.00	75.00
Columbia GL-101	(10")	**Gene Norman Concert At Shrine Auditorium, May 1949**	1952	60.00	150.00
Columbia CL-6301	(10")	**An Art Tatum Concert**	1954	30.00	75.00
Columbia CL-2565	(10")	**The Tatum Touch**	1956	20.00	50.00
		(Columbia 2565 is a reissue of 6301.)			
Harmony HL-7006	(M)	**An Art Tatum Concert**	1957	8.00	20.00
Clef MGC-612	(M)	**The Genius Of Art Tatum #1**	1954	30.00	75.00
		(Clef 612 features cover art by David Stone Martin.)			
Clef MGC-613	(M)	**The Genius Of Art Tatum #2**	1954	30.00	75.00
		(Clef 613 features cover art by David Stone Martin.)			

Art Tatum began his professional career playing for radio stations before moving to New York in 1932 to play and record as accompanist to Adelaide Hall. From 1933-43 he performed and recorded as a solo. His first trio featured Slam Stewart and Tiny Grimes and it was this format that he favored through most of his life. While he is generally looked back upon as a traditionalist, his playing in the early '30s was truly innovative, placing him at the pinnacle of jazz musicians.

Label & Catalog #		Title	Year	VG+	NM
Clef MGC-614	(M)	**The Genius Of Art Tatum #3**	1954	30.00	75.00
		(Clef 614 features cover art by David Stone Martin.)			
Clef MGC-615	(M)	**The Genius Of Art Tatum #4**	1954	30.00	75.00
		(Clef 615 features cover art by David Stone Martin.)			
Clef MGC-616	(M)	**The Genius Of Art Tatum**	1954	*Unreleased*	
Clef MGC-617	(M)	**The Genius Of Art Tatum**	1954	*Unreleased*	
Clef MGC-618	(M)	**The Genius Of Art Tatum #5**	1954	30.00	75.00
		(Clef 618 features cover art by David Stone Martin.)			
Clef MGC-619	(M)	**The Genius Of Art Tatum**	1954	*Unreleased*	
Clef MGC-620	(M)	**The Genius Of Art Tatum**	1954	*Unreleased*	
Clef MGC-621	(M)	**The Genius Of Art Tatum**	1954	*Unreleased*	
Clef *(No number)*	(M)	**Art Tatum**	1954	125.00	250.00
		(Boxed set of Volumes 2, 3, 4 and 5 of the "genius" series with cover art by David Stone Martin.)			
Clef MGC-657	(M)	**The Genius Of Art Tatum #6**	1955	30.00	75.00
		(Clef 657 features cover art by David Stone Martin.)			
Clef MGC-658	(M)	**The Genius Of Art Tatum #7**	1955	30.00	75.00
		(Clef 658 features cover art by David Stone Martin.)			
Clef MGC-659	(M)	**The Genius Of Art Tatum #8**	1955	30.00	75.00
		(Clef 659 features cover art by David Stone Martin.)			
Clef MGC-660	(M)	**The Genius Of Art Tatum #9**	1955	30.00	75.00
		(Clef 660 features cover art by David Stone Martin.)			
Clef MGC-661	(M)	**The Genius Of Art Tatum #10**	1955	30.00	75.00
		(Clef 661 features cover art by David Stone Martin.)			
Clef MGC-712	(M)	**The Genius Of Art Tatum #11**	1956	30.00	75.00
		(Clef 712 features cover art by David Stone Martin.)			
Clef MGC-741	(M)	**The Art Tatum Trio**	1955	*Unreleased*	
Clef MGC-746	(M)	**Presenting The Art Tatum Trio**	1955	*Unreleased*	
		("Presenting The Art Tatum Trio" was issued as Verve 8118.)			
Verve MGV-8036	(M)	**The Genius Of Art Tatum #1**	1957	20.00	50.00
Verve MGV-8037	(M)	**The Genius Of Art Tatum #2**	1957	20.00	50.00
Verve MGV-8038	(M)	**The Genius Of Art Tatum #3**	1957	20.00	50.00
Verve MGV-8039	(M)	**The Genius Of Art Tatum #4**	1957	20.00	50.00
Verve MGV-8040	(M)	**The Genius Of Art Tatum #5**	1957	20.00	50.00
Verve MGV-8055	(M)	**The Genius Of Art Tatum #6**	1957	20.00	50.00
Verve MGV-8056	(M)	**The Genius Of Art Tatum #7**	1957	20.00	50.00
Verve MGV-8057	(M)	**The Genius Of Art Tatum #8**	1957	20.00	50.00
Verve MGV-8058	(M)	**The Genius Of Art Tatum #9**	1957	20.00	50.00
Verve MGV-8059	(M)	**The Genius Of Art Tatum #10**	1957	20.00	50.00
Verve MGV-8095	(M)	**The Genius Of Art Tatum #11**	1957	20.00	50.00
		(Verve 8036-95 are reissues of Clef 612-712 with the DSM covers.)			
Verve MGV-8101-5	(M)	**Art Tatum, Volume 1**	1957	70.00	175.00
		(Boxed set of Volumes 1-5 of the "Genius" series with cover art by David Stone Martin.)			
Verve MGV-8102-5	(M)	**Art Tatum, Volume 2**	1957	70.00	175.00
		(Boxed set of Volumes 6-10 of the "Genius" series with cover art by David Stone Martin.)			
Verve MGV-8118	(M)	**Presenting The Art Tatum Trio**	1957	20.00	50.00
		(Verve 8059 is a reissue of Clef 746.)			
Verve MGV-8220	(M)	**The Art Tatum-Ben Webster Quartet**	1958	20.00	50.00
Verve MGV-8323	(M)	**The Greatest Piano Of Them All**	1959	20.00	50.00
Verve MGV-8332	(M)	**The Incomparable Music Of Art Tatum**	1959	20.00	50.00
Verve MGV-8347	(M)	**More Of The Greatest Piano Of Them All**	1959	20.00	50.00
Verve MGV-8360	(M)	**Still More Of The Greatest Piano Of Them All**	1960	20.00	50.00
		—Verve albums above have black labels with "Verve Records, Inc." on the bottom.—			
Verve V-8036	(M)	**The Genius Of Art Tatum #1**	1961	8.00	20.00
Verve V-8037	(M)	**The Genius Of Art Tatum #2**	1961	8.00	20.00
Verve V-8038	(M)	**The Genius Of Art Tatum #3**	1961	8.00	20.00
Verve V-8039	(M)	**The Genius Of Art Tatum #4**	1961	8.00	20.00
Verve V-8040	(M)	**The Genius Of Art Tatum #5**	1961	8.00	20.00
Verve V-8055	(M)	**The Genius Of Art Tatum #6**	1961	8.00	20.00
Verve V-8056	(M)	**The Genius Of Art Tatum #7**	1961	8.00	20.00
Verve V-8057	(M)	**The Genius Of Art Tatum #8**	1961	8.00	20.00
Verve V-8058	(M)	**The Genius Of Art Tatum #9**	1961	8.00	20.00
Verve V-8059	(M)	**The Genius Of Art Tatum #10**	1961	8.00	20.00
Verve V-8095	(M)	**The Genius Of Art Tatum #11**	1961	8.00	20.00
Verve V-8118	(M)	**Presenting The Art Tatum Trio**	1961	8.00	20.00
Verve V-8220	(M)	**The Art Tatum-Ben Webster Quartet**	1961	8.00	20.00

Label & Catalog #		Title	Year	VG+	NM
Verve V-8323	(M)	**The Greatest Piano Of Them All**	1961	8.00	20.00
Verve V-8332	(M)	**The Incomparable Music Of Art Tatum**	1961	8.00	20.00
Verve V-8347	(M)	**More Of The Greatest Piano Of Them All**	1961	8.00	20.00
Verve V-8360	(M)	**Still More Of The Greatest Piano Of Them All**	1961	8.00	20.00
Verve V-8433	(M)	**The Essential Art Tatum**	1962	8.00	20.00
		—Verve albums above have black labels with "MGM Records" on the bottom.—			
Decca DL-8715	(M)	**The Art Of Tatum**	1958	20.00	50.00
20th Century FTM-3029	(M)	**Piano Discoveries**	1960	10.00	25.00
20th Century FTS-3029	(E)	**Piano Discoveries**	1960	6.00	15.00
20th Century FTM-3033	(M)	**Piano Discoveries**	1960	10.00	25.00
20th Century FTS-3033	(E)	**Piano Discoveries**	1960	6.00	15.00
20th Century FTM-102-2	(M)	**Piano Discoveries** *(2 LPs)*	1961	12.00	30.00
20th Century FTS-102-2	(E)	**Piano Discoveries** *(2 LPs)*	1961	8.00	20.00
		(20th Century 102 is a reissue of 3029 and 3033.)			

TATUM, ART, & BENNY CARTER & LOUIS BELLSON

Clef MGC-643	(M)	**Tatum-Carter-Bellson**	1955	30.00	75.00
		(Clef 643 features cover art by David Stone Martin.)			
Verve MGV-8013	(M)	**The Three Giants**	1957	20.00	50.00
		(Verve 8013 is a reissue of Clef 643.)			
Verve MGV-8227	(M)	**Makin' Whoopee**	1958	20.00	50.00
		—Verve albums above have black labels with "Verve Records, Inc." on the bottom.—			
Verve V-8013	(M)	**The Three Giants**	1961	8.00	20.00
Verve V-8227	(M)	**Makin' Whoopee**	1961	8.00	20.00
		—Verve albums above have black labels with "MGM Records" on the bottom.—			

TATUM, ART & BUDDY DeFRANCO

Clef MGC-715	(M)	**The Art Tatum-Buddy DeFranco Quartet**	1955	*Unreleased*	
American Rec. Soc. G-412	(M)	**The Art Tatum-Buddy DeFranco Quartet**	1956	16.00	40.00
Verve MGV-8229	(M)	**The Art Tatum-Buddy DeFranco Quartet**	1958	20.00	50.00
		(Verve 8229 is a reissue of A.R.S. 412.)			
		—Verve albums above have black labels with "Verve Records, Inc." on the bottom.—			
Verve V-8229	(M)	**The Art Tatum-Buddy DeFranco Quartet**	1961	8.00	20.00
		—Verve albums above have black labels with "MGM Records" on the bottom.—			

TATUM, ART, & ROY ELDRIDGE & ALVIN STOLLER & JOHN SIMMONS

Clef MGC-679	(M)	**The Art Tatum-Roy Eldridge-Alvin Stoller-John Simmons Quartet**	1955	50.00	125.00
		(Clef 679 features cover art by David Stone Martin.)			
Verve MGV-8064	(M)	**The Art Tatum-Roy Eldridge-Alvin Stoller-John Simmons Quartet**	1957	30.00	75.00
		(Verve 8064 is a reissue of Clef 679 with the DSM cover.)			
		—Verve albums above have black labels with "Verve Records, Inc." on the bottom.—			
Verve V-8064	(M)	**The Art Tatum-Roy Eldridge-Alvin Stoller-John Simmons Quartet**	1961	10.00	25.00
		—Verve albums above have black labels with "MGM Records" on the bottom.—			

TATUM, ART / ERROLL GARNER

Roost LP-2213	(M)	**Giants Of The Piano**	1956	20.00	50.00
Jazztone J-1203	(M)	**Kings Of The Keyboard**	1956	16.00	40.00

TATUM, ART / MARY LOU WILLIAMS

Jazztone J-1280	(M)	**The King And Queen**	1958	16.00	40.00

TAYLOR, ART

Arthur Taylor is a modern jazz drummer. For additional listings refer to Les Jazz Modes and the Various Artists section under Prestige and Signal.

Prestige PRLP-7117	(M)	**Taylor's Wailers**	1957	40.00	100.00
		—Prestige albums above have yellow labels with a W. 50th Street, NYC address.—			
New Jazz NJLP-8219	(M)	**Taylor's Tenors**	1959	20.00	50.00
		—New Jazz albums above have purple labels.—			
New Jazz NJLP-8219	(M)	**Taylor's Tenors**	1965	10.00	25.00
		—New Jazz albums above have blue labels with a trident logo on the right side.—			
Blue Note BLP-4047	(M)	**A.T.'s Delight** *(Deep groove)*	1960	50.00	125.00
Blue Note BLP-4047	(M)	**A.T.'s Delight**	1960	30.00	75.00
Blue Note BST-84047	(S)	**A.T.'s Delight**	1960	20.00	50.00
		—Blue Note albums above have blue on white labels with a W. 63rd Street, NYC address.—			

Label & Catalog #		Title	Year	VG+	NM

TAYLOR, BILLY

William Taylor Jr. is a modern jazz pianist. For additional listings refer to Erroll Garner / Billy Taylor; Joe Holiday / Billy Taylor; Mundell Lowe & Billy Taylor & Gene Quill; Johnnie Ray; the "Jazz At 16 2/3 RPM" article; and the Jazzy Soundtracks section under Heritage and Mercury.

Savoy MG-9035	(10")	**Billy Taylor Piano**	1953	50.00	125.00
Atlantic ALR-113	(10")	**Piano Panorama**	1951	50.00	125.00
Atlantic 1277	(M)	**The Billy Taylor Touch**	1958	20.00	50.00
		(Atlantic 1277 is a reissue of 113.)			
Atlantic 1329	(M)	**One For Fun**	1960	20.00	50.00
Atlantic SD-1329	(S)	**One For Fun**	1960	16.00	40.00
		—Atlantic albums above have black mono or green stereo labels.—			
Atlantic 1277	(M)	**The Billy Taylor Touch**	1961	10.00	25.00
		—Atlantic albums above have multi-color labels with a white fan logo.—			
Roost R-406	(10")	**Jazz At Storyville**	1952	50.00	125.00
Roost R-409	(10")	**Taylor Made Jazz**	1952	50.00	125.00
Prestige PRLP-139	(10")	**Billy Taylor Trio, Volume 1**	1953	100.00	200.00
Prestige PRLP-165	(10")	**Billy Taylor Trio, Volume 2**	1953	100.00	200.00
Prestige PRLP-168	(10")	**Billy Taylor Trio, Volume 3**	1953	100.00	200.00
Prestige PRLP-184	(10")	**Billy Taylor Trio**	1954	70.00	175.00
Prestige PRLP-188	(10")	**Billy Taylor Trio**	1954	70.00	175.00
Prestige PRLP-194	(10")	**Billy Taylor Trio In Concert At Town Hall, December 17, 1954**	1955	70.00	175.00
Prestige PRLP-7001	(M)	**A Touch Of Taylor**	1955	30.00	75.00
Prestige PRLP-7015	(M)	**Billy Taylor Trio, Volume 1**	1956	30.00	75.00
		(Prestige 7105 is a reissue of 139.)			
Prestige PRLP-7016	(M)	**Billy Taylor Trio, Volume 2**	1956	30.00	75.00
		(Prestige 7016 is a reissue of 165 and 168.)			
Prestige PRLP-7051	(M)	**The Billy Taylor Trio With Candido**	1956	30.00	75.00
		(Prestige 7051 is a reissue of 188.)			
Prestige PRLP-7071	(M)	**Cross Section**	1956	30.00	75.00
		(Prestige 7071 is a reissue of 184.)			
Prestige PRLP-7093	(M)	**Billy Taylor Trio At Town Hall**	1957	30.00	75.00
		(Prestige 7093 is a reissue of 194.)			
		—Prestige albums above have yellow labels with a W. 50th Street, NYC address.—			
ABC-Paramount ABC-112	(M)	**Evergreens**	1956	20.00	50.00
ABC-Paramount ABC-134	(M)	**Billy Taylor At The London House**	1956	20.00	50.00
ABC-Paramount ABC-162	(M)	**Billy Taylor Introduces Ira Sullivan**	1957	20.00	50.00
ABC-Paramount ABC-177	(M)	**My Fair Lady Loves Jazz**	1957	20.00	50.00
ABC-Paramount ABC-226	(M)	**The New Trio**	1958	20.00	50.00
ABC-Paramount ABCS-226	(S)	**The New Trio**	1958	16.00	40.00
Argo LP-650	(M)	**Taylor Made Flute**	1959	20.00	50.00
Argo LPS-650	(S)	**Taylor Made Flute**	1959	16.00	40.00
SeSac N-3001	(M)	**Custom Taylored**	1959	20.00	50.00
SeSac SN-3001	(S)	**Custom Taylored**	1959	16.00	40.00
Riverside RLP-12-306	(M)	**Billy Taylor With Four Flutes**	1959	20.00	50.00
Riverside RLP-1151	(S)	**Billy Taylor With Four Flutes**	1959	16.00	40.00
Riverside RLP-12-319	(M)	**Billy Taylor Trio Uptown**	1960	20.00	50.00
Riverside RLP-1168	(S)	**Billy Taylor Trio Uptown**	1960	16.00	40.00
Riverside RLP-12-339	(M)	**Warming Up**	1960	20.00	50.00
Riverside RLP-1195	(S)	**Warming Up**	1960	16.00	40.00
		—Riverside albums above have blue mono or black stereo labels with a reel & mike logo on top.—			
Moodsville MVLP-16	(M)	**Interlude**	1961	20.00	50.00
		—Moodsville mono albums above have green labels with silver print.—			
Moodsville MVLP-16	(M)	**Interlude**	1965	10.00	25.00
		—Moodsville albums above have blue labels with a trident logo on the right side.—			
Mercury MG-20722	(M)	**Impromptu**	1962	10.00	25.00
Mercury SR-60722	(S)	**Impromptu**	1962	8.00	20.00
Capitol T-2039	(M)	**Right Here, Right Now**	1963	10.00	25.00
Capitol ST-2039	(S)	**Right Here, Right Now**	1963	8.00	20.00
Capitol T-2302	(M)	**Midnight Piano**	1965	10.00	25.00
Capitol ST-2302	(S)	**Midnight Piano**	1965	8.00	20.00
New Jazz NJLP-8313	(M)	**Live! At Town Hall**	1963	*Unreleased*	
Status ST-8313	(M)	**Live! At Town Hall**	1965	16.00	40.00
		(Status 8313 is a reissue of Prestige 7093.)			
Surrey S-1033	(M)	**Easy Life**	1966	12.00	30.00
Surrey SS-1033	(S)	**Easy Life**	1966	10.00	25.00
Tower ST-5111	(S)	**I Wish I Knew**	1968	10.00	25.00

Billy Taylor started with Ben Webster in 1942 then worked with Dizzy Gillespie, Eddie South, and Stuff Smith before joining Cozy Cole (1945), Machito, Slam Stewart, and Don Redman (1946). He formed a duo with Bob Wyatt in '48 and a quartet (1949-50), that was briefly fronted by Artie Shaw as his Gramercy 5 (1950). He played Birdland with everyone and formed a successful trio in 1952. Aside from his many recordings as a leader, he has appeared as a featured guest with Erroll Garner and Ira Sullivan and as a sideman on LPs by Mundell Lowe on Riverside, Johnny Ray on Columbia, Ernie Royal on Urania, Jackie Paris on Brunswick, and with the Metronome All Stars on Verve.

Label & Catalog #		Title	Year	VG+	NM
Prestige PRST-7664	(E)	**A Touch Of Taylor**	1969	5.00	12.00
		(Prestige 7664 is a reissue of 7001.)			

—Prestige albums above have blue labels with a trident logo on top.—

TAYLOR, CECIL

Cecil Taylor is a modern jazz piano player and composer. For additional listings refer to Donald Byrd & Gigi Gryce / Cecil Taylor; Jazz Composers Orchestra.

Label & Catalog #		Title	Year	VG+	NM
Transition TRLP-19	(M)	**Jazz Advance**	1956	60.00	150.00
		(Transition 19 was issued with a booklet, worth an additional $25.)			
United Arts. UAL-4014	(M)	**Hard Driving Jazz**	1959	20.00	50.00
United Arts. UAS-5014	(S)	**Stereo Drive**	1959	16.00	40.00
		("Stereo Drive" is the stereo version of "Hard Driving Jazz." U.A. 4014 was reissued as 14001, John Coltrane's "Coltrane Time.")			
United Arts. UAL-4046	(M)	**Love For Sale**	1959	20.00	50.00
United Arts. UAS-5046	(S)	**Love For Sale**	1959	16.00	40.00
Contemporary C-3562	(M)	**Looking Ahead!**	1959	20.00	50.00
Contemporary S-7562	(S)	**Looking Ahead!**	1959	16.00	40.00
		—Contemporary stereo albums have gold & black labels.—			
Candid CD-8006	(M)	**The World Of Cecil Taylor**	1960	20.00	50.00
Candid CS-9006	(S)	**The World Of Cecil Taylor**	1960	16.00	40.00
Fantasy 6014	(M)	**Live At The Cafe Montmarte**	1964	10.00	25.00
Fantasy 86014	(S)	**Live At The Cafe Montmarte**	1964	8.00	20.00
Blue Note BLP-4237	(M)	**Unit Structures**	1966	12.00	30.00
Blue Note BST-84237	(S)	**Unit Structures**	1966	10.00	25.00
		—Blue Note albums above have blue on white labels with a New York, USA address.—			
Blue Note BST-84237	(S)	**Unit Structures**	196?	5.00	12.00
Blue Note BLP-4260	(M)	**Conquistador**	1967	12.00	30.00
Blue Note BST-84260	(S)	**Conquistador**	1967	10.00	25.00
		—Blue Note albums above have blue on white labels with "A Division of Liberty Records."—			

TAYLOR, DICK

Label & Catalog #		Title	Year	VG+	NM
Skylark SKLP-18	(10")	**Blue Moon**	1954	30.00	75.00

TAYLOR, LYNN

Lynn Taylor is a jazz-based vocalist.

Label & Catalog #		Title	Year	VG+	NM
Grand Award GA-33-???	(M)	**Lynn Taylor Sings**	195?	150.00	300.00

TAYLOR, SAM "THE MAN"

Samuel "The Man" Taylor is a traditional jazz-based tenor and baritone saxophone and clarinet player.

Label & Catalog #		Title	Year	VG+	NM
Metrojazz E-1008	(M)	**Jazz For Commuters**	1958	20.00	50.00
Metrojazz SE-1008	(S)	**Jazz For Commuters**	1958	16.00	40.00
Lion L-70054	(M)	**Sam "The Man" Taylor**	1958	10.00	25.00
MGM E-3973	(M)	**Blue Mist**	1961	12.00	30.00
MGM SE-3973	(S)	**Blue Mist**	1961	10.00	25.00
Moodsville MVLP-24	(M)	**The Bad And The Beautiful**	1962	20.00	50.00
		—Moodsville mono albums above have green labels with silver print.—			
Moodsville MVLP-24	(M)	**The Bad And The Beautiful**	1965	10.00	25.00
		—Moodsville albums above have blue labels with a trident logo on the right side.—			
Decca DL-4302	(M)	**Misty Mood**	1962	8.00	20.00
Decca DL-74302	(S)	**Misty Mood**	1962	6.00	15.00
Decca DL-4417	(M)	**It's A Blue World**	1963	8.00	20.00
Decca DL-74417	(S)	**It's A Blue World**	1963	6.00	15.00

TEAGARDEN, JACK

Weldon "Jack" Teagarden is a traditional jazz trombone player and vocalist. For additional listings refer to Red Allen & Jack Teagarden & Kid Ory; Benny Goodman & Jack Teagarden; Lionel Hampton & Jack Teagarden; Bobby Hackett; Rex Stewart; and the Various Artists section under Verve.

Label & Catalog #		Title	Year	VG+	NM
Royale 18156	(10")	**The Blues**	195?	30.00	75.00
Commodore 20015	(10")	**Big T**	195?	30.00	75.00
Urania UJLP-1001	(10")	**Meet The New Jack Teagarden**	1954	30.00	75.00
Urania UJLP-1002	(10")	**Jack Teagarden Sings And Plays**	1954	30.00	75.00
Period SLP-1106	(10")	**Meet Me Where They Play The Blues**	1955	30.00	75.00
Period SLP-1110	(10")	**Original Dixieland**	1955	30.00	75.00
Jolly Roger 5026	(10")	**Jack Teagarden**	1955	20.00	50.00
Bethlehem BCP-32	(M)	**Jazz Great**	1955	20.00	50.00
Decca DL-8304	(M)	**Big T's Jazz**	1956	16.00	40.00

Label & Catalog #		Title	Year	VG+	NM
Decca DL-4540	*(M)*	**The Golden Horn Of Jack Teagarden**	*1964*	**6.00**	**15.00**
Decca DL-74540	*(S)*	**The Golden Horn Of Jack Teagarden**	*1964*	**5.00**	**12.00**
Capitol T-721	*(M)*	**This Is Teagarden**	*1956*	**16.00**	**40.00**
Capitol T-820	*(M)*	**Swing Low Sweet Spiritual**	*1957*	**16.00**	**40.00**
		— Capitol albums above have turquoise labels.—			
Capitol T-1095	*(M)*	**Big T's Dixieland Band**	*1959*	**10.00**	**25.00**
Capitol ST-1095	*(S)*	**Big T's Dixieland Band**	*1959*	**8.00**	**20.00**
Capitol T-1143	*(M)*	**Shades Of Night**	*1959*	**10.00**	**25.00**
Capitol ST-1143	*(S)*	**Shades Of Night**	*1959*	**8.00**	**20.00**
		— Capitol albums above have black "rainbow" labels with the logo on the left side.—			
Rondo-lette A-18	*(M)*	**The Blues And Dixie**	*1958*	**10.00**	**25.00**
Verve V-8416	*(M)*	**Mis'ry And The Blues**	*1961*	**8.00**	**20.00**
Verve V6-8416	*(S)*	**Mis'ry And The Blues**	*1961*	**6.00**	**15.00**
Verve V-8465	*(M)*	**Think Well Of Me**	*1962*	**8.00**	**20.00**
Verve V6-8465	*(S)*	**Think Well Of Me**	*1962*	**6.00**	**15.00**
Verve V-8495	*(M)*	**Jack Teagarden!!**	*1962*	**8.00**	**20.00**
Verve V6-8495	*(S)*	**Jack Teagarden!!**	*1962*	**6.00**	**15.00**
		— Verve albums above have black labels with "MGM Records" on the bottom.—			
Roulette R-25091	*(M)*	**Jack Teagarden At The Round Table**	*1960*	**8.00**	**20.00**
Roulette SR-25091	*(S)*	**Jack Teagarden At The Round Table**	*1960*	**6.00**	**15.00**
Roulette R-25119	*(M)*	**Jazz Maverick**	*1961*	**8.00**	**20.00**
Roulette SR-25119	*(S)*	**Jazz Maverick**	*1961*	**6.00**	**15.00**
Roulette R-25177	*(M)*	**Dixie Sound**	*1962*	**8.00**	**20.00**
Roulette SR-25177	*(S)*	**Dixie Sound**	*1962*	**6.00**	**15.00**
Roulette R-25243	*(M)*	**Portrait Of Mr. T**	*1963*	**8.00**	**20.00**
Roulette SR-25243	*(S)*	**Portrait Of Mr. T**	*1963*	**6.00**	**15.00**
Epic LN-6044	*(M)*	**King Of The Blues Trombone** *(3 LPs)*	*1963*	**30.00**	**75.00**
Epic LN-24045	*(M)*	**King Of The Blues Trombone—Vol. 1**	*1963*	**10.00**	**25.00**
Epic LN-24046	*(M)*	**King Of The Blues Trombone—Vol. 2**	*1963*	**10.00**	**25.00**
Epic LN-24047	*(M)*	**King Of The Blues Trombone—Vol. 3**	*1963*	**10.00**	**25.00**
		(Epic 24045-47 reissue 6044.)			
Columbia JSN-6044	*(M)*	**King Of The Blues Trombone** *(3 LPs)*	*196?*	**10.00**	**25.00**
		(Columbia Special Products reissue of Epic 6044.)			
RCA Victor LPV-528	*(M)*	**Jack Teagarden**	*1965*	**8.00**	**20.00**

TEAGARDEN, JACK / BOBBY HACKETT

Commodore FL-30012	*(M)*	**Jack Teagarden And Bobby Hackett**	*1959*	**12.00**	**30.00**

TEAGARDEN, JACK / JONAH JONES

Bethlehem BCP-6042	*(M)*	**Dixieland**	*1959*	**16.00**	**40.00**

TEAGARDEN, JACK / PEE WEE RUSSELL

Riverside RLP-12-141		**Jack Teagarden's Big Eight / Pee Wee Russell's Rhythmakers**	*1956*	**24.00**	**60.00**
		— Riverside albums above have blue on white labels.—			

TEMPLETON, ALEC

Alec Templeton is a traditional jazz-based pianist.

Atlantic 1222	*(M)*	**The Magic Piano**	*1956*	**16.00**	**40.00**
		— Atlantic albums above have black mono or green stereo labels.—			
Atlantic 1222	*(M)*	**The Magic Piano**	*1961*	**8.00**	**20.00**
		— Atlantic albums above have multi-color labels with a white fan logo.—			

TERRACE, PETE

Fantasy 3203	*(M)*	**Going Loco** *(Dark red vinyl)*	*1956*	**20.00**	**50.00**
Fantasy 3203	*(M)*	**Going Loco**	*195?*	**10.00**	**25.00**
Fantasy 3215	*(M)*	**Invitation To The Mambo** *(Dark red vinyl)*	*1956*	**20.00**	**50.00**
Fantasy 3215	*(M)*	**Invitation To The Mambo**	*195?*	**10.00**	**25.00**
Fantasy 3234	*(M)*	**The Pete Terrace Quintet** *(Dark red vinyl)*	*1957*	**20.00**	**50.00**
Fantasy 3234	*(M)*	**The Pete Terrace Quintet**	*195?*	**10.00**	**25.00**
		— Fantasy albums above have red labels on non-flexible vinyl.—			

TERRY, BUDDY

Prestige PRLP-7525	*(M)*	**Electric Soul**	*1967*	**10.00**	**25.00**
Prestige PRST-7525	*(S)*	**Electric Soul**	*1967*	**8.00**	**20.00**
Prestige PRLP-7541	*(M)*	**Natural Soul**	*1967*	**10.00**	**25.00**
Prestige PRST-7541	*(S)*	**Natural Soul**	*1967*	**8.00**	**20.00**
		— Prestige albums above have blue labels with a trident logo on the right side.—			

Clark Terry played briefly with Lionel Hampton before joining George Hudson in 1945. Moving to California, he played with Charlie Barnett, Eddie Vinson, Charlie Ventura, again with Hudson, and then Count Basie from 1948-51. This was followed by a lengthy stay with Duke Ellington (1951-59) before moving onto Quincy Jones. He has recorded with Coleman Hawkins, as a member of The Riverside Jazz Stars, and as a featured guest with Clea Bradford, Al Caiola, Budd Johnson, and Teri Thornton. As a sideman he can be heard on LPs by Basie on Columbia, Ellington on Columbia, Capitol and Bethlehem, Billy Taylor, Paul Gonsalves, and Jimmy Woods, each on Argo, Wardell Grey on Prestige, and both Dinah Washington and Quincy Jones on Mercury.

Label & Catalog #		Title	Year	VG+	NM

TERRY, CLARK

Clark Terry is a modern jazz trumpet and flugel horn player. For additional listings refer to Clea Bradford; Gary Burton / Sonny Rollins / Clark Terry; Al Caiola; Kenny Dorham & Clark Terry; Coleman Hawkins & Clark Terry; Budd Johnson; The Riverside Jazz Stars; Shirley Scott & Clark Terry; Teri Thornton.

Label & Catalog #		Title	Year	VG+	NM
Wing MGW-60002	(M)	**The Jazz School**	1955	30.00	75.00
EmArcy MG-36007	(M)	**Clark Terry**	1955	30.00	75.00
EmArcy MG-36093	(M)	**The Jazz School**	1956	24.00	60.00
		(EmArcy 30093 is a reissue of Wing 60002.)			
		—EmArcy albums above have blue labels with silver print.—			
Argo LP-620	(M)	**Out On A Limb**	1957	20.00	50.00
Riverside RLP-12-237	(M)	**Serenade To A Bus Seat**	1957	60.00	150.00
		—Riverside albums above have blue on white labels.—			
Riverside RLP-12-237	(M)	**Serenade To A Bus Seat**	1957	16.00	40.00
Riverside RLP-12-246	(M)	**Duke With A Difference**	1957	40.00	100.00
Riverside RLP-1108	(S)	**Duke With A Difference**	1959	30.00	75.00
Riverside RLP-12-271	(M)	**In Orbit**	1958	40.00	100.00
		(Riverside 271 also features Thelonoius Monk.)			
Riverside RLP-12-295	(M)	**Top And Bottom Brass**	1959	40.00	100.00
Riverside RLP-1137	(S)	**Top And Bottom Brass**	1959	30.00	75.00
		—Riverside albums above have blue mono or black stereo labels with a reel & mike logo on top.—			
Candid CD-8009	(M)	**Color Changes**	1960	20.00	50.00
Candid CS-9009	(S)	**Color Changes**	1960	16.00	40.00
Moodsville MVLP-20	(M)	**Everything's Mellow**	1961	20.00	50.00
Moodsville MVLP-26	(M)	**The Jazz Version Of "All American"**	1962	20.00	50.00
		—Moodsville mono albums above have green labels with silver print.—			
Moodsville MVLP-20	(M)	**Everything's Mellow**	1965	10.00	25.00
Moodsville MVLP-26	(M)	**The Jazz Version Of "All American"**	1965	10.00	25.00
		—Moodsville albums above have blue labels with a trident logo on the right side.—			
20th Cent. Fox TFM-3137	(M)	**What Makes Sammy Swing**	1963	10.00	25.00
20th Cent. Fox TFS-4137	(S)	**What Makes Sammy Swing**	1963	8.00	20.00
Cameo C-1064	(M)	**More**	1964	16.00	40.00
Cameo CS-1064	(S)	**More**	1964	12.00	30.00
Cameo C-1071	(M)	**Tread Ye Lightly**	1964	16.00	40.00
Cameo CS-1071	(S)	**Tread Ye Lightly**	1964	12.00	30.00
Mainstream 56043	(M)	**Clark Terry Tonight**	1965	10.00	25.00
Mainstream S-6043	(S)	**Clark Terry Tonight**	1965	8.00	20.00
		(Mainstram 56043 also features Bob Brookmeyer.)			
Mainstream 56054	(M)	**The Power Of Positive Swinging**	1965	10.00	25.00
Mainstream S-6054	(S)	**The Power Of Positive Swinging**	1965	8.00	20.00
Mainstream 56066	(M)	**Mumbles**	1966	10.00	25.00
Mainstream S-6066	(S)	**Mumbles**	1966	8.00	20.00
Impulse A-64	(M)	**The Happy Horn Of Clark Terry**	1964	12.00	30.00
Impulse AS-64	(S)	**The Happy Horn Of Clark Terry**	1964	10.00	25.00
Impulse A-9127	(M)	**Spanish Rice**	1966	12.00	30.00
Impulse AS-9127	(S)	**Spanish Rice**	1966	10.00	25.00
		—Impulse albums above have orange & black labels.—			
Impulse AS-64	(S)	**The Happy Horn Of Clark Terry**	1968	4.00	10.00
Impulse AS-9127	(S)	**Spanish Rice**	1968	4.00	10.00
Impulse AS-9157	(S)	**It's What's Happenin'**	1968	6.00	15.00
		—Impulse albums above have red & black labels with the "abc" logo on top.—			
Riverside RS-3009	(M)	**C.T. Meets Monk**	1967	8.00	20.00
Riverside RS-3009	(S)	**C.T. Meets Monk**	1967	6.00	15.00
		(Riverside 3009 is a reisue of 271.)			

TERRY, CLARK / COLEMAN HAWKINS

Label & Catalog #		Title	Year	VG+	NM
Colpix CP-450	(M)	**Eddie Costa Memorial Concert**	1963	16.00	40.00
Colpix SCP-450	(S)	**Eddie Costa Memorial Concert**	1963	20.00	50.00

TESCHEMACHER, FRANK

Frank "Tesch" Teschemacher is a traditional jazz clarinet, alto saxophone and violin player and arranger. For additional listings refer to Muggsy Spanier.

Label & Catalog #		Title	Year	VG+	NM
Brunswick BL-58017	(10")	**Tesch Plays Jazz Classics**	1950	30.00	75.00

THESELIUS, GOESTA

Swedish born Goesta Theselius is a traditional jazz-based piano and tenor saxophone player and composer.

Label & Catalog #		Title	Year	VG+	NM
Bally BAL-12002	(M)	**Swedish Jazz**	1956	20.00	50.00

Label & Catalog #		Title	Year	VG+	NM

THIELEMANS, TOOTS

Belgium born Jean "Toots" Thielmans is a jazz-based harmonica player.

Columbia CL-658	(M)	**The Sound**	1955	20.00	50.00

—Columbia albums above have six white on black "eye" logos on each label.—

Riverside RLP-12-257	(M)	**Man Bites Harmonica**	1958	40.00	100.00

—Riverside albums above have blue mono or black stereo labels with a reel & mike logo on top.—

Decca DL-9204	(M)	**Time Out For Toots**	1958	20.00	50.00
Decca DL-79204	(S)	**Time Out For Toots**	1958	16.00	40.00
Signature SM-6006	(M)	**The Soul Of Toots Thielmans**	1960	30.00	75.00
Signature SS-6006	(S)	**The Soul Of Toots Thielmans**	1960	20.00	50.00
ABC-Paramount ABC-482	(M)	**The Whistler And His Guitar**	1965	12.00	30.00
ABC-Paramount ABCS-482	(S)	**The Whistler And His Guitar**	1965	10.00	25.00

THIGPEN, ED

Edward Thigpen is a modern jazz drummer. For additional listings refer to the Various Artists section under Prestige.

Verve V-8663	(M)	**Out Of The Storm**	1966	8.00	20.00
Verve V6-8663	(S)	**Out Of The Storm**	1966	6.00	15.00

(Verve 8663 also features Kenny Burrell.)

THOMAS, JEANNIE

Jeanne Thomas is a jazz-based vocalist,

Strand SL-1030	(M)	**Jeannie Thomas Sings For The Boys**	1961	16.00	40.00
Strand SLS-1030	(S)	**Jeannie Thomas Sings For The Boys**	1961	16.00	40.00

THOMAS, JOE: *Refer to* VIC DICKENSON & JOE THOMAS

THOMAS, PAT

Singer Pat Thomas is backed by a small jazz group.

Strand SL-1015	(M)	**Jazz Patterns**	1960	20.00	50.00
Strand SLS-1015	(S)	**Jazz Patterns**	1960	20.00	50.00

THOMAS, RENE

Rene Thomas is a modern jazz-based guitarist.

Jazzland JLP-27	(M)	**Guitar Groove**	1960	16.00	40.00
Jazzland JLP-927	(S)	**Guitar Groove**	1960	12.00	30.00

THOMPSON, "SIR" CHARLES

Charles Thompson is a traditional jazz piano and organ player and arranger. For additional listings refer to The Manhattan Jazz All-Stars.

Apollo 103	(10")	**Sir Charles Thompson And His All Stars**	1951	240.00	400.00
Vanguard VRS-8003	(10")	**Sir Charles Thompson Sextet**	1953	40.00	100.00
Vanguard VRS-8006	(10")	**Sir Charles Thompson Quartet**	1954	40.00	100.00
Vanguard VRS-8009	(10")	**Sir Charles Thompson And His Band**	1954	50.00	125.00
Vanguard VRS-8018	(10")	**Sir Charles Thompson Trio**	1955	40.00	100.00
Columbia CL-1364	(M)	**Sir Charles Thompson And The Swing Organ**	1959	12.00	30.00
Columbia CS-8205	(S)	**Sir Charles Thompson And The Swing Organ**	1959	10.00	25.00
Columbia CL-1663	(M)	**Rockin' Rhythm**	1961	12.00	30.00
Columbia CS-8463	(S)	**Rockin' Rhythm**	1961	10.00	25.00

—Columbia albums above have six white on black "eye" logos on each label.—

THOMPSON, LES

RCA Victor LPT-3102	(10")	**Gene Norman Presents "Just Jazz"**	1952	60.00	150.00

THOMPSON, LUCKY

Eli "Lucky" Thompson is a big band and modern jazz tenor and soprano saxophone player. For additional listings refer to The Modern Jazz Society.

Top L-928	(10")	**Jazz At The Auditorium**	1954	50.00	125.00
Urania UJLP-1206	(M)	**Accent On Tenor**	1955	40.00	100.00
Transition TRLP-21	(M)	**Lucky Strikes**	1956	100.00	200.00

(Transition 21 was issued with a booklet, worth an additional $25.)

London D-93098	(10")	**Recorded In Paris '56**	1956	30.00	75.00
ABC-Paramount ABC-111	(M)	**Lucky Thompson Featuring Oscar Pettiford—Volume 1**	1956	30.00	75.00
ABC-Paramount ABC-171	(M)	**Lucky Thompson Featuring Oscar Pettiford—Volume 2**	1957	30.00	75.00
Dawn DLP-1113	(M)	**Lucky Thompson**	1957	30.00	75.00

Label & Catalog #		Title	Year	VG+	NM
Moodsville MVLP-39	(M)	**Lucky Thompson Plays Jerome Kern And No More**	1963	20.00	50.00
Moodsville MVST-39	(S)	**Lucky Thompson Plays Jerome Kern And No More**	1963	16.00	40.00
		—Moodsville mono albums above have green labels with silver print.—			
Moodsville MVLP-39	(M)	**Lucky Thompson Plays Jerome Kern And No More**	1965	10.00	25.00
Moodsville MVST-39	(S)	**Lucky Thompson Plays Jerome Kern And No More**	1965	8.00	20.00
		—Moodsville albums above have blue labels with a trident logo on the right side.—			
Prestige PRLP-7365	(M)	**Lucky Strikes**	1965	12.00	30.00
Prestige PRST-7365	(S)	**Lucky Strikes**	1965	10.00	25.00
Prestige PRLP-7394	(M)	**Happy Days Are Here Again**	1965	12.00	30.00
Prestige PRST-7394	(S)	**Happy Days Are Here Again**	1965	10.00	25.00
		—Prestige albums above have blue labels with a trident logo on the right side.—			
Rivoli 40	(M)	**Lucky Is Back!**	1965	12.00	30.00
Rivoli 40	(S)	**Lucky Is Back!**	1965	10.00	25.00
Rivoli 44	(M)	**Kinfolk's Corner**	1965	12.00	30.00
Rivoli 44	(S)	**Kinfolk's Corner**	1965	10.00	25.00

THORNE, FRAN

Francis Thorne Jr. is a modern jazz pianist.

Label & Catalog #		Title	Year	VG+	NM
Transition TRLP-27	(M)	**Piano Reflections**	1956	60.00	150.00
		(Transition 27 was issued with a booklet, worth an additional $25.)			

THORNHILL, CLAUDE

Claude Thornhill is a traditional jazz pianist, arranger, composer and band leader.

Label & Catalog #		Title	Year	VG+	NM
Columbia CL-6035	(10")	**Piano Reflections**	1949	30.00	75.00
Columbia CL-6050	(10")	**Dance Parade**	1949	30.00	75.00
Columbia CL-6164	(10")	**Claude Thornhill Encores**	1951	30.00	75.00
Trend TL-1001	(10")	**Dream Stuff**	1953	30.00	75.00
Trend TL-1002	(10")	**Claude Thornhill Plays The Great Jazz Arrangements Of Gerry Mulligan And Ralph Aldrich**	1953	30.00	75.00
Columbia CL-709	(M)	**Dancing After Midnight**	1955	16.00	40.00
		—Columbia albums above have three white on black "eye" logos on each side of each label.—			
Harmony HL-7088	(M)	**The Thornhill Sound**	1957	10.00	25.00
Camden CAL-307	(M)	**Dinner For Two**	1958	10.00	25.00
Kapp KL-1058	(M)	**Two Sides Of Claude Thornhill**	1958	12.00	30.00
Kapp KS-5058	(S)	**Two Sides Of Claude Thornhill**	1958	10.00	25.00
Decca DL-8722	(M)	**Claude On A Cloud**	1958	12.00	30.00
Decca DL-78722	(S)	**Claude On A Cloud**	1958	10.00	25.00
Decca DL-8878	(M)	**Dance To The Sound Of Claude Thornhill**	1958	12.00	30.00
Decca DL-78878	(S)	**Dance To The Sound Of Claude Thornhill**	1958	10.00	25.00

THORNTON, CLIFFORD

Label & Catalog #		Title	Year	VG+	NM
Third World 9636	(S)	**Freedom And Unity**	1969	6.00	15.00

THORNTON, TERI

Teri Thornton is a jazz-based vocalist.

Label & Catalog #		Title	Year	VG+	NM
Riverside RLP-352	(M)	**Devil May Care**	1961	16.00	40.00
Riverside RS-9352	(S)	**Devil May Care**	1961	12.00	30.00
		(Riverside 352 also features Seldon Powell and Clark Terry.)			
		—Riverside albums above have blue mono or black stereo labels with a reel & mike logo on top.—			
Columbia CL-2094	(M)	**Open Highway**	1963	16.00	40.00
Columbia CS-8894	(S)	**Open Highway**	1963	12.00	30.00
		—Columbia albums above have "Guaranteed High Fidelity" or "360 Sound Stereo" in black on the label.—			
Dauntless DM-4306	(M)	**Somewhere In The Night**	1963	12.00	30.00
Dauntless DS-6306	(S)	**Somewhere In The Night**	1963	10.00	25.00
Riverside RM-3525	(M)	**Lullabye Of The Leaves**	1964	12.00	30.00
Riverside RS-93525	(S)	**Lullabye Of The Leaves**	1964	10.00	25.00

THREE SOULS, THE

The Three Souls—Henry Cain, Albert Coleman and Will Scott—are a modern jazz group.

Label & Catalog #		Title	Year	VG+	NM
Argo LP-4005	(M)	**Almost Like Being In Love**	1960	10.00	25.00
Argo LPS-4005	(S)	**Almost Like Being In Love**	1960	8.00	20.00
Argo LP-4036	(M)	**Dangerous Dan Express**	1964	10.00	25.00
Argo LPS-4036	(S)	**Dangerous Dan Express**	1964	8.00	20.00

Label & Catalog #		Title	Year	VG+	NM
Argo LP-4044	(M)	**Soul Sounds**	1965	10.00	25.00
Argo LPS-4044	(S)	**Soul Sounds**	1965	8.00	20.00

THREE SOUNDS, THE

The Three Sounds—Bill Dowdy, Gene Harris and Andrew Simpkins—are a modern jazz vocal group. For additional listings refer to Nat Adderley; Lou Donaldson; Anita O'Day; Stanley Turrentine.

Label & Catalog #		Title	Year	VG+	NM
Blue Note BLP-1600	(M)	**Introducing The Three Sounds** *(Deep groove)*	1958	50.00	125.00
Blue Note BLP-1600	(M)	**Introducing The Three Sounds**	1958	30.00	75.00
Blue Note BST-1600	(S)	**Introducing The Three Sounds** *(Deep groove)*	1959	30.00	75.00
Blue Note BST-1600	(S)	**Introducing The Three Sounds**	1959	20.00	50.00
Blue Note BLP-4014	(M)	**Bottoms Up** *(Deep groove)*	1959	50.00	125.00
Blue Note BLP-4014	(M)	**Bottoms Up**	1959	30.00	75.00
Blue Note BST-4014	(S)	**Bottoms Up** *(Deep groove)*	1959	30.00	75.00
Blue Note BST-4014	(S)	**Bottoms Up**	1959	20.00	50.00
Blue Note BLP-4020	(M)	**Good Deal** *(Deep groove)*	1959	50.00	125.00
Blue Note BLP-4020	(M)	**Good Deal**	1959	30.00	75.00
Blue Note BST-84020	(S)	**Good Deal**	1959	20.00	50.00
Blue Note BLP-4044	(M)	**Moods** *(Deep groove)*	1960	50.00	125.00
Blue Note BLP-4044	(M)	**Moods**	1960	30.00	75.00
Blue Note BST-84044	(S)	**Moods**	1960	20.00	50.00
Blue Note BLP-4072	(M)	**Feelin' Good**	1961	30.00	75.00
Blue Note BST-84072	(S)	**Feelin' Good**	1961	20.00	50.00
—Blue Note albums above have blue on white labels with a W. 63rd St., NYC address.—					
Blue Note BLP-4088	(M)	**Here We Come**	1961	30.00	75.00
Blue Note BST-84088	(S)	**Here We Come**	1961	20.00	50.00
—Blue Note albums above have blue on white labels with a 61st St., NYC address.—					
Blue Note BLP-1600	(M)	**Introducing The Three Sounds**	1963	10.00	25.00
Blue Note BST-1600	(S)	**Introducing The Three Sounds**	1963	8.00	20.00
Blue Note BLP-4014	(M)	**Bottoms Up**	1963	10.00	25.00
Blue Note BST-4014	(S)	**Bottoms Up**	1963	8.00	20.00
Blue Note BLP-4020	(M)	**Good Deal**	1963	10.00	25.00
Blue Note BST-84020	(S)	**Good Deal**	1963	8.00	20.00
Blue Note BLP-4044	(M)	**Moods**	1963	10.00	25.00
Blue Note BST-84044	(S)	**Moods**	1963	8.00	20.00
Blue Note BLP-4072	(M)	**Feelin' Good**	1963	10.00	25.00
Blue Note BST-84072	(S)	**Feelin' Good**	1963	8.00	20.00
Blue Note BLP-4088	(M)	**Here We Come**	1963	10.00	25.00
Blue Note BST-84088	(S)	**Here We Come**	1963	8.00	20.00
Blue Note BLP-4102	(M)	**Hey! There**	1962	12.00	30.00
Blue Note BST-84102	(S)	**Hey! There**	1962	10.00	25.00
Blue Note BLP-4120	(M)	**It Just Got To Be**	1963	12.00	30.00
Blue Note BST-84120	(S)	**It Just Got To Be**	1963	10.00	25.00
Blue Note BLP-4155	(M)	**Black Orchid**	1963	12.00	30.00
Blue Note BST-84155	(S)	**Black Orchid**	1963	10.00	25.00
Blue Note BLP-4197	(M)	**Out Of This World**	1965	12.00	30.00
Blue Note BST-84197	(S)	**Out Of This World**	1965	10.00	25.00
Blue Note BLP-4248	(M)	**Vibrations**	1966	12.00	30.00
Blue Note BST-84248	(S)	**Vibrations**	1966	10.00	25.00
—Blue Note albums above have blue on white labels with a New York, USA address.—					
Blue Note BST-81600	(S)	**Introducing The Three Sounds**	196?	5.00	12.00
Blue Note BST-84014	(S)	**Bottoms Up**	196?	5.00	12.00
Blue Note BST-84020	(S)	**Good Deal**	196?	5.00	12.00
Blue Note BST-84044	(S)	**Moods**	196?	5.00	12.00
Blue Note BST-84072	(S)	**Feelin' Good**	196?	5.00	12.00
Blue Note BST-84088	(S)	**Here We Come**	1961	5.00	12.00
Blue Note BST-84102	(S)	**Hey! There**	196?	5.00	12.00
Blue Note BST-84120	(S)	**It Just Got To Be**	196?	5.00	12.00
Blue Note BST-84155	(S)	**Black Orchid**	196?	5.00	12.00
Blue Note BST-84197	(S)	**Out Of This World**	196?	5.00	12.00
Blue Note BST-84248	(S)	**Vibrations**	196?	5.00	12.00
Blue Note BLP-4265	(M)	**Live At The Lighthouse**	1967	10.00	25.00
Blue Note BST-84265	(S)	**Live At The Lighthouse**	1967	8.00	20.00
Blue Note BST-84285	(S)	**Coldwater Flat**	1968	8.00	20.00
Blue Note BST-84301	(S)	**Elegant Soul**	1968	8.00	20.00
		(Blue Note 84301 credits Gene Harris & His Three Sounds.)			
Blue Note BST-84341	(S)	**Soul Symphony**	1969	8.00	20.00
—Blue Note albums above have blue on white labels with "A Division of Liberty Records."—					

Label & Catalog #		Title	Year	VG+	NM
Verve V-8513	(M)	**Blue Genes**	1963	12.00	30.00
Verve V6-8513	(S)	**Blue Genes**	1963	10.00	25.00
		—Verve albums above have black labels with "MGM Records" on the bottom.—			
Mercury MG-20776	(M)	**Jazz On Broadway**	1963	12.00	30.00
Mercury SR-60776	(S)	**Jazz On Broadway**	1963	10.00	25.00
Mercury MG-20839	(M)	**Some Like It Modern**	1963	12.00	30.00
Mercury SR-60839	(S)	**Some Like It Modern**	1963	10.00	25.00
Mercury MG-20921	(M)	**Live At The Living Room**	1963	12.00	30.00
Mercury SR-60921	(S)	**Live At The Living Room**	1963	10.00	25.00
		—Mercury albums above have silver on black labels.—			
Limelight LM-82014	(M)	**Three Moods**	1965	10.00	25.00
Limelight LS-86014	(S)	**Three Moods**	1965	8.00	20.00
Limelight LM-82026	(M)	**Beautiful Friendship**	1965	10.00	25.00
Limelight LS-86026	(S)	**Beautiful Friendship**	1965	8.00	20.00

TIMMONS, BOBBY

Robert Timmons is a modern jazz pianist. For additional listings refer to Joe Alexander & Bobby Timmons; Art Blakey & The Jazz Messengers; John Jenkins & Cliff Jordan & Bobby Timmons; The Riverside Jazz Stars; The Young Lions.

Label & Catalog #		Title	Year	VG+	NM
Riverside RLP-12-317	(M)	**This Here Is Bobby Timmons**	1960	16.00	40.00
Riverside RLP-1164	(S)	**This Here Is Bobby Timmons**	1960	12.00	30.00
Riverside RLP-334	(M)	**Soul Time**	1960	16.00	40.00
Riverside RS-9334	(S)	**Soul Time**	1960	12.00	30.00
Riverside RLP-363	(M)	**Easy Does It**	1961	12.00	30.00
Riverside RS-9363	(S)	**Easy Does It**	1961	10.00	25.00
Riverside RLP-391	(M)	**The Bobby Timmons Trio In Person— Recorded 'Live' At The Village Vanguard**	1961	12.00	30.00
Riverside RS-9391	(S)	**The Bobby Timmons Trio In Person— Recorded 'Live' At The Village Vanguard**	1961	10.00	25.00
Riverside RLP-422	(M)	**Sweet And Soulful Sounds**	1962	12.00	30.00
Riverside RS-9422	(S)	**Sweet And Soulful Sounds**	1962	10.00	25.00
Riverside RLP-468	(M)	**Born To Be Blue!**	1963	12.00	30.00
Riverside RS-9468	(S)	**Born To Be Blue!**	1963	10.00	25.00
		—Riverside albums above have blue mono or black stereo labels with a reel & mike logo on top.—			
Prestige PRLP-7335	(M)	**Little Barefoot Soul**	1964	12.00	30.00
Prestige PRST-7335	(S)	**Little Barefoot Soul**	1964	10.00	25.00
Prestige PRLP-7351	(M)	**Chun-King**	1965	12.00	30.00
Prestige PRST-7351	(S)	**Chun-King**	1965	10.00	25.00
Prestige PRLP-7387	(M)	**Workin' Out**	1966	12.00	30.00
Prestige PRST-7387	(S)	**Workin' Out**	1966	10.00	25.00
Prestige PRLP-7414	(M)	**Holiday Soul**	1966	10.00	25.00
Prestige PRST-7414	(S)	**Holiday Soul**	1966	8.00	20.00
Prestige PRLP-7429	(M)	**Chicken & Dumplin's**	1966	8.00	20.00
Prestige PRST-7429	(S)	**Chicken & Dumplin's**	1966	6.00	15.00
Prestige PRLP-7465	(M)	**Soul Man**	1967	8.00	20.00
Prestige PRST-7465	(S)	**Soul Man**	1967	6.00	15.00
Prestige PRLP-7483	(M)	**Soul Food**	1967	8.00	20.00
Prestige PRST-7483	(S)	**Soul Food**	1967	6.00	15.00
		—Prestige albums above have blue labels with a trident logo on the right side.—			
Milestone MSP-9011	(S)	**Got To Get It**	1969	6.00	15.00
Milestone MSP-9020	(S)	**Do You Know The Way**	1969	6.00	15.00

TJADER, CAL

Callen Tjader Jr. is a modern jazz vibraphone player associated with Latin jazz. For additional listings refer to Dave Brubeck; Don Elliott / Cal Tjader; Anita O' Day; Mary Stallings.

Label & Catalog #		Title	Year	VG+	NM
Savoy MG-9036	(10")	**Cal Tjader—Vibist**	1954	40.00	100.00
Fantasy 3-9	(10")	**The Cal Tjader Trio** *(Colored vinyl)*	1953	60.00	150.00
Fantasy 3-9	(10")	**The Cal Tjader Trio**	1953	40.00	100.00
Fantasy 3-17	(10")	**Ritmo Caliente** *(Colored vinyl)*	1954	60.00	150.00
Fantasy 3-17	(10")	**Ritmo Caliente**	1954	40.00	100.00
Fantasy 3202	(M)	**Mambo With Tjader**	1955	30.00	75.00
Fantasy 3211	(M)	**Tjader Plays Tjazz**	1956	30.00	75.00
Fantasy 3216	(M)	**Ritmo Caliente**	1956	30.00	75.00
Fantasy 3221	(M)	**Tjader Plays Mambo**	1956	30.00	75.00
Fantasy 3227	(M)	**Cal Tjader Quartet**	1956	30.00	75.00
Fantasy 3232	(M)	**The Cal Tjader Quintet**	1956	30.00	75.00
		—Fantasy 12" albums above have red labels on dark red, non-flexible vinyl.—			

Label & Catalog #		Title	Year	VG+	NM
Fantasy 3202	(M)	**Mambo With Tjader**	195?	10.00	25.00
Fantasy 3211	(M)	**Tjader Plays Tjazz**	195?	10.00	25.00
Fantasy 3216	(M)	**Ritmo Caliente**	195?	10.00	25.00
Fantasy 8077	(E)	**Ritmo Caliente** *(Blue vinyl)*	1962	12.00	30.00
Fantasy 8077	(E)	**Ritmo Caliente**	1962	6.00	15.00
Fantasy 3221	(M)	**Tjader Plays Mambo**	1956	10.00	25.00
Fantasy 3232	(M)	**The Cal Tjader Quintet**	1956	10.00	25.00
Fantasy 3241	(M)	**Jazz At The Blackhawk** *(Red vinyl)*	1958	20.00	50.00
Fantasy 3241	(M)	**Jazz At The Blackhawk**	1957	12.00	30.00
Fantasy 3250	(M)	**Latin Kick** *(Red vinyl)*	1958	20.00	50.00
Fantasy 3250	(M)	**Latin Kick**	1957	12.00	30.00
Fantasy 8033	(S)	**Latin Kick** *(Blue vinyl)*	1962	12.00	30.00
Fantasy 8033	(S)	**Latin Kick**	1962	8.00	20.00
Fantasy 3262	(M)	**Mass Ritmo Caliente** *(Red vinyl)*	1958	20.00	50.00
Fantasy 3262	(M)	**Mass Ritmo Caliente**	1958	12.00	30.00
Fantasy 8003	(S)	**Mass Ritmo Caliente** *(Blue vinyl)*	1962	12.00	30.00
Fantasy 8003	(S)	**Mass Ritmo Caliente**	1962	8.00	20.00
Fantasy 3266	(M)	**Cal Tjader-Stan Getz Sextet** *(Red vinyl)*	1958	20.00	50.00
Fantasy 3266	(M)	**Cal Tjader-Stan Getz Sextet**	1958	12.00	30.00
Fantasy 8005	(S)	**Cal Tjader-Stan Getz Sextet** *(Blue vinyl)*	1962	12.00	30.00
Fantasy 8005	(S)	**Cal Tjader-Stan Getz Sextet**	1962	8.00	20.00
Fantasy 3271	(M)	**San Francisco Moods** *(Red vinyl)*	1958	20.00	50.00
Fantasy 3271	(M)	**San Francisco Moods**	1958	12.00	30.00
Fantasy 8017	(S)	**San Francisco Moods** *(Blue vinyl)*	1962	12.00	30.00
Fantasy 8017	(S)	**San Francisco Moods**	1962	8.00	20.00
Fantasy 3275	(M)	**Latin Concert** *(Red vinyl)*	1958	20.00	50.00
Fantasy 3275	(M)	**Latin Concert**	1959	12.00	30.00
Fantasy 8014	(S)	**Latin Concert** *(Blue vinyl)*	1962	12.00	30.00
Fantasy 8014	(S)	**Latin Concert**	1962	8.00	20.00
Fantasy 3278	(M)	**Tjader Plays Tjazz** *(Red vinyl)*	1958	20.00	50.00
Fantasy 3278	(M)	**Tjader Plays Tjazz**	1958	12.00	30.00
		(Fantasy 3278 is a reissue of 11.)			
Fantasy 8097	(E)	**Tjader Plays Tjazz** *(Blue vinyl)*	1962	12.00	30.00
Fantasy 8097	(E)	**Tjader Plays Tjazz**	1962	6.00	15.00
Fantasy 3279	(M)	**Latin For Lovers** *(Red vinyl)*	1958	20.00	50.00
Fantasy 3279	(M)	**Latin For Lovers**	1958	12.00	30.00
Fantasy 8016	(S)	**Latin For Lovers** *(Blue vinyl)*	1962	12.00	30.00
Fantasy 8016	(S)	**Latin For Lovers**	1962	8.00	20.00
Fantasy 8019	(S)	**Latin For Dancers**	1962	*See below*	
		(This stereo title was listed in catalogs but may not have been released.)			
Fantasy 3283	(M)	**Jazz At Blackhawk** *(Red vinyl)*	1959	20.00	50.00
Fantasy 3283	(M)	**Jazz At Blackhawk**	1959	12.00	30.00
Fantasy 8026	(S)	**Jazz At The Blackhawk** *(Blue vinyl)*	1962	12.00	30.00
Fantasy 8026	(S)	**Jazz At The Blackhawk**	1962	8.00	20.00
Fantasy 3289	(M)	**Tjader Goes Latin** *(Red vinyl)*	1959	20.00	50.00
Fantasy 3289	(M)	**Tjader Goes Latin**	1959	12.00	30.00
Fantasy 8030	(S)	**Tjader Goes Latin** *(Blue vinyl)*	1962	12.00	30.00
Fantasy 8030	(S)	**Tjader Goes Latin**	1962	8.00	20.00
Fantasy 3295	(M)	**Concert By The Sea** *(Red vinyl)*	1959	20.00	50.00
Fantasy 3295	(M)	**Concert By The Sea**	1959	12.00	30.00
Fantasy 8035	(S)	**Concert By The Sea** *(Blue vinyl)*	1962	12.00	30.00
Fantasy 8035	(S)	**Concert By The Sea**	1962	8.00	20.00
Fantasy 3299	(M)	**Concert On The Campus** *(Red vinyl)*	1960	16.00	40.00
Fantasy 3299	(M)	**Concert On The Campus**	1960	10.00	25.00
Fantasy 8044	(S)	**Concert On The Campus** *(Blue vinyl)*	1962	12.00	30.00
Fantasy 8044	(S)	**Concert On The Campus**	1962	8.00	20.00
Fantasy 3307	(M)	**Cal Tjader Quartet** *(Red vinyl)*	1960	16.00	40.00
Fantasy 3307	(M)	**Cal Tjader Quartet**	1960	10.00	25.00
Fantasy 8083	(S)	**Cal Tjader Quartet** *(Blue vinyl)*	1962	12.00	30.00
Fantasy 8083	(S)	**Cal Tjader Quartet**	1962	8.00	20.00
Fantasy 3309	(M)	**Demasado Caliente** *(Red vinyl)*	1960	16.00	40.00
Fantasy 3309	(M)	**Demasado Caliente**	1960	10.00	25.00
Fantasy 8053	(S)	**Demasado Caliente** *(Blue vinyl)*	1962	12.00	30.00
Fantasy 8053	(S)	**Demasado Caliente**	1962	8.00	20.00
Fantasy 3310	(M)	**West Side Story** *(Red vinyl)*	1960	16.00	40.00
Fantasy 3310	(M)	**West Side Story**	1960	10.00	25.00
Fantasy 8054	(S)	**West Side Story** *(Blue vinyl)*	1962	12.00	30.00
Fantasy 8054	(S)	**West Side Story**	1962	8.00	20.00

Label & Catalog #		Title	Year	VG+	NM
Fantasy 3313	(M)	**Cal Tjader** *(Red vinyl)*	1961	16.00	40.00
Fantasy 3313	(M)	**Cal Tjader**	1961	10.00	25.00
Fantasy 8084	(S)	**Cal Tjader** *(Blue vinyl)*	1962	12.00	30.00
Fantasy 8084	(S)	**Cal Tjader**	1962	8.00	20.00
Fantasy 3315	(M)	**Cal Tjader Live And Direct** *(Red vinyl)*	1961	16.00	40.00
Fantasy 3315	(M)	**Cal Tjader Live And Direct**	1961	10.00	25.00
Fantasy 8059	(S)	**Cal Tjader Live And Direct** *(Blue vinyl)*	1962	12.00	30.00
Fantasy 8059	(S)	**Cal Tjader Live And Direct**	1962	8.00	20.00
Fantasy 3326	(M)	**Mambo With Tjader** *(Red vinyl)*	1961	16.00	40.00
Fantasy 3326	(M)	**Mambo With Tjader**	1961	10.00	25.00
Fantasy 8057	(S)	**Mambo With Tjader** *(Blue vinyl)*	1962	12.00	30.00
Fantasy 8057	(S)	**Mambo With Tjader**	1962	8.00	20.00
Fantasy 3330	(M)	**Cal Tjader Plays Harold Arlen** *(Red vinyl)*	1961	16.00	40.00
Fantasy 3330	(M)	**Cal Tjader Plays Harold Arlen**	1961	10.00	25.00
Fantasy 8072	(S)	**Cal Tjader Plays Harold Arlen** *(Blue vinyl)*	1962	12.00	30.00
Fantasy 8072	(S)	**Cal Tjader Plays Harold Arlen**	1962	8.00	20.00
Fantasy 3339	(M)	**Latino** *(Red vinyl)*	1962	16.00	40.00
Fantasy 3339	(M)	**Latino**	196?	10.00	25.00
Fantasy 8079	(S)	**Latino** *(Blue vinyl)*	1962	12.00	30.00
Fantasy 8079	(S)	**Latino**	196?	8.00	20.00
Fantasy 3341	(M)	**Concert By The Sea, Volume 2** *(Red vinyl)*	1961	16.00	40.00
Fantasy 3341	(M)	**Concert By The Sea, Volume 2**	1961	10.00	25.00
Fantasy 8098	(S)	**Concert By The Sea, Volume 2** *(Blue vinyl)*	1962	12.00	30.00
Fantasy 8098	(S)	**Concert By The Sea, Volume 2**	1962	8.00	20.00
		—Fantasy albums above have red mono or blue stereo labels on non-flexible vinyl.—			
Fantasy 3202	(M)	**Mambo With Tjader**	195?	5.00	12.00
Fantasy 3211	(M)	**Tjader Plays Tjazz**	195?	5.00	12.00
Fantasy 3216	(M)	**Ritmo Caliente**	195?	5.00	12.00
Fantasy 8077	(E)	**Ritmo Caliente**	1962	5.00	12.00
Fantasy 3221	(M)	**Tjader Plays Mambo**	1956	5.00	12.00
Fantasy 3232	(M)	**The Cal Tjader Quintet**	1956	5.00	12.00
Fantasy 3241	(M)	**Jazz At The Blackhawk**	1957	5.00	12.00
Fantasy 3250	(M)	**Latin Kick**	1957	5.00	12.00
Fantasy 8033	(S)	**Latin Kick**	1962	4.00	10.00
Fantasy 3262	(M)	**Mass Ritmo Caliente**	1958	5.00	12.00
Fantasy 8003	(S)	**Mass Ritmo Caliente**	1962	4.00	10.00
Fantasy 3266	(M)	**Cal Tjader-Stan Getz Sextet**	1958	5.00	12.00
Fantasy 8005	(S)	**Cal Tjader-Stan Getz Sextet**	1962	4.00	10.00
Fantasy 3271	(M)	**San Francisco Moods**	1958	5.00	12.00
Fantasy 8017	(S)	**San Francisco Moods**	1962	4.00	10.00
Fantasy 3275	(M)	**Latin Concert**	1959	5.00	12.00
Fantasy 8014	(S)	**Latin Concert**	1962	4.00	10.00
Fantasy 3278	(M)	**Tjader Plays Tjazz**	1958	5.00	12.00
Fantasy 8097	(E)	**Tjader Plays Tjazz**	1962	4.00	10.00
Fantasy 3279	(M)	**Latin For Lovers**	1958	5.00	12.00
Fantasy 8016	(S)	**Latin For Lovers**	1962	4.00	10.00
Fantasy 3283	(M)	**Jazz At Blackhawk**	1959	5.00	12.00
Fantasy 8026	(S)	**Jazz At The Blackhawk**	1962	4.00	10.00
Fantasy 3289	(M)	**Tjader Goes Latin**	1959	5.00	12.00
Fantasy 8030	(S)	**Tjader Goes Latin**	1962	4.00	10.00
Fantasy 3295	(M)	**Concert By The Sea**	1959	5.00	12.00
Fantasy 8035	(S)	**Concert By The Sea**	1962	4.00	10.00
Fantasy 3299	(M)	**Concert On The Campus**	1960	5.00	12.00
Fantasy 8044	(S)	**Concert On The Campus**	1962	4.00	10.00
Fantasy 3307	(M)	**Cal Tjader Quartet**	1960	5.00	12.00
Fantasy 8083	(S)	**Cal Tjader Quartet**	1962	4.00	10.00
Fantasy 3309	(M)	**Demasado Caliente**	1960	5.00	12.00
Fantasy 8053	(S)	**Demasado Caliente**	1962	4.00	10.00
Fantasy 3310	(M)	**West Side Story**	1960	5.00	12.00
Fantasy 8054	(S)	**West Side Story**	1962	4.00	10.00
Fantasy 3313	(M)	**Cal Tjader**	1961	5.00	12.00
Fantasy 8084	(S)	**Cal Tjader**	1962	4.00	10.00
Fantasy 3315	(M)	**Cal Tjader Live And Direct**	1961	5.00	12.00
Fantasy 8059	(S)	**Cal Tjader Live And Direct**	1962	4.00	10.00
Fantasy 3326	(M)	**Mambo With Tjader**	1961	5.00	12.00
Fantasy 8057	(S)	**Mambo With Tjader**	1962	4.00	10.00
Fantasy 3330	(M)	**Cal Tjader Plays Harold Arlen**	1961	5.00	12.00
Fantasy 8072	(S)	**Cal Tjader Plays Harold Arlen**	1962	4.00	10.00

Label & Catalog #		Title	Year	VG+	NM
Fantasy 3339	(M)	**Latino**	196?	5.00	12.00
Fantasy 8079	(S)	**Latino**	196?	4.00	10.00
Fantasy 3341	(M)	**Concert By The Sea, Volume 2**	1961	5.00	12.00
Fantasy 8098	(S)	**Concert By The Sea, Volume 2**	1962	4.00	10.00
Fantasy 3348	(M)	**The Cal Tjader-Stan Getz Sextet**	1963	8.00	20.00
Fantasy 8348	(S)	**The Cal Tjader-Stan Getz Sextet**	1963	6.00	15.00
Fantasy 3366	(M)	**Cal Tjader's Greatest Hits**	1965	8.00	20.00
Fantasy 8366	(S)	**Cal Tjader's Greatest Hits**	1965	5.00	12.00
Fantasy 3374	(M)	**Latin For Dancers**	1966	8.00	20.00
Fantasy 8374	(S)	**Latin For Dancers**	1966	6.00	15.00
		—Fantasy albums above have red mono or blue stereo labels on flexible vinyl.—			
Verve V-8419	(M)	**In A Latin Bag**	1961	8.00	20.00
Verve V6-8419	(S)	**In A Latin Bag**	1961	6.00	15.00
Verve V-8459	(M)	**Saturday Night-Sunday Night At The Blackhawk**	1962	8.00	20.00
Verve V6-8459	(S)	**Saturday Night-Sunday Night At The Blackhawk**	1962	6.00	15.00
Verve V-8470	(M)	**The Contemporary Music Of Mexico & Brazil**	1962	6.00	15.00
Verve V6-8470	(S)	**The Contemporary Music Of Mexico & Brazil**	1962	5.00	12.00
Verve V-8507	(M)	**Several Shades Of Jade**	1963	6.00	15.00
Verve V6-8507	(S)	**Several Shades Of Jade**	1963	5.00	12.00
Verve V-8531	(M)	**Sona Libre**	1963	6.00	15.00
Verve V6-8531	(S)	**Sona Libre**	1963	5.00	12.00
Verve V-8575	(M)	**Breeze From The East**	1964	6.00	15.00
Verve V6-8575	(S)	**Breeze From The East**	1964	5.00	12.00
Verve V-8585	(M)	**Warm Wave**	1964	6.00	15.00
Verve V6-8585	(S)	**Warm Wave**	1964	5.00	12.00
Verve V-8614	(M)	**Soul Sauce**	1965	6.00	15.00
Verve V6-8614	(S)	**Soul Sauce**	1965	5.00	12.00
Verve V-8626	(M)	**Soul Bird/Whiffenpoof**	1966	6.00	15.00
Verve V6-8626	(S)	**Soul Bird/Whiffenpoof**	1965	5.00	12.00
Verve V-8637	(M)	**Soul Burst**	1965	6.00	15.00
Verve V6-8637	(S)	**Soul Burst**	1965	5.00	12.00
Verve V-8651	(M)	**El Sonid Nuevo—The New Soul Sound**	1966	6.00	15.00
Verve V6-8651	(S)	**El Sonid Nuevo—The New Soul Sound**	1966	5.00	12.00
Verve V-8671	(M)	**Along Comes Cal**	1966	6.00	15.00
Verve V6-8671	(S)	**Along Comes Cal**	1966	5.00	12.00
Verve V-8725	(M)	**The Best Of Cal Tjader**	1967	6.00	15.00
Verve V6-8725	(S)	**The Best Of Cal Tjader**	1967	5.00	12.00
Verve V-8730	(M)	**Hip Vibrations**	1967	6.00	15.00
Verve V6-8730	(S)	**Hip Vibrations**	1967	5.00	12.00
Verve V6-8769	(S)	**The Prophet**	1969	5.00	12.00
		—Verve albums above have black labels with "MGM Records" on the bottom.—			

TOGAWA, PAUL

Paul Togawa is a West Coast jazz drummer known for his TV and movie session work.

Mode LP-104	(M)	**Paul Togawa Quartet**	1957	30.00	75.00

TORME, MEL

Melvin Torme is a modern jazz pianist and drummer, vocalist and composer. For additional listings refer to the Jazzy Soundtracks section under Reprise.

Capitol P-200	(10")	**California Suite**	1950	40.00	100.00
MGM 552	(10")	**Songs**	1952	40.00	100.00
Coral CRL-57012	(M)	**Gene Norman Presents Mel Torme "Live" At The Crescendo**	1956	20.00	50.00
Coral CRL-57044	(M)	**Musical Sounds Are The Best Songs**	1956	20.00	50.00
Bethlehem BCP-34	(M)	**It's A Blue World**	1955	20.00	50.00
Bethlehem BCP-52	(M)	**Mel Torme And The Marty Paich Dektette**	1956	20.00	50.00
Bethlehem BCP-6013	(M)	**Mel Torme Sings Fred Astaire**	1957	20.00	50.00
Bethlehem BCP-6016	(M)	**California Suite**	1957	20.00	50.00
		(Bethlehem 6016 also features Marty Paich.)			
Bethlehem BCP-6020	(M)	**Mel Torme Live At The Crescendo**	1958	20.00	50.00
		(Bethlehem 6020 also features Marty Paich.)			
Bethlehem BCP-6031	(M)	**SongS For Any Taste**	1959	20.00	50.00
		(Bethlehem 6031 also features Marty Paich.)			
Tops L-1615	(M)	**Prelude To A Kiss**	1958	10.00	25.00
		(Tops 1615 also features Marty Paich.)			

Label & Catalog #		Title	Year	VG+	NM
Verve MGV-2105	(M)	**Torme**	1958	20.00	50.00
Verve MGVS-6015	(S)	**Torme**	1960	20.00	50.00
		(Verve 2105 also features Marty Paich.)			
Verve MGV-2117	(M)	**Ole' Torme—Mel Torme Goes South Of The Border With Billy May**	1959	20.00	50.00
Verve MGVS-6058	(S)	**Ole' Torme—Mel Torme Goes South Of The Border With Billy May**	1960	20.00	50.00
Verve MGV-2120	(M)	**Back In Town**	1959	20.00	50.00
Verve MGVS-6063	(S)	**Back In Town**	1960	20.00	50.00
		(Verve 2120 also features Marty Paich.)			
Verve MGV-2132	(M)	**Mel Torme Swings Schubert Alley**	1960	20.00	50.00
Verve MGVS-6146	(S)	**Mel Torme Swings Schubert Alley**	1960	20.00	50.00
		(Verve 2132 also features Marty Paich.)			
Verve MGV-2144	(M)	**Swingin' On The Moon**	1960	20.00	50.00
		(Verve 2144 also features Russ Garcia.)			
Verve MGV-2146	(M)	**Broadway, Right Now**	1961	20.00	50.00
		(Verve 2146 also features Margaret Whiting and Russ Garcia.)			
Verve MGV-2153	(M)	**I Dig The Duke! I Dig The Count!**	1960	*Unreleased*	
—Verve albums above have black labels with "Verve Records, Inc." on the bottom.—					
Verve V-2105	(M)	**Torme**	1961	8.00	20.00
Verve V6-2105	(S)	**Torme**	1961	10.00	25.00
Verve V-2117	(M)	**Ole' Torme— Mel Torme Goes South Of The Border**	1961	8.00	20.00
Verve V6-2117	(S)	**Ole' Torme— Mel Torme Goes South Of The Border**	1961	8.00	20.00
Verve V-2120	(M)	**Back In Town**	1961	8.00	20.00
Verve V6-2120	(S)	**Back In Town**	1961	10.00	25.00
Verve V-2132	(M)	**Mel Torme Swings Schubert Alley**	1961	8.00	20.00
Verve V6-2132	(S)	**Mel Torme Swings Schubert Alley**	1961	10.00	25.00
Verve V-2144	(M)	**Swingin' On The Moon**	1961	8.00	20.00
Verve V6-2144	(S)	**Swingin' On The Moon**	1961	10.00	25.00
Verve V-2146	(M)	**Broadway, Right Now**	1961	8.00	20.00
Verve V6-2146	(S)	**Broadway, Right Now**	1961	10.00	25.00
Verve V-8440	(M)	**My Kind Of Music**	1962	10.00	25.00
Verve V6-8440	(S)	**My Kind Of Music**	1962	12.00	30.00
Verve V-8491	(M)	**I Dig The Duke! I Dig The Count!**	1962	10.00	25.00
Verve V6-8491	(S)	**I Dig The Duke! I Dig The Count!**	1962	12.00	30.00
Verve V-8593	(M)	**Verve's Choice—The Best Of Mel Torme**	1964	5.00	12.00
Verve V6-8593	(S)	**Verve's Choice—The Best Of Mel Torme**	1964	6.00	15.00
—Verve albums above have black labels with "MGM Records" on the bottom.—					
Strand SL-1076	(M)	**Mel Torme Sings**	1960	6.00	15.00
Strand SLS-1076	(S)	**Mel Torme Sings**	1960	8.00	20.00
Atlantic 8066	(M)	**Mel Torme At The Red Hill Inn**	1962	12.00	30.00
Atlantic SD-8066	(S)	**Mel Torme At The Red Hill Inn**	1962	16.00	40.00
Atlantic 8069	(M)	**Comin' Home, Baby**	1962	12.00	30.00
Atlantic SD-8069	(S)	**Comin' Home, Baby**	1962	16.00	40.00
		(Atlantic 8069 also features Shorty Rogers.)			
Atlantic 8091	(M)	**Sunday In New York**	1963	12.00	30.00
Atlantic SD-8091	(S)	**Sunday In New York**	1963	16.00	40.00
—Atlantic albums above have multi-color labels with a black fan logo.—					
Metro 523	(M)	**I Wished On The Moon**	1965	4.00	10.00
Metro S-523	(S)	**I Wished On The Moon**	1965	5.00	12.00
Columbia CL-2318	(M)	**That's All—A Lush Romantic Album**	1965	6.00	15.00
Columbia CS-9118	(S)	**That's All—A Lush Romantic Album**	1965	8.00	20.00
—Columbia albums above have "Guaranteed High Fidelity" or "360 Sound Stereo" in black on the label.—					
Columbia CL-2535	(M)	**Mel Torme Right Now**	1966	5.00	12.00
Columbia CS-9335	(S)	**Mel Torme Right Now**	1966	6.00	15.00
—Columbia albums above have "360 Sound" in white on the bottom of the label.—					
Liberty LST-7560	(S)	**A Day In The Life Of Bonnie And Clyde**	1968	8.00	20.00

TOSHIKO (TOSHIKO AKIYOSHI)

Chinese born Toshiko Akiyoshi is a modern jazz pianist Toshiko Akiyoshi later recorded under her married name, Toshiko Mariano. For additional listings refer to Steve Kuhn & Toshiko Akiyoshi.

Label & Catalog #		Title	Year	VG+	NM
Norgran MGN-22	(10")	**Toshiko's Piano**	1954	60.00	150.00
		(Norgran 22 features cover art by David Stone Martin.)			
Verve MGV-8273	(M)	**The Many Sides Of Toshiko**	1958	20.00	50.00
—Verve albums above have black labels with "Verve Records, Inc." on the bottom.—					

Cy Touff left the army after the war and played with Jimmy Dale, Jay Burkhardt, Charlie Ventura, Shorty Sherock, Ray McKinley and Boyd Raeburn before joining Woody Herman (1953-55). Aside from his own LPs, he can be heard as a sideman with Herman on Capitol, Columbia and Verve, Chubby Jackson on Argo, and Nat Pierrce on Fantasy.

Label & Catalog #		Title	Year	VG+	NM
Verve V-8273	(M)	**The Many Sides Of Toshiko**	1961	8.00	20.00
		—Verve albums above have black labels with "MGM Records" on the bottom.—			
Storyville STLP-912	(M)	**The Toshiko Trio**	1956	20.00	50.00
Storyville STLP-918	(M)	**Toshiko Akiyoshi Her Trio-Her Quartet**	1957	20.00	50.00
Metrojazz E-1001	(M)	**United Notions**	1958	20.00	50.00
Metrojazz SE-1001	(S)	**United Notions**	1958	16.00	40.00
Candid CD-8015	(M)	**Toshiko Mariano**	1960	20.00	50.00
Candid CS-9015	(S)	**Toshiko Mariano**	1960	16.00	40.00
Dauntless DM-4308	(M)	**The Country & Western Sounds Of Jazz**	1963	20.00	50.00
Dauntless DS-6308	(S)	**The Country & Western Sounds Of Jazz**	1963	16.00	40.00

TOSHIKO-MARIANO

The wife-husband team of Toshiko Akiyoshi and Charlie Mariano.

Candid CD-8012	(M)	**Toshiko-Mariano Quartet**	1960	20.00	50.00
Candid CS-9012	(S)	**Toshiko-Mariano Quartet**	1960	16.00	40.00
Vee Jay LP-2505	(M)	**Jazz In Japan**	1964	12.00	30.00
Vee Jay LPS-2505	(S)	**Jazz In Japan**	1964	12.00	30.00

TOSHIKO / LEON SASH

Verve MGV-8236	(M)	**Toshiko And Leon Sash At Newport**	1958	20.00	50.00
		—Verve albums above have black labels with "Verve Records, Inc." on the bottom.—			
Verve V-8236	(M)	**Toshiko And Leon Sash At Newport**	1961	8.00	20.00
		—Verve albums above have black labels with "MGM Records" on the bottom.—			

TOUFF, CY

Cyril Touff is a West Coast jazz bass and trumpet player.

Pacific Jazz PJ-1211	(M)	**Cy Touff, His Octet And Quintet**	1956	40.00	100.00
		(Pacific Jazz 1211 also features Richie Kamuca.)			
World Pacific PJM-410	(M)	**Havin' A Ball**	1958	24.00	60.00
		(World Pacific 410 is an abridged reissue of Pacific Jazz 1211.)			
Pacific Jazz PJ-42	(M)	**Keester Parade**	1962	16.00	40.00
		(Pacific Jazz 42 is a reissue of World Pacific 410.)			
Argo LP-606	(M)	**Doorway To Dixie**	1956	16.00	40.00
		(Argo 606 also features Miff Mole.)			
Argo LP-641	(M)	**Touff Assignment**	1959	12.00	30.00
Argo LPS-641	(S)	**Touff Assignment**	1959	10.00	25.00

TRACEY, STAN

London LL-3107	(M)	**Showcase**	195?	12.00	30.00

TRAVIS, NICK

Nicholas Travascio, aka Nick Travis, is a modern jazz trumpet player. For additional listings refer to Boots Brown; Kent Harian; The Manhattan Jazz All Stars; Johnny Mathis.

RCA Victor LPM-1010	(M)	**The Panic Is On**	1954	30.00	75.00
		—RCA albums above have black labels with "Long Play" on the bottom.—			

TREVOR, JEANNIE

Mainstream 56075	(M)	**Jeannie Trevor Sings!!**	1965	10.00	25.00
Mainstream S-6075	(S)	**Jeannie Trevor Sings!!**	1965	12.00	30.00

TRIO, THE

The Trio is Kenny Clarke, Wendell Marshall and Hank Jones.

Savoy MG-12023	(M)	**The Trio**	1955	40.00	100.00

TRISTANO, LENNIE

Leonard Tristano is a modern jazz pianist and composer. For additional listings refer to Lee Wiley.

New Jazz NJLP-101	(10")	**Lennie Tristano With Lee Konitz**	1950	125.00	250.00
Prestige PRLP-101	(10")	**Lennie Tristano With Lee Konitz**	1951	100.00	200.00
		(Prestige 101 is a reissue of New Jazz 101.)			
EmArcy MG-26029	(10")	**Holiday In Piano**	1954	50.00	125.00
Atlantic 1224	(M)	**Lennie Tristano**	1955	35.00	75.00
		—Atlantic albums above have black mono or green stereo labels.—			
Atlantic 1224	(M)	**Lennie Tristano**	1960	10.00	25.00
Atlantic 1357	(M)	**The New Tristano**	1960	20.00	50.00
		—Atlantic albums above have multi-color labels with a white fan logo.—			
Atlantic 1224	(M)	**Lennie Tristano**	196?	4.00	10.00
Atlantic 1357	(M)	**The New Tristano**	196?	4.00	10.00
		—Atlantic albums above have multi-color labels with a black fan logo.—			

Label & Catalog #		Title	Year	VG+	NM

TRISTANO, LENNIE / JOE BUSHKIN / BOBBY SCOTT / MARIAN McPARTLAND

Savoy MG-12043	(M)	**The Jazz Keyboards Of Lennie Tristano, Joe Bushkin, Bobby Scott & Marian McPartland**	1955	20.00	50.00

TRISTANO, LENNIE / ARNOLD ROSS

EmArcy MG-26029	(10")	**Holiday Piano**	1953	50.00	100.00

TROUP, BOBBY

Robert Troup is a traditional jazz-based pianist, vocalist and composer.

Capitol H-484	(10")	**Bobby**	1953	30.00	75.00
Capitol T-484	(M)	**Bobby**	1955	20.00	50.00
Bethlehem BCP-1030	(10")	**Bobby Troup**	1955	20.00	50.00
Bethlehem BCP-19	(M)	**Bobby Troup Sings Johnny Mercer**	1955	20.00	50.00
Bethlehem BCP-35	(M)	**The Distinctive Style Of Bobby Troup**	1955	20.00	50.00
Liberty LRP-3002	(M)	**Bobby Troup And His Trio**	1955	20.00	50.00
Liberty LRP-3026	(M)	**Do Re Mi**	1957	20.00	50.00
Liberty LRP-3078	(M)	**Here's To My Lady**	1958	20.00	50.00
		—Liberty albums above have turquoise labels.—			
Mode LP-111	(M)	**Bobby Swings Tenderly**	1957	40.00	100.00
Interlude MO-501	(M)	**Cool**	1959	16.00	40.00
Interlude ST-1001	(S)	**Cool**	1959	12.00	30.00
		(Interlude 501 is a reissue of Mode 111.)			
RCA Victor LPM-1959	(M)	**Bobby Troup And His Jazz All-Stars**	1959	20.00	50.00
RCA Victor LSP-1959	(S)	**Bobby Troup And His Jazz All-Stars**	1959	16.00	40.00

—RCA albums above have black labels with "Long Play" or "Living Stereo" on the bottom.—

TURNER, "BIG" JOE

Joseph Turner is a traditional jazz and rhythm 'n' blues-based vocalist.

Decca DL-8044	(M)	**Joe Turner Sings Kansas City Jazz**	1953	100.00	200.00
Atlantic 1234	(M)	**The Boss Of The Blues**	1956	50.00	125.00
Atlantic SD-1234	(S)	**The Boss Of The Blues**	1958	70.00	175.00
Atlantic 8005	(M)	**Joe Turner**	1958	50.00	125.00
Atlantic 8023	(M)	**Rockin' The Blues**	1959	60.00	150.00
Atlantic 8033	(M)	**Big Joe Is Here**	1959	60.00	150.00
		—Atlantic albums above have black mono or green stereo labels.—			
Atlantic 1234	(M)	**The Boss Of The Blues**	1960	16.00	40.00
Atlantic SD-1234	(S)	**The Boss Of The Blues**	1960	20.00	50.00
Atlantic 8005	(M)	**Joe Turner**	1960	16.00	40.00
Atlantic 8023	(M)	**Rockin' The Blues**	1960	16.00	40.00
Atlantic 8033	(M)	**Big Joe Is Here**	1960	16.00	40.00
Atlantic 1332	(M)	**Big Joe Rides Again**	1960	30.00	75.00
Atlantic SD-1332	(S)	**Big Joe Rides Again**	1960	40.00	100.00
		—Atlantic albums above have multi-color labels with a white fan logo.—			
Atlantic 1234	(M)	**The Boss Of The Blues**	196?	6.00	15.00
Atlantic SD-1234	(S)	**The Boss Of The Blues**	196?	8.00	20.00
Atlantic 8005	(M)	**Joe Turner**	196?	6.00	15.00
Atlantic 8023	(M)	**Rockin' The Blues**	196?	6.00	15.00
Atlantic 8033	(M)	**Big Joe Is Here**	196?	6.00	15.00
Atlantic 1332	(M)	**Big Joe Rides Again**	196?	6.00	15.00
Atlantic SD-1332	(S)	**Big Joe Rides Again**	196?	8.00	20.00
Atlantic 8081	(M)	**The Best Of Joe Turner**	1963	20.00	50.00
		—Atlantic albums above have multi-color labels with a black fan logo.—			
Savoy MG-14012	(M)	**Joe Turner And The Blues**	1960	40.00	100.00
Savoy MG-14106	(M)	**Careless Love**	1963	30.00	75.00

TURNER, JOE, & PETE JOHNSON

Joseph Turner and Peter Johnson are traditional jazz pianists.

EmArcy MG-36014	(M)	**Joe Turner And Pete Johnson**	1955	30.00	75.00

TURNER, RAY

Raymond Turner is a jazz-based pianist.

Capitol H-306	(10")	**Kitten On The Keys**	1952	20.00	50.00

TURRENTINE, STANLEY

Stanley Turrentine is a modern jazz tenor sax player. For additional listings refer to Les McCann; Shirley Scott; Jimmy Smith.

Time 52086	(M)	**Stan The Man**	1960	20.00	50.00
Time S-2086	(S)	**Stan The Man**	1960	16.00	40.00

Label & Catalog #		Title	Year	VG+	NM
Blue Note BLP-4039	(M)	**Look Out!** *(Deep groove)*	1960	50.00	125.00
Blue Note BLP-4039	(M)	**Look Out!**	1960	30.00	75.00
Blue Note BST-84039	(S)	**Look Out!**	1960	20.00	50.00
Blue Note BLP-4057	(M)	**Blue Hour**	1961	30.00	75.00
Blue Note BST-84057	(S)	**Blue Hour**	1961	20.00	50.00
		(Blue Note 4057 also features The Three Sounds.)			
Blue Note BLP-4065	(M)	**Comin' Your Way**	1961	*Unreleased*	
Blue Note BST-84065	(S)	**Comin' Your Way**	1961	*Unreleased*	
Blue Note BLP-4069	(M)	**Up At Minton's, Volume 1**	1961	30.00	75.00
Blue Note BST-84069	(S)	**Up At Minton's, Volume 1**	1961	20.00	50.00
Blue Note BLP-4070	(M)	**Up At Minton's, Volume 2**	1961	30.00	75.00
Blue Note BST-84070	(S)	**Up At Minton's, Volume 2**	1961	20.00	50.00
		—Blue Note albums above have blue on white labels with W. 63rd St, NYC address.—			
Blue Note BLP-4081	(M)	**Dearly Beloved**	1961	30.00	75.00
Blue Note BST-84081	(S)	**Dearly Beloved**	1961	20.00	50.00
Blue Note BLP-4096	(M)	**That's Where It's At**	1962	30.00	75.00
Blue Note BST-84096	(S)	**That's Where It's At**	1962	20.00	50.00
		—Blue Note albums above have blue on white labels with a 61st St, NYC address.—			
Blue Note BLP-4039	(M)	**Look Out!**	1963	10.00	25.00
Blue Note BST-84039	(S)	**Look Out!**	1963	8.00	20.00
Blue Note BLP-4057	(M)	**Blue Hour**	1963	10.00	25.00
Blue Note BST-84057	(S)	**Blue Hour**	1963	8.00	20.00
Blue Note BLP-4069	(M)	**Up At Minton's, Volume 1**	1963	10.00	25.00
Blue Note BST-84069	(S)	**Up At Minton's, Volume 1**	1963	8.00	20.00
Blue Note BLP-4070	(M)	**Up At Minton's, Volume 2**	1963	10.00	25.00
Blue Note BST-84070	(S)	**Up At Minton's, Volume 2**	1963	8.00	20.00
Blue Note BLP-4081	(M)	**Dearly Beloved**	1963	10.00	25.00
Blue Note BST-84081	(S)	**Dearly Beloved**	1963	8.00	20.00
Blue Note BLP-4096	(M)	**That's Where It's At**	1963	10.00	25.00
Blue Note BST-84096	(S)	**That's Where It's At**	1963	8.00	20.00
Blue Note BLP-4122	(M)	**Jubilee Shout!!!**	1963	*Unreleased*	
Blue Note BST-84122	(S)	**Jubilee Shout!!!**	1963	*Unreleased*	
Blue Note BLP-4129	(M)	**Never Let Me Go**	1963	16.00	40.00
Blue Note BST-84129	(S)	**Never Let Me Go**	1963	12.00	30.00
Blue Note BLP-4150	(M)	**A Chip Off The Old Block**	1963	16.00	40.00
Blue Note BST-84150	(S)	**A Chip Off The Old Block**	1963	12.00	30.00
Blue Note BLP-4162	(M)	**Hustlin'**	1964	16.00	40.00
Blue Note BST-84162	(S)	**Hustlin'**	1964	12.00	30.00
Blue Note BLP-4201	(M)	**Joyride**	1965	12.00	30.00
Blue Note BST-84201	(S)	**Joyride**	1965	10.00	25.00
Blue Note BLP-4234	(M)	**Stanley Turrentine**	1965	*Unreleased*	
Blue Note BST-84234	(S)	**Stanley Turrentine**	1965	*Unreleased*	
Blue Note BLP-4240	(M)	**Rough 'n Tumble**	1966	12.00	30.00
Blue Note BST-84240	(S)	**Rough 'n Tumble**	1966	10.00	25.00
		—Blue Note albums above have blue on white labels with a New York, USA address.—			
Blue Note BST-84039	(S)	**Look Out!**	196?	5.00	12.00
Blue Note BST-84057	(S)	**Blue Hour**	196?	5.00	12.00
Blue Note BST-84069	(S)	**Up At Minton's, Volume 1**	196?	5.00	12.00
Blue Note BST-84070	(S)	**Up At Minton's, Volume 2**	196?	5.00	12.00
Blue Note BST-84081	(S)	**Dearly Beloved**	196?	5.00	12.00
Blue Note BST-84096	(S)	**That's Where It's At**	196?	5.00	12.00
Blue Note BST-84129	(S)	**Never Let Me Go**	196?	5.00	12.00
Blue Note BST-84150	(S)	**A Chip Off The Old Block**	196?	5.00	12.00
Blue Note BST-84162	(S)	**Hustlin'**	196?	5.00	12.00
Blue Note BST-84201	(S)	**Joyride**	196?	5.00	12.00
Blue Note BST-84240	(S)	**Rough 'n Tumble**	196?	5.00	12.00
Blue Note BLP-4256	(M)	**The Spoiler**	1967	10.00	25.00
Blue Note BST-84256	(S)	**The Spoiler**	1967	10.00	20.00
Blue Note BLP-4268	(M)	**Easy Walker**	1967	12.00	30.00
Blue Note BST-84268	(S)	**Easy Walker**	1967	10.00	20.00
Blue Note BST-84286	(S)	**In The Look Of Love**	1968	10.00	20.00
Blue Note BST-84298	(S)	**Always Something There**	1968	10.00	20.00
Blue Note BST-84315	(S)	**Common Touch!**	1969	10.00	20.00
Blue Note BST-84336	(S)	**Another Story**	1969	10.00	20.00
		—Blue Note albums above have blue on white labels with "A Division of Liberty Records."—			
Mainstream 56041	(M)	**Tiger Tail**	1965	10.00	25.00
Mainstream S-6041	(S)	**Tiger Tail**	1965	10.00	20.00

Label & Catalog #		Title	Year	VG+	NM
TURRENTINE, TOMMY					
Thomas Turrentine is a modern jazz trumpet player.					
Time T-70008	*(M)*	**Tommy Turrentine**	*1960*	**20.00**	**50.00**
Time ST-70008	*(S)*	**Tommy Turrentine**	*1960*	**16.00**	**40.00**
TWARDZIK, RICHARD					
Richard Twardzik is a West Coast jazz pianist. For additional listings refer to Russ Freeman.					
Pacific Jazz PJ-37	*(M)*	**The Last Set**	*1962*	**20.00**	**50.00**
TYLE, TEDDY					
Theodore Tyle is a modern jazz tenor saxophone player.					
Golden Crest GC-3060	*(M)*	**Moon Shot**	*1959*	**16.00**	**40.00**
TYLER, CHARLES					
Charles Tyler is a modern jazz alto saxophone player.					
ESP-Disk' 1029	*(M)*	**The Charles Tyler Ensemble**	*1966*	**10.00**	**25.00**
ESP-Disk' 1029	*(S)*	**The Charles Tyler Ensemble**	*1966*	**8.00**	**20.00**
ESP-Disk' 1025	*(S)*	**Eastern Man Alone**	*1968*	**8.00**	**20.00**
TYNER, McCOY					
McCoy Tyner is a modern jazz pianist. For additional listings refer to Elvin Jones & Jimmy Garrison.					
Impulse A-18	*(M)*	**Inception**	*1962*	**12.00**	**30.00**
Impulse AS-18	*(S)*	**Inception**	*1962*	**10.00**	**25.00**
Impulse A-33	*(M)*	**Reaching Fourth**	*1963*	**12.00**	**30.00**
Impulse AS-33	*(S)*	**Reaching Fourth**	*1963*	**10.00**	**25.00**
Impulse A-39	*(M)*	**A Night Of Ballads**	*1963*	**12.00**	**30.00**
Impulse AS-39	*(S)*	**A Night Of Ballads**	*1963*	**10.00**	**25.00**
Impulse A-48	*(M)*	**McCoy Tyner Live At Newport**	*1963*	**12.00**	**30.00**
Impulse AS-48	*(S)*	**McCoy Tyner Live At Newport**	*1963*	**10.00**	**25.00**
Impulse A-63	*(M)*	**Today And Tomorrow**	*1964*	**12.00**	**30.00**
Impulse AS-63	*(S)*	**Today And Tomorrow**	*1964*	**10.00**	**25.00**
Impulse A-79	*(M)*	**McCoy Tyner Plays Ellington**	*1965*	**12.00**	**30.00**
Impulse AS-79	*(S)*	**McCoy Tyner Plays Ellington**	*1965*	**10.00**	**25.00**
—Impulse albums above have orange & black labels.—					
Impulse AS-18	*(S)*	**Inception**	*1968*	**4.00**	**10.00**
Impulse AS-33	*(S)*	**Reaching Fourth**	*1968*	**4.00**	**10.00**
Impulse AS-39	*(S)*	**A Night Of Ballads**	*1968*	**4.00**	**10.00**
Impulse AS-48	*(S)*	**McCoy Tyner Live At Newport**	*1968*	**4.00**	**10.00**
Impulse AS-63	*(S)*	**Today And Tomorrow**	*1968*	**4.00**	**10.00**
Impulse AS-79	*(S)*	**McCoy Tyner Plays Ellington**	*1968*	**4.00**	**10.00**
—Impulse albums above have red & black labels with the "abc" logo on top.—					
Blue Note BLP-4264	*(M)*	**The Real McCoy**	*1967*	**10.00**	**25.00**
Blue Note BST-84264	*(S)*	**The Real McCoy**	*1967*	**8.00**	**20.00**
Blue Note BST-84275	*(S)*	**Tender Moments**	*1968*	**8.00**	**20.00**
Blue Note BST-84307	*(S)*	**Time For Tyner**	*1969*	**8.00**	**20.00**
Blue Note BST-84338	*(S)*	**Expansions**	*1969*	**8.00**	**20.00**
— Blue Note albums above have blue on white labels with "A Division of Liberty Records."—					

U.

ULANO, SAM

Lane LP-140	*(M)*	**Sam Ulano**	*195?*	**20.00**	**50.00**
Lane LP-151	*(M)*	**Sam Ulano Is Mr. Rhythm**	*195?*	**20.00**	**50.00**

UPCHURCH, PHIL

Milestone MSP-9010	*(S)*	**Feeling Blue**	*1968*	**6.00**	**15.00**

URSO, PHIL

Phillip Urso is a West Coast jazz tenor saxophonist.

Savoy MG-15041	*(10")*	**Bob Brookmeyer With Phil Urso**	*1954*	**60.00**	**150.00**
Savoy MG-12056	*(M)*	**The Philosophy Of Urso**	*1956*	**20.00**	**50.00**
		(Savoy 12056 is a reissue of 15041.)			
Regent MG-6003	*(M)*	**Sentimental Journey**	*1956*	**20.00**	**50.00**

URTREGER, RENE: ***Refer to*** **DICK KATZ / DEREK SMITH / RENE URTREGER**

USSELTON, BILLY

William Usselton is a modern jazz tenor saxophone player.

Kapp KL-1051	*(M)*	**Billy Usselton—His First Album**	*1957*	**20.00**	**50.00**

V.

VAN DAMME, ART

Arthur Van Damme is a traditional jazz accordion player. For additional listings refer to Frances Faye; and Jo Stafford.

Capitol H-178	*(10")*	**Cocktail Capers**	*1950*	**16.00**	**40.00**
Capitol L-300	*(10")*	**More Cocktail Capers**	*1952*	**16.00**	**40.00**
Capitol T-178	*(M)*	**Cocktail Capers**	*1954*	**12.00**	**30.00**
Capitol T-300	*(M)*	**More Cocktail Capers**	*1954*	**12.00**	**30.00**
		—Capitol albums above have turquoise labels.—			
Columbia CL-6265	*(10")*	**Martini Time**	*1953*	**16.00**	**40.00**
Columbia CL-544	*(M)*	**The Van Damme Sound**	*1955*	**12.00**	**30.00**
Columbia CL-630	*(M)*	**Martini Time**	*1955*	**12.00**	**30.00**
		—Columbia albums above have "Long LP Playing" on the bottom of the label.—			
Columbia CL-801	*(M)*	**Manhattan Time**	*1956*	**12.00**	**30.00**
Columbia CL-876	*(M)*	**The Art Of Van Damme**	*1956*	**12.00**	**30.00**
Columbia CL-2585	*(10")*	**Art Van Damme Quintet**	*1956*	**16.00**	**40.00**
Columbia C2L-7	*(M)*	**They're Playing Our Song** *(2 LPs)*	*1958*	**16.00**	**40.00**
Columbia CL-1382	*(M)*	**Everything's Coming Up Music**	*1959*	**12.00**	**30.00**
Columbia CS-8177	*(S)*	**Everything's Coming Up Music**	*1959*	**10.00**	**25.00**
Columbia CL-1563	*(M)*	**Accordion Ala Mode**	*1960*	**12.00**	**30.00**
Columbia CS-8363	*(S)*	**Accordion Ala Mode**	*1960*	**10.00**	**25.00**
		—Columbia albums above have six white on black "eye" logos on each label.—			
Columbia CL-1794	*(M)*	**Art Van Damme Swings Sweetly**	*1962*	**6.00**	**15.00**
Columbia CS-8594	*(S)*	**Art Van Damme Swings Sweetly**	*1962*	**5.00**	**12.00**
Columbia CL-2013	*(M)*	**A Perfect Match**	*1963*	**6.00**	**15.00**
Columbia CS-8813	*(S)*	**A Perfect Match**	*1963*	**5.00**	**12.00**
Columbia CL-2192	*(M)*	**The New Sound Of The Art Van Damme Septet**	*1964*	**6.00**	**15.00**
Columbia CS-8992	*(S)*	**The New Sound Of The Art Van Damme Septet**	*1964*	**5.00**	**12.00**
		—Columbia albums above have "Guaranteed High Fidelity" or "360 Sound Stereo" in black on the label.—			
Design DLP-905	*(M)*	**3 Of A Kind**	*196?*	**4.00**	**10.00**
Design SDLP-905	*(E)*	**3 Of A Kind**	*196?*	**2.00**	**5.00**

Label & Catalog #		Title	Year	VG+	NM
Pickwick PC-3009	(M)	**Best Of Art Van Damme**	196?	4.00	10.00
Pickwick PCS-3009	(E)	**Best Of Art Van Damme**	196?	2.00	5.00
Harmony HL-7439	(M)	**Music For Lovers**	196?	4.00	10.00
Harmony HS-11439	(S)	**Music For Lovers**	196?	2.00	5.00

VAN EPS, GEORGE

George Van Eps is a traditional jazz-based guitar player. For additional listings refer to Eddie Miller / George Van Eps; The Rampart Street Serenaders; and the Jazzy Soundtracks section under RCA Victor.

Label & Catalog #		Title	Year	VG+	NM
Columbia CL-929	(M)	**Mellow Guitar**	1956	16.00	40.00
— Columbia albums above have six white on black "eye" logos on each label.—					
Capitol T-2533	(M)	**My Guitar**	1966	8.00	20.00
Capitol ST-2533	(S)	**My Guitar**	1966	6.00	15.00

VAUGHAN, SARAH

Sarah "Sassy" Vaughan is a big band-based singer. For additional listings refer to Count Basie; Billy Eckstine & Sarah Vaughan.

Label & Catalog #		Title	Year	VG+	NM
Columbia CL-6133	(10")	**Sarah Vaughan**	1950	50.00	125.00
Columbia CL-660	(M)	**After Hours With Sarah Vaughan**	1955	20.00	50.00
Columbia CL-745	(M)	**Sarah Vaughan In Hi Fi**	1956	20.00	50.00
		(Columbia 745 is a reissue of 6133.)			
Columbia CL-914	(M)	**Linger Awhile**	1956	20.00	50.00
— Columbia albums above have six white on black "eye" logos on each label.—					
MGM E-165	(10")	**Tenderly**	1952	50.00	125.00
MGM E-544	(10")	**Sarah Vaughan Sings**	1951	50.00	125.00
MGM E-3274	(M)	**My Kinda Love**	1955	20.00	50.00
		(MGM 3274 is a reissue of 165 and 544.)			
Remington RLP-1024	(10")	**Hot Jazz**	1953	100.00	200.00
		(Remington 1024 collects Sarah's first sides for Continental in 1944.)			
Allegro 3080	(10")	**Early Sarah**	1953	30.00	75.00
Allegro 1592	(M)	**Sarah Vaughan**	1955	20.00	50.00
Allegro 1608	(M)	**Sarah Vaughan**	1955	20.00	50.00
EmArcy MG-26005	(10")	**Images**	1954	30.00	75.00
EmArcy MG-36004	(M)	**Sarah Vaughan**	1955	30.00	75.00
EmArcy MG-36058	(M)	**In The Land Of Hi-Fi**	1956	30.00	75.00
EmArcy MG-36089	(M)	**Sassy**	1956	20.00	50.00
EmArcy MG-36109	(M)	**Swingin' Easy**	1957	20.00	50.00
		(EmArcy 36109 is a reissue of 26005.)			
—EmArcy albums above have blue labels with silver print.—					
Riverside RLP-2511	(10")	**Sarah Vaughan Sings With John Kirby**	1955	40.00	100.00
Mercury MG-25188	(10")	**Divine Sarah**	1955	40.00	100.00
Mercury MG-20094	(M)	**Sarah Vaughan At The Blue Note**	1956	16.00	40.00
Mercury SR-60020	(S)	**Sarah Vaughan At The Blue Note**	1958	16.00	40.00
Mercury MGP-2-100	(M)	**Great Songs From Hit Shows** *(2 LPs)*	1957	30.00	75.00
Mercury MGP-2-101	(M)	**Sarah Vaughan Sings George Gershwin** *(2 LPs)*	1957	30.00	75.00
Mercury MG-20219	(M)	**Wonderful Sarah**	1957	16.00	40.00
Mercury MG-20223	(M)	**In A Romantic Mood**	1957	16.00	40.00
Mercury MG-20244	(M)	**Great Songs From Hit Shows, Vol. 1**	1958	12.00	30.00
Mercury MSR-60041	(S)	**Great Songs From Hit Shows, Vol. 1**	1959	16.00	40.00
Mercury MG-20245	(M)	**Great Songs From Hit Shows, Volume 2**	1958	12.00	30.00
Mercury SR-60078	(S)	**Great Songs From Hit Shows, Volume 2**	1959	16.00	40.00
		(Mercury 20244 and 20244 are reissues of 2-100.)			
Mercury MG-20310	(M)	**Sarah Vaughan Sings George Gershwin, Vol. 1**	1958	12.00	30.00
Mercury SR-60045	(S)	**Sarah Vaughan Sings George Gershwin, Vol. 1**	1959	16.00	40.00
Mercury MG-20311	(M)	**Sarah Vaughan Sings George Gershwin, Vol. 2**	1958	12.00	30.00
Mercury SR-60046	(S)	**Sarah Vaughan Sings George Gershwin, Vol. 2**	1959	16.00	40.00
		(Mercury 20310 and 20311 are reissues of 2-101.)			
Mercury MG-20326	(M)	**Sarah Vaughan & Her Trio At Mr. Kelly's**	1958	16.00	40.00
Mercury MG-20370	(M)	**Vaughan And Violins**	1958	16.00	40.00
Mercury SR-60038	(S)	**Vaughan And Violins**	1959	16.00	40.00
Mercury MG-20383	(M)	**After Hours At The London House**	1958	16.00	40.00
Mercury SR-60020	(S)	**After Hours At The London House**	1959	16.00	40.00
Mercury MG-20438	(M)	**The Magic Of Sarah Vaughan**	1959	12.00	30.00
Mercury SR-60110	(S)	**The Magic Of Sarah Vaughan**	1959	16.00	40.00
Mercury MG-20441	(M)	**No 'Count Sarah**	1959	12.00	30.00
Mercury SR-60116	(S)	**No 'Count Sarah**	1959	16.00	40.00
Mercury MG-20540	(M)	**The Divine Sarah Vaughan**	1960	10.00	25.00
Mercury SR-60255	(S)	**The Divine Sarah Vaughan**	1960	12.00	30.00

Sarah Vaughan debuted as a professional singer and pianist with Earl Hines' orchestra in 1943, joined Billy Eckstine's band in 1944 and cut her first solo sides the same year. After leaving Eckstine, she sang with John Kirby in 1945-46, but has carried on as a solo since. As a vocalist she earned the raves of Dizzy and Bird but, like many jazz-based singers, slowly moved into mainstream pop recordings as the '50s wore on. . .

Label & Catalog #		Title	Year	VG+	NM
Mercury MG-20580	(M)	**Close To You**	1960	10.00	25.00
Mercury SR-60240	(S)	**Close To You**	1960	12.00	30.00
Mercury MG-20617	(M)	**My Heart Sings**	1961	10.00	25.00
Mercury SR-60617	(S)	**My Heart Sings**	1961	12.00	30.00
Mercury MG-20645	(M)	**Sarah Vaughan's Golden Hits**	1961	8.00	20.00
Mercury SR-60645	(S)	**Sarah Vaughan's Golden Hits**	1961	10.00	25.00
Mercury MG-20831	(M)	**Sassy Swings The Tivoli**	1963	8.00	20.00
Mercury SR-60831	(S)	**Sassy Swings The Tivoli**	1963	10.00	25.00
Mercury MG-20882	(M)	**Vaughan With Voices**	1963	8.00	20.00
Mercury SR-60882	(S)	**Vaughan With Voices**	1963	10.00	25.00
		—Mercury albums above have silver on black labels.—			
Mercury MG-20941	(M)	**Viva Vaughan**	1964	6.00	15.00
Mercury SR-60941	(S)	**Viva Vaughan**	1964	8.00	20.00
Mercury MG-21009	(M)	**Sarah Vaughan Sings The Mancini Songbook**	1965	6.00	15.00
Mercury SR-61009	(S)	**Sarah Vaughan Sings The Mancini Songbook**	1965	8.00	20.00
Mercury MG-21069	(M)	**The Pop Artistry Of Sarah Vaughan**	1966	6.00	15.00
Mercury SR-61069	(S)	**The Pop Artistry Of Sarah Vaughan**	1966	8.00	20.00
Mercury MG-21079	(M)	**The New Scene**	1966	6.00	15.00
Mercury SR-61079	(S)	**The New Scene**	1966	8.00	20.00
Mercury MG-21116	(M)	**Sassy Swings Again**	1967	6.00	15.00
Mercury SR-61116	(S)	**Sassy Swings Again**	1967	8.00	20.00
		—Mercury albums above have red labels.—			
Concord 3018	(M)	**Sarah Vaughan Concert**	1957	12.00	30.00
Lion L-70052	(M)	**Tenderly**	1958	10.00	25.00
Rondo-lette A-35	(M)	**Songs Of Broadway**	1958	10.00	25.00
Rondo-lette A-53	(M)	**Sarah Vaughan Sings**	1959	10.00	25.00
Masterseal MS-55	(M)	**Sarah Vaughan Sings**	195?	10.00	25.00
		(Masterseal 55 collects Sarah's first sides for Continental in 1944.)			
Roulette R-52046	(M)	**Dreamy**	1960	12.00	30.00
Roulette SR-52046	(S)	**Dreamy**	1960	14.00	35.00
		—Roulette albums above have black labels.—			
Roulette R-52060	(M)	**Divine One**	1960	10.00	25.00
Roulette SR-52060	(S)	**Divine One**	1960	12.00	30.00
Roulette R-52070	(M)	**After Hours**	1961	10.00	25.00
Roulette SR-52070	(S)	**After Hours**	1961	12.00	30.00
Roulette R-52082	(M)	**You're Mine, You**	1962	10.00	25.00
Roulette SR-52082	(S)	**You're Mine, You**	1962	12.00	30.00
Roulette SR-52082	(S)	**You're Mine, You** *(Red vinyl)*	1962	20.00	50.00
Roulette R-52091	(M)	**Snowbound**	1962	8.00	20.00
Roulette SR-52091	(S)	**Snowbound**	1962	10.00	25.00
Roulette R-52092	(M)	**The Explosive Side Of Sarah**	1962	8.00	20.00
Roulette SR-52092	(S)	**The Explosive Side Of Sarah**	1962	10.00	25.00
		—Roulette albums above have white labels with criss-crossed color bars.—			
Roulette R-52100	(M)	**Star Eyes**	1963	6.00	15.00
Roulette SR-52100	(S)	**Star Eyes**	1963	8.00	20.00
Roulette R-52104	(M)	**Lonely Hours**	1963	6.00	15.00
Roulette SR-52104	(S)	**Lonely Hours**	1963	8.00	20.00
Roulette R-52109	(M)	**The World Of Sarah Vaughan**	1964	6.00	15.00
Roulette SR-52109	(S)	**The World Of Sarah Vaughan**	1964	8.00	20.00
Roulette R-52112	(M)	**Sweet 'N Sassy**	1964	6.00	15.00
Roulette SR-52112	(S)	**Sweet 'N Sassy**	1964	8.00	20.00
Roulette R-52116	(M)	**Sarah Sings Soulfully**	1965	6.00	15.00
Roulette SR-52116	(S)	**Sarah Sings Soulfully**	1965	8.00	20.00
Roulette R-52118	(M)	**Sarah Plus Two**	1965	6.00	15.00
Roulette SR-52118	(S)	**Sarah Plus Two**	1965	8.00	20.00
		—Roulette albums above have orange roulette wheel labels.—			
Wing MGW-12123	(M)	**All Time Favorites**	1963	4.00	10.00
Wing SRW-16123	(S)	**All Time Favorites**	1963	5.00	12.00
Wing MGW-12280	(M)	**The Magic Of Sarah Vaughan**	1964	4.00	10.00
Wing SRW-16280	(S)	**The Magic Of Sarah Vaughan**	1964	5.00	12.00
Metro M-539	(M)	**Tenderly**	1965	4.00	10.00
Metro MS-539	(S)	**Tenderly**	1965	5.00	12.00

VAUGHAN, SARAH, & DINAH WASHINGTON, & JOE WILLIAMS

Roulette R-52108	(M)	**We Three**	1964	6.00	15.00
Roulette SR-52108	(S)	**We Three**	1964	8.00	20.00

VAUGHN, "FATHER" TOM

Label & Catalog #		Title	Year	VG+	NM
RCA Victor LPM-3577	*(M)*	**Jazz In Concert At The Village Gate**	*1966*	**8.00**	**20.00**
RCA Victor LSP-3577	*(S)*	**Jazz In Concert At The Village Gate**	*1966*	**6.00**	**15.00**
RCA Victor LPM-3845	*(M)*	**Motor City Soul**	*1967*	**8.00**	**20.00**
RCA Victor LSP-3845	*(S)*	**Motor City Soul**	*1967*	**6.00**	**15.00**
		—RCA albums above have black labels with "Monaural" or "Stereo" on the bottom.—			

VEGA, AL

Al Vega is a modern jazz pianist.

Label & Catalog #		Title	Year	VG+	NM
Prestige PRLP-152	*(10")*	**Al Vega Piano Solos With Bongos**	*1953*	**60.00**	**150.00**

VENTURA, CAROL

Carol Ventura is a modern jazz vocalist.

Label & Catalog #		Title	Year	VG+	NM
Prestige PRLP-7358	*(M)*	**Carol!**	*1965*	**12.00**	**30.00**
Prestige PRST-7358	*(S)*	**Carol!**	*1965*	**10.00**	**25.00**
Prestige PRLP-7405	*(M)*	**I Love To Sing!**	*1965*	**12.00**	**30.00**
Prestige PRST-7405	*(S)*	**I Love To Sing!**	*1965*	**10.00**	**25.00**
		—Prestige albums above have blue labels with a trident logo on the right side.—			

VENTURA, CHARLIE

Charles Venturo, aka Charlie Ventura, is a traditional jazz saxophone(s) player. For additional listings refer to Gene Krupa; Gene Krupa & Charlie Ventura.

Label & Catalog #		Title	Year	VG+	NM
Crystalette 5000	*(10")*	**Stomping With The Sax**	*1950*	**50.00**	**125.00**
Coral CRL-56067	*(10")*	**Open House**	*1952*	**50.00**	**125.00**
Mercury MGC-117	*(10")*	**Charlie Ventura Collates**	*1952*	**100.00**	**200.00**
Clef MGC-117	*(10")*	**Charlie Ventura Collates**	*1953*	**70.00**	**175.00**
		(Clef 117 is a reissue of Mercury 117.)			
Norgran MGN-8	*(10")*	**Charlie Ventura Quartet**	*1953*	**70.00**	**175.00**
Norgran MGN-1041	*(M)*	**Charlie Ventura's Carnegie Hall Concert**	*1955*	**50.00**	**125.00**
		(Norgran 1041 features cover art by David Stone Martin.)			
Norgran MGN-1073	*(M)*	**In A Jazz Mood**	*1956*	**40.00**	**100.00**
		(Norgran 1073 is a reissue of Clef 117.)			
Norgran MGN-1075	*(M)*	**Blue Saxophone**	*1956*	**40.00**	**100.00**
		(Norgran 1075 is a reissue of 8.)			
Norgran MGN-1103	*(M)*	**Charley's Parley**	*1956*	**40.00**	**100.00**
Verve MGV-8132	*(M)*	**Charlie Ventura's Carnegie Hall Concert**	*1957*	**30.00**	**75.00**
		(Verve 8132 is a reissue of Norgran 1041 with the DSM cover.)			
Verve MGV-8163	*(M)*	**Charlie Ventura In A Jazz Mood**	*1957*	**20.00**	**50.00**
		(Verve 8163 is a reissue of Norgran 1073.)			
Verve MGV-8165	*(M)*	**Blue Saxophone**	*1957*	**20.00**	**50.00**
		(Verve 8165 is a reissue of Norgran 1075.)			
		—Verve albums above have black labels with "Verve Records, Inc." on the bottom.—			
Verve V-8132	*(M)*	**Charlie Ventura's Carnegie Hall Concert**	*1961*	**8.00**	**20.00**
Verve V-8163	*(M)*	**Charlie Ventura In A Jazz Mood**	*1961*	**8.00**	**20.00**
Verve V-8165	*(M)*	**Blue Saxophone**	*1961*	**8.00**	**20.00**
		—Verve albums above have black labels with "MGM Records" on the bottom.—			
Imperial IM-3002	*(10")*	**Charlie Ventura And His Sextet**	*1953*	**70.00**	**175.00**
Decca DL-8046	*(M)*	**Charlie Ventura Concert**	*1954*	**40.00**	**100.00**
Gene Norman GNP-1	*(M)*	**Charlie Ventura In Concert**	*1954*	**40.00**	**100.00**
		(Gene Norman 1 also features Jackie Cain and Roy Kral.)			
EmArcy MG-26028	*(10")*	**F.Y.I. Ventura**	*1954*	**50.00**	**125.00**
EmArcy MG-36015	*(M)*	**Jumping With Ventura**	*1955*	**30.00**	**75.00**
		—EmArcy albums above have blue labels with silver print.—			
RCA Victor LPM-1135	*(M)*	**It's All Bop To Me**	*1955*	**40.00**	**100.00**
		—RCA albums above have black labels with "Long Play" on the bottom.—			
Brunswick BL-54025	*(M)*	**Here's Charlie**	*1957*	**30.00**	**75.00**
Baton 1202	*(M)*	**New Charlie Ventura In Hi Fi**	*1957*	**20.00**	**50.00**
Regent MG-6064	*(M)*	**East Of Suez**	*1958*	**20.00**	**50.00**
		(Regent 6064 is a reissue of EmArcy 26028.)			
King 395-543	*(M)*	**Adventure With Charlie Ventura**	*1958*	**30.00**	**75.00**
		—King albums above have silver on black labels.—			
Tops L-1528	*(M)*	**Charlie Ventura Plays Hi Fi Jazz**	*1958*	**10.00**	**25.00**
Craftsman 8039	*(M)*	**Charlie Ventura Plays For The People**	*1960*	**8.00**	**20.00**
		(Craftsmen 8039 is a reissue of Top 1528.)			

VENTURA, CHARLIE / CHARLIE KENNEDY

Label & Catalog #		Title	Year	VG+	NM
Regent MG-6047	*(M)*	**Crazy Rhythms**	*1957*	**24.00**	**60.00**
		—EmArcy albums above have blue labels with silver print.—			

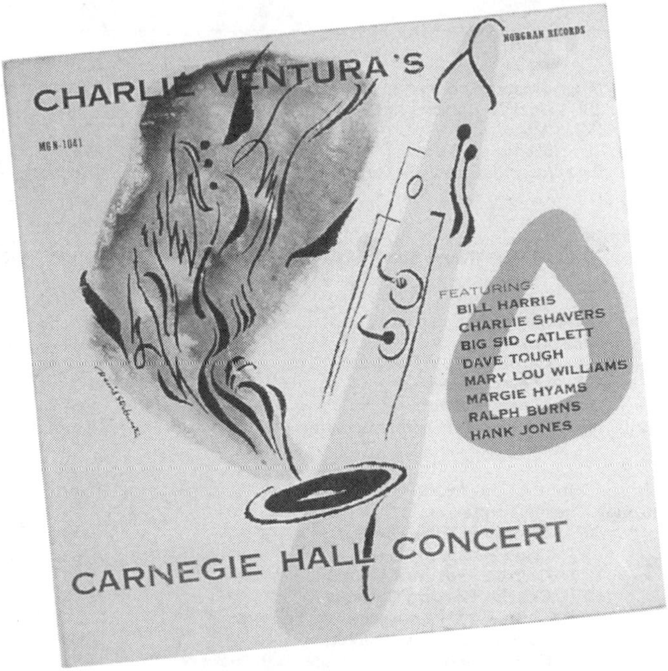

Charlie Ventura played with Gene Krupa (1942-43), Teddy Powell (1943-44) and Krupa again (1945-46) before forming his own band in 1946, often featuring new bop singers, such as Jackie Cain and Roy Kral. His playing can also be found on albums by Krupa on Columbia and Verve, The Metronome All Stars on Camden, and the JATP on Verve.

Label & Catalog #		Title	Year	VG+	NM
Savoy MG-12200	(M)	**Crazy Rhythms**	1969	8.00	20.00
		(Savoy 12200 is a reissue of Regent 6047.)			
		— Savoy albums above have red labels with silver print.—			

VENTURA, CHARLIE, & MARY ANN McCALL

Norgran MGN-20	(10")	**An Evening With Mary Ann McCall & Charlie Ventura**	1954	60.00	150.00
Norgran MGN-1013	(M)	**Another Evening With Charlie Ventura & Mary Ann McCall**	1954	40.00	100.00
		(Norgran 1013 features cover art by David Stone Martin.)			
Norgran MGN-1053	(M)	**An Evening With Mary Ann McCall & Charlie Ventura**	1955	40.00	100.00
		(Norgran 1053 is a reissue of 20. with cover art by David Stone Martin.)			
Verve MGV-8143	(M)	**An Evening With Mary Ann McCall & Charlie Ventura**	1957	30.00	75.00
		(Verve 8143 is a reissue of Norgran 1053 with the DSM cover.)			
		— Verve albums above have black labels with "Verve Records, Inc." on the bottom.—			
Verve V-8143	(M)	**An Evening With Mary Ann McCall & Charlie Ventura**	1961	10.00	25.00
		— Verve albums above have black labels with "MGM Records" on the bottom.—			

VENUTI, JOE / EDDIE LANG

Salvatore Massaro, aka Eddie Lang, is a traditional jazz guitar player.

"X" LVA-3036	(M)	**Joe Venuti And Eddie Lang**	1955	16.00	40.00

VENUTI, JOE

Giuseppi "Joe" Venuti is a traditional jazz violin player.

Grand Award GA-33-351	(M)	**Fiddle On Fire**	1956	16.00	40.00
Golden Crest GC-3100	(M)	**Joe Venuti Plays Gershwin**	1959	12.00	30.00
Golden Crest GC-3101	(M)	**Joe Venuti Plays Jerome Kern**	1959	12.00	30.00

VER PLANK, BILLY

John "Billy" Ver Plank is a traditional jazz trombone player and composer.

Savoy MG-12101	(M)	**Dancing Jazz**	1957	16.00	40.00
Savoy MG-12121	(M)	**Jazz For Playgirls**	1957	16.00	40.00
		— Savoy albums above have red labels with silver print.—			

VERNON, MILLI

Millie Vernon is a jazz-based vocalist.

Storyville STLP-910	(M)	**Introducing Milli Vernon**	1956	125.00	250.00

VICK, HAROLD

Harold Vick is a modern jazz tenor saxophone player.

Blue Note BLP-4138	(M)	**Steppin' Out**	1963	20.00	50.00
Blue Note BST-84138	(S)	**Steppin' Out**	1963	16.00	40.00
		— Blue Note albums above have blue on white labels with a New York, USA address.—			
Blue Note BST-84138	(S)	**Steppin' Out**	196?	5.00	12.00
		— Blue Note albums above have blue on white labels with "A Division of Liberty Records."—			
RCA Victor LPM-3677	(M)	**The Caribbean Suite**	1966	8.00	20.00
RCA Victor LSP-3677	(S)	**The Caribbean Suite**	1966	6.00	15.00
RCA Victor LPM-3761	(M)	**Straight Up**	1967	8.00	20.00
RCA Victor LSP-3761	(S)	**Straight Up**	1967	6.00	15.00
		— RCA albums above have black labels with "Mono Dynagroove" or "Stereo Dynagroove" on the bottom.—			

VIDEO ALL STARS, THE

The All Stars include Bob Cooper, Shelly Manne, Red Mitchell and Frank Rosolino.

Somerset SF-????	(M)	**The Video All Stars Play To TV Themes**	1956	50.00	125.00

VIG, TOMMY

Milestone MSP-9007	(S)	**Sounds Of The Seventies**	1968	6.00	15.00

VILLEGAS

Easy listening pianist Villegas is backed by Milt Hinton and Cozy Cole.

Columbia CL-787	(M)	**Introducing Villegas**	1956	12.00	30.00
Columbia CL-???	(M)	**Very, Very Villegas**	195?	12.00	30.00
		— Columbia albums above have six white on black "eye" logos on each label.—			

Label & Catalog #		Title	Year	VG+	NM
VINNEGAR, LEROY					
Leroy Vinegar is a West Coast jazz bassist For additional listings refer to Leonard Feather; Shelly Manne.					
Contemporary C-3542	*(M)*	**Leroy Walks!**	*1957*	**30.00**	**75.00**
Stereo Records S-7003	*(S)*	**Leroy Walks!**	*1958*	**20.00**	**50.00**
Contemporary S-7003	*(S)*	**Leroy Walks!**	*1959*	**16.00**	**40.00**
Contemporary M-3608	*(M)*	**Leroy Walks Again!**	*1962*	**16.00**	**40.00**
Contemporary S-7608	*(S)*	**Leroy Walks Again!**	*1962*	**12.00**	**30.00**
		– Contemporary stereo albums have gold & black labels. –			
Vee Jay LP-2502	*(M)*	**Jazz's Great Walker**	*1965*	**12.00**	**30.00**
Vee Jay LPS-2502	*(S)*	**Jazz's Great Walker**	*1965*	**12.00**	**30.00**
VINSON, EDDIE "CLEANHEAD"					
Edward Vinson is a traditional jazz and R&B-based alto saxophone player and vocalist. For additional listings refer to Jimmy Witherspoon & Eddie Vinson.					
Bethlehem BCP-5005	*(M)*	**Cleanhead's Back In Town**	*1957*	**20.00**	**50.00**
Aamco 312	*(M)*	**Cleanhead's Back In Town**	*196?*	**12.00**	**30.00**
		(Aamco 312 is a reissue of Bethlehem 5005.)			
Riverside RLP-502	*(M)*	**Back Door Blues**	*1965*	**16.00**	**40.00**
Riverside RS-9502	*(S)*	**Back Door Blues**	*1965*	**12.00**	**30.00**
		– Riverside albums above blue labels with "Orpheum Productions" on the bottom. –			
VIOLA, AL					
Al Viola is a modern jazz guitarist.					
Mode LP-121	*(M)*	**Solo Guitar**	*1957*	**30.00**	**75.00**

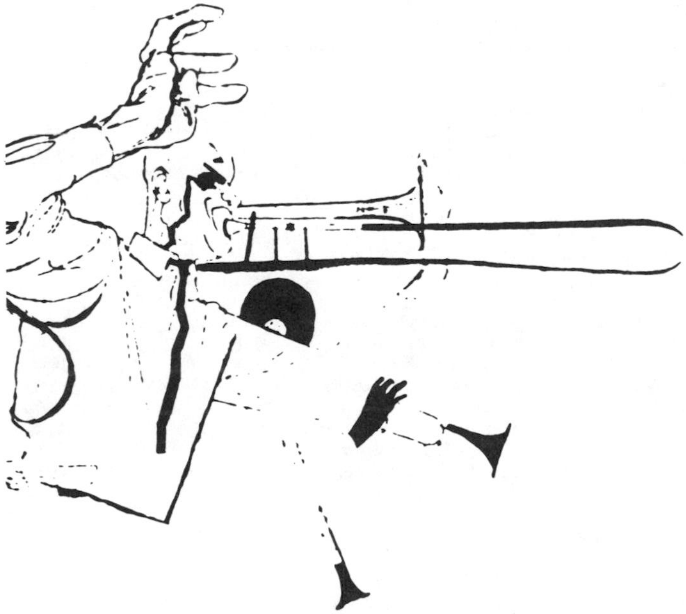

Lu Watters by David Stone Martin.

W.

WAGNER, LARRY

"A44" AP-501	(10")	**Larry Wagner**	1954	20.00	50.00

WALD, JERRY

Jerry Wald is a traditional jazz clarinet player and band leader.

Kapp KL-1043	(M)	**Listen To The Music Of Jerry Wald**	1956	16.00	40.00
Lion L-70014	(M)	**Tops In Pops—Designed For Dancing**	1958	10.00	25.00

WALDRON, MAL

Malcolm Waldron is a modern jazz pianist and composer. For additional listings refer to Ron Carter; Eric Dolphy; The Prestige Jazz Quartet; the Jazzy Soundtracks section under Impulse and Philips; and the Various Artists section under New Jazz and Prestige.

Prestige PRLP-7090	(M)	**Mal-1**	1957	30.00	75.00
Prestige PRLP-7111	(M)	**Mal-2**	1957	30.00	75.00
		(Prestige 7111 also features John Coltrane.)			
		—Prestige albums above have yellow labels with a W. 50th Street, NYC address.—			
New Jazz NJLP-8201	(M)	**Mal/3: Sounds**	1958	40.00	100.00
		—New Jazz albums above have yellow Prestige labels.—			
New Jazz NJLP-8201	(M)	**Mal/3: Sounds**	1958	20.00	50.00
New Jazz NJLP-8208	(M)	**Mal/4: Trio**	1958	20.00	50.00
New Jazz NJLP-8242	(M)	**Impressions**	1960	20.00	50.00
New Jazz NJLP-8269	(M)	**The Quest**	1962	20.00	50.00
		(New Jazz 9269 also features Eric Dolphy and Booker Ervin.)			
New Jazz NJLP-8316	(M)	**The Dealers**	1963	*Unreleased*	
		—New Jazz albums above have purple labels.—			
New Jazz NJLP-8201	(M)	**Mal/3: Sounds**	1965	10.00	25.00
New Jazz NJLP-8208	(M)	**Mal/4: Trio**	1965	10.00	25.00
New Jazz NJLP-8242	(M)	**Impressions**	1965	10.00	25.00
New Jazz NJLP-8269	(M)	**The Quest**	1965	10.00	25.00
		—New Jazz albums above have blue labels with a trident logo on the right side.—			
Status ST-8316	(M)	**The Dealers**	1965	16.00	40.00
		(Status 8316 also features John Coltrane.)			
Prestige PRST-7579	(S)	**The Quest**	1969	6.00	15.00
		(Prestige 7579 is a reissue of New Jazz 8269.)			
		—Prestige albums above have blue labels with a trident logo on top.—			
Music Minus One 1012	(M)	**Moonglow & Stardust**	1960	8.00	20.00
Music Minus One 1015	(M)	**Music Of Duke Ellington**	1960	8.00	20.00
Music Minus One 1016	(M)	**Music Of McHugh**	1960	8.00	20.00
Music Minus One 1017	(M)	**Mal Waldron**	1960	8.00	20.00
Music Minus One 1018	(M)	**For Singers 'N Singer**	1960	8.00	20.00
Music Minus One 4005	(M)	**Blue Drums**	1961	8.00	20.00
Music Minus One 4007	(M)	**For Pianists Only**	1961	8.00	20.00
Music Minus One 4008	(M)	**They Laughed When I Sat Down To Play**	1961	8.00	20.00
Music Minus One 175	(M)	**Fun With Brushes**	1960	8.00	20.00
Bethlehem BCP-6045	(M)	**Left Alone**	1960	16.00	40.00
Bethlehem SBCP-6045	(S)	**Left Alone**	1960	16.00	40.00

WALI & THE AFRO-CARAVAN

Solid State SS-18065	(S)	**Home Lost And Found**	1969	6.00	15.00

WALKER, T-BONE

Aaron Thibaud "T-Bone" Walker is a traditional jazz and R&B guitar and piano player and vocalist.

Capitol H-370	(10")	**Classics In Jazz**	1953	240.00	400.00
Capitol T-370	(M)	**Classics In Jazz**	1956	125.00	250.00

WALLER, FATS

Thomas "Fats" Waller is a traditional jazz piano and organ player, vocalist and composer.

RCA Victor WPT-8	(10")	**Fats Waller 1934-42**	1951	50.00	125.00
RCA Victor LPT-14	(10")	**Fats Waller Favorites**	1951	50.00	125.00
RCA Victor LPT-3040	(10")	**Swingin' The Organ**	1953	50.00	125.00
RCA Victor LPT-1001	(M)	**Fats Waller Plays And Sings**	1954	30.00	75.00

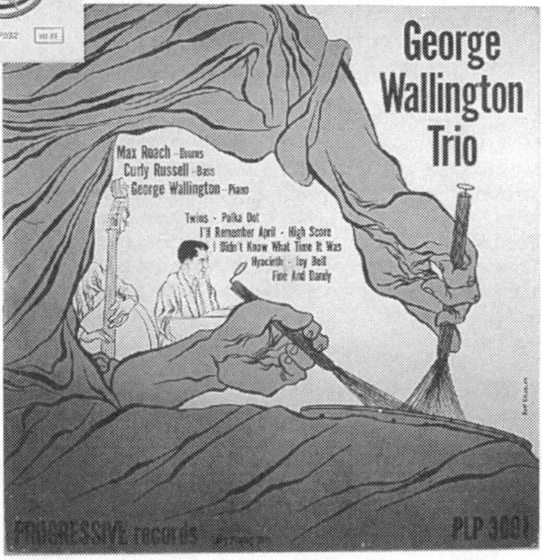

George Wallington played with Dizzy Gillespie's first combo on 52nd Street in 1944. He then gigged with Joe Marsala, Georgie Auld, Allan Eager, Charlie Parker, and Red Rodney. Forming his own group, he recorded first for Progressive and then Prestige. He also shares an album each with James Moody and Jimmy Raney and can be heard as a sideman on LPs by Gerry Mulligan on Prestige, Thomas Talbert on Atlantic, Bobby Jaspar on Riverside, Al Cohn on Savoy, and as a member of The Metronome All Stars on Verve.

Label & Catalog #		Title	Year	VG+	NM
RCA Victor LPT-6001	(M)	**Fats Waller Radio Transcriptions**	1954	40.00	100.00
		(Boxed set of two albums with a booklet.)			
RCA Victor LPM-1246	(M)	**Ain't Misbehavin'**	1956	20.00	50.00
RCA Victor LPM-1502	(M)	**Handful Of Keys**	1957	20.00	50.00
RCA Victor LPM-6000	(M)	**Fats** (2 LPs)	1960	20.00	50.00
		—RCA albums above have black labels with "Long Play" on the bottom.—			
RCA Victor LPV-473	(M)	**The Real Fats Waller**	1965	8.00	20.00
RCA Victor LPV-516	(M)	**Fats Waller '34/'35**	1965	8.00	20.00
RCA Victor LPV-525	(M)	**Valentine Stomp**	1965	8.00	20.00
RCA Victor LPV-550	(M)	**Smashing Thirds**	1966	8.00	20.00
RCA Victor LPV-562	(M)	**African Riplets**	1966	8.00	20.00
"X" LVA-3035	(10")	**The Young Fats Waller**	1955	50.00	125.00
Riverside RLP-1010	(10")	**Rediscovered Fats Waller Piano Solos**	1953	50.00	125.00
Riverside RLP-1021	(10")	**Fats Waller At The Organ**	1953	50.00	125.00
Riverside RLP-1022	(10")	**Jiving With Fats Waller**	1953	50.00	125.00
Riverside RLP-12-103	(M)	**The Young Fats Waller**	1955	24.00	60.00
Riverside RLP-12-109	(M)	**The Amazing Mr. Waller**	1955	24.00	60.00
		—Riverside albums above have blue on white labels.—			

WALLINGTON, GEORGE

Sicilian born Giorgio Filia, aka George Wallington, is a modern jazz pianist and composer. For additional listings refer to Bobby Jaspar; James Moody / George Wallington; Jimmy Raney / George Wallington.

Label & Catalog #		Title	Year	VG+	NM
Progressive 3001	(10")	**The George Wallington Trio**	1952	125.00	250.00
Prestige PRLP-136	(10")	**The George Wallington Trio**	1952	125.00	250.00
Prestige PRLP-158	(10")	**The George Wallington Trio, Volume 2**	1953	125.00	250.00
Prestige PRLP-7032	(M)	**Jazz For The Carriage Trade**	1956	240.00	400.00
		(Prestige 7032 also features Donald Byrd and Phil Woods.)			
		—Prestige albums above have yellow labels with a W. 50th Street, NYC address.—			
Savoy MG-15037	(10")	**The George Wallington Trio**	1954	40.00	100.00
		(Savoy 15037 is a reissue of Progressive 3001.)			
Blue Note BLP-5045	(10")	**George Wallington And His All Star Band**	1954	240.00	400.00
Norgran MGN-24	(10")	**The Workshop Of The George Wallington Trio**	1954	60.00	150.00
Norgran MGN-1010	(M)	**George Wallington With Strings**	1954	40.00	100.00
Verve MGV-2017	(M)	**Variations**	1956	30.00	75.00
		—Verve albums above have black labels with "Verve Records, Inc" on the bottom.—			
Progressive PLP-1001	(M)	**George Wallington Quintet At The Bohemia**	1955	660.00	1,000.00
Savoy MG-12081	(M)	**The George Wallington Trio**	1956	30.00	75.00
Savoy MG-12122	(M)	**Jazz At Hotchkiss**	1957	30.00	75.00
New Jazz NJLP-8207	(M)	**The New York Scene**	1958	60.00	150.00
		(New Jazz 8207 is a reissue of one side of "Modern Jazz Survey 1," listed in the "Jazz At 16 2/3 RPM" article.)			
		—New Jazz albums above have purple labels.—			
New Jazz NJLP-8207	(M)	**The New York Scene**	1965	16.00	40.00
		—New Jazz albums above have blue labels with a trident logo on the right side.—			
East-West 4004	(M)	**The Prestidigitator**	1958	60.00	150.00
Atlantic 1275	(M)	**Knight Music**	1958	30.00	75.00
Atlantic SD-1275	(S)	**Knight Music**	1958	24.00	60.00
		—Atlantic albums above have black mono or green stereo labels.—			
Atlantic 1275	(M)	**Knight Music**	1961	10.00	25.00
Atlantic SD-1275	(M)	**Knight Music**	1961	8.00	20.00
		—Atlantic albums above have multi-color labels with a white fan logo.—			
Prestige PRST-7587	(E)	**The George Wallington Trios**	1968	6.00	15.00
		(Prestige 7587 is a reissue of 136 and 158.)			
		—Prestige albums above have blue labels with a trident logo on top.—			

WALTER, CY

Label & Catalog #		Title	Year	VG+	NM
Atlantic 1236	(M)	**Rodgers Revisited**	1956	16.00	40.00
		—Atlantic albums above have black mono or green stereo labels.—			
Atlantic 1236	(M)	**Rodgers Revisited**	1961	8.00	20.00
		—Atlantic albums above have multi-color labels with a white fan logo.—			

WANDERLEY, WALTER

Label & Catalog #		Title	Year	VG+	NM
Verve V-8658	(M)	**Rain Forest**	1966	5.00	12.00
Verve V6-8658	(S)	**Rain Forest**	1966	4.00	10.00
		—Verve albums above have black labels with "MGM Records" on the bottom.—			

Label & Catalog #		Title	Year	VG+	NM
WARD, HELEN					
Helen Ward is a traditional jazz-based vocalist.					
Columbia CL-6271	(10")	**It's Been So Long**	1954	20.00	50.00
Pax 6004	(10")	**Wild Bill Davison With Helen Ward**	1954	20.00	50.00
WARDELL, ROOSEVELT					
Roosevelt Ward is a modern jazz pianist.					
Riverside RLP-350	(M)	**The Revelation**	1960	12.00	30.00
Riverside RS-9350	(S)	**The Revelation**	1960	10.00	25.00
		—Riverside albums above have blue mono or black stereo labels with a reel & mike logo on top.—			
WARE, WILBUR					
Wilbur Ware is a modern jazz bassist.					
Riverside RLP-12-252	(M)	**Chicago Sounds**	1957	30.00	75.00
		—Riverside albums above have blue mono or black stereo labels with a reel & mike logo on top.—			
WARE, WILBUR, & JOHNNY GRIFFIN & JUNIOR MANCE					
Jazzland JLP-12	(M)	**The Chicago Cookers**	1960	16.00	40.00
		(Jazzland 12 is a reissue of Riverside 252.)			
WASHINGTON, DINAH					
Ruth Jones, aka Dinah Washington, is a R&B/jazz singer. For additional listings refer to Sarah Vaughan & Dinah Washington.					
Mercury MG-25060	(10")	**Dinah Washington Songs**	1950	60.00	150.00
Mercury MG-25138	(10")	**Dynamic Dinah**	1952	50.00	125.00
Mercury MG-25140	(10")	**Blazing Ballads**	1952	50.00	125.00
Mercury MG-20119	(M)	**Music For A First Love**	1957	20.00	50.00
Mercury MG-20120	(M)	**Music For Late Hours**	1957	20.00	50.00
Mercury MG-20247	(M)	**The Best In Blues**	1958	20.00	50.00
Mercury MG-20439	(M)	**The Queen**	1959	12.00	30.00
Mercury SR-60111	(S)	**The Queen**	1959	16.00	40.00
Mercury MG-20479	(M)	**What A Diff'rence A Day Makes!**	1959	12.00	30.00
Mercury SR-60158	(S)	**What A Diff'rence A Day Makes!**	1959	16.00	40.00
Mercury MG-20523	(M)	**Newport '58**	1959	12.00	30.00
Mercury SR-60200	(S)	**Newport '58**	1959	16.00	40.00
Mercury MG-20525	(M)	**Dinah Washington Sings Fats Waller**	1959	12.00	30.00
Mercury SR-60202	(S)	**Dinah Washington Sings Fats Waller**	1959	16.00	40.00
		(Mercury 20525 is a reissue of EmArcy 36119.)			
Mercury MG-20572	(M)	**Unforgettable**	1960	10.00	25.00
Mercury SR-60232	(S)	**Unforgettable**	1960	12.00	30.00
Mercury MG-20604	(M)	**I Concentrate On You**	1960	10.00	25.00
Mercury SR-60604	(S)	**I Concentrate On You**	1960	12.00	30.00
Mercury MG-20614	(M)	**For Lonely Lovers**	1961	10.00	25.00
Mercury SR-60614	(S)	**For Lonely Lovers**	1961	12.00	30.00
Mercury MG-20638	(M)	**September In The Rain**	1961	10.00	25.00
Mercury SR-60638	(S)	**September In The Rain**	1961	12.00	30.00
Mercury MG-20661	(M)	**Tears & Laughter**	1962	10.00	25.00
Mercury SR-60661	(S)	**Tears & Laughter**	1962	12.00	30.00
Mercury MG-20729	(M)	**I Wanna Be Loved**	1962	10.00	25.00
Mercury SR-60729	(S)	**I Wanna Be Loved**	1962	12.00	30.00
Mercury MG-20788	(M)	**Dinah Washington's Golden Hits, Volume 1**	1963	8.00	20.00
Mercury SR-60788	(S)	**Dinah Washington's Golden Hits, Volume 1**	1963	10.00	25.00
Mercury MG-20789	(M)	**Dinah Washington's Golden Hits, Volume 2**	1963	8.00	20.00
Mercury SR-60789	(S)	**Dinah Washington's Golden Hits, Volume 2**	1963	10.00	25.00
Mercury MG-20829	(M)	**The Good Old Days**	1963	8.00	20.00
Mercury SR-60829	(S)	**The Good Old Days**	1963	10.00	25.00
		—Mercury albums above have silver on black labels.—			
Mercury MG-20928	(M)	**The Queen And Quincy**	1965	6.00	15.00
Mercury SR-60928	(S)	**The Queen And Quincy**	1965	8.00	20.00
		(Mercury 20928 also featues Quincy Jones.)			
Mercury MG-21119	(M)	**Dinah Discovered**	1967	8.00	20.00
Mercury SR-61119	(S)	**Dinah Discovered**	1967	6.00	15.00
Mercury PKW-2-121	(S)	**The Original Queen Of Soul** *(2 LPs)*	1969	6.00	15.00
Wing MGW-12140	(M)	**The Late, Late Show**	1963	4.00	10.00
Wing SRW-16140	(S)	**The Late, Late Show**	1963	5.00	12.00
Wing MGW-12271	(M)	**Dinah Washington Sings Fats Waller**	1964	4.00	10.00
Wing SRW-16271	(S)	**Dinah Washington Sings Fats Waller**	1964	5.00	12.00

Dinah Washington kicked off her career with Lionel Hampton in 1943, cutting her first sides by the end of the year with members of the band. By 1946 she had established herself in both the jazz and the R&B fields before moving into a more mainstream style that included standards and pop tunes. Unfortunately, while her eclecticism may have sold a few more records, it ultimately diluted her strength, which was not as a jazz singer but as an R&B diva.

Label & Catalog #		Title	Year	VG+	NM
EmArcy MG-26032	(10")	**After Hours With Miss D**	1954	50.00	125.00
EmArcy MG-36000	(M)	**Dinah Jams**	1955	20.00	50.00
EmArcy MG-36011	(M)	**For Those In Love**	1955	20.00	50.00
EmArcy MG-36028	(M)	**After Hours With Miss D**	1955	20.00	50.00
		(EmArcy 36028 is a reissue of 26032.)			
EmArcy MG-36065	(M)	**Dinah**	1956	20.00	50.00
EmArcy MG-36073	(M)	**In The Land Of Hi-Fi**	1956	20.00	50.00
EmArcy MG-36104	(M)	**The Swingin' Miss "D"**	1956	20.00	50.00
EmArcy MG-36119	(M)	**The Fats Waller Songbook**	1957	20.00	50.00
EmArcy MG-36130	(M)	**Dinah Washington Sings Bessie Smith**	1958	20.00	50.00
		– EmArcy albums above have blue labels with silver print.–			
Grand Award GA-33-318	(M)	**Dinah Washington Sings The Blues**	1955	30.00	75.00
		(G.A. 321 was issued with a removable "second" cover of a David Stone Martin painting that could be peeled off and framed.)			
Grand Award GA-33-318	(M)	**Dinah Washington Sings The Blues**	1955	20.00	50.00
		(Without the removable second cover.)			
Roulette R-25170	(M)	**Dinah '62**	1962	8.00	20.00
Roulette SR-25170	(S)	**Dinah '62**	1962	10.00	25.00
Roulette R-25180	(M)	**In Love**	1962	8.00	20.00
Roulette SR-25180	(S)	**In Love**	1962	10.00	25.00
		– Roulette albums above have black labels.–			
Roulette R-25183	(M)	**Drinking Again**	1962	6.00	15.00
Roulette SR-25183	(S)	**Drinking Again**	1962	8.00	20.00
Roulette R-25189	(M)	**Back To The Blues**	1962	6.00	15.00
Roulette SR-25189	(S)	**Back To The Blues**	1962	8.00	20.00
Roulette R-25220	(M)	**Dinah '63**	1963	6.00	15.00
Roulette SR-25220	(S)	**Dinah '63**	1963	8.00	20.00
Roulette R-25244	(M)	**In Tribute**	1963	6.00	15.00
Roulette SR-25244	(S)	**In Tribute**	1963	8.00	20.00
Roulette R-25253	(M)	**Stranger On Earth**	1964	6.00	15.00
Roulette SR-25253	(S)	**Stranger On Earth**	1964	8.00	20.00
Roulette R-25269	(M)	**Dinah Washington**	1964	6.00	15.00
Roulette SR-25269	(S)	**Dinah Washington**	1964	8.00	20.00
Roulette R-25289	(M)	**The Best Of Dinah Washington**	1965	6.00	15.00
Roulette SR-25289	(S)	**The Best Of Dinah Washington**	1965	8.00	20.00
		– Roulette albums above have orange & pink labels.–			

WASHINGTON, DINAH / TERRY GIBBS & MAX ROACH & DON ELLIOTT

EmArcy MG-36141	(M)	**Newport '58**	1958	16.00	40.00
		– EmArcy albums above have blue labels with silver print.–			
Mercury SR-60200	(S)	**Newport '58**	1959	12.00	30.00
		(Mercury 60200 is a stereo reissue of EmArcy 36141.)			

WASHINGTON, EARL

Earl Washington is a modern jazz pianist and composer.

Jazz Workshop JWS-202	(M)	**All Star Jazz**	1963	20.00	50.00
Jazz Workshop JWS-213	(M)	**Reflections**	1963	20.00	50.00

WASHINGTON, ERNESTINE

Disc DLP-712	(10")	**Ernestine Washington With Bunk Johnson**	195?	70.00	175.00
		(Disc 712 features cover art by David Stone Martin.)			

WASHINGTON, TYRONE

Tyrone Washington is a modern jazz tenor saxophone player.

Blue Note BST-84274	(S)	**Natural Essence**	1968	8.00	20.00
		– Blue Note albums above have blue on white labels with "A Division of Liberty Records."–			

WATERS, ETHEL

Ethel Waters is a traditional jazz vocalist.

Remington RLP-1025	(10")	**Ethel Waters**	1950	20.00	50.00
Mercury MG-20051	(M)	**Ethel Waters**	1954	20.00	50.00
"X" LVA-1009	(M)	**Ethel Waters**	1955	20.00	50.00

WATERS, PATTY

Patty Waters is a modern jazz vocalist.

ESP-Disk' 1025	(M)	**Patty Waters Sings**	1966	12.00	30.00
ESP-Disk' 1025	(S)	**Patty Waters Sings**	1966	10.00	25.00
ESP-Disk' 1055	(S)	**Patty Waters College Tour**	1968	20.00	50.00

Label & Catalog #		Title	Year	VG+	NM
WATKINS, DOUG					
Douglas Watkins is a modern jazz bass player. For additional listings refer to Art Blakey & The Jazz Messengers; The Manhattan Jazz All-Stars.; and the Various Artists section under Prestige.					
Transition TRLP-20	(M)	**Watkins At Large**	1956	600.00	900.00
		(Transition 20 was issued with a booklet, worth an additional $100.)			
New Jazz NJLP-8238	(M)	**Soulnik**	1960	20.00	50.00
		—New Jazz albums above have purple labels.—			
New Jazz NJLP-8238	(M)	**Soulnik**	1965	10.00	25.00
		—New Jazz albums above have blue labels with a trident logo on the right side.—			
Philips PHM-200-001	(M)	**French Horns For My Lady**	1962	10.00	25.00
Philips PHS-600-001	(S)	**French Horns For My Lady**	1962	8.00	20.00
WATKINS, JULIUS					
Julius Watkins is a modern jazz French horn player and composer. For additional listings refer to Les Jazz Modes; Thelonious Monk.					
Blue Note BLP-5053	(10")	**Julius Watkins Sextet**	1954	150.00	300.00
Blue Note BLP-5064	(10")	**Julius Watkins Sextet, Volume 2**	1955	150.00	300.00
WATT, TOMMY					
Bethlehem BCP-6052	(M)	**Watts Cooking**	1961	12.00	30.00
WATTERS, LU, & THE YERBA BUENA JAZZ BAND					
Lu Watters is a traditional jazz trumpet player. For additional listings refer to Clancy Hayes; Bob Helm; Bunk Johnson.					
Mercury MG-35013	(10")	**Lu Watters & The Yerba Buena Jazz Band**	1950	50.00	125.00
Mercury MGC-103	(10")	**Lu Watters & The Yerba Buena Jazz Band**	1950	40.00	100.00
		(Mercury 103 is a reissue of 35013.)			
Mercury MGC-503	(10")	**Lu Watters Jazz**	1951	40.00	100.00
		(Mercury 503 features cover art by David Stone Martin.)			
Mercury MGC-510	(10")	**Lu Watters And His Yerba Buena Jazz Band**	1952	40.00	100.00
		(Mercury 510 features cover art by David Stone Martin.)			
Clef MGC-103	(10")	**Lu Watters Jazz**	1954	*Unreleased*	
Clef MGC-503	(10")	**Lu Watters Jazz**	1954	30.00	75.00
		(Clef 503 is a reissue of Mercury 503 with the DSM cover.)			
Clef MGC-510	(10")	**Lu Watters And His Yerba Buena Jazz Band**	1954	30.00	75.00
		(Clef 510 is a reissue of Mercury 510 with the DSM cover.)			
Down Home MGD-5	(M)	**Lu Watters And His Yerba Buena Jass Band**	1955	24.00	60.00
		(Down Home 5 features cover art by David Stone Martin.)			
Verve MGV-1005	(M)	**Lu Watters And The Yerba Buena Jazz Band**	1956	20.00	50.00
		(Verve 1005 is a reissue of Down Home 5 with the DSM cover.)			
		—Verve albums above have black labels with "Verve Records, Inc" on the bottom.—			
Verve V-1005	(M)	**Lu Watters And The Yerba Buena Jazz Band**	1961	6.00	15.00
		—Verve albums above have black labels with "MGM Records" on the bottom.—			
Good Time Jazz L-8	(10")	**Lu Watters And The Yerba Buena Jazz Band**	1952	20.00	50.00
Good Time Jazz L-12001	(M)	**Dawn Club Favorites**	1954	16.00	40.00
Good Time Jazz L-12002	(M)	**Originals And Ragtime**	1954	16.00	40.00
Good Time Jazz L-12003	(M)	**Stomps, Etc. & The Blues**	1954	16.00	40.00
Good Time Jazz L-12007	(M)	**1942 Series**	1955	16.00	40.00
Good Time Jazz L-A	(M)	**San Francisco Style** *(3 LPs)*	195?	20.00	50.00
Riverside RLP-2513	(10")	**Lu Watters 1947**	1955	30.00	75.00
Riverside RLP-12-213	(M)	**San Francisco Style**	1956	24.00	60.00
		—Riverside albums above have blue on white labels.—			
WATTERS, LU / SANTO PECORA					
Verve MGV-1008	(M)	**Dixieland Jamboree**	1956	20.00	50.00
		(Verve 1008 features cover art by David Stone Martin.)			
		—Verve albums above have "Verve Records, Inc" on the bottom of the label.—			
Verve V-1008	(M)	**Dixieland Jamboree**	1961	8.00	20.00
		—Verve albums above have black labels with "MGM Records" on the bottom.—			
WATTS, ERNIE					
Pacific Jazz PJ-20155	(S)	**Planet Love**	1969	10.00	25.00
WATTS, MARZETTE					
Marzette Watts is a modern jazz multi-instrumentalist and composer.					
Savoy MG-12193	(S)	**Marzette Watts Ensemble**	1969	6.00	15.00
ESP-Disk' 1044	(S)	**Marzette Watts**	1971	6.00	15.00

Label & Catalog #		Title	Year	VG+	NM
WAYNE, CHUCK					
Charles Jagelka, aka Chuck Wayne, is a traditional jazz-based guitar player.					
Progressive 3003	(10")	**The Chuck Wayne Quintet**	1953	70.00	175.00
Savoy MG-12077	(M)	**The Jazz Guitarist**	1956	20.00	50.00
Vik LX-1098	(M)	**String Fever**	1957	20.00	50.00
Focus FL-333	(M)	**Tapestry**	1965	12.00	30.00
Focus FS-333	(S)	**Tapestry**	1965	10.00	25.00
Prestige PRLP-7367	(M)	**Morning Mist**	1965	10.00	25.00
Prestige PRST-7367	(S)	**Morning Mist**	1965	8.00	20.00
		—Prestige albums above have blue labels with a trident logo on the right side.—			
WAYNE, FRANCES					
Chiarina Francesca Bertocci, aka Frances Wayne, is a jazz-based vocalist.					
Coral CRL-56019	(10")	**Salute To Ethel Waters**	195?	24.00	60.00
Epic LN-3222	(M)	**Songs For My Man**	1956	20.00	50.00
		(Epic 5222 also features Neal Hefti.)			
Atlantic 1263	(M)	**The Warm Sound Of Frances Wayne**	1957	20.00	50.00
		—Atlantic albums above have black mono or green stereo labels.—			
Atlantic 1263	(M)	**The Warm Sound Of Frances Wayne**	1961	8.00	20.00
		—Atlantic albums above have multi-color labels with a white fan logo.—			
Brunswick BL-54022	(M)	**Frances Wayne**	1958	16.00	40.00
		(Brunswick 54022 also features Neal Hefti.)			
WEBB, CHICK					
William "Chick" Webb is a traditional jazz drummer and big band leader.					
Decca DL-9223	(M)	**Chick Webb 1937-39**	1958	20.00	50.00
Decca DL-79223	(E)	**Chick Webb 1937-39**	1958	14.00	35.00
Columbia CL-2639	(M)	**The Immortal Chick Webb**	1967	10.00	25.00
Columbia CS-9439	(E)	**The Immortal Chick Webb**	1967	4.00	10.00
		—Columbia albums above have "360 Sound" in white on the bottom of the label.—			
WEBB, ROGER					
Swan SW-516	(M)	**John, Paul & All That Jazz**	1964	12.00	30.00
Swan SWS-516	(S)	**John, Paul & All That Jazz**	1964	10.00	25.00
WEBSTER, BEN					
Benjamin "Frog" Webster is a traditional jazz-based tenor saxophone and piano player and arranger. For additional listings refer to Don Byas; Benny Carter; Coleman Hawkins; Coleman Hawkins / Ben Webster; Richard Holmes; Illinois Jacquet & Ben Webster; Gerry Mulligan & Ben Webster; Jo Stafford; Art Tatum.					
Brunswick BL-58031	(10")	**Tenor Sax Stylings**	1952	150.00	300.00
EmArcy MG-26006	(10")	**Big Tenor**	1954	125.00	250.00
Norgran MGN-1001	(M)	**The Consummate Artistry Of Ben Webster**	1954	60.00	150.00
Norgran MGN-1018	(M)	**Music For Loving**	1955	70.00	175.00
		(Norgran 1018 features cover art by David Stone Martin.)			
Norgran MGN-1039	(M)	**Ben Webster Plays Music With Feeling**	1955	70.00	175.00
		(Norgran 1039 features cover art by David Stone Martin.)			
Norgran MGN-1089	(M)	**King Of The Tenors**	1956	50.00	125.00
		(Norgran 1089 is a reissue of 1001.)			
Verve MGV-2026	(M)	**Sophisticated Lady—Ben Webster With Strings**	1956	20.00	50.00
		(Verve 2026 is a reissue of Norgran 1018.)			
Verve MGV-8020	(M)	**King Of The Tenors**	1957	20.00	50.00
		(Verve 8020 is a reissue of Norgran 1001.)			
Verve MGV-8130	(M)	**Music With Feeling—Ben Webster With Strings**	1957	20.00	50.00
		(Verve 8130 is a reissue of Norgran 1039.)			
Verve MGV-8274	(M)	**Soulville**	1958	20.00	50.00
Verve MGV-8318	(M)	**Ben Webster And Associates**	1959	20.00	50.00
Verve MGVS-6056	(S)	**Ben Webster And Associates**	1959	16.00	40.00
Verve MGV-8349	(M)	**Ben Webster Meets Oscar Peterson**	1959	20.00	50.00
Verve MGVS-6114	(S)	**Ben Webster Meets Oscar Peterson**	1960	16.00	40.00
Verve MGV-8359	(M)	**The Soul Of Ben Webster**	1960	20.00	50.00
Verve MGVS-6124	(S)	**The Soul Of Ben Webster**	1960	*Unreleased*	
		(Verve 8359 was reissued in the '60s with a stereo version, V6-8359.)			
		—Verve albums above have "Verve Records, Inc." on the bottom of the label.—			
Verve V-2026	(M)	**Sophisticated Lady—Ben Webster With Strings**	1961	8.00	20.00
Verve V-8020	(M)	**King Of The Tenors**	1961	8.00	20.00
Verve V-8130	(M)	**Music With Feeling—Ben Webster With Strings**	1961	8.00	20.00
Verve V-8274	(M)	**Soulville**	1961	8.00	20.00

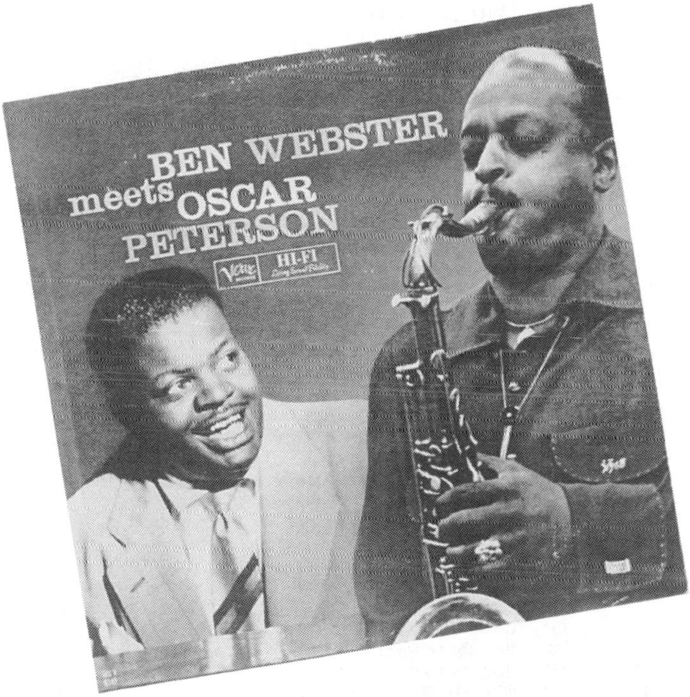

Ben Webster played piano with Dutch Campbell and as a tenorman with Gene Coy, Jap Allen, Blanche Calloway, and Andy Kirk before moving to New York with Bennie Moten in 1932. He then worked with Benny Carter, Fletcher Henderson, Willie Bryant, Cab Calloway, and Stuff Smith. He was associated with Duke Ellington on and off from 1935 through 1948. He has recorded album projects with Coleman Hawkins, Illinois Jacquet and Gerry Mulligan and appeared as a featured guest with Don Byas, Benny Carter, Hawkins, Groove Holmes, and Art Tatum. As a sideman he appears on LPs by Harry Edison, Woody Herman, and Buddy Rich, each on Verve, Bill Harris on Fantasy, Ellington and Red Norvo, both on RCA Victor, Georgie Auld on Grand Award, Jo Stafford on Columbia, and as a member of the JATP.

Label & Catalog #		Title	Year	VG+	NM
Verve V-8318	(M)	**Ben Webster And Associates**	1961	8.00	20.00
Verve V6-8318	(S)	**Ben Webster And Associates**	1961	6.00	15.00
Verve V-8349	(M)	**Ben Webster Meets Oscar Peterson**	1961	8.00	20.00
Verve V6-8349	(S)	**Ben Webster Meets Oscar Peterson**	1961	6.00	15.00
Verve V-8359	(M)	**The Soul Of Ben Webster**	1961	8.00	20.00
—Verve albums above have black labels with "MGM Records" on the bottom.—					
Reprise R-2001	(M)	**The Warm Moods Of Ben Webster**	1961	12.00	30.00
Reprise R9-2001	(S)	**The Warm Moods Of Ben Webster**	1961	10.00	25.00
Impulse A-65	(M)	**See You At The Fair**	1964	12.00	30.00
Impulse AS-65	(S)	**See You At The Fair**	1964	10.00	25.00
—Impulse albums above have orange & black labels.—					
Impulse AS-65	(S)	**See You At The Fair**	1968	4.00	10.00
—Impulse albums above have red & black labels with the "abc" logo on top.—					

WEBSTER, BEN, & HARRY "SWEETS" EDISON

Columbia CL-1891	(M)	**Ben Webster-Sweets Edison**	1962	12.00	30.00
Columbia CS-8691	(S)	**Ben Webster-Sweets Edison**	1962	10.00	25.00
—Columbia albums above have "Guaranteed High Fidelity" or "360 Sound Stereo" in black on the label.—					

WEBSTER, BEN, & JOE ZAWINUL

Riverside RLP-476	(M)	**Soulmates**	1964	12.00	30.00
Riverside RS-9476	(S)	**Soulmates**	1964	10.00	25.00
—Riverside albums above have blue mono or black stereo labels with a reel & mike logo on top.—					

WECHTER, JULIUS

Jazz: West LP-9	(M)	**Linear Sketches**	1956	100.00	200.00

WEED, BUDDY

Harold "Buddy" Weed is a traditional jazz pianist, composer and band leader.

Columbia CL-6160	(10")	**Piano Moods**	1951	20.00	50.00
Coral CRL-57087	(M)	**Piano Solos With Rhythm Accompaniment**	1957	16.00	40.00

WEIN, GEORGE

George Wein is a traditional jazz pianist and vocalist.

Atlantic 1221	(M)	**Wein, Women And Song**	1955	20.00	50.00
—Atlantic albums above have black mono or green stereo labels.—					
Atlantic 1221	(M)	**Wein, Women And Song**	1961	8.00	20.00
—Atlantic albums above have multi-color labels with a white fan logo.—					
RCA Victor LPM-1332	(M)	**The Magic Horn Of George Wein**	1956	16.00	40.00
—RCA albums above have black labels with "Long Play" on the bottom.—					
Bethlehem BCP-6050	(M)	**George Wein & The Storyville Sextet—Jazz At The Modern**	1960	16.00	40.00
Bethlehem SBCP-6050	(S)	**George Wein & The Storyville Sextet—Jazz At The Modern**	1960	16.00	40.00
Impulse A-31	(M)	**George Wein & The Newport All-Stars**	1963	10.00	25.00
Impulse AS-31	(S)	**George Wein & The Newport All-Stars**	1963	8.00	20.00
Columbia CS-9631	(S)	**Alive And Well In Mexico**	1968	6.00	15.00
—Columbia albums above have "360 Sound" on the bottom of the label.—					
Atlantoc SD-1533	(S)	**George Wein & The Newport All-Stars**	1969	5.00	12.00

WELLS, DICKY

William "Dicky" Wells is a traditional jazz trombone player, vocalist, arranger and composer. For additional listings refer to Rex Stewart & Dickie Wells.

Felsted 7006	(M)	**Bones For The King**	1958	16.00	40.00
Felsted 2006	(S)	**Bones For The King**	1958	12.00	30.00
Felsted 7009	(M)	**Trombone Four In Hand**	1958	16.00	40.00
Felsted 2009	(S)	**Trombone Four In Hand**	1958	12.00	30.00
Prestige PRST-7593	(E)	**Dicky Wells In Paris 1937**	1968	10.00	25.00
—Prestige albums above have blue labels with a trident logo on top.—					

WELLSTOOD, DICK

Richard Wellstood is a traditional jazz-based pianist.

Riverside RLP-2506	(10")	**Dick Wellstood**	1955	30.00	75.00

WELLSTOOD, DICK, & CLIFF JACKSON

Clifton Jackson is a traditional jazz pianist.

Swingville SVLP-2026	(M)	**Uptown And Downtown**	1961	20.00	50.00
—Swingville mono albums above have purple mono or red stereo labels.—					

Label & Catalog #		Title	Year	VG+	NM
Swingville SVLP-2026	(M)	**Uptown And Downtown**	1965	10.00	25.00
		—Swingville albums above have blue labels with a trident logo on the right side.—			

WESS, FRANK

Frank Wess is a modern jazz tenor saxophone and flute player and composer. For additional listings refer to Doro-thy Ashby; John Coltrane & Frank Wess; Herbie Mann; and the Various Artists section under Prestige and Savoy.

Commodore FL-20031	(10")	**Frank Wess Quintet**	1952	50.00	125.00
Commodore FL-20032	(10")	**Frank Wess**	1952	50.00	125.00
Savoy MG-12022	(M)	**Flutes And Reeds**	1955	30.00	75.00
		(Savoy 12022 also features Ernie Wilkins.)			
Savoy MG-12072	(M)	**North, South, East, Wess**	1956	30.00	75.00
Savoy MG-12095	(M)	**Jazz For Playboys**	1956	30.00	75.00
		—Savoy albums above have silver on red labels.—			
Moodsville MVLP-8	(M)	**Frank Wess Quartet**	1960	20.00	50.00
		—Moodsville mono albums above have green labels with silver print.—			
Moodsville MVLP-8	(M)	**Frank Wess Quartet**	1965	10.00	25.00
		—Moodsville albums above have blue labels with a trident logo on the right side.—			
Prestige PRLP-7231	(M)	**Southern Comfort**	1962	16.00	40.00
Prestige PRST-7231	(S)	**Southern Comfort**	1962	16.00	40.00
Prestige PRLP-7266	(M)	**Yo Ho! Poor You, Little Me**	1963	16.00	40.00
Prestige PRST-7266	(S)	**Yo Ho! Poor You, Little Me**	1963	16.00	40.00
		—Prestige albums above have yellow mono or silver stereo labels with a Bergenfield, NJ address .—			
Mainstream 56033	(M)	**Award Winner**	1965	10.00	25.00
Mainstream S-6033	(E)	**Award Winner**	1965	5.00	12.00
		(Mainstream 56033 is a reissue of Commodore 20031 and 20032)			

WESS, FRANK, & THAD JONES

New Jazz NJLP-8310	(M)	**Touche**	1963	*Unreleased*	
Status ST-8310	(M)	**Touche**	1965	16.00	40.00
		(Status 8310 is a reissue of Prestige 7084, a various artists album.)			

WESS, FRANK, & KENNY BURRELL

Prestige PRLP-7278	(M)	**Steamin'**	1963	16.00	40.00
Prestige PRST-7278	(E)	**Steamin'**	1963	12.00	30.00
		(Prestige 7278 is a reissue of 7118, Thad Jones' "After Hours.")			
		—Prestige albums above have yellow mono or silver stereo labels with a Bergenfield, NJ address .—			

WEST, ALVY

Columbia CL-6062	(10")	**Alvy West & His Little Band**	1949	20.00	50.00

WESTCHESTER WORKSHOP, THE

Unique LP-103	(M)	**Unique Jazz**	1957	20.00	50.00

WESTON, RANDY

Randolph Weston is a modern jazz pianist and composer.

Riverside RLP-2508	(10")	**Cole Porter In A Modern Mood**	1954	50.00	125.00
Riverside RLP-2515	(10")	**Randy Weston Trio**	1955	50.00	125.00
Riverside RLP-12-203	(M)	**Get Happy**	1956	24.00	60.00
Riverside RLP-12-214	(M)	**With These Hands...**	1956	24.00	60.00
Riverside RLP-12-227	(M)	**Randy Weston Trio And Solo**	1957	24.00	60.00
		(Riverside 227 is a reissue of 2515.)			
Riverside RLP-12-232	(M)	**Jazz A La Bohemia**	1957	24.00	60.00
		—Riverside albums above have blue on white labels.—			
Dawn DLP-1116	(M)	**The Modern Art Of Jazz**	1957	30.00	75.00
Jubilee JLP-1060	(M)	**Piano Ala Mode**	1957	16.00	40.00
United Arts. UAL-4011	(M)	**Little Niles**	1959	20.00	50.00
United Arts. UAS-5011	(S)	**Little Niles**	1959	16.00	40.00
United Arts. UAL-4045	(M)	**Destry Rides Again**	1959	20.00	50.00
United Arts. UAS-5045	(S)	**Destry Rides Again**	1959	16.00	40.00
United Arts. UAL-4066	(M)	**Live At The Five Spot**	1959	20.00	50.00
United Arts. UAS-5066	(S)	**Live At The Five Spot**	1959	16.00	40.00
Jazzland JLP-4	(M)	**Zulu!**	1960	16.00	40.00
		(Jazzland 4 is a reissue of Riverside 227.)			
Roulette R-65001	(M)	**Uhuru Afrika**	1960	16.00	40.00
Roulette RS-65001	(S)	**Uhuru Afrika**	1960	12.00	30.00
Colpix CP-456	(M)	**Highlight**	1963	12.00	30.00
Colpix SCP-456	(S)	**Highlight**	1963	20.00	50.00

Label & Catalog #		Title	Year	VG+	NM
WESTON, RANDY, & CECIL PAYNE					
Jazzland JLP-13	(M)	**Greenwich Village Jazz**	1960	16.00	40.00
		(Jazzland 13 is a reissue of Riverside 232.)			
WESTON, RANDY / LEM WINCHESTER					
Metrojazz E-1005	(M)	**New Faces At Newport**	1958	20.00	50.00
Metrojazz SE-1005	(S)	**New Faces At Newport**	1958	16.00	40.00
WETMORE, DICK					
Richard Wetmore is a modern jazz violinist.					
Bethlehem BCP-1035	(10")	**Dick Wetmore**	1955	40.00	100.00
WETTLING, GEORGE					
George Wettling is a traditional jazz drummer.					
Weathers Ind. 5501	(M)	**High Fidelity Rhythms**	1955	16.00	40.00
Kapp KL-1005	(M)	**Ragtime Duo**	1955	16.00	40.00
		(Kapp 1005 also features Frank Signorelli.)			
Kapp KL-1028	(M)	**Jazz Trios**	1956	16.00	40.00
Columbia CL-2559	(10")	**George Wettling's Jazz Band**	1956	16.00	40.00
Harmony HL-7080	(M)	**Dixieland In Hi-Fi**	1957	6.00	15.00
WHITE, KITTY					
Kathryn "Kitty" White is a modern jazz-based vocalist.					
Pacifica PL-802	(10")	**Kitty White**	1955	30.00	75.00
EmArcy MG-36020	(M)	**A New Voice In Jazz**	1955	20.00	50.00
EmArcy MG-36068	(M)	**Kitty White**	1955	20.00	50.00
		—EmArcy albums above have blue labels with silver print.—			
WHITE, MIKE					
Seeco SLP-4420	(M)	**Dixieland Jazz**	1960	10.00	25.00
Seeco SLP-4420	(S)	**Dixieland Jazz**	1960	8.00	20.00
WHITE, STEVE					
Liberty LJH-6006	(M)	**Jazz Mad—The Unpredictable Steve White**	1955	16.00	40.00
WHITEMAN, PAUL					
Paul Whiteman is a traditional jazz violin player and band leader. For additional listings refer to Bix Beiderbecke.					
"X" LVA-3040	(10")	**Paul Whiteman's Orchestra Featuring Bix Beiderbecke**	1955	30.00	75.00
Capitol T-622	(M)	**Classics In Jazz**	1955	20.00	50.00
		—Capitol albums above have turquoise labels.—			
Grand Award GA-33-901	(M)	**Paul Whiteman: 50th Anniversary** *(2 LPs)*	1956	20.00	50.00
Grand Award GA-33-503	(M)	**The Greatest Stars Of My Life**	195?	20.00	50.00
		(Grand Award 503 was issued in a red velvet jacket.)			
WIGGINS, GERALD					
Gerald Wiggins is a modern jazz pianist. For additional listings refer to the Various Artists section under Tampa.					
Discovery DL-2003	(10")	**Gerald Wiggins Trio**	1953	50.00	125.00
Dig LP-102	(M)	**Gerald Wiggins Trio**	1956	24.00	60.00
Motif 504	(M)	**Reminiscin' With Wig**	1956	24.00	60.00
Challenge CHP-604	(M)	**The King And I**	1957	24.00	60.00
Tampa TP-1	(M)	**The Loveliness Of You** *(Colored vinyl)*	1957	40.00	100.00
Tampa TP-1	(M)	**The Loveliness Of You**	1958	20.00	50.00
Tampa TP-33	(M)	**Gerald Wiggins Trio** *(Colored vinyl)*	1957	40.00	100.00
Tampa TP-33	(M)	**Gerald Wiggins Trio**	1958	20.00	50.00
Contemporary M-3595	(M)	**Relax And Enjoy It**	1961	16.00	40.00
Contemporary S-7595	(S)	**Relax And Enjoy It**	1961	12.00	30.00
		—Contemporary stereo albums have gold & black labels.—			
Hifijazz J-618	(M)	**Wiggin' Out**	1961	16.00	40.00
Hifijazz JS-618	(S)	**Wiggin' Out**	1961	12.00	30.00
Specialty SP-2101	(S)	**Around The World**	1969	6.00	15.00
WIGGS, JOHNNY					
John Wigginton Hyman, aka Johnny Wiggs, is a traditional jazz cornet player.					
Southland LP-200	(10")	**Johnny Wiggs**	1954	20.00	50.00

As a teenager, Lee Wiley had established her credentials with Leo Reisman's orchestra by 1932. Her career as both a singer extraordinaire (Bud Freeman claimed she sang like Bix played) and a crafty songwriter included pop along with her jazz associations, including Eddie Condon, Paul Whiteman, and husband Jess Stacy. Her recording career of the '50s included stays with Columbia, where she was accompanied by Bobby Hackett and Joe Bushkin, and RCA Victor, which features brillaint arrangements by Ralph Burns, along with Storyville.

Label & Catalog #		Title	Year	VG+	NM
WIGGS, JOHNNY, & RAYMOND BURKE					
Paramount LP-107	(10")	**New Orleans Jazz Chamber Music Session**	1954	20.00	50.00
"S/D" LP-1001	(10")	**Chamber Jazz**	1955	20.00	50.00
WILBUR, BOB					
Robert Wilbur is a traditional jazz clarinet and soprano saxophone player.					
Circle L-406	(10")	**Bob Wilbur Jazz Band**	1951	20.00	50.00
Riverside RLP-2501	(10")	**Young Men With Horns**	1952	30.00	75.00
WILCOX, LARRY					
Columbia CL-2147	(M)	**Hot Rod Jazz**	1964	12.00	30.00
Columbia CS-8947	(S)	**Hot Rod Jazz**	1964	12.00	30.00
Columbia CSRP-8947	(M)	**Hot Rod Jazz** *(Columbia Special Products)*	196?	6.00	15.00
WILDER, ALEC					
Alexander "Alec" Wilder is jazz-based composer. For additional listings refer to Frank Sinatra.					
Mercury MG-25008	(10")	**Alec Wilder And His Octet**	1949	20.00	50.00
Columbia CL-6181	(10")	**Alec Wilder Octet**	1951	20.00	50.00
WILDER, JOE					
Joseph Wilder is a traditional jazz-based trumpet player. For additional listings refer to Ernie Wilkins.					
Savoy MG-12063	(M)	**'N' Wilder...**	1956	16.00	40.00
Columbia CL-1319	(M)	**Jazz From "Peter Gunn"**	1959	16.00	40.00
Columbia CS-8121	(S)	**Jazz From "Peter Gunn"**	1959	12.00	30.00
Columbia CL-1372	(M)	**The Pretty Sound Of Joe Wilder**	1959	12.00	30.00
Columbia CS-8173	(S)	**The Pretty Sound Of Joe Wilder**	1959	10.00	25.00
		— Columbia albums above have six white on black "eye" logos on each label. —			
WILEY, LEE					
Lee Wiley is a jazz-based vocalist and composer. For additional listings refer to Ellis Larkins / Lee Wiley.					
Liberty Music Shop 1003	(10")	**Cole Porter Songs By Lee Wiley**	195?	150.00	300.00
Liberty Music Shop 1004	(10")	**George Gershwin Songs By Lee Wiley**	195?	150.00	300.00
Columbia CL-6169	(10")	**Night In Manhattan**	1951	40.00	100.00
		(Columbia 6169 also features Bobby Hackett and Joe Bushkin.)			
Columbia CL-6215	(10")	**Lee Wiley Sings Vincent Youmans**	1952	40.00	100.00
Columbia CL-6216	(10")	**Lee Wiley Sings Irving Berlin**	1952	40.00	100.00
Columbia CL-656	(M)	**Night In Manhattan**	1955	40.00	100.00
		(Columbia 656 is a reissue of 6196 plus additional tracks.)			
		— Columbia albums above have six white on black "eye" logos on each label. —			
Allegro-Elite 4019	(10")	**Lee Wiley Sings—Lennie Tristano Plays**	195?	40.00	100.00
Storyville STLP-312	(10")	**Lee Wiley Sings Rodgers And Hart**	1954	70.00	175.00
Jazztone J-1248	(M)	**The Songs Of Rodgers & Hart—Intimate Jazz**	1956	20.00	50.00
		(Jazztone 1248 is a various artists album crediting Lee Wiley & Friend.)			
RCA Victor LPM-1408	(M)	**West Of The Moon**	1957	30.00	75.00
RCA Victor LPM-1566	(M)	**Touch Of The Blues**	1957	24.00	60.00
		— RCA albums above have black labels with "Long Play" on the bottom. —			
"JJC" M-2002	(M)	**The One And Only Lee Wiley**	195?	20.00	50.00
"JJC" M-2003	(M)	**The Classics Interpretations Of The Immortal Cole Porter**	195?	20.00	50.00
Ric M-2002	(M)	**The One And Only Lee Wiley**	1964	8.00	20.00
Ric S-2002	(S)	**The One And Only Lee Wiley**	1964	10.00	25.00
WILKERSON, DON					
Donald Wilkerson is a modern jazz tenor saxophone player.					
Riverside RLP-332	(M)	**Texas Twister**	1960	16.00	40.00
Riverside RLP-1186	(S)	**Texas Twister**	1960	12.00	30.00
		— Riverside albums above have blue mono or black stereo labels with a reel & mike logo on top. —			
Blue Note BLP-4107	(M)	**Preach, Brother!**	1962	16.00	40.00
Blue Note BST-84107	(S)	**Preach, Brother!**	1962	12.00	30.00
Blue Note BLP-4121	(M)	**Elder Don**	1963	16.00	40.00
Blue Note BST-84121	(S)	**Elder Don**	1963	12.00	30.00
Blue Note BLP-4145	(M)	**Shoutin'**	1963	16.00	40.00
Blue Note BST-84145	(S)	**Shoutin'**	1963	12.00	30.00
		— Blue Note albums above have blue on white labels with a New York, USA address. —			
Blue Note BST-84107	(S)	**Preach, Brother!**	196?	5.00	12.00
Blue Note BST-84121	(S)	**Elder Don**	196?	5.00	12.00
Blue Note BST-84145	(S)	**Shoutin'**	196?	5.00	12.00
		— Blue Note albums above have blue on white labels with "A Division of Liberty Records.". —			

Label & Catalog #		Title	Year	VG+	NM

WILKINS, ERNIE

Ernest Wilkins is a traditional jazz alto and tenor sax player and composer. For additional listings refer to Kenny Clarke & Ernie Wilkins; Frank Wess.

Label & Catalog #		Title	Year	VG+	NM
Savoy MG-12044	(M)	**Top Brass Featuring 5 Trumpets**	1955	24.00	60.00
		(Savoy 12044 features Donald Byrd, Ray Copeland, Ernie Royal, Idrees Sulieman and Joe Wilder.)			
		—Savoy albums above have maroon labels.—			
Everest LPBR-5077	(M)	**Here Comes The Swingin' Mr. Wilkins**	1959	12.00	30.00
Everest SDBR-1077	(S)	**Here Comes The Swingin' Mr. Wilkins**	1959	10.00	25.00
Everest LPBR-5104	(M)	**The Big New Band Of The '60s**	1960	12.00	30.00
Everest SDBR-1104	(S)	**The Big New Band Of The '60s**	1960	10.00	25.00

WILLETTE, BABY FACE

"Baby Face" Willette is a modern jazz organ player.

Label & Catalog #		Title	Year	VG+	NM
Blue Note BLP-4068	(M)	**Face To Face**	1961	60.00	150.00
Blue Note BST-84068	(S)	**Face To Face**	1961	50.00	125.00
		—Blue Note albums above have blue on white labels with a W. 63rd St., NYC address.—			
Blue Note BLP-4084	(M)	**Stop And Listen**	1962	50.00	125.00
Blue Note BST-84084	(S)	**Stop And Listen**	1962	40.00	100.00
		—Blue Note albums above have blue on white labels with a 61st St, NYC address.—			
Blue Note BLP-4068	(M)	**Face To Face**	1963	10.00	25.00
Blue Note BST-84068	(S)	**Face To Face**	1963	8.00	20.00
Blue Note BLP-4084	(M)	**Stop And Listen**	1963	10.00	25.00
Blue Note BST-84084	(S)	**Stop And Listen**	1963	8.00	20.00
		—Blue Note albums above have blue on white labels with a New York, USA address.—			
Blue Note BST-84068	(S)	**Face To Face**	196?	5.00	12.00
Blue Note BST-84084	(S)	**Stop And Listen**	196?	5.00	12.00
		—Blue Note albums above have blue on white labels with "A Division of Liberty Records.".—			
Argo LP-739	(M)	**No Rock**	1964	12.00	30.00
Argo LPS-739	(S)	**No Rock**	1964	10.00	25.00
Argo LP-749	(M)	**Behind The 8 Ball**	1965	12.00	30.00
Argo LPS-749	(S)	**Behind The 8 Ball**	1965	10.00	25.00

WILLIAMS, ANN

Ann Williams is a modern jazz vocalist.

Label & Catalog #		Title	Year	VG+	NM
Charlie Parker PLP-807	(M)	**First Time Out**	1963	16.00	40.00
Charlie Parker PLP-807S	(S)	**First Time Out**	1963	14.00	35.00

WILLIAMS, ANTHONY: ***Refer to*** **TONY WILLIAMS**

WILLIAMS, COOTIE

Charles "Cootie" Williams is a traditional jazz trumpet player. For additional listings refer to Rex Stewart.

Label & Catalog #		Title	Year	VG+	NM
RCA Victor LPM-1718	(M)	**Cootie Williams In Hi Fi**	1958	30.00	75.00
		—RCA albums above have black labels with "Long Play" on the bottom.—			
Jaro 5001	(M)	**Around Midnight**	1959	40.00	100.00
Jaro 8001	(S)	**Around Midnight**	1959	30.00	75.00
		(Jaro 5001 also features Wini Brown.)			
Warwick W-2027	(M)	**Do Nothing Till You Hear From Me**	1960	16.00	40.00
Warwick W-2027ST	(S)	**Do Nothing Till You Hear From Me**	1960	24.00	60.00
Moodsville MVLP-27	(M)	**The Solid Trumpet Of Cootie Williams**	1962	20.00	50.00
		—Moodsville mono albums above have green labels with silver print.—			
Moodsville MVLP-27	(M)	**The Solid Trumpet Of Cootie Williams**	1965	10.00	25.00
		—Moodsville albums above have blue labels with a trident logo on the right side.—			

WILLIAMS, COOTIE / JIMMY PRESTON

Label & Catalog #		Title	Year	VG+	NM
Allegro Elite 4109	(10")	**Rock 'N' Roll**	195?	20.00	50.00

WILLIAMS, GEORGE

George "The Fox" Williams is a traditional jazz-based composer and band leader.

Label & Catalog #		Title	Year	VG+	NM
RCA Victor LPM-1205	(M)	**We Could Make Such Beautiful Music**	1956	16.00	40.00
		—RCA albums above have black labels with "Long Play" on the bottom.—			

WILLIAMS, HERBIE

Herbert Williams is a modern jazz soprano saxophone player.

Label & Catalog #		Title	Year	VG+	NM
Jazz Workshop JWS-216	(M)	**The Soul And Sound Of Herbie Williams**	1963	20.00	50.00

Label & Catalog #		Title	Year	VG+	NM

WILLIAMS, JOE

Joseph Goreed, aka Joe Williams, is a traditional jazz and big band vocalist. For additional listings refer to Count Basie & Joe Williams; Sarah Vaughan & Dinah Washington & Joe Williams.

Label & Catalog #		Title	Year	VG+	NM
Regent MG-6002	(M)	**Joe Williams Sings Everyday**	1956	20.00	50.00
Savoy MG-12216	(S)	**Joe Williams Sings**	196?	6.00	15.00
		(Savoy 12216 is a reisue of Regent 6002.)			
Roulette R-52005	(M)	**Man Ain't Supposed To Cry**	1958	16.00	40.00
Roulette SR-52005	(S)	**Man Ain't Supposed To Cry**	1958	20.00	50.00
Roulette R-52030	(M)	**Joe Williams Sings About You!**	1959	16.00	40.00
Roulette SR-52030	(S)	**Joe Williams Sings About You!**	1959	20.00	50.00
Roulette R-52039	(M)	**That Kind Of Woman**	1960	16.00	40.00
Roulette SR-52039	(S)	**That Kind Of Woman**	1960	20.00	50.00
		—Roulette albums above have white labels.—			
Roulette R-52066	(M)	**Sentimental And Melancholy**	1961	10.00	25.00
Roulette SR-52066	(S)	**Sentimental And Melancholy**	1961	12.00	30.00
Roulette R-52069	(M)	**Together**	1961	10.00	25.00
Roulette SR-52069	(S)	**Together**	1961	12.00	30.00
Roulette R-52071	(M)	**Have A Good Time**	1961	10.00	25.00
Roulette SR-52071	(S)	**Have A Good Time**	1961	12.00	30.00
Roulette R-52085	(M)	**Swingin' Night At Birdland**	1962	10.00	25.00
Roulette SR-52085	(S)	**Swingin' Night At Birdland**	1962	12.00	30.00
Roulette R-52102	(M)	**One Is A Lonesome Number**	1963	10.00	25.00
Roulette SR-52102	(S)	**One Is A Lonesome Number**	1963	12.00	30.00
Roulette R-52105	(M)	**New Kind Of Love**	1963	10.00	25.00
Roulette SR-52105	(S)	**New Kind Of Love**	1963	12.00	30.00
		—Roulette albums above have orange & pink labels.—			
RCA Victor LPM-2713	(M)	**Jump For Joy**	1963	10.00	25.00
RCA Victor LSP-2713	(S)	**Jump For Joy**	1963	12.00	30.00
		—RCA albums above have black labels with "Long Play" or "Living Stereo" on the bottom.—			
RCA Victor LPM-2762	(M)	**Joe Williams At Newport '63**	1963	10.00	25.00
RCA Victor LSP-2762	(S)	**Joe Williams At Newport '63**	1963	12.00	30.00
RCA Victor LPM-2879	(M)	**Me And The Blues**	1964	10.00	25.00
RCA Victor LSP-2879	(S)	**Me And The Blues**	1964	12.00	30.00
		—RCA mono albums above have black labels with "Mono" or "Living Stereo" on the bottom.—			
RCA Victor LPM-3433	(M)	**Song Is You**	1965	8.00	20.00
RCA Victor LSP-3433	(S)	**Song Is You**	1965	10.00	25.00
RCA Victor LPM-3461	(M)	**The Exciting Joe Williams**	1965	8.00	20.00
RCA Victor LSP-3461	(S)	**The Exciting Joe Williams**	1965	10.00	25.00
		—RCA mono albums above have black labels with "Monaural" or "Stereo" on the bottom.—			
Solid State SM-17008	(M)	**Presenting Joe Williams & The Jazz Orchestra**	1967	8.00	20.00
Solid State SS-18008	(S)	**Presenting Joe Williams & The Jazz Orchestra**	1967	6.00	15.00
Solid State SM-17015	(M)	**Something Old, New And Blue**	1968	10.00	25.00
Solid State SS-18015	(S)	**Something Old, New And Blue**	1968	6.00	15.00

WILLIAMS, JOHN

John Williams is a modern jazz pianist and composer.

Label & Catalog #		Title	Year	VG+	NM
EmArcy MG-26047	(10")	**John Williams**	1955	40.00	100.00
EmArcy MG-36061	(M)	**John Williams Trio**	1956	20.00	50.00
		—EmArcy albums above have blue labels with silver print.—			

WILLIAMS, JOHN TOWNER

Label & Catalog #		Title	Year	VG+	NM
Bethlehem BCP-6025	(M)	**World On A String**	1958	20.00	50.00

WILLIAMS, KEITH

Keith Williams is a trumpet player and arranger with this sole jazz outing in his work.

Label & Catalog #		Title	Year	VG+	NM
Edison 501	(M)	**Big Band Jazz Themes**	1960	8.00	20.00

WILLIAMS, MARY LOU

Mary Elfreida Winn, aka Mary Lou Williams, is a traditional jazz pianist and composer. For additional listings refer to Barbara Carroll / Mary Lou Williams; Al Haig / Mary Lou Williams; Art Tatum / Mary Lou Williams.

Label & Catalog #		Title	Year	VG+	NM
Asch ALP-345	(10")	**Mary Lou Williams Trio**	1950	60.00	150.00
		(Asch 345 features cover art by David Stone Martin.)			
Stinson SLP-24	(10")	**Mary Lou Williams**	1950	60.00	150.00
		(Stinson 24 features cover art by David Stone Martin.)			
Stinson SLP-29	(10")	**Jazz Variation**	1950	50.00	125.00
Folkways FP-32	(10")	**Rehearsal—Jazz Session/ Footnotes To Jazz, Vol. 3**	1951	40.00	100.00

Label & Catalog #		Title	Year	VG+	NM
Atlantic ALR-114	(10")	**Piano Panorama—Volume 2**	1951	50.00	125.00
Circle 412	(10")	**Piano Contempo**	1951	50.00	125.00
King 295-85	(10")	**Progressive Piano Stylings**	1953	60.00	150.00
Contemporary C-2507	(10")	**Piano '53**	1953	40.00	100.00
EmArcy MG-26033	(10")	**Mary Lou**	1954	40.00	100.00
Concert Hall Jazz 1007	(10")	**A Keyboard History**	1955	20.00	50.00
Jazztone J-1206	(M)	**A Keyboard History**	1955	16.00	40.00
Mary 32843	(M)	**Black Christ Of The Andes**	1964	12.00	30.00
Mary 32843	(S)	**Black Christ Of The Andes**	1964	10.00	25.00
Mary 282489	(M)	**Music For Peace**	1964	12.00	30.00
Mary 282489	(S)	**Music For Peace**	1964	10.00	25.00

(Mary 32843 and 282489 feature cover art by David Stone Martin.)

WILLIAMS, MARY LOU / RALPH BURNS

Jazztone J-1255	(M)	**Composres—Pianists**	1956	16.00	40.00

WILLIAMS, MARY LOU, & DON BYAS / BUCK CLAYTON & ALIX COMBELLE

Storyville STLP-906	(M)	**Messin' 'Round In Montmarte**	1956	20.00	50.00

WILLIAMS, RICHARD

Richard Williams is a modern jazz trumpet player and composer.

Candid CD-8003	(M)	**New Horn In Town**	1960	20.00	50.00
Candid CS-9003	(S)	**New Horn In Town**	1960	16.00	40.00

WILLIAMS, TONY

Anthony Williams is a modern jazz drummer.

Blue Note BLP-4180	(M)	**Life Time**	1964	12.00	30.00
Blue Note BST-84180	(S)	**Life Time**	1964	10.00	25.00
Blue Note BLP-4216	(M)	**Spring**	1965	12.00	30.00
Blue Note BST-84216	(S)	**Spring**	1965	10.00	25.00
—Blue Note albums above have blue on white labels with a New York, USA address.—					
Blue Note BST-84180	(S)	**Life Time**	196?	5.00	12.00
Blue Note BST-84216	(S)	**Spring**	196?	5.00	12.00
—Blue Note albums above have blue on white labels with "A Division of Liberty Records."—					
Polydor 25-3001	(S)	**Emergency** (2 LPs)	1969	6.00	15.00

WILLIAMS, VALDO

Savoy MG-12188	(M)	**New Advanced Jazz**	1969	12.00	30.00

WILLIAMSON, CLAUDE

Claude Williamson is a West Coast jazz pianist. For additional listings refer to Bud Shank.

Capitol H-6502	(10")	**Claude Williamson**	1954	20.00	50.00
Capitol H-6511	(10")	**Keys West**	1955	20.00	50.00
Capitol T-6511	(M)	**Keys West**	1956	16.00	40.00
Bethlehem BCP-54	(M)	**Claude Williamson**	1956	16.00	40.00
Bethlehem BCP-69	(M)	**'Round Midnight**	1957	16.00	40.00
Criterion 601	(M)	**Claude Williamson Mulls The Mulligan Scene**	195?	16.00	40.00
Contract 15001	(M)	**The Fabulous Claude Williamson Trio**	196?	12.00	30.00
Contract 15003	(M)	**Theatre Party**	196?	12.00	30.00

WILLIAMSON, STU

Stuart Williamson is a West Coast jazz trumpet and valve trombone player.

Bethlehem BCP-1024	(10")	**Stu Williamson Plays**	1955	50.00	125.00
Bethlehem BCP-31	(M)	**Stu Williamson Plays**	1955	30.00	75.00
		(Bethlehem 31 is a reissue of 1024.)			
Bethlehem BCP-55	(M)	**Stu Williamson**	1956	30.00	75.00

WILSON, GERALD

Gerald Wilson is a traditional jazz trumpet player, arranger and composer associated with West Coast jazz. For additional listings refer to Carmell Jones; Tricky Lofton & Carmell Jones; Les McCann.

Federal 295-93	(10")	**Gerald Wilson**	1953	125.00	250.00
Audio Lab AL-1538	(M)	**Big Band Modern**	1959	60.00	150.00
		(Audio Lab 1538 is a reissue of Federal 93.)			
Pacific Jazz PJ-34	(M)	**You Better Believe It**	1961	12.00	30.00
Pacific Jazz ST-34	(S)	**You Better Believe It**	1961	10.00	25.00
		(Pacific Jazz 34 also features Groove Holmes.)			
Pacific Jazz PJ-61	(M)	**Moment Of Truth**	1962	12.00	30.00
Pacific Jazz ST-61	(S)	**Moment Of Truth**	1962	10.00	25.00

Label & Catalog #		Title	Year	VG+	NM
Pacific Jazz PJ-80	(M)	**Portraits**	1961	12.00	30.00
Pacific Jazz ST-80	(S)	**Portraits**	1964	10.00	25.00
Pacific Jazz PJ-88	(M)	**Gerald Wilson On Stage**	1964	12.00	30.00
Pacific Jazz ST-88	(S)	**Gerald Wilson On Stage**	1964	10.00	25.00
Pacific Jazz PJ-10099	(M)	**Feelin' Kinda Blue**	1964	8.00	20.00
Pacific Jazz ST-20099	(S)	**Feelin' Kinda Blue**	1966	6.00	15.00
Pacific Jazz PJ-10111	(M)	**Golden Sword**	1966	8.00	20.00
Pacific Jazz ST-20111	(S)	**Golden Sword**	1966	6.00	15.00
Pacific Jazz PJ-10118	(M)	**Live And Swinging**	1967	8.00	20.00
Pacific Jazz ST-20118	(S)	**Live And Swinging**	1967	6.00	15.00
Pacific Jazz ST-20132	(S)	**Everywhere**	1968	6.00	15.00
Pacific Jazz ST-20135	(S)	**California Soul**	1968	6.00	15.00
Pacific Jazz ST-20160	(S)	**Eternal Equinox**	1968	6.00	15.00

WILSON, JACK

John Wilson is a jazz-based pianist.

Label & Catalog #		Title	Year	VG+	NM
Atlantic 1406	(M)	**Jack Wilson Quartet**	1963	16.00	40.00
Atlantic SD-1406	(S)	**Jack Wilson Quartet**	1963	12.00	30.00
Atlantic 1427	(M)	**The Two Sides Of Jack Wilson**	1964	16.00	40.00
Atlantic SD-1427	(S)	**The Two Sides Of Jack Wilson**	1964	12.00	30.00
		—Atlantic albums above have multi-color labels with a black fan logo.—			
Vault LP-9001	(M)	**Brazilian Mancini**	1964	12.00	30.00
Vault LPS-9001	(S)	**Brazilian Mancini**	1964	10.00	25.00
Vault LP-9002	(M)	**Ramblin'**	1964	12.00	30.00
Vault LPS-9002	(S)	**Ramblin'**	1964	10.00	25.00
		(Vault 9002 also features Roy Ayers.)			
Vault LP-9008	(M)	**Jazz Organs**	1965	12.00	30.00
Vault LPS-9008	(S)	**Jazz Organs**	1965	10.00	25.00
Blue Note BLP-4251	(M)	**Something Personal**	1967	12.00	30.00
Blue Note BST-84251	(S)	**Something Personal**	1967	10.00	25.00
		— Blue Note albums above blue on white labels with a New York, USA address.—			
Blue Note BST-84251	(S)	**Something Personal**	196?	5.00	12.00
Blue Note BST-84270	(S)	**Easterly Winds**	1968	6.00	15.00
Blue Note BST-84328	(S)	**Song For My Daughter**	1969	6.00	15.00
		— Blue Note albums above blue on white labels with "A Division of Liberty Records."—			

WILSON, NANCY

Nancy Wilson is a jazz-based pop vocalist.

Label & Catalog #		Title	Year	VG+	NM
Capitol T-1319	(M)	**Like In Love**	1960	8.00	20.00
Capitol ST-1319	(S)	**Like In Love**	1960	10.00	25.00
Capitol T-1440	(M)	**Something Wonderful**	1960	8.00	20.00
Capitol ST-1440	(S)	**Something Wonderful**	1960	10.00	25.00
Capitol T-1524	(M)	**The Swingin's Mutual**	1961	8.00	20.00
Capitol ST-1524	(S)	**The Swingin's Mutual**	1961	10.00	25.00
		(Capitol 1524 also features George Shearing.)			
Capitol T-1657	(M)	**Nancy Wilson/Cannonball Adderley**	1961	8.00	20.00
Capitol ST-1657	(S)	**Nancy Wilson/Cannonball Adderley**	1961	10.00	25.00
		— Capitol albums above have black "rainbow" labels with the logo on the left side.—			
Capitol T-1319	(M)	**Like In Love**	1960	4.00	10.00
Capitol ST-1319	(S)	**Like In Love**	1960	5.00	12.00
Capitol T-1440	(M)	**Something Wonderful**	1960	4.00	10.00
Capitol ST-1440	(S)	**Something Wonderful**	1960	5.00	12.00
Capitol T-1524	(M)	**The Swingin's Mutual**	1961	4.00	10.00
Capitol ST-1524	(S)	**The Swingin's Mutual**	1961	5.00	12.00
Capitol T-1657	(M)	**Nancy Wilson/Cannonball Adderley**	1961	4.00	10.00
Capitol ST-1657	(S)	**Nancy Wilson/Cannonball Adderley**	1961	5.00	12.00
Capitol T-1767	(M)	**Hello, Young Lovers**	1962	5.00	12.00
Capitol ST-1767	(S)	**Hello, Young Lovers**	1962	6.00	15.00
Capitol T-1828	(M)	**Broadway My Way**	1963	5.00	12.00
Capitol ST-1828	(S)	**Broadway My Way**	1963	6.00	15.00
Capitol T-1934	(M)	**Hollywood My Way**	1963	5.00	12.00
Capitol ST-1934	(S)	**Hollywood My Way**	1963	6.00	15.00
Capitol T-2012	(M)	**Yesterday's Love Songs... Today's Blues**	1963	5.00	12.00
Capitol ST-2012	(S)	**Yesterday's Love Songs... Today's Blues**	1963	6.00	15.00
Capitol T-2082	(M)	**Today, Tomorrow, Forever**	1964	5.00	12.00
Capitol ST-2082	(S)	**Today, Tomorrow, Forever**	1964	6.00	15.00
		— Capitol albums above have black "rainbow" labels with the logo on top.—			

WILSON, REG

Label & Catalog #		Title	Year	VG+	NM
Herald HLP-0104	(M)	**All By Himself**	1956	16.00	40.00

WILSON, REUBEN

Reuben Wilson is a modern jazz organ player.

Label & Catalog #		Title	Year	VG+	NM
Blue Note BST-84295	(S)	**On Broadway**	1968	10.00	25.00
Blue Note BST-84317	(S)	**Love Bug**	1969	10.00	25.00

— Blue Note albums above blue on white labels with "A Division of Liberty Records."—

WILSON, TEDDY

Theodore Wilson is a traditional jazz pianist and arranger. For additional listings refer to Benny Goodman; Gene Krupa & Lionel Hampton; the Jazzy Soundtracks section under Decca.

Label & Catalog #		Title	Year	VG+	NM
Columbia CL-6040	(10")	**Teddy Wilson Featuring Billie Holiday**	1949	150.00	300.00
Columbia CL-6098	(10")	**Teddy Wilson And His Piano**	1950	100.00	200.00
Columbia CL-6153	(10")	**Piano Moods**	1950	50.00	125.00
Columbia CL-748	(M)	**Mr. Wilson**	1956	20.00	60.00
Columbia CL-1318	(M)	**Mr. Wilson And Mr. Gershwin**	1959	16.00	40.00
Columbia CL-1352	(M)	**Gypsy**	1959	16.00	40.00
Columbia CS-8160	(S)	**Gypsy**	1959	12.00	30.00
Columbia CL-1442	(M)	**And Then They Wrote**	1960	16.00	40.00
Columbia CS-8242	(S)	**And Then They Wrote**	1960	12.00	30.00

— Columbia albums above have six white on black "eye" logos on each label.—

Label & Catalog #		Title	Year	VG+	NM
Dial LP-213	(10")	**Teddy Wilson All Stars**	1950	125.00	250.00
Commodore FL-20029	(10")	**Town Hall Concert**	1952	70.00	175.00
MGM E-129	(10")	**Runnin' Wild**	1951	70.00	175.00
Allegro 4024	(10")	**All Star Sextet**	1954	40.00	100.00
Allegro 4031	(10")	**All Star Sextet**	1954	40.00	100.00
Royale 18169	(10")	**Teddy Wilson And His All Stars**	195?	40.00	100.00
Mercury MG-25172	(10")	**Piano Pastries**	1953	50.00	125.00
Clef MGC-140	(10")	**The Didactic Mr. Wilson**	1953	50.00	125.00
Clef MGC-156	(10")	**Soft Moods With Teddy Wilson**	1954	50.00	125.00
Norgran MGN-1019	(M)	**The Creative Teddy Wilson**	1955	40.00	100.00

(Norgran 1019 features cover art by David Stone Martin.)

Label & Catalog #		Title	Year	VG+	NM
Verve MGV-2011	(M)	**Intimate Listening**	1956	20.00	50.00
Verve MGV-2029	(M)	**For Quiet Lovers**	1956	30.00	75.00

(Verve 2029 is a reissue of Norgran 1019 with the DSM cover.)

Label & Catalog #		Title	Year	VG+	NM
Verve MGV-2073	(M)	**I Got Rhythm**	1957	20.00	50.00
Verve MGV-8272	(M)	**The Impeccable Mr. Teddy Wilson**	1958	20.00	50.00
Verve MGV-8299	(M)	**These Tunes Remind Me Of You**	1959	20.00	50.00
Verve MGV-8330	(M)	**The Touch Of Teddy Wilson**	1959	20.00	50.00

— Verve albums above have "Verve Records, Inc." on the bottom of the label.—

Label & Catalog #		Title	Year	VG+	NM
Verve V-2011	(M)	**Intimate Listening**	1961	8.00	20.00
Verve V-2029	(M)	**For Quiet Lovers**	1961	8.00	20.00
Verve V-2073	(M)	**I Got Rhythm**	1961	8.00	20.00
Verve V-8272	(M)	**The Impeccable Mr. Teddy Wilson**	1961	8.00	20.00
Verve V-8299	(M)	**These Tunes Remind Me Of You**	1961	8.00	20.00
Verve V-8330	(M)	**The Touch Of Teddy Wilson**	1961	8.00	20.00

— Verve albums above have black labels with "MGM Records" on the bottom.—

Label & Catalog #		Title	Year	VG+	NM
Cameo C-1059	(M)	**Teddy Wilson 1964**	1964	12.00	30.00
Cameo CS-1059	(S)	**Teddy Wilson 1964**	1964	12.00	30.00
Prestige PRST-7696	(S)	**The Teddy Wilson Trio In Europe**	1969	5.00	12.00

— Prestige albums above have blue labels with a trident logo on top.—

WILSON, TEDDY / GERRY MULLIGAN

Label & Catalog #		Title	Year	VG+	NM
Verve MGV-8235	(M)	**The Teddy Wilson Trio And The Gerry Mulligan Quartet At Newport**	1958	20.00	50.00

— Verve albums above have black labels with "Verve Records, Inc." on the bottom.—

Label & Catalog #		Title	Year	VG+	NM
Verve V-8235	(M)	**The Teddy Wilson Trio And The Gerry Mulligan Quartet At Newport**	1961	8.00	20.00

— Verve albums above have black labels with "MGM Records" on the bottom.—

WINCHESTER, LEM

Lemuel Winchester is a modern jazz vibraphone player. For additional listings refer to Randy Weston / Lem Winchester.

Label & Catalog #		Title	Year	VG+	NM
Argo LP-642	(M)	**Lem Winchester With The Ramsey Lewis Trio**	1959	20.00	50.00
Argo LPS-642	(S)	**Lem Winchester With The Ramsey Lewis Trio**	1959	16.00	40.00
New Jazz NJLP-8223	(M)	**Winchester Special**	1959	30.00	75.00

(New Jazz 8223 also features Benny Golson.)

Label & Catalog #		Title	Year	VG+	NM
New Jazz NJLP-8239	(M)	**Lem's Beat**	1960	30.00	75.00
New Jazz NJLP-8244	(M)	**Another Opus**	1960	30.00	75.00
		—New Jazz albums above have purple labels.—			
New Jazz NJLP-8223	(M)	**Winchester Special**	1965	10.00	25.00
New Jazz NJLP-8239	(M)	**Lem's Beat**	1965	10.00	25.00
New Jazz NJLP-8244	(M)	**Another Opus**	1965	10.00	25.00
		—New Jazz albums above have blue labels with a trident logo on the right side.—			
Moodsville MVLP-11	(M)	**Lem Winchester With Feeling**	1960	20.00	50.00
		—Moodsville mono albums above have green labels with silver print.—			
Moodsville MVLP-11	(M)	**Lem Winchester With Feeling**	1965	10.00	25.00
		—Moodsville albums above have blue labels with a trident logo on the right side.—			
MGM E-1005	(M)	**New Faces At Newport**	1960	16.00	40.00
Argo LP-642	(M)	**Lem Winchester With The Ramsey Lewis Trio**	1959		

WINDHURST, JOHNNY

John Windhurst is a traditional jazz-based trumpet player.

Label & Catalog #		Title	Year	VG+	NM
Transition TRLP-2	(M)	**Jazz At Columbus Ave.**	1956	60.00	150.00
		(Transition 2 was issued with a booklet, worth an additional $25.)			

WINDING, KAI

Danish born Kai Winding is a modern jazz trombone player and composer. For additional listings refer to Stan Getz / Red Rodney / Kai Winding; J.J. Johnson & Kai Winding; Gerry Mulligan & Kai Winding; Fats Navarro / Kai Winding / Brew Moore; Zoot Sims; and the "Jazz At 16 2/3 RPM" article.

Label & Catalog #		Title	Year	VG+	NM
Roost LP-408	(10")	**Kai Winding All Stars**	1952	50.00	125.00
Savoy MG-9017	(10")	**New Trends Of Jazz**	1952	50.00	125.00
Columbia CL-936	(M)	**Trombone Sound**	1956	20.00	50.00
Columbia CL-999	(M)	**Trombone Panorama**	1957	20.00	50.00
Columbia CL-1264	(M)	**Swingin' State**	1958	20.00	50.00
Columbia CS-8062	(S)	**Swingin' State**	1958	16.00	40.00
Columbia CL-1329	(M)	**Dance To The City Beat**	1959	16.00	40.00
Columbia CS-8136	(S)	**Dance To The City Beat**	1959	12.00	30.00
		—Columbia albums above have six white on black "eye" logos on each label.—			
Harmony HL-7341	(M)	**The Great Kai Winding Sound**	1962	6.00	15.00
Harmony HS-7341	(S)	**The Great Kai Winding Sound**	1962	5.00	12.00
Impulse A-3	(M)	**The Incredible Kai Winding Trombones**	1960	12.00	30.00
Impulse AS-3	(S)	**The Incredible Kai Winding Trombones**	1960	10.00	25.00
		—Impulse albums above have orange & black labels.—			
Impulse AS-3	(S)	**The Incredible Kai Winding Trombones**	1968	4.00	10.00
		—Impulse albums above have red & black labels with the "abc" logo on top.—			
Verve V-8427	(M)	**Kai Ole'**	1962	10.00	25.00
Verve V6-8427	(S)	**Kai Ole'**	1962	8.00	20.00
Verve V-8493	(M)	**Suspense Themes In Jazz**	1962	10.00	25.00
Verve V6-8493	(S)	**Suspense Themes In Jazz**	1962	8.00	20.00
Verve V-8525	(M)	**Kai Winding Solo**	1963	10.00	25.00
Verve V6-8525	(S)	**Kai Winding Solo**	1963	8.00	20.00
Verve V-8551	(M)	**More!!!**	1963	10.00	25.00
Verve V6-8551	(S)	**More!!!**	1963	8.00	20.00
		(Verve 8551 also features Kenny Burrell.)			
Verve V-8556	(M)	**The Lonely One**	1963	10.00	25.00
Verve V6-8556	(S)	**The Lonely One**	1963	8.00	20.00
Verve V-8573	(M)	**Mondo Cane #2**	1964	12.00	30.00
Verve V6-8573	(S)	**Mondo Cane #2**	1964	10.00	25.00
Verve V-8602	(M)	**Modern Country**	1964	8.00	20.00
Verve V6-8602	(S)	**Modern Country**	1964	6.00	15.00
Verve V-8620	(M)	**Rainy Day**	1965	6.00	15.00
Verve V6-8620	(S)	**Rainy Day**	1965	5.00	12.00
Verve V-8639	(M)	**The "In" Instrumentals**	1965	6.00	15.00
Verve V6-8639	(S)	**The "In" Instrumentals**	1965	5.00	12.00
Verve V-8657	(M)	**More Brass**	1966	6.00	15.00
Verve V6-8657	(S)	**More Brass**	1966	5.00	12.00
Verve V-8661	(M)	**Dirty Dog**	1966	6.00	15.00
Verve V6-8661	(S)	**Dirty Dog**	1966	5.00	12.00
Verve V-8691	(M)	**Penny Lane & Time**	1967	6.00	15.00
Verve V6-8691	(S)	**Penny Lane & Time**	1967	5.00	12.00
		—Verve albums above have black labels with "MGM Records" on the bottom.—			
A&M SP-3008	(S)	**Israel**	1969	4.00	10.00

Label & Catalog #		Title	Year	VG+	NM
WINDY CITY SEVEN, THE					
Dolphin 9	(M)	**Windy City Seven**	195?	20.00	50.00
WINTER, PAUL					
Paul Winter is a modern jazz alto saxophone player and composer.					
Columbia CL-1925	(M)	**Jazz Meets The Bossa Nova**	1963	6.00	15.00
Columbia CS-8725	(S)	**Jazz Meets The Bossa Nova**	1963	5.00	12.00
Columbia CL-1997	(M)	**Jazz Premiere: Washington**	1963	6.00	15.00
Columbia CS-8797	(S)	**Jazz Premiere: Washington**	1963	5.00	12.00
Columbia CL-2064	(M)	**New Jazz On Campus**	1963	6.00	15.00
Columbia CS-8864	(S)	**New Jazz On Campus**	1963	5.00	12.00
Columbia CL-2155	(M)	**Jazz Meets The Folk Song**	1964	6.00	15.00
Columbia CS-8955	(S)	**Jazz Meets The Folk Song**	1964	5.00	12.00
Columbia CL-2272	(M)	**The Sound Of Ipanema**	1965	6.00	15.00
Columbia CS-9072	(S)	**The Sound Of Ipanema**	1965	5.00	12.00
Columbia CL-2315	(M)	**Rio**	1965	6.00	15.00
Columbia CS-9115	(S)	**Rio**	1965	5.00	12.00
		(Columbia 2315 also features Luiz Bonfa.)			
—Columbia albums above have "Guaranteed High Fidelity" or "360 Sound Stereo" in black on the label.—					
WINTERS, JERRI					
Jerri Winters is a jazz-based vocalist.					
Bethlehem BCP-76	(M)	**Somebody Loves Me**	1957	20.00	50.00
WINTERS, PINKY					
Creative LP-604	(M)	**Lonely One**	1956	24.00	60.00
Argo LP-604	(M)	**Lonely One**	1956	16.00	40.00
		(Argo 604 is a reissue of Creative 604.)			
WINTERS, SMILEY					
Arhoolie 8004/5	(S)	**Smiley Etc.** *(2 LPs)*	1969	6.00	15.00
WISNER, JIMMY					
Chancellor CHJ-5014	(M)	**Aper-Sepshun**	1960	12.00	30.00
Chancellor CHJS-5014	(S)	**Aper-Sepshun**	1960	10.00	25.00
Felsted FL-7509	(M)	**Blues For Harvey**	1962	12.00	30.00
Felsted FL-2509	(S)	**Blues For Harvey**	1962	10.00	25.00
WITHERSPOON, JIMMY					
James Witherspoon is a rhythm 'n' blues-based vocalist. For additional listings refer to Wilbur DeParis.					
RCA Victor LPM-1639	(M)	**Goin' To Kansas City Blues**	1957	40.00	100.00
—RCA albums above have black labels with "Long Play" on the bottom.—					
Hifijazz J-421	(M)	**At The Monterey Jazz Festival**	1959	40.00	100.00
Hifijazz J-422	(M)	**Feelin' The Spirit**	1959	40.00	100.00
Hifijazz J-426	(M)	**Jimmy Witherspoon At The Renaissance**	1959	40.00	100.00
World Pacific WP-1267	(M)	**Singin' The Blues**	1959	30.00	75.00
World Pacific WP-1402	(M)	**There's Good Rockin' Tonight**	1961	24.00	60.00
		(World Pacific 1402 is a reissue of 1267.)			
Reprise R-2008	(M)	**Spoon**	1961	16.00	40.00
Reprise R9-2008	(S)	**Spoon**	1961	20.00	50.00
Reprise R-6012	(M)	**Hey, Mrs. Jones**	1961	16.00	40.00
Reprise R9-6012	(S)	**Hey, Mrs. Jones**	1961	30.00	50.00
Reprise R-6059	(M)	**Roots**	1962	12.00	30.00
Reprise R9-6059	(S)	**Roots**	1962	16.00	40.00
Prestige PRLP-7290	(M)	**Baby, Baby, Baby**	1963	16.00	40.00
Prestige PRST-7290	(S)	**Baby, Baby, Baby**	1963	16.00	40.00
Prestige PRLP-7300	(M)	**Evenin' Blues**	1964	16.00	40.00
Prestige PRST-7300	(S)	**Evenin' Blues**	1964	16.00	40.00
Prestige PRLP-7314	(M)	**Blues Around The Clock**	1964	16.00	40.00
Prestige PRST-7314	(S)	**Blues Around The Clock**	1964	16.00	40.00
Prestige PRLP-7327	(M)	**Blue Spoon**	1964	16.00	40.00
Prestige PRST-7327	(S)	**Blue Spoon**	1964	16.00	40.00
—Prestige albums above have yellow mono or silver stereo labels with a Bergenfield, NJ address .—					
Prestige PRLP-7356	(M)	**Some Of My Best Friends Are The Blues**	1965	8.00	20.00
Prestige PRST-7356	(S)	**Some Of My Best Friends Are The Blues**	1965	10.00	25.00
Prestige PRLP-7418	(M)	**Spoon In London**	1966	8.00	20.00
Prestige PRST-7418	(S)	**Spoon In London**	1966	10.00	25.00

Phil Woods left Juiliard to play with Richard Hayman and Charlie Barnett (1954), Jimmy Raney (1955), George Wallington, Friedrich Gulda, and Dizzy Gillespie (1956) before forming a combo with Gene Quill in 1956. He also gigged with Buddy Rich (1958-59) before joining Quincy Jones in 1959. Woods can be found as a sideman on albums by Gillespie on Verve, Wallington on Prestige, New Jazz and Savoy, Leonard Feather on Mode, George Russell on Decca, Joe Newman on RCA Victor, Jackie Cain & Roy Kral on ABC-Paramount, Quincy Jones on ABC-Paramount and Mercury, Manny Albam on Coral, Sahib Shibab on Savoy, and Zoot Sims on United Artists.

Label & Catalog #		Title	Year	VG+	NM
Prestige PRLP-7475	(M)	**Blues For Easy Livers**	1967	8.00	20.00
Prestige PRST-7475	(S)	**Blues For Easy Livers**	1967	10.00	25.00
		—Prestige albums above have blue labels with a trident logo on the right side.—			
Prestige PRST-7713	(S)	**The Best Of Jimmy Witherspoon**	1969	6.00	15.00
		—Prestige albums above have blue labels with a trident logo on top.—			
Constellation C-1422	(M)	**Take This Hammer**	1964	12.00	30.00
Constellation CS-1422	(E)	**Take This Hammer**	1964	6.00	15.00
Verve V-5007	(M)	**Blue Point Of View**	1966	8.00	20.00
Verve V6-5007	(S)	**Blue Point Of View**	1966	10.00	25.00
Verve V6-5050	(S)	**A Spoonful Of Soul**	1968	8.00	20.00
		—Verve albums above have black labels with "MGM Records" on the bottom.—			

WITHERSPOON, JIMMY, & GROOVE HOLMES

Surrey S-1106	(M)	**Blues For Spoon And Groove**	1965	10.00	25.00
Surrey SS-1106	(S)	**Blues For Spoon And Groove**	1965	12.00	30.00

WITHERSPOON, JIMMY / EDDIE "CLEANHEAD" VINSON

King 395-634	(M)	**Battle Of The Blues, Volume 3**	1959	660.00	1,000.00

WITTWER, JOHNNY: ***Refer to*** **KID ORY / JOHNNY WITTWER**

WOFFORD, MIKE

Epic LN-24225	(M)	**Strawberry Wine**	1967	8.00	20.00
Epic BN-26225	(S)	**Strawberry Wine**	1967	6.00	15.00
Milestone MPS-9012	(S)	**Summer Night**	1968	6.00	15.00

WOOD, JOHN

Ranwood RLP-8036	(S)	**Introducing The John Wood Trio**	1969	5.00	12.00

WOODEN JOE: ***Refer to*** **WOODEN JOE NICHOLAS**

WOODS, JIMMY

James Woods is a West Coast jazz alto saxophone player.

Contemporary M-3605	(M)	**Awakening**	1962	12.00	30.00
Contemporary S-7605	(S)	**Awakening**	1962	10.00	25.00
Contemporary M-3612	(M)	**Conflict**	1963	12.00	30.00
Contemporary S-7612	(S)	**Conflict**	1963	10.00	25.00
		(Contemporary 3812 also features Elvin Jones.)			
		—Contemporary stereo albums have gold & black labels.—			

WOODS, PHIL

Philip Woods is a modern jazz alto and soprano saxophone and clarinet player. For additional listings refer to The Manhattan Jazz All Stars; Orchestra USA; Jimmy Raney; Zoot Sims; and the Various Artists section under Prestige and Signal.

New Jazz NJLP-1104	(10")	**Phil Woods New Jazz Quintet**	1954	125.00	250.00
Prestige PRLP-191	(10")	**Phil Woods New Jazz Quartet**	1954	100.00	200.00
Prestige PRLP-204	(10")	**Phil Woods New Jazz Quintet**	1955	100.00	200.00
		(Prestige 204 is a reissue of New Jazz 1104.)			
Prestige PRLP-7018	(M)	**Woodlore**	1956	40.00	100.00
Prestige PRLP-7046	(M)	**Paring Off**	1956	40.00	100.00
Prestige PRLP-7080	(M)	**The Young Bloods**	1957	40.00	100.00
		(Prestige 7080 also features Donald Byrd.)			
		—Prestige albums above have yellow labels with a W. 50th Street, NYC address.—			
Epic LN-3436	(M)	**Warm Woods**	1958	20.00	50.00
Candid CD-8016	(M)	**Rights Of Swing**	1960	20.00	50.00
Candid CS-9016	(S)	**Rights Of Swing**	1960	16.00	40.00
New Jazz NJLP-8291	(M)	**Pot Pie**	1962	30.00	75.00
		(New Jazz 8291 is a reissue of Prestige 191 and 204.)			
New Jazz NJLP-8304	(M)	**Sugan**	1963	*Unreleased*	
		—New Jazz albums above have purple labels.—			
New Jazz NJLP-8291	(M)	**Pot Pie**	1965	10.00	25.00
		—New Jazz albums above have blue labels with a trident logo on the right side.—			
Status ST-8304	(M)	**Sugan**	1965	16.00	40.00
		(Status 8304, which also features Red Garland, is a reissue of one half of "Modern Jazz Survey 1," listed in the "Jazz At 16 2/3 RPM" article..)			
Impulse A-9143	(M)	**Greek Cooking**	1967	12.00	30.00
Impulse AS-9143	(S)	**Greek Cooking**	1967	10.00	25.00
		—Impulse albums above have orange & black labels.—			

Label & Catalog #		Title	Year	VG+	NM
Impulse AS-9143	(S)	**Greek Cooking**	1968	4.00	10.00

—Impulse albums above have red & black labels with the "abc" logo on top.—

Label & Catalog #		Title	Year	VG+	NM
Prestige PRST-7673	(E)	**Early Quintets**	1969	6.00	15.00

—Prestige albums above have blue labels with a trident logo on top.—

Label & Catalog #		Title	Year	VG+	NM
Verve V6-8791	(S)	**Round Trip**	1969	6.00	15.00

—Verve albums above have black labels with "MGM Records" on the bottom.—

WOODS, PHIL, & GENE QUILL

Label & Catalog #		Title	Year	VG+	NM
RCA Victor LPM-1284	(M)	**The Woods-Quill Sextet**	1956	30.00	75.00

—RCA albums above have black labels with "Long Play" on the bottom.—

Label & Catalog #		Title	Year	VG+	NM
Prestige PRLP-7115	(M)	**Phil & Quill With Prestige**	1957	30.00	75.00

—Prestige albums above have yellow labels with a W. 50th Street, NYC address.—

Label & Catalog #		Title	Year	VG+	NM
Epic LN-3521	(M)	**Phil Talks With Quill**	1959	20.00	50.00
Epic BN-554	(S)	**Phil Talks With Quill**	1959	16.00	40.00

WOODS, PHIL, & GENE QUILL / JACKIE McLEAN & JOHN JENKINS / HAL McKUSICK

Label & Catalog #		Title	Year	VG+	NM
New Jazz NJLP-8204	(M)	**Bird Feathers**	1958	40.00	100.00

—New Jazz albums above have yellow Prestige labels.—

Label & Catalog #		Title	Year	VG+	NM
New Jazz NJLP-8204	(M)	**Bird Feathers**	1959	20.00	50.00

—New Jazz albums above have purple labels.—

Label & Catalog #		Title	Year	VG+	NM
New Jazz NJLP-8204	(M)	**Bird Feathers**	1965	10.00	25.00

—New Jazz albums above have blue labels with a trident logo on the right side.—

WRICE, LARRY "WILD"

Label & Catalog #		Title	Year	VG+	NM
Pacific Jazz PJ-24	(M)	**Wild!**	1961	12.00	30.00
Pacific Jazz ST-24	(S)	**Wild!**	1961	10.00	25.00

WRIGHT, DEMPSEY

Label & Catalog #		Title	Year	VG+	NM
Andex A-3006	(M)	**The Wright Approach**	1958	24.00	60.00
Andex AS-3006	(S)	**The Wright Approach**	1958	20.00	50.00

WRIGHT, FRANK

Frank Wright is a modern jazz tenor saxophone player.

Label & Catalog #		Title	Year	VG+	NM
ESP-Disk' 1023	(M)	**Frank Wright Trio**	1966	10.00	25.00
ESP-Disk' 1023	(S)	**Frank Wright Trio**	1966	8.00	20.00
ESP-Disk' 1053	(S)	**Your Prayer**	1968	8.00	20.00

WRIGHT, JOHN

John Wright is a modern jazz pianist.

Label & Catalog #		Title	Year	VG+	NM
Prestige PRLP-7190	(M)	**South Side Soul**	1960	16.00	40.00
Prestige PRLP-7197	(M)	**Nice 'N' Nasty**	1961	16.00	40.00
Prestige PRLP-7212	(M)	**Makin' Out**	1961	16.00	40.00
Prestige PRLP-7233	(M)	**Mr. Soul**	1962	16.00	40.00
Prestige PRST-7233	(S)	**Mr. Soul**	1962	16.00	40.00

—Prestige albums above have yellow mono or silver stereo labels with a Bergenfield, NJ address .—

Label & Catalog #		Title	Year	VG+	NM
New Jazz NJLP-8322	(M)	**The Last Amen**	196?	*Unreleased*	
Status ST-8322	(M)	**The Last Amen**	1965	16.00	40.00

WRIGHT, LEO

Leo Wright is a modern jazz alto saxophone, clarinet and flute player.

Label & Catalog #		Title	Year	VG+	NM
Atlantic 1358	(M)	**Blues Shout**	1960	12.00	30.00
Atlantic SD-1358	(S)	**Blues Shout**	1960	10.00	25.00

—Atlantic albums above have a white fan logo on the right side of the label.—

Label & Catalog #		Title	Year	VG+	NM
Atlantic 1358	(M)	**Blues Shout**	196?	5.00	12.00
Atlantic SD-1358	(S)	**Blues Shout**	196?	4.00	10.00
Atlantic 1393	(M)	**Suddenly The Blues**	1962	10.00	25.00
Atlantic SD-1393	(S)	**Suddenly The Blues**	1962	8.00	20.00

—Atlantic albums above have multi-color labels with a black fan logo.—

WRIGHT, MARVIN

Marvin "Lefty" Wright is a traditional jazz-based pianist.

Label & Catalog #		Title	Year	VG+	NM
"X" LXA-3028	(10")	**Boogie Woogie Piano**	1954	20.00	50.00

WRIGHT, NAT

Nathaniel Wright is a modern jazz vocalist.

Label & Catalog #		Title	Year	VG+	NM
Warwick W-2040	(M)	**The Biggest Voice In Jazz**	1961	20.00	50.00
Warwick W-2040ST	(S)	**The Biggest Voice In Jazz**	1961	30.00	75.00

Label & Catalog #		Title	Year	VG+	NM
WYNN, ALBERT					
Albert Wynn is a traditional jazz trombone player.					
Riverside RLP-426	(M)	**Albert Wynn And His Gutbucket Seven**	1962	**12.00**	**30.00**
Riverside RS-9426	(E)	**Albert Wynn And His Gutbucket Seven**	1962	**6.00**	**15.00**

—Riverside albums above have blue mono or black stereo labels with a reel & mike logo on top.—

This illustration of Charlie Shavers, done by David Stone Martin, is now the logo used by Clef Records.

Y.

YAGED, SOL

Solomon Yaged is a traditional jazz clarinet player.

Herald HLP-0103	(M)	**It Might As Well Be Swing**	1956	16.00	40.00
Lane LP-149	(M)	**Live At The Gaslight Club**	195?	20.00	50.00
Lane LP-154	(M)	**One More Time**	195?	20.00	50.00
Lane LPS-154	(S)	**One More Time**	195?	20.00	50.00
Lane LP-155	(M)	**Sol Yaged At The Gaslight Club**	195?	20.00	50.00
Lane LPS-155	(S)	**Sol Yaged At The Gaslight Club**	195?	20.00	50.00
Philips PHM-200-002	(M)	**Jazz At The Metropole**	1961	8.00	20.00
Philips PHS-600-002	(S)	**Jazz At The Metropole**	1961	6.00	15.00

YALE DIXIELAND BAND, THE

Columbia CL-736	(M)	**Eli's Chosen Six**	1955	16.00	40.00

—Columbia albums above have six white on black "eye" logos on each label.—

YANCEY, JIMMY (JIMMY YANCEY & MAMA)

Mr. Yancey is a traditional jazz pianist; Mrs. Yancey, a vocalist. For additional listings refer to Jim Ewell.

Atlantic ALS-103	(10")	**Yancey Special**	1950	30.00	75.00
Paramount CJS-101	(10")	**Yancey Special**	1951	30.00	75.00
Atlantic ALS-130	(10")	**Yancey Special**	1952	30.00	75.00
Atlantic ALS-134	(10")	**Piano Solos**	1952	30.00	75.00
"X" LX-3000	(10")	**Blues And Boogie**	1954	30.00	75.00
Pax LP-6011	(10")	**1943 Mixture**	1954	30.00	75.00
Pax LP-6012	(10")	**Evening With The Yanceys**	1954	30.00	75.00
Riverside RLP-1028	(10")	**Lost Recording Date**	1954	30.00	75.00
Riverside RLP-12-124	(M)	**Yancey's Getaway**	1956	24.00	60.00

—Riverside albums above have blue on white labels.—

Atlantic 1283	(M)	**Pure Blues**	1958	20.00	50.00

—Atlantic albums above have black mono or green stereo labels.—

Atlantic 1283	(M)	**Pure Blues**	1961	6.00	15.00

—Atlantic albums above have multi-color labels with a white fan logo.—

Atlantic 1283	(M)	**Pure Blues**	196?	4.00	10.00

—Atlantic albums above have multi-color labels with a black fan logo.—

YERBA BUENA JAZZ BAND, THE: ***Refer to*** **LU WATTERS**

YOUNG, CECIL

King 295-1	(10")	**A Concert Of Cool Jazz**	1952	30.00	75.00

YOUNG, ELDEE

Eldee Young is a modern jazz bassist.

Argo LP-1003	(M)	**Eldee Young And Company**	1962	10.00	25.00
Argo LPS-1003	(S)	**Eldee Young And Company**	1962	8.00	20.00
Argo LP-699	(M)	**Just For Kicks**	1962	8.00	20.00
Argo LPS-699	(S)	**Just For Kicks**	1962	6.00	15.00

YOUNG, JOHN

John Young is a modern jazz pianist.

Argo LP-612	(M)	**Young John Young**	1957	16.00	40.00
Argo LP-692	(M)	**Themes And Things**	1962	12.00	30.00
Argo LPS-692	(S)	**Themes And Things**	1962	10.00	25.00
Argo LP-713	(M)	**A Touch Of Pepper**	1962	12.00	30.00
Argo LPS-713	(S)	**A Touch Of Pepper**	1962	10.00	25.00
Delmark DL-403	(M)	**The John Young Trio**	1961	16.00	40.00
Delmark DS-403	(S)	**The John Young Trio**	1961	12.00	30.00

YOUNG, LARRY

Lawrence Young is a modern jazz organist and composer.

New Jazz NJLP-8249	(M)	**Testifying**	1960	20.00	50.00
New Jazz NJLP-8264	(M)	**Young Blues**	1961	20.00	50.00

—New Jazz albums above have purple labels.—

Label & Catalog #		Title	Year	VG+	NM
New Jazz NJLP-8249	(M)	**Testifying**	1965	10.00	25.00
New Jazz NJLP-8264	(M)	**Young Blues**	1965	10.00	25.00
		—New Jazz albums above have blue labels with a trident logo on the right side.—			
Prestige PRLP-7237	(M)	**Groove Street**	1962	16.00	40.00
Prestige PRST-7237	(S)	**Groove Street**	1962	16.00	40.00
		—Prestige albums above have yellow mono or silver stereo labels with a Bergenfield, NJ address .—			
Blue Note BLP-4187	(M)	**Into Somethin'**	1964	16.00	40.00
Blue Note BST-84187	(S)	**Into Somethin'**	1964	12.00	30.00
Blue Note BLP-4221	(M)	**Unity**	1966	16.00	40.00
Blue Note BST-84221	(S)	**Unity**	1966	12.00	30.00
Blue Note BLP-4242	(M)	**Of Love And Peace**	1966	16.00	40.00
Blue Note BST-84242	(S)	**Of Love And Peace**	1966	12.00	30.00
		—Blue Note albums above have blue on white labels with a New York, USA address.—			
Blue Note BST-84187	(S)	**Into Somethin'**	196?	5.00	12.00
Blue Note BST-84221	(S)	**Unity**	196?	5.00	12.00
Blue Note BST-84242	(S)	**Of Love And Peace**	196?	5.00	12.00
Blue Note BLP-4266	(S)	**Contrasts**	1967	16.00	40.00
Blue Note BST-84266	(S)	**Contrasts**	1967	12.00	30.00
Blue Note BST-84304	(S)	**Heaven On Earth**	1968	12.00	30.00
		—Blue Note albums above blue on white labels with "A Division of Liberty Records."—			

YOUNG, LESTER

Lester "Pres" or "Prez" Young is a traditional jazz-based tenor saxophone and clarinet player who will forever be associated with Billie Holiday, who coined his nickname for "The President." For additional listings refer to Count Basie; Coleman Hawkins / Howard McGhee / Lester Young.

Label & Catalog #		Title	Year	VG+	NM
Savoy MG-9002	(10")	**Lester Young**	1951	150.00	300.00
Commodore FL-20021	(10")	**Kansas City Style**	1952	150.00	300.00
Aladdin AL-705	(10")	**King Cole—Lester Young—Red Callender Trio**	1953	150.00	300.00
Aladdin AL-706	(10")	**Lester Young—His Tenor Sax**	1953	150.00	300.00
Aladdin AL-801	(M)	**Lester Young And His Tenor Sax, Volume 1**	1956	50.00	125.00
Aladdin AL-802	(M)	**Lester Young And His Tenor Sax, Volume 2**	1956	50.00	125.00
Savoy MG-12068	(M)	**The Immortal Lester Young**	1956	40.00	100.00
		(Savoy 12068 is a reissue of 9002.)			
Savoy MG-12071	(M)	**The Master's Touch**	1956	40.00	100.00
		(Savoy 12071 also features Count Basie.)			
Mercury MGC-104	(10")	**The Lester Young Trio**	1951	150.00	300.00
		(Mercury 104 also features Nat Cole and Buddy Rich with cover art by David Stone Martin.)			
Mercury MGC-108	(10")	**Lester Young Collates**	1951	150.00	300.00
Mercury MGC-124	(10")	**Lester Young Collates #2**	1953	*Unreleased*	
		(Jackets of Mercury 124 apparently contain copies of Clef 124.)			
Clef MGC-104	(10")	**The Lester Young Trio**	1953	125.00	250.00
		(Clef 104 features cover art by David Stone Martin.)			
Clef MGC-108	(10")	**Lester Young Collates**	1953	125.00	250.00
		(Clef 108 is a reissue of Mercury 108.)			
Clef MGC-124	(10")	**Lester Young Collates #2**	1953	125.00	250.00
		(Clef 124 is a reissue of Mercury 124 with the DSM cover.)			
Clef MGC-135	(10")	**Lester Young Trio #2**	1953	125.00	250.00
		(Clef 135 is a reissue of Mercury 104.)			
Norgran MGN-5	(10")	**Lester Young With The Oscar Peterson Trio #1**	1954	125.00	250.00
		(Norgran 5 features cover art by David Stone Martin.)			
Norgran MGN-6	(10")	**Lester Young With The Oscar Peterson Trio #2**	1954	125.00	250.00
Norgran MGN-1005	(M)	**The President**	1954	100.00	200.00
Norgran MGN-1022	(M)	**Lester Young**	1955	100.00	200.00
		(Norgran 1022 features cover art by David Stone Martin.)			
Norgran MGN-1043	(M)	**Pres And Sweets**	1955	100.00	200.00
		(Norgran 1043 also features Sweets Edison with cover art by David Stone Martin.)			
Norgran MGN-1054	(M)	**The Pres-ident Plays With The Oscar Peterson Trio**	1955	50.00	125.00
		(Norgran 1054 is a reissue of 5 and 6.)			
Norgran MGN-1071	(M)	**Lester's Here**	1956	50.00	125.00
		(Norgran 1071 is a reissue of Clef 124.)			
Norgran MGN-1072	(M)	**Pres**	1956	50.00	125.00
		(Norgran 1072 is a reissue of Clef 108.)			
Norgran MGN-1074	(M)	**Lester Young—Nat "King" Cole—Buddy Rich Trio**	1956	50.00	125.00
		(Norgran 1074 is a reissue of Clef 104 and 135.)			

Lester Young's first big job was with The Bostonians in 1929-30. By 1936 he had played with King Oliver, Walter Page, Benny Moten, Count Basie, Fletcher Henderson, and Andy Kirk. He rejoined Basie (1936-40), formed a famed trio with Nat "King" Cole and Red Callender (their rare 10" album for Aladdin is pictured here), and revolutionized tenor saxophone playing in jazz, in effect becoming the pivotal musician in the transition from hot jazz to cool. To many, he is remembered for his sensitive accompaniments to Billie Holiday, who nicknamed him "The Pres." Mr. Young can also be found on many albums by Holiday, Count Basie on Savoy, Epic and Verve, Billy Eckstine on MGM, Benny Goodman on Columbia, and as a mainstay with the JATP.

Label & Catalog #		Title	Year	VG+	NM
Norgran MGN-1093	(M)	**Lester Swings Again**	1956	40.00	100.00
		(Norgran 1093 is a reissue of 1005.)			
Norgran MGN-1100	(M)	**Lester Young**	1956	40.00	100.00
		(Norgran 1100 is a reissue of 1022.)			
American Rec. Soc. G-417	(M)	**Pres And Teddy**	1956	20.00	50.00
		(American Recording Society 417 also features Teddy Wilson.)			
Verve MGV-8134	(M)	**Pres And Sweets**	1957	30.00	75.00
		(Verve 8134 is a reissue of Norgran 1043.)			
Verve MGV-8144	(M)	**The Pres-ident Plays With The Oscar Peterson Trio**	1957	30.00	75.00
		(Verve 8144 is a reissue of Norgran 1054.)			
Verve MGV-8161	(M)	**Lester's Here**	1957	30.00	75.00
		(Verve 8161 is a reissue of Norgran 1071.)			
Verve MGV-8162	(M)	**Pres**	1957	30.00	75.00
		(Verve 8162 is a reissue of Norgran 1072.)			
Verve MGV-8164	(M)	**Lester Young—Buddy Rich Trio**	1957	30.00	75.00
		(Verve 8164 is a reissue of Norgran 1074.)			
Verve MGV-8181	(M)	**Lester Swings Again**	1957	30.00	75.00
		(Verve 8181 is a reissue of Norgran 1093.)			
Verve MGV-8187	(M)	**It Don't Mean A Thing (If It Ain't Got That Swing)**	1957	30.00	75.00
		(Verve 8187 is a reissue of Norgran 1022.)			
Verve MGV-8205	(M)	**Pres And Teddy**	1957	30.00	75.00
		(Verve 8205 is a reissue of A.R.S. 417.)			
Verve MGV-8308	(M)	**The Lester Young Story**	1959	24.00	60.00
Verve MGV-8378	(M)	**Lester Young In Paris**	1960	24.00	60.00
Verve MGV-8398	(M)	**The Essential Lester Young**	1961	24.00	60.00
		—Verve albums above have black labels with "Verve Records, Inc." on the bottom.—			
Verve V-8134	(M)	**Pres And Sweets**	1961	10.00	25.00
Verve V-8144	(M)	**The Pres-ident Plays With The Oscar Peterson Trio**	1961	10.00	25.00
Verve V-8161	(M)	**Lester's Here**	1961	10.00	25.00
Verve V-8162	(M)	**Pres**	1961	10.00	25.00
Verve V-8164	(M)	**Lester Young—Buddy Rich Trio**	1961	10.00	25.00
Verve V-8181	(M)	**Lester Swings Again**	1961	10.00	25.00
Verve V-8187	(M)	**It Don't Mean A Thing (If It Ain't Got That Swing)**	1961	10.00	25.00
Verve V-8205	(M)	**Pres And Teddy**	1961	10.00	25.00
Verve V-8308	(M)	**The Lester Young Story**	1961	10.00	25.00
Verve V-8378	(M)	**Lester Young In Paris**	1961	10.00	25.00
Verve V-8398	(M)	**The Essential Lester Young**	1961	10.00	25.00
		—Verve albums above have black labels with "MGM Records" on the bottom.—			
Verve VSP-27	(M)	**Pres And His Cabinet**	1966	6.00	15.00
Verve VSPS-27	(E)	**Pres And His Cabinet**	1966	3.00	7.50
Verve VSP-30	(M)	**Giants 3**	1966	6.00	15.00
Verve VSPS-30	(E)	**Giants 3**	1966	3.00	7.50
		(Verve 30 is a reissue of 8164.)			
Intro 602	(M)	**Swingin' Lester Young**	1957	40.00	100.00
Intro 603	(M)	**The Greatest**	1957	40.00	100.00
Score SLP-4019	(M)	**Lester Young—Nat King Cole Trio**	1958	40.00	100.00
		(Score 4019 is a reissue of Aladdin 705.)			
Score SLP-4028	(M)	**Lester Young's Greatest**	1958	60.00	150.00
Score SLP-4029	(M)	**Swinging Lester Young**	1958	60.00	150.00
Epic LN-6031	(M)	**Lester Young Memorial Album** *(2 LPs)*	1959	60.00	150.00
Epic LN-3576	(M)	**Lester Young Memorial Album, Volume 1**	1959	20.00	50.00
Epic LN-3577	(M)	**Lester Young Memorial Album, Volume 2**	1959	20.00	50.00
Commodore FL-30014	(M)	**Kansas City Style**	1959	40.00	100.00
		(Commodore 30014 is a reissue of 20021.)			
Savoy MG-12155	(M)	**Lester Warms Up—Jazz Immortals Series, Vol. 2**	1961	16.00	40.00
Charlie Parker CLP-402	(M)	**Pres**	1961	20.00	50.00
Charlie Parker CLP-405	(M)	**Pres Is Blue**	1961	20.00	50.00
Imperial LP-9181	(M)	**The Immortal Lester Young, Volume 1**	1962	20.00	50.00
Imperial LP-12181	(E)	**The Immortal Lester Young, Volume 1**	1962	12.00	30.00
Imperial LP-9187	(M)	**The Immortal Lester Young, Volume 2**	1962	20.00	50.00
Imperial LP-12187	(E)	**The Immortal Lester Young, Volume 2**	1962	12.00	30.00
Crown CLP-5305	(M)	**Nat "King" Cole Meets Lester Young**	196?	10.00	25.00
Crown CST-305	(E)	**Nat "King" Cole Meets Lester Young**	196?	4.00	10.00
		(Crown 5305 is a reissue of Aladdin 705 plus two by Red Callender.)			

Label & Catalog #		Title	Year	VG+	NM
Mainstream 56002	(M)	**The Influence Of Five**	1965	10.00	25.00
Mainstream S-6002	(E)	**The Influence Of Five**	1965	4.00	10.00
Mainstream 56004	(M)	**Town Hall Concert**	1965	10.00	25.00
Mainstream S-6004	(E)	**Town Hall Concert**	1965	4.00	10.00
Mainstream 56008	(M)	**Chairman Of The Board**	1965	10.00	25.00
Mainstream S-6008	(E)	**Chairman Of The Board**	1965	4.00	10.00
Mainstream 56009	(M)	**52nd Street**	1965	10.00	25.00
Mainstream S-6009	(E)	**52nd Street**	1965	4.00	10.00
Mainstream 56012	(M)	**Prez**	1965	10.00	25.00
Mainstream S-6012	(E)	**Prez**	1965	4.00	10.00

YOUNG, LESTER / COUNT BASIE

Mercury MG-25015	(10")	**Lester Young Quartet And Count Basie Seven**	1950	125.00	250.00

YOUNG, LESTER / CHU BERRY

Jazztone J-1218	(M)	**Tops On Tenor**	1956	20.00	50.00

YOUNG, LESTER, & ROY ELDRIDGE & HARRY EDISON

Verve MGV-8298	(M)	**Going For Myself**	1959	24.00	60.00
Verve MGV-8316	(M)	**Laughin' To Keep From Cryin'**	1959	24.00	60.00
Verve MGVS-6054	(S)	**Laughin' To Keep From Cryin'**	1960	20.00	50.00

—Verve albums above have black labels with "Verve Records, Inc." on the bottom.—

Verve V-8298	(M)	**Going For Myself**	1961	10.00	25.00
Verve V-8316	(M)	**Laughin' To Keep From Cryin'**	1961	10.00	25.00
Verve V6-8316	(S)	**Laughin' To Keep From Cryin'**	1961	8.00	20.00

—Verve albums above have black labels with "MGM Records" on the bottom.—

YOUNG, LESTER, & ILLINOIS JACQUET

Aladdin LP-701	(10")	**Battle Of The Saxes**	1953	150.00	300.00

YOUNG, LESTER, & PAUL QUINICHETTE

EmArcy MG-26021	(10")	**Pres Meets Vice-Pres**	1954	125.00	250.00

YOUNG, WEBSTER

Webster Young is a modern jazz trumpet player. For additional listings refer to the Various Artists section under Prestige.

Prestige PRLP-7106	(M)	**For Lady**	1957	40.00	100.00

—Prestige albums above have yellow labels with a W. 50th Street, NYC address.—

YOUNG LIONS, THE

The Young Lions are Bob Cranshaw, Louis Hayes, Albert Heath, Lee Morgan, Wayne Shorter, Frank Strozier and Bobby Timmons.

Vee Jay LP-3013	(M)	**The Young Lions**	1960	20.00	50.00
Vee Jay SR-3013	(S)	**The Young Lions**	1960	20.00	50.00

YOUNG MEN FROM MEMPHIS

The Yonung Men include Booker Little, Phineas Newborn and Frank Strozier.

United Arts. UAL-4029	(M)	**Down Home Reunion**	1959	20.00	50.00
United Arts. UAS-5029	(S)	**Down Home Reunion**	1959	16.00	40.00

YOUNG TUXEDO BRASS BAND, THE

Atlantic 1297	(M)	**Jazz Begins**	1958	16.00	40.00
Atlantic SD-1297	(M)	**Jazz Begins**	1958	12.00	30.00

—Atlantic albums above have black mono or green stereo labels.—

Atlantic 1297	(M)	**Jazz Begins**	1961	8.00	20.00
Atlantic SD-1297	(M)	**Jazz Begins**	1961	6.00	15.00

—Atlantic albums above have multi-color labels with a white fan logo.—

Atlantic 1297	(M)	**Jazz Begins**	196?	5.00	12.00
Atlantic SD-1297	(M)	**Jazz Begins**	196?	4.00	10.00

—Atlantic albums above have multi-color labels with a black fan logo.—

Z.

ZACK, GEORGE

George Zack is a traditional jazz pianist and vocalist.

Commodore FL-20001	*(10")*	**Party Piano Of The Roaring '20s**	*1950*	**20.00**	**50.00**

ZAWINUL, JOE

Joseph Zawinul is a modern jazz keyboard player. For additional listings refer to Ben Webster & Joe Zawinul.

Atlantic 3004	*(M)*	**Money In The Pocket**	*1966*	**10.00**	**25.00**
Atlantic SD-3004	*(S)*	**Money In The Pocket**	*1966*	**8.00**	**20.00**
Vortex 2002	*(S)*	**The Rise And Fall Of The 3rd Stream**	*1968*	**8.00**	**20.00**

ZEITLIN, DENNY

Denny Zeitlin is a modern jazz-based piano player.

Columbia CL-2182	*(M)*	**Cathexis**	*1964*	**10.00**	**25.00**
Columbia CS-8982	*(S)*	**Cathexis**	*1964*	**8.00**	**20.00**
Columbia CL-2340	*(M)*	**Carnival**	*1965*	**10.00**	**25.00**
Columbia CS-9140	*(S)*	**Carnival**	*1965*	**8.00**	**20.00**

—Columbia albums above have "Guaranteed High Fidelity" or "360 Sound Stereo" in black on the label.—

Columbia CL-2463	*(M)*	**Shining Hour**	*1966*	**6.00**	**15.00**
Columbia CS-9263	*(S)*	**Shining Hour**	*1966*	**5.00**	**12.00**
Columbia CL-2748	*(M)*	**Zeitgeist**	*1966*	**6.00**	**15.00**
Columbia CS-9548	*(S)*	**Zeitgeist**	*1966*	**5.00**	**12.00**

—Columbia albums above have "360 Sound" in white on the bottom of the label.—

ZITO, PHIL

Columbia CL-6110	*(10")*	**International City Dixielanders**	*1950*	**20.00**	**50.00**

ZITRO, JAMES

James Zitro is a modern jazz drummer.

ESP-Disk' 1052	*(S)*	**Zitro**	*1968*	**8.00**	**20.00**

ZOLLER, ATTILLA

EmArcy SPE-66013	*(S)*	**The Horizon Beyond**	*1968*	**10.00**	**25.00**

ZURKE, BOB

Robert Zurke is a traditional jazz pianist.

RCA Victor LPM-1013	*(M)*	**The Tom Cat On The Keys**	*1955*	**30.00**	**75.00**

—RCA albums above have black labels with "Long Play" on the bottom.—

Jazzy Soundtracks

This section includes movie and television soundtracks that either feature a jazz artist or artists (as composer or performer) or "jazzy" arrangements and/or performances by otherwise non-jazz artists. This section does not [intentionally] include albums by jazz artists that interpret soundtrack or show tunes in a jazz manner. For readers interested in these, the following artists have recorded such "Jazz Interpretations Of" followed by the label on which at lest one such undertaking exists: Cannonball Adderley on Capitol; Bill Barron on Dauntless; Aaron Bell on Lion; Charlie Byrd on Columbia; Barbara Carroll on Kapp and Warner Bros.; Bobby Bryant on World Pacific; John Carisi on Columbia; Benny Carter on United Artists; Bob Cooper on World Pacific; Wild Bill Davis on Everest; Miles Davis on Columbia; Walter Dickerson on Dauntless and MGM; and Kenny Drew on Riverside.

Stan Freeman on Columbia; Terry Gibbs on Verve; Benny Goodman on Capitol; Vince Guaraldi on Fantasy; Chico Hamilton on World Pacific and Columbia; Eddie Harris on Vee Jay; Hamp Hawes on Vault; Paul Horn on Columbia; Ahmad Jamal on Argo; The Jazz Modes on Atlantic; Hank Jones on Golden Crest and Capitol; Jonah Jones on Capitol; Quincy Jones on Mercury; Barney Kessell on Contemporary; the Krupa-Hampton-Wilson Trio on Clef; Mundell Lowe on Camden; Henry Mancini on RCA Victor; The Manhattan Jazz All-Stars on Columbia; Shelly Manne on Contemporary, Capitol and Atlantic; The Mastersounds on World Pacific; Gary McFarland on Verve; The Mitchell-Ruff Duo on Roulette; and The Modern Jazz Quartet on Atlantic.

Morris Nanton on Warner Bros.; Frankie Ortega on Jubilee; Bernard Peiffer on Laurie; Oscar Peterson on Verve; Dave Pike on Moodsville; Bill Potts on United Artists and Colpix; Andre Previn on Contemporary; Freddie Redd on Blue Note; Jerome Richardson on United Artists; The Riverside Jazz Stars on Riverside; Shorty Rogers on RCA Victor; Tony Scott on Signature and ABC-Paramount; Bud Shank on Pacific Jazz; The Soundstage All-Stars on Dot; Billy Taylor on ABC-Paramount; Clark Terry on Moodsville; Cal Tjader on Fantasy; The Video All Stars on Somerset; Randy Weston on United Artists; Joe Wilder on Columbia; The Gilbert & Sullivan Jazz Workshop on Andex; Tupper Saussy on Monument; and Tom Scott on Flying Dutchman.

Atlantic 1284	*(M)*	**No Sun In Venice**	*1958*	**12.00**	**30.00**
Atlantic SD-1284	*(S)*	**No Sun In Venice**	*1958*	**12.00**	**30.00**
		(Atlantic 1284 features The Modern Jazz Quartet playing compositions by conductor John Lewis.)			
		—Atlantic albums above have black mono or green stereo labels.—			
Atlantic 1284	*(M)*	**No Sun In Venice**	*196?*	**8.00**	**20.00**
Atlantic SD-1284	*(S)*	**No Sun In Venice**	*196?*	**6.00**	**15.00**
		—Atlantic albums above have multi-color labels with a white fan logo.—			
Atlantic 1284	*(M)*	**No Sun In Venice**	*196?*	**5.00**	**12.00**
Atlantic SD-1284	*(S)*	**No Sun In Venice**	*196?*	**4.00**	**10.00**
Atlantic 1388	*(M)*	**A Milanese Story**	*1962*	**8.00**	**20.00**
Atlantic SD-1388	*(S)*	**A Milanese Story**	*1962*	**8.00**	**20.00**
		(Atlantic 1388 features compositions by conductor John Lewis.)			
		—Atlantic albums above have multi-color labels with a black fan logo.—			
Capitol L-355	*(M)*	**St. Louis Woman**	*1955*	**30.00**	**75.00**
		(Capitol 355 features Pearl Bailey and Harold Nicholas.)			
Capitol W-881	*(M)*	**The James Dean Story**	*1957*	**30.00**	**75.00**
		(Capitol 881 features compositions by conductor Leith Stevens.)			
Capitol W-993	*(M)*	**Saint Louis Blues**	*1958*	**20.00**	**50.00**
		(Capitol 993 features performances by Nat King Cole.)			
		—Original Capitol albums above have turquoise labels.—			
Capitol W-993	*(M)*	**Saint Louis Blues**	*195?*	**10.00**	**25.00**
Capitol T-1160	*(M)*	**Hey Boy, Hey Girl**	*1959*	**20.00**	**50.00**
		(Capitol 1160 features performances by Louis Prima and Keely Smith.)			
		—Capitol albums above have black "rainbow" labels with the logo on the left side.—			
Capitol W-993	*(M)*	**Saint Louis Blues**	*196?*	**6.00**	**15.00**
		—Capitol albums above have black "rainbow" labels with the logo on top.—			
Chancellor CHL-5016	*(M)*	**College Confidential**	*1960*	**16.00**	**40.00**
Chancellor CHLS-5016	*(S)*	**College Confidential**	*1960*	**20.00**	**50.00**
		(Chancellor 5016 features Milt Bernhart, Bob Cooper, Shelly Manne, Jimmy Rowles and Bud Shank playing compositions by Dean Elliott.)			

Songs From Pete Kelly's Blues (1955), directed by and starring Jack Webb as a troubled trumpet player, gave Peggy Lee and Ella Fitzgerald roles in the film and, of course, on the soundtrack. John Lewis was quite at home providing the score for *No Sun In Venice* (1958), which Atlantic inexplicably listed in its catalogs and inner sleeves for years as *One Never Knows*, a title of one the album's songs.

Label & Catalog #		Title	Year	VG+	NM
Charlie Parker PLP-406	(M)	**Satan In High Heels** *(Gatefold cover)*	1962	24.00	60.00
Charlie Parker PLP-406S	(S)	**Satan In High Heels** *(Gatefold cover)*	1962	30.00	75.00
Charlie Parker PLP-406	(M)	**Satan In High Heels** *(Standard cover)*	1962	16.00	40.00
Charlie Parker PLP-406S	(S)	**Satan In High Heels** *(Standard cover)*	1962	20.00	50.00
		(C.P. 406 features compositions by conductor Mundell Lowe.)			
Charlie Parker PLP-806	(M)	**The Music From "The Connection"**	1962	16.00	40.00
Charlie Parker PLP-806S	(S)	**The Music From "The Connection"**	1962	20.00	50.00
		(C.P. 806 features compositions by Kenny Drew and conductor Cecil Payne.)			
Charlie Parker PLP-813	(M)	**Music Of The Original Soundtrack From The Motion Picture "Les Liaisons Dangereuses"**	1962	10.00	25.00
Charlie Parker PLP-813S	(S)	**Music Of The Original Soundtrack From The Motion Picture "Les Liaisons Dangereuses"**	1962	12.00	30.00
		(C.P. 813 features compositions by conductor Duke Jordan.)			
Colpix CP-427	(M)	**The Interns**	1962	12.00	30.00
Colpix SCP-427	(S)	**The Interns**	1962	20.00	50.00
		(Colpix 427 features compositions by conductor Leith Stevens.)			
Colpix CP-478	(M)	**Selections From The Film "Golden Boy"**	1965	12.00	30.00
Colpix CST-478	(S)	**Selections From The Film "Golden Boy"**	1965	20.00	50.00
		(Colpix 478 features Art Blakey & The Jazz Messengers.)			
Colpix CP-492	(M)	**Gone With The Wave**	1965	12.00	30.00
Colpix CST-492	(S)	**Gone With The Wave**	1965	20.00	50.00
		(Colpix 492 features compositions by Lalo Schifrin and performances by Laurindo Almeida and Shelly Manne.)			
Columbia CL-6106 (10")	(M)	**Young Man With A Horn**	1950	30.00	75.00
		(Columbia 6106 features performances by Harry James & Doris Day.)			
Columbia CL-6151 (10")	(M)	**Destination Moon**	1950	30.00	75.00
		(Columbia 6151 features compositions by conductor Leith Stevens.)			
Columbia CL-582	(M)	**Young Man With A Horn**	1955	16.00	40.00
Columbia CL-690	(M)	**Pete Kelly's Blues**	1955	16.00	40.00
		(Columbia 690 features performances by Matty Matlock.)			
Columbia CL-958	(M)	**Baby Doll**	1956	40.00	100.00
		(Columbia 958 features compositions by Kenyon Hopkins.)			
Columbia CL-1360	(M)	**Anatomy Of A Murder**	1959	16.00	40.00
Columbia CS-8166	(S)	**Anatomy Of A Murder**	1959	20.00	50.00
		(Columbia 1360 features compositions by conductor Duke Ellington.)			
— Columbia albums above have white on black "six" eye logos on each label.—					
Columbia CL-2123	(M)	**East Side, West Side**	1963	10.00	25.00
Columbia CS-8923	(S)	**East Side, West Side**	1963	12.00	30.00
		(Col. 2123 features compositions by conductor Kenyon Hopkins.)			
Columbia CL-2269	(M)	**The Reporter**	1963	8.00	20.00
Columbia CS-9069	(S)	**The Reporter**	1963	10.00	25.00
		(Col. 2269 features compositions by conductor Kenyon Hopkins.)			
Columbia CL-2275	(M)	**Mr. Broadway**	1964	8.00	20.00
Columbia CS-9075	(S)	**Mr. Broadway**	1964	10.00	25.00
		(Columbia 2275 features Dave Brubeck and his quartet.)			
— Columbia albums above have "Guaranteed High Fidelity" or "360 Sound Stereo" in black on the label.—					
Columbia OL-6770	(M)	**Blackbirds Of 1928**	1968	6.00	15.00
		(Columbia 6770 is a reissue of Sutton 270 plus two tracks.)			
Commentary CYN-02	(M)	**Clara / Beg, Borrow And Steal**	1960	30.00	75.00
		(Commentary 2 features compositions by Bud Freeman.)			
Contact C-1	(M)	**My People**	1966	8.00	20.00
Contact CS-1	(S)	**My People**	1966	10.00	25.00
		(Contact 1 features compositions by Duke Ellington with a performance by Joya Sherrill.)			
Contemporary M-3587	(M)	**The Proper Time**	1960	16.00	40.00
Contemporary S-7587	(S)	**The Proper Time**	1960	20.00	50.00
		(Contemporary 3587 features performances by Shelly Manne.)			
Coral CRL-56122 (10")	(M)	**Private Hell 36**	1954	30.00	75.00
		(Coral 56122 eatures compositions by conductor Leith Stevens.)			
Coral-57132	(M)	**The Strange One**	1957	20.00	50.00
		(Coral 57132 eatures compositions by conductor Kenyon Hopkins.)			

Label & Catalog #		Title	Year	VG+	NM
Decca DL-5515 (10")	(M)	**The Wild One**	1954	40.00	100.00
		(Decca 5515 features compositions by conductor Leith Stevens.)			
Decca DL-5519 (10")	(M)	**The Glenn Miller Story**	1954	30.00	75.00
Decca DL-8166	(M)	**Songs From "Pete Kelly's Blues"**	1955	30.00	75.00
		(Decca 8166 eatures performances by Peggy Lee and Ella Fitzgerald.)			
Decca DL-8610	(M)	**The Sweet Smell Of Success**	1957	20.00	50.00
		(Decca 8610 features compositions by Chico Hamilton and Fred Katz.)			
Decca DL-8614	(M)	**Jazz Themes Recorded For The Soundtrack Of The Motion Picture "The Sweet Smell Of Success"**	1957	20.00	50.00
		(Decca 8614 features performances by Chico Hamilton.)			
Decca DL-8226	(M)	**The Glenn Miller Story**	1958	16.00	40.00
Decca DL-78226	(E)	**The Glenn Miller Story**	1958	10.00	25.00
		(Decca 8226 features a score by Henry Mancini with Miller, Louis Armstrong and Gene Krupa.)			
Decca DL-8252	(M)	**The Benny Goodman Story, Volume 1**	1956	16.00	40.00
Decca DL-78252	(E)	**The Benny Goodman Story, Volume 1**	1958	12.00	30.00
Decca DL-8253	(M)	**The Benny Goodman Story, Volume 2**	1956	16.00	40.00
Decca DL-78253	(E)	**The Benny Goodman Story, Volume 2**	1958	12.00	30.00
Decca DL-8257	(M)	**The Man With The Golden Arm**	1956	20.00	50.00
Decca DL-8257	(E)	**The Man With The Golden Arm**	1959	12.00	30.00
		(Decca 8257 features performances by Shorty Rogers with Shelly Manne and Bud Shank.)			
Decca DL-8349	(M)	**The Wild One**	1956	24.00	60.00
		(Decca 8349 is a reissue of 5515.)			
Decca DX-188	(M)	**The Benny Goodman Story** *(2 Lps)*	1959	20.00	50.00
Decca DXSB7-188	(E)	**The Benny Goodman Story** *(2 LPs)*	1959	14.00	35.00
		(Decca 188 is a reissue of 8252 and 8253. "The Benny Goodman Story" was scored by Henry Mancini and features performances by Goodman with Lionel Hampton, Stan Getz, Gene Krupa, and Teddy Wilson.)			
		—Original Decca albums above have silver on black labels.—			
Decca DL-9123	(M)	**The Glenn Miller Story**	1965	8.00	20.00
Decca DL-79123	(E)	**The Glenn Miller Story**	1965	5.00	12.00
Dot DLP-9500	(M)	**The Five Pennies**	1959	16.00	40.00
Dot DLP-29500	(S)	**The Five Pennies**	1959	20.00	50.00
		(Dot 9500, a biography of Red Nichols, features compositions by conductor Leith Stevens with performances by Nichols, Louis Armstrong and Bob Crosby.)			
Dot DLP-3306	(M)	**The Rat Race**	1960	16.00	40.00
Dot DLP-25306	(S)	**The Rat Race**	1960	24.00	60.00
		(Dot 3306 features performances by Sam Butera.)			
Dot DLP-3831	(M)	**Music From "Mission: Impossible"**	1967	6.00	15.00
Dot DLP-25831	(S)	**Music From "Mission: Impossible"**	1967	8.00	20.00
		(Dot 3381 features compositions by conductor Lalo Schifrin.)			
EmArcy MG-36162	(M)	**Music From "Richard Diamond"**	1959	16.00	40.00
EmArcy SR-80045	(S)	**Music From "Richard Diamond"**	1959	20.00	50.00
		(EmArcy 36132 features compositions by conductor Pete Rugolo.)			
		—Original EmArcy albums above have blue labels. with silver print—			
Epic LN-3672	(M)	**Black Orpheus**	1959	16.00	40.00
		(Epic 3672 features compositions by Antonio Jobim and Luiz Bonfa. Reissued as Fontana 27520.)			
Epic LA-16022	(M)	**Les Liaisons Dangereuses**	1961	12.00	30.00
Epic BA-17022	(S)	**Les Liaisons Dangereuses**	1961	16.00	40.00
		(Epic 16022 features Art Blakey & The Jazz Messengers. Reissued as Fontana 27539)			
Epic LA-16032	(M)	**All Night Long**	1961	10.00	25.00
Epic BA-17032	(S)	**All Night Long**	1961	12.00	30.00
		(Epic 16032 features Dave Brubeck and Charles Mingus.)			
Felsted 7512	(M)	**Music From "The Connection"**	1960	30.00	75.00
Felsted 2512	(S)	**Music From "The Connection"**	1960	40.00	100.00
		(Felsted 7512 features performances by Howard McGhee.)			
Fontana MGF-27520	(M)	**Black Orpheus**	1965	8.00	20.00
Fontana SRF-67520	(E)	**Black Orpheus**	1965	6.00	15.00
		(Fontana 27520 is a reissue of Epic 3672.)			

Label & Catalog #		Title	Year	VG+	NM
Fontana MGF-27532	(M)	**Jazz On The Screen**	1965	16.00	40.00
Fontana SRF-67532	(S)	**Jazz On The Screen**	1965	12.00	30.00
		(Fontana 27532 features compositions and performances by Miles Davis for the film "L'Ascenseur Pour l' Echafaud" and by Art Blakey for "The Women Disappear.")			
Fontana MGF-27539	(M)	**Les Liaisons Dangereuses**	1965	8.00	20.00
Fontana SRF-67539	(E)	**Les Liaisons Dangereuses**	1965	6.00	15.00
		(Fontana 27539 is a reissue of Epic 16022.)			
Heritage 600	(M)	**Love Life**	195?	20.00	50.00
		(Heritage 600 features Billy Taylor.)			
Impulse S-9111	(M)	**Alfie**	1966	12.00	30.00
Impulse AS-9111	(S)	**Alfie**	1966	12.00	30.00
		(Impulse 9111 features compositions by Sonny Rollins conducted by Oliver Nelson.)			
Impulse S-9141	(M)	**Sweet Love, Bitter**	1967	12.00	30.00
Impulse AS-9141	(S)	**Sweet Love, Bitter**	1967	12.00	30.00
		(Impulse 9141 features performances by composer Mal Waldron.)			
		— Original Impulse albums above have orange & brown labels.—			
Impulse AS-9111	(S)	**Alfie**	1968	4.00	10.00
Impulse AS-9141	(S)	**Sweet Love, Bitter**	1968	4.00	10.00
		— Impulse albums above have red & brown labels with the "abc" logo on top.—			
Kimberly 2016	(M)	**Swinging Soundtrack**	1960	20.00	50.00
Kimberly 11016	(S)	**Swinging Soundtrack**	1960	24.00	60.00
		(Kimberly 2016 is a reissue of World Pacific 2005.)			
Mercury MG-20654	(M)	**The Original Jazz Score Of "Kwamina"**	1961	12.00	30.00
Mercury SR-60654	(S)	**The Original Jazz Score Of "Kwamina"**	1961	16.00	40.00
		(Mercury 20654 features performances by Billy Taylor.)			
Mercury MG-20859	(M)	**A New Kind Of Love**	1963	8.00	20.00
Mercury SR-60859	(S)	**A New Kind Of Love**	1963	10.00	25.00
		(Mercury 20859 features performances by Erroll Garner with conductor Leith Stevens.)			
Mercury MG-21016	(M)	**The Gentle Rain**	1966	10.00	25.00
Mercury SR-61016	(S)	**The Gentle Rain**	1966	12.00	30.00
		(Mercury 21016 features compositions by Luiz Bonfa.)			
MGM E-3812	(M)	**The Subterraneans**	1960	20.00	50.00
MGM SE-3812	(S)	**The Subterraneans**	1960	24.00	60.00
		(MGM 3812 features compositions by conductor Andre Previn with performances by Art Farmer, Carmen McRae, Gerry Mulligan and Art Pepper.)			
MGM E-4184	(M)	**The V.I.P.s Theme**	1963	8.00	20.00
MGM SE-4184	(S)	**The V.I.P.s Theme**	1963	10.00	25.00
		(MGM 4184 features performances by Bill Evans.)			
MGM E-4312	(M)	**Mickey One**	1965	10.00	25.00
MGM SE-4312	(S)	**Mickey One**	1965	12.00	30.00
		(MGM 4312 features Eddie Sauter compositions played by Stan Getz.)			
MGM E-4447	(M)	**Blow-Up**	1966	10.00	25.00
MGM SE-4447	(S)	**Blow-Up**	1966	12.00	30.00
		(MGM 4477 features compositions by conductor Herbie Hancock.)			
MGM CH-1043	(M)	**Daktari**	1967	6.00	15.00
MGM CHS-1043	(M)	**Daktari**	1967	5.00	12.00
		(MGM 1043 features compositions by conductor Shelly Manne.)			
Omega OL-3	(M)	**Destination Moon**	1959	24.00	60.00
Omega OSL-3	(E)	**Destination Moon**	1959	12.00	30.00
		(Omega 3 features compositions by Leith Stevens.)			
Pacific Jazz PJ-35	(M)	**Barefoot Adventure**	1961	10.00	25.00
Pacific Jazz ST-35	(S)	**Barefoot Adventure**	1961	12.00	30.00
		(P.J. 35 features Bud Shank compositions performed by Shank with Carmell Jones and Shelly Manne.)			
Paramount PAS-5002	(S)	**More Music From "Mission: Impossible"**	1969	6.00	15.00
		(Paramount 5002 features compositions by conductor Lalo Schifrin.)			

With *The Music From Peter Gunn* (1959), Henry Mancini and his jazz combo featuring Pete Candoli, Shelly Manne and Art Pepper, introduced millions of Americans to the sounds of "modern jazz" through the medium of television. *The Cool World* (1964), "the first film ever to be made completely in Harlem," featured Dizzy Gillespie's quintet with James Moody, Kenny Barron, Chris White and Rudy Collins.

Label & Catalog #		Title	Year	VG+	NM
Philips PHM-200-138	(M)	**Cool World**	1964	12.00	30.00
Philips PHS-600-138	(S)	**Cool World**	1964	16.00	40.00
		(Philips 138 features Dizzy Gillespie playing music composed and arranged by Mal Waldron.)			
RCA Victor LPT-3064 (10")	(M)	**Sun Valley Serenade**	1954	30.00	75.00
		(RCA 3064 features performances by Glenn Miller.)			
RCA Victor LPT-3065 (10")	(M)	**Orchestra Wives**	1954	30.00	75.00
		(RCA 3065 features performances by Glenn Miller.)			
RCA Victor LPM-1126	(M)	**Pete Kelly's Blues**	1955	20.00	50.00
		(RCA 1126 features Matty Matlock and George Van Eps.)			
RCA Victor LPM-1618	(M)	**Eleven Against The Ice**	1958	30.00	75.00
		(RCA 1618 features compositions by conductor Kenyon Hopkins.)			
		—RCA albums above have black labels with "Long Play" or "Living Stereo" on the bottom.—			
RCA Victor LPM-2795	(M)	**The Pink Panther**	1964	5.00	12.00
RCA Victor LSP-2795	(S)	**The Pink Panther**	1964	6.00	15.00
		(RCA 2795 features compositions by conductor Henry Manicini. The "Pink Panther" theme is blown by Plas Johnson.)			
		—RCA albums above have black labels with "Mono" or "Stereo" on the bottom.—			
Reprise R-6180	(M)	**A Man Called Adam**	1966	10.00	25.00
Reprise RS-6180	(S)	**A Man Called Adam**	1966	12.00	30.00
		(Reprise 6180 features compositions by conductor Benny Carter, with Nat Adderley, Louis Armstrong and Mel Torme.)			
Revue 1	(M)	**Blackbirds Of 1928**	196?	12.00	30.00
		Revue 1 features Duke Ellington and Don Redman. Reissued as Sutton 270.)			
Sutton SU-270	(M)	**Blackbirds Of 1928**	196?	8.00	20.00
Sutton SSU-270	(E)	**Blackbirds Of 1928**	196?	5.00	12.00
		(Sutton 270 is a reissue of Revue 1 plus two tracks. Reissued as Columbia OL-6770.)			
Time 52034	(M)	**Thriller**	1960	12.00	30.00
Time S-2034	(S)	**Thriller**	1960	16.00	40.00
		(Time 52034 features compositions by conductor Pete Rugolo.)			
20th Cent. Fox TCF-100	(M)	**The Glenn Miller Story** *(2 LPs)*	1959	16.00	40.00
20th Cent. Fox TCFS-100	(E)	**The Glenn Miller Story** *(2 LPs)*	1959	10.00	25.00
20th Cent. Fox TCF-3159	(M)	**The Glenn Miller Story, Volume 1**	1965	8.00	20.00
20th Cent. Fox TCFS-3159	(E)	**The Glenn Miller Story, Volume 1**	1965	5.00	12.00
20th Cent. Fox TCF-3160	(M)	**The Glenn Miller Story, Volume 2**	1965	8.00	20.00
20th Cent. Fox TCFS-3160	(E)	**The Glenn Miller Story, Volume 2**	1965	5.00	12.00
		(TCF 3159 and 3160 are reissues of 100.)			
United Arts. UAL-4006	(M)	**I Want To Live**	1958	16.00	40.00
United Arts. UAS-5006	(S)	**I Want To Live**	1958	20.00	50.00
		(U.A. 4006 collects the jazz score from the film featuring Art Farmer, Shelly Manne and Gerry Mulligan.)			
United Arts. UXL-1	(M)	**I Want To Live** *(2 LPs)*	1958	20.00	50.00
United Arts. UXS-51	(S)	**I Want To Live** *(2 LPs)*	1958	24.00	60.00
		(Two album set collects United Artists 4005 and 4006.)			
United Arts. UAL-4061	(M)	**Odds Against Tomorrow**	1959	12.00	30.00
United Arts. UAS-5061	(S)	**Odds Against Tomorrow**	1959	16.00	40.00
		(U.A. 4061 features The Modern Jazz Quartet playing compositions by conductor John Lewis.)			
United Arts. UAL-4065	(M)	**The Fugitive Kind**	1960	16.00	40.00
United Arts. UAS-5065	(M)	**The Fugitive Kind**	1960	20.00	50.00
		(U.A. 4065 features compositions by conductor Kenyon Hopkins.)			
United Arts. UAL-4092	(M)	**Paris Blues**	1960	12.00	30.00
United Arts. UAS-5092	(S)	**Paris Blues**	1960	16.00	40.00
		(U.A. 4092 features compositions by Duke Ellington and performances by Louis Armstrong.)			
United Arts. DF-3	(M)	**I Want To Live / Odds Against Tomorrow**	1963	8.00	20.00
United Arts. DFS-3	(E)	**I Want To Live / Odds Against Tomorrow**	1963	10.00	25.00
		(One side features music from United Artists 4006; the other, 4061, "Odds Against Tomorrow.")			

Label & Catalog #		Title	Year	VG+	NM
United Arts. UAS-5199	(S)	**Young Billy Young**	1969	6.00	15.00
		(U.A. 5199 features compositions by conductor Shelly Manne.)			
Verve MGV-15010	(M)	**The Gene Krupa Story**	1959	16.00	40.00
Verve MGVS-6105	(S)	**The Gene Krupa Story**	1959	12.00	30.00
		(Verve 15010 features performances by Gene Krupa with Shelly Manne, Red Nichols and Anita O'Day.)			
Verve MGV-4043	(M)	**Let No Man Write My Epitaph**	1960	20.00	50.00
		(Verve 4043 features performances by Ella Fitzgerald and Paul Smith.)			
		— Original Verve albums above have black labels with "Verve Records, Inc." on the bottom.—			
Verve V-15010	(M)	**The Gene Krupa Story**	1961	6.00	15.00
Verve V6-15010	(S)	**The Gene Krupa Story**	1961	5.00	12.00
Verve V-8548	(M)	**The Yellow Canary**	1963	8.00	20.00
Verve V6-8548	(S)	**The Yellow Canary**	1963	10.00	25.00
		(Verve 15010 features compositions by conductor Kenyon Hopkins.)			
Verve V-8624	(M)	**"Once A Thief" & Other Film Themes**	1965	8.00	20.00
Verve V6-8624	(S)	**"Once A Thief" & Other Film Themes**	1965	10.00	25.00
		(Verve 8624 features compositions by conductor Lalo Schifrin.)			
Verve V-8638	(M)	**Mr. Buddwing**	1965	6.00	15.00
Verve V6-8638	(S)	**Mr. Buddwing**	1965	8.00	20.00
		(Verve 8638 features compositions by conductor Kenyon Hopkins.)			
Verve V-8664	(M)	**This Property Is Condemned**	1966	10.00	25.00
Verve V6-8664	(S)	**This Property Is Condemned**	1966	12.00	30.00
		(Verve 8664 features compositions by conductor Kenyon Hopkins.)			
Verve V-8679	(M)	**The Deadly Affair**	1966	6.00	15.00
Verve V6-8679	(S)	**The Deadly Affair**	1966	8.00	20.00
		(Verve 8679 features compositions by conductor Quincy Jones, with a performance by Astrud Gilberto.)			
		— Verve albums above have black labels with "MGM Records" on the bottom.—			
Warner Bros. W-1289	(M)	**77 Sunset Strip**	1959	12.00	30.00
Warner Bros. WS-1289	(S)	**77 Sunset Strip**	1959	16.00	40.00
		(W.B. 1289 features jazzy compositions and performances by Warren Barker's orchestra and combo.)			
Warner Bros. WS-1747	(S)	**Oh Good Grief!**	1968	6.00	15.00
		(W.B 1747 features jazzy background music by Vince Guaraldi from sundry "Peanuts" cartoons.)			
Warner Bros. WS-1777	(S)	**Bullitt**	1968	10.00	25.00
		(W.B. 1777 features compositions by conductor Lalo Schifrin.)			
Warwick W-2030	(M)	**Hell To Eternity**	1960	24.00	50.00
Warwick W-2030ST	(S)	**Hell To Eternity**	1960	30.00	75.00
		(Warwick 2030 features compositions by conductor Leith Stevens.)			
World Pacific P-2005	(M)	**Theme Music From "The James Dean Story"**	1958	40.00	100.00
		(W.P. 2005 features performances by Chet Baker and Bud Shank. Reissued as Kimberly 2016.)			
World Pacific WP-1265	(M)	**Slippery When Wet**	1959	24.00	60.00
		(W.P. 265 features performances by composer Bud Shank with Bob Cooper.)			

Jazz at the Philharmonic

Jazz impresario Norman Granz was one of the first to recognize the inherent possibilities for music in the 33 1/3 RPM long playing album. This new format, introduced by Columbia and Decca in 1949, allowed musicians to stretch outside of the restrictive time limits imposed by 78s. Granz was thus able to capture extended performances for the first time, a rather novel listening experience for jazz aficionados in those heady times. His first releases to take advantage of this were the *Jazz At The Philharmonic* series (or *JATP*, as they were affectionately referred), introduced in 1950 and essentially in print in one form or another since. While they no longer enjoy a large audience—primarily because they are *not* the most exciting of recordings and their novelty has long since worn off—they nonetheless play a relatively important role in the development of recorded jazz. And, as collectibles, while they are not big ticket items, the many reissues the various volumes went through has made the series both perplexing and exciting to pursue. One would have had to have religiously purchased each new volume as it was issued to be sure at this point in time of the absolutely correct chronology of the next few volumes.

The first *JATP* album was issued on Moses Asch's Stinson label with Asch retaining the rights to the tapes, a procedural error that Granz would not replicate in his later dealings. This 10" album was issued on translucent red vinyl with cover art by David Stone Martin. It was subsequently reissued on black vinyl and again on a dark, opaque red vinyl. *Volumes 2 Volume 3* then appeared as 10" albums on Arco Records in 1950. At this point Granz signed a distribution deal with Mercury Records. The first title was *How High The Moon* (Mercury MG-35001), which would serve as the first volume of the series from this point on, Granz basically ignoring the existence of the Stinson release. Eight more *JATPs* followed as part of the 35000 series in 1950: *Volumes 4-11*, all 10" albums, designated by Mercury exclusively for Granz' productions.

By 1951 Granz had established his own Clef Records, to be distributed by Mercury as Mercury/Clef. Naturally, the first order of business was to reissue (again) each of the *JATP* albums; *How High The Moon* and *Volumes 2-11* were issued as Clef 10" albums in 1951. In lieu of actual catalog numbers each title was numbered MGC-Vol. 1 through 11. Then followed three new titles, *Volumes 12, 13* and *14*. In 1953 *HHTM* was issued by Mercury as a 12" album, MGC-508, and Clef appeared for the first time as a solo label. That is, it was simply Clef Records, no longer Mercury/Clef and, *once again*, each of the titles was reissued as a 10" album carrying the same "MGC-Vol." catalog number.

In 1954-55 Granz issued the *JATP* series on 12" albums, each new title combining two of the earlier discs. That is, the new 12" albums had one 10" album on each of its sides. These were known as *Jazz At The Philharmonic, New Volumes 2-7* with *New Volume 2* containing old volumes 2 and 3; *New Volume 3* was the old 4 and 5; *New Volume 4* was the old 6 and 14; *New Volume 5* was the old 7, 10 and 11; *New Volume 6* was the old 8 and 9; and *New Volume 7* was the old 12 and 13. Each of these new volumes featured a previously used DSM cover. These were then followed by volumes 15 through 18, boxed three-album sets with new material. Each box featured cover art from Martin and contained a bonus booklet.

In 1956 Granz consolidated his labels (along with Clef he issued albums on Norgran and Down Home) into Verve Records and, ahem, reissued all of the older titles on the new imprint as 12" albums. While the first seven volumes kept their old catalog number, the three-album sets were now numbered consecutively as *JATP, Volume 8* (formerly 15), *Volume 9* (formerly 16), *Volume 10* (formerly 17), and *11* (formerly 18). These were kept in print by MGM after they acquired the label in 1960. They may not set turntables on fire in the '90s, but these were immensely popular discs in their day and most copies for sale are worn. Finally, a twelfth volume featuring Ella Fitzgerald was announced and advertised but apparently never appeared; it's possible that *Ella At The Opera House* (Verve 8264, 1958), which features the JATP All-Stars, was culled from these recordings.

The chart below shows the history of the *JATP* series with the column on the left listing the various volumes by number ("HHTM" standing for *How High The Moon* while "JACH" means *Jazz At Carnegie Hall*) while the row across the tops lists the possible record companies with which the individual volumes could have been released. The chart is followed by the actual listings, which includes other Granz endeavors, the *Jam Session* series and *The Jazz Scene*.

—Stinson 10" Albums—

Stinson SLP-23	*(10")*	**Jazz At The Philharmonic**	*1950*	**40.00**	**100.00**
		(Rranslucent red vinyl with cover art by David Stone Martin.)			
Stinson SLP-23	*(10")*	**Jazz At The Philharmonic**	*195?*	**30.00**	**75.00**
		(Second pressings are on black vinyl with the DSM cover.)			
Stinson SLP-23	*(10")*	**Jazz At The Philharmonic**	*195?*	**30.00**	**75.00**
		(Later pressings are on dark red vinyl with the DSM cover.)			

Three examples of 10" albums from the *Jazz at the Philharmonic* confusing incarnations: First on Stinson with a nice cover by David Stone Martin, then on Arco with no cover art and no back cover, and then on Granz' own Clef label, again with attractive art by DSM.

Label & Catalog #		Title	Year	VG+	NM
		—Arco 10" Albums—			
Arco AL-1	*(10")*	**Jazz At The Philharmonic, Vol. 2**	*1950*	**30.00**	**75.00**
Arco AL-2	*(10")*	**Jazz At The Philharmonic, Vol. 3**	*1950*	**30.00**	**75.00**
Arco AL-4	*(10")*	**Jazz At Carnegie Hall**	*1950*	**30.00**	**75.00**
Arco AL-8	*(10")*	**Jazz At Carnegie Hall, Vol. 2**	*195?*	**30.00**	**75.00**
		—Mercury 10" Albums—			
Mercury MG-35001	*(10")*	**How High The Moon**	*1950*	**30.00**	**75.00**
Mercury MG-35002	*(10")*	**Jazz At The Philharmonic, Vol. 10**	*1950*	**40.00**	**100.00**
		(Mercury 35002 features cover art by David Stone Martin.)			
Mercury MG-35003	*(10")*	**Jazz At The Philharmonic, Vol. 2**	*1950*	**30.00**	**75.00**
Mercury MG-35004	*(10")*	**Jazz At The Philharmonic, Vol. 3**	*1950*	**30.00**	**75.00**
		(Mercury 35003 and 35004 are reissues of Arco 1 and 2 and 4.)			
Mercury MG-35005	*(10")*	**Jazz At The Philharmonic, Vol. 4**	*1950*	**40.00**	**100.00**
		(Mercury 35005 features cover art by David Stone Martin.)			
Mercury MG-35006	*(10")*	**Jazz At The Philharmonic, Vol. 5**	*1950*	**30.00**	**75.00**
Mercury MG-35007	*(10")*	**Jazz At The Philharmonic, Vol. 6**	*1950*	**30.00**	**75.00**
Mercury MG-35008	*(10")*	**Jazz At The Philharmonic, Vol. 7**	*1950*	**30.00**	**75.00**
Mercury MG-35000	*(10")*	**Jazz At The Philharmonic, Vol. 8**	*1950*	**30.00**	**75.00**
Mercury MG-35009	*(10")*	**Jazz At The Philharmonic, Vol. 9**	*1950*	**30.00**	**75.00**
Mercury MG-35010	*(10")*	**Jazz At Carnegie Hall**	*1950*	**30.00**	**75.00**
		(Mercury 35010 is a reissue of Arco 4.)			
Mercury MG-35011	*(10")*	**Jazz At The Philharmonic, Vol. 11**	*1950*	**30.00**	**75.00**
		—Mercury Clef 10" Albums—			
Mercury MGC-Vol. 1	*(10")*	**How High The Moon**	*1951*	**24.00**	**60.00**
Mercury MGC-Vol. 2	*(10")*	**Jazz At The Philharmonic, Vol. 2**	*1951*	**24.00**	**60.00**
Mercury MGC-Vol. 3	*(10")*	**Jazz At The Philharmonic, Vol. 3**	*1951*	**24.00**	**60.00**
Mercury MGC-Vol. 4	*(10")*	**Jazz At The Philharmonic, Vol. 4**	*1951*	**24.00**	**60.00**
Mercury MGC-Vol. 5	*(10")*	**Jazz At The Philharmonic, Vol. 5**	*1951*	**24.00**	**60.00**
Mercury MGC-Vol. 6	*(10")*	**Jazz At The Philharmonic, Vol. 6**	*1951*	**24.00**	**60.00**
Mercury MGC-Vol. 7	*(10")*	**Jazz At The Philharmonic, Vol. 7**	*1951*	**24.00**	**60.00**
Mercury MGC-Vol. 8	*(10")*	**Jazz At The Philharmonic, Vol. 8**	*1951*	**24.00**	**60.00**
Mercury MGC-Vol. 9	*(10")*	**Jazz At The Philharmonic, Vol. 9**	*1951*	**24.00**	**60.00**
Mercury MGC-Vol. 10	*(10")*	**Jazz At The Philharmonic, Vol. 10**	*1951*	**30.00**	**75.00**
		(Mercury 10 features cover art by David Stone Martin.)			
Mercury MGC-Vol. 11	*(10")*	**Jazz At The Philharmonic, Vol. 11**	*1951*	**24.00**	**60.00**
		(Mercury Vol. 1-11 are reissues of 35000-35011.)			
Mercury MGC-Vol. 12	*(10")*	**Jazz At The Philharmonic, Vol. 12**	*1951*	**24.00**	**60.00**
Mercury MGC-Vol. 13	*(10")*	**Jazz At The Philharmonic, Vol. 13**	*1951*	**24.00**	**60.00**
Mercury MGC-Vol. 14	*(10")*	**Jazz At The Philharmonic, Vol. 14**	*1952*	**24.00**	**60.00**
Mercury MGC-Vol. 15	*(10")*	**Jazz At The Philharmonic, Vol. 15**	*1953*	**24.00**	**60.00**
		—Mercury 12" Albums—			
Mercury MGC-601	*(M)*	**Jam Session #1**	*1953*	**30.00**	**75.00**
Mercury MGC-602	*(M)*	**Jam Session #2**	*1953*	**30.00**	**75.00**
Mercury MGC-608	*(M)*	**How High The Moon**	*1953*	**30.00**	**75.00**
		(Mercury 608 is a reissue of Vol. 1.)			
Mercury MGJC-1	*(M)*	**Jazz Concert** *(2 LPs)*	*1953*	**50.00**	**125.00**
		(Boxed set of 2501 and 2502 with cover art by David Stone Martin.)			
		—Clef 10" Albums—			
Clef Special Edition	*(10")*	**Jazz Scene** *(2 LPs)*	*1953*	**30.00**	**75.00**
		(Purchasers of this boxed set also had the option to buy an "attractive separate folio at $5 of 31 superb photographs prepared by Gjon Mill's for the original 78 rpm album," worth an additional $25.)			
Clef MGC-Vol .2	*(10")*	**Jazz At The Philharmonic, Vol. 2**	*1953*	**24.00**	**60.00**
Clef MGC-Vol. 3	*(10")*	**Jazz At The Philharmonic, Vol. 3**	*1953*	**24.00**	**60.00**
Clef MGC-Vol. 4	*(10")*	**Jazz At The Philharmonic, Vol. 4**	*1953*	**30.00**	**75.00**
		(Clef 4 features cover art by David Stone Martin.)			
Clef MGC-Vol. 5	*(10")*	**Jazz At The Philharmonic, Vol. 5**	*1953*	**24.00**	**60.00**
Clef MGC-Vol. 6	*(10")*	**Jazz At The Philharmonic, Vol. 6**	*1953*	**24.00**	**60.00**
Clef MGC-Vol. 7	*(10")*	**Jazz At The Philharmonic, Vol. 7**	*1953*	**24.00**	**60.00**
Clef MGC-Vol. 8	*(10")*	**Jazz At The Philharmonic, Vol. 8**	*1953*	**24.00**	**60.00**
Clef MGC-Vol. 9	*(10")*	**Jazz At The Philharmonic, Vol. 9**	*1953*	**24.00**	**60.00**
Clef MGC-Vol. 10	*(10")*	**Jazz At The Philharmonic, Vol. 10**	*1953*	**24.00**	**60.00**
		(Clef 10 features cover art by David Stone Martin.)			

Label & Catalog #		Title	Year	VG+	NM
Clef MGC-Vol. 11	(10")	**Jazz At The Philharmonic, Vol. 11**	1953	24.00	60.00
		(Clef 11 features cover art by David Stone Martin.)			
Clef MGC-Vol. 12	(10")	**Jazz At The Philharmonic, Vol. 12**	1953	24.00	60.00
Clef MGC-Vol. 13	(10")	**Jazz At The Philharmonic, Vol. 13**	1953	24.00	60.00
		(Clef 13 features cover art by David Stone Martin.)			
Clef MGC-Vol. 14	(10")	**Jazz At The Philharmonic, Vol. 14**	1953	24.00	60.00
		Clef Vol. 1-14 are reissues of Mercury Vol. 1-14.)			
Clef MGC-Vol. 15 (12")	(M)	**Jazz At The Philharmonic, Vol. 15**	1953	24.00	60.00
		(Clef Vol. 15 is a reisue of Mercury Vol. 15.)			
		– Clef 12" Albums–			
Clef MGC-4001	(M)	**Jam Session #1**	1953	20.00	50.00
Clef MGC-4002	(M)	**Jam Session #2**	1953	20.00	50.00
		(Clef 4001 and 4002 are reissues of Mercury 601 and 602.)			
Clef MGC-4003	(M)	**Jam Session #3**	1953	20.00	50.00
Clef MGC-4004	(M)	**Jam Session #4**	1953	20.00	50.00
Clef MGC-4005	(M)	**Jam Session #5**	1953	20.00	50.00
Clef MGC-4006	(M)	**Jam Session #6**	1953	20.00	50.00
Clef MGC-4007	(M)	**Jazz Scene**	1953	20.00	50.00
Clef MGC-601	(M)	**Jam Session #1**	1954	16.00	40.00
Clef MGC-602	(M)	**Jam Session #2**	1954	16.00	40.00
		(Clef 601 and 602 are reissues of 4001 and 4002.)			
Clef MGC-608	(M)	**How High The Moon**	1955	16.00	40.00
		(Clef 608 is a reissue of Mercury 508.)			
Clef MGC-651	(M)	**Jam Session #1**	1955	16.00	40.00
Clef MGC-652	(M)	**Jam Session #2**	1955	16.00	40.00
Clef MGC-653	(M)	**Jam Session #3**	1955	16.00	40.00
Clef MGC-654	(M)	**Jam Session #4**	1955	16.00	40.00
Clef MGC-655	(M)	**Jam Session #5**	1955	16.00	40.00
Clef MGC-656	(M)	**Jam Session #6**	1955	16.00	40.00
		(Clef 651-656 are reissues of 4001-4006.)			
Clef MGC-674	(M)	**The Jazz Scene**	1955	16.00	40.00
Clef MGC-677	(M)	**Jam Session #7**	1955	16.00	40.00
Clef MGC-711	(M)	**Jam Session #8**	1955	16.00	40.00
		("Jam Session" 1-8 feature cover art by David Stone Martin.)			
Clef MGC-Vol. 1	(M)	**How High The Moon**	1955	20.00	50.00
		(Clef Vol. 1 is a reissue of 608.)			
Clef MGC-Vol. 2	(M)	**Jazz At The Philharmonic, New Vol.** 2	1955	20.00	50.00
		(Clef Vol. 2 is a reissue of the 10" Vol. 2 and 3 with cover art by David Stone Martin.)			
Clef MGC-Vol. 3	(M)	**Jazz At The Philharmonic, New Vol.** 3	1955	20.00	50.00
		(Clef Vol. 3 is a reissue of the 10" Vol. 4 and 5 with cover art by David Stone Martin.)			
Clef MGC-Vol. 4	(M)	**Jazz At The Philharmonic, New Vol.** 4	1955	20.00	50.00
		(Clef Vol. 4 is a reissue of the 10" Vol. 6 and 14 with cover art by David Stone Martin.)			
Clef MGC-Vol. 5	(M)	**Jazz At The Philharmonic, New Vol.** 5	1955	20.00	50.00
		(Clef Vol. 5 is a reissue of the 10" Vol. 7, 10 and 11 with cover art by David Stone Martin.)			
Clef MGC-Vol. 6	(M)	**Jazz At The Philharmonic, New Vol.** 6	1955	20.00	50.00
		(Clef Vol. 6 is a reissue of the 10" Vol. 8 and 9.)			
Clef MGC-Vol. 7	(M)	**Jazz At The Philharmonic, New Vol.** 7	1955	20.00	50.00
		(Clef Vol. 3 is a reissue of the 10" Vol. 12 and 13 with cover art by David Stone Martin.)			
Clef MGC-Vol. 15	(M)	**Jazz At The Philharmonic, Vol. 15**	1954	30.00	75.00
		(3 LPs with souvenir program and cover art by David Stone Martin.)			
Clef MGC-Vol. 16	(M)	**Jazz At The Philharmonic, Vol. 16**	1954	30.00	75.00
		(3 LPs with souvenir program and cover art by David Stone Martin.)			
Clef MGC-Vol. 17	(M)	**Jazz At The Philharmonic, Vol. 17**	1955	30.00	75.00
		(3 LPs with photo album and cover art by David Stone Martin.)			
Clef MGC-Vol. 18	(M)	**Jazz At The Philharmonic, Vol. 18**	1955	30.00	75.00
		(3 LPs with booklet.)			
Clef MGC-4001/7	(M)	**Jam Session**	1953	125.00	250.00
		(Boxed set of the first six Vol.s of "Jam Session," 4001-4006 and "Jazz Scene," 4007 with cover art by David Stone Martin.)			

Label & Catalog #		Title	Year	VG+	NM
		—Norgran 12" Albums—			
Norgran MGN-2501	(M)	**Norman Granz Jazz Concert**	1954	30.00	75.00
Norgran MGN-2502	(M)	**Norman Granz Jazz Concert**	1954	30.00	75.00
Norgran MGN-3501-2	(M)	**Jazz Concert** *(2 LPs)*	1956	50.00	125.00
		(Norgran 3501 is a reissue of Mercury JC-1 with the DSM cover.)			
		—Verve 12" Albums—			
Verve MGV-8049	(M)	**Jam Session #1**	1956	12.00	30.00
Verve MGV-8050	(M)	**Jam Session #2**	1956	12.00	30.00
Verve MGV-8051	(M)	**Jam Session #3**	1956	12.00	30.00
Verve MGV-8052	(M)	**Jam Session #4**	1956	12.00	30.00
Verve MGV-8053	(M)	**Jam Session #5**	1956	12.00	30.00
Verve MGV-8054	(M)	**Jam Session #6**	1956	12.00	30.00
Verve MGV-8060	(M)	**The Jazz Scene**	1957	12.00	30.00
Verve MGV-8062	(M)	**Jam Session #7**	1957	12.00	30.00
Verve MGV-8094	(M)	**Jam Session #8**	1957	12.00	30.00
		(Verve 8049-54, 8060, 8062 and 8094 are reissues of Clef 651-656, 674, 677 and 711.)			
Verve MGV-8196	(M)	**Jam Session #9**	1957	12.00	30.00
Verve MGC-Vol. 1	(M)	**How High The Moon**	1957	12.00	30.00
Verve MGC-Vol. 2	(M)	**Jazz At The Philharmonic, Vol. 2**	1957	12.00	30.00
Verve MGC-Vol. 3	(M)	**Jazz At The Philharmonic, Vol. 3**	1957	12.00	30.00
Verve MGC-Vol. 4	(M)	**Jazz At The Philharmonic, Vol. 4**	1957	12.00	30.00
Verve MGC-Vol. 5	(M)	**Jazz At The Philharmonic, Vol. 5**	1957	12.00	30.00
Verve MGC-Vol. 6	(M)	**Jazz At The Philharmonic, Vol. 6**	1957	12.00	30.00
Verve MGC-Vol. 7	(M)	**Jazz At The Philharmonic, Vol. 7**	1957	12.00	30.00
		(Verve Vol. 1-7 are reissues of Clef Vol. 1-7.)			
Verve MGC-Vol. 8	(M)	**Jazz At The Philharmonic, Vol. 8** *(3 LPs)*	1957	20.00	50.00
		(Verve Vol. 8 is a reissue of Clef New Vol. 15.)			
Verve MGC-Vol. 9	(M)	**Jazz At The Philharmonic, Vol. 9** *(3 LPs)*	1957	20.00	50.00
		(Verve Vol. 9 is a reissue of Clef New Vol. 16.)			
Verve MGC-Vol. 10	(M)	**Jazz At The Philharmonic, Vol. 10** *(3 LPs)*	1957	20.00	50.00
		(Verve Vol. 10 is a reissue of Clef New Vol. 17.)			
Verve MGC-Vol. 11	(M)	**Jazz At The Philharmonic, Vol. 11** *(2 LPs)*	1957	16.00	40.00
		(Verve Vol. 11 is a reissue of Clef New Vol. 18 with the DSM cover.)			
Verve MGC-Vol. 12	(M)	**Jazz At The Philharmonic, Vol. 12** *(2 LPs)*	195?		*See below*
		(Vol. 12 was advertised— "Ella Fitzgerald sings in her first JATP concert recorded on Verve. Two Twelve-inch Long Play Records $9.96"— but I have no verification of its having been released. . .)			
Verve MGV-8060	(M)	**The Jazz Scene**	1957	14.00	35.00
		(Verve 8060 is a reissue of Clef 674.)			
Verve MGV-8267	(M)	**The JATP All-Stars At The Opera House**	1958	14.00	35.00
Verve MGVS-6029	(S)	**The JATP All-Stars At The Opera House**	1960	12.00	30.00
Verve MGV-8284	(M)	**The JATP All-Stars At The Opera House**	1959		*Unreleased*
		—Original Verve albums above have "Verve Records, Inc." on the bottom of the label.—			
Verve V-8060	(M)	**The Jazz Scene**	1961	6.00	15.00
Verve V-8267	(M)	**The JATP All-Stars At The Opera House**	1961	8.00	20.00
Verve V6-8267	(S)	**The JATP All-Stars At The Opera House**	1961	6.00	15.00
Verve V-8486	(M)	**The JATP All-Stars—Funky Blues**	1962	12.00	30.00
Verve V6-8486	(S)	**The JATP All-Stars—Funky Blues**	1962	10.00	25.00
		(Verve 8486 is a reissue of Mercury 602.)			
Verve V-8489	(M)	**The JATP All-Stars At The Opera House**	1962	10.00	25.00
Verve V6-8489	(S)	**The JATP All-Stars At The Opera House**	1962	8.00	20.00
		(Verve 8489 is a reissue of 8267.)			
Verve V-8539	(M)	**Jazz At The Philharmonic In Europe, Vol. 1**	1963	10.00	25.00
Verve V6-8539	(S)	**Jazz At The Philharmonic In Europe, Vol. 1**	1963	8.00	20.00
Verve V-8540	(M)	**Jazz At The Philharmonic In Europe, Vol. 2**	1963	10.00	25.00
Verve V6-8540	(S)	**Jazz At The Philharmonic In Europe, Vol. 2**	1963	8.00	20.00
Verve V-8541	(M)	**Jazz At The Philharmonic In Europe, Vol. 3**	1963	10.00	25.00
Verve V6-8541	(S)	**Jazz At The Philharmonic In Europe, Vol. 3**	1963	8.00	20.00
Verve V-8542	(M)	**Jazz At The Philharmonic In Europe, Vol. 4**	1963	10.00	25.00
Verve V6-8542	(S)	**Jazz At The Philharmonic In Europe, Vol. 4**	1963	8.00	20.00
		—Verve albums above have black labels with "MGM Records" on the bottom.—			
Verve VSP-15	(M)	**The JATP All Stars—How High The Moon**	1966	5.00	12.00
Verve VSPS-15	(E)	**The JATP All Stars—How High The Moon**	1966	4.00	10.00
Verve VSP-16	(M)	**The JATP All Stars—Perdido**	1966	5.00	12.00
Verve VSPS-16	(E)	**The JATP All Stars—Perdido**	1966	4.00	10.00
		(Verve 15 and 16 repackage material from previous JATP releases.)			

Various Artists Compilations & All-Star Sessions

This section collects various artists compilations with the records listed by label. In most of the musical genres– pop, rock, country, etc.– the typical various artists album is a compilation of tracks compiled by the record company as a sampler of their product or as a showcase of their stars or accomplishments. Most various artists albums allow each artist only one track but exceptions are plentiful. (In this book, an album that collects tracks from three artists is listed in the main section of the book; albums from four or more artists are listed here.) The tracks may be from singles or albums by they are almost always assembled from previously released material. While this system holds true for the major labels handling of jazz collections, anthologies and compilations, a whole other type of album exists courtesy of the smaller, more or less exclusively jazz labels: These are the leaderless "blowing" sessions featuring an "all-star" cast called into the studio to cut some sides that will sell some records (Prestige and Savoy contribute the bulk of these albums).

While there may be a featured soloist or two, since there are no real leaders, these albums cannot be listed under an artist in the main section of the book. Exceptions are primarily among the listings for Prestige, notable for reissuing leaderless albums with a new catalogue number (often retaining the original title and cover) and crediting the album to an artist from the session who had since achieved significant sales status. Rather than list the same record in two different parts of the book, I have listed the original blowing session under the artist later credited, although I kept the original issue below with a reference. The only instance where this has any real affect on the integrity of an artist's discography is with John Coltrane: "Tenor Conclave" is listed first in his discography because it was reissued by Prestige as his album years later. His first *real* album as a leader, *Coltrane*, is therefore listed second.

A second type of compilation consists of collecting previously unrelated tracks into a cohesive anthology that makes a statement, such as all vocals, pianos, trumpets, etc. These most often consist of sessions to small to fill an album or of outtakes from a previously released session. Some albums take the form of "duals" and are usually between two artists, one to a side. Since both of the above are often dealt with as various artists sets by collectors and dealers alike, theys are listed below (when known) with notes referring the reader to the individual (actually, dual) listings in the book. Examples include Brunswick's "Battle of Jazz" series or King's "Battle of the Blues." Aside from filling missing holes in collectors running a label, there is very little demand for various artists records that do not contain material unavailable elsewhere.

ABC-Paramount ABC-109	*(M)*	**The Four Most Guitars**	*1956*	**10.00**	**25.00**
ABC-Paramount ABC-115	*(M)*	**Know Your Jazz**	*1956*	**10.00**	**25.00**
Adventures/Sound WL-127	*(M)*	**Modern Jazz Concert**	*1958*	**16.00**	**40.00**
Adventures/Sound WL-162	*(M)*	**One World Jazz**	*1959*	**20.00**	**50.00**
Adventures/Sound WS-314	*(S)*	**One World Jazz**	*1959*	**16.00**	**40.00**
Aladdin LP-701	*(10")*	**Battle Of The Saxes**	*1950*	**100.00**	**200.00**
Aladdin LP-703	*(10")*	**Party After Hours**	*1950*	**100.00**	**200.00**
Allegro 1590	*(10")*	**Bushkin-Safranski-Wilson Groups**	*1955*	**20.00**	**50.00**
Allegro ALL-737	*(M)*	**Jazz Greats!**	*1958*	**12.00**	**30.00**
American Rec. Soc. LP-100	*(M)*	**Three Roads To Jazz**	*1956*	**12.00**	**30.00**
American Rec. Soc. G-401	*(M)*	**Giants Of Jazz**	*1956*	**12.00**	**30.00**
American Rec. Soc. G-404	*(M)*	**Funky Blues No. 2**	*1956*	**12.00**	**30.00**
American Rec. Soc. G-424	*(M)*	**All Star Tribute To Tatum**	*1957*	**12.00**	**30.00**
Angel ANG-60001	*(10")*	**Italian Jazz Stars**	*1955*	**20.00**	**50.00**
Angel ANG-60004	*(10")*	**London Broil**	*1955*	**20.00**	**50.00**
Angel ANG-60007	*(10")*	**Cats And Jammer Kids**	*1955*	**20.00**	**50.00**
Angel ANG-60009	*(10")*	**French Toast**	*1956*	**20.00**	**50.00**
Atlantic ALS-139	*(10")*	**Dixieland At Jazz, Ltd.—Vol. 1**	*1952*	**24.00**	**60.00**
Atlantic ALS-140	*(10")*	**Dixieland At Jazz, Ltd.—Vol. 2**	*1952*	**24.00**	**60.00**
Atlantic 1261	*(M)*	**Dixieland At Jazz, Ltd.**	*1957*	**16.00**	**40.00**
Atlantic 1296	*(M)*	**Voodoo Drums In Hi-Fi**	*1958*	**16.00**	**40.00**
Atlantic 1298	*(M)*	**Historic Jazz Concert At Music Inn**	*1958*	**16.00**	**40.00**

—Atlantic albums above have black mono or green stereo labels.—

Label & Catalog #		Title	Year	VG+	NM
Atlantic 1261	(M)	**Dixieland At Jazz, Ltd.**	1961	10.00	25.00
Atlantic 1296	(M)	**Voodoo Drums In Hi-Fi**	1961	8.00	20.00
Atlantic 1298	(M)	**Historic Jazz Concert At Music Inn**	1961	8.00	20.00
Atlantic 1331	(M)	**Newport Jazz Festival All Stars**	1961	10.00	25.00
Atlantic SD-1331	(S)	**Newport Jazz Festival All Stars**	1961	8.00	20.00
Atlantic 1337	(M)	**The Blues In Modern Jazz**	1961	8.00	20.00
Atlantic 1338	(M)	**Jazz At Jazz Ltd.**	1961	10.00	25.00
		—Atlantic albums above have multi-color labels with a white fan logo.—			
Atlantic 1296	(M)	**Voodoo Drums In Hi-Fi**	196?	6.00	15.00
Atlantic 1298	(M)	**Historic Jazz Concert At Music Inn**	196?	6.00	15.00
Atlantic 1337	(M)	**The Blues In Modern Jazz**	196?	6.00	15.00
Atlantic SD-1337	(E)	**The Blues In Modern Jazz**	1969	2.50	7.50
		—Atlantic albums above have multi-color labels with a white fan logo.—			
Audiophile AP-23	(M)	**Swing Potpourri**	1953	12.00	30.00
Audiophile AP-24	(M)	**Jazz Potpourri**	1953	12.00	30.00
Audiophile AP-27	(M)	**Easy Listening**	1953	12.00	30.00
Audiophile AP-28	(M)	**Piano Artistry**	1953	12.00	30.00
Audiophile AP-38	(M)	**Easy Listening**	1953	12.00	30.00
Audiophile AP-43	(M)	**Unexpurgated Jazz**	1953	12.00	30.00
Audiophile XL-325	(M)	**Dixieland Jazz**	1954	12.00	30.00
Audiophile XL-327	(M)	**Easy Listening**	1954	12.00	30.00
Audiophile XL-330	(M)	**Dixieland Jazz**	1954	12.00	30.00
Bethlehem EXLP-1	(M)	**Porgy & Bess** *(3 LPs)*	1956	24.00	60.00
Bethlehem EXLP-2	(M)	**Bethlehem's Grab Bag**	1958	16.00	40.00
Bethlehem EXLP-6	(M)	**Bethlehem's Best** *(3 LPs)*	1958	24.00	60.00
Bethlehem BCP-80	(M)	**Jazz City Presents**	1957	12.00	30.00
Bethlehem BCP-82	(M)	**Just For Variety—Bethlehem's Best, Vol. 1**	1957	12.00	30.00
Bethlehem BCP-83	(M)	**Just For Variety—Bethlehem's Best, Vol. 2**	1957	12.00	30.00
Bethlehem BCP-84	(M)	**Just For Variety—Bethlehem's Best, Vol. 3**	1957	12.00	30.00
		(Bethlehem 82-84 are reissues of 6.)			
Bethlehem BCP-85	(M)	**Nothing Cheesy About This Jazz**	1958	12.00	30.00
Bethlehem BCP-86	(M)	**We Cut This Album For Bread**	1958	12.00	30.00
Bethlehem BCP-87	(M)	**Double Barrel Jazz**	1958	12.00	30.00
Bethlehem BCP-88	(M)	**Jazz Music For People Who Don't Care About Money**	1958	12.00	30.00
Bethlehem BCP-89	(M)	**We Built A Jazz Album For You**	1958	12.00	30.00
Bethlehem BCP-90	(M)	**Handful Of Cool Jazz**	1959	12.00	30.00
Bethlehem BCP-91	(M)	**A Lot Of Yarn But A Well-Knitted Jazz Album**	1959	12.00	30.00
Bethlehem BCP-92	(M)	**No Sour Grapes—Just Pure Jazz**	1959	12.00	30.00
Bethlehem BCP-6024	(M)	**Winner's Circle**	1958	16.00	40.00
Bethlehem BCP-6034	(M)	**Smart, Luscious, Beautiful**	1959	12.00	30.00
Bethlehem BCP-6035	(M)	**Fifteen Star Saxophones**	1959	12.00	30.00
Bethlehem BCP-6036	(M)	**Trombone Bandstand**	1959	12.00	30.00
Bethlehem BCP-6037	(M)	**Big Band Contrast**	1959	12.00	30.00
Bethlehem BCP-6038	(M)	**Blues Ville**	1959	12.00	30.00
Bethlehem BCP-6039	(M)	**Jazz Music For Birds**	1959	12.00	30.00
Bethlehem BCP-6040	(M)	**Porgy & Bess**	1959	12.00	30.00
Bethlehem BCP-6056	(M)	**Motor City Scene**	1961	20.00	50.00
		(Beth. 6056 is an all-star session with Pepper Adams, Donad Byrd, Kenny Burrell, Tommy Flanagan, Louis Hayes and Paul Chambers.)			
Bethlehem BCP-6060	(M)	**Award Album Jazz Vocals**	1961	10.00	25.00
Bethlehem BCP-6065	(M)	**Golden Jazz Instrumentals**	1961	10.00	25.00
Bethlehem BCP-6066	(M)	**John Coltrane In The Winner's Circle**	1961	10.00	25.00
		(Bethlehem 6066 is a reissue 6024, a various artists album.)			
Bethlehem BCP-6068	(M)	**Award Album Jazz Vocals**	1961	10.00	25.00
Bethlehem BCP-6071	(M)	**Blues 'N' Folk**	1961	10.00	25.00
Bethlehem BCP-6073	(M)	**Jazz For Surf-Niks**	1961	10.00	25.00
Blue Note BLP-5001	(10")	**Mellow The Mood/Jazz In A Mellow Mood**	1951	100.00	200.00
Blue Note BLP-5026	(10")	**Memorable Sessions In Jazz**	1953	100.00	200.00
Blue Note BLP-5027	(10")	**Swing Hi, Swing Lo**	1953	100.00	200.00
Blue Note BLP-5059	(10")	**Best From The West— Modern Sounds From California, Vol. 1**	1955	100.00	200.00
Blue Note BLP-5060	(10")	**Best From The West— Modern Sounds From California, Vol. 2**	1955	100.00	200.00

Label & Catalog #		Title	Year	VG+	NM
Blue Note B-6507	(M)	**Swing Hi, Swing Lo**	1969	6.00	15.00
		(Blue Note 6507 is a reissue of 5027.)			
Blue Note B-6509	(M)	**Blue Note Classics**	1969	6.00	15.00
Bluesville BVLP-1009	(M)	**Soul Jazz, Vol. 1**	1960	16.00	40.00
Bluesville BVLP-1010	(M)	**Soul Jazz, Vol. 2**	1960	16.00	40.00
		—Bluesville albums above have blue labels with silver print.—			
Bluesville BVLP-1009	(M)	**Soul Jazz, Vol. 1**	1965	8.00	20.00
Bluesville BVLP-1010	(M)	**Soul Jazz, Vol. 2**	1965	1800	20.00
		—Bluesville albums above have blue labels with a trident logo on the right side.—			
Brunswick BL-58018	(10")	**Boogie Woogie Piano**	1950	20.00	50.00
Brunswick BL-58024	(10")	**Harlem Jazz 1930**	1951	20.00	50.00
Brunswick BL-58026	(10")	**New Orleans To Chicago**	1951	20.00	50.00
Brunswick BL-58037	(10")	**Battle Of Jazz, Vol. 1: *Refer to* Bud Freeman / Joe Marsala**			
Brunswick BL-58038	(10")	**Battle Of Jazz, Vol. 2: *Refer to* Art Tatum / Zutty Singleton**			
Brunswick BL-58039	(10")	**Battle Of Jazz, Vol. 3:**	1953	20.00	50.00
Brunswick BL-58042	(10")	**Battle Of Jazz, Vol. 4: *Refer to* Edmond Hall / Miff Mole**			
Brunswick BL-58043	(10")	**Battle Of Jazz, Vol. 5: *Refer to* Bobby Hackett / Max Kaminsky**			
Brunswick BL-58044	(10")	**Battle Of Jazz, Vol. 6: *Refer to* Red Allen / Red Norvo**			
Brunswick BL-58045	(10")	**Battle Of Jazz, Vol. 7: *Refer to* Roy Eldridge / Sammy Price**			
Brunswick BL-58046	(10")	**Battle Of Jazz, Vol. 8: *Refer to* Johnny Dodds / Jimmy Noone**			
Brunswick BL-58048	(10")	**Jazz On The Air**	1953	20.00	50.00
Brunswick BL-58050	(10")	**Big Band Jazz**	1953	20.00	50.00
Brunswick BL-58058	(10")	**Hi-Fi Jazz**	1954	20.00	50.00
Brunswick BL-54000	(M)	**Jazztime, USA—Vol. 1**	1952	12.00	30.00
Brunswick BL-54001	(M)	**Jazztime, USA—Vol. 2**	1953	12.00	30.00
Brunswick BL-54002	(M)	**Jazztime, USA—Vol. 3**	1953	12.00	30.00
Brunswick BL-54003	(M)	**The Orchestra "House Of Sound"**	1954	12.00	30.00
Brunswick BL-54014	(M)	**Piano Jazz—Vol. 1**	1955	12.00	30.00
Brunswick BL-54015	(M)	**Piano Jazz—Vol. 2**	1955	12.00	30.00
Camden CAL-328	(M)	**Great Jazz Pianists**	1958	10.00	25.00
Camden CAL-339	(M)	**Great Jazz Reeds**	1958	10.00	25.00
Camden CAL-368	(M)	**Best Of The Big Name Bands**	1958	10.00	25.00
Camden CAL-371	(M)	**Rhythm & Blues**	1958	20.00	50.00
Camden CAL-383	(M)	**Great Jazz Brass**	1958	10.00	25.00
Camden CAL-384	(M)	**Modern Jazz Piano**	1958	10.00	25.00
Camden CAL-426	(M)	**Metronome All Stars**	1958	10.00	25.00
Camden CAL-882	(M)	**Great Jazz Pianists Of Our Time**	1965	6.00	15.00
Camden CAS-882	(E)	**Great Jazz Pianists Of Our Time**	1965	4.00	10.00
Candid CD-8019	(M)	**The Jazz Life**	1960	16.00	40.00
Candid CS-9019	(S)	**The Jazz Life**	1960	12.00	30.00
Capitol H-235	(10")	**Battle Of Bands**	1950	20.00	50.00
Capitol H-239	(10")	**History Of Jazz, Vol. 1—The Solid South**	1950	20.00	50.00
Capitol H-240	(10")	**History Of Jazz, Vol. 2—The Golden Era**	1950	20.00	50.00
Capitol H-241	(10")	**History Of Jazz, Vol. 3—Then Came Swing**	1950	20.00	50.00
Capitol H-242	(10")	**History Of Jazz, Vol. 4—Enter The Cool**	1950	20.00	50.00
Capitol H-312	(10")	**Dixieland Detour**	1952	20.00	50.00
Capitol H-321	(10")	**Classics In Jazz—Dixieland Stylists**	1952	20.00	50.00
Capitol H-322	(10")	**Classics In Jazz—Small Combos**	1952	20.00	50.00
Capitol H-323	(10")	**Piano Stylists**	1952	20.00	50.00
Capitol H-325	(10")	**The Modern Idiom**	1952	20.00	50.00
Capitol H-326	(10")	**Trumpet Stylists**	1952	20.00	50.00
Capitol H-328	(10")	**Sax Stylists**	1952	20.00	50.00
Capitol H-371	(10")	**Classics In Jazz—Cool And Quiet**	1953	20.00	50.00
Capitol T-320	(M)	**Classics In Jazz**	1954	12.00	30.00
Capitol T-667	(M)	**Battle Of The Big Bands**	1956	12.00	30.00
Capitol T-707	(M)	**Session At Midnight**	1956	12.00	30.00
Capitol TBO-727	(M)	**Dance To The Bands** *(2 LPs)*	1956	14.00	35.00
Capitol T-761	(M)	**Session At Riverside**	1956	10.00	25.00
Capitol T-793	(M)	**History Of Jazz, Vol. 1—N' Orleans Origins**	1956	10.00	25.00
Capitol T-794	(M)	**History Of Jazz, Vol. 2—The Turbulent '20s**	1956	10.00	25.00
Capitol T-795	(M)	**History Of Jazz, Vol. 3—Everybody Swings**	1956	10.00	25.00
Capitol T-796	(M)	**History Of Jazz, Vol. 4—Enter The Cool**	1956	10.00	25.00

—Capitol albums above have turquoise labels.—

Label & Catalog #		Title	Year	VG+	NM
Capitol T-1057	(M)	**K.C. In The '30s**	1958	10.00	25.00
Capitol T-1386	(M)	**Swing Again!**	1960	8.00	20.00
Capitol DT-1386	(E)	**Swing Again!**	1960	4.00	10.00
Capitol TBO-1970	(M)	**Esquire's World Of Jazz** *(2 LPs)*	1963	8.00	20.00
Capitol STBO-1970	(S)	**Esquire's World Of Jazz** *(2 LPs)*	1963	6.00	15.00
Circle L-402	(M)	**All-Star Stompers**	1951	16.00	40.00
Circle L-407	(M)	**Jamming At Rudi's, Vol. 1**	1951	16.00	40.00
Circle L-410	(M)	**Jamming At Rudi's, Vol. 2**	1951	16.00	40.00
Clef MGC-639	(M)	**Our Best**	1955	20.00	50.00
Clef MGC-742	(M)	**Down Beat Critics Poll Winners**	1955	*Unreleased*	
Clef MGC-743	(M)	**Metronome All Stars 1956**	1956	24.00	60.00
Colosseum CRLP-171	(M)	**Jazz And Pops From The Soviet Union**	1955	12.00	30.00
Columbia CL-6016	(10")	**Theme Songs**	1949	16.00	40.00
Columbia CL-6057	(10")	**Popular Favorites**	1949	16.00	40.00
Columbia CL-2511	(10")	**Soft Pedal**	1949	16.00	40.00
Columbia CL-2528	(10")	**The Metronome All Stars**	1949	16.00	40.00
Columbia CL-2534	(10")	**Hot Canaries**	1949	16.00	40.00
Columbia CL-547	(M)	**Jam Session Coast-To-Coast**	1954	12.00	30.00
Columbia CL-557	(M)	**Jam Session At Carnegie Hall**	1954	16.00	40.00
Columbia JZ-1	(M)	**I Like Jazz**	1955	12.00	30.00
Columbia JJ-1	(M)	**Columbia Jazz Festival**	1959	10.00	25.00
Columbia GB-4	(M)	**Winners Circle Limited Edition**	1959	10.00	25.00
Columbia CL-599	(M)	**Saturday Night Mood**	1955	10.00	25.00
Columbia CL-602	(M)	**Piano Music For Two**	1955	10.00	25.00
Columbia CL-603	(M)	**Piano Music For Parties**	1955	10.00	25.00
Columbia CL-607	(M)	**Requested By You**	1955	10.00	25.00
Columbia CL-611	(M)	**Ballroom Bandstand**	1955	10.00	25.00
Columbia CL-632	(M)	**Chicago Style Jazz**	1955	10.00	25.00
		— Columbia albums above have "Long Playing" on the bottom of the label. —			
Columbia CL-685	(M)	**Upright And Lowdown**	1955	8.00	20.00
Columbia CL-717	(M)	**Gary Moore Presents "My Kind Of Music"**	1956	8.00	20.00
Columbia CL-736	(M)	**College Jazz—Dixieland**	1956	8.00	20.00
Columbia CL-777	(M)	**$64,000 Jazz**	1956	8.00	20.00
Columbia CL-908	(M)	**Add-A-Part Jazz**	1956	8.00	20.00
Columbia CL-931	(M)	**American Jazz Festival At Newport '56, No. 1:** ***Refer to*** **Louis Armstrong / Eddie Condon**			
Columbia CL-932	(M)	**American Jazz Festival At Newport '56, No. 2:** ***Refer to*** **Dave Brubeck / J.J. Johnson**			
Columbia CL-933	(M)	**American Jazz Festival At Newport '56, No. 3:** ***Refer to*** **Duke Ellington / Buck Clayton**			
Columbia CL-934	(M)	**American Jazz Festival At Newport '56, No. 4:** ***Refer to*** **Duke Ellington**			
Columbia CL-967	(M)	**Dance, Be Happy!**	1957	8.00	20.00
Columbia CL-1020	(M)	**Jazz Omnibus**	1957	8.00	20.00
Columbia CL-1036	(M)	**The Jazz Makers**	1957	8.00	20.00
Columbia CL-1098	(M)	**The Sound Of Jazz**	1957	8.00	20.00
Columbia CL-1388	(M)	**Something New Something Blue**	1959	8.00	20.00
Columbia CL-1610	(M)	**Jazz Poll Winners**	1960	8.00	20.00
		— Columbia albums above have six white on black "eye" logos on each label. —			
Columbia C3L-30	(M)	**Jazz Odyssey—The Sound Of New Orleans** *(3 LP box with booklet.)*	196?	12.00	30.00
Columbia C3L-32	(M)	**Jazz Odyssey—The Sound Of Chicago** *(3 LP box with booklet.)*	196?	12.00	30.00
Columbia CL-1893	(M)	**Jingle Bell Jazz**	1962	8.00	20.00
Columbia CS-8693	(S)	**Jingle Bell Jazz**	1962	6.00	15.00
Columbia CL-2018	(M)	**4 To Go**	1963	6.00	15.00
Columbia CS-8818	(S)	**4 To Go**	1963	5.00	12.00
		— Columbia albums above have "Guaranteed High Fidelity" or "360 Sound Stereo" in black on the label. —			
Columbia CLP-119	(M)	**Cool And Carefree**	1964	5.00	12.00
Columbia CSP-119	(E)	**Cool And Carefree** *(Special Products 119 manufactured for Carrier Air Conditioners.)*	1964	3.20	8.00
Columbia CLP-298	(M)	**The Jazz Sound**	1966	5.00	12.00
Columbia CSP-298	(S)	**The Jazz Sound**	1966	4.00	10.00
Columbia CSS-524	(S)	**The Jazz World**	196?	4.00	10.00
Columbia XTV-68933/4	(M)	**The Four Roses Dance Party** *(Sampler)*	1962	6.00	15.00

Label & Catalog #		Title	Year	VG+	NM
Commodore FL-20010	(10")	**Dixieland Jazz Gems**	1950	20.00	50.00
Commodore FL-30006	(M)	**Jam Session At Commodore**	1951	16.00	40.00
Concord 3012	(M)	**Tenor Sax**	195?	12.00	30.00
Cook LP-1084	(M)	**Blowout At Mardi Gras**	1955	16.00	40.00
Cook LP-1085	(10")	**Clambake On Bourbon Street**	1955	20.00	50.00
Coral CRL-57035	(M)	**The East Coast Jazz Scene, Vol. 1**	1956	20.00	50.00
Coral CRL-57149	(M)	**Jazz Cornucopia**	1958	12.00	30.00
Coral CJE-100	(M)	**The Jazz Story**	195?	40.00	100.00
		(Boxed set of 3 LPs narrated by Steve Allen.)			
Core 100	(M)	**A Jazz Salute To Freedom** *(2 LPs)*	196?	10.00	25.00
		(Core 101 collects Roost and Roulette material.)			
Crown CLP-5008	(M)	**Jazz Surprise**	1957	8.00	20.00
Crown CLP-5056	(M)	**Jazz Confidential**	1959	8.00	20.00
Dawn DLP-1125	(M)	**New Voices**	1956	30.00	75.00
Debut	(M)	**Jazz At Massey Hall:** ***Refer to*** **The Quintet**			
Debut DEB-198	(M)	**Autobiography In Jazz**	1955	60.00	150.00
Decca DL-5133	(10")	**Gems Of Jazz, Vol. 1**	1950	20.00	50.00
Decca DL-5134	(10")	**Gems Of Jazz, Vol. 2**	1950	20.00	50.00
Decca DL-5191	(10")	**The Man With A Horn**	1950	20.00	50.00
Decca DL-5248	(10")	**Boogie Woogie**	1950	20.00	50.00
Decca DL-5249	(10")	**Boogie Woogie—Kings & Queens**	1950	20.00	50.00
Decca DL-5383	(10")	**Gems Of Jazz, Vol. 3**	1952	20.00	50.00
Decca DL-5384	(10")	**Gems Of Jazz, Vol. 4**	1952	20.00	50.00
Decca DL-5422	(10")	**British Festival Of Jazz Concert**	1952	20.00	50.00
Decca DL-5424	(10")	**British Jazz Festival**	1952	20.00	50.00
Decca DL-5483	(10")	**New Orleans Jazz**	1953	20.00	50.00
Decca DL-5486	(10")	**The Feminine Touch**	1953	20.00	50.00
Decca DL-8039	(M)	**Gems Of Jazz, Vol. 1**	1954	12.00	30.00
Decca DL-8040	(M)	**Gems Of Jazz, Vol. 2**	1954	12.00	30.00
Decca DL-8041	(M)	**Gems Of Jazz, Vol. 3**	1954	12.00	30.00
Decca DL-8042	(M)	**Gems Of Jazz, Vol. 4**	1954	12.00	30.00
Decca DL-8043	(M)	**Gems Of Jazz, Vol. 5**	1954	12.00	30.00
Decca DL-8044	(M)	**Kansas City Jazz**	1954	12.00	30.00
Decca DL-8045	(M)	**Five Feet Of Swing**	1954	12.00	30.00
Decca DL-8058	(M)	**Jazz Studio 1:** ***Refer to*** **Paul Quinichette & Frank Foster**			
Decca DL-8067	(M)	**Record Hop**	1955	12.00	30.00
Decca DL-8079	(M)	**Jazz Studio 2:** ***Refer to*** **John Graas & Herb Geller**			
Decca DL-8104	(M)	**Jazz Studio 3:** ***Refer to*** **John Graas & Gerry Mulligan**			
Decca DL-8156	(M)	**Jazz Studio 4:** ***Refer to*** **Jack Millman**			
Decca DL-8229	(M)	**Das Is Jazz!**	1956	12.00	30.00
Decca DL-8235	(M)	**Jazz Studio 5:** ***Refer to*** **Ralph Burns & Joe Newman**			
Decca DL-8244	(M)	**Introduction To Jazz**	1956	12.00	30.00
Decca DL-8281	(M)	**A Night At Eddie Condon's**	1956	12.00	30.00
Decca DL-8282	(M)	**Ivy League Jazz**	1956	12.00	30.00
Decca DL-8283	(M)	**New Orleans Jazz**	1956	12.00	30.00
Decca DL-8314	(M)	**Music For The Boy Friend... He Really Digs Jazz**	1956	12.00	30.00
Decca DL-8316	(M)	**The Feminine Touch**	1956	12.00	30.00
Decca DXF-140	(M)	**The Encyclopedia Of Jazz On Records** *(4 LPs)*	1957	40.00	100.00
Decca DL-8398	(M)	**The Encyclopedia Of Jazz On Records, Vol. 1— Jazz Of The Twenties**	1957	8.00	20.00
Decca DL-8399	(M)	**The Encyclopedia Of Jazz On Records, Vol. 2— Jazz Of The Thirties**	1957	8.00	20.00
Decca DL-8400	(M)	**The Encyclopedia Of Jazz On Records, Vol. 3— Jazz Of The Forties**	1957	8.00	20.00
Decca DL-8401	(M)	**The Encyclopedia Of Jazz On Records, Vol. 4— Jazz Of The Fifties**	1957	8.00	20.00
		—Decca albums above have black labels with silver print.—			
Design DLP-29	(M)	**Modern Jazz Hall Of Fame**	196?	4.00	10.00
Design DLPS-29	(E)	**Modern Jazz Hall Of Fame**	196?	1.00	5.00

Label & Catalog #		Title	Year	VG+	NM
Discovery DL-3014	(10")	**Songs By Rodgers & Hart & Johnny Green**	1951	20.00	50.00
Discovery DL-2001	(10")	**Panorama Of British Jazz**	1953	20.00	50.00
Discovery DL-2002	(10")	**Jazz From Sweden**	1953	20.00	50.00
Discovery DL-2008	(10")	**Swedish Pastry**	1954	20.00	50.00
Discovery DL-2010	(10")	**Isles Of Jazz**	1954	20.00	50.00
Dot DLP-3009	(M)	**Native New Orleans Jazz**	1956	12.00	30.00
Dot DLP-9003	(M)	**Downbeat Jazz Concert**	1958	14.00	35.00
Dot DLP-29003	(S)	**Downbeat Jazz Concert**	1958	10.00	25.00
Dot DLP-3188	(M)	**Downbeat Jazz Concert, Vol. 2**	1959	14.00	35.00
Dot DLP-25188	(S)	**Downbeat Jazz Concert, Vol. 2**	1959	10.00	25.00
Dotted Eighth 101	(M)	**Jazz For Art's Sake**	195?	12.00	30.00
Elektra SMP-3	(M)	**Folk, Pop 'N Jazz Sampler**	196?	6.00	15.00
EmArcy MG-26001	(10")	**The Young At Bop**	1954	30.00	75.00
EmArcy MG-26015	(10")	**Holiday In Trumpet**	1954	30.00	75.00
EmArcy MG-26019	(10")	**Holiday In Sax**	1954	30.00	75.00
EmArcy MG-36002	(M)	**Jam Session**	1954	20.00	50.00
EmArcy MG-36016	(M)	**The Advance Guard Of The '40s**	1955	20.00	50.00
EmArcy MG-36017	(M)	**Trumpet Interlude**	1955	20.00	50.00
EmArcy MG-36018	(M)	**Alto Altitude**	1955	20.00	50.00
EmArcy MG-36023	(M)	**Battle Of The Saxes—Tenor All Stars**	1955	20.00	50.00
EmArcy MG-36038	(M)	**Boning Up On 'Bones**	1955	20.00	50.00
EmArcy MG-36039	(M)	**Best Coast Jazz**	1955	30.00	75.00
		(EmArcy 36039 is an all-star session featuring Walter Benton, Clifford Brown, Herb Geller, Curtis Counce, Kenny Drew, Joe Maini and Max Roach.)			
EmArcy MG-36048	(M)	**Jazz Giants, Vol. 1**	1955	16.00	40.00
EmArcy MG-36049	(M)	**Jazz Giants, Vol. 2—The Piano Players**	1955	16.00	40.00
EmArcy MG-36050	(M)	**Jazz Giants, Vol. 3—Reeds, Part 1**	1955	16.00	40.00
EmArcy MG-36051	(M)	**Jazz Giants, Vol. 3—Reeds, Part 2**	1955	16.00	40.00
EmArcy MG-36052	(M)	**Jazz Giants, Vol. 4—Folk Blues**	1955	16.00	40.00
EmArcy MG-36053	(M)	**Jazz Giants, Vol. 5—Brass**	1955	16.00	40.00
EmArcy MG-36054	(M)	**Jazz Giants, Vol. 6—Modern Swedes**	1955	16.00	40.00
EmArcy MG-36055	(M)	**Jazz Giants, Vol. 7—Dixieland**	1955	16.00	40.00
EmArcy DEM-2	(M)	**Jazz Of Two Decades**	1956	16.00	40.00
EmArcy MG-36071	(M)	**Jazz Giants, Vol. 8—Drum Role**	1956	16.00	40.00
EmArcy MG-36085	(M)	**The Young Ones Of Jazz**	1956	16.00	40.00
EmArcy MG-36086	(M)	**For Jazz Lovers**	1956	16.00	40.00
EmArcy MG-36087	(M)	**Bargain Day**	1956	16.00	40.00
EmArcy MG-36088	(M)	**Under One Roof**	1956	16.00	40.00
		—EmArcy albums above have blue labels with silver print.—			
EmArcy MGE-26002	(M)	**International Jazz Workshop**	1964	12.00	30.00
EmArcy SRE-66002	(S)	**International Jazz Workshop**	1964	10.00	25.00
		(EmArcy 26012 is a reissue of 26003.)			
Epic LN-1126	(10")	**Cool Jazz From Holland**	1955	20.00	50.00
Epic LN-1124	(10")	**New Chamber Jazz**	1955	20.00	50.00
Epic LN-3120	(M)	**For Dancers Only**	1955	12.00	30.00
Epic LN-3127	(M)	**Pick Up The Beat**	1955	12.00	30.00
Epic LN-3136	(M)	**Dancing With The Stars**	1955	12.00	30.00
Epic LN-320?	(M)	**After Hour Jazz**	1955	12.00	30.00
Epic LN-3252	(M)	**Trumpeter's Holiday**	1956	12.00	30.00
Epic LN-3271	(M)	**The Rhythm Section**	1956	12.00	30.00
Epic LN-3278	(M)	**The Sax Section**	1956	16.00	40.00
Epic LN-3295	(M)	**The Art Of Jazz Piano**	1956	12.00	30.00
Epic LN-3297	(M)	**Rhythm Plus One**	1956	12.00	30.00
Epic LN-3309	(M)	**Swedes From Jazzville**	1957	20.00	50.00
Esoteric ESJ-2	(10")	**Jazz Off The Air, Vol. 1**	1952	30.00	75.00
Esoteric ESJ-3	(10")	**Jazz Off The Air, Vol. 2**	1952	30.00	75.00
Fantasy FS-654	(M)	**Fantasy Sampler** *(Dark red vinyl)*	195?	6.00	15.00
Flying Dutchman FDS-104	(S)	**Head Start—Bob Thiele Emergency** *(2 LPs)*	1969	6.00	15.00

Label & Catalog #		Title	Year	VG+	NM
FM LP-303	(M)	**Jazz Committee For Latin American Affairs**	1963	20.00	50.00
Folkways FP-712	(10")	**First Album Of Jazz**	1951	20.00	50.00
Folkways FP-30	(10")	**Footnotes To Jazz, Vol. 1:** *Refer to* **Johnny Dodds**			
Folkways FP-31	(10")	**Footnotes To Jazz, Vol. 2— Anatomy Of A Jazz Composition**	1951	20.00	50.00
Folkways FP-32	(10")	**Footnotes To Jazz, Vol. 3:** *Refer to* **Mary Lou Williams**			
Folkways FP-53/4	(M)	**Jazz, Vol. 1—The South**	1951	10.00	25.00
Folkways FP-55/6	(M)	**Jazz, Vol. 2—The Blues**	1951	10.00	25.00
Folkways FP-57/8	(M)	**Jazz, Vol. 3—New Orleans**	1951	10.00	25.00
Folkways FP-59/60	(M)	**Jazz, Vol. 4—Jazz Singers**	1951	10.00	25.00
Folkways FP-63/4	(M)	**Jazz, Vol. 5—Chicago**	1951	10.00	25.00
Folkways FP-65/6	(M)	**Jazz, Vol. 6—Chicago #2**	1951	10.00	25.00
Folkways FP-67/8	(M)	**Jazz, Vol. 7—New York 1922-1934**	1951	10.00	25.00
Folkways FP-69/70	(M)	**Jazz, Vol. 8—Big Bands Before 1938**	1951	10.00	25.00
Folkways FP-71/2	(M)	**Jazz, Vol. 9—Piano**	1951	10.00	25.00
Folkways FP-73/4	(M)	**Jazz, Vol. 10—Boogie, Jump, K.C.**	1951	10.00	25.00
Folkways FP-75/6	(M)	**Jazz, Vol. 11—Addenda**	1951	10.00	25.00
Folkways FA-2464	(M)	**The Music Of New Orleans, Vol. 4— The Birth Of Jazz**	195?	6.00	15.00
Folkways FA-2650	(M)	**Music From The South, Vol. 1— Country Brass Bands**	195?	6.00	15.00
Gene Norman GNP-20	(M)	**Be Our Guest**	1955	10.00	25.00
Gene Norman GNP-27	(M)	**Escape**	1958	8.00	20.00
Golden Crest GC-3021	(M)	**Dixieland In Old New Orleans**	1958	8.00	20.00
Golden Crest GC-3039	(M)	**Ivy League Jazz**	1958	8.00	20.00
Good Time Jazz L-12005	(M)	**Jazz Band Ball**	1954	8.00	20.00
Good Time Jazz L-12019	(M)	**Recorded In New Orleans, Vol. 1**	1955	8.00	20.00
Good Time Jazz L-12020	(M)	**Recorded In New Orleans, Vol. 2**	1955	8.00	20.00
Grand Award GA-33-310	(M)	**Dixieland Jazz** *(G.A. 310 was issued with a removable "second" cover of a David Stone Martin painting that could be peeled off and framed.)*	1955	24.00	60.00
Grand Award GA-33-310	(M)	**Dixieland Jazz** *(Without the removable second cover by DSM.)*	1955	10.00	25.00
Grand Award GA-33-322	(M)	**A Musical History Of Jazz**	1955	8.00	20.00
Groove LG-1003	(M)	**Cool Gabriels**	1956	20.00	50.00
Halo 50223	(M)	**All Star Jazz**	195?	12.00	30.00
Harmony HL-7042	(M)	**Yours**	1957	6.00	15.00
Harmony HL-7044	(M)	**Metronome All Stars**	1957	8.00	20.00
Harmony HL-7196	(M)	**Modern Jazz Festival**	1958	6.00	15.00
Harmony HL-7255	(M)	**Greatest Hits**	1960	6.00	15.00
Imperial LP-9246	(M)	**Just Jazz**	1963	8.00	20.00
Imperial LP-12246	(S)	**Just Jazz**	1963	6.00	15.00
Impulse A-36	(M)	**Americans In Europe, Vol. 1**	1963	10.00	25.00
Impulse AS-36	(S)	**Americans In Europe, Vol. 1**	1963	8.00	20.00
Impulse A-37	(M)	**Americans In Europe, Vol. 2**	1963	10.00	25.00
Impulse AS-37	(S)	**Americans In Europe, Vol. 2**	1963	8.00	20.00
Impulse A-90	(M)	**The New Wave In Jazz**	1966	8.00	20.00
Impulse AS-90	(S)	**The New Wave In Jazz**	1966	6.00	15.00
Impulse A-9	(M)	**The Definitive Jazz Scene, Vol. 1**	1966	8.00	20.00
Impulse AS-99	(S)	**The Definitive Jazz Scene, Vol. 1**	1966	6.00	15.00
Impulse A-100	(M)	**The Definitive Jazz Scene, Vol. 2**	1966	8.00	20.00
Impulse AS-100	(S)	**The Definitive Jazz Scene, Vol. 2**	1966	6.00	15.00
Impulse A-9101	(M)	**Definitive Jazz Scene, Vol. 3**	1966	8.00	20.00
Impulse AS-9101	(S)	**Definitive Jazz Scene, Vol. 3**	1966	6.00	15.00
Impulse A-9145	(M)	**Intercollegiate Music Festival, Vol. 1**	1967	8.00	20.00
Impulse AS-9145	(S)	**Intercollegiate Music Festival, Vol. 1**	1967	6.00	15.00

—Impulse albums above have orange & black labels.—

Label & Catalog #		Title	Year	VG+	NM
Impulse AS-36	(S)	**Americans In Europe, Vol. 1**	1968	4.00	10.00
Impulse AS-37	(S)	**Americans In Europe, Vol. 2**	1968	4.00	10.00
Impulse AS-90	(S)	**The New Wave In Jazz**	1968	4.00	10.00
Impulse AS-99	(S)	**The Definitive Jazz Scene, Vol. 1**	1968	4.00	10.00
Impulse AS-100	(S)	**The Definitive Jazz Scene, Vol. 2**	1968	4.00	10.00
Impulse AS-9101	(S)	**Definitive Jazz Scene, Vol. 3**	1968	4.00	10.00
Impulse AS-9145	(S)	**Intercollegiate Music Festival, Vol. 1**	1968	4.00	10.00
		—Impulse albums above have red & black labels with the "abc" logo on top.—			
Jaguar JP-801	(10")	**Jazz Dance**	1954	20.00	50.00
Jaguar JP-803	(10")	**Jazz From Down Under**	1954	20.00	50.00
Jazz: West Coast JWC-500	(M)	**An Anthology Of California Music**	1955	60.00	150.00
Jazz: West Coast JWC-501	(M)	**An Anthology Of California Music, Vol. 2**	1956	60.00	150.00
Jazz: West Coast JWC-506	(M)	**Jazz Pianists Galore**	1956	60.00	150.00
Jazzland JLP-7	(M)	**Cruisin'**	1960	12.00	30.00
Jazzland JLP-97	(S)	**Cruisin'**	1960	10.00	25.00
Jazzman LJ-334	(M)	**Dixieland Contrasts**	1954	12.00	30.00
Jazztone J-SPEC-100	(10")	**Jazztone Sampler**	1955	16.00	40.00
		(Jazztone 100 was issued with a 7 x 7" booklet "this music called jazz" by Nat Shapiro, worth an additional $10.)			
Jazztone J-1215	(M)	**Happy Jazz**	1956	12.00	30.00
Jazztone J-1216	(M)	**Dixieland Classics**	1956	12.00	30.00
Jazztone J-1219	(M)	**Jazz Concert**	1956	12.00	30.00
Jazztone J-1221	(M)	**Combo Jazz**	1956	12.00	30.00
Jazztone J-1231	(M)	**Modern Jazz Spectacular**	1956	12.00	30.00
Jazztone J-1243	(M)	**An Anthology Of West Coast Jazz**	1957	12.00	30.00
Jazztone J-1245	(M)	**The Great Swing Bands**	1957	12.00	30.00
Jazztone J-1249	(M)	**Early Jazz Greats, Vol. 1**	1957	12.00	30.00
Jazztone J-1252	(M)	**Early Jazz Greats, Vol. 2**	1957	12.00	30.00
Jazztone J-12??	(M)	**West Coast Jazz, Vol. 2**	1957	12.00	30.00
Jazztone J-1254	(M)	**Jazz a la Mood**	1957	12.00	30.00
Jazztone J-1258	(M)	**Comparative Blues**	1957	12.00	30.00
Jazztone J-1254	(M)	**Jazz a la Mood**	1957	12.00	30.00
Jazztone J-1265	(M)	**Swing Lightly**	1957	12.00	30.00
Jazztone J-1282	(M)	**Jazz A La Midnight**	1957	12.00	30.00
Kapp KS-1	(M)	**Jazz Festival**	1956	8.00	20.00
Kapp KL-1007	(M)	**Jazz Goes To Broadway**	1956	8.00	20.00
Kapp KXL-5001	(M)	**Modern Jazz Gallery**	195?	8.00	20.00
Kimberly 2016	(M)	**Swinging Soundtrack**	1963	10.00	25.00
Kimberly 11016	(S)	**Swinging Soundtrack**	1963	8.00	20.00
Kimberly 2017	(M)	**Southern Meetin'**	1963	10.00	25.00
Kimberly 11017	(S)	**Southern Meetin'**	1963	8.00	20.00
Kimberly 2020	(M)	**This Is The Blues**	1963	10.00	25.00
Kimberly 11020	(S)	**This Is The Blues**	1963	8.00	20.00
Kimberly 2022	(M)	**Percussion Unabridged**	1963	10.00	25.00
Kimberly 11022	(S)	**Percussion Unabridged**	1963	8.00	20.00
Kimberly 2024	(M)	**Swinging Broadway**	1963	10.00	25.00
Kimberly 11024	(S)	**Swinging Broadway**	1963	8.00	20.00
		(Kimberly 2024 is a reissue of World Pacific 404.)			
Liberty LJH-6001	(M)	**Jazz In Hollywood**	1955	12.00	30.00
Liberty SL-9005	(M)	**Escapade Reviews The Jazz Scene**	1957	12.00	30.00
Limelight LM-82017	(M)	**Charlie Parker 10th Memorial Concert**	1965	8.00	20.00
Limelight LS-86017	(S)	**Charlie Parker 10th Memorial Concert**	1965	6.00	15.00
London LL-1184	(M)	**Traditional Jazz At The Royal Festival Hall**	1955	8.00	20.00
London LL-1185	(M)	**Modern Jazz**	1955	8.00	20.00
London LL-1242	(M)	**Traditional Jazz**	1955	8.00	20.00
London LL-1337	(M)	**Dixie, London Style**	1956	8.00	20.00
London LL-1444	(M)	**A Scrapbook Of British Jazz, 1926-1956**	1956	8.00	20.00

Label & Catalog #		Title	Year	VG+	NM
Mainstream 56025	(M)	**A Look At Yesterday**	1965	10.00	25.00
Mainstream S-6025	(E)	**A Look At Yesterday**	1965	5.00	12.00
Mercury MG-20016	(10")	**Tenor Jazz** *(Issued in a paper sleeve)*	1950	40.00	100.00
Mercury MG-20133	(M)	**Swinging For The King**	1956	20.00	50.00
Metrojazz E-1005	(M)	**New Faces At Newport**	1959	16.00	40.00
Metrojazz SE-1005	(S)	**New Faces At Newport**	1959	12.00	30.00
Metrojazz 2-E-1009	(M)	**The Seven Ages Of Jazz** *(2 LPs)*	1959	20.00	50.00
Metrojazz 2-SE-1009	(S)	**The Seven Ages Of Jazz** *(2 LPs)*	1959	16.00	40.00
MGM E-100	(10")	**Keyboard Kings**	1951	20.00	50.00
MGM E-194	(10")	**Pop Parade**	1953	20.00	50.00
MGM E-211	(10")	**Hot Vs. Cool—A Battle Of Jazz**	1953	20.00	50.00
MGM E-231	(10")	**Dixieland Vs. Birdland**	1954	20.00	50.00
MGM E-255	(10")	**Cats Vs. Chicks**	1954	20.00	50.00
MGM E-3157	(M)	**Cool Europe**	1955	12.00	30.00
MGM E-3262	(M)	**Strictly From Dixie**	1956	12.00	30.00
MGM E-3325	(M)	**A Hi Fi Salute To The Great Ones**	1956	12.00	30.00
MGM E-3354	(M)	**A Hi Fi Salute To The Great Ones, Vol. 2**	1956	12.00	30.00
MGM E-3390	(M)	**West Coast Vs. East Coast**	1956	12.00	30.00
Monarch LP-201	(10")	**Monarch All Star Jazz, Vol. 1**	1952	20.00	50.00
Monarch LP-202	(10")	**Monarch All Star Jazz, Vol. 2**	1952	20.00	50.00
Monarch LP-203	(10")	**Monarch All Star Jazz, Vol. 3**	1952	20.00	50.00
Monarch LP-204	(10")	**Monarch All Star Jazz, Vol. 4**	1952	20.00	50.00
Monarch LP-205	(10")	**Monarch All Star Jazz, Vol. 5**	1952	20.00	50.00
Moodsville MVLP-2	(M)	**Modern Moods**	1961	16.00	40.00
Moodsville MVLP-33	(M)	**America's Greatest Jazzmen Play George Gershwin**	1963	16.00	40.00
Moodsville MVST-33	(S)	**America's Greatest Jazzmen Play George Gershwin**	1963	12.00	30.00
Moodsville MVLP-34	(M)	**America's Greatest Jazzmen Play Cole Porter**	1963	16.00	40.00
Moodsville MVST-34	(S)	**America's Greatest Jazzmen Play Cole Porter**	1963	12.00	30.00
Moodsville MVLP-35	(M)	**America's Greatest Jazzmen Play Richard Rodgers**	1963	16.00	40.00
Moodsville MVST-35	(S)	**America's Greatest Jazzmen Play Richard Rodgers**	1963	12.00	30.00
Moodsville MVLP-37	(M)	**Lusty Moods**	1963	16.00	40.00
Moodsville MVST-37	(S)	**Lusty Moods**	1963	12.00	30.00
Moodsville MVLP-38	(M)	**America's Greatest Jazzmen Play The Broadway Scene**	1963	16.00	40.00
Moodsville MVST-38	(S)	**America's Greatest Jazzmen Play The Broadway Scene**	1963	12.00	30.00
—Moodsville mono albums above have green labels with silver print.—					
Moodsville MVLP-2	(M)	**Modern Moods**	1965	8.00	20.00
Moodsville MVLP-33	(M)	**America's Greatest Jazzmen Play George Gershwin**	1965	8.00	20.00
Moodsville MVST-33	(S)	**America's Greatest Jazzmen Play George Gershwin**	1965	6.00	15.00
Moodsville MVLP-34	(M)	**America's Greatest Jazzmen Play Cole Porter**	1965	8.00	20.00
Moodsville MVST-34	(S)	**America's Greatest Jazzmen Play Cole Porter**	1965	6.00	15.00
Moodsville MVLP-35	(M)	**America's Greatest Jazzmen Play Richard Rodgers**	1965	8.00	20.00
Moodsville MVST-35	(S)	**America's Greatest Jazzmen Play Richard Rodgers**	1965	6.00	15.00
Moodsville MVLP-37	(M)	**Lusty Moods**	1965	8.00	20.00
Moodsville MVST-37	(S)	**Lusty Moods**	1965	6.00	15.00
Moodsville MVLP-38	(M)	**America's Greatest Jazzmen Play The Broadway Scene**	1965	8.00	20.00
Moodsville MVST-38	(S)	**America's Greatest Jazzmen Play The Broadway Scene**	1965	6.00	15.00

—Moodsville albums above have blue labels with a trident logo on the right side.—

Label & Catalog #		Title	Year	VG+	NM
New Jazz NJLP-8202	(M)	**Roots: *Refer to* Idrees Sulieman**			
New Jazz NJLP-8204	(M)	**Bird Feathers: *Refer ot* Phil Woods & Gene Quill / Jackie McLean / Hal McKusick**			
New Jazz NJLP-8216	(M)	**Coolin'**	1959	24.00	60.00
		(New Jazz 8216 is an all-star session featuring Teddy Charles, John Jenkins, Idrees Sulieman and Mal Waldron.)			
New Jazz NJLP-8217	(M)	**The Cats**	1959	30.00	75.00
		(New Jazz 8217 is an all-star session featuring Tommy Flanagan, John Coltrane, Kenny Burrell and Idrees Sulieman.)			
New Jazz NJLP-8292	(M)	**Jazz Soul Of "Cleopatra"**	1962	16.00	40.00
New Jazz NJLP-8295	(M)	**Ezz-Thetic: *Refer to* Lee Konitz / Miles Davis / Teddy Charles**			
New Jazz NJLP-8315	(M)	**My Fair Lady**	1963	Unreleased	
New Jazz NJLP-8318	(M)	**Guitar Soul**	1963	Unreleased	
New Jazz NJLP-8319	(M)	**Lusty Moods**	1963	Unreleased	
		—New Jazz albums above have purple labels.—			
New Jazz NJLP-8216	(M)	**Coolin'**	1965	8.00	20.00
New Jazz NJLP-8217	(M)	**The Cats**	1965	12.00	30.00
New Jazz NJLP-8292	(M)	**Jazz Soul Of "Cleopatra"**	1965	8.00	20.00
		—New Jazz albums above have blue labels with a trident logo on the right side.—			
Norgran MGN-1021	(M)	**Our Best**	1955	30.00	75.00
Norgran MGN-1033	(M)	**Swing Guitars**	1955	30.00	75.00
		(Norgran 1033 features cover art by David Stone Martin.)			
Norgran MGN-1034	(M)	**Tenor Saxes**	1955	30.00	75.00
		(Norgran 1034 features cover art by David Stone Martin.)			
Norgran MGN-1035	(M)	**Alto Saxes**	1955	30.00	75.00
		(Norgran 1035 features cover art by David Stone Martin.)			
Norgran MGN-1036	(M)	**Piano Interpretations**	1955	30.00	75.00
		(Norgran 1036 features cover art by David Stone Martin.)			
Norgran MGN-1056	(M)	**The Jazz Giants**	1956	30.00	75.00
Norgran MGN-1065	(M)	**An Evening Of Jazz**	1956	30.00	75.00
		(Norgran 1065 is a reissue of Norgran 25, "The Six," with cover art by David Stone Martin.)			
Pacific Jazz PJM-404	(M)	**Jazz Swings Broadway**	1956	20.00	50.00
Pacific Jazz JWC-500	(M)	**Jazz West Coast, Vol. 1**	1956	20.00	50.00
Pacific Jazz JWC-501	(M)	**Jazz West Coast, Vol. 2**	1956	20.00	50.00
Pacific Jazz JWC-502	(M)	**The Blues, Vol. 2**	1956	20.00	50.00
Pacific Jazz JWC-504	(M)	**Rogers & Hart Gems**	1956	20.00	50.00
Pacific Jazz JWC-505	(M)	**Solo Flight**	1956	20.00	50.00
Pacific Jazz JWC-506	(M)	**Pianists Galore**	1957	20.00	50.00
Pacific Jazz JWC-507	(M)	**Jazz West Coast, Vol. 3**	1957	20.00	50.00
Pacific Jazz JWC-508	(M)	**The Hard Swing**	1957	20.00	50.00
Pacific Jazz HFS-1	(M)	**Assorted Flavors Of Pacific Jazz**	1956	20.00	50.00
Pacific Jazz PJ-13	(M)	**This Is The Blues, Vol. 1**	1961	12.00	30.00
Pacific Jazz PJ-30	(M)	**This Is The Blues, Vol. 2**	1962	12.00	30.00
Pacific Jazz ST-30	(S)	**This Is The Blues, Vol. 2**	1962	10.00	25.00
Paradox LP-6002	(10")	**Dixieland Rhythm Kings**	1951	20.00	50.00
Paradox LP-6003	(10")	**Jazz At Storyville**	1951	20.00	50.00
Paramount LP-104	(10")	**Informal Session At Squirrel's By The Sons Of Bix's** *(2 LPs)*	1954	24.00	60.00
Paramount LP-108	(10")	**Second Session At Squirrel's**	1954	20.00	50.00
Paramount LP-109	(10")	**The Four Most Guitars**	1954	20.00	50.00
Paramount LP-110	(10")	**A Third Session At Squirrel's**	1954	20.00	50.00
Pax LP-6006	(10")	**Jazz Duplex**	1954	12.00	30.00
Pax LP-6009	(10")	**Americans Abroad, Vol. 1**	1955	16.00	40.00
Pax LP-6015	(10")	**Americans Abroad, Vol. 2**	1955	16.00	40.00
Period SPL-302	(M)	**Period's Jazz Digest** *(Sampler)*	1956	20.00	50.00
Period SPL-304	(M)	**Period's Jazz Digest Vol. 2** *(Sampler)*	1955	20.00	50.00
Playboy PB-1957	(M)	**Playboy All Stars —Volume 1** *(2 LPs)*	1957	12.00	30.00
Playboy PB-1958	(M)	**Playboy All Stars —Volume 2** *(2 LPs)*	1958	12.00	30.00
Playboy PB-1959	(M)	**Playboy All Stars —Volume 3** *(3 LPs)*	1959	16.00	40.00

Label & Catalog #		Title	Year	VG+	NM
Prestige PRLP-113	(10")	**Modern Jazz Trumpets**	1951	100.00	200.00
Prestige PRLP-119	(10")	**New Sounds From Sweden, Vol. 1— The Daring Young Swedes**	1951	100.00	200.00
Prestige PRLP-121	(10")	**New Sounds From Sweden, Vol. 2: *Refer to* Bengt Hallberg / Lars Gullin**			
Prestige PRLP-133	(10")	**New Sounds From Sweden, Vol. 3: *Refer to* Arne Domnerus / Lars Gullin**			
Prestige PRLP-134	(10")	**New Sounds From Sweden, Vol. 4: *Refer to* Arne Domnerus**			
Prestige PRLP-135	(10")	**Mambo Jazz**	1952	60.00	150.00
Prestige PRLP-141	(10")	**Relaxed Saxophone Moods**	1953	40.00	100.00
Prestige PRLP-144	(10")	**New Sounds From Sweden, Vol. 5: *Refer to* Lars Gullin**			
Prestige PRLP-145	(10")	**New Sounds From Sweden, Vol. 6: *Refer to* Bengt Hallberg / Arne Domnerus**			
Prestige PRLP-151	(10")	**New Sounds From Sweden, Vol. 7: *Refer to* Lars Gullin**			
Prestige PRLP-155	(10")	**New Sounds From Sweden, Vol. 8: *Refer to* Reinhold Svensson**			
Prestige PRLP-7013	(M)	**Conception**	1956	40.00	100.00
Prestige PRLP-7073	(M)	**All Night Long**	1957	40.00	100.00
		(Prestige 7073 is an all-star session with Donald Byrd, Jerome Richardson, Kenny Burrell, Hank Mobley, Mal Waldron, Doug Watkins and Art Taylor. Reissued as 7289, Burrell's "All Night Long.")			
Prestige PRLP-7074	(M)	**Tenor Conclave**	1957	40.00	100.00
		(Prestige 7074 is an all-star session featuring Hank Mobley, Al Cohn, John Coltrane, and Zoot Sims. Reissued as 7249, Coltrane's "Tenor Conclave.")			
Prestige PRLP-7081	(M)	**All Day Long**	1957	40.00	100.00
		(Prestige 7081 is an all-star session with Donald Byrd, Frank Foster, Kenny Burrell, Doug Watkins and Art Taylor. Reissued as 7277, Burrell's "All Day Long.")			
Prestige PRLP-7084	(M)	**Olio**	1957	40.00	100.00
		(Prestige 7084 is an all-star session with Thad Jones, Frank Wess, Teddy Charles, Mal Waldron, Doug Watkins and Elvin Jones. Reissued as Status 8310, Wess & Jones' "Touche.")			
Prestige PRLP-7102	(M)	**Earthy!**	1957	40.00	100.00
		(Prestige 7102 is an all-star session with Kenny Burrell, Al Cohn, Art Farmer, Hal McKusick, Mal Waldron, Teddy Kotick and Ed Thigpen.)			
Prestige PRLP-7112	(M)	**Interplay For 2 Trumpets And 2 Tenors**	1957	40.00	100.00
		(Prestige 7112 is an all-star session featuring Idrees Sulieman, Webster Young, John Coltrane and Bobby Jaspar with Mal Waldron, Kenny Burrell, Paul Chambers and Art Taylor.)			
Prestige PRLP-7116	(M)	**Four Altos**	1957	40.00	100.00
		(Prestige 7116 is an all-star session featuring Phil Woods, Gene Quill, Sahib Shibab, Hal Stein, Mal Waldron, Tommy Potter & Louis Hayes.)			
Prestige PRLP-7131	(M)	**Wheelin' & Dealin'**	1957	40.00	100.00
		(Prestige 7131 is an all-star session with Frank Wess, John Coltrane, Paul Quinichette, Mal Waldron, Doug Watkins and Art Taylor. Reissued as Status 8327, Coltrane & Wess' "Wheelin' & Dealin'.")			
		—Prestige albums above have yellow labels with a W. 50th Street, NYC address.—			
Prestige PRLP-7167	(M)	**Very Saxy**	1959	24.00	60.00
		(Prestige 7167 is an all-star session featuring Eddie Davis, Buddy Tate, Coleman Hawkins and Arnett Cobb.)			
Prestige PRLP-7298	(M)	**Prestige Groovy Goodies, Vol. 1**	1964	12.00	30.00
Prestige PRST-7298	(E)	**Prestige Groovy Goodies, Vol. 1**	1964	8.00	20.00
		—Prestige albums above have yellow mono or silver stereo labels with a Bergenfield, NJ address .—			
Prestige PRLP-7341	(M)	**Jazz Interplay** *(2 LPs)*	1964	16.00	40.00
Prestige PRST-7341	(E)	**Jazz Interplay** *(2 LPs)*	1964	10.00	25.00
		(Prestige 7341 is a reissue of 7111, Mal Waldron's "Mal-2," and 7112.)			
		—Prestige albums above have blue labels with a trident logo on the right side.—			
Prestige PRLP-7342	(M)	**Hard Cookin': *Refer to* Art Farmer / Art Taylor**			
Prestige PRLP-7344	(M)	**Trumpets All Out: *Refer to* Art Farmer**			
Prestige PRST-7604	(S)	**Swing 1946**	1969	6.00	15.00
Prestige PRST-7631	(S)	**The Violin Summit**	1969	6.00	15.00
Prestige PRST-7645	(S)	**The Big Bands 1933**	1969	6.00	15.00
Prestige PRST-7646	(S)	**Swing Classics 1935**	1969	6.00	15.00
Prestige PRST-7647	(S)	**Jazz Pioneers 1933-36**	1969	6.00	15.00
Prestige PRST-7684	(S)	**Alto Summit**	1969	6.00	15.00
		—Prestige albums above have blue labels with a trident logo on top.—			
RCA Victor LPT-1	(10")	**Theme Songs**	1951	16.00	40.00
RCA Victor LPT-2	(10")	**Dance Band Hits**	1951	16.00	40.00
RCA Victor LPT-3	(10")	**Small Combo Hits**	1951	16.00	40.00

Label & Catalog #		Title	Year	VG+	NM
RCA Victor LPT-4	(10")	**Keyboard Kings Of Jazz**	1951	16.00	40.00
RCA Victor LPT-12	(10")	**Up Swing**	1951	16.00	40.00
RCA Victor LPT-13	(10")	**Smoke Rings**	1951	16.00	40.00
RCA Victor LPT-21	(10")	**All-Star Dates**	1951	20.00	50.00
RCA Victor LPT-26	(10")	**Great Trumpet Artists**	1951	16.00	40.00
RCA Victor LPT-35	(10")	**Great Trumpet Artists**	1952	20.00	50.00
RCA Victor LJM-3001	(10")	**Progressive Piano**	1952	20.00	50.00
RCA Victor LPM-3102	(10")	**Gene Norman Presents Just Jazz**	1953	20.00	50.00
RCA Victor LPT-1000	(M)	**Ragtimers Immortal Performances**	1954	12.00	30.00
RCA Victor LJM-1008	(M)	**Jazz For People Who Hate Jazz**	1954	12.00	30.00
RCA Victor LPM-1070	(M)	**Perfect For Dancing—Fox Trots**	1954	12.00	30.00
RCA Victor LPM-1071	(M)	**Perfect For Dancing—Jitterbug Or Lindy**	1954	12.00	30.00
RCA Victor LPM-1072	(M)	**Perfect For Dancing—All Tempos**	1954	12.00	30.00
RCA Victor LPM-1146	(M)	**Lullaby Of Birdland**	1955	20.00	50.00
RCA Victor LPM-1325	(M)	**The Wide, Wide World Of Jazz**	1956	12.00	30.00
RCA Victor LPM-1327	(M)	**The Birdland Stars On Tour, Vol. 1**	1956	16.00	40.00
RCA Victor LPM-1328	(M)	**The Birdland Stars On Tour, Vol. 2**	1956	16.00	40.00
RCA Victor LPM-1332	(M)	**The Magic Horn**	1956	16.00	40.00
RCA Victor LPM-1365	(M)	**The Mellow Moods Of Jazz**	1956	16.00	40.00
RCA Victor LPM-1373	(M)	**A String Of Swingin' Pearls**	1956	12.00	30.00
RCA Victor LPM-1393	(M)	**Guide To Jazz**	1956	12.00	30.00
RCA Victor LPM-1508	(M)	**Chicago / Austin High School**	1957	12.00	30.00
		—RCA Victor albums above have black labels with "Long Play" on the bottom.—			
RCA Victor LEJ-1	(10")	**Encyclopedia Of Recorded Jazz, Album 1**	1956	16.00	40.00
RCA Victor LEJ-2	(10")	**Encyclopedia Of Recorded Jazz, Album 2**	1956	16.00	40.00
RCA Victor LEJ-3	(10")	**Encyclopedia Of Recorded Jazz, Album 3**	1956	16.00	40.00
RCA Victor LEJ-4	(10")	**Encyclopedia Of Recorded Jazz, Album 4**	1956	16.00	40.00
RCA Victor LEJ-5	(10")	**Encyclopedia Of Recorded Jazz, Album 5**	1956	16.00	40.00
RCA Victor LEJ-6	(10")	**Encyclopedia Of Recorded Jazz, Album 6**	1956	16.00	40.00
RCA Victor LEJ-7	(10")	**Encyclopedia Of Recorded Jazz, Album 7**	1956	16.00	40.00
RCA Victor LEJ-8	(10")	**Encyclopedia Of Recorded Jazz, Album 8**	1956	16.00	40.00
RCA Victor LEJ-9	(10")	**Encyclopedia Of Recorded Jazz, Album 9**	1956	16.00	40.00
RCA Victor LEJ-10	(10")	**Encyclopedia Of Recorded Jazz, Album 10**	1956	16.00	40.00
RCA Victor LEJ-11	(10")	**Encyclopedia Of Recorded Jazz, Album 11**	1956	16.00	40.00
RCA Victor LEJ-12	(10")	**Encyclopedia Of Recorded Jazz, Album 12**	1956	16.00	40.00
RCA Victor PR-112	(M)	**Music From The Dancing Years** *(Sampler for Dole Pineapple)*	1961	6.00	15.00
RCA Victor LPM-3499	(M)	**The Jazz Piano**	1966	10.00	25.00
RCA Victor LSP-3499	(S)	**The Jazz Piano**	1966	8.00	20.00
RCA Victor LPM-3738	(M)	**Tribute To Charlie Parker— From The Newport Jazz Festival**	1967	12.00	30.00
RCA Victor LSP-3738	(S)	**Tribute To Charlie Parker— From The Newport Jazz Festival**	1967	8.00	20.00
		—RCA albums above have black labels with "Monaural" or "Stereo" on the bottom.—			
RCA Victor LPV-544	(M)	**Esquire's All-American Hot Jazz**	1967	8.00	20.00
Regal LP-11	(10")	**Jazz Ltd.**	1951	20.00	50.00
Regent MG-6001	(M)	**Jazz South Pacific**	1956	20.00	50.00
Reprise R-6089	(M)	**Portraits In Jazz**	1963	6.00	15.00
Reprise R9-6089	(S)	**Portraits In Jazz**	1963	5.00	12.00
Riverside RLP-1005	(10")	**New Orleans Horns**	1953	30.00	75.00
Riverside RLP-1006	(10")	**Ragtime Piano Roll, Vol. 1**	1953	30.00	75.00
Riverside RLP-1009	(10")	**Pioneers Of Boogie Woogie**	1953	30.00	75.00
Riverside RLP-1025	(10")	**Ragtime Piano Roll, Vol. 2**	1954	30.00	75.00
Riverside RLP-1032	(10")	**The Great Blues Singers**	1954	30.00	75.00
Riverside RLP-1034	(10")	**Pioneers Of Boogie Woogie, Vol. 2**	1954	30.00	75.00
Riverside RLP-1039	(10")	**Backwood Blues**	1954	30.00	75.00
Riverside RLP-1040	(10")	**Collectors Items, Vol. 2**	1954	30.00	75.00
Riverside RLP-1047	(10")	**New Orleans Revival**	1954	30.00	75.00
Riverside RLP-1048	(10")	**New York Jazz Of The Twenties**	1954	30.00	75.00
Riverside RLP-1049	(10")	**Ragtime Piano Roll, Vol. 3**	1954	30.00	75.00
Riverside RLP-1052	(10")	**Classic Blues Accompanists**	1955	30.00	75.00
Riverside RLP-1074	(10")	**Great Blues**	1955	30.00	75.00
Riverside RLP-2503	(10")	**New Orleans Encore**	1954	30.00	75.00

Label & Catalog #		Title	Year	VG+	NM
Riverside SDP-11	(M)	**History Of Classic Jazz**	1956	150.00	300.00
		(Five records issued in a leatherette album with an illustrated booklet.)			
Riverside RLP-12-801	(M)	**Jazz Of The Roaring 20's**	195?	16.00	40.00
Riverside RLP-12-808	(M)	**This Could Lead To Love**	195?	16.00	40.00
Riverside RLP-12-102	(M)	**New Orleans Rhythm Kings**	195?	16.00	40.00
Riverside RLP-12-106	(M)	**Giants Of Boogie Woogie**	1956	16.00	40.00
Riverside RLP-12-108	(M)	**Jazz Of The Roaring Twenties— Dance Music Of The Charleston Era**	1956	16.00	40.00
Riverside RLP-12-110	(M)	**Piano Roll Transcriptions**	1956	16.00	40.00
Riverside RLP-12-112	(M)	**History Of Classic Jazz, Vol. 1**	1957	16.00	40.00
Riverside RLP-12-113	(M)	**History Of Classic Jazz, Vol. 2**	1957	16.00	40.00
Riverside RLP-12-114	(M)	**History Of Classic Jazz, Vol. 3**	1957	16.00	40.00
Riverside RLP-12-115	(M)	**History Of Classic Jazz, Vol. 4**	1957	16.00	40.00
Riverside RLP-12-116	(M)	**History Of Classic Jazz, Vol. 5**	1957	16.00	40.00
		(Riverside 112-116 are reissues from SPD-11.)			
Riverside RLP-12-119	(M)	**New Orleans Legends**	1957	16.00	40.00
Riverside RLP-12-121	(M)	**Great Blues Singers**	1957	16.00	40.00
Riverside RLP-12-126	(M)	**Piano Roll Transcriptions**	1957	16.00	40.00
Riverside RLP-12-127	(M)	**On-The-Road Jazz**	1957	16.00	40.00
Riverside RLP-12-131	(M)	**Kings Of Classic Jazz**	1957	16.00	40.00
Riverside RLP-12-143	(M)	**Giants Of Small Band Swing, Vol. 1**	1957	16.00	40.00
Riverside RLP-12-243	(M)	**Blues For Tomorrow**	1957	16.00	40.00
Riverside RLP-12-244	(M)	**Jazz For Lovers**	1957	16.00	40.00
		— Riverside albums above have blue on white labels.—			
Riverside RLP-12-267	(M)	**Riverside Drive**	1958	12.00	30.00
Riverside RLP-12-272	(M)	**Eight Ways To Jazz**	1958	12.00	30.00
Riverside RLP-12-284	(M)	**Saxophone Revolt**	1958	12.00	30.00
Riverside RLP-12-294	(M)	**New Blue Horns**	1958	12.00	30.00
Riverside RLP-3503	(M)	**The Compositions Of Thelonious Monk**	1962	8.00	20.00
Riverside RS-93503	(S)	**The Compositions Of Thelonious Monk**	1962	6.00	15.00
Riverside RLP-3504	(M)	**The Compositions Of Miles Davis**	1962	8.00	20.00
Riverside RS-93504	(S)	**The Compositions Of Miles Davis**	1962	6.00	15.00
Riverside RLP-3505	(M)	**The Compositions Of Benny Golson**	1962	8.00	20.00
Riverside RS-93505	(S)	**The Compositions Of Benny Golson**	1962	6.00	15.00
Riverside RLP-3506	(M)	**The Compositions Of Charlie Parker**	1962	8.00	20.00
Riverside RS-93506	(S)	**The Compositions Of Charlie Parker**	1962	6.00	15.00
Riverside RLP-3507	(M)	**The Compositions Of Duke Ellington**	1962	8.00	20.00
Riverside RS-93507	(S)	**The Compositions Of Duke Ellington**	1962	6.00	15.00
Riverside RLP-3508	(M)	**The Compositions Of Dizzy Gillespie**	1962	8.00	20.00
Riverside RS-93508	(S)	**The Compositions Of Dizzy Gillespie**	1962	6.00	15.00
Riverside RLP-3509	(M)	**The Compositions Of Horace Silver**	1962	8.00	20.00
Riverside RS-93509	(S)	**The Compositions Of Horace Silver**	1962	6.00	15.00
Riverside RLP-3510	(M)	**The Compositions Of Duke Ellington, Vol. 2**	1962	8.00	20.00
Riverside RS-93510	(S)	**The Compositions Of Duke Ellington, Vol. 2**	1962	6.00	15.00
Riverside RLP-3511	(M)	**The Compositions Of Tadd Dameron**	1962	8.00	20.00
Riverside RS-93511	(S)	**The Compositions Of Tadd Dameron**	1962	6.00	15.00
Riverside RLP-3512	(M)	**The Compositions Of Bobby Timmons**	1962	8.00	20.00
Riverside RS-93512	(S)	**The Compositions Of Bobby Timmons**	1962	6.00	15.00
Riverside RM-3514	(M)	**The Compositions Of Richard Rodgers**	1963	8.00	20.00
Riverside RS-93514	(S)	**The Compositions Of Richard Rodgers**	1963	6.00	15.00
Riverside RM-3515	(M)	**The Compositions Of Cole Porter**	1963	8.00	20.00
Riverside RS-93515	(S)	**The Compositions Of Cole Porter**	1963	6.00	15.00
Riverside RM-3516	(M)	**The Compositions Of Jerome Kern**	1963	8.00	20.00
Riverside RS-93516	(S)	**The Compositions Of Jerome Kern**	1963	6.00	15.00
Riverside RM-3517	(M)	**The Compositions Of George Gershwin**	1963	8.00	20.00
Riverside RS-93517	(S)	**The Compositions Of George Gershwin**	1963	6.00	15.00
Riverside RM-3518	(M)	**The Compositions Of Harold Arlen**	1963	8.00	20.00
Riverside RS-93518	(S)	**The Compositions Of Harold Arlen**	1963	6.00	15.00
Riverside RM-3519	(M)	**The Compositions Of Irving Berlin**	1963	8.00	20.00
Riverside RS-93519	(S)	**The Compositions Of Irving Berlin**	1963	6.00	15.00
Riverside RLP-356	(M)	**New Orleans—The Living Legends, Vol. 1**	196?	8.00	20.00
Riverside RS-9356	(E)	**New Orleans—The Living Legends, Vol. 1**	196?	5.00	12.00
Riverside RLP-357	(M)	**New Orleans—The Living Legends, Vol. 2**	196?	8.00	20.00
Riverside RS-9357	(E)	**New Orleans—The Living Legends, Vol. 2**	196?	5.00	12.00
Riverside RLP-389	(M)	**Chicago—The Living Legends, Vol. 1**	196?	8.00	20.00
Riverside RS-9389	(E)	**Chicago—The Living Legends, Vol. 1**	196?	5.00	12.00
Riverside RLP-390	(M)	**Chicago—The Living Legends, Vol. 2**	196?	8.00	20.00
Riverside RS-9390	(E)	**Chicago—The Living Legends, Vol. 2**	196?	5.00	12.00

Label & Catalog #		Title	Year	VG+	NM
Roost LP-1201	(M)	**5th Anniversary Album**	1955	20.00	50.00
Roulette R-52015	(M)	**Monday Night At Birdland**	1958	12.00	30.00
Roulette SR-52015	(S)	**Monday Night At Birdland**	1958	10.00	25.00
Roulette R-52022	(M)	**Another Monday Night At Birdland**	1959	12.00	30.00
Roulette SR-52022	(S)	**Another Monday Night At Birdland**	1959	10.00	25.00
Roulette R-52049	(M)	**Gretsch Drum Night At Birdland**	1960	12.00	30.00
Roulette SR-52049	(S)	**Gretsch Drum Night At Birdland**	1960	10.00	25.00
Savoy MG-9008	(10")	**Tenor Sax Solos, Vol. 1**	1952	50.00	125.00
Savoy MG-9013	(10")	**Tenor Sax Solos, Vol. 2**	1952	50.00	125.00
Savoy MG-9021	(10")	**Tenor Sax Solos, Vol. 3**	1953	50.00	125.00
Savoy MG-9022	(10")	**The Birth Of Bop, Vol. 1**	1953	50.00	125.00
Savoy MG-9023	(10")	**The Birth Of Bop, Vol. 2**	1953	50.00	125.00
Savoy MG-9024	(10")	**The Birth Of Bop, Vol. 3**	1953	50.00	125.00
Savoy MG-9025	(10")	**The Birth Of Bop, Vol. 4**	1953	50.00	125.00
Savoy MG-9026	(10")	**The Birth Of Bop, Vol. 5**	1953	50.00	125.00
Savoy MG-15001	(10")	**Jazz At Storyville**	1952	30.00	75.00
Savoy MG-15005	(10")	**Dixieland Series, Vol. 1**	1952	30.00	75.00
Savoy MG-15008	(10")	**Rhythm And Blues**	1952	30.00	75.00
Savoy MG-15009	(10")	**Dixieland Series, Vol. 2**	1952	30.00	75.00
Savoy MG-15014	(10")	**Jazz At Storyville**	1952	30.00	75.00
Savoy MG-15015	(10")	**The Golden Era Of Jazz, Vol. 1**	1952	30.00	75.00
Savoy MG-15016	(10")	**Jazz At Storyville, Vol. 2**	1952	30.00	75.00
Savoy MG-15018	(10")	**The Golden Era Of Jazz, Vol. 2**	1952	30.00	75.00
Savoy MG-15019	(10")	**Jazz At Storyville, Vol. 3**	1953	30.00	75.00
Savoy MG-15020	(10")	**Jazz At Storyville, Vol. 4**	1953	30.00	75.00
Savoy MG-15029	(10")	**Ringside At Condon's**	1954	30.00	75.00
Savoy MG-12012	(M)	**Jazz Concert West Coast**	1955	30.00	75.00
		(Savoy 12012 is an all-star session with Dexter Gordon, Wardell Gray, Sonny Criss, Hampton Hawes, Barney Kessell, Howard McGhee and Al Killian.)			
Savoy MG-12029	(M)	**Montage**	1955	30.00	75.00
		(Savoy 12029 is an all-star session with two bands, both driven by Kenny Clarke and Hank Jones.)			
Savoy MG-12036	(M)	**Opus De Jazz**	1955	30.00	75.0
		(Savoy 12036 is an all-star session with Milt Jackson, Frank Wess, Kenny Clarke, Hank Jones, and Eddie Jones.)			
Savoy MG-12045	(M)	**Deep People: *Refer to* Shelly Manne / Bill Russo**			
Savoy MG-12060	(M)	**Singin' 'N Swingin': *Refer to* Annie Ross / Dorothy Dunn / Shelby Davis**			
Savoy MG-12062	(M)	**Swing... Not Spring!**	1956	20.00	50.00
Savoy MG-12074	(M)	**Loaded**	1956	20.00	50.00
Savoy MG-12078	(M)	**No 'Count**	1956	24.00	60.00
		(Savoy 12078 is an all-star session featuring the basic Basie band—Henry Coker, Frank Foster, Eddie Jones and Benny Powell and Frank Wess—with Kenny Burrell and Kenny Clarke.)			
Savoy MG-12083	(M)	**Jazzmen—Detroit**	1956	30.00	75.00
		(Savoy 120083 is an all-star session of Detroit-based musicians: Pepper Adams, Kenny Burrell, Paul Chambers, Kenny Clarke and Tommy Flanagan.)			
Savoy MG-12085	(M)	**Opus In Swing**	1956	24.00	60.00
		(Savoy 120085 is an all-star session with Kenny Burrell, Kenny Clarke, Freddie Green, Eddie Jones and Frank Wess.)			
Savoy MG-12086	(M)	**Trombones**	1956	24.00	60.00
		(Savoy 12086 is an all-star session featuring Henry Coker, Bill Hughes, Benny Powell and Jimmy Cleveland with Frank Wess.)			
Savoy MG-12096	(M)	**Trumpets All Out**	1957	24.00	60.00
		(Savoy 12096 is an all-star session featuring Art Farmer, Ernie Royal, Charlie Shavers, Emmett Berry and Harold Baker.)			
Savoy MG-12097	(M)	**Lookin' For A Boy: *Refer to* Adelaide Robbins / Marian McPartland / Barbara Carroll**			
Savoy MG-12100	(M)	**I Just Love Jazz Piano!: *Refer to* Hampton Hawes / John Mehegan / Herbie Nichols / Paul Smith**			
Savoy MG-12105	(M)	**Lestorian Mode: *Refer to* Stan Getz / Red Rodney / Kai Winding**			
Savoy MG-12114	(M)	**Opus De Bop: *Refer to* Stan Getz / Sonny Stitt / Fats Navarro**			
Savoy MG-12115	(M)	**Stable Mates**	1957	20.00	50.00
Savoy MG-12119	(M)	**In The Beginning... Bebop: *Refer to* Fats Navarro / Kai Winding / Brew Moore**			

Label & Catalog #		Title	Year	VG+	NM
Savoy MG-12123	(M)	**Jazz Is Busting Out All Over**	1957	20.00	50.00
Savoy MG-12125	(M)	**The Many Faces Of The Blues**	1957	20.00	50.00
Savoy MG-12126	(M)	**The Jazz Hour**	1957	20.00	50.00
Savoy MG-12138	(M)	**Bird's Night—The Music Of Charlie Parker**	1958	20.00	50.00
		(Savoy 12138 is a reissue of Signal 1204.)			
Savoy MG-12142	(M)	**Opus De Blues**	1959	24.00	60.00
		(Savoy 12142 is an all-star session with Curtis Fuller, Charles Fowkes, Eddie, Hank and Thad Jones, Gus Johnson and Frank Wess.)			
Savoy MG-12173	(M)	**Four French Horns**	1961	20.00	50.00
Savoy MG-12196	(M)	**Jazz Concert West Coast**	1961	20.00	50.00
		(Savoy 12196 is an all-star session with Dexter Gordon, Barney Kessell, Wardell Gray, Sonny Criss, Hampton Hawes, Harry Babasin and Howard McGhee.)			
Savoy MG-12199	(M)	**House Rent Party**	1961	20.00	50.00
Savoy MG-12205	(M)	**Jazz South Pacific**	196?	6.00	15.00
		(Savoy 12205 is a reissue of Regent 6001.)			
Savoy MG-12213	(M)	**Dixieland Main Stream**	196?	6.00	15.00
Savoy MG-12217	(M)	**Singin' & Swingin'**	196?	6.00	15.00
Savoy MG-12220	(M)	**The Girls Sing**	196?	6.00	15.00
Signal S-1204	(M)	**A Night At The Five Spot—A Memorial Concert Dedicated To The Music Of Charlie Parker**	1957	40.00	100.00
		(Signal 104 is an all-star session with Cecil Payne, Phil Woods, Frank Socolow, Duke Jordan, Wendell Marshall and Art Taylor.)			
Skylark SKLP-12	(10")	**Jam Session, Vol. 2**	1954	60.00	250.00
Solid State SS-94	(S)	**You've Got To Hear It To Believe It** *(Sampler)*	1966	6.00	15.00
Solid State SS-180??	(S)	**Jazz For A Sunday Afternoon**	1968	5.00	12.00
Solid State SS-18028	(S)	**Jazz For A Sunday Afternoon, Vol. 2**	1968	5.00	12.00
Solid State SS-180??	(S)	**Jazz For A Sunday Afternoon, Vol. 3**	1968	5.00	12.00
Solid State SS-18037	(S)	**West Coast Scene**	1968	5.00	12.00
Solid State SS-18052	(S)	**Jazz For A Sunday Afternoon, Vol. 4**	1969	5.00	12.00
Southland SLP-211	(M)	**New Orleans Jazz Stars**	1955	10.00	25.00
Southland SLP-214	(M)	**New Orleans Jazz Babies**	1955	10.00	25.00
Southland SLP-215	(M)	**New Orleans To Los Angeles**	1955	10.00	25.00
Southland SLP-216	(M)	**New Orleans Dixieland**	1955	10.00	25.00
Southland SLP-217	(M)	**New Orleans Jazz Kings**	1955	10.00	25.00
Specialty LP-2010	(M)	**Dizzy Atmosphere**	1957	12.00	30.00
Starlite ST-7003	(M)	**Jazz Lab**	1955	20.00	50.00
Status ST-8315	(M)	**My Fair Lady**	1965	12.00	30.00
Status ST-8318	(M)	**Guitar Soul:** ***Refer to*** **Kenny Burrell / Tiny Grimes / Bill Jennings**			
Status ST-8319	(M)	**Lusty Moods**	1965	12.00	30.00
		(Status 8319 is a reissue of Moodsville 37.)			
Storyville STLP-311	(10")	**Jazz At The Boston Arts Festival**	1954	30.00	75.00
Storyville STLP-319	(10")	**Jazz At Storyville**	1955	30.00	75.00
Storyville STLP-916	(M)	**The Women In Jazz**	1956	20.00	50.00
Swingville SVLP-2010	(M)	**The Swingville All Stars**	1960	16.00	40.00
Swingville SVLP-2040	(M)	**Dixieland Hits**	1962	16.00	40.00
		—Swingville mono albums above have purple labels; stereo albums have red labels.—			
Swingville SVLP-2010	(M)	**The Swingville All Stars**	1965	8.00	20.00
Swingville SVLP-2040	(M)	**Dixieland Hits**	1965	8.00	20.00
		—Swingville albums above have blue labels with a trident logo on the right side.—			
Tampa TP-2	(M)	**A Swingin' Gig** *(Colored vinyl)*	1957	32.00	80.00
Tampa TP-2	(M)	**A Swingin' Gig**	1958	16.00	40.00
		(Tampa 2 is an all-star session with Buddy Collette, Curtis Counce, Max Albright, Chuck Gentry, William Green, John Anderson, Gerald Wiggins, Dave Wells, Gene Cipriano and Joe Comfort.)			
Tampa TP-11	(M)	**Jazz Americana** *(Colored vinyl)*	1957	32.00	80.00
Tampa TP-11	(M)	**Jazz Americana**	1958	16.00	40.00

Label & Catalog #		Title	Year	VG+	NM
Tone 1	(M)	**Primitive Piano**	195?	12.00	30.00
Tops L-1508	(M)	**Jazz Greats**	1958	8.00	20.00
Tops L-1521	(M)	**Modern Jazz**	1958	8.00	20.00
Tops L-1532	(M)	**Concert In Jazz**	1958	8.00	20.00
Transition TRLP-30	(M)	**Jazz In Transition**	1956	60.00	150.00
		(Transition 30 was issued with a booklet, worth an additional $25.)			
United Arts. X-71	(M)	**Some Like It Cool**	1959	16.00	40.00
United Arts. SX-71	(S)	**Some Like It Cool**	1959	12.00	30.00
United Arts. UAL-4023	(M)	**Stretching Out**	1959	40.00	100.00
United Arts. UAS-5023	(S)	**Stretching Out**	1959	30.00	75.00
		(United Artists 4023 is an all-star session with Zoot Sims, Al Cohn, Bob Brookmeyer, Harry Edison, Nat Pierce and Freddie Green.)			
Urania UJLP-1205	(M)	**Accent On Trombone**	1955	12.00	30.00
Urania UJLP-1207	(M)	**Accent On Piano**	1955	12.00	30.00
Urania UJLP-1209	(M)	**Mood In Blue**	1955	12.00	30.00
Vanguard VRS-8523	(M)	**John Hammond Presents "Spirituals To Swing" At Carnegie Hall 1938**	1959	16.00	40.00
Vanguard VRS-8524	(M)	**John Hammond Presents "Spirituals To Swing" At Carnegie Hall 1939**	1959	16.00	40.00
Vee Jay LP-3026	(M)	**Summit Meeting**	1962	8.00	20.00
Vee Jay LPS-3026	(S)	**Summit Meeting**	1962	6.00	15.00
Vee Jay LP-2501	(M)	**Encyclopedia Of Jazz Of The '60s— Giants Of The Saxophone**	1964	8.00	20.00
Vee Jay LPS-2501	(S)	**Encyclopedia Of Jazz Of The '60s— Giants Of The Saxophone**	1964	6.00	15.00
Vee Jay LP-2506	(M)	**Encyclopedia Of Jazz Of The '60s—Blues Bag**	1964	8.00	20.00
Vee Jay LPS-2506	(S)	**Encyclopedia Of Jazz Of The '60s—Blues Bag**	1964	6.00	15.00
Verve MGV-2032	(M)	**A Potpourri Of Jazz**	1956	14.00	35.00
Verve MGV-2036	(M)	**Here Come The Girls**	1956	14.00	35.00
Verve MGV-8030	(M)	**Metronome All Stars 1956**	1957	14.00	35.00
Verve MGV-8124	(M)	**Swing Guitars**	1957	14.00	35.00
		(Verve 8124 is a reissue of Norgran 1033 with the DSM cover.)			
Verve MGV-8125	(M)	**Piano Interpretations**	1957	14.00	35.00
		(Verve 8125 is a reissue of Norgran 1036 with the DSM cover.)			
Verve MGV-8126	(M)	**Alto Saxes**	1957	14.00	35.00
		(Verve 8126 is a reissue of Norgran 1035 with the DSM cover.)			
Verve MGV-8127	(M)	**Tenor Saxes**	1957	14.00	35.00
		(Verve 8127 is a reissue of Norgran 1034 with the DSM cover.)			
Verve MGV-8146	(M)	**The Jazz Giants '56**	1957	14.00	35.00
		(Verve 8146 is a reissue of Norgran 1056)			
Verve MGV-8155	(M)	**An Evening Of Jazz**	1957	14.00	35.00
		(Verve 8155 is a reissue of Norgran 1065 with the DSM cover.)			
Verve MGV-8189-2	(M)	**Midnight Jazz At Carnegie Hall** *(2 LPs)*	1957	14.00	35.00
Verve MGV-8194	(M)	**The Verve Compendium Of Jazz, No. 1**	1957	14.00	35.00
Verve MGV-8195	(M)	**The Verve Compendium Of Jazz, No. 2**	1957	14.00	35.00
Verve MGV-8207	(M)	**Here Come The Swinging Bands**	1957	14.00	35.00
Verve MGV-8225	(M)	**Sittin' In**	1958	20.00	50.00
		(Verve 8225 is an all-star session with Stan Getz, Dizzy Gillespie, Coleman Hawkins, Paul Gonzalvez, Wynton Kelly, Wendell Marshall and J.C. Heard.)			
Verve MGV-8230	(M)	**The Anatomy Of Improvisation**	1958	14.00	35.00
Verve MGV-8231-2	(M)	**Jazz At The Hollywood Bowl** *(2 LPs)*	1958	20.00	50.00
Verve MGV-8248	(M)	**Jazz Giants '58**	1958	20.00	50.00
		(Verve 8248 is an all-star session with Stan Getz, Gerry Mulligan, Harry Edison, Louis Bellson and the Oscar Peterson Trio.)			
Verve MGV-8320	(M)	**Down Beat's Hall Of Fame, Vol. 1**	1959	20.00	50.00
Verve MGV-8341	(M)	**College Album**	1959	*Unreleased*	
		—Verve albums above have "Verve Records, Inc." on the bottom of the label.—			
Verve V-2032	(M)	**A Potpourri Of Jazz**	1961	6.00	15.00
Verve V-2036	(M)	**Here Come The Girls**	1961	6.00	15.00
Verve V-8030	(M)	**Metronome All Stars 1956**	1961	6.00	15.00

Label & Catalog #		Title	Year	VG+	NM
Verve V-8124	(M)	**Swing Guitars**	1961	6.00	15.00
Verve V-8125	(M)	**Piano Interpretations**	1961	6.00	15.00
Verve V-8126	(M)	**Alto Saxes**	1961	6.00	15.00
Verve V-8127	(M)	**Tenor Saxes**	1961	6.00	15.00
Verve V-8146	(M)	**The Jazz Giants '56**	1961	6.00	15.00
Verve V-8155	(M)	**An Evening Of Jazz**	1961	6.00	15.00
Verve V-8189-2	(M)	**Midnight Jazz At Carnegie Hall** *(2 LPs)*	1961	8.00	20.00
Verve V-8194	(M)	**The Verve Compendium Of Jazz, No. 1**	1961	6.00	15.00
Verve V-8195	(M)	**The Verve Compendium Of Jazz, No. 2**	1961	6.00	15.00
Verve V-8207	(M)	**Here Come The Swinging Bands**	1961	6.00	15.00
Verve V-8225	(M)	**Sittin' In**	1961	8.00	20.00
Verve V-8230	(M)	**The Anatomy Of Improvisation**	1961	6.00	15.00
Verve V-8231-2	(M)	**Jazz At The Hollywood Bowl** *(2 LPs)*	1961	8.00	20.00
Verve V-8248	(M)	**Jazz Giants '58**	1961	8.00	20.00
Verve V-8320	(M)	**Down Beat's Hall Of Fame, Vol. 1**	1961	6.00	15.00
Verve V-8408	(M)	**Collectors' Choice**	1961	*Unreleased*	
Verve V-8441	(M)	**Chicago And All That Jazz!**	1961	12.00	30.00
Verve V6-8441	(S)	**Chicago And All That Jazz!**	1962	10.00	25.00
		(Verve 8441 is an all-star session with Eddie Condon, Bud Freeman, Bob Haggart, Gene Krupa, Jimmy McPartland, Pee Wee Russell, Joe Sullivan and Jack Teagarden.)			
Verve V-8505	(M)	**The Essential Jazz Vocals**	1963	10.00	25.00
Verve V6-8505	(S)	**The Essential Jazz Vocals**	1963	8.00	20.00
Verve V-8579	(M)	**Winners All! The Down Beat Jazz Poll '64**	1964	10.00	25.00
Verve V6-8579	(S)	**Winners All! The Down Beat Jazz Poll '64**	1964	8.00	20.00
Verve V-8677	(M)	**Encyclopedia Of Jazz In The '60s, Vol. 1**	1966	6.00	15.00
Verve V6-8677	(S)	**Encyclopedia Of Jazz In The '60s, Vol. 1**	1966	5.00	12.00
		— Verve albums above have black labels with "MGM Records" on the bottom.—			
Verve V6-201	(M)	**The Hits Are On Verve**	1964	8.00	20.00
Verve V6S-201	(S)	**The Hits Are On Verve**	1964	6.00	15.00
Verve VSP-13	(M)	**Piano Modern**	1966	4.00	10.00
Verve VSPS-13	(E)	**Piano Modern**	1966	1.00	5.00
Verve VSP-17	(M)	**The Art Of The Ballad**	1966	4.00	10.00
Verve VSPS-17	(E)	**The Art Of The Ballad**	1966	1.00	5.00
Verve VSP-24	(M)	**The Jazz Round**	1966	4.00	10.00
Verve VSSP-24	(E)	**The Jazz Round**	1966	1.00	5.00
Verve VSP-38	(M)	**The Art Of The Ballad 2**	1966	4.00	10.00
Verve VSPS-38	(E)	**The Art Of The Ballad 2**	1966	1.00	5.00
Vik LX-1057	(M)	**Dixieland Festival, Vol. 1**	1956	12.00	30.00
Vik LX-1070	(M)	**Birdland Dream Band, Vol. 1**	1957	12.00	30.00
Vik LX-1077	(M)	**Birdland Dream Band, Vol. 2**	1957	12.00	30.00
Vik LX-1087	(M)	**Trombone Scene**	1957	12.00	30.00
Waldorf Music Hall 33-141	(10")	**Red Hot And Blue Jazz**	195?	100.00	200.00
Warner Bros. W-1272	(M)	**The Trombones, Inc.**	1959	12.00	30.00
Warner Bros. WS-1272	(S)	**The Trombones, Inc.**	1959	10.00	25.00
Warner Bros. W-1281	(M)	**Jazz Festival In Hi-Fi—Near In And Far Out**	1959	12.00	30.00
Warner Bros. WS-1281	(S)	**Jazz Festival In Stereo—Near In And Far Out**	1959	10.00	25.00
Warwick W-5003	(M)	**The Soul Of Jazz Percussion**	1960	12.00	30.00
Warwick W-5003ST	(S)	**The Soul Of Jazz Percussion**	1960	16.00	40.00
WGM 2-B	(M)	**World's Greatest Music Series Pop/Jazz**	196?	12.00	30.00
		(5 LP box collects Roulette material.)			
World Pacific PJM-404	(M)	**Jazz Swings Broadway**	1958	16.00	40.00
World Pacific JWC-500	(M)	**Jazz West Coast, Vol. 1**	1958	16.00	40.00
World Pacific JWC-501	(M)	**Jazz West Coast, Vol. 2**	1958	16.00	40.00
World Pacific JWC-502	(M)	**The Blues, Vol. 2**	1958	16.00	40.00
World Pacific JWC-504	(M)	**Rogers & Hart Gems**	1958	16.00	40.00
World Pacific JWC-505	(M)	**Solo Flight**	1958	16.00	40.00
World Pacific JWC-506	(M)	**Pianists Galore**	1958	16.00	40.00
World Pacific JWC-507	(M)	**Jazz West Coast, Vol. 3**	1958	16.00	40.00
World Pacific JWC-508	(M)	**The Hard Swing**	1958	16.00	40.00
World Pacific JWC-509	(M)	**The Blues, Vol. 2—Have Blues, Will Travel**	1958	16.00	40.00

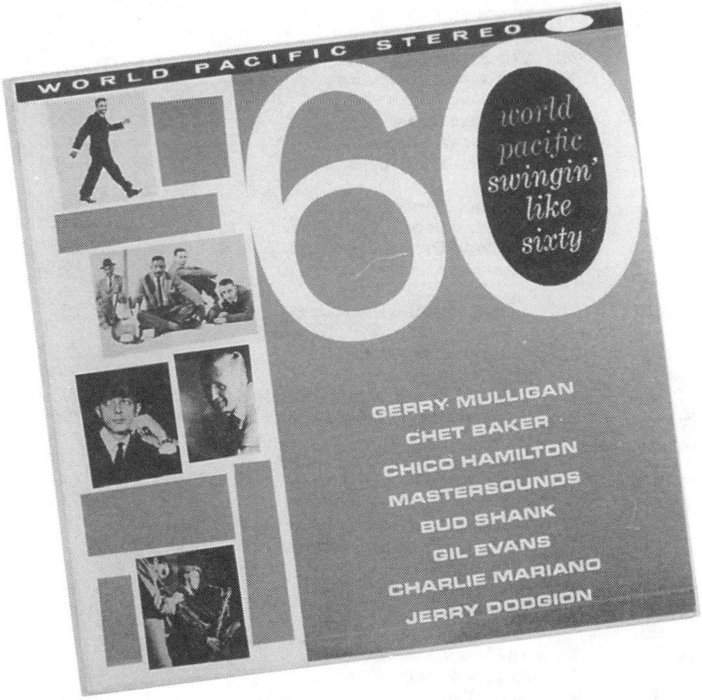

World Pacific's *Something For Both Ears!* was first issued through mail-order ads as a stereo sampler in 1959; check the manufacturers list price prominently displayed as part of the cover graphics. It was reissued a year later as *Swingin' Like Sixty* with a new catalog number and a new, full list price for sale in stores.

Label & Catalog #		*Title*	*Year*	*VG+*	*NM*
World Pacific JWC-510	*(M)*	**Jazz West Coast, Vol. 4**	*1958*	**16.00**	**40.00**
World Pacific ST-1009	*(S)*	**Jazz West Coast, Vol. 4**	*1959*	**12.00**	**30.00**
World Pacific JWC-511	*(M)*	**Jazz West Coast, Vol. 5**	*1958*	**16.00**	**40.00**
World Pacific JWC-512	*(M)*	**The Blues, Vol. 3—Blowin' The Blues**	*1958*	**16.00**	**40.00**
World Pacific ST-1029	*(S)*	**The Blues, Vol. 3—Blowin' The Blues**	*1959*	**12.00**	**30.00**
World Pacific WP-1247	*(M)*	**Drums On Fire**	*1958*	**16.00**	**40.00**
World Pacific HFS-2	*(S)*	**Something For Both Ears** *(Stereo sampler)*	*1958*	**14.00**	**35.00**
World Pacific ST-1021	*(S)*	**The Blues In Stereo**	*1959*	**12.00**	**30.00**
World Pacific WP-1257	*(M)*	**The Sound Of Big Band Jazz In Hi-Fi**	*1960*	**16.00**	**40.00**
World Pacific ST-1015	*(S)*	**The Sound Of Big Band Jazz In Stereo**	*1960*	**12.00**	**30.00**
World Pacific WP-1261	*(M)*	**More Drums On Fire**	*1960*	**16.00**	**40.00**
World Pacific ST-1022	*(S)*	**More Drums On Fire**	*1960*	**12.00**	**30.00**
World Pacific ST-1289	*(S)*	**Swingin' Like Sixty, Vol. 1**	*1960*	**12.00**	**30.00**
World Pacific ST-1290	*(S)*	**Swingin' Like Sixty, Vol. 2**	*1960*	**12.00**	**30.00**
World Pacific ST-1291	*(S)*	**Swingin' Like Sixty, Vol. 3**	*1960*	**12.00**	**30.00**
		(World Pacific 1291 is a reissue of HFS 2.)			
World Pacific KBIG-1	*(S)*	**KBIG Choices**	*1964*	**10.00**	**25.00**
World Wide MGS-20002	*(S)*	**The Soul Of Jazz**	*1958*	**24.00**	**60.00**
"X" LX-3009	*(10")*	**Backgrounds Of Jazz, Vol. 1— The Jug Bands**	*1954*	**30.00**	**75.00**
"X" LVA-3016	*(10")*	**Backgrounds Of Jazz, Vol. 1— Country & Urban Blues**	*1954*	**30.00**	**75.00**
"X" LVA-3021	*(10")*	**Washboard Rhythm Kings, Vol. 1**	*1954*	**30.00**	**75.00**
"X" LVA-3029	*(10")*	**New Orleans Style**	*1954*	**30.00**	**75.00**
"X" LVA-3030	*(10")*	**The Swing Era, Vol. 1**	*1955*	**30.00**	**75.00**
"X" LVA-3032	*(10")*	**Backgrounds Of Jazz, Vol. 3— Kings Of The Blues**	*1955*	**30.00**	**75.00**
"X" LVA-1003	*(M)*	**Composers At Play— Harold Arlen And Cole Porter**	*1955*	**16.00**	**40.00**

David Stone Martin & The Art Of Jazz

There is an artist in the world of jazz who never blew a single note but whose every work is avidly collected by aficionados around the world. An artist with no musical ability who left an indelible stamp on the world of jazz in the '50s and who has inspired notable artists since. The hundreds of drawings and paintings by David Stone Martin that grace the covers of record albums from the '50s virtually define jazz art. While there are many wonderful jacket designs from this period, including the graphics department for Capitol and the sharp-as-Madison-Avenue paintings of William Claxton for Contemporary, Martin stands head and shoulders above the others. His drawing for Clef 4001, *Jam Session*, may be the single most reproduced and recognized drawing in the world of jazz.

Born David Livingstone Martin, he graduated from the Art Institute of Chicago. While working for CBS in 1940 he fell under the influence of Ben Shahn, from which a deep and lasting social relevance would permeate his work. (For examples, refer to Stinson 21, James P. Johnson's *New York Jazz*, or Disc 660, Leadbelly's *Negro Folksongs*.) Martin made his first marks on the record collecting world in the late '40s when he began designing and executing the covers for 78 RPM albums for Moses Asch's labels, Stinson, Disc and Asch. But it was under entrepreneur and jazz impresario Norman Granz that he came into his own.

Both Asch and Granz were independent, liberal wills—plainly against segregation—and both were art collectors who appreciated DSM's genius, giving him full reign with his work. DSM worked in a basic "graphics" format—black ink drawing with two or three primary colors—that often seemed like artifacts of the Twilight Zone. On Clef 507, *Bud Powell Piano*, a third hand appears, floating spider-like over the keyboards. The drawing used for both Clef 4003 and 4004, *Jam Session #3* and *#4*, needs only a mysteriously cast shadow to fit comfortably with the moods of proto-surrealist Georgio de Chirico's haunting canvases.

Martin had an immediate impact, both on record collectors and other jacket designers. When Andy Warhol ventured into the world of record jacket design with Blue Note, his drawings and color emulated almost exactly those of DSM. When fans turned into active collectors and began circulating sale and auction lists, albums bearing David Stone Martin's work were noted, certainly an unusual occurrence for a field of aural appreciators.

During his career he was responsible for over 250 covers along with designing the original labels for Clef, Norgran, Down Home, Verve (whose familiar trumpet player logo was based on Charlie Shavers) and Progressive. The signature of David Stone Martin on a cover means that the art for that jacket was entirely the work of one man. This stands in contrast to other companies, where the jackets were usually designed and executed by a staff. He produced an enormous body of work outside of the jazz field, including poster art for Broadway productions and a parade of covers for *Time*, and, in 1968, he was the subject of a special program by Canadian Television.

During this same period he was responsible for several non-jazz titles: For Asch he did Burl Ives' *Wayfaring Stranger* and, for Disc, *Josh White;* Woody Guthrie's *Ballads From The Dust Bowl; Calypso*; Leadbelly's *Negro Folk Songs*; Richard Dyer-Bennett's *Love Songs; A Stan Wilson Recital;* Ralph Page's *Square*

Illustrations from a book on Jelly Roll Morton by David Stone Martin.

Dances; the *Favorite Songs* and *Calypso* compilations; Rachmilovich's *The Bells;* Prokofieff's *Romeo & Juliet;* and, for Dial, William Masselos and Maro Ajemian's *Bartok Sonata For Two Pianos And Percussion* and Stravinsky's *Renard,* conducted by Robert Craft. For RCA Victor he painted Harry Belafonte's *Love Is A Gentle Thing.*

In a novel move, Grand Award Records issued several albums with Martin paintings that came with a "removable cover" over the regular printed jacket, allowing the customer to peel off the "painting" for framing. He also contributed cover art to *down beat* magazine, all of which are also collectible as DSM artifacts. Other work includes Coleman Hawkins' *Sirius* on Pablo and *The Verve Collector's Item,* an anthology from the mid '70s. In 1981 he provided a nice black & white wash drawing for Frank Strazzeri's *Relaxin'* album on Sea Breeze Records. When Gus Stratiras started Progressive and Stratiras Records in the '80s, he commissioned eighteen covers from Martin, although these are noticeably different from his '50s work, especially in the more elaborate use of color. And while they are unique and attractive, except for one or two instances (Progressive 7010, Carmen Leggio's *Smile,* is the standout), they lack the verve of his earlier work.

Through the years, as albums were reissued and the covers reproduced, the original art source was not always available and a sometimes not-too-subtle metamorphosis occurred. In these cases, owning a copy of the first pressing LP with the art as Martin intended it is as close to the real thing as collectors can get. The novice collector needs to be aware that several other artists emulated Martin to the point of actually being confused by some. At least four albums, Clef 110, 127, 511 and 600, were done by Elizabeth Dauber in a style identical to DSM's and were, in fact, commissioned by Martin for Granz.

A book devoted to both original covers from the '50s and later portraits of notable jazz figures has been compiled by Manek Daver from his personal collection. *Jazz Graphics-David Stone Martin* (Graphic-sha Publishing, 1991) includes several essays in both English and Japanese and is available through Books Nippon, San Francisco, CA, should your local retail outlet not carry it.

An entirely different tack to cover design was taken at Blue Note: co-owner Frank Wolff began shooting a series of extraordinary portraits of the artists, their mood and ambience perfect for the jazz world, but in stark contrast to the posed (and sterile) photos of the major labels. While these early albums were quite attractive with Wolff's atmospheric shots, the graphics reached fruition in 1956 when Reid Miles, a commercial artist with a keen sense of design, joined the team. His layouts incorporated Wolff's shots perfectly, combining them with the mood of the album and a playful graphic sense that allowed each album to have its own unique look. (Miles also did cover design's for Bob Weinstock's Prestige label.) The body of work that accumulated allowed a style to develop that was exclusively Blue Note's. To this day, a Blue Note album is immediately recognizable.

As these albums are hard to find, we are fortunate to have *Blue Note—The Album Cover Art* (Chronicle Books, San Francisco, 1991), a book that displays this always innovative and often gorgeous cover art. Edited by Graham Marsh, Felix Cromley and Glyn Callingham for Chronicle Books with a foreword by Horace Silver, there are over 230 covers illustrated in full color and, as the book measures the same size as an album, more than 50 are reproduced full scale!

Illustrations from a book on Jelly Roll Morton by David Stone Martin.

Obviously, Chronicle knows a good thing and Marsh and Callingham have followed with two new books: *California Cool: West Coast Jazz Of The 50s & 60s—The Album Cover Art* features a foreword by artist/photographer William Claxton, whose 1955 book of photographs, *Jazz West Coast*, helped inspire the Eastern media's obsession with the musicians on the other side of the continent. The book is divided into more or less thematic sections, such as "Girls," "Hats" and "Location," which makes for fun viewing but a lot of flipping back and forth for anyone trying to get a sense of each company's graphic identity.

New York Hot: East Coast Jazz Of The 50s & 60s—The Album Cover Art, is more straightforward, dividing the book into sections on Prestige, Riverside and Atlantic with a fourth section covering other East Coast based labels. These books are a great introduction and could lead a beginner into collecting jazz just by looking at the covers. The two newer titles have 112 pages with more than 50 full-size reproductions. All three, are currently in-print and available at your favorite book seller for a mere $24.95.

Collecting The Finest In Jazz Since 1939

Entering the world of collecting jazz records is fraught with suspense and anticipation, as, excepting this book, there is little in the way of published information for the novice. *And* most long-time collectors would rather undergo various forms of torture usually reserved for old Fu Manchu films than willingly part with whatever shred of arcana they possess. Nonetheless, one becomes immediately familiar with a note. . . a Blue Note. This one label is revered by almost every collector of "modern" jazz and for good reason: From the artists signed to the sessions held, from the pressing of the vinyl to the graphics of the cover, Blue Note was a labor of love.

"Blue Note Records are designed simply to serve the uncompromising expressions of hot jazz, or swing in general. Any particular style of playing which represents an authentic way of musical feeling is genuine expression. By virtue of its significance in place, time and circumstance, it possesses its own tradition, artistic standards and audience that keeps it alive. Hot jazz, therefore, is expression and communication, a musical and social manifestation, and Blue Note records are concerned with identifying its impulse, not it sensational and commercial adornments."

While this healthy attitude plastered on the company's first brochure prior to World War II dealt with "hot jazz," the same spirit was maintained throughout the label's life as an independent producer of jazz recordings. Blue Note was the brainchild of Alfred Lion, a young German immigrant who had discovered the music in 1925 via Sam Woodyard & His Chocolate Dandies and, as an importer and exporter, had sought to introduce his fellow countrymen to these exciting American sounds.

Traveling to the United States in 1930, Lion returned with more than 300 jazz records. Unfortunately, the rise to power of Adolf Hitler and his brown shirts made Lion's permanent departure (1938) necessary and his goal of bringing jazz to the Fatherland futile.

After attending the "Spirituals to Swing" concert at Carnegie Hall on December 23, 1938, Lion approached boogie woogie piano legends Albert Ammons and Meade Lux Lewis with a session offer. In early '39, in a relaxed and convivial setting, these two men provided the would-be entrepreneur with the music that was to appear on his first records, two 78 rpm singles, of which Lion pressed fifty each. Shortly after that, a session with Sidney Bechet led to the label's first hit, "Summertime." Even with these humble beginnings, Lion established his difference: Instead of the normal 10," the discs were 12," allowing the players a little latitude to stretch out of the 2:30 limitations of the smaller disc. While the label design Lion would use for decades was on these two discs, the colors were black on pink instead of the now familiar blue on white.

When childhood friend Francis "Frank" Wolff emigrated to the New World in 1941, he joined Lion with both his love for the music and his photographer's sense of image. Together they recorded several sessions before being interrupted by the war: Lion was drafted and Blue Note's operations discontinued. Wolff took employ with Milt Gabler, who ran his own independent jazz label, Commodore, and the two men kept both labels in print and on turntables.

With Lion's return from the service in 1943, the partners set up leg residence in their now legendary 767 Lexington Avenue, NYC, offices. After se eral sessions with small groups attempting to survive the death of swing and t big band, tenor saxophonist Ike Quebec introduced Lion and Wolff to such bop pers as Bud Powell and Thelonious Monk, hardly household names at the time. Thus they entered the world of modern jazz, immediately learning that this new music often received less than overwhelming support from distributors and consumers. Nonetheless, Alfred and Frank remained committed to these new artists and their music, steadfastly recording and issuing new titles deemed "too far out" for the marketplace.

Most independent labels were run as cost effectively as possible. Sessions were often of the "blowing" sorts, where, unrehearsed (not of the musicians choice, but the owners were not about to pay these cats to play for "no one"), a group got together before their regular night gigs to cut as many sides as possible, often with a nominal leader whose name and figure could be used on the album. And, as session time was expensive, little if anything was discarded, thus many musicians lived to see their less than best released on record.

Lion and Wolff turned all of this around, planning each date and allowing several paid rehearsals. Thus, along with providing an environment conducive to creativity, and treating their artists with the graciousness they deserved, Blue Note was able to record not only better executed sessions but also allowed and encouraged a far greater ambition in what the artists attempted, keeping the label in the vanguard of new jazz.

In 1953, Lion and Wolff were introduced to engineer extraordinaire Dr. Rudolph Van Gelder. An optometrist by day, when the sun set Rudy ran the most famous jazz recording studio on the East Coast from his home in Hackensack, NJ. He was already well known for getting a great sound for other labels, but after working with Lion—who knew *exactly* how he wanted each artist, each instrument, to sound—he developed a system of placement of musicians and mikes and recording that became known as the "Van Gelder sound," even though Rudy insists that "his" sound would not be possible without Alfred's ears!

A 1954 session for pianist Horace Silver marked another turning point in the development of the Blue Note legend: Silver requested Art Blakey, Kenny Dorham, Hank Mobley and Doug Watkins for this session. The men found both the session and the experience so rewarding that they formed a loose aggregate for the expressed purpose of communicating modern jazz by combining the idiom of bop with the soul of the blues. Calling themselves the Jazz Messengers, their sound came to be associated with Blue Note's as much as Van Gelder's.

Thus, with Lion in charge of the music, its selection and recording, Van Gelder over-seeing the control board, and a solid group of interchangeable musicians led by Blakey and Silver, Blue Note entered its "classic" period, producing a body of work that, artistically and commercially, dominated the jazz record scene for almost a decade. In 1959, Ike Quebec signed on not only as a performer, but also as A&R man, musical director and producer, bringing such older luminaries as Dexter Gordon back to the jazz scene. After Ike's untimely death in 1961, his position was filled by pianist Duke Pearson.

As the enormous responsibilities entailed in running a record label increasingly took their toll on the no-longer-young men, the demand from distributors for more product mounted (in response to the unexpected sales of this funkier, more accessible sound). In 1966, Blue Note was sold to Liberty Records, with Alfred remaining in charge of the label's output for a year, at which point he retired. Wolff and Pearson continued to produce the sessions, but much of the charm left when the indie joined the majors and the new sound of funk began to dominate. The covers were now turned out by liberty's art department and while they were competent, the difference was obvious.

By the beginning of the '70s, Wolff was dead and Pearson withdrawn. The label's increasing reliance on funk led to fusion, abandoning the classic sound that they had brought to the mainstream. While the original albums remained in print, fan-turned-producer Michael Cuscuna began researching unreleased sessions, initially through the reminiscences of musicians he was then producing. Beginning in 1975, he searched through the company vaults, locating and listening to every session Blue Note had recorded, cataloguing them for future use. From his work over one hundred "new" titles were issued, many in Japan. It is these reissues that kept the Blue Note magic alive for collectors.

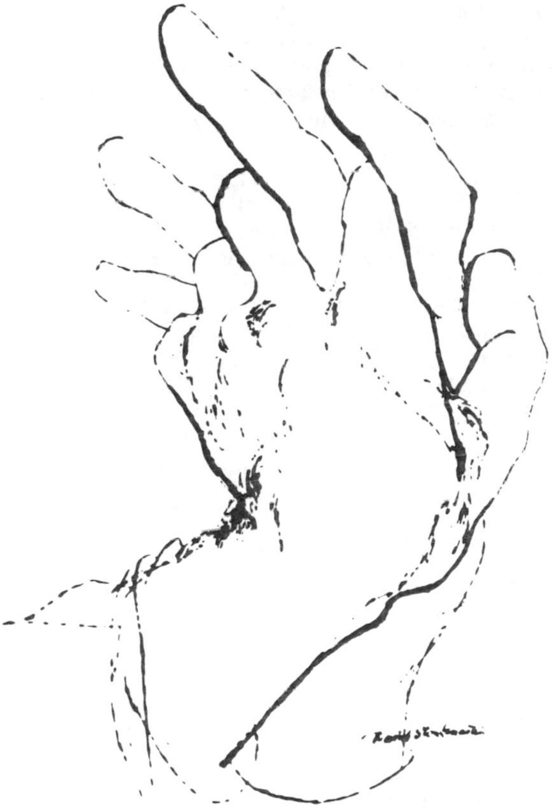

Mary Lou Williams by David Stone Martin. All rights reserved.

Jazz & The Audiophile

Emerging from the early hi-fi, there were those who were not simply satisfied with whatever technology was available on a mass-produced basis for a reasonable price. These hobbyists pursued a more perfect medium, through the selection of the correct gear, the placement of speakers, the "tweaking" of each and every facet of their equipment and the environment in which it was enjoyed. Often perceived as obsessed by the more relaxed majority, many of the innovations now taken for granted, both in the hardware (the electronics and other playback equipment) and the software (the recording and actual manufacturing of the records), can be traced directly to the interventions, insights and perseverance of these pioneers.

Originally dubbed "golden ears," their primary concern was an accurate recreation of the musical event as it occurred in its natural environment. Many of these listeners placed a primary emphasis on "sound field" recordings, those that, by use of the most appropriate equipment in the proper environment, with mikes properly placed and, most importantly, no post-recording manipulation of the signal, come closest to achieving the idealized sound presentation. In record collecting today, the term "audiophile" is generally applied to those who specialize in high-quality *stereo* recordings on high-quality vinyl.

While every album *could* be an audiophile pressing, very few are and the standard of quality, especially in the amount of pressings done from each stamper to the quality of the vinyl used, dropped dramatically during the '70s. Thus the door was open for several independent companies to enter the field and provide the market with better records. The most popular of these have been the half-speed mastered "Original Master Recordings" from Mobile Fidelity Sound Laboratories. Virtually the entire catalog of this small label is now collectible. The Nautilus label half-speed "Super Disks" were less successful on the market than MFSL and consequently their titles are a bit harder to find, although the demand is not as great from the collectors.

There are smaller labels, such as Sheffield Labs, Wilson Audio and Reference Recordings, that also specialized in audiophile pressings—and have a deserved reputation among said 'philes. Other collectible audiophile labels exist outside the boundaries of the increasingly xenophobic U.S., such as Cube (West Germany), Vertigo (U.K.), CBS (Canada, Germany and Japan), Nimbus (U.K.) and A&M (Canada). Again, while these pressings are outside the scope of this particular book, these companies' products were often available domestically and sought out by the audiophiliac.

Among the majors, CBS poured out a large number of their Columbia and Epic catalog in this format, but these were done in relatively small printings, did not fare well on the retail racks and thus, the demand for certain titles is increasing. The actual pressings themselves, from inception through mastering and pressing, were qualitatively far behind the smaller companies, leaving a great deal to be desired. When the relative failure of this line was obvious, rather than simply delete the titles and make them available to cut-out bins nationwide, CBS simply recalled them and recycled the vinyl for future use, making many of the CBS titles difficult indeed to track down. Thus their value as collectibles outstrips their value as vehicles for a truly pleasing listening experience.

The prices for audiophile oriented collectibles that overlap with the interests of the general jazz market will continue to rise steadily if not always dramatically. The prices on a few items listed in this book– Miles Davis' *Kind Of Blue* (Columbia CS-8163, 1959), Oliver Nelson's *The Blues And The Abstract Truth* (Impulse AS-5, 1961) and Eric Dolphy's *Out To Lunch* (Blue Note BST-84163, 1964) are examples– have been influenced by this market, which does exert an undeniable affect on the market. *The Absolute Sound*, one of several magazines geared to these tastes, needs only review a stereo album favorably and the demand among the audiophile faithful can push the value of the record way over the previously established norm. *Clap Hands, Hear Comes Charlie* (Verve V6-4053, 1962) went from just another Ella album of the early '60s to a $200+ item in the gold ear community, due to one rave review!

Finally, there is the issue of still-sealed copies of audiophile recordings, which often sell for many times the assumed value of a mint copy. The demand issue here, which may be, with individual collectors, far in excess of that of the mainstream collector, best placed in context by considering that many audiophiles have cartridges on their tone arms worth more than the average collector's entire sound system. The idea of subjecting said cartridge to the trauma of a worn record makes obvious sense. Please note that not all audiophiles want sealed copies; many demand opened, examined copies in mint condition; this way any defects originated at the manufacturer's level may be observed by both the seller and the buyer.

Bibliography

Aside from the obvious—the records themselves and other domestically printed discographies, many sources were used: Record company brochures and catalogs; lists advertised in trade journals of the time (particularly *Downbeat* and *Metronome*). Many Japanese publications were made available to me, both magazines and books. Particularly valuable were *Jazz Hero's Data Bank* (JICC, 1991) and the *Swing Journal*, Special Issue Vol. 41, No. 526, 1987. A scholarly Japanese publication, this special issue is a book documenting the entire Jazz issues of Blue Note, Prestige, Riverside, EmArcy/Mercury, Savoy and Verve. While countless jazz books and biographies were referenced for this project, a good many proved virtually useless from a discographer's perspective.

Most jazz books are anecdotal and filled with interesting tales from the careers of the musicians, generally concerning specific gigs. When records are referred to at all (at least in the books on the classic jazz), it is about a particular side (78), not on LPs. In fact, with some biographers, the reader might get the impression that LPs have had little to do with the history and development of the music! However, the following books played a role in the generation of this book:

John Chilton, *Who's Who Of Jazz—Storyville To Swing Street*, Time/Life Records 1978

Manek Daver, *David Stone Martin: Jazz Graphics*, Graphic-Sha 1991

Leonard Feather, *The Book Of Jazz*, Meridian 1959

Leonard Feather, *The Encyclopedia Of Jazz*, Horizon Press 1960

Ferguson & Johnson, *Mainstream Jazz Reference & Price Guide*, O'Sullivan Woodside 1984

Ted Fox, *In The Groove*, St. Martin's Press, 1985

Robert Gordon, *Jazz West Coast*, Quartet Books 1990

Richard Hadlock, *Jazz Masters Of The Twenties*, Collier Books 1965

Max Harrison, Charles Fox & Eric Thacker, *The Essential Jazz Records*, Greenwood Books 1984

Terry Leonard, *Goldmine's Jazz Price Guide*, Krause Publications 1990

Joe Lindsay, *Record Label Guide For Domestic LPs*, BioDisc 1986

Len Lyons, *The 101 Best Jazz Albums*, Morrow/Quill 1980

Len Lyons & Don Perlo, *Jazz Portraits—The Lives And Music Of The Jazz Masters*, William Morrow & Co. 1989

Graham Marsh, Felix Cromley & Gynn Callingham, *Blue Note—The Album Cover Art*, Chronicle Books 1991

Graham Marsh & Gynn Callingham, *California Cool: West Coast Jazz Of The 50s & 60s—The Album Cover Art*, Chronicle Books 1993

Graham Marsh & Gynn Callingham, *New York Hot: East Coast Jazz Of The 50s & 60s—The Album Cover Art*, Chronicle Books 1993

Brian Priestly, *Mingus—A Critical Biography*, Quartet Books, 1982

Brian Priestly, *Jazz On Record—A History*, Billboard Books 1991

George T. Simon, *The Big Bands*, The MacMillan Co. 1967

John Wilson, *The Collectors Jazz: Traditional And Swing*, Keystone 1958

The Rolling Stone Jazz Record Guide, Straight Arrow

An Author's Bio

Born to a modest family of registered Democrats in Wilkes-Barre General Hospital in 1951 (Virgo by birth, radical by inclination), I can honestly count Marcel Duchamp and burning culm-banks as pivotal influences on my developing psyche. While my baby-book, long since lost in the Great Flood of '72, claimed my favorite song in my preliterate years was "Sh-Boom," I remember "Hound Dog". . . Growing up, Wilkes-Barre seemed more a part of the past than the present: I can recall going to the movies on a Saturday afternoon for 15¢ with my brother Charles and good bud Donny Flynn, spending hours absorbing such seminal works of art as *Earth Vs The Flying Saucers* and *The Atomic Submarine, The Mask* and *Dementia 13, The Delicate Delinquent* and *Abbott & Costello Meet The Wolfman*, and the other staples of '50s and '60s matinees.

Way back then, comic books were 32 pages for a dime, 16 oz. RC Colas were 13¢, Tastycakes were, er, tasty, and I whiled many a day away readin' and sippin' in awe of The Fantastic Four, Batman, and especially Steve Ditko's Dr. Strange and Spiderman. By the age of twelve I had passed through dinosaurs (a phase I joyfully find my five-year old daughter, Ananda, locked in today), the Civil War, military aircraft of the War To End All Wars (ho ho), and baseball cards. I was ready for something new. . .

My record collecting career began with the atrocious "electronically reprocessed stereo" reissues of *Elvis' Golden Records 1, 2* and *3*, and greatest hits collections of Chuck Berry, Little Richard, Fats Domino, Jerry Lee Lewis, and The Platters. As Northeastern Pennsylvania was a dumping grounds for cut-outs (all most of us could afford), I was able to pick up anything deleted, which is where my exposure to jazz came from. Buying Louis Armstrong, Duke Ellington, Ella Fitzgerald and Count Basie for less than $2 made it easy to broaden my horizons on a shoestring allowance.

In 1965 The Byrds' "Mr. Tambourine Man" turned my entire perception of pop music inside out and I spent the next fifteen years or so listening exclusively to the Rock-With-A-Capital-R of the '60s: *Pet Sounds, Sgt. Pepper, Blonde On Blonde, Surrealistic Pillow, Younger Than Yesterday, Face To Face, Beggar's Banquet*, etc. all of which remain favorites decades later. Jazz re-entered the picture with the early fusion excursions of Miles Davis & Co; *Bitches Brew* was heady listening, even in the still psychedelic years of the early '70s. From fusion I worked my way back, usually at the behest of my then room-mate John Styklunas, who introduced me to the many wonders of modern jazz, especially Charles Mingus and Eric Dolphy.

Jazz that gets the most plays in my apartment these days include the Time/Life "Giants Of Jazz" boxed set, *Billie Holiday*, Duke Ellington's *Jazz party* and *In The Uncommon Market*, Miles' Prestige albums (all of them), *Mingus Ah Um* (from which comes Ananda's favorite jazz piece, "Fables Of Faubus") and *Mingus Dynasty*, Eric Dolphy's *Outward Bound* and *Out There*, and lotsa Coltrane, especially *Blue Train, Giant Steps* and *Coltrane* on Impulse.

Current non-musical obsessions include but are not limited to hiking the mountains of the Pacific Northwest; dreaming of pizza from Arcaro & Jenell's in Old Forge, PA; old movies with Fred Astaire, Jean Arthur, Carol Lombard and particularly Cary Grant; tall women who work out; books on mind-manifesting agents; rereading all of James Clavell's novels and the complete *Cerebus The Aardvark*; and ranting at the lunatic behavior of the owners of Major League Baseball teams.

As for my origins as record collecting's "pricing guru," well. . . In 1983 I was drafted out of art classes for duty on the O' Sullivan Woodside line of record collectors price guides. This was caused by the the departure of the former editor and the need for someone who knew the field in a broad sense; was capable of doing the necessary work; and, most importantly, was readily available! I authored the controversial and iconoclastic *1985-86 Rock Records Album Price Guide* and the *1985-86 Elvis Presley Record Price Guide* before that company's premature demise. In 1985 I inaugurated the *Goldmine* line of price guides for record collectors: *Goldmine's Price Guide To Collectible Record Album, Goldmine 45RPM Rock'n Roll Record Price Guide*, and this jazz book you are holding (with more in the future).

I am also associated with White Dragon Press, for whom I produced *A Touch Of Gold: The Elvis Presley Record & Memorabilia Price Guide* and for whom I am completing *Rhythm & Blues: A Discography & Price Guide 1949-1959*, due in the summer of 1994, and, in the not too distant future, *Movie Music: A Discography & Price Guide To Soundtrack Albums*, which will also cover television and original cast recordings. WDP and I are also considering more jazz projects, primarily the Blue Note project discussed in this book's Foreword, to be followed by a similar project for Prestige, Verve, and Impulse. But that may be looking *too* far into the future. . .